MW01363219

Nicholas Copernicus
1473-1543

Galileo Galilei
1564-1642

Johannes Kepler
1571-1630

Leonard Euler
1703-1783

Joseph Louis Lagrange
1736-1813

Pierre-Simon Marquis de Laplace
1749-1827

Pierre de Fermat
1608-1665

Sir Isaac Newton
1642-1727

Gottfried Wilhelm Leibniz
1646-1716

Augustine-Louis Cauchy
1789-1867

Carl Gustav Jacob Jacobi
1804-1851

Sir William Rowan Hamilton
1805-1865

(Adapted from David Eugene Smith, *Portraits of Eminent Mathematicians with Biographical Sketches,* Vol. I & II, Scripta Mathematica, New York, 1938)

CLASSICAL MECHANICS

CLASSICAL MECHANICS

Narayan Chandra Rana
Tata Institute of Fundamental Research, Bombay

Pramod Sharadchandra Joag
University of Poona, Pune

McGraw Hill Education (India) Private Limited
CHENNAI

McGraw Hill Education Offices
Chennai New York St Louis San Francisco Auckland Bogotá Caracas
Kuala Lumpur Lisbon London Madrid Mexico City Milan Montreal
San Juan Santiago Singapore Sydney Tokyo Toronto

McGraw Hill Education (India) Private Limited

Copyright © 1991, by McGraw Hill Education (India) Private Limited

43rd reprint 2016
RZALCDLQRYLBL

No part of this publication may be reproduced or distributed in any form or by any means, electronic, mechanical, photocopying, recording, or otherwise or stored in a database or retrieval system without the prior written permission of the publishers. The program listings (if any) may be entered, stored and executed in a computer system, but they may not be reproduced for publication.

This edition can be exported from India only by the publishers,
McGraw Hill Education (India) Private Limited.

ISBN (13 digits): 978-0-07-460315-4
ISBN (10 digits): 0-07-460315-9

Published by McGraw Hill Education (India) Private Limited,
444/1, Sri Ekambara Naicker Industrial Estate, Alapakkam, Porur, Chennai 600 116, Tamil Nadu, India.
Text and cover printed at Pushp Print Services, Maujpur, Shahdara, New Delhi–110053.

Visit us at: www.mheducation.co.in

Dedicated to

Professor Amal Kumar Raychaudhuri
of Presidency College, Calcutta

Generations of Indian students owe their
Classical Mechanics to you!

Foreword

One may ask why one should have one more book on a time-worn subject like Classical Mechanics, on which there are so many books available in the international market. The reason is that while science and the market of books are international, the practice of science, and in particular its teaching, is national, and one does need books specially prepared taking into account the specific backgrounds of students and curricula in our country. Production of high-quality books is also an important part of the development of self-reliant science capability in the country. The book by Dr. N. C. Rana is therefore most welcome.

The book has grown out of the lecture course given by Dr. Rana at the Poona University under the joint M.Sc. programme of the Poona University and Tata Institute of Fundamental Research. In this programme we had on the one hand some students selected on the basis of a national test, and others who came in the normal course from various colleges affiliated to the University of Poona, including the colleges in the districts. The lectures were held in common, but the tutorials, with an emphasis on problem-solving, tried to cater to the different backgrounds and capabilities of the students.

I shared an office with Dr. Rana during this period (1986 – 87) and watched with fascination his intensive interaction with the students — how he was most of the time surrounded by students of both categories, and the way he handled their difficulties at different levels. Most of the students, especially those from Poona colleges, had no experience of problem-solving during their undergraduate years, and they gradually developed a self-confidence in the process. Seeing this, I thought Dr. Rana should convert his lecture notes into a textbook, so that other students elsewhere could also benefit from his pedagogic approach. I am glad that he has accepted my suggestion and has written this book in collaboration with Dr. P. S. Joag, who has had a long experience with the students of Poona University.

I am sure this book will be found not only useful to but also stimulating by students in India and outside.

B. M. Udgaonkar

Professor of Physics
Tata Institute of Fundamental Research
Bombay

Preface

This book has grown out of a course of 65 lectures on classical mechanics delivered by one of us to the first year M.Sc. students at the Department of Physics, University of Poona. The course was part of a new M.Sc. programme which was jointly run for three successive years by the Tata Institute of Fundamental Research, Bombay and the University of Poona, Pune, in order to attract the best talents to research.

The outline of the course followed the standard post-graduate syllabi of most of the Indian universities. However, while shaping the lectures into this book, the scope was sufficiently widened to enable undergraduates majoring in physics in all universities (including the ones in Western countries) and post-graduates of Indian universities to use it as a standard textbook.

It may not be out of place to say a few words about the new features of this book compared to, say, the most popular textbook on the subject written by Herbert Goldstein. In our book we have included the results of many new experiments on the methods of teaching different topics of classical mechanics, that were published in the international fora of physics teachers, such as the *American Journal of Physics* and *Physics Education*, and in magazines like *Physics Today* and *Scientific American.* Such material from about 250 articles, which we did not find in any standard textbook on the subject, has been incorporated laying emphasis on historical developments, and including short biographical notes on the relevant eminent personalities. Above all, we have attempted a unified approach to physics through the doorway of classical mechanics. We have tried to coin as many lively and interesting problems as possible with sufficient hints and answers to most of the problems given at the end of the book. New topics like dynamics of sports, physics of tides, theory of friction, and so on have been included with the hope that some day these will become part of the standard syllabus. In Indian universities, a typical course on classical mechanics includes not only the particle and rigid body dynamics but also bits of continuum mechanics and fluid dynamics. As a result a student is forced to buy at least three books for a single course. So we have included two chapters, one on elasticity and the other on fluid dynamics, to meet the minimum requirement.

It was the kind suggestion of Professor B. M. Udgaonkar, the man behind the introduction of the above M. Sc. programme, that motivated us to take up the project of writing this book. Professor V. Singh, Director of Tata Institute of Fundamental Research, has kindly given us the permission to use all the facilities required for preparing the camera-ready copy of the manuscript on a laser printer. Professor J. V. Narlikar, Director of the Inter University Centre for Astronomy and Astrophysics, has kindly helped us find a suitable publisher. Professor G. Rajasekaran, Co-director of the Institute for Mathematical Sciences, and the anonymous referees with great pains have done a critical reading of the manuscript and have given valuable suggestions. It is indeed a great pleasure for us to thank all these gentlemen for their kind suggestions and gestures.

We also gratefully acknowledge the help and assistance in many different ways towards the preparation of the manuscript extended by our students and friends, particularly Dr. Banashree Mitra, Mr. Sukamal Dutta, Ms. Vandana Nanal, Mr. Sukalyan Chattopadhyay, Mr. Debashis Ghoshal, Mr. Peter Thomas, Ms. Pratibha Joag, Dr. Anil Gangal, Dr. H. M. Antia, Dr. Sanjeev Dhurandhar, Dr. G. H. Keswani, Dr. Satyajit Saha, Dr. Chinmoy Ghosh and Dr. Achintya Pal.

We shall highly appreciate receiving valuable comments and suggestions from the users and the reviewers of the book for further improvements.

Narayan Chandra Rana
Pramod Sharadchandra Joag

Contents

Values of Fundamental Physical Constants

Universal Constants

speed of light in vacuum	c	299 792 458	$\mathrm{ms^{-1}}$
permeability of vacuum	μ_0	$4\pi \times 10^{-7}$	$\mathrm{NA^{-2}}$
		$= 12.566\ 370\ 614...$	$10^{-7}\ \mathrm{NA^{-2}}$
permittivity of vacuum, $1/\mu_0 c^2$	ϵ_0	8.854 187 817...	$10^{-12}\ \mathrm{Fm^{-1}}$
Newtonian constant of gravitation	G	6.672 59(85)	$10^{-11}\ \mathrm{m^3\ kg^{-1}\ s^{-2}}$
Planck constant	h	6.626 075 5(40)	10^{-34} J s
in electron volts, h/e		4.135 669 2(12)	10^{-15} eV s
$h/2\pi$	$\hbar$	1.054 572 66(63)	10^{-34} J s
in electron volts, $\hbar/e$		6.852 122 0(20)	10^{-16} eV s

Atomic and Nuclear Constants

elementary charge	e	1.602 177 33(49)	10^{-19} C
fine-structure constant, $\mu_0 c e^2/2h$	α	7.297 353 08(33)	10^{-3}
Bohr radius, $\alpha/4\pi R_\infty$	a_0	0.529 177 249(24)	10^{-10} m
electron mass	m_e	9.109 389 7(54)	10^{-31} kg
		5.485 799 03(13)	10^{-4} amu
in electron volts, $m_e c^2/e$		0.510 999 06(15)	MeV
Compton wavelength, $h/m_e c$	λ_c	2.426 310 58(22)	10^{-12} m
$\lambda_c/2\pi = \alpha a_0 = \alpha^2/4\pi R_\infty$	$\bar{\lambda}_c$	3.861 593 23(35)	10^{-13} m
classical electron radius, $\alpha^2 a_0$	r_e	2.817 940 92(38)	10^{-15} m
Thomson cross-section, $(8\pi/3)r_e{}^2$	σ_e	0.665 246 16(18)	$10^{-28}\ \mathrm{m^2}$
electron magnetic moment	μ_e	928.477 01(31)	$10^{-26}\ \mathrm{JT^{-1}}$
in Bohr magnetons	μ_e/μ_B	1.001 159 652 193(10)	
proton mass	m_p	1.672 623 1(10)	10^{-27} kg
		1.007 276 470(12)	amu
in electron volts, $m_p c^2/e$		938.272 31(28)	MeV
neutron mass	m_n	1.674 928 6(10)	10^{-27} kg
		1.008 664 904(14)	amu
in electron volts, $m_n c^2/e$		939.565 63(28)	MeV
Avogadro constant	N_A, L	6.022 136 7(36)	$10^{23}\ \mathrm{mol^{-1}}$

atomic mass constant			
$m_u = \frac{1}{12}m(^{12}C)$	m_u	1.660 540 2(10)	10^{-27} kg
in electron volts, $m_u c^2/e$		931.494 32(28)	MeV
molar gas constant	R	8.314 510(70)	J mol^{-1} K^{-1}
Boltzmann constant, R/N_A	k	1.380 658(12)	10^{-23} J K^{-1}
in electron volts, k/e		8.617 385(73)	10^{-5} eV K^{-1}
in hertz, k/h		2.083 674(18)	10^{10} Hz K^{-1}
in wavenumbers, k/hc		69.503 87(59)	m^{-1} K^{-1}
Stefan-Boltzmann constant, $(\pi^2/60)k^4/\hbar^3c^2$	σ	5.670 51(19)	10^{-8} W m^{-2} K^{-4}

Astronomical Constants

heliocentric gravitational constant	$GM_\odot$	1.327 124 38	10^{20} m^3 s^{-2}
geocentric gravitational constant	$GM_\oplus$	3.986 004 48	10^{14} m^3 s^{-2}
Astronomical unit	1 AU	1.495 978 706 6	10^{11} m
equatorial radius of sun	$R_\odot$	6.959 9	10^8 m
equatorial radius of earth	$R_\oplus$	6.378 137	10^6 m
angular velocity of earth	$\omega_\oplus$	7.292 115 146 7	10^{-5} s^{-1}
ratio of earth's mass to moon's mass	$M_\oplus/M_{☾}$	81.300 813	
radius of moon	$R_{☾}$	1.738 2	10^6 m

I

Introduction

I.1 WHAT IS THIS CHAPTER ABOUT?

The present chapter is devoted to briefly recapitulating the topics that are usually covered at the lower levels. The first two sections are quite formal, and at places may even appear to be pedantic. However, the reader need not lose heart if lost in too many definitions or concepts. The reader may as well omit these two sections in the first reading. In the third section one would find a brief historical note on the development of ideas, mostly related to mechanics up to the time of Newton. Even though it is quite brief, reading it may be found amusing. We really come to the business from the fourth section onwards. It is presumed that a student would have already spent a number of years studying various aspects of Newton's laws of motion. Even writing a summary of all that would surely take many more pages than we have spent. Nevertheless, we have tried to emphasize the significant aspects of Newton's laws of motion, and some of their applications. Should any more important items be included, the authors would appreciate receiving specific suggestions.

We plan to give in the introduction to every chapter, a brief note about the most eminent person, if any, marked for the development of material that is covered in that chapter. In this chapter, it is obviously Newton.

Born prematurely, a physical weakling, Sir Isaac Newton (1642 – 1727) had to wear a bolster to support his neck during his first months; and no one expected him to live. Newton's father died three months before he was born, his mother remarried and he was left with his aged grandmother. He entered Trinity College in 1661. Not so distinguished as a student, he failed in 1663 in a scholarship examination due to awful inadequacy in geometry. The fateful Plague years of 1665 – 1666, he spent away from Cambridge and these were the most fruitful years of his life, laying the foundation for his future greatness in optics, dynamics and mathematics. Returning to Cambridge, he first became a minor fellow at Trinity in 1667 and a major fellow the next year. His mathematics professor, Isaac Barrow recognised his genius, and in a rare act of self-abnegation, Barrow resigned his professorship so that the young and more promising Newton could have it. So Newton was offered the Lucasian Chair of Mathematics in 1669. At Cambridge, Newton became the very model of an absent-minded professor. He was never known to indulge in any recreation or pastime, either in riding out or taking the air, walking, bowling, or any other exercise whatever, thinking hours lost in such activities, were better spent in studies. He often worked until two to three o'clock in the morning, ate sparingly and sometimes forgot to eat altogether.

He presented his first paper, in optics, in 1672 to the Royal Society, and was immediately elected a fellow of the Society. However, his theory of light and colour brought him into great controversy with Christiaan Huygens and Robert Hooke, and he vowed not to publish any of his discoveries. During the Plague years, he completely solved the problem of colliding bodies, discovered the law of centrifugal force and got the idea of gravitation. He solved the Kepler problem (actually the inverse of it) in 1679, and the wonderful theorem proving that a homogeneous gravitating sphere attracts all points outside it as if its mass were concentrated at its centre in 1685. It is only at the insistence of Sir Edmond Halley that he finally decided to publish his works. He composed his magnum opus the *Principia* sometime between autumn 1684 and spring 1686, which was finally published in July 1687 in three volumes. Since then *Principia* has been regarded as the Bible of mechanics.

In 1696, he abandoned the academic life for the position of a Warden, later the Master, of Mint. In 1705, he was knighted by the King and later served many years as the President of the Royal Society. His book on optics was published in 1704.

The plan of the present book is given in the sixth section with specific reference to the limitations of Newton's program. The concept of the whole book is to present most of the important post-Newtonian developments of classical mechanics. So please do not miss this section. The chapter ends with a set of fifty problems, with some hints for the solutions, at the end of the book. We expect that an average student would be able to solve half of the problems even without looking at the hints.

I.2 WHAT IS CLASSICAL MECHANICS ?

Classical mechanics is that branch of physics which deals with the description and explanation of the motion of point-like as well as extended, rigid as well as deformable objects embedded in a three-dimensional Euclidean space. The part of mechanics which deals only with the geometrical description of the motion, such as Galileo's laws of falling bodies, or Kepler's laws of planetary motion, is called *kinematics.* The part which offers causal explanation of the motion along with its description, such as the application of Newton's laws of motion, Newton's law of gravitation, etc., is called *dynamics.* The present book is primarily concerned with classical dynamics of Newton and his followers.

I.3 THE PLACE OF CLASSICAL MECHANICS IN PHYSICS AND SOME BASIC DEFINITIONS

Classical mechanics is the oldest branch of physics. Some of the greatest minds of all times, such as Sir Isaac Newton, Joseph Lagrange, Leonhard Euler, Simon Laplace, Henry Poincare, Sir William Hamilton and Carl Jacobi, laid the foundation and built the theoretical structure of the subject. The well formulated structure of classical mechanics has in fact provided an ideal paradigm for the structural development of the relatively new branches of physics, such as electrodynamics, relativistic mechanics, quantum mechanics and statistical mechanics. In this section we would like to explain briefly what is meant by classical in classical mechanics, in reference to other modern branches of mechanics and while doing so, introduce a few related concepts and definitions.

A particle is ideally defined to be any point-like object or entity; however, it can have any finite extension provided its extension is irrelevant to the study of the motion of the object as a whole. For example, the motion of the earth around the sun can be studied assuming the whole earth to be a particle, while the motion of a billiard ball or a disc will require a knowledge of its shape and distribution of matter within and therefore cannot be regarded as a particle. Even an atom or a molecule may or may not be regarded as a particle; it all depends on the requirement whether its extension is relevant to the study of its motion or not. Classically, a particle is endowed with some mass and electric charge (if it is not electrically neutral), whereas an extended object is characterised by not only its total mass and charge, but also their distributions throughout the body, giving rise to concepts such as moment of inertia, electric dipole and multipole moments, etc. Classically, the spin of a body can be imagined only if it has got an extension and therefore the concepts of moment of inertia and spin are inseparable in classical mechanics. However, in quantum mechanics a particle can have mass, charge and also spin; that is why the spin of an elementary particle is said to be a purely quantum concept. This is one of the major differences between the concepts of particle in classical and quantum mechanics.

The concept of a classical particle endowed with mass and electric charge represents its ontological (existential) status. Next comes the concept of motion of the particle, which requires introduction of two more fundamental concepts, namely space and time. The concept of space is inherent in the idea of the extension of any object and also in the idea of separation between two particles. Essentially, the mere allowance for the discreteness of an entity in the form of more than one particle in the universe necessitates the introduction of the concept of space. Up to this point space and matter together give only a static organisation of matter in space. If this organisation of matter is not found to be static, that is, if a change in the total organisation is perceived, one can retain the same space as the common substratum for the description of the changes that occur continuously and these continuous changes in the organisation of matter constitute the motion of the constituent objects or entities. Time is the parameter that characterises the changes in (or, equivalently, the motion of) the organisation of matter in space. Space and time do not have any ontological status. They are merely concepts in the mind of a conscious observer. These concepts allow motion to be possible and entities to have both extensions and coexistensibility in plural forms. However, in classical mechanics there is hardly any place for mind and consciousness and therefore, the observer is most conveniently replaced by the idea of a frame of reference. But in quantum mechanics, the role of a conscious observer in the process of measurement has been one of the central issues right from its inception.

Now with respect to a given reference frame S_o, the so called impersonalised observer of classical mechanics, one postulates the existence of a *three dimensional Euclidean space* E_3, such that the position of any particle with respect to S_o can be represented by a point in E_3. The motion of a particle is defined to be the change of its position relative to S_o. In classical mechanics, motion is assumed to be continuous and hence each particle describes a continuous *orbit* or *trajectory* in E_3. Since time is to be a measure of motion, a physical clock that measures time has to measure the motion of some particle in it. An *instant* is defined to be the cursory position of this chosen particle of the physical clock, such as the tip of the 'second' hand of a clock, or the position of the sun's centre in the sky, or the state of an electrically charged particle in a piece of suitably-cut quartz crystal, etc. Now, by making a one-to-one correspondence between the continuous orbit of this particle of the clock and the orbit of any other given particle in the universe we can ascertain that at every instant, each particle in the universe has a unique position with respect to any given frame of reference. This continuous nature of space, time and the orbit or trajectory of any classical particle is often implied by the use of the phrase classical, as opposed to quantum which necessarily allows indeterminacy in position and time at the cost of continuity and sharpness of the orbit of so called quantum particles, the latter behaving like packets of waves diffused in space and time. Thus in classical mechanics every real object, be it a particle or an extended body which is rigid, elastic or fluid, has a *continuous* history in space and time.

So far we have defined space, time and motion in terms of geometry, but physics is also concerned with the quantitative description of nature. This means that one has to associate geometry with numbers. It was a German mathematician, Georg Cantor, who proved in 1873 that there is a one-to-one correspondence between the set of all real numbers and the set of all points in any finite or infinite line, surface area, 3-D or higher (up to countable infinite) dimensional volumes. The whole is then equal to a part of itself! For example, for every possible real number x that lies between 0 and ∞ the value of e^{-x} always lies between 0 and 1. Again, whatever numbers you choose between 0 and 1, you can multiply all of them by any arbitrarily chosen small number ϵ, so that the number of real numbers between 0 and ϵ is exactly the same as those between 0 and 1, which is also precisely the same as the number of real numbers between 0 and ∞. The same is true for the total number of points in any infinitesimally small but finite or infinitely large segment of a line or of an area or of a volume. This exact equivalence between geometry and real numbers has made the geometrical representation of algebraic equations possible, together with the freedom to arbitrarily choose the scale, that is, the length of the segment of any axis one chooses to represent the intervals between $0, 1, 2, \ldots,$ etc. Because of the above freedom, two persons never draw a graph identically even though the two graphs representing the same equations are mathematically equivalent. To a physicist, this freedom has, first of all, given an opportunity to express space, time, mass and charge in a quantitative fashion and second, an absolute freedom to choose the units of measurements. The International Bureau of Standards (BIH) in Paris has adopted some arbitrary definitions of the SI units. The four primary units are, M,K,S, and I, namely, to quantify matter (mass and charge or electric current) and motion (space and time). There are three other primary units, kelvin, mole and candela for measuring absolute temperature, number of atoms and luminous intensity of any radiating source, respectively. All other concepts in physics and their corresponding units are defined by prescribing implicit or explicit relations among the already defined ones. All laws of physics are merely some statements of these inter-relations among various concepts, each of which is quantifiable with some uniquely defined units. If any of the above seven primary units is redefined by the BIH, for the sake of consistency, all the related derived units will have to be accordingly redefined.

Once the units are defined, position, time, etc. can be exactly quantified. At any instant, the position of any particle in any n dimensional Euclidean space E_n with respect to any given reference frame is expressed by an ordered set of n independent real numbers $(x_1, x_2, \ldots, x_n)$, say, each being called a position coordinate. The very fact that we can draw at most three mutually perpendicular axes at any given point in our real world, and that the transverse electromagnetic (elastic) waves exist and can freely propagate in space (in the elastic medium), show that the dimensions of the space embedding classical and electromagnetic phenomena are to be three, or more precisely, at least three. Similarly, the time t at a given instant, as read by a clock, is expressed as a real number. Thus the equation of the orbit of any classical particle in E_3 is given by the explicit functions $x_1(t)$, $x_2(t)$ and $x_3(t)$. Now, what happens when we go to another frame which has got its own clock and meter stick, calibrated in the same units as those in the original frame ? We make the following two assumptions in classical mechanics while going from one frame of reference to another:

(i) All instantaneous readings of the clocks identically calibrated but located in different frames are absolutely identical.

(ii) The individual position coordinates of any given particle at any given instant may be different in different frames, but must satisfy the basic Euclidean condition, that is, the distance between any pair of particles in any given frame at a given instant is the same.

We know that these assumptions are violated in frames which have got bodies moving with extremely high velocities, comparable to that of light in vacuum (c = 299792.458 km/s, exact by definition). At such high speeds, the time differences between any two given instants are measured differently in different reference frames, and these deviating time differences are related to their Euclidean distance measurements by certain rules. These rules were prescribed by a new theory, the special theory of relativity, advanced by Albert Einstein in 1905. The measurements of space, time and mass thus become frame-dependent quantities in this new theory, and classical mechanics is replaced by relativistic mechanics. However, at speeds less than, say, 1000 km/s, the results obtained using the laws of classical mechanics differ from their relativistic counterparts at the fifth significant digit at the most, and hence are not significantly different. Usually, relativistic mechanics is treated separately, but we shall occasionally pick up some interesting problems or examples from relativistic mechanics as illustrations.

The most important point about the theory of relativity is the union of space and time forming a single continuum (Someone found it in the very name of Einstein, whose break up is suggested to be EIN+ST+EIN, 'ein' meaning 'one' in German and ST being the abbreviation for space and time !) In his general theory of relativity, Einstein has gone one step further and combined space-time and matter, one being able to influence the other. As a result, a local fluctuation in space-time can propagate as a gravitational wave, which is an entity as real as the electromagnetic waves. So in Einstein's hand, not only have space and time united to form a single continuum, but they have also been promoted to having an ontological status, which, in the premise of classical mechanics is enjoyed by matter alone and in electrodynamics by charged particles and their fields. Furthermore, the question of the physical reality of the above trinity of space, time and matter, as Einstein had perceived it, is now undergoing the acid tests of quantum mechanical experiments. It is doubtful whether quantum reality can be at all independent of any conscious observer, in which case quantum mechanics may not be all that mechanical ! In this respect, classical mechanics is absolutely mechanical. With this mechanical view of the world in mind, we shall proceed for the rest of the book.

I.4 A BRIEF HISTORY OF THE DEVELOPMENT OF MECHANICS UP TO NEWTON

The Greek philosopher-scientist Aristotle (384 – 322 BC) was the first to suggest in his book *Physics* a quantitative law of motion, which states that the velocity of any object (v) is proportional to the applied force (F) and inversely proportional to the resistance (R), that is,

$$v = k\frac{F}{R}$$

where k is a constant. Till the beginning of the fourteenth century, Aristotlian ideas prevailed throughout Europe, though not without criticisms — particularly, noting that some minimum force is normally needed in order to impart motion to any body that rests on some other body. One of the early medieval scholars, Avempace (1106 – 1138) gave an alternative law to replace Aristotle's, which states that

$$v = k(F - R)$$

according to which a minimum of force $F = R$ is required to initiate motion. It is now known that the same law was proposed by Johannes Philoponus at the end of the sixth century AD.

From AD 1300 onwards, two medieval schools, one centred around Merton college, Oxford, and the other centred in Paris, began to contribute substantially to the development of mechanics. Richard Swinehead was the first to define *uniform local motion* to be 'one in which in every equal part of the time an equal distance is described'. William Heytesbury correctly conceived the idea of acceleration: 'any motion whatsoever is uniformly accelerated if in each of any equal parts of time, it acquires an equal increment of velocity'. He was also the first to define instantaneous velocity. By 1350 the Mertonian school arrived at the correct mean speed theorem, which simply states that the mean speed over any interval of time for a uniformly accelerated motion starting from rest is exactly the half of the final speed. The proof of this theorem readily came from Nicole de Oresme (1325 – 1382) of the Parisian school.

Meanwhile Thomas Bradwardine (1290 – 1349) in his *Tractatus de Proportionibus* gave in 1328 another law of motion, which reads as *The proportions of the proportions of motive to resistive powers is equal to the proportion of their resistive speeds of motion, and conversely.* In effect this means

$$v = k\log\frac{F}{R}$$

It should however be remembered that the idea of logarithm was introduced by John Napier in 1614. Jean Buridan of the Parisian school introduced a term *impetus* (I) to represent the impressed force of moving bodies, which was defined as the product of velocity and the quantity of matter. He also explained the cause of free fall as the increase in the *impetus*. Subsequently, Marsilius of Inghen (1340 – 1396) distinguished between rectilinear and the circular *impetus*. William of Ockham (1300 – 1350) was the first to separate the problem of kinematics from that of dynamics. According to him, *kinematics* deals with the definition and measurement of motion, whereas *dynamics*, with the measurement of forces and their effects.

The next stage of major developments took place in the arena of celestial mechanics. The Polish astronomer Nicolaus Copernicus (1473 – 1531) put forward the heliocentric theory of the solar system, replacing the astronomer Claudius Ptolemy's geocentric one (150 AD). Not long after Copernicus' death, a Danish nobleman Tycho de Brahe (1546 – 1601) began a series of observations on Mars and the other planets but died before he could properly analyse the data. It was one of his young assistants, Johannes Kepler (1571 – 1630) who, having got access to these data could finally formulate his three celebrated laws of planetary motion (the first two were published in 1609 and the third in 1618) which can be stated as follows.

(i) The planets orbit the sun in ellipses with the sun at one focus

(ii) The line joining the sun and the planet sweeps equal areas in equal intervals of time; and

(iii) The squares of the orbital periods of the planets are directly proportional to the cubes of the mean distances of the planets from the sun.

While Kepler was busy in formulating these laws, Galileo Galilei (1564 – 1642), the famous Italian scientist, made a telescope in 1610. By observing Jupiter's moons and the phases of Venus, he confirmed the Copernican heliocentric theory of the solar system. He also performed the famous 'Tower of Pisa' experiment during 1589 – 1632, but in the beginning supported Aristotle's view namely the downward movement of any body endowed with weight is quicker in inverse proportion to its size. In doing so he was in fact giving due respect to his raw observational results, *viz.*, due to air resistance, one actually finds that heavy and dense bodies descend faster than the bulky and lighter ones. It was around 1638 that he finally formulated the *three laws of falling bodies* which go by his name, basically asserting that if one completely removes the resistance of air, all materials would descend with equal acceleration. In 1632 he published the principle of conservation of motion on any frictionless horizontal plane. This law is often referred to as the Galilean law of inertia. Galileo was also the first to note the isochronous motion of simple pendula, that is the period of a simple pendulum is independent of its amplitude of oscillation. He is regarded as the true father of physical science since he totally broke the age old tradition of accepting the supremacy of pedagogical arguments. He put every scientific assertion to direct experimental or observational test as a necessary condition for its viability as a scientific statement. Following this spirit of scientific investigation, Europe soon became the birthplace of practically all the scientific and technological developments that were to follow. The Italian Academy of Sciences was established in 1607, the Royal Society of London in 1660 and the French Academy of Sciences in 1666.

The French philosopher René Descartes (1596 – 1650) strongly opposed any possibility of action at a distance. Every action, according to him, has to be transmitted necessarily through the physical contact of material bodies. However, he is chiefly remembered for his idea of Cartesian coordinates. The Dutch mathematician Willebrord Snell (1591 – 1626) gave the laws of refraction of light (1621) and also determined the radius of the earth quite accurately (1625). The Italian physicist Evangelista Torricelli (1608 – 1647) developed parabolic ballistics (1640) as a consequence of Galileo's laws of falling bodies. He also invented the mercury barometer (1643). Another French amateur mathematician Pierre de Fermat (1601 – 1665) gave the principle of least time for the propagation of light rays in any medium (1657), based on Snell's law of refraction. Blaise Pascal (1623 – 1662), a French mathematician, developed the theory of hydrostatics in 1637. Sir Christopher Wren (1632 – 1723), the famous English architect and mathematician, formulated some laws of collision of elastic bodies, introduced parabolic mirrors in telescopes (1669), and fixed the standard length of oscillation of a pendulum clock (1671). The Dutch physicist Christiaan Huygens (1629 – 1695) gave the correct laws of colliding bodies (1656) and the kinematics of circular and the isochronal motion along a cycloidal track (1673) and, of course, his theory of light propagation in the form of undulatory waves (1678). The English physicist Robert Hooke (1635 – 1703), proposed the so-called Hooke's law of elasticity (1675) and correctly guessed the inverse square law of force between the sun and the planets (1679). The Italian physicist Giovanni Borelli (1608 – 1679) talked about the *centrifugal forces* acting on bodies moving in circular orbits. Most of these people were in fact aware of Kepler's laws of planetary motion and wanted to understand the dynamics behind them. However, they were so much influenced by the Cartesian antithesis of any kind of action-at-a-distance, that they found it difficult to imagine any force operative between the sun and the planets across the cosmic void.

Sir Isaac Newton (1642 – 1727), the greatest scientific genius of all time, was the first to successfully explain not only Kepler's laws of motion but also myriads of other phenomena and problems of that time. He was one of the co-inventors of the calculus. He formulated the laws of motion, the law of gravitation, studied the motion of particles — both in free space and in presence of resistive media, just to name a few topics which now form the basis of classical mechanics. The book he wrote, in three volumes, The *Philosophiae Naturalis Principia Mathematica* (in short, *Principia*) was published by the Royal Society of London on July 5, 1687, on the insistence and kind patronage of Sir Edmond Halley, and is said to be a mark of the most original creativity ever produced by a single person in the history of mankind.

I.5 NEWTON'S LAWS OF MOTION

According to Newton, any change in the motion of an object, described with respect to a given frame of reference, is the result of the mutual interaction between the object and its environment. The central problem of mechanics is to understand and quantify the connection between these interactions and the resulting motion. Regarding these interactions as the cause, and the motion as the effect, one is to quantify the relation between cause and effect. It is natural to expect that the interactions causing the motion can be quantified in terms of the measurable physical properties of the body and its environment, e.g., mass, electric charge, magnetic dipole moment, etc.

Newton gave a programme to attack this problem which comprises two steps:

(i) A vector quantity called *force* ($\boldsymbol{F}$) is regarded as the cause of change in the state of motion of a body, or in other words, the vehicle of interaction between the moving object and its environment. The force acting on the body can cause acceleration ($\boldsymbol{a}$) which is a vector quantity, like the force. (Vectors are briefly dealt with in appendix A2.)

(ii) The forces acting on the body are calculated on the basis of the properties of the body and its environment, requiring determination of the appropriate force laws.

Newton's formulation of step (i) above forms the basis of his laws of motion. These laws of motion are valid in a class of reference frames called *inertial frames*. In fact, we can turn around and define the inertial frames to be those frames of reference in which Newton's laws of motion are valid. Newton's laws can be stated as follows:

(i) Law of Inertia

In an inertial frame, every free particle (that is, a particle not acted upon by a net external force) has a constant velocity.

The original version of this law written in Latin was slightly different. When translated into English, it reads: 'every body free of impressed forces either preserves a state of rest or continues in uniform rectilinear motion *ad infinitum*.'

In an inertial system a free particle undergoes equal displacements in equal intervals of time. This fact defines a time scale or a clock for inertial frames called inertial time scale.

Motion of free particles in inertial frames will be in straight lines. For, if this motion were on a curve with non-vanishing curvature, the velocity of this free particle, which is a vector tangent to the path of the particle, would change with time, contradicting the first law. Thus, a path traced by a free particle in an inertial frame defines a straight line in that frame.

Since a free particle covers an equal measure of space in equal measure of time, *ad infinitum*, it implies that along the straight line of the path, space is uniform or homogeneous, and so also time. Again, since the direction of the straight line path could have been any, it also implies that space is isotropic. So an inertial frame is also interpreted to stand for the homogeneity and isotropy of space, and *homogeneity of time*.

Since free particles travel in straight lines, an ideal inertial frame would be the one that has all the axes as straight lines. Only the oblique and rectangular Cartesian coordinate systems satisfy this requirement. Other coordinate systems, for example, a spherical polar coordinate system has as coordinates the polar angle θ and the azimuthal angle ϕ, which cannot change without violating the rectilinear property of inertial motion.

We see that the first law requires the notion of a free particle, which depends on the definition of force given by the second law.

(ii) Law of Causality

If the total force exerted on a particle by other objects at any specified time is represented by a vector $\boldsymbol{F}$, then

$$\boldsymbol{F} = m\boldsymbol{a} = d\boldsymbol{p}/dt \tag{I.1}$$

where $\boldsymbol{a} = d\boldsymbol{v}/dt$ is the acceleration of the particle at the given instant, m is the mass of the particle, $\boldsymbol{v}$ is the velocity of the particle at that instant and $\boldsymbol{p} = m\boldsymbol{v}$ is the linear momentum. The vector quantity $\boldsymbol{F}$ is called force and Eq. (I.1) above, is taken to be its definition. This law is a complete law.

Newton's original version of the second law also reads somewhat differently: 'The change of motion Δv is proportional to the motive force ΔI impressed, and is made in the direction of the right line in which that force is impressed.' Thus if we consider all these changes to take place in time Δt, and take the constant of proportionality to be $1/m$, in the limit of $\Delta t \rightarrow 0$, we get the usual form. It should be noted that vector notations were formally introduced in physics by Willard Gibbs in 1901; Newton and many others did not use vector quantities as such. Every time, they wrote out all the Cartesian or polar components explicitly, depending on the coordinate system that they were using.

Through this law, the study of the motions of bodies became part of a new branch of science called dynamics. By itself it is not a verifiable law, to start with. For the first time it defined the notion of force through a directly measurable quantity called acceleration and another quantity called mass. Measurement of mass, or the quantity of matter, in a given body would have been extremely difficult, had we lived on a planet where uniformity of gravity could not be assumed as an approximation. Again, since Newton had to develop the science of mechanics from almost nothing other than his three laws of motion, he could not initially check the validity of his laws of motion. He derived the first universal law of force, that is, the inverse distance-square law of the gravitational force, from a combination of Kepler's laws of planetary motion and his own three laws of motion. Having obtained a law of force, he could then have many situations where he would know the values of mass, acceleration and force, independent of his second law of motion, and therefore test its validity. Actually he had been working on these ideas since 1665 or so, but published with great confidence only after 22 years, when he became sure that these were the laws of nature.

The second law is a prescription for formulating the dynamical equations of motion in inertial frames. The first law has already defined what inertial frames are. They are rectangular Cartesian frames in which a free particle either stays at rest or continues with uniform rectilinear motion *ad infinitum*.

It is now important to note that the force of gravitation is all pervading. It is called a body force, since this force acts at each point of the body. It is also called external or applied force for obvious reasons. However, in real life situations we very often come across various kinds of contact or surface forces, forces produced due to collision, or hindrance to natural motion. Since Newton's second law demands the *a priori* knowledge of the total force that a body experiences, this total force must also include all the forces of reactions that it experiences; in the third law, Newton prescribes the general nature of the forces of reaction in relation to the forces of action.

(iii) Law of Reciprocity

To the force exerted by every object on a particle, there corresponds an equal and opposite force exerted by the particle on that object.

For two interacting particles, if $\boldsymbol{F}_{21}$ is the force exerted by the first particle on the second, and $\boldsymbol{F}_{12}$ is the force exerted by the second particle on the first, we must have

$$\boldsymbol{F}_{12} = -\boldsymbol{F}_{21}$$

Using the second law, we have, then

$$\frac{d}{dt}(\boldsymbol{p}_1 + \boldsymbol{p}_2) = \boldsymbol{0}$$

where $\boldsymbol{p}_1$ and $\boldsymbol{p}_2$ are the linear momenta of the two particles 1 and 2 respectively. This means that the total linear momentum $\boldsymbol{p}_1 + \boldsymbol{p}_2$ is a constant of motion. In other words, the total linear momentum of any isolated pair of mutually interacting particles, expressed as a vector sum of quantities $\boldsymbol{p}_1$ and $\boldsymbol{p}_2$, is conserved.

If all the possible actions and reactions are found to be totally confined within a system, such a system is, by definition, called a *closed* system. By the third law, such a system must conserve the total linear momentum. Again, a closed system is not acted upon by any externally applied forces. Hence, by the first law, a closed system as a whole must act as an inertial frame. Thus, we can have even a time bomb at rest as a closed system which, on explosion, can disintegrate apart, but it would happen in such a way that its centre of mass still continues to remain stationary and the system as a whole can still be regarded as a closed system. However in the process we have released some potent chemical energy in the form of systemic motions of the splinters.

The third law says that if there exists some action on some particle, then the rest of the universe, or the remaining part of the closed system under consideration must experience the reaction. So if you raise your hand, the rest of the universe is going to share its reaction. Therefore all possible motions in the universe are constantly getting modified due to some or other ongoing actions and reactions that take place here and there. But then how to begin or trigger an action? By nature a trigger is always a kind of *spontaneous action*, be it in the form of spontaneous decay of particle, or a nuclear or chemical reaction, always releasing some potent energy in the form of kinetic energy. Even today, trigger or spontaneous actions are still considered to be mysterious processes of nature. However, if this is the only ultimate process of generating motion, then the third law is the most fundamental law of nature.

(iv) Law of Superposition

The total force $\boldsymbol{F}$ due to several objects acting simultaneously on a particle is equal to the vector sum of the forces $\boldsymbol{F}_k$, due to each object acting independently, that is,

$$\boldsymbol{F} = \sum_k \boldsymbol{F}_k \tag{I.2}$$

This is a 'divide and conquer' rule for solving mechanical problems involving complex forces. There is no unique way of dividing the total $\boldsymbol{F}$ into a number of components. In other words, for a given $\boldsymbol{F}$ there are, in general, infinity of solutions of Eq. (I.2), though, of course, all $\boldsymbol{F}_k$'s cannot be mutually orthogonal. Newton did not write this law as a separate one, but it is independent of the first three laws, and was first explicitly mentioned by Daniel Bernoulli in 1738.

During the past three hundred years, Newton's laws of motion have been critically examined over and again, particularly to see whether all the three laws are independent or not. The most widely argued point is that the first law is a special case of the second law, because as we put $\boldsymbol{F} = 0$ in Eq. (I.1), it implies that the acceleration $\boldsymbol{a}$ is zero and therefore guarantees rectilinear motion with constant velocity. Why then had Newton put it as a separate law of nature?

At the time of Newton, there was perhaps an intellectual tradition following the divine idea of the Trinity in the theological framework of Christianity, that any law must have three aspects or three components for its perfection and completeness. There were three laws of the falling bodies, due to Galileo, three laws of Kepler, for the motion of planets, three laws of motion and three components of the law of universal gravitation, due to Newton, three laws of motion of the moon, due to Cassini, and so on. People were so obsessed with the number three, a book had to have three volumes; for example, we have three volumes of *Principia*, three volumes of the work of Copernicus, and so on. Nevertheless, Newton would have had sufficient arguments in favour of the first law as a law independent of the other two.

Basically, there exist four different pictures or viewpoints forwarded by different people at different times:

(a) *Gustav Kirchhoff's picture (1876):* The second law is simply a definition of force. The first law is a special case of the second law and therefore is not an independent law. The whole of Newtonian mechanics is regarded as an axiomatic formulation from the definition of force as given by the second law alone.

(b) *Isaac Newton's picture (1687):* Newton does not consider the first law derivable from the second law. The first law gives the phenomenological definition of an inertial frame. A reference frame, attached to a free particle, whose phenomenological behaviour would be to maintain a constant velocity vector for all time, is called an inertial frame. However, inside a freely falling lift, which is acted upon by an external force, all objects seem to behave as free particles. But Newton would then argue, since these particles do not continue their uniform rectilinear motion for ever, the freely falling lift can not be regarded as an inertial frame. The second law represents the behaviour of the real world with respect to an 'inertial frame'. If the observed acceleration is not explained in terms of all the known real forces, or in other words the second law is found to be not valid, Newton would declare that the frame with respect to which accelerations are measured is noninertial. And he would not agree that his laws of motion are not universal. So he suggests that one should, along with the real forces, include some fictitious forces such as the centrifugal forces or the Coriolis forces and so on, depending upon the particular type of the noninertial behaviour, and use the second law for the noninertial frames also. The equations of motion (see below) can be solved and their detailed predictions can be tested by doing experiments. So the second law is a law of nature.

So far as the limiting behaviour of the first law to the second is concerned, the limit is, in this case, asymptotic in nature. The asymptotic limits are something that a correct theory must satisfy, but the limits themselves must be provided from some other independent sources. For example, without the prior knowledge of Newtonian physics, Einstein's field theory would not have anything to test under asymptotic limits. Once you have these limits properly set, you have the theory to proceed with. In the case of Newton's laws the asymptotic limit of the second law is asserted by the statement of the first law. Once that is justified the first law reduces to the definition of inertial frames. In fact, according to Newton, the validity of all the three laws put together consistently defines the total concept of the inertial frames.

(c) *Bishop Berkeley (1710) and Ernst Mach's (1883) picture:* Here the assertion is that the second law is a law of nature and that the first law is a special case of the second law. They however make an additional postulate that the inertial frames are fixed or moving with uniform velocity with respect to the distant stars and galaxies in the universe. Without such a distant background reference in the sky, they argue that no one can have an idea of an inertial frame, let alone the idea of velocity and acceleration of a lone particle in the universe. If there is only one particle in the universe, the applied force is of course zero, acceleration is, strictly speaking, indeterminate, in which case the validity of the second law would demand that the mass of the lone particle in an otherwise empty universe be zero. So they insist that the measurement of true or inertial acceleration is possible only if there is a significant number of distant and heavy objects in the background.

(d) *Albert Einstein's picture (1907):* Newton's laws of motion are valid in co-ordinate frames fixed or moving with constant velocity relative to a freely falling observer. The phenomenon of weightlessness allows one, in principle, to identify such a reference frame. So he argues that all the freely falling observers can serve as 'inertial' frames. In fact, the sun is falling freely in space under the action of the gravity of the Milky Way for ever — even the galaxies have been falling freely in the field of every other body in the universe since the big bang. In his general theory of relativity, the classical idea of gravitation as a force has been dispensed with. Thus, in Einstein's view, the gravitational force joins the centrifugal and Coriolis force in the category of fictitious forces.

All these four viewpoints are distinctly different but are all equally feasible. One has to stick to any one of the viewpoints and we choose Newton's viewpoint for writing the rest of the book.

In general, the force on a particle may vary as it moves in space, that is, if the particle's position is described by the vector function $\boldsymbol{r}(t)$ of time and its velocity by another vector function $\boldsymbol{v}(t)$ of time, then the force on the particle in its successive positions is a (given) vector function $\boldsymbol{F}(\boldsymbol{r}(t), \boldsymbol{v}(t), t)$. Assuming that the first and second order time derivatives of $\boldsymbol{r}(t)$ exist, we have, for acceleration,

$$\boldsymbol{a}(t) = \ddot{\boldsymbol{r}}(t) \tag{I.3}$$

where, the number of overhead dots denotes the order of total differentiation with respect to time t. Substituting in Eq. (I.1), we get an ordinary second order differential equation in $\boldsymbol{r}(t)$:

$$m\ddot{\boldsymbol{r}}(t) = \boldsymbol{F}(\boldsymbol{r}(t), \boldsymbol{v}(t), t) \tag{I.4}$$

If $\boldsymbol{r}$ is a vector in 3-D space, Eq. (I.4) stands for three equations, one in each of its rectangular Cartesian components x, y and z. Each of these requires the specification of two constants (initial conditions) for a complete solution. Thus, if the position and velocity of the particle at any instant t (say $t = 0$) is known, its subsequent motion can be completely described, provided we can solve Eq. (I.4). Furthermore, if $\boldsymbol{F}$ does not depend explicitly on t, that is, $\boldsymbol{F} = \boldsymbol{F}(\boldsymbol{r}(t), \boldsymbol{v}(t))$, then the vector Eq. (I.4) is necessarily invariant under the change of the sign of t so that Eq. (I.4) completely determines the motion of the particle in the past ($t < 0$). Furthermore, if the sign of time can be actually reversed, the particle will retrace the same trajectory (as it has traced for the positive direction of time) in the opposite direction. Eq. (I.4) or any of their equivalents are called Newton's equations of motion.

I.5.1 Some Examples of Force Laws and the Corresponding Motions

From the mechanical standpoint, forces can be divided into two broad classes : (a) *body forces* which act on each point on the body (inside as well as on the surface) such as gravitation, and (b) *surface* or *contact forces* acting at the surface only, for example, pressure, tension, elastic forces at the contact, all reactions due to mutual contact between two bodies. We shall give here a few specific examples of force laws:

(i) Hooke's Law (1675)

Within a certain specified domain of space, the force $\boldsymbol{F}$ acting on a particle is attractive in nature and is linearly proportional to the displacement ($\boldsymbol{r}$) from the position of equilibrium. That is,

$$\boldsymbol{F} = -k\boldsymbol{r}$$

where k is the constant of proportionality, called Hooke's constant, and $\boldsymbol{r}$ is measured from the position of equilibrium. Following Newton's programme, the equation of motion of any particle under the above force law is,

$$m\ddot{\boldsymbol{r}} = -k\boldsymbol{r} \tag{I.5}$$

the general solution being

$$\boldsymbol{r} = \boldsymbol{a}\cos(\sqrt{k/m}\, t) + \boldsymbol{b}\sin(\sqrt{k/m}\, t) \tag{I.6}$$

where $\boldsymbol{a}$ and $\boldsymbol{b}$ are the constants of integration, which can be related to the initial position $\boldsymbol{r}_o$ and initial velocity $\boldsymbol{v}_o$ by

$$\boldsymbol{r}_o = \boldsymbol{a} \quad \text{and} \quad \boldsymbol{v}_o = \sqrt{k/m}\,\boldsymbol{b} \tag{I.7}$$

The motion is, in general, elliptical with the centre of the ellipse at the position of equilibrium.

(ii) Newton's Law of Gravitation (1687)

All particles in the universe attract all other particles along the line joining the two mass centres with a force directly proportional to the product of their masses (m_1, m_2 say) and inversely proportional to the square of the distance between them, that is,

$$\boldsymbol{F}_{12} = -\frac{Gm_1m_2}{|\boldsymbol{r}_{12}|^3}\boldsymbol{r}_{12} = -\boldsymbol{F}_{21} \tag{I.8}$$

where $\boldsymbol{r}_{12} = \boldsymbol{r}_1 - \boldsymbol{r}_2$, $\boldsymbol{F}_{12}$ is the force on particle number 1 (having mass m_1) exerted by the particle number 2 (having mass m_2) and G is the universal constant of gravitation. The general motion under this law has been discussed in chapter 4. A similar inverse square law but with a provision for both attraction and repulsion holds good for any two static electric charges or two static magnetic poles, given by the French physicist Charles Coulomb (1784).

(iii) Lorentz's Law of Electromagnetic Force (1892)

Any charged particle having mass m and electric charge e moving under the action of an electric field $\boldsymbol{E}(\boldsymbol{r}, t)$ and a magnetic field of induction $\boldsymbol{B}(\boldsymbol{r}, t)$ experiences a force $\boldsymbol{F}$ given by

$$\boldsymbol{F} = e(\boldsymbol{E} + \boldsymbol{v} \times \boldsymbol{B}) \tag{I.9}$$

This is essentially a two-component force, the first term representing the electric force and the second term the magnetic force. The latter acts perpendicular to the direction of the instantaneous motion of the particle. For constant $\boldsymbol{E}$ and $\boldsymbol{B}$, the equation of motion is

$$\ddot{\boldsymbol{r}} = (e/m)(\boldsymbol{E} + \boldsymbol{v} \times \boldsymbol{B})$$

whose exact solution has been given, for example, by F. R. Gantmakher (1960) as follows:

$$\begin{aligned}\boldsymbol{r}(t) = \boldsymbol{r}_o + \boldsymbol{v}_o t + \frac{1}{2}\boldsymbol{g}t^2 &+ \left(\frac{\cos\omega t - 1}{\omega^2}\right)(\boldsymbol{\omega} \times \boldsymbol{v}_o) \\ &+ \left(\frac{\cos\omega t - 1 + \omega^2 t^2/2}{\omega^4}\right)(\boldsymbol{\omega} \times (\boldsymbol{\omega} \times \boldsymbol{g})) \\ &- \left(\frac{\omega t - \sin\omega t}{\omega^3}\right)[\boldsymbol{\omega} \times \boldsymbol{g} - \boldsymbol{\omega} \times (\boldsymbol{\omega} \times \boldsymbol{v}_o)]\end{aligned} \tag{I.10}$$

where $\boldsymbol{r}_o$ and $\boldsymbol{v}_o$ are the initial position and velocity of the particle, $\boldsymbol{g} = e\boldsymbol{E}/m$ is a constant, $\boldsymbol{\omega} = (e/m)\boldsymbol{B}$ is the cyclotron frequency vector, which is again a constant. This path represents a spiralling orbit, the guiding centre of which describes a parabola due to the action of the constant $\boldsymbol{E}$ field.

(iv) Law of Constant Force (Torricelli's ballistics, 1640)

Near the surface of the earth, the gravitational force of the earth on a given particle is taken to be approximately constant, say $\boldsymbol{F} = m\boldsymbol{g}$, where $\boldsymbol{g}$ is a constant. The equation of motion is given by $\ddot{\boldsymbol{r}} = \boldsymbol{g} =$ constant, with a solution

$$\boldsymbol{r} = \boldsymbol{r}_o + \boldsymbol{v}_o t + \frac{1}{2}\boldsymbol{g}t^2$$

representing a parabolic trajectory, in general.

(v) Stokes' Law of Viscous Drag (1850)

The drag force acting on a homogeneous sphere moving inside a viscous fluid with very low velocities is given by $\boldsymbol{F} = -6\pi\eta R\boldsymbol{v}$, where η is the coefficient of viscosity of the fluid, R is the radius of the sphere, and $\boldsymbol{v}$ its velocity. This is a linear drag force, also applicable to the slow motion of dust particles and aerosols in air, or to the slow motion of electrons in a conductor. In the presence of uniform gravity $\boldsymbol{g}$, the equation of motion becomes

$$\ddot{\boldsymbol{r}} = -\lambda\dot{\boldsymbol{r}} + \boldsymbol{g} \tag{I.11}$$

where the drag part of the force is $-\lambda \boldsymbol{v}$, λ being a constant. The general solution is given by

$$\boldsymbol{r} = \left(\frac{1 - e^{-\lambda t}}{\lambda}\right)\boldsymbol{v}_o + \left(\frac{e^{-\lambda t} + \lambda t - 1}{\lambda^2}\right)\boldsymbol{g} \tag{I.12}$$

However, for moderate and high speed motion in air, a quadratic drag law is applicable, for which

$$\boldsymbol{F} = -C_D \rho A v \boldsymbol{v}$$

C_D ($\simeq 0.5$) being the drag coefficient, ρ the mass density of the fluid medium and A the cross-sectional area of the body. Finding an exact solution for a ballistic missile moving under constant gravity and a quadratic drag force is a formidable task.

In fact many kinds of drag forces are possible. The drag forces proportional to v, v^2, and $av + bv^2$ were considered by Newton himself. Later on, many others tried various other forms and quickly exhausted the list of all those for which the motion was analytically integrable.

(vi) Coulomb's Law of Friction (1779)

The maximum static force of friction $\boldsymbol{F}$, developed at the surface of contact between two bodies, due to a normal force of reaction $\boldsymbol{N}$, that can prevent any motion along the boundary of the two surfaces in contact, is given by

$$|\boldsymbol{F}| = \mu_s |\boldsymbol{N}|$$

where μ_s is a constant, called the coefficient of static friction between the two given surfaces. The force of friction acts in a direction opposite to that of the applied force. This law was originally proposed by G. Amontons in 1699.

If the two surfaces begin to slide, the same law applies, but the coefficient of sliding friction μ_k is slightly lower than μ_s. However, more experiments done recently, suggest a small departure from Coulomb's law, and a better empirical law, obeyed by a large variety of rough surfaces seems to follow the equation

$$F = K' N^{0.91}$$

where the constant K' depends on the nature of the two surfaces. When the forces are expressed in SI units, the value of K', is found to be 0.24 for glass sliding on wood, 0.35 for metal on wood or metal on metal, 0.49 for wood on mica, 0.58 for glass on glass, and so on. Rolling friction is also assumed to follow a law quite similar to Coulomb's law, the coefficient, generally, being smaller than that for sliding.

I.5.2 An Extension of Newton's Second Law to a System of Particles

Consider a system of N particles having masses $m_1, m_2, \ldots, m_N$, positions $\boldsymbol{r}_1(t), \ldots, \boldsymbol{r}_N(t)$ at any instant t and moving under forces $\boldsymbol{f}_1, \boldsymbol{f}_2, \cdots, \boldsymbol{f}_N$ externally applied on them, along with their mutual interaction forces $\boldsymbol{f}_{ij}$ (= the force on the ith particle produced by the jth particle). Newton's programme can now be slightly modified so that the ensemble of these N particles may dynamically behave as an aggregate of total mass

$$M = \sum_{i=1}^{N} m_i$$

One defines the centre of mass of such a system to be located at $\boldsymbol{R}$, through the relation

$$M\boldsymbol{R} = \sum_{i=1}^{N} m_i \boldsymbol{r}_i$$

The velocity $\boldsymbol{V}$ of the centre of mass is similarly defined through

$$M\boldsymbol{V} = \sum_{i=1}^{N} m_i \dot{\boldsymbol{r}}_i = M\dot{\boldsymbol{R}}$$

Now it is very simple to see that

$$M\ddot{\boldsymbol{R}} = \sum_{i=1}^{N} m_i \ddot{\boldsymbol{r}}_i = \sum_{i=1}^{N} \boldsymbol{f}_i + \sum_{i=1}^{N} \sum_{\substack{j=1 \\ j \neq i}}^{N} \boldsymbol{f}_{ij} = \boldsymbol{F} \tag{I.13}$$

where $\boldsymbol{F}$ is the total force, which is the vector sum of all the forces that are experienced by the individual particles. However, by the third law, the ***internal forces*** satisfy $\boldsymbol{f}_{ij} = -\boldsymbol{f}_{ji}$ so that all $\boldsymbol{f}_{ij}$ cancel pairwise. Thus, $\boldsymbol{F}$ is reduced to merely the vector sum of all the external forces, for which the knowledge of only the external forces suffices. Therefore, with the quantities M, $\boldsymbol{R}$, $\boldsymbol{V}$ and $\boldsymbol{F}$ defined as above, the dynamical behaviour of the aggregate can be represented by a single vector equation

$$M\ddot{\boldsymbol{R}} = \boldsymbol{F}$$

replacing N vector equations given by

$$m_i \ddot{\boldsymbol{r}}_i = \boldsymbol{f}_i + \sum_{j \neq i} \boldsymbol{f}_{ij} \quad (i \text{ not summed}, j \text{ summed})$$

Obviously it is easier to solve one (vector) differential equation than N such equations, but of course, at the cost of the details of the motion of individual particles. This is an important result. We can successfully talk about the motion of a body as a whole without requiring any knowledge of the internal forces. So the earth or a ball or a piece of stone or a molecule can be treated as particle in its full right guaranteed by the Eq. (I.13) whenever structural details are not required.

Now in the absence of any external force $\boldsymbol{F}$, $\boldsymbol{V}$ becomes a constant of motion and

$$\boldsymbol{R} = \boldsymbol{R}_o + \boldsymbol{V}t$$

that is, the centre of mass moves with a constant velocity $\boldsymbol{V}$.

One further defines the moment of momentum $\boldsymbol{L}$ of the system about the origin (of any given inertial frame) by,

$$L = \sum_{i=1}^{N} m_i \boldsymbol{r}_i \times \boldsymbol{v}_i \tag{I.14}$$

and the torque $\boldsymbol{\Gamma}$ by the *total moment of the force* about the origin, given by

$$\boldsymbol{\Gamma} = \sum_{i=1}^{N} \boldsymbol{r}_i \times (\boldsymbol{f}_i + \sum_{j \neq i}^{N} \boldsymbol{f}_{ij}) = \sum_{i=1}^{N} \boldsymbol{r}_i \times \boldsymbol{f}_i + \sum_{i=1}^{N} \sum_{j>i}^{N} (\boldsymbol{r}_i - \boldsymbol{r}_j) \times \boldsymbol{f}_{ij} \tag{I.15}$$

It is now easy to see that

$$\boldsymbol{\Gamma} = \sum_{i=1}^{N} m_i \boldsymbol{r}_i \times \ddot{\boldsymbol{r}}_i = \frac{d}{dt}(\sum_{i=1}^{N} m_i \boldsymbol{r}_i \times \boldsymbol{v}_i) = \frac{d\boldsymbol{L}}{dt} \tag{I.16}$$

This is called the torque-angular momentum relationship for a system of particles.

Equation (I.16) is not an independent law of motion as it is derived from Newton's laws of motion. Like Eq. (I.13), the validity of Eq. (I.16) is also independent of the internal forces, even though there is no guarantee that internal forces of non-central in character would not have a non-zero contribution to the measured torque given by Eq. (I.15). Thus, the basis of profound claims such as the connections of homogeneity and isotropy of space to the conservations of linear and angular momenta of closed systems (namely, the value of V being independent of the choice of the origin, and the value of $\boldsymbol{L}$ being independent of rotation of the combined set of vectors $\boldsymbol{R}$ and $\boldsymbol{P}$ in their plane, an inherent property of the vector product, by its definition) should be taken with caution (see p. 80). In the latter case, because of the explicit dependence on $\boldsymbol{R}$, the tanslational symmetry is lost.

I.5.3 Work, Power, and Kinetic and Potential Energies

If the point of application of force $\boldsymbol{F}$ which is in general a function of $\boldsymbol{r}$, $\boldsymbol{v}$ and t, that is , $\boldsymbol{F} = \boldsymbol{F}(\boldsymbol{r}, \boldsymbol{v}, t)$, is displaced by an infinitesimal amount $d\boldsymbol{r}$, an infinitesimal amount of work dW done by the force is defined by the scalar product

$$dW = \boldsymbol{F} \cdot d\boldsymbol{r} \tag{I.17}$$

For any finite displacement between $\boldsymbol{r} = \boldsymbol{r}_1$ to say $\boldsymbol{r} = \boldsymbol{r}_2$, a finite amount of work is done and is given by integrating Eq. (I.17) over the given path connecting $\boldsymbol{r}_1$ and $\boldsymbol{r}_2$ as its end points. Unless $\boldsymbol{F}$ is uniform over the path, $W = \boldsymbol{F} \cdot \boldsymbol{r}$ is as incorrect as $\boldsymbol{r} = \boldsymbol{v}t$, or, $\boldsymbol{v} = \boldsymbol{a}t$. (But $\boldsymbol{F}$ can be assumed to be uniform only over an infinitesimal displacement $d\boldsymbol{r}$. Had we strictly defined $W = \boldsymbol{F} \cdot \boldsymbol{r}$, it would have meant $dW = \boldsymbol{F} \cdot d\boldsymbol{r} + d\boldsymbol{F} \cdot \boldsymbol{r}$, which is non-sense. Similarly, the mass element must be defined as $dm = \rho\, dr^3$.)

The power P attained at any instant by the agency that produces the above force $\boldsymbol{F}$, is defined by

$$P = \frac{dW}{dt} = \boldsymbol{F} \cdot \boldsymbol{v} \tag{I.18}$$

Applying Newton's second law and assuming a constant mass,

$$P = m\frac{d\boldsymbol{v}}{dt}\cdot\boldsymbol{v} = \frac{d}{dt}(\frac{1}{2}m\boldsymbol{v}\cdot\boldsymbol{v}) = \frac{dT}{dt} \tag{I.19}$$

through which the kinetic energy is defined as

$$T = \frac{1}{2}mv^2 \tag{I.20}$$

where m is the mass of the particle on which the force $\boldsymbol{F}$ is applied. The quantity mv^2 used to be called *vis viva* by Leibniz (1695). Later on someone coined the term 'kinetic energy'. The definition given by Eq. (I.20) is however taken to be true irrespective of the fact whether m is a constant or not.

For any arbitrary force function $\boldsymbol{F} = \boldsymbol{F}(\boldsymbol{r},\boldsymbol{v},t)$, dW in Eq. (I.17) cannot be a perfect differential, and W_{12} is not only the function of the end points $\boldsymbol{r}_1$, $\boldsymbol{r}_2$ but also of the path chosen to connect $\boldsymbol{r}_1$ and $\boldsymbol{r}_2$. Now suppose, $\boldsymbol{F}$ is independent of $\boldsymbol{v}$, then there can exist a potential energy function $V(\boldsymbol{r},t)$ such that,

$$\boldsymbol{F}(\boldsymbol{r},t) = -\nabla V(\boldsymbol{r},t) \tag{I.21}$$

in which case, Eq. (I.17) becomes

$$dW = -\nabla V(\boldsymbol{r},t)\cdot d\boldsymbol{r} = -\left(\frac{dV}{dt} - \frac{\partial V}{\partial t}\right)dt = -dV(\boldsymbol{r},t) + \frac{\partial V}{\partial t}dt \tag{I.22}$$

So, the condition for $\boldsymbol{F}\cdot d\boldsymbol{r}$ to become a perfect differential is that $\boldsymbol{F}$ should be independent of both $\boldsymbol{v}$ and t and the corresponding potential energy function given by $V(\boldsymbol{r})$ is called a *conservative potential energy function.* From Eqs (I.19) and (I.22) with $\partial V/\partial t = 0$, one finds,

$$\frac{d}{dt}(T + V) = 0 \tag{I.23}$$

or, in other words, the sum of the kinetic energy and the conservative potential energy, called by definition the *total energy of the system*,

$$E = T + V \tag{I.24}$$

is a constant of motion. Galileo had noticed that the speed of a particle on an inclined plane starting from rest depends only on the vertical height through which it has descended. The principle of the conservation of total energy has, since then, been gradually develope-d through the works of Huygens, Newton, Bernoulli(s) and Lagrange. Its link with the symmetry with respect to time translation is apparent from the requirement of $\partial V/\partial t = 0$.

The zero of the potential energy function can, however, be chosen arbitrarily. If the zero of any conservative potential energy is chosen to be at $\boldsymbol{r} = \boldsymbol{r}_o$, then

$$V(\boldsymbol{r}) = -\int_{\boldsymbol{r}_o}^{\boldsymbol{r}} \boldsymbol{F}(\boldsymbol{r})\cdot d\boldsymbol{r} \tag{I.25}$$

For the inverse square law of gravitational fields, the tip of $\boldsymbol{r}_o$ is usually chosen to be at ∞, but for Hooke's type of the force field, at the origin. The idea of the potential function was first introduced by Lagrange in 1773 and the term 'potential' is due to Green (1828).

I.5.4 Equations of Motions for Variable Mass

Since Newton's second law is given by

$$\frac{d\boldsymbol{p}}{dt} = \boldsymbol{F}_{\text{ext}}$$

where $\boldsymbol{p} = m\boldsymbol{v}$; these two can be combined to give

$$m\frac{d\boldsymbol{v}}{dt} + \boldsymbol{v}\frac{dm}{dt} = \boldsymbol{F}_{\text{ext}} \tag{I.26}$$

If the mass of the system under consideration is changing with time $dm/dt \neq 0$, the Eq. (I.26) is the equation of motion of such a system.

However, for the motion of a rocket of mass $m(t)$, that burns fuel and ejects the burnt gas with relative velocity $\boldsymbol{u}$ and at a rate $-\ dm/dt$, the equation of the motion of the rocket is simply given by

$$m\frac{d\boldsymbol{v}}{dt} - \boldsymbol{u}\frac{dm}{dt} = \boldsymbol{F}_{\text{ext}} \tag{I.27}$$

I.6 LIMITATIONS OF NEWTON'S PROGRAMME

The direct application of Newton's laws in solving problems of mechanics has many limitations.

1. Newton's laws are valid only in inertial frames, which are by definition rectangular Cartesian-like. Therefore, the equations of motion have to be set up and solved in rectangular Cartesian-like coordinates. The equations of motion would then look like $m\ddot{x}_i = F_i$, $i = 1, 2, 3$; where F_i is the ith component of the external force applied on a particle of mass m. Now suppose we want to write down the equations of motion in spherical polar coordinates, which have got the polar axis as the third axis of the Cartesian system. We may intuitively imagine that the radial coordinate r measuring distance in the radial direction might be as good as any one of the Cartesian axes, and be tempted to write the equation of motion in the radial coordinate as $m\ddot{r} = F_r$, where F_r is the component of the external force in the radial direction. But obviously this equation cannot be right; for if it was, a planet could never, in principle, revolve around the sun in a circular orbit, in which case $F_r \neq 0$ will imply $\ddot{r} \neq 0$, $\dot{r} \neq 0$ and hence the value of r must change with time. So Newton's second law is not valid even for the r coordinate of a spherical polar coordinate system. If we now force it to be valid, we have no other choice than to invent and add an imaginary force term to the real external force term in order to totally nullify the latter, thus justifying a constant value of r. Such imaginary forces, which have to be incorporated because of the noninertial nature of the coordinate frames used, are called pseudoforces or inertial forces.

However noninertial frames cannot be avoided in many of the most important applications of mechanics. For example, a reference frame attached to the earth rotates with it around its axis of rotation and is hence noninertial. The motion of any object with respect to the earth is, strictly speaking, a motion in a noninertial frame. This situation is handled by establishing a connection between the noninertial and any one inertial frame. As a result, some inertial force terms do appear in the transformed version of Newton's equations of motion in the noninertial frames. Pseudoforces cannot be associated with the interactions of the object and its environment as the real forces can be. Real forces never change as a result of transformation of reference frames. Examples of pseudoforces are centrifugal force, Coriolis force, etc. We shall deal with this problem in the chapter on rotating frames. Extended bodies, being rigid or elastic or fluid in nature, can move in any manner allowing very complicated rotations in them. Newton's second law of motion has to be modified for such systems. The last three chapters are devoted to the dynamics of rigid, elastic and fluid bodies.

2. The most inconvenient aspect of the use of Newton's laws of motion is that they are restricted to Cartesian frames and that they deal with the dynamical problems in terms of the forces only. In the subsequent chapters we shall present treatments that do not refer to forces at all and coordinates that are more natural (to the given situation) than the Cartesian ones, can be chosen. In these formulations, the force function is replaced by a suitable potential function. Chapter 2 deals with such a formulation.

3. As we have seen, each of the three Eqs (I.4), being a second order differential equation, always requires two initial values to be specified. At each point of the orbit the differential equations tell us how the state changes differentially over an infinitesimally small interval of time. Since the classical world is totally deterministic, it allows us to predict the dynamical evolution of a system both by differential and integral techniques. Such integral and variational techniques seem to be far more general than the differential ones. Chapter 6 has been devoted to the development of Hamilton's principle and the variational approach to classical mechanics.

4. The Newtonian definition of linear momentum, that is, $\boldsymbol{p} = m\boldsymbol{v}$ and his third law of motion together suggest that the total momentum of a pair of mutually interacting particles is conserved. It was later found that for two charged particles moving under the mutual forces of action given by Lorentz force (see Eq. (I.9)), the quantity $\boldsymbol{p}_1 + \boldsymbol{p}_2 = m_1\boldsymbol{v}_1 + m_2\boldsymbol{v}_2$ is no longer a constant of motion. What happens is the following: When a charged particle moves, it behaves like an electric current and therefore, produces a magnetic field around it. This magnetic field exerts a magnetic force on the other charged particle if the latter is moving. So the momentum of the second particle changes, but not the energy. Now what agent transfers this momentum? Surely it is the magnetic field produced by the first particle, which would not have existed had the first particle been at rest with respect to the second particle. The net result is that the magnetic field itself must carry some momentum so that it can impart some momentum to the charged particle. So if we want to save the third law of motion or the principle of conservation of momentum for the motion of charged particles, the Newtonian concept of momentum has to be revised. We shall see in the following chapters how this problem is resolved in the Lagrangian and the Hamiltonian formulations, through the definition of canonical momentum.

5. Application of Newton's laws of motion requires the specification of all forces acting on the object at all instants of time. In real situations, particularly when the constraint forces are involved, this can be a formidable task. The problem is dealt with in the next chapter, that is chapter 1.

6. Newton's laws are based on the concepts of absolute time, absolute space, absolute simultaneity of events and infinite speed of propagation of information. These are not supported by current theories, which require, in particular, that the measure of inertia or mass is not an absolute quantity but that only the rest mass is an invariant characteristic of material objects. In this book we have not given any systematic development of special relativistic mechanics, although occasionally examples and results are given just to stress the important differences that they lead to.

I.7 SUMMARY

Certain key points have been emphasized in this chapter. A classically defined particle is always assumed to have no structure, and hence can have no moment of inertia, and no spin. But a quantum particle can have spin without a structure. Another point we have made is that in physics, very often we plot graphs for representing the motion of a particle using any arbitrary scale for graduating the axes. This is possible because any finite length of a line contains as many points as there are real numbers between any two real numbers. Since physical quantities are all expressed in terms of some numbers, they can be geometrically plotted on a graph. Moreover, the choice of units can also be absolutely arbitrary because there can be an exact one to one correspondence of the total set of real numbers between any two arbitrary intervals of real numbers, as also of the total number of points between any two segments of arc, surface or volume elements.

In the history part, we want to emphasize one point; Galileo was the father of modern science, and he broke the age long tradition of accepting pedagogical reasoning in preference to directly testable results of experiments. His successor Newton had the best combination of both a theoretical mind and experimental hands.

Newton's laws of motion are accepted as a set of axioms. The first law like the other two is an axiom, that is, an unproved and unprovable assumption, which Newton proposed as a useful way of thinking about the world in order to make sense of the vast variety of motions that are observed. An axiom is judged by its proposer to be so basic and so fundamental that there is nothing more basic or fundamental with which it can be proved. It is a concept invented for the purpose of proving a starting point of thinking about the phenomena at hand. In fact any attempt to justify an axiom is ultimately bound to be circular, for how can one begin other than at the beginning? The ultimate test of whether or not the axioms achieve what is hoped to be achieved is, how successful they are at predicting observable results that can be checked with actual phenomena. They represent a complete strategy for solving a variety of dynamical problems, not all however. The concepts of inertial frame, conservation of linear momentum, closed systems, and symmetries of space and time were explained.

Nevertheless, it is apparent that Newton's programme is tedious and far from simple, particularly in noninertial situations. The motion of rigid bodies, or of continuous elastic or fluid media does not lend itself to simple ways of tackling it. The greatest disadvantage, however, was that Newton had always tried to resolve most problems geometrically, rather than analytically. For the constrained motions, the determination of all the unimportant reaction forces was a great nuisance, which Newton was fully aware of, but apparently could not suggest practical solutions to.

The rest of the book aims at presenting a number of alternative and superior techniques that have been invented and mastered by Lagrange, Euler, Hamilton, Poisson, Jacobi, and others. The analytical formulation of dynamics has literally begun with the works of Euler and Lagrange.

In many Indian universities, the undergraduate syllabi for classical mechanics include topics like dynamics with constraints, Lagrangian and Hamiltonian formulations, central force and rigid body dynamics. The first five chapters and the first 9 sections of chapter 12 are devoted to these topics. However, we discovered that many colleges did not teach these advanced topics in spite of their being an essential part of the undergraduate honours course. The time allocated for teaching classical mechanics at the Master's level is also not sufficient to cover all the required back logs. This book can be of use in this context also.

At the end of each chapter, a number of problems and exercises are suggested, with some hints and answers at the end of the book. Since the intended level of the book is a non-elementary one, a pre-requisite is a knowledge of classical dynamics to the level of, say, Halliday and Resnick's treatise on the same subject. We offer 50 introductory problems right below to be solved without (take full credit, say 2 points each) or with the help of the hints provided (take half credit, say 1 point each) before starting with chapter 1 of the book. One may, of course, read Appendices A1, A2 and A3 and parts of chapters 3, 4, 12 and 14 even before beginning with the chapter 1, which may help solve some of the following problems. The sequence of the problems is not chosen in order of increasing or decreasing difficulty, so don't stop even if you cannot solve any particular ones in the beginning. The problems are of two kinds; some are precise, while others are approximate, so that only order of magnitude calculations would suffice to serve the purpose of posing the problem. This is also true of the problems given at the end of all other chapters.

PROBLEMS

I.1 A system of natural units formed out of $\hbar$, c, G and k (Boltzmann's constant) is called Planck units. Find the Planck units of length, time, mass and temperature. Compare the Planck length with the Compton wavelength of a Planck mass particle and the peak wavelength of blackbody radiation having a temperature equal to the Planck temperature.

I.2 A car is naturally sliding down on an incline that makes an angle α with the horizontal. A ball is thrown out from the moving car in a direction perpendicular to the plane of the incline. Will it return to the car ? What if the wheels share a mass $\tan^2 \alpha$ times the mass of the car ?

I.3 Sit on a chair which is connected to a rope of negligible mass passing through a pulley fixed on the ceiling and hold the other end of the rope in your hand. Can you pull yourself up ? What is the force N that you exert on the chair ? Under what circumstances can N vanish ?

I.4 A massive object is suspended by a cord and an identical cord is attached to the bottom of the object and dangles below it. A downward force may be applied to the lower end of the lower cord. Show that the upper cord breaks with a slow steady pull (on the lower cord) and that the lower cord breaks with a quick jerk.

I.5 Describe the 3-D motion of a pendulum bob hung by a rubber band. What are the frequencies of its vertical and horizontal oscillations ?

I.6 Two particles in a uniform gravitational field have initial positions and velocities $\boldsymbol{r}_1$, $\boldsymbol{v}_1$, $\boldsymbol{r}_2$ and $\boldsymbol{v}_2$ respectively. Using these initial conditions alone, state a test for determining whether the particles will collide.

I.7 A basketball is thrown vertically downward from the top of a tall building and it lands on the street below. How high will it bounce ? Take the diameter of the ball to be 0.3 m, its mass 0.7 kg, density of air 1.29 kg/m^3, the drag coefficient for the quadratic drag law $C_D = 0.5$ (Drag force, $F = C_D A \rho v^2/2$, A = area of the body that faces the drag, ρ = density of the fluid, v = speed of the body).

I.8 A stone of mass m is projected vertically upward from the ground level with an initial speed v_1. Assuming a quadratic law of drag force, show that
(1) the speed of return to the ground v_2 is always less than v_1, and
(2) the time of descent t_2 is always greater than the time of ascent t_1.

I.9 A normal human heart pumps about 5 litres of blood per minute at a systolic pressure of 120 torr. What is the minimum power of the heart required for pumping blood alone ?

I.10 Suppose we sweat away 2.5 litres of water every day at a normal body temperature of 37°C (take the outside temperature to be 25°C). What would then be the minimum calorie requirement of the body ? Assume the heat of combustion for food or fuel carbon to be 10 Kcal/gm. How much oxygen is to be breathed to digest our daily food ? If we breathe 16 times a minute with 30% efficiency in the consumption of oxygen, what is the required lung capacity of an average human being ?

I.11 If you remove all the electrons from a rain drop (diameter = 1 mm), what would be the gain in the electrostatic potential of the entire earth ? Take the radius of the earth to be R = 6378.14 km.

I.12 The standard speed of the tape in play mode is about 4.76 cm/s. The thickness of the tape is 1.15×10^{-2} mm. There is an index meter which reads in proportion with the length of the tape run. The maximum index reading is 730 for a tape run of 45 minutes. The inner hub radius of the tape mount is 1.35 cm. If a particular song starts at the index number 220, find the outer radii of the two discs of the tape at that moment.

I.13 Two vehicles are bumper to bumper at a stop signal. The lead vehicle moves with a constant acceleration a for time T. The second vehicle follows the first but maintains a separation distance proportional to its own speed. Describe the motion of the second vehicle during time T.

I.14 The famous astrophysicist from Cambridge, Steven Hawking, suggested in 1975 that a black hole of mass M and radius R (= $2GM/c^2$) emits like a black body with a temperature $T = \hbar c^3/8GMk$ ($\hbar$ = Planck's constant/2π, k = Boltzmann's constant, c = speed of light in vacuum). How long will it survive ?

I.15 The most distant object that we have seen so far is a quasar sitting at a distance of about 15×10^9 light years away from us. Assuming that the universe is a big black hole of the above radius, find the average mass density of the universe. How many galaxies are there in the universe if the mass of individual object is about 5×10^{41} kg ?

I.16 Show that time taken for unhindered gravitational collapse of any homogeneous spherical body does not depend on its size or mass, but only on the density. Find the collapse times for the earth, sun, moon, an interstellar cloud and the universe, the densities being 5.51, 1.41, 3.34, 10^{-23}, and 10^{-29} (in units of gm/cm^3), respectively.

I.17 Suppose the sun contracts to a pulsar. Estimate the minimum radius of the pulsar and its period of rotation. Assume the period of rotation of the sun to be 25.38 days. Compare the kinetic energy of rotation of the star with that of the pulsar. What is the source of this increased kinetic energy? Take the radius and the mass of the sun to be 7×10^8 m and 2×10^{30} kg, respectively.

I.18 From a 100 m high tower, a boy stretches the rubber cord of his catapult so that it becomes 10 cm longer, and projects a stone of mass 20 gm at an angle 30 degrees with the horizon. Find the amount of heat generated when the stone hits the ground. Stretching of the cord by 1 cm requires a force of 1 kgf. Disregard the resistance of air.

I.19 Find the optimum speed (v_o) and angle (θ_o) with the horizontal for netting a basket ball at height h and distance L. Show that θ_o is greater than $\pi/4$ by an amount $\tan^{-1}(h/L)$.

I.20 A ballistic missile is fired with an initial speed v_o up the slope of a hill that has an angular elevation ϕ with the horizontal. Find the maximum range of the missile along the hill slope and show that it ensures that the direction of hitting the target is normal to the direction of firing.

I.21 Use the same quadratic law of drag force as in problem number I.7 above (but with C_D = 0.7) to calculate the power required for swimming under water at speed 1.7 m/s. What would be the speed of a cyclist (C_D = 0.9) if he consumes only a tenth as much power in combating the air drag ? (Assume the total surface area of an average athlete's body =1.1 m^2.)

I.22 For non-spinning high speed golf balls the force of air drag is roughly linear with velocity ($F_D = Cv$). Assume that $C/m = 0.25\ s^{-1}$, $m = 46$ g and that the maximum horizontal range of 152 m is obtained with an initial speed of 61 m/s. Show that the angle of striking has to be 32 degrees with the horizontal, whereas in absence of any air drag it would have been 45 degrees.

I.23 Find the kinetic energy of a cyclist riding at a speed of 9 km/h. The cyclist with his bicycle weighs 78 kgf, and the wheels 3 kgf. Consider the bicycle wheels as hoops.

I.24 Find the maximum deflection of a leaf spring caused by a load placed on its middle, if the static deflection of the spring due to the same load is $x_o = 2$ cm. What will the maximum initial deflection be if the same load is dropped onto the middle of the spring from a height of h = 1 m with zero initial velocity.

I.25 The kinetic energy of a neutron diminishes 1.4 times when it collides elastically and centrally with the stationary nucleus of a moderating material. What is the moderating element ?

I.26 In the reaction $N^{14}(\alpha\ ,\ p)O^{17}$ (Q value = – 1.18 MeV), the kinetic energy of an alpha particle, $E = 7.7$ MeV. Show that the angle with the direction of motion of the alpha particle at which proton escapes if its kinetic energy $E_p = 5.5$ MeV, is about 54 degrees (Take the mass data from any book on nuclear physics).

I.27 A centrifuge is used for the separation of isotopes of Uranium in one of its natural gas compounds, called Uranium hexafluoride (UF_6). The gas in natural isotopic mixtures (^{238}U : $^{235}U = 139 : 1$) is placed inside a cylindrical vessel rotating at a high speed. The centrifugal potential determines the Boltzmann-like barometric distribution of the gas isotopes. Compare the concentrations of light and heavy Uranium isotopes near the centrifuge walls, if the diameter of the cylinder is 10 cm, the rotation speed is 2000 rps, and the temperature of UF_6 compound is 27°C.

I.28 A centrifugal governor is of the form shown in Fig. I.1. The mass of each weight is m and the spring constant k. Will this device work in a condition of weightlessness? What is the dependence of angle α on the speed of rotation of the system ?

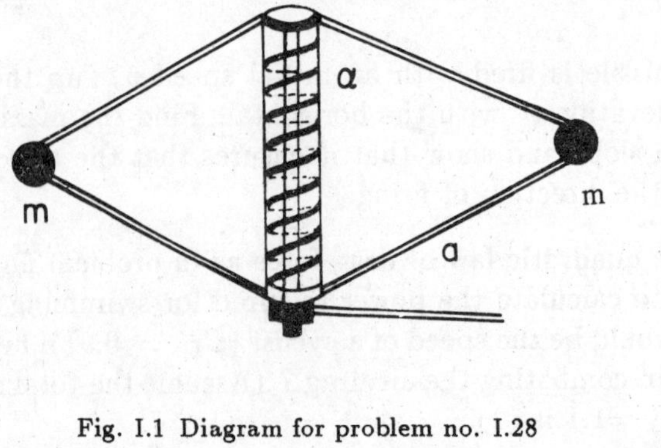

Fig. I.1 Diagram for problem no. I.28

I.29 The surfaces of two cylinders made of aluminium (solid) and of lead (hollow) having the identical radius ($r = 6$ cm) and weight ($W = 0.5$ kgf) are painted with the same colour (the densities of Al and Pb being 2.7 and 11.2 times that of water).
(1) How can the cylinders be distinguished by observing their translational velocities at the base of an inclined plane?
(2) Find their moments of inertia.
(3) How much time does it take for each cylinder to roll down the inclined plane without slipping ? Height of the inclined plane $h = 0.5$ m, the angle of inclination $\alpha = 30$ degrees, and the initial velocity = 0.

I.30 A spherical bowl of radius R rotates about the vertical diameter. The bowl contains a small object whose radius vector in the course of rotation makes an angle α with the vertical. What would be the minimum angular velocity ω of the bowl in order to prevent the object from sliding down, if the coefficient of static friction is μ_s?

I.31 Twenty drops of lead were formed when the lower end of a vertically suspended lead wire of 1 mm in diameter was melted. By how much did the wire become shorter ? The coefficient of surface tension of liquid lead is 0.47 N/m. Assume that the diameter of the neck of a drop at the moment it breaks away is equal to the diameter of the wire, and the density of lead = 11,200 kg/m^3 in both the phases.

I.32 A 'hula hoop' of mass M and radius R is started across a level lawn with its centre of mass moving at linear speed v_o and a backspin ω_o. The coefficient of sliding friction is a constant. Show that if the hoop is to come back toward the starting point, it is necessary that $\omega_o > v_o/R$.

I.33 A uniform cylinder of radius R is spun about its axis, to the angular velocity ω_o, and then placed in a rectangular corner. The coefficient of friction between the corner walls and the cylinder is K. Show that the cylinder accomplishes n turns before it stops, where

$$n = \frac{(1 + K^2)\omega_o^2 R}{8\pi g K(1 + K)}$$

I.34 A uniform solid cylinder of radius R rolls over a horizontal plane passing into an inclined plane forming an angle of depression α with the horizontal. Find the maximum value of the speed v_o which still permits the cylinder to roll onto the inclined plane without a jump. The sliding is assumed to be absent. Show that there will always be a jump if $\alpha \geq \cos^{-1}(4/7)$, no matter how slowly the cylinder rolls down across the slant.

I.35 A uniform ball of radius r rolls without slipping down the top of a sphere of radius R. Show that the angular velocity of the ball at the moment it breaks off the sphere is given by

$$\omega = \left[10g(R + r)/17r^2\right]^{1/2}$$

The initial velocity of the ball is assumed to be negligible.

I.36 A chain AB of length l is located in a smooth horizontal tube AC so that its fraction of length h hangs freely and touches the surface of the table with its lower end B. At a certain moment, end A of the chain is set free. With what velocity will this end of the chain slip out of the tube ?

I.37 A spaceship of mass m_o moves in the absence of external forces with a constant velocity $\boldsymbol{v}_o$. To change the motion direction, a jet engine is switched on. It starts ejecting a gas jet with velocity $\boldsymbol{u}$ which is constant relative to the spaceship and at right angles to the spaceship motion. The engine is shut down when the mass of the spaceship decreases to m. Through what angle α did the direction of the motion of the spaceship deviate due to the jet engine operation ?

I.38 A rocket of initial mass M_i (which is equal to the sum of the payload mass M_f and the fuel) and velocity $\boldsymbol{v}_i$ ignites all its fuel with a constant velocity of ejection $-u_o(\boldsymbol{v}_i/v_i)$ with respect to the rocket. Find its final velocity $\boldsymbol{v}_f$ if it is moving
(1) in free space,
(2) against a constant gravity field $\boldsymbol{g}$, and
(3) against the earth's gravity field (obeying the inverse square law of distance with respect to the centre of earth).

I.39 A horizontal plane supports a stationary vertical cylinder of radius R and a vertical disc A attached to the cylinder by a horizontal thread AB of length l_o. An initial velocity $\boldsymbol{v}_o$ is imparted to the disc perpendicular to the straightened string. How long will it move along the plane until it strikes against the cylinder ? The friction is assumed to be negligible.

I.40 A wheel of radius b is rolling over level ground at a constant forward speed v_o. A bit of mud breaks loose from the rim of the wheel. What is the greatest height above the ground that a piece of mud can reach ? Is there any critical speed of the wheel below which the mud will not leave the wheel at all ?

I.41 A vertically oriented uniform rod of mass M and length l can rotate about its upper end. A horizontally flying bullet of mass m strikes the lower end of the rod and gets stuck in it; as a result, the rod swings through an angle. Assuming that m is very much less than M, find
(a) the velocity $\boldsymbol{v}$ of the flying bullet;
(b) the momentum increment in the system 'bullet-rod' during the impact, what causes the changes of that momentum;
(c) at what distance x from the upper end of the rod the bullet must strike for the momentum of the 'bullet-rod' system to remain constant during the impact ?

I.42 A rigid symmetrical dumbbell having two spheres of mass $m/2$ each and connected by a rigid rod of length l, is floating freely inside a spaceship under 'no-gravity' condition. Now a ball of mass m and speed v_o collides elastically with one of the spheres of the dumbbell at an angle 90 degrees to the axis of the dumbbell. Show that the resultant angular momentum of the dumbbell with respect to its centre of mass is exactly two thirds of the initial angular momentum of the ball with respect to the centre of mass of the dumbbell. Neglect the mass of the rod.

I.43 A point moves in the plane so that its tangential acceleration $f_t = a$, and its normal acceleration $f_n = bt^4$, where a, b are positive constants and t is the time. At $t = 0$, the point was at rest. Find the curvature and the total acceleration f as function of the distance covered s. (If necessary, read Appendix A2 before trying the problem.)

I.44 When a small ball of mass m is placed on top of a large ball of mass M and they are dropped together, the small ball rebounds much higher than its original height. If the coefficients of restitution be e_1 and e_2 for the collisions of the large ball and the small ball respectively, show that the height amplification is given by A^2, where

$$A = \frac{(1 + e_1)(1 + e_2)}{1 + m/M} - 1$$

For ideal elastic rebounds of a stack of 3 balls of masses $m_1 \ll m_2 \ll m_3$ with m_1 on the top and dropped from the height h,show that the maximum height attained by the top ball is 49 times h. (The coefficient of restitution of any elastic collision is defined to be the ratio of the relative velocities of the two bodies immediately after the collision to that immediately before the collision. This is an experimental law first given by John Wallis in 1668.)

I.45 For a vertical free fall from rest under a constant g, the air drag force, be it linear or quadratic, leads to a terminal speed, say v_t. For a given v_t, find the speed and distance traveled as functions of t and show that the quadratic drag law leads to a larger velocity and larger displacement at any time t than the linear drag law.

I.46 Show that the value of g should increase as we go deeper into the earth's crust because the density of the crust is less than two thirds of the average density of the earth.

I.47 Suppose there is a fifth force in the universe, due to which Newton's law of gravitation is modified by a Yukawa type potential, so that the potential due to a point mass m at a distance r is,

$$V(r) = -\frac{G_\infty m}{r}\left(1 + \alpha e^{-r/\lambda}\right)$$

where G_∞ is the usual Newtonian constant of gravitation valid here for $r \to \infty$, λ is the range of short range gravitation and α is its strength. Because of this modified form of the potential, there will be a local gravity anomaly $\Delta g(z)$, z being the depth below the surface of the earth. Obtain an expression for $g(z)$ and show that the effective constant of gravitation deep inside any mine, that is, for $z \gg \lambda$, would be given by $G_{\text{mine}} = G_\infty(1 + \alpha)$.

I.48 Two particles of mass m_1 and m_2 having velocities (in one dimension) u_1 and u_2 respectively, collide and their velocities after collision become v_1 and v_2. If you write the results in matrix notation with $u = (u_1, u_2)$ and $v = (v_1, v_2)$, then show that there exists a 2×2 matrix M such that $v = Mu$. Show that $M^2 = I$ (Identity matrix) with real eigenvalues $\lambda = \pm 1$. What is the significance of the characteristic vectors ?

I.49 A cylinder rolls down a rough incline PC, moves on to a horizontal plane (made up of same material as that of the incline) up to distance say CB, and stops at B. If the foot of perpendicular for P is A on the line CB, show that the coefficient of friction of the incline and the plane is given by the ratio of the lengths AP and AB.

I.50 A damped harmonic oscillator has the equation of motion of the form $\ddot{x} + 2\lambda\dot{x} + \omega^2 x = 0$. Construct matrices $X = (x, \dot{x})$ and

$$A = \begin{pmatrix} 0 & 1 \\ -\omega^2 & -2\lambda \end{pmatrix}$$

so that the equation of motion reduces to a matrix equation $\dot{X} = AX$ with matrix solution

$$X = e^{At} X_o$$

Find the matrix e^{At}. What happens when $\omega \to \lambda$?

1

Constrained Motions in Cartesian Coordinates

1.0 INTRODUCTION

Sir Isaac Newton conceived the greater part of his monumental work, *The Principia* before he was 23, even though it got finally published when he was 44. After the publication of *The Principia* in 1687, he lived for another 40 years, during which time he paid little attention to improvise his scheme of dynamics, in order to make it usable under the circumstances of constrained motions. There was one great weakness in Newton's personality, because of which he cultivated a jealous proprietary interest in every object he studied, and almost every achievement of his creative life was accompanied by some quarrel. He got himself bitterly engaged in fighting out issues like who between him and Robert Hooke was the real discoverer of the inverse square law of gravitation or who between him and Leibnitz was the true inventor of the differential calculus. He had a heated exchange of abuse with Jean Bernoulli on the deficiencies of the *Principia*, with Giovanni Rizzetti for the latter's challenge of Newton's optical experiments, with Johann von Hatzfeld on perpetual motion, and so on. He was also deeply religious, and spent a reasonable portion of the last 20 years of his life in preparing a book on the *Chronology of Ancient Kingdom Amended.* We shall see in this chapter, how incomplete was the scheme he gave for tackling dynamical problems, particularly the ones involving hindered motions, that is, motions hindered by the presence of hard surfaces. A genius as he was, could have suggested practical remedies, and perhaps one did not have to wait for the first remedy to come from Jean le Rond D'Alembert as late as in 1743.

Newton's approach was highly geometrical. At that time, mathematics was of course in such a primitive state that an analytical treatment of dynamics was virtually impossible. Differential calculus was made available to the scientific community through the publication of Leibniz in 1686. The integral calculus was formulated by Jean Bernoulli around 1690. In 1718, Jean Bernoulli formally defined 'functions' as variables; the notation $f(x)$ was introduced by Euler a few years later; Taylor's series was published by Brook Taylor in 1715; partial differentiations and partial differential equations were introduced by Euler in 1734; the hyperbolic functions were introduced by Riccatti in 1757 and the trigonometric functions by Wallis and Lambert in 1768.

Born in Paris as an illegal son of aristocrats and found near the Church of St. Jean le Rond, D'Alembert (1717 – 1783) spent his childhood and youth in the house of his foster-father, a glazier. His natural father, Chevalier Destouches, was forced by the law to support the boy with an annuity. When it became apparent that the boy was a genius, his mother wanted to take him back, but the boy refused to accept her as his mother and continued to live with his foster-parents. At the age of 24, he was admitted to the French Academy of Sciences, and within two years he published his book on mechanics, *Traité de Dynamique.* He believed in actions only by gravity or impact and devised a method of reducing practically all problems of dynamics to ones of statics by superposing additional forces corresponding to those which represent the actual accelerations. The present chapter is meant to elucidate the basic problems of constrained motions in the Newtonian scheme and some practical solutions to them, as suggested over the past three hundred years by people like D'Alembert, Lagrange, Gauss, Gibbs, Hertz and Appell. Paul Appell's magnum opus was *Traité de Mecanique Rationnelle*, published in 1909.

1.1 CONSTRAINTS AND THEIR CLASSIFICATION

In many real-life situations the object in motion is restricted or constrained to move in such a way that its coordinates and or velocity components must satisfy some prescribed relations at every instant of time. These relations can be expressed in the form of either equations or inequalities. For example, the motion of the centre of mass of a billiard ball of radius R moving on a billiard table of length and breadth, $2a$ and $2b$ respectively, must satisfy

$$-a + R \leq x \leq a - R \qquad -b + R \leq y \leq b - R \qquad z = R$$

assuming that the origin of the coordinate axes is at the centre of the rectangular table and x and y axes are parallel to length and breadth respectively. This is a set of one equation and two inequalities, which the motion of a billiard ball is to satisfy at all instants of time.

Most physical realizations of constrained motion involve surfaces of other bodies, for example, that of the billiard table in the above example. Similarly, a train running along the rails or the motion of a simple pendulum in a vertical plane define a constrained motion in one dimension. Physically, constrained motion is realised by the forces which arise when the object in motion is in contact with the constraining surfaces or curves. These forces, called *constraint forces*, are usually stiff elastic forces at the contact. The basic properties of constraint forces can be summarised with the following points:

(i) They are elastic in nature and appear at the surface of contact. They arise because the motion defined by the external applied forces is hindered by the contact.

(ii) They are so strong that they barely allow the body under consideration to deviate even slightly from a prescribed path or surface. This prescribed path or surface is called a *constraint.* The scalar equations that describe or prescribe the surface of constraint are called *constraint equations.*

(iii) The sole effect of constraint force is to keep the constraint relations satisfied.

Constraints are classified into different types and classes, based on four criteria, namely (I) whether they are time dependent or time independent, (II) whether they are integrable algebraic relations among the coordinates or nonintegrable ones, (III) whether they are conservative or dissipative, and (IV) whether they are algebraic equations or algebraic inequalities. Every constraint relation must be characterised by these four labels each of which has got a binary option. Table 1.1 summarises the classifications of the constraint relations.

Table 1.1 Classification of Constraints

A constraint is

I. Either **Scleronomic** : constraint relations do not explicitly depend on time,
or **Rheonomic** : constraint relations depend explicitly on time,

and

II. Either **Holonomic** : constraint relations are or can be made independent of velocities $(\dot{x}, \dot{y}, \dot{z})$,
or **Nonholonomic** : constraint relations are not holonomic,

and

III. Either **Conservative** : total mechanical energy of the system is conserved while performing the constrained motion. Constraint forces do not do any work,
or **Dissipative** : constraint forces do work and total mechanical energy is not conserved,

and

IV. Either **Bilateral** : at any point on the constraint surface both the forward and backward motions are possible. Constraint relations are not in the form of inequalities but are in the form of equations,
or **Unilateral** : at some points no forward motion is possible. Constraint relations are expressed in the form of inequalities.

Properties of constraints:

(i) Just by looking at the constraint relation it may be possible to determine the type qualification for the classes I, II and IV, but the determination of the type qualification for class III depends on whether the constraint forces do any work while maintaining the constraint relation throughout all stages of motion.

(ii) It may so happen that the constraint relation contains velocities but can be integrated with respect to time so that the resulting relation is made free of velocities. In such cases the constraint is holonomic. For example, the constraint equation

$$(yz - 2x + y)\dot{x} + (xz - 2y + x)\dot{y} + xy\dot{z} = 0$$

can be integrated to

$$(1 + z)xy = x^2 + y^2 + c$$

so that this constraint is holonomic.

(iii) The general form of the unilateral constraint can be written as

$$f(\boldsymbol{r}_1,\ldots,\boldsymbol{r}_n,\dot{\boldsymbol{r}}_1,\ldots,\dot{\boldsymbol{r}}_n,t) \geq 0 \tag{1.1}$$

where $\boldsymbol{r}_i$ and $\dot{\boldsymbol{r}}_i$ are the position and velocity of the ith particle of the system in motion. Whenever the state of motion of the system is such that, for the scalar function f above, the condition $f = 0$ is satisfied we say that the constraint is taut. The motion of a system with unilateral constraints can be divided into portions so that in certain portions the constraint is taut and the motion occurs as if the constraint were bilateral, and in other portions the constraint is not taut and the motion occurs as if there were no constraints.

However, in this book, we shall be considering constraints that are almost exclusively bilateral, unless stated otherwise.

(iv) Forces of constraints: We have already mentioned in the Introduction chapter that Newton's second law of motion is a complete law of nature. The relation between the observed acceleraticn of an object, and the total force it is subjected to, is fixed in any inertial frame. But somehow one has to specify this total force which Newton has not been able to for arbitrary dynamical systems. By the law of superposition of forces, one can divide the total force into as many components as one wishes. So for a given problem, one first tries to make a list of all the 'obvious' forces. Usually they are the ones that are defined by the universally recognised laws of forces, such as Newton's law of gravitation, Coulomb's law of electrostatics, and so on. They really do not depend on the nature of constraint relations, e.g., the sort of surfaces on which the particles are constrained to move. It is customary to identify all such externally applied universal forces and include them under the category of externally applied forces. The rest of the forces are assumed to originate from contact with the constraining surfaces. Such forces are categorically classified as the forces of constraints. Unfortunately, Newton has not given any prescription for calculating these forces of constraints. Hence, in absence of the knowledge of the total force, Newton's second law in its differential form cannot be formulated let alone finding a solution to dynamical problems involving constraints.

(v) Work done by the constraint forces: Usually the constraint forces act in a direction perpendicular to the surface of constraints at every point on it, while the motion of the object is parallel to the surface at every point. In such cases the work done by constraint forces is zero. One obvious exception is, of course, the frictional force due to sliding which does work for real displacements. Another exception is the rheonomic constraint for which the constraint force need not act perpendicular to the real displacement. This can be easily seen from Fig. 1.1 where the real path of the bob of pendulum with variable string length $l = l(t)$ is shown. We see from the figure that $\boldsymbol{T}\cdot\Delta\boldsymbol{r} \neq O$, where $\boldsymbol{T}$ is the tension in the string (constraint force) and $\Delta\boldsymbol{r}$ is the real displacement. However the work done by the tension in the simple pendulum is zero as the length of the string remains constant, allowing the bob to move perpendicular to the constraint force of tension that acts along the string. Generally speaking, rheonomic constraints are dissipative, although there are exceptions.

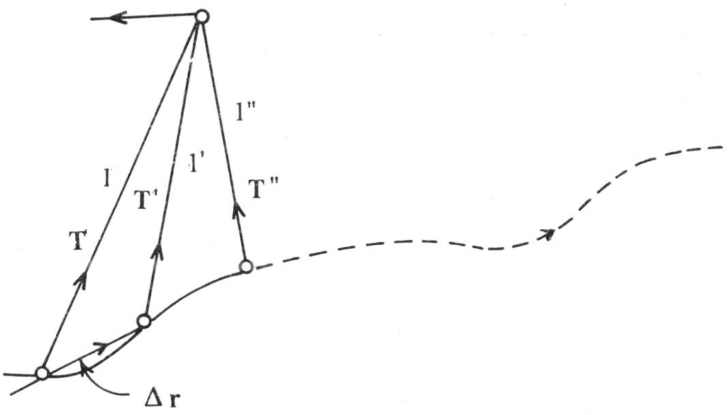

Fig. 1.1 An example of work done by constraint force being nonzero when the constraint is rheonomic

1.2 EXAMPLES OF CONSTRAINTS

We now give examples illustrating various types of constraints.

1. Rigid body

A rigid body is, by definition, a system of particles such that the distance between any pair of particles remains constant in time. Thus the motion of a rigid body is constrained by the equations

$$|\boldsymbol{r}_i - \boldsymbol{r}_k| = \text{const.} \tag{1.2}$$

where the pair of subscripts (i, k) run over all distinct pairs of particles forming the body. Obviously this constraint is scleronomic. The constraint is also holonomic and bilateral. We prove that this constraint is also conservative, that is, the work done by the internal forces (which are the forces of constraint) in the rigid body is zero. This is shown as follows. The constraint relations (1.2) can be written as

$$|\boldsymbol{r}_i - \boldsymbol{r}_k|^2 = \text{const.}$$

Taking differentials,

$$(\boldsymbol{r}_i - \boldsymbol{r}_k)\cdot\Delta(\boldsymbol{r}_i - \boldsymbol{r}_k) = 0 \tag{1.3}$$

Now let the internal force of constraint on the ith particle due to the kth particle be represented by $\boldsymbol{F}_{ik}$. By Newton's third law we have,

$$\boldsymbol{F}_{ik} = -\boldsymbol{F}_{ki}$$

Thus we have for the work done by $\boldsymbol{F}_{ik}$ due to a displacement $\Delta\boldsymbol{r}_i$ of the ith particle,

$$\boldsymbol{F}_{ik}\cdot\Delta\boldsymbol{r}_i = -\boldsymbol{F}_{ki}\cdot\Delta\boldsymbol{r}_i \tag{1.4}$$

where $\Delta\boldsymbol{r}_i$ is a possible displacement (consistent with all the constraint relations) given by

Eq. (1.3). By virtue of Eq. (1.4) we can write for the total work done by the system

$$\Delta W = \sum_{\substack{i,k \\ k \neq i}} \boldsymbol{F}_{ik} \cdot \Delta \boldsymbol{r}_i = \sum_{\substack{i,k \\ k > i}} \{\boldsymbol{F}_{ik} \cdot \Delta \boldsymbol{r}_i + \boldsymbol{F}_{ki} \cdot \Delta \boldsymbol{r}_k\} = \sum_{\substack{i,k \\ k > i}} \boldsymbol{F}_{ik} \cdot \Delta(\boldsymbol{r}_i - \boldsymbol{r}_k)$$

Again, since all $\boldsymbol{F}_{ik}$ are the internal forces which arise purely due to interaction between all possible pairs of particles, it is only natural that $\boldsymbol{F}_{ik}$ will act parallel to the line joining the ith and jth particles. Thus we can write,

$$\boldsymbol{F}_{ik} = C_{ik}(\boldsymbol{r}_i - \boldsymbol{r}_k)$$

where C_{ik}'s are real constants and symmetric in i and k. Substituting in the above expression for the total work, we have

$$\Delta W = \sum_{\substack{i,k \\ k > i}} C_{ik}(\boldsymbol{r}_i - \boldsymbol{r}_k) \cdot \Delta(\boldsymbol{r}_i - \boldsymbol{r}_k)$$

Now by Eq. (1.3) each individual term of the summand is zero. Thus the constraint of rigidity is conservative in nature, apart from its being scleronomic, holonomic and bilateral.

2. Deformable Bodies

As opposed to rigid bodies we have deformable bodies, that is, bodies whose shape can change. Suppose that the deformation of the body is changing in time according to a certain prescribed function of time. Then the motion of such a body is constrained by the equation

$$|\boldsymbol{r}_i - \boldsymbol{r}_k| = f(t) \tag{1.5}$$

where, again $\boldsymbol{r}_i$ and $\boldsymbol{r}_k$ are position vectors and the pair of subscripts (i, k) runs over all distinct pairs of particles in the body. It is easy to show that these constraint relations cannot give the total work $\Delta W = 0$, as it did in the previous case. This is a case of rheonomic, holonomic, bilateral and dissipative constraint.

3. Simple Pendulum with Rigid Support

The position of the bob at any time must satisfy

$$|\boldsymbol{r}|^2 = x^2 + y^2 + z^2 = l^2 \tag{1.6}$$

where l is the constant length of the string connecting the bob to the fulcrum (which is taken to be the origin). The tension in the string $\boldsymbol{T}$ is parallel to $-\boldsymbol{r}$, giving the work done by the constraint force $\Delta W = \boldsymbol{T} \cdot \Delta \boldsymbol{r} = 0$, as $\boldsymbol{r} \cdot \Delta \boldsymbol{r} = 0$ from Eq. (1.6). This is a scleronomic, holonomic, bilateral and conservative constraint.

4. Pendulum with Variable Length

Suppose the length of the string is changing according to a given function $l(t)$. Then the constraint equation is

$$|\boldsymbol{r}(t)|^2 = l^2(t) \tag{1.7}$$

where $\boldsymbol{r}(t)$ is the position vector of the bob at time t (the origin being at the fixed fulcrum). Hence we have $\boldsymbol{r} \cdot \Delta \boldsymbol{r} \neq 0$, but since $\boldsymbol{T}$ is parallel to $-\boldsymbol{r}$, the work done by the constraint force $\boldsymbol{T}$ is $\Delta W = \boldsymbol{T} \cdot \Delta \boldsymbol{r} \neq 0$. This is a case of a rheonomic, holonomic, bilateral and dissipative constraint. Such a pendulum can increase or decrease its amplitude of oscillation depending on the time of pulling and releasing of the string of the pendulum through its fulcrum.

5. A Spherical Container of Fixed Radius R Filled with a Gas

The constraint relations for the gas particles inside the container are

$$|\boldsymbol{r}_i| \leq R \tag{1.8}$$

where $\boldsymbol{r}_i$ is measured from the centre of the container. The equality in Eq. (1.8) corresponds to the equation of the surface of the container, that is, for the situation when the particle is about to bounce off the surface. This is a case of a scleronnomic, holonomic, conservative and unilateral constraint.

6. An Expanding or Contracting Spherical Container of Gas

Suppose the radius R of the container is changing with time so that the position of any particle at any instant will satisfy

$$|\boldsymbol{r}| \leq R(t) \tag{1.9}$$

where the equality holds when the particle is just about to bounce off from the wall. If the chamber is expanding, the kinetic energy of the bouncing particle decreases at each bounce. This is a case of a rheonomic, holonomic, unilateral and dissipative constraint.

7. A Simple Pendulum with its Bob Sliding on a Circular Track

Here the constraint forces involve frictional forces due to sliding of the bob on the track. Since frictional forces due to sliding are nonconservative (they do nonzero work on the bob as it moves from one end to the other) the pendulum loses energy as its motion is hindered due to friction. This is therefore, an example of a dissipative constraint.

8. Rolling without Sliding

Suppose a spherical ball or a cylinder is rolling on a plane without sliding. We assume that the surfaces in contact are perfectly rough. Thus the frictional forces are not negligible. Since the point of contact is not sliding, the frictional forces do not do any work, and hence the total mechanical energy of the rolling body is conserved. Thus the constraint is conservative. To obtain the constraint equation we note that rolling without sliding means that the relative velocity of the point of contact with respect to the plane is zero. Then the velocity $\boldsymbol{V}$ of any point P in the rolling body, as seen from a fixed frame of reference, is given by

$$\boldsymbol{V} = \boldsymbol{V}_{\text{cm}} + \boldsymbol{\omega} \times \boldsymbol{r} \tag{1.10}$$

where $\boldsymbol{V}_{\text{cm}}$ is the velocity of the centre of mass and $\boldsymbol{r}$ is measured from the CM to the point P under consideration. Thus the velocity of the point of contact (nearest to the axis in the case of cylinder) is obtained by putting

$$\boldsymbol{r} = -r\,\hat{\boldsymbol{n}}$$

in Eq. (1.10) where $\hat{\boldsymbol{n}}$ is the unit vector along the outward normal to the plane and r is the radius of the sphere (or cylinder). Since there is no sliding of this point (or the line) we must have the instantaneous velocity $\boldsymbol{V}$ at the contact

$$\boldsymbol{V} = \boldsymbol{V}_{\text{cm}} - r(\boldsymbol{\omega} \times \hat{\boldsymbol{n}}) = \boldsymbol{0} \tag{1.11}$$

This is the required vector equation of constraint representing actually three scalar equations. For a sphere this constraint is nonintegrable because $\boldsymbol{\omega}$ is generally not expressible in the form of a total time derivative of any single coordinate. Thus the constraint is non-holonomic. However, for a cylinder, $\omega = (d\theta/dt)$ where θ is the angle of rotation of the cylinder about its axis. Therefore this equation of constraint can be integrated and reduced to a holonomic form, giving a relation between $\boldsymbol{r}$ and the coordinates of the centre of mass.

1.3 PRINCIPLE OF VIRTUAL WORK

1.3.1 Virtual Displacement

Any imaginary displacement which is consistent with the constraint relation at a given instant (that is, without allowing the real time to change) is called a *virtual displacement.*

Thus, given a system in a positional configuration $\boldsymbol{r}(t)$ at time t, the set of all virtual displacements is a particular subset of the set of all possible displacements. Physically such displacements are the displacements that would occur if the system was frozen in its motion at time t, and the system was then moved without violating any of the constraints operating on the system at that instant. A virtual displacement is finite in magnitude, but in this book a virtual displacement actually means an infinitesimal virtual displacement that does not violate any of the constraints operative at the given instant t. So by definition, a virtual infinitesimal displacement is given by

$$\delta x_i = dx_i \Big|_{dt = 0}$$

Example

Consider a simple pendulum with variable string length $l(t)$. At any instant the string length is $l(t)$ and the real displacement of the bob $\Delta\boldsymbol{r}$ in time Δt is not perpendicular to the string direction (see Fig. 1.1). A virtual displacement $\delta\boldsymbol{r}$ is thought to be an imaginary displacement consistent with the constraint $l(t)$ for time t. For the whole of $\delta\boldsymbol{r}$ the value of $l(t)$ is kept the same as that for the instant t. Hence the virtual displacement $\delta\boldsymbol{r}(t)$ constructed in the above way is perpendicular to the string direction prevailing at time t, whereas the real displacement $\Delta\boldsymbol{r}(t)$ is defined as usual by $\boldsymbol{r}(t + \Delta t) - \boldsymbol{r}(t)$, with the fact that $\boldsymbol{r}(t + \Delta t)$ is consistent with the constraint relation at $t + \Delta t$ and that $\boldsymbol{r}(t)$ is consistent with the constraint relation at t.

1.3.2 Virtual Work

Work done by any force on a particle due to its virtual displacement is called *virtual work.* We can express this definition through the equation

$$\delta W = \boldsymbol{F} \cdot \delta\boldsymbol{r} \tag{1.12}$$

Here $\boldsymbol{F}$ is the vector sum of the constraint force $\boldsymbol{f}$ and the applied forces $\boldsymbol{F}^{(a)}$ and an infinitesimally small element of all virtual quantities are usually denoted by a prefix δ, reserving Δ or d for the real ones.

1.3.3 Principle of Virtual Work

We know that for a system in static equilibrium the total force on the system vanishes, by definition. Hence the virtual work done on such systems due to any arbitrary virtual displacement must identically vanish. Thus the total force $\boldsymbol{F}$ on the system given by

$$\boldsymbol{F} = \boldsymbol{f} + \boldsymbol{F}^{(a)} = \boldsymbol{0}$$

where $\boldsymbol{f}$ is the sum total of the constraint forces and $\boldsymbol{F}^{(a)}$ that of the the applied forces, must yield, for the virtual work

$$\delta W = \boldsymbol{F} \cdot \delta \boldsymbol{r} = 0 \tag{1.13}$$

Furthermore, if the virtual work done by the constraint forces also vanishes, that is,

$$\boldsymbol{f} \cdot \delta \boldsymbol{r} = 0 \tag{1.14}$$

then the virtual work done by the applied force on a system in static equilibrium also vanishes, or in other words, the condition for static equilibrium reduces to

$$\delta W_a = \boldsymbol{F}^{(a)} \cdot \delta \boldsymbol{r} = 0 \tag{1.15}$$

For a system of n particles we should have

$$\delta W_a = \sum_{i=1}^{n} \boldsymbol{F}_i^{(a)} \cdot \delta \boldsymbol{r}_i = 0 \tag{1.16}$$

The above equation states that the necessary condition for static equilibrium is that the virtual work done by all the applied forces should vanish, provided the virtual work done by all the constraint forces vanishes. This is called the *principle of virtual work.*

The strength of the above principle lies in the fact that for a dynamical system one can determine the amount of force one needs to apply to the system in order to make it static (which is essential for making the principle of virtual work applicable to the system under consideration). We shall discuss this point in a later section devoted to what is known as D'Alembert's principle.

An Example

This is shown in the accompanying Fig. 1.2. The motion of two blocks having masses M_1 and M_2 is constrained by the fact that the string connecting them has a constant length l. Obviously, this is a case of a scleronomic, holonomic, bilateral and conservative constraint, provided friction due to the pulley can be neglected. Elementary considerations without involving virtual work show that the accelerations of the blocks are given by

$$\ddot{\boldsymbol{x}}_{M1} = \frac{(M_1 - M_2)\boldsymbol{g}}{M_1 + M_2} = -\ddot{\boldsymbol{x}}_{M2}$$

where $\boldsymbol{x}_{M1}$ and $\boldsymbol{x}_{M2}$ are measured downward from the horizontal plane passing through the centre of the pulley. Thus, for a static situation one must have $\ddot{\boldsymbol{x}}_{M1} = -\ddot{\boldsymbol{x}}_{M2} = 0$ requiring $M_1 = M_2$.

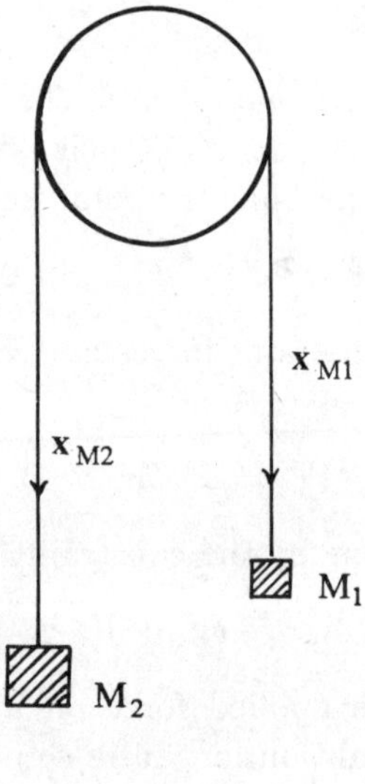

Fig. 1.2 Simple Atwood's machine

To apply the principle of virtual work to the above case we first note that, since the constraint $|\boldsymbol{x}_{M1}| + |\boldsymbol{x}_{M2}| = l$ is scleronomic, the virtual and real displacements are one and the same. Next, a displacement of one block causes an equal and opposite displacement of the other block. Thus the vanishing of virtual work done by the applied forces requires that

$$M_1 g|\Delta \boldsymbol{x}_{M1}| - M_2 g|\Delta \boldsymbol{x}_{M2}| = 0$$

or, $M_1 = M_2$, which is quite obvious. One can verify that in this case the work done by the constraint forces also vanishes.

1.4 THE BASIC PROBLEM WITH THE CONSTRAINT FORCES

Take the simplest case of one particle motion under a general velocity dependent constraint given by the relation,

$$g(\boldsymbol{r}, \dot{\boldsymbol{r}}, t) = 0 \tag{1.17}$$

To fulfill the requirement of the constraint, an unknown constraint force $\boldsymbol{f}$ must be introduced in addition to the known applied force $\boldsymbol{F}^{(a)}$ on the particle. Thus Newton's second law takes the form

$$m\ddot{\boldsymbol{r}} = \boldsymbol{F}^{(a)} + \boldsymbol{f} \tag{1.18}$$

The vector Eq. (1.18) is a set of three scalar equations and the Eq. (1.17) is a single scalar equation so that we have in total four equations. The total number of unknowns are the three functions $x(t)$, $y(t)$, $z(t)$ (or any other set of three independent Cartesian coordinate functions represented by the vector $\boldsymbol{r}$) and the three components of $\boldsymbol{f}$, that is, six in all. Thus we have four equations in six unknowns, a problem which does not possess a unique solution. This is the basic problem in dealing with constraint forces.

Earlier we noticed that unless we can analytically express the forces of constraint on the same footing as the externally applied forces, the content of the right hand side of Newton's second law remains incomplete and therefore one could not proceed any further. Now we discover an additional problem, that is, even if the constraint relation is completely specified, we have too few equations to solve for all the unknowns. At this point, one may begin to wonder as to how one solved so many problems of constrained motions using Newton's method. Well, you can now scrutinise all the details of the methods you had applied, and find for yourself that some extra equations were indeed formulated in each case. There exists no particular rule as to how to formulate such new equations. Usually the torque equations and sometimes the energy equations act as supplements to the usual second law. But we are now interested in obtaining a precise method of tackling any given dynamical problem of constrained motions, so that even a blind can solve the problem. It is like inventing algebra (mechanical prescriptions) to replace intuition based arithmetic.

1.5 LAGRANGE'S EQUATIONS OF MOTION OF THE FIRST KIND

In order to circumvent the situation noted in the previous section, let us claim (and hope) that the constraint relation must contain complete information regarding the restriction put on the motion of the system. This cannot be otherwise, because, given a kinematical description of the motion we should not need anything more than the constraint relation to check whether the motion is consistent with that constraint. This consideration suggests that the constraint forces should be derivable solely from the constraint relations. To achieve this, one proceeds as follows.

First consider a nonholonomic constraint, say, the one given by Eq. (1.17). Let us define $h = dg/dt$. Since $g(\boldsymbol{r}, \dot{\boldsymbol{r}}, t) = 0$, $h(\boldsymbol{r}, \dot{\boldsymbol{r}}, \ddot{\boldsymbol{r}}, t)$ must also be equal to zero, that is,

$$h = \frac{dg}{dt} = \frac{\partial g}{\partial t} + \frac{\partial g}{\partial \boldsymbol{r}} \cdot \dot{\boldsymbol{r}} + \frac{\partial g}{\partial \dot{\boldsymbol{r}}} \cdot \ddot{\boldsymbol{r}} = 0$$

Again, since none of dg/dt, $\partial g/\partial \boldsymbol{r}$, $\partial g/\partial \dot{\boldsymbol{r}}$ contains $\ddot{\boldsymbol{r}}$ explicitly, we have

$$\frac{\partial h}{\partial \ddot{\boldsymbol{r}}} = \frac{\partial g}{\partial \dot{\boldsymbol{r}}} \tag{1.19}$$

and h depends linearly on $\ddot{\boldsymbol{r}}$, where $\ddot{\boldsymbol{r}}$ is the total acceleration of the particle.

Now if the constraint were holonomic, say of the form $g(\boldsymbol{r}, t) = 0$, we would like to define the function h by $h = d^2g/dt^2$. Arguing as before, as $g(\boldsymbol{r},t) = 0$, $h = 0$, that is,

$$0 = h = \frac{d^2 g}{dt^2} = \frac{d}{dt}\left(\frac{\partial g}{\partial t} + \frac{\partial g}{\partial \boldsymbol{r}} \cdot \dot{\boldsymbol{r}}\right)$$

$$= \frac{\partial^2 g}{\partial t^2} + \frac{\partial^2 g}{\partial \boldsymbol{r} \partial t} \cdot \dot{\boldsymbol{r}} + \frac{d}{dt}\left(\frac{\partial g}{\partial \boldsymbol{r}}\right) \cdot \dot{\boldsymbol{r}} + \frac{\partial g}{\partial \boldsymbol{r}} \cdot \ddot{\boldsymbol{r}}$$

The first three terms on the RHS of the previous equation do not contain any $\ddot{\boldsymbol{r}}$ explicitly and so also the factor $\partial g/\partial \boldsymbol{r}$ of the fourth term. Therefore,

$$\frac{\partial h}{\partial \ddot{\boldsymbol{r}}} = \frac{\partial g}{\partial \boldsymbol{r}} \tag{1.20}$$

and h is once again linearly related to the total acceleration $\ddot{\boldsymbol{r}}$.

Note that in both the cases, $(\partial h/\partial \ddot{\boldsymbol{r}})$ is a vector function of $\boldsymbol{r}$ and t (and may as well be a function of $\dot{\boldsymbol{r}}$, if the constraint is nonholonomic) and h is linearly dependent on $\ddot{\boldsymbol{r}}$. The equations

$$h = \frac{dg}{dt} = 0 \quad \text{for the nonholonomic case} \quad \text{and}$$

$$h = \frac{d^2 g}{dt^2} = 0 \quad \text{for the holonomic case}$$

are the additional constraint equations on the total acceleration (or equivalently, the total force). This has the general form

$$0 = (\text{some function of } \boldsymbol{r},\ \dot{\boldsymbol{r}} \text{ and } t) + \left(\frac{\partial h}{\partial \ddot{\boldsymbol{r}}}\right) \cdot \ddot{\boldsymbol{r}}$$

where $\ddot{\boldsymbol{r}}$ is the total acceleration of the particle and $(\partial h/\partial \ddot{\boldsymbol{r}})$ is a vector quantity determined purely from the constraint relation and is itself independent of the total acceleration.

The above constraint relation on total acceleration is therefore directly affected by the vector $(\partial h/\partial \ddot{\boldsymbol{r}})$. Only the component of total acceleration parallel to the vector $(\partial h/\partial \ddot{\boldsymbol{r}})$ enter the above constraint relation, because of the scalar nature of the scalar product $(\partial h/\partial \ddot{\boldsymbol{r}}) \cdot \ddot{\boldsymbol{r}}$. Therefore, the constraint force cannot have any component perpendicular to $(\partial h/\partial \ddot{\boldsymbol{r}})$, because if it had, it ought to have contradicted our legitimate expectation that forces of constraints be solely derivable from the constraint relations. Or in other words, $\boldsymbol{f}$ must be parallel to $(\partial h/\partial \ddot{\boldsymbol{r}})$, that is,

$$\boldsymbol{f} = \lambda \frac{\partial h}{\partial \ddot{\boldsymbol{r}}} \tag{1.21}$$

where λ is an unknown scalar, that takes care of the required dimension and magnitude of $\boldsymbol{f}$.

Since $g(\boldsymbol{r}, \dot{\boldsymbol{r}}, t)$ is given, h and hence $\boldsymbol{f}$ are known except for λ. Now there are four unknowns and four independent equations giving simultaneous solutions for $\boldsymbol{r}$ and hence, along with λ, $\boldsymbol{f}$ is uniquely determined. Newton's equations of motion now acquire the form,

$$m\ddot{\boldsymbol{r}} - \boldsymbol{F}^{(a)} - \lambda \frac{\partial h}{\partial \ddot{\boldsymbol{r}}} = \boldsymbol{0} \tag{1.22}$$

More explicitly, that is, in terms of the given constraint relation, we have for holonomic one-particle systems

$$m\ddot{\boldsymbol{r}} - \boldsymbol{F}^{(a)} - \lambda\frac{\partial g(\boldsymbol{r},t)}{\partial \boldsymbol{r}} = \boldsymbol{0}$$

and for nonholonomic one-particle systems,

$$m\ddot{\boldsymbol{r}} - \boldsymbol{F}^{(a)} - \lambda\frac{\partial g(\boldsymbol{r},\dot{\boldsymbol{r}},t)}{\partial \dot{\boldsymbol{r}}} = \boldsymbol{0}$$

These are sometimes called *Lagrange's equations of the first kind*, and λ is called *Lagrange's undetermined multiplier*.

It may be mentioned that the concept of undetermined multiplier was introduced in physics by Joseph Louis Lagrange in 1764. Today even school children use the idea, quite unknowingly though, when they try to solve simultaneous algebraic linear equations involving two or more unknowns. When we find the equations $ax + by = p$ and $cx + dy = q$ with x and y as unknowns, we multiply the first equation by c and the second by a and then subtract the first from the second in order to eliminate x and thereby evaluate y. Here the Lagrange multipliers are c and a respectively.

1.5.1 Generalization to a System of N Particles with k Constraint Relations

The above considerations can be easily generalized to the motion of a system of N particles, with k constraints; namely

$$g_i(\boldsymbol{r}_j,\dot{\boldsymbol{r}}_j,t) = 0 \qquad \text{for} \quad i = 1,\ldots,k$$

where j in $\boldsymbol{r}_j$ and $\dot{\boldsymbol{r}}_j$ runs over all or a fraction of the particles. Let us define

$$h_i = \frac{dg_i}{dt} \quad \text{for the nonholonomic constraints, and}$$

$$h_i = \frac{d^2 g_i}{dt^2} \quad \text{for holonomic ones}$$

The force of constraint on the jth particle due to the imposition of the ith constraint is

$$\boldsymbol{f}_{ji} = \lambda_i \frac{\partial h_i}{\partial \ddot{\boldsymbol{r}}_j}$$

so that the total force of constraint on the jth particle is given by

$$\boldsymbol{f}_j = \sum_{i=1}^{k} \lambda_i \frac{\partial h_i}{\partial \ddot{\boldsymbol{r}}_j}$$

where $\lambda_1,\ldots,\lambda_k$ are the k Lagrange multipliers that are introduced. Thus Newton's equation of motion for the jth particle having mass m_j becomes

$$m_j\ddot{\boldsymbol{r}}_j - \boldsymbol{F}_j^{(a)} - \sum_{i=1}^{k} \lambda_i \frac{\partial h_i}{\partial \ddot{\boldsymbol{r}}_j} = \boldsymbol{0} \qquad j = 1,\ldots,N \tag{1.23}$$

where $\boldsymbol{F}_j^{(a)}$ is the total external force applied on the jth particle.

These N vector equations (or, $3N$ scalar equations) apply to the cases of holonomic or nonholonomic, and scleronomic or rheonomic constraints that are expressible in the bilateral forms only. Note that the total number of equations one has to deal with is $3N + k$, as the number of dynamical equations is $3N$ and the number of constraint equations is k. Moreover, these are coupled equations (see the last summand in Eq. (1.23)) and hence their integration is quite involved. For this reason Lagrange's equations of the first kind find little use in actual practice. Nevertheless, once solved, they provide a complete solution to the dynamical problems of most diverse nature. The method is precise and complete.

1.5.2 An Example

Let us study the motion of a simple pendulum oscillating in the $x - z$ plane. For this system, the holonomic constraints are

$$g_1 \equiv y = 0$$

$$\text{and} \quad g_2 \equiv x^2 + y^2 + z^2 - l^2 = 0$$

The applied forces are $F_x = 0 = F_y$ and $F_z = mg$. Since there are two constraints g_1 and g_2, two multipliers say λ_1 and λ_2 are needed. The equations of motion are

$$m\ddot{x} - \lambda_1 \frac{\partial g_1}{\partial x} - \lambda_2 \frac{\partial g_2}{\partial x} = 0$$

$$m\ddot{y} - \lambda_1 \frac{\partial g_1}{\partial y} - \lambda_2 \frac{\partial g_2}{\partial y} = 0$$

$$m\ddot{z} - mg - \lambda_1 \frac{\partial g_1}{\partial z} - \lambda_2 \frac{\partial g_2}{\partial z} = 0$$

Substituting for the partial derivatives

$$\begin{aligned} m\ddot{x} - 2\lambda_2 x &= 0 \\ m\ddot{y} - \lambda_1 - 2\lambda_2 y &= 0 \\ m\ddot{z} - mg - 2\lambda_2 z &= 0 \end{aligned} \tag{1.24}$$

Let us assume that the oscillations are of small amplitude, giving for

$$z^2 = l^2 - x^2 - y^2$$

$$z = l\sqrt{1 - \frac{x^2 + y^2}{l^2}} \simeq l\left(1 - \frac{x^2 + y^2}{2l^2}\right) \simeq l$$

as $x^2 + y^2 \ll l^2$ (second order of smallness). Thus to the first order of smallness of the amplitude, $z =$ constant, and therefore $\dot{z}$ and $\ddot{z}$ are negligibly small compared to $\dot{x}$ and $\ddot{x}$. Putting $z = l$, $\ddot{z} = 0$, we get from the last of Eqs (1.24),

$$\lambda_2 = -\frac{mg}{2l}$$

Since $y = 0$ at every instant of time, $\dot{y} = \ddot{y} = 0$, giving $\lambda_1 = 0$ from the middle one of Eq. (1.24). Finally the first equation of (1.24) gives

$$\ddot{x} + \frac{g}{l}x = 0$$

which describes an SHM in the x-coordinate with angular frequency $\omega = \sqrt{g/l}$. Moreover, $\lambda_1 = 0$ and $\lambda_2 = -mg/2l$ imply that:
the x-component of the constraint force $= 2\lambda_2 x = -mgx/l = -mg\sin\theta \simeq -mg\theta$
where, θ is the angular position of of the bob with respect to the local vertical,
the y-component of the constraint force $= \lambda_1 + 2\lambda_2 y = 0$ and
the z-component of the constraint force $= 2\lambda_2 z = -mgz/l = -mg\cos\theta \simeq -mg$.
These are nothing but the components of the tension in the string.

1.6 GIBBS-APPELL'S PRINCIPLE OF LEAST CONSTRAINT

Willard Gibbs (1879) and later Paul Appell (1899) gave a new meaning to Lagrange's equations of motion of the first kind. Following their suggestions, let us define a quantity called the *kinetic energy of acceleration* of a system of N particles, given by

$$S = \frac{1}{2}\sum_{j=1}^{N} m_j|\ddot{\boldsymbol{r}}_j|^2 \tag{1.25}$$

where velocity is replaced by acceleration in the usual expression for kinetic energy. Now Lagrange's equations of the first kind as given in Eq. (1.23) reduce to the form

$$\frac{\partial G}{\partial \ddot{\boldsymbol{r}}_j} = 0 \tag{1.26}$$

where

$$G = S - \sum_{j=1}^{N} \boldsymbol{F}_j^{(a)} \cdot \ddot{\boldsymbol{r}}_j - \sum_{i=1}^{k} \lambda_i h_i \tag{1.27}$$

is a scalar point function of acceleration formed out of known quantities such as externally applied forces and constraint equations. This is called Gibbs-Appell's form of the equations of motion. More recently, T. R. Kane (1969) has developed a new scheme of setting up of equations of motion, which are in spirit quite similar to Gibbs-Appell's.

Furthermore, it is easy to check that

$$\frac{\partial^2 G}{\partial \ddot{\boldsymbol{r}}_j^2} = \frac{\partial^2 S}{\partial \ddot{\boldsymbol{r}}_j^2} = m_j > 0$$

So the function G is such that its first derivative with respect to acceleration $\ddot{\boldsymbol{r}}_j$ is zero by requirement of the equation of motion and its second derivative with respect to $\ddot{\boldsymbol{r}}_j$ is positive as the mass of any particle is greater than zero. This means that Gibbs-Appell's form of equations of motion is a minimum for G with respect to all possible variations of $\ddot{\boldsymbol{r}}_j$. The function G is called Gibbs-Appell's *least constraint function.* Gibbs-Appell's principle of least constraint states that for a given set of position vectors $\boldsymbol{r}_j$ and velocities $\dot{\boldsymbol{r}}_j$, $j = 1,\ldots,N$, the Gibbs-Appell function $G(\boldsymbol{r},\dot{\boldsymbol{r}},\ddot{\boldsymbol{r}})$ is a minimum if and only if the accelerations $\ddot{\boldsymbol{r}}_j$ $(j = 1,\ldots,N)$ are chosen to be the measured or the actual ones. This effort of Gibbs and Appell can be viewed as an early attempt to geometrise dynamics.

1.7 D'ALEMBERT'S PRINCIPLE

So far our approach has been to evaluate the forces of constraints and solve Newton's equations of motion. This is obviously a tedious procedure as is apparent in the example worked out above. Now, the question is, can we totally eliminate or bypass the determination of the forces of constraints? The answer as we know today is an affirmative one, provided we stop referring to forces, and deal directly with work, or kinetic or potential energy, and/or introduce non-Cartesian coordinates, if such coordinates appear to be more natural than the Cartesian ones. Following the historical sequence of developments, first we move on to a picture based on the concept of work, or more precisely, virtual work.

We have seen that constraint forces do work in dissipative and rheonomic systems. For a dissipative system such as one having friction, the constraint forces can be taken care of by promoting them to the list of externally applied forces. The real problem would then lie only with rheonomic systems. These systems can be handled by using the idea of virtual work.

1.7.1 Conditions for Vanishing Virtual Work due to Constraint Forces Alone

We have seen earlier that the principle of virtual work involving only applied forces holds good if the virtual work done by the constraint forces vanishes identically. We now proceed to obtain general conditions under which this is valid. The work done by the constraint forces arising due to the specified constraints, under arbitrary but infinitesimally small virtual displacements of the particles compatible with the constraints is

$$\delta W = \sum_{j=1}^{N} \boldsymbol{f}_j \cdot \delta\boldsymbol{r}_j = \sum_{j=1}^{N} \delta\boldsymbol{r}_j \cdot \left(\sum_{i=1}^{k} \lambda_i \frac{\partial h_i}{\partial \ddot{\boldsymbol{r}}_j}\right) \tag{1.28}$$

Now δW vanishes identically for the following two types of constraints, namely, for

1. all holonomic constraints: We have, by virtue of Eq. (1.20)

$$\delta W = \sum_j \delta\boldsymbol{r}_j \cdot \left(\sum_i \lambda_i \frac{\partial g_i}{\partial \boldsymbol{r}_j}\right) = \sum_i \lambda_i \delta g_i = 0$$

because all $\delta g_i = 0$ trivially by virtue of the constraint equations $g_i = 0$.

2. those nonholonomic constraints which are homogeneous functions of velocities except for an additive function of position and time: By virtue of the definition of homogeneous function of velocities of order n, we must have

$$g_i(\boldsymbol{r},\alpha\dot{\boldsymbol{r}},t) = \alpha^n\, g_i(\boldsymbol{r},\dot{\boldsymbol{r}},t) \tag{1.29}$$

where α is any scalar constant and n is a non-negative integer. For example,

$$g \equiv a(x,y,t)\dot{x}^3 + b(x,y,t)\dot{y}^3 + c(x,y,t)\dot{x}^2\dot{y} + d(x,y,t)\dot{x}\dot{y}^2 + 3e(x,y,t)$$

satisfies this required condition for $n = 3$, except for the additive function e of coordinates and time. For such *nonholonomic* cases, consider

$$\delta W = \sum_j \delta\boldsymbol{r}_j \cdot \left(\sum_i \lambda_i \frac{\partial g_i}{\partial \dot{\boldsymbol{r}}_j}\right) \tag{1.30}$$

To ensure

$$\sum_j \delta\boldsymbol{r}_j \cdot \frac{\partial g_i}{\partial \dot{\boldsymbol{r}}_j} = 0 \tag{1.31}$$

the function $\partial g_i / \partial \dot{\boldsymbol{r}}_j$ must satisfy

$$\sum_j \frac{\partial g_i}{\partial \dot{\boldsymbol{r}}_j} \cdot d\boldsymbol{r}_j + nJ_i(\boldsymbol{r}_j, t)dt = 0$$

for any real displacement $d\boldsymbol{r}_j$ in real time dt, because the above equation reduces to Eq. (1.31) when the displacement $d\boldsymbol{r}_j$ is replaced by a virtual displacement $\delta\boldsymbol{r}_j$ as it presumes a condition $dt = 0$ for all virtual displacements. Here $J_i(\boldsymbol{r}_j, t)$ can be any arbitrary function of coordinates and time. The above condition can now be rewritten as

$$g \equiv \sum_j \frac{\partial g_i}{\partial \dot{\boldsymbol{r}}_j} \cdot \dot{\boldsymbol{r}}_j + nJ_i(\boldsymbol{r}_j, t) = 0$$

The first summand will cancel with $J_i(\boldsymbol{r}_j, t)$ if the g_i's are purely homogeneous functions of velocities of any order n plus a term $J_i(\boldsymbol{r}_j, t)$. Thus those nonholonomic constraints which are homogeneous functions of velocities plus a suitable additive function of coordinates and time can have a set of nonzero $J_i(\boldsymbol{r}_j, t)$ such that a total of zero virtual work is done by all the constraint forces.

Under these two types of situations, the virtual work done by the constraint forces vanishes. Therefore, the necessary condition for static equilibrium becomes

$$\sum_j \boldsymbol{F}_j^{(a)} \cdot \delta\boldsymbol{r}_j = 0 \tag{1.16}$$

where $\boldsymbol{F}_j^{(a)}$ is the total applied force on jth particle.

1.7.2 D'Alembert's Principle

We can use the above condition for vanishing virtual work done by the constraint forces for any dynamical system, not necessarily in static equilibrium. For the jth particle in such a system, Newton's equation of motion reads as

$$\boldsymbol{F}_j^{(a)} + \boldsymbol{f}_j = \dot{\boldsymbol{p}}_j \tag{1.32}$$

where $\boldsymbol{f}_j$ is the constraint force, $\boldsymbol{F}_j^{(a)}$ is the applied force and $\boldsymbol{p}_j$ is the linear momentum, all pertaining to the jth particle. Now the system also satisfies, by requirement of vanishing virtual work done by all constraint forces,

$$\delta W = \sum_j \boldsymbol{f}_j \cdot \delta \boldsymbol{r}_j = 0 \tag{1.33}$$

Taking the scalar product of each term in Eq. (1.32) with the infinitesimal virtual displacement of the jth particle $\delta \boldsymbol{r}_j$ and summing over all particles of the system, we get after accounting for Eq. (1.33)

$$\sum_{j=1}^{N} \left(\boldsymbol{F}_j^{(a)} - \dot{\boldsymbol{p}}_j \right) \cdot \delta \boldsymbol{r}_j = 0 \tag{1.34}$$

where $-\dot{\boldsymbol{p}}_j$ appears as an effective force called the *reverse force of inertia* on the jth particle, supplementing the already existing externally applied force $F_j^{(a)}$. The key point is that in Eq. (1.34) we have got rid of the constraint forces $\boldsymbol{f}_j$. Equation (1.34) generalises the principle of virtual work to a far wider class that inched the dynamical systems encompassing all holonomic and a large class of nonholonomic systems for which the virtual work vanishes. Equation (1.34) is commonly called D'Alembert's principle after its propounder, who published it in 1743.

Remarks: (i) Unlike Newton's $3N$ equations of motion, D'Alembert's principle is just one equation of motion.

(ii) D'Alembert's principle does not involve the forces of constraints in any way. So it is sufficient to specify all the applied forces only.

(iii) It is so general that even a knowledge of the constraint relations is not explicitly required except for determining $\delta \boldsymbol{r}_j$.

(iv) Its validity extends to all rheonomic and scleronomic systems that are either holonomic, or homogeneous nonholonomic (see the previous subsection). All such systems for which D'Alembert's principle is valid may be called *D'Alembertian* systems.

(v) The inertial force $-\dot{\boldsymbol{p}}_j$ is introduced to reduce the problem of dynamics to one of statics (compare Eq. (1.34) with Eq. (1.16)).

(vi) The force of inertia can be regarded as an inertial force arising in an accelerated frame of reference. In this sense, this is a forerunner of the *equivalence principle* of the general theory of relativity. In a freely falling accelerated frame $\boldsymbol{F}_j^{(a)} - \dot{\boldsymbol{p}}_j = 0$, gravity is nullified by the inertial force even though the whole system is in motion and not in either static or dynamic equilibrium.

(vii) D'Alembert's principle, it is often said, gives a complete solution to the problems of mechanics. All the different principles of mechanics are merely mathematically different formulations of D'Alembert's principle. Hamilton's principle (see chapter 6) can also be obtained from D'Alembert's principle. However, one should remember that Lagrange's equations of the first kind in the form given above, are even more general as they are valid for all holonomic and nonholonomic systems.

(viii) D'Alembert's principle is more elementary than the variational principles on another account; it requires no integration with respect to time. However the disadvantage is that the virtual work of the inertial force is polygenic and thus is not reducible to a single scalar function. This makes the principle most unsuitable for the use of curvilinear coordinates.

1.7.3 Some Applications of D'Alembert's Principle

(i) A spherical pendulum of varying length: A particle of mass m is suspended by a massless wire of length

$$r = a + b\cos(\omega t) \qquad (a > b > 0) \tag{1.35}$$

to form a spherical pendulum. Below we find the virtual displacements and the equations of motion using D'Alembert's principle.

Let r, θ and ϕ be the spherical polar coordinates of the particle. The acceleration of the particle is given by (see Appendix A2)

$$\begin{aligned}\ddot{\boldsymbol{r}} &= (\ddot{r} - r\dot{\theta}^2 - r\dot{\phi}^2\sin^2\theta\,)\hat{\boldsymbol{r}} + (r\ddot{\theta} + 2\dot{r}\dot{\theta} - r\dot{\phi}^2\sin\theta\cos\theta)\hat{\boldsymbol{\theta}} \\ &\quad + (r\ddot{\phi}\sin\theta + 2\dot{r}\dot{\phi}\sin\theta + 2r\dot{\theta}\dot{\phi}\cos\theta)\hat{\boldsymbol{\phi}}\end{aligned} \tag{1.36}$$

Virtual displacement must be consistent with the instantaneous constraint, namely $r =$ constant, therefore,

$$\delta\boldsymbol{r} = r\delta\theta\hat{\boldsymbol{\theta}} + r\sin\theta\delta\phi\hat{\boldsymbol{\phi}} \tag{1.37}$$

The external force on the system is

$$\boldsymbol{F} = -mg\hat{\boldsymbol{k}} = -mg(\cos\theta\hat{\boldsymbol{r}} - \sin\theta\hat{\boldsymbol{\theta}}) \tag{1.38}$$

By D'Alembert's principle, we must have

$$(\boldsymbol{F} - m\ddot{\boldsymbol{r}})\cdot\delta\boldsymbol{r} = 0 \tag{1.39}$$

which when coupled with Eqs .(1.35 – 1.38) gives the equations of motion in θ and ϕ.

(ii) An incline that makes an angle α with the horizontal is given a horizontal acceleration of magnitude a in the vertical plane of the incline, in order to prevent the sliding of any frictionless block placed on the incline. We want to find the value of a.

Virtual displacement must be consistent with the instantaneous constraint, that is, $\delta x = \delta l\cos\alpha$, $\delta y = \delta l\sin\alpha$, where δl is a possible virtual displacement along the incline. The forces applied on the system are $F_x = 0$ and $F_y = mg$. We do not bother about constraint forces. By D'Alembert's principle, we have

$$F_x\delta x + F_y\delta y - ma_x\delta x - ma_y\delta y = 0$$

or

$$0 + mg\,\delta l\sin\alpha - ma\,\delta l\cos\alpha - 0 = 0$$

since $a_y = 0$ (given) and $a_x = a$ (also given). This gives

$$a = g\tan\alpha$$

which is the required horizontal acceleration of the incline in order to prevent the sliding of the block placed on the incline.

1.8 SOME ADDITIONAL REMARKS

(i) We have already seen that systems having rheonomic constraints are nonconservative. Real work done by forces due to, say, holonomic, rheonomic constraints can be calculated as follows. We have

$$\frac{dW}{dt} = \sum_j \boldsymbol{f}_j \cdot \frac{d\boldsymbol{r}_j}{dt} = \sum_i \sum_j \lambda_i \frac{\partial g_j}{\partial \boldsymbol{r}_j} \cdot \frac{d\boldsymbol{r}_j}{dt} = \sum_i \lambda_i \left(\frac{dg_i}{dt} - \frac{\partial g_i}{\partial t} \right)$$

Since $g_i = 0$, $dg_i/dt = 0$, and the constraints being rheonomic, that is, $\partial g_i/\partial t \neq 0$, we have

$$\frac{dW}{dt} \neq 0$$

Therefore any holonomic but rheonomic system is in general nonconservative. Note, however, that the sum $\Sigma\lambda_i(\partial g_i/\partial t)$ may still vanish even if none of the individual $\partial g_i/\partial t$'s is zero. This makes some room for exceptional cases.

The real work done by the constraint forces can be obtained by integrating the above equation. The negative sign in the equation does not mean that work is always done on the system by the constraint forces, as the actual sign will depend on the signs of individual factors and terms in the summand.

(ii) Consider a system with unilateral constraints in equilibrium. Physically, a unilateral constraint is realised by a surface which divides the total space into two regions. The motion of the system is restricted to only one of the two regions and the system is not allowed to move across the surface. Therefore, when the system is on this dividing surface, the virtual displacements cannot have components in the direction of the unit normal pointing inside the prohibited region. However, since the system is driven to this surface under the action of the applied forces, these must have components in the direction of the unit normal defined above. Therefore, allowed virtual displacement can have only negative components in the direction of the applied forces. This means that the condition for equilibrium, Eq. (1.16) gets replaced by

$$\delta W_a = \sum \boldsymbol{F}_i^{(a)} \cdot \delta \boldsymbol{r}_i \leq 0$$

Equality is applied when the system is not on the constraint surface. Thus for example, for a ball hung from a ceiling by a string, a downward virtual displacement from its equilibrium position is not allowed while an upward virtual displacement is allowed in which case work done by the applied force of gravity is negative. Note that for a 1-D motion, the constraining 'surface' is a point, for a 2-D motion it is a curve and for 3-D motion, it is a closed surface.

1.9 WORK-ENERGY RELATION FOR CONSTRAINT FORCES OF SLIDING FRICTION

Friction plays a great role in our day to day life. Without friction, we could not walk, the cars could not move on the roads unless fired by a rocket, we could not hang a thing on or stick to the wall, and so on. The force of friction between two surfaces depends simultaneously on how hard they are pressed against each other by a force normal to the surface of contact and on the forces of pull or push that act parallel to the surface of contact. The forces of pull or push remain exactly balanced by the forces of friction that develop at the interface, up to limits set by the coefficient of static friction and the normal component of the pressure force. Since the point of contact does not move till the sliding occurs, the force of friction does not find a chance to do work on the bodies and the energy of the system remains unaffected. However, in the presence of sliding friction, the mechanical energy of the system gets gradually converted into heat, and therefore it is the first law of thermodynamics, rather than the simple conservation of mechanical energy that would be the most appropriate conservation law to be applied. A usual paradox goes like this: suppose a block is dragged at constant speed across a table with friction. The applied force of magnitude f acting through a distance d does an amount of work fd. The frictional force $\mu_k N$ ($= f$, since no acceleration is observed) does an amount of work $-\mu_k N d = -fd$, thus suggesting the total work $= fd - fd = 0$. For a point particle, the work done is equal to the change in kinetic energy, leading to the result that $fd - fd = 0 = \Delta(mv^2/2)$, that is, v does not change. This is fine, but where is the energy term representing the increased internal energy of the block? Thus the above treatment gives a right answer for the speed of the block, but not the correct work-energy relation. It ought to incorporate the first law of thermodynamics.

Moreover, for calculating the frictional work, the d used for the work done by the applied forces cannot be used. It is true that the block has moved through a distance d, but the frictional force at the interface has not worked through all that distance. Sherwood and Bernard (1984) suggest that d should be replaced by $d_{\text{eff}} \leq d$ for calculating the frictional work; the exact relation between d_{eff} and d should depend on the nature of the two surfaces at contact of sliding. When two surfaces are of identical nature $d_{\text{eff}} = d/2$, when the sliding upper block is soft and the resting lower block is very hard $d_{\text{eff}} = 0$, and when the sliding upper block is hard and the resting lower block is soft $d_{\text{eff}} = d$. One should also consider the heat exchange across the surface, depending on the thermal conductivity of the sliding blocks.

When a block slides through a distance d down an incline (angle of inclination α) with friction, the block's hot teeth are continually transferring heat to the new cold regions of the incline, so that the possible heat transfer from block to incline $|Q|$ is not negligible. Newton's method would suggest the work energy relation be given by

$$(mg\sin\alpha - \mu_k N)d = \Delta\left(\frac{1}{2}mv^2\right) \tag{1.39}$$

but from the first law of thermodynamics, the Sherwood equation would give

$$(mg\sin\alpha)d - \mu_k N d_{\text{eff}} - |Q| = \Delta\left(\frac{1}{2}mv^2\right) + \Delta E_{\text{thermal of block}} \tag{1.40}$$

However, Eq. (1.40) alone is also incomplete as the effective displacement d_{eff} of the frictional force is unknown. So one has to combine the Eqs (1.39) and (1.40), giving

$$\mu_k N(d - d_{\text{eff}}) = \Delta E_{\text{thermal of block}} + |Q|$$

Since the right hand side is positive, $d_{\text{eff}} < d$. Further, if we consider the universe as the closed system (that is, block + incline + earth) the total change in the thermal energy of the universe would be simply $\mu_k N d$.

1.10 SUMMARY

Constraints are defined and classified. In holonomic cases, these are algebraic equations of the surfaces on which motion of the system is constrained. In nonholonomic cases, the constraint equations are irreducible functions of velocities. If the surfaces of constraints in a given problem change with time, the constraints are rheonomic, otherwise scleronomic. Other classifications are not so essential.

Forces are broadly classified into two main types. Forces that appear to be capable of producing actions due to some well known external force-bearing agents are grouped into external or externally applied forces. The rest, arising from the details of constraining are grouped into forces of constraints.

Since by definition, the external or applied forces are all known forces, the key problem of dynamics is either to determine all the forces of constraints or eliminate them from the final equations of motion. In any case, if we want to retain Newton's form of the equations of motion, we have to determine the forces of constraints. Demanding that the constraint relations must contain all the necessary information on the forces of constraints, it is possible to have a satisfactory formulation commonly known as Lagrange's equations of motion of the first kind.

The other approach, namely, eliminating all the terms bearing the forces of constraints from the final equation of motion, using notions of virtual displacements and virtual work is due to D'Alembert. It is shown that virtual work done by constraint forces vanishes totally for all holonomic constraints and also for a subset of nonholonomic constraints. D'Alembert's principle is therefore considered to be far more powerful than Newton's equations of motion.

In Gibbs-Appell's form, dynamical problems involving constraints find a direct geometrical interpretation in the sense that natural paths under the given constraints maintain Gibbs-Appell's function at their minima.

Finally, the section on constraint forces due to sliding friction tries to convey the message that the phenomenon of sliding friction is still not well understood. The work energy relation cannot just be handled by dynamics alone, the first law of thermodynamics has to step in and this must require the knowledge of the quality of roughness of the sliding surfaces.

PROBLEMS

1.1 Write down the equations of constraints in Cartesian coordinates for the following dynamical systems and categorize them according to the classification of the constraints: (i) A small rigid rod of length l is allowed to move in any manner inside a balloon of fixed radius $R > l$, the end parts of the rod always touching the balloon's surface. What changes would it have, if R is now $R(t) = R + at$, say, a being a small

constant.
(ii) A piece of flexible but nonextensible string of length l_o is tied to the ceiling at a horizontal separation of $l < l_o$. A heavy bead is allowed to slide in any manner without any friction along the string. Because of the weight of the bead the string is all the time stretched into a 'V' shape.
(iii) The motion of a ship on the surface of the earth when the earth is expanding slowly with time. What would be the general nature of the constraints if the earth is further assumed to rotate 20 times faster than its present rate?
(iv) A pair of cartwheels of radius R, the centres of which are connected by a rigid shaft of length l is allowed to roll without slipping down an incline that makes an angle α with the horizontal.
(v) The motion of the filament of a bulb that is socketed in a table lamp stand which consists of a fixed base and two rigid stems with two flexible spherical joints before meeting the bulb holder. Does it make any difference if the filament is assumed to be a part of a rigid line or a coiled piece of wire?
(vi) The motion of a crank-shaft connecting a moving piston on one side and the spoke of a wheel on the other.

1.2 Prove that D'Alembert's equation represents the conservation of energy, if virtual displacements are regarded as real ones.

1.3 A mass point moves on the outside surface of the upper hemisphere of a globe. Let its initial position $\boldsymbol{r}$ and initial velocity $\boldsymbol{v}$ be arbitrary, except that the latter is to be tangential to the surface of the sphere. The motion is to be frictionless, occurring solely under the influence of gravity. Investigate the problem in terms of the Cartesian coordinates only and find at what height from the centre the particle should jump off the sphere.

1.4 A block of mass m slides down on a frictionless incline. Solve for its equations of motion using D'Alembert's principle and Lagrange's method.

1.5 Find the equations of motion of a solid sphere rolling down on an incline using Lagrange multipliers for the rolling constraints. What would be the work energy relation if there is slipping as well as rolling?

1.6 A particle of mass m is suspended by a massless wire of length $r = a + b\cos\omega t$, $(a > b > 0)$ to form a spherical pendulum. Find the virtual displacements and the equations of motion using D'Alembert's principle.

1.7 Inspired by Gibbs-Appell's principle of least constraint, Heinrich Hertz in 1896 derived his principle of least curvature for systems under the action of no external forces. Take the mass of all the particles to be unity and use Gibbs-Appell's principle of least constraint to derive Hertz's *principle of least curvature* which states that 'every free system remains in a state of rest or of uniform motion along the path of the least curvature'. The curvature of the trajectory, is defined as $\sqrt{K}$, where

$$K = \sum_{k=1}^{N} \left(\frac{d^2 x_k}{ds^2} \right)^2$$

ds being the line element in a $3N$ dimensional Euclidean space, given by $ds^2 = \sum_k dx_k^2$, and N being the number of particles.

1.8 A bead of mass m is constrained to slide down a frictionless right circular helical wire under the influence of gravity. Assume the axis of the helix to be vertical (z-axis), a the radius of the helix, $2\pi b$ the constant pitch length, so that the parametric equation of the helix can be written as $\mathbf{r}(\lambda) = a\cos\lambda\hat{\imath} + a\sin\lambda\hat{\jmath} + b\lambda\hat{k}$. Find the constraint force and an explicit solution to the equations of motion. If the wire had been in the shape of a parabola, say $x^2 = 4az$, $a > 0$, what would have been the equation of motion?

2

Lagrangian Formulation in Generalised Coordinates

2.0 INTRODUCTION

In the previous chapter, we have seen with great relief that D'Alembert's principle does not require a knowledge of the forces of constraints, although the constraint equations are of course needed for providing the virtual displacements. This is fine, but our problem is to obtain the solutions for $3N$ Cartesian coordinates (N being the number of particles involved). Lagrange's equations of the first kind are $3N$ in number, whereas D'Alembert's principle is a single equation. Coupled with the given constraint equations, the former set of equations but not the latter is capable of providing us with the complete solution to the problem. This is the basic limitation of D'Alembert's principle.

It was once again Joseph Louis Lagrange (1736 – 1813) who at the age of 19 conceived of, and at the age of 23 formulated, an ingenious analytical method that allowed him to extract a sufficient number of independent equations from just the one, D'Alembert's principle. He finally published the work in the form of a book entitled *Mechanique Analytique*, although he had finished the manuscript 6 years earlier. Breaking the tradition of all his predecessors, Lagrange did not put in his book a single diagram, or a construction, or geometrical or mechanical reasoning. The book was just full of algebraic operations. Sir William Rowan Hamilton later described the book as a 'scientific poem'; E. T. Bell called it 'the finest example in all science of the art of getting something out of nothing'.

At Turin, the boyish professor Lagrange used to lecture to the students, all older than himself, and founded the Turin Academy of Sciences at the age of 22. Lagrange sent some of his works to Euler when he was still in his teens. Euler had baffled for long with his semigeometrical methods to tackle the problem of isoperimetry, found Lagrange's new scheme straightforward and elegant and solved the problem immediately. He and D'Alembert schemed to get Lagrange at the Berlin Academy. On the invitation of the king the Great Frederick, Lagrange joined the Berlin Academy in 1766 to succeed Euler, and Euler returned to St. Peterburg in Russia.

Lagrange got the grand prize of the French Academy of Sciences in 1764 for solving the problem of libration of the moon, that is, why we see the same face of the moon all the time. He again captured the prestigious prize in 1766 by explaining the inequalities in the motion of the satellites of Jupiter. He captured it for the third time in 1772 by solving the three body problem in gravitation, for the fourth time in 1774 for his theory of the motion of the moon, and for the fifth time in 1778 for the calculations of the perturbations of planets on cometary orbits. Lagrange joined the French Academy in 1787 on the invitation of Louis XVI; the French revolution began and his close friend Lavoisier was guillotined, but Lagrange was saved because he never criticised anybody. He was famous for his standard reply 'I do not know' to anything and everything that was controversial. After the French revolution, 'École Normale' was established in 1795 and Lagrange was appointed a professor of mathematics. This institute was closed in 1797 and instead 'École Polytechnique' was founded in the same year, where Lagrange found a position, which he held till he died in 1813. He finished another two books, *The Theory of Analytic Functions* in 1797 and *The Lectures on the Calculus of Functions* in 1801, whose limitations made young Cauchy develop the theory of complex variables.

2.1 CHANGE OF NOTATION

Consider a system of N particles. We rename and arrange the Cartesian coordinates and masses of all the particles in the following order.

Particle no 1 :	Coordinates	Mass
	$x_1 \to x_1$	$m_1 \to m_1$
	$y_1 \to x_2$	$m_1 \to m_2$
	$z_1 \to x_3$	$m_1 \to m_3$

Particle no 2 :	Coordinates	Mass
	$x_2 \to x_4$	$m_2 \to m_4$
	$y_2 \to x_5$	$m_2 \to m_5$
	$z_2 \to x_6$	$m_2 \to m_6$

and so on. Finally, for

Particle no N :	Coordinates	Mass
	$x_N \to x_{3N-2}$	$m_N \to m_{3N-2}$
	$y_N \to x_{3N-1}$	$m_N \to m_{3N-1}$
	$z_N \to x_{3N}$	$m_N \to m_{3N}$

The rth particle has Cartesian coordinates $(x_{3r-2}, x_{3r-1}, x_{3r})$ and mass $m_{3r-2} = m_{3r-1} = m_{3r}$ (the original mass m_r). With this notation D'Alembert's principle (see Eq. 1.34) takes the following form:

$$\sum_{i=1}^{3N}\left(F_i^{(a)}-m_i\frac{d^2x_i}{dt^2}\right)\delta x_i=0 \tag{2.1}$$

This is a single equation with $3N$ bracketed terms in series, the sum being equated to zero. Because of the constraint relations δx_i are not all arbitrary. In other words, all the δx_i are not linearly independent, and the expression within each parenthesis need not vanish separately.

In the above notation, Lagrange's equations of the first kind become

$$m_i\frac{d^2x_i}{dt^2}-F_i^{(a)}-\sum_{r=1}^{k+k'}\lambda_r\frac{\partial h_r}{\partial\ddot{x}_i}=0 \tag{2.2}$$

where k and k' are the total number of holonomic and nonholonomic constraints respectively. These are $3N$ differential equations each containing a maximum of $k+k'+2$ terms. There are further, $k+k'$ equations of constraints. Thus $3N+k+k'$ equations are to be solved for the $3N$ unknowns in x_i and $k+k'$ unknowns in λ_r. In most treatments, D'Alembert's principle is obtained first and then Lagrange's equations of the first kind are derived from it. We have reversed the order because Lagrange's equations of the first kind are more general than D'Alembert's principle. However neither method is economical except for a few specific cases, because there are too many unknowns to be solved for. Now the question is, can one minimise the number of unknown variables. The answer is, in general, 'yes'. There comes the concept of degrees of freedom of a dynamical system and with it a powerful technique for solving dynamical problems developed by Euler and Lagrange.

2.2 DEGREES OF FREEDOM

The minimum number of independent variables (say $u_1, u_2, \ldots u_n$), required to fix the position and the configuration of a dynamical system which are compatible with the given constraints is called the number of *degrees of freedom* (DOF) of the system. These independent variables must be sufficient in number to describe all possible positions and configurations of the system consistent with the given constraints. By independent we mean that for the n variables given by $u_1,\ldots,u_n$, if we have n constants $c_1,\ldots,c_n$ satisfying

$$\sum_{i=1}^{n}c_i\,du_i=0$$

at any point, then it necessarily follows that

$$c_1=c_2=\cdots=c_n=0$$

Thus the differential change of the value of any one of a given set of independent variables cannot be obtained by any linear combination of the differentials of the other variables at any point. In other words there cannot exist any constraint relation for any given set of independent variables.

We now give examples to enumerate the number of degrees of freedom.

1. A free particle : Since we are dealing with the motion of particles in three dimensional Euclidean space (E_3), a free particle can have the maximum degrees of freedom bounded by the dimensionality of its position space, which is 3 for E_3. The three Cartesian coordinates of a free particle are independent variables, each varying between $-\infty$ and $+\infty$. So the number of DOF for a free particle is 3.
2. N free particles : Each particle requires 3 independent coordinates to be specified, Hence N particles require $3N$ independent coordinates to completely describe them. Thus the number of DOF is $3N$.
3. N particles with k constraint relations : When the values of any of $3N - k$ coordinates are known, the values of the remaining k coordinates are fixed by the requirement that at every instant of time all the $3N$ coordinates must satisfy the given k constraint relations. Thus only $3N - k$ independent variables are needed to completely specify the state of the system. This is a standard procedure of finding the number of DOF of any dynamical system, namely, first find the number of particles in the system and second, the number of constraints. Of course one has to make sure that each of these k constraints is independent of all the others. So in this case the number of DOF is $3N - k$.
4. The fixed fulcrum of a simple pendulum : This is a point fixed on a ceiling. It requires three coordinates, say (x_0, y_0, z_0), to represent its position. But all these coordinates are fixed, not variable. Hence its number of DOF is 0. We can express this fact in terms of constraints. This is done as follows: $x = x_0$, $y = y_0$ and $z = z_0$ are the three constraint relations. Thus according to the standard procedure, the number of DOF is $3 \times$ (number of particles) - (number of constraints) $= 3 \times 1 - 3 = 0$.
5. The bob of a conical pendulum : Assume that the bob is a particle. The constraint is the fixed length l between the moving bob and the fixed fulcrum, that is, $x^2 + y^2 + z^2 = l^2$, if the fulcrum is taken to be the origin. Hence the number of DOF is $3 \times 1 - 1 = 2$.
6. A dumbbell : The idealization of this is two heavy point particles joined together by a massless rigid rod. Thus this system consists of two particles ($N = 2$) with one constraint $(x_2 - x_1)^2 + (y_2 - y_1)^2 + (z_2 - z_1)^2 = l^2$, where l is the length of the connecting rod, and the points (x_1, y_1, z_1) and (x_2, y_2, z_2) are the coordinates of the two massive particles. Hence the number of DOF is $3 \times 2 - 1 = 5$
7. Three point masses connected by three rigid massless rods : In this system there are three particles and three constraints between them, due to the rigid rods. Thus the number of DOF is $3 \times 3 - 3 = 6$.
8. A rigid body : The mathematical idealization of a rigid body is a system with a large number of particles (point masses) not all lying on one line, and with all its particles at fixed distances from each other. Take any three points which are not collinear, their number of DOF $= 6$ according to the previous example. If one fixes these three points, the body (consisting of N particles) is immovable. Hence the number of DOF of a rigid body having $N \geq 3$ is 6, which is independent of N.
9. A rigid body fixed at one point : Since it is fixed at one point we lose 3 degrees of freedom. Hence the number of DOF of this system is $6 - 3 = 3$. The body can rotate freely about this fixed point with these degrees of freedom.

10. A rigid body rotating about a fixed axis in space : In this case, the number of DOF is 1.

2.3 GENERALISED COORDINATES

We have seen that for a system of N particles with k independent constraints, the number of independent variables required to specify its configuration and position is $n = 3N - k$, which is less than the total number of Cartesian coordinates involved. The question is how to specify these independent variables. We can of course, choose any $3N - k$ out of the $3N$ Cartesian coordinates to be the independent variables. However, this choice is by no means binding on us. We can choose any set of the required number of independent quantities say $(q_1, q_2, \ldots, q_n)$ such that all Cartesian coordinates are known functions of the q_i variables:

$$\begin{aligned} x_1 &= x_1(q_1, q_2, \ldots, q_n, t) \\ x_2 &= x_2(q_1, q_2, \ldots, q_n, t) \\ &\vdots \\ x_i &= x_i(q_1, q_2, \ldots, q_n, t) \\ &\vdots \\ x_{3N} &= x_{3N}(q_1, q_2, \ldots, q_n, t) \end{aligned} \tag{2.3}$$

One should note that if there is an explicit time dependence in some or all of the functions defined in Eq. (2.3), the system is called *rheonomic*. Otherwise the system is called *scleronomic*.

Obtaining a solution of the mechanical problem now involves two steps. First, set up the equations of motion in terms of the q_i variables and integrate them to obtain their time dependence. Then the functions $x_i(t)$ can be obtained using Eq. (2.3). This can simplify the problem, because integrating the equations of motion in the q_i variables may be simpler. In fact, choice of good q_i variables is guided by this requirement. These variables defined through Eq. (2.3) are called *generalised coordinates*.

Thus we can define *generalised coordinates* as the independent coordinates sufficient to completely specify the configuration of a dynamical system. They are not necessarily rectangular Cartesian coordinates.

For example, consider the central force problem. For a particle revolving around a fixed attracting centre, it is easier to work with spherical polar coordinates, which are related to Cartesian coordinates through the equations (see Appendix A1)

$$\begin{aligned} x &= r \sin\theta \cos\phi \\ y &= r \sin\theta \sin\phi \\ z &= r \cos\theta \end{aligned}$$

Similarly, for a spherical pendulum, θ and ϕ are the most suitable generalised coordinates, and so on.

2.3.1 Remarks

1. The generalised coordinates do not necessarily belong to any conventional coordinate system. They can be any curvilinear coordinates, dimensionless parameters such as angles or their combinations, etc.

2. For holonomic systems, the number of generalised coordinates is exactly equal to the number of DOF of the system, that is, for a system of N particles having k holonomic constraints, the total number of generalised coordinates is $3N - k$. Hence they are strictly independent of each other.

3. For nonholonomic systems, the number of generalised coordinates required is larger than the number of DOF. If there are k holonomic and k' nonholonomic constraints, the number of DOF of the system is $3N - k - k'$. However the required number of generalised coordinates is $3N - k$. Hence these generalised coordinates are called *quasi-generalised* coordinates, in order to reserve the term *generalised* for the holonomic cases only.

Example 1. A rigid spherical ball is rolling without slipping on a table. A spherical ball, being a rigid body, has a total of six degrees of freedom. But it has to satisfy the constraints of rolling without slipping which are given by $\boldsymbol{v}_{\text{cm}} = r\boldsymbol{\omega} \times \hat{\boldsymbol{n}}$ (see example 8 in section 1.2), a vector equation equivalent to three scalar equations. Thus the number of DOF is $6 - 3 = 3$. Of these three constraints, at least one will turn out to be nonholonomic. Hence the minimum number of quasi-generalised coordinates is 4 (for example, two Cartesian coordinates for the centre of mass and two angular coordinates with respect to the CM for the relative orientation of the point of contact on the sphere).

Example 2. The problem of a disc rolling without slipping on a table is exactly similar to the one above. There is one nonholonomic rolling constraint. Although the number of DOF is 3, the required number of quasi-generalised coordinates is 4 (the two Cartesian coordinates for the location of the CM and two angular coordinates, namely one for the orientation of the disc with respect to the vertical and the other the angle of rolling).

4. The total time derivative of any generalised coordinate is called the *generalised coordinate velocity* or the *generalised velocity* in short. It is denoted by $\dot{q}_i$, that is,

$$\dot{q}_i = \frac{dq_i}{dt} \qquad i = 1, \ldots, n \tag{2.4}$$

5. The set of all q_i, $i = 1, 2, ..., n$, span an n-dimensional space R^n called the *configuration space* of the system. At any given time t, the system is located at some point in its configuration space, so the time evolution of the system is represented by a definite trajectory in its configuration space. The n-dimensional configuration space R^n contains ∞^{n-1} curves through each point — each curve being a possible path of the system — each of which can be traversed at any speed. The space is a dynamical one in the sense that motions do actually take place in it. The velocity of a point moving along a trajectory in the configuration space has n components $\dot{q}_i$, $i = 1, \ldots, n$.

6. The *extended configuration space* $R^n \times R^1(t) \longrightarrow R^{n+1}$ is geometrical, the extra dimension being that for the time parameter t. There are ∞^n curves through each point — each curve again being a possible path. But these paths do not traverse in time, there is no motion in the space, there do however exist simply mathematical relations between curves.

2.4 LAGRANGE'S EQUATIONS OF MOTION OF THE SECOND KIND

These are also known as *Lagrange's equations of motion.*

Consider a rheonomic, holonomic system having N particles and k holonomic constraints. Thus it has $n = 3N - k$ degrees of freedom. Choose n generalised coordinates $(q_1, q_2, \ldots, q_n)$. These are related to Cartesian coordinates through Eq. (2.3). Therefore, the Cartesian velocity components are

$$\dot{x}_i = \frac{dx_i}{dt} = \frac{\partial x_i}{\partial t} + \sum_{j=1}^{n} \frac{\partial x_i}{\partial q_j}\dot{q}_j \tag{2.5}$$

From now on, we will use the *Einstein summation convention*, in which whenever there is a repeated index in any term, there is an implicit summation over that index, unless otherwise mentioned. For example, in the above equation, the index j is repeated in the second term on the RHS, and there is a summation from $j = 1$ to $j = n$. Thus it is possible to dispense with the summation sign, and we can write that term as $(\partial x_i/\partial q_j)\,\dot{q}_j$. Equation (2.5) gives

$$\frac{\partial \dot{x}_i}{\partial \dot{q}_j} = \frac{\partial x_i}{\partial q_j} \tag{2.6}$$

Next consider

$$\begin{aligned}\frac{d}{dt}\left(\frac{\partial x_i}{\partial q_j}\right) &= \frac{\partial}{\partial t}\left(\frac{\partial x_i}{\partial q_j}\right) + \frac{\partial}{\partial q_l}\left(\frac{\partial x_i}{\partial q_j}\right)\dot{q}_l \\ &= \frac{\partial}{\partial q_j}\left(\frac{\partial x_i}{\partial t} + \frac{\partial x_i}{\partial q_l}\dot{q}_l\right) \\ &= \frac{\partial \dot{x}_i}{\partial q_j}\end{aligned} \tag{2.7}$$

We have started to use the summation convention, so there is a summation over the index l. The relations (2.6) and (2.7) are true for both rheonomic and scleronomic systems, that is, irrespective of whether x_i depends explicitly on time or not. Now since any infinitesimal virtual displacement is given by

$$\delta x_i = [dx_i]_{dt=0} = \frac{\partial x_i}{\partial q_j}\delta q_j \tag{2.8}$$

we can begin to transform D'Alembert's principle for this system, which at present is of the Cartesian (or Newtonian) form, that is,

$$\left(m_i \frac{d^2 x_i}{dt^2} - F_i^{(a)}\right)\delta x_i = 0 \tag{2.9}$$

to a form expressed totally in terms of the generalised coordinates. Consider the first term on the LHS (summation over i implied) of Eq. (2.9):

$$m_i \frac{d^2 x_i}{dt^2}\delta x_i = m_i \left(\frac{d^2 x_i}{dt^2}\right)\left(\frac{\partial x_i}{\partial q_j}\right)\delta q_j$$

$$
\begin{aligned}
&= \frac{d}{dt}\left(m_i \frac{dx_i}{dt}\frac{\partial x_i}{\partial q_j}\right)\delta q_j - m_i\left(\frac{dx_i}{dt}\right)\frac{d}{dt}\left(\frac{\partial x_i}{\partial q_j}\right)\delta q_j \\
&= \frac{d}{dt}\left(m_i \dot{x}_i \frac{\partial \dot{x}_i}{\partial \dot{q}_j}\right)\delta q_j - \left(m_i \dot{x}_i \frac{\partial \dot{x}_i}{\partial q_j}\right)\delta q_j \\
&= \frac{d}{dt}\left[\frac{\partial}{\partial \dot{q}_j}\left(\frac{1}{2}m_i \dot{x}_i^2\right)\right]\delta q_j - \frac{\partial}{\partial q_j}\left(\frac{1}{2}m_i\dot{x}_i^2\right)\delta q_j \\
&= \left[\frac{d}{dt}\left(\frac{\partial T}{\partial \dot{q}_j}\right) - \frac{\partial T}{\partial q_j}\right]\delta q_j
\end{aligned} \tag{2.10}
$$

where $T = \frac{1}{2}m_i\dot{x}_i^2$ is the total kinetic energy of the system, by its standard definition in terms of the Cartesian coordinates.

The second term on the LHS of D'Alembert's equation is

$$
\begin{aligned}
-F_i^{(a)}\delta x_i &= -F_i^{(a)}\left(\frac{\partial x_i}{\partial q_j}\right)\delta q_j \\
&= -Q_j \delta q_j
\end{aligned} \tag{2.11}
$$

which defines

$$
Q_j = F_i^{(a)}\left(\frac{\partial x_i}{\partial q_j}\right) \tag{2.12}
$$

as the jth component of the *generalised force*. Suppose q_j is an angle, then Q_j would be the torque corresponding to that angle.

Combining Eqs (2.9), (2.10) and (2.12), D'Alembert's equation becomes

$$
\left[\frac{d}{dt}\left(\frac{\partial T}{\partial \dot{q}_j}\right) - \frac{\partial T}{\partial q_j} - Q_j\right]\delta q_j = 0 \tag{2.13}
$$

Since the q_j coordinates are independent, the values of all the δq_j's can be arbitrary. Therefore, the above equality can hold good if and only if the individual coefficient of each δq_j is separately zero. This implies

$$
\frac{d}{dt}\left(\frac{\partial T}{\partial \dot{q}_j}\right) - \frac{\partial T}{\partial q_j} = Q_j \tag{2.14}
$$

for every generalised coordinate q_j and its generalised velocity $\dot{q}_j$. These $n = 3N - k$ differential equations are called Lagrange's equations of motion of the second kind, published by him in 1788. This is how Lagrange recovered the requisite minimum possible number of independent equations of motion from just one, namely D'Alembert's principle.

It is worth noting that the constraint relations are not at all apparent in Eq. (2.14) but the choice of the generalised coordinates and the determination of the kinetic energy function T in terms of q_j, $\dot{q}_j$ and t depend on the knowledge of the constraint relations.

In the next section we shall see that Lagrange's equations are n second-order ordinary, linear, coupled differential equations. A general solution of these equations involves $2n$ arbitrary constants of integration. The values of these $2n$ constants can only be determined if we know the state of the system (the values of all the generalised coordinates and velocities) at some instant of time. Once determined, the motion of the system gets completely specified for all time in the past as well as in the future.

Now, the ultimate justification for any law to exist in physics lies with experiments. Thus the verification of the above formalism (a restatement of Newtonian mechanics) lies with our ability (or failure) to match it with experience. It so happens, that the above is true to a good approximation when compared with reality. However, one of the principal assumptions, that is implicit, is that the exact measurability of the positions and velocities of all the particles in a system at some point of time is possible. At the turn of this century, physicists found it impossible to explain certain phenomena at the microscopic scale within this framework. This led them to question this fundamental assumption of classical mechanics, and to the concept of what is now known as Heisenberg's uncertainty principle, which roughly states that it is impossible even in principle to simultaneously find out the positions and velocities of particles to an arbitrary accuracy. An investigation of the consequences of this led to the formulation of quantum mechanics which is a far more satisfactory theory of reality. It can be shown that at the macroscopic scale, classical mechanics is the limiting case of quantum mechanics, which explains its success.

Even within the framework of classical mechanics, there are many systems where a slight difference in the initial state of the system leads to totally different behaviour in a very short period of time. For such systems, a quantitative prediction of their time evolution makes little sense. For example, consider drops of water falling out of a tap. The way they splash seems totally random. This is because of very tiny vortices and turbulence inside the tap just before the drop falls. These small differences cause each drop to splash differently. In other words, even if classical mechanics applies to such systems, since it is impossible in practice to find out the state of a system with absolute certainty, it will not take very long for us to lose all information about the initial conditions. A study of such systems is now one of the exciting areas of research in modern classical mechanics, called dynamics of deterministic chaos.

2.5 PROPERTIES OF KINETIC ENERGY FUNCTION T

By Eq. (2.10) the *kinetic energy function* is $T = \frac{1}{2}m_i\dot{x}_i^2$ where for a generally rheonomic system the Cartesian coordinates and velocities are given by Eqs (2.3) and (2.5) namely,

$$x_i = x_i(q_1, q_2, ..., q_n, t) \qquad \text{and} \qquad \dot{x}_i = \frac{\partial x_i}{\partial t} + \frac{\partial x_i}{\partial q_j}\dot{q}_j$$

This gives

$$\begin{aligned} T &= \frac{1}{2}m_i\left(\frac{\partial x_i}{\partial t} + \frac{\partial x_i}{\partial q_j}\dot{q}_j\right)^2 \\ &= \frac{1}{2}m_i\left(\frac{\partial x_i}{\partial t}\right)^2 + m_i\left(\frac{\partial x_i}{\partial t}\right)\left(\frac{\partial x_i}{\partial q_j}\right)\dot{q}_j + \frac{1}{2}m_i\left(\frac{\partial x_i}{\partial q_j}\right)\left(\frac{\partial x_i}{\partial q_l}\right)\dot{q}_j\dot{q}_l \\ &= T_0 + T_1 + T_2 \end{aligned} \tag{2.15}$$

This equation defines T_0, T_1 and T_2. T_0 is only a function of the q_i's and t. We can then write

$$T_0 = \frac{1}{2}m_i\left(\frac{\partial x_i}{\partial t}\right)^2 = a_0 \qquad \text{(say)} \tag{2.16}$$

T_1 is a linear combination of $\dot{q}_j$'s

$$T_1 = a_j\dot{q}_j \qquad \text{(say)} \tag{2.17}$$

where

$$a_j = m_i\left(\frac{\partial x_i}{\partial t}\right)\left(\frac{\partial x_i}{\partial q_j}\right) \tag{2.18}$$

a_j's, like a_0, are only functions of q_i's and t. The third term can similarly be written as

$$T_2 = \frac{1}{2}a_{jl}\dot{q}_j\dot{q}_l \tag{2.19}$$

where

$$a_{jl} = m_i\left(\frac{\partial x_i}{\partial q_j}\right)\left(\frac{\partial x_i}{\partial q_l}\right) \tag{2.20}$$

Again a_{jl}'s are functions of q_i's and t only. Combining the above together, we have

$$T = a_0 + a_j\dot{q}_j + \frac{1}{2}a_{jl}\dot{q}_j\dot{q}_l \tag{2.21}$$

which makes all the dependences of T on generalised coordinate velocities explicit.

Thus the kinetic energy is in general made up of a term that is independent of the generalised velocities, a term linear, and a term that is quadratic in them. For scleronomic systems $T = T_2$ as $T_0 = T_1 = 0$, since x_i's do not depend explicitly on time.

It can be shown that T, T_0 and T_2 are non-negative definite quantities, that is, $T \geq 0$, $T_0 \geq 0$ and $T_2 \geq 0$. For T and T_0, this is evident from their definitions (see Eq. (2.15)). T_2 is non-negative because the matrix $[a_{jl}]$ is symmetric and non-negative definite (all its eigen-values are greater than or equal to 0). T_2 vanishes only if all the $\dot{q}_i$'s are zero. T_1 can be either positive or negative.

Substituting for the full expression for T in Lagrange's equations (Eq. (2.14)) we get

$$\frac{d}{dt}\left[\frac{\partial}{\partial \dot{q}_j}(T_0 + T_1 + T_2)\right] - \frac{\partial}{\partial q_j}(T_0 + T_1 + T_2) = Q_j$$

Thus Lagrange's equations are second order linear coupled differential equations in q_i provided the Q_j's are not explicit functions of $\ddot{q}_i$'s. We now discuss some of the important types of Q_j's that can exist.

Case 1: $Q_j = Q_j(q_1, ..., q_n, t)$

Here Q_j's are functions of the q_i's and t and not of the generalised velocities. In such cases there exists an *ordinary potential energy function* $V(q_1, \ldots, q_n, t)$ such that by definition

$$Q_j = -\frac{\partial V}{\partial q_j} \qquad j = 1, \ldots, n \tag{2.22}$$

Lagrange's equations then become

$$\frac{d}{dt}\left(\frac{\partial T}{\partial \dot{q}_j}\right) - \frac{\partial T}{\partial q_j} + \frac{\partial V}{\partial q_j} = 0$$

or we can write,

$$\frac{d}{dt}\left(\frac{\partial L}{\partial \dot{q}_j}\right) - \frac{\partial L}{\partial q_j} = 0 \qquad j = 1, \ldots, n \tag{2.23}$$

where

$$L = T - V \tag{2.24}$$

$L = L(q_1, \ldots, q_n, \dot{q}_1, \ldots, \dot{q}_n)$ is called by definition the *Lagrangian* of the system. The n equations in Eq. (2.23) are called the *Euler-Lagrange equations of motion.* These are a system of second order coupled linear differential equations in the q_i variables.

Case 2: $Q_j = Q_j(q_1, \ldots, q_n, \dot{q}_1, \ldots, \dot{q}_n, t)$, also derivable from a velocity dependent potential energy function in the following way.

When the Q_j's are derivable from a potential energy function U (the more general case will be discussed later) satisfying the equations by definition,

$$Q_j = \frac{d}{dt}\left(\frac{\partial U}{\partial \dot{q}_j}\right) - \frac{\partial U}{\partial q_j} \qquad j = 1, \ldots, n \tag{2.25}$$

where $U = U(q_1, \ldots, q_n, \dot{q}_1, \ldots, \dot{q}_n, t)$ is called a *generalised potential energy function*, then we get from Lagrange's equations of motion (Eq. (2.14)),

$$\frac{d}{dt}\left(\frac{\partial L}{\partial \dot{q}_j}\right) - \frac{\partial L}{\partial q_j} = 0 \qquad j = 1, \ldots, n \tag{2.26}$$

where

$$L = T - U \tag{2.27}$$

is also called the *Lagrangian* of the system as before. Note that Eqs (2.23) and (2.26) are identical in form, except for the difference in the definition of L depending on the nature of Q_j's.

Case 3: Existence of nonpotential forces

It is possible that there exist some *nonpotential forces* Q'_j apart from the potential force component (derivable either from a velocity independent ordinary potential V or a velocity dependent generalised potential U). In this case Euler-Lagrange's equations take the following most general form

$$\frac{d}{dt}\left(\frac{\partial L}{\partial \dot{q}_j}\right) - \frac{\partial L}{\partial q_j} = Q'_j \qquad j = 1, \ldots, n \tag{2.28}$$

Here $Q'_j = Q'_j(q_1, \ldots, q_n, \dot{q}_1, \ldots, \dot{q}_n, t)$ in general, and $L = T - V$ or $= T - U$ as the case may be. However, it is usually preferable to use $L = T - V$ and keep all velocity dependent forces included in Q'_j, if the inclusion of a nonpotential part is essentially unavoidable.

2.6 THEOREM ON TOTAL ENERGY

Let us consider a system which satisfies Lagrange's equations in the following form (see Eq. (2.14))

$$\frac{d}{dt}\left(\frac{\partial T}{\partial \dot{q}_j}\right) - \frac{\partial T}{\partial q_j} = Q_j$$

where in general,

$$Q_j = -\frac{\partial V}{\partial q_j} + Q'_j \tag{2.29}$$

V being the ordinary potential energy function and Q'_j the jth component of the generalised nonpotential forces.

By definition, the total energy of the system (E) is the sum of its ordinary potential energy and kinetic energy. We want to determine its time dependence. Now, since $T = T(q_1, \ldots, q_n, \dot{q}_1, \ldots, \dot{q}_n, t)$,

$$\begin{aligned}\frac{dT}{dt} &= \frac{\partial T}{\partial t} + \frac{\partial T}{\partial q_j}\dot{q}_j + \frac{\partial T}{\partial \dot{q}_j}\ddot{q}_j \\ &= \frac{\partial T}{\partial t} + \frac{\partial T}{\partial q_j}\dot{q}_j + \frac{d}{dt}\left(\frac{\partial T}{\partial \dot{q}_j}\dot{q}_j\right) - \frac{d}{dt}\left(\frac{\partial T}{\partial \dot{q}_j}\right)\dot{q}_j \\ &= \frac{\partial T}{\partial t} + \frac{d}{dt}\left(\frac{\partial T}{\partial \dot{q}_j}\dot{q}_j\right) + \left(\frac{\partial V}{\partial q_j} - Q'_j\right)\dot{q}_j\end{aligned} \tag{2.30}$$

using Euler-Lagrange's equation in the last step. Substituting $T = T_0 + T_1 + T_2$ (Eq. (2.15)) in Eq. (2.30), and using Euler's theorem on homogeneous functions,

$$\begin{aligned}\frac{dT}{dt} &= \frac{\partial T}{\partial t} + \frac{d}{dt}(T_1 + 2T_2) + \left(\frac{\partial V}{\partial q_j} - Q'_j\right)\dot{q}_j \\ &= 2\frac{dT}{dt} - \frac{d}{dt}(2T_0 + T_1) + \frac{\partial T}{\partial t} + \left(\frac{dV}{dt} - \frac{\partial V}{\partial t}\right) - Q'_j\dot{q}_j\end{aligned} \tag{2.31}$$

Since by definition $E = T + V$, we have for the time rate of variation of total energy,

$$\frac{dE}{dt} = \frac{d}{dt}(T + V) = \frac{d}{dt}(2T_0 + T_1) - \frac{\partial T}{\partial t} + \frac{\partial V}{\partial t} + Q'_j\dot{q}_j \tag{2.32}$$

This is the most general result for rheonomic systems. Some special cases are considered below.

Case (i) Scleronomic Systems

For all such systems, $\partial T/\partial t = 0$, $T_0 = 0$ and $T_1 = 0$. Thus we have

$$\frac{dE}{dt} = \frac{\partial V}{\partial t} + Q'_j\dot{q}_j \tag{2.33}$$

Suppose V does not explicitly depend on time, then

$$\frac{dE}{dt} = Q'_j \dot{q}_j = P'$$

where P' is the power associated with the nonpotential forces. This equation tells us that nonconservation of total energy is directly associated with the existence of nonpotential forces Q'_j's, even though the Lagrangian $L = T - V$ does not have any explicit dependence on time in this case.

Case (ii) Conservative Systems

Here we consider systems which are scleronomic with no nonpotential forces. We also assume further that the ordinary potential energy function does not explicitly depend on time. It is only then

$$\frac{dE}{dt} = 0 \quad \text{or} \quad E \equiv T + V = E_0 \quad \text{(say)} \tag{2.34}$$

or in words, throughout the motion, the energy of the system is conserved. Such systems are by definition called *conservative systems*. This integral of motion for any conservative system is called the *energy integral.*

Case (iii) Systems for which the Nonpotential Forces Q'_j do not Consume Power

For such systems, Q'_j's exist, and the power associated with them

$$P' = Q'_j \dot{q}_j = 0 \tag{2.35}$$

At least some Q'_j's must be non-zero, but the above summation has to vanish. All the velocity dependent forces that have this property are known as *gyroscopic forces*. For scleronomic systems under the actions of gyroscopic forces and an ordinary potential energy function that is not explicitly time dependent, the energy integral $E = E_0$ exists. We shall show in the next section that certain kinds of gyroscopic forces can be included in and promoted to the class of generalised velocity dependent potential energy functions U.

Case (iv) Systems Experiencing Dissipative Forces that Consume Power

In this case, by definition of the *dissipative forces* $Q'_j \dot{q}_j < 0$. Note that dissipative forces like the forces of friction are included, even though sometimes they do not do any work. However, the energy is generally lost in the form of heat, sound, etc. All scleronomic systems incurring dissipative losses should satisfy the energy condition:

$$\frac{dE}{dt} < 0 \tag{2.36}$$

Thus not all scleronomic systems are necessarily conservative. We now consider an important kind of situation which also serves to illustrate Eqs (2.35) and (2.36).

Case (v) Systems Experiencing Nonpotential Forces that have Linear Dependence on Generalised Velocities

In general, such forces can be represented by the linear matrix equation

$$Q'_j = B_{jk} \dot{q}_k \tag{2.37}$$

where B_{jk} are constants (the most general case is when there is also an additive part, and that is discussed in the next section). $B = [B_{jk}]$ is an $n \times n$ matrix and can be symmetrised in the following way

$$B = \frac{1}{2}(B + \tilde{B}) + \frac{1}{2}(B - \tilde{B}) \equiv -S + A \tag{2.38}$$

Here $\tilde{B}$ is the transpose of matrix B. The negative sign is chosen for convenience. S is a symmetric matrix and A is antisymmetric, that is,

$$S = \tilde{S} \quad \text{and} \quad A = -\tilde{A} \tag{2.39}$$

Thus the associated power is

$$P' = Q'_j \dot{q}_j = [-S + A]_{jk}\, \dot{q}_j \dot{q}_k = -S_{jk}\dot{q}_j\dot{q}_k + A_{jk}\dot{q}_j\dot{q}_k \tag{2.40}$$

The second term identically vanishes because A is antisymmetric. Thus the antisymmetric part of B does not cause any dissipation of energy, and $Q'_j(\text{anti}) = A_{jk}\dot{q}_k$, $j = 1, \ldots, n$, are therefore, gyroscopic forces. The Coriolis force $\boldsymbol{F}_c = 2m(\boldsymbol{v} \times \boldsymbol{w})$ and the Lorentz force on a charged particle moving in a magnetic field $\boldsymbol{F}_m = e(\boldsymbol{v} \times \boldsymbol{B})$ are examples of gyroscopic forces. In fact, any vector cross product is equivalently an antisymmetric tensor of the second rank. The power associated with these forces is $\boldsymbol{F} \cdot \boldsymbol{v} = 0$, as we would expect. We will discuss more about these forces in section 2.8.

On the other hand, the symmetric component of Eq. (2.40) does not in general vanish as $-S_{jk}\dot{q}_j\dot{q}_k \neq 0$. So the forces $Q'_j(\text{sym})$ are dissipative, that is, the total energy of the system decreases with time, and the algebraic sign of power is negative,

$$P' = -S_{jk}\dot{q}_j\dot{q}_k < 0 \tag{2.41}$$

This means that

$$S_{jk}\dot{q}_j\dot{q}_k > 0$$

or **S** is positive definite. Therefore,

$$-\frac{dE}{dt} \equiv -P' > 0 \tag{2.42}$$

is the rate of energy dissipation of this system. Now, $-\frac{1}{2}P'$ is traditionally called the *Rayleigh dissipation function* R, that is,

$$R = \frac{1}{2}S_{jk}\dot{q}_j\dot{q}_k \tag{2.43}$$

This is always positive and satisfies the equation

$$Q'_j = -\frac{\partial R}{\partial \dot{q}_j} \tag{2.44}$$

corresponding to the symmetric (dissipative) part of **B**. The rate of increase of energy in the system is

$$\frac{dE}{dt} = P' = -2R \tag{2.45}$$

So for dissipative systems where the nonpotential forces are linear in the generalised velocities (that is, air resistance to a good approximation or, Stokes' law of viscosity), Euler-Lagrange's equations of motion have the form

$$\frac{d}{dt}\left(\frac{\partial L}{\partial \dot{q}_j}\right) - \frac{\partial L}{\partial q_j} + \frac{\partial R}{\partial \dot{q}_j} = 0 \tag{2.46}$$

2.7 SOME REMARKS ABOUT THE LAGRANGIAN

At this stage, we emphasize a few important properties of Lagrangian:

1. L is a scalar function of q_j's,$\dot{q}_j$'s and t. The q_j variables costitute the basis vectors of an abstract n-dimensional configuration space. Any point in this space along with a tangent direction ($\dot{q}_j$'s at that point) completely determines the state, and the future of the dynamical system is determined by Euler-Lagrange's equations of motion.
2. L is not unique in its functional form because it is possible to preserve the form of the Euler-Lagrange equations of motion for a variety of choices of the Lagrangian. In fact, given a Lagrangian, it is possible to construct any number of other equivalent Lagrangians (see section 2.9).
3. For any classical holonomic system L can be constructed either from $T - V$ or from $T-U$, as the case may be, with the condition that both T and V (or U) must be initially expressed with respect to an *inertial frame* in which the predecessor equations namely, D'Alembert's principle and Newton's laws are valid. However, it may be noted that in the special relativistic dynamics, the classical definition of $L = T - V$ or $L = T - U$ is no longer valid.

2.8 LINEAR GENERALISED POTENTIALS

By definition from Eq. (2.25), of the generalised force corresponding to the jth generalised coordinate,

$$\begin{aligned} Q_j &= \frac{d}{dt}\left(\frac{\partial U}{\partial \dot{q}_j}\right) - \frac{\partial U}{\partial q_j} \\ &= \frac{\partial^2 U}{\partial \dot{q}_i \partial \dot{q}_j}\ddot{q}_i + (\text{terms that do not contain } \ddot{q}_i) \end{aligned} \tag{2.47}$$

For a large number of realistic situations, Q_j's do not explicitly depend on the generalised accelerations, hence for such systems, $\partial^2 U/\partial \dot{q}_i \partial \dot{q}_j$ must vanish. Thus for such systems the generalised potential energy can be given by

$$U = V_i \dot{q}_i + V \tag{2.48}$$

where V_i (that is, $V_1, \ldots, V_n$) and the ordinary potential energy function V are all functions of q_i's and t only. We then have

$$Q_j = \frac{d}{dt}\left(\frac{\partial U}{\partial \dot{q}_j}\right) - \frac{\partial U}{\partial q_j} = \frac{dV_j}{dt} - \frac{\partial V_i}{\partial q_j}\dot{q}_i - \frac{\partial V}{\partial q_j} = -\frac{\partial V}{\partial q_j} + \frac{\partial V_j}{\partial t} + \left(\frac{\partial V_j}{\partial q_i} - \frac{\partial V_i}{\partial q_j}\right)\dot{q}_i \quad (2.49)$$

Suppose further that the coefficients V_j do not depend explicitly on time,

$$Q_j = -\frac{\partial V}{\partial q_j} + \left(\frac{\partial V_j}{\partial q_i} - \frac{\partial V_i}{\partial q_j}\right)\dot{q}_i$$

that is, under circumstances, the generalised force can be thought of as a sum of an ordinary type of potential force $\partial V/\partial q_j$ and a gyroscopic force $Q_j = A_{ij}\dot{q}_i$, since the second term in the RHS is antisymmetric with respect to i and j. Thus all such gyroscopic forces can be included in the definition of a generalised potential energy function U, leaving only the dissipative forces to be included in the category of the nonpotential forces Q'_j's. The latter can be handled by defining a suitable Rayleigh's dissipation function, provided the drag forces are linear with respect to velocity.

Charged Particle in an Electromagnetic Field

A classic example of this case is the Lorentz force experienced by a charged particle in an electromagnetic field, given by

$$\boldsymbol{F} = e(\boldsymbol{E} + \boldsymbol{v} \times \boldsymbol{B}) \quad (2.50)$$

where

$$\boldsymbol{E} = -\nabla\phi - \frac{\partial \boldsymbol{A}}{\partial t} \quad \text{and} \quad \boldsymbol{B} = \nabla \times \boldsymbol{A} \quad (2.51)$$

Here, $\phi = \phi(\boldsymbol{r}, t)$ is the scalar electromagnetic potential and $\boldsymbol{A} = \boldsymbol{A}(\boldsymbol{r}, t)$ is the vector electromagnetic potential. We leave it as an exercise to show that with the choice of a generalised potential energy function of the form

$$U = e\phi - e(\boldsymbol{v} \cdot \boldsymbol{A}) \quad (2.52)$$

that is, by setting $V_i = eA_i$ and $V = e\phi$, we get the correct equations of motion, namely Eq. (2.50). The key point here is that the magnetic force is gyroscopic in nature, and is of the type discussed in this section, so it can be incorporated in a suitably defined generalised potential U, such as the one given by Eq. (2.52).

2.9 GENERALISED MOMENTA AND ENERGY

In the Lagrangian dynamics, it would be proper to define both momentum and energy in terms of the given Lagrangian. We know that the Newtonian momentum is, by definition, $p_i = mv_i = \partial T/\partial \dot{x}_i$ in Cartesian coordinates. In terms of the Lagrangian, this p_i would correspond to $\partial L/\partial \dot{x}_i$, provided the potential energy part of L is independent of both $\dot{x}_i$s and t. By this analogy, the *generalised momentum* p_i corresponding to a generalised coordinate q_i is defined as

$$p_i \equiv \frac{\partial L}{\partial \dot{q}_i} \quad (2.53)$$

The generalised momentum defined in the above way is also known as the *canonical momentum*. Now suppose $L = T - V$, where V does not depend on the $\dot{q}_i$'s, then

$$p_i = \frac{\partial L}{\partial \dot{q}_i} = \frac{\partial T}{\partial \dot{q}_i} = \frac{\partial}{\partial \dot{q}_i}(T_1 + T_2) \tag{2.54}$$

giving

$$\dot{q}_i p_i = 2T_2 + T_1 = 2T - T_1 - 2T_0 \tag{2.55}$$

Therefore for scleronomic systems having ordinary potential forces,

$$\dot{q}_i p_i = 2T \tag{2.56}$$

If, on the other hand, $L = T - U$, where $U = V_i \dot{q}_i + V$, we get

$$p_i = \frac{\partial (T - U)}{\partial \dot{q}_i} = \frac{\partial T}{\partial \dot{q}_i} - V_i \tag{2.57}$$

Thus the generalised momentum does not arise totally from the kinetic energy term, but also from the generalised potential energy term, which in the most general case being velocity dependent, carries some amount of canonical momentum. If the generalised potential energy function is linear in $\dot{q}_i$, as noted in the previous section (see Eq. (2.48)), then from Eq. (2.57),

$$\dot{q}_i p_i = 2T_2 + T_1 - U + V = 2T - U + V - T_1 - 2T_0 \tag{2.58}$$

Hence, for a scleronomic system having both gyroscopic and ordinary potential forces,

$$\dot{q}_i p_i = 2T - U + V \tag{2.59}$$

Obviously, neither of the pairs of Eqs (2.55) and (2.58), and Eqs (2.56) and (2.59) is identical, the difference clearly arising from the two different definitions of L.

We have already seen in section 2.5 that energy is a well-defined, conserved quantity for systems which are conservative in nature. A system is conservative when it is non-dissipative and scleronomic in nature and does not have any explicit time dependence on its ordinary potential energy function. Let us now see whether under the same conditions, a given Lagrangian can also specify the same energy integral. For a given $L = L(q_i, \dot{q}_i, t)$, using the most general form of Euler-Lagrange's equations of motion, its total time derivative is

$$\begin{aligned} \frac{dL}{dt} &= \frac{\partial L}{\partial t} + \frac{\partial L}{\partial q_i}\dot{q}_i + \frac{\partial L}{\partial \dot{q}_i}\ddot{q}_i = \frac{\partial L}{\partial t} + \frac{\partial L}{\partial q_i}\dot{q}_i + \frac{d}{dt}\left(\frac{\partial L}{\partial \dot{q}_i}\dot{q}_i\right) - \frac{d}{dt}\left(\frac{\partial L}{\partial \dot{q}_i}\right)\dot{q}_i \\ &= \frac{\partial L}{\partial t} + \frac{d}{dt}\left(\frac{\partial L}{\partial \dot{q}_i}\dot{q}_i\right) - Q'_i \dot{q}_i \end{aligned}$$

If the system is non-dissipative ($Q'_i \dot{q}_i = 0$) and the Lagrangian is explicitly time independent, then

$$\frac{d}{dt}\left(\frac{\partial L}{\partial \dot{q}_i}\dot{q}_i - L\right) = 0$$

Thus the quantity

$$J \equiv \frac{\partial L}{\partial \dot{q}_i}\dot{q}_i - L = p_i\dot{q}_i - L = \text{ const. } = J_o \quad \text{(say)} \tag{2.60}$$

is a constant of motion. This integral of motion J_o is by definition called the *Jacobi integral* of the system, and the function J, we shall see later, corresponds to nothing else but the Hamiltonian, provided all $\dot{q}_i$s are sustituted properly by functions of p_is. From Eqs (2.55) and (2.58), the Jacobi integral in general corresponds to

$$J_o \equiv \frac{\partial L}{\partial \dot{q}_i}\dot{q}_i - L = T + V - T_1 - 2T_0 = E - T_1 - 2T_0 \tag{2.61}$$

and is identical for both the definitions of L, namely $L = T - V$ and $L = T - U$. Furthermore, $\partial L/\partial t = 0$ would also imply $\partial T/\partial t = 0$, and as an anticedent, $T_1 = T_0 = 0$. Thus, $J_o = E_o$, if L is defined as either $T - V$ or $T - U$, with the only required condition that $\partial L/\partial t = 0$.

However, the Lagrangian L need not always be defined as $T - V$ or $T - U$, and the existence of a Jacobi integral would not necessarily mean that the system be conservative. In fact, there are examples of non-dissipative rheonomic systems (see problem nos. 2.11 and 2.12), which have their Lagrangians explicitly independent of time, thus defining a Jacobi integral instead of an energy integral. However, for any conservative system, irrespective of its potential energy functions (U or V), its total energy is always given by $T + V$, never by $T + U$, which is justified from the expression (2.61). The velocity dependent part of the potential energy U does not enter into the expression for the total energy, simply because the work done by gyroscopic forces is zero.

Thus for a charged particle moving in a static magnetic field, the generalised momentum of the particle can be obtained from Eqs (2.52) and (2.53):

$$\boldsymbol{p} = m\boldsymbol{v} + e\boldsymbol{A} \tag{2.62}$$

The first term is the mechanical or the Newtonian momentum of the charged particle and the second term is a contribution from the value of the vector potential $\boldsymbol{A}$ at the point where the particle is presently located. Moreover, the vectors $\boldsymbol{p}$ and $\boldsymbol{v}$ are no longer collinear. For this system, $\boldsymbol{p} \cdot \boldsymbol{v} = mv^2 + e(\boldsymbol{v} \cdot \boldsymbol{A})$ and the total energy $E = T + V = \frac{1}{2}mv^2 + e\phi$ is an integral of motion. The electromagnetism is thus well described by the Lagrangian scheme.

However, for a relativistically moving free particle, $T = (m - m_0)c^2$, where $m = m_0/\sqrt{1 - v^2/c^2}$, m_0 being the rest mass. If we proceed to define L as $L = T - V$ with $V = 0$, the canonical momentum $\boldsymbol{p} \equiv \partial L/\partial \boldsymbol{r} \neq m\boldsymbol{v}$ leads to a point of contradiction. It is therefore advisable to relax the idea of defining L as $T - V$ or $T - U$ as a necessary condition, and one is let free to choose a Lagarangian which would produce the correct set of equations of motion and the canonical momentum (see Eq. (5.15) for example).

2.10 GAUGE FUNCTION FOR LAGRANGIAN

Let $L(q_i, \dot{q}_i, t)$ be the Lagrangian of a system and $F(q_i, t)$ be any differentiable function.

Then $L + dF/dt$ also satisfies Euler-Lagrange's equations of motion. For,

$$\begin{aligned}\frac{d}{dt}\left(\frac{\partial(dF/dt)}{\partial \dot{q}_i}\right) - \frac{\partial}{\partial q_i}\left(\frac{dF}{dt}\right) &= \frac{d}{dt}\left[\frac{\partial}{\partial \dot{q}_i}\left(\frac{\partial F}{\partial t} + \frac{\partial F}{\partial q_j}\dot{q}_j\right)\right] - \frac{\partial}{\partial q_i}\left(\frac{\partial F}{\partial t} + \frac{\partial F}{\partial q_j}\dot{q}_j\right) \\ &= \frac{\partial}{\partial t}\left(\frac{\partial F}{\partial q_i}\right) + \frac{\partial}{\partial q_j}\left(\frac{\partial F}{\partial q_i}\right)\dot{q}_j - \frac{\partial^2 F}{\partial q_i \partial t} - \frac{\partial^2 F}{\partial q_i \partial q_j}\dot{q}_j \\ &= 0\end{aligned}$$

$F(q_i, t)$ is called the *gauge function* for the Lagrangian. This introduces an arbitrariness in the form of the Lagrangian that can preserve the same form of the equations of motion written in terms of L. So if $L = L(q_i, \dot{q}_i, t)$ can produce a set of equations of motion through Euler-Lagrange equations of motion, then any other Lagrangian $L' = L(q_i, \dot{q}_i, t) + dF(q_i, t)/dt$ formed from any arbitrary choice of $F(q_i, t)$ can be plugged in the same Euler-Lagrange equations of motion replacing the original L. The explicit forms of the equations of motion in q_i and t would not be different for these two different Lagrangians.

However, the generalised momenta corresponding to $L' = L + dF/dt$ are

$$p'_i = \frac{\partial L'}{\partial \dot{q}_i} = \frac{\partial L}{\partial \dot{q}_i} + \frac{\partial}{\partial \dot{q}_i}\left(\frac{\partial F}{\partial t} + \frac{\partial F}{\partial q_j}\dot{q}_j\right) = p_i + \frac{\partial F}{\partial q_i} \tag{2.63}$$

Similarly for the Jacobi integral (or the energy in case the system is conservative) we have

$$J' = \dot{q}_i\frac{\partial L'}{\partial \dot{q}_i} - L' = J + \dot{q}_i\frac{\partial F}{\partial q_i} - \frac{dF}{dt} = J - \frac{\partial F}{\partial t} \tag{2.64}$$

Thus, under Lagrangian gauge transformation, the canonical momenta and the Jacobi integral change in the above manner. The momenta change due to explicit spatial variation of the gauge function F and the energy-like Jacobi integral changes due to the explicit time variation of F. In the process the new Lagrangian effectively acquires a new gyroscopic potential energy and its ordinary potential energy is also modified.

2.11 INVARIANCE OF THE EULER-LAGRANGE EQUATIONS OF MOTION UNDER GENERALISED COORDINATE TRANSFORMATIONS

Let $q_1, \ldots, q_n$, be the old set of generalised coordinates and $Q_1, \ldots, Q_n$ be the new set (keeping the same time parameter t for both) so that an admissible transformation between these two sets of coordinates be given by

$$\begin{aligned} q_1 &= q_1(Q_1, \ldots, Q_n, t) \\ \vdots\ &\quad \vdots \\ q_n &= q_n(Q_1, \ldots, Q_n, t) \end{aligned} \tag{2.65}$$

So we can still retain the same n-dimensional (R^n) configuration space, but the new set of the n curvilinear coordinate axes Q_j's must all be suitably reoriented according to the inverse of the transformation Eqs (2.65). Now we have, from Eq. (2.65),

$$\dot{q}_i = \frac{\partial q_i}{\partial t} + \frac{\partial q_i}{\partial Q_j}\dot{Q}_j$$

which gives

$$\frac{\partial \dot{q}_i}{\partial \dot{Q}_j} = \frac{\partial q_i}{\partial Q_j}$$

Further,

$$\frac{d}{dt}\left(\frac{\partial q_i}{\partial Q_j}\right) = \frac{\partial \dot{q}_i}{\partial Q_j}$$

and

$$0 = \frac{\partial t}{\partial \dot{Q}_j} = \frac{\partial t}{\partial Q_j} = \frac{\partial q_i}{\partial \dot{Q}_j}$$

All these conditions are derived from Eqs (2.65), and they merely restate the same transformation Eqs (2.65) in the differential form. Actually, these differential conditions will be used to carry out the necessary transformations for the Euler-Lagrange equations of motion. Being differential in nature, any generalised coordinate transformation representing a constant translation in the coordinates will in no way affect the Euler-Lagrange equations of motion. Usually such uniform coordinate translations are ignored. This is the reason why one restricts oneself to a class of admissible transformations devoid of any uniform translation. Such transformations are called ***point transformations***, by definition. Translations are eliminated by demanding that at least one point in the configuration space must remain unchanged.

Now on substitution of $q_i = q_i(Q_1, \ldots, Q_n, t)$ and $\dot{q}_i = \dot{q}_i(Q_1, \ldots, Q_n, \dot{Q}_1, \ldots, \dot{Q}_n, t)$ in $L(q_1, \ldots, q_n, \dot{q}_1, \ldots, \dot{q}_n, t)$ we get the transformed Lagrangian as $\tilde{L}(Q_1, \ldots, Q_n, \dot{Q}_1, \ldots, \dot{Q}_n, t)$ which retains the old value of L at the corresponding points. Only the functional form of L changes to $\tilde{L}$ in the new coordinates. Now consider,

$$\begin{aligned}
\frac{d}{dt}\left(\frac{\partial \tilde{L}}{\partial \dot{Q}_j}\right) - \frac{\partial \tilde{L}}{\partial Q_j} &= \frac{d}{dt}\left(\frac{\partial L}{\partial q_i}\frac{\partial q_i}{\partial \dot{Q}_j} + \frac{\partial L}{\partial \dot{q}_i}\frac{\partial \dot{q}_i}{\partial \dot{Q}_j} + \frac{\partial L}{\partial t}\frac{\partial t}{\partial \dot{Q}_j}\right) \\
&\quad - \left(\frac{\partial L}{\partial q_i}\frac{\partial q_i}{\partial Q_j} + \frac{\partial L}{\partial \dot{q}_i}\frac{\partial \dot{q}_i}{\partial Q_j} + \frac{\partial L}{\partial t}\frac{\partial t}{\partial Q_j}\right) \\
&= \frac{d}{dt}\left(\frac{\partial L}{\partial \dot{q}_i}\frac{\partial q_i}{\partial Q_j}\right) - \left[\frac{\partial L}{\partial q_i}\frac{\partial q_i}{\partial Q_j} + \frac{\partial L}{\partial \dot{q}_i}\frac{d}{dt}\left(\frac{\partial q_i}{\partial Q_j}\right)\right] \\
&= \frac{d}{dt}\left(\frac{\partial L}{\partial \dot{q}_i}\right)\frac{\partial q_i}{\partial Q_j} + \frac{\partial L}{\partial \dot{q}_i}\frac{d}{dt}\left(\frac{\partial q_i}{\partial Q_j}\right) - \frac{\partial L}{\partial q_i}\frac{\partial q_i}{\partial Q_j} - \frac{\partial L}{\partial \dot{q}_i}\frac{d}{dt}\left(\frac{\partial q_i}{\partial Q_j}\right) \\
&= \left[\frac{d}{dt}\left(\frac{\partial L}{\partial \dot{q}_i}\right) - \frac{\partial L}{\partial q_i}\right]\frac{\partial q_i}{\partial Q_j}
\end{aligned}$$

Thus if the most general Euler-Lagrange's equations of motion with Cartesian components of nonpotential forces as F'_k are valid in terms of the old set of coordinates, that is, if

$$\frac{d}{dt}\left(\frac{\partial L}{\partial \dot{q}_i}\right) - \frac{\partial L}{\partial q_i} = F'_k \frac{\partial x_k}{\partial q_i} \qquad \text{for every} \quad q_i$$

then

$$\frac{d}{dt}\left(\frac{\partial \tilde{L}}{\partial \dot{Q}_j}\right) - \frac{\partial \tilde{L}}{\partial Q_j} = F'_k \frac{\partial x_k}{\partial Q_j}$$

is also valid for every Q_j coordinate.

Therefore, Euler-Lagrange's equations of motion, in their most general form, remain invariant in form under the most general (that is, time dependent) generalised coordinate transformation.

This is simply a remarkable result. While introducing the idea of the generalised coordinates towards the beginning of this chapter, we could not prescribe any method by which one can choose a set of generalised coordinates. Now it is obvious that if n be the number of the DOF of a holonomic (and bilateral) system, one can choose any set of n independent coordinate variables with some explicit prescribed relations given in the form of Eq. (2.1), express the Lagrangian in terms of these n independent coordinates and time and yet can write the same Euler-Lagrange's equations motion (given in the form of the Eq. (2.14)) in order to derive the equations of motion in these coordinates. So far as the basic form of Euler-Lagrange's equations of motion are concerned, it really does not matter at all what set of generalised coordinates are chosen for describing the motion. But if we want to write Newton's laws of motion in a given set of generalised coordinates, there is no standard or unique form of the equation of motion available except for the rectangular Cartesian coordinates, where we ought to worry about the constraint forces. In the Euler-Lagrange formalism, the basic equations of motion have got a unique form given by the Eq. (2.14), which must remain strictly valid for any *complete set* of generalised coordinates. Only major task is then to formulate the explicit form of L in term of the chosen set of generalised coordinates.

Next consider the quantity

$$\begin{aligned}
P_j\dot{Q}_j &= \frac{\partial \tilde{L}}{\partial \dot{Q}_j}\dot{Q}_j = \left(\frac{\partial L}{\partial \dot{q}_i}\frac{\partial \dot{q}_i}{\partial \dot{Q}_j}\right)\left(\frac{\partial Q_j}{\partial q_l}\dot{q}_l + \frac{\partial Q_j}{\partial t}\right) \\
&= \frac{\partial L}{\partial \dot{q}_i}\frac{\partial q_i}{\partial Q_j}\frac{\partial Q_j}{\partial q_l}\dot{q}_l + \frac{\partial L}{\partial \dot{q}_i}\frac{\partial q_i}{\partial Q_j}\frac{\partial Q_j}{\partial t} \\
&= \frac{\partial L}{\partial \dot{q}_i}\frac{\partial q_i}{\partial q_l}\dot{q}_l - \frac{\partial L}{\partial \dot{q}_i}\frac{\partial q_i}{\partial t} \\
&= \frac{\partial L}{\partial \dot{q}_i}\dot{q}_i - p_i\frac{\partial q_i}{\partial t} \\
&= p_i\dot{q}_i - p_i\frac{\partial q_i}{\partial t}
\end{aligned}$$

Therefore the quantity $P_j\dot{Q}_j$ remains invariant only if $q_i = q_i(Q_j)$, that is, the transformation does not depend explicitly on time. Again since $P_j = p_i(\partial q_i/\partial Q_j)$, the transformed momenta, change from the original ones because of the pure (time independent) coordinate transformation, the transformed energy-like Jacobi integral $P_j\dot{Q}_j - \tilde{L}$ can differ form its original Jacobi integral $J = p_i\dot{q}_i - L$, only if the coordinate transformations are explicitly time dependent (that is, $(\partial q_i/\partial t) \neq 0$). So this provides a way by which one can preserve the value of L and the form of Euler-Lagrange's equations of motion, but the values of the Jacobi integral and canonical momenta may change simply due to the imposed coordinate transformation leading to reorientation and differential expansion/contraction of the coordinate axes drawn in the same old n-dimensional configuration space.

2.12 CYCLIC OR IGNORABLE COORDINATES

The Lagrangian of any physical system is generally expected to have explicit dependence on all the generalised coordinates q_i, all the generalised velocities $\dot{q}_i$ and time t, that is,

$$L = L(q_1, \ldots, q_n, \dot{q}_1, \ldots, \dot{q}_n, t)$$

where n is the total number of generalised coordinates. Due to some reason if some of the generalised coordinates do not appear explicitly in the expression for the Lagrangian, these coordinates are by definition called *cyclic* or *ignorable* coordinates. Any change in these coordinates cannot affect the Lagrangian.

Example: The Lagrangian for a projectile, moving under the earth's approximately constant field of gravity is given by

$$L = \frac{1}{2}mv^2 - mgz = \frac{1}{2}m(\dot{x}^2 + \dot{y}^2 + \dot{z}^2) - mgz$$

where g is the constant acceleration due to gravity. Here (x, y, z) is the set of the Cartesian coordinates of the projectile of mass m, z being the vertical component (upward positive). Obviously, in this example, x and y are the cyclic coordinates.

We now prove the following theorem.

Theorem: In absence of any nonpotential forces, the generalised momentum corresponding to any cyclic coordinate is a conserved quantity.

Proof: Let q_i be a cyclic coordinate, then by its definition

$$\frac{\partial L}{\partial q_i} = 0$$

Euler-Lagrange's equation for the same coordinate reduces to

$$\frac{d}{dt}\left(\frac{\partial L}{\partial \dot{q}_i}\right) = Q'_i \equiv 0$$

Therefore,

$$p_i = \frac{\partial L}{\partial \dot{q}_i} \quad \text{is a constant of motion}$$

In the above example, $p_y = \partial L/\partial \dot{y} = m\dot{y}$ and $p_x = \partial L/\partial \dot{x} = m\dot{x}$ are the two conserved components of linear momentum, corresponding to the cyclic coordinates y and x respectively. As expected, the horizontal components of the linear momentum of the projectile are conserved.

2.13 INTEGRALS OF MOTION

For any mechanical system there exist some functions of q_i's and $\dot{q}_i$'s, whose values remain constant throughout the motion of the system, in spite of the fact that the values of q_i's and $\dot{q}_i$'s are all changing with time. The former set of functions are by definition called the integrals of motion.

The general solution of Euler-Lagrange's equations of motion, for any mechanical system having the number of DOF $= n$ has the form

$$q_i = q_i(t, c_1, \ldots, c_{2n}) \qquad i = 1, \ldots, n$$

and

$$\dot{q}_i = \dot{q}_i(t, c_1, \ldots, c_{2n}) \qquad i = 1, \ldots, n$$

where $c_1, \ldots, c_{2n}$ are the $2n$ constants of integration. One can arbitrarily choose any one of these $2n$ functions and construct an expression for t by inverting the relation and then substitute this expression for t in the rest $2n - 1$ functions. Therefore, one can have a maximum number of $2n - 1$ independent integrals of motion for any mechanical system having n degrees of freedom. To see that these $2n - 1$ expressions are the constants of motion, note that these expressions can be inverted to express the constants $c_1, \ldots, c_{2n-1}$ as functions of $(q_i, \dot{q}_i,\ i = 1, \ldots, n)$, which are also the integrals of motion. There can be infinitely many ways of expressing the constants of motion, but only a maximum of $2n - 1$ would be independent of each other and have no explicit dependence on time. Of course, there would always remain one more independent constant of motion, which will have an explicit dependence on time.

The significance of the existence of $2n - 1$ constants of motion will become clear when we talk about the phase space of $2n$ dimensions. The specification of $2n - 1$ functions in that space would simply mean that only one degree of freedom will be left, which will of course be a curve in the $2n$ -dimensional space. Obviously, this curve ought to represent the unique trajectory of the system in the phase space subject to the specification of all the $2n - 1$ integrals of motion. Along the trajectory time will change, and this is going to be fixed by the one remaining, namely the explicitly time dependent constant of motion. In the n -dimensional configuration space, the system will also describe a unique trajectory, but for a given trajectory, there would be n independent choices of the initial conditions that would lead to the same final trajectory. This tells us how important it would be to consider phase space for it uniquely (or canonically, meaning providentially destined) defines the trajectories.

2.14 CONCEPT OF SYMMETRY: HOMOGENEITY AND ISOTROPY

If any system or any function representing a property of the system does not change under some operation (defined on the system), the system is said to possess a *symmetry* with respect to the given operation.

2.14.1 Examples

1. When a cylinder is rotated about its axis by an arbitrary angle its apparent shape does not change. The cylinder is said to have rotational symmetry about its axis.
2. The size, shape and position of a homogeneous sphere remains invariant under any arbitrary rotation about any axis passing through its centre. By measuring any property of the sphere, it is impossible to detect whether such a rotation has at all taken place. As a consequence, the form of the equation of a sphere with respect to an origin coinciding with its centre does not change no matter how we choose the directions of the x, y, z axes.
3. We wish to give this example of symmetry operation expressed in an abstract manner. We know that Euler-Lagrange's equations of motion do neither change their form under point transformations nor do they change if we add to the Lagrangian a total time derivative of any arbitrary function $F(q,t)$. The latter is called the Lagrangian gauge symmetry of Euler-Lagrange's equations of motion.

Homogeneity of space: If for any arbitrary displacement of the origin of any reference frame the physical properties of all closed systems remain unaffected, we say that space is *homogeneous*. Thus every point in space is equivalent to every other point for the description of the state of motion of any closed system, such as the universe. A *closed system*, by definition is the one that is not acted upon by any field of force, whose source is external to the system.

Isotropy of space: If for any arbitrary rotation about the origin of any reference frame the physical properties of any closed system remain unaffected, we say that space is *isotropic*. Thus every direction in space is as good as any other direction for the description of any closed system, and the choice of the Cartesian axes can be arbitrary in direction.

Homogeneity of time: If for any arbitrary displacement of the origin of time, the physical properties of any closed system remain unaffected we say that time is *homogeneous*. Every moment of time is as good as any other moment of time for the description of a closed system.

Note that the above properties of space and time mean the invariance of physical properties under certain kinds of symmetry operations. The configuration and states of motion related by these operations are equivalent. These symmetries correspond to invariance under arbitrary translation, arbitrary rotation about arbitrary axis and the operation of 'waiting', that is, the passage of time, respectively. Conversely, space can be said to be homogeneous and isotropic, and time as homogeneous, only if the states of motion of all closed systems are found to be invariant under these operations. Thus the homogeneity of space and time and isotropy of space are guaranteed only for a system which is not acted upon by any external force.

A closed system is described as any other system by its Lagrangian. In particular, we require that the Lagrangian of a closed system should be invariant under the operations of translation and rotation in space and that it should not change just by waiting, that is, it should not depend explicitly on time.

Consider a frame of reference in which space and time are not homogeneous and space is not isotropic. Such a frame may be realised if it is accelerating with respect to some fixed frame. In this frame, the physical state of motion of a closed system may change by mere translation in space or by mere passage of time. A change in the physical state of motion of a system will, in general, involve a change in its acceleration. Thus a system which was at rest at some time may suddenly start moving after some time, seemingly without experiencing any action of the external force of any kind. This means that Newton's laws of motion are not valid in such a frame. We have defined inertial frame of reference to be the frame in which Newton's laws of motion are valid. Thus we require that in an inertial frame space and time must be homogeneous and isotropic, for the description of any closed system. This can be taken to be an alternative definition of the inertial frame.

We have seen that the Lagrangian of a closed system must be invariant under the translations and rotations in space. In other words, these are the symmetry operations for the Lagrangian. These symmetries in Lagrangian have very important consequences. Each of these symmetries corresponds to a conservation law, giving rise to a conserved quantity or an integral of motion which is additive. Additivity means that the value of the integral of motion for the whole system is the sum of its values for various parts of the system.

It turns out that every symmetry in the Lagrangian corresponds to a conservation law. This statement was rigorously proved by Emmy Noether in 1918, and is called *Noether's theorem*. We shall prove Noether's theorem later in chapter 6. At the moment we wish to obtain the conservation laws bred by the homogeneity of time and space, and the isotropy of space.

(a) Homogeneity of Time and Conservation of Energy

The Lagrangian of a closed system should not have any explicit dependence on time so that $(\partial L/\partial t) = 0$ and hence, using Lagrange's equations involving nonpotential forces of external origin,

$$\frac{dJ}{dt} = \frac{d}{dt}\left(\frac{\partial L}{\partial \dot{q}_i}\dot{q}_i - L\right) = Q'_i\dot{q}_i$$

However, for a closed system, all the components of the external forces are zero including the nonpotential ones giving $Q'_i = 0$ so that the Jacobi integral becomes a constant of motion.

Now since there is no external force, V (and/or U) reduce(s) to a constant, say V_o, and $L = T - V_o$. Since L is independent of time, so is T as V is a constant, and therefore, $T_o = T_1 = 0$ giving $T = T_2$. The system is therefore totally scleronomic, implying that

$$J = E = T + V_o = \text{const.}$$

Hence total energy is conserved for any closed system due to homogeneity of time.

(b) Homogeneity of Space and Conservation of Linear Momentum

The Lagrangian of a closed system should not change due to any arbitrarily small uniform translation for all particles. In Cartesian rectangular coordinates this translation can be written, for the ith particle

$$\boldsymbol{r}_i \longrightarrow \boldsymbol{r}_i + \delta\boldsymbol{r}_i$$

where $\delta\boldsymbol{r}_i = \boldsymbol{\epsilon}$ is a constant vector, infinitesimally small in magnitude. We have

$$\delta L = \sum_i \frac{\partial L}{\partial \boldsymbol{r}_i} \cdot \delta\boldsymbol{r}_i = \sum_i \left(\boldsymbol{\epsilon} \cdot \frac{\partial L}{\partial \boldsymbol{r}_i}\right) = \boldsymbol{\epsilon} \cdot \left(\sum_i \frac{\partial L}{\partial \boldsymbol{r}_i}\right)$$

We require that $\delta L = 0$ for any arbitrary translation $\boldsymbol{\epsilon}$ which implies, for the whole system

$$\sum_i \frac{\partial L}{\partial \boldsymbol{r}_i} = 0$$

Adding the corresponding terms in Euler-Lagrange's equations of motion for all particles,

$$\sum_i \frac{d}{dt}\left(\frac{\partial L}{\partial \boldsymbol{v}_i}\right) - \sum_i \frac{\partial L}{\partial \boldsymbol{r}_i} = 0$$

or

$$\sum_i \frac{d}{dt}\left(\frac{\partial L}{\partial \boldsymbol{v}_i}\right) = 0 \quad \text{or} \quad \frac{d}{dt}\left(\sum_i \boldsymbol{p}_i\right) = 0$$

Therefore, the total linear momentum

$$\sum_i \boldsymbol{p}_i = \boldsymbol{P} \quad \text{(say)} \tag{2.66}$$

is the quantity that is conserved. Thus the total linear momentum of any closed system is conserved due to the homogeneity of space.

(c) Isotropy of Space and the Conservation of Angular Momentum

The Lagrangian for a closed system should not change due to any arbitrary small rotation of reference frame about some arbitrary direction.

An arbitrary small rotation $\delta\theta$ about some direction $\hat{\boldsymbol{n}}$ passing through the origin brings about a change in any vector $\boldsymbol{A}$ given by

$$\delta\boldsymbol{A} = (\delta\theta\hat{\boldsymbol{n}}) \times \boldsymbol{A} \tag{2.67}$$

Therefore all position vectors $\boldsymbol{r}_i$ will change by

$$\delta\boldsymbol{r}_i = (\delta\theta\hat{\boldsymbol{n}}) \times \boldsymbol{r}_i$$

and the velocity vectors $\boldsymbol{v}_i$ by

$$\delta\boldsymbol{v}_i = (\delta\theta\hat{\boldsymbol{n}}) \times \boldsymbol{v}_i$$

Since all vectors ought to change in the above fashion, the following proof is going to be valid only if L for the closed system does not contain any vectors other than $\boldsymbol{r}$ and $\boldsymbol{p}$; not even a constant vector such as the dipole moment vector is allowed to be present in L, though L remains always as a scalar.

Therefore for any closed system

$$\begin{aligned}\delta L &= \sum_i \left(\frac{\partial L}{\partial \boldsymbol{r}_i} \cdot \delta \boldsymbol{r}_i + \frac{\partial L}{\partial \boldsymbol{v}_i} \cdot \delta \boldsymbol{v}_i \right) \\ &= \sum_i (\dot{\boldsymbol{p}}_i \cdot \delta \boldsymbol{r}_i + \boldsymbol{p}_i \cdot \delta \boldsymbol{v}_i) \\ &= \delta\theta \sum_i [\dot{\boldsymbol{p}}_i \cdot (\hat{\boldsymbol{n}} \times \boldsymbol{r}_i) + \boldsymbol{p}_i \cdot (\hat{\boldsymbol{n}} \times \boldsymbol{v}_i)] \\ &= \delta\theta \sum_i \left[\frac{d}{dt} (\boldsymbol{r}_i \times \boldsymbol{p}_i) \cdot \hat{\boldsymbol{n}} \right] \\ &= \delta\theta \hat{\boldsymbol{n}} \cdot \frac{d}{dt} \left(\sum_i \boldsymbol{r}_i \times \boldsymbol{p}_i \right)\end{aligned}$$

Since $\delta\theta$ is arbitrary and $\delta L = 0$ due to the required isotropy of space for the description of a closed system, we have

$$\frac{d}{dt} \left(\sum_i \boldsymbol{r}_i \times \boldsymbol{p}_i \right) = \boldsymbol{0}$$

or

$$\sum_i \boldsymbol{r}_i \times \boldsymbol{p}_i = \boldsymbol{L} \qquad \text{(say)}$$

is the conserved quantity which, by definition, is the total moment of momentum or the total angular momentum about the origin of the closed system.

2.15 INVARIANCE UNDER GALILEAN TRANSFORMATIONS

We have defined inertial frames as those in which Newton's laws of motion are valid, or alternatively, in which the space and time are homogeneous and space is isotropic. Consider two inertial frames S and S′ in relative motion. In general, various kinematical and physical quantities pertaining to the system will have different values in these two inertial frames. The problem is to obtain relations between the values of a given quantity measured with respect to these two inertial frames.

An immediate consequence of the requirement that Newton's laws be valid in both the frames is that the forces acting on the system must be the same in both the frames, that is, for the ith particle

$$m_i \frac{d^2 \boldsymbol{r}'_i}{dt^2} = \boldsymbol{F}_i = m_i \frac{d^2 \boldsymbol{r}_i}{dt^2}$$

where i is not summed over and we have assumed that the time is universal, that is, it always has the same value in both the frames. $\boldsymbol{r}_i$ and $\boldsymbol{r}'_i$ are the position vectors of the ith particle in S and S′ respectively, that is, $\boldsymbol{r}$ becomes $\boldsymbol{r}'$ as we go from S to S′. Thus we must have

$$\frac{d^2(\boldsymbol{r}_i - \boldsymbol{r}'_i)}{dt^2} = \boldsymbol{0} \quad \text{or} \quad \boldsymbol{r}_i - \boldsymbol{r}'_i = \boldsymbol{u}_o(t - t_o) = \boldsymbol{u}_o t$$

if the origins of S and S′ coincided at $t = 0$, rather than at $t = t_o$. The constant of integration, $\boldsymbol{u}_o$ stands for the constant relative velocity of S′ with respect to S. Thus we get the basic transformation equations

$$\boldsymbol{r}'_i = \boldsymbol{r}_i - \boldsymbol{u}_o t \tag{2.68}$$

with the implicit assumption $t' = t$. The frames S and S′ are said to be connected by a *Galilean transformation* if the transformation equations are by definition given by the Eq. (2.68).

Let us now see how the Lagrangian of any system transforms between S and S′. In the case of the motion of a single particle moving under an external field of force due to an ordinary potential V, the Lagrangian in S′ is given by

$$\begin{aligned} L' &= \frac{1}{2}mv'^2 - V \\ &= \frac{1}{2}m|\boldsymbol{v} - \boldsymbol{u}_o|^2 - V \\ &= \frac{1}{2}mv^2 - V - m\boldsymbol{v}\cdot\boldsymbol{u}_o + \frac{1}{2}mu_o^2 \\ &= L + \frac{d}{dt}\left(\frac{1}{2}mu_o^2 t - m\boldsymbol{u}_o\cdot\boldsymbol{r}\right) \\ &= L + \frac{dF(\boldsymbol{r},t)}{dt} \quad \text{(say)} \end{aligned}$$

Note that V has remained the same because V is normally a function of $\boldsymbol{r}_2 - \boldsymbol{r}_1$ and $\boldsymbol{r}_2 - \boldsymbol{r}_1 = \boldsymbol{r}'_2 - \boldsymbol{r}'_1$ at all instants by Eq. (2.68). Thus through the above gauge function $F(\boldsymbol{r},t)$ (see section 2.9) both L and L' must satisfy the same Euler-Lagrange's equations of motion, that is, the latter preserve their form in S′. This is effected by the Lagrangian gauge function

$$F(\boldsymbol{r},t) = \frac{1}{2}mu_o^2 t - m\boldsymbol{u}_o\cdot\boldsymbol{r} \tag{2.69}$$

provided $\boldsymbol{u}_o$ is the constant relative velocity of S′ with respect to S. So the coordinate transformation corresponding to any Galilean transformation can be viewed as a Lagrangian gauge transformation. Thus instead of performing the coordinate transformation given by Eq. (2.68) we can also directly transform the Lagrangian using the gauge function given by Eq. (2.69) and obtain the same results.

It is also easy to see that in Eq. (2.68) one can eliminate $\boldsymbol{u}_o$ to obtain

$$\boldsymbol{r}'_i - \boldsymbol{r}_i = (\dot{\boldsymbol{r}}'_i - \dot{\boldsymbol{r}}_i)t$$

so that

$$\boldsymbol{r}'_i - \boldsymbol{v}'_i t = \boldsymbol{r}_i - \boldsymbol{v}_i t$$

For the whole system this appears to suggest that the quantity $\sum_i m_i(\boldsymbol{r}_i - \boldsymbol{v}_i t)$ has the same value in all inertial frames, which are of course, connected by Galilean transformations. Or in other words,

$$\sum_i m_i \boldsymbol{r}_i - \sum_i \boldsymbol{p}_i t = M\boldsymbol{R} - \boldsymbol{P}t \tag{2.70}$$

is a constant of motion arising out of the symmetry implied by the Galilean invariance of Newton's equations of motion. Here $M = \sum_i m_i$ is the total mass, $\boldsymbol{R}$ is the position vector of the centre of mass and $\boldsymbol{P}$ is the total linear momentum of the system.

Thus for a *closed system* we have constructed in all *ten additive constants of motion*, of which three are due to linear momentum, three are due to angular momentum, three are due to Galilean invariance and one due to energy.

Now if $\boldsymbol{u}_o$ were a function of t so that frame S$'$ becomes noninertial and if we insist to write for single particle motion

$$L' = \frac{1}{2}m|\boldsymbol{v}'|^2 - V$$

so that the equations of motion in S$'$ are then given by

$$\frac{d}{dt}\left(\frac{\partial L'}{\partial \boldsymbol{v}'}\right) - \frac{\partial L'}{\partial \boldsymbol{r}'} = \boldsymbol{0}$$

which means

$$m\dot{\boldsymbol{v}}' + \nabla V = \boldsymbol{0} \tag{2.71}$$

But at any instant t, $\boldsymbol{v}' = \boldsymbol{v} - \boldsymbol{u}_o$, so that the Eq. (2.71) implies

$$m\dot{\boldsymbol{v}} - m\dot{\boldsymbol{u}}_o + \nabla V = \boldsymbol{0} \tag{2.72}$$

So we do not get back the original equations of motion of the system in S if we define L' in a noninertial frame in the same way as we define in the inertial frames. We have an extra force term $-m\dot{\boldsymbol{u}}_o$ added to the system, consequently violating Newton's second law which must apply only to the inertial frames such as S. Equation (2.72) is different from the original $m\dot{\boldsymbol{v}} + \nabla V = \boldsymbol{0}$. Thus the form of Euler-Lagrange's equation is not preserved in a noninertial frame. Since Newton's laws are not preserved, D'Alembert's principle is also not valid in the noninertial frames and hence the Lagrangian cannot be constructed simply from $T = mv'^2/2$, even if V remains unchanged.

It is then important to note that the Lagrangian must always be constructed with respect to an inertial frame, although it may involve quantities referring to a noninertial frame. An expression for kinetic energy must be constructed in an inertial frame first, and then by substituting for inertial velocities in terms of the velocities and coordinates of the noninertial frame, one would finally obtain a Lagrangian, to be used in terms of the coordinates and velocities with reference to the noninertial frame. This point will be more fully discussed in chapter 3, for a particular class of noninertial frames, called the rotating frames of reference.

2.16 LAGRANGIAN FOR FREE PARTICLE MOTION

A free particle is one which is not acted upon by any external force at all. Hence the potential functions V or U can be taken as zero, or at most a constant. Therefore, the Lagrangian L for any free particle is essentially equal to its kinetic energy T. Let us see how the expression for T takes different forms in different coordinate systems. In this case, the number of DOF is three, so the number of independent integrals of motion is five.

2.16.1 Rectangular Cartesian Coordinate System

The Lagrangian is

$$L = T = \frac{1}{2}m(\dot{x}^2 + \dot{y}^2 + \dot{z}^2)$$

All the three coordinates are cyclic giving

$$p_x = \frac{\partial L}{\partial \dot{x}} = m\dot{x} \qquad p_y = \frac{\partial L}{\partial \dot{y}} = m\dot{y} \qquad \text{and} \qquad p_z = \frac{\partial L}{\partial \dot{z}} = m\dot{z}$$

as the constants of motion. The energy integral is

$$E = \frac{\partial L}{\partial \dot{x}}\dot{x} + \frac{\partial L}{\partial \dot{y}}\dot{y} + \frac{\partial L}{\partial \dot{z}}\dot{z} - L = \frac{1}{2m}(p_x^2 + p_y^2 + p_z^2)$$

and is obviously a constant of motion. But if p_x, p_y, p_z are assumed to be independent integrals of motion, then E is not. The other two independent integrals of motion, though not obvious, are any two components of the angular momentum.

2.16.2 Cylindrical Polar Coordinate System

In this system the Lagrangian is

$$L = T = \frac{1}{2}mv^2 = \frac{1}{2}m\left(\frac{ds}{dt}\right)^2$$
$$= \frac{1}{2}m(\dot{r}^2 + r^2\dot{\theta}^2 + \dot{z}^2)$$

Here, for the same free particle, only θ and z are cyclic coordinates giving $p_\theta = (\partial L/\partial\dot{\theta}) = mr^2\dot{\theta}$ = angular momentum about the z-axis passing through the origin and $p_z = m\dot{z}$ as two independent constants of motion. Therefore this coordinate system is not as good as the Cartesian system for the description of a free particle motion so far as the number of the cyclic coordinates are concerned, but the Cartesian frame did not make it obvious that the angular momentum about the z-axis can be a constant of motion.

2.16.3 Spherical Polar Coordinate System

With respect to this frame of reference the Lagrangian is

$$L = T = \frac{1}{2}mv^2 = \frac{1}{2}m\left(\frac{ds}{dt}\right)^2$$
$$= \frac{1}{2}m(\dot{r}^2 + r^2\dot{\theta}^2 + r^2\sin^2\theta\dot{\phi}^2)$$

Here, only ϕ is cyclic giving $p_\phi = mr^2 \sin^2\theta\dot{\phi} = \text{constant}$, which is the angular momentum about the z-axis. Other constants of motion are hidden.

One can write down the equations of motion in each case and solve them. Obviously, these will be the parametric equations of straight lines in different coordinate systems, with t as the parameter.

Throughout the book, we shall come across the expressions for Lagrangians for a number of physical situations. So we refrain from working out examples in this chapter. The problems suggested at the end of the chapter can be worked out with the help of the hints given at the end of the book.

2.17 LAGRANGE'S EQUATIONS OF MOTION FOR NONHOLONOMIC SYSTEMS

We have noted in section 2.3 that for a nonholonomic bilateral system having k' nonholonomic constraint relations and n degrees of freedom, the number of quasi-generalised coordinates required is $n + k'$, where $n = 3N - k - k'$, N being the number of particles and k being the number of holonomic constraints.

If all the nonholonomic constraints are given by

$$g_i = g_i(q_1, \ldots, q_{n+k'}, \dot{q}_1, \ldots, \dot{q}_{n+k'}, t) = 0 \tag{2.73}$$

where $i = 1, \ldots, k'$, following the argument given in section 1.5, the generalised constraint forces arising out of Eq. (2.73) would be given by

$$(Q_j)_c = \sum_{i=1}^{k'} \lambda_i \frac{\partial g_i}{\partial \dot{q}_j} \tag{2.74}$$

where λ_i are the Lagrange multipliers. Equations ((2.14) or (2.28)) have so far been the most general form of Euler-Lagrange equations of motion for a holonomic system having nonpotential forces $Q'_j(q, \dot{q}, t)$. Now Eqs ((2.14) or (2.28)) can further be generalised to include any nonholonomic system experiencing forces of both the potential and nonpotential types to take the form,

$$\frac{d}{dt}\left(\frac{\partial L}{\partial \dot{q}_j}\right) - \frac{\partial L}{\partial q_j} = Q'_j + (Q_j)_c = Q'_j + \sum_{i=1}^{k'} \lambda_i \frac{\partial g_i}{\partial \dot{q}_j}$$

or

$$\frac{d}{dt}\left(\frac{\partial L}{\partial \dot{q}_j}\right) - \frac{\partial L}{\partial q_j} - \sum_{i=1}^{k'} \lambda_i \frac{\partial g_i}{\partial \dot{q}_j} = Q'_j \tag{2.75}$$

Here L is as usual defined to be either $T - V$ or $T - U$ depending on the nature of the potential forces with

$$T = \frac{1}{2}\sum_{i=1}^{3N} m_i \dot{x}_i^2$$

$$\begin{aligned} x_i &= x_i(q_1,\ldots,q_{3N-k},t) \quad \text{for} \quad i = 1,\ldots,3N \\ V &= V(q_1,\ldots,q_{3N-k},t) \qquad \text{or} \\ U &= U(q_1,\ldots,q_{3N-k},\dot{q}_1,\ldots,\dot{q}_{3N-k},t) \qquad \text{and} \\ g_i &= 0 \qquad \text{for} \quad i = 1,\ldots,k' \qquad \text{as given by Eq. (2.73)} \end{aligned}$$

Equation (2.75) is valid for any type of nonholonomic constraints. But we know that certain classes of nonholonomic constraint forces do not do any virtual work, provided they are expressible as homogeneous functions of velocities except for an additive arbitrary function of coordinates and time (see section 1.7). For such simple nonholonomic D'Alembertian systems, Eq. (2.75) takes the following form:

$$\sum_{j=1}^{n+k'}\left[\frac{d}{dt}\left(\frac{\partial L}{\partial \dot{q}_j}\right) - \frac{\partial L}{\partial q_j}\right]\cdot \delta q_j = \delta W' = \sum_{j=1}^{n+k'} Q'_j \delta q_j \tag{2.76}$$

where not all δq_j's but only n of them can be arbitrary. This is of course the most general form of D'Alembert's principle expressed in terms of the quasi-generalised coordinates. Obviously, in absence of any nonpotential generalised forces, $\delta W' = 0$. This extension of Lagrange's formalism to nonholonomic systems was first done by Ferrers in 1871.

A worked out example of a case of the nonholonomic constraints:

The motion of a village cart wheel that is rolling on an incline without slipping.

Let us assume that the wheels of the cart have radius b, the separation between the wheels is a, the angle of inclination of the incline α, the incline runs down along $-y$ axis, x axis is horizontal.

Now the coordinates to describe the motion are as follows:

$(x, y) =$ the rectangular Cartesian coordinates for the location of the centre of mass of the entire cart wheel system projected on the plane of the incline,

$\theta =$ the angle between the axle and y axis, and

$\phi_1, \phi_2 =$ angles of rotations in the planes of the wheels.

So these constitute five coordinates.

Then come the constraints: The vector condition for no slipping gives rise to the following constraints

(i) an integrable or holonomic constraint given by $a\, d\theta = b(d\phi_1 + d\phi_2)$, or

$$\dot{\theta} = \frac{b}{a}(\dot{\phi}_1 + \dot{\phi}_2)$$

(ii) the differential displacement ds of the centre of mass has a direction always perpendicular to the axle, or

$$ds = \frac{b}{2}(d\phi_1 - d\phi_2)$$

This second constraint is not integrable as ds is not a coordinate. Actually, this constraint is equivalent to two nonholonomic constraints, given by

$$dx = \frac{b}{2}(d\phi_1 - d\phi_2)\cos\theta \quad \text{and} \quad dy = \frac{b}{2}(d\phi_1 - d\phi_2)\sin\theta$$

So there are three constraints in five coordinates, giving the number of DOF = 2. But because of 2 nonholonomic constraints the minimum number of quasi-generalised coordinates required is 4.

The gravitational force on the system is $F_y = -Mg\sin\alpha$, M being the total mass of the system, the potential energy is $Mgy\sin\alpha$. The kinetic energy is

$$T = \frac{1}{2}M\dot{s}^2 + \frac{1}{2}I_z\dot{\theta}^2 + \frac{1}{2}I_c(\dot{\phi}_1^2 + \dot{\phi}_2^2)$$

where $I_z = I_a + 2I_b + ma^2/2$, $I_c = mb^2/2$, m being the mass of individual wheels.

The constraint relations are found to satisfy $a^2\dot{\theta}^2 + 4\dot{s}^2 = 2b^2(\dot{\phi}_1^2 + \dot{\phi}_2^2)$, thus eliminating $\dot{\theta}^2$, we have,

$$T = \frac{1}{2}\mu\dot{s}^2 + \frac{1}{2}\beta(\dot{\phi}_1^2 + \dot{\phi}_2^2)$$

where $\mu = M + 2I_c/b^2$, $\beta = I_z + a^2I_c/2b^2$, and hence the Lagrangian

$$L = \frac{1}{2}\mu(\dot{x}^2 + \dot{y}^2) + + \frac{1}{2}\beta(\dot{\phi}_1^2 + \dot{\phi}_2^2) - Mgy\sin\alpha$$

now being describable in terms of 4 quasi-generalised coordinates x, y, ϕ_1, ϕ_2.

Writing Lagrange's equation in the form of D'Alembert's principle in quasi-generalised coordinates,

$$\sum_{j=1}^{4}\left(\frac{d}{dt}\frac{\partial L}{\partial \dot{q}_j} - \frac{\partial L}{\partial q_j}\right)\delta q_j = 0$$

on rewriting

$$\mu\ddot{x}\delta x + (\mu\ddot{y} + Mg\sin\alpha)\delta y + \beta(\ddot{\phi}_1 + \ddot{\phi}_2)(\delta\phi_1 + \delta\phi_2) = 0$$

Now if we eliminate δx and δy using the nonholonomic constraint relations, $\delta\phi_1$ and $\delta\phi_2$ become arbitrary, and hence their coefficients vanish, giving

$$\dot{\phi}_1 + \dot{\phi}_2 = \dot{\theta} = \text{const.} = \omega \text{ (say)}$$

and

$$\ddot{s} = -\frac{Mg}{\mu}\sin\alpha\sin\theta$$

where $\dot{x} = \dot{s}\cos\theta$ and $\dot{y} = \dot{s}\sin\theta$ are used. The second equation has a solution

$$\dot{s} = \frac{Mg}{\mu\omega}\sin\alpha\cos\theta + v_o$$

v_o being the constant of integration, implying the speed of the centre of mass when the axle is moving parallel to the x axis. Thus the solutions for $\dot{x}$ and $\dot{y}$ are

$$\dot{x} = \dot{s}\cos\theta = \frac{Mg\sin\alpha}{2\mu\omega}(1 + \cos 2\theta) + v_o\cos\theta$$

and

$$\dot{y} = \dot{s}\sin\theta = \frac{Mg\sin\alpha}{2\mu\omega}\sin 2\theta + v_o\sin\theta$$

So the motion in $\dot{y}$ is purely oscillatory, but that in $\dot{x}$ has a constant time average, $Mg\sin\alpha/2\mu\omega$. Therefore, the cartwheel will be drifting horizontally but oscillating along the slope of the incline. Recall that $\theta = \omega t +$ constant.

The general solution for x and y now becomes

$$x = \frac{Mg\sin\alpha}{4\mu\omega^2}(2\theta + \sin 2\theta) + x_o$$

and

$$y = -\frac{Mg\sin\alpha}{4\mu\omega^2}\cos 2\theta + y_o$$

These equations describe a cycloid with cusps pointing along the $+y$ axis, the total vertical amplitude $= Mg\sin\alpha/4\mu\omega^2$ and the horizontal separation between the consecutive cusps as π times the vertical amplitude.

Now if $\alpha = 0$, that is, the cartwheel is moving in a horizontal plane instead of an incline without allowing its wheels to slip, the centre of mass will execute a purely circular motion.

2.18 LAGRANGE'S EQUATIONS OF MOTION FOR IMPULSIVE FORCES

Consider a holonomic system containing N particles, described by n generalised coordinates $q_1, \ldots, q_n$. Let a large external force $\boldsymbol{F}(t)$ act on this system for a very short time say between t and $t + \Delta t$. $\boldsymbol{F}(t)$ may also vary rapidly within the time interval Δt over which it acts. This situation is realised during collisions of material bodies. Instead of dealing with the impulsive force $\boldsymbol{F}(t)$, whose variation with time during t is generally unknown, it is advantageous to deal with a quantity called *impulse* of $\boldsymbol{F}(t)$ defined as

$$\boldsymbol{P}(t, t + \Delta t) = \int_t^{t+\Delta t} \boldsymbol{F}(t')\,dt' \qquad (2.77)$$

Since the duration of impact is very short we can assume displacements to remain unchanged during the impact whereas the velocities can be assumed to change almost instantaneously. This is because, in response to finite changes in velocities, displacements take a finite time to develop. This means that the following limit exists

$$\hat{\boldsymbol{P}}(t) = \lim \boldsymbol{P}(t, t + \Delta t) \qquad (2.78)$$

where

$$\lim \equiv \text{limit as } \Delta t \longrightarrow 0 \quad |\boldsymbol{F}(t)| \longrightarrow \infty \quad \text{and } \boldsymbol{P}(t, t + \Delta t) \text{ is held const.}$$

The quantity $\hat{\boldsymbol{P}}(t)$ is called the *instantaneous impulse* (or *impulse* for short) and has the dimension [F] [T].

The formulation of the above problem in terms of generalised coordinates can be done as follows. Let the holonomic system mentioned above be acted upon by a force between the time t and $t + \Delta t$ and let Q_i be the generalised component of the force corresponding to the generalised coordinate q_i. Then the generalised component of the impulse corresponding to the generalised coordinate q_i applied to the system between t and $t + \Delta t$ is defined as

$$Q_i(t, t + \Delta t) \equiv \int_t^{t + \Delta t} Q_i(t')\, dt' \tag{2.79}$$

Again we define an instantaneous impulse associated with $Q_i(t, t + \Delta t)$ as

$$\hat{Q}_i(t) = \lim Q_i(t, t + \Delta t) \tag{2.80}$$

where

$$\lim \equiv \text{limit as } \Delta t \longrightarrow 0, \quad |Q_i(t)| \longrightarrow \infty \quad \text{and } Q_i(t, t + \Delta t) \text{ is held constant} \tag{2.81}$$

We can now modify Euler-Lagrange's equations to allow for the impulsive forces. Euler-Lagrange's equations of motion for a holonomic system can be written as

$$\frac{d}{dt}\left(\frac{\partial T}{\partial \dot{q}_i}\right) - \frac{\partial T}{\partial q_i} = Q_i \tag{2.82}$$

If we integrate Eq. (2.82) from t to $t + \Delta t$ take the limit defined in Eq. (2.81) we get

$$\lim \int_t^{t + \Delta t} \frac{d}{dt'}\left(\frac{\partial T}{\partial \dot{q}_i}\right) dt' - \lim \int_t^{t + \Delta t} \frac{\partial T}{\partial q_i} dt' = \lim \int_t^{t + \Delta t} Q_i\, dt'$$

The first term can be reduced to

$$\lim \int_t^{t + \Delta t} \frac{d}{dt'}\left(\frac{\partial T}{\partial \dot{q}_i}\right) dt' = \lim \left[\left.\frac{\partial T}{\partial \dot{q}_i}\right|_t^{t + \Delta t}\right]_{\Delta t \to 0} = \Delta p_i \tag{2.83}$$

where $p_i = \partial T/\partial \dot{q}_i$ is the generalised momentum corresponding to the generalised coordinate q_i.

Now the integrand in the second term in Eq. (2.82) remains finite during the impulse, therefore

$$\lim \int_t^{t + \Delta t} \frac{\partial T}{\partial q_i} dt' = 0$$

and from Eq. (2.80) the term on RHS is just the instantaneous impulse $\hat{Q}_i(t)$ or $\hat{Q}_i$ for brevity. Thus Eq. (2.82) reduces to

$$\Delta p_i = \hat{Q}_i \tag{2.84}$$

Equation (2.84) states that *the incremental change in the generalised momentum is equal to the generalised impulse.*

The value of the generalised impulse can be obtained from the expression for virtual work done by the impulsive forces. Let $\boldsymbol{F}_1, \ldots, \boldsymbol{F}_N$ be the impulsive forces on the system of N particles. Then

$$\sum_{k=1}^{n} \hat{Q}_k \delta q_k = \sum_{j=1}^{N} \boldsymbol{F}_j \cdot \delta \boldsymbol{r}_j = \sum_{j=1}^{N} \sum_{k=1}^{n} \boldsymbol{F}_j \cdot \frac{\partial \boldsymbol{r}_j}{\partial q_k} \delta q_k = \sum_{k=1}^{n} \left(\sum_{j=1}^{N} \boldsymbol{F}_j \cdot \frac{\partial \boldsymbol{r}_j}{\partial q_k} \right) \delta q_k$$

where n is the number of degrees of freedom. Comparing term by term we get

$$\hat{Q}_k = \sum_{j=1}^{N} \boldsymbol{F}_j \cdot \frac{\partial \boldsymbol{r}_j}{\partial q_k} \tag{2.85}$$

In the above formulation we have assumed that the constraint forces are not impulsive.

Finally we note that systems subjected to impulsive forces are not generally conservative since energy is dissipated during impact of bodies.

Example

Consider a double pendulum in which the masses m_1 and m_2 are connected by massless rigid links of lengths l_1 and l_2 respectively. We obtain Euler-Lagrange's equation of motion for the case in which a source of an impulsive force $\hat{P}$ strikes horizontally at a distance d from the support when the links are at rest in the vertical position. Consider the case in which $l_1 < d < l_1 + l_2$.

The value of the kinetic energy corresponding to the vertical position is

$$T = \frac{1}{2} m_1 (l_1 \dot{\theta}_1)^2 + \frac{1}{2} m_2 (l_1 \dot{\theta}_1 + l_2 \dot{\theta}_2)^2 \tag{2.86}$$

Denoting by $\hat{Q}_1$ and $\hat{Q}_2$ the impulsive forces associated with the generalised coordinates θ_1 and θ_2, we can write the expression for the virtual work

$$\hat{P}\delta[l_1\theta_1 + (d - l_1)\theta_2] = \hat{P}[l_1\delta\theta_1 + (d - l_1)\delta\theta_2] = \hat{Q}_1\delta\theta_1 + \hat{Q}_2\delta\theta_2 \tag{2.87}$$

which gives

$$\hat{Q}_1 = \hat{P} l_1 \quad \text{and} \quad \hat{Q}_2 = \hat{P}(d - l_1) \tag{2.88}$$

and we note that $\hat{Q}_1$, $\hat{Q}_2$ are impulsive moments rather than forces. Since the momentum before the application of $\hat{P}$ is zero, we have

$$\Delta p_i = p_i = \frac{\partial T}{\partial \dot{\theta}_i} \qquad i = 1, 2 \tag{2.89}$$

so that using Eq. (2.84) in conjunction with Eqs (2.86) and (2.88) we obtain

$$\begin{aligned} m_1 l_1^2 \dot{\theta}_1 + m_2 l_1 (l_1 \dot{\theta}_1 + l_2 \dot{\theta}_2) &= \hat{P} l_1 \\ m_2 l_2 (l_1 \dot{\theta}_1 + l_2 \dot{\theta}_2) &= \hat{P}(d - l_1) \end{aligned} \tag{2.90}$$

which are the desired equations.

2.19 SUMMARY

D'Alembert's principle is not of much use unless the possible displacements δx_i are made absolutely independent of each other. In the presence of constraints, the constraint relations have to be satisfied by the δx_i's, making them dependent on one another. If there are k holonomic constraints and N particles, $3N - k$ should be the maximum number of possible independent coordinate displacements. $3N - k$ is called the number of degrees of freedom of the system. Any set of $3N - k$ independent coordinates, called the generalised coordinates for the holonomic system, are defined and used by Lagrange to break up the single equation of D'Alembert's principle into $3N - k$ independent equations of motion. These equations are called Lagrange's equations of motion of the second kind. At about the same time Euler also developed variational calculus and obtained Lagrange's equations of motion from general principles, and hence these equations are often regarded as Euler-Lagrange's equations of motion.

The Lagrangian L is a scalar point function described in a $3N - k$ -dimensional configuration space, but it cannot be uniquely specified because of the functional dependence of L on the coordinate velocities and time. The generalised momenta p_i were defined in terms of the Lagrangian, which is either given or constructed from its definitions $L = T - V$, or $L = T - U$, where T is the kinetic energy, V is the ordinary potential energy and U is the generalised potential energy, as the case may be, for defining L.

For every particular generalised coordinate that is absent or cyclic in the expression for the Lagrangian, Euler-Lagrange's equation of motion for that particular coordinate leads to the conservation of the generalised momentum, conjugate to the cyclic coordinate. If the Lagrangian is time independent, it must conserve an energy-like quantity called the Jacobi integral, which can be identified with the actual energy provided both the ordinary potential energy function and the kinetic energy function are independent of both velocity and time. Such systems are called conservative systems. It is shown that the generalised potential energy functions can in most cases be conveniently represented by a sum of ordinary potential energy function and a term originating due to some gyroscopic forces of antisymmetric nature.

The preservation of the explicit form of the Euler-Lagrangian equations of motion in terms of the Lagrangian does not require that the Lagrangian be unique. In fact one can add a total time derivative of any scalar point function of coordinates and time to the physical Lagrangian and still retain the same form of the Euler-Lagrangian equations of motion in terms of the new Lagrangian. Such an invariance, duly recognised as a symmetry property of the Lagrangian functions, is sometimes referred to as invariance under Lagrangian gauge transformation. Such changed Lagrangians would not give the equations of motion when explicitly written out in terms of the coordinates, differing from those written out for the original Lagrangian. It is also shown that Euler-Lagrange's form of the equations of motion remains invariant under any generalised coordinate transformation connecting one to the transformed set.

Expected symmetries of the Lagrangian for any closed system under, say, infinitesimal translation, rotation, shift in the origin of time or Galilean transformation between two moving inertial frames, by Noether's theorem, result in the conservation of ten quantities — linear momentum, angular momentum, energy and centre of mass motion.

The Lagrangian formalism is extended to incorporate dissipation of the Rayleigh type and further to include the nonholonomic systems by Ferrers. For nonholonomic systems, the generalised coordinates are not sufficient. The total number of coordinates required is still $3N - k$, even though an extra number of k' nonholonomic constraints are present. Such coordinates are called quasi-generalised coordinates, or simply quasi-coordinates.

PROBLEMS

2.1 Find the number of degrees of freedom of the dynamical systems described in problem number 1.1. What are the suitable generalised coordinates that one can select for these?

2.2 During the boiling of any liquid, a phase transition takes place from its liquid to the vapour state. Assume that during the process of boiling individual molecules do not change their vibrational state of motion, but all their possible translational and rotational degrees of freedom are suddenly restored. Using Boltzmann's law of equipartition of energy, namely an increase in energy by $\frac{1}{2}kT_b$ per molecule per degree of freedom, calculate the contributions to the latent heat of vaporisation of water, liquid nitrogen and liquid helium at their respective boiling points, $T_b = 373$ K, 77 K and 4.2 K, k being the Boltzmann's constant $= 1.38 \times 10^{-23}$ J/K.

2.3 Show that

$$(i)\ \delta L = \frac{d}{dt}(p_i \delta q_i) \qquad (ii)\ \frac{\partial T}{\partial p_i} = \dot{q}_i \qquad \text{and} \qquad (iii)\ \delta T + \delta V = 0$$

for conservative systems.

2.4 Show that Appell's equations of motion are valid for generalised coordinates, that is, they can take the form

$$\frac{\partial S}{\partial \ddot{q}_i} = Q_i = F_j \frac{\partial x_j}{\partial q_i} \qquad \text{where} \qquad S = \sum_{k=1}^{3N} m_k (\ddot{x}_k)^2 \quad \text{is the energy of}$$

acceleration of the system.

Consider a bead of mass m sliding under gravity on a uniform smooth circular wire of mass M radius r_o, which rolls on a horizontal plane keeping its plane always vertical. Deduce Appell's equations of motion for the systems and confirm that they are none other than the Euler-Lagrange equations of motion.

2.5 Consider in detail the transformation $x = r\cos\theta$ and $y = r\sin\theta$. F_x and F_y are the Cartesian components of the external force $\boldsymbol{F}$. Derive the components of the generalised forces Q_r and Q_θ in terms of the generalised coordinates r and θ, and compare with the force components F_r and F_θ, the latter being the radial and transverse components of $\boldsymbol{F}$. Show that $F_r = Q_r$, but $F_\theta \neq Q_\theta$. Explain why this is so. Using the spherical polar coordinates, interpret the meanings of Q_θ and Q_ϕ.

2.6 Find the generalised forces for the generalised coordinates describing the small amplitude oscillation of a double pendulum. Use D'Alembert's principle to find the equations of motion.

2.7 Construct the Lagrangians for the following dynamical systems and find the first integrals for all the cyclic coordinates:
(i) A system of two particles having masses m_1 and m_2 are connected by an inextensible, massless string of length l passing through a small hole in a horizontal table.
(ii) A block of mass M constrained to slide along a smooth horizontal bar and another mass m ($< M$) is connected to M by a massless, stretchless, flexible string of length l. The second mass can swing freely in any direction.
(iii) A rigid and smooth circular wire of radius R is constrained to rotate in its plane (horizontal) about a fixed point on the wire with constant angular speed ω. Consider the motion of a bead of mass m sliding freely on the wire.
(iv) A disc of radius R rolling on a perfectly rough horizontal plane and constrained to remain vertical. This is a nonholonomic case. Take it as a separate problem and solve it.
(v) A charged particle moving under the Lorentz force law given $\boldsymbol{f} = e\boldsymbol{E} + e\boldsymbol{v} \times \boldsymbol{B}$, where $\boldsymbol{E} = -\nabla\phi - \partial\boldsymbol{A}/\partial t$ and $\boldsymbol{B} = \nabla \times \boldsymbol{A}$ are the electric field and magnetic induction respectively, $\boldsymbol{A}(\boldsymbol{r},t)$ and $\phi(\boldsymbol{r},t)$ being the vector and scalar electromagnetic potentials .

2.8 A flexible tape of length L and thickness k is tightly wound and is then allowed to unwind as it rolls down on an incline that makes an angle α with the horizontal. Form the Lagrangian, determine the energy integral of the system. Solve the equation of motion to find the time to completely unwind the tape.

2.9 A pendulum bob of radius r is rolling on a circular track of radius R ($> r$). Construct the Lagrangian, derive the equation of motion and compare its period of oscillation (of small amplitude only) with that of a simple pendulum of string length $R - r$.

2.10 Assume the Lagrangian for a relativistic pendulum motion to be $L(x,v) = m_o c^2\{(1 - v^2/c^2)^{-1/2} - 1\} - kx^2/2$, k being the spring constant. How is its period modified for a semi-relativistic speed $v \simeq 0.1c$?

2.11 We know that the energy like Jacobi integral $\dot{q}_i(\partial L/\partial \dot{q}_i) - L$ exists whenever t does not explicitly occur in L. Show that the following rheonomic system is nonconservative although it still has a Jacobi integral. A bead of unit mass is moving under gravity on a smooth rigid circular wire of radius r_o, the wire being driven with a steady angular speed ω about a vertical diameter. Show that in this case the Jacobi integral is not equal to $T + V$. Prove that only for conservative systems does the Jacobi integral equal $T + V$.

2.12 Sometimes a rheonomic system can be conservative. Consider the following case. Two particles are connected by a rigid massless rod of length l which rotates in a horizontal plane with a constant angular velocity ω. Knife-edge supports at the two particles prevent either particle from having a velocity component along the rod, but the particles can slide without friction in a direction perpendicular to the rod. Find the equations of motion. Solve for x and y, the coordinates of the centre of mass, and the constraint force as functions of time, if the centre of mass is initially at the origin and has a velocity v_o in the positive y- direction. Show that the system is conservative, even though it is rheonomic. Find the Jacobi integral.

2.13 Find the equation of motion corresponding to the Lagrangian

$$L(x, \dot{x}) = e^{-x^2}\left(e^{-\dot{x}^2} + 2\dot{x}\int_0^{\dot{x}} e^{-\alpha^2}\,d\alpha\right)$$

Find the energy integral for the system. Construct another Lagrangian which can give rise to the same equation of motion.

2.14 A rough and heavy horizontal disc rotates with a constant angular velocity ω about a stationary vertical axis passing through its centre. A spherical ball of mass m and radius R is let loose on the rotating disc and the ball starts rolling on the disc without slipping. Find the trajectory of the ball with respect to the outside fixed frame of reference.

2.15 A child's swing of variable string length $l(t)$, the length being manipulated by pulling or releasing it through the hinge point, is oscillating in a vertical plane. Using the Lagrangian method, make a study of this non-conservative system. Under what circumstances may the energy of the system accumulate with time?

2.16 Show that the total number of independent integrals of motion (I) for a closed system embedded in an n-dimensional Euclidean space is given $I = (n^2 + 3n + 2)/2$. How many of these are additive in nature? Now for 3–D Euclidean space, $n = 3$ gives $I = 10$. Even if we consider the $3 + 1$ -dimensional space time continuum from the point of view of special theory of relativity, justify that I should still be 10 only. How many more integrals of motion are needed for a closed system of 3 particles interacting with one another gravitationally or for that of a freely moving rigid body?

2.17 Show that the following are the integrals of motion:
(i) $\boldsymbol{A} = \boldsymbol{v} \times \boldsymbol{L} - K\boldsymbol{r}/r$ for the motion of particle in the potential $V = -K/r$, $\boldsymbol{L}$ being the angular momentum $= \boldsymbol{r} \times \boldsymbol{p}$, and $K =$ const.
(ii) $\boldsymbol{L}\cdot\boldsymbol{B} + e|\boldsymbol{r} \times \boldsymbol{B}|^2/2$ for a charged particle moving in a uniform field of magnetic induction $\boldsymbol{B}$.
(iii) $\boldsymbol{L}\cdot\hat{\boldsymbol{k}} + eM/\sqrt{r^2 - (\boldsymbol{r}\cdot\hat{\boldsymbol{k}})^2}$ for the motion of a charged particle in the field of

a magnetic dipole having a constant moment $\boldsymbol{M} = M\hat{\boldsymbol{k}}$, which can be produced by a vector potential $\boldsymbol{A} = M(\hat{\boldsymbol{k}} \times \boldsymbol{r})/r^3$

(iv) $\boldsymbol{F}\cdot(\boldsymbol{v} \times \boldsymbol{L}) - K(\boldsymbol{F}\cdot\boldsymbol{r})/r + (\boldsymbol{F} \times \boldsymbol{r})^2/2$ for a particle moving in a combined fields due to a uniform force field $\boldsymbol{F}$ and a Newtonian field, given by the potential $V(\boldsymbol{r}) = -K/r - \boldsymbol{F}\cdot\boldsymbol{r}$

2.18 How do the energy and momenta change under

(i) the Galilean transformation between two inertial frames of reference which have a constant relative velocity $\boldsymbol{V}$, that is, $\boldsymbol{r} = \boldsymbol{r}' + \boldsymbol{V}t$

(ii) a rotating coordinate transformation given by

$$x = x'\cos\omega t - y'\sin\omega t \qquad y = x'\sin\omega t + y'\cos\omega t \qquad \text{and} \qquad z = z'$$

where ω is a constant.

(iii) translation with constant acceleration given by $\boldsymbol{r} = \boldsymbol{r}' + \boldsymbol{u}_o t + \boldsymbol{g}t^2/2$, $\boldsymbol{u}_o$ and $\boldsymbol{g}$ being constant vectors. Could all such changes be accommodated by some suitable Lagrangian gauge terms dF/dt?

3

Rotating Frames of Reference

3.0 INTRODUCTION

We have seen earlier that the equations of motion due to Newton, D'Alembert, or Lagrange are valid only if the forces or the Lagrangian is formulated in some inertial frame of reference. However, many systems in nature are found to be naturally rotating or accelerating and it may be more convenient to use the coordinates that directly refer to such noninertial frames. For example, the earth is rotating about an axis passing through its geographical north pole. So any reference frame that is firmly attached to earth is a rotating (noninertial) frame. Therefore, it is necessary to develop methods for writing down the Lagrangian or the Newtonian equations of motion using the coordinates of a rotating frame. Taking the rotating frames as an example, we have in this chapter discussed in detail the consequences of changing over from an inertial to a noninertial frame. The transformation laws for rotating frames were given by a French engineer Gustave Gaspard de Coriolis (1792 – 1843) in his book entitled *Traité de la mechanique des corps solides* published in 1831. It was Coriolis who changed Leibniz's definition of *vis viva*, mv^2 to $\frac{1}{2}mv^2$, which is today's kinetic energy.

3.1 INERTIAL FORCES IN THE ROTATING FRAME

Let there be a fixed frame S with $\hat{\boldsymbol{i}}$, $\hat{\boldsymbol{j}}$, $\hat{\boldsymbol{k}}$, as the fixed unit vectors forming a rectangular Cartesian triad and the frame S$'$ with its triad $(\hat{\boldsymbol{i}}', \hat{\boldsymbol{j}}', \hat{\boldsymbol{k}}')$, originally coincident with S be rotating with velocity $\boldsymbol{\omega}\ (= \hat{\boldsymbol{n}}\omega)$ about their common origin O (see Fig. 3.1). Given any vector $\boldsymbol{G}$, how do we see it and its time derivative in the two frames? Physically, the $\boldsymbol{G}$ vector is the same in both the frames so that

$$\boldsymbol{G}\big|_{\text{fixed}} = \boldsymbol{G}\big|_{\text{rot}} \tag{3.1}$$

But the components of $\boldsymbol{G}$ in S and S$'$ are different because the unit vectors in both the frames are pointing differently. Hence,

$$\boldsymbol{G}\big|_{\text{fixed}} = G_1\hat{\boldsymbol{i}} + G_2\hat{\boldsymbol{j}} + G_3\hat{\boldsymbol{k}} = G_1'\hat{\boldsymbol{i}}' + G_2'\hat{\boldsymbol{j}}' + G_3'\hat{\boldsymbol{k}}' = \boldsymbol{G}\big|_{\text{rot}}$$

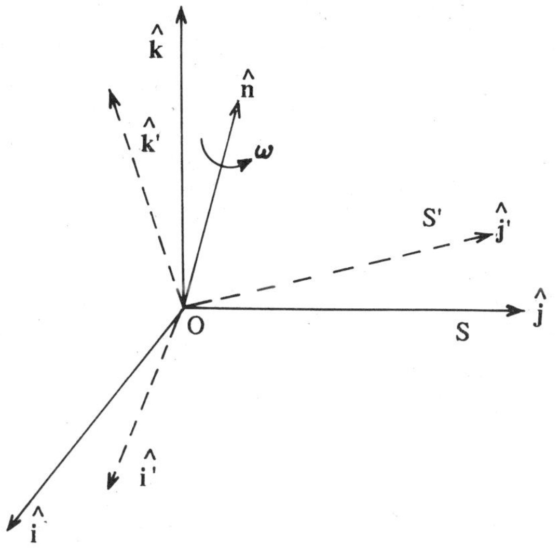

Fig. 3.1 Cartesian axes of an inertial (S) and a rotating (S′) frames of reference, S′ rotating about their common origin O with an instantaneous angular velocity of rotation $\boldsymbol{\omega}$ with respect to S

The time derivatives of $\boldsymbol{G}_{\text{fixed}}$ and $\boldsymbol{G}_{\text{rot}}$ must also be equal, because they are also one and the same physical vector. Thus,

$$\frac{d}{dt}\left[\boldsymbol{G}_{\text{fixed}}\right] = \frac{d}{dt}\left[\boldsymbol{G}_{\text{rot}}\right]$$

One usually denotes

$$\frac{d}{dt}\left[\boldsymbol{G}_{\text{fixed}}\right] \text{ by } \left[\frac{d\boldsymbol{G}}{dt}\right]_{\text{fixed}}$$

because this is the rate of variation of $\boldsymbol{G}$ as *measured* by an observer in the fixed frame. Since the unit vectors $\hat{\boldsymbol{i}}$, $\hat{\boldsymbol{j}}$, $\hat{\boldsymbol{k}}$, of the fixed frame S do not change with time, we can write

$$\left[\frac{d\boldsymbol{G}}{dt}\right]_{\text{fixed}} = \frac{dG_1}{dt}\hat{\boldsymbol{i}} + \frac{dG_2}{dt}\hat{\boldsymbol{j}} + \frac{dG_3}{dt}\hat{\boldsymbol{k}}$$

which must be equal to $(d\left[\boldsymbol{G}_{\text{rot}}\right]/dt)$ given by,

$$\begin{aligned}\left[\frac{d\boldsymbol{G}}{dt}\right]_{\text{fixed}} &= \frac{d}{dt}\left[\boldsymbol{G}_{\text{rot}}\right] \\ &= \frac{d}{dt}\left(G_1'\hat{\boldsymbol{i}}' + G_2'\hat{\boldsymbol{j}}' + G_3'\hat{\boldsymbol{k}}'\right) \\ &= \frac{dG_1'}{dt}\hat{\boldsymbol{i}}' + \frac{dG_2'}{dt}\hat{\boldsymbol{j}}' + \frac{dG_3'}{dt}\hat{\boldsymbol{k}}' + G_1'\frac{d\hat{\boldsymbol{i}}'}{dt} + G_2'\frac{d\hat{\boldsymbol{j}}'}{dt} + G_3'\frac{d\hat{\boldsymbol{k}}'}{dt}\end{aligned}$$

One denotes the first three terms by $[d\boldsymbol{G}/dt]_{\text{rot}}$ because this is precisely the time derivative of $\boldsymbol{G}$ as measured by an observer in the rotating frame S′. We are defining all these concepts explicitly for reasons of clarity.

Now using Eq. (2.67) for any arbitrary vector $\boldsymbol{A}$, we have

$$\frac{\Delta \boldsymbol{A}}{\Delta t} = \hat{\boldsymbol{n}}\frac{\Delta \theta}{\Delta t} \times \boldsymbol{A}$$

Taking the limit as $\Delta t \to 0$,

$$\frac{d\boldsymbol{A}}{dt} = \omega \hat{\boldsymbol{n}} \times \boldsymbol{A} = \boldsymbol{\omega} \times \boldsymbol{A} \tag{3.2}$$

Applying this to $\hat{\boldsymbol{i}}', \hat{\boldsymbol{j}}', \hat{\boldsymbol{k}}'$ we get

$$\frac{d\hat{\boldsymbol{i}}'}{dt} = \boldsymbol{\omega} \times \hat{\boldsymbol{i}}' \qquad \frac{d\hat{\boldsymbol{j}}'}{dt} = \boldsymbol{\omega} \times \hat{\boldsymbol{j}}' \qquad \frac{d\hat{\boldsymbol{k}}'}{dt} = \boldsymbol{\omega} \times \hat{\boldsymbol{k}}'$$

Using these in the expression for $([d\boldsymbol{G}/dt]_{\text{fixed}})$ we get

$$\left[\frac{d\boldsymbol{G}}{dt}\right]_{\text{fixed}} = \left[\frac{d\boldsymbol{G}}{dt}\right]_{\text{rot}} + \boldsymbol{\omega} \times \left(G_1'\hat{\boldsymbol{i}}' + G_2'\hat{\boldsymbol{j}}' + G_3'\hat{\boldsymbol{k}}'\right)$$

or

$$\left[\frac{d\boldsymbol{G}}{dt}\right]_{\text{fixed}} = \left[\frac{d\boldsymbol{G}}{dt}\right]_{\text{rot}} + \boldsymbol{\omega} \times \boldsymbol{G} \tag{3.3}$$

Thus we have an operator identity

$$\left[\frac{d}{dt}\right]_{\text{fixed}} = \left[\frac{d}{dt}\right]_{\text{rot}} + \boldsymbol{\omega} \times \tag{3.4}$$

where the meanings of the brackets and suffixes are as stated above. This result is valid for any arbitrary vector $\boldsymbol{G}$ and any arbitrary $\boldsymbol{\omega}$ passing through the common origin.

Putting $\boldsymbol{G} = \boldsymbol{r}$, the position vector of a particle, we get

$$\left[\frac{d\boldsymbol{r}}{dt}\right]_{\text{fixed}} = \left[\frac{d\boldsymbol{r}}{dt}\right]_{\text{rot}} + \boldsymbol{\omega} \times \boldsymbol{r}$$

or

$$[\boldsymbol{v}]_{\text{fixed}} = [\boldsymbol{v}]_{\text{rot}} + \boldsymbol{\omega} \times \boldsymbol{r}$$

Denoting $[\boldsymbol{v}]_{\text{fixed}} = \boldsymbol{v}_o$ and $[\boldsymbol{v}]_{\text{rot}} = \boldsymbol{v}$ we write

$$\boldsymbol{v}_o = \boldsymbol{v} + \boldsymbol{\omega} \times \boldsymbol{r} \tag{3.5}$$

Again, putting $\boldsymbol{G} = \boldsymbol{v}_o$ in Eq. (3.3),

$$\left[\frac{d\boldsymbol{v}_o}{dt}\right]_{\text{fixed}} = \left[\frac{d\boldsymbol{v}_o}{dt}\right]_{\text{rot}} + \boldsymbol{\omega} \times \boldsymbol{v}_o$$
$$= \frac{d}{dt}(\boldsymbol{v} + \omega \times \boldsymbol{r}) + \omega \times (\boldsymbol{v} + \omega \times \boldsymbol{r})$$
$$= \frac{d\boldsymbol{v}}{dt} + \dot{\omega} \times \boldsymbol{r} + 2\omega \times \boldsymbol{v} + \omega \times (\omega \times \boldsymbol{r})$$

where $d\boldsymbol{v}/dt$ is the acceleration as *measured* in the S′ frame. If we are to consider the motion of a particle of mass m, its equations of motion from the point of view of an observer who is at rest with respect to S′ can be expressed as

$$m\frac{d\boldsymbol{v}}{dt} = m\frac{d\boldsymbol{v}_o}{dt} + m\boldsymbol{r} \times \dot{\omega} + 2m\boldsymbol{v} \times \omega + m(\boldsymbol{\omega} \times \boldsymbol{r}) \times \boldsymbol{\omega} \tag{3.6}$$

The first term on RHS of Eq. (3.6) corresponds to the product of mass and the inertial acceleration in the fixed frame, that is, the actual forces applied on the system, or the true external forces. Other terms correspond to the psuedoforces or the fictitious or inertial forces that arise due to the fact that the rotating frame is noninertial. They are called, from left to right, Euler force, Coriolis force, (named after Gustov Coriolis who derived formulae for the rotating frame of reference in 1829) and centrifugal force respectively. These forces appear to exist only in a rotating frame of reference.

Equation (3.6) can also be obtained in the Lagrangian formulation. Consider the Lagrangian of the system, which has to be evaluated in the inertial frame only, and then should be expressed in terms of quantities defined in the rotating frame. Thus one can write

$$\begin{aligned} L &= \frac{1}{2}m|\boldsymbol{v}_o|^2 - V = \frac{1}{2}m|\boldsymbol{v} + \boldsymbol{\omega} \times \boldsymbol{r}|^2 - V \\ &= \frac{1}{2}m|\boldsymbol{v}|^2 + m\boldsymbol{v}\cdot(\omega \times \boldsymbol{r}) + \frac{1}{2}m(\omega \times \boldsymbol{r})\cdot(\omega \times \boldsymbol{r}) - V \end{aligned} \tag{3.7}$$

To construct various terms occurring in the Euler– Lagrange equations of motion, consider

$$\frac{\partial L}{\partial v} = m\boldsymbol{v} + m(\omega \times \boldsymbol{r}) = m(\boldsymbol{v} + \boldsymbol{\omega} \times \boldsymbol{r}) = \boldsymbol{p}$$

where $\boldsymbol{p}$ is the generalised momentum corresponding to $\boldsymbol{r}$. So the true momentum of the particle is not just mv but mv_o which is the momentum observed in a fixed frame, say $\boldsymbol{p}_o$. Next consider,

$$\frac{\partial L}{\partial \boldsymbol{r}} = m(\boldsymbol{v} \times \boldsymbol{\omega}) - m\omega \times (\omega \times \boldsymbol{r}) - \nabla V$$

Substituting in the Euler– Lagrange equations of motion

$$\frac{d}{dt}\left[\frac{\partial L}{\partial v}\right] - \frac{\partial L}{\partial \boldsymbol{r}} = 0$$

we get

$$m\frac{d\boldsymbol{v}}{dt} + 2m\boldsymbol{\omega} \times \boldsymbol{v} - m(\omega \times \boldsymbol{r}) \times \boldsymbol{\omega} + m\dot{\omega} \times \boldsymbol{r} + \nabla V = 0$$

which is the same as Eq. (3.6), provided we identify $-\nabla V$ with the externally applied forces, which must be equal to $m(d\boldsymbol{v}_o/dt)$.

The total energy of the particle in the rotating frame can be calculated as follows:

$$\begin{aligned} E &= \boldsymbol{p}\cdot\boldsymbol{v} - L = m\boldsymbol{v}_o\cdot(\boldsymbol{v}_o - \boldsymbol{\omega}\times\boldsymbol{r}) - \frac{1}{2}mv_o^2 + V \\ &= \frac{1}{2}mv_o^2 + V - m\boldsymbol{v}_o\cdot(\boldsymbol{\omega}\times\boldsymbol{r}) = E_o - \boldsymbol{p}\cdot(\boldsymbol{\omega}\times\boldsymbol{r}) \\ &= E_o - \boldsymbol{\omega}\cdot\boldsymbol{L} \end{aligned} \tag{3.8}$$

where E_o is the total energy measured in the fixed frame and $\boldsymbol{L}$ is the angular momentum of the system measured in the rotating frame. (Note however that $\boldsymbol{L} = \boldsymbol{L}_o$). Both E and E_o are the constants of motion in S$'$ and S respectively, as the Langrangian does not have any explicit dependence on time, but E can be greater than or less than E_o depending on the relative orientations of $\boldsymbol{L}$ and $\boldsymbol{\omega}$.

3.2 ELECTROMAGNETIC ANALOGY OF THE INERTIAL FORCES

We note in Eq. (3.7) that the Coriolis force $\boldsymbol{f}_{\text{cr}} = 2m(\boldsymbol{v}\times\boldsymbol{\omega})$ is a velocity dependent force and it does not do any work, as the instantaneous velocity $\boldsymbol{v}$ is always perpendicular to the force $\boldsymbol{f}_{\text{cr}}$. This is a gyroscopic force and therefore, can be included in a generalised potential energy U defined in Eqs (2.47) and (2.48) which satisfies the Euler– Lagrange equation of motion (2.26). One can, in fact, rewrite Eq. (3.7) as $L = T - U$ with

$$T = \frac{1}{2}mv^2 \quad \text{and} \quad U = V - \frac{1}{2}m|\boldsymbol{\omega}\times\boldsymbol{r}|^2 - m\boldsymbol{v}\cdot(\boldsymbol{\omega}\times\boldsymbol{r}) \tag{3.9}$$

The first two terms in U are velocity independent potential energies and can be put together in the form of an effective ordinary potential energy $V_{\text{eff}} = V - \frac{1}{2}m|\boldsymbol{\omega}\times\boldsymbol{r}|^2$ The new term $-\frac{1}{2}m|\boldsymbol{\omega}\times\boldsymbol{r}|^2$ is called the centrifugal potential energy (say V_{cf}) because the centrifugal force is simply equal to $-\nabla V_{\text{cf}}$. Now, from the definition of energy E in the rotating frame as given in Eq. (3.8) it can easily be shown that

$$E = T + V_{\text{eff}} = \frac{1}{2}mv^2 - \frac{1}{2}m|\boldsymbol{\omega}\times\boldsymbol{r}|^2 + V \tag{3.10}$$

The velocity dependent part of U does not enter the expression for energy. On comparison with the generalised electromagnetic potential energy given in Eq. (2.52) one can verify the following correspondences: (find out what would electric field correspond to)

(1) The scalar potential energy $e\phi \longleftrightarrow V_{\text{eff}}$
(2) The velocity-dependent potential energy $e(\boldsymbol{v}\cdot\boldsymbol{A}) \longleftrightarrow m\boldsymbol{v}\cdot(\boldsymbol{\omega}\times\boldsymbol{r})$, implying further,
(3) The vector potential (momentum) $e\boldsymbol{A} \longleftrightarrow m(\boldsymbol{\omega}\times\boldsymbol{r})$,
(4) The magnetic induction $\boldsymbol{B} = (\nabla\times\boldsymbol{A}) \longleftrightarrow (m/e)\nabla\times(\boldsymbol{\omega}\times\boldsymbol{r}) = (2m/e)\boldsymbol{\omega}$, if $\boldsymbol{\omega}$ does not vary from point to point,
(5) Magnetic force $e(\boldsymbol{v}\times\boldsymbol{B}) \longleftrightarrow 2m(\boldsymbol{v}\times\boldsymbol{\omega})$ = Coriolis force,
(6) Canonical momentum $m\boldsymbol{v} + e\boldsymbol{A} \longleftrightarrow m(\boldsymbol{v} + \boldsymbol{\omega}\times\boldsymbol{r})$ and

(7) Energy $\frac{1}{2}mv^2 + e\phi \longleftrightarrow \frac{1}{2}mv^2 + V_{\text{eff}}$.

The analogy seems to be quite appropriate; particularly striking is the analogy between the magnetic field $\boldsymbol{B}$ and the angular velocity vector $\boldsymbol{\omega}$. The magnetic field results, in fact, from the vortices of the charge motions; and surprisingly enough, the cyclotron frequency of revolution of a charged particle in a uniform magnetic induction B is given by $\omega_c = eB/m\ (= 2|\boldsymbol{\omega}|$, from the above analogy)!

3.3 EFFECTS OF CORIOLIS FORCE

First we make a few general comments. The earth rotates from west towards east, so that at any place on earth the angular velocity vector $\boldsymbol{\omega}$ is directed towards the north and is parallel to the axis of rotation of the earth, that is, the polar axis (see Fig. 3.2). In any frame attached to the earth, an object moving with velocity $\boldsymbol{v}$ will experience a Coriolis force $2m\boldsymbol{v} \times \boldsymbol{\omega}$. The direction of this force is perpendicular to both $\boldsymbol{v}$ and $\boldsymbol{\omega}$ and the magnitude of the Coriolis acceleration can never exceed

$$2\omega v = 1.46 \times 10^{-4} v \tag{3.11}$$

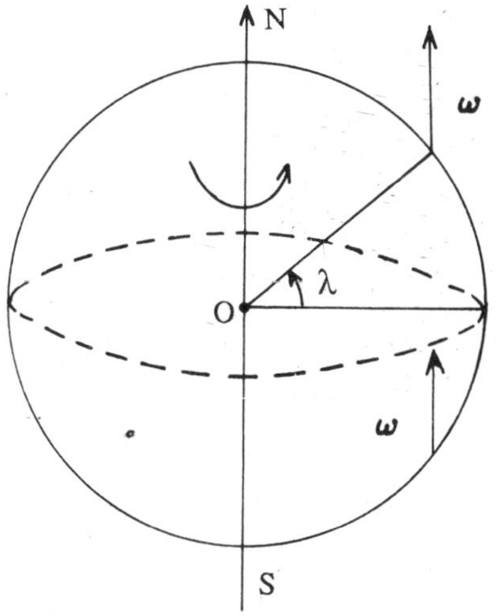

Fig. 3.2 The direction of $\boldsymbol{\omega}$ at any arbitrary point on the surface of the earth

where we have used the value of ω for earth (one complete rotation takes place in $23^{\text{h}}\ 56^{\text{m}}\ 4^{\text{s}}.01$) given by

$$\omega = \left[\frac{2\pi}{23.9345 \times 3600}\right] \simeq 7.292 \times 10^{-5}\ \text{rad/s}. \tag{3.12}$$

For an object moving even with a speed of 1km/sec, this upper limit is only $0.15\text{m/s}^2 \simeq$

$0.015g$. Thus the magnitude of the effect of Coriolis force is extremely small compared to g, the acceleration due to earth's gravity. However, in many natural circumstances, the period of time over which this tiny acceleration acts, can be quite long leading to substantial deflections. We now describe a few such instances.

3.3.1 When A River Flows on the Surface of the Earth

Rivers flow approximately in a horizontal plane. However, a nominal downward slope in the direction of their flow is important for maintaining the speed of the flow. So the gravitational force acting primarily downward has also a small component in the forward direction of flow depending on the magnitude of the slope of the downstream. But there is absolutely no component of $\boldsymbol{g}_{\text{eff}}$ (see below) acting along the breadth of a river. Hence the component of the Coriolis force, however small, can act freely on the moving water across the direction of the stream.

In order to find out this transverse horizontal component of the Coriolis acceleration, let us choose the direction of the flow to be the x-axis, the transverse horizontal axis to the left of the flow direction as the y-axis and the local vertical (up) as the z-axis. Let the direction of the flow at a place having geographical latitude λ , make an angle ϕ (in the anticlockwise sense) with respect to the geographical north direction. Therefore the earth's angular velocity vector $\boldsymbol{\omega}$, with respect to the above reference frame can be expressed

$$\boldsymbol{\omega} = \omega(\sin\lambda\hat{\boldsymbol{k}} + \cos\lambda\cos\phi\hat{\boldsymbol{i}} - \cos\lambda\sin\phi\hat{\boldsymbol{j}})$$

The velocity of the flow is

$$\boldsymbol{v} = v\hat{\boldsymbol{i}}$$

giving the Coriolis acceleration

$$\boldsymbol{a}_c = 2\boldsymbol{v}\times\boldsymbol{\omega} = -2v\omega[\sin\lambda\hat{\boldsymbol{j}} + \cos\lambda\sin\phi\hat{\boldsymbol{k}}] \tag{3.13}$$

The small vertical component of $\boldsymbol{a}_c$ is lost in comparison with $\boldsymbol{g}_{\text{eff}}$ as $\boldsymbol{g}_{\text{eff}} = -g_{\text{eff}}\hat{\boldsymbol{k}}$, but along the $\hat{\boldsymbol{j}}$-axis the only acceleration is $-2v\omega\sin\lambda$. This quantity is independent of ϕ and hence does not depend on whether the flow is towards north or south or east or west. But it depends on λ. It is negative (that is, to the right of the flow) for $\lambda > 0$ (that is, in the northern hemisphere), positive (that is, to the left of the flow) for $\lambda < 0$ (that is, in the southern hemisphere) and vanishes for $\lambda = 0$. Thus the effect is absent for river flowing past or along the geographical equator.

Thus, a Coriolis force will be experienced by the water in the rivers flowing in any direction, causing a deviation towards the right of the flow direction in the northern hemisphere and to the left of the flow direction in the southern hemisphere. As a result, the corresponding banks of the river will be denuded more, which is actually observed. The other effect of this jth component of the Coriolis force is to raise the right banks of the rivers in the northern hemisphere to a slightly higher level than the left banks. The opposite is true for the rivers flowing in the southern hemisphere.

3.3.2 Air Flow on the Surface of the Earth

(a) Cyclones

When a low pressure zone is created at any place on earth, pressure gradients are set up and air flows towards the low pressure zone to equalise the pressure difference. In the absence of Coriolis force the direction of wind velocity would be perpendicular to the isobars (the equipressure lines) as shown in Fig. 3.3. However, in the northern hemisphere, Coriolis force acts on the wind to deviate its direction towards its right and the wind now flows spirally towards the centre of low pressure in a counter-clockwise direction. Since the Coriolis force acts perpendicular to the trajectory, it will provide the centripetal force, that is, $v^2/R \simeq 2\omega v$, where R is the radius of curvature of the wind trajectory. This gives $R \simeq v/2\omega$. For wind speed $v = 30$ m/sec (that is, 108 km/hr), $R \simeq 210$ km. The radius of the cyclonic activity is directly proportional to the speed of the wind. Of course, the eye of the cyclone also moves along with the centre of low pressure. In the southern hemisphere the cyclonic direction about the eye of the cyclone is clockwise and the magnitudes of the cyclonic activity are all similar.

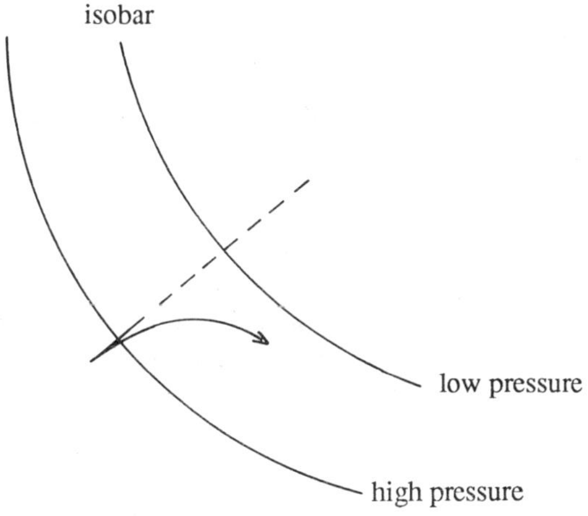

Fig. 3.3 Coriolis deflection of the direction of wind motion between two atmospheric isobars

(b) Trade Winds and Tropical Winds

These occur, again, due to moderate (as compared to cyclonic case) pressure gradients in the atmosphere set up over large distances. Again, the winds would tend to flow perpendicular to isobars but the Coriolis force makes the flow direction deviate towards the right or left depending upon whether the phenomenon is occurring in the northern or southern hemisphere . Since in this case Coriolis force is comparable in magnitude to that due to the pressure gradients, winds continue to deviate until their flow is parallel to isobars and the resulting Coriolis force just balances the pressure gradient force. The wind then continue to flow parallel to the isobars circulating in the northern hemisphere counter clockwise around the centre of low pressure. The corresponding winds flow clockwise in the southern hemisphere. The same type of analysis goes for the oceanographic water currents.

It must be emphasised that this is a simplified picture of the real phenomenon where, for example, we have not bothered about the way the pressure gradients are set up which involves complicated hydrodynamic equations. We have also neglected the effect of viscosity.

3.3.3 Projectile Motion

We now analyse the effect of the Coriolis force on a projectile.

The acceleration of a projectile, with respect to the earth measured at any place on the earth is given by Eq. (3.6), where $\boldsymbol{\omega}$ is the constant angular velocity of earth's rotation about its polar axis. In general, we have,

$$\dot{\boldsymbol{v}} = 2\boldsymbol{v} \times \boldsymbol{\omega} + (\boldsymbol{\omega} \times \boldsymbol{r}) \times \boldsymbol{\omega} + \boldsymbol{g} \tag{3.14}$$

where $\boldsymbol{g}$ is the acceleration purely due to gravity of the earth ($m\boldsymbol{g} = -\nabla V$, V is the actual gravitational potential energy of the projectile due to the earth at the point under consideration). We define

$$\boldsymbol{g}_{\text{eff}} = (\boldsymbol{\omega} \times \boldsymbol{r}) \times \boldsymbol{\omega} + \boldsymbol{g} \tag{3.15}$$

to be the effective local acceleration (due to combined gravity and centrifugal force of the earth's rotation), which can be derived from the effective potential

$$V_{\text{eff}} = V - \frac{m}{2}|\boldsymbol{\omega} \times \boldsymbol{r}|^2$$

in the form of $m\boldsymbol{g}_{\text{eff}} = -\nabla V_{\text{eff}}$.

Before cooling down to the present form, the earth was once in fluid state rotating about its axis. The free surface of any fluid in stationary state assumes an equipotential surface corresponding to the superposition of all the potentials due to, say, the gravitational force and the centrifugal force due to rotation, if any. If it were not an equipotential surface, the forces tangent to the surface would have caused the actual transport of the fluid mass in order to nullify them and generate a mechanical equilibrium. On such a surface, called the *geoid*, $\boldsymbol{g}_{\text{eff}}$ defined through Eq. (3.15) must be normal at every point. In fact, the present surface of the earth is, to a very good approximation, a geoid. Therefore at every point $\boldsymbol{g}_{\text{eff}}$ is normal to the earth's surface defined by the mean sea level, which is, by property of water an equipotential surface. The contribution due to centrifugal acceleration is maximum on the equator of the earth (magnitude = 0.03392 m/sec^2) and acts directly against the local gravity, giving $g_{\text{eff}} = 9.7803$ m/sec^2 on the equator. At the poles, the centrifugal acceleration vanishes, but g_{eff} at the poles increases by 0.05173 m/sec^2, the excess over the centrifugal correction being a contribution coming from the oblateness of the geoid, which amounts to 0.0178 m/sec^2.

Equation (3.14) now reads as

$$\dot{\boldsymbol{v}} = 2\boldsymbol{v} \times \boldsymbol{\omega} + \boldsymbol{g}_{\text{eff}} \tag{3.16}$$

To solve this equation we note that the magnitude of Coriolis acceleration is much smaller than $\boldsymbol{g}_{\text{eff}}$. Therefore we can adopt the method of successive approximation (iterative process) as our strategy to solve Eq. (3.16).

Suppose $\boldsymbol{v}(t)$ satisfies Eq. (3.16). Then we write,

$$\boldsymbol{v}(t) = \boldsymbol{v}_1(t) + \boldsymbol{v}_2(t)$$

such that

$$|\boldsymbol{v}_1(t)| \gg |\boldsymbol{v}_2(t)| \qquad \dot{\boldsymbol{v}}_1 = \boldsymbol{g}_{\text{eff}} \qquad \text{and} \qquad \dot{\boldsymbol{v}}_2 = 2\boldsymbol{v}_1 \times \boldsymbol{\omega}$$

Assuming $\boldsymbol{g}_{\text{eff}} =$ constant over the trajectory of the projectile, the first of these equations gives, on integration,

$$\boldsymbol{v}_1 = \boldsymbol{g}_{\text{eff}}t + \boldsymbol{v}_o$$

with $\boldsymbol{v}_o$ as the constant of integration. And then , on substitution of this $\boldsymbol{v}_1$, the second equation gives, on further integration,

$$\boldsymbol{v}_2 = (\boldsymbol{g}_{\text{eff}} \times \boldsymbol{\omega})t^2 + 2(\boldsymbol{v}_o \times \boldsymbol{\omega})t$$

Therefore,

$$\boldsymbol{v}(t) = \boldsymbol{v}_1 + \boldsymbol{v}_2 = \boldsymbol{v}_o + (\boldsymbol{g}_{\text{eff}} + 2\boldsymbol{v}_o \times \boldsymbol{\omega})t + (\boldsymbol{g}_{\text{eff}} \times \boldsymbol{\omega})t^2 \tag{3.17}$$

Since $\boldsymbol{v} = d\boldsymbol{r}/dt$, we integrate this equation with respect to time to get an approximate solution correct up to the order $g\omega t^3$,

$$\boldsymbol{r}(t) = \boldsymbol{r}_o + \boldsymbol{v}_o t + \frac{1}{2}(\boldsymbol{g}_{\text{eff}} + 2\boldsymbol{v}_o \times \boldsymbol{\omega})t^2 + \frac{1}{3}(\boldsymbol{g}_{\text{eff}} \times \boldsymbol{\omega})t^3 \tag{3.18}$$

where $\boldsymbol{r}_o$ and $\boldsymbol{v}_o$ are the initial position and velocity of the projectile.

For constant $\boldsymbol{g}_{\text{eff}}$, an exact solution to Eq. (3.16) has, however been provided by F. R. Gantmakher (1960) called Gantmakher's formula for deflection due to Coriolis force and is given by

$$\begin{aligned}\boldsymbol{r}(t) = \boldsymbol{r}_o + \boldsymbol{v}_o t + \frac{1}{2}\boldsymbol{g}_{\text{eff}}t^2 + \left\{\frac{\cos(2\omega t) - 1}{2\omega^2}\right\}(\boldsymbol{\omega} \times \boldsymbol{v}_o) \\ + \left\{\frac{-1 + 2\omega^2 t^2 + \cos(2\omega t)}{4\omega^4}\right\}[\boldsymbol{\omega} \times (\boldsymbol{\omega} \times \boldsymbol{g}_{\text{eff}})] \\ - \left\{\frac{2\omega t - \sin(2\omega t)}{2\omega^3}\right\}\left\{\frac{1}{2}(\boldsymbol{\omega} \times \boldsymbol{g}_{\text{eff}}) - \boldsymbol{\omega} \times (\boldsymbol{\omega} \times \boldsymbol{v}_o)\right\}\end{aligned} \tag{3.19}$$

Let us now consider the projectile motion over a given geographical latitude λ (see Fig. 3.4). There can be various cases:

(a) The projectile dropped from a height h with initial velocity zero:

Thus $\boldsymbol{v}_o = 0$, $\boldsymbol{r}_o = h\hat{\boldsymbol{k}}$, $\boldsymbol{g}_{\text{eff}} = -g_{\text{eff}}\hat{\boldsymbol{k}}$, and $\boldsymbol{\omega} = \omega(\cos\lambda\hat{\boldsymbol{j}} + \sin\lambda\hat{\boldsymbol{k}})$, where $\hat{\boldsymbol{i}}$ is towards east, $\hat{\boldsymbol{j}}$ towards north and $\hat{\boldsymbol{k}}$ vertically upwards over the place under consideration. Substituting these in the approximate solution (3.18), one obtains

$$\boldsymbol{r}(t) = h\hat{\boldsymbol{k}} - \frac{1}{2}g_{\text{eff}}t^2\hat{\boldsymbol{k}} + \frac{1}{3}\omega\cos\lambda g_{\text{eff}}t^3\hat{\boldsymbol{i}}$$

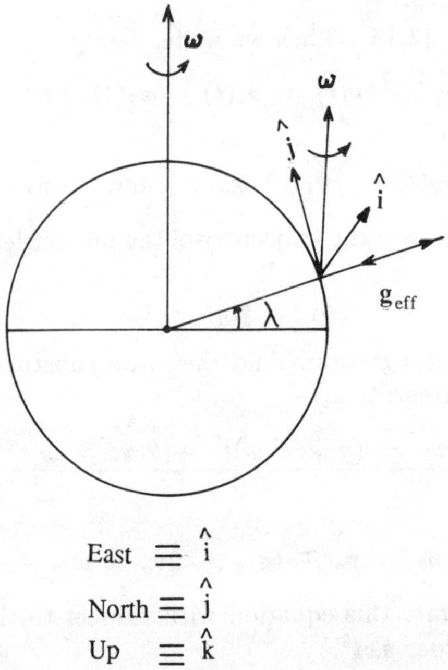

Fig. 3.4 Natural set of rectangular Cartesian coordinates at any point on the surface of the rotating earth, representing the relevant rotating frame of reference

Now the projectile will hit the earth as soon as the condition $h = g_{\rm eff}t^2/2$ is satisfied and at that moment

$$\boldsymbol{r} = \frac{1}{3}\omega g_{\rm eff}\cos\lambda\left(\frac{2h}{g_{\rm eff}}\right)^{3/2}\hat{\boldsymbol{i}}$$

It does not reach to the origin, but is shifted from the origin by the above amount to the east irrespective of the sign of λ. The Coriolis deflection is therefore towards east at all latitudes in both the hemispheres (as $\cos\lambda > 0$ for $-\pi/2 < \lambda < \pi/2$) and the amount of deflection from the local vertical is given by

$$d = \frac{1}{3}\omega g_{\rm eff}\cos\lambda\left(\frac{2h}{g_{\rm eff}}\right)^{3/2} \tag{3.20}$$

For $h = 300$ m and $\lambda = 40°$, $d \simeq 9$ cm but for $h = 30$ m, d is smaller by a factor $10\sqrt{10}$ giving only about 3 mm, which is very difficult to detect.

Newton was the first to propose an experiment of this kind to detect the rotation of the earth. After about 100 years in 1791, Gugliemini of Bologna had made an attempt to carry out the experiment from a 300 ft high tower but the results were disappointing due to sway in wind. Meanwhile Gauss and Coriolis did extensive calculations on the Coriolis deflection. Reich's experiments in 1831 – 33 in the mines of Frieberg, in fact, resulted in $d = 2.58$ cm for $h = 158$ m. Later on in 1903, E. H. Hall made 948 trials at the 23 meter high tower at the Harvard University and got the expected result $d \simeq 1.50$ mm. But he also got a southerly deflection of about 0.045 mm. In 1912, J. G. Hagen used Atwood's machine to artificially reduce the g_{eff} by a factor of about 10 and proved the Coriolis effect beyond doubt and also observed no appreciable southerly deflections.

One, in fact, arrives at very small southerly deflection of order $\frac{1}{6}g_{\text{eff}}\omega^2 t^4 \sin\lambda\cos\lambda$ from the formula in Eq. (3.19) together with the usual easterly deflection given by d in Eq. (3.20). But this is too small to be observed and also the effect of non-uniformity in g_{eff} becomes important at that level.

(b) A projectile is sent vertically up with velocity $\boldsymbol{v}_o$ to reach a height h above the ground and it returns to the ground:

In this case, we have

$$\boldsymbol{v}_o = v_o\hat{\boldsymbol{k}} = \sqrt{2g_{\text{eff}}h}\,\hat{\boldsymbol{k}} \quad \boldsymbol{r}_o = 0 \quad \boldsymbol{g}_{\text{eff}} = -\,g_{\text{eff}}\hat{\boldsymbol{k}} \quad \text{and} \quad \boldsymbol{\omega} = \omega(\cos\lambda\hat{\boldsymbol{j}} + \sin\lambda\hat{\boldsymbol{k}})$$

Then Eq. (3.18) gives us

$$\boldsymbol{r}(t) = (v_o t - \frac{1}{2}g_{\text{eff}}t^2)\hat{\boldsymbol{k}} - \sqrt{2g_{\text{eff}}h}\,t^2\omega\cos\lambda\hat{\boldsymbol{i}} + \frac{1}{3}\omega\cos\lambda g_{\text{eff}}t^3\hat{\boldsymbol{i}} \tag{3.21}$$

The coefficient of $\hat{\boldsymbol{k}}$ in Eq. (3.21) must vanish as the projectile returns to the ground. Therefore,

$$\boldsymbol{r}(t) = -\frac{4}{3}\frac{v_o^3}{g_{\text{eff}}^2}\omega\cos\lambda\hat{\boldsymbol{i}} \tag{3.22}$$

Thus the deflection is to the west in both the hemispheres and vanishes at the poles.

When compared with Eq. (3.20) the deflection given by Eq. (3.22) is exactly $4d$ and its sign is just the opposite. Qualitatively this can be understood in the following way.

The earth is rotating from west to east with an equatorial speed of rotation of about 465 m/sec. This speed reduces by a factor of $\cos\lambda$ as we go to any latitude λ, nevertheless the sense of rotation remains the same everywhere. Now as we climb a tall tower, the speed of rotation of the tip of the tower is slightly higher than that of its base. So when we drop a stone from the top of a tower, its initial easterly speed is higher than that of anything at the base. With this slightly higher speed any particle dropped from a height reaches the ground with a net easterly deflection. This is true for all latitudes. Now, when we project a stone up from the ground its initial horizontal speed due to earth's rotation is lower than that for any point above the ground. Hence the projectile gradually lags behind the earth's rotation, and returns to the ground with a net westerly deflection, and it is larger because it has spent longer time in flight and has lagged behind the earth's rotation all the time.

3.3.4 Coriolis Effect in Atomic Nuclei

We have seen that in a rotating frame the energy of any particle E is less than its inertial value E_o by an amount $\boldsymbol{\omega}\cdot\boldsymbol{L}$ (see Eq. (3.8)), where $\boldsymbol{\omega}$ is the angular velocity of rotation of the rotating frame and $\boldsymbol{L}$ is the angular momentum of the particle as defined in the rotating frame. So a particle in the rotating frame has the lowest energy when the angular momentum vector $\boldsymbol{L}$ aligns with the angular velocity vector $\boldsymbol{\omega}$ of the rotating frame. Usually in nuclei having an odd number of nucleons, the odd nucleon is found to rotate about the even numbered nucleon with a high orbital angular momentum . In such cases the $\boldsymbol{\omega} \cdot \boldsymbol{L}$ term becomes quite important in their Hamiltonian and the lowest energy states are found to be associated with the maximally aligned angular momenta to the rotationally aligned bands of nuclear states. This has been observationally verified.

3.3.5 Coriolis Phenomenon in the Planetary Atmospheres

For a fast rotating planet, the Coriolis effect can be quite prominent and may give rise to gross atmospheric structures on the planet. Jupiter and Saturn are more than or about 10 times bigger in size than the earth, and rotate with an angular speed of about two and a half times that of the earth and show a number of bands parallel to their respective equators. The vertical currents of air due to convection are subjected to a large Coriolis force which acts in the horizontal direction, and they finally start encircling the planet in the rotationally aligned orbits.

3.4 FOUCAULT'S PENDULUM

A French physicist Lèon Foucault, noticed that the small effect of the Coriolis force could be greatly amplified by using a pendulum, an idea which had escaped the notice of Gauss, Laplace, D'Alembert, Poisson and others. He noticed that the rightward Coriolis deflection on one swing of the pendulum could not be undone in the return swing: the effect would accumulate! Thus the effect of Coriolis force of terrestrial origin moved from the domain of theory and outdoor observations to that of observation in a laboratory experiment. A simple set up is shown in Fig. 3.5.

The equation of motion for the pendulum including the Coriolis term is

$$\ddot{\boldsymbol{r}} + k^2\boldsymbol{r} = 2(\boldsymbol{v} \times \boldsymbol{\omega}) \tag{3.23}$$

where $k^2 = g_{\text{eff}}/l$, l being the effective length of swing. Written in terms of Cartesian components, these are

$$\begin{aligned} \ddot{x} + k^2 x &= 2(\dot{y}\omega_z - \dot{z}\omega_y) \simeq 2\dot{y}\omega_z \\ \text{and} \qquad \ddot{y} + k^2 y &= 2(\dot{z}\omega_x - \dot{x}\omega_z) \simeq -2\dot{x}\omega_z \end{aligned} \tag{3.24}$$

The last two approximations are justified because $\dot{z}$ and $\ddot{z}$ are negligible compared to $\dot{x}$, $\dot{y}$, and $\ddot{x}$, $\ddot{y}$. Equations (3.24) are coupled equations of motion in x and y. To solve, choose complex variable $u = x + iy$, $i = \sqrt{-1}$. Then multiplying the second of Eqs (3.24) by i and adding to the first, we get

$$\ddot{u} + k^2 u = -2i\omega_z \dot{u}$$

or

$$\ddot{u} + 2i\omega_z \dot{u} + k^2 u = 0$$

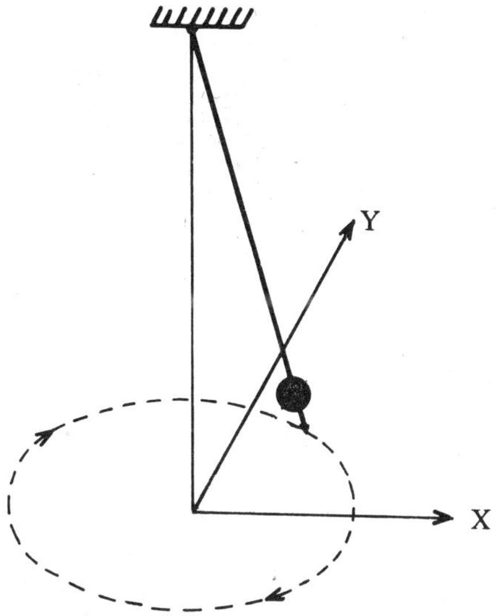

Fig. 3.5 Foucault's pendulum: its plane of oscillation, while passing always through the origin, rotates slowly in the clockwise sense

The general solution of the above equation is

$$u = \exp(-i\omega_z t)[A_1 \exp(ik't) + A_2 \exp(-ik't)]$$

where $k'^2 = k^2 + \omega_z^2$. Thus we have

$$x + iy = (x_o + iy_o)\exp(-i\omega_z t) \tag{3.25}$$

where x_o and y_o are solutions when Coriolis force is absent, $k' \simeq k$ is assumed as $k \gg \omega_z$.

Equation (3.25) tells us that the plane of oscillation of the pendulum rotates with an angular velocity $-\omega_z \hat{\boldsymbol{k}}$, that is, opposite to the sense of rotation of the earth. The period for a complete rotation of the plane of oscillation is

$$T = \frac{2\pi}{\omega_z} = \frac{2\pi}{\omega \sin \lambda} \tag{3.26}$$

where λ is the geographical latitude of the place. At the poles, $T = 24$ hrs, while at the equator $T = \infty$ so that no rotation of the plane of oscillation is observed. Foucault had demonstrated the truth of Eqs (3.25) and (3.26) through his historic pendulum experiment in 1851, that goes by his name.

Note that by measuring T Foucault measured the period of rotation of the earth. Thus we get the terrestrial demonstration of the earth's axial rotation. This was the first experimental proof that the earth is in fact rotating with respect to the inertial frame in which Newton's laws are to be valid, with an angular velocity which is precisely the same as that inferred from the apparent diurnal rotation of the sun, moon, and the star sphere.

It is straightforward to understand the mathematical logic behind the appearance of ω_z rather than $\boldsymbol{\omega}$ in Eqs (3.25) and (3.26), but it is not so easy to intuitively comprehend the same. If Foucault's experiment be performed at the poles, $\omega_z = \omega$, and we can follow why the plane of oscillation of the pendulum does not change in the inertial frame — it is because the earth rotates beneath the support of the pendulum exactly once a day. But what is difficult to understand is that while every other place on earth is also rotating back to the same point at an interval of one day, Foucault's pendulum hanging over the place is found to return to its original plane of oscillation much later, for example, over a place with geographical latitude, say $\lambda = 30^o$, $T = 48$ hours. Why are these two events not synchronised at all points on earth?

Apparently, the reason is that the pendulum does not understand the curvature of the earth. It thinks as if its bob is always lying on a plane surface which can be constructed by making a huge cone, with its base touching the small circle for a given λ and having the apex of the cone at some point above the nearer geographic pole. Only with a radial cut, such a cone can be flattened on to a plane to form a disc of radius $R \cot \lambda$ (R being the radius of the earth), with a missing segment of the disc. (The outer perimeter of this cone-turned-into-a-flat-disc is not $2\pi R \cot \lambda$ but $2\pi R \cos \lambda$). In the time the earth completes one diurnal rotation, Foucault's pendulum at latitude λ completes a precession up to an angle covered by the arc perimeter of the flattened disc, which is smaller than 2π by a factor of $\sin \lambda$, which is what appears in Eq. (3.26).

Foucault's precessing pendulum makes use of the horizontal component of the Coriolis force. The existence of the vertical component of the Coriolis force was first demonstrated by another ingeneous experiment devised by the Hungarian physicist Rolland Eötvos in 1922. He took a chemical balance, removed its pans and allowed the rotation of the beam in the horizontal plane. The Coriolis force on the two arms of the beam acts up and down producing a horizontal torque on the beam which brings the balance into forced vibration. Although this effect was very small, Eötvos was also able to demonstrate the rotation of the earth.

3.5 VELOCITY AND ACCELERATION OF A PARTICLE WITH RESPECT TO A SYSTEM HAVING TWO INDEPENDENT ROTATIONS ABOUT A COMMON POINT

This situation is realised in a precessing flywheel (see Fig. 3.6). Let S_o be the inertial frame with (x_o, y_o, z_o) axes fixed in space and origin at the centre of the wheel. z_o is the vertical axis about which the precession of the rotating wheel as a whole takes place.

Let S_1 with axes (x_1, y_1, z_1) be the intermediate rotating frame rotating with angular velocity $\boldsymbol{\omega}_o$ about the z_o axis so that z_o and z_1 axes are common but x_1 and y_1 axes are rotating in the plane of x_o and y_o axes with the angular speed ω_o. The x_1 axis is chosen to be along the normal to the plane of the wheel.

Let S_2 having axes (x_2, y_2, z_2) be the body frame fixed to the body of the wheel. x_1 and x_2 axes are common. The wheel rotates about this common $x_1 - x_2$ axis with angular

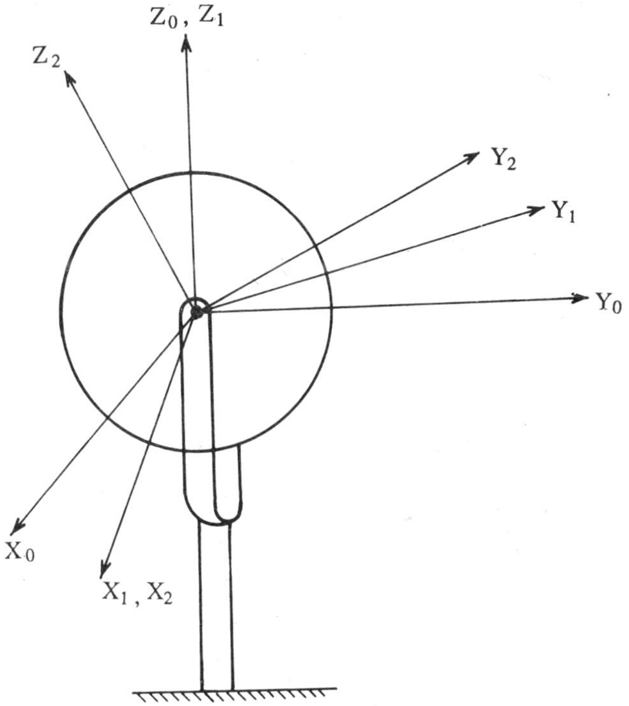

Fig. 3.6 Precession of a rotating flywheel

velocity $\boldsymbol{\omega}_1$. Thus the axes y_2 and z_2 rotate in the plane of the axes y_1 and z_1 with the same angular speed ω_1. The origins of all the frames, S_o, S_1 and S_2 coincide.

In order to deal with the most general case of rigid body rotations about a fixed point we need to add one more rotation and that is about the z_2 axis, passing to a new frame say S_3, which will then be the body frame, and S_1 and S_2 will play the role of intermediate frames. The resulting three rotations are called the Eulerian rotations.

However, for the present, the problem we wish to deal with is to calculate the velocity and acceleration of any point fixed in the rotating body of the wheel with reference to the inertial reference frame S_o. There are essentially two methods of doing this.

Method A

Calculate the velocity and acceleration in the frame S_1 and then transform to the velocity and acceleration in the frame S_o.

Method B

Calculate the composite angular velocity and angular acceleration of the entire system and then transform from S_2 to S_o directly.

The relevant equations for the consideration of the above methods are Eqs (3.4), (3.5) and (3.6).

Method A

The velocity and acceleration of any fixed point in the frame S_2 measured in the S_1 frame (that is, in terms of the unit vectors of the S_1 frame) is

$$\boldsymbol{v}_1 = \boldsymbol{\omega}_1 \times \boldsymbol{r}\big|_1$$

and

$$\boldsymbol{a}_1 = \dot{\boldsymbol{\omega}}_1 \times \boldsymbol{r}\big|_1 + \boldsymbol{\omega}_{11} \times (\boldsymbol{\omega} \times \boldsymbol{r})\big|_1$$

where $\big|_1$ means that the quantities are expressed with respect to the unit vectors (triad) of S_1. Note that $\boldsymbol{r}$ is the same in all the three frames.

Now the velocity and acceleration of the same point with respect to the fixed S_o frame in terms of the unit vectors of the frame S_1 are

$$\boldsymbol{v}_o = \boldsymbol{v}_1 + \boldsymbol{\omega}_o \times \boldsymbol{r}\big|_1 \tag{3.27}$$

and

$$\boldsymbol{a}_o = \boldsymbol{a}_1 + \dot{\boldsymbol{\omega}}_o \times \boldsymbol{r}\big|_1 + 2\boldsymbol{\omega}_o \times \boldsymbol{v}_1\big|_1 + \boldsymbol{\omega}_o \times (\boldsymbol{\omega}_o \times \boldsymbol{r})\big|_1 \tag{3.28}$$

Method B

The composite angular velocity of the entire system expressed in terms of the unit vectors of S_1 is

$$\boldsymbol{\Omega} = \boldsymbol{\omega}_o\big|_1 + \boldsymbol{\omega}_1\big|_1 \tag{3.29}$$

The angular acceleration of the composite system with respect to S_o as expressed in terms of the unit vectors S_1 is

$$\boldsymbol{\alpha} = \dot{\boldsymbol{\Omega}}\big|_1 + \boldsymbol{\omega}_o \times \boldsymbol{\Omega}\big|_1 \tag{3.30}$$

Then the velocity and acceleration of any point fixed with respect to S_2 and measured directly in S_o but expressed in unit vectors of S_1 are

$$\boldsymbol{v}_o = \boldsymbol{\Omega} \times \boldsymbol{r}\big|_1 \tag{3.31}$$

and

$$\boldsymbol{a}_o = \boldsymbol{\alpha} \times \boldsymbol{r}\big|_1 + \boldsymbol{\Omega} \times (\boldsymbol{\Omega} \times \boldsymbol{r})\big|_1 \tag{3.32}$$

It is now straightforward to check that both the methods give identical results.

3.6 MORE GENERAL CASE OF TWO ROTATIONS SEPARATED BY ONE TRANSLATION

As shown in Fig. 3.7, let the frame S_1 rotate about the common origin O of S_1 and the fixed frame S_o with angular velocity $\boldsymbol{\omega}_o$. Let S_1' and S_1 be the frames having directions of their axes identical but their origins O and O′ separated by a translation $\boldsymbol{R}$. Let the frame S_2 be rotating with respect to S_1' about their common origin at O′ with angular velocity ω_1. The problem is to relate the velocity and acceleration of any particle with respect to S_2 frame to those with respect to S_o frame in unit vectors of S_1 or S_1', for example.

There exist, again, two methods of solution as described in the previous article.

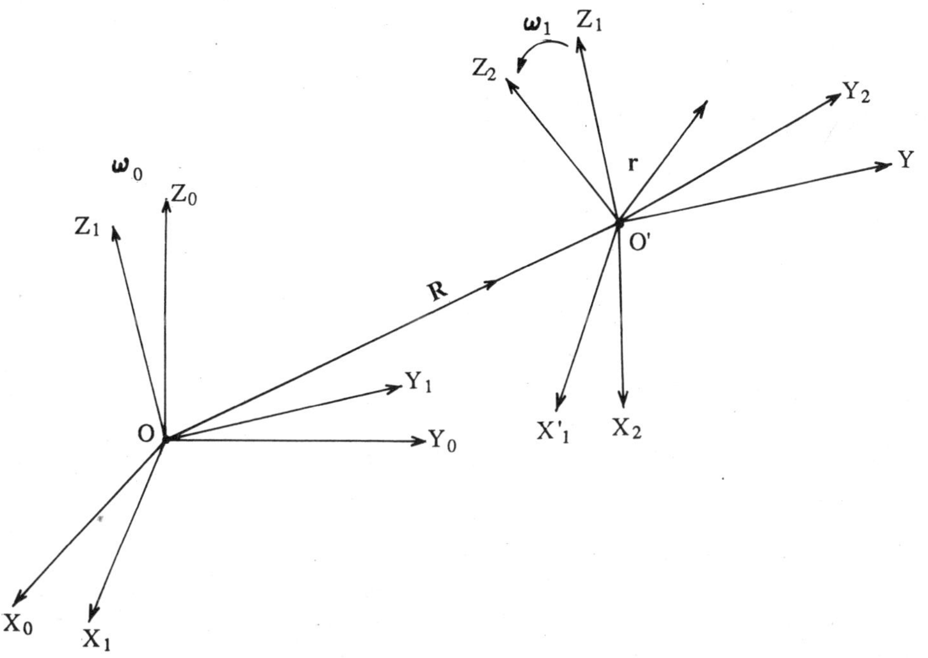

Fig. 3.7 Two rotating frames of reference connected by a translation between their origins O and O′

Method A:

Velocity and acceleration in S_1' frame are (assuming $\boldsymbol{v}_2 \neq 0$ in general)

$$\boldsymbol{v}'_1 = \boldsymbol{v}_2\big|_1 + \boldsymbol{\omega}_1 \times \boldsymbol{r}\big|_1$$

$$\boldsymbol{a}'_1 = \boldsymbol{a}_2\big|_1 + \dot{\boldsymbol{\omega}} \times \boldsymbol{r}\big|_1 - 2\boldsymbol{v}_2 \times \boldsymbol{\omega}_1\big|_1 + \boldsymbol{\omega}_1 \times (\boldsymbol{\omega}_1 \times \boldsymbol{r})\big|_1$$

In the S_1 frame these quantities are respectively

$$\boldsymbol{v}_1 = \dot{\boldsymbol{R}}\big|_1 + \boldsymbol{v}'_1\big|_1, \qquad \text{and} \qquad \boldsymbol{a}_1 = \ddot{\boldsymbol{R}}\big|_1 + \boldsymbol{a}'_1\big|_1$$

Finally these quantities with respect to the S_o frame expressed in the unit vectors of S_1 will be

$$\boldsymbol{v}_o = \boldsymbol{v}_1\big|_1 + \boldsymbol{\omega}_o \times (\boldsymbol{r} + \boldsymbol{R})\big|_1 \tag{3.33}$$

and

$$\boldsymbol{a}_o = \boldsymbol{a}_1\big|_1 + \dot{\boldsymbol{\omega}}_o \times (\boldsymbol{r} + \boldsymbol{R})\big|_1 + 2\boldsymbol{\omega}_o \times \boldsymbol{v}_1\big|_1 + \boldsymbol{\omega}_o \times (\boldsymbol{\omega}_o \times (\boldsymbol{r} + \boldsymbol{R}))\big|_1 \tag{3.34}$$

Method B:

The composite angular velocity of the whole system with respect to S_o is

$$\boldsymbol{\Omega} = \boldsymbol{\omega}_o\big|_1 + \boldsymbol{\omega}_1\big|_1 \tag{3.35}$$

The angular acceleration of composite system with respect to S_o is

$$\boldsymbol{\alpha} = \dot{\boldsymbol{\Omega}}\big|_1 + \boldsymbol{\omega}_o \times \boldsymbol{\Omega}\big|_1 \tag{3.36}$$

Therefore,

$$\boldsymbol{v}_o = \dot{\boldsymbol{R}}\big|_1 + \boldsymbol{\omega}_o \times \boldsymbol{R}\big|_1 + \dot{\boldsymbol{r}}\big|_1 + \boldsymbol{\Omega} \times \boldsymbol{r}\big|_1 \tag{3.37}$$

Finally we can write

$$\begin{aligned}\boldsymbol{a}_o = \ddot{\boldsymbol{R}}\big|_1 &+ \dot{\boldsymbol{\omega}}_o \times \boldsymbol{R}\big|_1 + 2\boldsymbol{\omega}_o \times \dot{\boldsymbol{R}}\big|_1 + \boldsymbol{\omega}_o \times (\boldsymbol{\omega}_o \times \boldsymbol{R})\big|_1 \\ &+ \ddot{\boldsymbol{r}}\big|_1 + \boldsymbol{\alpha} \times \boldsymbol{r}\big|_1 + 2\boldsymbol{\Omega} \times \dot{\boldsymbol{r}}\big|_1 + \boldsymbol{\Omega} \times (\boldsymbol{\Omega} \times \boldsymbol{r})\big|_1\end{aligned} \tag{3.38}$$

where $\ddot{\boldsymbol{r}} = \boldsymbol{a}_2$ and $\dot{\boldsymbol{r}} = \boldsymbol{v}_2$.

Following are two physical examples conforming to the situations described above.

1. A turnable table fan rotates about a vertical shaft with the blades rotating about an origin which does not lie on this shaft.
2. The earth is rotating about its own axis and at the same time revolving around the sun. Any point on the surface of the earth has a complicated motion with respect to the centre of the solar system. Generalising further, how does the motion of any point on the surface of a rotating planet, such as Jupiter, appear to a person sitting on earth? Such problems involve complicated rotations of more than one rotating frame of reference with their origins also separated. The methods described in the present section are adequate to tackle such complicated problems. One has to follow either method A or method B.

3.7 SUMMARY

In order to go from an inertial to a noninertial frame, the initial position vectors $\boldsymbol{r}_i$, velocities $\boldsymbol{v}_i$ in the Lagrangian scheme and $\boldsymbol{r}_i$, $\boldsymbol{v}_i$ and $\boldsymbol{a}_i$, the acceleration in the Newtonian scheme are to be expressed in terms of the respective quantities in the noninertial frame.

For frames rotating about a fixed point, the position vectors like any other vector in the two frames are identical, except that the components of the vectors along the respective coordinate axes (Cartesian) would be different. But if we consider any given vector , say $\boldsymbol{G}$, and then take the time derivative of the respective components in the two frames rather than the time derivative of the vector as a whole, the answers would differ by a term $\boldsymbol{\omega} \times \boldsymbol{G}$ as shown in Eq. (3.3). It is this extra term that finally brings about differences in the expressions for the acceleration in the two frames.

The fictitious force terms that appear with reference to an observer in the rotating frame of reference are readily classified into centrifugal force, Coriolis force and Euler force — the first one being position dependent, the second one being velocity dependent and the third one being due to nonuniformity of rotation of the rotating frame, if any.

The centrifugal force can readily be grouped into the class of gravity as it can be derived from an effective ordinary potential energy function. The Coriolis force is however found to be gyroscopic in nature, and therefore is not capable of doing work. It can be derived from a vector potential instead. One can draw a nice analogy between these inertial force terms and the components of the Lorentz force on electrically charged particles. The centrifugal force resembles the electric force, and the Coriolis force is the exact replica of the magnetic force. In fact the link between the two is quite realistic in the sense that magnetic field itself originates in circulation of electric charge, and that the Larmor frequency is directly linked with our $\boldsymbol{\omega}$.

The effect of the Coriolis force due to rotation of the earth on projectiles, large scale air circulation on the surface of the earth, flow of rivers, etc. is studied in detail. The general rule is that in the northern hemisphere, the Coriolis deflection on a horizontally moving object takes place always to the right of the instantaneous direction of motion. Foucault had constructed a huge pendulum and demonstrated for the first time in 1851 that the earth is rotating with the same angular speed of rotation as was already inferred from the apparent diurnal motion of the stars around the earth.

More general cases of rotations, such as two rotations about a common point, or two rotations separated by a time varying translation are considered, and general methods of handling such, and even more complicated, situations are outlined.

PROBLEMS

3.1 A smooth disc is rotating in a horizontal plane with uniform angular speed ω about a vertical axis passing through its centre. A particle is allowed to slide on the disc with negligible friction. Since the motion is in two dimensions and takes place in a rotating frame, analyse the motion from the point of view of the disc using a complex variable for denoting the position $z = x + iy$ of the particle on the disc. Show that the equation of motion in the rotating frame reduces to $\ddot{z} + 2i\omega\dot{z} - \omega^2 z = 0$. Find the solution for the track if the initial position and velocities are supplied.

3.2 Show that two infinitesimal rotations $\delta\boldsymbol{\theta}_1$ $(= \delta\theta_1\hat{\boldsymbol{n}}_1)$ and $\delta\boldsymbol{\theta}_2$ $(= \delta\theta_2\hat{\boldsymbol{n}}_2)$ commute, but not the finite ones, say $\boldsymbol{\theta}_1$ and $\boldsymbol{\theta}_2$, where $\boldsymbol{\theta} = \theta\hat{\boldsymbol{n}}$ means rotation by an angle θ about an axis implied by the direction of the unit vector $\hat{\boldsymbol{n}}$. Since the infinitesimal rotations commute, construct a finite rotation $\boldsymbol{\theta}$ by superposing a large number N of infinitesimal rotation $\Delta\boldsymbol{\theta} = \boldsymbol{\theta}/N$. Following this procedure show that in the limit $N \to \infty$, a finite rotation of $\boldsymbol{r}_o$ by $\boldsymbol{\theta}$ leading to $\boldsymbol{r}$ such that

$$\boldsymbol{r} = \boldsymbol{r}_o + \frac{\sin\theta}{\theta}(\boldsymbol{\theta} \times \boldsymbol{r}_o) + \frac{1 - \cos\theta}{\theta^2}(\boldsymbol{\theta} \times (\boldsymbol{\theta} \times \boldsymbol{r}_o))$$

or in matrix notation $\boldsymbol{r} = S\boldsymbol{r}_o$, where S is given by a matrix

$$S_{ij} = \cos\theta\delta_{ij} + \frac{\sin\theta}{\theta}\epsilon_{ijk}\theta_k + \frac{1 - \cos\theta}{\theta^2}\theta_i\theta_j$$

Show further that S is orthogonal, that is, $S^T S = S^{-1}S$, and that $\dot{S}S^{-1} = \Omega$ is an antisymmetric matrix. Since all 3×3 antisymmetric matrices can be represented by an axial vector, in this case say by $\boldsymbol{\omega}$, such that $\epsilon_{ijk}\omega_j = \Omega_{ik}$.
Prove that $\dot{\boldsymbol{r}} = \Omega\boldsymbol{r}_o = \boldsymbol{\omega} \times \boldsymbol{r}$, where $\boldsymbol{\omega}$ is in general not the same as $d\boldsymbol{\theta}/dt$. It is

given by

$$\boldsymbol{\omega} = \frac{d\boldsymbol{\theta}}{dt} + \frac{1 - \cos\theta}{\theta^2}\left(\boldsymbol{\theta} \times \frac{d\boldsymbol{\theta}}{dt}\right) + \frac{\theta - \sin\theta}{\theta^3}\left[\boldsymbol{\theta} \times \left(\boldsymbol{\theta} \times \frac{d\boldsymbol{\theta}}{dt}\right)\right]$$

3.3 Using the Gantmakher formula, derive the above relation between $\boldsymbol{r}$ and $\boldsymbol{r}_o$ connected by a finite rotation $\boldsymbol{\theta} = \theta\hat{\boldsymbol{n}}$, that is, the relation

$$\boldsymbol{r} = \boldsymbol{r}_o + \frac{\sin\theta}{\theta}(\boldsymbol{\theta} \times \boldsymbol{r}_o) + \frac{1 - \cos\theta}{\theta^2}(\boldsymbol{\theta} \times (\boldsymbol{\theta} \times \boldsymbol{r}_o))$$

Use Gantmakher formula to write the solution for the motion of a charged particle in a constant electric field $\boldsymbol{E}$ and a constant magnetic field $\boldsymbol{B}$. Find the motion for the case with $\boldsymbol{B} = B_z\hat{\boldsymbol{k}}$, $\boldsymbol{E} = E_x\hat{\boldsymbol{i}} + E_y\hat{\boldsymbol{j}}$, $\boldsymbol{v}_o = v_o\hat{\boldsymbol{k}}$, $\boldsymbol{r}_o = \boldsymbol{0}$.

3.4 Find the Lagrangian of a rigid symmetrical dumbbell (that is, two equal point masses connected a rigid and massless rod) rotating freely about its centre of mass and the centre of mass is moving in a circular track, not necessarily horizontal.

3.5 Using the principle of conservation of angular momentum about the centre of the earth, show that the stone dropped from rest and from a height h above the ground will produce the same easterly deviation as would be given by a consideration of the Coriolis force.

3.6 The Coriolis deflection of a falling stone might be significantly affected by the presence of air drag. Assume a quadratic drag force $f = kv^2$ and show that in fact the ratio of the modified displacement δ and the displacement without any air drag δ_o is given by

$$\frac{\delta}{\delta_o} = \frac{3}{2}\sqrt{\alpha h}\int_0^1 \frac{x\,dx}{\sqrt{1 - e^{-\alpha x}}} \simeq 1 + \frac{3}{20}\alpha h \qquad \text{for } \alpha h \ll 1$$

where $\alpha = 2k/m$, $m =$ mass of the stone, $h =$ height above the ground from which the stone is dropped. For a stone of radius 1 cm and density 2600 kg/m^3, $\alpha \simeq 0.02\ \text{m}^{-1}$. Find the ratio δ/δ_o for $h = 200$ m.

3.7 If a projectile is fired due east from a point on the surface of the earth at a geographical latitude λ, with a velocity v_o and at an angle of elevation above the horizontal of α, show that the lateral deflection of the projectile when the projectile strikes the earth is

$$d = \frac{4v_o^3}{g^2}\omega\sin\lambda\sin^2\alpha\cos\alpha$$

where ω is the angular frequency of the earth and g is the acceleration due to gravity. If the range of the projectile is R_o for the case $\omega = 0$, show also that the change of range due to the rotation of the earth is

$$R - R_o = \sqrt{\frac{2R^3}{g}}\,\omega\cos\lambda\left[\cot^{1/2}\lambda - \frac{1}{3}\tan^{3/2}\alpha\right]$$

3.8 Find the velocity and acceleration of the tips of the horizontal and vertical blades of an ordinary revolving table fan. Assume that the blades revolve with a constant angular speed ω_1, and that the horizontal shaft holding the motor rotates about a vertical axis sinusoidally with an angular speed $\omega = \omega_o \cos \Omega t$.

3.9 Suppose we have an inertial system S_o with respect to which another system S_1 is rotating about their common z-axis with an angular speed $\dot{\phi}$ in their $x-y$ plane. A further system S_2 is rotating about the common x-axis of S_1 and S_2 with an angular speed $\dot{\theta}$ in their common plane of $y-z$ axes. Find the net angular velocity $\boldsymbol{\Omega}$ and net angular acceleration $\boldsymbol{\alpha}$ in the basis sets of S_o, S_1, and S_2.

3.10 A perfectly elastic ping pong ball is colliding back and forth along a horizontally aligned diameter of a hollow sphere. Show that due to the Coriolis force acting on the ball at that place (due to the earth's rotation), the path of the ping pong ball will be rotating about the centre of the sphere at a rate exactly twice the rate of rotation of the plane of oscillation of Foucault's pendulum, over a place of the same geographical latitude.

4
Central Force

4.0 INTRODUCTION

Central force is one of the oldest and richest topics of classical mechanics. The first two correct laws of force, Hooke's law of elasticity and Newton's inverse square law of gravitation are central forces by nature. Coulomb's electrostatic force between two charges, the van der Waal forces between neutral atoms and molecules in a gas, or even the Yukawa force between the nucleons in the nucleus of atoms are but other examples of central forces.

Details of the central forces are usually taught at lower levels, except for adequate emphasis on phenomena like tides, dynamical manipulations of the orbits of spaceships in this space age, the geometry of the orbits of planets, natural examples of virialised systems, etc., which are duly covered in this chapter. Of course, for the sake of completeness, the planetary laws of motion, the closure properties of orbits under central forces and the dynamics of collisions and scattering are included.

Practically all great minds have, at one time or another, explored the problems of central force. Thus we find Kepler in Kepler's laws of motion and Kepler's equation, Newton in prescribing the law of gravitation, Bernoulli, Laplace, Hamilton and Lenz in finding out all the constants of motion for Keplerian orbits, Bertrand to find the conditions of closure under the action of general central forces, Halley, Euler and Gauss to study the orbits of planets and comets, Laplace to prove the stability of the solar system, Lagrange to solve three body problems, D'Alembert to solve the precession of earth's axis of rotation, Jacobi to formulate the inverse square law problems in parabolic coordinates, Darwin to tackle the problem of tides, Delaunay to calculate precise orbit of the moon, Rutherford to study the scattering under inverse square law of forces, Clausius to find virial properties of central force systems, Poisson to give the differential equation for gravitational potential, and so on.

4.1 DEFINITION AND PROPERTIES OF THE CENTRAL FORCE

In this chapter we deal with a class of force laws having a particular kind of dependence on space variables (r, θ, ϕ). We start with the definition of a field of force, or in short, a force field.

By a *force field*, or for that matter any vector field, we mean a rule (equivalently, a vector function $\boldsymbol{f} \; : \; R^3 \;\rightarrow\; R^3$) which assigns a unique force to every point in space, or in a specific domain, if it is not ubiquitous.

If the force field is derivable from a scalar potential energy field, then we have an *ordinary potential energy function* $V(\boldsymbol{r})$ defined in all real space, or if restricted, on the domain of $\boldsymbol{f}(\boldsymbol{r})$, such that

$$\boldsymbol{f}(\boldsymbol{r}) \;=\; -\,\nabla V(\boldsymbol{r}) \tag{4.1}$$

We are interested in the case where the potential energy function is a function of the scalar distance $r \;=\; |\boldsymbol{r}|$ from a fixed point in space. This fixed point is the source of the force field and is called the *centre of force*. If we choose this fixed point to be the origin, the potential energy function satisfies

$$V(\boldsymbol{r}) \;=\; V(|\boldsymbol{r}|) \tag{4.2}$$

where $\boldsymbol{r}$ is the position vector of any arbitrary point. When this happens we say that the potential energy function is centrally symmetric and the corresponding force field is *central.*

Using polar coordinates to describe the central force field, Eq. (4.1), coupled with Eq. (4.2) reduces to

$$\boldsymbol{f}(\boldsymbol{r}) \;=\; -\,\frac{\partial V(r)}{\partial r}\hat{\boldsymbol{r}} \tag{4.3}$$

that is, the force is always directed towards or away from the centre (origin). We denote the magnitude of the central force at r by $f(r)$. In general any given $f(r)$ could be uniquely represented by a power in r, that is,

$$f(r) \;=\; \sum_{n\,=\,-\,\infty}^{\infty} \; k_n \, r^{-n} \tag{4.4}$$

where k_n's are either constants including zeros, or at most functions of time.

4.1.1 Properties of the Conservative Central Force

If a central force does not depend on time explicitly, it is called a *Conservative central force.*

1. Such central forces preserve homogeneity of time which implies the existence of an energy integral, that is, the total energy of a system driven by the field of a central force is a constant of motion. In order to see this more explicitly, we take a scalar product of Eq. (4.1) and the velocity of any particle in the system $\boldsymbol{v}$ to get

$$m\dot{\boldsymbol{v}}\cdot\boldsymbol{v} \;+\; \nabla V\cdot\boldsymbol{v} \;=\; 0$$

or

$$\frac{d}{dt}\left(\frac{1}{2}\,mv^2 \;+\; V\right) \;=\; 0$$

which implies that the sum of the kinetic energy

$$T \;=\; \frac{1}{2}\,mv^2$$

and the potential energy ($= V$) is a constant say E such that

$$T + V = E$$

2. Only radial (r) dependence and no angular (θ, ϕ) dependence in $\boldsymbol{f}(\boldsymbol{r})$ implies that the isotropy of space is preserved by $\boldsymbol{f}(\boldsymbol{r})$ about its origin. This means that the total angular momentum of the system about the origin is conserved. To see this explicitly we note that the torque about the origin ($\boldsymbol{\Gamma} = \boldsymbol{r} \times \boldsymbol{f}(\boldsymbol{r})$) vanishes; hence the angular momentum $\boldsymbol{h}$ ($= m\,(\boldsymbol{r} \times \boldsymbol{v})$) is a constant of motion.

3. Suppose the initial velocity of a particle moving under central force is not parallel to the force direction. The force is always directed towards a fixed point in space, so it has no component perpendicular to the plane defined by the partial velocity vector and the direction of the force. Hence the particle continues to move in this plane only. Thus motion under central force is planar. A simple proof of this would be as follows : Since the angular momentum is conserved, $\boldsymbol{h} = m\,\boldsymbol{r} \times \boldsymbol{v}$ is a constant vector, implying that both $\boldsymbol{r}$ and $\boldsymbol{v}$ must always lie in the plane perpendicular to the fixed vector $\boldsymbol{h}$.

4. Once the orbital plane is known, the complete trajectory of the particle moving under the central force field is described by any two independent coordinates as parametric functions of time such as $r(t)$ and $\theta(t)$. However one can eliminate t from these two relations to get $r(\theta)$, which is just the equation of the orbit. The equation of the orbit, of course, cannot tell us where the particle is at any instant t.

5. The initial position and velocity ($\boldsymbol{r}_o, \boldsymbol{v}_o$) ; or the total energy, the angular momentum and the initial position of the particle in the plane of motion ($E, \boldsymbol{h}, r_o, \theta_o$) ; or the six orbital elements (a, e, n, i, Ω, Γ see article 4.8 for definition) fix the whole problem to a specific state of motion. In other words, any six independent constants are required for a complete description of any particle's motion under any central force.

4.2 TWO-BODY CENTRAL FORCE PROBLEM

Consider the motion of two particles, each of which is a source of a central force field and the potential energy of the system is a function only of their separation, that is, $V = V(|\boldsymbol{r}_1 - \boldsymbol{r}_2|)$, where $\boldsymbol{r}_1$ and $\boldsymbol{r}_2$ are the position vectors of particles number 1 and 2 having masses m_1 and m_2 respectively (see Fig. 4.1).

The position vector of the centre of mass ($\boldsymbol{R}$) is defined through the equation

$$m_1\,\boldsymbol{r}_1 + m_2\,\boldsymbol{r}_2 = (m_1 + m_2)\,\boldsymbol{R} \tag{4.5}$$

and the relative position vector of the particle 2 with respect to particle 1 is

$$\boldsymbol{r} = \boldsymbol{r}_2 - \boldsymbol{r}_1 \tag{4.6}$$

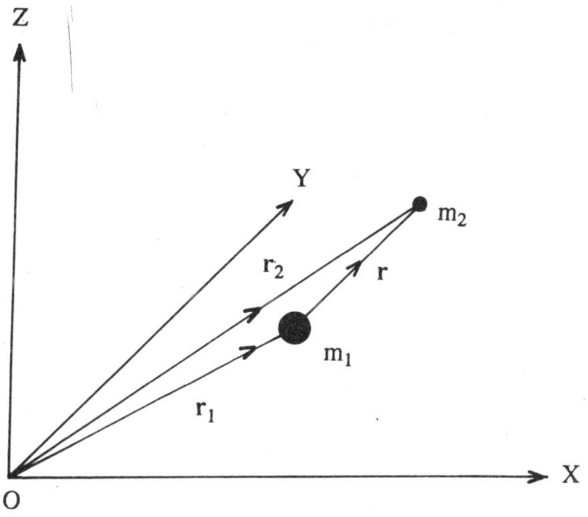

Fig. 4.1 Motion of two point masses under the action of a central force between them

The Lagrangian of the system is given by

$$L = \frac{1}{2}(m_1 |\dot{\boldsymbol{r}}_1|^2 + m_2 |\dot{\boldsymbol{r}}_2|^2) - V(|\boldsymbol{r}_1 - \boldsymbol{r}_2|) \tag{4.7}$$

We can eliminate $\boldsymbol{r}_1$ and $\boldsymbol{r}_2$ from Eq. (4.7) and write it in terms of $\boldsymbol{r}$ and $\boldsymbol{R}$ using Eqs (4.5) and (4.6) and get the Lagrangian in the form

$$L = \frac{1}{2} M \dot{\boldsymbol{R}}^2 + \frac{1}{2}\mu \dot{\boldsymbol{r}}^2 - V(r) \tag{4.8}$$

where $M = m_1 + m_2$ is the total mass of the system, and

$$\mu = \frac{m_1 m_2}{m_1 + m_2} = \left(\frac{1}{m_1} + \frac{1}{m_2}\right)^{-1} \tag{4.9}$$

is called the *reduced mass* of the system.

Since L is cyclic in $\boldsymbol{R}$, $\dot{\boldsymbol{R}}$ is a constant of motion and therefore the centre of mass can act as the origin of an inertial system. Again, since $\dot{\boldsymbol{R}}$ is a constant of motion $1/2\, M\dot{\boldsymbol{R}}^2$ is a constant which can be dropped from Eq. (4.8). Since $\boldsymbol{r}$ is measured from particle 1, the latter serves as the origin of a noninertial frame. This does not bother us, however, because we have first constructed the Lagrangian in an inertial frame (Eq. (4.7)) and then expressed it in terms of quantities defined with respect to a noninertial frame. Dropping the constant term $1/2\, M\dot{\boldsymbol{R}}^2$ from Eq. (4.8) we can thus write,

$$L = \frac{1}{2}\mu \dot{\boldsymbol{r}}^2 - V(r) \tag{4.10}$$

where $\boldsymbol{r}$ is given by Eq. (4.6) and $r = |\boldsymbol{r}|$.

The above form of Lagrangian is such that it effectively corresponds to single particle motion with an effective mass equal to the reduced mass of the system, and the source of the central force seems to act effectively as an immovable source situated at the origin. Actually this origin is moving with nonuniform velocity and acceleration. However, one may not be aware of this fact merely by looking at the explicit form of the Lagrangian given by Eq. (4.10).

Because of the conservation of angular momentum (see p. 120), the orbit must lie in a plane. Expressing Eq. (4.10) in the plane polar coordinates (r, θ) defined in the plane of the orbit,

$$L = \frac{1}{2}\,\mu\,(\dot{r}^2 + r^2\dot{\theta}^2) - V(r) \tag{4.11}$$

Here θ is a cyclic coordinate, therefore the generalised momentum conjugate to θ is conserved. We have,

$$p_\theta = \frac{\partial L}{\partial \dot{\theta}} = \mu r^2 \dot{\theta} = \text{const.} = h \text{ (say)} \tag{4.12}$$

As expected, p_θ, the angular momentum of the system by definition, is conserved.

Euler-Lagrange's equation of motion in r is

$$\frac{d}{dt}(\mu\dot{r}) - \mu r\dot{\theta}^2 + \frac{\partial V}{\partial r} = 0 \tag{4.13}$$

This is a second order differential equation in r, and hence needs to be integrated twice in order to obtain the complete solution. However, it is always profitable to look for the existence of the first integrals of motion, and if they exist, one can take, for example, the energy integral, which is essentially a first order differential equation, and solve for the motion. The first integrals require the specification of the values of the respective integrals, so one set of initial conditions are in fact already utilised through these, namely h and E. The actual energy integral for the above problem is (see Eq. (2.60)) given by

$$E = \frac{\partial L}{\partial \dot{r}}\,\dot{r} + \frac{\partial L}{\partial \dot{\theta}}\,\dot{\theta} - L = \frac{1}{2}\,\mu(\dot{r}^2 + r^2\dot{\theta}^2) + V(r)$$

Since $\dot{\theta}$ and r are related through Eq. (4.12) ($\dot{\theta} = h/\mu r^2$) we can reduce the energy integral corresponding to a one-dimensional motion in r

$$E = \frac{1}{2}\mu\dot{r}^2 + \left[\frac{1}{2}\frac{h^2}{\mu r^2} + V(r)\right] = \frac{1}{2}\mu\dot{r}^2 + V_{\text{eff}}(r) \tag{4.14}$$

where

$$V_{\text{eff}}(r) = V(r) + \frac{1}{2}\frac{h^2}{\mu r^2} \tag{4.15}$$

Equation (4.14) for energy suggests that the radial kinetic energy is $1/2\,(\mu\dot{r}^2)$ and the effective potential energy for the radial motion is $V_{\text{eff}}(r)$. It consists of two parts namely, $V(r)$, which is the actual potential energy and $1/2(h^2/\mu r^2) = 1/2(\mu r^2\dot{\theta}^2)$ which is the centrifugal potential energy for the radial motion (compare with Eq. (3.10)).

The centrifugal potential energy increases indefinitely as $1/r^2$ for $r \to 0$ (see Fig. 4.2).

For attractive forces $V(r)$ is negative for all values of r and asymptotically vanishes as $r \rightarrow \infty$.

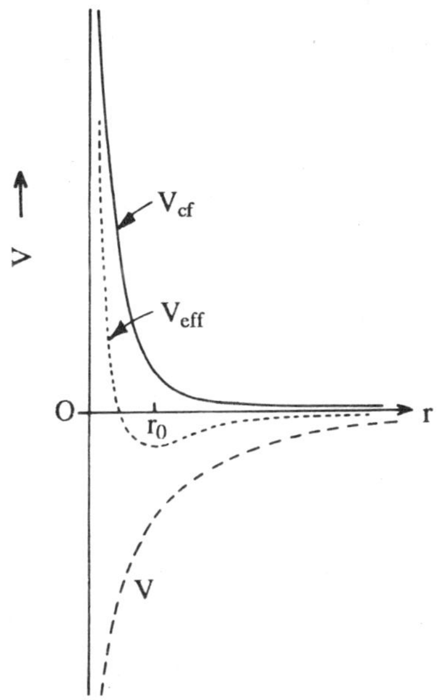

Fig. 4.2 The monotonic gravitational (dashed line) and centrifugal (solid line) potential energies of a particle as functions of r, for its motion considered in the radial coordinate only, even though the actual motion taking place in a 2-D plane. The sum of the two, V_{eff} can have a minimum with a finite negative value, thus allowing a range of bounded orbits

A motion is called *bounded* in r, if $\dot{r}$ vanishes at the extreme values of r say $r = r_{min}$ and $r = r_{max}$. Both of these bounds must exist for a bounded motion. Thus from equation (4.14) $E = V_{eff}(r)$ for both $r = r_{max}$ and $r = r_{min}$. Next, note that

$$E - V_{eff}(r) = \frac{1}{2}\mu\dot{r}^2 > 0$$

for all r. Therefore for any physically possible radial motion we must have

$$V_{eff}(r) \leq E$$

for every value of r accessible to the system. In other words, some portion of $V_{eff}(r)$ curve must lie below the curve $V_{eff}(r) = E$ in order to have an allowed radial motion.

4.3 STABILITY OF ORBITS

By an orbit we mean a scheduled path of any object moving under a central force. An orbit is called ***stable*** if, when a slight perturbation is given to the initial position, the orbit is perturbed only slightly. The perturbation is usually given to the radial coordinate keeping either the energy or the angular momentum unchanged.

The condition for stability in radial motion is given by the existence of a local minimum in $V_{\text{eff}}(r)$, that is, we require

$$\frac{\partial^2 V_{\text{eff}}(r)}{\partial r^2} > 0 \text{ at the value of } r, \text{ say } r = r_o, \text{ given by } \frac{\partial V_{\text{eff}}(r)}{\partial r} = 0 \qquad (4.16)$$

If for any central force, potential energy function $V(r) = br^{n+1}$, b being a constant, and centrifugal potential energy $V_{\text{cf}}(r) = ar^{-2}$, $(a > 0)$, where a is again, a constant, and $\frac{\partial V_{\text{eff}}(r)}{\partial r} = 0$ at $r = r_o$, so that

$$(n + 1)\, b = 2a\, r_o^{-3-n}$$

Hence

$$\left[\frac{d^2 V_{\text{eff}}}{dr^2}\right]_{r = r_o} = 2ar_o^{-4}(3 + n)$$

Therefore, any circular orbit with $r = r_o$ under any central force can satisfy the stability condition if

$$n > -3$$

This can also be proved from more elementary considerations given below without using the conditions given in Eq. (4.16).

The second order differential equation for an orbit under any central force $f(r)$, obtained from Eq. (4.13) is given by

$$\frac{d^2 u}{d\theta^2} + u = -\frac{\mu F(u)}{h^2 u^2} \qquad (4.17)$$

where $u = 1/r$ and $F(u) = f(1/u)$.

Assume a circular orbit so that $r = r_o$ which means $u = u_o = r_o^{-1}$. This gives, for the total energy,

$$E_o = (V_{\text{eff}})_o = \frac{1}{2}\frac{h^2}{\mu} u_o^2 + V_o$$

and from Eq. (4.17)

$$u_o = -\frac{\mu F(u_o)}{h^2 u_o^2} \qquad (4.18)$$

Now we add a small perturbation to u, given by $u = u_o + \xi$ ($\xi << u_o$). The equation of the orbit becomes,

$$\frac{d^2 \xi}{d\theta^2} + u_o + \xi = -\frac{\mu F(u_o + \xi)}{h^2 (u_o + \xi)^2}$$

Expanding $F(u_o + \xi)$ in Taylor's series around u_o we get

$$\frac{d^2\xi}{d\theta^2} + u_o + \xi = -\frac{\mu[F(u_o) + \xi F'(u_o) + (\xi^2/2)\,F''(u_o) + \cdots]}{h^2\,(u_o^2 + 2\,\xi u_o + \xi^2)}$$

$$= -\frac{\mu F(u_o)}{h^2\,u_o^2}\left[1 + \xi\left(\frac{F'(u_o)}{F(u_o)} - \frac{2}{u_o}\right) + \cdots\right]$$

Keeping the angular momentum constant and all the terms up to only the first order in ξ, the above equation becomes, using Eq. (4.18),

$$\frac{d^2\xi}{d\theta^2} + A\xi = 0 \tag{4.19}$$

where

$$A = 1 + \frac{\mu F(u_o)}{h^2\,u_o^2}\left(\frac{F'(u_o)}{F(u_o)} - \frac{2}{u_o}\right)$$

or using Eq. (4.18) again,

$$A = 1 - u_o\left(\frac{F'(u_o)}{F(u_o)} - \frac{2}{u_o}\right) = 3 - u_o\left(\frac{F'(u_o)}{F(u_o)}\right) \tag{4.20}$$

The general solution of Eq. (4.19) is

$$\begin{aligned} \xi &= C_1\cos(\sqrt{A}\,\theta) + C_2\sin(\sqrt{A}\,\theta) \qquad \text{for } A > 0 \\ &= C_1\cosh(\sqrt{-A}\,\theta) + C_2\sinh(\sqrt{-A}\,\theta) \ \text{ for } A < 0 \\ &= C_1\theta + C_2 \qquad \text{for } A = 0 \end{aligned} \tag{4.21}$$

Of the above solutions only the first one remains finite while the others increase indefinitely with θ. Therefore, a circular orbit of radius $r_o = 1/u_o$ is stable if and only if $A > 0$, that is,

$$3 - \frac{u_o F'(u_o)}{F(u_o)} > 0 \qquad \text{or} \qquad \left.\frac{d\ln F(u)}{du}\right|_{u = u_o} < \frac{3}{u_o} = 3r_o$$

Now, if $F(u) = Ku^{-n}$ then $uF'(u)/F(u) = -n$, where K and n are constants.

This means that for $f(r) = kr^n$, the circular orbits are stable, if and only if $n > -3$.

4.4 CONDITIONS FOR CLOSURE

An orbit is said to be *closed* if the particle eventually retraces its path (orbit). Or, in other words, closure of an orbit requires the period of radial oscillation to match with that of the θ oscillation. By the time u or r returns to its original value, θ must complete an integral number of revolutions. This means that $\sqrt{A}$ in Eq. (4.21) must be a rational number, say p/q, where p and q are integers. In that case after q revolutions of the radius vector (that is, the rotation in θ by $2\pi q$), the value of u completes p oscillations about its mean value u_o. However, this condition is not sufficient for closure of a general noncircular orbit. To obtain the relevant conditions one has to consider arbitrarily large deviations from a circular orbit. These, in turn, impose further restrictions which the orbit must satisfy, in order to be closed.

It was proved by Bertrand, in 1873, that *stable as well as closed orbits are possible only for* $A = 1$ *and* $A = 4$. This fact is known as Bertrand's theorem. The proof can be found in Appendix A of Goldstein's book. Referring to the end of the previous section we note that $A = 1$ corresponds to $n = -3 + A = -2$, that is, $f(r) \propto 1/r^2$, which is the familiar inverse square law. The case $A = 4$ corresponds to $n = -3 + A = 1$ or, $f(r) \propto r$ which is Hooke's law or the law of harmonic forces.

Let us summarise the above in the following points:

1. All bounded orbits are closed only for the inverse square law of force of the Coulombian or Newtonian type and for the linear laws of force of Hooke's type.

2. $A = 1$ implies inverse square law, for which one oscillation in r is completed as soon as θ changes by 2π. Thus the radial and angular oscillations are degenerate. However for Hooke's type of the laws of forces $\sqrt{A} = 2$, so that one complete rotation in θ by 2π implies two complete radial oscillations.

3. Both gravitation and electrostatic attraction provide situations where both these force laws are realised; an inverse square law outside any spherically symmetric homogeneous body (uniformly charged or neutral) and the Hooke's law inside it.

4. The condition for bounded motion is that there is a bounded domain of r in which $V_{\text{eff}}(r) \leq E$, the energy. The condition for stability of circular orbits is $n > -3$, where $f(r) \propto r^n$. The closed orbits exist only for $n = 1$ and $n = -2$.

4.5 INTEGRABLE POWER LAWS OF THE CENTRAL FORCE

We now obtain a first order differential equation for the orbit and write its formal solution. We start with the energy integral,

$$E = \frac{1}{2}\mu(\dot{r}^2 + r^2\,\dot{\theta}^2) + V(r)$$

We can write

$$\dot{r} = \frac{dr}{d\theta}\,\dot{\theta} = \frac{dr}{d\theta}\left(\frac{h}{\mu r^2}\right)$$

so that

$$E = \frac{1}{2}\left(\frac{h^2}{\mu r^4}\right)\left(\frac{dr}{d\theta}\right)^2 + \frac{1}{2}\frac{h^2}{\mu r^2} + V(r)$$

or

$$\frac{dr}{d\theta} = \sqrt{\frac{2\mu r^4}{h^2}[E - V(r)] - r^2}$$

Its formal solution can be written as

$$\theta = \theta_o + \int_{r_o}^{r} \frac{dr'}{r'^2\sqrt{\frac{2\mu}{h^2}[E - V(r')] - \frac{1}{r'^2}}} = \theta_o - \int_{u_o}^{u} \frac{du'}{\sqrt{\frac{2\mu}{h^2}\left[E - V\left(\frac{1}{u'}\right)\right] - u'^2}} \tag{4.22}$$

where, as before, $u = 1/r$.

Now the following points may be noted:

1. For given E, h and the form of $V(r)$, the orbit is fixed. u_o and θ_o refer merely to the starting point on the orbit.

2. If $V(r) \propto r^{n+1}$, the above integral can be directly integrated for $n = 1, -2$ and -3.

3. For $n = 5, 3, 0, -4, -5$ and -7, the results can be expressed in terms of elliptic integrals where, by definition, an elliptic integral is $\int R(x,w)dx$ with R being any rational function of x and w is defined by

$$w = \sqrt{\alpha x^4 + \beta x^3 + \gamma x^2 + \delta x + \eta}$$

such that α and β cannot be simultaneously zero, and γ, δ and η are constants. We are not giving any proof of the statements, for which one may consult Goldstein's book.

4. For other values of n, the equation of the orbit cannot be expressed in closed form.

4.6 DERIVATION OF FORCE LAWS FROM KINEMATICAL LAWS OF MOTION

Kepler's laws of planetary motion do not provide any explanation for planetary motions; instead, they are merely the descriptions of the motion. Velocity, acceleration and areal velocity are kinematical quantities, the corresponding dynamical quantities being linear momentum, force and angular momentum respectively. The difference between these two sets of quantities is primarily the mass factor. We know that acceleration, a kinematical quantity, is defined as $\boldsymbol{a} = d\boldsymbol{v}/dt$. Its dynamical equivalent, Newton's second law of motion, given by $\boldsymbol{F} = d\boldsymbol{p}/dt$ is far more significant than its kinematical counterpart, although both are merely definitions. Similarly Kepler's second law of constant areal velocity can be explained by a dynamically very significant conservation law, that is, the conservation of orbital angular momentum of the planets. However, historically it was a giant step forward when Newton derived a fundamental force law of nature from Kepler's laws of planetary motion, using his laws of motion. Here we shall present two examples of derivation of force laws from given kinematical laws.

4.6.1 Newton's Law of Gravitation From Kepler's Laws of Planetary Motion

Kepler's first law suggests that the equation of the orbit in plane polar coordinates about the focus is (see Fig. 4.3) given by

$$r = \frac{a(1 - e^2)}{1 + e\cos\theta} \tag{4.23}$$

where a is the semimajor axis and e the eccentricity of the orbit. Kepler's second law states that the areal velocity is constant, that is,

$$r^2\dot{\theta} = \text{const.} = H \text{ (say)} \tag{4.24}$$

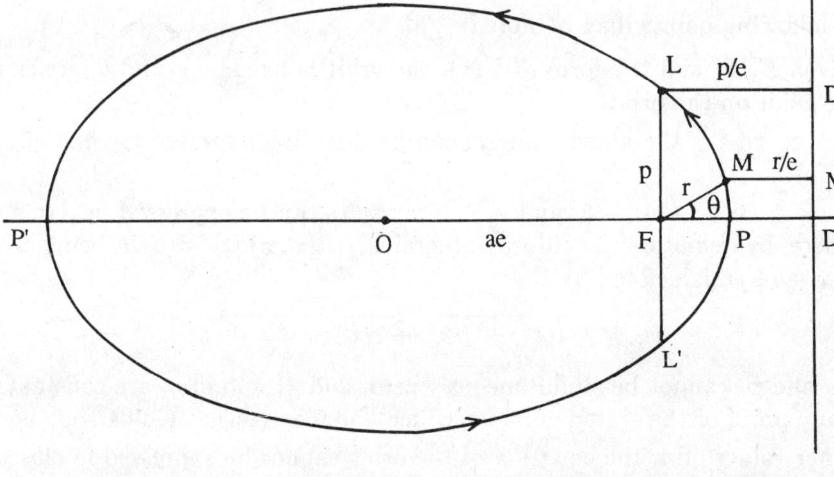

Fig. 4.3 Finding the general equation of a conic section. From the above construction LD = MM′ + FM cos θ, M being any point on the conic, the extended line DD_o the directrix, LL′ the latus rectum, P the pericenter, and F the primary focus

The force on the planet at any instant (using Newton's second law of motion) is

$$\boldsymbol{F} = m\ddot{\boldsymbol{r}} = m(\ddot{r} - r\dot{\theta}^2)\,\hat{\boldsymbol{r}} + m(r\ddot{\theta} + 2\dot{r}\dot{\theta})\,\hat{\boldsymbol{\theta}} \tag{4.25}$$

Differentiating Eqs (4.23) and (4.24) with respect to t one can express the RHS of Eq. (4.25) in terms of r and θ variables to give,

$$\boldsymbol{F} = -\frac{mH^2}{a(1 - e^2)r^2}\,\hat{\boldsymbol{r}} \tag{4.26}$$

Since for any planet, m, a, H^2 and e are all positive constants and $e < 1$, the force is not only central but also attractive in nature and follows an inverse square law of distance from the sun.

Now one has to check whether the constant of proportionality between F and $1/r^2$ would be the same for all planets because m, a, e, H are all different for different planets. Here comes in the use of the third law.

Kepler's third law says that the orbital period $P \propto a^{3/2}$ or,

$$P^2 = K_o{}^2 a^3 \tag{4.27}$$

K_o being the same for all planets . Now from the definition of areal velocity and its constancy,

$$r^2\dot{\theta} = H = 2\pi ab/P = (2\pi a^2\sqrt{1 - e^2})/P \tag{4.28}$$

Combining Eqs (4.27) and (4.28) we get

$$H^2 = \frac{4\pi^2 a(1 - e^2)}{K_o^2}$$

so that

$$\boldsymbol{F} = -\frac{4\pi^2 m}{K_o{}^2 r^2}\hat{\boldsymbol{r}}$$

where K_o is the same constant for all planets. Therefore it turns out that apart from the inverse square dependence on distance and a constant factor, the force of attraction between any planet and the sun is also proportional to the mass of the planet.

Now one uses Newton's third law of motion, that is, the planet must be attracting the sun with the same but opposite force. This is possible only if the factor $1/K_o^2$ is proportional to the mass of the sun $M_\odot$, leading finally to Newton's law of Gravitation

$$\boldsymbol{F} = -\frac{GM_\odot m}{r^2}\hat{\boldsymbol{r}}$$

where G is a universal constant. However, Newton could become sure of the universality of this law only after finding that it gave him the right value of the acceleration due to gravity on the surface of the earth, and also quantitatively explained Galileo's kinematical laws of freely falling bodies, the observed relationship between the length and period of oscillation of any simple pendulum and the motion of the moon around the earth. Thus, during Newton's lifetime, the universality of Newton's laws of gravitation extended at least up to the scale size of the solar system, or more precisely, up to then known outermost planet Saturn.

4.6.2 Force Law Corresponding To Ptolemy's Epicyclic Model

Basically Ptolemy's epicyclic model suggests that each planet including the sun and the moon is moving in a circle called *epicycle*, the centre of which is again moving in a circle called *deferent*. In the most primitive forms of the *geocentric* models the earth was assumed to be at the centre of all deferents and the angular speeds on the deferent (ω_1) and on the epicycle (ω_2) were assumed to be constants. (However, in the actual models of Ptolemy, of Aryabhata I and of others, the earth was assumed to be slightly displaced from the respective centres of the deferents, and the origin about which ω_1 was assumed to be constant was yet another point called the *equant* as shown in Fig. 4.4).

Essentially the orbit of a planet can be represented by

$$\boldsymbol{r} = \boldsymbol{r}_1 + \boldsymbol{r}_2$$

where

$$\boldsymbol{r}_1 = a[\cos(\omega_1 t)\hat{\boldsymbol{i}} + \sin(\omega_1 t)\hat{\boldsymbol{j}}], \quad \text{and} \quad \boldsymbol{r}_2 = b[\cos(\omega_2 t)\hat{\boldsymbol{i}} + \sin(\omega_2 t)\hat{\boldsymbol{j}}]$$

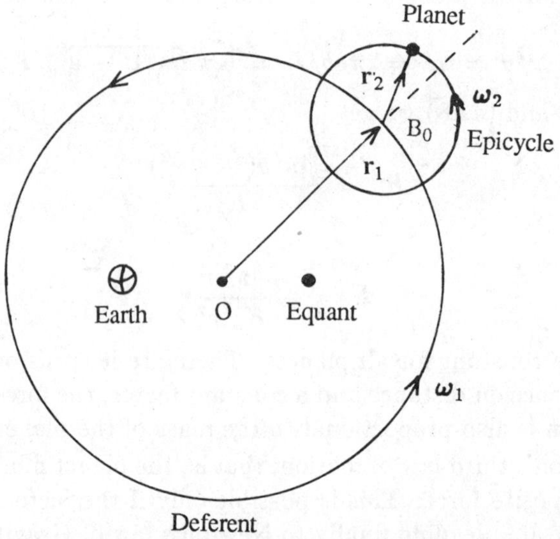

Fig. 4.4 **Motion of a planet in Ptolemy's geocentric model of a rigid body with respect to an outside inertial frame at O and a body frame at B_o**

a being the radius of the planet's orbital deferent and b the radius of the planet's orbital epicycle (see Fig. 4.4). Now, $\dot{\boldsymbol{r}}_1 = \boldsymbol{\omega}_1 \times \boldsymbol{r}_1$, where $\boldsymbol{\omega}_1 = \omega_1 \hat{\boldsymbol{k}}$, say, $\hat{\boldsymbol{k}}$ pointing in a direction perpendicular to the orbital plane of the planet, and similarly $\dot{\boldsymbol{r}}_2 = \boldsymbol{\omega}_2 \times \boldsymbol{r}_2$, with $\boldsymbol{\omega}_2 = \omega_2 \hat{\boldsymbol{k}}$, giving

$$\dot{\boldsymbol{r}} = \boldsymbol{\omega}_1 \times \boldsymbol{r}_1 + \boldsymbol{\omega}_2 \times \boldsymbol{r}_2$$
$$\ddot{\boldsymbol{r}} = \boldsymbol{\omega}_1 \times (\boldsymbol{\omega}_1 \times \boldsymbol{r}_1) + \boldsymbol{\omega}_2 \times (\boldsymbol{\omega}_2 \times \boldsymbol{r}_2)$$

It is now easy to show that

$$(\boldsymbol{\omega}_1 + \boldsymbol{\omega}_2) \times \dot{\boldsymbol{r}} = \ddot{\boldsymbol{r}} - (\boldsymbol{\omega}_1 \cdot \boldsymbol{\omega}_2)\boldsymbol{r}$$

or

$$\ddot{\boldsymbol{r}} = (\boldsymbol{\omega}_1 \cdot \boldsymbol{\omega}_2)\boldsymbol{r} + (\boldsymbol{\omega}_1 + \boldsymbol{\omega}_2) \times \dot{\boldsymbol{r}}$$

Since $\boldsymbol{\omega}_1$ and $\boldsymbol{\omega}_2$ are taken to be constants and are either parallel or antiparallel, this force law corresponds to an isotropic (charged) oscillator (represented by the first term) placed in a uniform magnetic field (represented by the second term). Even though such a force law is not totally unphysical, as it corresponds to an oscillating charged particle inside a magnetron, it would be extremely difficult to justify such a physical scenario for the motion of planets in the solar system. Hence Ptolemy's epicyclic model was not considered a viable physical model of the solar system, even if its kinematical descriptions were proved to be correct.

4.7 KEPLER'S PROBLEM

Kepler's problem is the inverse of Newton's problem; starting with Newton's law of gravitation, one now has to deduce Kepler's laws of planetary motion. This is a central force problem with the law of force given by the Newtonian inverse square law, namely

$$\boldsymbol{f}(\boldsymbol{r}) = -\frac{GM_\odot m}{r^2}\hat{\boldsymbol{r}} \quad \text{and} \quad V(r) = -\frac{GM_\odot m}{r} \tag{4.29}$$

where $\boldsymbol{r}$ is the radius vector of the planet measured from the centre of the sun. $M_\odot$ and m are the masses of the sun and the planet respectively. It was not Newton but Jacob Hermann, a student of Johannes Bernoulli, obtained for the first time in 1710 the orbit equation for Newton's law of gravitation.

The equation of motion under Newton's law of gravitation is given by

$$\mu\frac{d^2\boldsymbol{r}}{dt^2} = f(r)\hat{\boldsymbol{r}} = -\frac{GM_\odot m}{r^2}\hat{\boldsymbol{r}}$$

or

$$\frac{d^2\boldsymbol{r}}{dt^2} = -\frac{G(M_\odot + m)}{r^2}\hat{\boldsymbol{r}} = -\frac{K}{r^2}\hat{\boldsymbol{r}} \tag{4.30}$$

with

$$K = G(M_\odot + m) = GM_\odot\left(1 + \frac{m}{M_\odot}\right)$$

Taking vector product with $\boldsymbol{r}$ on both sides of Eq. (4.30), we get,

$$\boldsymbol{r} \times \frac{d^2\boldsymbol{r}}{dt^2} = \boldsymbol{0}$$

which means that the vector

$$\boldsymbol{H} = \boldsymbol{r} \times \frac{d\boldsymbol{r}}{dt} = 2\boldsymbol{A}' \text{ (say)} \tag{4.31}$$

is a constant of motion. One can easily identify $\boldsymbol{A}'$ as the *areal velocity vector*. Thus Eq. (4.31) states that the radius vector of the planet sweeps equal areas in equal intervals of time, proving Kepler's second law.

Since $\boldsymbol{r}\cdot\boldsymbol{H} = 0$, $\boldsymbol{r}$ is always perpendicular to the $\boldsymbol{H}$ vector, that is, $\boldsymbol{r}$ is confined to the plane perpendicular to the $\boldsymbol{H}$ vector. Now consider,

$$\frac{d^2\boldsymbol{r}}{dt^2} \times \boldsymbol{H} = -\frac{K}{r^3}\boldsymbol{r} \times \left(\boldsymbol{r} \times \frac{d\boldsymbol{r}}{dt}\right) = K\frac{d}{dt}\left(\frac{\boldsymbol{r}}{r}\right)$$

Using the fact that $d\boldsymbol{H}/dt = 0$, we can transform the LHS to get after integration

$$\frac{d\boldsymbol{r}}{dt} \times \boldsymbol{H} - K\frac{\boldsymbol{r}}{r} = \text{const.} = \boldsymbol{A} \tag{4.32}$$

where Eq. (4.32) defines the constant vector $\boldsymbol{A}$. Thus we get another constant of motion $\boldsymbol{A}$ called the *Runge-Lenz vector*. It is also called the Laplace vector or even sometimes the Laplace-Runge-Lenz vector. However, the actual credit should have gone to Jacob Hermann who was the first to obtain the correct magnitude of this vector in 1710, and to Johannes Bernoulli who found its direction in 1713.

Since $\boldsymbol{A} \cdot \boldsymbol{H} = 0$, we see that $\boldsymbol{A}$ is perpendicular to $\boldsymbol{H}$ or, $\boldsymbol{A}$ is a fixed vector lying in the plane of the orbit.

Let us now proceed to obtain the equation of the orbit. We start with,

$$H^2 = \boldsymbol{H} \cdot \boldsymbol{H} = \boldsymbol{H} \cdot \left(\boldsymbol{r} \times \frac{d\boldsymbol{r}}{dt} \right) = \boldsymbol{r} \cdot \left(\frac{d\boldsymbol{r}}{dt} \times \boldsymbol{H} \right)$$

$$= \boldsymbol{r} \cdot \left(\boldsymbol{A} + \frac{K\boldsymbol{r}}{r} \right) = \boldsymbol{r} \cdot \boldsymbol{A} + Kr$$

Therefore, we get for r

$$r = \frac{H^2/K}{1 + \frac{|\boldsymbol{A}|}{K} \cos\theta} \tag{4.33}$$

where θ is the angle between the $\boldsymbol{r}$ and $\boldsymbol{A}$. Equation (4.33) is the equation of the orbit. It has the form

$$r = \frac{p}{1 + e\cos\theta} \tag{4.34}$$

Equation (4.34) has the form of the equation for a general conic section (cf. Eq. 4.23). Thus Kepler's first law is proved. The planetary orbit is a conic section with $p = H^2/K$ as the *semilatus rectum*, $e = |\boldsymbol{A}|/K = A/K$ as the *eccentricity*. θ, which is the angle between $\boldsymbol{r}$ and $\boldsymbol{A}$ is called the *true anomaly*, that is, the angle between the *perihelion* (by definition, a point on the orbit closest to the sun) and the radius vector. This identification makes it clear that $\boldsymbol{A}$ lies in the direction of the perihelion (as r is minimum for $\theta = 0$) and aligns with the major axis of the conic section. *Aphelion* is defined to be a point on the orbit farthest from the sun, that is, corresponding to $\theta = \pi$ in Eq. (4.34).

If the orbit is not referred to any specific central object, one usually refers to these two points as *pericenter* and *apocenter*. If the orbit is around the earth instead of the sun one uses the terms *perigee* and *apogee* instead of perihelion and aphelion. Similarly, for the orbit of a star around another star, astronomers use the terms *periastron* and *apoastron* respectively. The line of the major axis is also called the *apsidal* line or simply *apsis*, to include the cases of unbound (parabolic and hyperbolic) orbits as well.

We further have,

$$|\boldsymbol{A}| = A = Ke = GM_\odot e \left(1 + \frac{m}{M_\odot} \right) \tag{4.35}$$

Because its magnitude is proportional to e, $\boldsymbol{A}$ is sometimes called the *eccentricity vector*. Historically it was so named by Hamilton (1845).

In order to know which of the conic sections can possibly represent a planetary orbit, it is necessary to obtain a relation between the orbital eccentricity and the *specific energy* (E') of the planet, that is, energy per unit reduced mass of the planet. We get from Eq. (4.32),

$$A^2 = \left| \frac{d\boldsymbol{r}}{dt} \right|^2 H^2 + K^2 - \frac{2K}{r} H^2$$

and then, differentiating with respect to t,

$$\frac{1}{2}\frac{d}{dt}(v^2) = \frac{d\mathbf{r}}{dt} \cdot \frac{d^2\mathbf{r}}{dt^2} = \frac{d}{dt}\left(\frac{K}{r}\right)$$

giving

$$\frac{d}{dt}\left(\frac{1}{2}v^2 - \frac{K}{r}\right) = \frac{d}{dt}\left(\frac{E}{\mu}\right) = 0$$

However, the expression in the bracket is the specific energy, denoted by $E' = E/\mu$. Using this expression for E' we get

$$A^2 = 2E'H^2 + K^2 \tag{4.36}$$

Therefore, from Eq. (4.35)

$$e = \frac{A}{K} = \sqrt{1 + \frac{2E'H^2}{K^2}} \tag{4.37}$$

Thus the specific energy $E' < 0$ implies $e < 1$, $E' > 0$ implies $e > 1$, $E' = 0$ implies $e = 1$ and $E' = -K^2/2H^2$ gives $e = 0$. It is well known that for $0 < e < 1$ the conic section is an *ellipse*, for $e = 1$ it is a *parabola*, for $e > 1$ it is a *hyperbola*, and for $e = 0$ it is a *circle*. But we know that, for the attractive inverse square law, the requirement that the orbit be bounded corresponds to $-K^2/2H^2 < E' < 0$ implying $0 < e < 1$. Thus the planetary orbits must be elliptical. (However, for a repulsive inverse square law, $K < 0$, hence always $E' > 0$ implying $e > 1$ or no bounded orbits.)

For elliptical orbits (see Fig. 4.3), the length of semilatus rectum is

$$p = a(1 - e^2)$$

a being the length of the semimajor axis. Hence, from Eqs (4.33), (4.34) and (4.37)

$$a = -\frac{K}{2E'} \tag{4.38}$$

Using the expression for E' we get

$$v^2 = K\left(\frac{2}{r} - \frac{1}{a}\right) \tag{4.39}$$

This relation is pictorially illustrated in Fig. 4.5. The expression (4.39) can be rewritten as

$$\frac{1}{2}v^2 = \frac{K}{r} - \frac{K}{2a}$$

which is the gain in specific kinetic energy of any particle dropped from rest from a height $2a$ from the force centre to a height r from the force centre . If we draw a circle of radius $2a$ about the force centre O, the actual elliptical orbit lies inside this circle. The actual speed of the particle at any point on the orbit is the same as that gained by a free fall from $r' = 2a$ to $r' = r$, where r' is also measured from the force centre O.

Note that we have proved the first two of Kepler's laws namely the ellipticity of the planetary orbits and constancy of areal velocity. We shall now prove the third law which

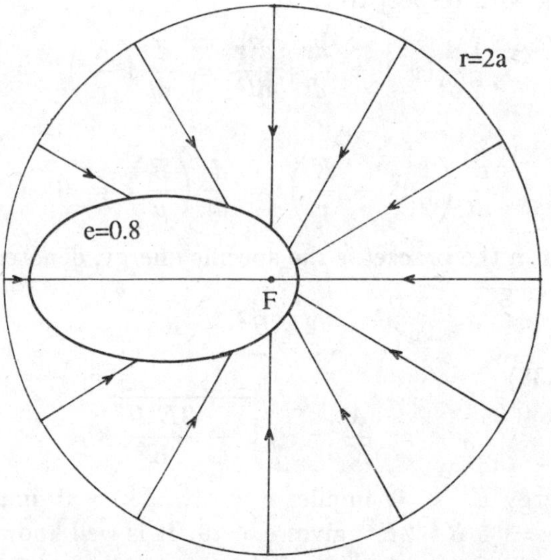

Fig. 4.5 The variation of the Keplerian orbital speed along the orbit of a planet can be viewed as that due to the differential gain from free fall from the rest from a circle of radius equal to the length of the major axis of the orbit, to the location on the orbit, shown by the arrowed paths of the assumed free fall

states that the square of the period of revolution is proportional to the cube of the semimajor axis. Since the areal speed $H/2$ is constant, we can write

$$\frac{1}{2}H\int_0^P dt = \text{total area of the ellipse} = \pi a^2 \sqrt{1 - e^2}$$

where P is the period of the orbital motion. This gives

$$P = \frac{2\pi a^2\sqrt{1 - e^2}}{H} \tag{4.40}$$

Using $H^2/K = p = a(1 - e^2)$, we get

$$\frac{P^2}{a^3} = \frac{4\pi^2}{G(M_\odot + m)} \tag{4.41}$$

which is the required law, provided we neglect m in comparison with $M_\odot$.

We conclude this section with the following remarks:

1. Planetary laws of motion can only evaluate K and less precisely $m/M_\odot$ (by using Kepler's third law and Eq. (4.41)).

2. Using these laws, one cannot evaluate G and $M_\odot$ separately; only the product $GM_\odot$ can be evaluated. Thus, only if G has been determined by an independent method, say by

any laboratory method, the mass of the sun, $M_\odot$, can be determined. The value of $GM_\odot$ is known quite precisely from Newton's time, but even now the best accuracy of G hardly goes beyond four significant digits. Carl Gauss had adopted, in 1809, a value of $GM_\odot$ defined by $k^2 = GM_\odot$. Here k is called *Gauss' constant of gravitation* for the sun. Its value is fixed by his choice

$$k = \sqrt{GM_\odot} = 0.01720209895 \text{ AU}^{3/2}\text{day}^{-1} \text{ exactly}$$

so that the period of revolution of a test particle orbiting around the sun at a distance of 1 AU is $P = 2\pi/k$. This provides a definition of AU, the *astronomical unit*. So 1 AU need not be exactly the average distance of the earth from the sun. Since k has been fixed for all time, any revision for the mass of the earth (actually $m/M_\odot$ ratio) would call for a revision in the actual length of AU in SI units. According to the best estimate to this date, $M_\odot = 328900.55$ times the mass of earth plus moon, giving the length of the semimajor axis of the earth's orbit $a = 1.000000034$ AU, where 1 AU = 149597870.66 km, and $GM_\odot = 1.32712438 \times 10^{20}$ m^{3}s^{-2}.

3. We must remember $K = k^2(1 + m/M_\odot)$. It differs slightly from planet to planet. So Kepler's third law is not exact, since K is not the same for all planets.

4.8 ACTUAL GEOMETRY OF ORBITS AND ORBITAL ELEMENTS

The plane of the earth's revolution around the sun, called the *ecliptic*, is taken to be the reference plane for the ecliptic (polar) coordinate system (see Fig. 4.6). *Celestial longitude* is measured along the ecliptic in an anticlockwise sense and the *celestial latitude* is the angular elevation or depression with respect to the ecliptic. The origin of the longitude is set by the line of intersection of the ecliptic and the *celestial equator*, the latter being the extended plane of the earth's equator. This origin defines the direction of the *Vernal equinox* (♈) or the *First Point of Aries*. The orbital plane of any other planet may make an angle i, called the *angle of inclination*, with the ecliptic. The two orbital planes, namely, those of the earth and of the planet concerned, intersect along a line called the *nodal line* or simply the *orbital node*. There are obviously two nodes: through one the planet moves from the south of the ecliptic to the north of it, called the *ascending* node, and through the other the planet moves from the north to the south of the ecliptic, called the *descending* node. The location of the ascending node on the ecliptic with respect to its standard origin (♈) is given by the angular quantity Ω, defining the *longitude of the ascending node*. Similarly, the location of the perihelion of the planet's orbit is expressed by the *longitude of the perihelion* (Γ), and the true distance of the perihelion from the sun by $q \equiv a(1 - e)$. Specifying further the orbital *eccentricity* e, and the *length of the semimajor axis* a (or equivalently, the *orbital period* P) determines the orbit precisely in space. The initialisation of the orbit is done by supplying the *epoch of the perihelion passage* of the planet, which is usually denoted by T_o.

In order to fix the orbit of a planet in space we thus require six independent quantities called the *orbital elements*. The six orbital elements are a (or P), e, Γ, Ω, i and T_o, all of which have been defined in the preceding paragraph. We list them again for a quick

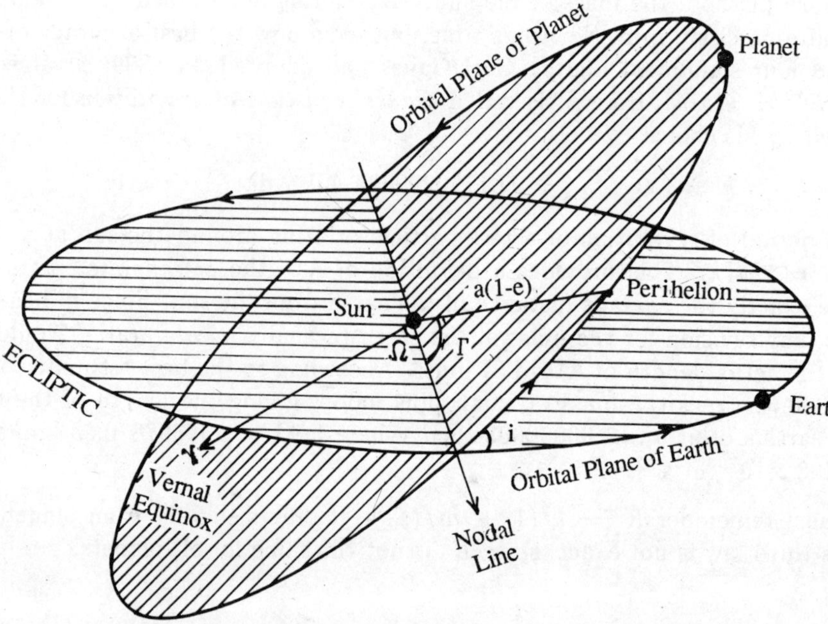

Fig. 4.6 Orbital elements of planetary orbits explained

reference.

a = semimajor axis, or P = orbital period = $2\pi\sqrt{a^3/K}$

e = eccentricity

Γ = longitude of the perihelion

Ω = longitude of the node

i = inclination of the orbit with respect to the ecliptic, and

T_o = epoch of a perihelion passage.

We now define the concept of *anomaly*. Anomaly, by definition is a measure of the angular advance of the planet centred at the sun, from its last perihelion passage. Usually, the following kinds of anomalies are defined:

True anomaly (ν) = actual angle at the focus = ∠HFM in Fig. 4.7 = same as θ in Eq. (4.33).

Mean anomaly (g) = $2\pi(t - T_o)/P$, where t is any instant of time, and

Eccentric anomaly (E) = ∠POM′ in Fig. 4.7.

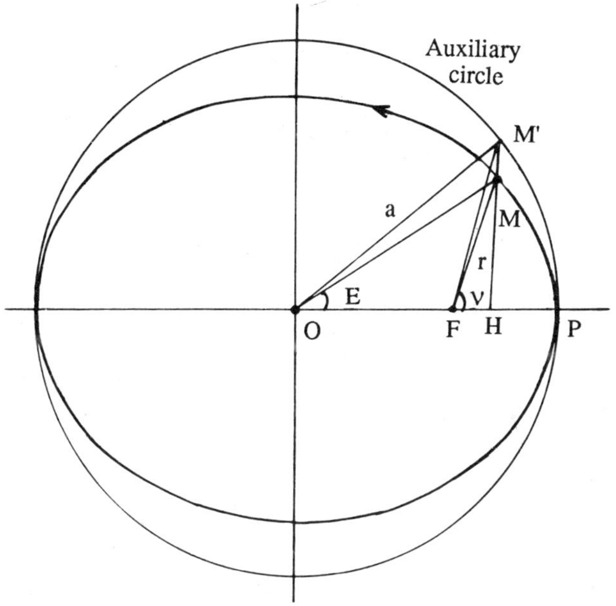

Fig. 4.7 The eccentric and true anomalies (E and ν) explained with reference to the auxiliary circle

Figure 4.7 shows an elliptic orbit with its auxiliary circle. An ellipse is known to be an *affine* transform of its auxiliary circle in the ratio $\sqrt{1 - e^2}$ to 1.

The three kinds of anomalies defined above are not independent. The relation between E and ν can be obtained as follows (refer to Fig. 4.7). We have

$$\begin{aligned} x &= \text{FH} = r\cos\nu = a(\cos E - e) \\ y &= \text{HM} = r\sin\nu = (a\sin E)\,(\text{HM}/\text{HM}') = a\sqrt{1 - e^2}\,\sin E \\ r &= \sqrt{x^2 + y^2} = a(1 - e\cos E) \end{aligned} \tag{4.42}$$

and from the 1st and the 3rd of Eq. (4.42)

$$\tan\frac{\nu}{2} = \sqrt{\frac{1 - \cos\nu}{1 + \cos\nu}} = \sqrt{\frac{1 + e}{1 - e}}\tan\frac{E}{2} \tag{4.43}$$

which is one of the required relations, namely the relation between the eccentric and true anomalies.

4.9 KEPLER'S EQUATION

Kepler's equation represents the relation between the eccentric and mean anomalies. This can be geometrically obtained as follows.

Referring to Fig. 4.7 one can write

$$\text{The sector area PFM} = \text{Areal velocity} \times (t - T_o) = \frac{1}{2}H(t - T_o) = \frac{1}{2}\frac{HgP}{2\pi}$$

Using Eq. (4.40) we get,

$$\text{The sector area PFM} = \frac{1}{2}a^2\sqrt{1 - e^2}\, g$$

Again, since,

$$\frac{\text{Sector area PFM}}{\text{Sector area PFM}'} = \sqrt{1 - e^2}$$

$$\text{the sector area PFM}' = \frac{1}{2}a^2\, g$$

It is easy to see, however, that

$$\text{sector area PFM}' = \text{sector area POM}' - \text{triangular area FOM}' = \frac{1}{2}a^2 E - \frac{1}{2}\,a^2 e \sin E$$

or

$$E - e\sin E = g = \frac{2\pi(t - T_o)}{P} \tag{4.44}$$

This is the famous Kepler's equation relating E to g, or equivalently E to t.

In the above we have derived Kepler's equation for an elliptic orbit. Equivalent forms for hyperbolic and parabolic orbits exist. We summarise them in Table 4.1 ($p = H^2/K$, Eq. (4.34)). In the parabolic case, the expression can be found in closed form and the equivalent of Kepler's equation is what is known as Barker's equation.

Table 4.1 Equivalent Forms of Kepler's Equation for Parabolic, Elliptic and Hyperbolic Cases

Quantity	*Elliptic case*	*Hyperbolic case*	*Parabolic case*
			$(s = \tan \nu/2)$
$r\cos\nu$	$a(\cos E - e)$	$a(\cosh F - e)$	$p(1 - s^2)/2$
$r\sin\nu$	$a\sqrt{1 - e^2}\,\sin E$	$a\sqrt{e^2 - 1}\,\sinh F$	ps
$t - T_o$	$P(E - e\sin E)/2\pi$	$\sqrt{a^3/K}(-F + e\sinh F)$	$\sqrt{p^3/K}\,s(1 + s^2/3)/2$

The entries in the last row are the equivalents of Kepler's equations for the above three cases. Usually one wants to determine the values of r and ν for a given value of t. Of course, all the orbital elements are usually known. So the first step is to use Kepler's Eq.

(4.44) or its approximate equivalent for hyperbolic and parabolic cases, for evaluating an intermediate quantity E, F or s. Since Kepler's equation is transcendental in E or F, it has to be evaluated numerically (or using any series expansion for E or F). Once E, F or s is determined, the first two rows of the above table give the values of $r\cos\nu$ and $r\sin\nu$ from which r and ν can be easily evaluated, thus specifying the location of the object on the orbit at any instant t.

4.10 CONSTRUCTION OF AN ORBIT FROM GIVEN SET OF INITIAL CONDITIONS

Any two-body problem in celestial mechanics is basically a two-dimensional problem, which means that only four independent initial conditions are to be specified. Let us suppose that the given or specified quantities are r_o and $\boldsymbol{v}_o$. Assuming $m \ll M_\odot$, we can take $K = GM_\odot$. The geometrical construction of the orbit in the plane of the drawing sheet involves the following steps:

(i) We can write the conditions for the nature of the orbit (see section 4.7) in terms of v_o and r_o and test which of the following conditions is satisfied.

$$\begin{aligned} v_o^2 &> \frac{2GM_\odot}{r_o} \quad \Rightarrow \quad \text{hyperbola} \\ &= \frac{2GM_\odot}{r_o} \quad \Rightarrow \quad \text{parabola} \\ &< \frac{2GM_\odot}{r_o} \quad \Rightarrow \quad \text{ellipse} \\ &= \frac{GM_\odot}{r_o} \quad \Rightarrow \quad \text{circle} \end{aligned}$$

The quantity $\sqrt{2GM_\odot/r_o}$ is called the *escape velocity* at r_o. Since G, $M_\odot$, r_o and v_o ($= |\boldsymbol{v}_o|$) are known, we can thus determine the nature of the orbit.

(ii) If the orbit is elliptical, the length of the semimajor axis is obtained from Eq. (4.39) and then do the following.

(iia) Draw a normal PN to the initial velocity direction $\boldsymbol{v}_o$ at P and join the point P to the force centre F (see Fig. 4.8). Now it is a *property* of the conic sections that the normal PN bisects the angle ∠FPF′, F′ being the other focus. Draw the line showing the direction of the secondary focus PF′ from P. Now, use another property of the ellipse namely FP + F′P $= 2a$. Since we know a and FP we can calculate the length F′P $= 2a - r_o = r_o'$, say. This gives the location of the secondary focus F′ on the line PF′.

(iib) Join FF′ by a line and extend it. This will be the major axis.

(iic) Again from the relation FF′ $= 2ae$, we can obtain the eccentricity e of the orbit. However we can complete the drawing of the ellipse using a piece of string with ends tied at F′ and F, and running a pencil through P with the cords always stretched to maximum.

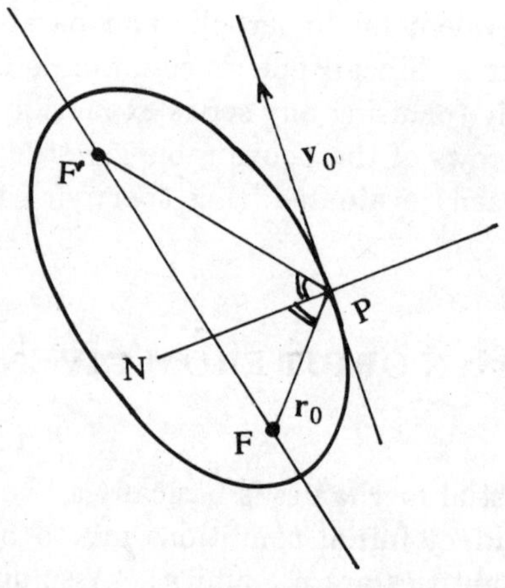

Fig. 4.8 Construction of the unique Keplerian orbit from the given initial position and velocity with respect to the force centre, whose strength in terms of GM is known.

For hyperbolic orbits rules (iia – c) are quite similar except that FP – FP$'$ = $2a$. For drawing a hyperbola, take a zipper tape instead of a piece of string. Open it half way though, nail at two points of the open arms. These two points must be the foci. Push the pencil through the zipper to draw the hyperbola.

4.11 KEPLER'S PROBLEM IN VELOCITY SPACE

We now obtain expressions for the radial and transverse velocities of the planet.

(i) Radial Velocity

Taking Eq. (4.34) as the equation of a conic section, the radial component of velocity of any planet is given by

$$v_r = \frac{dr}{dt} = \frac{He\sin\theta}{p} = \sqrt{\frac{K}{a(1-e^2)}}\, e\sin\theta$$

Thus v_r changes periodically as $\sin\theta$ does. The amplitude of variation is $\sqrt{K/a(1-e^2)}\,e$. Also, v_r is maximum when the particle is on the latus rectum ($\theta = \pm\pi/2$) and $v_r = 0$ at the pericenter and the apocenter.

(ii) Transverse Velocity

We have, for the transverse velocity v_θ,

$$v_\theta = r\,\dot{\theta} = \frac{\sqrt{pK}}{r} = \sqrt{\frac{K(1-e^2)}{a}}\,\frac{a}{r} \tag{4.46}$$

The speed of the planet is given by Eq. (4.39). Therefore,

$$a = \frac{Kr}{(2K - rv^2)} \quad \text{and} \quad e = \sqrt{1 - \frac{v_\theta^2 r^2}{Ka}}$$

(iii) Representations of a and e in Velocity Space

Since the circular velocity for a given r is $v_c = \sqrt{K/r}$, one can conveniently express all the velocity components in units of v_c and a in units of r. Thus, defining

$$\tilde{v}_r = \frac{v_r}{v_c} \quad \tilde{v}_\theta = \frac{v_\theta}{v_c} \quad \text{and } \tilde{a} = \frac{a}{r}$$

we finally have

$$\tilde{a} = \frac{1}{2 - \tilde{v}^2} \quad \text{and} \quad e = \sqrt{1 - \tilde{v}_\theta^2(2 - \tilde{v}^2)} \tag{4.47}$$

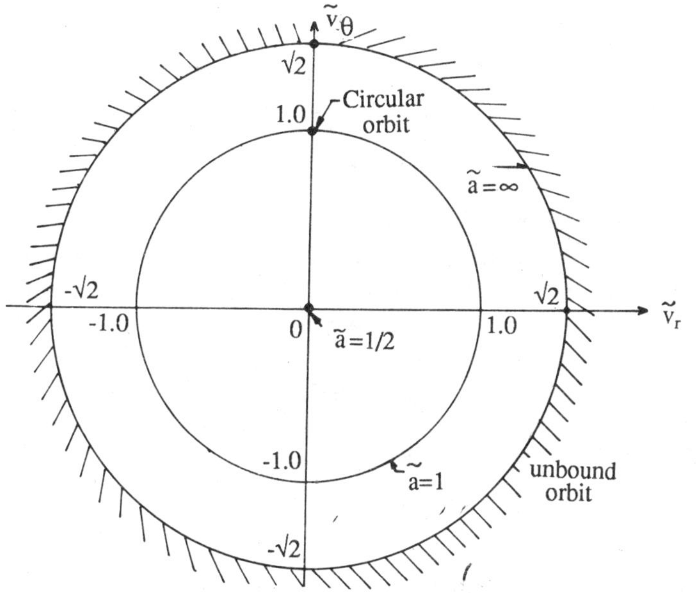

Fig. 4.9(a) Contours of constant lengths of semimajor axes of Keplerian orbits, drawn in the polar mapping of the velocity space

The range of $\tilde{a}$ is from 1/2 (for $\tilde{v} = 0$) to ∞ (for $\tilde{v} = \sqrt{2}$). The curves of constant semimajor axes are therefore circles as shown in Fig. 4.9(a). All circular orbits have $\tilde{v}_r = 0$ and $\tilde{v}_\theta = 1$ so they are all crowded at $y = 1$ on the y-axis. Orbits with $\tilde{v} \simeq \sqrt{2}$ (from below) have speeds very close to that of the escape speed. The curves of equal eccentricity intersect the y-axis twice, once at pericenter (top) and the other at apocenter (bottom). The pericenter has higher $\tilde{v}_\theta$ than the apocenter (see Fig. 4.9(b)). Since the pericenter is close to the boundary of the bounded orbits, the speed at pericenter approaches the escape speed that is why the motion of a comet can be approximated by a parabola when it comes very close to the sun.

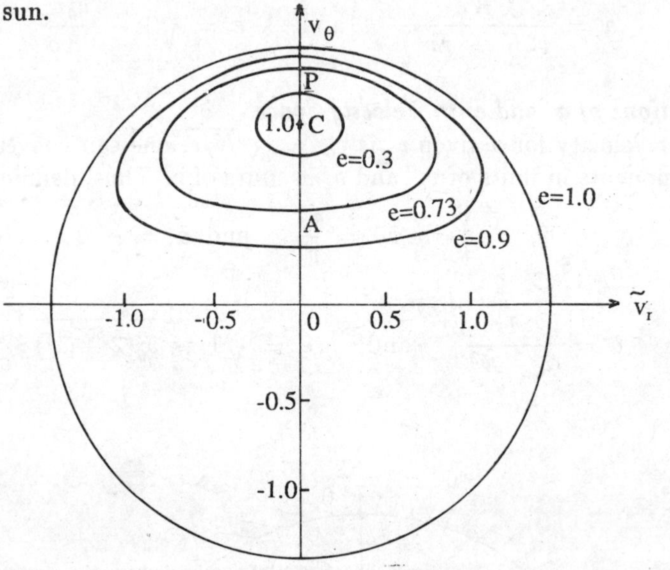

Fig. 4.9(b) Contours of iso-eccentricities of Keplerian orbits in the velocity space

(iv) Equation of Orbit in terms of v_θ

Since $H = r^2\dot{\theta}$ and $v_\theta = r\dot{\theta}$, one gets $v_\theta = H/r = Hu$, where H is a constant (see also Eq. (4.46)). So both u and v_θ will satisfy similar differential equations for orbits under any central force. We know that for attractive inverse square law, u satisfies

$$\frac{d^2u}{d\theta^2} + u = \frac{K}{H^2}$$

Hence v_θ should satisfy

$$\frac{d^2v_\theta}{d\theta^2} + v_\theta = \frac{K}{H}$$

which has a solution

$$v_\theta = \frac{K}{H} + D\cos(\theta - \theta_o)$$

D and θ_o being constants of integration. The value of v_θ simply oscillates about its mean value K/H with an amplitude D. As $v_\theta = H/r$, the above solution in v_θ corresponds to the equation for conic section $r = r(\theta)$. On comparison it turns out that $D = Ke/H$, e being the eccentricity of the actual orbit.

4.12 ORBITS OF ARTIFICIAL SATELLITES

(i) Geosynchronous Orbit

The orbit of any satellite around the earth that has an orbital period the same as that of the earth's diurnal rotation ($P_\oplus$) is called a *geosynchronous* orbit. Any such orbit must satisfy the condition,

$$P_\oplus = 23 \text{ hours } 56 \text{ minutes } 4.099(\pm 0.003) \text{ seconds}$$

From Kepler's third law applied to earth's satellites, the semimajor axis of the geosynchronous orbits are

$$a_s = \left(\frac{GM_\oplus}{4\pi^2}\right)^{1/3} \times P_\oplus^{2/3} = 42,164.2 \text{ km}$$

where $M_\oplus$ is the mass of the earth.

Given that the orbit is geosynchronous, it can have any eccentricity and any orientation with respect to the earth's equator.

(ii) Geostationary Orbit

The *geostationary* orbit of the satellite around the earth is such that the satellite remains stationary with respect to all points on the surface of the earth. This requires that the orbit must

(a) be geosynchronous, (b) be circular, and (c) stay over the geographical equator of the earth.

The height of such an orbit from the surface of the earth is therefore given by

$$a_s - R_\oplus = 35,786 \text{ km}$$

(iii) How to Put a Geostationary Satellite into Orbit

This is done in two steps :

(a) The satellite is directly launched into a low altitude orbit called the transfer orbit, having perigee $\sim$ 200 km above the earth's surface and apogee touching the geostationary orbit at a height of 35,786 km. This requires the eccentricity of the transfer orbit to be about 0.73.

(b) Since the final orbit has to be circular with radius $r = 42,164$ km a suitable thrust at the apogee of the transfer orbit is required. Referring to Fig. 4.9(b) and using Eq. (4.47), for $e = 0.73$ one obtains AC = OC/2 = 1.5 km/s. Thus for raising from A to C one needs to raise the velocity from 1.5 km/s to 3 km/s. The European rocket Ariane V is launched on the basis of the above principle.

The American Space Shuttle follows a different procedure. It starts orbiting the earth in a nearly circular orbit at a height of about 200 km from the ground (see Fig. 4.9(c)). Next, to put the satellite into an elongated transfer orbit would require an impulse to be given at the perigee. With reference to Fig. 4.9(b), the required move is to push the satellite from C to P which requires imparting $\tilde{v}_o = 0.3$, that is, 0.3 times the circular velocity corresponding to the initially put low orbit. Since $v_c = 7.9$ km/s for all circular orbits close to the surface of the earth, the required $v_o \simeq 2.4$ km/s. The final step, namely pushing from point A to C in Fig. 4.9(b) in order to transfer the satellite from its highly elliptical transfer orbit to the perfectly circular geostationary orbit the second step, is identical for both the European Ariane and American Space Shuttle programmes.

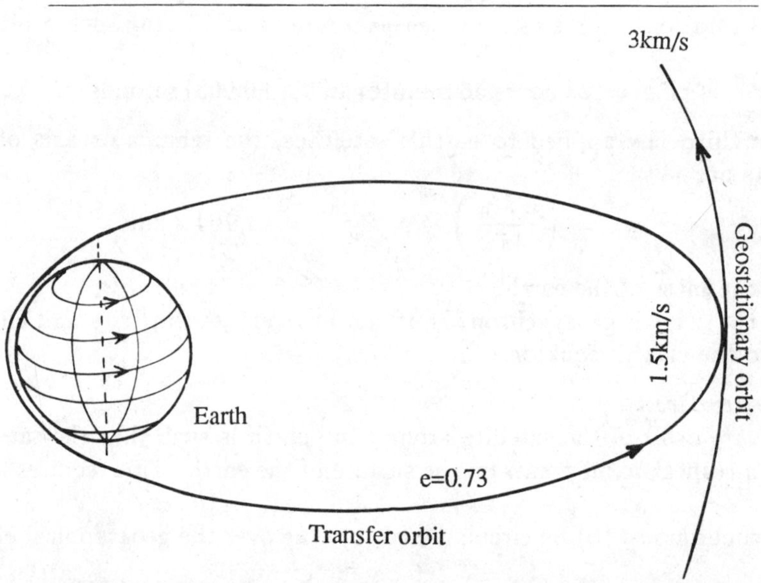

Fig. 4.9(c) Transfer orbit for launching an artificial satellite to the geostationary orbit

(iv) Why Should Rockets be Fired off from the Perigee rather than the Apogee ?

The equation of motion of a rocket, having a variable mass, moving in the free space under the rocket action of its own, is given by equation (I.27),

$$\boldsymbol{F} = m\frac{d\boldsymbol{v}}{dt} = \boldsymbol{u}_o \frac{dm}{dt}$$

where dm/dt is the rate of change of the total mass due to fuel consumption, $\boldsymbol{u}_o$ is the velocity of the ejected gas relative to the rocket, m is the mass of the rocket at any instant and $\boldsymbol{v}$ is the velocity of the rocket. The power gained at any instant due to the rocket action is given by

$$\boldsymbol{F} \cdot \boldsymbol{v} = (\boldsymbol{v} \cdot \boldsymbol{u}_o) \frac{dm}{dt}$$

For a constant rate of fuel consumption and the speed of the ejecta, the power gain is proportional to $\boldsymbol{v} \cdot \boldsymbol{u}_o = u_o v \cos\theta$, where θ is the angle between $\boldsymbol{v}$ and $\boldsymbol{u}_o$. In order to maximise the power gain, we need $\theta = 180^o$ (since $dm/dt < 0$) and v as large as possible. Since the speed of the satellite or of the rocket is highest at perigee, the rocket should be fired when it passes through the perigee for a maximum gain in kinetic energy in minimum possible time, that is, with the minimum expenditure of fuel.

4.13 PRECESSION OF THE PERIHELIA OF PLANETARY ORBITS DUE TO SMALL PERTURBING NONINVERSE SQUARE LAW OF FORCE

In this book, we have not dealt with the general theory of perturbation. We take this opportunity to introduce the readers to perturbative analysis, by way of studying the effect of small perturbation in a central force field. The theory of perturbation is based on the main premise that the perturbing component of force is negligibly small compared to the force contributed by the main source of force. Since we have already analysed in great detail the motion of particles under an inverse square law of central force, we take the main source of force as due to an agent producing the field of force that follows a perfect inverse square law of distance. The perturbing force is assumed to be sufficiently weaker in strength, and itself a central force obeying a different power law of distance.

The effect of including a small component of non-inverse-square-law of central force is that it would be directly related to the departure from the condition of orbital closure, or equivalently, to the nonconservation of the Runge-Lenz vector which always points towards the instantaneous pericenter of the orbit.

We know that for any central force,

$$r^2\dot{\theta} = H = \text{const.}$$

and

$$\ddot{r} - r\dot{\theta}^2 = F(r) \quad \left[= -\frac{K}{r^2} \text{ for the inverse square law}\right]$$

Therefore,

$$\ddot{r} - \frac{H^2}{r^3} = F(r)$$

We take a circular orbit of radius a so that $\ddot{r} = \dot{r} = 0$, which means $F(a) = -H^2/a^3$. Now for a small perturbation $r = a + \xi$, $\xi \ll a$, we have, to the first order of ξ/a,

$$\ddot{r} = \ddot{\xi}, \qquad F(a + \xi) = F(a) + \xi F'(a)$$

and

$$r^{-3} = (a + \xi)^{-3} = a^{-3}\left(1 - \frac{3\xi}{a}\right)$$

leading to

$$\ddot{\xi} - \left[F'(a) + \frac{3}{a}F(a)\right]\xi = 0$$

Hence the period of radial oscillation τ_r is given by that of ξ, that is,

$$\tau_r = 2\pi\left[-F'(a) - \frac{3}{a}F(a)\right]^{-1/2}$$

We know that r takes the extreme values on the line of apse. Let ψ be the apsidal angle swept by the radius vector $\boldsymbol{r}$ between the two consecutive passages through the line of apse in the same direction. We must then have,

$$\psi = \frac{1}{2}\tau_r\dot{\theta}$$

Since

$$F(a) = -\frac{H^2}{a^3} \quad \text{and} \quad \dot{\theta} = \frac{H}{a^2} = \sqrt{-\frac{F(a)}{a}}$$

we can express ψ as

$$\psi = \pi \left[3 + \frac{aF'(a)}{F(a)}\right]^{-1/2}$$

For an inverse square law, $F(r) = -K/r^2$ so that $aF'(a)/F(a) = -2$, giving,

$$\psi = \pi$$

This happens because the orbital period is equal to the period of radial oscillation.

Now let us allow some perturbation in the force term which follows a noninverse square law, namely

$$F(r) = F_o(r) + F_1(r)$$

say, where $F_o(r) = -K/r^2$ and $F_1(r)$ is any small correction to $F_o(r)$ with any other power law of r. Then upon substitution in the expression for ψ, and further simplification, we find

$$\psi = \pi \left[1 - \frac{F_1(a) + \frac{1}{2}aF_1'(a)}{F_o(a)}\right]$$

Thus the amount of precession per half period is $\psi - \pi$, and therefore, the angular velocity of precession is given by,

$$-\frac{2\pi}{P}\left[\frac{F_1(a) + \frac{1}{2}aF_1'(a)}{F_o(a)}\right] \equiv \Omega_p \tag{4.48}$$

where $2\pi/P$ is the orbital angular velocity $= \omega_p$. The sign of precession depends on those of the factors $[aF_1'(a)/F_1(a)]$ and $F_o(r)$. Thus, for attractive inverse square law of the main force $F_o(a)$,

$$\frac{aF_1'(a)}{F_1(a)} > -2$$

corresponds to the advance of perihelion, while

$$\frac{aF_1'(a)}{F_1(a)} < -2$$

gives retrograde motion of the perihelion.

Equation (4.48) is valid for nearly circular orbits for which eccentricity e can be neglected. We need a more general treatment for moderately eccentric orbits. This can be done using the Runge-Lenz vector in the following way.

Let us define the specific Runge-Lenz vector by,

$$\boldsymbol{A} = \boldsymbol{v} \times \boldsymbol{H} - K\hat{\boldsymbol{r}} \tag{4.49}$$

where $K = G(M_\odot + m)$, $\boldsymbol{H}$ = specific angular momentum $= \boldsymbol{r} \times \boldsymbol{p}/\mu$, μ = reduced mass, $\hat{\boldsymbol{r}} = \hat{\boldsymbol{i}}\cos\theta + \hat{\boldsymbol{j}}\sin\theta$ and $\hat{\boldsymbol{\theta}} = -\hat{\boldsymbol{i}}\sin\theta + \hat{\boldsymbol{j}}\cos\theta$, θ being the true anomaly measured from the perihelion and $\hat{\boldsymbol{i}}$ the unit vector along the major axis pointing from focus to the perihelion. On differentiation, Eq. (4.49) gives,

$$\frac{d\boldsymbol{A}}{dt} = \frac{d\boldsymbol{v}}{dt} \times \boldsymbol{H} - K\frac{d\hat{\boldsymbol{r}}}{dt} \tag{4.50}$$

since $\boldsymbol{H}$ is conserved for all types of central forces. Now, using the the vector equation of motion, $d\boldsymbol{v}/dt = -\nabla V(r)$, where the total gravitational potential

$$V(r) = -\frac{K}{r} + V_1(r) \tag{4.51}$$

with $V_1(r)$ = the potential for the small perturbing noninverse square law of force, Eq. (4.50) can be reduced to

$$\frac{d\boldsymbol{A}}{dt} = H\frac{\partial V_1}{\partial r}\hat{\boldsymbol{\theta}} \tag{4.52}$$

or

$$\frac{d\boldsymbol{A}}{d\theta} = \frac{d\boldsymbol{A}}{dt}\Big/\frac{d\theta}{dt} = r^2\frac{\partial V_1}{\partial r}\hat{\boldsymbol{\theta}}$$

Therefore, the change in the direction of the perihelion, say $\Delta\phi$, in the time in which θ changes from 0 to 2π (that is, during one orbital revolution) is given by the magnitude of the change in $\boldsymbol{A}$:

$$|d\boldsymbol{A}|\hat{\boldsymbol{k}} = |\boldsymbol{A}|\Delta\phi\hat{\boldsymbol{k}} = Ke\Delta\phi\,\hat{\boldsymbol{k}} = \int_0^{2\pi}\hat{\boldsymbol{i}} \times \left(\frac{d\boldsymbol{A}}{d\theta}\right)d\theta = \int_0^{2\pi} r^2\left(\frac{\partial V_1}{\partial r}\right)\cos\theta\, d\theta\,\hat{\boldsymbol{k}}$$

noting that $|d\boldsymbol{A}|\hat{\boldsymbol{k}} = \hat{\boldsymbol{i}} \times d\boldsymbol{A}$. So the angular velocity of precession of perihelion is

$$\Omega_p = \frac{\Delta\phi}{P} = -\frac{1}{2\pi e\sqrt{Ka^3}}\int_0^{2\pi} r^2 F_1(r)\cos\theta\, d\theta \tag{4.53}$$

where

$$F_1(r) = -\frac{\partial V_1(r)}{\partial r} \qquad r = \frac{a(1-e^2)}{1+e\cos\theta} \qquad \text{and} \qquad P = \frac{2\pi}{\omega_p} = 2\pi\sqrt{\frac{a^3}{K}}$$

Equation (4.53) is the most general expression for studying the effect on the motion of the perihelion of orbits in presence of any small perturbations of a perfect inverse square law of the main driving force.

4.13.1 Applications

(i) Precession of Perihelion of Equatorial Orbits of Earth's Satellites due to the Flattening of the Earth

The gravitational potential due to the flattened earth can be written as

$$V(r) = -\frac{\alpha}{r} - \frac{\beta}{r^3}$$

where

$$\alpha = GM_{\oplus}$$

and

$$\beta = \frac{1}{2}G(C - A)(1 - 3\cos^2\phi)$$

$\phi = 90^o - \lambda$, λ being the latitude, A and C are the two principal moments of inertia of the earth (for its derivation, see section 12.25), $(C - A)/A$ being the measure of the flattening. β is positive for orbits lying close to the equator.

The second term in $V(r)$ is our $V_1(r)$, which corresponds to a central force component having an inverse fourth power dependence on r, that is,

$$F_1(r) = -\frac{3\beta}{r^4}$$

This leads to the angular velocity of precession of the perihelion of the orbit of any geocentric object, be it an artificial geosatellite or the moon, to be given by

$$\Omega_p = \frac{3\beta}{\alpha^{1/2}a^{3/2}(1 - e^2)} \qquad (4.54a)$$

Actually, the moon's orbital perigee precesses due to the oblateness of the earth at a rate of about one complete revolution in every 8.8 years. The orbits of artificial satellites, being much closer to the earth and having appreciable eccentricity, can precess at a very fast rate, sometimes a few degrees of arc a day. Thus, if you spot a satellite moving across the sky in the twilight hours, it may be seen next day (or after a few days depending on the exact period of its revolution) but with a changed orientation in the sky.

Not only the orbits of satellites around the earth, but also the orbits of planets around the sun would show this effect, since the sun must have an oblate spheroid configuration, however small, due to its axial rotation. Brans Dicke had once proposed that the solar oblateness will measurably contribute to the precession of the perihelion of Mercury's orbit in space. When Dicke proposed it, sun's oblateness was reported to be a few parts in 10^{-5}, but the current estimates of the solar oblateness suggest an oblateness possibly no more than a few parts in 10^{-7}, in which case, the effect is quantitatively negligible compared to other factors that lead to the precession of the perihelion of Mercury's orbit.

(ii) The General Relativistic Correction to the Newtonian Force

The general theory of relativity, as proposed by Albert Einstein in 1916, suggested that Newton's law of gravitation is only approximately correct. When interpreted in terms of the force that acts on any test particle moving under the influence of the sun, the general relativistic equations of motion are found to contain some terms which are non-Newtonian, one of which is given by

$$F_1(r) = -\frac{4G^2M_\odot^2}{r^3c^2} = -\frac{\beta'}{r^3} \quad \text{(say)}$$

Hopefully, you can also derive this term without knowing much of the general theory of relativity, if you attempt to work out the problem no 6.9. The Keplerian orbits in general relativity are still planar in nature, but because of the above force term, there will be a precession of the line of apsis, the angular velocity of precession amounting to

$$\Omega_p = \frac{\beta'}{2(Ka)^{1/2}(1 - e^2)} \tag{4.54b}$$

The sun is so massive that this kind of general relativistic effect is discernible in the eccentric motions of all the inner planets. Mercury's orbit being closest to the sun and being highly eccentric compared to other planet's, the magnitude of this effect is quite appreciable. Even though the concept of general relativity was not there in the nineteenth century, this effect in the form of a discrepancy was first observationally estimated by Leverrier in 1860. By the turn of the nineteenth century, people had devised at least half a dozen explanations for this discrepancy, all of which turned out to be mere guess work and wrong, once Einstein came up with a prediction from his general theory of relativity in 1916, that exactly matched with this discrepancy, amounting to only 43 arc seconds per century.

(iii) Perturbation due to Other Planets on a Given Planet

In the presence of a third object a Keplerian pair experiences a perturbative force due to the third object. Since there are nine planets in the solar system the motion of any planet is disturbed by the eight other planets. The long term effect on the perihelion motion of any planet will be due to these extra perturbations, suitably smoothened over sufficiently long period of time.

We know that a lighted joss stick appears as a continuous streak of light when the lighted end is moved fast. Following this analogy, a planet of mass m orbiting in a circular orbit of radius R can be viewed as a ring of radius R with mass per unit length $\lambda = m/(2\pi R)$ to an observer who perceives centuries as short as blinks of an eye. The force field due to such a planetary ring can be shown to have the form

$$F_1(r) = \frac{\pi G\lambda r}{R^2 - r^2} \tag{4.55}$$

where R is the orbital radius of the perturbing planet (or equivalently, of the ring), r is the radial distance to any arbitrary point from the centre of the ring, and λ is the linear mass density of the perturbing planet along the ring (orbit). The value of the total perturbing force at the location of the perturbed planet (having an orbital radius a) then becomes,

$$F_1(a) = \pi G \sum_i \lambda_i \frac{a}{R_i^2 - a^2}$$

giving

$$F_1'(a) = \pi G \sum_i \lambda_i \frac{R_i^2 + a^2}{(R_i^2 - a^2)^2}$$

where the sum extends over all the perturbing planets: the ith one having mass m_i, orbital radius R_i and $\lambda_i = m_i/2\pi R_i$. The inverse square law of force due to the sun on the concerned planet is, of course,

$$F_o = -\frac{GM_\odot}{a^2}$$

We now apply this formulation to the study of the perihelion precession of the orbit of

Mercury around the sun. When put all the relevant numbers, taking from any elementary book on astronomy, the bracketed quantity in Eq. (4.48) becomes for Mercury's orbit,

$$\frac{F_1(a)}{F_o} + \frac{aF_1'(a)}{2F_o} = -9.84 \times 10^{-7}$$

due to all other planets, which results in $\Omega_p = 529$ arcsec/century. The general relativistic correction as given by Eq. (4.54b) gives another 43 arcsec/century. The secular motion of the ecliptic adds further to this 2.3 arcsec/century. Precession of the origin namely the Vernal equinox (for definition see section 4.8, and for calculation see section 12.24) adds -5029 arcsec/century. So the observed rate with respect to the moving equinox is

$$529 + 43 + 2.3 - (-5029) = 5603.3 \text{ arcsec/century}$$

However, the true advance of perihelion of Mercury in space (in an inertial frame) is only

$$529 + 43 = 572 \text{ arcsec/century}$$

Thus, the general relativistic contribution to the rate of advance of the perihelion of Mercury is quite insignificant compared to the total amount that one observes while sitting on the earth. Even so, this effect is considered to be one of the five major observable effects that the general theory of relativity has proposed so far and the first one to be tested straightway at the time of the proposition of the theory in 1916.

4.14 THE BASIC PHYSICS OF TIDES

The shore line of water over any sea beach is seen to advance and recede twice a day. This phenomenon is known as ocean tides. We aim to formulate the laws of ocean tides in the present section. Newton was the first person to give the correct reasoning for this phenomenon. However, his treatment lacked rigour, and was satisfactorily improved by Sir G. N. Darwin in 1883. The treatment is far from simple, even though its essence can be brought out in terms of simple laws of physics. In some text books, a discussion of tides is available, but it is either too simplified, or erroneously presented. More modern and sophisticated treatments are provided by A. T. Doodson (1921) and G. Godin (1972). In fact, all the quantitative details of oceanic tides have begun to be understood only very recently. The long term effects of tides on the motion of the satellites is one of the current interests of planetary scientists, as it is connected to the origin and internal structures of the planets and satellites. Tidal effects are also important in the studies of accretion discs around massive black holes, neutron stars, etc. So it is desirable that we have some proper introduction to the basic physics of tides.

A central force cannot be totally uniform inside any finite volume of space, be it far or near, large or small. Hence over the extent of any physical body, the applied gravitational force cannot be totally uniform. A rigid body can withstand this nonuniformity of force but a fluid body cannot. A fluid will gradually shift to a place where the applied force is relatively stronger. This is the basic cause of tides produced in any non-rigid body of finite size.

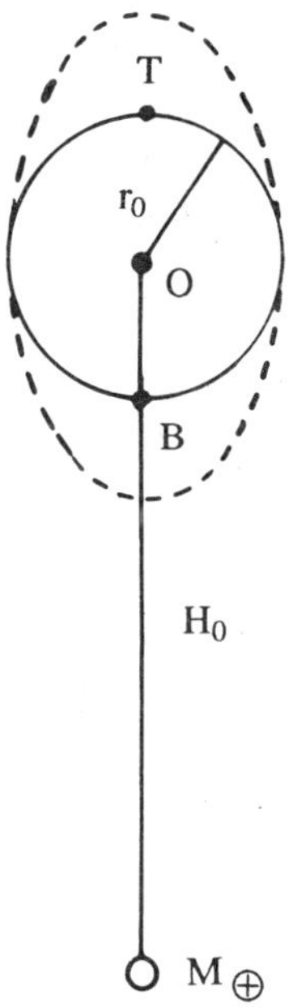

Fig. 4.10 Origin of tidal bulges explained

(i) Tidal Bulge

Let us now see the effect of the inverse square law of gravitation. Let there be a freely falling small spherical observatory in space under the action of the gravitational force of the earth (see Fig. 4.10). The field outside the earth is effectively due to a point mass placed at the centre of the earth. Let H_o be the distance from the centre of the earth to the centre of the observatory O and r_o be the radius of the freely falling observatory. The downward acceleration due to gravity at O is given by

$$g_o = \frac{GM_\oplus}{H_o^2} \qquad [M_\oplus \ : \ \text{mass of the earth}]$$

The downward acceleration due to gravity at the topmost point T of the observatory is

$$g_t = \frac{GM_\oplus}{(H_o + r_o)^2} = g_o\left(1 - \frac{2r_o}{H_o} + \cdots\right) < g_o \tag{4.56}$$

The downward acceleration due to gravity at the bottommost point B of the observatory is

$$g_b = \frac{GM_\oplus}{(H_o - r_o)^2} = g_o\left(1 + \frac{2r_o}{H_o} + \cdots\right) > g_o \tag{4.57}$$

Thus if a particle is released at O it will fall uniformly with the observatory with the downward acceleration g_o and always remain at the centre of the freely falling observatory. But if the particle is released at the top it will have less downward acceleration than at O and therefore it will start lagging behind O, with the result that its distance from O will be increasing with time with a relative acceleration $2r_o g_o/H_o$. On the other hand, if the particle had been released at B, it would have accelerated at a relatively higher rate than the one at O, the difference in the acceleration being again $2r_o g_o/H_o$. So the distance between T and B would gradually increase with time, while the centre and the equatorial plane remaining essentially unchanged. Or in other words, had the wall of the freely falling observatory been made up of fluid material or loose particles, the sphericity of the laboratory would have been destroyed and it would have assumed the shape of a prolate spheroid. This effect is called the *tidal bulging* of a large enough fluid sphere. The axis of the bulge is always aligned along the line of action of the externally acting perturbing central force, which again corresponds to the direction of the source of the tide raising perturbation.

(ii) Tidal Forces on the Earth due to the Moon

The earth is about 81 times more massive than the moon, their centre to centre separation is about 60 times the radius of the earth and their diameters are roughly in the r[illegible] 1:3. Since we are considering the tidal forces on earth due to moon, the surface of the earth now behaves like a freely falling observatory in the gravitational field of the moon.

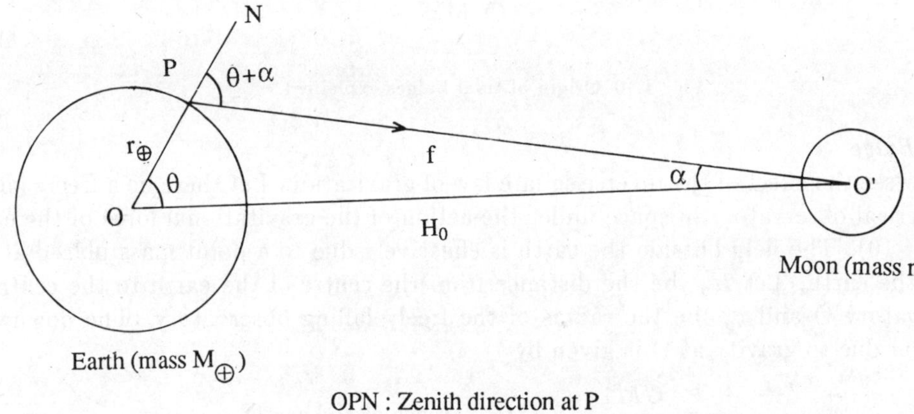

OPN : Zenith direction at P

∠ NPO'= Zenith distance of the moon

α = ∠ OOP : Angle subtended at moon by the radius vector OP

Fig. 4.11 The Gravitational force of the moon's attraction on a particle on the surface of the earth, depending on the zenithal angle and distance of the moon from the location of the particle

At any arbitrary point P on the surface of the earth (see Fig. 4.11) the magnitude of the gravitational acceleration due to the moon is

$$f = \frac{Gm}{R^2}$$

where m is the mass of the moon and

$$R = \text{distance O}'\text{P} = \sqrt{H_o^2 + r_o^2 - 2H_o r_o \cos\theta}$$

$$H_o = \text{OO}', \; r_o = \text{OP (earth's radius) and } \theta = \angle \text{O}'\text{OP}$$

Now the zenithal (or the radial) component of the acceleration at P is (see Fig. 4.11)

$$f_r = \frac{Gm}{R^2}\cos(\theta + \alpha)$$

and the horizontal (or the tangential) component is

$$f_\theta = -\frac{Gm}{R^2}\sin(\theta + \alpha)$$

which is algebraically positive in the direction of increasing θ. Using the following Taylor series expansion

$$\frac{1}{R^2} = \frac{1}{H_o^2}\left[1 - \frac{2r_o\cos\theta}{H_o} + \frac{r_o^2}{H_o^2}\right]^{-1} \simeq \frac{1}{H_o^2}\left[1 + \frac{2r_o\cos\theta}{H_o} + \cdots\right]$$

to the first order of approximation, and using

$$\sin\alpha = \frac{r_o\sin\theta}{R} \simeq \frac{r_o\sin\theta}{H_o} \quad \text{and} \quad \cos\alpha = \sqrt{1 - \sin^2\alpha} \simeq 1$$

and

$$\cos(\theta + \alpha) = \cos\theta\cos\alpha - \sin\theta\sin\alpha \simeq \cos\theta - \frac{r_o\sin^2\theta}{H_o}$$

$$\sin(\theta + \alpha) = \sin\theta\cos\alpha + \cos\theta\sin\alpha \simeq \sin\theta + \frac{r_o\sin\theta\cos\theta}{H_o}$$

we get, for f_r and f_θ,

$$\begin{aligned} f_r &= \frac{Gm}{H_o^2}\left[\cos\theta - \frac{r_o}{H_o}(1 - 3\cos^2\theta) + \cdots\right] \\ f_\theta &= \frac{Gm}{H_o^2}\left[-\sin\theta - \frac{r_o}{H_o}(3\sin\theta\cos\theta) + \cdots\right] \end{aligned} \tag{4.58}$$

The magnitude of the total acceleration at P due to the moon is given by,

$$f = \frac{Gm}{R^2} = \frac{Gm}{H_o^2}\left[1 + \frac{2r_o\cos\theta}{H_o} + \cdots\right] = f_o\left[1 + \frac{2r_o\cos\theta}{H_o} + \cdots\right] \tag{4.59}$$

where $f_o = Gm/H_o^2$ is the acceleration at O due to the moon at O′. We can write f_r and f_θ in terms of f_o:

$$\begin{aligned} f_r &= f_o\cos\theta - f_o\left(\frac{r_o}{H_o}\right)(1 - 3\cos^2\theta) \\ f_\theta &= -f_o\sin\theta - f_o\left(\frac{r_o}{H_o}\right)(3\sin\theta\cos\theta) \end{aligned} \tag{4.60}$$

These equations specify all the extra force components due to the presence of the moon in its orbit around the earth, acting at any point on the surface of the earth, apart from the earth's own gravitational and centrifugal forces that act at the same point. Obviously, the magnitude of f_r and f_θ are extremely tiny compared to g_{eff}, being only of the order of 2 – $4 \times 10^{-6} g_{\text{eff}}$.

(iii) The Equilibrium Tidal Heights due to the Moon

The first terms in f_r and f_θ are merely the two components of $\boldsymbol{f}_o$ and they correspond to the same free fall acceleration of P as of O. They are like the first term g_o appearing in the expressions for g_t and g_b in the example of the freely falling observatory. We have seen that this term does not correspond to the tidal force. However if the observatory were held fixed in space with respect to the force centre, then O would no longer have been accelerated and therefore g_t and g_b would have been fully manifested. Since neither the moon nor the earth is fixed in space, they are all truly freely falling observatories (remember that all free orbits including the circular ones are freely falling trajectories, falling due to the action of the centripetal force) and the first terms in the expressions for f_r and f_θ correspond to the commonly shared acceleration of all points of the body, that is, of the earth as a whole. But by definition, tidal forces are the nonuniform part of the total force, so any constant force can be subtracted or added to the total force without affecting the tidal behaviour in the slightest. So the truly differential accelerations are given by the second term in the expressions for f_r and f_θ and are called the primary terms of tidal acceleration.

Again, by definition, f_r acts radially at P and merely adds (insignificantly though !) to the local gravity of the earth so that the weight of all bodies resting at P increases by the amount $[-f_o(r_o/H_o)(1 - 3\cos^2\theta)]$ per unit mass of the bodies and hence this component cannot produce any visible change in the value of g_{eff}, the change occurring only at the eighth significant digit. However, the other tidal component f_θ is not counteracted by any reaction force in that direction. This is therefore bound to produce a free motion of any fluid at P along the tangential direction. Hence the primary component of the tide producing acceleration is given by the second term in the second expression in Eq. (4.60),

$$f_\theta\Big|_{\text{tide}} = -\frac{3}{2}\frac{Gmr_o}{H_o^3}\sin(2\theta) \tag{4.61}$$

where θ is roughly the zenith angle of the moon as seen from the point P on the earth. The distribution of this force is shown in Fig. 4.12. The magnitude of the tidal force becomes maximum at $\theta = 45^o$ and 135° and it vanishes at $\theta = 0^o$, 90° and 180°. Basically the fluid is pulled in two opposite directions in the two hemispheres divided by the plane passing through the centre of the earth and perpendicular to the earth moon synodic line. Fluid will tend to accumulate in both the sublunar and antilunar regions.

The work done by the tidal force per unit mass of the fluid between $\theta = \pi/2$ and

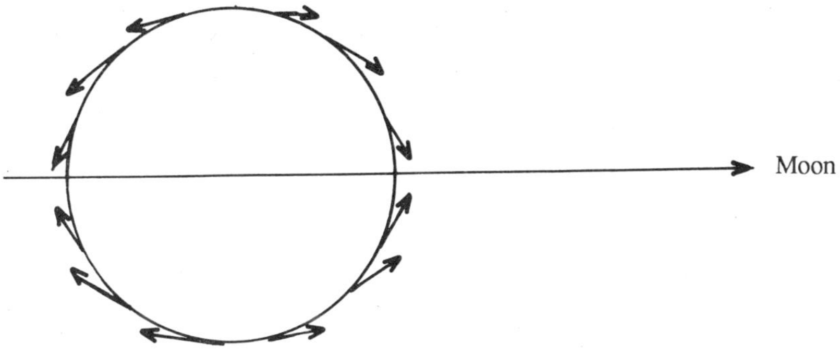

Fig. 4.12 The angular distribution of the θ-component of the lunar tidal acceleration over the surface of the earth in a meridional plane of the moon

$\theta = z =$ the zenithal angle of the moon when it reaches the highest point in the sky,

$$\begin{aligned} W_t &= \int_{\pi/2}^{z} f_\theta\Big|_{\text{tide}} r_o \, d\theta \\ &= -\frac{3}{2}\frac{Gmr_o^2}{H_o^3}\cos^2 z \end{aligned} \tag{4.62}$$

This work must be equal to $-gh_{\text{tide}}$, where h_{tide} is the *height of tide* measured from its lowest level

$$\begin{aligned} h_{\text{tide}} &= \frac{3}{2}\left(\frac{m}{M_\oplus}\right)\left(\frac{r_o}{H_o^3}\right)^3 r_o \cos^2 z \\ &\simeq 0.54 \text{ metres for } z = 0 \end{aligned} \tag{4.63}$$

Thus as obtained in Eq. (4.63), about 0.5 m would have been the maximum tidal height (that is, the height difference between the low and the high tides) if the earth was not rotating (which is the condition for equilibrium tide) and was covered uniformly with water. Because of the fast rotation of the earth, the equilibrium tidal configuration is never achieved, there always remains a lag as a huge mass of oceanic water has to move physically from one region to another in order to keep the tidal bulge aligning as close to the direction of the moon as possible. The *tidal lag* is represented by an angle δ, which amounts to about 2.16 degrees of arc for the oceanic tides on the earth.

There is another big effect due to the nonequilibrium nature of the oceanic tides. While the huge mass of water physically transports itself from one place to another, it interacts dynamically with the bottom surface of the sea as well as the topography of the shore line. During the process of filling and emptying various cavity like regions, the phenomenon of cavity resonance on large scale becomes an important factor in locally enhancing the height of tides over and above the height of the equilibrium tide. The enhancement due to the peculiarities of the land profile, resonance due to shallow water trapped near fjords, gravity waves, etc. can be as large as a factor of 10 – 50 compared to the height of the equilibrium tide. The calculations of all these effects are not at all easy to perform, and therefore, some semiempirical fits for the amplitudes of different modes of tides are obtained for each place separately, which are used to prepare the charts for the tidal prediction.

(iv) Why are there Two Tides a Day?

The earth rotates about its spin axis passing through the geographical north pole once a day, while the moon orbits the earth only once every 27.32 days. Therefore every point on the earth's surface, particularly the equatorial and midlatitude regions must pass through one sublunar and one antilunar bulge every day, thereby experiencing two tides a day. Since the moon advances by about 13° eastward every day, the sublunar point also advances in space by the same amount and the earth has to rotate this extra 13° (which takes about 52 minutes) to reach the sublunar point the next day. Hence two consecutive high tides are on an average separated by 12 hrs and 26 mins and two consecutive sublunar high tides by 24 hrs and 52 mins. The sublunar tides are known as primary tides and the antilunar tides as the secondary tides.

When the tides over a given place achieve their maximum heights during any time of the day or night depending on the time of the upper and lower meridional passages of the moon over that place, they are called high tides and when the water recedes to the lowest levels such tides are called low tides. Usually the tidal heights are measured from the zero level set by the lowest possible of all low tides, observed through years. The amplitudes of the high and low tides are not the same every day. It follows a monthly as well as yearly cycle. The monthly variation of the tidal amplitude of the high and low tides is due to the interference of the solar contribution of tide to the lunar one. Since the sun and the moon do not come over the meridian at the same time everyday, their tides are not added in phase; so sometimes the effects are cancelling and at other times enhancing the lunar tide. The seasonal and yearly variations are due to the change in the relative orientation of the diurnal track of the moon over any place, and the variation of its distance from the earth.

The height of the highest of all high tides on the east coast of the Arabian sea is about 5.5 m during the quiet conditions of the climate. Inside the fjords, or between a big island and its nearest mainland, or during storms, the tidal heights can reach anywhere between 10 m and 50 m.

(v) Relative Tidal Heights due to the Moon and the Sun

The relative tidal forces are determined essentially by the factor mr_o/H_o^3, where m is the mass of the tide raising body, r_o is the radius of the object on which tide is raised and H_o is the distance between them. Therefore,

$$\frac{\text{Tidal forces due to moon}}{\text{Tidal forces due to sun}} = \frac{[m/H_o^3]_{\text{moon}}}{[m/H_o^3]_{\text{sun}}} = \frac{\rho_m}{\rho_s}\left(\frac{\theta_m}{\theta_s}\right)^3 \tag{4.64}$$

where θ_m and θ_s are the angular radii of the moon and the sun respectively (as seen from the earth) and ρ_m, ρ_s their average mass densities. Since the sun and the moon have almost equal angular sizes as seen from the earth, that is,

$$\theta_m \simeq \theta_s$$

and therefore,

$$\frac{\text{Tidal forces due to moon on earth}}{\text{Tidal forces due to sun on earth}} = \frac{\rho_m}{\rho_s} = \frac{3.34 \times 10^3 \text{ kg/m}^3}{1.41 \times 10^3 \text{ kg/m}^3} \simeq 2.5$$

During the new moons and the full moons the sun, the moon and the earth are nearly aligned and the two tidal forces add to each other. But during the quarters, the sun and the moon are at right angles with respect to the earth and as a result produce an opposing tidal effect. The high tides during any new moon and full moon are called *spring* tides and are supposed to be $(2.5 + 1.0)/(2.5 - 1.0) = 7/3$ times higher than the *neap* tides that occur during the quarter moons. There are also seasonal and other long term variations in the tidal heights due to the variation in the maximum altitude and distance of the sun and the moon from any given place on the surface of the earth.

(vi) Solid Tides

Since no object is perfectly rigid, there will always be some tidal distortions in the solid earth too, due to the moon (and also the sun). But the distortions due to solid tides hardly amounts to a few centimetres and occur inside the body of the earth. However, for the satellites of Jupiter or of Saturn, these distortions (caused by the respective planets) can be quite substantial, so much so that no satellite can even survive inside a certain distance from the parent planet. More distant ones, such as the Io of Jupiter, can show volcanic effects purely due to tidal heating of their mantle. It is believed that the rings of Saturn, Jupiter, Uranus and Neptune have formed due to tidal disruption in the past of some of their regular satellites. The limiting distance from the planet within which a liquid satellite disrupts completely due to tidal effects is called the *Roche limit* which was first deduced by Roche and was found by him to be about 2.46 times the radius of the parent planet. In fact, all the major rings of Saturn lie within this critical Roche limit for Saturn. A simplified idea of how this limit can be derived has been outlined in the problem no 4.25.

(vii) Tidal Torque, Tidal Dissipation and Lengthening of Day

Since the earth is rotating, the tidal bulge produced by the moon has to shift continually on the surface of the earth in order to keep itself up in phase with the moon. The axis of the bulge, which should always point toward the moon, has to shift with time at a rate of about 1° every 4 minutes carrying the required amount of oceanic water with it. In the process the motion of water experiences the viscous forces of drag within itself and at its contact surface with the sea bed. This has got two effects. (a) The tidal bulge lags behind the arrival of the moon on the meridian (Meridian is the vertical plane passing through the north south points). (b) This angular lag (δ) is the cause of the tidal torque that acts on the earth and is of course produced by the moon. The moon experiences the reaction in the form of an equal and opposite tidal torque. The magnitude of the tidal torque is given by

$$\Gamma \propto \frac{Gmr_o^5}{2H_o^6} \sin 2\delta \tag{4.65}$$

The constant of proportionality, called the Love number (usually denoted by k_2), differs from object to object; for the earth it is 0.9, for the moon it is about 0.06. The value of δ for the earth due to lunar tide is about $2^o.16$. This torque results in a secular (meaning longterm) increase of the earth's period of rotation by about 2.4 millisecond/century or about an hour every 160 million years. So about 160 million years ago, the length of the day was about 23 hours! However over smaller time intervals, say over a few months, years, or even decades, earth's rotation period fluctuates with an amplitude approximately 100 times larger than the above secular one. Such short-term fluctuations are possibly due to atmospheric motions, oceanic currents, tectonic movements inside the earth, moon's orbital nutation, etc. Consequently we have to add or subtract 1 leap second every few months or even few years. However the secular slowing down of the earth's angular speed of rotation will continue until a steady state is reached for which $\delta = 0$ (see Eq. (4.65), the tidal torque vanishes, that is, the tidal bulge is always pointing toward the moon). This will be identically satisfied only when the length of the day on earth becomes equal to the length of the month, which is the orbital period of revolution of the moon around the earth. The moon has already attained this state because of the tidal torques of far greater amplitude produced by the earth on the moon during its early phases, and now from the earth we always see the same face of the moon. The moon is tidally locked to the earth. Similarly, there will also come a day when the moon will see the same face of the earth. For this to happen, we may have to wait for another 4 billion years or so.

4.15 SCATTERING IN A CONSERVATIVE CENTRAL FORCE FIELD

(i) Scattering Cross-section

Scattering is a process in which an entity changes its direction of motion due to its close approach to or encounter with an agent which interacts via its own force fields. Usually classical particles as well as quantum objects like photons, electrons, etc. are subject to scattering by suitable agents called scatterers. In any physical encounter, two things may happen; the particle is either scattered or absorbed by the agent. If there is any stream (or flux or beam) of particles, the total loss from the incident stream must be the sum of the losses due to scattering and absorption. This sum effect is called the extinction, and by definition,

$$\text{extinction} = \text{scattering} + \text{absorption}$$

Now we define a few quantities.

Flux density: This is also called the intensity. It is the number of particles that are emitted in a direction implied by their velocity $\boldsymbol{v}$, through unit area normal to $\boldsymbol{v}$ and per unit solid angle around the direction of $\boldsymbol{v}$.

If the incident beam is sent in a particular direction with some definite velocity $\boldsymbol{v}$ of each particle and the number density at any instant of time inside the beam, say n_o, then the *incident intensity I* is defined to be

$$\begin{aligned} I(v) &= n_o\,|v| \\ &= \text{total number of particles passing through a unit area} \\ &\quad \text{normal to } v \text{ per unit time.} \end{aligned} \tag{4.66}$$

However, if the incident beam has got a spread in the solid angle then the incident intensity has to be defined as

$$I(\Omega, v) = n(\Omega)\,|v| \tag{4.67}$$

For the unidirectional beams, after the interaction with the scattering agent some of the particles are deflected, some might even be absorbed by the agent itself and the rest will still follow the incident direction. The intensity of the last component called the emergent intensity is always less than or at most equal to the incident intensity, assuming that the speed of the particles remains the same at large distances from the force centre of scattering.

Total scattering cross-section: The actual time rate of loss of particles due to scattering in different directions may be characterised by the effective loss of the area normal to the direction of the beam that originally contained these scattered particles. This loss of total effective area from the incident beam cross-section is called the ***cross-section*** of scattering. In other words, if the total cross-section of scattering is said to be σ_T, it simply means that the number of particles that were incident (per unit time) through the cross-sectional area σ_T are now missing due to the fact that they are continually scattered away in directions other than the incident beam direction. So by definition

$$\begin{aligned}\sigma_T &= \frac{\text{Total number of particles scattered per unit time}}{\text{Total number of particles incident per unit normal area per unit time}} \\ &= \frac{\text{Total number of particles scattered per unit time}}{\text{Incident intensity}}.\end{aligned} \tag{4.68}$$

Differential scattering cross-section: One may also define a *differential* scattering cross-section $\sigma(\Omega)$ if the scattering in a particular direction is to be estimated. By definition,

$$\sigma(\Omega)\,d\Omega = \frac{\begin{array}{l}\text{Total number of particles scattered per unit time into the solid angle}\\ d\Omega \text{ around the direction defined by } \mathbf{\Omega}\end{array}}{\text{Incident intensity}} \tag{4.69}$$

Basically $\sigma(\Omega)d\Omega$ corresponds to the effective loss of normal area from the incident beam, from which particles are continually scattered into the solid angle $d\Omega$ around the direction implied by $\mathbf{\Omega}$. It is easy to see that

$$\sigma_T = \int \sigma(\Omega)\,d\Omega \qquad \text{or} \qquad \frac{d\sigma_T}{d\Omega} = \sigma(\Omega) \tag{4.70}$$

It is to be noted that in the spherical polar coordinates with its polar axis coinciding with the incident beam direction, $d\Omega = \sin\theta\, d\theta\, d\phi$. If there is ϕ-symmetry in the problem $d\phi$ can be integrated from 0 to 2π and $d\Omega$ can be expressed as a function of θ alone, and it will no longer represent a particular direction but a particular conical section between $\theta = \theta$ and $\theta = \theta + d\theta$. In this case $d\Omega$ becomes

$$d\Omega = 2\pi \sin\theta\, d\theta \tag{4.71}$$

(ii) Scattering in a Conservative Central Force Field

The scattering of individual particles is a two body problem, one partner of which is the force centre and the other partner is the particle itself. We know that a two body problem can always be reduced to a one body problem with the net result that the scattering agent (force centre) can be assumed to be fixed in space and the scattered particle has to assume the reduced mass of the system. Using this one particle formulation we represent F as the force centre in Fig. 4.13, which remains fixed and the scattered particles fly past F following different trajectories. Since the particles are coming from infinity with some nonzero velocity $\boldsymbol{v}_o$, the original specific energy of individual particles $E' = v_o^2/2 > 0$. If a particle has to avoid hitting the force centre directly it must not travel in the direction passing through the force centre when it is at infinity. Vectorially speaking, this would mean that $\boldsymbol{r} \times \boldsymbol{v}_o$ should not be equal to zero for that particle ($\boldsymbol{r}$ measured from the force centre). But $\boldsymbol{r} \times \boldsymbol{v}_o = \boldsymbol{H}$, which is the specific angular momentum of the system and is a constant of motion for any kind of the conservative central force. This enables us to define a parameter s such that

$$H = |\boldsymbol{H}| = v_o s$$

s is called the *impact parameter* of the particle and is simply the minimum distance of separation between F and the trajectory of the particle, had there been no force field operative at F. We thus have

$$H = v_o s = s\sqrt{2E'} \tag{4.72}$$

E', which is the specific energy (energy per unit reduced mass), is also a constant of motion, provided, of course, that the force field is conservative which we have assumed it to be.

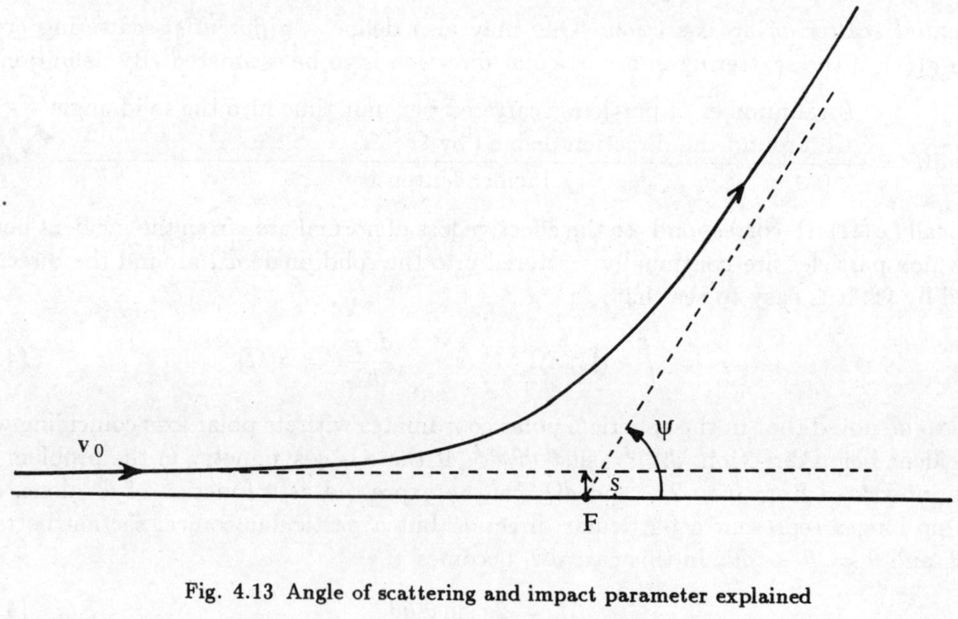

Fig. 4.13 Angle of scattering and impact parameter explained

The angle of scattering, ψ, is defined to be the angle between the incident and the scattered directions. Now, if θ is the angle between the radius vector of the particle at any instant and its initial radius vector while at infinity or at very large distance, then θ varies from 0 to $\pi - \psi$. From Eq. (4.22) we know that

$$\theta_{max} = 2 \int_{r_{min}}^{\infty} \frac{dr}{r^2 \sqrt{2H^{-2}\{E' - V(r)\} - r^{-2}}}$$

where $V(r)$ is the potential at r due to the central force acting at F, and r_{min} = minimum distance of approach of the particle with respect to F (see Fig. 4.13). Obviously $r_{min} \neq s$, but in general $r_{min} = r_{min}(s)$. Therefore, we get for the angle of scattering

$$\psi = \pi - \theta_{max} = \pi - 2 \int_{r_{min}}^{\infty} \frac{dr}{r^2 \sqrt{2E'H^{-2} - 2V(r)H^{-2} - r^{-2}}} \tag{4.73}$$

For a given incident intensity, $\boldsymbol{v}_o$ and hence E' are the same for all particles but the specific angular momentum $\boldsymbol{H}$ will differ from particle to particle as the impact parameter s varies. From Eq. (4.73) it is now apparent that, as $r_{min} = r_{min}(s)$,

$$\psi = \psi(s)$$

that is, the angle of scattering is different for different impact parameters and the same for particles with the same impact parameter, provided E' (or v_o) remains the same for all the incident particles. The geometry of this situation has got an azimuthal symmetry about the direction of v_o passing through the force centre F. Now, from the definition of the differential scattering cross-section we see that, due to azimuthal symmetry, the area lost from the incident beam due to scattering at an interval of the scattering angles ψ and $\psi + d\psi$, is the same as the area of the annular ring corresponding to the range of impact parameters s and $s - ds$, so that,

$$\sigma(\psi) 2\pi \sin\psi |d\psi| = 2\pi\, s\, |ds|$$

or

$$\sigma(\psi) = \frac{s}{\sin\psi} \left| \frac{ds}{d\psi} \right| \tag{4.74}$$

where $\psi = \psi(s)$ is given by Eq. (4.73).

(iii) Scattering by Inverse Square Law of Force

We know that $E' > 0$ corresponds to a hyperbolic orbit, for a force field given by $F(r) = -K/r^2$, where K can be negative or positive according to the repulsive or attractive nature of the force field. In Fig. 4.14, the left hand track represents the path of the particle moving in an attractive type of the inverse square law of force fields, operative at F. For the same set of parameters, the right hand track would correspond to the path to be followed by the particle in a repulsive force field, operative also at the same location F. These two curves are symmetric about their common directrix, except that the signs of the curvature are the opposite. The equations for such a pair of orbits are given by (cf. Eq. (4.34) for the generality of the solutions)

$$r = \frac{p}{e\cos\nu \pm 1}$$

where the + sign corresponds to the attractive field and the − sign to the repulsive field.

The asymptotes $r \to \infty$ correspond to $\nu \to \nu_o$ given by, $\cos\nu_o = \pm e^{-1}$, where the + sign is for the repulsive field and the − sign for the attractive field. For the attractive force field we have $\psi = 2\nu_o - \pi$, but for the repulsive field $\psi = \pi - 2\nu_o$. Substituting the respective expressions for ν_o, we find for both the cases

$$\psi = \pi - 2\cos^{-1}\left(\frac{1}{e}\right) \tag{4.76}$$

Thus for both the repulsive and the attractive cases, the deflection is the same (which is obvious from Fig. 4.14), and it depends only on the eccentricity of the hyperbolic track of the particle under consideration. Using Eq. (4.37) in Eq. (4.76), we can eliminate e and express ψ as a function of E' and H :

$$\cot^2\left(\frac{\psi}{2}\right) = e^2 - 1 = \frac{2E'H^2}{K^2}$$

Since $H = v_o s = s\sqrt{2E'}$, we can write for the impact parameter

$$s = \frac{H}{\sqrt{2E'}} = \frac{K\cot(\psi/2)}{2E'} \tag{4.77}$$

Equation (4.77) represents our long sought for explicit functional form of $\psi(s)$, a result obtained without performing the integration for evaluating the integral in Eq. (4.73).

Using the expression given in Eq. (4.77) for s the RHS of Eq. (4.74) is evaluated to give

$$\sigma(\psi) = \frac{1}{4}\left(\frac{K}{2E'}\right)^2 \csc^4(\psi/2) \tag{4.78}$$

Equation (4.78) is the Rutherford formula for the differential scattering of particles in the force field of an inverse square law of force (derived by Ernst Rutherford in 1909).

Obviously, $\sigma(\psi)$ given by Eq. (4.78) blows up as $\psi \to 0$, the reason being that *all* particles are scattered, however nominal be their angle of scattering. Note that $s \to \infty$ as $\psi \to 0$ implying that particles that are incident through an infinite cross-section are bound to be scattered through a vanishingly small angle ($\psi \sim 0$). Thus we have,

$$\sigma_T = \int_{\psi_o}^{\pi} \sigma(\psi)\, 2\pi \sin\psi\, d\psi \longrightarrow \infty, \qquad \text{as } \psi_o \to 0$$

This divergence exists for any central force with $f(r) \propto r^{-n}$, n being any positive exponent.

For further study of small angle scattering, one is referred to two articles in the *American Journal of Physics*: volume 43, page 328, and volume 45, page 1122.

(iv) Enhancement of Geometrical Scattering Cross-section due to Inverse Square Law of Attraction and the Cross-section for Capture

We describe it by way of giving an worked out example. The idea is that, if a swarm of particles is intercepted by a rigid sphere, it is the geometrical cross-section of the sphere that causes the interception. But if the sphere is massive enough to have its escape velocity

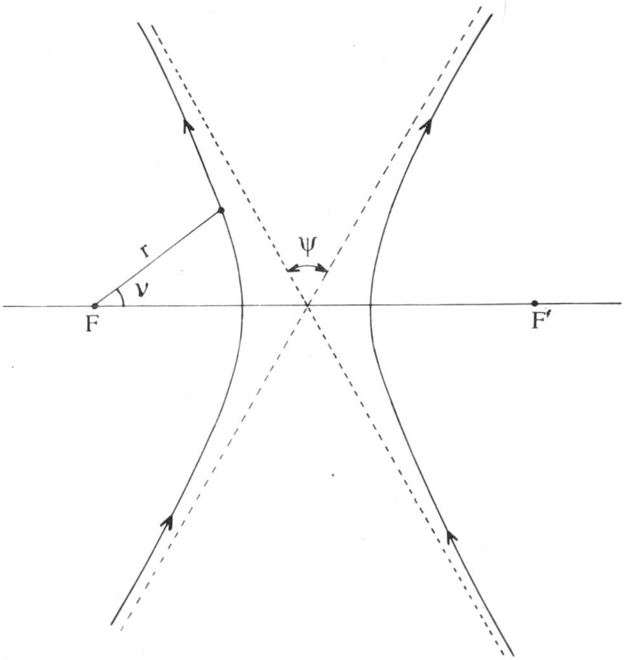

Fig. 4.14 Symmetry of the paths of scattering in a repulsive (right track) and an attractive (left track) force fields of identical strength situated at F, for particles incident with identical impact parameter and identical initial speed

compared to the velocity of projectile particles, then the effective cross-section of interception is enhanced. In fact, as would be shown below, the massive body can simply swallow all particles that have an impact parameter much larger than the geometrical radius of the body. The cross-section for swallowing is called the capture cross-section.

Let the earth be streaming through a swarm of meteorites with a relative speed v_o. Because of the conservation of specific angular momentum we get,

$$v_o s = v_m r_o$$

v_m being the speed at closest approach (see Fig. 4.15), s the impact parameter, $r_o = r_{\min}$ ($= r_{\oplus}$ here) and

$$v_m^2 = v_o^2 + \frac{2Gm}{r_o} = v_o^2 + v_e^2$$

by the law of the conservation of energy. Here v_e is the earth's escape speed at r_o. Hence,

$$\pi s^2 = \pi r_o^2 \left[1 + \frac{v_e^2}{v_o^2}\right] \tag{4.79}$$

So the capture cross-section is enhanced compared to its geomerical value by a factor > 1.
Since the sun is speeding through the local interstellar medium with a speed of about 23

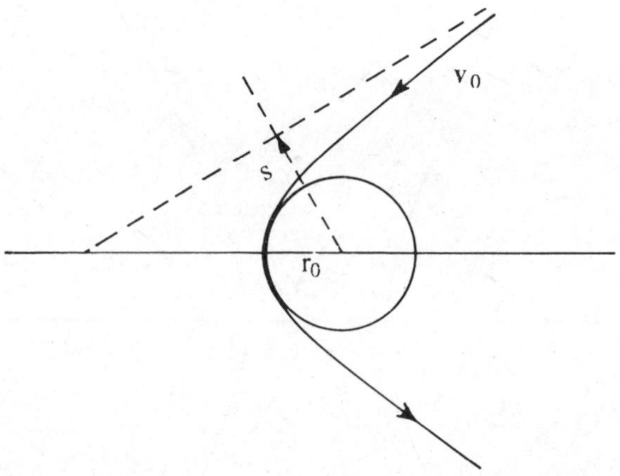

Fig. 4.15 Critical impact parameter for gravitational capture

km/s (towards the constellation Hercules) compared to its own escape speed which is about 617.6 km/s, it will gobble up everything that comes within a radius $s \approx 26.9\ R_\odot$, that is, within about 27 times its geometrical radius, but for the earth $v_e = 11.2$ km/s, and hence this enhancement will hardly be 10% of its own radius.

(v) Conserved Quantities in a Two Body Collision driven by a Central Force

As we have seen in section 4.2, for the two body central force problem the velocity of the centre of mass (CM) is a constant of motion. Let $\boldsymbol{r}_s$ and $\boldsymbol{r}_t$ denote the position vectors of the scatterer and the particle respectively and $\boldsymbol{R}$ be the position vector of the centre of mass at any given instant of time, as measured in some fixed inertial frame. Then the value of the expression

$$M\dot{\boldsymbol{R}} = (m_t + m_s)\dot{\boldsymbol{R}} = m_s\dot{\boldsymbol{r}}_s + m_t\dot{\boldsymbol{r}}_t \tag{4.80}$$

remains constant for all time. Here, m_s and m_t are the masses of the scatterer and the particle respectively. Now let $\boldsymbol{p}_s$ and $\boldsymbol{p}'_s$ be the initial and final momenta of the scatterer, that is, the asymptotic values of $m_s\dot{\boldsymbol{r}}_s$ before and after collision. Similarly $\boldsymbol{p}_t$ and $\boldsymbol{p}'_t$ be the initial and final momenta of the particle. By Eq. (4.80) we get

$$\boldsymbol{p}_s + \boldsymbol{p}_t = M\dot{\boldsymbol{R}} = \boldsymbol{p}'_s + \boldsymbol{p}'_t \tag{4.81}$$

Equation (4.81) simply states the law of conservation of linear momentum for the process of two body collision. Note the additivity of linear momenta in Eq. (4.81). The principle of momentum conservation is the most general conservation principle for collisions as it is independent of the forces involved. If we assume that the forces operative between the scatterer and the particle are conservative in nature, the total energy of this system of two particles must also be conserved.

In order to obtain this conservation law we consider the magnitude of momentum of one of the particles in the CM frame $\mu|\dot{\boldsymbol{r}}|$, where μ is the reduced mass of the system and $\boldsymbol{r} = \boldsymbol{r}_s - \boldsymbol{r}_t$ is the relative displacement between the scatterer and the particle. (In the

CM frame centre of mass is stationary, yielding its momentum to be zero while the value of $\boldsymbol{r}$ and hence $\dot{\boldsymbol{r}}$ remains the same in all frames) It is easy to see that,

$$\mu\dot{\boldsymbol{r}} = m_s(\dot{\boldsymbol{r}}_s - \dot{\boldsymbol{R}}) = -m_t(\dot{\boldsymbol{r}}_t - \dot{\boldsymbol{R}}) \tag{4.82}$$

If $\boldsymbol{p}_{\rm cm}$ and $\boldsymbol{p}'_{\rm cm}$ are the initial and final values of $\mu\dot{\boldsymbol{r}}$ then

$$\begin{aligned} \boldsymbol{p}_{\rm cm} &= \boldsymbol{p}_s - m_s\dot{\boldsymbol{R}} = -(\boldsymbol{p}_t - m_t\dot{\boldsymbol{R}}) \\ \text{and} \quad \boldsymbol{p}'_{\rm cm} &= \boldsymbol{p}'_s - m_s\dot{\boldsymbol{R}} = -(\boldsymbol{p}'_t - m_t\dot{\boldsymbol{R}}) \end{aligned} \tag{4.83}$$

Now if the forces are conservative the energy of the two body system must be conserved and in particular, the asymptotic values of the energy must be equal. Thus, we have

$$p^2_{\rm cm} = p'^2_{\rm cm} \tag{4.84}$$

Equation (4.84) expresses energy conservation for the system. It can be expressed in terms of the individual particles' momenta by using the relation

$$\frac{1}{2}m_s\dot{\boldsymbol{r}}_s^2 + \frac{1}{2}m_t\dot{\boldsymbol{r}}_t^2 = \frac{1}{2}M\dot{\boldsymbol{R}}^2 + \frac{1}{2}\mu\dot{\boldsymbol{r}}^2 \tag{4.85}$$

Equation (4.85) follows from Eq. (4.82) and holds irrespective of whether energy is conserved or not. Evaluating Eq. (4.85) in the asymptotic region and using Eq. (4.84) we get the energy conservation in the form

$$\frac{p_s^2}{2m_s} + \frac{p_t^2}{2m_t} = \frac{p'^2_s}{2m_s} + \frac{p'^2_t}{2m_t} \tag{4.86}$$

A collision is said to be *elastic* if it obeys Eq. (4.86), that is, if it conserves kinetic energy and the masses involved. Equations (4.84) and (4.86) apply to any binary elastic collision. It is obvious from Eq. (4.84) that an elastic collision simply rotates the initial CM momentum $\boldsymbol{p}_{\rm cm}$ through some angle ψ into its final value $\boldsymbol{p}'_{\rm cm}$. Thus, we can write,

$$\boldsymbol{p}'_{\rm cm} = \boldsymbol{p}_{\rm cm}\cos\psi + (\boldsymbol{p}_{\rm cm} \times \hat{\boldsymbol{i}})\sin\psi \tag{4.87}$$

where $\hat{\boldsymbol{i}}$ is the unit vector in the triad $(\hat{\boldsymbol{i}}, \hat{\boldsymbol{j}}, \hat{\boldsymbol{k}})$, $\hat{\boldsymbol{j}}$ and $\hat{\boldsymbol{k}}$ defining the plane of scattering. The angle ψ is called the CM scattering angle. The velocities of the particles with respect to the CM are $\dot{\boldsymbol{r}}_s - \dot{\boldsymbol{R}}$ and $\dot{\boldsymbol{r}}_t - \dot{\boldsymbol{R}}$ respectively, which are always oppositely directed according to Eq. (4.82). Thus relations between the initial and final states can be shown as in Fig. 4.15.

(vi) Momentum and Energy Transfer in Scattering

The momentum transferred between the scatterer and the particle say $\Delta\boldsymbol{p}$, can be obtained from Eq. (4.83). We have

$$\Delta\boldsymbol{p} = \boldsymbol{p}'_{\rm cm} - \boldsymbol{p}_{\rm cm} = \boldsymbol{p}'_s - \boldsymbol{p}_s = -(\boldsymbol{p}'_t - \boldsymbol{p}_t) \tag{4.88}$$

Thus $\Delta\boldsymbol{p}$ is independent of CM velocity $\dot{\boldsymbol{R}}$. However, the energy transfer ΔE defined by

$$\Delta E = \frac{1}{2m_t}(p'^2_t - p_t^2) = \frac{1}{2m_s}(p'^2_s - p_s^2) \tag{4.89}$$

depends on the CM velocity $\dot{R}$, because, again with the help of Eq. (4.83), we can express ΔE in the form

$$\Delta E = -\dot{R} \cdot \Delta p \tag{4.90}$$

Equation (4.88) tells us that ΔE is positive if the scatterer loses energy in the collision, and negative if the scatterer gains energy.

Equation (4.90) has important applications in astromechanics as well as atomic physics. A spacecraft traveling from the earth to any of the outer planets, say Saturn, Uranus, Neptune or pluto, can be given a large boost in velocity by scattering it off Jupiter. For the Jupiter-spacecraft system we can place the origin of the 'Lab frame' on the sun so that $\dot{R}$ is nothing else but the velocity of Jupiter relative to the sun. Since the mass of Jupiter is too huge compared to that of the spacecraft, the CM stays on the Jupiter. In order to maximise the boost available to the spacecraft we must maximise $\dot{R} \cdot \Delta p = \dot{R} \cdot (p'_{cm} - p_{cm})$. However, the initial momentum of the spacecraft, p_t as it is launched from the earth also fixes p_{cm} through the equation,

$$p_{cm} = p_t - m_t \dot{R}$$

Since p_{cm} is fixed the maximum boost is achieved by adjusting the impact parameter for the collision so that p'_{cm} is parallel to $\dot{R}$, giving $\dot{R} \cdot p'_{cm}$ its maximum value. This is achieved by appropriate timing of the launch and maneuvering of the spacecraft. Note that this is an instance of scattering by an attractive inverse square law of force due to Jupiter's gravity. Since the force is conservative and the scattering is elastic we can use the Eq. (4.90). The amount of energy gained by the spacecraft equals the amount of energy lost by Jupiter. However, this energy is too small to perturb Jupiter's orbit around the sun in any way. In other words, Jupiter and the spacecraft can be considered to form a closed system, as far as the scattering process is concerned.

A gravity-assisted trajectory from the earth to Uranus is shown in Fig. 4.16. The transit time from the earth to Uranus is about 5 years on the assisted orbit as compared to 16 years on an unassisted orbit with the same initial conditions.

(vii) Relation Between Lab Scattering Variables and CM Scattering Variables

Until now we were primarily concerned with the effectively one body problem, of scattering of a particle with a fixed centre of force. In an actual laboratory experiment scattering involves two bodies and the scatterer or the target particle is not stationary, but recoils as a result of scattering. The scattering angle, actually measured in the laboratory, say ψ', (see below) is the angle between the final and incident directions of the scattered particle. The scattering angle ψ, defined in the one body problem is the angle between the final and initial directions of the relative vector $r = r_s - r_t$ of the two particles. These two angles would be the same only if the second particle remains stationary throughout the scattering process. Thus it is imperative, to establish quantitative relationships between the scattering variables in the CM frame (which corresponds to the equivalent one particle problem) and the scattering variables in the lab frame.

In a typical scattering experiment one particle with initial momentum p_t is shot at a

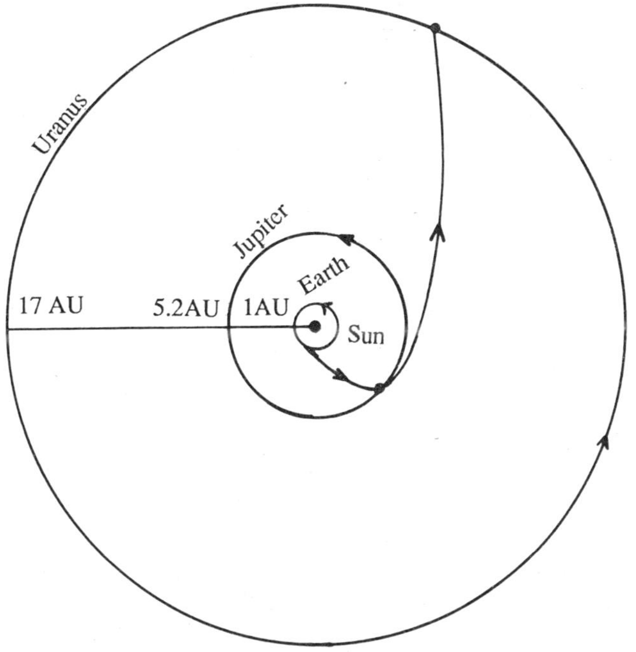

Fig. 4.16 A schematic orbital configuration for supplying gravitational boost to a spacecraft while it passes by Jupiter

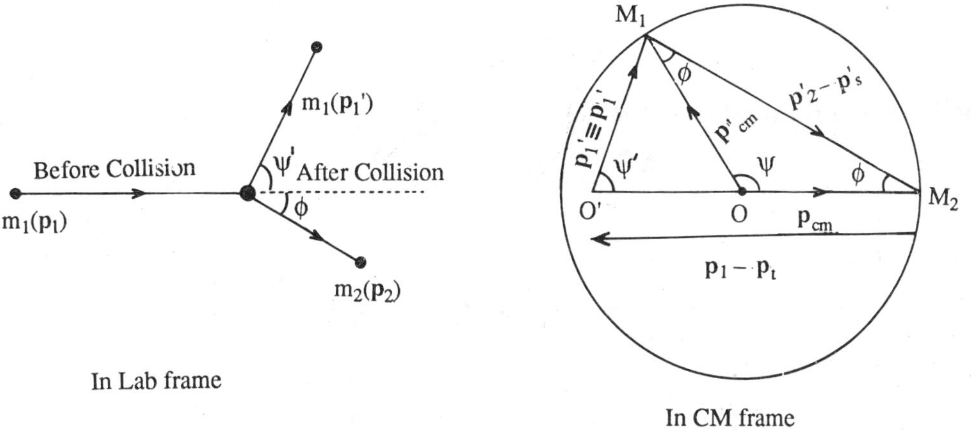

Fig. 4.17 Kinematics of binary collision in the lab and CM frames

target particle at rest in the laboratory with initial momentum $\boldsymbol{p}_s = 0$. Both $\boldsymbol{p}_s$ and $\boldsymbol{p}_t$ are measured with respect to a frame fixed in the laboratory in which the experiment is carried out. Fig. 4.17 shows the scattering variables which can be measured in a laboratory. Angle ψ' is called the *lab scattering angle* and ϕ is called the *recoil angle*. With the lab condition $\boldsymbol{p}_s = 0$, the first of Eq. (4.83) gives the relation between lab and CM momenta before collision:

$$\boldsymbol{p}_t = \frac{M}{m_s}\boldsymbol{p}_{\text{cm}} = M\dot{\boldsymbol{R}} \tag{4.91}$$

Using this to eliminate $\dot{\boldsymbol{R}}$ from the second of equation (4.83) and solving for the final LAB momenta in terms of the CM momenta we get,

$$\boldsymbol{p}'_t = \frac{m_t}{m_s}\boldsymbol{p}_{\text{cm}} + \boldsymbol{p}'_{\text{cm}} \tag{4.92}$$

$$\boldsymbol{p}'_s = \boldsymbol{p}_{\text{cm}} - \boldsymbol{p}'_{\text{cm}} = -\Delta\boldsymbol{p} \tag{4.93}$$

Equations (4.91-93) describe all the relations between lab and CM variables. These relations, along with the conservation laws are depicted in Fig. 4.17.

Let us now express the lab energy transfer ΔE and LAB scattering angle ψ' in terms of the CM variables. The total energy E_o of the two particle system equals the initial kinetic energy of the projectile. This, in turn, can be expressed in terms of the CM momentum using Eq. (4.91). Thus,

$$E_o = \frac{p_t^2}{2m_t} = \frac{M^2 p_{\text{cm}}^2}{2m_t m_s^2} \tag{4.94}$$

Since the total energy is conserved, during the collision, E_o (see Eq. (4.93)) will be redistributed among the particles. Since the scatterer is at rest initially, the energy transferred ΔE is equal to its kinetic energy after collision. Using Eqs (4.89) and (4.93), this fact can be expressed as

$$\Delta E = \frac{p_s'^2}{2m_s} = \frac{(\boldsymbol{p}'_{\text{cm}} - \boldsymbol{p}_{\text{cm}})^2}{2m_s} \tag{4.95}$$

The fractional energy transfer is, therefore,

$$\frac{\Delta E}{E_o} = \frac{\mu(\boldsymbol{p}'_{\text{cm}} - \boldsymbol{p}_{\text{cm}})^2}{M p_{\text{cm}}^2}$$

Now $(\boldsymbol{p}'_{\text{cm}} - \boldsymbol{p}_{\text{cm}})^2$ can be written as

$$(\boldsymbol{p}'_{\text{cm}} - \boldsymbol{p}_{\text{cm}})^2 = p'^2_{\text{cm}} + p^2_{\text{cm}} - 2p'_{\text{cm}}\, p_{\text{cm}} \cos\psi$$

By Eq. (4.84) this becomes

$$(\boldsymbol{p}'_{\text{cm}} - \boldsymbol{p}_{\text{cm}})^2 = 2p^2_{\text{cm}}(1 - \cos\psi) = 4p^2_{\text{cm}}\sin^2(\psi/2)$$

which finally gives

$$\frac{\Delta E}{E_o} = \frac{\mu(\boldsymbol{p}'_{\text{cm}} - \boldsymbol{p}_{\text{cm}})^2}{M p^2_{\text{cm}}} = \frac{4m_t m_s}{(m_t + m_s)^2}\sin^2(\psi/2) \tag{4.96}$$

Since Eq. (4.96) is independent of CM velocity $\dot{\boldsymbol{R}}$, it must apply to moving targets as well as the stationary targets as we have considered here.

Note that the energy transfer is maximum for $\psi = \pi$ giving

$$\left(\frac{\Delta E}{E_o}\right)_{\max} = \frac{4m_s m_t}{(m_s + m_t)^2} \leq 1 \tag{4.97}$$

This means that all of the energy can be transferred to the target (scatterer) only if $m_t = m_s$. Thus, for example, hydrogen rich materials are more effective in slowing down neutrons than heavy materials like lead, because the mass of a hydrogen atom is nearly the same as the mass of a neutron. Electrons passing through a material lose most of their energy to other electrons in the material, rather than atomic nuclei. Since the proton to electron mass ratio is about 1836, the maximum energy transferred by an electron to a nucleus with n nucleons corresponds to

$$\left(\frac{\Delta E}{E_o}\right)_{\max} = \frac{0.002}{n}$$

In order to relate lab scattering angle to the CM scattering angle we treat the plane containing all the momentum vectors to be the complex plane. Further, let a hat on a vector denote a unit vector in the direction of that vector. Then the lab and the CM scattering angles can be defined through the relations

$$\begin{aligned} \hat{p}'_{\text{cm}} &= \hat{p}_{\text{cm}} \exp(i\psi) \\ \hat{p}'_t &= \hat{p}_t \exp(i\psi') \qquad \text{where } i = \sqrt{-1} \end{aligned} \tag{4.98}$$

From Eq. (4.91) we see that

$$\hat{p}_t = \hat{p}_{\text{cm}}$$

so if we take a scalar product of Eq. (4.92) and $\hat{p}_{\text{cm}}$ and introduce the scattering angles defined through Eq. (4.98) we get

$$p'_t \exp(i\psi') = p_{\text{cm}} \left(\frac{m_t}{m_s} + \exp(i\psi)\right) \tag{4.99}$$

To eliminate p'_t and p_{cm} from the above relation consider

$$\begin{aligned} \left(\frac{p'_t}{p_{\text{cm}}}\right)^2 &= \left(\frac{m_t}{m_s} + \exp(i\psi)\right)\left(\frac{m_t}{m_s} + \exp(-i\psi)\right) \\ &= 1 + \left(\frac{m_t}{m_s}\right)^2 + \frac{2m_t}{m_s}\cos\psi \end{aligned}$$

which, on substituting back into Eq. (4.99) gives

$$\exp(i\psi') = \frac{(m_t/m_s) + \exp(i\psi)}{\left[1 + (m_t/m_s)^2 + 2\,(m_t/m_s)\cos\psi\right]^{1/2}} \tag{4.100}$$

Equating the real and imaginary parts of Eq. (4.100) and taking their ratio, we get finally,

$$\tan\psi' = \frac{\sin\psi}{m_t/m_s + \cos\psi} \tag{4.101}$$

To interpret this formula for $m_t < m_s$ refer to Fig. 4.17. For fixed initial CM momentum p_{cm} the final CM momentum p'_{cm} must lie on a sphere of radius p_{cm}. It is clear from Fig. 4.17 that there is a unique value of ψ' for every value of ψ in the range $0 \leq \psi \leq \pi$ covering all possibilities. For the limiting case of the stationary target ($m_t \ll m_s$) Eq. (4.101) reduces to $\tan\psi' = \tan\psi$ whence $\psi' = \psi$. For the case of equal masses $m_s = m_t$ the origin O in Fig. 4.17 lies on the circle and Eq. (4.101) reduces to $\tan\psi' = \tan(\psi/2)$ whence $\psi' = \psi/2$.

For a light target $m_t > m_s$, the origin O lies outside the circle as shown in Fig. 4.17. In this case there are two values ψ_1 and ψ_2 of the CM scattering angle for each value of the Lab scattering angle. The two values ψ_1 and ψ_2 can be distinguished in the lab by measuring the kinetic energy of the scattered particle. The lab scattering angle has a maximum value $\psi'_{\max}$ given by

$$\sin(\psi'_{\max}) = \frac{m_s}{m_t} \tag{4.102}$$

which can be read off from the figure. Eq. (4.102) tells us, for example, that a proton cannot be scattered by more than $0^o.03$ by an electron. Therefore, any significant deflection of protons or heavier atomic nuclei passing through matter is due to collision with nuclei rather than electrons. This is how Lord Rutherford could conclude about the existence as well as the size of a heavy nucleus in an atom, from the experiments he did on the scattering of α-particles by the atoms of gold.

(viii) Lab and CM Cross-sections

We have already evaluated the differential scattering cross-section in terms of the CM variables (see Eq. (4.74)). In order to obtain a relation between the CM cross-section and the lab cross-section consider the real part of Eq. (4.100) giving the relation between scattering angles:

$$\cos\psi' = \frac{(m_t/m_s) + \cos\psi}{\left[1 + (m_t/m_s)^2 + 2\,(m_t/m_s)\cos\psi\right]^{1/2}} \tag{4.103}$$

Lab scattering through an angle ψ' into $d\omega = \sin\psi' d\psi' d\phi$ corresponds to CM scattering through an angle ψ into $d\Omega = \sin\psi d\psi d\phi$. The relation between the two functional forms of the differential cross-section say $\sigma(\psi)$ and $\sigma'(\psi')$ is obtained by observing that in a particular experiment the number of particles scattered into a given solid angle must be the same whether we express the event in terms of ψ' or ψ. Therefore,

$$2\pi I\sigma(\psi)\sin\psi\,|d\psi| = 2\pi I\sigma'(\psi')\sin\psi'\,|d\psi'|$$

or

$$\sigma'(\psi') = \sigma(\psi)\,\frac{\sin\psi}{\sin\psi'}\left|\frac{d\psi}{d\psi'}\right| = \sigma(\psi)\left|\frac{d(\cos\psi)}{d(\cos\psi')}\right| \tag{4.104}$$

From Eq. (4.103) we obtain

$$\frac{d\omega}{d\Omega} = \frac{d(\cos\psi')}{d(\cos\psi)} = \frac{1 + (m_t/m_s)\cos\psi}{\left[1 + (m_t/m_s)^2 + 2(m_t/m_s)\cos\psi\right]^{3/2}}$$
$$= \frac{(1 + (m_t/m_s)\sin\psi)^{1/2}}{\left[(m_t/m_s)\cos\psi + (1 + (m_t/m_s)\sin\psi)^{1/2}\right]^2} \tag{4.105}$$

For $m_s = m_t$ this reduces to,

$$\frac{d\omega}{d\Omega} = \frac{1}{4\cos\frac{1}{2}\psi} = \frac{1}{4\cos\psi'} \tag{4.106}$$

For a heavy target $m_s \gg m_t$ the Eq. (4.105) reduces to unity, and hence the lab and CM cross-sections are nearly equal. For $m_t = m_s$,

$$\sigma'(\psi') = 4\cos\psi'\sigma(\psi)$$

Even when scattering is isotropic in terms of ψ (that is, $\sigma(\psi)$ is a constant independent of ψ) the cross-section in terms of ψ' varies as the cosine of the angle! Note, again, that $\psi' \leq \pi/2$ when $m_t = m_s$.

Lastly we point out that $\sigma(\psi)$ is not the the cross-section that an observer in the CM frame would measure. Both $\sigma(\psi)$ and $\sigma'(\psi')$ are cross-sections measured in the Lab frame and are merely the expressions for the cross-section in terms of different coordinates. An observer sitting on the centre of mass would see a different incident intensity from that measured in the lab frame. Therefore, the corresponding transformation has to be included to relate the cross-sections as measured in the CM and the lab frames.

4.16 VIRIAL THEOREM

The virial theorem expresses a conservation law for a system of interacting particles, which has already achieved a dynamical equilibrium. The virial theorem was first given by Rudolf Clausius in 1870. The interaction is assumed to be of a central force type in general.

Consider a system of N interacting particles that has achieved dynamical equilibrium through some kind of central force interactions. Let T be the total translational kinetic energy of such a system and W be the virial of the system defined as

$$W = \sum_{i=1}^{N} \boldsymbol{F}_i \cdot \boldsymbol{r}_i \tag{4.107}$$

where, $\boldsymbol{F}_i$ is the net force on ith particle and $\boldsymbol{r}_i$ is the position vector of the same particle. The virial theorem states that under dynamical equilibrium,

$$2T + W = 0 \tag{4.108}$$

Proof: The equation of motion of the ith particle is

$$m_i \frac{d^2\boldsymbol{r}_i}{dt^2} = \boldsymbol{F}_i$$

Now consider the virial of the system

$$\begin{aligned}
W &= \sum_{i=1}^{N} \boldsymbol{F}_i \cdot \boldsymbol{r}_i = \sum_{i=1}^{N} m_i \frac{d^2\boldsymbol{r}_i}{dt^2} \cdot \boldsymbol{r}_i \\
&= \sum_{i=1}^{N} m_i \frac{d}{dt}\left(\frac{d\boldsymbol{r}_i}{dt} \cdot \boldsymbol{r}_i\right) - \sum_{i=1}^{N} m_i \frac{d\boldsymbol{r}_i}{dt} \cdot \frac{d\boldsymbol{r}_i}{dt} \\
&= \frac{1}{2} \sum_{i=1}^{N} \frac{d^2}{dt^2} (m_i\, \boldsymbol{r}_i \cdot \boldsymbol{r}_i) - 2T \\
&= \frac{1}{2} \frac{d^2}{dt^2}(I) - 2T
\end{aligned}$$

where I = moment of inertia of the whole system about the origin, and T = total translational kinetic energy. If the system has achieved dynamical equilibrium its moment of inertia should not change with time so that $dI/dt = 0 = d^2I/dt^2$, giving

$$W + 2T = 0$$

and therefore, proving the theorem. The term d^2I/dt^2 does not vanish till process of virialisation continues. The time scale over which this process of virialisation takes place is called the virial time scale of the system. Virial W is connected with the total potential energy of the system. If the central force law between any two particles i and j is of the type

$$\begin{aligned}
\boldsymbol{F}_{ij} &= \text{force on the } i\text{th particle due to the } j\text{th particle} \\
&= f_{ij}(\boldsymbol{r}_i - \boldsymbol{r}_j) \qquad i \neq j
\end{aligned}$$

where

$$f_{ij} = \frac{k_{ij}}{|\boldsymbol{r}_i - \boldsymbol{r}_j|^{n+1}} \qquad i \neq j$$

and where k_{ij} may depend on m_i, m_j etc., but not on the mutual separation of the particles or on time. We can write the virial due to these forces as

$$W = \sum_{i} \sum_{j \neq i} \boldsymbol{F}_{ij} \cdot \boldsymbol{r}_i$$

or

$$\begin{aligned}
W &= \sum_{i} \sum_{j \neq i} f_{ij}\,(\boldsymbol{r}_i - \boldsymbol{r}_j) \cdot \left[\frac{1}{2}(\boldsymbol{r}_i - \boldsymbol{r}_j) + \frac{1}{2}(\boldsymbol{r}_i + \boldsymbol{r}_j)\right] \\
&= \frac{1}{2} \sum_{i} \sum_{j \neq i} f_{ij} |\boldsymbol{r}_i - \boldsymbol{r}_j|^2 + \frac{1}{2} \sum_{i} \sum_{j \neq i} f_{ij}(\boldsymbol{r}_i - \boldsymbol{r}_j) \cdot (\boldsymbol{r}_i + \boldsymbol{r}_j)
\end{aligned}$$

The second term vanishes because the summand is the product of antisymmetric and symmetric expressions with respect to (i, j). Therefore,

$$W = \frac{1}{2}\sum_i \sum_{j \neq i} f_{ij}|\boldsymbol{r}_i - \boldsymbol{r}_j|^2 = \frac{1}{2}\sum_i \sum_{j \neq i} \frac{k_{ij}}{|\boldsymbol{r}_i - \boldsymbol{r}_j|^{n-1}} = (n-1)\,V \tag{4.109}$$

where

$$V = \frac{1}{2}\sum_i \sum_{j \neq i} \int_{\infty}^{\boldsymbol{r}_i - \boldsymbol{r}_j} \boldsymbol{F}_{ij} \cdot d\,(\boldsymbol{r}_i - \boldsymbol{r}_j)$$

is the total potential energy of the system. So, in the absence of any external forces the virial theorem for a system of N mutually interacting particles in dynamical equilibrium is given by

$$2T + (n-1)\,V = 0 \tag{4.110}$$

provided the force of interaction between any pair of particles follows a law $|\boldsymbol{F}_{ij}| \propto |\boldsymbol{r}_i - \boldsymbol{r}_j|^{-n}$. If the forces of interaction obey the attractive inverse square law, from Eq. (4.109) we get $W = V$ and hence

$$2T + V = 0 \tag{4.111}$$

This is a special case of the virial theorem (Eq. (4.110)), which, in turn, is a special case of the most general virial theorem (Eq. (4.108)).

Examples

(i) A virialised homogeneous and spherical cluster of galaxies (or of stars) of the cluster radius R and the cluster mass M has a gravitational potential energy V and total kinetic energy T, given by

$$V = -\frac{3}{5}\frac{GM^2}{R} \qquad T = \frac{1}{2}M\bar{v^2}$$

where $\bar{v^2}$ is the mean square speed of the individual galaxies (or stars). Thus from the virial theorem (Eq. (4.111)) we get

$$M = \frac{5}{3}\frac{R\bar{v^2}}{G} \tag{4.112}$$

If we can measure the mean square speed from the observed Doppler spread of the spectral lines and the radius from its known distance and measured angular size of the virialised cluster, we can infer the mass of the cluster from the above formula.

(ii) Consider an ideal gas. It does not have any forces acting between its particles. The only force on the particles is the reaction force due to the impact on the walls of the container. For this force we can write

$$dF = -p'dA'$$

where p' is the pressure of the gas and dA' an element of area on the surface of the container (the direction of dA' being chosen +ve for the outward normal). Thus we get, for the virial,

$$W = -p' \oint \boldsymbol{r} \cdot d\boldsymbol{A}' = -p' \int_{V'} (\nabla \cdot \boldsymbol{r})\, dV' = -3p'V'$$

where V' is the volume of the container. From the most general virial theorem, we have

$$2T + W = 0$$

so that,

$$T = -\frac{1}{2}W = \frac{3}{2}p'V'$$

Now it is well known that the total translational kinetic energy of an ideal gas comprising N particles is $(3/2)NkT'$ where T' is the temperature of the gas and k, Boltzmann's constant. Substituting this in the above equation we get the well-known result namely the equation of state

$$p'V' = NkT'$$

(iii) Let us apply the results of example (ii) to a star. A star is supposed to be made up of ideal gas. Let a small mass dm of a perfect gas consisting of dN particles have translational kinetic energy associated with it, given by,

$$dT = \frac{3}{2}p'\, dV' = \frac{3}{2}kT'dN = \frac{3}{2}R'\, T'\frac{dm}{\mu}$$

where μ is the mean molecular weight and R' is the gas constant. (Note: $dN = N_A\, dm/\mu$, N_A = Avogadro's number). Now since,

$$C_p - C_v = R' = kN_A$$

and C_vT'/μ = internal energy per unit mass = dU/dm we can write dT as

$$dT = \frac{3}{2}(C_p - C_v)\, T'\frac{dm}{\mu} = \frac{3}{2}\frac{C_vT'}{\mu}\left(\frac{C_p}{C_v} - 1\right) dm$$

$$= \frac{3}{2}(\gamma - 1)dU$$

Therefore, for the whole star,

$$T = \frac{3}{2}(\gamma - 1)U \tag{4.113}$$

γ being the ratio of the two specific heats, C_p and C_v.

For an ideal monatomic gas $\gamma = 5/3$ giving $T = U$. This result is obvious from the fact that for a monatomic ideal gas all the internal energy is translational kinetic energy of the atoms. For diatomic gases, $\gamma = 7/5$, giving $T = (3/5)U$, and so on.

But in general, for any gravitating system, such as a star, the virial theorem (Eq. (4.111)) gives

$$U = \frac{2T}{3(\gamma - 1)} = \frac{-V}{3(\gamma - 1)} \tag{4.114}$$

Therefore, the total internal energy

$$E = U + V = \frac{\gamma - 4/3}{\gamma - 1} V \tag{4.115}$$

For $\gamma > 4/3$, $E < 0$ (since $V < 0$) and therefore the star is ***stable***. A star is ***unstable*** if $\gamma < 4/3$. Hence a gaseous planet entirely made up of triatomic gases such as CO_2, H_2O or NO_2 with $\gamma = 9/7$ will become virially unstable.

(iv) The virial for a system of charged particles moving in a magnetic field is given by

$$\text{The magnetic virial } W_m = \sum_i \boldsymbol{F}_i \cdot \boldsymbol{r}_i$$

where $\boldsymbol{F}_i$ is the magnetic force on the ith particle having charge e_i, given by $\boldsymbol{F}_i = e_i (\boldsymbol{v}_i \times \boldsymbol{B})$, $\boldsymbol{B}$ being the magnetic induction. Therefore,

$$W_m = \sum_{i=1}^{N} e_i \boldsymbol{r}_i \cdot (\boldsymbol{v}_i \times \boldsymbol{B}) = \sum_i \frac{e_i}{m_i} (m_i \boldsymbol{r}_i \times \boldsymbol{v}_i) \cdot \boldsymbol{B} = \frac{e}{m} \boldsymbol{L} \cdot \boldsymbol{B} \tag{4.116}$$

provided all changed particles have the same e/m ratio. $\boldsymbol{L}$ is the total angular momentum of the system. This virial should be added to the gravitational virial, if any.

4.17 SUMMARY

Central force is a class of prescribed laws of forces that defines a point acting as a central origin of force, the magnitude of the force being a function of only the distance from this origin and the direction being either parallel (repulsive) or antiparallel (attractive) to the radius vector. For the conservative central forces, the energy and the vector angular momentum are the first integrals of motion. The two body problem can always be reduced to a single body problem but at the cost of the conservation of linear momentum and the inertial nature of the frame. A third integral of motion belonging to the class of the first integrals, called the Runge-Lenz vector, exists only for two special types of central forces: one being the inverse square law (both attractive and repulsive) and the other Hooke's linear law. By Bertrand's theorem, all stable and bounded orbits become also closed only under these two types of central forces. Any deviation from these two types of the force laws makes all noncircular orbits precess about their apsidal lines and fill the space densely like the space-filling curves.

Newton derived the law of gravitation from Kepler's laws of planetary motions combined with his own laws of motion. Later on, Kepler's laws were also derived back from Newton's laws of motion and of gravitation. In the theory of planetary motions, the product of the gravitational constant and the mass of the central body (GM) comes always as a unit, and therefore, neither the gravitational constant nor the mass of the central body can be determined separately. Planets which do not have any satellites could not have their masses determined except from the weak perturbations that they produce on other nearby planets.

It is easy to fix the orbit of a planet from the knowledge of the five time independent constants of motion, but not so easy to calculate the exact position in the orbit at a given time. This requires the solution of Kepler's equation which is not integrable in closed form except for the parabolic orbits.

The transfer orbits between two orbits are most economic if the firing from the inner orbit takes place at the perigee rather than at the apogee. The geostationary orbit is a unique orbit around the earth and is a very special case of the infinitely many possible geosynchronous orbits.

Tides are produced on any extended body basically due to the nonuniformity of the (central) force of the tide-raising source over the physical extension of the body, the rear parts being less attracted than the central part and the central part being less attracted than the front parts. Only fluids and plastic solids can respond to tidal forces. It is the tiny tangential component of the tidal force that acts on the fluid elements, makes it work against the local gravity and gain height. The tidal bulge actually fills the deformed equipotential surface, which assumes the shape of a prolate spheroid in presence of an orbiting satellite.

Scattering in the field of a central force is a process that makes an incident beam of particles lose the sense of their original directions. The actual area of cross-section of the incident beam that is lost once the beam is well past the scatterer, is called the total cross-section of scattering. The differential cross-section is the loss of area from the incident beam per unit solid angle of the angle of scattering. Rutherford scattering in a field of force obeying an inverse square law of distance suggests an extremely rapid increase in the angle of deflection at close enough encounters, which enabled Rutherford to measure the smallness of the atomic nuclei. In astronomical situations with attractive force fields, the sun-like stars gobble up, instead of deflecting away, practically anything that is originally targeted within a radius of about 25 times the radius of the star. The scattering of any small object such as a spaceship by Jupiter can be so arranged that Jupiter's orbital momentum is imparted to the spaceship profitably enough to send the latter out of the solar system.

The virialisation of a dynamical system can be viewed as a dynamical process of relaxing in which an equilibrium ratio between the kinetic and the potential energy is achieved. This equilibrium ratio depends on the exponent of the power law of central forces. For the gravitational fields, the equilibrium share of the kinetic energy is only one half of its potential energy, no matter how one prepares the original system, subject however to the condition that the system does not disperse away before it is virialised.

PROBLEMS

4.1 A radially stretched and self supported vertically hanging rope is in circular orbit around the Earth's equator. Find the length, maximum tension and total energy of the rope, if its lower end remains hanging just over the ground and never touches.

4.2 Consider a Keplerian two body system having unequal masses. Set up the Lagrangian of the system with respect to the centre of mass frame. Show that both the particles describe respective conic sections but with identical eccentricity. Find the share of the angular momentum and energy for each particle.

4.3 (a) Find the conditions for stability of circular orbits in a screened Coulomb potential given by

$$V(r) = -\frac{K}{r}\exp\left\{-\frac{r}{a}\right\} \qquad K = Ze^2 > 0 \qquad a > 0$$

Illustrate graphically the radial variation of the effective potential.

(b) How are the stable circular orbits on the surface of a cone, if the cone is put upside down with its vertex pointing downward?

4.4 Suppose an astronomer finds a light object orbiting a motionless heavy one in a circle that has the heavy one located on its circumference, instead of at the centre. Deduce the force law and the system's energy. Assume H_o = const.

4.5 Show that if the equation of the orbit is $\theta = f(r)$ and the force is central, that is, $r^2\dot{\theta}$ = constant = H, the radial acceleration is given by

$$\ddot{r} - r\dot{\theta}^2 = -\frac{H^2}{r^3}\left\{\frac{2}{r^2[f'(r)]^2} + \frac{f''(r)}{r[f'(r)]^3} + 1\right\}$$

Find the exponent of the power law nature of the central force if the orbit is

(i) spiral, that is, $\theta \propto r^{-1}$ and

(ii) $r = a \tanh(\theta/\sqrt{2})$

4.6 (i) If jerk $\boldsymbol{j}$ is defined by $\boldsymbol{j} = \ddot{\boldsymbol{v}}(t)$, find an expression for jerk for Keplerian orbits.

(ii) We know that the speed, acceleration and angular speed of a planet are all maximum at the perihelion and minimum at the aphelion. Find the locations where angular accelerations and decelerations are maximum.

(iii) Show that the synodic period (return to the same configurational positions relative to the earth and sun) S for both superior (outside the earth's orbit) and inferior (inside earth's orbit) planets is given by

$$S^2 = \frac{a^3}{(1 - a^{1.5})^2}$$

where a is the semimajor axis of the planet in AU and S measured in yr.

4.7 Show that the equivalent of Kepler's equation for the parabolic orbits is analytically integrable. Use the result to calculate how long a comet approaching the sun in a parabolic orbit would spend inside earth's orbit (radius = 1 AU = 1.496×10^{11} m), assuming the perihelion distance of the comet from the sun to be 0.587 AU. Take $M_\odot = 1.987 \times 10^{30}$ kg.

4.8 (a) Derive Kepler's equation analytically with the definition of E given by Eqs (4.42).

(b) Expand it in terms of g and find a series expansion for ν in terms of g and eccentricity e.

4.9 Would an electron exposed to solar radiation pressure and gravity be expelled from the solar system? What is the critical luminosity for doing this job ?

4.10 Calculate the minimum velocity a spacecraft needs in order to escape from the solar gravitational field, starting from the surface of the earth.

4.11 As the moon is revolving round the earth and the earth round the sun, one would expect the moon's path to be convex towards the sun while the moon is in her crescent phases. Show that this can actually never happen, even under the circumstances of the new moon.

4.12 Find the time-average of r, θ-average of r and the arc-length-average of r for a Keplerian elliptical orbit having semimajor axis a and eccentricity e.

4.13 Science fiction writers such as John Norman writing 'Chronicles of Counter Earth', have described a sister planet which shares the same orbit with the earth. When the earth is at perihelion, the sister planet is at aphelion. How could earthlings launch a spacecraft to explore this counter earth? (The problem is to find a satisfactory transfer orbit). When the earth is at one end of the semilatus rectum (given $a = 1.00$ AU and $e = 0.01674$), find the angle between the sun and the counter earth.

4.14 A space vehicle moving in a circular orbit of radius r_1 transfers to a circular orbit of radius r_2 by means of an elliptical transfer orbit, called the ***Hohman transfer orbit.*** With what speed should the spacecraft be launched from the earth's surface in order to send it to Mars in least possible time ? How long is the in-flight time ?

4.15 It is planned to launch a satellite (of mass m) in a circular orbit in the central inverse square gravitational force field of the earth. The satellite is to be 'rocketed' to a point P at altitude h and given the proper value of the kinetic energy with direction of motion perpendicular to the line joining P and the centre of the earth. Everything goes as planned, except the direction of motion is at the angle $\theta \neq 90^o$. Show that (a) the orbit is an ellipse with its semimajor axis length equal to the radius $R_\oplus + h$ of the intended circular orbit ($R_\oplus$ = radius of the earth), (b) the point P is at one end of the minor axis of the ellipse, and (c) the eccentricity of the ellipse is $\cos\theta$.

4.16 How large is the classical deflection of the light rays that grazes past a neutron star (mass = 3×10^{30} kg, radius = 10 km)?

4.17 Show that elastic scattering by a hard paraboloidal surface follows the same law of angular distribution as that of the Rutherford scattering in a repulsive inverse square law of force field. Find the effective focal length of the latter.

4.18 The supernova 1987A is situated about 170,000 light years away from the earth and expected to have released 10^{46} J of energy in the form of neutrinos. If the average energy of neutrinos is about 10 MeV and the Čerenkov detector containing about 2000 metric tons of water at Kamiokande in Japan catches about 10 neutrinos coming from the supernova through reactions of the type $\bar{\nu}_e + p \rightarrow n + e^+$, find the cross-section for this neutrino (actually antineutrino) reaction.

4.19 Show that the difference between the scattering angles in the lab frame and the CM frame is $\sin^{-1}(x \sin\psi_{\rm lab})$, where x = the mass ratio of the scattered particle and the force centre.

4.20 Find the angular frequency of the precession of the pericenter of the orbit of any planet if it experiences a small perturbation due to the following noninverse square

law forces:
(i) Yukawa type of short range potential $V(r) = -\frac{K}{r}e^{-r/d}$, where $r \gg d$, K and d are constants.
(ii) Hall type of potential $V(r) = -K/r^{1+\delta}$, $(\delta \ll 1)$, δ being a small constant.
(iii)$V(r) = -K/r - K'/r^4$.

4.21 Given the Runge-Lenz vector $\boldsymbol{A} = (-2\mu E)^{-1/2}(K\boldsymbol{r}/r + \boldsymbol{L} \times \boldsymbol{p})$, where $\boldsymbol{L} = \boldsymbol{r} \times \boldsymbol{p}$, $K = GMm$, $\mu = mM/(m+M)$, and energy $E = mv^2/2 + V(r)$. Now if the force field is a combination of inverse square and inverse cubic attractive forces, say $F(\boldsymbol{r}) = -K\,\boldsymbol{r}/r^3 - K'\boldsymbol{r}/r^4$, we know that the perihelion will be precessing at a steady rate. This means that it is possible to eliminate precession and the effect of the cubic law of force if we move to a suitable rotating frame of reference. Show that $L'^2 = L^2 - K'$, and $e' = \sqrt{1 + (2EL'^2/K^2)}$, where L' and e' are the angular momentum and the eccentricity as seen from this rotating frame.

4.22 The nucleus of an atom of gold is bombarded with alpha particles each having a kinetic energy 7.6 MeV. Determine the spatial domain around the gold nucleus, which is not accessible to the alpha particles.

4.23 If the sun is moving through the interstellar cloud with a speed of 23 km/s and the interstellar cloud has a density of 5 hydrogen atoms per cm^3, how much would be the yearly increase in the mass of the sun due to accretion ?

4.24 Show that when measured with respect to the mean sea level the gain in tidal height at the (sublunar) high tide is about twice the drop in tidal height at its low tide.

4.25 Assume that a close pair of identical satellites of radius r_s and mass density ρ_s is revolving around a primary planet of radius R_p and mass density ρ_p. If the pair touches each other physically and are radially aligned for a moment, can there be a situation for which the mutual gravitational attraction between the pair will not be sufficient to resist the tidal force of the primary acting on them? Show that the condition for winning over the tidal disruption does not depend on the size of the satellites, but only on the ratios of densities and the orbital radius to R_p. The latter ratio, called the Roche lobe ratio, is an ideal ratio for ring formation inside the Roche lobe of any homogeneous spherical object.

4.26 A rotating and self-gravitating interstellar cloud is in virial equilibrium having a magnetic field trapped inside. Find the virial for the system.

5

Hamilton's Equations of Motion

5.0 INTRODUCTION

In chapter 2, we were concerned exclusively with Lagrangian dynamics, that is, the equations of motion were obtained from a knowledge of the Lagrangian of the system. For a holonomic system described by a set of n generalised coordinates, there exists an equivalent formulation of its dynamics, a formulation in terms of its Hamilton's function or the Hamiltonian. Just like the Lagrangian, the Hamiltonian of a system can be used to obtain the equations of motion of the system. The chief disadvantage of Lagrange's equations of motion is that they are second order total differential equations in generalised coordinates. Hamilton's equations of motion, on the other hand, are first order total differential equations in generalised coordinates and generalised momenta.

Sir William Rowan Hamilton (1805 – 1865), born in Dublin, was said to be a child prodigy. Having been brought up by his uncle, a distinguished philologist, William could read English at the age of three, became a good geographer at the age of four, could translate Latin, Greek and Hebrew at the age of five, and by 13, he mastered 13 languages that included Hindi, Marathi, Bengali, Sanskrit, Malayalam and Chinese. All his life he loved animals and, what is regrettably rarer, respected them as equals. Up to the age of 15, he showed little sign of interest in science or mathematics. However, he started reading *Principia* at the age of 16, and by 17 he mastered mathematics through integral calculus, gained enough knowledge in mathematical astronomy to enable him to calculate the timings of eclipses, and wrote Part I of his book, *A Theory of Systems of Rays*, which got published when he was 22. Hamilton never attended any school before going to university, through his admission to Trinity college at 18, on scoring the highest marks in the admission test, which was contested by about 100 candidates.

By 21, he remodeled geometrical optics entirely. He demonstrated that all researches on any system of optical rays can be reduced to the study of a single function, called 'characteristic function' (we shall read more about it in chapters 6 and 10). He became the Royal Astronomer of Ireland, the most prestigious Professor's Chair won by an undergraduate of 22. Within a couple of years, he turned towards mechanics and remodeled it entirely in terms of his 'characteristic function'. His contemporaries had mixed feelings about his works; some said his whole scheme was just an intellectual exercise, others thought him to be a genius and a real pioneer. It was only after the advent of quantum mechanics in the twentieth century, that his works got proper attention. Now every one knows how crucial is the role played by the concept of the Hamiltonian in quantum mechanics, Hamilton's principle in all field theories, Hamilton's principal function in the path integral formulation of quantum mechanics, and the Hamilton-Jacobi differential equation for a complete classical solution to dynamical problems. Through the works of Gibbs, his incipient idea of phase space became the only useful way of studying statistical mechanics.

However, for the purpose of the present chapter, the logical connection between the Lagrangian and Hamiltonian is formally established through the so called Legendre transformation, which we now proceed to describe.

5.1 LEGENDRE'S DUAL TRANSFORMATION

Theorem: Let a function $F(u_1, u_2, \ldots, u_n)$ have an explicit dependence on the n independent variables $u_1, u_2, \ldots, u_n$. Let the function F be transformed to another function $G = G(v_1, v_2, \ldots, v_n)$ expressed explicitly in terms of a new set of n independent variables $v_1, v_2, \ldots, v_n$, where these new variables are connected to the old variables by a given set of relations

$$v_i = \frac{\partial F}{\partial u_i} \qquad i = 1, \ldots, n \tag{5.1}$$

and the form of G is given by $G(v_1, v_2, \ldots, v_n) = u_i v_i - F(u_1, u_2, \ldots, u_n)$. Then the variables $u_1, \ldots, u_n$ satisfy the dual transformation, namely, the relations

$$u_i = \frac{\partial G}{\partial v_i} \qquad i = 1, \ldots, n \tag{5.2}$$

and

$$F(u_1, \ldots, u_n) = u_i v_i - G(v_1, \ldots, v_n)$$

This duality of transformation between the two functions $F(u_1, \ldots, u_n)$ and $G(v_1, \ldots, v_n)$ and also between the two sets of variables given by the Eqs (5.1) and (5.2) are referred to as *Legendre's dual transformation*.

Proof: Since the form of G is given by

$$G(v_1, \ldots, v_n) = u_i v_i - F(u_1, \ldots, u_n)$$

from the left-hand side, $\delta G = (\partial G/\partial v_i)\delta v_i$, and from the right-hand side

$$\delta G = u_i \delta v_i + v_i \delta u_i - \frac{\partial F}{\partial u_i}\delta u_i$$

so that

$$\frac{\partial G}{\partial v_i}\delta v_i = u_i \delta v_i + \left(v_i - \frac{\partial F}{\partial u_i}\right)\delta u_i$$

Since it is given that, $v_i = (\partial F/\partial u_i)$, one must have its dual

$$u_i = \frac{\partial G}{\partial v_i}$$

as δv_i's are arbitrary because all v_i's are independent. Thus the duality of the transformation is proved. Note that $G = u_i v_i - F$ can simply be rearranged to write $F = u_i v_i - G$. Further, it is easy to see that we could have started from Eq. (5.2) and $F = u_i v_i - G$ and proved Eq. (5.1) and $G = u_i v_i - F$ in exactly the same way.

5.1.1 Extension of the Theorem to Include Passive Variables

Now suppose that there is a further set of m independent passive variables $w_1, \ldots, w_m$ which are present in both F and G. Then there would be some extra conditions for Legendre's dual transformation to be satisfied. These conditions are

$$\frac{\partial F}{\partial w_i} = -\frac{\partial G}{\partial w_i} \qquad i = 1, \ldots, m \tag{5.3}$$

This can be proved as follows. Consider

$$G = G(v_1, \ldots, v_n, w_1, \ldots, w_m) = u_i v_i - F(u_1, \ldots, u_n, w_1, \ldots, w_m)$$

Therefore

$$\delta G = \frac{\partial G}{\partial v_i}\delta v_i + \frac{\partial G}{\partial w_i}\delta w_i$$

$$\delta G = u_i \delta v_i + v_i \delta u_i - \frac{\partial F}{\partial u_i}\delta u_i - \frac{\partial F}{\partial w_i}\delta w_i$$

so that $v_i = \partial F/\partial u_i$ are all satisfied provided,

$$u_i = \frac{\partial G}{\partial v_i} \qquad \text{and} \qquad \frac{\partial G}{\partial w_i} = -\frac{\partial F}{\partial w_i}$$

which proves the assertion. Note that the latter relations have acquired a negative sign.

Example

In thermodynamics the four thermodynamic potentials, namely,

$$\begin{aligned} \text{the internal energy} \quad U' &= U'(S', V') \\ \text{the free energy} \quad F' &= F'(V', T') \\ \text{the enthalpy} \quad H' &= H'(S', P') \\ \text{and Gibb's potential} \quad G' &= G'(P', T') \end{aligned}$$

are all connected by Legendre's dual transformation. Here the independent variables are any two, out of the entropy S', volume V', temperature T' and pressure P'. A change in the pair of independent variables defines a new potential function which is connected to the old one by a suitable Legendre's dual transformation.

For example, a dual transformation of $U'(S', V')$ can be the free energy $F'(V', T')$ where V' remains as the passive variable and the variable S' is transformed to T'. Of course, this is possible if a relation like

$$T' = \frac{\partial U'}{\partial S'}$$

exists for a change over of the active variable S' in U' to T' in F'. Then by Legendre's dual transformation theorem (except for a negative sign), we shall have

$$F'(V',T') = U'(S',V') - T'S'$$

$$S' = -\frac{\partial F'}{\partial T'} \quad \text{and} \quad \frac{\partial F'}{\partial V'} = \frac{\partial U'}{\partial V'}$$

Similarly one can find that

$$H' = U' + P'V' \quad \text{with} \quad P' = -\frac{\partial U'}{\partial V'} \quad \text{and} \quad V' = \frac{\partial H'}{\partial P'}$$

and

$$G' = F' + P'V' \quad \text{with} \quad P' = -\frac{\partial F'}{\partial V'} \quad \text{and} \quad V' = \frac{\partial G'}{\partial P'}$$

as dual transforms of U' and F' respectively.

5.2 HAMILTON'S FUNCTION AND HAMILTON'S EQUATIONS OF MOTION

Let us now apply Legendre's dual transformation to the Lagrangian of a system $L(q_1, \ldots, q_n, \dot{q}_1, \ldots, \dot{q}_n, t)$ with $\dot{q}_i$ as the active variables and q_i and t as the passive variables. The dual variables of $\dot{q}_i$, $i = 1, \ldots, n$ are given by the generalised momenta

$$p_i = \frac{\partial L}{\partial \dot{q}_i} \qquad i = 1, \ldots, n \tag{5.4}$$

Hence the dual function of the Lagrangian L is

$$H = p_i \dot{q}_i - L(q, \dot{q}, t) \tag{5.5}$$

where

$$H = H(q_1, \ldots, q_n, p, \ldots, p_n, t) = H(q, p, t)$$

and in short, is called *Hamilton's function* or the *Hamiltonian* of the system. The dual transformation of Eq. (5.4) is

$$\dot{q}_i = \frac{\partial H}{\partial p_i} \qquad i = 1, \ldots, n \tag{5.6}$$

and the Eqs (5.3) for the passive variables take the form

$$\frac{\partial L}{\partial t} = -\frac{\partial H}{\partial t} \tag{5.7}$$

and

$$\frac{\partial L}{\partial q_i} = -\frac{\partial H}{\partial q_i} \qquad i = 1, \ldots, n \tag{5.8}$$

We know that provided (i) there are no non-potential forces, (ii) the system is holonomic and bilateral, and (iii) Euler– Lagrange's equations of motion are valid, one can write

$$\frac{\partial L}{\partial q_i} = \frac{d}{dt}\left(\frac{\partial L}{\partial \dot{q}_i}\right) = \dot{p}_i$$

Substituting in Eq. (5.8) we get

$$\dot{p}_i = -\frac{\partial H}{\partial q_i} \qquad i = 1, \ldots, n \tag{5.9}$$

The set of Eqs (5.6) and (5.9) together is called the Hamilton's equations of motion or the canonical equations of motion. Sir William Hamilton derived these equations in 1835.

5.3 PROPERTIES OF THE HAMILTONIAN AND OF HAMILTON'S EQUATIONS OF MOTION

1. If the Lagrangian does not have any explicit dependence on time, the Hamiltonian also does not depend explicitly on time. This simply follows from Eq. (5.7) above.

2. Consider

$$\begin{aligned}\frac{dH}{dt} &= \frac{d}{dt}H(q_1, \ldots, q_n, p_1, \ldots, p_n, t)\\ &= \frac{\partial H}{\partial t} + \frac{\partial H}{\partial q_i}\dot{q}_i + \frac{\partial H}{\partial p_i}\dot{p}_i\\ &= \frac{\partial H}{\partial t} - \dot{p}_i\dot{q}_i + \dot{p}_i\dot{q}_i\\ &= \frac{\partial H}{\partial t}\end{aligned} \tag{5.10}$$

where we have used Hamilton's equations of motion. Thus if the Lagrangian or equivalently the Hamiltonian does not explicitly depend on time, the Hamiltonian is a constant of motion. In fact, in this case,

$$H = p_i\dot{q}_i - L = E$$

is the energy integral for conservative systems, for which $H = T + V = E$. Otherwise, in general if $H \neq H(t)$ and $L \neq L(t)$, there will exist a constant of motion, called the *Jacobi integral* given by the function

$$H = \text{a const.} = J$$

which need not be identical with the actual energy E.

3. Hamilton's equations of motion are first order total differential equations. But the total number of equations of motion is $2n$, unlike the n second order total differential equations for Euler-Lagrange's equations of motion. Thus, even in the Hamiltonian formulation, a

system with the number of DOF $= n$ has $2n - 1$ independent constants of motion, as it should.

4. Hamilton's equations of motion are symmetric in q_i and p_i except for a change in sign in the second set. Thus it does not make any essential difference, which of the two sets of quantities q_i's and p_i's is called the coordinates or the momenta. Their roles can be trivially interchanged just by making a change of (relative) sign. Thus the new set of variables, say (Q_i, P_i) defined by

$$Q_i = -p_i \quad \text{and} \quad P_i = q_i$$

should leave Hamilton's equations of motion unchanged and hence are equivalent to the set (q_i, p_i) for the description of the dynamics of the system. Thus generalised momenta and coordinates are dynamically equivalent sets of variables. This is quite explicit in quantum mechanics, even though this point was never appreciated during Hamilton's life time, and some people even branded him as a crazy man, with crazy ideas, that are purely mathematical and which have no relevance to meaningful physics!

5. The Hamiltonian and Hamilton's equations of motion can be derived only for holonomic systems. This is a cognisable restriction for the dynamics of bodies of large mass, whose motion is constrained by hard and immovable surfaces of various kinds. However, for the dynamics of microscopic systems like the atoms, molecules, etc. the forces involved are the known definite forces exerted by microscopic particles on one another and can be accounted for as the applied forces on the system. In these circumstances, the above restriction, and indeed the whole concept of constraints and constraint forces, becomes artificial and unnecessary. So the Hamiltonian dynamics can fundamentally enjoy an unrestricted applicability in the domain of microcosms.

6. The knowledge of the Hamiltonian of a system is extremely important, particularly if we are interested in quantising a dynamical system. As a rule, one starts with the classical Hamiltonian function and then replaces the generalised coordinates and momenta by the corresponding differential operators or the matrices, for setting up the Schrödinger equation or Heisenberg's matrix equation.

5.4 ROUTHIAN

This is another potential function constructed out of the Lagrangian and plays a role somewhat intermediate between the Lagrangian and the Hamiltonian. The *Routhian* is a function of mixed variables q_i, $\dot{q}_i$ and p_i, where the number of q_i coordinates is $n =$ the number of DOF and the rest n velocity-like independent variables are shared by $\dot{q}$'s and p's. The construction of a Routhian is meaningful only if there are some cyclic coordinates in the Lagrangian. If the first k out of n coordinates are cyclic in L then the Routhian for such a system is defined as

$$\begin{aligned} R &= R(q_1, \ldots, q_n, p_1, \ldots, p_k, \dot{q}_{k+1}, \ldots, \dot{q}_n, t) \\ &= \sum_{i=1}^{k} p_i \dot{q}_i - L(q_1, \ldots, q_n, \dot{q}_1, \ldots, \dot{q}_n, t) \end{aligned} \tag{5.11}$$

where $\dot{q}_i$, $i = 1, \ldots, k$ are constants of motion. Obviously the first equality, which is merely a functional definition of R gives

$$dR = \sum_{i=1}^{n} \frac{\partial R}{\partial q_i} dq_i + \sum_{i=1}^{k} \frac{\partial R}{\partial p_i} dp_i + \sum_{i=k+1}^{n} \frac{\partial R}{\partial \dot{q}_i} d\dot{q}_i + \frac{\partial R}{\partial t} dt$$

but the second equality in Eq. (5.11), that is, the defined explicit expression for R gives

$$dR = \sum_{i=1}^{k} (p_i d\dot{q}_i + \dot{q}_i dp_i) - \frac{\partial L}{\partial t} dt - \sum_{i=1}^{n} \left[\frac{\partial L}{\partial q_i} dq_i + \frac{\partial L}{\partial \dot{q}_i} d\dot{q}_i \right]$$

$$= - \sum_{i=k+1}^{n} p_i d\dot{q}_i + \sum_{i=1}^{k} \dot{q}_i dp_i - \frac{\partial L}{\partial t} - \sum_{i=1}^{n} \dot{p}_i dq_i$$

Now, comparing these two expressions for dR and treating the arguments of R as independent variables, we have, for the first k coordinates

$$\dot{q}_i = \frac{\partial R}{\partial p_i} \quad \text{and} \quad \dot{p}_i = \frac{\partial R}{\partial q_i} \quad \text{for } i = 1, \ldots, k \tag{5.12}$$

But for the rest $n - k$ coordinates, that is, from $i = k + 1$ to $i = n$, we get

$$\dot{p}_i = -\frac{\partial R}{\partial q_i} \quad \text{and} \quad p_i = -\frac{\partial R}{\partial \dot{q}_i}$$

Combining the last two equations, we then get

$$\frac{d}{dt}\left[\frac{\partial R}{\partial \dot{q}_i}\right] = \frac{\partial R}{\partial q_i} \quad \text{for } i = k + 1, \ldots, n \tag{5.13}$$

Finally for the t variable

$$\frac{\partial R}{\partial t} = -\frac{\partial L}{\partial t}$$

Hence for the first k coordinates which are supposed to be cyclic, Eqs (5.12) are like the Hamilton's equations of motion with H replaced by R. They would directly conserve momenta p_i since R is cyclic in the corresponding q_i. The rest $n - k$ coordinates in R are seen in Eq. (5.13) to satisfy Lagrange like equations of motion in R instead of L. The total energy in terms of the Routhian is therefore given by

$$E = \sum_{i=1}^{n} p_i \dot{q}_i - L = R + \sum_{i=k+1}^{n} p_i \dot{q}_i = R - \frac{\partial R}{\partial \dot{q}_i} \dot{q}_i \tag{5.14}$$

Since the first k coordinates are cyclic in R, the first k momenta are just constants of motion and cease to remain as variables. So the Routhian function will then effectively behave like a Lagrangian of a system having the number of DOF $= n - k$. In fact the Routhian satisfies the Lagrange-like equations of motion in all these $n - k$ coordinates. This effective reduction in the number of DOF is the chief advantage of the use of Routhian. It is because of this reduction in the number of DOF that the Kepler problem in three dimensions can be reduced to a planar problem with an effective number of DOF = 2, even though the orbit still remains describable in terms of all the three coordinates, r, θ and ϕ. Thus the number of DOF of a system, basically determined by the number of constraint relations, can effectively get reduced further, by the dynamical symmetries of the system. The constants of motion can indeed serve as extra constraints, which when expressed in terms of q's and $\dot{q}$'s, may look like nonholonomic constraints. For example, in the Kepler problem above, one can always define an arbitrary set of spherical polar coordinates, that will lead to $p_\phi = mr^2\dot{\phi} =$ constant, which can be viewed as a nonholonomic constraint in r and ϕ, but in reality the motion is free from any mechanical constraints.

5.5 CONFIGURATION SPACE, PHASE SPACE AND STATE SPACE

The n-dimensional space spanned by all the n generalised coordinates of any dynamical system is called the *configuration space* of that dynamical system.

The *phase space* is, on the other hand, spanned by all the n generalised coordinates and the corresponding n generalised momenta forming a $2n$-dimensional space.

The *state space* is a $2n + 1$ -dimensional space where one more dimension is added to the phase space to include the parameter time. This is also sometimes called it extended phase space.

One can also define a $n + 1$ -dimensional *extended configuration space* or *event space* by extending the n-dimensional configuration space to include the parameter time. This might look like a space-time continuum, but it is generally not so, as it is not a metric space. In fact none of the above types of fictitious mathematical constructs of hyperspaces defines any measure of scalar distance between two neighbouring points, so as to be called a metric, which should remain invariant under admissible coordinate transformations.

The Lagrangian $L(q_1, \ldots, q_n, \dot{q}_1, \ldots, \dot{q}_n, t)$ is always described in the configuration space of the requisite dimension set by the total number of generalised coordinates (including cyclic ones) of the system. The set $(q_1, \ldots, q_n)$ specifies a definite point in the configuration space which is the location of the system in the same space. The set of generalised velocities $\dot{q}_1, \ldots, \dot{q}_n$ represents the instantaneous direction and magnitude of the motion of the point $(q_1, \ldots, q_n)$ at time t. Euler-Lagrange's equations of motion determine only the curvature and torsion of the trajectory of the system in the configuration space provided the system is represented by a particular point in this space at time t.

On the other hand, the Hamiltonian $H(q_1, \ldots, q_n, p_1, \ldots, p_n, t)$ is described in a $2n$-dimensional phase space where each point has got coordinates and momenta uniquely specified so that Hamilton's equations of motion determine the course of evolution of the system in the form of a definite trajectory (or ray) in the phase space. This trajectory (and hence the motion of the system) is literally canonical, as it is predetermined, as if providentially, by the specified Hamiltonian. But in the case of the Lagrangian and Euler-Lagrange's equations of motion, the generalised velocities can be arbitrarily specified through the initial conditions for any given point in the configuration space and hence the course of evolution is not determined by the choice of the point alone. In a phase space the trajectory of phase point is analogous to the trajectory of a fluid particle in the motion of a fluid system. This is the reason why the occupant of a dynamical system in a phase space is often called a phase fluid.

In the phase space or the configuration space the trajectories may or may not be closed. But in the state space, however, two different trajectories may intersect in case of collisions, but a single trajectory never forms a closed loop. All trajectories in state space are open. A closed system evolves like a bundle of fibres in the time direction.

Example

Let us take a simple pendulum of fixed length l and bob mass m (Fig. 5.1). Take θ to be the generalised coordinate. For small θ the Lagrangian of this system can be written as

$$L(\theta,\dot{\theta}) = \frac{1}{2}m(l^2\dot{\theta}^2 - gl\theta^2)$$

where g is the constant acceleration due to gravity. This Lagrangian can be used to obtain Euler-Lagrange's equation of motion which has the form

$$\ddot{\theta} + \frac{g}{l}\theta = 0$$

Again the Lagrangian gives the generalised momentum as

$$p_\theta = \frac{\partial L}{\partial \dot{\theta}} = ml^2\dot{\theta}$$

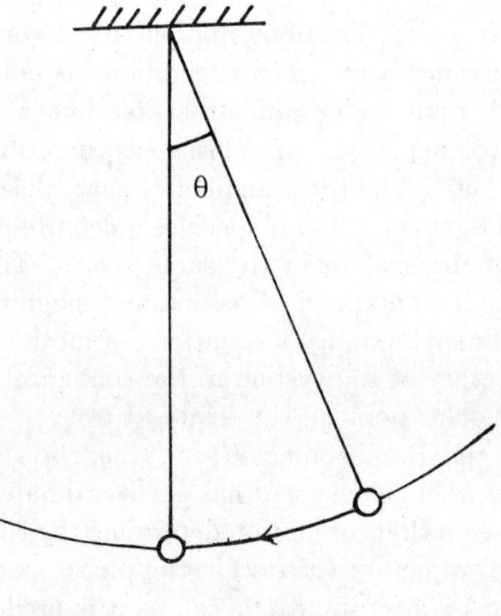

Fig. 5.1 Motion of a simple pendulum in real space

Finally the expressions for the total energy and the Hamiltonian are easily obtained as

$$E = \frac{1}{2}m(l^2\dot{\theta}^2 + gl\theta^2) \quad \text{and} \quad H(\theta,p_\theta) = \frac{p_\theta^2}{2ml^2} + \frac{1}{2}mgl\theta^2$$

The Hamiltonian yields Hamilton's equations of motion as

$$\dot{p}_\theta = -\frac{\partial H}{\partial \theta} = -mgl\theta \quad \text{and} \quad \dot{\theta} = \frac{\partial H}{\partial p_\theta} = \frac{p_\theta}{ml^2}$$

These are the two first order total differential equations. One can combine these two coupled equations and eliminate dt. We then get

$$\frac{dp_\theta}{d\theta} = \frac{m^2 g l^3 \theta}{p_\theta}$$

which can be easily integrated to give

$$p_\theta^2 + m^2 g l^3 \theta^2 = \text{const.}$$

This is the equation of an ellipse in coordinates p_θ and θ. Figure 5.2 shows the configuration space, the phase space and the state space diagrams of this system.

5.6 LAGRANGIAN AND HAMILTONIAN OF RELATIVISTIC PARTICLES AND LIGHT RAYS

One of the most famous equations of special relativistic mechanics, that is quoted even by a layman is $E = mc^2$, given by Albert Einstein in 1905. Here E is the total energy associated with mass m of a particle, both measured in a given inertial frame of reference. The relativistic momentum of a free particle is $\boldsymbol{p} = m\boldsymbol{v}$. In both these expressions mass is a frame dependent quantity. If a particle has got a rest mass m_o, its mass measured in a frame moving with a relativistic velocity $\boldsymbol{v}$ is given by $m = m_o/\sqrt{1 - v^2/c^2}$, c being the speed of light in vacuum.

Now, for a free particle the energy is

$$E = \boldsymbol{p}\cdot\boldsymbol{v} - L(\boldsymbol{r},\boldsymbol{v}) \quad \text{or} \quad mc^2 = mv^2 - L(\boldsymbol{r},\boldsymbol{v})$$

which gives

$$L(\boldsymbol{r},\boldsymbol{v}) = m(v^2 - c^2) = -m_o c\sqrt{c^2 - v^2} \tag{5.15}$$

This is the Lagrangian of a relativistic free particle.

If the particle is moving in a conservative potential field given by $V(\boldsymbol{r})$, the relativistic Lagrangian of the particle may be written as

$$L(\boldsymbol{r},\boldsymbol{v}) = -m_o c^2\sqrt{1 - v^2/c^2} - V(\boldsymbol{r}) \tag{5.16}$$

In the non-relativistic limit, ($v \ll c$), one gets from Eq. (5.16)

$$L(\boldsymbol{r},\boldsymbol{v}) = \frac{1}{2}m_o v^2 - V(\boldsymbol{r}) - m_o c^2$$

Except for the constant term, $-m_o c^2$, this is the expected classical Lagrangian for a particle moving in $V(\boldsymbol{r})$.

If a relativistic charged particle is moving in an electromagnetic field, the Lagrangian for

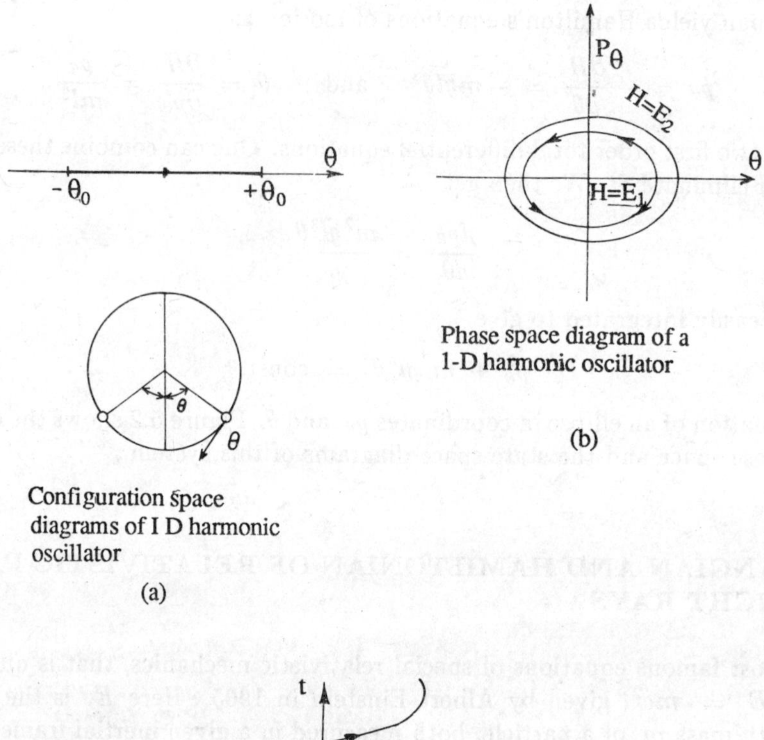

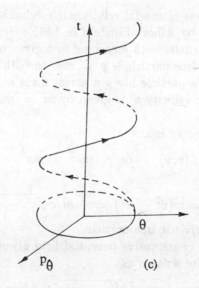

Fig. 5.2 Motion of a simple pendulum in its 1-D configuration space (a), 2-D phase space (b), and 3-D state space (c)

this particle can be obtained by subtracting the generalised potential $U(\boldsymbol{r}, \boldsymbol{v}) \ = \ e\phi \ - \ e(\boldsymbol{A} \cdot \boldsymbol{v})$ from the Lagrangian of a relativistic free particle given by Eq. (5.15). Thus we get, for

a relativistic charged particle

$$L(\boldsymbol{r},\boldsymbol{v}) = -m_o c\sqrt{c^2 - v^2} - e\phi + e\boldsymbol{A}\cdot\boldsymbol{v} \tag{5.17}$$

where e is the electric charge on the particle, $\boldsymbol{A} = \boldsymbol{A}(\boldsymbol{r},t)$ is the electromagnetic vector potential and $\phi = \phi(\boldsymbol{r},t)$ is the scalar electric potential at the location $(\boldsymbol{r})$ of the particle at time t.

Next, we wish to derive the Lagrangian for light rays. For a freely propagating beam of light, whether traveling in a transparent optical medium or in vacuum, according to the special theory of relativity, the rest mass associated with the photon is zero. Hence from Eq. (5.15) the Lagrangian for light rays is

$$L(\boldsymbol{r},\boldsymbol{v}) = 0 \tag{5.18}$$

However, this is not valid for a trapped beam of light, say inside a hot plasma. In that case the photon has a finite range, thus having a non-zero effective rest mass.

Once the Lagrangian is known, it is fairly easy to derive the corresponding Hamiltonian. As an illustration of the procedure of constructing a Hamiltonian from a given Lagrangian, we take the case of a relativistic free particle. First we define the canonical momentum

$$\boldsymbol{p} = \frac{\partial L}{\partial \boldsymbol{v}} = \frac{m_o\boldsymbol{v}}{\sqrt{1 - v^2/c^2}} \tag{5.19}$$

Since the Hamiltonian $H(\boldsymbol{r},\boldsymbol{p}) = \boldsymbol{p}\cdot\boldsymbol{v} - L$ is a function of $\boldsymbol{r}$ and $\boldsymbol{p}$ alone, we must express $\boldsymbol{v}$ as a function of $\boldsymbol{r}$ and $\boldsymbol{p}$ only so that

$$H(\boldsymbol{r},\boldsymbol{p}) = \boldsymbol{p}\cdot\boldsymbol{v}(\boldsymbol{r},\boldsymbol{p}) - L(\boldsymbol{r},\boldsymbol{v}(\boldsymbol{r},\boldsymbol{p}))$$

From Eq. (5.19)

$$p^2 = \frac{m_o^2 v^2}{1 - v^2/c^2} \qquad \text{or} \qquad \boldsymbol{v} = \frac{\boldsymbol{p}}{m_o}\left[1 + \frac{p^2}{m_o^2 c^2}\right]^{-1/2}$$

Therefore

$$H(\boldsymbol{r},\boldsymbol{p}) = \sqrt{p^2c^2 + m_o^2c^4} \tag{5.20}$$

Hence, corresponding to the Lagrangian (Eq. (5.16)), the Hamiltonian should be

$$H(\boldsymbol{r},\boldsymbol{p}) = \sqrt{p^2c^2 + m_o^2c^4} + V(\boldsymbol{r}) \tag{5.21}$$

In a similar manner it can easily be shown that the Hamiltonian of a relativistic charged particle moving in an electromagnetic field is

$$H(\boldsymbol{r},\boldsymbol{p}) = \sqrt{(\boldsymbol{p} - e\boldsymbol{A})^2c^2 + m_o^2c^4} + e\phi \tag{5.22}$$

where the canonical momentum is given by

$$\boldsymbol{p} = \frac{m_o\boldsymbol{v}}{\sqrt{1 - v^2/c^2}} + e\boldsymbol{A} = m\boldsymbol{v} + e\boldsymbol{A} \tag{5.23}$$

Similarly for light rays the Hamiltonian is given by

$$H(\boldsymbol{r}, \boldsymbol{v}) = \boldsymbol{p} \cdot \boldsymbol{v} - L = \boldsymbol{p} \cdot \boldsymbol{v}$$

But $\boldsymbol{v}$ should now be expressed as a function of $(\boldsymbol{r}, \boldsymbol{p})$. In an optically transparent medium, the speed of light is $v = c/\mu$, where μ is the refractive index of the medium. In general μ is a function of position $(\boldsymbol{r})$ and wavelength (λ). In the photon picture of light, the wavelength λ is related to the momentum $\boldsymbol{p}$ of the photon by $|\boldsymbol{p}| = h/\lambda$, where h is Planck's constant. Hence, one can write

$$H(\boldsymbol{r}, \boldsymbol{p}) = pv = \frac{pc}{\mu(\boldsymbol{r}, \boldsymbol{p})} \tag{5.24}$$

Using this Hamiltonian, one can obtain the equations of motion for propagation of light rays in any optical medium, given by

$$\dot{\boldsymbol{r}} = \frac{\partial H}{\partial \boldsymbol{p}} = \frac{c\boldsymbol{p}}{p\mu(\boldsymbol{r}, \boldsymbol{p})} - \frac{cp}{\mu^2}\left[\frac{\partial \mu(\boldsymbol{r}, \boldsymbol{p})}{\partial \boldsymbol{p}}\right] \tag{5.25}$$

and

$$\dot{\boldsymbol{p}} = -\frac{\partial H}{\partial \boldsymbol{r}} = \frac{pc}{\mu^2}\nabla \mu(\boldsymbol{r}, \boldsymbol{p}) \tag{5.26}$$

where $p = |\boldsymbol{p}|$.

It can be shown that $\dot{\boldsymbol{r}}$ in Eq. (5.25) corresponds to the group velocity of the wave packet associated with the photon. Equations (5.26) can be used to derive the trajectory of any light beam in any dispersive medium characterised by a given $\mu(\boldsymbol{r}, \boldsymbol{p})$, or equivalently $\mu(\boldsymbol{r}, \lambda)$.

5.7 RELATIVISTIC MASS TENSORS

The idea of tensors has been introduced in Appendix A3, and the reader is asked to refer to it before continuing with the present section.

In the previous section, we have already derived various forms of the Lagrangian for a particle moving with relativistic speeds under the action of some external force fields. The relativistic dynamics can also be studied by covariantly expressing Newton's second law of motion, that is, by forcing the validity of the Newtonian definition of force, $\boldsymbol{F} = d\boldsymbol{p}/dt$ where $\boldsymbol{p} = m\boldsymbol{v}$ is the relativistic momentum of the particle moving with velocity $\boldsymbol{v}$, the relativistic mass $m = m_o\gamma$, m_o being the rest mass of the particle, and $\gamma = (1 - v^2/c^2)^{-1/2}$ is the so called Lorentz γ-factor. Hence the ith component of the force can be expressed as

$$F_i = \frac{d}{dt}(mv_i) = \gamma^3 m_o \left[\frac{\delta_{ij}}{\gamma^2} + \frac{1}{c^2}\frac{dx_i}{dt}\frac{dx_j}{dt}\right]\frac{d^2x_j}{dt^2} = m_{ij}\frac{d^2x_j}{dt^2} \tag{5.27}$$

where the *relativistic mass tensor*

$$m_{ij} = m_o\left[\frac{\delta_{ij}}{\gamma^2} + \frac{v_iv_j}{c^2}\right]\gamma^3 \tag{5.28}$$

Obviously the direction of the force is no longer parallel to the direction of the acceleration, because of the presence of the second term in Eq. (5.28) which can be neglected only if $v_i v_j/c^2$ is small compared to γ^{-2}.

There are of course certain special cases in which m_{ij} behaves like a scalar and the force becomes parallel to the acceleration. For example, when the force $\boldsymbol{F}$ is acting parallel to the direction of motion of the particle, that is, $\boldsymbol{F}$ is parallel to $\boldsymbol{v}$

$$F_i = \gamma^3 m_o \frac{d^2 x_i}{dt^2} = m_l \frac{d^2 x_i}{dt^2} \tag{5.29}$$

where $m_l = \gamma^3 m_o$ is called the *longitudinal mass* of the particle. Again, when the force $\boldsymbol{F}$ is acting in a direction normal to the direction of the motion

$$F_i = \gamma m_o \frac{d^2 x_i}{dt^2} = m_t \frac{d^2 x_i}{dt^2} \tag{5.30}$$

with $m_t = \gamma m_o =$ the *transverse mass* of the particle. All it means is that the mass tensor m_{ij} in the form of Eq. (5.28) is in general not diagonalisable for any arbitrary direction of motion with respect to the direction of the applied force. It becomes so only when one of the principal axes (or the characteristic vectors) is aligned parallel or transverse to the direction of the force, which produces the diagonal elements as m_l, m_t and m_t, the transverse components being doubly degenerate. In this way, the mass tensor now can be reduced to behave as a vector. Finally, one can form a scalar out of the mass tensor by way of contraction of indices and the mass scalar for the Lorentz frame will turn out to be m_o, the rest mass of the particle.

Now let us formulate a possible form for the mass tensor m_{ij} for any given Lagrangian $L = L(q_1, \ldots, q_n, \dot{q}_1, \ldots, \dot{q}_n, t)$, for a nonrelativistic system. Using the operational identity,

$$\frac{d}{dt} = \frac{\partial}{\partial t} + \dot{q}_j \frac{\partial}{\partial q_j} + \ddot{q}_j \frac{\partial}{\partial \dot{q}_j}$$

the usual Euler-Lagrange's equations of motion namely,

$$\frac{d}{dt}\left(\frac{\partial L}{\partial \dot{q}_i}\right) - \frac{\partial L}{\partial q_i} = 0$$

can be reduced to

$$\ddot{q}_j \left[\frac{\partial^2 L}{\partial \dot{q}_i \partial \dot{q}_j}\right] = \frac{\partial L}{\partial q_i} \tag{5.31}$$

where we have assumed that $\partial L/\partial \dot{q}_i \ (= p_i)$ is not an explicit function of $q_1, \ldots, q_n$ and t. Since Euler-Lagrange's equations of motion can be written as

$$\frac{dp_i}{dt} = \frac{\partial L}{\partial q_i}$$

so that $(\partial L/\partial q_i)$ can be regarded as the Newtonian equivalent of some kind of generalised force and $\ddot{q}_i$ as the corresponding generalised acceleration, an effective mass tensor can be defined from Eq. (5.31) as

$$m_{ij} = \frac{\partial^2 L}{\partial \dot{q}_i \partial \dot{q}_j} \tag{5.32}$$

One can now easily see that the Lagrangian for the relativistic particle moving in a potential field $V(\boldsymbol{r}, t)$, as given by Eq. (5.16) or the one moving in an electromagnetic field with the generalised potential given by Eq. (5.17) yields the same result for the mass tensor as given in Eq. (5.28) (see problem 5.11), provided the definition of m_{ij} is taken to be the one given above, namely in Eq. (5.32). In fact, for the motion of the relativistic charged particle having charge e and moving in an electromagnetic field, one can show that

$$m_o\gamma(\delta_{ij} + \gamma^2 v_i v_j)\frac{d^2 r_j}{dt^2} = eE_i + e(\boldsymbol{v} \times \boldsymbol{B})_i \tag{5.33}$$

where $\boldsymbol{E}$ and $\boldsymbol{B}$ are the electric field and the magnetic induction respectively at the location of the moving particle as seen by any inertial observer.

The first term on the LHS of Eq. (5.33) is $m_o\gamma(d^2r_i/dt^2)$ which is nothing but the ordinary relativistic force with mass $m = m_o\gamma$. The corresponding acceleration is in the direction parallel to the forces expressed on the RHS of Eq. (5.33). But the second term on the LHS of Eq. (5.33) can be rewritten in the vector notation as $m_o\gamma^3(\boldsymbol{v}\cdot\boldsymbol{a})\boldsymbol{v}/c^2$, where $\boldsymbol{a} = d^2\boldsymbol{r}/dt^2$ denotes the acceleration vector. This term can be taken to the RHS of Eq. (5.33) and interpreted as a relativistic constraint force $\boldsymbol{f}_c = -m_o\gamma^2(\boldsymbol{v}\cdot\boldsymbol{a})\boldsymbol{v}/c^2$. This force is antiparallel to $\boldsymbol{v}$ when the angle between $\boldsymbol{v}$ and $\boldsymbol{a}$ is acute, and is parallel to $\boldsymbol{v}$ otherwise. Now the angle between $\boldsymbol{a}$ and $\boldsymbol{v}$ is acute only when the particle is accelerating forward or speeding up and in that case the component of $\boldsymbol{v}$ perpendicular to $\boldsymbol{a}$ will undergo a negative acceleration.

It is also possible to consistently define a mass tensor from a given Hamiltonian $H = H(q_1, \ldots, q_n, p_1, \ldots, p_n, t)$ in the following way. From Hamilton's equations of motion,

$$\begin{aligned}\ddot{q}_i &= \frac{d\dot{q}_i}{dt} = \frac{d}{dt}\left[\frac{\partial H}{\partial p_i}\right] = \frac{\partial^2 H}{\partial p_i \partial p_j}\dot{p}_j + \frac{\partial^2 H}{\partial p_i \partial q_j}\dot{q}_j + \frac{\partial^2 H}{\partial p_i \partial t} \\ &= -\frac{\partial^2 H}{\partial p_i \partial p_j}\frac{\partial H}{\partial q_j} + \frac{\partial^2 H}{\partial p_i \partial q_j}\frac{\partial H}{\partial p_j} + \frac{\partial^2 H}{\partial p_i \partial t}\end{aligned} \tag{5.34}$$

From the first term on the RHS, the inverse mass tensor m_{ij}^{-1} can be defined as

$$m_{ij}^{-1} = \frac{\partial^2 H}{\partial p_i \partial p_j} \tag{5.35}$$

because, when H does not depend explicitly on time, the system is conservative with the generalised force $\partial H/\partial q_i = Q_i$. Here again, we have assumed that $\partial H/\partial q_i$ is not a function of p_i so that the last two terms on the RHS of Eq. (5.34) vanish. We thus have

$$\ddot{q}_i = -\frac{\partial^2 H}{\partial p_i \partial p_j}Q_j = m_{ij}^{-1}Q_j$$

Furthermore, one can also verify that

$$\frac{\partial^2 L}{\partial \dot{q}_i \partial \dot{q}_j} \frac{\partial^2 H}{\partial p_i \partial p_j} = \delta_{ij} \tag{5.36}$$

provided m_{ij} is itself nonsingular. For example, if we consider the Lagrangian and the Hamiltonian for a relativistic particle moving in a conservative force field we can easily verify Eq. (5.36) using Eq. (5.28) and the expression for m_{ij}^{-1} from its definition (Eq. (5.35))

$$m_{ij}^{-1} = \frac{\partial^2 H}{\partial p_i \partial p_j} = m_o^{-1} \gamma^{-1} \left(\delta_{ij} - \frac{v_i v_j}{c^2} \right)$$

Equation (5.35) is, however, most profitably used in the calculation of the effective mass of an electron or hole moving inside a solid lattice for which the dispersion relation $\omega(\boldsymbol{k})$ or $E(\boldsymbol{p})$ is known. Taking $p_i = \hbar k_i$ and $H = E$, Eq. (5.35) transforms into

$$m_{ij}^{-1} = \frac{1}{\hbar^2} \frac{\partial^2 E}{\partial k_i \partial k_j} \tag{5.37}$$

where $\boldsymbol{k}$ is the wave vector associated with the motion of an electron or hole in the lattice, and E is the energy of the same electron or hole as a function of $\boldsymbol{k}$.

5.8 SUMMARY

Hamilton derived the equations of motion in 1835 in terms of a function called the Hamiltonian $H = H(q, p, t)$, which can geometrically describe a surface in phase space. If one draws a normal to this surface $H(q, p, t) = E$ (say, a constant) at a point (q, p) in the phase space, its projections onto the individual coordinate and momentum axes represent the time rate of increment of the respective coordinates and momenta. So unlike the case with the Lagrangian described in configuration space, the evolution at all points of the phase space is completely specified with the specification of the Hamiltonian.

For conservative systems, this Hamiltonian function represents a constant of motion, which can readily be identified with the total energy of the system. Moreover, the paths of evolution in phase space always lie on the surface of the given constant energy.

The description in terms of the Hamiltonian is extremely useful even for quantising any dynamical system under consideration. The knowledge of the explicit Hamiltonian is required to construct Schrödinger's equation, as that of the Lagrangian is required for developing field theory.

The concept of relativistic and electromagnetic mass tensors is introduced in the last section, which elucidates some aspects of the motion of relativistic and charged particles that are not found in usual text books. Also the construction of the Lagrangian and Hamiltonian for such systems in section 5.6 gives an idea of how the same results, namely the same equations of motion, can be derived using so many different techniques. While reading this chapter, one must keep in mind that Einstein's summation convention is implied wherever it applies, unless stated otherwise.

PROBLEMS

5.1 If the Lagrangian $L = L_o + L_1 + L_2 + \cdots$, where L_r is a homogeneous function of degree r in $\dot{q}_i$ with coefficients as any function of q_i, prove that
(a) the Hamiltonian is given by

$$H = -L_o + L_2 + 2L_3 + \cdots$$

(b) $H = 0$, for $L = L_1$

5.2 Write down the complete set of Hamilton's equations of motion for a dynamical system for which the Lagrangian is given by

$$L = \frac{1}{2}a_{ij}\dot{q}_i\dot{q}_j - V(q) \qquad i, j = 1, \ldots, n$$

5.3 If $z_k = \frac{1}{\sqrt{2}}(q_k + ip_k)$ and $\bar{z}_k = \frac{1}{\sqrt{2}}(q_k - ip_k)$, show that Hamilton's equations of motion can be expressed in the following compact form

$$\frac{dz_k}{dt} + i\frac{\partial H}{\partial \bar{z}_k} = 0$$

where $i = \sqrt{-1}$.

5.4 If a dynamical system is subject to constraints of the form $X_i^j \delta q_i = 0$ $(j = 1, \ldots, k;\ i = 1, \ldots, n;\quad n > k)$, deduce Hamilton's equations

$$\dot{x}_m = \frac{\partial H}{\partial p_m} + \sum_{j=1} k\lambda_j X_m^j$$

where X_m^j are suitably constructed from X_i^j and λ_j are Lagrange's undetermined multipliers.

5.5 The Hamiltonian for a 3-D isotropic harmonic oscillator is given by

$$H = \frac{1}{2}\sum_{i=1}^{3}(p_i^2 + \mu q_i^2)$$

Show that,

$$F_1 = q_2p_3 - q_3p_2$$
$$F_2 = q_3p_1 - q_1p_3$$
$$F_3 = q_1p_2 - q_2p_1$$
$$G_1 = \mu q_1 \cos(\mu t) - p_1 \sin(\mu t)$$
$$G_2 = \mu q_2 \cos(\mu t) - p_2 \sin(\mu t)$$
$$G_3 = \mu q_3 \cos(\mu t) - p_3 \sin(\mu t)$$

are the constants of motion.

5.6 For the following Lagrangians, find the corresponding Hamiltonians:
(i) $L(x, \dot{x}) = \frac{1}{2}\dot{x}^2 - \frac{1}{2}\omega^2 x^2 - \alpha x^3 + \beta x \dot{x}^2$, for an anharmonic oscillator,
(ii) $L(\theta, z, \dot{\theta}, \dot{z}) = \frac{1}{2}m(l^2\dot{\theta}^2 - 2l\dot{\theta}\dot{z}\sin\theta) + mgl\cos\theta + \frac{1}{2}\dot{z}^2 + mgz$, for a pendulum (l, θ) hung from the ceiling of a moving lift, the instantaneous position of the fulcrum being denoted by $z(t)$.
(iii) $L(q, \dot{q}, t) = \frac{1}{2}G(q,t)\dot{q}^2 + F(q,t)\dot{q} - V(q,t)$, for particle motion in resistive media embedded in a conservative field.
(iv) $L(x, \dot{x}) = \frac{1}{2}m\dot{x}^2\left[1 + (df/dx)^2\right] - mgf(x)$, for a bead of mass m sliding smoothly along a wire of shape $z = f(x)$, z-axis and x-axis being respectively horizontal and vertical.

5.7 Find the Routhian for the following Lagrangians:
(i) $L = \frac{1}{2}\mu(\dot{r}^2 + r^2\dot{\theta}^2) + GMm/r$; $\mu = mM/(m + M)$, G, M, m are constants.
(ii) $L = \frac{1}{2}I_3(\dot{\psi} + \dot{\phi}\cos\theta)^2 + \frac{1}{2}I_1(\dot{\theta}^2 + \dot{\phi}^2\sin^2\theta) - mgl\cos\theta$;
I_1, I_3, m, g, l are constants. Find also the effective potentials for the r-motion in the first case and for the θ-motion in the second case.

5.8 Show that for any closed system, the translational and rotational invariance of the Hamiltonian $H(\boldsymbol{r}, \boldsymbol{p})$ for infinitesimal translation and rotation leads to the conservation of the total linear and angular momentum respectively.

5.9 Set up Hamilton's equations of motion for the following Lagrangians:
(i) $L(\boldsymbol{r}, \boldsymbol{v}) = -m_o c\sqrt{c^2 - v^2} + e\boldsymbol{A}\cdot\boldsymbol{v} - e\phi$
(ii) $L(q, \dot{q}, t) = m(\dot{q}^2\sin^2\omega t + q\dot{q}\omega\sin 2\omega t + q^2\omega^2)/2$.

5.10 Find the equation for the trajectory of light ray through the atmosphere for which the refractive index (μ) decreases linearly with height z as $\mu(z) = 1 + n_o\exp(-z/H)$ and explain the phenomenon of mirage. Take $n_o = 1.000292$, $H = 8.0$ km.

5.11 Using the definition of m_{ij} given by Eq. (5.32) and the Lagrangian for the motion of a relativistic charged particle, as given in (i) of problem 5.9, show that it satisfies the equation of motion given by Eq. (5.33).

6

Principle of Least Action and Hamilton's Principle

6.0 INTRODUCTION

In this chapter we are going to introduce a new way of formulating dynamical problems. This technique goes by the name of the variational principle. It involves a good deal of variational calculus. We know that Leibniz and Newton had independently invented differential calculus some time before 1675. The foundation of integral and variational calculus was laid by Jean Bernoulli around 1690, and further developed by Euler in 1734 and by Lagrange and Euler in 1762.

Suppose we ask the following question: how do you define a circle? In fact, it can be defined in many different ways. For example, one of you may define the circle as a locus of points in a plane equidistant from a given point. When expressed mathematically it may read as $(x - x_1)^2 + (y - y_1)^2 = a^2$, where (x_1, y_1) is the given point called the centre of the circle, and a the given distance called the radius of the circle. In polar coordinates with the origin at the centre, the equation looks very simple, $r = a$. Another one of you may define it as a locus of a point at which the angle made with two given points in a plane is always a right angle. If the distance between the two given points is $2a$, and one of the points is chosen to be the origin of a plane polar coordinate system, the equation of the circle becomes $r = 2a\cos\theta$. One of you may also define a circle as a curve of constant curvature drawn in a plane. Mathematically speaking, this definition implies the equation of circle to be $d\theta/ds = a^{-1}$ or, $a\, d^2y/dx^2 = \{1 + (dy/dx)^2\}^{3/2}$. Unlike the first two, this one is a differential representation. In the same spirit, the variational definition of a circle would be the one that encloses an area of given magnitude with the smallest possible arc length drawn in a plane. Again, mathematically speaking, the equation would be $\delta \oint \sqrt{r^2 + (dr/d\theta)^2}\, d\theta = 0$, with the constraint relation for the area given by $\oint r^2\, d\theta$ = constant. This is known as the problem of isoperimetry proposed by Jean Bernoulli around 1690. It should be noted that all the four definitions are equivalent.

In order to make the analogy complete with our business of dynamics, we can readily recognise the differential form to represent Newton's second law of motion, or Euler– Lagrange's equations of motion or even Hamilton's equations of motion. The first two forms of our example look like algebraic solutions to the differential equations. The motivation for the search for a possible variational form of the equations of motion came from the work of Fermat, who in 1657 suggested that given the initial and final points, light follows a path through any given optical medium in such a way that the sum of the piecewise product of the refractive index n and the path lengths is an extremum. The question was, for matter particles can there be a suitable replacement for the refractive index, so that the sum of the piecewise product of this replaced quantity and the path length over the entire path between two fixed points could be an extremum? Maupertuis was the first person who got an answer to it. However, it was later known that Leibniz also had thought of Maupertuis' principle a few decades earlier than Maupertuis.

Nevertheless, this problem was so exciting that it involved people like Euler, Lagrange, Hamilton, Jacobi and Noether, each contributing substantially to the field. Today, Hamilton's principle plays a key role in field theory, be it classical, quantum mechanical, or relativistic quantum mechanical. Their starting point is Hamilton's principle.

6.1 PRINCIPLE OF LEAST ACTION

A French mathematician Pierre de Maupertuis in 1740 enunciated the famous principle of least action. This can be stated as follows. Consider a particle moving from point 1 to point 2 in space. Then out of all possible paths between these two fixed points in space, the actual path traversed by the particle is the one for which the integral called the action,

$$S = \int_1^2 mv\, ds \tag{6.1}$$

is an extremum, that is, this integral has the largest or the smallest value for the actual path. This can also be expressed by requiring that for the actual path taken by the particle the first variation of the above integral should vanish, that is,

$$\delta S = \delta \int_1^2 mv\, ds = 0 \tag{6.2}$$

Here of course we impose the condition that a particle's energy is a constant of motion.

This principle was first published as an exact dynamical theorem by Leonard Euler in 1744, who proved it for a single particle moving in a plane. Finally, Joseph Lagrange formulated the principle of least action in a form applicable to general cases like many particle systems (1760 – 61). Lagrange stated this principle as follows,

$$\delta \left(m_1 \int_1^2 v_1\, ds_1 + m_2 \int_1^2 v_2\, ds_2 + \ldots \right)_{E\,=\,\text{const.}} = 0$$

or

$$\delta \left(m_i \int v_i\, ds_i \right)_{E\,=\,\text{const.}} = 0 \tag{6.3}$$

Before we proceed with Lagrange's proof we make a study of the basics of calculus of variation.

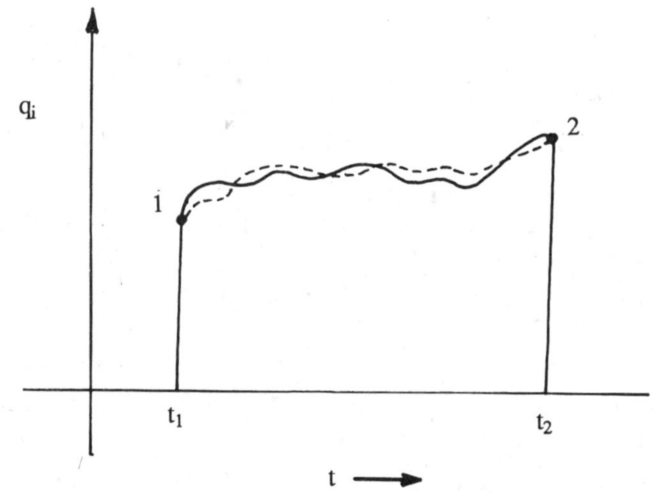

Fig. 6.1 Variation of path between two fixed terminal points

A variation of the path from any given path in configuration space is always considered to be infinitesimal and the variation in the (generalised) coordinates is always taken at the same instant. At any given instant of time, for every point on any given path, there exists a corresponding point on a neighboring path that differs from the original point by an infinitesimal separation in the generalised coordinates, the two points having the coordinates $q_i(t)$ and $q_i(t) + \delta q_i(t)$. This $\delta q_i(t)$ is called the variation in the generalised coordinate $q_i(t)$ at time t. In Fig. 6.1 the solid curve is the curve q_i between $t = t_1$, and $t = t_2$ and the dotted curve is the variation of the above curve. So at any instant t in the range $t_1 < t < t_2$, the varied path has slightly different coordinates from its value for the original curve. Any change in the coordinate that occurs naturally with time, be it represented by the solid curve or the dotted curve in Fig. 6.1, is the real change in the coordinate and is represented by dq_i along the respective path. Figure 6.2 is a magnified view of a small portion of the two paths shown in Fig 6.1 so that the paths AB and CD are the segments of any two varied paths where point C corresponds to the variation of point A at time t and point D stands for the variation of point B at time $t + dt$. We can now reach point D from point A via two routes : either by the route ACD or by the route ABD. The coordinates of the points A,B and C in Fig. 6.2 are as follows

$$\begin{array}{ll} \text{Point A :} & (t, \quad q_i) \\ \text{Point B :} & (t + dt, \quad q_i + dq_i) \\ \text{Point C :} & (t, \quad q_i + \delta q_i) \end{array}$$

Now point D can have its coordinates as either $\{t + dt, (q_i + dq_i) + \delta(q_i + dq_i)\}$ if we move from B to D, or $\{t + dt, (q_i + \delta q_i) + d(q_i + \delta q_i)\}$ if we move from C to D. But they should physically correspond to the same quantity. Hence, equating these two expressions we can easily get,

$$\delta(dq_i) = d(\delta q_i) \tag{6.4}$$

Hence δ and d commute. Again all the variations take place at the same instant t, therefore the variation of t is identically zero, that is, $\delta t = 0$, by definition for any value of t.

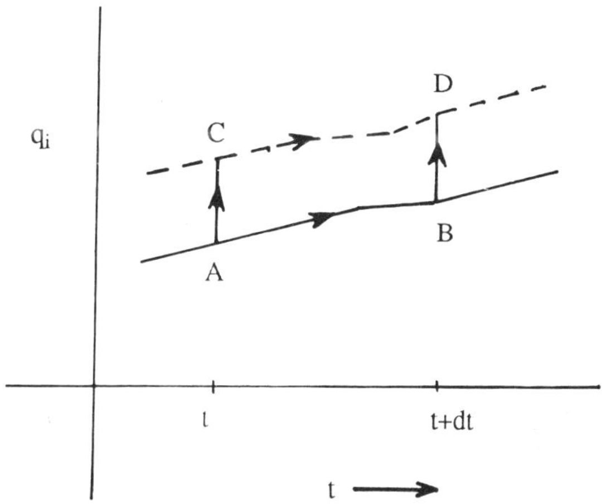

Fig. 6.2 Infinitesimal segments of the real and varied paths

Now

$$\delta(dq_i) = \delta(\dot{q}_i\, dt) = \delta\dot{q}_i\, dt + \dot{q}_i\, \delta(dt) = \delta\dot{q}_i\, dt$$

Since $\delta(dq_i) = d(\delta q_i)$, we thus have

$$d(\delta q_i) = \delta\dot{q}_i\, dt$$

or

$$\frac{d}{dt}(\delta q_i) = \delta\dot{q}_i \tag{6.5}$$

Thus the variation in $\dot{q}_i$ is related to the variation in q_i by the total time derivative of the latter.

We must now understand what we mean by the first variation of the integral

$$\int_{P_1}^{P_2} F(q_1, \ldots, q_n; \dot{q}_1, \ldots, \dot{q}_n, t)\, dt \tag{6.6}$$

Here F is a differentiable function over the n-dimensional configuration space and P_1, P_2 are two fixed points in the configuration space and the integral is to be carried out along a path C joining P_1 and P_2. The parameter t parametrises the path C. We are interested in the variation of the value of the above integral as the path C is varied slightly, keeping the end points P_1 and P_2 fixed and also keeping the values of the parameter t at P_1 and P_2

fixed (that is, all varied paths start from P_1 at the same initial value of t and end at P_2 at the same final value of t).

Now choosing one path in the configuration space is equivalent to fixing the functional dependences $q_i(t)$, $i = 1, \ldots, n$. Since the path passes through P_1 and P_2, we must have,

$$q_i(t_1) = q_i' \qquad \text{and} \qquad q_i(t_2) = q_i'' \tag{6.7}$$

where q_i' and q_i'' are the coordinates of the points P_1 and P_2, and t_1 and t_2 are the values of parameter t at P_1 and P_2 respectively, on the given path. In order to account for the possible variations in path, we make the functions q_i depend on an additional parameter u such that a given value of u corresponds to a unique path, that is, in general,

$$q_i = q_i(t, u) \qquad i = 1, \ldots, n \tag{6.8}$$

with

$$q_i = q_i(t, 0) = q_i(t)$$

for a special path characterised by $u = 0$. A neighbouring path or a curve $C(u)$ corresponding to the parameter value u is given by

$$q_i = q_i(t, u) = q_i(t) + u\eta_i(t) \tag{6.9}$$

where

$$\eta_i(t) = \left(\frac{\partial q_i}{\partial u}\right)_{u=0}$$

Here we have expanded $q_i(t, u)$ in a Taylor series around $u = 0$ and kept the terms up to the first order only, since the variation is small. In order that $C(u)$ also pass through P_1 and P_2, we require,

$$\eta_i(t_1) = \eta_i(t_2) = 0 \tag{6.10}$$

Further, differentiating Eq. (6.9) with respect to t, we get

$$\dot{q}_i(t, u) = \dot{q}_i(t) + u\dot{\eta}_i(t) \tag{6.11}$$

where we have put

$$\dot{\eta}_i = \left(\frac{\partial \dot{q}_i}{\partial u}\right)_{u=0}$$

The integral evaluated along the curve $C(u)$ between P_1 and P_2 is obviously a function of u so that we should write

$$I(u) = \int_{t_1}^{t_2} F(q_i(t, u), \dot{q}_i(t, u), t)\, dt$$

or, using Eqs (6.9) and (6.11),

$$I(u) = \int_{t_1}^{t_2} F(t,\, q_i(t) + u\eta_i(t),\, \dot{q}_i(t) + u\dot{\eta}_i(t))dt \tag{6.12}$$

The integral (6.6) can be denoted as $I(0)$ and hence, expanding $I(u)$ in Taylor's series around $u = 0$ we get

$$I(u) = I(0) + u\left(\frac{\partial I}{\partial u}\right)_{u=0} + O(u^2) \tag{6.13}$$

where $O(u^2)$ represents terms of order of magnitude of u^2. This suggests the definition of δI, the first order variation in I due to an infinitesimal change in the path characterised by u, and is given by

$$\delta I = \delta\int_{t_1}^{t_2} F(q_i, \dot{q}_i, t)dt = u\left(\frac{\partial I}{\partial u}\right)_{u=0} \tag{6.14}$$

Differentiating the RHS of Eq. (6.12) with respect to u (assuming t_1, t_2 fixed) and then putting $u = 0$ we get

$$\left(\frac{\partial I}{\partial u}\right)_{u=0} = \int_{t_1}^{t_2}\left\{\frac{\partial F}{\partial q_i}\eta_i + \frac{\partial F}{\partial \dot{q}_i}\dot{\eta}_i\right\}dt$$

Therefore,

$$\delta I = u\left(\frac{\partial I}{\partial u}\right)_{u=0} = \int_{t_1}^{t_2}\left\{\frac{\partial F}{\partial q_i}u\eta_i + \frac{\partial F}{\partial \dot{q}_i}u\dot{\eta}_i\right\}dt$$

Now it is easy to see from Eqs (6.9) and (6.11) that

$$\delta q_i(t) = u\eta_i(t) \quad \text{and} \quad \delta\dot{q}_i(t) = u\dot{\eta}_i(t) \tag{6.15}$$

giving

$$\delta I = \int_{t_1}^{t_2}\left\{\frac{\partial F}{\partial q_i}\delta q_i + \frac{\partial F}{\partial \dot{q}_i}\delta\dot{q}_i\right\}dt = \int_{t_1}^{t_2}\delta F dt \tag{6.16}$$

The quantity δI is called the first variation of the integral (6.6). Now consider the variation of the following integral given by

$$\delta I' = \delta\int_{P_1}^{P_2} F(q, \dot{q}, t)dq = \delta\int_{P_1}^{P_2} F\frac{dq}{dt}dt$$

Using Eq. (6.16) we get

$$\begin{aligned}\delta I' &= \int_{P_1}^{P_2}\delta\left(F\frac{dq}{dt}\right)dt = \int_{P_1}^{P_2}\delta F dq + \int_{P_1}^{P_2} F\delta(\dot{q})dt \\ &= \int_{P_1}^{P_2}\delta F dq + \int_{P_1}^{P_2} F\frac{d}{dt}(\delta q)dt = \int_{P_1}^{P_2}\delta F dq + \int_{P_1}^{P_2} Fd(\delta q) \\ &= \int_{P_1}^{P_2}\delta F dq + \int_{P_1}^{P_2} F\delta(dq)\end{aligned} \tag{6.17}$$

where we have used Eqs (6.5) and (6.4) (in that order).

The results expressed in Eqs (6.16) and (6.17) can be easily appreciated if we recall the definition of the integral as the summed products of F and Δt or F and Δq over the entire interval under consideration. In that case, the variation of the integral with the fixed limits of integration will legitimately be transferred to the possible variation of the products $F\Delta t$ or $F\Delta q$. Since the variation of dt is zero, we have only one term in Eq. (6.16) and two terms in Eq. (6.17).

We shall use Eqs (6.16) and (6.17) extensively in this chapter. Note that while calculating $(\partial I/\partial u)_{u=0}$ we have assumed that the limits of integration (that is, end points of all the paths) are constants independent of u. Otherwise, according to Leibniz's rule of differentiation under the integral, derivatives of these limits have to be accounted for. Indeed, as we shall see in section 6.2 , the variations at the end points need not always vanish, in which case the corresponding differentials appear in the expression for the first variation of the integral. If the end points of all the varied paths are not the same we have $(\delta q_i)_{\text{initial}} \neq 0$. Moreover under more general situations the two varied paths need not even start precisely at the same instant nor may they end at the same instant. The allowance for such variations in the timings of the initial and final instants (though generally very small and usually denoted by $(\Delta t)_{\text{initial}}$ and $(\Delta t)_{\text{final}}$) sometimes play a crucial role in the variational studies. Now we come back to Lagrange's proof of the principle of least action. This involves the Cartesian coordinates x_i in spite of the fact that the motions may take place in presence of constraints, so that the arbitrary variations of all x_i are not strictly allowed, as x_i 's are not all independent of one another. So only if there are no constraints, is the proof given below mathematically flawless.

Let $\hat{\boldsymbol{t}}_i$ be the unit tangent vector to the ith curve representing the path for the ith particle at the point under consideration. Thus the variation of Lagrange's action for the whole system of N particles can be written as (as the Einsteinian summation convention implies)

$$
\begin{aligned}
\delta\left(m_i \int v_i ds_i\right) &= \delta\left(m_i \int (v_i\hat{\boldsymbol{t}}_i)\cdot(ds_i\hat{\boldsymbol{t}}_i)\right) = \delta\left(m_i \int \boldsymbol{v}_i \cdot d\boldsymbol{r}_i\right) \\
&= \left(m_i \int \delta\boldsymbol{v}_i \cdot d\boldsymbol{r}_i\right) + m_i \int \boldsymbol{v}_i \cdot \delta(d\boldsymbol{r}_i) \\
&= m_i \int \delta\dot{\boldsymbol{r}}_i \cdot d\boldsymbol{r}_i + m_i \int \dot{\boldsymbol{r}}_i \cdot d(\delta\boldsymbol{r}_i) \\
&= m_i \int \delta\dot{\boldsymbol{r}}_i \cdot d\boldsymbol{r}_i + m_i \int d(\dot{\boldsymbol{r}}_i \cdot \delta\boldsymbol{r}_i) - m_i \int d\dot{\boldsymbol{r}}_i \cdot \delta\boldsymbol{r}_i \\
&= m_i \int \delta\dot{\boldsymbol{r}}_i \cdot \dot{\boldsymbol{r}}_i\, dt + m_i \int d(\dot{\boldsymbol{r}}_i \cdot \delta\boldsymbol{r}_i) - m_i \int (\ddot{\boldsymbol{r}}_i \cdot \delta\boldsymbol{r}_i)\, dt \\
&= \left[\int m_i\dot{\boldsymbol{r}}_i \cdot \delta\dot{\boldsymbol{r}}_i dt + \int \boldsymbol{\nabla}_i V \cdot \delta\boldsymbol{r}_i dt\right] - \int \boldsymbol{\nabla}_i V \cdot \delta\boldsymbol{r}_i dt \\
&\qquad + \int m_i d(\dot{\boldsymbol{r}}_i \cdot \delta\boldsymbol{r}_i) - \int m_i(\ddot{\boldsymbol{r}}_i \cdot \delta\boldsymbol{r}_i) dt \\
&= \int (\delta T + \delta V) dt - \int (m_i\ddot{\boldsymbol{r}}_i + \boldsymbol{\nabla}_i V)\cdot \delta\boldsymbol{r}_i dt + \int m_i d(\dot{\boldsymbol{r}}_i \cdot \delta\boldsymbol{r}_i) \\
&= \int \delta E dt + \int m_i d(\dot{\boldsymbol{r}}_i \cdot \delta\boldsymbol{r}_i) - \int (m_i\ddot{\boldsymbol{r}}_i - \boldsymbol{F}_i)\cdot \delta\boldsymbol{r}_i dt
\end{aligned}
\tag{6.18}
$$

Here $\boldsymbol{F}_i = -\boldsymbol{\nabla}_i V$ is the conservative external force that is applied on the ith particle, and E is the total energy of the system, $E = T + V$. Now, if

(i) the energy is kept constant for all the varied paths, that is, only those variations are taken for which total energy E of the system is the same for all the varied paths and is a constant of motion for each of the paths,

(ii) the end points are fixed, that is, $\delta \boldsymbol{r}_i = 0$ at both the ends,that is,

$$\int_1^2 m_i d(\dot{\boldsymbol{r}}_i \cdot \delta \boldsymbol{r}_i) = m_i(\dot{\boldsymbol{r}}_i \cdot \delta \boldsymbol{r}_i)\Big|_1^2 = 0$$

and

(iii) D'Alembert's principle is valid, that is,

$$(m_i \ddot{\boldsymbol{r}}_i - \boldsymbol{F}_i) \cdot \delta \boldsymbol{r}_i = 0$$

then all the three terms on RHS of Eq. (6.18) vanish giving

$$\delta \int_1^2 m_i v_i ds_i = 0 \tag{6.19}$$

Again since $m_i v_i ds_i = m_i \boldsymbol{v}_i \cdot d\boldsymbol{r}_i = \boldsymbol{p}_i \cdot \boldsymbol{v}_i dt$, Eq. (6.18) can also be expressed as

$$\delta \int_1^2 (\boldsymbol{p}_i \cdot \boldsymbol{v}_i) dt \Big|_{E\, =\, \text{const.}} = 0$$

In terms of generalised coordinates this means

$$\delta \int_1^2 p_i \dot{q}_i dt \Big|_{E\, =\, \text{const.}} = \delta \int_1^2 p_i dq_i \Big|_{E\, =\, \text{const.}} = 0 \tag{6.20}$$

The principle of least action expressed as in Eq. (6.19) is sometimes called Lagrange's principle of least action. Since $p_i \dot{q}_i = 2T$, another equivalent form of Eq. (6.20) is

$$\int_1^2 2T dt \Big|_{E\, =\, \text{const.}} = 0 \tag{6.21}$$

which is sometimes called Jacobi's principle of least action. One more equivalent form that ensues from Eq. (6.19) is

$$\int_1^2 \sqrt{2m_i(E_i - V_i)}\, ds_i \Big|_{E\, =\, \text{constant}} = 0 \tag{6.22}$$

where $E_i = \frac{1}{2} m_i v_i^2 + V_i$, and V_i are the total energy and the potential energy respectively of the ith particle. Some books refer to this as Jacobi's principle of least action.

Remarks:

1. The condition (iii) for the applicability of the principle of least action should not be interpreted as a validity check on Newton's second law of motion as $\boldsymbol{F}_i$ in Eq. (6.18) do not contain any constraint forces and hence do not represent the total force. The above forces $\boldsymbol{F}_i$ are the externally applied forces and are conservative in nature. The validity of D'Alembert's

principle requires that (i) the quantities must be evaluated in the inertial frames only, and (ii) the system must be D'Alembertian, that is, holonomic or at most a special class of non-holonomic systems in which the velocity dependence in the constraint relation is homogeneous. One should, however, remember that Lagrange's proof itself becomes invalid for any constrained system.

2. The end points do not have the same interpretation for all the principles of least action. For example, $\delta \int_1^2 p_i dq_i = 0$ means that the integration is to be performed over dq_i and the end points are $(q_i)_i$ and $(q_i)_f$ respectively, whereas for Jacobi's principle of least action $\int_1^2 2T dt = 0$, the integration is to be perfomed with respect to time and the end point timings are fixed. Moreover, it is also required that the condition (ii) be satisfied, that is, the terminal coordinates must be fixed.

3. We also require that $\int_1^2 \delta E dt = 0$. The easiest way to satisfy this condition is to set $\delta E = 0$ for the entire route, implying that the system must be conservative.

4. Most of these principles of least action can be expressed as $\delta \int_1^2 mv ds = 0$, i.e., the specification of the integrand requires the knowledge of the momentum p as a function of E and spatial coordinate $\boldsymbol{r}$, but not the knowledge of the explicit time dependence of $\boldsymbol{r}(t)$. So if one is basically interested in the trajectories of the particles, rather than a complete solution to the motion, these principles of least action are ideal for such a purpose.

6.2 HAMILTON'S PRINCIPLE

We have seen that all the principles of least action stated above in different forms have very limited applicability. These seem to be far more restricted than D'Alembert's principle. First, one has to do away with the requirement that the system should be conservative. In other words, the term $\int_1^2 \delta E dt$ in Eq. (6.18) should be expressed in a different way. This is done in the following way.

Consider a term like $\delta \int_1^2 E dt$. Obviously a definite integral $\int_1^2 E dt$ should be a function of the limits of integration. Mathematically speaking, the variation of this integral can, in general, have two contributions : one coming from a term $\int_1^2 \delta E dt$ = the variation in energy between the real and the varied path integrated between the time limits and the second, $E_f \Delta_f t - E_a \Delta_a t$, originating from the time variation, if any, between the two paths at the terminal points. Therefore,

$$\int_1^2 \delta E dt = \delta \int_1^2 E dt - [E_f \Delta_f t - E_a \Delta_a t]$$

where $\Delta_f t$ and $\Delta_a t$ are the variations in the limits of integration over t. In the derivation of Eq. (6.18) we have everywhere used the criterion that all δ variations are virtual (no change in real time). Here we have relaxed the condition only for the end points (in time).

Now writing the LHS of Eq. (6.18) as

$$\delta \int_1^2 m_i \boldsymbol{v}_i \cdot d\boldsymbol{r}_i = \delta \int_1^2 m_i \boldsymbol{v}_i \cdot \boldsymbol{v}_i dt = \delta \int_1^2 2T dt$$

and rearranging Eq. (6.18) and using $T + V = E$, we get

$$\delta \int_1^2 (T - V)dt = \int_1^2 m_i d(\dot{\boldsymbol{r}}_i \cdot \delta \boldsymbol{r}_i) - \int_1^2 (m_i \ddot{\boldsymbol{r}}_i - \boldsymbol{F}_i) \cdot \delta \boldsymbol{r}_i dt - [E_f \Delta_f t - E_a \Delta_a t] \tag{6.23}$$

the left-hand side of which is $\int_1^2 Ldt$, where L is the Lagrangian of the system.

Now we can have $\delta \int_1^2 Ldt = 0$, from Eq. (6.23) provided the following conditions are simultaneously satisfied namely,

(i) all the coordinates of the end points are fixed $\delta \boldsymbol{r}_i \Big|_f = \delta \boldsymbol{r}_i \Big|_a$,

(ii) $\Delta_a t = \Delta_f t = 0$, that is, both the terminal time instants are fixed but now it does not matter whether energy is varied between the real and the varied paths or not, and

(iii) D'Alembert's principle of motion is valid (tentatively); the exact requirement of this third condition needs further investigation.

The above Lagrangian $L = T - V$ can easily be generalised to $L = T - U$ as we know that U differs from V by a gyroscopic force term which does not do any work, so its inclusion on both sides of Eq. (6.23) is permissible. Unless given *a priori*, one always calculates L from its Cartesian description of velocities which are known functions of generalised coordinates and velocities. But as soon as one writes L in terms of the generalised coordinates and velocities, all q_i and $\dot{q}_i$'s become independent of one another for all holonomic bilateral systems, and the use of the variational principle with all δq_i 's being mutually independent becomes fully justified. However, since one cannot, in principle, start with a quantity $\delta \boldsymbol{r}_i$ for a constrained system, it is impossible to rigorously prove this principle.

The above form of the least action principle, namely,

$$\delta \int_1^2 L(q, \dot{q}, t)dt = 0 \tag{6.24}$$

is called Hamilton's principle of least action (or Hamilton's principle in short) where the end points of the paths are fixed both in space and time but the energy at any point of the varied path need not be the same as at the corresponding point on the real path. Hamilton suggested this principle in 1834. This principle is so important that it is worth stating again in words.

Hamilton's principle:

A dynamical system moves from one configuration to another in such a way that the variation of the integral, $\int_1^2 Ldt$ (L being the given Lagrangian of the system) between the actual path taken and any neighbouring virtual path, coterminous in both space and time with the actual path, is zero, or in other words, $\int_1^2 Ldt$ is stationary.

The point to be noted here is that Hamilton introduced it as a principle to be obeyed by nature and did not specify the exact domain of its validity. From its inception, this principle has assumed an axiomatic status. It is certainly valid for an unconstrained system which is obviously D'Alembertian, but whether or not it applies to the general D'Alembertian systems is yet to be seen.

Thus there are basically two working forms of the principle of least action.

1. Lagrange's principle of least action

$$\left[\delta\int_{q_{ka}}^{q_{kf}} p_k dq_k\right]_{E\,=\,\text{const.}} = 0 \tag{6.25}$$

which is restricted to the conservative systems only, and

2. Hamilton's principle

$$\delta\int_{t_1}^{t_2} L(q,\dot{q},t)dt = 0 \tag{6.24}$$

which is certainly restricted to the D'Alembertian systems. Whether further restrictions are to be imposed or not is considered in section 6.4.

6.3 COMPARISON BETWEEN FERMAT'S PRINCIPLE OF LEAST ACTION IN OPTICS AND MAUPERTUIS' PRINCIPLE OF LEAST ACTION IN MECHANICS

The famous French mathematician Pierre de Fermat (1657) gave his principle of least action for the path of light rays, which states simply that

$$\delta\int_1^2 \frac{ds}{v} = 0 \tag{6.26}$$

where v is the speed of light at a point in an optical medium and ds is the displacement measured along the path of the ray at the corresponding point. Since light travels with a fantastically great speed, one need not bother about its actual motion in time; the determination of its trajectory is sufficient, which is what Fermat's principle offers us.

Maupertuis' principle of least action for material particles, on the other hand, requires the condition

$$\delta\int_1^2 v\,ds = 0 \tag{6.27}$$

to be satisfied if the particle is moving in a conservative force field and if the varied paths correspond to the same energy of the system as the real path. So this principle can be used to determine the trajectory of a material particle. Now the most interesting thing to note is that these two principles of least action have exactly opposite dependence on the speed v in their integrands. It certainly raises the doubt as to whether or not light can be regarded as a particle in the true mechanical sense.

In the last quarter of the seventeenth century, the Dutch physicist Christiaan Huygens and the English physicist Sir Isaac Newton were caught in a debate as to the nature of light rays; whether light rays are propagating waves or traveling corpuscles. Snell's law of refraction of light (given by the Dutch physicist Willebrord Snell in 1621) was found to be derivable not only from Fermat's principle and Huygens' wave theory of light but also from Newton's corpuscular theory. Now the question is, how could it happen? In order to satisfy Snell's law of refraction, Fermat's principle suggests that the speed of light has to be lower in the denser medium and the refractive index of any homogeneous medium $n = (c/v) > 1$, where c is the speed of light in vacuum and v the speed of light in the refractive medium. On the other hand, the corpuscular theory of light following Maupertuis' principle of least action, suggested an opposite relation, namely higher speed of corpuscular light beam in the denser medium (see problem 6.6). This debate remained unsettled until Fizeau in 1851 did an experiment to measure the actual speed of light in water and Newton's corpuscular theory was abandoned thereafter. So the trajectory of the light rays follows from Fermat's principle of least action, not from Maupertuis'.

6.4 DERIVATION OF EULER-LAGRANGE EQUATIONS OF MOTION FROM HAMILTON'S PRINCIPLE

In order to use Hamilton's principle as expressed in Eq. (6.24), namely,

$$\delta \int_1^2 L(q, \dot{q}, t)dt = 0$$

where q and $\dot{q}$ stand for the sets of n generalised coordinates and n generalised coordinate velocities respectively, the only thing one needs is the specification of the Lagrangian of the system in its explicit form. Thus we construct an n-dimensional configuration space and varied paths are drawn in it. As the end points of all varied paths are coterminous both in coordinates and time, we get, as in Eq. (6.17)

$$\delta \int_1^2 Ldt = \int_1^2 \delta L dt + \int_1^2 L\delta(dt)$$

The second term on RHS vanishes because $\delta(dt) = 0$ for all points of the varied paths including the end points. We have,

$$\delta L = \frac{\partial L}{\partial q_i}\delta q_i + \frac{\partial L}{\partial \dot{q}_i}\delta \dot{q}_i + \frac{\partial L}{\partial t}\delta t$$

provided all q_i, $\dot{q}_i$ and t are strictly independent arguments, which is true only for a bilateral holonomic system. Again, the third term on RHS vanishes as $\delta t = 0$ and we can write

$$\begin{aligned}\delta L &= \frac{\partial L}{\partial q_i}\delta q_i + \frac{\partial L}{\partial \dot{q}_i}\frac{d}{dt}(\delta q_i) \\ &= \frac{\partial L}{\partial q_i}\delta q_i + \frac{d}{dt}\left(\frac{\partial L}{\partial \dot{q}_i}\delta q_i\right) - \frac{d}{dt}\left(\frac{\partial L}{\partial \dot{q}_i}\right)\delta q_i \\ &= \frac{d}{dt}\left(\frac{\partial L}{\partial \dot{q}_i}\delta q_i\right) - \left[\frac{d}{dt}\left(\frac{\partial L}{\partial \dot{q}_i}\right) - \frac{\partial L}{\partial q_i}\right]\delta q_i\end{aligned}$$

It should be noted here that although q_i and $\dot{q}_i$ are all independent of one another, δq_i and $\delta \dot{q}_i$ are not because of the variational identities $\delta \dot{q}_i = d(\delta q_i)/dt$. Hence even though $L = L(q, \dot{q}, t)$, $\delta \int_1^2 Ldt$ becomes finally dependent on δq_i's, t_a, t_f, q_{ia} and q_{if} . Thus we get,

$$\delta \int_1^2 L dt = \int_1^2 \delta L dt = \frac{\partial L}{\partial \dot{q}_i}\delta q_i \bigg|_1^2 - \int_1^2 \left[\frac{d}{dt}\left(\frac{\partial L}{\partial \dot{q}_i}\right) - \frac{\partial L}{\partial q_i}\right] \delta q_i dt$$

The first term on RHS vanishes because δq_i at the terminal points 1 and 2 are zero. Thus Hamilton's principle requires

$$\int_1^2 \left[\frac{d}{dt}\left(\frac{\partial L}{\partial \dot{q}_i}\right) - \frac{\partial L}{\partial q_i}\right] \delta q_i dt = 0$$

Since q_i 's are all independent of each other, δq_i can be arbitrary and the above equality is satisfied only if

$$\frac{d}{dt}\left(\frac{\partial L}{\partial \dot{q}_i}\right) - \frac{\partial L}{\partial q_i} = 0 \qquad i = 1, \ldots, n$$

which are the well-known Euler–Lagrange's equations of motion for any bilateral holonomic system having no nonpotential forces and n DOF. Obviously the definition of L does not and cannot contain any effect of nonpotential forces. Euler had used the above variational procedure in order to derive the same equations of motion as were derived by Lagrange starting from D'Alembert's principle. This is the reason why we call them Euler-Lagrange's equations of motion.

For nonholonomic systems, the q_i 's are not all independent of each other and hence δq_i 's cannot be taken as independent variations of q_i 's. So Hamilton's principle is unusable, and hence in practice cannot be applied to nonholonomic systems. In this sense Hamilton's principle is more restricted than D'Alembert's principle for tackling mechanical problems. However, the variational principles do not exclude their applicability to systems having infinite DOF. All modern field theories, being examples of infinite DOF and spanning almost the entire physics, are, in fact, founded upon the versatile use of Hamilton's principle. This is considered to be the greatest advantage of Hamilton's principle over D'Alembert's principle.

6.5 DERIVATION OF HAMILTON'S EQUATIONS OF MOTION FOR HOLONOMIC SYSTEMS FROM HAMILTON'S PRINCIPLE

We start by requiring that

$$\delta \int_1^2 L dt = \int_1^2 (\delta L) dt = 0$$

The relation between the Lagrangian and the Hamiltonian is given by the usual Legendre transformation

$$L(q, \dot{q}, t) = p_i \dot{q}_i - H(q, p, t)$$

Therefore, in terms of the Lagrangian and the Hamiltonian variables,

$$\begin{aligned} \delta L &= p_i \delta \dot{q}_i + \dot{q}_i \delta p_i - \frac{\partial H}{\partial q_i}\delta q_i - \frac{\partial H}{\partial p_i}\delta p_i \\ &= \frac{d}{dt}(p_i \delta q_i) - \left(\dot{p}_i + \frac{\partial H}{\partial q_i}\right)\delta q_i + \left(\dot{q}_i - \frac{\partial H}{\partial p_i}\right)\delta p_i \end{aligned}$$

the variations of L now being expressible in terms of δq_i and δp_i through the Hamiltonian function. Both can be arbitrary, provided we consider the variation of the paths in a $2n$-dimensional phase space and no longer in the n-dimensional configuration space. Through this, we are now allowing $\delta \dot{p}_i = d(\delta p_i)/dt$ together with $\delta \dot{q}_i = d(\delta q_i)/dt$. Thus we have,

$$\delta \int_1^2 L dt = \int_1^2 (\delta L) dt = [p_i \delta q_i]_1^2 - \int_1^2 \left(\dot{p}_i + \frac{\partial H}{\partial q_i}\right) \delta q_i + \int_1^2 \left(\dot{q}_i - \frac{\partial H}{\partial p_i}\right) \delta p_i$$

The first term on RHS vanishes since $\delta q_i = 0$ at the terminal points 1 and 2. Since the system is holonomic and is now described in the phase space, q_i's and p_i's are all independent, and, δq_i's and δp_i's are arbitrary at all points of the path. It should be noted that the vanishing of δq_i at the terminal points does not imply that δp_i's are also zero at the terminal points. In fact they do not generally vanish. All the above integrals can vanish, only if

$$\dot{p}_i = -\frac{\partial H}{\partial q_i} \quad \text{and} \quad \dot{q}_i = \frac{\partial H}{\partial p_i}$$

which are Hamilton's equations of motion.

6.6 INVARIANCE OF HAMILTON'S PRINCIPLE UNDER GENERALISED COORDINATE TRANSFORMATION

We have already seen earlier that if we add the total time derivative of any function of the form $F(q_1, \ldots, q_n, t)$ to the Lagrangian of a holonomic system, Euler-Lagrange's equations of motion remain unchanged. This fact can be demonstrated in a more straightforward manner in the following way. Let

$$L'(q_1, \ldots, q_n; \dot{q}_1, \ldots, \dot{q}_n; t) = L(q_1, \ldots, q_n; \dot{q}_1, \ldots, \dot{q}_n; t) + \frac{dF(q_1, \ldots, q_n, t)}{dt}$$

Therefore,

$$\delta \int_1^2 L' dt = \delta \int_1^2 L dt + \delta \int_1^2 \left[\frac{dF(q_1, \ldots, q_n, t)}{dt}\right] dt$$

$$= \delta \int_1^2 L dt + \delta \left[F(q_1, \ldots, q_n, t)\right]_1^2$$

The last term on the RHS vanishes because

$$\delta F = \frac{\partial F}{\partial q_i} \delta q_i + \frac{\partial F}{\partial t} \delta t$$

is zero when evaluated at both the end points. Therefore,

$$\delta \int_1^2 L' dt = \delta \int_1^2 L dt = 0$$

Thus the Lagrangian $L' = L + dF/dt$ is also subject to Hamilton's principle and therefore must lead to the same form of Euler-Lagrange's equations of motion as L.

Let us consider a general coordinate transformation from a set of independent coordinates and time $(q_1, \ldots, q_n, t)$ to another independent set $(Q_1, \ldots, Q_n, \tau)$ given by

$$q_i = q_i(Q_1, \ldots, Q_n, \tau) \quad \text{and} \quad t = t(Q_1, \ldots, Q_n, \tau) \quad i = 1, \ldots, n \tag{6.28}$$

The same old Lagrangian L changes only its form to $\tilde{L}(Q_1, \ldots, Q_n, \tau)$ on mere substitution of Eq. (6.28) in L. Now, if the total physical content or the message of Hamilton's principle is not to change under this transformation (6.28), then we must have

$$\delta \int_1^2 L(q_1, \ldots, q_n, t)dt = \delta \int_1^2 \tilde{L}(Q_1, \ldots, Q_n, \tau)\frac{dt}{d\tau}d\tau = \delta \int_1^2 L^*(Q_1, \ldots, Q_n, \tau)d\tau$$

with the result that the new Lagrangian L^* must be given by

$$L^*(Q_1, \ldots, Q_n, \tau) = \tilde{L}(Q_1, \ldots, Q_n, \tau)\frac{dt}{d\tau} = L(q_1, \ldots, q_n, t)\frac{dt}{d\tau} \tag{6.29}$$

This is the required condition on the Lagrangian for any generalised coordinate and time transformation, which ought to preserve the form of Euler-Lagrange's equations of motion.

6.7 HAMILTON'S PRINCIPAL AND CHARACTERISTIC FUNCTIONS

Let us write Hamilton's principle for any holonomic bilateral system as

$$\delta W = \delta \int_1^2 L dt = 0$$

The first of the above equalities defines a function

$$W = \int_1^2 L dt \tag{6.30}$$

The function W as defined above is called *Hamilton's principal function.* We have already seen that Hamilton's principle is valid if both the terminal points are fixed in space and time. Hence W must be a function of the sets of generalised coordinates of the initial and final points (that is, of points 1 and 2) in the n-dimensional configuration space and of the initial and final instants of time at which the particle was at the initial and final points respectively. Thus we can write,

$$W = W(q_{1a}, \ldots, q_{na}; q_{1f}, \ldots, q_{nf}; t_a, t_f) \tag{6.31}$$

for any bilateral holonomic system having the number of DOF $= n$. However, this is also valid if we are working with a phase space of dimension $2n$.

In terms of generalised coordinates and momenta, we can now evaluate the general variation of W in the phase space in the following way. First we start with,

$$\begin{aligned}
\delta \int_1^2 p_i dq_i &= \int_1^2 \delta p_i dq_i + \int_1^2 p_i \delta(dq_i) = \int_1^2 \delta p_i \dot{q}_i dt + \int_1^2 p_i d(\delta q_i) \\
&= \int_1^2 \delta p_i \frac{\partial H}{\partial p_i} dt + \int_1^2 d(p_i \delta q_i) - \int_1^2 \dot{p}_i \delta q_i dt \\
&= \int_1^2 \left(\frac{\partial H}{\partial p_i} \delta p_i + \frac{\partial H}{\partial q_i} \delta q_i \right) dt + [p_i \delta q_i]_1^2 \\
&= \int_1^2 \delta H dt + [p_i \delta q_i]_1^2
\end{aligned}$$

Now,

$$\begin{aligned}
\delta W &= \delta \int_1^2 [p_i dq_i - H dt] \\
&= \int_1^2 \delta H dt - \delta \int_1^2 H dt + [p_i \delta q_i]_1^2 \qquad (6.32) \\
&= -[H_f \Delta_f t - H_a \Delta_a t] + [p_i \delta q_i]_f - [p_i \delta q_i]_a
\end{aligned}$$

where the suffix f corresponds to the final terminal point and the suffix a corresponds to the initial terminal point. Here $\Delta_f t$, $\Delta_a t$, $(\delta q_i)_f$ and $(\delta q_i)_a$ for $i = 1, \ldots, n$ can be arbitrary and hence are independent of each other. Therefore, any arbitrary variation of W can be fully interpreted using a subset of the phase space. In fact the n-dimensional configuration space will suffice to describe the complete time evolution of the function W. Hence, we must have, for δW, from Eq. (6.31),

$$\delta W = \frac{\partial W}{\partial q_{ia}} \delta q_{ia} + \frac{\partial W}{\partial q_{if}} \delta q_{if} + \frac{\partial W}{\partial t_a} \Delta t_a + \frac{\partial W}{\partial t_f} \Delta t_f \qquad (6.33)$$

Comparing term by term for Eqs (6.32) and (6.33), we get,

$$\frac{\partial W}{\partial q_{ia}} = -p_{ia} \qquad (6.34a)$$

$$\frac{\partial W}{\partial q_{if}} = p_{if} \qquad (6.34b)$$

$$\frac{\partial W}{\partial t_f} + H\left(q_{if}, \frac{\partial W}{\partial q_{if}}\right) = 0 \qquad (6.34c)$$

and $$\frac{\partial W}{\partial t_a} - H\left(q_{ia}, \frac{\partial W}{\partial q_{ia}}\right) = 0 \qquad (6.34d)$$

Thus Hamilton's principal function can be obtained by solving (simultaneously) the last two of the above equations which are the first order partial differential equations, and using the first two as supplements.

Now *Hamilton's characteristic function* is defined in a similar way from Lagrange's principle of least action, namely, $\delta \int_1^2 p_i dq_i = 0$ which is valid if $\delta H = 0$, or $H = E =$ const. over the varied paths whose end point coordinates are fixed. Hamilton's characteristic function is defined as

$$\left[\int_1^2 p_i dq_i\right]_{H=E} = S(q_{1a}, \ldots, q_{na}; q_{1f}, \ldots, q_{nf}; E)$$

with the differential conditions

$$\frac{\partial S}{\partial q_{ia}} = -p_{ia} \tag{6.35a}$$

and

$$\frac{\partial S}{\partial q_{if}} = p_{if} \tag{6.35b}$$

and $H = E$ corresponding to the first order partial differential equation

$$H\left(q_{ra}; \frac{\partial S}{\partial q_{ra}}\right) = E \tag{6.36a}$$

and

$$H\left(q_{rf}; \frac{\partial S}{\partial q_{rf}}\right) = E \tag{6.36b}$$

It should be pointed out that the notations S and W are just the opposite in Goldstein's book.

It was initially Hamilton who suggested that a pair of the partial differential equations (consisting of the initial and final sets of coordinates and time as independent variables) as given by Eqs (6.34c,d) or (6.36a,b) are to be solved for either the W function or S function, as the case may be. One has to first obtain the correct complete integral for the required set of simultaneous partial differential equations. Because, a complete integral to the initial-value-related equation will contain n arbitrary nontrivial constants, and similarly the final-value-related equation will also contain another n arbitrary nontrivial constants. The form of the integral has to be such that the constants of integration do exactly take the place of the initial values q_{ia} and p_{ia}, thus duly satisfying the other two sets of the equations, namely, Eqs (6.34a,b) or Eqs (6.35a,b). This is really a very difficult task, making Hamilton's prescription the most formidable onc, even though the solution, if obtained, would represent the most complete one indeed.

At this point of impasse, Jacobi (1845) demonstrated two things: one that for conservative systems, one can choose either of the W formalism and the S formalism without sacrificing any degree of completeness of the solutions thus obtaied, and the other that for a given formalism, two partial differential equations, namely the initial and the final value-related equations need not be solved simultaneously. Without losing generality, he claimed, it is sufficient to solve only the final-value-related equations as the equations in the running variables, so that the final solutions would look like either $S = S(q_i, E)$ or $W = W(q_i, t)$, as the case may be. The initial-value-related equations are therefore all redundant. Jacobi further pointed out that there was also no need to look for any special complete integral with the right type of the constants of motion. In fact, any complete integral with a set of

$n + 1$ arbitrary constants coupled with the equations

$$\frac{\partial W}{\partial q_i} = p_i \quad \text{and} \quad \frac{\partial W}{\partial \alpha_i} = \beta_i$$

was shown to be equivalent to Hamilton's $2n$ equations of motion, both solving the problem equally exactly and completely. Here α_i are the n nontrivial constants of integration that come with the complete integral for W. The proof and details of Jacobi's method will be considered in chapter 10.

Therefore, we have, for the S formalism:

$$\frac{\partial S}{\partial q_i} = p_i \tag{6.37a}$$

and

$$H\left(q_i, \frac{\partial S}{\partial q_i}\right) = E \tag{6.37b}$$

and for the W formalism:

$$\frac{\partial W}{\partial q_i} = p_i \tag{6.38a}$$

and

$$H\left(q_i, \frac{\partial W}{\partial q_i}, t\right) + \frac{\partial W}{\partial t} = 0 \tag{6.38b}$$

The first-order partial differential equations given by Eqs (6.37b) and (6.38b) are respectively called the *time-independent* and the *time-dependent Hamilton-Jacobi equations.*

6.8 NOETHER'S THEOREM

We have already introduced Noether's theorem in section 2.13. Here we shall give its formal statement and the proof.

Theorem

If for an infinitesimal transformation of the generalised coordinates q_i of a holonomic system and of time t of the form

$$\begin{aligned} q_i' &= q_i + \epsilon\Psi_i(q_i, t) \\ t' &= t + \epsilon\chi(q_i, t) \qquad \epsilon \to 0 \end{aligned} \tag{6.39}$$

Hamilton's principal function is invariant, that is,

$$\delta \int_{t_1}^{t_2} L\left(q_i, \frac{dq_i}{dt}, t\right) dt = \delta \int_{t_1'}^{t_2'} L\left(q_i', \frac{dq_i'}{dt'}, t'\right) dt'$$

then the quantity

$$\frac{\partial L}{\partial q_i}(\dot{q}_i\chi - \Psi_i) - L\chi \tag{6.40}$$

is an integral of motion.

Proof

We know that the variation of Hamilton's principal function stands for the variation of the terminal coordinates and time, that is,

$$\delta W = \delta \int_{t_1}^{t_2} L(q, \dot{q}, t) dt = \left[\frac{\partial W}{\partial q_i} \delta q_i + \frac{\partial W}{\partial t} \delta t \right]_a^f$$

If we now interpret δq_i and δt which are infinitesimal variations or displacements in the values of the coordinates and time of the original frame, to be effectively equivalent to the ones generated by the infinitesimal coordinate and time transformations given by Eq. (6.39), then $\delta q_i = -\epsilon \Psi_i(q,t)$ and $\delta t = -\epsilon \chi(q,t)$ for all points of the path including the end points. This is called a changeover from an active to a passive viewpoint. Let us digress here for a moment in order to clarify this point with an example.

Suppose a rigid body rotates about an axis represented by the unit vector $\hat{\boldsymbol{n}}$ by an amount $\Delta\theta$ in time Δt. The position vector of any particle at $\boldsymbol{r}$ will now actively change to $\boldsymbol{r} + \Delta \boldsymbol{r} = \boldsymbol{r} + (\hat{\boldsymbol{n}} \times \boldsymbol{r})\Delta\theta$. But the same change in coordinates can be effected by rotating the coordinate axes about $\hat{\boldsymbol{n}}$ by an angle $-\Delta\theta$. The former viewpoint is called an *active viewpoint* and the latter a *passive* one. Note that there will be a change of sign.

So the requirement of the invariance of W under a passive coordinate and time transformation given by Eq. (6.39) can be effectively viewed as one under an active displacement in both coordinates and time, with a change of sign. Thus, $\delta W = 0$ under the transformation Eq. (6.39) will effectively mean

$$\left[\frac{\partial W}{\partial q_i} \epsilon \Psi_i(q,t) + \frac{\partial W}{\partial t} \epsilon \chi(q,t) \right]_{\text{final}} = \left[\frac{\partial W}{\partial q_i} \epsilon \Psi_i(q,t) + \frac{\partial W}{\partial t} \epsilon \chi(q,t) \right]_{\text{initial}}$$

Now since ϵ is arbitrary, $p_i = \partial W / \partial q_i$ and $H = -\partial W / \partial t$, we must have, for all points of the path,

$$p_i \Psi_i(q,t) - H\chi(q,t) = \text{const.}$$

or

$$\frac{\partial L}{\partial \dot{q}_i} \Psi_i(q,t) - \left(\frac{\partial L}{\partial \dot{q}_i} \dot{q}_i - L \right) \chi(q,t) = \text{const.}$$

or

$$\frac{\partial L}{\partial \dot{q}_i} (\dot{q}_i \chi(q,t) - \Psi(q,t)) - L\chi(q,t) = \text{const.}$$

This theorem is valid for all bilateral holonomic systems. Noether's theorem in the above form can further be generalised to the case when the transformation of coordinates and time changes Hamilton's principal function in the following way;

$$\int_{t_1}^{t_2} L\left(q, \frac{dq}{dt}, t\right) dt = \int_{t_1'}^{t_2'} \left[L\left(q', \frac{dq'}{dt'}, t'\right) + \epsilon \frac{dF(q', t')}{dt'} \right] dt'$$

that is, when W is invariant under the Lagrangian gauge transformation, to a new set of coordinates and time. Obviously, this would simply add $F(q,t)$ to Eq. (6.40) giving

$$\frac{\partial L}{\partial \dot{q}_i}(\dot{q}_i\chi - \Psi_i) - L\chi + F = \text{const.} \tag{6.41}$$

This is the most general form of Noether's theorem first given by Emmy Noether in 1918.

Now for any closed system, all the conservation laws due to homogeneity of space and time and isotropy of space would follow immediately from Eqs (6.40) and (6.41), as shown below.

(i) For the homogeneity of time, we put $q_i' = q_i$ and $t' = t + \epsilon$ so that $\Psi_i = 0$ and $\chi = 1$ and the Eq. (6.40) gives

$$\frac{\partial L}{\partial \dot{q}_i}\dot{q}_i - L = \text{const.}$$

This is the law of conservation of energy for a closed system.

(ii) For the homogeneity of space, we use Cartesian coordinates with the infinitesimal coordinate transformation $x_i' = x_i + \epsilon$ and $t' = t$, that is, $\Psi_i = 1$ and $\chi = 0$ for any particular i, giving

$$\frac{\partial L}{\partial \dot{x}_i} = \text{const.} \quad \text{or} \quad p_i = \text{const.}$$

So the component p_i of the linear momentum corresponding to any Cartesian coordinate x_i is conserved for a closed system.

(iii) For the isotropy of space, we choose any particular generalised coordinate q_i as the angle θ and $q_i' = q_i + \epsilon$, $t' = t$ with $\Psi_i = 1$ and $\chi = 0$ giving

$$\frac{\partial L}{\partial \dot{q}_i} = \text{const.} = \frac{\partial L}{\partial \dot{\theta}}$$

Thus the angular momentum corresponding to the θ-rotation is constant.

(iv) For invariance under the Galilean transformation, we must use the form given by Eq. (6.41). Taking $t' = t$, $x' = x - \epsilon t$ so that $\chi = 0$, $\Psi_i = -t$, and the required $F = -m\dot{x}$, for a single particle moving in the x-direction, Noether's theorem in the form of Eq. (6.41) says that

$$-m\dot{x}t + mx = \text{const.}$$

Actually, for a system of particles,

$$\Sigma m_i x_i - \Sigma p_i t = \text{const.}$$

which is known as Galilean translational invariance.

6.9 LORENTZ INVARIANCE OF HAMILTON'S PRINCIPAL FUNCTION FOR THE RELATIVISTIC MOTION OF A FREE PARTICLE

The special relativistic metric in 4-space is given by

$$ds^2 = c^2 dt^2 - dx^2 - dy^2 - dz^2 = c^2 dt^2 \left(1 - \frac{v^2}{c^2}\right)$$

Therefore,

$$ds = c\sqrt{1 - \frac{v^2}{c^2}}\, dt \tag{6.42}$$

Define

$$W_{12} = \int_1^2 dW = \int_1^2 L\, dt$$

and use the expression for the Lagrangian for a free particle given by Eq. (5.15) to get

$$W_{12} = -\int_1^2 m_0 c^2 \sqrt{1 - \frac{v^2}{c^2}}\, dt = -\int_1^2 m_0 c\, ds \tag{6.43}$$

Since m_0 and ds are Lorentz invariants and c is a constant, W_{12} for the motion of a free particle is an invariant quantity.

Now $\delta W = 0$ for the motion of any free particle would imply

$$\delta \int_1^2 ds = 0 \tag{6.44}$$

which is the condition for motion along the 'straightest' or *geodesic* paths, by definition. Thus all free particles follow geodesics in the space-time continuum. In fact, it can be shown that Euler-Lagrange's equations of motion for a free particle, described in the configuration space (which is now a metric space, by default), are also mathematically equivalent to the geodesic equations of motion of the same test particle in the metric space. This is how the dynamics and the geometry fused together in the hands of Einstein.

6.10 SIGNIFICANCE OF HAMILTON'S PRINCIPLE

1. Hamilton's principle is a novel and powerful technique for solving a wide variety of dynamical problems. Unlike all the other techniques, this one does not start with a differential equation, rather it starts with an integral which is then optimised against some possible variations of the path. The original motivation of Maupertuis was to glorify God's grand design through his action principle. He argued that differential equations, such as Newton's equations of motion (or Euler-Lagrange's or Hamilton's equations of motion of later days), assign the system under consideration the amount of force or acceleration at every instant of time so that the system evolves in time bit by bit, not knowing where exactly it will finally arrive. On the other hand, the action principles require the end points be known first, then out of all possible paths, nature follows the one for which a particular integral is an extremum. Any such explanation of natural events is called a *teleological* explanation, in which a well-defined purpose works behind every perceptible motion or change.

However, a purely mechanistic explanation for this kind of teleological arguments is also possible. Mathematically speaking, the process of integration is the inverse of that of differentiation. The very process of taking the 'variation' of an integral returns the original differential equation. It is not surprising that they yield the same result mathematically. Physically speaking the principles of classical mechanics are time symmetric and deterministic. One would have been surprised, had the integral variational techniques not provided the same results as their differential counterparts.

2. Hamilton's principle can be used for holonomic systems as well as for systems having infinite degrees of freedom.

3. Once the Lagrangian is correctly formulated, Hamilton's principle brings out all the essential dynamical features of the system, even though the choice of Lagrangian is not unique. In chapter 2, we have seen that changing the Lagrangian by a gauge term essentially implies changing the energy and momenta while keeping the basic form of Euler-Lagrange's equations of motion intact. Hence, the specification of the Lagrangian ought to convey more complete information than merely the differential equations of motion. A dynamical system chooses the natural path in such a way that the variations of the kinetic energy integral $\int_1^2 T dt$ and that of the potential energy integral $\int_1^2 V dt$ between two different, closely separated paths are equalised as closely as possible. By no means is this to mean that the system cannot be conservative. One may recall that for conservative systems $T + V = E$ is conserved along any path of evolution, but we are considering $\delta \int (T - V) dt = 0$ for two neighbouring paths, the former change being along the path, the latter change being across the path. The former may or may not preserve $(T + V)$, whereas the latter always preserves $(T - V)$ at any given point on the real path under infinitesimal variations. This is the microscopic essence of Hamilton's principle.

6.11 SUMMARY

Maupertuis' principle of least action can be viewed as generating the equations for the trajectories of particles, rather than the time evolution of their orbits. This is not surprising, because the main inspiration came from Fermat's principle and from the fact that light rays travel so fast that they leave only their tracks behind. The time evolution of the trajectories become irrelevant for light rays. Jacobi's principle of action also leads to the equations for the trajectories of particles of matter in phase space. It is only Hamilton's principle that deals with the time evolution of the trajectories and is capable of giving the complete information.

It is shown that Hamilton's principle can generate Euler-Lagrange's equations of motion and also Hamilton's equations of motion. In the first case, the varied paths are chosen in extended configuration space, but in the second in extended phase space. In both cases, only the variations in terminal coordinates (not in the terminal momenta in general) vanish.

Hamilton's principal function for fixed initial values of generalised coordinates and time represents evolving surfaces in the configuration space. At any instant, the system is located at a definite point on this constantly evolving surface. The momentum of this system at the given instant points in a direction perpendicular to this surface, and therefore the trajectory of the particle always remains perpendicular to the evolving surface of the principal function.

However, if we plot Hamilton's principal function in the extended configuration space, it becomes a fixed surface. Any two points on this surface are assured of having connected by at least one real path among all the possible varied ones. This natural path is invariably a kind of geodesic described on the surface between the two given points.

PROBLEMS

6.1 Using the variational principles, derive the equations for a stable equilibrium configuration of a uniform rope or a necklace hung between any two given points in the constant gravity field of the earth.

6.2 Show that the arc of least distance, called the geodesic, between two given points on the earth's surface having the same nonzero geographical latitude always appears to be convex towards the nearer geographical pole. Assume the earth to be spherical.

6.3 A particle of mass m moving in the potential field due to constant gravity, $V(z) = -mgz$ travels from the point $z = 0$ to the point $z = z_0$ in time t_0. Find the exact time dependence of the position of the particle, assuming it to be of the form $z(t) = At^2 + Bt + C$, and determining the constants A, B and C such that Hamilton's principle is obeyed.

6.4 For a coordinate and time transformation of the Minkowskian type given by $x = X \cosh\theta + T \sinh\theta$, $t = X \sinh\theta + T/ \cosh\theta$, θ being a constant, show that the relativistic Lagrangian for a free particle $L = -m_o\sqrt{1-(dx/dt)^2}$, ($c$ is taken to be unity) remains invariant.

6.5 Show that for a given Lagrangian of the from

$$L(q,\dot{q},t) = a_{ij}(q)\dot{q}_i\dot{q}_j - V(q_1,\ldots,q_n)$$

and a time transformation given by $t = \lambda T$, with a scaling factor λ, the invariance of Hamilton's principal function $W = \int_1^2 L dt$ with respect to λ variation leads to the vanishing of the Hamiltonian of the system.

6.6 Show that Maupertuis' principle of least action $\delta\int_1^2 v ds = 0$ for any particle of mass m and energy E passing through a surface of discontinuity that induces an abrupt change in the potential energy from a constant value V_1 to another constant value V_2 leads to instantaneous changes in the speeds across the boundary given by $v_2 : v_1 = \sin i : \sin r$, where i is the angle of incidence and r the angle of emergence, both measured with respect to the normal. Derive the result from first principles also.

6.7 A particle is moving in a plane wave like external field given by the Lagrangian $L = \frac{1}{2}mv^2 - V(\boldsymbol{r} - \boldsymbol{u}t)$, $\boldsymbol{u}$ being the velocity of wave propagation. Use a transformation that leaves the potential V invariant and show that the ensuing conservation law is $E - \boldsymbol{u}\cdot\boldsymbol{p} = \text{const.}$

6.8 Suppose that a particle is moving in a potential field that is a homogeneous function of $\boldsymbol{r}$ and is given by $U(\alpha\boldsymbol{r}) = \alpha^n U(\boldsymbol{r})$, α being arbitrary and n the degree of homogeneity. If action has to remain invariant under transformations $\boldsymbol{r}' = \beta_1\boldsymbol{r}$ and $t' = \beta_2 t$, show that $\boldsymbol{p}\cdot\boldsymbol{r} - 2Et$ is a conserved quantity.

6.9 Take the Schwarzschild metric

$$ds^2 = c^2\left(1 - \frac{2GM}{rc^2}\right)dt^2 - \frac{dr^2}{1 - (2GM/rc^2)} - r^2(d\theta^2 + \sin^2\theta d\phi^2)$$

around a static body of mass M, and calculate the Lagrangian for the motion of a test particle of mass m moving in the field of M.

6.10 Taking the Lagrangian for a free particle in the form

$$L = \frac{1}{2}mv^2 = \frac{1}{2}m\left(\frac{ds}{dt}\right)^2 = \frac{1}{2}mg_{ik}\left(\frac{dx_i}{dt}\right)\left(\frac{dx_k}{dt}\right)$$

apply Hamilton's principle or straightway use Euler-Lagrange's equations of motion to show that $\ddot{x}_i + C_{ijk}\dot{x}_j\dot{x}_k = 0$ become the equations of motion, where

$$C_{ijk} = \frac{1}{2}g_{il}\left[\frac{\partial g_{kl}}{\partial x_j} + \frac{\partial g_{lj}}{\partial x_k} - \frac{\partial g_{jk}}{\partial x_l}\right]$$

are the so called Riemann-Christoffel symbols.

7

Brachistochrones, Tautochrones and the Cycloid Family

7.0 INTRODUCTION

About thirty years before Newton's *Principia* was published, Fermat proposed his principle of least action in optics. It was then not known whether light propagated as waves or as streams of particles. About twenty years after Fermat's proposition, Huygens hypothesised that light travels as waves, and the Fermat's principle took the form as shown in Eq. (6.26). Obviously, $\delta \int ds/v = \delta \int dt = 0$, suggesting that the paths of light rays are the quickest possible routes between any two given points. For matter particles, this can be realised through Hamilton's principle if and only if the Lagrangian of the matter particle is a constant of motion. For natural motions in the presence of external fields, the above condition is usually not satisfied, but the motion can be constrained to follow paths of widely varying shapes. It then became an interesting problem to find the required shape of the constrained path in the field of uniform gravity that would take minimum time to cover between two given points. Within ten years of the publication of the *Principia*, this problem came as an open challenge from Jean Bernoulli. One evening, Newton also came to know about it and sent the solution to the proposer without signing the reply. Finding paths of quickest descent is an interesting topic by itself. We plan to present it in the form of a separate chapter, rather than as a section to the previous chapter.

One comes across the name of Bernoulli so often that one forgets that not all Bernoullis are the same person. There are essentially three Bernoullis, father, uncle and son, who continued to exist from the late seventeenth century through the late eighteenth century. Their first names are not spelt consistently in the existing literatures. Jacques (also spelt as Jacob or Jakob) (1654 – 1705) and Jean (or John or Johannes) (1667 – 1748) are the two brothers born in Basle, Switzerland. The elder brother was the discoverer of logarithmic spirals, caustics and evolutes, transcendental curves, isoperimetry, infinite series and finite sums, the problems of catenary and isochrones, etc. The younger brother is known to be the inventor of integral calculus, calculus of variations, the problem of brachistochrones, and he defended Leibniz very strongly in his controversial claim of being the true inventor of differential calculus. Jean is the father of Daniel (1700 – 1782) who gave us the famous Bernoulli equation of motion of perfect fluids.

7.1 THE 'CHRONE' FAMILY OF CURVES

In 1696, Jean Bernoulli proposed the famous brachistochrone problem (brachisto = shortest; chrone = time):

Given two points, to find the curve(s) joining them along which a particle starting from rest slides under constant gravitational force, in the least possible time.

The solution, namely a cycloid, was obtained by Jean Bernoulli himself, his elder brother Jacques Bernoulli, Leibniz, Newton and L'Hospital. In order to tackle this problem more rigorously the calculus of variation was further developed by Euler and Lagrange.

More generally, *a brachistochrone is a curve joining two points along which a particle moves under the action of a given conservative force field in the least possible time.*

In 1686, Leibniz posed the problem of *tautochrone* or *isochrone* (*tauto* or *iso* meaning same or identical). This is *a curve such that a particle starting from rest takes the same time to slide along the curve to a special point on that curve, irrespective of its starting point on the curve.*

The tautochrone problem was also solved analytically by Leibniz and Jacob Bernoulli in 1690. However, Huygens used the idea of tautochronous motion in devising pendulum in 1657 and gave a geometrical proof of this curve being a cycloid in 1673.

Brachistochrones and tautochrones are found to be identical for only three types of conservative force fields. One is the constant gravity field near the surface of the earth, the other two are the attractive and repulsive Hooke's type of force field. For example, the attractive Hooke's type of force field is found inside a homogeneous and spherically symmetric gravitating body, whereas the repulsive type is the centrifugal force field in a plane perpendicular to the axis of rotation. In a constant force field the required curve is a cycloid, whereas it is a hypocycloid for an attractive type of Hooke's force and an epicycloid for a repulsive force field, the magnitude of the force being proportional to the distance from a fixed point.

7.2 BRACHISTOCHRONE FOR UNIFORM FORCE FIELD

A particle of mass m is released from rest in a uniform field of force $\boldsymbol{F} = m\boldsymbol{g}$, $\boldsymbol{g}$ being a constant vector. The time taken for the particle to move from point 1 to point 2 (see Fig. 7.1) is given by

$$t_{12} = \int_1^2 \frac{ds}{v} = \int_1^2 \sqrt{\frac{1 + y'^2}{2gx}}\, dx$$

where $y' = dy/dx$, $ds = \sqrt{dx^2 + dy^2}$ and $v = \sqrt{2gx}$, x being measured in the downward direction (that is along $\boldsymbol{g}$) from point 1 and y in the horizontal direction to the right (see Fig. 7.1). The path is, by definition, a brachistochrone if the variation

$$\delta t_{12} = 0 \tag{7.1}$$

or

$$\delta \int_1^2 \sqrt{\frac{1 + y'^2}{2gx}}\, dx = 0$$

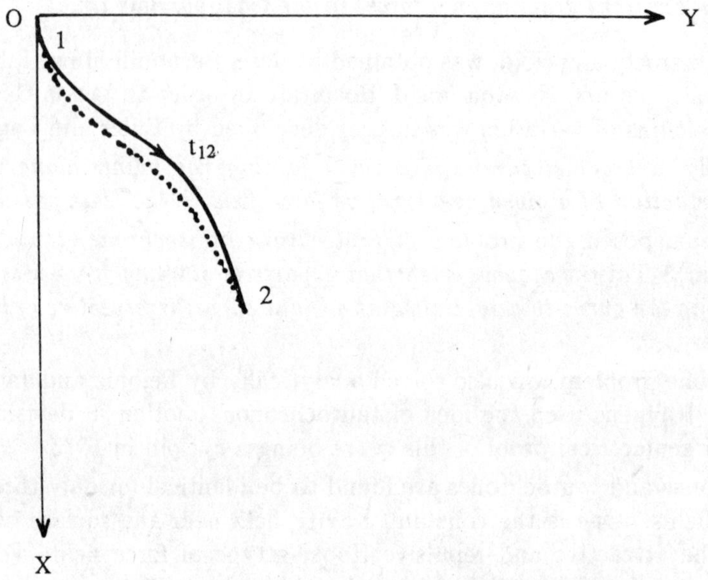

Fig. 7.1 Possible variational changes in the travel time t_{12} between two fixed terminal points, marked by 1 and 2

Now, from the Euler-Lagrange theorem we know that for any given function $f(y, dy/dx, x)$, the variation

$$\delta \int_1^2 f\left(y, \frac{dy}{dx}, x\right) dx = 0$$

if and only if the function f satisfies the following differential equation

$$\frac{d}{dx}\left(\frac{\partial f}{\partial y'}\right) - \frac{\partial f}{\partial y} = 0$$

Here $f(y, y', x)$ replaces the Lagrangian $L(q, \dot{q}, t)$, x replaces the time t and y behaves as a coordinate and hence $y' = dy/dx$ is a velocity component in the usual Euler– Lagrange equation of motion.

In the present case,

$$f(y, y', x) = \sqrt{\frac{1 + y'^2}{x}}$$

disregarding the constant factor $\sqrt{2g}$. We thus have

$$\frac{\partial f}{\partial y} = 0 \qquad \text{and} \qquad \frac{\partial f}{\partial y'} = \frac{y'}{\sqrt{x(1 + y'^2)}}$$

Therefore the Euler-Lagrange condition reduces to

$$\frac{d}{dx}\left(\frac{\partial f}{\partial y'}\right) = 0$$

or

$$\frac{\partial f}{\partial y'} = \text{constant (independent of } x\text{)}$$

or

$$\frac{y'}{\sqrt{x(1 + y'^2)}} = \frac{1}{\sqrt{2a}} \qquad \text{say}$$

where a is a constant. Therefore,

$$\frac{dy}{dx} = y' = \sqrt{\frac{x}{2a - x}}$$

or

$$y = \int_0^x \sqrt{\frac{x}{2a - x}}\, dx$$

Substituting

$$x = 2a \sin^2 \frac{\theta}{2}$$

we get

$$y = a(\theta - \sin\theta)$$

Therefore, a brachistochrone in a constant gravity field is given by the following parametric equations:

$$x = a(1 - \cos\theta),$$

and

$$y = a(\theta - \sin\theta) \tag{7.2}$$

The function (7.2) is displayed in Fig. 7.2. It is called a cycloid. A cycloid is a path traced by a point on the circumference of a disc rolling with a constant speed along a line. The cycloid given in Fig. 7.2 has the cusps pointing upwards and touching the y-axis at an interval of $2a$. In this case the disc has to roll upside down on the y-axis which is, here, a horizontal line marked on a ceiling like plane.

7.3 CYCLOID AS A TAUTOCHRONE

We now show that a cycloidal slide track (sliding without friction) in a constant gravity field

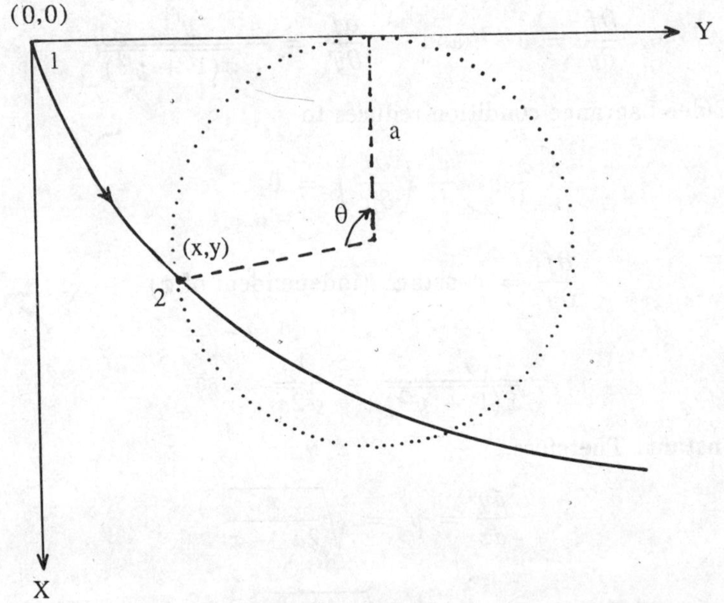

Fig. 7.2 A circle rolling, without slipping, on a straight line act as the generator of a cycloid

corresponds to a tautochrone provided the special point is chosen so as to satisfy $y' = 0$, y being the measure of the ordinate. This is any one of the bottom most points of the cycloid, symmetrically situated between any two consecutive cusps of the cycloid. Let us now shift the origin of the previous cycloid (the one shown in Fig. 7.2) to the special point chosen above and define x as the horizontal axis and y as the vertically upward axis. The resulting cycloid (shown in Fig. 7.3) is described by the functions

$$x = a(\theta + \sin\theta)$$

and

$$y = a(1 - \cos\theta)$$

where θ is the amount of roll of the generating disc of radius a.

Let the coordinate of any point P on the track be described by the arclength s measured from the origin and the tangent at P make an angle β with the x axis. We have, for the differential arclength,

$$ds = \sqrt{dx^2 + dy^2} = 2a\cos\frac{\theta}{2}\,d\theta$$

or

$$s = \int_0^s ds = 4a\sin\frac{\theta}{2} \tag{7.4}$$

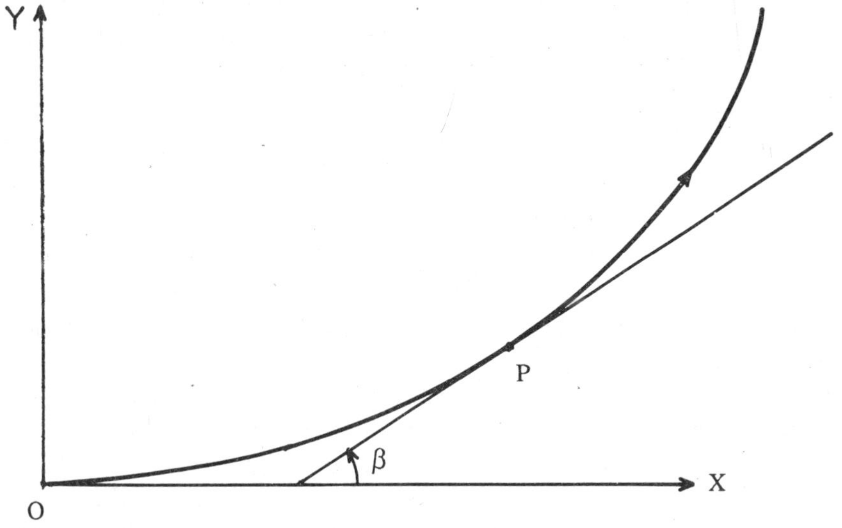

Fig. 7.3 Change in the angle of slope of the cycloid (β) is related to the angle of rotation (θ) of the generating circle, in the ratio 1 : 2

Again, by definition of the slope of the track at the point P (see Fig. 7.3)

$$\tan\beta = \frac{dy}{dx} = \tan\frac{\theta}{2}$$

Therefore, we have

$$\beta = \frac{\theta}{2}$$

implying that the tangent at any point on the track makes an angle $\theta/2$, where θ is the angle of rotation of the generating disc, due to which the reference point has moved from the origin O to the present location P.

Now the equation of motion of any particle running down the track can be obtained from the knowledge of the acceleration of the particle at any arbitrary point of the track, say at P, which is given by

$$\begin{aligned} \ddot{s} &= -g\sin\beta \\ &= -g\sin\frac{\theta}{2} \\ &= -\frac{g\,s}{4a} \qquad \text{by Eq. (7.4)} \end{aligned}$$

or

$$\ddot{s} + \frac{g\,s}{4a} = 0$$

which represents a simple harmonic motion in s with a period

$$T = 2\pi\sqrt{\frac{4a}{g}} \tag{7.5}$$

We know that the period of a simple harmonic motion is independent of its amplitude s. Hence the time taken by a particle to slide (from rest) from any point on the track to its bottommost point must be independent of the location of the starting point. This time is given by

$$\frac{1}{4}T = \pi\sqrt{\frac{a}{g}}$$

Hence any cycloidal track, oriented in the above mentioned manner, becomes a tautochrone for the constrained motion in a constant force field.

This is obviously an important result. We know that a simple pendulum describes a circular arc rather than a cycloidal track. So its period of oscillation is amplitude-dependent, although the dependence is very weak for smaller amplitudes. Now if the bob of a simple pendulum could be made to follow a cycloidal track about its bottom most point O which must be situated at a point equidistant from the vertically oriented cusp as shown in Fig. 7.2, rather than a circular track, its motion will be perfectly tautochronous (under the constant gravity field of the earth). The radius of curvature of the cycloid near the point O is $4a$, hence one understands why the complete period of oscillation for the above tautochronous motion has an equivalent suspension length of $4a$, as obtained in Eq. (7.5).

It was Galileo who while seated in a dinner party sometime in 1583, observed that the lamp hanging from the ceiling oscillates with a period independent of the amplitude of its oscillation, provided the amplitude was not too large. Later in 1657, Christiaan Huygens deduced from geometrical arguments that the required curve for a truly tautochronous motion of a pendulum is a cycloid. But then the question was how to make a pendulum describe a cycloid rather than a circular arc? Fortunately, the trick lies in a definite property of the cycloids. It is known that the involute of a cycloid is another cycloid and we know that generally an involute is generated by the free end of a taut thread wrapped against its evolute curve (see problem number I.39 and Appendix A2). So an idealised suspension thread of a simple pendulum can be wrapped and unwrapped against cheeks of appropriate shape. Actually the point of suspension is chosen to be any one cusp of an evolute cycloid with the cusp pointing upward. The other end of the thread that holds the heavy bob keeps the thread always straight and describes the involute of the curve defined by the cheek. In this case both are cycloids, and hence such a pendulum will execute perfectly tautochronous oscillations at all amplitudes.

Given a curve, it can be used as an evolute in order to generate its involute, which again can be used as an evolute in order to generate its own involute. This process leads to a family of curves called tesserals. Obviously, cycloids belong to a family of tesserals.

7.4 BRACHISTOCHRONE FOR SPHERICALLY SYMMETRIC POTENTIAL FIELD $V(r)$

Consider a region of space in which there acts a spherically symmetric potential $V(r)$. We give here a formulation (solution) of the brachistochrone problem for a particle moving under such a general central force.

The equation for the brachistochrone is generated by the variational equation

$$0 = \delta \int_1^2 dt = \delta \int_1^2 \frac{ds}{v}$$
$$= \delta \int_1^2 \sqrt{\frac{dr^2 + r^2 d\theta^2}{2[E - V(r)]}}$$
$$= \delta \int_1^2 \sqrt{\frac{r'^2 + r^2}{2[E - V(r)]}}\, d\theta$$

where $r' = dr/d\theta$, E = total energy per unit mass, $V(r)$ being the potential. Having defined

$$f(r, r', \theta) = \sqrt{\frac{r'^2 + r^2}{E - V(r)}}$$

the above variational equation would now hold only if it satisfies the Euler-Lagrange equations in f, given by

$$\frac{d}{d\theta}\left(\frac{\partial f}{\partial r'}\right) - \frac{\partial f}{\partial r} = 0$$

or

$$r'' - \left(\frac{2}{r} + \frac{V'}{2(E - V)}\right) r'^2 - r - \frac{V'}{2(E - V)} r^2 = 0 \tag{7.6}$$

where $r'' = d^2 r/d\theta^2$ and $V' = dV/dr$.

Equation (7.6) is a second order differential equation in θ and not very easy to solve for the equation of the brachistochrone $r = r(\theta)$. However, we know that the Euler-Lagrange equation must lead to an energy like integral of motion called the Jacobi integral, if $f(r, r', \theta)$ is not an explicit function of θ, which means that in the present case such an integral exists in the form of

$$r'\frac{\partial f}{\partial r'} - f = \text{const.}$$

This integral being a function of the first order differential coefficients readily corresponds to

$$r'^2 = \frac{K r^4}{E - V(r)} - r^2 \tag{7.7}$$

where

$$K = \frac{E - V(r_o)}{r_o^2} = \text{const.}$$

r_o being the distance from the centre of the potential to the nearest (in some cases, farthest) point on the trajectory at which point $r' = dr/d\theta = 0$. Being a first order differential equation, Eq. (7.7) is easy to solve for the brachistochrones in any given spherically symmetric potential $V(r)$, by the method of quadratures, for example.

7.5 BRACHISTOCHRONES AND TAUTOCHRONES INSIDE A GRAVITATING HOMOGENEOUS SPHERE

Let us now analyse the nature of brachistochrones and tautochrones for a special case of the central forces, namely for the one under the action of the gravitational potential inside a homogeneous sphere of radius R and mass M, the gravitational potential at any distance $r \leq R$ from the centre of the sphere being given by

$$V(r) = \frac{GM}{2R}\left(-3 + \frac{r^2}{R^2}\right) \qquad r \leq R$$

If a particle starts from rest from any point on the surface of the sphere, its specific energy is $E = V(R) = -GM/R$. Therefore, at any point on the curve which lies totally inside the sphere, the energy condition is,

$$E - V(r) = \frac{GM}{2R^3}(R^2 - r^2)$$

Thus the equation for the brachistochrone inside a gravitating homogeneous sphere will have the form given by Eq. (7.7),

$$r'^2 = \frac{K'r^4}{R^2 - r^2} - r^2$$

where

$$K' = \frac{2KR^3}{GM} = \frac{R^2 - r_o^2}{r_o^2}$$

and as before r_o refers to that point on the track for which $r' = dr/d\theta = 0$. Now

$$\frac{R^2 - r^2}{r^2}\left[1 + \frac{r'^2}{r^2}\right] = \text{const.} \tag{7.8}$$

is the required equation for the brachistochrone, defining the track of the brachistochrone if the particle starts from rest on the surface of a homogeneous sphere of radius R.

Integration of Eq. (7.8) gives the equation of the track as that of a hypocycloid which can be generated by the locus of a point fixed on a smaller circle of radius $(R - r_o)/2$, which is made to roll without slipping in the same plane but on the inside of a firmly fixed bigger circle of radius R (see Fig. 7.4). If the ratio R/r_o is irrational, the repeating arches of the hypocycloid never close on themselves.

If the above procedure is taken to be the formal geometrical definition of a hypocycloid, we have R as the radius of the fixed circle, and define $a = (R - r_o)/2$ to be the radius of the rolling circle, a parameter $\alpha = a/R \leq 1$, and an angle θ between the x axis and the line joining the centres of the fixed and the rolling circle, so that the parametric

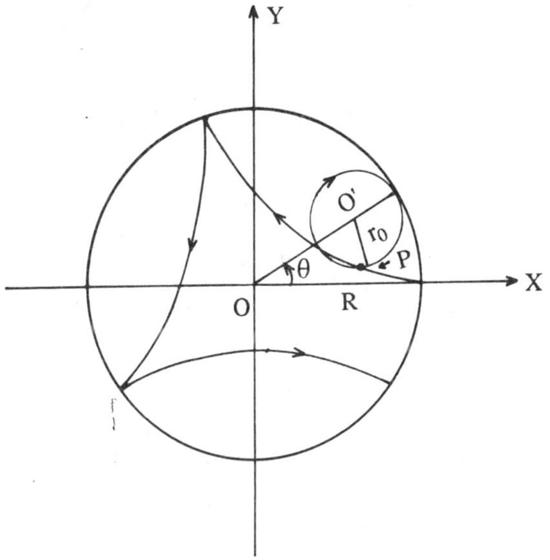

Fig. 7.4 A circle rolling on the inside of a bigger circle generates a hypocycloid

equation of the hypocycloid is given by

$$\begin{aligned} x(\theta) &= R\left\{(1 - \alpha)\cos\theta + \alpha\cos\left(\frac{1 - \alpha}{\alpha}\theta\right)\right\} \\ y(\theta) &= R\left\{(1 - \alpha)\sin\theta - \alpha\sin\left(\frac{1 - \alpha}{\alpha}\theta\right)\right\} \end{aligned} \tag{7.9}$$

Here (x, y) are the Cartesian coordinates of the locus, measured from the centre of the fixed circle. Also note that in terms of the plane polar coordinates (r, θ) the centre of the rolling circle is at $r = R - a$, and $\theta = \theta$. The first terms in Eq. (7.9) correspond to the coordinates of the centre of the rolling circle, and the second terms are the coordinates of a fixed point on the rim of the rolling circle with respect to the centre of the rolling circle. By the time the centre of the rolling circle rotates by an angle θ the rolling circle itself rotates in its own frame by an angle $R\theta/a = \theta\alpha = \phi$, say, but with respect to an outside inertial frame the amount of rotation is only $\phi - \theta$, hence the odd argument in the second terms of (7.9).

However we shall use here another form of the hypocycloid equation given in terms of the radial coordinate r (measured from the centre of the fixed circle to the point on the path) and the arclength s along the path (measured from the point of closest approach to the centre of the fixed circle):

$$r^2 = \frac{s^2}{4\alpha(1 - \alpha)} + (1 - 2\alpha)^2 R^2 \tag{7.10}$$

The speed of the particle starting from rest on the boundary of the fixed circle is given by

$$\dot{s}^2 = \frac{g}{R}(R^2 - r^2) \tag{7.11}$$

Replacing r^2 in Eq. (7.11) by Eq. (7.10) and differentiating Eq. (7.11) with respect to time one gets,

$$\ddot{s} + \frac{g\,s}{4\alpha(1 - \alpha)R} = 0 \tag{7.12}$$

This again, being the equation of a simple harmonic motion, represents a tautochronous motion executed on the above hypocycloid, where g is the value of the acceleration due to gravity on the surface of a nonrotating homogeneous sphere of radius R.

Like the cycloids, hypocycloids also belong to a family of tesserals, that is, the curves of the same family serving as both evolutes and involutes. If someday our technology permits us to run a locomotive service along a hypocycloid tunnel joining any two points on the surface of the earth, it will then make us save the maximum possible time for shuttling between these two points at the minimum expense of fuel. When compared with straight line tunnels between any two points on the surface of the earth, the saving of time may sometimes be by a factor of 1.5 or more (see problem 7.4). It should be further noted that motion along a straight tunnel is also tautochronous, but such a track is not a brachistochrone. Hence all tautochrones are not brachistochrones, and all brachistochrones are tautochrones only under three special types of force fields mentioned in Section 7.1.

7.6 TAUTOCHRONOUS MOTION IN A CENTRIFUGAL FORCE FIELD AND EPICYCLOIDS

In this case also, the brachistochrones and tautochrones are identical and describe an epicycloid generated by the rolling of a circle of radius a along the outside of a fixed circle of radius R, that is concentric with the axis of rotation, both the circles lying in the same plane perpendicular to the axis of rotation (see Fig. 7.5).

The equations are similar except for some changes in the +/− signs. For example, the parametric equation for an epicycloid would be

$$\begin{aligned} x(\theta) &= R\left\{(1 + \alpha)\cos\theta - \alpha\cos\left(\frac{1 + \alpha}{\alpha}\theta\right)\right\} \\ y(\theta) &= R\left\{(1 + \alpha)\sin\theta - \alpha\sin\left(\frac{1 + \alpha}{\alpha}\theta\right)\right\} \end{aligned} \tag{7.13}$$

where R is the radius of the fixed circle on the outer periphery of which another circle of radius $a = \alpha R$ is made to roll without slipping. θ is the angle of transportation of the centre of this rolling circle measured at the centre of the fixed circle with respect to the direction of the x-axis. It is obvious from Fig. 7.5 as well as from Eq. (7.13) that R is the radial distance of the cusps of the epicycloid and $r_o = R(1 + 2\alpha)$ is the radial distance for the farthest point on the epicycloid measured from the centre of the fixed circle.

Now the centrifugal potential field generated by a rotating disc is given by $V(r) =$

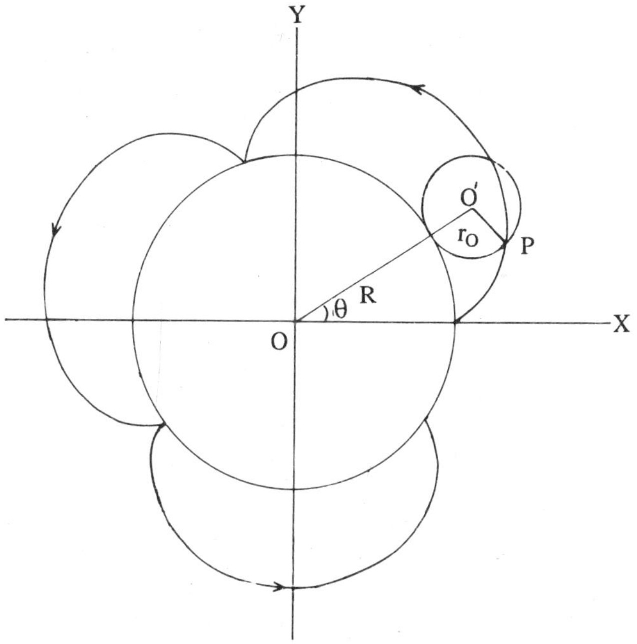

Fig. 7.5 A circle rolling on the outside of a bigger circle generates a epicycloid

$-\frac{1}{2}\omega_o^2 r^2$, ω_o being the angular speed of rotation of the disc. A particle dropped gently on this rotating disc at $r = R$ with no initial relative motion will trace an epicycloid on the surface of the disc, having cusps always at $r = R$, and the equation for the tautochronous motion along the epicycloid will be given by

$$\ddot{s} + \frac{\omega^2 s}{4\alpha(1 + \alpha)} = 0 \qquad (7.14)$$

where

$$s = \frac{\sqrt{(r_o^2 - r^2)(r_o^2 - R^2)}}{R}$$

Epicycloids also belong to a family of tesserals.

7.7 SUMMARY

Brachistochrones and tautochrones are the curves of constraints for respectively 'least' and 'equal' travel times for material particles moving under any given force field. They can be identical only for three types of force fields, namely cycloids for constant force fields, hypocycloids for attractive Hooke's type of force fields, and epicycloids for centrifugal force fields in the equatorial plane.

PROBLEMS

7.1 Two identical cycloids made of wood are fixed next to each other on the ceiling of a room, with all the cusps touching the ceiling. A simple pendulum with a flexible but inextensible cord is suspended from the wedge like meeting point of the two adjacent cusps. In order to make the pendulum swing with a period totally independent of the amplitude, what would be length of suspension l of the pendulum if the cycloids are generated from the rolling of a circle of radius R?

7.2 Derive the equation for the hypocycloids and epicycloids as given by Eq. (7.9) and Eq. (7.12) from geometrical considerations, that is, just considering the rolling of a circle of radius $a = \alpha R$ on inside/outside periphery of a fixed circle of radium of R. Prove that the length s measured from any central point (equidistant from any pair of two consecutive cusps) satisfies an identical relation

$$r^2 = r_o^2 + \frac{a^2 s^2}{a^2 - r^2}$$

r_o being the distance of the central point from O, the centre of the fixed circle, and r being the radial distance to any point on the hypocycloid/epicycloid measured from O.

7.3 It is shown in the text that Eq. (7.9) for the hypocycloid corresponds to a tautochrone in an attractive Hooke's type of external force field. Now show that they also satisfy the condition for brachistochrone, namely Eq. (7.8).

7.4 Assume that the earth is spherical with radius R and that its interior is homogeneous having a uniform density ρ. A deep underground hypocycloidal tunnel is made through the earth connecting two given places on the surface of the earth at an angular separation of θ (with respect to the centre of the earth). Find the total length L, and the maximum depth H of the tunnel as a function of R and θ only. Compare the time of transit of any freely moving bogie of a train along this hypocycloidal track to that along the straight tunnel connecting the same two points.

7.5 If, instead of a particle sliding down without sliding friction, a thin disc of radius r rolls down without slipping under the action of the constant gravity field, show that the track should still be cycloidal for executing a tautochronous motion.

7.6 How does the combined force field of the earth due to its own gravitation and axial rotation acting at any interior point of the earth affect the period of tautochronous motion, (in the equatorial plane) that satisfies the brachistochrone condition? If the earth be given sufficient angular speed of rotation, could the brachistochrones ever change from hypocycloids to epicycloids?

7.7 A bead of mass m subject to the force $\boldsymbol{F} = cy\hat{\jmath}$ slides from $x = -x_o$, $y = y_o$ to $x = x_o$, $y = y_o$ on a frictionless wire fixed in the x-y plane. The initial speed is $v_o = y_o\sqrt{c/m}$. Show that the trip time is minimised if the shape of the wire is circular with radius $\sqrt{x_o^2 + y_o^2}$. Determine the travel time and find a physical situation where the above can be realised.

7.8 Solve the problem of brachistochrone for the surface constraint as a vertical cylinder between two points (ρ_o, ϕ_o, z_o) and $(\rho_o, 0, 0)$, $z_o > 0$, in the earth's uniform field of gravitation.

8

Canonical Transformations

8.0 INTRODUCTION

We now move to a new topic. This and the next chapter are supposed to complement each other. In most textbooks they are dealt with in a single chapter. So it would be advisable to read both the chapters first, before trying to solve the problems.

We have already seen that the generalised coordinates and their corresponding generalised momenta could be physically or dimensionally anything except for their pairwise conjugate relationship, which maintains the dimension of the product of any pair of conjugate variables to that of action, or simply $[ML^2T^{-1}]$. In this chapter, we shall in the name of so-called canonical transformations, transform more freely, not only the generalised coordinates and generalised momenta but also the value and the form of the Hamiltonian. The only requirement we shall respectfully mete out is to retain the form of Hamilton's canonical equations of motion, so that the new or transformed Hamiltonian also satisfies the $2n$ equations of motion in the new coordinates and new momenta. The Hamiltonian is regarded merely as a mathematical function of a set of coordinate and momentum like parameters.

In the process we can hit by chance or by some systematic procedure, a canonical transformation that can transform the old or normal looking Hamiltonian to any desired simple form of our choice, say proportional to the new momentum or the new coordinate. Naturally in such cases, solving the new Hamilton's equations of motion becomes trivial. Then using the inverse transformations, these solutions can readily be transformed to represent the solutions in the old coordinates and old momenta. In this way we can spare ourselves from solving directly Hamilton's equations of motion written in terms of the old coordinates and momenta. This is a kind of technical revolution for solving dynamical problems much like the invention of the Laplace transforms for solving complicated differential equations.

Canonical transformations were introduced by Hamilton, but developed more fully by Jacobi at about the same time as Hamilton was doing them by himself. Their generality and far-reaching consequences were not immediately appreciated by the scientific community. It was only when group properties of transformations in general became well-known to the physicists that the importance of canonical transformations was fully realised. Nevertheless, through the use of phase space in statistical mechanics, the idea of energy (Hamiltonian) as a constant of motion played a key role in realising the microcanonical ensemble representations of the thermodynamical systems. We shall briefly discuss the nature of Hamiltonian flows towards the end of the chapter.

8.1 BACKGROUND AND DEFINITION

For a holonomic bilateral dynamical system with n degrees of freedom, the choice of the n generalised coordinates is quite arbitrary. A given set of generalised coordinates need not reflect all the cyclic coordinates in the Lagrangian or the Hamiltonian expressed in terms of these generalised coordinates and generalised velocities or momenta. It is, therefore, very often needed to transform from one set of generalised coordinates, say $(q_1, \ldots, q_n)$, to another set of generalised coordinates, say $(Q_1, \ldots, Q_n)$, connected by what is called a *point transformation* given by

$$Q_i = Q_i(q_1, \ldots, q_n) \qquad i = 1, \ldots, n \tag{8.1}$$

The Jacobian of this transformation should not vanish in order that the inverse transformations,

$$q_i = q_i(Q_1, \ldots, Q_n) \qquad i = 1, \ldots, n \tag{8.2}$$

also exist.

Since the set $(q_1, \ldots, q_n)$ represents a definite point in the configuration space spanned by these n $q-$coordinates, it will lead to another definite point expressed by the transformations (8.1) in the configuration space spanned by the n $Q-$coordinates.

The Lagrangian $L(q_1, \ldots, q_n; \dot{q}_1, \ldots, \dot{q}_n; t)$ can be expressed in terms of the new coordinates and coordinate velocities so that (see section 6.6)

$$L(q, \dot{q}, t) = \tilde{L}(Q, \dot{Q}, t)$$

The new momenta are given by

$$P_i = \frac{\partial \tilde{L}}{\partial \dot{Q}_i} = P_i(q_1, \ldots, q_n; p_1, \ldots, p_n; t)$$

Note that the new momenta are defined in terms of the old coordinates, old momenta and time only. Thus the general form of the point transformation is

$$Q_i = Q_i(q_1, \ldots, q_n; t) \qquad \text{and} \qquad P_i = P_i(q_1, \ldots, q_n; p_1, \ldots, p_n; t) \tag{8.3}$$

with the corresponding inverse transformations

$$q_i = q_i(Q_1, \ldots, Q_n; t) \qquad \text{and} \qquad p_i = p_i(Q_1, \ldots, Q_n; P_1, \ldots, P_n; t) \tag{8.4}$$

We must also require that Eqs (8.1) and (8.2) leave the form of Lagrange's equations of motion invariant. It can easily be shown that Eqs (8.1) and (8.2) satisfy this requirement.

Point transformations (8.1) and (8.2) are defined over the configuration space. Hamilton's equations of motion, however, describe the evolution of the state of a system in its phase space. Thus, whenever Hamilton's equations of motion are used to describe the system's dynamics, the transformations (8.3) and (8.4) must be replaced by a suitable phase space transformation, namely

$$Q_i = Q_i(q_1, \ldots, q_n; p_1, \ldots, p_n; t) \qquad \text{and} \qquad P_i = P_i(q_1, \ldots, q_n; p_1, \ldots, p_n; t) \tag{8.5}$$

If we now want to have a physically meaningful phase space transformation, it would be quite logical to demand that the transformations (8.5) should leave the form of Hamilton's canonical equations of motion invariant. Equivalently, we may require the invariance of Hamilton's principle under the transformations (8.5), that is,

$$0 = \delta \int_{t_o}^{t} \left[\sum_i p_i \dot{q}_i - H(q,p,t) \right] dt = \delta \int_{t_o}^{t} \left[\sum_i P_i \dot{Q}_i - K(Q,P,t) \right] dt \tag{8.6}$$

where $K(Q, P, t)$ is the transformed Hamiltonian. The condition given by Eq. (8.6) leads immediately to Hamilton's canonical equations of motion

$$\dot{P}_i = -\frac{\partial K}{\partial Q_i} \quad \text{and} \quad \dot{Q}_i = \frac{\partial K}{\partial P_i} \tag{8.7}$$

which must be satisfied by the new coordinates and momenta (Q_i, P_i).

The phase space transformations (8.5) that preserve the forms of the *canonical* equations of motion, (that is, of the Hamiltonian equations of motion) are called *Canonical Transformations (CT)*. Some textbooks however, prefer to define CTs through the invariance of elementary Poisson Brackets. The two definitions are equivalent.

We can also think of transformations

$$q_i = q_i(Q_1, \ldots, Q_n, t) \quad \text{and} \quad p_i = P_i$$

such that only coordinates are transformed in the phase space without touching the sector for momenta. Such transformations are by nature point transformations, and are called extended point transformations.

8.2 GENERATING FUNCTIONS

The essential requirement for the canonical transformation is that every natural path in the phase space spanned by (p, q) should, when mapped onto the transformed phase space spanned by (P, Q), again be a natural path satisfying the corresponding Hamilton's equations of motion.

We know that Hamilton's equations of motion result from Hamilton's principle which requires that both the terminal coordinates and the terminal times be kept fixed and the path at all other points be arbitrarily varied from the natural one. Hence we can always add to the integrand of the transformed quantities in Eq. (8.6), namely $P_i\dot{Q}_i - K(P, Q, t)$, a total time derivative of any function whose variations vanish at the limits of the integration. Since the variation of $t, q_1, \ldots, q_n$, and hence of $t, Q_1, \ldots, Q_n$ have to vanish at the end points, for the validity of Hamilton's principle, such a function must be the time derivative of a suitable function that depends on $t, q_1, \ldots, q_n; Q_1, \ldots, Q_n$, say $F_1(q_1, \ldots, q_n; Q_1, \ldots, Q_n; t)$, which automatically satisfies

$$\delta \int_{t_o}^{t} \frac{d}{dt} F_1(q_1, \ldots, q_n; Q_1, \ldots, Q_n; t) dt = \delta \left[F_1(q_1, \ldots, q_n; Q_1, \ldots, Q_n; t) \right]_{t_o}^{t} = 0$$

Thus we can generalise the requirement given by Eq. (8.6) on transformations (8.5) as

$$0 = \delta \int_{t_o}^{t} [\Sigma_i p_i \dot{q}_i - H(p,q,t)]\, dt$$
$$= \delta \int_{t_o}^{t} \left[\Sigma_i P_i \dot{Q}_i - K(P,Q,t) + \frac{d}{dt}F_1(q,Q,t)\right] dt$$

where the two integrands are in general related by

$$\lambda\, [\Sigma_i p_i \dot{q}_i - H(q_1,\ldots,q_n;p_1,\ldots p_n;t)]$$
$$= \Sigma_i P_i \dot{Q}_i - K(Q_1,\ldots,Q_n;P_1,\ldots,P_n;t) + \frac{d}{dt}F_1(q,Q,t) \qquad (8.8)$$

Here λ is a constant scale factor, called the *valence* of CT. When $\lambda \neq 1$, the transformations (8.8) are called the *extended canonical* transformations. Normally λ is set to unity and the transformation (8.8) is called *univalent* or *ordinary canonical* or simply *canonical* transformation. Henceforth we shall use $\lambda = 1$ for which the conditional requirement (8.8) becomes

$$p_i \dot{q}_i - H(q,p,t) = P_i \dot{Q}_i - K(Q,P,t) + \frac{dF_1(q,Q,t)}{dt}$$
$$= P_i \dot{Q}_i - K(Q,P,t) + \frac{\partial F_1}{\partial t} + \frac{\partial F_1}{\partial q_i}\dot{q}_i + \frac{\partial F_1}{\partial Q_i}\dot{Q}_i \qquad (8.9)$$

Henceforth Einstein's summation convention is implied for all the repeated indices used in any term. Rewriting Eq. (8.9) in differential form

$$p_i dq_i - H(q,p,t)dt = P_i dQ_i - K(Q,P,t)dt + \frac{\partial F_1}{\partial t}dt + \frac{\partial F_1}{\partial q_i}dq_i + \frac{\partial F_1}{\partial Q_i}dQ_i$$

and treating q, Q, t as independent variables, we now get

$$p_i = \left(\frac{\partial F_1}{\partial q_i}\right)_{Q,t}$$
$$P_i = -\left(\frac{\partial F_1}{\partial Q_i}\right)_{q,t} \qquad \text{for} \quad i = 1,\ldots,n \qquad (8.10)$$
$$K(Q,P,t) = H(q,p,t) + \frac{\partial F_1}{\partial t},$$

The function $F_1(q,Q,t)$ is called the *generating function* of the canonical transformation because it specifies the required equations of the transformation, namely the ones given by Eq. (8.5).

Therefore, for univalent CTs, the physical dimension of the transformed Hamiltonian remains unchanged.

Furthermore, if F_1 is not an explicit function of time, that is, $F_1 = F_1(q,Q)$, the value of K, the transformed Hamiltonian (also jocularly called 'Kamiltonian') is the same as that of the Hamiltonian H in the original phase space, for every point of the phase space spanned by (Q, P). But in general, the value of the Hamiltonian changes under any time dependent canonical transformations.

8.2.1 How to Obtain the Required CT When the Generating Function is Given

When the generating function is given one can uniquely construct the transformations (8.5) and the transformed Hamiltonian in the following four steps:

(a) Construct the n equations of the old momenta using the first of the set of relations (8.10), that is, obtain

$$p_i(q, Q, t) = \left(\frac{\partial F_1}{\partial q_i}\right)_{Q,t} \qquad i = 1, \ldots, n \tag{8.11}$$

From these relations by algebraic manipulation try to solve for Q_i's, so that Q_i's are now expressed as $Q_i = Q_i(q, p, t)$. This is possible because the transformations (8.5) are supposed to be invertible, at least locally. So we obtain the new coordinates as the functions of the old coordinates, old momenta and time, that is, half of the required equations for the CT are constructed.

(b) Take the second group of n independent equations of the new momenta in Eq. (8.10), given by

$$P_i = -\frac{\partial F_1}{\partial Q_i} = P_i(q; Q, t) \qquad i = 1, \ldots, n$$

and substitute for all $Q_i = Q_i(q, p, t)$ that are obtained from the step (a) above in each of these P_i equations in order to obtain $P_i = P_i(q, p, t)$. So we get all new momenta as the functions of the old coordinates, old momenta and time.

(c) Find the inverse transformations $p_i = p_i(Q, P, t)$ and $q_i = q_i(Q, P, t)$.

(d) Now find $K(Q, P, t)$ from $H(p, q, t) + \partial F_1/\partial t$ by substituting all p's and q's as functions of Q, P, t only, in both these terms.

An example: Consider the harmonic oscillator problem with $H = p^2/2m + kq^2/2$ and a generating function $F_1 = 1/2\sqrt{km}\, q^2 \cot Q$. The above procedure as in part (a) yields

$$Q = \tan^{-1}(\sqrt{km}\, q/p)$$

part (b) gives

$$P = \sqrt{m/4k}\,(kq^2 + p^2/m)$$

part (c) prescribes the inverse transformations,

$$p = (km)^{1/4}\sqrt{2P}\,\cos Q \qquad \text{and} \qquad q = (km)^{-1/4}\sqrt{2P}\,\sin Q$$

and finally part (d) gives the transformed Hamiltonian

$$K = \sqrt{k/m}P$$

One may note that the original Hamiltonian which was quadratic in both q and p, has been transformed to a form which is linear in P with no dependence on Q. With such a simple form of the Hamiltonian, it is very easy to solve the equations of motion in P, Q and then, if necessary, one can substitute back for P and Q and get the solutions for q and p, which would be the same as those, obtained by solving the original Hamilton's equations in q and p directly.

8.2.2 How to Obtain the Generating Function F_1 when the CT is Given

In this case $F_1(q, Q, t)$ is not given but the transformation Eqs (8.5) are given. The following procedure may be adopted in order to find $F_1(q, Q, t)$.

(a) Invert Eqs (8.5) in order to obtain $p_i = p_i(Q, P, t)$ and $q_i = q_i(Q, P, t)$.

(b) Again take Eqs (8.5) and eliminate all p_i's so that after rearranging one obtains $P_i = P_i(q, Q, t)$. Similarly again take Eqs (8.5) and eliminate all P_i's so that this time on rearrangement, one obtains $p_i = p_i(q, Q, t)$.

(c) Write these newly obtained expressions for $p_i = p_i(q, Q, t)$ and $P_i = P_i(q, Q, t)$ in the partial differential equations

$$p_i(q, Q, t) = \frac{\partial F_1}{\partial q_i} \qquad \text{and} \qquad P_i(q, Q, t) = -\frac{\partial F_1}{\partial Q_i}$$

respectively, and integrate both these partial differential equations separately. The first one will result in a solution to $F_1(q, Q, t)$ except for the constant of integration, which would be a function of $Q's$ and t only. Similarly, the second one will also result in another solution to $F_1(q, Q, t)$ except for its constant of integration which will now be a function of q_i and t only. These two expressions for F_1 can be suitably combined to find the correct solution for $F_1(q, Q, t)$.

(d) Once $F_1(q, Q, t)$ is obtained, find K from $H(p, q, t) + \partial F_1/\partial t$ by substituting for p's and q's from the inverse transformations to Eqs (8.5).

An example:

Given $Q = \log[(1/q) \sin p]$, $P = q \cot p$ and $H = p^2/2m + kq^2/2$, find $F_1(q, Q, t)$ and $K(Q, P, t)$.

Following the above procedure one first obtains the inverse transformations as $p = \cos^{-1}(P \exp Q)$; $q = [\exp(-2Q) - P^2]^{1/2}$ which can be used to finally obtain $F_1(q, Q) = q \cos^{-1}[(1 - q^2 \exp 2Q)^{1/2}] + [\exp(-2Q) - q^2]^{1/2}$

8.2.3 Other Principal Forms of the Generating Function

The generating function need not always be an explicit function of q, Q, t only. In fact one can apply Legendre's transformations to $F_1(q, Q, t)$ and obtain generating functions as explicit functions of other variables. Apart from the passive coordinate t, the other two independent coordinates in a generating function can be any two (one old and the other new) out of q, Q, p and P, but never more than two because the third one can always be expressed in terms of the first two.

Sometimes a generating function of the form $F_2 = F_2(q, P, t)$ is more useful than F_1. In order to go from F_1 to F_2 using Legendre's transformation, we must note that the new variables $P_i = -\partial F_1/\partial Q_i$ are as independent as Q_i's, hence Legendre's dual transformation of F_1 will be

$$F_2(q, P, t) = F_1(q, Q, t) + P_i Q_i$$

Therefore,

$$\begin{aligned} p_i dq_i - H dt &= P_i dQ_i - K dt + dF_1 \\ &= P_i dQ_i - K dt + dF_2 - d(P_i Q_i) \\ &= -K dt + \frac{\partial F_2}{\partial t} dt + \frac{\partial F_2}{\partial q_i} dq_i + \frac{\partial F_2}{\partial P_i} dP_i - Q_i dP_i \end{aligned}$$

Since in this case q, P and t are all regarded as independent, one obtains,

$$\begin{aligned} p_i &= \left(\frac{\partial F_2}{\partial q_i}\right)_{P,t} \\ Q_i &= \left(\frac{\partial F_2}{\partial P_i}\right)_{q,t} \qquad i = 1, \ldots, n, \qquad (8.12) \\ K &= H + \frac{\partial F_2}{\partial t} \end{aligned}$$

Similarly one can form a third generating function $F_3(Q, p, t)$ from F_1 by replacing q_i's by p_i's given by $p_i = \partial F_1/\partial q_i$, in which case, Legendre's dual transformation becomes

$$F_3(Q, p, t) = F_1(q, Q, t) - p_i q_i$$

Following the same procedure as in the case of F_2, we obtain

$$\begin{aligned} P_i &= -\left(\frac{\partial F_3}{\partial Q_i}\right)_{p,t} \\ q_i &= -\left(\frac{\partial F_3}{\partial p_i}\right)_{Q,t} \qquad i = 1, \ldots, n \qquad (8.13) \\ K &= H + \frac{\partial F_3}{\partial t} \end{aligned}$$

Similarly, a fourth generating function $F_4(p, P, t)$ can be constructed either from F_2 or F_3 or even from F_1 where

$$\begin{aligned} F_4(p, P, t) &= F_1(q, Q, t) - q_i p_i + P_i Q_i \\ &= F_3(Q, p, t) + P_i Q_i \\ &= F_2(q, P, t) - p_i q_i \end{aligned}$$

giving finally,

$$\begin{aligned} q_i &= -\left(\frac{\partial F_4}{\partial p_i}\right)_{P,t} \\ Q_i &= \left(\frac{\partial F_4}{\partial P_i}\right)_{p,t} \qquad i = 1,\ldots,n \\ K &= H + \frac{\partial F_4}{\partial t} \end{aligned} \tag{8.14}$$

These four generating functions have striking similarities with the four thermodynamic potentials U', H', F' and G' described earlier in connection with Legendre's transformations in section 5.1. These four generating functions also satisfy Maxwell-like relations which can be obtained by differentiating once more the first two relations of each of the sets of Eqs (8.10), (8.12), (8.13) and (8.14). We quote the final results

$$\begin{aligned} \left(\frac{\partial p_i}{\partial Q_k}\right)_{q,t} &= -\left(\frac{\partial P_k}{\partial q_i}\right)_{Q,t} \qquad i,k = 1,\ldots,n \\ \left(\frac{\partial p_i}{\partial P_k}\right)_{q,t} &= \left(\frac{\partial Q_k}{\partial q_i}\right)_{P,t} \qquad i,k = 1,\ldots,n \\ \left(\frac{\partial P_i}{\partial p_k}\right)_{Q,t} &= \left(\frac{\partial q_k}{\partial Q_i}\right)_{p,t} \qquad i,k = 1,\ldots,n \\ \left(\frac{\partial q_i}{\partial P_k}\right)_{p,t} &= -\left(\frac{\partial Q_k}{\partial p_i}\right)_{P,t} \qquad i,k = 1,\ldots,n \end{aligned} \tag{8.15}$$

each one obtained in sequel from the four distinct forms of the generating functions, namely $F_1(q,Q,t)$, $F_2(q,P,t)$, $F_3(p,Q,t)$ and $F_4(p,P,t)$.

Equations (8.15) are to be satisfied by all univalent canonical transformations. The beauty of these equations lies in their symmetrical forms, which are totally independent of the Hamiltonian or the generating functions. Given a set of canonical transformations either in the form of Eqs (8.1) or in the form of Eqs (8.5), they must satisfy all the four sets of equations given in Eqs (8.15).

An interesting point to note is that in all four cases the value of the transformed Hamiltonian K is related to the value of the old Hamiltonian by a similar relation, the value differs by the partial time derivative of any one of the generating functions. If there is an explicit time dependence in the transformations themselves the generating functions must also have explicit time dependence because $Q = Q(t)$ and $P = P(t)$ imply moving frames of reference and hence energy or Hamiltonian cannot be the same in the two frames, even though with respect to either frame they may be a constant of motion.

8.2.4 Conditions for Canonicality

The property of the canonical transformations, namely the occurrence of the same time parameter t in both the phase spaces spanned by (q,p) and (Q,P), should in principle allow us to test the condition for canonical transformation in terms of q, p, Q, P and their differentials only. Time can be treated as an independent parameter. In fact this is quite obvious in all the four sets of Eqs (8.15) that can be used for testing the canonicality of a given phase space transformation. All these conditions are also seen to be evaluated at constant t, which signifies the purely geometrical nature of the canonical transformations that take place in terms of the phase space coordinates alone. Although the conditions for canonicality by definition must be such as to preserve the form of Hamilton's equations of motion, the conditions themselves in the form of Eqs (8.15) are intrinsically independent of the Hamiltonian. In order to appreciate this point further, let us recall the condition for canonicality in terms of the generating function $F_1(q,Q,t)$ from Eq. (8.9) given by

$$p_i dq_i - H(p,q,t)dt = P_i dQ_i - K(P,Q,t)dt + dF_1(q,Q,t) \tag{8.16}$$

Here dq_i and dQ_i are the differential (perfect) changes in the coordinates in real time dt. Since the transformations in the phase space between two sets of coordinates q_i's and Q_i's are essentially geometrical (that is, without involving $t \to t'$), we can look upon dq_i and dQ_i as the elements of static geometrical curves rather than evolving paths, so far as the testing of the canonical condition is concerned. This leads to setting $dt = 0$ in Eq. (8.16) which gives

$$p_i\,\delta q_i - P_i\,\delta Q_i = \text{an exact differential} \tag{8.17}$$

where t in $P_i(q,p,t), Q_i(q,p,t)$ and $F_1(q,Q,t)$ is held constant while finding the differentials δq_i and δQ_i. This is analogous to the testing of a geometrical condition on rheonomic constraints which can proceed with the contemporaneous variations of the coordinates. Here in the above condition $P_i = P_i(q,p,t)$ and $Q_i = Q_i(q,p,t)$ are already used to evaluate $P_i dQ_i$ in terms of (p,q,t) only, so that the exactness can be tested in either the (q,p) space or the (Q,P) space but not in any mixed space. Also note that the process of setting $dt = 0$ automatically removes all the Hamiltonian dependent terms from Eq. (8.16).

Now such a set of equations in terms of differentials is said to have the property of contact transformations, which are defined as follows.

If the equations connecting two sets of variables $(q_1,\ldots,q_n,\ p_1,\ldots,p_n)$ and $(Q_1,\ldots,Q_n,\ P_1,\ldots,P_n)$ are such that the differential form

$$P_1 dQ_1 + \ldots + P_n dQ_n - \{p_1 dq_1 + \ldots + p_n dq_n\}$$

is, when expressed in terms of $(q_1,\ldots,q_n,\ p_1,\ldots,p_n)$ and their differentials, the perfect differential of a function of $(q_1,\ldots,q_n,\ p_1,\ldots,p_n)$, then the change from the set of variables from $(q_1,\ldots,q_n,\ p_1,\ldots,p_n)$ to $(Q_1,\ldots,Q_n,\ P_1,\ldots,P_n)$ is called a *contact* transformation. Its essential geometrical property is that if one draws two curves which meet tangentially at some point then in the transformed phase space the corresponding curves are also bound to meet tangentially at the corresponding phase space point, thus emphasizing the meaning of the adjective 'contact'.

Now the condition (8.17) does satisfy this property, and hence *all canonical transformations are nothing but contact transformations*, so long as the time parameter itself is not transformed. The condition (8.17) can also be derived from the first of Maxwell's relations, that is,

$$\left(\frac{\partial p_i}{\partial Q_k}\right)_{q,t} = -\left(\frac{\partial P_k}{\partial q_i}\right)_{Q,t}$$

because we know that if

$$\left(\frac{\partial M}{\partial y}\right)_x = \left(\frac{\partial N}{\partial x}\right)_y$$

then $Mdx + Ndy$ is a perfect differential, which gives the condition (8.17).

Similar conditions can be derived from the other three equations of Maxwell, and they are

$$p_i\delta q_i + Q_i\delta P_i = \text{a perfect differential}$$

$$q_i\delta p_i + P_i\delta Q_i = \text{a perfect differential}$$

and

$$q_i\delta p_i - Q_i\delta P_i = \text{a perfect differential}$$

Some more tests of canonicality will be given in the next chapter and in problem 8.6.

8.3 PROPERTIES OF CANONICAL TRANSFORMATIONS

1. The Jacobian determinant of the univalent canonical transformations is unity, with the result that any finite volume of the phase space before and after the transformation remains the same. (Canonical transformations preserve volume in the phase space.)

Let

$$Q_i = Q_i(q,p,t) \qquad \text{and} \qquad P_i = P_i(q,p,t) \qquad i = 1,\ldots,n$$

be a univalent canonical transformation. The Jacobian of the transformation is defined to be

$$J_{(q,p)\to(Q,P)} = \frac{\partial(Q_1,\ldots,Q_n;P_1,\ldots,P_n)}{\partial(q_1,\ldots,q_n;p_1,\ldots,p_n)} \equiv \det\begin{bmatrix} \frac{\partial Q_1}{\partial q_1} & \cdots & \cdots & \frac{\partial Q_1}{\partial p_n} \\ \cdots & \cdots & \cdots & \cdots \\ \cdots & \cdots & \cdots & \cdots \\ \frac{\partial P_n}{\partial q_1} & \cdots & \cdots & \frac{\partial P_n}{\partial p_n} \end{bmatrix} \tag{8.18}$$

Introducing an intermediate pair of sets of independent coordinates (q, Q) we can write

$$J = \frac{\partial(Q_1,\ldots,Q_n;P_1,\ldots,P_n)}{\partial(q_1\ \ldots,q_n;Q_1,\ldots,Q_n)}\cdot\frac{\partial(q_1,\ldots,q_n;Q_1,\ldots,Q_n)}{\partial(q_1,\ldots,q_n;p_1,\ldots,p_n)}$$

We now interchange the left and the right halves of columns in the first factor and write the second factor in terms of the corresponding inverse transformations. We get

$$J = -\left[\frac{\partial(Q_1,\ldots,Q_n;P_1,\ldots,P_n)}{\partial(Q_1,\ldots,Q_n;q_1,\ldots,q_n)}\right]\left[\frac{\partial(q_1,\ldots,q_n;p_1,\ldots,p_n)}{\partial(q_1,\ldots,q_n;Q_1,\ldots,Q_n)}\right]^{-1}$$

These two determinants have the following general forms respectively:

$$\begin{pmatrix} I & \left(\frac{\partial Q}{\partial q}\right)_p \\ O & \left(\frac{\partial P}{\partial q}\right)_p \end{pmatrix} \quad \text{and} \quad \begin{pmatrix} I & \left(\frac{\partial q}{\partial Q}\right)_P \\ O & \left(\frac{\partial p}{\partial Q}\right)_P \end{pmatrix}$$

From these general forms, it is easy to deduce that

$$\begin{aligned} J &= \left[-\frac{\partial(P_1,\ldots,P_n)}{\partial(q_1,\ldots,q_n)} \right]_{Q's} \left[\frac{\partial(p_1,\ldots,p_n)}{\partial(Q_1,\ldots,Q_n)} \right]_{q's}^{-1} \\ &= \left[\frac{\partial(\partial F_1/\partial Q_1,\ldots,\partial F_1/\partial Q_n)}{\partial(q_1,\ldots,q_n)} \right]_{Q's} \left[\frac{\partial(\partial F_1/\partial q_1,\ldots,\partial F_1/\partial q_n)}{\partial(Q_1,\ldots,Q_n)} \right]_{q's}^{-1} \end{aligned}$$

It is now obvious that these two determinants are identical, and therefore, J $= 1$. Hence,

$$\begin{aligned} dq_1 \ldots dq_n dp_1 \ldots dp_n &= J\, dQ_1 \ldots dQ_n dP_1 \ldots dP_n \\ &= dQ_1 \ldots dQ_n dP_1 \ldots dP_n \end{aligned}$$

In other words, the volume element of the phase space remains unchanged for any univalent canonical transformation. This is generally valid when the phase space is constructed in a Cartesian fashion. Note that a change from the Cartesian to the spherical polar coordinates, has the Jacobian

$$J_{(x,y,z)\to(r,\theta,\phi)} = r^2 \sin\theta \neq 1 \tag{8.19}$$

So this extended point transformation $(x, y, z, p_x, p_y, p_z) \to (r, \theta, \phi, p_x, p_y, p_z)$ is not canonical. Try to solve problem number 8.5 for further clarification.

2. All univalent canonical transformations form a group. For this we need to show that

(a) The identity transformation $(q, p) \to (Q, P)$ where $q = Q$ and $p = P$ is a canonical transformation.

(b) Two canonical transformations performed in sequence correspond to a single canonical transformation (closure condition).

(c) The inverse of a given canonical transformation exists and is itself a canonical transformation.

(d) The CTs performed in order $(C_1C_2)C_3$ and $C_1(C_2C_3)$ are identical, that is, the composition of CTs is associative.

To show (a) we choose a generating function $F_2(q, P) = q_iP_i$. Therefore,

$$p_i = \frac{\partial F_2}{\partial q_i} = P_i \quad \text{and} \quad Q_i = \frac{\partial F_2}{\partial P_i} = q_i$$

which demonstrates the existence of an identity transformation which is canonical.

To show (b), let

$$\begin{aligned} \tilde{Q} &= \tilde{Q}(Q, P, t) \qquad \tilde{P} = \tilde{P}(Q, P, t) \\ \text{and} \qquad Q &= Q(q, p, t) \qquad P = P(q, p, t) \end{aligned}$$

be the canonical transformations. Therefore at any fixed time t_o, we can write, using Eq. (8.17)

$$d\tilde{F}(Q,\tilde{Q},t_o) = P_i\delta Q_i - \tilde{P}_i\delta\tilde{Q}_i \quad \text{and} \quad dF(q,Q,t_o) = p_i\delta q_i - P_i\delta Q_i$$

Adding these equations we get

$$d(F + \tilde{F}) = p_i\delta q_i - \tilde{P}_i\delta\tilde{Q}_i \tag{8.20}$$

which proves the assertion.

To prove (c) let

$$Q = Q(q,p,t) \text{ and } P = P(q,p,t) \tag{8.21}$$

be a canonical transformation. We want to prove that the inverse transformation

$$q = q(Q,P,t) \text{ and } p = p(Q,P,t) \tag{8.22}$$

exists and is canonical.

For this we assume that the derivatives of Q and P are continuous. Then a well-known theorem in calculus, the inverse mapping theorem, states that Eq. (8.22) exists at every point in the range of Eq. (8.21) provided the Jacobian determinant of Eq. (8.21) (Eq. 8.18) is nonzero at every point in the domain of Eq. (8.21). We have already proved that the Jacobian determinant of Eq. (8.21) is unity over the domain of Eq. (8.21). This proves the existence of Eq. (8.22).

Since the transformation (8.21) is canonical, by Eqs (8.16) and (8.17) we get, for every t_o

$$dF(q,p,t_o) = p_i\delta q_i - P_i\delta Q_i \tag{8.23}$$

If we substitute the inverse transformations (8.22) in Eq. (8.23) we find that the transformed function $-\tilde{F}(Q,P,t_o)$ satisfies the relation

$$d[-\tilde{F}(Q,P,t_o)] = P_i\delta Q_i - p_i\delta q_i$$

which shows that the transformation (8.22) is canonical.

To prove (d) consider the following canonical transformations

$$C : (q^{(o)},p^{(o)}) \xrightarrow{F^{(o)}} (q^{(1)},p^{(1)})$$

$$B : (q^{(1)},p^{(1)}) \xrightarrow{F^{(1)}} (q^{(2)},p^{(2)})$$

and

$$A : (q^{(2)},p^{(2)}) \xrightarrow{F^{(2)}} (q^{(3)},p^{(3)})$$

Using the procedure leading to Eq. (8.20) we see that the generating function for both the compositions, $A(BC)$ and $(AB)C$, are $F^{(o)} + F^{1)} + F^{(2)}$ showing that $(AB)C = A(BC)$.

Therefore, ***all univalent CTs form a group***, or in other words, the algebra of the group are uniformly applicable to all the possible examples of CTs.

8.4 SOME EXAMPLES OF CANONICAL TRANSFORMATIONS

The examples given below are picked in order to demonstrate how versatile the CTs are and how the hidden symmetries become quite transparent in many cases.

1. Let us study the canonical transformation generated by $F_1(q, Q, t) = q_i Q_i$. It immediately gives

$$p_i = \frac{\partial F_1}{\partial q_i} = Q_i \quad \text{and} \quad P_i = -\frac{\partial F_1}{\partial Q_i} = -q_i \tag{8.24}$$

Equations (8.24) show that momenta and coordinates are canonically equivalent. They can be exchanged except for a sign. This fact can be appreciated by noting that Hamilton's equations of motion are symmetric in p_i's and q_i's except for a change of sign. Thus generalised momenta and coordinates are completely equivalent in the description of the phase trajectories of a system obeying Hamilton's equations of motion. The coordinate sector of the phase space can interchangeably be read as the momentum sector except for the flip of sign to be introduced.

2. The extended point transformations are in general *not* canonical transformations. It should be cautioned that most textbooks claim the opposite.

Usually the generating function is chosen to be

$$F_2 = \sum_i f_i(q_1, \ldots, q_n; t)\, P_i$$

giving

$$Q_i = \frac{\partial F_2}{\partial P_i} = f_i(q_1, \ldots, q_n; t)$$

This justifies only a partial requirement of a point transformation. Now the above form of F_2 also gives

$$p_i = \frac{\partial F_2}{\partial q_i} = P_i \frac{\partial f_i}{\partial q_i}$$

which means that $p_i \neq P_i$. Hence the above transformation is in general not an extended point transformation.

3. The gauge transformations for the electromagnetic potentials are merely canonical transformations in the phase space.

It is well known that Maxwell's equations of electromagnetism do not specify the electromagnetic potentials $\boldsymbol{A}(\boldsymbol{r}, t)$ and $\phi(\boldsymbol{r}, t)$ uniquely. If the potentials are changed as

$$\boldsymbol{A}'(\boldsymbol{r}, t) = \boldsymbol{A}(\boldsymbol{r}, t) + \nabla f(\boldsymbol{r}, t) \quad \text{and} \quad \phi'(\boldsymbol{r}, t) = \phi(\boldsymbol{r}, t) - \frac{\partial f(\boldsymbol{r}, t)}{\partial t} \tag{8.25}$$

where $f(\boldsymbol{r}, t)$ is any arbitrarily chosen scalar point function; both the sets $(\boldsymbol{A}', \phi')$ and $(\boldsymbol{A}, \phi)$ satisfy the same Maxwell's equations. The transformations (8.25) are called *electromagnetic gauge transformations*, under which Maxwell's equations remain invariant.

We now show that the gauge transformations (8.25) can be effected through a canonical transformation of coordinates $\boldsymbol{r}$ and momenta $\boldsymbol{p}$ to $(\boldsymbol{Q},\ \boldsymbol{P})$ as defined below.

Choose a generating function

$$F_2(\boldsymbol{r}, \boldsymbol{P}) = \boldsymbol{r} \cdot \boldsymbol{P} - e\, f(\boldsymbol{r}, t)$$

This gives

$$\boldsymbol{p} = \frac{\partial F_2}{\partial \boldsymbol{r}} = \boldsymbol{P} - e\,\nabla f \quad \text{and} \quad \boldsymbol{Q} = \frac{\partial F_2}{\partial \boldsymbol{P}} = \boldsymbol{r} \tag{8.26}$$

which means that $\boldsymbol{Q} = \boldsymbol{r}$ and $\dot{\boldsymbol{Q}} = \dot{\boldsymbol{r}}$. The new Hamiltonian is

$$K(\boldsymbol{P}, \boldsymbol{Q}) = H + \frac{\partial F_2}{\partial t} = H - e\,\frac{\partial f}{\partial t} \tag{8.27}$$

Now we know that the canonical momentum is

$$\boldsymbol{p} = m\boldsymbol{v} + e\boldsymbol{A}$$

and if the gauge transformations (8.25) correspond to the canonical transformations (8.26) then the canonically new momentum $\boldsymbol{P}$ which is equal to $\boldsymbol{p} + e\nabla f$ must correspond to $m\dot{\boldsymbol{Q}} + e\boldsymbol{A}'$, that is its gauge equivalent. This is shown as follows:

$$\begin{aligned} \boldsymbol{P} &= \boldsymbol{p} + e\,\nabla f = m\dot{\boldsymbol{r}} + e\boldsymbol{A} + e\,\nabla f \\ &= m\dot{\boldsymbol{Q}} + e(\boldsymbol{A} + \nabla f) = m\dot{\boldsymbol{Q}} + e\boldsymbol{A}' \end{aligned}$$

giving the first of the Eqs (8.25).

Similarly from Eq. (8.27) we get

$$\begin{aligned} K &= H - e\,\frac{\partial f}{\partial t} = \frac{1}{2}m\dot{\boldsymbol{r}}^2 + e\,\phi - e\,\frac{\partial f}{\partial t} \\ &= \frac{1}{2}m\dot{\boldsymbol{Q}}^2 + e\left[\phi - \frac{\partial f}{\partial t}\right] = \frac{1}{2}m\dot{\boldsymbol{Q}}^2 + e\,\phi' \end{aligned}$$

giving the second of Eqs (8.25). Thus the new canonical momentum and energy are the gauge transforms of the old canonical momentum and energy respectively, showing that the electromagnetic gauge transformations can be viewed as a univalent canonical transformation (8.26).

4. The Lagrangian gauge transformation given by

$$L'(q, \dot{q}, t) = L(q, \dot{q}, t) + \frac{df(q,t)}{dt}$$

can also be viewed as a canonical transformation effected by the generating function,

$$F_2(q, P) = q_i P_i - f(q,t)$$

giving

$$p_i = \frac{\partial F_2}{\partial q_i} = P_i - \frac{\partial f}{\partial q_i} \quad \text{and} \quad Q_i = \frac{\partial F_2}{\partial P_i} = q_i \tag{8.28}$$

and

$$K = H + \frac{\partial F_2}{\partial t} = H - \frac{\partial f}{\partial t} \tag{8.29}$$

Note that $q_i = Q_i$ and hence $\dot{q}_i = \dot{Q}_i$.

Now one has to see whether the new momenta P_i and Hamiltonian K obtained via canonical transformation are the same as those expected from the new Lagrangian L', that is, whether

$$P_i = \frac{\partial L'}{\partial \dot{Q}_i} \quad \text{and} \quad K = \frac{\partial L'}{\partial \dot{Q}_i}\dot{Q}_i - L'$$

In order to prove this, consider

$$\frac{\partial L'}{\partial \dot{Q}_i} = \frac{\partial L'}{\partial \dot{q}_i} = \frac{\partial L}{\partial \dot{q}_i} + \frac{\partial}{\partial \dot{q}_i}\left(\frac{df}{dt}\right)$$

$$= p_i + \frac{\partial}{\partial \dot{q}_i}\left[\frac{\partial f}{\partial t} + \frac{\partial f}{\partial q_i}\dot{q}_i\right] = p_i + \frac{\partial f}{\partial q_i} = P_i$$

Further,

$$\dot{Q}_i \frac{\partial L'}{\partial \dot{Q}_i} - L' = \dot{q}_i\left(p_i + \frac{\partial f}{\partial q_i}\right) - L - \frac{\partial f}{\partial t} - \dot{q}_i\frac{\partial f}{\partial q_i}$$

$$= (\dot{q}_i p_i - L) - \frac{\partial f}{\partial t} = H - \frac{\partial f}{\partial t} = K$$

which proves the assertion.

5. Any infinitesimal coordinate transformation is a canonical transformation.

Choose the generating function to be

$$F_2(\boldsymbol{r}, \boldsymbol{P}) = \boldsymbol{r} \cdot \boldsymbol{P} + \Delta\boldsymbol{a} \cdot \boldsymbol{P}$$

where $\Delta\boldsymbol{a}$ is a constant vector representing an infinitesimal coordinate transformation,

$$\boldsymbol{Q} \rightarrow \boldsymbol{r} + \Delta\boldsymbol{a} \tag{8.30}$$

or equivalently, a shift in the origin of the coordinate system by $-\Delta\boldsymbol{a}$. The above generating function gives

$$\boldsymbol{Q} = \frac{\partial F_2}{\partial \boldsymbol{P}} = \boldsymbol{r} + \Delta\boldsymbol{a} \qquad \boldsymbol{p} = \frac{\partial F_2}{\partial \boldsymbol{r}} = \boldsymbol{P} \quad \text{and} \quad K = H \tag{8.31}$$

leaving momentum and Hamiltonian unchanged as expected. Equations (8.31) obviously correspond to the infinitesimal coordinate transformation (8.30), which is now proved to be a CT.

6. Any infinitesimal rotation by $\Delta\phi$ of the coordinate frame about an axis passing through the origin and pointing in the direction of the unit vector $\hat{\boldsymbol{n}}$ corresponds to a canonical transformation.

Take as the generating function,

$$F_2(\boldsymbol{r}, \boldsymbol{P}) = \boldsymbol{r} \cdot \boldsymbol{P} + \Delta\phi\, \hat{\boldsymbol{n}} \cdot (\boldsymbol{r} \times \boldsymbol{P})$$

Hence

$$Q = \frac{\partial F_2}{\partial \boldsymbol{P}} = \boldsymbol{r} + \Delta\phi\,(\hat{\boldsymbol{n}} \times \boldsymbol{r})$$
$$\boldsymbol{p} = \frac{\partial F_2}{\partial \boldsymbol{r}} = \boldsymbol{P} - \Delta\phi\,(\hat{\boldsymbol{n}} \times \boldsymbol{P}) \tag{8.32}$$

Equations (8.32) correspond to an infinitesimal rotation $\Delta\phi$ of the system around any arbitrary direction ($\hat{\boldsymbol{n}}$) or equivalently to the rotation of the coordinate frame by $-\hat{\boldsymbol{n}}\,\Delta\phi$ around the same direction.

7. Any infinitesimal transformation involving a shift only in time by Δt is also a canonical transformation that connects the evolution of the coordinates and momenta in time.

Since the time evolution of a conservative system over any interval of time is governed by the Hamiltonian, we choose as the generating function

$$F_2(q, P) = qP + \Delta t\, H(q, P) \tag{8.33}$$

This gives

$$Q(t) = \frac{\partial F_2}{\partial P} = q + \Delta t \frac{\partial H}{\partial P} = q + \Delta t \dot{Q}$$
$$\simeq q(t) + \Delta t \dot{q} \simeq q(t + \Delta t)$$

correct to the first order of smallness of Δt. The above approximations are possible because of the smallness of Δt. Again,

$$p(t) = \frac{\partial F_2}{\partial q} = P + \Delta t\,\frac{\partial H}{\partial q} = P(t) - \dot{p}\Delta t$$

Thus we get

$$Q(t) = q(t + \Delta t) \qquad \text{and} \qquad P(t) = p(t) + \dot{p}\,\Delta t = p(t + \Delta t) \tag{8.34}$$

and also

$$K = H(q(t + \Delta t), p(t + \Delta(t))) \tag{8.35}$$

Equations (8.34) and (8.35) show that an infinitesimal change in time by Δt leads to the evolution of the conservative system from $q(t)$ to $Q(t) = q(t + \Delta t)$, $p(t)$ to $P(t) = p(t + \Delta t)$ and $H(q(t), p(t))$ to $K(Q, P) = H(q(t + \Delta t), p(t + \Delta t))$. This transformation can be viewed as an infinitesimal canonical transformation generated by the generating function (8.33) which involves the Hamiltonian in the infinitesimal term. This is the reason why the Hamiltonian is called *the generator of evolution.*

Since canonical transformations are associative, a large number of infinitesimal transformations of the above kind can be applied in succession. Thus, any general solution $q = q(q_o, p_o, t)$ and $p = p(q_o, p_o, t)$ from the initial values (q_o, p_o) can be regarded as a canonical transformation between the initial and final values, that is, directly from (q_o, p_o) to (q, p).

8. The canonical transformation generated by

$$F_2(\boldsymbol{r}, \boldsymbol{P}) = \boldsymbol{r} \cdot \boldsymbol{P} + (\boldsymbol{V} \cdot \boldsymbol{P})t - m\,(\boldsymbol{r} \cdot \boldsymbol{V})$$

also represents a physical situation.

In this case, we have

$$p = \frac{\partial F_2}{\partial r} = P - mV \qquad \text{or} \qquad P = p + mV$$

$$Q = \frac{\partial F_2}{\partial P} = r + Vt \tag{8.36}$$

and

$$K = H + \frac{\partial F_2}{\partial t} = H + P \cdot V \tag{8.37}$$

We know that Eqs (8.36) and (8.37) represent a Galilean transformation from (r, p) to (Q, P), where the origin of the (r, p) system is moving in real space with a constant velocity V with respect to the origin of the (Q, P) system.

9. A changeover to a uniformly rotating frame of reference from a stationary frame can also be shown to be canonical using the following generating function,

$$F_2(r, P) = r \cdot P - t\,\omega \cdot (r \times P)$$

because this generating function gives

$$\begin{aligned} p &= \frac{\partial F_2}{\partial r} = P + (\omega \times P)\,t \\ Q &= \frac{\partial F_2}{\partial P} = r + (r \times \omega)\,t \end{aligned} \tag{8.38}$$

and

$$\begin{aligned} K &= H + \frac{\partial F_2}{\partial t} = H - \omega \cdot (r \times P) \\ &= H - \omega \cdot (Q \times P) = H - \omega \cdot L \end{aligned} \tag{8.39}$$

where L is the angular momentum measured in the rotating frame. These results can be verified from the ones given in chapter 3, namely Eq. (3.8).

8.5 CANONICAL TRANSFORMATION TO THE FREE PARTICLE HAMILTONIAN

The principal utility of the canonical transformation is to transform the physical Hamiltonian $H(q, p, t)$ to a new Hamiltonian $K(Q, P, t)$ such that the corresponding equations of motion become easier to solve and also display all possible cyclic coordinates and conserved quantities. As an illustration we shall present here examples in which the transformed Hamiltonian of a non-free system may look like that of a free particle.

Let us consider the motion of an electrically charged particle having charge e and mass m in a uniform electric field E with E pointing along the one-dimensional positive q-axis. The Hamiltonian is

$$H(q, p) = \frac{p^2}{2m} - eEq$$

giving the complete solutions of Hamilton's equations of motion as

$$p = eEt + p_o$$

$$q = \left(\frac{eE}{2m}\right) t^2 + \left(\frac{p_o}{m}\right) t + q_o$$

We want to canonically transform (q,p) to (Q,P) such that the transformed Hamiltonian $K(Q,P)$ assumes the form of a free particle Hamiltonian for mass m, that is,

$$K(Q,P) = \frac{P^2}{2m}$$

with a complete solution,

$$Q = \left(\frac{P_o}{2m}\right) t + Q_o \quad \text{and} \quad P = P_o$$

Now eliminating t between these two sets of solutions and setting $q_o = Q_o = 0$ and $p_o = P_o = P$ we get,

$$q = \frac{eE}{2m}\left(\frac{mQ}{P}\right)^2 + Q \quad \text{and} \quad p = eE\left(\frac{mQ}{P}\right) + P \tag{8.40}$$

This is the required canonical transformation.

Similarly, the Hamiltonian for a simple 1–D harmonic oscillator in (q,p) is given by

$$H(q,p) = \frac{p^2}{2m} + \frac{1}{2}m\omega^2 q^2$$

with a complete solution

$$p = p_o \cos(\omega t) - m\omega q_o \sin(\omega t)$$

and

$$q = \frac{p_o}{m\omega}\sin(\omega t) + q_o \cos(\omega t)$$

On the elimination of t between these solutions and the required free particle solution in (Q,P) with $Q_o = q_o = 0$ and $p_o = P_o = P$, one obtains

$$p = P\cos\left(\frac{m\omega Q}{P}\right) \quad \text{and} \quad q = \left(\frac{P}{m\omega}\right)\sin\left(\frac{m\omega Q}{P}\right) \tag{8.41}$$

In some extreme cases it is even possible to make the transformed Hamiltonian totally vanish, that is, $K(Q,P,t) = 0$, irrespective of the given form of $H(q,p,t)$. When we use Hamilton's principal function $W(q_1,\ldots,q_n;t)$ (see Eq. 6.38b) as a generating function, the transformed Hamiltonian vanishes automatically because of the identities

$$K \equiv H + \frac{\partial W}{\partial t} \equiv 0$$

Such a class of solutions and the corresponding CTs will be of utmost importance, and in fact forms the basis of chapter 10.

It may not be out of place to make comment on Eq. (6.38a). It is obvious that the normal to the equi-action surface for W in the n-dimensional configuration space is defining the canonical momentum as a vector in the same configuration space. The Hamiltonian being a surface in the phase space finds a place also in the configuration space through the function W, through the relation Eq. (6.38b). The partial time derivative of W at a given point in the configuration space defines the form of the Hamiltonian.

8.6 LIOUVILLE'S THEOREM

We know that every possible state of a system is represented by a unique point in its phase space. Let us call this point in the phase space to be the image point of the system. Since the state of the system at any given time (through Hamilton's equations of motion) determines uniquely its state at any other time, the motion of the image point in the phase space (determining the changes of state the system with time) is uniquely determined by its initial position. The path traced by the image point in the phase space as it moves in accordance with the time evolution of the system is called a trajectory. Obviously, one and only one trajectory passes through each point of the phase space as Hamilton's equations of motion fix the local gradients uniquely.

Suppose at some time t_o, the image point of the system in its phase space is at M_o and at some other time t (succeeding or preceding t_o) at some other point M. We know that the points M_o and M determine each other uniquely. So we can say that, during the time interval $t_o - t$ the point M_o of the phase space goes over to M. During the same interval of time, every other point of the phase space goes over to a definite new position. In other words, the entire phase space is transformed into itself. Moreover, this transformation is one to one because the position of a point at time t also determines its position at the time t_o. If we keep t_o fixed and vary t arbitrarily then by the example 7 of section 8.4 we see that the set of all possible changes of state (during $t_o - t$) of the given system is represented as an infinite (continuous) sequence of canonical transformations of the phase space into itself, such that each transformation in the sequence involves an infinitesimal increment in time. We call the above described motion of the phase space in itself, its *natural motion* .

Let M' denote a set of points in phase space with volume $V(0) \neq 0$ at time $t = 0$. During the natural motion of phase space this set goes over to a set $M'(t)$ in a time interval t with volume $V(t)$. *Liouville's theorem* then asserts that

$$V(0) = V(t)$$

Proof

The transformation from M' to $M'(t)$ is a canonical transformation which is a composition of an infinite sequence of infinitesimal canonical transformations. We have already proved that every canonical transformation preserves volume in phase space by virtue of the fact that its Jacobian is unity. This completes the proof.

However, one should remember that Liouville's theorem does not apply to the dissipative systems for which the constant energy surface containing the trajectories in the phase space keeps on shrinking in volume due to dissipation.

8.7 AREA CONSERVATION PROPERTY OF HAMILTONIAN FLOWS

We shall now prove a fundamental property of Hamiltonian systems. Let (q, p) denote some convenient coordinates in the phase space of the system. Consider a closed curve (loop) C in the phase space. Then the area in the closed loop C is defined as

$$A = \sum_k \oint_C p_k dq_k \equiv \oint_C < p, dq > \tag{8.42}$$

where $< p, dq >$ denotes the scalar product $\sum_k p_k dq_k$. This means that the area A in Eq. (8.42) is the algebraic sum of all the projected partial areas on the coordinate planes defined by the conjugate pairs of q_k, p_k (see Fig. 8.1). Every point on C moves in accordance with Hamilton's equations of motion, with the Hamiltonian $H(q, p, t)$. In other words, the loop C moves according to the natural motion of the phase space. The change in its area A is given by

$$\frac{dA}{dt} = \frac{d}{dt}\oint_C < p, dq > = \oint_C < \dot{p}, dq > + \oint_C < p, d\dot{q} >$$

Integrating second term on RHS by parts, we get,

$$\frac{dA}{dt} = \oint_C < \dot{p}, dq > - \oint_C < \dot{q}, dp > + [< p, \dot{q} >]_C \tag{8.43}$$

The last term vanishes because C is a closed loop and $< p, \dot{q} >$ is single valued. Using Hamilton's equations, we get

$$\frac{dA}{dt} = - \oint_C < \frac{\partial H}{\partial q}, dq > - \oint_C < \frac{\partial H}{\partial p}, dp > = - [H]_C = 0$$

as H is single valued.

Thus the natural motion of the phase space (governed by Hamilton's equations) leaves invariant the area enclosed by an arbitrary closed loop in the phase space.

The converse of the above result is also true. Thus if a continuous transformation of the phase space onto itself conserves areas for all closed loops for all time then that transformation must be generated by a Hamiltonian $H(p, q, t)$. This can be proved as follows.

Since we are now given that $dA/dt = 0$, using Eq. (8.43) we can write

$$\oint_C < \dot{p}, dq > - \oint_C < \dot{q}, dp > + [< p, \dot{q} >]_C = 0 \tag{8.44}$$

Since Eq. (8.44) must hold for any closed loop C in the phase space we must have,

$$- < \dot{p}, dq > + < \dot{q}, dp > = 0 \tag{8.45}$$

Equation (8.45) is an equation to some hypersurface in the $2n$-dimensional phase space. The vector $\boldsymbol{X} = (-\dot{p}, \dot{q})$ is normal to this surface at every point on it. Now at any given instant

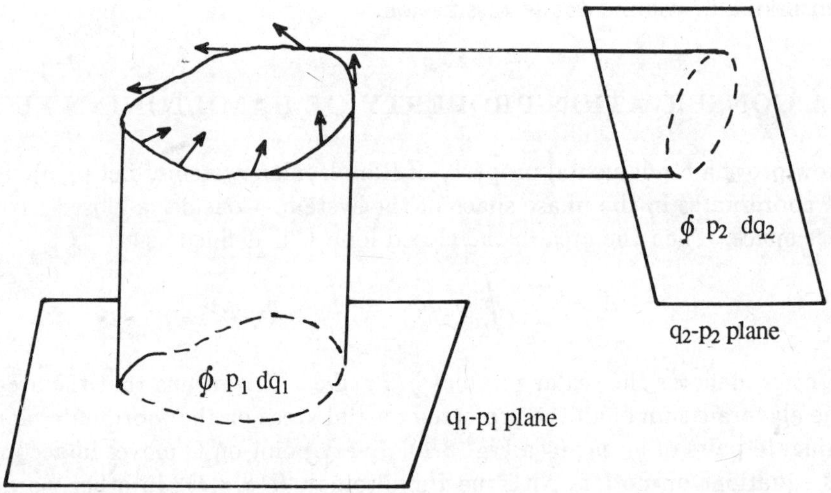

Fig. 8.1 Projections of the bounding surface of a given phase space volume on to the elementary phase planes

t, let $H(p, q, t)$ denote a single valued scalar function which is constant on the hypersurface defined by Eq. (8.45). Then it is well known that

$$\boldsymbol{X} \equiv (-\dot{p}, \dot{q}) = \nabla H \equiv \left(\frac{\partial H}{\partial q}, \frac{\partial H}{\partial p}\right) \tag{8.46}$$

where

$$\frac{\partial}{\partial p} \equiv \left(\frac{\partial}{\partial p_1}, \frac{\partial}{\partial p_2}, \ldots, \frac{\partial}{\partial p_n}\right) \quad \text{and} \quad \frac{\partial}{\partial q} \equiv \left(\frac{\partial}{\partial q_1}, \frac{\partial}{\partial q_2}, \ldots, \frac{\partial}{\partial q_n}\right)$$

Equations (8.46) are nothing but Hamilton's equations of motion, which proves what we wanted.

Thus we have proved the important result that a system is Hamiltonian if and only if the corresponding continuous transformation of the phase space onto itself conserves areas in the sense described above.

Any continuous (usually one parameter) transformation of the phase space onto itself is called a flow. If a flow conserves areas then it is called a Hamiltonian flow.

Note that the above proof did not depend in any way on whether the Hamiltonian of the system is time dependent or time independent, that is whether the energy of the system is conserved or not. Thus the area preserving property holds good for both time dependent and time independent Hamiltonian systems. Therefore, the net result is that if $(q(t), p(t))$ represents the state of the system at time t and

$$T_t : (q(0), p(0)) \rightarrow (q(t), p(t)) \tag{8.47}$$

denotes the phase space transformation generated by the Hamiltonian, the transformation T_t conserves areas in phase space.

We shall now show that any continuous phase space transformation is canonical if and only if it conserves areas in the phase space.

We know that a transformation

$$Q = Q(q,p,t) \qquad \text{and} \qquad P = P(q,p,t) \tag{8.48}$$

is canonical if and only if there exists a function $F(q,p,t)$ such that for every instant of time,

$$dF(q,p,t) = <p,dq> - <P(q,p,t)\,,\,dQ(q,p,t)> \tag{8.49}$$

Integrate both sides around any closed loop C in the phase space, say counter-clockwise. Since F is single valued and C is a closed curve, the integral of the LHS gives zero so that

$$\oint_C <p,dq> = \oint_C <P(q,p,t),dQ(q,p,t)> = \oint_{C'} <P,dQ> \tag{8.50}$$

where the loop C gets transformed into C′ under the transformation (8.48). Thus we have proved that if the transformation (8.48) satisfies Eq. (8.49) then it conserves areas in the phase space. Now suppose we are given that (8.48) conserves areas in the phase space then it is trivial to show that it must satisfy Eq. (8.49). We leave this as an exercise.

Thus, in fact we can define a canonical transformation as a phase space transformation (8.48) which conserves areas in the phase space. It is also well known that a transformation is area preserving if and only if its Jacobian is unity. Thus a transformation is canonical if and only if its Jacobian is unity. This statement is stronger than the one proved in section 8.3 where only the necessity was proved.

The area preserving property of the Hamiltonian flows is more fundamental than its volume preserving property (Liouville's theorem). Thus Liouville's theorem can be proved using the fact that the transformation T_t (see Eq. (8.47)) is area preserving (that is, canonical) but the area preserving property of T_t cannot be proved using Liouville's theorem.

8.8 SUMMARY

This is an interesting chapter. It gives us a handle to transform the Hamiltonian to have any desired form so that solving Hamilton's equations in the transformed set of the generalised coordinates and generalised momenta becomes quite trivial. So the basic requirement for this has been to allow only those phase space transformations that leave the form of Hamilton's equations of motion invariant. The class of such transformations are called canonical, or equivalently, contact transformations. These two connotations differ only in the style of their definitions. They are called canonical to signify that the canonical equations of motion remain by condition invariant in form. The connotation contact signifies continuation of the property of touching any two curves in both the original and transformed phase spaces. The definition of the second type is in fact independent of the knowledge of any Hamiltonian, which it should be, because the transformation equations themselves do not have anything to do with any Hamiltonian. However, one can easily check that the use of an Hamiltonian in testing canonicality is like the use of litmus paper in testing the acidity of a given solution, which is not supposed to influence the nature of the solution it tests. In fact one can use any Hamiltonian, that is, any arbitrary function of momenta and coordinates to test the canonicality. The contact behaviour does not involve time, and this property being geometrical must be satisfied at any given instant.

All canonical transformations form a group, which means that for any given canonical transformation an inverse CT exists, that an identity transformation is a CT, that any two successive CTs can be regarded as a single CT, and that three consecutive CTs also satisfy the associative property. The group properties of the CTs essentially give all CTs a feeling of belonging to a family.

All the various examples of CTs in different contexts of physics show their versatility. Obviously from the examples given in section 8.4 it is apparent that all these CTs define some kind of momenta and Hamiltonian, which may or may not have any connection with our regular notions of momentum and energy, yet they all are seen to satisfy a set of first order differential equations called Hamilton's equations of motion. So these merely constitute a unified viewpoint that the CTs have brought into physics. Once again, we must remember that all CTs form a group, and therefore, so many isolated events of physics given in the form of examples of CTs in section 8.4 are assembled into a family.

The seventh of the above examples uses a CT that can transform the initial coordinates and momenta to the coordinates and momenta at a later instant infinitesimally next to it. So the whole course of evolution of a dynamically conservative system can be regarded as the gradual unfolding of a contact transformation. The Hamiltonian quietly changes from $H(q(t), p(t))$ to $H(q(t+\Delta t), p(t+\Delta t))$, as is expected in such a case.

In section 8.5, we have illustrated with an example how the motion of a charged particle in a uniform electric field could be viewed as a motion of a free particle in a new system of phase space coordinates effected by a suitable CT.

The last two sections deal with general theorems regarding the behaviour of phase space under CTs. Certain properties do remain invariant. Liouville's theorem guarantees the invariance of the volume of phase space spanned by a conservative dynamical system. The other theorem, namely the area theorem, is more general, and it asserts that the sum of all the projected areas on the individual conjugate planes in a phase space under any given closed curve remains unchanged as the system evolves with time.

PROBLEMS

8.1 Show that the identity transformations can exist only in the form of $F_2(P, q) = P_i q_i$ and $F_3(p, Q) = -p_i Q_i$, not for $F_1 = F_1(q, Q)$ and $F_4 = F_4(p, P)$.

8.2 If two CTs

$$(q, p) \overset{F_2}{\rightarrow} (Q, P)$$

and

$$(Q, P) \overset{G_2}{\rightarrow} (Q', P')$$

are generated by $F_2(q, P)$ and $G_2(Q, P')$, show that

$$(q, p) \overset{H_2}{\rightarrow} (Q', P')$$

is also a CT generated by $H_2(q, P') = F_2(q, P) + G_2(Q, P') - \Sigma_i P_i Q_i$.

8.3 The reflection about the x_2–x_3 plane passing through the origin, that is, $x_1' = -x_1$, $x_2' = x_2$ and $x_3' = x_3$ is canonical and is generated by $F_2(x, P) = -x_1P_1 + x_2P_2 + x_3P_3$. How does the momentum vector transform?

8.4 A general rotation about the origin, $x_i \xrightarrow{R} x_i' = \sum_i R_{ij}x_j$, is described by the rotation matrix $R = [R_{ij}]$, $i, j = 1, 2, 3$. Find the generating function $F_2(x_i, p_i')$ and the transformation equations for the momentum components.

8.5 Show that the Cartesian to polar coordinate transformations in phase space if introduced only for the coordinate sector given by $(x_1, x_2, x_3, p_1\ p_2, p_3) \rightarrow (r, \theta, \phi, p_1, p_2, p_3)$, is not canonical, but the transformation $(x_1, x_2, x_3, p_1\ p_2, p_3) \rightarrow (r, \theta, \phi, p_r, p_\theta, p_\phi)$ is, being effected through a generating function $F_3 = F_3(p_1, p_2, p_3, r, \theta, \phi) = -(p_1 r \sin\theta\cos\phi + p_2 r\sin\theta\sin\phi + p_3 r\cos\theta)$. Find p_r, p_θ, p_ϕ and evaluate for $p^2 = p_1^2 + p_2^2 + p_3^2$ in terms of p_r, p_θ, p_ϕ. Also check whether the Jacobian for the second transformation is unity.

8.6 Apart from the conditions of canonicality stated already in section 8.2.4, prove that the following conditions are also valid for testing canonicality of a phase space transformation given by $Q_i = Q_i(q,p,t)$ and $P_i = P_i(q,p,t)$:
(i)

$$\sum_k \left(\frac{\partial Q_i}{\partial q_k}\frac{\partial P_j}{\partial p_k} - \frac{\partial Q_i}{\partial p_k}\frac{\partial P_j}{\partial q_k}\right) = \delta_{ij}$$

$$\sum_k \left(\frac{\partial Q_i}{\partial q_k}\frac{\partial Q_j}{\partial p_k} - \frac{\partial Q_i}{\partial p_k}\frac{\partial Q_j}{\partial q_k}\right) = 0$$

$$\sum_k \left(\frac{\partial P_i}{\partial q_k}\frac{\partial P_j}{\partial p_k} - \frac{\partial P_i}{\partial p_k}\frac{\partial P_j}{\partial q_k}\right) = 0$$

The meaning of these expressions in terms of the Poisson's brackets will be clear when we move on to the next chapter.

(ii) If δ be a symbol for an independent set of small increments (of coordinates and momenta) and d be a symbol for total increments in the sense of the total differentials (of coordinates and momenta), then show that

$$\sum_k (\delta P_k dQ_k - dP_k \delta Q_k) = \sum_k (\delta p_k dq_k - dp_k \delta q_k)$$

This is called the bilinear covariance of the Pfaffians $\Sigma_k P_k dQ_k$ and $\Sigma_k p_k dq_k$, where $P_k = P_k(Q_1, \ldots, Q_n)$ and $p_k = p_k(q_1, \ldots, q_n)$.

8.7 Prove that the following transformations are canonical:
(i) $Q = p^{-1}$ $\quad P = qp^2$
(ii) $Q = q^\alpha \cos\beta p$ $\quad P = q^\alpha \sin\beta p$ $\quad$ only if $\alpha = \frac{1}{2}$ and $\beta = 2$
(iii) $Q = \tan^{-1}(\alpha q/p)$ $\quad P = \frac{1}{2}\alpha q^2(1 + p^2/\alpha^2 q^2)$ $\quad$ for any constant α
(iv) $Q = \ln(1 + \sqrt{q}\cos p)$ $\quad P = 2(1 + \sqrt{q}\cos p)\sqrt{q}\sin p$
(v) $Q = \sqrt{2q}\, e^t \cos p$ $\quad P = \sqrt{2q}\, e^{-t}\sin p$
(vi) $Q = aq + bp$ $\quad P = cq + dp$ $\quad$ only if $ad - bc = 1$

(vii) $Q = q\tan p \quad P = \ln\sin p$
(viii) $Q_i = p_i \tan t \quad P_i = q_i \tan t$
(ix) $q = P^2 + Q^2 \qquad p = \frac{1}{2}\tan^{-1}(P/Q)$
(x) $p_i = P_i \Sigma p_j^2 \qquad Q_i = q_i \Sigma p_j^2 - 2p_i \Sigma p_j q_j$

8.8 Determine the canonical transformations defined by the following generating functions:
(i) $F_1(q, Q, t) = \frac{1}{2} m\omega(t) q^2 \cot Q$
(ii) $F_1(q, Q, t) = \frac{1}{2} m\omega [q - F(t)/m\omega^2]^2 \cot Q$
(iii) $F_1(q, Q) = qQ - \frac{1}{2} m\omega q^2 - Q^2/4m\omega$
(iv) $F_3(Q, p) = -(e^Q - 1)^2 \tan p$
What happens to the Hamiltonian of a simple harmonic oscillator when transformed from p, q coordinates to P, Q coordinates for each of these transformations?

8.9 (a) Show that the transformation defined by the equations,

$$Q_1 = q_1^2 + \lambda^2 p_1^2$$

$$Q_2 = \frac{1}{2\lambda^2}(q_1^2 + q_2^2 + \lambda^2 p_1^2 + \lambda^2 p_2^2)$$

$$2\lambda P_1 = \tan^{-1}(q_1/\lambda p_1) - \tan^{-1}(q_2/\lambda p_2)$$

$$P_2 = \lambda \tan^{-1}(q_2/\lambda p_2)$$

is a contact transformation, and that it reduces the original Hamiltonian

$$H = \frac{1}{2}(p_1^2 + p_2^2 + q_1^2/\lambda^2 + q_2^2/\lambda^2)$$

to its transformed form

$$K = Q_2$$

(b) Similarly show that the transformation defined by

$$q_1 = \lambda_1^{-1/2}(2Q_1)^{1/2}\cos P_1 + \lambda_2^{-1/2}(2Q_2)^{1/2}\cos P_2$$

$$q_2 = -\lambda_1^{-1/2}(2Q_1)^{1/2}\cos P_1 + \lambda_2^{-1/2}(2Q_2)^{1/2}\cos P_2$$

$$p_1 = \frac{1}{2}(2\lambda_1 Q_1)^{1/2}\sin P_1 + \frac{1}{2}(2\lambda_2 Q_2)^{1/2}\sin P_2$$

$$p_2 = -\frac{1}{2}(2\lambda_1 Q_1)^{1/2}\sin P_1 + \frac{1}{2}(2\lambda_2 Q_2)^{1/2}\sin P_2$$

changes the Hamiltonian

$$H = p_1^2 + p_2^2 + \lambda_1^2(q_1 - q_2)^2/8 + \lambda_2^2(q_1 + q_2)^2/8$$

to $\qquad K = \lambda_1 Q_1 + \lambda_2 Q_2$.
Integrate the equations of motion and express the solution in terms of the original equations.

8.10 Show that the generating function $F_1(q, Q) = -\frac{1}{2} mg\tau(q + Q) - \frac{1}{2} m(q - Q)^2/\tau$ produces a canonical transformation which consists in changing the coordinate $q(t)$ and momentum $p(t)$ to $Q(t) = q(t + \tau)$ and $P(t) = p(t + \tau)$, where g and

τ are both constants, for the 1-D motion of a particle of mass m moving in a field of uniform gravity having the potential energy $V(q) = -mgq$.

8.11 Consider the Hamiltonian for small oscillations of an anharmonic oscillator of unit mass to be $H(q,p) = p^2/2 + \omega^2 q^2/2 + \alpha q^3 + \beta q p^2$ under the assumption that $\alpha q \ll \omega^2$ and $\beta q \ll 1$. Find the parameters a, b for the canonical transformation produced by the generating function $F_2(q,P) = qP + aq^2 P + bP^3$ such that the new Hamiltonian does not contain any anharmonic terms up to the first order in $\alpha Q/\omega^2$ and βQ. Determine the solution for $q(t)$.

8.12 If an infinitesimal segment of a curve (dy, dx) in a 2-D space, having slope p is transformed to (dY, dX) with a new slope P, find the transformation and justify why such a transformation should be called a contact transformation.

9
The Poisson Bracket

9.0 INTRODUCTION

Usually the Poisson bracket relations are included in the chapter dealing with the canonical transformations. In fact one of the test criteria for the canonicality of a given phase space transformation is a set of fundamental Poisson bracket relations. So we would recommend reading both these chapters before solving some of the problems suggested at the end of the last chapter. Again, since the Poisson bracket relations have been used in toto in defining the commutator relations in quantum mechanics, one should really read this chapter with care. At the end of chapter 10, we have included a section that deals exclusively with some of the classical-quantum analogies, where we shall show the link between the two. The important aspect of the Poisson bracket relations is that they are invariant under the canonical transformations.

Siméon Denis Poisson (1781 – 1840) is one of the few people who in the early nineteenth century contributed to dynamics not just as a mathematician but also as a physicist. When he was 17, his genius was quickly recognised by Lagrange, whose course in analysis was attended by Poisson. He is celebrated for his theoretical contributions to electricity and magnetism, elasticity, calculus of variation, differential geometry, theory of probability, surface tension, diffusion of heat, celestial mechanics, etc. He joined as a demonstrator at the École Polytechnique in 1800, became an assistant to Fourier and immediately succeeded the latter to his professorial chair. In 1808, he was appointed astronomer at the Bureau des Longitudes and succeeded Laplace as its chief mathematician in 1827. Among other contributors to the field of Poisson's bracket, the notable ones are Jacobi and Lagrange, but only in the present century did the topic enjoy extreme popularity, because of its quantum correspondence, mainly through the works of Heisenberg, Ehrenfest and Dirac.

9.1 DEFINITION

A Poisson bracket (PB in short) is a special kind of relation between a pair of dynamical variables (that is, measurable physical attributes) of any holonomic system, which is found to remain invariant under any canonical transformation. Their main utility lies in the fact that they can be used to construct new integrals of motion from the known ones. Poisson brackets are the classical analogues of commutation relations between operators in quantum mechanics. Historically the commutator relations in quantum mechanics were defined in analogy with the already existing classically defined Poisson brackets. The concept of the Poisson bracket was introduced by S. D. Poisson as early as 1809 and is defined as follows:

Given any two dynamical variables $u(p,q,t)$ and $v(p,q,t)$, the Poisson bracket of u and v is defined as

$$[u,v]_{(p,q)} = \sum_{i=1}^{n} \left(\frac{\partial u}{\partial q_i}\frac{\partial v}{\partial p_i} - \frac{\partial u}{\partial p_i}\frac{\partial v}{\partial q_i} \right) \tag{9.1}$$

where the suffix (p,q) refers to the set (p_i, q_i, t) of independent variables pertaining to a holonomic system with the number of DOF $= n$, with respect to which the PB is evaluated. The suffix (p,q) can be dropped, provided no ambiguity arises from doing so. (Some books define PB as a negative of the definition given in Eq. (9.1), that is, with each term having the opposite sign.)

9.2 SOME USEFUL IDENTITIES

Throughout this chapter $u(p,q,t)$, $v(p,q,t)$ and $w(p,q,t)$ are assumed to be any three dynamical variables pertaining to a holonomic system with the number of DOF $= n$ whose generalised coordinates and momenta are denoted by the set (q_i, p_i). The following identities can be easily proved.

(i) The PB of any two dynamical variables is anticommutative.

$$[u,v] = -[v,u] \tag{9.2}$$

As a corollary we have

$$[u,u] = -[u,u] = 0$$

(ii) If c is a constant, that is, not a function of (p,q,t) then,

$$[cu,v] = [u,cv] = c\,[u,v] \tag{9.3}$$

(iii) The PBs also satisfy the distributive property

$$[u+v, w] = [u,w] + [v,w] \quad \text{and} \quad [u,vw] = [u,v]w + v[u,w] \tag{9.4}$$

(iv) The partial derivative of any PB relation can be shown to satisfy

$$\frac{\partial}{\partial t}[u,v] = [\frac{\partial u}{\partial t}, v] + [u, \frac{\partial v}{\partial t}] \tag{9.5}$$

(v) A famous identity called *Jacobi's identity* is given by

$$[u,[v,w]] + [v,[w,u]] + [w,[u,v]] = 0 \tag{9.6}$$

(vi) Let $w_1, w_2, \ldots, w_n$ be a set of dynamical quantities (all functions of p,q,t) and let $F(w_1, \ldots, w_n)$ be a differentiable function of $w_1, w_2, \ldots, w_n$. Then,

$$[u, F(w_1, w_2, \ldots, w_n)] = \frac{\partial F}{\partial w_1}[u, w_1] + \frac{\partial F}{\partial w_2}[u, w_2] + \ldots + \frac{\partial F}{\partial \omega_n}[u, \omega_n] \tag{9.7}$$

9.3 ELEMENTARY PBs

The PBs constructed out of the canonical coordinates and momenta themselves are called elementary PBs. It is trivial to show that

$$[q_i, q_j] = 0 = [p_i, p_j] \quad \text{and} \quad [q_i, p_j] = -[p_j, q_i] = \delta_{ij} \tag{9.8}$$

We also have

$$[u, q_i] = -\frac{\partial u}{\partial p_i} \quad \text{and} \quad [u, p_i] = \frac{\partial u}{\partial q_i} \tag{9.9}$$

Equations (9.9) imply, for Cartesian coordinates

$$[u, \boldsymbol{r}] = -\boldsymbol{\nabla}_p u \quad \text{and} \quad [u, \boldsymbol{p}] = \boldsymbol{\nabla}_r u \tag{9.10}$$

Thus, by replacing $u(q, p, t)$ in Eq. (9.9) by the Hamiltonian function $H(q, p, t)$ one obtains Hamilton's equations of motion in terms of the PBs:

$$\dot{q}_i = [H, q_i] \quad \text{and} \quad \dot{p}_i = [H, p_i] \tag{9.11}$$

For a single particle, and in terms of Cartesian coordinates, Eqs (9.11) take the following form

$$\dot{\boldsymbol{r}} = [H, \boldsymbol{r}] \quad \text{and} \quad \dot{\boldsymbol{p}} = [H, \boldsymbol{p}] \tag{9.12}$$

Now, since p_i, q_i are explicit functions of time it is possible to invert these relations, namely $p_i = p_i(t)$ and $q_i = q_i(t)$ to get t as a function if p_i and q_i. Thus for t as a dynamical variable expressed as $t(p_i, q_i)$, we can write

$$[t, H] = \frac{\partial t}{\partial q_i}\frac{\partial H}{\partial p_i} - \frac{\partial t}{\partial p_i}\frac{\partial H}{\partial q_i} = \frac{\partial t}{\partial q_i}\frac{dq_i}{dt} + \frac{\partial t}{\partial p_i}\frac{dp_i}{dt} = \frac{dt}{dt} = 1 \tag{9.13}$$

One can easily identify all the quantum analogues of the PBs expressed in Eqs (9.8) – (9.13). We shall now prove two important theorems.

9.4 POISSON'S THEOREM

The total time rate of evolution of any dynamical variable $u(p, q, t)$ is given by

$$\frac{du}{dt} = \frac{\partial u}{\partial t} + [u, H] \tag{9.14}$$

Proof: Starting with the left-hand side,

$$\frac{du}{dt} = \frac{\partial u}{\partial t} + \frac{\partial u}{\partial q_i}\dot{q}_i + \frac{\partial u}{\partial p_i}\dot{p}_i = \frac{\partial u}{\partial t} + \frac{\partial u}{\partial q_i}\frac{\partial H}{\partial p_i} - \frac{\partial u}{\partial p_i}\frac{\partial H}{\partial q_i} = \frac{\partial u}{\partial t} + [u, H]$$

Thus if u is a constant of motion so that $du/dt = 0$, then by Poisson's theorem,

$$\frac{\partial u}{\partial t} + [u, H] = 0$$

Furthermore, if u does not contain time explicitly, that is, $\partial u/\partial t = 0$, then $[u, H] = 0$

is the required condition for u to be a constant of motion.

Now it is easy to check for any given Hamiltonian of the form $H = H(q,p,t)$ that one has

$$\frac{\partial H}{\partial t} = \frac{dH}{dt} \tag{9.15}$$

apart from Hamilton's equations of motion as obtained from Eq. (9.11).

9.5 JACOBI-POISSON THEOREM (OR POISSON'S SECOND THEOREM) ON PBs

If u and v are any two constants of motion of any given holonomic dynamical system, their PB $[u,v]$ is also a constant of motion. This is called Jacobi-Poisson's theorem or Poisson's second theorem on the PB relations.

Proof : Consider

$$\frac{d}{dt}[u,v] = \frac{\partial}{\partial t}[u,v] + [[u,v],H]$$

Using Eqs (9.5) and (9.6), we get

$$\begin{aligned}\frac{d}{dt}[u,v] &= [\frac{\partial u}{\partial t},v] + [u,\frac{\partial v}{\partial t}] - [[v,H],u] - [[H,u],v] \\ &= [\frac{\partial u}{\partial t} + [u,H],v] + [u,\frac{\partial v}{\partial t} + [v,H]] \\ &= [\frac{du}{dt},v] + [u,\frac{dv}{dt}] \\ &= 0\end{aligned}$$

because both du/dt and dv/dt vanish by the requirement that u and v are both constants of motion.

This theorem has profound significance for determining new constants of motion. To start with if we have got any two independent constants of motion, then a third one can be constructed from the PB of these two, which may result in either a new (that is, independent) constant of motion, or trivially either of the first two. If the former is true, we may make another pair of new PBs and if we are lucky, we can, in this way generate all the hidden constants of the motion. It should be remembered that a dynamical system having n degrees of freedom can have at the most $2n-1$ independent constants of motion, which are functions of p_i and q_i's only, and one constant of motion that must involve time explicitly.

Examples

1. Consider an isotropic 2-D harmonic oscillator that has the Hamiltonian of the form

$$H(x,y,p_x,p_y) = \frac{1}{2m}(p_x^2 + p_y^2) + \frac{1}{2}k(x^2 + y^2)$$

Being two dimensional it has only three independent integrals of motion. One is of course the energy integral E, since H does not contain time explicitly. Again, since the force field here is a central one, the angular momentum perpendicular to the $x-y$ plane

$$L = xp_y - yp_x$$

is also conserved. To construct a third one, note that H can be decomposed into two parts each corresponding to a 1–D harmonic oscillator and conserving its own energy component so that the difference of energies of these two components is also a constant of motion. Therefore,

$$\frac{1}{2m}(p_x^2 - p_y^2) + \frac{1}{2}k(x^2 - y^2) = B \qquad \text{(say)} \tag{9.16}$$

is a constant of motion.

Now let us construct a new integral of motion say C from L and B, using the Jacobi-Poisson theorem given by

$$C = [L, B] = [xp_y - yp_x, B] = \frac{2}{m}(p_x p_y + mkxy) \tag{9.17}$$

C is obviously independent of L and B, but not simultaneously of L, B and H, as

$$H^2 = E^2 = B^2 + \frac{1}{4}C^2 + \omega^2 L^2 \tag{9.18}$$

where $\omega = \sqrt{k/m}$. One can also check that

$$[C, L] = 4B \qquad \text{and} \qquad [C, B] = -4kL/m$$

We get back B and L respectively, and hence no further independent constants of motion can be generated in this process.

In order to find the nature of C one has to write down the complete solution for x and y, given by

$$x = a\sin[\omega(t - t_0)] \qquad y = b\sin[\omega(t - t_0) + \beta] \tag{9.19}$$

where β is the constant phase difference between the two. The four constants of motion here are a, b, β and t_0. One should remember that only three of these can have no explicit time dependence in their expressions. Now from Eqs (9.17) and (9.19), we get

$$C = 2abm\omega^2 \cos\beta$$

2. The constants of motion of a 2–D isotropic harmonic oscillator are, however, best studied by the Runge-Lenz tensor of second rank defined by

$$A_{ij} = \frac{1}{2m}p_i p_j + \frac{1}{2}kx_i x_j \tag{9.20}$$

Since we know that $dp_i/dt = -kx_i$ are the equations of motion of this system, they would immediately satisfy $dA_{ij}/dt = 0$, which means that A_{ij}'s are all constants of motion. For a 2–D isotropic harmonic oscillator as expected, A_{11}, A_{12} $(= A_{21})$ and A_{22} are the only three independent constants of motion. Therefore,

The trace of the A matrix $= A_{11} + A_{22} = H =$ constant and

$$\text{The determinant of the } A \text{ matrix} = A_{11}A_{22} - A_{12}^2 = \frac{\omega^2 L^2}{4} = \text{const.}$$

are just two other dependent constants of motion.

9.6 INVARIANCE OF PB UNDER CANONICAL TRANSFORMATIONS

Consider a canonical transformation (8.5) and two dynamical variables $u(p,q,t)$ and $v(p,q,t)$, so that they transform into $\tilde{u}(P,Q,t)$ and $\tilde{v}(P,Q,t)$, given by

$$u(p,q,t) = u\left(p(P,Q,t), q(P,Q,t), t\right) = \tilde{u}(P,Q,t)$$

and

$$v(p,q,t) = v\left(p(P,Q,t), q(P,Q,t), t\right) = \tilde{v}(P,Q,t)$$

We want to show that

$$[u,v]_{(p,q)} = [\tilde{u},\tilde{v}]_{(P,Q)} \tag{9.22}$$

Proof

In what follows we use Maxwell's relations (8.15) to obtain

$$\frac{\partial u}{\partial q_i} = \frac{\partial \tilde{u}}{\partial Q_j}\frac{\partial Q_j}{\partial q_i} + \frac{\partial \tilde{u}}{\partial P_j}\frac{\partial P_j}{\partial q_i} = \frac{\partial \tilde{u}}{\partial Q_j}\frac{\partial p_i}{\partial P_j} - \frac{\partial \tilde{u}}{\partial P_j}\frac{\partial p_i}{\partial Q_j}$$

and

$$\frac{\partial u}{\partial p_i} = \frac{\partial \tilde{u}}{\partial Q_j}\frac{\partial Q_j}{\partial p_i} + \frac{\partial \tilde{u}}{\partial P_j}\frac{\partial P_j}{\partial p_i} = -\frac{\partial \tilde{u}}{\partial Q_j}\frac{\partial q_i}{\partial P_j} + \frac{\partial \tilde{u}}{\partial P_j}\frac{\partial q_i}{\partial Q_j}$$

Therefore,

$$\begin{aligned}
[u,v]_{(p,q)} &= \frac{\partial u}{\partial q_i}\frac{\partial v}{\partial p_i} - \frac{\partial u}{\partial p_i}\frac{\partial v}{\partial q_i} \\
&= \frac{\partial \tilde{u}}{\partial Q_j}\frac{\partial p_i}{\partial P_j}\frac{\partial v}{\partial p_i} - \frac{\partial \tilde{u}}{\partial P_j}\frac{\partial p_i}{\partial Q_j}\frac{\partial v}{\partial p_i} + \frac{\partial \tilde{u}}{\partial Q_j}\frac{\partial q_i}{\partial P_j}\frac{\partial v}{\partial q_i} - \frac{\partial \tilde{u}}{\partial P_j}\frac{\partial q_i}{\partial Q_j}\frac{\partial v}{\partial q_i} \\
&= \frac{\partial \tilde{u}}{\partial Q_j}\left[\frac{\partial p_i}{\partial P_j}\frac{\partial v}{\partial p_i} + \frac{\partial q_i}{\partial P_j}\frac{\partial v}{\partial q_i}\right] - \frac{\partial \tilde{u}}{\partial P_j}\left[\frac{\partial p_i}{\partial Q_j}\frac{\partial v}{\partial p_i} + \frac{\partial q_i}{\partial Q_j}\frac{\partial v}{\partial q_i}\right] \\
&= \frac{\partial \tilde{u}}{\partial Q_j}\frac{\partial \tilde{v}}{\partial P_j} - \frac{\partial \tilde{u}}{\partial P_j}\frac{\partial \tilde{v}}{\partial Q_j} \\
&= [\tilde{u},\tilde{v}]_{(P,Q)}
\end{aligned}$$

which is what we wanted to prove.

This result has also got far reaching significance. We know that the electromagnetic gauge transformation, Lorentz and Galilean transformations are all CTs. Hence any PB defined for a pair of dynamical variables must remain unchanged for all the above general transformations. So any vector or scalar quantity that is expressible as a PB must remain invariant under rotation, translation, GT, Lorentz transformation and so on.

9.7 PBs INVOLVING ANGULAR MOMENTUM

We know that the canonically conjugate momentum corresponding to any angle variable represents a component of angular momentum. Nevertheless, the total angular momentum of a system is best defined in terms of the Cartesian coordinates and momenta of the individual particles. Let us consider a one-particle (or at most an effectively one-particle) system with the ith Cartesian component of its total angular momentum vector, given by $L_i = \epsilon_{ijk} x_j p_k$. Now PBs formed between any pair of the components, say L_i and L_j are found to satisfy the relation

$$[L_i, L_j] = \epsilon_{ijk} L_k \tag{9.22}$$

When expressed in terms of x, y, z components, the relation (9.22) actually stands for

$$[L_x, L_y] = L_z \qquad [L_y, L_z] = L_x \qquad [L_z, L_x] = L_y \qquad \text{and}$$

$$[L_x, L_x] = [L_y, L_y] = [L_z, L_z] = 0$$

The PBs between a Cartesian component of $\boldsymbol{L}$ and any of the Cartesian components of $\boldsymbol{r}$ and $\boldsymbol{p}$ also satisfy the following additional relations:

$$[L_i, x_j] = \epsilon_{ijk} x_k \qquad \text{and} \qquad [L_i, p_j] = \epsilon_{ijk} p_k \tag{9.23}$$

All the PBs that are expressed in Eqs (9.22) and (9.23) are proved as follows. For example,

$$\begin{aligned}[L_i, x_j] &= [\epsilon_{ikl} x_k p_l, x_j] = -\epsilon_{ikl} x_k \delta_{jl} \qquad \text{(using Eq. (9.7))} \\ &= -\epsilon_{ikj} x_k = \epsilon_{ijk} x_k\end{aligned}$$

and

$$\begin{aligned}[L_i, L_j] &= [\epsilon_{ink} x_n p_k, \epsilon_{jlm} x_l p_m] \\ &= \epsilon_{ink} \epsilon_{jlm} [x_n p_k, x_l p_m] \\ &= \epsilon_{nki} \epsilon_{jlm} \{x_l p_k [x_n, p_m] + x_n p_m [p_k, x_l]\} \\ &= \epsilon_{nki} \epsilon_{jlm} \{\delta_{nm} x_l p_k - \delta_{kl} x_n p_m\} \\ &= \epsilon_{nki} \epsilon_{jln} x_l p_k - \epsilon_{nki} \epsilon_{jkm} x_n p_m \\ &= \epsilon_{nmi} \epsilon_{jln} x_l p_m - \epsilon_{lki} \epsilon_{jkm} x_l p_m \\ &= (\epsilon_{nmi} \epsilon_{njl} - \epsilon_{kil} \epsilon_{kmj}) x_l p_m \\ &= (\delta_{mj} \delta_{il} - \delta_{ml} \delta_{ij} - \delta_{im} \delta_{lj} + \delta_{ij} \delta_{lm}) x_l p_m \\ &= (\delta_{il} \delta_{jm} - \delta_{im} \delta_{jl}) x_l p_m \\ &= \epsilon_{kij} \epsilon_{klm} x_l p_m \\ &= \epsilon_{ijk} L_k\end{aligned}$$

One simple meaning of this last result is that if we have any two Cartesian components of $\boldsymbol{L}$ as constants of motion, then the third component and hence $\boldsymbol{L}$ as a whole must be constants of motion. This result can further be generalised because of the following PB relation, given by

$$[\boldsymbol{a} \cdot \boldsymbol{L}, \boldsymbol{b} \cdot \boldsymbol{L}] = (\boldsymbol{a} \times \boldsymbol{b}) \cdot \boldsymbol{L} \tag{9.24}$$

where $\boldsymbol{a}$ and $\boldsymbol{b}$ are any two constant vectors. So if $\boldsymbol{a}$ and $\boldsymbol{b}$ represent any two unit vectors along which the components of $\boldsymbol{L}$ are separately conserved, the component of $\boldsymbol{L}$ perpendicular to the plane formed by $\boldsymbol{a}$ and $\boldsymbol{b}$ is also conserved.

Next we would like to show the connection between rotation and angular momentum through the PB relations. Consider any scalar function $\phi = \phi(\boldsymbol{r}, \boldsymbol{p})$, and an infinitesimal rotation of the coordinate system about any arbitrary direction $\hat{n}$ passing through the origin, by an angle $\delta\theta$. This results in

$$\boldsymbol{r} \to \boldsymbol{r} + \delta\boldsymbol{r} = \boldsymbol{r} - \delta\theta\, \hat{\boldsymbol{n}} \times \boldsymbol{r}$$

$$\boldsymbol{p} \to \boldsymbol{p} + \delta\boldsymbol{p} = \boldsymbol{p} - \delta\theta\, \hat{\boldsymbol{n}} \times \boldsymbol{p}$$

and

$$\phi \to \phi(\boldsymbol{r} + \delta\boldsymbol{r},\, \boldsymbol{p} + \delta\boldsymbol{p}) = \phi(\boldsymbol{r},\, \boldsymbol{p})$$

as the scalar function ϕ by definition should remain unchanged under rotation of coordinates. Now, if the scalar function ϕ does not contain any other vectors than $\boldsymbol{r}$, and $\boldsymbol{p}$,

$$0 = \delta\phi = \frac{\partial\phi}{\partial x_i}\delta x_i + \frac{\partial\phi}{\partial p_i}\delta p_i = -\,\delta\theta\epsilon_{ijk}\left(\frac{\partial\phi}{\partial x_i}x_k + \frac{\partial\phi}{\partial p_i}p_k\right)n_j$$

$$= -\,\delta\theta\left[\frac{\partial\phi}{\partial x_i}\frac{\partial(\epsilon_{ijk}x_k p_i)}{\partial p_i} - \frac{\partial\phi}{\partial p_i}\frac{\partial(\epsilon_{jik}x_i p_k)}{\partial x_i}\right]n_j = -\,\delta\theta\,[\phi, L_j n_j]$$

Since $\delta\theta$ is arbitrary, for any systemic scalar function $\phi = \phi(\boldsymbol{r},\, \boldsymbol{p})$,

$$[\phi, \boldsymbol{L}\cdot\hat{\boldsymbol{n}}] = 0 \tag{9.25}$$

Similarly, for any systemic vector function $\boldsymbol{f} = \boldsymbol{f}(\boldsymbol{r},\, \boldsymbol{p})$, it can be shown that

$$[\boldsymbol{f},\, \boldsymbol{L}\cdot\hat{\boldsymbol{n}}] = \hat{\boldsymbol{n}} \times \boldsymbol{f} \tag{9.26}$$

as $\delta\boldsymbol{f} = -\,\delta\theta\,\hat{\boldsymbol{n}} \times \boldsymbol{f}$. In terms of the i, j, k notation, Eqs (9.25) and (9.26) may be written as

$$[\phi, L_j] = 0 \tag{9.27}$$

$$[f_i, L_j] = \epsilon_{ijk} f_k \tag{9.28}$$

Since these results are valid for any arbitrary small rotation of the coordinate system, as well as for any arbitrary choice of the functions $\phi(\boldsymbol{r},\, \boldsymbol{p})$ and $\boldsymbol{f}(\boldsymbol{r},\, \boldsymbol{p})$, the PB relations given by Eqs (9.27) and (9.28) do in fact reflect the fundamental structural properties of the 3–D Euclidean space. Furthermore, the PBs expressed in Eqs (9.22) – (9.24) are merely some special cases of the relation (9.28). Some more examples of the use of the relation (9.27) would be

$$[\boldsymbol{r}\cdot\boldsymbol{p}, L_i] = 0 \tag{9.29}$$

and

$$[L_i, H] = 0 \tag{9.30}$$

provided H is a scalar function of only vectors $\boldsymbol{r}$ and $\boldsymbol{p}$, which is obviously satisfied by a central force problem, otherwise see Prob no. 9.1 (iii) for general solution.

9.8 DIRAC'S FORMULATION OF THE GENERALISED HAMILTONIAN

For a holonomic system having the number of DOF $= n$, we have $2n$ linearly independent generalised coordinates and velocities $q_1, q_2, \cdots, q_n; \dot{q}_1, \dot{q}_2, \cdots, \dot{q}_n$. In order to pass from the Lagrangian to the Hamiltonian formulation one requires that all the conjugate momenta defined by

$$p_i = \frac{\partial L}{\partial \dot{q}_i} \qquad i = 1, 2, \cdots, n$$

be linearly independent of one another. The above requirement is, however, not always fulfilled. For example, in the covariant formulation of the (special) relativistic dynamics, the four coordinates x_μ ($\mu = 1, 2, 3, 4$) are linearly independent but the corresponding four momenta p_μ ($\mu = 1, 2, 3, 4$) are not, simply because of the constraint relation, $p_\mu p_\mu = -m_0^2 c^2$. Dirac in 1950 gave a general formulation for the Hamiltonian dynamics of such systems.

Suppose that there are m independent constraint relations involving momenta and coordinates only, to be given by

$$g_i(q_1, q_2, \ldots, q_n; p_1, p_2, \ldots, p_n) = 0 \qquad i = 1, \ldots, m \leq n \tag{9.31}$$

and

$$p_j = \frac{\partial L(q_1, q_2, \ldots, q_n; \dot{q}_1, \dot{q}_2, \cdots, \dot{q}_n)}{\partial \dot{q}_j} \qquad j = 1, \ldots, n \tag{9.32}$$

For small arbitrary variations δq_j and $\delta \dot{q}_j$ in the coordinates and velocities, the relations (9.31) will impose m restrictions on the variations of δp_j:

$$\frac{\partial g_i}{\partial q_j}\delta q_j + \frac{\partial g_i}{\partial p_j}\delta p_j = 0 \qquad i = 1, \ldots, m \tag{9.33}$$

Now since the Hamiltonian $H = H(q_1, \ldots, q_n; p_1, \ldots, p_n) = p_j \dot{q}_j - L$, we have,

$$\begin{aligned} \frac{\partial H}{\partial q_j}\delta q_j + \frac{\partial H}{\partial p_i}\delta p_i &= \delta H \\ &= p_j \delta \dot{q}_j + \dot{q}_j \delta p_j - \frac{\partial L}{\partial q_j}\delta q_j - \frac{\partial L}{\partial \dot{q}_j}\delta \dot{q}_j \\ &= \dot{q}_j \delta p_j - \frac{\partial L}{\partial q_j}\delta q_j \end{aligned} \tag{9.34}$$

where all δp_j are not arbitrary. In order to make all δp_j and δq_j arbitrary one may combine Eqs (9.33) and (9.34) with the introduction of m Lagrange multipliers say $C_1, \ldots, C_m$, such that

$$\dot{q}_j = \frac{\partial H}{\partial p_j} + C_i \frac{\partial g_i}{\partial p_j} = [q_j, H + C_i g_i]$$

and

$$-\dot{p}_j = -\frac{\partial L}{\partial q_j} = \frac{\partial H}{\partial q_j} + C_i \frac{\partial g_i}{\partial q_j} = [H + C_i g_i, p_j] \tag{9.35}$$

Equations (9.35) are called Dirac's generalised form of Hamilton's equations of motion in which the Hamiltonian $H = q_i p_i - L$ is effectively replaced by $H + C_i g_i = p_i \dot{q}_i - L + C_i g_i$.

Now for any dynamical variable $f = f(q_1, q_2, \ldots, q_n; p_1, \ldots, p_n, t)$,

$$\frac{df}{dt} = \frac{\partial f}{\partial t} + \frac{\partial f}{\partial q_j}\dot{q}_j + \frac{\partial f}{\partial p_j}\dot{p}_j = \frac{\partial f}{\partial t} + [f, H + C_i g_i] \tag{9.36}$$

Finally one may note that in order to quantise any classical system, a general formulation in terms of PBs and the Hamiltonian is quite essential, as it becomes very easy to write Schrödinger's equation once the explicit form of the Hamiltonian is known, or the commutation relations can be formulated, provided the classical PB relations are known.

9.9 LAGRANGE BRACKET (LB)

Another class of useful relations between dynamical variables are the so called *Lagrange brackets* introduced by Lagrange in 1808. For any two independent dynamical variables $u(p, q, t)$ and $v(p, q, t)$ pertaining to a dynamical system with the number of DOF $= n$, their Lagrange bracket is defined as

$$(u, v)_{(p,q)} = \sum_{i=1}^{n}\left(\frac{\partial q_i}{\partial u}\frac{\partial p_i}{\partial v} - \frac{\partial q_i}{\partial v}\frac{\partial p_i}{\partial u}\right) = \sum_{i=1}^{n}\frac{\partial(q_i, p_i)}{\partial(u, v)} \tag{9.37}$$

Clearly the Lagrange bracket is antisymmetric:

$$(u, v) = -(v, u) \tag{9.38}$$

Let us suppose that there are $2n$ independent functions $u_1, u_2, \ldots, u_{2n}$ of the variables (q_i, p_i). Conversely, $q_1, \ldots, q_n; p_1, \ldots, p_n$ may be regarded as functions of $u_1, u_2, \ldots, u_{2n}$. From their definitions one may suspect that there is some relation between Poisson brackets $[u_r, u_s]$ and Lagrange brackets (u_r, u_s). Indeed so; for let us consider

$$\sum_{r=1}^{2n}[u_r, u_i](u_r, u_j)$$

$$= \sum_{r=1}^{2n}\sum_{k=1}^{n}\sum_{l=1}^{n}\left(\frac{\partial u_r}{\partial q_k}\frac{\partial u_i}{\partial p_k} - \frac{\partial u_r}{\partial p_k}\frac{\partial u_i}{\partial q_k}\right)\left(\frac{\partial q_l}{\partial u_r}\frac{\partial p_l}{\partial u_j} - \frac{\partial q_l}{\partial u_j}\frac{\partial p_l}{\partial u_r}\right) \tag{9.39}$$

But

$$\sum_{r=1}^{2n}\frac{\partial u_r}{\partial q_k}\frac{\partial q_l}{\partial u_r} = \sum_{r=1}^{2n}\frac{\partial u_r}{\partial p_k}\frac{\partial p_l}{\partial u_r} = \delta_{kl} \tag{9.40}$$

where δ_{kl} is the Kronecker delta matrix. Moreover,

$$\sum_{r=1}^{2n}\frac{\partial u_r}{\partial q_k}\frac{\partial p_l}{\partial u_r} = \sum_{r=1}^{2n}\frac{\partial u_r}{\partial p_k}\frac{\partial q_l}{\partial u_r} = 0 \tag{9.41}$$

Hence, Eq. (9.39) reduces to

$$\sum_{r=1}^{2n} [u_r, u_i](u_r, u_j) = \sum_{r=1}^{n} \left(\frac{\partial u_i}{\partial p_k} \frac{\partial p_k}{\partial u_j} + \frac{\partial u_i}{\partial q_k} \frac{\partial q_k}{\partial u_j} \right) = \delta_{ij} \tag{9.42}$$

If we regard the PB $[u_r, u_i]$ as the element P_{ri} of the $2n \times 2n$ matrix $[P]$ and the LB (u_r, u_j) as the element L_{rj} of the $2n \times 2n$ matrix $[L]$, then Eq. (9.42) can be written in the matrix form.

$$[P]^T[L] = [I_{2n}] \tag{9.43}$$

where $[I_{2n}]$ is the unit matrix of order $2n$ and $[P]^T$ means the transpose of $[P]$. Since the determinant of the product of two matrices is the product of their determinants, it follows from Eq. (9.43) that the determinants of matrices $[P]$ and $[L]$ are reciprocals of each other. It is also clear from Eq. (9.43) that one type of bracket determines the other so that if the Poisson bracket is invariant under canonical transformation the Lagrange bracket is also invariant.

The Lagrange or Poisson brackets can be used to test whether a given transformation is canonical. If the transformation $Q_i = Q_i(q, p, t,)$, $P_i = P_i(q, p, t)$, $i = 1, 2, \ldots, n$ is to be canonical, the new variables Q_i and P_i must satisfy Eq. (8.17). Since the old variables (q_i, p_i) may be regarded as functions of the new variables, the necessary and sufficient condition for a transformation to be canonical is that, for a fixed value of time, the expression

$$\sum_{r=1}^{n} \left[\left(\sum_{i=1}^{n} p_i \frac{\partial q_i}{\partial Q_r} - P_r \right) dQ_r + \left(\sum_{i=1}^{n} p_i \frac{\partial q_i}{\partial P_r} \right) dP_r \right] \tag{9.44}$$

be a perfect differential. The conditions for this are

$$\frac{\partial}{\partial Q_s} \left(\sum_{i=1}^{n} p_i \frac{\partial q_i}{\partial Q_r} - P_r \right) = \frac{\partial}{\partial Q_r} \left(\sum_{i=1}^{n} p_i \frac{\partial q_i}{\partial Q_s} - P_s \right)$$

$$\frac{\partial}{\partial P_s} \left(\sum_{i=1}^{n} p_i \frac{\partial q_i}{\partial P_r} \right) = \frac{\partial}{\partial P_r} \left(\sum_{i=1}^{n} p_i \frac{\partial q_i}{\partial P_s} \right)$$

and

$$\frac{\partial}{\partial P_s} \left(\sum_{i=1}^{n} p_i \frac{\partial q_i}{\partial Q_r} - P_r \right) = \frac{\partial}{\partial Q_r} \left(\sum_{i=1}^{n} p_i \frac{\partial q_i}{\partial P_s} \right) \tag{9.45}$$

However Q_i and P_i are independent variables, so that conditions (9.45) can easily be shown to reduce to

$$(Q_r, Q_s) = 0 \qquad (P_r, P_s) = 0 \qquad \text{and} \qquad (Q_r, P_s) = \delta_{rs} \tag{9.46}$$

The necessary and sufficient condition that a transformation be canonical can also be reduced to the requirement that for a fixed value of time the expression

$$\sum_{r=1}^{n}\left[\left(\sum_{i=1}^{n} P_i \frac{\partial Q_i}{\partial q_r} - p_r\right) dq_r + \left(\sum_{i=1}^{n} P_i \frac{\partial Q_i}{\partial p_r}\right) dp_r\right] \tag{9.47}$$

be a perfect differential. Proceeding in an exactly similar fashion as we did to obtain conditions (9.46) we can see that the requirement that expression (9.47) be a perfect differential is equivalent to the conditions

$$[Q_r, Q_s] = 0 \qquad [P_r, P_s] = 0 \qquad \text{and} \qquad [Q_r, P_s] = \delta_{rs} \tag{9.48}$$

We see that the conditions (9.48) for the canonicality of a given transformation are truly independent of the knowledge of any Hamiltonian or of any specific property of the dynamical system, except for its being holonomic with specified degrees of freedom.

9.10 SUMMARY

Poisson bracket relations and some of their properties (1809) were known about a quarter of a century before Hamilton's equations of motion were formulated (1835) or the properties of the contact transformations were proved by Jacobi (1837). The idea of the Lagrange brackets was introduced by Lagrange in 1808. In fact some books introduce them before the Poisson brackets.

It should be noted that some text books define the Poisson bracket relation in the reverse order of the partial derivatives with respect to q_i, and p_i. As a result there is an interchange of signs between the two sets of terms.

The fundamental Poisson brackets, such as $[Q_i, P_j] = \delta_{ij}$, $[P_i, P_j] = [Q_i, Q_j] = 0$, are extremely useful for testing the canonicality of any given phase space transformation.

Poisson brackets can be a useful tool for finding out some of the hidden constants of motion. They are also useful in describing the infinitesimal contact transformations for rotation, translation or even in terms of time evolution of a system.

An important application of the concept of PBs is illustrated in Dirac's formulation of generalised Hamiltonian systems, which is actually the starting point of the modern study of constrained dynamics. Dirac has written a book on this fascinating subject.

PROBLEMS

9.1 Show that operationally the vector product of any two vectors, the PB of any two dynamical variables and the multiplication of any two $n \times n$ matrices share all the rules in common without exception. Evaluate

$$[[[A, B], C], D] + [[[C, D], A], B] + [[[D, A], B], C]$$

and

$$[[[A, B], C], D] + [[[B, C], D], A] + [[[C, D], A], B] + [[[D, A], B], C]$$

9.2 Evaluate the following Poisson brackets,
(i) $[\boldsymbol{a}\cdot\boldsymbol{r}\,,\,\boldsymbol{b}\cdot\boldsymbol{p}]$
(ii) $[(\boldsymbol{a}\cdot\boldsymbol{r})^2,\,\boldsymbol{p}]$
(iii) $[\boldsymbol{L}\,,\,H]$ and
(iv) $[\boldsymbol{f}\cdot\boldsymbol{L}\,,\,\boldsymbol{g}\cdot\boldsymbol{L}]$
where $\boldsymbol{a}$ and $\boldsymbol{b}$ are constant vectors, and $\boldsymbol{f} = \boldsymbol{f}(\boldsymbol{r},\boldsymbol{p})$, $\boldsymbol{g} = \boldsymbol{g}(\boldsymbol{r},\boldsymbol{p})$ and $H = p^2/2m + V(\boldsymbol{r})$.

9.3 Evaluate $[L_i,\,A_{jk}]$ and $[A_{jk},\,A_{il}]$ where $\boldsymbol{L} = \boldsymbol{r}\times\boldsymbol{p}$ and $A_{ij} = x_i x_j + p_i p_j$.

9.4 A charged particle carrying an electric charge e is moving in an inhomogeneous field of magnetic induction $\boldsymbol{B}$. Show that any two Cartesian components of its velocity satisfy the following PB relation

$$[v_i\,,\,v_j] = \frac{e}{m^2}\epsilon_{ijk}B_k$$

9.5 Using PB relation show that the modified Runge-Lenz vector

$$\boldsymbol{A} = \frac{1}{\sqrt{(-2\mu E)}}(K\mu^2\boldsymbol{r}/r + \boldsymbol{L}\times\boldsymbol{p})$$

for planetary motion is a constant of motion, where $K = G(M + m)$, $\boldsymbol{p} = \mu\boldsymbol{v}$, $\boldsymbol{L} = \boldsymbol{r}\times\boldsymbol{p}$, and μ = reduced mass of the system = $mM/(M + m)$. Evaluate $[A_i,\,A_j]$, $[L_i,\,A_j]$ and $[A_i,\,H]$.

9.6 Prove that the value of any function $f(p(t),\,q(t))$ of coordinates and momenta of a system at time t can be expressed in terms of the values of p and q at $t = 0$ as follows :

$$f(p(t),\,q(t)) = f_0 + \frac{t}{1!}[f_0, H] + \frac{t^2}{2!}[[f_0, H], H] + \frac{t^3}{3!}[[[f_0, H], H], H] + \cdots$$

where $f_0 = f(p(t=0),\,q(t=0))$ and $H = H(p(t=0),\,q(t=0))$, the latter being the Hamiltonian at $t = 0$.

9.7 For an infinitesimal transformation $P_i = p_i + \Delta p_i$, $Q_i = q_i + \Delta q_i$, governed by $F_2 = F_2(P,q) = \Sigma P_i q_i + u(P,q)$, where $p_i = p_i(\theta)$ and $q_i = q_i(\theta)$ are functions of a continuous time like parameter θ, show that

$$\frac{dp_i}{d\theta} = -\frac{\partial w}{\partial q_i} = [p_i, w] \quad\text{and}\quad \frac{dq_i}{d\theta} = \frac{\partial w}{\partial p_i} = [q_i, w]$$

where w is defined through $u(p_i(\theta + \delta\theta),\,q_i(\theta)) = w(p_i(\theta),\,q_i(\theta))\delta\theta$, and is called the generator for the infinitesimal transformation. Using the above relation and the properties of PBs show that for any $f = f(q,p)$

$$\frac{df}{d\theta} = [f, w] \quad\text{and}\quad \frac{d^2 f}{d\theta^2} = [[f, w], w]$$

9.8 Given the canonical transformations $Q_i = Q_i(q,p,t)$, $P_i = P_i(q,p,t)$, and their inverse transformations effected through the generating function $F_2 = F_2(q,P,t)$, show that

$$\left[Q_i, \frac{\partial F_2}{\partial t}\right] = \frac{\partial Q_i}{\partial t} \quad \text{and} \quad \left[P_i, \frac{\partial F_2}{\partial t}\right] = \frac{\partial P_i}{\partial t}$$

Using these results show further that

$$\frac{dQ_i}{dt} = [Q_i, K] \quad \text{and} \quad \frac{dP_i}{dt} = [P_i, K]$$

where $K = H + \partial F_2/\partial t$.

9.9 Show that the time reversal transformation given by $Q = q$, $P = -p$ and $T = -t$, is canonical, in the sense that the form of Hamilton's equations of motion is preserved, but does not satisfy the invariance of the fundamental Poisson bracket relations. Hence these two criteria are not equal in all respects.

10

Hamilton-Jacobi Theory

10.0 INTRODUCTION

The Hamilton-Jacobi theory is usually considered to be the most intricate part of classical dynamics. So we have tried to explain the difficult parts as much at length as possible, with a sufficient number of worked out examples. We would like to urge you to acquaint yourself with this very important and most powerful analytical method of solving dynamical problems. No less a mathematical intellect than Jacobi has contributed significantly to simplifying the Hamiltonian approach to solve for the required characteristic function. About Jacobi it is said, 'for sheer manipulative ability in tangled algebra Euler and Jacobi have had no rival, unless it be the Indian mathematical genius, Srinivasa Ramanujan, in our century', quoted from E. T. Bell's *Men of Mathematics*.

Carl Gustov Jacob Jacobi (1804 – 1851) mainly worked on the theory of elliptic functions, elliptic integrals, determinants, numbers, etc. His investigations on first order partial differential equations were published posthumously (he contracted small pox and died suddenly) in his treatise on Dynamics. Other great minds who have contributed substantially to applying the HJ theory to conservative periodic systems were C. E. Delaunay, P. Stäckel, T. Levi-Civita, J. M. Burgers, P. Epstein and K. Schwarzschild.

10.1 SOLUTION TO THE TIME DEPENDENT HAMILTON-JACOBI EQUATION AND JACOBI'S THEOREM

We write the time dependent Hamilton-Jacobi (HJ) equation for a holonomic system having n DOF as

$$H\left(q_1, \ldots, q_n; \frac{\partial W}{\partial q_1}, \ldots, \frac{\partial W}{\partial q_n}\right) + \frac{\partial W}{\partial t} = 0$$

This is a partial differential equation of the first order in the unknown function W. It can have a complete solution (that is, W as a function of $q_1, \ldots, q_n, t$ and of course, the constants of integration) known as the *complete integral* which will contain as many arbitrary constants (that is, constants of integration) as there are independent variables.

For a system with n DOF we have n independent coordinate variables and the time variable t, so the complete integral W must contain $n + 1$ arbitrary constants, of which one would be simply an additive constant, since the equation contains only the derivatives in the form of $\partial W/\partial t$ and $\{\partial W/\partial q_i\}$ and not W tself. Thus the remaining n arbitrary constants must appear as arguments of W so that the solution (complete integral) has the form

$$W = W(q_1, \ldots, q_n; t; \alpha_1, \ldots, \alpha_n) + A \qquad (10.1)$$

where $\alpha_1, \ldots, \alpha_n$ and A are the constants of integration.

In 1845, Jacobi proved a theorem, now known as *Jacobi's theorem* which was published posthumously and which asserts that the system would dynamically evolve in such a way that the derivatives of W with respect to α's remain constant in time and the equations of motion would simply read as

$$\frac{\partial W}{\partial \alpha_i} = \beta_i \qquad i = 1, \ldots, n \qquad (10.2)$$

where β_i's are n constants of motion.

Usually α's are called the *first integrals* of motion and β's are called the *second integrals* of motion. Now given the complete solution W, Eqs (10.2) and those from the definition of (initial) momenta, that is,

$$\left.\frac{\partial W}{\partial q_i}\right|_{(q_{ia}, t=0)} = p_{ia} \qquad i = 1, \ldots, n \qquad (10.3)$$

make up two systems, each of n inhomogeneous simultaneous algebraic equations in n unknowns, respectively q_is and α_is.

Assuming that the Jacobian determinant for the transformation does not vanish, we can solve the Eqs (10.3) for α_is and substituting these α_is in Eqs (10.2) we finally solve for q_is giving

$$q_i = q_i(q_{1a}, \ldots, q_{na}; p_{ia}, \ldots, p_{na}; \beta_1, \ldots, \beta_n; t) = q_i(q_{1a}, \ldots, q_{na}; p_{1a}, \ldots, p_{na}; t)$$

because

$$\beta_i = \left.\frac{\partial W}{\partial \alpha_i}\right|_{(q_{ia}, t=0)} \qquad (10.4)$$

Substituting these expressions for q_is in the equations

$$\frac{\partial W}{\partial q_i} = p_i \qquad (10.5)$$

we get

$$p_i = p_i(q_{1a}, \ldots, q_{na}; p_{1a}, \ldots, p_{na}; \beta_1, \ldots, \beta_n; t) = p_i(q_{1a}, \ldots, q_{na}; p_{1a}, \ldots, p_{na}; t)$$

thus completely solving the problem in terms of the initial coordinates and momenta.

Proof of Jacobi's theorem

Given the complete integral solution for W given by Eq. (10.1), we wish to prove Eq.

(10.2). Consider,

$$\begin{aligned}
\frac{d}{dt}\left(\frac{\partial W}{\partial \alpha_i}\right) &= \frac{\partial}{\partial t}\left(\frac{\partial W}{\partial \alpha_i}\right) + \frac{\partial^2 W}{\partial q_j \partial \alpha_i}\dot{q}_j \\
&= \frac{\partial}{\partial \alpha_i}\left(\frac{\partial W}{\partial t}\right) + \frac{\partial}{\partial \alpha_i}\left(\frac{\partial W}{\partial q_j}\right)\dot{q}_j \\
&= \frac{\partial}{\partial \alpha_i}\left[-H\left(q_j; \frac{\partial W}{\partial q_j}\right)\right] + \frac{\partial^2 W}{\partial \alpha_i \partial q_j}\dot{q}_j \\
&= -\frac{\partial H}{\partial q_j}\frac{\partial q_j}{\partial \alpha_i} - \frac{\partial H}{\partial\left(\frac{\partial W}{\partial q_j}\right)}\frac{\partial^2 W}{\partial \alpha_i \partial q_j} + \frac{\partial^2 W}{\partial \alpha_i \partial q_j}\dot{q}_j
\end{aligned}$$

Note that since q_is and α_is are independent, $\partial q_j/\partial \alpha_i = 0$, so that we can finally write

$$\frac{d}{dt}\left(\frac{\partial W}{\partial \alpha_i}\right) = \left(-\frac{\partial H}{\partial p_j} + \dot{q}_j\right)\frac{\partial^2 W}{\partial \alpha_i \partial q_j} = 0$$

by Hamilton's equations of motion, and prove the theorem.

The method of solving dynamical problems involving holonomic systems via HJ equations is considered to be the most powerful method, provided one can indeed integrate the HJ equation to get a complete integral. It is worthwhile to state a formal stepwise procedure for tackling a dynamical problem using the HJ method.

1. Construct the Hamiltonian $H(p, q, t)$ of the system.

2. Set up the HJ equation by substituting all $p_i = (\partial W/\partial q_i)$ in the expression for the Hamiltonian.

3. Find the general solution of the HJ equation in the form of a complete integral (10.1). Usually one follows the method of separation of variables to solve the HJ equation.

4. Apply Jacobi's theorem to this solution, that is, set $\partial W/\partial \alpha_i = \beta_i$, where $\{\beta_i\}$ is another set of n arbitrary constants.

5. Now $\partial W/\partial \alpha_i = \beta_i$ are a set of n inhomogeneous simultaneous algebraic equations in n unknowns $\{q_i\}$ involving $2n$ constants ($\{\alpha_i\}$, $\{\beta_i\}$) and time t. Solve these for $\{q_i\}$ to get

$$q_i = q_i(\alpha_1, \ldots, \alpha_n; \beta_1, \ldots, \beta_n; t) \tag{10.6}$$

6. Now $\{\alpha_i\}$ and $\{\beta_i\}$ can be expressed in terms of initial coordinates and momenta by inverting the Eqs (10.3) and using Eqs (10.4) respectively, in that order. Substituting these expressions for $\{\alpha_i\}$ and $\{\beta_i\}$ into Eqs (10.6) gives $\{q_i\}$ as functions of initial coordinates $\{q_{ia}\}$, momenta $\{p_{ia}\}$ and time t:

$$q_i = q_i(q_{1a}, \ldots, q_{na}; p_{1a}, \ldots, p_{na}; t) \tag{10.7}$$

7. Now substitute the functions (10.7) into Eqs (10.5) to get

$$p_i = p_i(q_{1a}, \ldots, q_{na}; p_{1a}, \ldots, p_{na}; t) \tag{10.8}$$

Equations (10.7) and (10.8) constitute the complete solution of the given dynamical problem.

8. Now if one wishes, one can obtain an expression for the total energy of the system, which is in general not a constant of motion, from

$$E = -\frac{\partial W}{\partial t}$$

For conservative systems, one can in fact have two choices. One can either start with the time dependent HJ equation and solve by the method described above, or one can write down the time independent HJ equation in terms of Hamilton's characteristic function $S(q_1, \ldots, q_n; E)$, namely

$$H\left(q_1, \ldots, q_n; \frac{\partial S}{\partial q_1}, \ldots, \frac{\partial S}{\partial q_n}\right) = E \tag{10.9}$$

and follow a somewhat 'similar' procedure. This is left as an exercise. However, there would be a corresponding Jacobi's theorem, and the organisation of the constants of integration for the complete integral would be somewhat different.

10.2 CONNECTION WITH CANONICAL TRANSFORMATION

Let us now make a canonical transformation from (q, p) to (Q, P) via the generating function

$$F_2(q_1, \ldots, q_n; P_1, \ldots, P_n; t) = W(q_1, \ldots, q_n; \alpha_1, \ldots, \alpha_n; t)$$

Here we treat the new momenta $\{P_i = \alpha_i\}$. In order that the transformation be canonical we must have,

$$p_i = \frac{\partial F_2}{\partial q_i} \equiv \frac{\partial W}{\partial q_i} \quad \text{and} \quad Q_i = \frac{\partial F_2}{\partial P_i} \equiv \frac{\partial W}{\partial \alpha_i} \tag{10.10}$$

and

$$K = H + \frac{\partial F_2}{\partial t} \equiv H + \frac{\partial W}{\partial t} = 0$$

The first and the third equations in (10.10) clearly identify W to be Hamilton's principal function on one hand and the complete integral of the HJ equation on the other. The second set of Eqs (10.10) defines $\{Q_i\}$ in terms of $\{q_i\}, \{\alpha_i\}, t$. The first set of Eqs (10.10) does indeed satisfy the definition of momenta in terms of Hamilton's principal function. The second set of the Eqs (10.10) defines a set of new coordinates $\{Q_i\}$ in terms of $\{q_i\}, \{\alpha_i\}, t$. Note that the equalities in the last of the Eqs (10.10) are not only dictated by the requirement of canonicality but are also the consequence of the requirement that W be Hamilton's principal function.

Now since the transformed Hamiltonian $K(P, Q, t) = 0$, the corresponding Hamilton's equations of motion,

$$\dot{Q}_i = \frac{\partial K}{\partial P_i} = 0 \quad \text{and} \quad \dot{P}_i = -\frac{\partial K}{\partial Q_i} = 0$$

lead to solutions

$$P_i = \text{const.} \quad \text{and} \quad Q_i = \text{const.}$$

However, we already know that

$$P_i = \text{const.} = \alpha_i$$

where α_i are the constants of integration in the HJ equation. But $Q_i = \text{const.} = \partial W/\partial \alpha_i$ are the new results of the identification of W with the generating function F_2 of the above canonical transformation, that is, through $F_2 = W$. Therefore,

$$\frac{\partial W}{\partial \alpha_i} = \text{const.} = \beta_i \tag{10.11}$$

where $\beta_i \equiv Q_i$.

This is simply Jacobi's theorem. It is now further clear why $\{\beta_i\}$ are called the second integrals of motion. Using Eqs (10.10) and (10.11) the dynamical problem can be solved following the steps described in the last section. So the important result that we derive from this section is that the set (α_i, β_i) is canonically related to the set (p_i, q_i) through a generating function the same as Hamilton's principal function. Thus the transformed Hamiltonian simply vanishes. However, if we had started with the time independent HJ equation and tried to prove the corresponding Jacobi's theorem following the above method, we would have got back the first set of Eqs (10.10) as they are, but the last equation of (10.10) would not lead to the vanishing of the transformed Hamiltonian, rather we would have obtained $K = H = \text{constant} = E$. Jacobi's theorem follows from Hamilton's equations of motion in terms of the transformed quantities, with the fact that $K = \text{constant} = E$.

We can now see the role of Hamilton-Jacobi differential equation in a proper perspective. Our original problem was to solve the $2n$ Hamilton's first order differential equations for a system with n DOF:

$$\dot{p}_i = -\frac{\partial H}{\partial q_i} \quad \text{and} \quad \dot{q}_i = \frac{\partial H}{\partial p_i} \qquad i = 1, \ldots, n$$

To do this we seek a canonical transformation such that the new Hamiltonian is either zero, or more generally, depends exclusively on either the new momenta or the new coordinates (see section 10.5). Once this is done, the integration of Hamilton's equations becomes quite trivial. *The generating function for this canonical transformation is given by the solution of the HJ equation.* Thus the problem of solving the system of $2n$ ordinary differential equations (Hamilton's equations) is now reduced to finding a complete integral of a single partial differential equation in $(n+1)$ variables, namely the time dependent or time independent HJ equation. It is indeed surprising that this 'reduction' from the simple to the complicated provides an effective method for solving concrete problems. However, it turns out that this is the most powerful method known for exact integration, and many problems which were solved by Jacobi cannot be solved by other means.

10.3 HOW TO FIND THE COMPLETE INTEGRAL OF THE HJ EQUATION

Usually the generalised coordinates are so chosen that the HJ equation can be solved by the method of separation of variables. First if the Hamiltonian does not explicitly contain time one can linearly decouple time from the rest of the variables in W and write

$$W(q_1, \ldots, q_n, t) = W_o(q_1, \ldots, q_n) + W'(t) \tag{10.12}$$

so that the HJ equation becomes

$$\frac{dW'(t)}{dt} = -H\left(q_1, \ldots, q_n; \frac{\partial W_o}{\partial q_1}, \ldots, \frac{\partial W_o}{\partial q_n}\right) \tag{10.13}$$

Since the RHS and the LHS are now functions of totally different variables, they can be equal for all values of these variables only if the LHS and the RHS are separately equal to a constant independent of all the above variables. This is the reason why the method of separation of variables can be so powerful in solving partial differential equations. Sometimes the decoupling is done, not as a sum of two functions, but as a product of two functions. However in the present case we can write

$$\frac{dW'}{dt} = -E$$

and

$$H\left(q_1, \ldots, q_n, \frac{\partial W_o}{\partial q_1}, \ldots, \frac{\partial W_o}{\partial q_n}\right) = E \tag{10.14}$$

where E is the constant of separation. Equation (10.14) can be viewed as the time independent HJ equation with W_o to be identified as Hamilton's characteristic function. In any case the solution to the time dependent HJ equation for conservative dynamical systems thus has the form, apart from a trivial additive constant term,

$$W = W_o(q_1, \ldots, q_n, \alpha_1, \ldots, \alpha_{n-1}, E) - Et$$

We can now identify W_o with Hamilton's characteristic function and formally write

$$W_o \equiv S(q_1, \ldots, q_n, \alpha_1, \ldots, \alpha_{n-1}, E)$$

One should of course, remember that the function S is usually expressed explicitly in terms of the terminal coordinates, one set being $\{q_{ia}\}$ and the other say $\{q_i\}$, instead of the present set of arguments of W_o. Also note that the nth (or the first!) constant of integration, α_n, has been replaced by the energy integral E. If we regard $\{\alpha_i\}$ to be some kind of momenta, then energy seems to behave like a kind of momentum, a forerunner of a well accepted result in special relativistic mechanics.

10.3.1 Conditions for Separability of Coordinates

In 1887, O. Staude for systems with two degrees of freedom and later P. Stäckel (during 1891-

1895) for systems with an arbitrary but finite number of DOF, showed that the motion of a system whose HJ equation can be integrated by separation of variables is *multiply periodic*, or in astronomer's language *conditionally periodic*. The converse of this theorem will be proved in section 10.5. Stäckel also showed that for systems with a separable HJ differential equation, the integral of Jacobi's action $2\int T dt$ can be separated into a sum

$$\sum_{k=1}^{N} \int \sqrt{f_k(q_k)} dq_k$$

where N is the number of DOF, and f_k's are functions of only q_k's, and these oscillate between two fixed limits (libration, defined in section 10.5), or are such that their increase by a certain constant value leaves the configuration of the system unchanged (rotation).

However, the ***necessary and sufficient conditions for separability*** were first obtained by T. Levi-Civita in 1904. These are a set of $N(N-1)/2$ partial differential equations, given by

$$\begin{aligned} \frac{\partial H}{\partial p_k}\frac{\partial H}{\partial p_s}\frac{\partial^2 H}{\partial q_k \partial q_s} - \frac{\partial H}{\partial p_k}\frac{\partial H}{\partial q_s}\frac{\partial^2 H}{\partial q_k \partial p_s} - \frac{\partial H}{\partial q_k}\frac{\partial H}{\partial p_s}\frac{\partial^2 H}{\partial p_k \partial q_s} \\ + \frac{\partial H}{\partial q_k}\frac{\partial H}{\partial q_s}\frac{\partial^2 H}{\partial p_k \partial p_s} = 0 \end{aligned} \tag{10.15}$$

for $k = 1, \ldots, N$ and $s = 1, \ldots, k-1, k+1, \ldots, N$.

If any set of conjugate variables (q_k, p_k) satisfies the conditions of separability then any other set connected by a canonical transformation is also separable. A dynamical system which in addition to this class of variables is separable in still another set, was called by Schwarzschild a *degenerate* system.

Further studies on separability were carried out by Paul Epstein (1916), a student of Arnold Sommerfeld, and independently by Karl Schwarzschild (1916).

10.3.2 Separability of Coordinates for Systems under Central or Axisymmetric Forces

The dynamical problems that deal with central or axisymmetric forces can possibly be best handled in terms of spherical polar coordinates, in which case the Hamiltonian would assume the following general form:

$$H = H(r, \theta, \phi, \dot{r}, \dot{\theta}, \dot{\phi}) = \frac{1}{2\mu}\left[p_r^2 + \frac{p_\theta^2}{r^2} + \frac{p_\phi^2}{r^2 \sin^2\theta}\right] + V(r, \theta, \phi) \tag{10.16}$$

If V has an azimuthal symmetry, so that

$$V(r, \theta) = a(r) + \frac{b(\theta)}{r^2} \tag{10.17}$$

we can separate variables in the HJ equation. The Equation (10.14) takes the form

$$\frac{1}{2\mu}\left(\frac{\partial W_o}{\partial r}\right)^2 + a(r) + \frac{1}{2\mu r^2}\left[\left(\frac{\partial W_o}{\partial \theta}\right)^2 + 2\mu b(\theta)\right] + \frac{1}{2\mu r^2 \sin^2\theta}\left(\frac{\partial W_o}{\partial \phi}\right)^2 = E$$

Since the coordinate ϕ is cyclic, we seek a solution of the form

$$W_o = p_\phi \phi + W_1(r) + W_2(\theta)$$

so that

$$\left(\frac{dW_2}{d\theta}\right)^2 + 2\mu b(\theta) + \frac{p_\phi^2}{\sin^2\theta} = \beta$$

and

$$\frac{1}{2\mu}\left(\frac{dW_1}{dr}\right)^2 + a(r) + \frac{\beta}{2\mu r^2} = E$$

where β, p_ϕ and E are the constants of variable separations, for θ, ϕ and t respectively.

Finally, integrating these ordinary differential equations we get

$$W = -Et + p_\phi\phi + \int\left[\beta - 2\mu b(\theta) - \frac{p_\phi^2}{\sin^2\theta}\right]^{1/2} d\theta + \int\left\{2\mu[E - a(r)] - \frac{\beta}{r^2}\right\}^{1/2} dr \tag{10.18}$$

Similarly, depending on the symmetry in the potential one may need to write the Hamiltonian in parabolic, elliptical or cylindrical polar coordinates and try for the separability of the variables.

10.4 WORKED-OUT EXAMPLES

10.4.1 The Case of 1–D Simple Harmonic Oscillator

The form of the Hamiltonian given by

$$H(q,p) = \frac{p^2}{2m} + \frac{1}{2}kq^2$$

leads to the HJ equation in the form

$$\frac{\partial W}{\partial t} + \frac{1}{2m}\left(\frac{\partial W}{\partial q}\right)^2 + \frac{1}{2}kq^2 = 0 \tag{10.19}$$

Now let

$$W(q,t) = W_1(t) + W_2(q)$$

Putting this solution into Eq. (10.19) we get

$$\frac{dW_1}{dt} = -\frac{1}{2m}\left(\frac{dW_2}{dq}\right)^2 - \frac{1}{2}kq^2$$

Since W_1 depends only on t and W_2 depends only on q, Eq. (10.19) holds good provided

$$\frac{dW_1(t)}{dt} = -E \quad \text{and} \quad \frac{1}{2m}\left(\frac{dW_2}{dq}\right)^2 + \frac{1}{2}kq^2 = E \tag{10.20}$$

The first equation has a solution

$$W_1 = -Et + \text{const.}$$

and the second has

$$W_2(q) = \frac{1}{2}\sqrt{mk}\left[\frac{2E}{k}\sin^{-1}\sqrt{\frac{kq^2}{2E}} + q\sqrt{\frac{2E}{k} - q^2}\right] + \text{const.}$$

Therefore, the complete integral is

$$W(q,t) = -Et + W_2(q,E) + \text{const.}$$

Apart from an additive constant, a new constant E has appeared in the solution and since this is a one-variable problem, we expected only one constant in the class of α_is. Here $\alpha_1 = E$. Now by Jacobi's theorem

$$\frac{\partial W}{\partial E} = \beta_1 = -t + \sqrt{\frac{m}{k}}\sin^{-1}\sqrt{\frac{kq^2}{2E}} \tag{10.21}$$

where β_1 is a constant. Its value can be obtained by putting $t = 0$ and $q = q^{(0)}$ in Eq. (10.21). Let us denote it by t_o. Thus we get an algebraic relation involving constants t_o and E and the variable q:

$$t_o = -t + \sqrt{\frac{m}{k}}\sin^{-1}\sqrt{\frac{kq^2}{2E}} \tag{10.22}$$

Inverting Eq. (10.22) we get

$$q(E,t) = \sqrt{\frac{2E}{k}}\sin\left[\sqrt{\frac{k}{m}}(t + t_o)\right] \tag{10.23}$$

The momentum is given by

$$p = \frac{\partial W}{\partial q} = \frac{\partial W_2}{\partial q} = \sqrt{m(2E - kq^2)}$$

which can be expressed as a function of t if we substitute for $q = q(t)$ from Eq. (10.23). Finally for energy, we get

$$-\frac{\partial W}{\partial t} = E$$

10.4.2 The Case of Planetary Orbits in Two Dimensions (r, θ)

The detailed solution for the Keplerian problem in the HJ formulation was first obtained by Jacobi. He also solved for the motion under two fixed centres of Newtonian attraction (or Coulombian repulsion), a case which, according to Jacobi, is separable in elliptical coordinates (that is, in the parameters of families of confocal ellipses and hyperbolas whose centres are at the centres of forces).

The HJ equation for planetary orbits in plane polar coordinates described in the plane of the orbit has the following form

$$\frac{1}{2\mu}\left(\frac{\partial W_o}{\partial r}\right)^2 - \frac{k}{r} + \frac{1}{2\mu r^2}\left(\frac{\partial W_o}{\partial \theta}\right)^2 = E$$

Since this differential equation is cyclic in θ, the solution can be written as

$$W_o(r,\theta) = p_\theta \theta + W_1(r)$$

$$\frac{1}{2\mu}\left(\frac{dW_1}{dr}\right)^2 - \frac{k}{r} + \frac{p_\theta^2}{2\mu r^2} = E$$

or

$$W_1(r) = \int \left[2\mu\left(E + \frac{k}{r}\right) - \frac{p_\theta^2}{r^2}\right]^{1/2} dr$$

and therefore,

$$W(r,\theta,p_\theta,E,t) = -Et + p_\theta\theta + \int \left\{2\mu\left(E + \frac{k}{r}\right) - \frac{p_\theta^2}{r^2}\right\}^{1/2} dr \qquad (10.24)$$

Now by Jacobi's theorem

$$\frac{\partial W}{\partial p_\theta} = \text{const.} = \beta_\theta = \theta + \frac{\partial W_1}{\partial p_\theta} \qquad (10.25)$$

This gives equation of the orbit in θ. And finally,

$$\frac{\partial W}{\partial E} = \text{const.} = \beta_E = -t + \frac{\partial W_1}{\partial E} \qquad (10.26)$$

giving the equation of orbit in t.

A general prescription for finding the integral $W_1(r)$ is in section numbers 2.267, 2.261 and 2.266 of the *Table Of Integrals, Series, and Products* by I. S. Gradshsteyn and I. M. Ryzhik:

Given $R = a + bx + cx^2$

$$\int \sqrt{R}\frac{dx}{x} = \sqrt{R} + a\int \frac{dx}{x\sqrt{R}} + \frac{b}{2}\int \frac{dx}{\sqrt{R}}$$

$$\int \frac{dx}{\sqrt{R}} = \frac{1}{\sqrt{c}} \ln(2\sqrt{cR} + 2cx + b) \qquad c > 0$$
$$= \frac{1}{\sqrt{c}} \sinh^{-1}\left(\frac{2cx + b}{\sqrt{\Delta}}\right) \qquad c > 0 \quad \Delta > 0 \quad \Delta = 4ac - b^2$$
$$= \frac{-1}{\sqrt{-c}} \sin^{-1}\left(\frac{2cx + b}{\sqrt{-\Delta}}\right) \qquad c < 0 \quad \Delta < 0 \tag{10.27}$$
$$= \frac{1}{\sqrt{c}} \ln(2cx + b) \qquad c > 0 \ \Delta = 0$$

$$\int \frac{dx}{x\sqrt{R}} = -\frac{1}{\sqrt{a}} \ln \frac{2a + bx + 2\sqrt{aR}}{x} \qquad a > 0$$
$$= \frac{1}{\sqrt{-a}} \sin^{-1} \frac{2a + bx}{x\sqrt{-\Delta}} \qquad a < 0 \quad \Delta < 0 \quad \Delta = 4ac - b^2$$
$$= \frac{1}{\sqrt{-a}} \tan^{-1} \frac{2a + bx}{2\sqrt{-a}\sqrt{R}} \qquad a < 0$$
$$= -\frac{1}{\sqrt{a}} \sinh^{-1} \frac{2a + bx}{x\sqrt{\Delta}} \qquad a > 0 \quad \Delta > 0 \tag{10.28}$$
$$= -\frac{1}{\sqrt{a}} \tanh^{-1} \frac{2a + bx}{2\sqrt{a}\sqrt{R}} \qquad a > 0$$
$$= \frac{1}{\sqrt{a}} \ln \frac{x}{2a + bx} \qquad a > 0 \quad \Delta = 0$$
$$= -\frac{2\sqrt{bx + cx^2}}{bx} \qquad a = 0 \quad b \neq 0$$

The planetary motion can also be solved in parabolic coordinates $(u,\ v,\ \phi)$, defined by

$$x = \sqrt{uv}\ \cos\phi \qquad y = \sqrt{uv}\ \sin\phi \qquad \text{and} \qquad z = (u - v)/2$$

We know that the Lagrangian for planetary motion is

$$L = \frac{1}{2}\mu(\dot{x}^2 + \dot{y}^2 + \dot{z}^2) + \frac{GMm}{r}$$

where

$$r = \sqrt{x^2 + y^2 + z^2} \qquad \mu = \frac{Mm}{M + m}$$

The Lagrangian, in terms of the above parabolic coordinates, becomes

$$L(u, v, \phi, \dot{u}, \dot{v}, \dot{\phi}) = \frac{1}{8}\mu(u + v)\left(\frac{\dot{u}^2}{u} + \frac{\dot{v}^2}{v}\right) + \frac{1}{2}\mu uv\dot{\phi}^2 + \frac{2GMm}{u + v}$$

Hence the Hamiltonian becomes

$$H(u, v, \phi, p_u, p_v, p_\phi) = \frac{2}{\mu(u + v)}(up_u^2 + vp_v^2) + \frac{1}{2}\frac{p_\phi^2}{\mu uv} - \frac{2GMm}{u + v}$$

Thus the HJ equation is

$$\frac{\partial W}{\partial t} + \frac{2}{\mu(u+v)}\left[u\left(\frac{\partial W}{\partial u}\right)^2 + v\left(\frac{\partial W}{\partial v}\right)^2 + \frac{1}{4}\left(\frac{1}{u}+\frac{1}{v}\right)\right.$$
$$\left.\left(\frac{\partial W}{\partial \phi}\right)^2 - GMm\right] = 0$$

Now taking

$$W = -Et + \alpha_1\phi + W_1(u) + W_2(v)$$

one gets

$$u\left(\frac{dW_1}{du}\right)^2 - \frac{EMmu}{2(M+m)} + \frac{\alpha_1^2}{4u} - \alpha_2 - \frac{1}{2}\frac{GM^2m^2}{M+m} = 0$$

and

$$v\left(\frac{dW_2}{dv}\right)^2 - \frac{EMmv}{2(M+m)} + \frac{\alpha_1^2}{4v} + \alpha_2 - \frac{1}{2}\frac{GM^2m^2}{M+m} = 0$$

Thus, in terms of parabolic coordinates also, the planetary motion is decomposable into completely separable Hamilton's principal function. Normally two sets of coordinates, for each of which a dynamical problem is separable, do not occur. But the planetary motion has this facility because of its added symmetry in the form of the degeneracy of the frequencies of radial and azimuthal oscillations. This is more fully discussed in section 10.5.

10.4.3 Swinging Atwood's Machine

Two masses M and m connected via a pair of horizontally placed frictionless and weightless pulleys are tied at the ends of an inextensible string. The heavier mass M can move only up or down whereas the lighter mass m can oscillate in a vertical plane (r, θ) as shown in Fig. (10.1). We have,
the kinetic energy $T = \frac{1}{2}(M+m)\dot{r}^2 + \frac{1}{2}mr^2\dot{\theta}^2$
the potential energy $V = gr(M - m\cos\theta)$
the total energy $E = T + V$
the Lagrangian $L = T - V$ and
the generalised momenta

$$p_r = \frac{\partial L}{\partial \dot{r}} = (M+m)\,\dot{r} \qquad \text{and} \qquad p_\theta = \frac{\partial L}{\partial \dot{\theta}} = mr^2\dot{\theta}$$

so that the Hamiltonian is

$$H(r,\theta,p_r,p_\theta) = \frac{1}{2}\left(\frac{p_r^2}{M+m} + \frac{p_\theta^2}{mr^2}\right) + g\,r(M - m\cos\theta)$$

The form of the Hamiltonian is such that the HJ equations constructed out of this H will not satisfy the separability requirement for the solution of the HJ equation since in the last term both r and θ are mixed. Hence we must look for a suitable pair of generalised

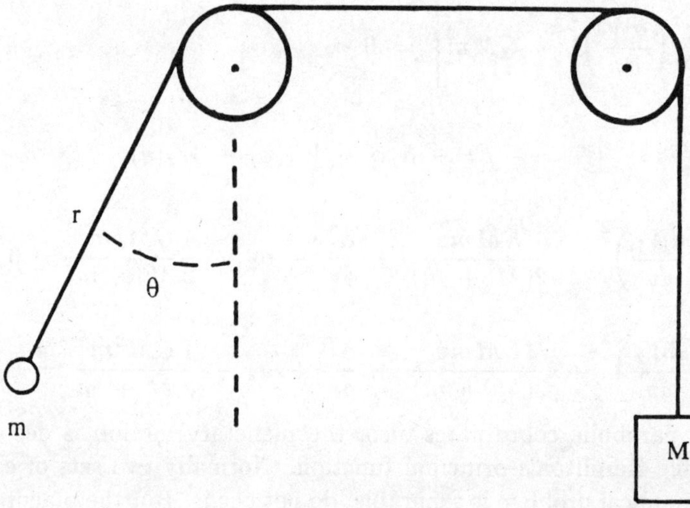

Fig. 10.1 A simple Atwood's pendulum

coordinates in terms of which the HJ equation would be separable in those new coordinates. In 1986 such a pair of the generalised coordinates has been found and reported in Am. J. Phys. **54**, 142 (1986), and we present the method below.

We have to transform (r, θ) to parabolic cylindrical coordinates (ξ, η) defined through

$$r = \frac{1}{2}(\xi^2 + \eta^2) \qquad \text{and} \qquad \theta = 2\tan^{-1}\left(\frac{\xi^2 - \eta^2}{2\xi\eta}\right)$$

with the inverse transformations

$$\xi^2 = r\left(1 + \sin\frac{\theta}{2}\right) \qquad \text{and} \qquad \eta^2 = r\left(1 - \sin\frac{\theta}{2}\right)$$

The energy integral now becomes

$$E = \left[\frac{1}{2}(M + m)\xi^2 + 2m\eta^2\right]\dot{\xi}^2 + \left[\frac{1}{2}(M + m)\eta^2 + 2m\xi^2\right]\dot{\eta}^2$$
$$+ (M - 3m)\xi\eta\dot{\xi}\dot{\eta} + \frac{g}{2}\frac{(M + m)(\xi^4 + \eta^4) + (M - 3m)\xi^2\eta^2}{\xi^2 + \eta^2}$$

This simplifies for the case with $M = 3m$ and henceforth we deal with this special case, with

$$p_\xi = 4\dot{\xi}(\xi^2 + \eta^2) \qquad \text{and} \qquad p_\eta = 4\dot{\eta}(\xi^2 + \eta^2)$$

and

$$H(\xi,\eta,p_\xi,p_\eta) = \frac{(p_\xi^2 + p_\eta^2)/8 + 2g(\xi^4 + \eta^4)}{\xi^2 + \eta^2} = E$$

assuming further $m = 1$. Hence the HJ equation becomes

$$\left(\frac{\partial W}{\partial \xi}\right)^2 + \left(\frac{\partial W}{\partial \eta}\right)^2 + 16g\left(\xi^4 + \eta^4\right) = 8E\left(\xi^2 + \eta^2\right)$$

To separate the variables put

$$W(\xi,\eta) = W_1(\xi) + W_2(\eta)$$

which, when substituted in the HJ equation, results in

$$\left(\frac{dW_1}{d\xi}\right)^2 + 16g\xi^4 - 8E\xi^2 = I = p_\xi^2 + 16g\xi^4 - 8E\xi^2$$

and

$$\left(\frac{dW_2}{d\eta}\right)^2 + 16g\eta^4 - 8E\eta^2 = -I = p_\eta^2 + 16g\eta^4 - 8E\eta^2$$

where I is the constant of separation which can be regarded as a new constant of motion apart from the energy integral E. From these two expressions for I it is easy to show that

$$I = \frac{16\left(\xi^2 + \eta^2\right)\left(\dot{\xi}^2\eta^2 - \xi^2\dot{\eta}^2\right) + 16g\left(\xi^2 - \eta^2\right)\xi^2\eta^2}{\left(\xi^2 + \eta^2\right)}$$

When translated into the old coordinates $r,\theta,\dot{r},\dot{\theta}$ one obtains

$$I(r,\theta,\dot{r},\dot{\theta}) = 16r^2\dot{\theta}\left(\dot{r}\cos\frac{\theta}{2} - \frac{r\dot{\theta}}{2}\sin\frac{\theta}{2}\right) + 16gr^2\sin\frac{\theta}{2}\cos^2\frac{\theta}{2}$$

This hidden symmetry would not have been obtained through the study of the problem in its original (r,θ) coordinates only, or through the study of the Poisson brackets, or the cyclic coordinates of the Hamiltonian. The separability of the solution of the HJ equation on any given dynamical problem into functions of its individual generalised coordinates is thus an extremely useful tool for evaluating all the hidden constants of motion. Unfortunately, one has to use a trial and error approach to hit the right coordinate system.

It has been found that the above problem is separable not only for $M = 3m$ but in general for $M = m(4n^2 - 1)$, where n is any integer. It is however not yet known why $M : m = 4n^2 - 1$ has such special symmetries.

10.4.4 1–D Damped Harmonic Oscillator

The equation of motion is

$$m\ddot{q} + \lambda\dot{q} + m\omega_o^2 q = 0 \tag{10.29}$$

For quantising such an oscillator one needs to formulate a suitable Lagrangian and Hamiltonian for this system. In the literature one finds a large number of papers justifying one or the other Lagrangian, but most of them defy a consistent physical picture of the system.

For example, if one starts with the energy condition, namely

$$E = T + V = \frac{1}{2}m\dot{q}^2 + \frac{1}{2}m\omega_o^2 q^2 \qquad \text{with } H = \dot{q}\frac{\partial L}{\partial \dot{q}} - L = E$$

on integration one would find,

$$L = \frac{1}{2}m\dot{q}^2 - \frac{1}{2}m\omega_o^2 q^2 + \dot{q}h(q,t)$$

No matter what $h(q,t)$ is, this L does not produce the right equation of motion (Eq. (10.29)).

Now suppose one forms a Lagrangian that correctly reproduces the equation of motion. One such Lagrangian is often quoted as

$$L(q,\dot{q},t) = e^{\lambda t/m}\left[\frac{1}{2}m\dot{q}^2 - \frac{1}{2}m\omega_o^2 q^2\right] \tag{10.30}$$

On solving the Lagrangian equation of motion one gets

$$q = A\, e^{-\lambda t/2m}\cos\omega t \tag{10.31}$$

where $\omega = \sqrt{\omega_o^2 - (\lambda^2/4m^2)} > 0$. Hence the Hamiltonian is

$$H = \dot{q}\frac{\partial L}{\partial \dot{q}} - L = \left(\frac{1}{2}m\dot{q}^2 + \frac{1}{2}m\omega_o^2 q^2\right)e^{\lambda t/m} \tag{10.32}$$

and, after using the expression for q in Eq. (10.31) the value of H becomes

$$H = \frac{1}{2}A^2 m\left[\left(\frac{\lambda^2}{4m^2} + \omega_o^2\right)\cos^2\omega t + \frac{1}{2}\frac{\lambda\omega}{m}\sin 2\omega t + \omega^2\sin^2\omega t\right]$$

We now see that even though the position and the velocities are damped in time, the Hamiltonian is not damped, but oscillates with period π/ω. The energy averaged over any full period is

$$\bar{H} = \frac{1}{4}mA^2\left[\frac{\lambda^2}{4m^2} + \omega_o^2 + \omega^2\right] = \frac{1}{2}mA^2\omega_o^2 \tag{10.33}$$

which is constant!

These kind of fallacies are known to exist with the above standard form of the Lagrangian even though it produces the correct equation of motion. So some people claim that the above Lagrangian does not correspond to the physical Lagrangian of a damped harmonic oscillator, but that it corresponds to that for a variable mass oscillator (for example, a bucket oscillating in the rain collecting water at a constant rate).

Recently, a suitable canonical transformation of the Hamiltonian in Eq. (10.32) has been found so that the transformed Hamiltonian does not have any explicit time dependence, hence an energy like Jacobi integral can be obtained for the system.

Starting with the equation of motion (10.29) and defining the canonical momentum by

$$p = \frac{\partial L}{\partial \dot{q}} = m\dot{q}\, e^{\lambda t/m}$$

the Hamiltonian in Eq. (10.32) becomes

$$H(q,p,t) = e^{-\lambda t/m}\frac{p^2}{2m} + \frac{m\omega_o^2}{2}q^2\, e^{\lambda t/m} \tag{10.34}$$

This form of H has explicit time dependence and hence it is not a constant of the motion. Herein lies the catch: while calculating $\bar{H}$ in Eq. (10.33) we tacitly assumed that H in Eq. (10.32) was a constant of motion, and that it represented the energy, like a Jacobi integral.

Now let us make a canonical transformation given by

$$Q = q\, e^{\lambda t/2m} \qquad \text{and} \qquad P = p\, e^{-\lambda t/2m}$$

with the generating function,

$$F_2(q,P,t) = e^{\lambda t/2m} qP$$

The transformed Hamiltonian becomes

$$K(P,Q,t) = H(q,p,t) + \frac{\partial F_2}{\partial t} = \frac{P^2}{2m} + \frac{m}{2}\omega_o^2 Q^2 + \frac{\lambda}{2m}QP$$

which is independent of time! Hence this Hamiltonian can be regarded as a constant of motion. In terms of the old variables this new Jacobi integral of motion becomes

$$J = e^{-\lambda t/m}\frac{p^2}{2m} + \frac{m\omega_o^2}{2}q^2 e^{\lambda t/m} + \frac{\lambda}{2m}qp$$

and not the old Hamiltonian given by Eq. (10.34) so that the amplitudes of both q and p diminish with time but not of the integral J as a whole.

One can then proceed to set up the HJ equation in terms of the new variables (Q,P)

$$\frac{\partial W}{\partial t} + \frac{1}{2m}\left(\frac{\partial W}{\partial Q}\right)^2 + \frac{m\omega_o^2 Q^2}{2} + \frac{\lambda}{2m}Q\left(\frac{\partial W}{\partial Q}\right) = 0$$

and seek a solution

$$W(Q,\alpha,t) = -\alpha t + W_o(Q,\alpha)$$

where α is the new energy-like Jacobi integral $J\ (= K)$. On substitution by $x = \sqrt{m\omega_o}Q$,

$$\left(\frac{dW_o}{dx}\right)^2 + ax\frac{dW_o}{dx} + (x^2 - b) = 0$$

where $a = \lambda/m\omega_o$ and $b = 2\alpha/\omega_o$, giving a solution

$$W_o(x) = -\frac{ax^2}{4} + \int\sqrt{b - \left(1 - \frac{a^2}{4}\right)x^2}\,dx$$

Now a can have values < 2, $= 2$, or > 2, having three different solutions, representing an underdamped, critically damped and overdamped oscillator. To illustrate one case we take $a < 2$ and define $c = \sqrt{1 - a^2/4}$ to give the solution,

$$W(x, \alpha) = -\alpha t - \frac{ax^2}{4} + \int \sqrt{b - c^2x^2}\, dx$$

Now

$$\beta = \frac{\partial W}{\partial \alpha} = -t + \frac{1}{\omega_o} \int \frac{dx}{\sqrt{b - c^2x^2}} = -t + \frac{1}{c\omega_o} \sin^{-1}\left(\frac{cx}{\sqrt{b}}\right)$$

or

$$\sin^{-1}\left(\frac{cx}{\sqrt{b}}\right) = c\omega_o(t + \beta) = \omega t + \delta \qquad \text{say.}$$

Therefore, the final solution is,

$$q = Q\, e^{-\lambda t/2m} = A\, e^{-\lambda t/2m} \sin(\omega t + \delta)$$

which is a physical solution admitting of no ambiguity or contradiction at any stage. Similarly the solutions for the other two cases follow in their expected forms.

10.5 ACTION-ANGLE VARIABLES

This is a versatile technique used for finding all the periodicities in a periodic system without completely solving the HJ equations, and was first devised by Delaunay in 1846 in connection with some problems in celestial mechanics. However, the name action-angle variables was suggested by Karl Schwarzschild in 1916.

Periodic systems are those which repeat their state of motion after a constant interval of time known as the period. In the phase space all such systems need not retrace their paths. Those which retrace their paths in phase space are called *librating* systems. On the other hand, for the *rotating* systems some momenta are periodic functions of their conjugate coordinates, but the latter do not return to their original value and increase or decrease monotonically with time. Thus libration corresponds to periodic systems having velocities $\dot{q}_i$ changing sign over any single period, otherwise q_i cannot return to their old values after completion of the period. Rotation leads to a situation where q_i changes monotonically or remains constant while the system returns, after each period in q_i, to its original configuration.

Action variables are useful parameters for systems which are *periodic, conservative* and *orthogonally decomposable*, that is, Hamilton's characteristic function is completely separable in all its variables. The *action variables* are defined as

$$J_i = \oint p_i dq_i \tag{10.35}$$

where i is not summed over and the cyclic integral is performed over a full periodic variation in q_i.

If the complete integral of the time independent HJ equation

$$H\left(q_1,\ldots,q_n,\frac{\partial S}{\partial q_1},\ldots,\frac{\partial S}{\partial q_n}\right) = E$$

is

$$S(q_1,\ldots,q_n;\alpha_1,\ldots,\alpha_n) = \sum_{i=1}^{n} S_i(q_i;\alpha_1,\ldots,\alpha_n)$$

where one of the $\{\alpha_i\}$ is the energy E, then

$$\begin{aligned} J_i &= \oint p_i dq_i = \oint \frac{\partial S}{\partial q_i} dq_i = \oint \frac{dS_i}{dq_i} dq_i \\ &= \text{a function independent of } q_i \\ &\quad \text{but dependent on } \alpha_1,\ldots,\alpha_n \text{ only} \end{aligned}$$

that is,

$$J_i = J_i(\alpha_1,\ldots,\alpha_n) \qquad i=1,\ldots,n$$

Now, these n relations can be inverted to obtain

$$\alpha_i = \alpha_i(J_1,\ldots,J_n) \qquad i=1,\ldots,n$$

so that the complete integral can also be written as

$$\tilde{S}(q_1,\ldots,q_n;J_1,\ldots,J_n)$$

instead of $S(q_1,\ldots,q_n;\alpha_1,\ldots,\alpha_n)$. $\{J_i\}$ are here the constants of motion (although called action 'variables'!). We can regard them as new momenta P_i for a canonical transformation with a new set of coordinates Q_i, conjugate to these momenta P_i, $(i=1,\ldots,n)$. This canonical transformation may be generated by a generating function of the type F_2, same as the complete integral of the time independent HJ equation or Hamilton's characteristic function $\tilde{S}(q_1,\ldots,q_n;J_1,\ldots,J_n)$. The conditions are

$$Q_i = \frac{\partial \tilde{S}}{\partial P_i} \equiv \frac{\partial \tilde{S}}{\partial J_i} \qquad \text{and} \qquad p_i = \frac{\partial \tilde{S}}{\partial q_i}$$

with the new Hamiltonian

$$K(P,Q) = H(p,q) = E(J_1,\ldots,J_n)$$

which does not depend on $\{Q_i\}$.

The canonical equations of motion corresponding to the new Hamiltonian K are

$$\dot{P}_i = -\frac{\partial K}{\partial Q_i} = 0$$

and

$$\dot{Q}_i = \frac{\partial K}{\partial P_i} = \frac{\partial E}{\partial J_i} = \text{const.} = \nu_i \quad \text{say}$$

where $\{\nu_i\}$ is another set of constants. Note that $Q_i \neq 0$ unlike its counterpart in the time dependent HJ equation, where Jacobi's theorem suggested $\{Q_i\}$ to be constants of motion. Here, the solution for $\{Q_i\}$ is

$$Q_i = \nu_i t + \beta_i$$

where

$$\nu_i = \frac{\partial E}{\partial J_i} = \text{const.} \tag{10.36}$$

and β_i are the constants of integration. Again Q_is are the coordinates conjugate to momenta J_is, and J_is are of the same dimension as that of angular momentum or action or Planck's constant $\hbar$. Hence Q_is are basically angle like variables and are therefore dimensionless. These Q_is are historically denoted by ω_is and are called *angle variables*, given by

$$\omega_i = \nu_i t + \beta_i \tag{10.37}$$

Obviously, ν_is look like frequencies of oscillation of the coordinate q_i which gives rise to J_i, and β_is are the phase constants.

Thus if the relation $E = E(J_1, \ldots, J_n)$ is known, the frequencies of oscillation ν_is for all the coordinates given by

$$\nu_i = \frac{\partial E}{\partial J_i}$$

can be obtained. If two or more frequencies of oscillation are identical, such a periodic system is called a *degenerate* periodic system. If further, all the frequencies $\{\nu_i\}$ are found to be identical, the system is termed as a *completely degenerate* periodic system.

Now, the new set of variables (ν_i, J_i) should completely specify the dynamical state of any conservative periodic system and

$$\omega_i = \frac{\partial \tilde{S}}{\partial J_i} = \nu_i t + \beta_i$$

can produce the general solution

$$q_k = q_k(J_1, \ldots, J_n; \omega_1, \ldots, \omega_n)$$

which can be represented by a multiple Fourier expansion of the fundamental frequencies $\{\nu_i\}$, given by

$$q_k = \sum_{n_1, \ldots, n_N = -\infty}^{\infty} A^{(k)}_{n_1 \ldots n_N}(J_1, \ldots, J_n) \exp\left\{ 2\pi\sqrt{-1} \sum_{j=1}^{N} (n_j \nu_j t + \beta_j) \right\} \tag{10.38}$$

where N is the number of DOF of the system, and where the summation in the front extends over all integer values of n_j.

The motion in general is not periodic, its orbit having the characteristics of an 'open' Lissajous figure. Only if the ν_i's are commensurate does the current point of the orbit ever return strictly to to its starting point.

The use of this technique was limited to astronomers only, until it was brought into physics by Stäckel, Epstein, and Schwarzschild. If these N frequencies of the system satisfy

$n \leq N$ linear equations with integral coefficients, the system is said to have an n-fold degeneracy. In this case, the orbit does not, as in the nondegenerate case, fulfill in the configuration space an N-fold, but only an $(N - n)$-fold continuum, and the system can be transformed by an appropriate change of variables into a system with $(N - n)$ degrees of freedom.

10.5.1 1–D Simple Harmonic Oscillator

The Hamiltonian for such a periodic system is given by

$$H = \frac{1}{2m}p^2 + \frac{1}{2}kq^2$$

which sets the time independent HJ equation as

$$\frac{1}{2m}\left(\frac{\partial S}{\partial q}\right)^2 + \frac{1}{2}kq^2 = E$$

Therefore,

$$J = \oint p dq = \oint \frac{\partial S}{\partial q} dq = \oint \sqrt{2m\left(E - \frac{1}{2}kq^2\right)} dq = 2\sqrt{\frac{m}{k}}E\pi \tag{10.39}$$

and hence the frequency of oscillation is

$$\nu = \frac{\partial E}{\partial J} = \frac{1}{2\pi}\sqrt{\frac{k}{m}} \tag{10.40}$$

10.5.2 The Kepler Problem

The motion is periodic if the energy $E < 0$. The Hamiltonian is

$$H = \frac{1}{2\mu}\left(p_r^2 + \frac{p_\theta^2}{r^2} + \frac{p_\phi^2}{r^2 \sin^2\theta}\right) + V(r)$$

Taking

$$S(r, \theta, \phi) = S_r(r) + S_\theta(\theta) + \alpha_\phi \phi$$

the HJ equation reduces to

$$\left(\frac{dS_\theta}{d\theta}\right)^2 + \frac{\alpha_\phi^2}{\sin^2\theta} = \alpha_\theta^2 \equiv p_\theta^2 + \frac{\alpha_\phi^2}{\sin^2\theta}$$

and

$$\left(\frac{dS_r}{dr}\right)^2 + \frac{\alpha_\theta^2}{r^2} = 2\mu\{E - V(r)\} \equiv p_r^2 + \frac{\alpha_\theta^2}{r^2}$$

Hence

$$J_\phi = \oint \left(\frac{\partial S}{\partial \phi}\right) d\phi = \oint \alpha_\phi d\phi = 2\pi\alpha_\phi = 2\pi p_\phi \tag{10.41}$$

$$J_\theta = \oint \left(\frac{\partial S}{\partial \theta}\right) d\theta = \oint \sqrt{\alpha_\theta^2 - \frac{\alpha_\phi 2}{\sin^2\theta}}\, d\theta = 2\pi(\alpha_\theta - \alpha_\phi) \tag{10.42}$$

and

$$J_r = \oint \left(\frac{\partial S}{\partial r}\right) dr = \oint \sqrt{2\mu\{E - V(r)\} - \frac{\alpha_\theta^2}{r^2}}\, dr$$

$$= \oint \sqrt{2\mu E + \frac{2\mu^2 K}{r} - \frac{(J_\theta + J_\phi)^2}{4\pi^2 r^2}}\, dr \qquad \text{putting} \quad V(r) = -\frac{K\mu}{r}$$

$$= -(J_\theta + J_\phi) + \pi K\mu\sqrt{\frac{2\mu}{-E}}$$

Therefore,

$$E = -\frac{2\pi^2\mu^3 K^2}{(J_r + J_\theta + J_\phi)^2} \tag{10.43}$$

Since this relation is completely symmetric in J_r, J_θ, J_ϕ, all the three frequencies are identical, that is,

$$\begin{aligned} \nu_r &= \nu_\theta = \nu_\phi \\ &= \frac{4\pi^2\mu^3 K^2}{(J_r + J_\theta + J_\phi)^3} \\ &= \frac{1}{\pi K}\sqrt{\frac{-2E^3}{\mu^3}} \qquad \text{where} \quad K = G(M_\odot + m) \end{aligned} \tag{10.44}$$

Thus we see that planetary motions are *completely degenerate* in all three coordinates r, θ and ϕ. In other words, all bounded orbits of any two body system moving under any inverse square law of an attractive central force are closed (Bertrand's theorem).

Now if the central force contains terms which are of non-inverse square law type, (say an r^{-3} term due to general relativistic correction) the orbit would no longer be closed, but would still satisfy the planar motion. As a result, one of the degeneracies will be removed and the motion will still be singly degenerate with $\nu_\phi = \nu_\theta \neq \nu_r$, for all kinds of central forces (except of course the inverse-square law and Hooke's law, for which the motion is completely degenerate). This (θ, ϕ) degeneracy can also be removed, for example, by applying some non-central forces such as switching on a constant magnetic field which produces a velocity dependent Lorentz force on an atomic system. This is the well-known Zeeman effect which removes the azimuthal degeneracy. The same is also true for the Stark effect. The HJ equations were completely solved for the Zeeman effect by P. Debye in 1915 and for the Stark effect by Schwarzschild in 1916, as a limiting case of Jacobi's solution to the motion under two central forces of the inverse square law type.

10.5.3 Integrable Systems

Consider a conservative system with n DOF and the Hamiltonian $H(q,p)$. We do not *a priori* require that its motion in the phase space be periodic. However, we assume the existence of a canonical transformation $(p,q) \longrightarrow (J,Q)$ such that the new Hamiltonian $E(J_1,\ldots,J_n)$ depends exclusively on the new momenta $\{J_i\}$ and not on the new coordinates $\{Q_i\}$. Hamilton's equations in the transformed coordinates read:

$$\dot{Q}_i = \frac{\partial E}{\partial J_i} = \nu_i(J_1,\ldots,J_n) \qquad \dot{J}_i = -\frac{\partial E}{\partial Q_i} = 0 \qquad i = 1,\ldots,n$$

These can readily be integrated to give

$$Q_i(t) = \nu_i t + \beta_i \qquad (\beta_i = Q_i(0)) \qquad J_i(t) = \alpha_i = J_i(0)$$

Now going back to the old variables, we get $2n$ combinations of $\{p_i, q_i\}$ and t:

$$\beta_i = Q_i(p_k(t), q_k(t), t) - \nu_i(\alpha_1,\ldots,\alpha_n)\, t \qquad \alpha_i = J_i(p_k(t), q_k(t)) \qquad i,k = 1,\ldots,n$$

which do not change with time. Thus we have solved the equations of motion completely and obtained $2n$ constants of motion. Such Hamiltonian systems are said to be *integrable.*

It will be interesting to analyse the motion of an integrable system in phase space. First, note that the transformed Hamiltonian is like a free particle Hamiltonian with coordinates $Q_i(t)$ changing monotonically with time just as in the case of a free particle. However, the actual motion of the system need not correspond to that of non-interacting free particles. In particular, the motion of the system may be bounded, that is, confined to a finite region of space and not unbounded like that of the free particles. Since all the momenta are finite, and are consistent with the conserved value of the energy, the phase space motion of such a system must also be bounded or confined to regions with finite volume in the $(2n-1)$-dimensional constant energy surface in the phase space. In general, the phase space (actually a subspace of the constant energy surface, see below) of such a system is divided into invariant parts, each with finite volume, such that a trajectory passing through a point in an invariant part remains in it for all time. Such an invariant part participates in the natural motion of the phase space by transforming onto itself and the structure remains invariant under any canonical transformation, since the image of an invariant part with finite volume under a canonical transformation will again be an invariant part with the same volume. Therefore, if the phase space motion of the system is bounded by an invariant region with finite volume with respect to one set of canonical variables (p,q) then it should be similarly bounded with respect to any other canonically transformed set (P,Q). However, our new coordinates $Q_i(t)$ change monotonically with time so that $Q_i(t) \longrightarrow \infty$ as $t \longrightarrow \infty$ giving an unbounded motion, leading to an apparent paradox. The only way to resolve this paradox is to treat new coordinates Q_i to be dimensionless quantities like angles with new momenta J_i having dimensions of angular momentum or action. Thus the phase space motion of a general integrable system turns out to be periodic or nearly periodic (see below). We shall not pause here to rigorously establish these results.

We can now develop a quantitative picture of the motion of a general integrable system in its phase space. When $n = 1$, the motion can be visualised as rotation around a circle of radius $\alpha = J(0)$ with constant angular velocity ν; therefore the bounded motion of a system with one DOF is always periodic. When $n = 2$, there are two radii determined by $\alpha_1 = J_1(0)$ and $\alpha_2 = J_2(0)$ with angular velocities ν_1 and ν_2; so the motion is confined to a two-dimensional toroidal surface or a 2-torus. Note that this 2-torus forms an invariant subspace of the phase space to which the motion of the system is confined. In order to understand the motion on this 2-torus we appeal to the so-called Poincaré recurrence theorem, which states that a trajectory passing through a point in an invariant part of the phase space returns to every neighbourhood of that point, however close, after a finite time. Two cases arise while applying this theorem to the 2-torus. First, when $\nu_1/\nu_2 = m'/n'$, a rational number, we see that the time taken, say T, to perform m' complete rotations around the circle with radius α_1 is the same as that taken for n' complete rotations around the circle with radius α_2 so that the motion on the torus becomes periodic with period T. Note that Poincaré's recurrence theorem is trivially satisfied in this case. Second, when ν_1/ν_2 is an irrational number, the motion on the 2-torus cannot be periodic, but applying Poincaré's recurrence theorem we can easily see that the trajectory should wind the 2-torus densely and endlessly. This kind of motion is called *quasi-periodic* or *conditionally periodic*. In general, the motion of an integrable Hamiltonian system with n DOF is quasi-periodic and is confined to an n-torus. As an immediate consequence of this fact we see that the integrable systems do not satisfy the requirements of statistical mechanics, since the dimension of the constant-energy surface $(2n-1)$ is larger than that of the torus whenever $n > 1$ and the trajectory cannot fill up the energy surface, not to mention the equal probability assumption of microcanonical ensemble.

A few questions may arise.

1. Do we have any necessary and sufficient condition for the integrability of the Hamiltonian systems?
It turns out that a Hamiltonian system with n DOF is integrable if we can find a set of n integrals of motion, say $\{F_i\}$, which are functionally independent and satisfy $[F_i, F_j] = 0$ $(i \neq j)$ $i, j = 1, \ldots, n$. It is easy to see that if the system is integrable, the transformed momenta $\{J_i\}$ provide the required set of n integrals of motion.

2. Are there many integrable systems among all Hamiltonian systems?
It is found that integrabilty is an exceptional property of Hamiltonian systems whenever $n > 2$. Integrable systems are so rare that in general it is impossible to approximate a nonintegrable Hamiltonian system by an associated series of integrable ones. This statement is to be compared with irrational numbers which can always be approached by sequences of rational numbers, because the latter are dense on the real axis, although the length associated with any set of rational numbers is zero.

3. What happens with the quantitative picture of motion when the system is made slightly nonintegrable, that is, when the Hamiltonian becomes $H = H_o + V$, where H_o is integrable and V contains a small parameter?
The answer to this question is provided by the KAM theorem, first enunciated by A. N. Kolmogorov in 1954 and completely proved by V. I. Arnold and E. Moser in the early sixties. The mathematical prerequisite goes well beyond this book; so we give only a loose formulation of the theorem.

If the following conditions hold:

(a) the perturbation V causing nonintegrability is small (we ignore the precise formulation of smallness)

(b) the frequencies $\{\nu_i\}$ of the unperturbed integrable Hamiltonian satisfy

$$\frac{\partial(\nu_1, \ldots, \nu_n)}{\partial(J_1, \ldots, J_n)} = 0$$

then the motion is still confined to an n-torus except for a negligible set of initial conditions, which may lead to wandering motion on the energy surface. These n-tori, called *KAM surfaces*, or *KAM curves*, if seen in plane sections, may be slightly distorted compared to that of the $V = 0$ case. Nevertheless, the quantitative picture of the motion remains much the same as that of the unperturbed integrable system.

10.6 ADIABATIC INVARIANTS

Here we consider the effect of slow variation of some characteristic parameter, say λ, of an initially conservative (implying a constant λ) and periodic system, to find whether certain quantities can remain invariant under such slow changes. By slow changes we mean the changes which are slow compared with the periodic variation, that is, $d\lambda/\lambda << dt/\tau$, τ being the period.

Adiabaticity in dynamical contexts was first explored by Boltzmann (1866) and Clausius (1870 – 71). Later Helmholtz (1884) and Hertz (1894) used the notion of the action integrals of periodic systems to define adiabatic motion. However, it was Lord Rayleigh who in 1902 showed that the energy of a simple pendulum (E) would remain proportional to its frequency (ν) if its length was altered continuously and infinitesimally slowly. Obviously, here the *adiabatic invariant* is claimed to be the ratio E/ν. The existence of adiabatic invariants for systems of N degrees of freedom was proved in statistical mechanics by P. Hertz in 1910. In the Solvay Congress of 1911, Lorentz asked whether a quantised pendulum whose string is being shortened remained in its quantised state; Einstein answered unhesitatingly — if the length of the pendulum is changed infinitesimally slowly, its energy remains equal to $h\nu$ if it was originally $h\nu$ – which was already proved by Lord Rayleigh.

It was indeed J. M. Burgers who in 1918 proved that *action variables are adiabatic invariants*, or more precisely, the time average of any action variable, $\bar{J}$, over a single period behaves like an adiabatic invariant. Since in the case of the simple pendulum, it has been shown earlier that $J = E/\nu$, Burgers' theorem is obeyed. We present his proof below.

Let us consider a dynamical system of n degrees of freedom and let λ be a parameter that effects the change in say the energy of the system. Let λ vary slowly with time such that $d\lambda/\lambda << dt/\tau_i$, τ_i being the longest period of oscillation of the system, say that of the ith coordinate. When λ is constant, the system remains conservative and can be completely described by the action angle variables (J_i, ω_i).

The Hamiltonian for the above system is given by

$$H = H(J_1, \ldots, J_n, \lambda)$$

If the time independent HJ equation has a solution $S(q_1,\ldots,q_n;J_1,\ldots,J_n,\lambda)$, which also behaves like a generating function for transforming (q,p) to (ω,J). Obviously, the transformed Hamiltonian $K(\omega_1,\ldots,\omega_n;J_1,\ldots,J_n;\lambda)$ would be

$$K(\omega_1,\ldots,\omega_n;J_1,\ldots,J_n;\lambda)$$

$$= H(q_1,\ldots,q_n;p_1,\ldots,p_n;\lambda) + \dot{\lambda}\frac{\partial S(q_1,\ldots,q_n;J_1,\ldots,J_n;\lambda)}{\partial\lambda}$$

Since we are interested in finding out the change in J_i s we have to consider the Hamiltonian equation of motion in J_i, which is,

$$\dot{J}_i = -\frac{\partial K}{\partial\omega_i}$$

But S is not an explicit function of ω_i, so it will be easier if we consider a Legendre transformation of S giving

$$\tilde{S}(q_1,\ldots,q_n;\omega_1,\ldots,\omega_n;\lambda) = S(q_1,\ldots,q_n;J_1,\ldots,J_n;\lambda) - \sum J_i\omega_i$$

for which

$$K(\omega_1,\ldots,\omega_n;J_1,\ldots,J_n;\lambda)$$

$$= H(q_1,\ldots,q_n;p_1,\ldots,p_n;\lambda) + \dot{\lambda}\frac{\partial\tilde{S}(q_1,\ldots,q_n;J_1,\ldots,J_n;\lambda)}{\partial\lambda}$$

and therefore,

$$\dot{J}_i = -\frac{\partial K}{\partial\omega_i} = -\dot{\lambda}\frac{\partial}{\partial\omega_i}\left(\frac{\partial\tilde{S}}{\partial\lambda}\right)$$

Note that the function $\tilde{S}$, like S, depends on t only through the parameter λ, which varies very slowly.

Therefore, the change of $\dot{J}_i$ (denoted by ΔJ_i) over a period τ_i of the ith angle variable ω_i, can be expressed as

$$\Delta J_i = -\int_0^{\tau_i}\dot{\lambda}\frac{\partial}{\partial\omega_i}\left(\frac{\partial\tilde{S}}{\partial\lambda}\right)dt$$

$$= -\dot{\lambda}\int_0^{\tau_i}\frac{\partial}{\partial\omega_i}\left(\frac{\partial\tilde{S}}{\partial\lambda}\right)dt + O\left(\dot{\lambda}^2,\ddot{\lambda}\right)$$

Before one starts with the action angle variables one has already assumed the complete separability of the coordinates and thus J_i is defined as

$$J_i = \oint p_i dq_i = \oint\frac{\partial S_i}{\partial q_i}dq_i = \oint\frac{\partial\tilde{S}_i}{\partial q_i}dq_i$$

where i is not summed and $S_i = \int p_i dq_i$, and $\tilde{S}_i = S_i - J_i\omega_i$. Hence,

$$\Delta J_i = -\dot{\lambda} \int_0^{\tau_i} \frac{\partial}{\partial \omega_i}\left(\frac{\partial \tilde{S}_i}{\partial \lambda}\right) dt + O\left(\dot{\lambda}^2, \ddot{\lambda}\right)$$

At the end of the period τ_i, S_i must change by J_i and ω_i change by unity, hence $\tilde{S}_i$ returns to the same value like a periodic function of ω_i, so also $(\partial \tilde{S}_i/\partial \lambda)$. Therefore $(\partial \tilde{S}_i/\partial \lambda)$ can be a Fourier sum for the fundamental frequency ω_i, that is,

$$\frac{\partial \tilde{S}_i}{\partial \lambda} = \sum_k A_k(J_1, \ldots, J_n, \lambda) \exp(2\pi\sqrt{-1}\, k\omega_i)$$

where k are integers, so that

$$\Delta J_i = -\dot{\lambda} \sum_k \int_0^{\tau_i} 2\pi A_k \sqrt{-1}\, k \exp(2\pi\sqrt{-1}\, k\omega_i) dt + O(\dot{\lambda}^2, \ddot{\lambda})$$

The first term obviously vanishes and since λ is a slowly varying parameter, and the second term can be neglected so that

$$\Delta J_i = 0 \tag{10.45}$$

for any periodic and marginally nonconservative system. This fact is usually stated as J_i is an adiabatic invariant for any secular (that is, long term) changes in the Hamiltonian function.

Of course, much later Levi-Civita (1934) rigorously laid the mathematical foundation of the theory of adiabatic invariants. Adiabatic invariants for more complex systems such as compound pendulum and electrically oscillating circuits were solved by P. L. Bhatnagar and D. S. Kothari in 1942.

Examples

(i) For a 1–D harmonic oscillator from Eqs (10.39) and (10.40), $J = E/2\pi\nu$. If the energy is slowly changed, the frequency will also change proportionately. If the length is changed slowly, this will simply lead to a slow change in frequency and a proportionate change in the energy.

(ii) In the Kepler problem, we have seen from Eqs (10.43) and (10.44)

$$J_r + J_\theta + J_\phi = \pi\sqrt{2\mu^3}\frac{G(M_\odot + m)}{\sqrt{-E}}$$

Thus for adiabatic changes, J_r, J_θ and J_ϕ should not change over any integral number of periods. For example, for a very slow variation in G, the orbital energy must vary as $|E| \propto G^2$, or for a very slow rate of loss of mass of the sun, the energy must change as $|E| \propto M_\odot^2$. Again, since $J_\phi = 2\pi p_\phi$, any adiabatic change of any kind would keep the ϕ-component of angular momentum (p_ϕ) constant.

(iii) Take another example. Suppose that there is a constant magnetic field in which a charged particle having an electric charge e is moving in a circle. The magnetic induction $\boldsymbol{B}$ is changed slowly. The adiabatic invariant for this case is

$$\begin{aligned} J &= \oint \boldsymbol{p}\cdot d\boldsymbol{l} = \oint (m\boldsymbol{v} + e\boldsymbol{A})\cdot d\boldsymbol{l} = 2\pi mvr + e\nabla\times\boldsymbol{A}\cdot d\boldsymbol{s} \\ &= 2\pi m\left(\frac{eB}{m}\right)r^2 + \pi e r^2 B = 3\pi e B r^2 \end{aligned} \tag{10.46}$$

using $mv^2/r = evB$ for circular orbits in a plane perpendicular to the direction of $\boldsymbol{B}$. Therefore, Br^2 must remain constant, that is, the total flux threading through the orbit must be conserved. If B increases slowly the orbit must slowly shrink as $r \propto B^{-1/2}$.

(iv) The idea of adiabatic invariants (that is, J_i = constant) is extremely useful in many practical situations. Historically it has also provided the major guideline for the formulation of the early quantisation rules for the atomic systems. The main idea that

$$J_r = n_r h \qquad J_\phi = n_\theta h \qquad J_\phi = n_\phi h \tag{10.47}$$

has been used to construct the stationary energy levels of an atom. If we do not perturb the stationary states of atoms by sufficiently strong electric and magnetic fields, atomic systems do not make a transition (in the Bohr model of atoms). Thus classical concepts like adiabatic invariants are helpful in making oneself comfortable with the idea of the existence of stationary states of an atom.

10.7 CLASSICAL-QUANTUM ANALOGIES

In this section, we would like to analyse some of the limitations of classical dynamics and see how far the latter can be regarded as a stepping stone towards developing more complete theories of nature, namely the relativistic and quantum theories.

10.7.1 Argument for Constancy of the Speed of Light in Vacuum

We know that Maxwell's electrodynamical equations in usual notations

$$\begin{aligned} \nabla\cdot\boldsymbol{D} &= \rho \qquad \nabla\times\boldsymbol{E} = -\frac{\partial\boldsymbol{B}}{\partial t} \\ \nabla\cdot\boldsymbol{B} &= 0 \qquad \nabla\times\boldsymbol{H} = \boldsymbol{j} + \frac{\partial\boldsymbol{D}}{\partial t} \end{aligned} \tag{10.48}$$

supplemented by the relations

$$\boldsymbol{D} = \varepsilon\boldsymbol{E} \qquad \boldsymbol{B} = \mu\boldsymbol{H} \qquad \boldsymbol{j} = \sigma\boldsymbol{E}$$

can give with a little vector manipulation

$$\nabla\times(\nabla\times\boldsymbol{H}) = \nabla(\nabla\cdot\boldsymbol{H}) - \nabla^2\boldsymbol{H} = -\mu\sigma\frac{\partial\boldsymbol{H}}{\partial t} - \varepsilon\mu\frac{\partial^2\boldsymbol{H}}{\partial t^2}$$

so that one obtains the wave equation in $\boldsymbol{H}$,

$$\frac{\partial^2 \boldsymbol{H}}{\partial t^2} - \frac{1}{\varepsilon\mu}\nabla^2 \boldsymbol{H} + \frac{\sigma}{\varepsilon}\frac{\partial \boldsymbol{H}}{\partial t} = \mathbf{0} \tag{10.49}$$

and similarly for the wave equation in $\boldsymbol{E}$,

$$\frac{\partial^2 \boldsymbol{E}}{\partial t^2} - \frac{1}{\varepsilon\mu}\nabla^2 \boldsymbol{E} + \frac{\sigma}{\varepsilon}\frac{\partial \boldsymbol{E}}{\partial t} = \mathbf{0} \tag{10.50}$$

Since for propagation in free space, the Ohmic conductivity $\sigma = 0$, the dielectric permittivity $\varepsilon = \varepsilon_o$ and the magnetic permeability $\mu = \mu_o$ are constants, the third term in both Eqs (10.49) and (10.50) vanishes, and we get the standard electromagnetic wave equation of the form

$$\frac{\partial^2 \boldsymbol{F}}{\partial t^2} - (v^2\nabla^2)\boldsymbol{F} = \mathbf{0} \tag{10.51}$$

where $v = (\varepsilon_o\mu_o)^{-1/2} = c$ is the constant speed of propagation of the $\boldsymbol{F}$ vector ($\boldsymbol{F}$ can be either $\boldsymbol{E}$ or $\boldsymbol{H}$). Taking the bracketed quantity in Eq. (10.51) as a space dependent operator, the general D'Alembertian solution of Eq.(10.51) is like that of an SHO with its spring constant replaced by the operator $\pm i(\boldsymbol{v}\cdot\nabla)$,

$$\begin{aligned}
\boldsymbol{F}(\boldsymbol{r},t) &= e^{t(\boldsymbol{v}\cdot\nabla)}\boldsymbol{f}_1(\boldsymbol{r}) + e^{-t(\boldsymbol{v}\cdot\nabla)}\boldsymbol{f}_2(\boldsymbol{r}) \\
&= \left(1 + t\boldsymbol{v}\cdot\nabla + \frac{t^2v^2}{2!}\nabla^2 + \cdots\right)\boldsymbol{f}_1(\boldsymbol{r}) + (1 - t\boldsymbol{v}\cdot\nabla + \cdots)\boldsymbol{f}_2(\boldsymbol{r}) \\
&= \boldsymbol{f}_1(\boldsymbol{r} + \boldsymbol{v}t) + \boldsymbol{f}_2(\boldsymbol{r} - \boldsymbol{v}t) \qquad \text{by Taylor's theorem}
\end{aligned}$$

The first one is a solution for backward propagation and the second one is a solution for propagation in the forward direction. The functional forms of $\boldsymbol{f}_1$ and $\boldsymbol{f}_2$ with respect to their arguments can be anything. However, as a particular solution, a monochromatic plane wave can propagate in the forward direction with a constant angular frequency ω and a constant wave vector $\boldsymbol{k}$, such that $\boldsymbol{f}_2$ is described by a cosine function and its argument $\boldsymbol{k}\cdot\boldsymbol{r} - \omega t$ is just $\boldsymbol{k}\cdot(\boldsymbol{r} - \boldsymbol{v}t)$, satisfying the property required by the general solution.

Since the speed of propagation in free space $v = (\varepsilon_o\mu_o)^{-1/2} = c$, depends only on the properties of vacuum, it should not change with respect to any motion of inertial observers. Supposing that it does, we can possibly think of riding on one of the crests of the plane monochromatic electromagnetic wave, which means that we should be able to see totally stationary solutions for the electric and magnetic fields described by

$$\boldsymbol{E} = \boldsymbol{E}_o\cos(\boldsymbol{k}\cdot\boldsymbol{r}) \qquad \boldsymbol{H} = \boldsymbol{H}_o\cos(\boldsymbol{k}\cdot\boldsymbol{r})$$

Putting these expressions in Maxwell's equations, we get

$$\nabla\times\boldsymbol{E} = \mathbf{0} = \nabla\times\boldsymbol{H} \qquad \text{and} \qquad \nabla\cdot\boldsymbol{E} = 0 = \nabla\cdot\boldsymbol{H}$$

When both the divergence and curl of a vector vanish, it is either a constant vector or a null one, implying that we can never ride on a freely propagating plane electromagnetic wave and make it appear stationary. The speed of light in vacuum is a property of vacuum and must be an observer-independent quantity, which is what was postulated by Albert Einstein in his special theory of relativity.

10.7.2 Planck's Quantum Law of Light

In chapter 6, we have seen that if $W(\boldsymbol{r}, t) = \int L dt$ is Hamilton's principal function and $S(\boldsymbol{r}) = \int \boldsymbol{p} \cdot d\boldsymbol{r}$ Hamilton's characteristic function, they should satisfy for free motions

$$W = S - Et = \boldsymbol{p} \cdot \boldsymbol{r} - Et \qquad S = \boldsymbol{p} \cdot \boldsymbol{r} \qquad \boldsymbol{p} = \nabla W \qquad E = -\frac{\partial W}{\partial t}$$

and

$$\frac{dW}{dt} = L = \boldsymbol{p} \cdot \boldsymbol{r} - E \tag{10.52}$$

where E is the constant energy of the particle and $\boldsymbol{p}$ its linear momentum pointing normally to the surfaces of constant W or constant S.

Now if we want to visualise the free propagation of a plane electromagnetic wave as a free motion of a particle, we can exploit the nice similarity between the form of the argument of the cosine wave and the form of the expression for W, as explicit linear functions of $\boldsymbol{r}$ and t. The comparison immediately suggests that

$$\boldsymbol{p} \propto \boldsymbol{k} \qquad \text{and} \qquad E \propto \omega$$

which must have an identical constant of proportionality. If we choose the constant of proportionality to be $\hbar = h/2\pi$, h being the Planck constant, we get the *Planck law of energy*, and Einstein's law of momentum of photons, the quantum of light in particle form, given by

$$E = \hbar\omega = h\nu \qquad \text{and} \qquad \boldsymbol{p} = \hbar\boldsymbol{k} = \frac{h}{\lambda}\hat{\boldsymbol{k}} \tag{10.53}$$

where λ is the wavelength of the monochromatic light. It is now easy to find that the Lagrangian for the motion of light particles is

$$L = pc - E = 0 \qquad \text{and} \qquad W = \hbar(\boldsymbol{k} \cdot \boldsymbol{r} - \omega t) \tag{10.54}$$

Here $W/\hbar$ is now to be interpreted as the phase angle of the electromagnetic wave at $t = 0$, and the vanishing of L is not new (see Eq. (5.18)).

Note also that the increment in the value of S, the Jacobi or Lagrange action, over one complete wavelength is simply h, the Planck constant.

10.7.3 Uncertainty Principle for Photons

Plane monochromatic electromagnetic waves are represented by ideal cosine functions of the phase angle, which have neither a beginning nor an end. In nature the process of emission of light, say by an atom or an accelerating charged particle, cannot be indefinitely long. Hence the best realization of a plane monochromatic beam of light must consist of truncated pieces of EM wave trains, called *packets of waves*. If the individual process of emission of an EM wave lasts for Δt, the length of individual wave packets would be then, $\Delta x = c\Delta t$. Now how to make a packet out of never-ending infinitely long and uniform cosine waves? We know that two propagating cosine waves with nearly equal wavelengths or frequencies can superimpose on each other to produce beats or an envelope of packets. The whole point is that monochromaticity has to be sacrificed. Let us allow a spread in ω as $\Delta\omega$, or equivalently, a spread in wavelength $\Delta\lambda = -c\Delta\nu/\nu^2$, such that across the distance $\Delta x/2$ the wave of wavelength $\lambda + \Delta\lambda$ lags behind that of wavelength λ by $\lambda/2$ and thus produces a totally destructive interference, at the two termini of the wave packet along the x-axis. Thus we minimally require

$$\frac{\Delta x}{\lambda}\Delta\lambda = \lambda \qquad \text{or} \qquad \Delta\nu\Delta t = 1$$

With the Planck law, this condition for photons reads as

$$\Delta E \cdot \Delta t = h = \Delta p \cdot \Delta x \tag{10.55}$$

This is in consistence with Heisenberg's uncertainty principle applied to photons.

10.7.4 Schrödinger's Wave Equation for Matter Particles

Since the linear momentum of a particle is given by ∇W, the particle always moves normal to the surfaces of constant W and its magnitude is given by the space rate of change of W, that is the change over unit distance along this normal, keeping of course time as constant. If W is expressed in units of $\hbar$ by defining an imaginary dimensionless parameter $-i\Psi$ through the relation $W = -i\hbar\Psi$, $i = \sqrt{-1}$, then we would have

$$\boldsymbol{p} = -i\hbar\nabla\Psi \tag{10.56}$$

$$E = H = -\frac{\partial W}{\partial t} = i\hbar\frac{\partial\Psi}{\partial t} \tag{10.57}$$

and the Hamilton-Jacobi equation would read as

$$-\frac{\hbar^2}{2m}\nabla^2\Psi + V\Psi = i\hbar\frac{\partial\Psi}{\partial t} \tag{10.58}$$

The classical-quantum correspondences are now transparent. *Schrödinger's wave equation* is the quantum mechanical form of the classical Hamilton-Jacobi equation of motion. Instead of finding a solution to the W function, one looks for a solution to the Ψ function. It is the interpretation of Ψ and the involvement of complex numbers in the Schrödinger equation that deviate from the spirit of classical descriptions.

10.7.5 Commutator Relations

Let us suppose that A, B, C and D are any four dynamical variables that are functions of coordinates and momenta. The Poisson bracket of the products AB and CD can be expressed in the following two equivalent ways:

$$[AB, CD] = A[B, CD] + [A, CD]B = AC[B, D] + A[B, C]D + [A, C]DB + C[A, D]B$$

and

$$[AB, CD] = [AB, C]D + C[AB, D] = A[B, C]D + [A, C]BD + CA[B, D] + C[A, D]B$$

keeping the proper order. On comparison, we find

$$AC[B, D] + [A, C]DB = [A, C]BD + CA[B, D]$$

or

$$(AC - CA)[B, D] = (BD - DB)[A, C]$$

This is satisfied provided

$$AC - CA = \alpha[A, C] \quad \text{and} \quad BD - DB = \alpha[B, D]$$

where α is any universal constant. The quantum-classical correspondences between quantum commutator relations and classical Poisson brackets suggest that $\alpha = i\hbar$, so that for any two dynamical variables A and B,

$$AB - BA = i\hbar[A, B] \tag{10.59}$$

Understandably, from the dimensional point of view, the Poisson bracket contains an extra dimension of the angular momentum or action in its denominator, which is killed by the dimension of $\hbar$ in Eq. (10.59).

The entire chapter 9 can be converted into a topic of quantum commutator relations, with $\boldsymbol{p}$ substituted by $-i\hbar\nabla$ and $\boldsymbol{r}$ for $\boldsymbol{x}$. For example, the angular momentum operator becomes $-i\hbar\boldsymbol{r} \times \nabla$.

Werner Heisenberg, Max Born and Pascal Jordan showed in 1925 that the ordinary Hamiltonian equations of dynamics were still valid in quantum theory, provided the symbols representing the coordinates and momentum in classical dynamics are interpreted as operators whose products did not commute. Two years later Heisenberg put forward the uncertainty principle which vindicated Hamilton's intuition of the duality between generalised coordinates and generalised momenta.

10.7.6 De Broglie Hypothesis

Let us consider the motion of a free particle both classically and quantum mechanically. The Hamilton-Jacobi equation

$$\frac{1}{2m}\left(\frac{\partial W}{\partial \boldsymbol{r}}\right)^2 + V = -\frac{\partial W}{\partial t} = E \quad \text{with} \quad \nabla W = \boldsymbol{p}$$

yields the usual solution $W = \boldsymbol{p}\cdot\boldsymbol{r} - Et$. Now its quantum mechanical equivalent, the Schrödinger equation

$$-\frac{\hbar^2}{2m}\nabla^2\Psi = i\hbar\frac{\partial \Psi}{\partial t} = E\Psi \quad \text{with} \quad \boldsymbol{p}\Psi = -i\hbar\nabla\Psi$$

produces a solution

$$\Psi(\boldsymbol{r},t) = \Psi_o\, e^{i(\boldsymbol{k}\cdot\boldsymbol{r} - \omega t)} \qquad k^2 = \frac{2mE}{\hbar^2}, \qquad \omega = \frac{E}{\hbar} \qquad \text{and}$$

$$\boldsymbol{p} = \hbar\boldsymbol{k} \qquad \text{or} \qquad \text{the wavelength} = \lambda = \frac{h}{p} \tag{10.60}$$

So the quantum solution for a free particle motion corresponds to a plane monochromatic wave propagating in the same direction as the momentum of the classical particle. If there is a beam of particles with a sufficiently small spread in energy, the assembly of waves turns into packets, the group velocity of which ($v_g = d\omega/dk$), from the above expressions for ω and k is found to be p/m = the classical speed of the particle. So Eq. (10.60) represents the mathematical form of De Broglie's hypothesis, namely a reciprocal relation between the momentum of a particle and its wavelength of propagation in its wave form. According to the above hypothesis every particle can be thought of as a moving train of waves having the wave vector $\boldsymbol{k}$ and angular frequency ω, as given above.

If we now closely scrutinize and compare the equations and solutions for the classical and quantum descriptions, we can note the following points:

(a) The classical equation is a second degree first order partial differential equation in W, whereas the quantum equation looks like a diffusion equation with its time part containing an imaginary coefficient.

(b) Both the equations are usually solved by the method of separation of variables, but the classical one as a sum and the quantum one as a product of two functions.

(c) The time part has a solution linearly varying with time for the classical equation, but has an oscillatory exponential behaviour for the quantum equation. The same is also true for the space part.

It is nevertheless nice to see that the classical free particle solution for W appears as a factor in the exponent of its quantum solution, namely the Ψ function, that is,

$$\Psi(\boldsymbol{r},t) = \Psi_o\, e^{iW/\hbar} \tag{10.61}$$

This particular classical to quantum correspondence has been fully exploited by Richard Feynman in developing his path integral formulation of quantum mechanics. Since the function $W = \int_1^2 L dt$, and its variation over different chosen paths keeping the end point coordinates (not momenta) fixed vanishes near the actual path, by Hamilton's principle, the correspondence becomes all the more meaningful.

10.7.7 Bohr-Sommerfeld Quantisations of Atomic States

This has already been hinted at the end of section 10.6. The main problem with classical atoms is that they are unstable. Classical electrodynamics predicts that any accelerating charged particle having electric charge e, mass m and acceleration $\boldsymbol{a}$ should radiate electromagnetic radiation with power $P = \mu_o e^2 a/6\pi c$. If in a hydrogen atom the electron is revolving in a circular orbit of radius about 0.05 nm with a speed of about 2200 km/s, it will be orbiting at a rate of about 7×10^{15} revolutions per second. But because of its tremendous centripetal acceleration of about 2.5×10^{21} times g, the electron will radiate and spiral into the nucleus in about 10^{-11} second. Why are then the atoms so stable?

The classical theories completely break down on this point. But if you use the De Broglie hypothesis, you can calculate the wavelength of the matter wave associated with the speeding electron around the nucleus, and compare it with the perimeter of the orbit ($2\pi r$). If they match by any exact integer factor, the waves would superimpose onto themselves all the time and form stationary states. Thus the condition for the occurrence of the stationary states would be

$$2\pi r = n\lambda = \frac{nh}{p}$$

or in terms of the orbital angular momentum J of the electron

$$J = pr = nh \tag{10.62}$$

where n is any positive integer. This condition is known as the ***Bohr condition*** for stationary states of all hydrogen like atoms, after its Danish inventor Niels Bohr (1913). However, Bohr proposed it as a hypothesis, and started calling n as the *principal quantum number*, years later. The angular momenta of the stationary orbits are discrete and jump only in integral multiple of h.

Within two years W. Wilson and Arnold Sommerfeld independently suggested that the circular orbits of the Bohr atom ought to be replaced by elliptic orbits. They were compelled to postulate a new, azimuthal quantum number to relate to the ratio of minor to major axes of the ellipse. They proposed the phase integrals $\oint p_i dq_i$ to be similarly quantised as Bohr's, and gave two quantum conditions instead of one given by Bohr in Eq.(10.62),

$$\oint p_r dr = n_r h \qquad \text{and} \qquad \oint p_\psi d\psi = n_k h \tag{10.63}$$

where n_r is called the *radial quantum number* and n_k the *azimuthal quantum number*, the ψ-motion being described in the plane of the orbit. They showed the ratio of the minor to major axis of the elliptical orbit is simply $k/(n_r + n_k)$, and the energy of the electron in that orbit is proportional to $(n_r + n_k)^{-2}$. The *principal quantum number* n is defined to be $n = n_r + n_k$, where $n \geq n_k > 0$, with $n_k = 1, 2, 3, 4, \ldots$ are spectroscopically identified as *sharp* (s), *principal* (p), *diffuse* (d), *fundamental* (f), ... series of spectral lines respectively. For a given n, the degeneracies in energy for the possible range of n_k were shown by Sommerfeld to be removed due to special relativistic variation of mass over elliptical orbits.

The connection of these phase integrals with the action variables and the link between action variables and adiabatic invariants were pointed out by Epstein (1916) and Schwarzschild (1916). This paper of Schwarzschild was published on the day he died. Schwarzschild showed that there should be three quantum conditions (10.47) for three adiabatic invariants or action integrals; with $n_k = n_\theta + n_\phi$, n_θ being the *latitudinal quantum number*, and n_ϕ the *equatorial* or *magnetic quantum number*. Since the Kepler problem could also be treated in parabolic coordinates, the question was whether parabolic quantum numbers should also give the same answer to the energy levels. This ambiguity was successfully resolved by both

Epstein and Schwarzschild, and the results of computation for the Stark effect in parabolic coordinates agreed well with those computed on the basis of the spherical polar coordinates (work out the problem no 10.6).

In a sense, all these developments glorified the accidental symmetries of the Coulomb field in atoms, as well the power of the well-developed classical techniques for handling such subtle issues.

10.8 SUMMARY

The standard method of formulating and solving any dynamical problem according to the Hamilton-Jacobi theory has been given. Like D'Alembert's principle, the formulated problem reduces to a single equation, in the present case a first order partial differential equation (of usually the second degree). By Jacobi's theorem any complete integral of this partial differential equation is capable of producing the full solution to the problem.

However, finding a complete integral is the most challenging part of this scheme. Complete separability of variables becomes a precondition to finding a complete integral, and therefore, only those problems can be fully studied for which complete separability in the chosen variables is achieved. Subject to this, all the hidden constants of motion, however complicated in form, can be found out. In the following chapter we shall see that for small oscillations, the separability is guaranteed, — obviously not for any arbitrary motion of the system but for small amplitude oscillations. The necessary and sufficient conditions for complete separability for any arbitrary dynamical system are given by Levi Civita.

Periodic systems can be studied with the help of action angle variables provided the systems are conservative and completely separable in coordinates. All the frequencies can easily be found out without solving the equations of motion. Only in degenerate cases can more than one set of coordinates make the characteristic function completely separable.

Adiabatic invariants are extremely useful for handling periodic systems that are subject to slow perturbation. In nature, no finite system can be considered as totally closed. Periodic systems react in such a way that all the action integrals of the system remain unchanged to the first order of perturbation. Even atoms do not make a transition unless a sufficiently strong perturbation is given to the system leading to a direct change in the action integrals that label the orbitals.

The final section on classical-quantum correspondences points out the fact that classical mechanics has indeed provided not only all the raw material but also a fully developed infrastructure needed for the early development of quantum mechanics at an extraordinarily fast pace.

PROBLEMS

10.1 Prove Jacobi's theorem for the time independent Hamilton-Jacobi theory.

10.2 Solve for the parabolic motion of projectiles under the constant force of earth's gravity by using the Hamilton-Jacobi method.

10.3 Consider the motion of a body of unit mass on the constrained path $y = \cosh x$ under a potential $V = x^2/2$. Solve Hamilton's equations of motion directly as well as by using the Hamilton-Jacobi method.

10.4 Find the canonical transformation through the solution of the Hamilton-Jacobi equation, the generating function for which is $F_2 = S(q, P)$ that transforms the Hamiltonian

$$H(q,p) = \frac{p^2}{2m} + \frac{m\omega^2 q^2}{2}$$

to $K(Q,P) = f(P)$ only.

10.5 Solve the Hamilton-Jacobi equation for a particle moving under a potential field given by

$$V(r) = \frac{\boldsymbol{a} \cdot \boldsymbol{r}}{r^3}$$

the field of a dipole, where $\boldsymbol{a}$ is the constant dipole moment vector. Choose the z-axis along $\boldsymbol{a}$. Find the integrals of motion and the total cross-section for particle absorption into the central region of $V(r)$.

10.6 Separate the variables in the Hamilton-Jacobi equations for the problem of the Stark effect with the potential

$$V(r, z) = \frac{k^2}{r} + Ez$$

where E is the applied constant electric field along the z-axis, using the parabolic coordinates u, v and ϕ:

$$x = \sqrt{uv} \cos\phi \qquad y = \sqrt{uv} \sin\phi \qquad z = (u - v)/2$$

10.7 Find the action and angle variables for the potential energy $V(q) = V_o \tan^2(\alpha q)$, where V_o and α are positive constants. What is the angular frequency of oscillation?

10.8 Show that the motion of a particle of mass m under a noncentral potential energy

$$V(\boldsymbol{r}) = \frac{\beta^2}{2mr^2} \sec^2\theta - \frac{k}{r}$$

leads to identical expressions for the action integrals J_r and J_ϕ as those of Kepler's problem. Find the energy function as $E(J_r, J_\theta, J_\phi)$ and show further that the frequencies $\nu_r = \nu_\phi$ but $\nu_\theta = 2\nu_\phi$.

10.9 A particle moves inside an elastic sphere, the radius of which changes slowly. How does its energy change?

10.10 Determine the change in the energy of a charged particle moving in a central field of potential $V(r)$ when a weak uniform magnetic field $\boldsymbol{B}$ is slowly switched on. Take the Hamiltonian

$$H = \frac{1}{2m}\left(p_r^2 + \frac{p_\theta^2}{r^2} + \frac{p_\phi^2}{r^2 \sin^2\theta}\right) + mV(r) - \frac{1}{2m} eBp_\phi$$

11
Small Oscillations

11.0 INTRODUCTION

So far we have been dealing with dynamical systems moving under given constraints, and sought for complete solutions as functions of the initial conditions and time. However, in many situations we notice that a dynamical system is apparently at rest or in some steady state condition. If we give a small perturbation to the system possibly by pushing or shaking it a little bit, only two things may happen: either the system as a whole or part of it settles in a to-and-fro oscillation about its original position or configuration, or it moves away and does not return to its original position at all. In this chapter, we shall study the fate of all possible small perturbations given to a dynamical system in mechanical equilibrium, and see under what circumstances oscillations are possible, and with what frequencies, phase lags, etc.

The theory of small oscillations was developed primarily by Lagrange, D'Alembert, Poincaré, and Liapounoff. In recent times, stability analysis has become an extremely important part of all kinds of dynamical investigations. The key question is, given a small perturbation, does it grow with time or, equivalently, what is the dispersion relation (see Eqs (11.23) and (11.24)) for imposed periodic solutions?

11.1 TYPES OF EQUILIBRIA AND THE POTENTIAL AT EQUILIBRIUM

An equilibrium state of a system is defined to be one in which all forces (internal as well as external) cancel for some configuration of the system. A system in a state of equilibrium, continues to be in that state for all times unless perturbed by an external agency. However, the concept of equilibrium can also be defined without making any reference to force. It can be defined as a state in which the time derivatives of physical variables (observables) vanish. Therefore, this definition can very well be used in the context of quantum mechanical descriptions.

Equilibria are classified in the following way.

Static Equilibrium

The state of zero kinetic energy continues for an indefinite period, and the immediate surrounding of the system is not changing with time. An example is a stone at the bottom of a valley.

Dynamic Equilibrium

The net force on the system is zero and the system continues with zero kinetic energy, but the immediate surroundings of the system change with time in such a way that it exerts a balancing force on the system which contributes to the nct force experienced by the system. Examples: charge neutrality of atoms, molecules and solids makes them exert zero electrical force on one another, but each of them is in dynamical equilibrium. To give another example, consider a ball static on the head of a fountain. It has zero kinetic energy, but its immediate surrounding is changing all the time, hence it is in dynamical equilibrium.

Stable Equilibrium

Given a small displacement, the system tends to return to the original equilibrium configuration. Example: the bob of a simple pendulum in its equilibrium state satisfies the above stability criterion.

Unstable Equilibrium

Given a small displacement, the system does not return to the original equilibrium configuration. Example: a large stone sitting on the upper edge of a cliff.

Metastable Equilibrium

Given a sufficiently large displacement, the system fails to return, although for smaller displacements it could return to the original equilibrium configuration. Example: a balloon which explodes above a certain gas pressure.

Let us now consider the dynamical configuration of the system from the point of view of energy, particularly potential energy. The total energy of a conservative system is given by

$$E = T + V = \text{kinetic energy} + \text{potential energy}$$

Since kinetic energy is always a non-negative quantity ($T \geq 0$), we must have $E \geq V$ for allowed motions, and the system can stay at the equilibrium state ($T = 0$) only if $E = V$. We know that for a conservative system the total energy E cannot change with time so that

$$E = E_o = \text{const.}$$

and for the system at rest and at equilibrium,

$$V = V_o = \text{const.} = E_o$$

Now in order to judge the stability of an equilibrium state, we have to give a small perturbation to the system. For simplicity, let us consider the motion in one dimension, and assume that the potential energy V is a given function of the space coordinate x. Let the system be in a state of static stable equilibrium with energy E_o and position x_o (see Fig. 11.1). Obviously the kinetic energy of the system in this state is zero ($T_o = 0$). Now let us displace the system to a nearby point x_1 (by applying some external force other than the given potential field) and release it. (The extra perturbing force is then switched off.) The potential energy of the system at x_1 is now $V(x_1)$ and the kinetic energy at x_1 is zero. So

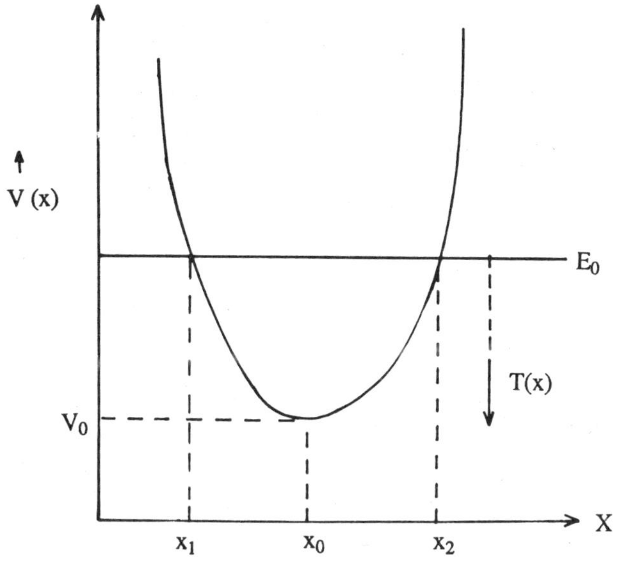

Fig. 11.1 Potential energy for a 1-D motion of a system, as a function of its position, and the limits of allowed motion for a given energy of the system

the total energy at x_1 is $E = V(x_1)$. By the definition of stable equilibrium the system should stay around x_o and should never go very much farther than $|x_1 - x_o|$. Since the motion has to be bounded on both sides of x_o, the kinetic energy of the system becomes zero at the two extreme points. Let the other extreme point be at $x = x_2$. The kinetic energy over the interval $x_1 \leq x \leq x_2$ is gained by the system through the difference of its potential energies at x and at x_1 (or x_2), that is,

$$T(x) = V(x_1) - V(x) = V(x_2) - V(x)$$

Since $V(x_1) = V(x_2)$, by Rolle's theorem there exists at least one point in $x_1 < x < x_2$ such that

$$\frac{dV}{dx} = 0 = \frac{dT}{dx}$$

and this is precisely the point x_o at which no force acts on the system as $\nabla V = 0$. But $T(x) > 0$ in $x_1 < x < x_2$, implying that $T(x)$ is maximum at x_o, or in other words, x_o must be a point of local minimum of the function $V(x)$. Conversely, if at some coordinate position of a conservative system, the potential energy has a strict minimum then this position is the position of stable equilibrium of the system. This is called *Lagrange's theorem of stable equilibrium.*

By the above considerations we must have, for a system in stable equilibrium at a position x_o

$$\left.\frac{dV}{dx}\right|_{x = x_o} = 0 \quad \text{and} \quad \left.\frac{d^2V}{dx^2}\right|_{x = x_o} > 0 \tag{11.1}$$

The first of these two equations follows simply from the requirement that the net external force on the system in equilibrium must vanish.

Now let us expand $V(x)$ in the vicinity of the stable equilibrium position x_o. This gives

$$V(x) = V(x_o) + \left(\frac{dV}{dx}\right)_{x = x_o} (x - x_o) + \frac{1}{2!}\left(\frac{d^2V}{dx^2}\right)_{x = x_o} (x - x_o)^2 + \ldots \qquad (11.2)$$

Let us further choose the origin of the coordinate system at the position of the equilibrium so that $x_o = 0$ and also choose $V(x_o) = V(0) = 0$. Using Eq. (11.1) and neglecting higher order terms in Eq. (11.2) we get

$$V(x) = \frac{1}{2}kx^2 \qquad (11.3)$$

where $k > 0$ is the constant value of (d^2V/dx^2) at $x = x_o = 0$. Now, the kinetic energy of the system is

$$T = \frac{1}{2}mv^2$$

so that the Lagrangian of the system *slightly* displaced from the position of stable equilibrium, for the 1-D case, becomes

$$L(x, \dot{x}) = \frac{1}{2}mv^2 - \frac{1}{2}kx^2 = \frac{1}{2}m\dot{x}^2 - \frac{1}{2}kx^2 \qquad (11.4)$$

This gives rise to the equation of motion in the form

$$m\ddot{x} + kx = 0 \qquad (11.5)$$

Since both k and m are positive constants, Eq. (11.5) is an equation of motion for a simple harmonic oscillator, whose solution is given by

$$x = c_1 \cos(\omega t) + c_2 \sin(\omega t)$$

where

$$\omega = \sqrt{\frac{k}{m}}$$

or

$$x = a\cos(\omega t + \delta) \qquad (11.6)$$

with

$$c_1 = a\cos\delta \qquad c_2 = -a\sin\delta \qquad a = \sqrt{c_1^2 + c_2^2}$$

and

$$\delta = \tan^{-1}\left(-\frac{c_2}{c_1}\right)$$

Therefore, the frequency of oscillation is simply the square root of the ratio of the coefficient of x^2 in the expression for potential energy and that of v^2 in the expression for kinetic energy.

In terms of the initial coordinate x_o and initial speed v_o, the expressions for the amplitude a and the phase δ become

$$a = \sqrt{x_o^2 + \frac{v_o^2}{\omega^2}} \qquad \text{and} \qquad \delta = \tan^{-1}\left(-\frac{v_o}{\omega x_o}\right)$$

The solution can be also expressed in terms of complex quantities, for example,

$$x = \text{Re}\left[Ae^{i\omega t}\right] \tag{11.7}$$

where

$$A = ae^{i\delta}$$

is the complex amplitude containing information on the phase.

The total energy of the system is

$$E = \frac{1}{2}m\omega^2 a^2 \tag{11.8}$$

Thus we see that a system in stable equilibrium, when displaced from its equilibrium configuration, performs, in the first approximation (that is, when the displacement and the resulting amplitude is small), harmonic oscillations about its equilibrium configuration, whose equation of motion is given by Eq. (11.5), and the general solutions by Eqs (11.6) or (11.7).

We now give some examples of the systems which perform small oscillations about their equilibrium configurations, and the ways in which these oscillations manifest themselves in practice.

1. Small natural oscillations of diatomic molecules in a mixture of different isotopes, say $^{12}C^{16}O$, $^{14}C^{16}O$, $^{12}C^{18}O$, etc. of carbon monoxide, for example.

The situation is depicted in Fig. 11.2a. The masses m_1 and m_2 of the two component atoms differ slightly for different isotopes of these two elements. Denoting by l_o the equilibrium distance between the nuclei of the atoms making the molecule, and by x the deviation of this distance from l_o, the Lagrangian for this vibrating system is

$$L = \frac{1}{2}\mu v^2 - \frac{1}{2}kx^2 \tag{11.9}$$

where μ is the reduced mass of the system given by

$$\frac{1}{\mu} = \frac{1}{m_1} + \frac{1}{m_2}$$

Here k is the spring constant of vibration of the molecule, which depends on the electronic distribution in the molecule and is approximately same for different isotopic combinations. Thus the frequency of vibration of the molecule is given by

$$\omega = \sqrt{\frac{k}{\mu}} = \sqrt{\frac{k(m_1 + m_2)}{m_1 m_2}} \tag{11.10}$$

The ratio ω'/ω of frequencies for the same orbital configurations in two different isotopic

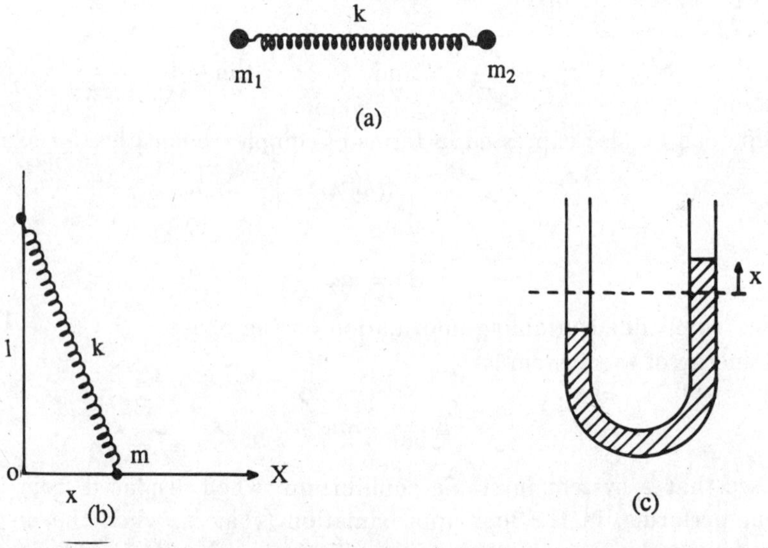

Fig. 11.2 Examples of oscillators: (a) a diatomic molecule, (b) 1-D constrained motion of a particle on a horizontal line when the particle is tied to one end of a spring (of length l in its relaxed state), the other end being fixed at a height l above the origin, (c) a column of liquid in a U-tube

combinations having reduced masses μ' and μ, is given by

$$\frac{\omega'}{\omega} = \sqrt{\frac{m_1 m_2 (m_1' + m_2')}{m_1' m_2' (m_1 + m_2)}} \tag{11.11}$$

Hence by measuring ω' and ω, the difference between the isotopic reduced masses can be determined, which will help identify the isotopes themselves.

2. The small oscillations of a massless spring fixed at one end A (see Fig. 11.2b) and the other end carrying a particle of mass m which is constrained to move on a horizontal axis.

The spring requires a force $\boldsymbol{F} = |\boldsymbol{F}|$ when its lower end is at B. We want to find the frequency of oscillation of the particle if the spring constant is k, and the length AB $= l$.

The potential energy of the spring at any point at a distance x from B, compared to that at B, is given by

$$V = \boldsymbol{F} \cdot \boldsymbol{\delta l}$$

For $x \ll l$, $|\delta l| = \sqrt{l^2 + x^2} - l \simeq x^2/2l$, and therefore $V = Fx^2/2l$. Thus the Lagrangian for the system is

$$L = \frac{1}{2} m\dot{x}^2 - \frac{1}{2}\frac{Fx^2}{l}$$

giving the frequency of oscillation

$$\omega = \sqrt{\frac{F/l}{m}} = \sqrt{\frac{F}{ml}}$$

3. The small amplitude oscillation of a column of mercury of total length L that partially fills a U tube (see Fig. 11.2c), having a cross sectional area A.

The tube is rocked gently so that the column of mercury begins to oscillate. We want to find the period of oscillation.

The magnitude of the force which restores the body to its equilibrium position is given by

$$F = \rho g \, \Delta(\text{volume}) = 2\rho g A x = kx \qquad \text{say}$$

Thus

$$\omega_o = \sqrt{\frac{k}{m}} = \sqrt{\frac{2\rho g A}{\rho A L}} = \sqrt{\frac{2g}{L}}$$

11.2 STUDY OF SMALL OSCILLATIONS USING GENERALISED COORDINATES

Consider a scleronomic and holonomic dynamical system having n DOF and the generalised coordinates $(q_1, \ldots, q_n)$. Let this system be in a state of stable equilibrium. We shift the origin of the coordinate system so that the equilibrium configuration corresponds to $0 = q_1 = \ldots = q_n$. The kinetic energy of the system in the state of stable equilibrium vanishes. Moreover, once in the state of stable equilibrium, the system remains in that state for an indefinite period of time. Therefore, the Lagrangian L of a system in a state of stable equilibrium reduces to $L = T - V = -V$. Now if V is a function of only $\{q_i\}$, the state of stable equilibrium would correspond to

$$\frac{d}{dt}\left(-\frac{\partial V}{\partial \dot{q}_i}\right)_o + \left(\frac{\partial V}{\partial q_i}\right)_o = 0 \tag{11.12}$$

where the lower suffix o implies that the derivatives are to be evaluated at the origin. Since V is assumed to depend only on $\{q_i\}$ the first term in Eq. (11.12) vanishes, reducing it to

$$\left(\frac{\partial V}{\partial q_i}\right)_o = 0 \tag{11.13}$$

In other words, the generalised forces evaluated at the position of equilibrium must vanish. Moreover, the stability of the equilibrium state requires that the equilibrium configuration correspond to a local minimum of the function $V(q_i)$, or, that in the δ-neighbourhood of the point of equilibrium (in the configuration space), the potential function $V(q_i)$ should monotonically increase from its value at the equilibrium point. Otherwise, if the system at the equilibrium position is disturbed infinitesimally, its kinetic energy can increase, keeping its total energy constant, and the system moves away from the state of equilibrium at the slightest possible perturbation. Thus we must have

$$V(q_1, \ldots, q_n) > V(0, \ldots, 0)$$

for all points in some neighbourhood of the origin. Setting $V(0, \ldots, 0) = 0$, without losing any generality, the above inequality becomes

$$V(q_1, \ldots, q_n) \geq 0 \tag{11.14}$$

with the equality applying only at the origin.

Expanding V in a Taylor's series in q_i for small values of q_i 's one gets

$$\begin{aligned} V(q_1, \ldots, q_n) &= V(0, \ldots, 0) + \left(\frac{\partial V}{\partial q_i}\right)_o q_i + \frac{1}{2!}\left(\frac{\partial^2 V}{\partial q_i \partial q_j}\right)_o q_i q_j \\ &+ \frac{1}{3!}\left(\frac{\partial^3 V}{\partial q_i \partial q_j \partial q_k}\right)_o q_i q_j q_k + \text{higher order terms} \end{aligned}$$

The first term vanishes by choice, the second term vanishes by condition (11.13), and by the inequality (11.14) we must have Writing

$$b_{ij} = \frac{1}{2}\left(\frac{\partial^2 V}{\partial q_i \partial q_j}\right)_o$$

which are constants strictly independent of q_i 's, the positivity condition on V given by Eq. (11.14) becomes

$$b_{ij} q_i q_j \geq 0 \tag{11.15}$$

with the equality holding only at the origin ($q_1 = q_2 = \ldots = q_n = 0$). Inequality (11.15) can be written, in terms of matrices as follows

$$(q_1 \ \cdots \ q_n)\begin{pmatrix} b_{11} & \cdots & b_{1n} \\ \vdots & & \vdots \\ b_{n1} & \cdots & b_{nn} \end{pmatrix}\begin{pmatrix} q_1 \\ \vdots \\ q_n \end{pmatrix} \geq 0 \tag{11.16}$$

Since q_i 's are arbitrary (except for being defined in some small neighbourhood of the origin) the Eq. (11.16) is really a condition on the nature of the matrix $[b_{ij}]$ requiring it to be ***positive definite*** (that is, determinants of all orders upto n formed out of $[b_{ij}]$ are non-zero and positive). Thus the stability of the equilibrium at the origin requires that $[b_{ij}]$ as defined by Eq. (11.15) be a positive definite matrix.

Similarly the kinetic energy of a scleronomic system is homogeneously quadratic in the generalised velocities and is given by

$$T = a'_{ij}\dot{q}_i\dot{q}_j$$

where $\{a'_{ij}\}$ in general, are functions of q_i 's. Expanding a'_{ij} around the origin (a point of stable equilibrium) in Taylor's series, we get

$$a'_{ij}(q_1, \ldots, q_n) = a'_{ij}(0, \ldots, 0) + \left(\frac{\partial a'_{ij}}{\partial q_k}\right)_o q_k + \frac{1}{2!}\left(\frac{\partial^2 a'_{ij}}{\partial q_k \partial q_l}\right)_o q_k q_l + \ldots$$

Now it turns out that in most of the cases, the quantities $(\partial a'_{ij}/\partial q_k)$ and their higher order derivatives evaluated at the origin are negligible. In the case of Cartesian coordinates these are exactly zero; for spherical polar coordinates these are of second order smallness.

Hence, to a good approximation, the a'_{ij}'s are taken to be their values at the position of stable equilibrium, that is, the origin, and are therefore set to

$$a_{ij} = a'_{ij}(0,\ldots,0)$$

Therefore, the kinetic energy is given by

$$T = a_{ij}\dot{q}_i\dot{q}_j \geq 0 \tag{11.17}$$

which is once again a non-negative quantity, the equality holding only for the case when all $\dot{q}_i$'s are zero.

Again, the inequality in (11.17) is a matrix inequality involving the matrix $[a_{ij}]$ and column vectors $[\dot{q}_i]$ and $[\dot{q}_j]$. Thus $[a_{ij}]$ is also a *positive definite matrix.* Further, we note that

$$b_{ij} \equiv \frac{1}{2}\left(\frac{\partial^2 V}{\partial q_i \partial q_j}\right)_o = b_{ji}$$

and

$$a_{ij} \equiv \frac{1}{2}\left(\frac{\partial^2 T}{\partial \dot{q}_i \partial \dot{q}_j}\right)_o = a_{ji} \tag{11.18}$$

Equations (11.18) imply that both $[a_{ij}]$ and $[b_{ij}]$ are symmetric matrices. Further, since all $\{q_i\}$ and $\{q_j\}$ are real, $[a_{ij}]$ and $[b_{ij}]$ must also be real by their definitions. Hence both $[a_{ij}]$ and $[b_{ij}]$ are *real symmetric positive definite matrices* of order $(n \times n)$, where n is the number of DOF of the system.

Now we can proceed to form the Lagrangian and Lagrange's equations of motion for small oscillations in the coordinates q_i 's. We have

$$L = T - V = (a_{ij}\dot{q}_i\dot{q}_j - b_{ij}q_iq_j) \tag{11.19}$$

where a_{ij} 's and b_{ij} 's are constants independent of time and coordinates, and the summation over i and j is implied. Lagrange's equations of motion are, therefore, given by

$$(a_{ij}\ddot{q}_j + b_{ij}q_j) = 0 \qquad i = 1,\ldots,n \tag{11.20}$$

These are n equations of coupled harmonic motion, each equation having n coupled terms involving, in general, all the n generalised coordinates and their second order total time derivatives.

Let us look for a solution corresponding to each of the n coordinates executing an SHM with a single period (or, equivalently, with the same angular frequency, say p) given by

$$q_j = A_j \exp(\sqrt{-1}\, pt) \qquad \text{for } j = 1,\ldots,n \tag{11.21}$$

with the amplitudes A_j which are in general complex (containing a phase factor $\exp\sqrt{-1}\theta$). If such a secular solution exists, it would correspond to what is called *normal mode* of small oscillations in which each and every generalised coordinate of the system (that is, the system as a whole) oscillates with a single frequency p, but the amplitudes (and phases) of oscillation might differ from coordinate to coordinate.

Let us now use the expressions (11.21) as the desired solutions to Eqs (11.20) and see under what conditions the system oscillates in a normal mode. So we substitute these might differ from coordinate to coordinate.

Let us now use the expressions (11.21) as the desired solutions to Eqs (11.20) and see under what conditions the system oscillates in a normal mode. So we substitute these required solutions in the differential equations of motion (Eq. (11.20)) which results in the following set of n simultaneous algebraic equations in A_j

$$- a_{ij}p^2 A_j + b_{ij} A_j = 0 \qquad i = 1, \ldots, n \tag{11.22}$$

Obviously the A_j 's occurring in Eq. (11.21) must be the solutions of the matrix Eq. (11.22).

A trivial solution of Eq. (11.22) is, of course, that all the A_j 's $= 0$, which means no oscillations at all. Existence of a non-trivial solution is guaranteed, however, subject to the condition that

$$\det \|b_{ij} - a_{ij}p^2\| = 0 \tag{11.23}$$

Equation (11.23) is a single algebraic equation involving an nth degree polynomial in p^2, which has n roots, of which some or all are distinct and by nature can be either real or complex. We are, of course, interested in the solutions corresponding to p^2 $(= \lambda$ say) that admit oscillatory modes. This means that out of all the n roots of the Eq. (11.23) we choose only the real and positive ones ($p^2 \geq 0$). (Otherwise, hyperbolic solutions would mean runaway solutions for stable equilibrium!) In fact we expect that all the n roots of p^2 must be ≥ 0 for any small perturbations about a stable equilibrium.

By now we know that $[a_{ij}]$ and $[b_{ij}]$ are real, symmetric and positive definite matrices in the expression for the Lagrangian near any stable equilibrium. What do these properties imply for the nature of p^2? To see this, consider the characteristic Eqs (11.22), assuming that p^2 is one of the roots of Eq. (11.23). Multiplying Eq. (11.22) by A_i^* and summing over i we get

$$(b_{ij} - p^2 a_{ij}) A_i^* A_j = 0$$

where A_i^* is the complex conjugate of A_i. Separating the two sets of terms we get (this time showing all the summations explicitly)

$$\sum_{i,j} b_{ij} A_i^* A_j = p^2 \sum_{i,j} a_{ij} A_i^* A_j$$

or

$$p^2 = \frac{\sum_{i,j} b_{ij} A_i^* A_j}{\sum_{i,j} a_{ij} A_i^* A_j} \tag{11.24}$$

From the symmetry of b_{ij}

$$b_{ij} A_i^* A_j = b_{ij} A_j^* A_i$$

Hence, $b_{ij} A_i^* A_j$ and similarly $a_{ij} A_i^* A_j$ are both real. So, p^2 is also real. From Eq. (11.22) it then follows that the ratio of any two A_k's are also real. Therefore

$$A_i = (A_i)_{\text{real, positive}}\, e^{\sqrt{-1}\theta}$$

which means that the phases are the same or opposite (that is, differ by π) so that

$$A_i = \pm\, (A_i)_{\text{real, positive}}\, e^{\sqrt{-1}\theta} \tag{11.25}$$

The binary solutions expressed in Eq. (11.25) imply that

$$A_i^* A_j \;=\; \pm\,(A_i)_{\text{real, positive}}\,(A_j)_{\text{real, positive}} \tag{11.26}$$

where the plus sign is for the pair having identical phases and the minus sign for the opposite phases.

Equations (11.24) and (11.26) together with the fact that $[b_{ij}]$ and $[a_{ij}]$ are positive definite, real and symmetric matrices guarantee that all $p^2 > 0$. Thus we see that normal modes of oscillations are possible. One can excite the whole system with a single frequency choosing any one of the n roots of Eq.(11.23). However, not all coordinates will execute the SHM with the same phase, but their mutual phases, if not same, must differ by π only. There could be a maximum of n distinct normal modes if all the n roots of Eq. (11.23) coupled with Eq. (11.25) are distinct. Otherwise some modes will have the same frequency. Such normal modes are said to be *degenerate.* The frequencies of normal modes, that is, the roots of Eq. (11.23) are called *eigen-frequencies of vibration* of the system.

To give an example, let us take a tight horizontal rope and hang from it a number of simple pendula of different lengths of suspension. Somehow we manage to make it oscillate with a single frequency for all the pendula (for example by putting a heavy pendulum in the system and enforcing a forced oscillation). To our surprise we will see either all of them oscillating in phase or at most some of them having an exactly opposite phase, but never with any other arbitrary relative phases.

Another classic example could be a system of two identical magnetic compasses set in a mode of coupled oscillations. Take two identical magnetic compasses. Set one of them on a table. Allow its needle to come to rest. Now bring the second compass close to the first, shake it so that its needle is set oscillating, and place it on the table close to one end of the needle of the first compass. There will be exchanging coupled oscillations: one dies away, the other picks up, and this goes on until they are damped out by friction. Now if you shake both the needles, it is possible to excite the two independent normal modes of oscillations whose superposition produces either of the two states: needles swing with equal amplitudes either in phase or with opposite phase. Other superpositions of the normal modes can give more complex behaviour.

The general solution for any normal mode of oscillation with the eigen-frequency, say p_α $(\alpha = 1, \ldots, n)$, is given by

$$q_i^{(\alpha)} \;=\; \text{Re}\left[A_i^{(\alpha)} e^{\sqrt{-1}p_\alpha t}\right] \;=\; A_{i\alpha}\cos(p_\alpha t \,+\, \theta_\alpha)$$

where $A_{i\alpha}$ is the real amplitude of oscillation of the ith coordinate in the αth normal mode corresponding to the eigen-frequency p_α and θ_α's are all different for different α's (that is, for different normal modes) but either same or differing by π for all the coordinates for the αth normal mode. However, if one arbitrarily excites the system, it will not respond with a single or pure normal mode of oscillation, but in general with a mixture of all possible modes on each of the coordinates so that

$$q_i \;=\; \sum_\alpha q_i^{(\alpha)} \;=\; \sum_\alpha A_{i\alpha}\cos(p_\alpha t \,+\, \theta_\alpha) \tag{11.27}$$

is the most general solution for any arbitrarily excited oscillation of the system, provided all the normal mode solutions are linearly independent. For example, when a string is arbitrarily excited it vibrates with all possible harmonics, but one can always excite it in such a special way that the whole string vibrates with a single frequency, corresponding to particular normal mode.

11.2.1 Properties of A_i for All the n Distinct Values of p^2

Let us select any two distinct eigen-frequencies for two distinct normal modes with $p^2 = p_\alpha^2$ and p_β^2 say. These would then satisfy

$$\sum_j -a_{ij}p_\alpha^2 A_{j\alpha} + \sum_j b_{ij}A_{j\alpha} = 0$$

and

$$\sum_i -a_{ij}p_\beta^2 A_{i\beta} + \sum_i b_{ij}A_{i\beta} = 0$$

α and β not being summed over. We retain the summation signs for reasons of clarity, albeit sacrificing brevity. These equations are each a set of n equations with the set of $n + n$ unknowns, $\{A_{j\alpha}\}$ and $\{A_{i\beta}\}$, respectively. Multiplying the first by $\{A_{i\beta}\}$ and the second by $\{A_{j\alpha}\}$ and summing over all the indices (except, of course, α and β), we get

$$\begin{aligned} -\sum_{i,j} a_{ij}p_\alpha^2 A_{i\beta}A_{j\alpha} + \sum_{i,j} b_{ij}A_{i\beta}A_{j\alpha} &= 0 \\ -\sum_{i,j} a_{ij}p_\beta^2 A_{i\beta}A_{j\alpha} + \sum_{i,j} b_{ij}A_{i\beta}A_{j\alpha} &= 0 \end{aligned} \tag{11.28}$$

Now subtracting the first from the second of the above sets of equations

$$\sum_{i,j} a_{ij}A_{i\beta}A_{j\alpha}\left(p_\alpha^2 - p_\beta^2\right) = 0 \tag{11.29}$$

Since by our assumption the two roots are distinct, $p_\alpha^2 \neq p_\beta^2$, we get

$$\sum_{i,j} a_{ij}A_{i\beta}A_{j\alpha} = 0 \qquad \text{for} \qquad \alpha \neq \beta \tag{11.30}$$

But if we had chosen the two roots p_α^2 and p_β^2 to be identical, we would then have got from Eq. (11.29)

$$\sum_{i,j} a_{ij}A_{i\beta}A_{j\alpha} \neq 0 \qquad \text{for} \qquad \alpha = \beta$$

However, since a_{ij} is a positive definite real symmetric matrix, we know that $\Sigma a_{ij}A_{i\alpha}A_{j\alpha} = \Delta_\alpha$ say, must be a positive quantity, if not equal to zero, which is the second case above. In fact one can easily normalise $A_{i\alpha}$ and $A_{j\alpha}$ by dividing them by $\sqrt{\Delta_\alpha} = C_\alpha$, say, such that

$$\sum_{i,j} a_{ij}\tilde{A}_{i\alpha}\tilde{A}_{j\alpha} = 1 \tag{11.31}$$

where $\{\tilde{A}_{i\alpha}\}$ are simply $\{A_{i\alpha}/\sqrt{\Delta_\alpha}\}$.

Combining Eqs (11.30) and (11.31) we can write

$$\sum_{i,j} a_{ij}\tilde{A}_{i\beta}\tilde{A}_{j\alpha} = \delta_{\alpha\beta} \tag{11.32a}$$

Now substituting Eq. (11.32a) in the first of Eq. (11.28), we get

$$\sum_{i,j} b_{ij}\tilde{A}_{i\beta}\tilde{A}_{j\alpha} = \sum_{i,j} a_{ij}\tilde{A}_{i\beta}\tilde{A}_{j\alpha}p_\alpha^2 = \delta_{\alpha\beta}p_\alpha^2 \tag{11.32b}$$

Equations (11.32a) and (11.32b) relate the matrix written in terms of the generalised coordinates to those written in terms of the eigen-values of the problem through very simple equations. The normalised amplitudes of the normal modes of oscillations are in fact seen to diagonalise both the $[a_{ij}]$ and $[b_{ij}]$ matrices. In the next subsection we shall exploit these extremely useful properties for obtaining the simplest possible representations of the problem of small amplitude oscillations.

11.2.2 Normal Coordinates and Principal Oscillations for Totally Non-Degenerate Systems

Since we have now normalised the $A_{i\alpha}$'s so as to satisfy Eq. (11.31), the general solution (11.27) for the ith generalised coordinate would appear as

$$q_i = \sum_\alpha \tilde{A}_{i\alpha}C_\alpha \cos(p_\alpha t + \theta_\alpha) \tag{11.33}$$

where $C_\alpha > 0$, for $\alpha = 1, \ldots, n$, are the same coefficients compensating for the factors of normalization introduced in Eq. (11.31).

Let us now consider a coordinate transformation given by

$$Q_\alpha = C_\alpha \cos(p_\alpha t + \theta_\alpha) \tag{11.34}$$

so that

$$q_i = \sum_\alpha \tilde{A}_{i\alpha}Q_\alpha \tag{11.35}$$

and

$$\dot{q}_i = \sum_\alpha \tilde{A}_{i\alpha}\dot{Q}_\alpha \tag{11.36}$$

Let us now obtain the expressions for the potential and kinetic energies of the system in terms of the new coordinates $\{Q_\alpha\}$ and their velocities $\{\dot{Q}_\alpha\}$. We get

$$V = \sum_{i,j} b_{ij}q_iq_j = \sum_{i,j,\alpha,\beta} b_{ij}\tilde{A}_{i\beta}\tilde{A}_{j\alpha}Q_\alpha Q_\beta = \sum_{\alpha,\beta} \delta_{\alpha\beta}p_\alpha^2 Q_\alpha Q_\beta = \sum_\alpha p_\alpha^2 Q_\alpha^2 \tag{11.37a}$$

and

$$T = \sum_{i,j} a_{ij}\dot{q}_i\dot{q}_j = \sum_{i,j,\alpha,\beta} a_{ij}\tilde{A}_{i\alpha}\dot{Q}_\alpha\tilde{A}_{j\beta}\dot{Q}_\beta = \sum_\alpha \dot{Q}_\alpha^2 \tag{11.37b}$$

where use has been made of the relations (11.32 a,b).

Thus in terms of these new coordinates $\{Q_\alpha\}$ and their corresponding coordinate velocities $\{\dot{Q}_\alpha\}$ the old $[a_{ij}]$ matrix has transformed into an identity matrix and $[b_{ij}]$ has turned into a diagonal matrix with the diagonal elements as $p_1^2, \ldots, p_n^2$, that is

$$[b_{ij}] = \text{diag}\,(p_1^2, \ldots, p_n^2)$$

We can say that the coordinate transformation (11.34) has completely diagonalised the matrices $[a_{ij}]$ and $[b_{ij}]$. Any transformation that diagonalises a matrix is called a *principal* transformation or a *similarity* transformation. Thus the transformation given by Eq. (11.34) is called the principal transformation and the coordinates $\{Q_\alpha\}$ are called the *normal* coordinates. In terms of these normal coordinates, the Lagrangian becomes

$$L = T - V = \sum_\alpha \dot{Q}_\alpha^2 - \sum_\alpha p_\alpha^2 Q_\alpha^2 \tag{11.38}$$

each coordinate term being orthogonally separated. The Lagrangian equations of motion expressed in the normal coordinates reduce to

$$\frac{d}{dt}\left(\frac{\partial L}{\partial \dot{Q}_\alpha}\right) - \left(\frac{\partial L}{\partial Q_\alpha}\right) = 0$$

or

$$\ddot{Q}_\alpha + p_\alpha^2 Q_\alpha = 0 \qquad \alpha = 1, \ldots, n \tag{11.39}$$

with the solution for each normal coordinate Q_α

$$Q_\alpha = C_\alpha \cos\,(p_\alpha t + \theta_\alpha) \tag{11.40}$$

which naturally justifies the principal transformations themselves as expressed in Eq. (11.34). So in terms of the normal coordinates $\{Q_\alpha\}$, the system is effectively decoupled into n independent simple harmonic oscillations in n normal coordinates.

The principal oscillation corresponding to each distinct α (or normal mode) is given by the n-dimensional vector in the configuration space of the dynamical system $\mathbf{q}_\alpha(q_{1\alpha}, \ldots, q_{n\alpha})$ with individual components

$$q_{i\alpha} = C_\alpha \tilde{A}_{i\alpha} \cos\,(p_\alpha t + \theta_\alpha) \tag{11.41}$$

where α is not to be summed over. There are n such principal oscillations, one for each normal mode, or equivalently for each α. These are n orthogonal vectors in the configuration space. A superposition of all these n principal oscillations for n distinct normal modes gives any arbitrary oscillation of the system, which is, as it should be, just an arbitrary vector in the configuration space.

It is to be noted that the expressions for the principal oscillations contain time dependent periodic terms. Does it then mean that the directions of principal oscillations when mapped in the configuration space are continually changing with time? Fortunately, they do not, simply because all the coordinates for a given principal oscillation have identical periods, and identical phases apart from a difference of 180 degrees for some coordinates. So each normal mode solution corresponds to an oscillation in a particular direction in the configuration space. The normal coordinate for a given principal oscillation represents the actual behaviour of the displacement along the direction of principal oscillation. We can of course imagine the normal coordinates to span a new n dimensional configuration space, in which the individual principal oscillations will execute simple harmonic motions with the respective normal mode frequencies along the respective new coordinate axes.

11.2.4 Degenerate Cases

For the case when degenerate roots, say p_α^2 , of Eq. (11.23) have multiplicity m, Lagrange had thought that the general solution of such problems of small oscillations might not be expressible as a linear combination of n normal mode solutions because the latter are not linearly independent. However, it was later demonstrated by Weierstrass that for each root of Eq. (11.23) with multiplicity $n \geq m \geq 2$ there exist exactly m linearly independent solutions of the system of n linear equations so that a total of n linearly independent amplitude vectors can be found including the ones for the degenerate modes. Hence the above form of the general solution remains valid even for a system having some degenerate modes of multiplicities $m \geq 2$.

11.2.5 An Example of Small Amplitude Oscillations : Compound Pendula

Two pendula having identical bobs of mass (m) and lengths of suspension (l) are hung from a horizontal ceiling some horizontal distance (l_o) apart and are connected by a spring (of constant k and length l_o at relaxation) the ends of which are tied with the strings of suspension at a distance h below their respective points of suspension. Let the angles of deflection ϕ_1 and ϕ_2 of the pendula from the respective vertical lines in their common plane of oscillation be the two independent generalised coordinates. Assume ϕ_1 and ϕ_2 to be small enough to be called small oscillations about their stable equilibrium configuration viz., $\phi_1 = \phi_2 = 0$. First we form the Lagrangian.

The kinetic energy $T = \frac{1}{2}ml^2(\dot{\phi}_1^2 + \dot{\phi}_2^2) = a_{ij}\dot{q}_i\dot{q}_j$, giving

$$a_{ij} = \begin{pmatrix} \frac{1}{2}ml^2 & 0 \\ 0 & \frac{1}{2}ml^2 \end{pmatrix}$$

The potential energy is, assuming ϕ_1 and ϕ_2 to be small,

$$\begin{aligned} V &= mgl(1 - \cos\phi_1) + mgl(1 - \cos\phi_2) + \frac{1}{2}kh^2(\phi_2 - \phi_1)^2 \\ &\simeq \frac{1}{2}(mgl + kh^2)(\phi_1^2 + \phi_2^2) - kh^2\phi_1\phi_2 \end{aligned}$$

giving

$$b_{ij} = \begin{pmatrix} \frac{1}{2}(mgl + kh^2) & -\frac{1}{2}kh^2 \\ -\frac{1}{2}kh^2 & \frac{1}{2}(mgl + kh^2) \end{pmatrix}$$

The matrices $[a_{ij}]$ and $[b_{ij}]$ are real, symmetric and positive definite; $[a_{ij}]$ is diagonal but not $[b_{ij}]$.

Therefore the secular Eq. (11.23) becomes, in this case, dropping all the factors 1/2

$$\det \begin{Vmatrix} (mgl + kh^2) - p^2ml^2 & -kh^2 \\ -kh^2 & (mgl + kh^2) - p^2ml^2 \end{Vmatrix} = 0$$

or

$$(mgl + kh^2 - p^2ml^2)^2 - k^2h^4 = 0$$

or

$$p_\alpha^2 = \frac{g}{l} \quad \text{and} \quad p_\beta^2 = \frac{mgl + 2kh^2}{ml^2} = \frac{g}{l} + \frac{2kh}{ml^2}$$

Thus these p_α and p_β are the frequencies of the two normal modes of oscillation.

The amplitudes of small oscillations for these two normal modes can be found from solving the respective sets of linear equations namely

$$(b_{ij} - p_\alpha^2 a_{ij})A\alpha j = 0$$

for the first normal mode (frequency p_α) and

$$(b_{ij} - p_\beta^2 a_{ij})A_{\beta j} = 0$$

for the second mode (frequency p_β).

For the first mode we have

$$\begin{aligned} (b_{11} - p_\alpha^2 a_{11})A_{\alpha 1} + (b_{12} - p_\alpha^2 a_{12})A_{\alpha 2} &= 0 \\ (b_{21} - p_\alpha^2 b_{21})A_{\alpha 1} + (b_{22} - p_\alpha^2 a_{22})A_{\alpha 2} &= 0 \end{aligned} \tag{11.42}$$

Solving these we get

$$A_{\alpha 1} = A_{\alpha 2} = \text{const. (say } C_1)$$

so that the oscillations in ϕ_1 and ϕ_2 for the normal mode frequency $p_\alpha = \sqrt{g/l}$ are

$$\phi_{1\alpha} = C_1 \cos(p_\alpha t + \theta_\alpha)$$

and

$$\phi_{2\alpha} = C_1 \cos(p_\alpha t + \theta_\alpha)$$

Thus both the pendula oscillate in phase with the same frequency as $p_\alpha = \sqrt{g/l}$, i.e., they oscillate together keeping the bobs always at the same separation as the distance between their points of suspension. An abstract vector formed out of the sum of these two components is a principal oscillation corresponding to the normal mode frequency p_α.

Similarly, for the second normal mode, one replaces p_α^2 in Eqs (11.42) by p_β^2 and $A_{\alpha 1}$, $A_{\alpha 2}$ by $A_{\beta 1}$, $A_{\beta 2}$ respectively, and obtains a solution

$$A_{\beta 1} = -A_{\beta 2} = C_2 \text{ say}$$

Hence

$$\phi_{1\beta} = C_2 \cos(p_\beta t + \theta_\beta)$$

and

$$\phi_{2\beta} = -C_2 \cos(p_\beta t + \theta_\beta) = C_2 \cos(p_\beta t + \theta_\beta + \pi$$

Thus in this normal mode of oscillation with frequency

$$p_\beta = \sqrt{\frac{g}{l} + \frac{2kh^2}{ml^2}} > p_\alpha$$

the pendula will oscillate 180 degrees out of phase, that is, both of them will approach each other for a while, then go apart and come back and so on. The second principal oscillation is represented by the linear superposition of these two individual oscillations in two different coordinates both executing in the second normal mode of frequency p_β.

Now any general oscillation would be a linear sum of these two principal oscillations, and obviously it would be a vector in the configuration space of this dynamical system. If we prefer to write this general solution in two of its generalised coordinate components, they would look like

$$\phi_1 = C_1 \cos(p_\alpha t + \theta_\alpha) + C_2 \cos(p_\beta t + \theta_\beta)$$

and

$$\phi_2 = C_1 \cos(p_\alpha t + \theta_\alpha) - C_2 \cos(p_\beta t + \theta_\beta)$$

It is also seen that the components of any particular principal oscillation have the same amplitude, same frequency and same argument for cosine function except for an occasional change by π. So it is better to define all these components by a single entity. This is done by introducing the normal coordinates, one normal coordinate for each normal mode or equivalently for each principal oscillation. In the present example, the two normal coordinates are

$$Q_\alpha = C_1 \cos(p_\alpha t + \theta_\alpha) \quad \text{and} \quad Q_\beta = C_2 \cos(p_\beta t + \theta_\beta)$$

so that

$$\phi_1 = (Q_\alpha + Q_\beta) \quad \text{and} \quad \phi_2 = (Q_\alpha - Q_\beta)$$

It is now easy to find out the directions of the principal oscillations in the configuration space. Since the components of the vectors (ϕ_1, ϕ_2) are, by definition, the generalised coordinates orthogonal to each other, the principal oscillations represent a pair of orthogonal vectors at an angle of 45 degrees to the former.

11.3 FORCED VIBRATIONS AND RESONANCE

Until now, we have considered the free oscillations of a system around its equilibrium configuration, that is, the oscillations of the system when slightly disturbed initially from the equilibrium configuration and then allowed to oscillate by itself. In a variety of situations, however, the system is set into oscillation about its equilibrium configuration by an external force varying periodically with time. These are the so-called forced oscillations whose frequency is determined by the frequency of the driving force rather than by the normal mode frequencies. However, the normal modes of free oscillations play a crucial role in the analysis of forced oscillations. In particular, the problem of obtaining the amplitudes of the forced oscillations is greatly simplified by use of the normal coordinates obtained from free oscillations.

Suppose F_β is the generalised force corresponding to the generalised coordinate, say q_β, then the generalised force corresponding to α^{th} normal coordinate Q_α is given by

$$f_\alpha = \sum_\beta F_\beta \frac{\partial q_\beta}{\partial Q_\alpha} \tag{11.43}$$

The equations of motion, when expressed in normal coordinates become (see Eq. (11.39))

$$\ddot{Q}_\alpha + p_\alpha^2 Q_\alpha = f_\alpha(t) \tag{11.44}$$

Equations (11.44) are a set of n inhomogeneous differential equations that can be solved only when we know the dependence of f on time. Note, however, that the normal coordinates preserve their advantage of separating the variables. Thus each of the Eqs (11.44) involves only a single variable and can be solved independent of others.

In many real systems the oscillations are damped by the resistance of the medium in which the system is oscillating (or by some other reason). The corresponding forces, acting on the system, are dissipative in nature and are proportional to the velocities of the particles of the system. As described in chapter 2, these can be obtained from a dissipation function

$$R = \frac{1}{2} h_{jk} \dot{q}_j \dot{q}_k \tag{11.45}$$

where h_{jk} is a symmetric matrix. In order that the normal coordinates exist, we must find out a principal axis transformation which simultaneously diagonalises the matrices $[a_{ij}]$, $[b_{ij}]$ and $[h_{ij}]$ defined by Eqs (11.18) and (11.45). Such a principal axis transformation does not necessarily exist in every case. However, henceforth we specialise in the case where a transformation to normal coordinates is possible. In such cases, Eqs (11.44) are replaced by

$$\ddot{Q}_\alpha + k_\alpha \dot{Q}_\alpha + p_\alpha^2 Q_\alpha = f_\alpha(t) \tag{11.46}$$

which again are n uncoupled differential equations, each involving a single coordinate, and hence can be solved independently of others.

Thus the problem of forced oscillations for each normal coordinate boils down to solving a differential equation of the form

$$\ddot{x} + 2\beta\dot{x} + \omega_o^2 x = \frac{f(t)}{m} \tag{11.47}$$

where Q_α is replaced by x, k_α by 2β, p_α^2 is replaced by $\omega_o^2 = p_\alpha^2$ and $f_\alpha(t)$ by $f(t)/m$. Here $m\omega_o^2 = k$ say, is the spring constant and m is the mass of the system. We shall refer to the physical system obeying Eq. (11.47) as an oscillator driven by a force function $f(t)$.

Now in many instances, the time dependence of the force function $f(t)$ is a simple sinusoid. For example, in an acoustic problem, the driving force might arise from the pressure of a sound wave impinging on the system and $f(t)$ then has the same frequency as the sound wave. Or, if the system is a poly-atomic molecule, a sinusoidal driving force is present if the molecule is illuminated by a monochromatic light beam. Each atom in the molecule is then subjected to an electromagnetic force whose frequency is that of the incident light. Even when $f(t)$ is not sinusoidal with a single frequency it can often be considered as a superposition of such sinusoidal terms. Thus if $f(t)$ is periodic it can be represented as Fourier series, otherwise a Fourier integral representation is suitable. Since Eq. (11.47) is linear, its solution corresponding to a given $f(t)$ can be obtained by superposing the solutions corresponding to the sinusoidal terms in its Fourier representation. It is therefore of general importance to study the nature of solutions of (11.47) with $f(t)$ having a sinusoidal variation with time. We consider, therefore,

$$\ddot{x} + 2\beta\dot{x} + \omega_o^2 x = \frac{f_o}{m}\cos\omega t \tag{11.48}$$

where f_o is a constant independent of x and t.

The complete solution of Eq. (11.48) is the sum of the complete solution of the homogeneous equation

$$\ddot{x} + 2\beta\dot{x} + \omega_o^2 x = 0 \tag{11.49}$$

and any particular solution of Eq. (11.48). The term consisting of the complete solution to the homogeneous equation will be damped out with time, as long as $\beta > O$ and is called the transient term. The remaining term in the solution persists in time and is called the steady state solution. We are interested in the steady state solution to Eq. (11.48) which is given by

$$x = A\cos(\omega t - \phi) \tag{11.50}$$

where

$$A = \frac{f_o/m}{\sqrt{(\omega_o^2 - \omega^2) + 4\beta^2\omega^2}} \tag{11.51}$$

and

$$\tan\phi = \frac{2\omega\beta}{\omega_o^2 - \omega^2}$$

We see that the motion is sinusoidal, with the angular frequency ω which is the same as that of the driving force. The phase $(\omega t - \phi)$ lags behind the phase ωt of the driving force by ϕ radians. The phase angle ϕ depends on the frequency of the driving force and ranges from zero to π as ω ranges from 0 to infinity. The amplitude A which depends on the magnitude and frequency of the driving force is considered in subsection 11.3.2.

11.3.1 Energy Considerations

In many problems we are interested in the amount of energy that is stored in the oscillator in the form of kinetic or potential energy and also in the amount of work that must be done by the driving force to maintain a given amount of energy in the oscillator.

The average potential energy and the average kinetic energy stored in the oscillator can be found by averaging the quantities $kx^2/2$ and $m\dot{x}^2/2$ over a single period. Thus we get

$$\begin{aligned}\left\langle \frac{1}{2}kx^2 \right\rangle &= \frac{1}{\tau}\int_t^{t+\tau} \frac{1}{2}k\left[A\cos(\omega t - \phi)\right]^2 dt \\ &= \frac{kA^2}{4} = \frac{m\omega_o^2 A^2}{4}\end{aligned} \tag{11.52}$$

and

$$\left\langle \frac{1}{2} m \dot{x}^2 \right\rangle = \frac{1}{\tau} \int_t^{t+\tau} \frac{1}{2} m [-A\omega \sin(\omega t - \phi)]^2 \, dt$$
$$= \frac{m\omega^2 A^2}{4} \tag{11.53}$$

where A is given in Eq. (11.51).

In the steady state, the values of both kinetic and potential energies at the beginning of a period are the same as those at the end of a period. Hence the driving force is needed to do work only to supply the energy dissipated due to the damping force. The energy dissipated by the damping force in one period or equivalently the negative of the work done by the damping force in one period is

$$-\Delta W = \int_{x(t)}^{x(t+\tau)} 2m\beta \dot{x} dx = 2m \int_t^{t+\tau} \beta \dot{x}^2 dt = \beta m \omega^2 A^2 \tau \tag{11.54}$$

A measure of the efficiency of a given oscillator for energy storage is given by the Q *factor* defined by

$$Q = 2\pi \frac{\text{average stored energy}}{\text{energy dissipated per cycle}} = 2\pi \frac{m\omega_o^2 A^2/4 + m\omega^2 A^2/4}{\beta m \omega^2 A^2 \tau}$$
$$= \frac{\omega_o^2 + \omega^2}{4\beta\omega} \tag{11.55}$$

Here we have used Eqs (11.52) and (11.53). So

$$Q \propto \beta^{-1}$$

and when $\omega \simeq \omega_o$,

$$Q \simeq \frac{\omega_o}{2\beta} \tag{11.56}$$

11.3.2 Resonance

We know that the normal coordinate $x(t)$ and the corresponding velocity $\dot{x}(t)$ are sinusoidal functions with amplitudes A and A' respectively given by Eq. (11.51), and that

$$A' = \omega A \tag{11.57}$$

If the magnitude f_o of the driving force is held fixed and the frequency ω is varied, and if $\beta < \omega_o$, the quantities A and A' will each have a maximum value for certain frequency. If $\beta \ll \omega_o$ the quantities A and A' are sharply peaked around their maximum values as illustrated in Fig. 11.3(a) and 11.3(b). This rapid enhancement in the value of A or A' in the neighborhood of a certain frequency is called a *resonance* and the frequency at which a resonance occurs is called the *resonant frequency*.

The frequency ω_R at which the amplitude A becomes maximum is called the displacement resonance frequency and is found by maximising Eq. (11.56) with respect to ω or

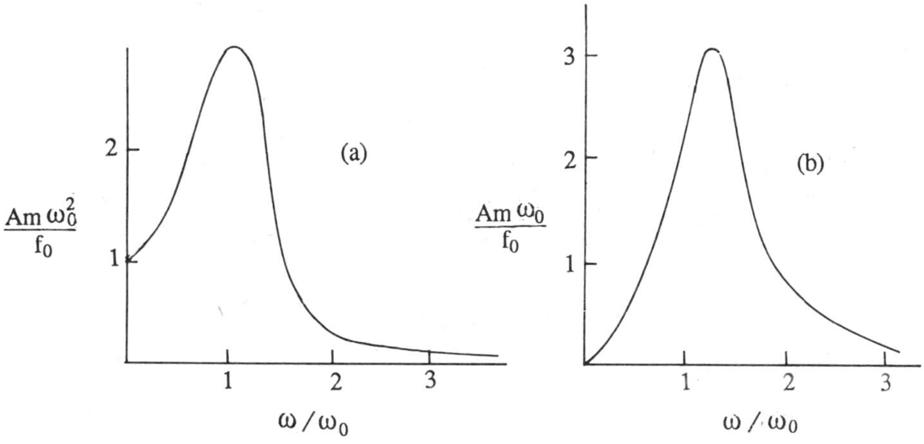

Fig. 11.3 Frequency dependence of (a) $Am\omega^2/f_o$, and (b) $Am\omega/f_o$, showing the peaks around the resonating frequency/par

more simply by minimising its denominator with respect to ω^2. Doing this we obtain

$$\omega_R = \sqrt{\omega_o^2 - 2\beta^2} \tag{11.58}$$

If $\beta \ll \omega_o$, then

$$\omega_R \simeq \omega_o \tag{11.59}$$

The frequency ω'_R at which A' becomes maximum is called the velocity resonance frequency and is given by

$$\omega'_R = \omega_o \tag{11.60}$$

When $\beta \ll \omega_o$ the resonance occurs in both the cases at the frequency ω_o. When the term resonance frequency is used without any adjective, it generally refers to ω_o.

It is easy to see that the average stored energy in the oscillator also shows resonant behaviour as the frequency of the driving force ω is changed. Indeed, the average potential energy is given by $m\omega_o^2 A^2/4$ and the average kinetic energy by $m\omega^2 A^2/4 = mA'^2/4$. It follows that the resonance curve for the average potential energy is just $m\omega_o^2/4$ times the square of the resonance cure for the displacement, and the resonance curve for the kinetic energy is $m/4$ times the square of the resonance curve for the velocity. Obviously the average potential energy has its maximum value at $\omega = \omega_R$ (Eq. (11.58)) and the average kinetic energy has its maximum value at $\omega = \omega'_R$ (Eq. (11.60)). For the total average energy of the oscillator the resonance occurs at $(\omega_R + \omega'_R)/2$ with the maximum value $(m/4)[\omega_o^2 A^2 + A'^2]$.

The sharpness of the resonance peak can be described by measuring its full width at the point where the amplitude has dropped to half of its maximum value. This is called ***full width at half maximum*** and is designated as $\Delta\omega$. The value of $\Delta\omega$ for the velocity resonance curve, and also, when $\beta \ll \omega_o$, for the displacement resonance curve is given by

$$\Delta\omega = 2\sqrt{3}\,\beta \tag{11.61}$$

Similarly the value of $\Delta\omega$ for the kinetic energy resonance, when $\beta \ll \omega_o$, for the potential energy resonance curve is 2β. Note that in all these cases the width of the resonance curve is a measure of the strength of damping. The greater the damping the wider is the resonance curve. Further, when $\omega = \omega_o$ the Q *factor* of the oscillator is

$$Q_o = \frac{\omega_o}{2\beta}$$

so that Q_o is inversely proportional to the width of the resonance curve. The sharper the resonance, the larger is the value of Q_o. It can be shown that, in the absence of the driving force, the amplitude of the damped oscillator decays with a time constant $1/\beta$. Thus the relaxation time is inversely proportional to the width.

The above analysis leads to the conclusion that a great deal of information about the oscillator can be obtained from one of its resonance curves. The location of the resonance gives its natural (normal mode) frequency ω_o and the width helps us determine the damping factor. These can further be related to the Q factor, the relaxation time, the restoring and the damping forces, etc. In many instances it is easier to obtain a resonance curve than to obtain the information on these quantities directly from their definitions.

Note that in principle, at resonance, only a single natural frequency of the system is excited. Indeed, at resonance the amplitude corresponding to resonant frequency far exceeds that corresponding to any other frequency that may be excited due to some stray disturbances or noise. Thus, at resonance, the signal to noise ratio becomes very high. Therefore the resonance phenomenon offers a very accurate and sensitive spectroscopic technique to study the natural excitations of the system. Electron Paramagnetic Resonance (EPR), Nuclear Magnetic Resonance (NMR) and Mössbauer spectroscopy, are but a few examples of highly sensitive and accurate spectroscopic techniques based on the phenomenon of resonance.

11.4 SUMMARY

The different types of equilibrium configurations are classified into stable, unstable and metastable states. Also the equilibrium itself could be static or dynamic.

Obviously, the form of the Lagrangian for small perturbations about any one of the equilibrium configurations is drastically simplified. If the equilibrium point under consideration is a stable one, there always exists a solution that represents oscillation. More surprisingly, such oscillations are invariably of the simple harmonic type, with periods independent of the amplitude of perturbation, provided of course, the amplitudes are small.

It is always possible to excite the system which may have an arbitrarily large number of degrees of freedom, in a manner to execute simple harmonic oscillations in all generalised coordinates with a single frequency. This is called a normal mode of oscillation. Using the Lagrangian method, it is shown that the equations of motion reduce to a set of linearly coupled algebraic equations in amplitudes, and that the solution for all possible normal modes reduces to one of the standard eigenvalue problems. If the the number of DOF is n, the maximum possible number of independent normal modes is obviously n. Furthermore, for each normal mode, the relative amplitudes of oscillation in individual generalised coordinates can be arbitrary, but not the relative phases, which are very strictly either 0° or 180°, and nothing in between.

Because of the last condition, for any given normal mode of small amplitude oscillation, the dynamical representation of the system in its n-dimensional configuration space corresponds to a simple harmonic motion in a straight line. This is called a principal oscillation corresponding to the given normal mode. A single coordinate, say Q, may also be defined as a measure of the total instantaneous displacement along this line from the equilibrium position in order to represent this oscillation in the configuration space. This is precisely the normal coordinate. Therefore, in a given normal mode, a suitably defined normal coordinate will execute the corresponding principal oscillation.

Hence, there can be at most n different principal oscillations and the corresponding normal coordinates. A linear superposition of these principal oscillations can represent any arbitrary oscillation produced by arbitrarily exciting the system.

In the presence of damping and externally impressed oscillations, the system responds in resonance whenever the frequency of the impressed oscillation is chosen very close to one of the natural frequencies of oscillation of the system. Since the power consumption due to damping increases as the amplitude of oscillation grows, the amplitude of the resonating system finally adjusts to a maximum value when the power fed by the impressing system exactly balances the power lost due to damping.

PROBLEMS

11.1 A piston of mass m divides a cylinder containing gas into two equal parts. Suppose the piston is displaced to the left a distance x and let go. Find the frequency of the piston's oscillation , if the process takes place
(i) at constant temperature and
(ii) adiabatically.

11.2 Find the differential equation for the contour of a constraining surface on which a point mass will oscillate with a period independent of the amplitude.

11.3 Professor I. Rabi was once running a cosmic ray experiment on a mountain top and noticed that his mechanical wrist watch (vibrating balance wheel type) started running slightly faster. He posed the problem to Professor Fermi during a train ride, who thought for a while and produced a fully quantitative explanation within an hour. Could you figure out the line of reasoning?

11.4 A spherical ball rolls in a quarter-circle track suspended as a pendulum bob. Solve for the coupled oscillations of the system and show that the dynamical coupling between the ball and the track produces some dramatic starts and stops.

11.5 Atwood's oscillator consists of a solid disc of mass M and radius R, pivoted at the centre, with an additional mass m placed at a distance r from the centre. The equilibrium is maintained by a mass m', which is suspended from a massless string wrapped around the disc. At the equilibrium position, the line from the centre of the disc to the mass m makes an angle ϕ with the vertical. If the system is displaced by a small angle θ, show that the ensuing motion is simple harmonic.

11.6 Find the first order correction to the period of a relativistic harmonic oscillator with the Lagrangian given by

$$L = \frac{m_o c^2}{\sqrt{1 - v^2/c^2}} - m_o c^2 - \frac{1}{2}kx^2$$

Also find the higher order correction to the period of finite amplitude oscillations of a classical harmonic oscillator.

11.7 Find the frequencies of small oscillation of a spherical pendulum (a particle of mass m suspended by a string of length l), if the angle of deflection from the vertical oscillates about the steady value θ_o.

11.8 Three particles each of mass m are in equilibrium and joined cyclically by unstretched massless springs, each with Hooke's law spring constant k. They are constrained to move in a circular track. Each mass is displaced from equilibrium by small displacements u_1, u_2 and u_3. Find the eigen-frequencies of oscillations.

11.9 Find the normal oscillations of a system of two identical particles moving only vertically but hanging from the ceiling by two equal springs in succession, with one particle between the springs and the other at the bottom.

11.10 Find the normal coordinates of the systems with the following Lagrangians

(i)

$$L = \frac{1}{2}(\dot{x}^2 + \dot{y}^2) - \frac{1}{2}(\omega_1^2 x^2 + \omega_2^2 y^2) + \alpha xy$$

(ii)

$$L = \frac{1}{2}(m_1\dot{x}^2 + m_2\dot{y}^2) + \beta\dot{x}\dot{y} - \frac{1}{2}(x^2 + y^2)$$

where α, β, ω_1, ω_2, m_1 and m_2 are constants.

11.11 We know that the value of 'g' on Jupiter is about 25.5 m/s^2. Can you devise a simple pendulum experiment on earth that would oscillate with the period adjusted to the value of g on Jupiter?

11.12 What is the best way to measure the mass of an object hanging from a practically weightless spring inside a transparent but totally enclosed box? The external shape of the box is, say, pyramidal. This practical question was posed at the 1982 Physics competition at the University of New South Wales. The best prize went to the person who utilised a method of the normal mode oscillations.

11.13 It is known that one has to apply some trick in order to hold a long stick vertically up on the tip of a finger and walk. In dynamics, this problem is known as the problem of the inverted pendulum. Under what condition does an inverted pendulum become stable?

12

Rigid Body Dynamics

12.0 INTRODUCTION

We have written a rather long chapter on this topic, the reason being our attempt to elaborate on the basics that involve conceptual clarity of the motions of rigid bodies. It has been our sad experience that most students appearing for the qualifying orals for admission to the Ph.D. programmes in physics at research institutions do fairly badly in the rigid body dynamics part. We have therefore covered parts of the undergraduate syllabus in great detail in the first half of the chapter, and more advanced topics are presented in the second half. Section 12.28 deals with a totally new but exciting topic, a brief treatise on the dynamics of sports and games. Have fun reading it!

After Newton, the most ingenious man to have exploited the full power of calculus in applying Newton's laws of motion to rigid body dynamics and continuum mechanics is said to be Leonhard Euler, the most prolific mathematician of all time. A straightforward list of Euler's works would occupy no less than 80 pages of this book, and all his works, altogether 866 papers, amount to 69 large volumes. Euler was one of the great mathematicians who could work anywhere under any conditions. He would dash off a mathematical paper in the half an hour or so between the first and second calls to dinner. The ease with which he wrote the most difficult mathematics is incredible. Publishers running short of material would come and pick up the top deck of his piled up manuscripts, so in most cases the actual chronology is lost.

Born in Switzerland in 1705, Euler joined St. Petersburg Academy in Russia in 1725, lost the sight of one eye in 1736, joined Berlin Academy at the invitation of the King Frederick, became totally blind in 1766 and returned to St. Petersburg Academy, and worked with full enthusiasm till he died in 1783. He just finished the calculation of the orbit of Uranus, which was recently discovered by William Herschel, and died following a heart attack.

He introduced analytical methods into mechanics as early as 1736 and made quasi-axiomatic use of the principle of virtual work. He deduced the differential equation for the problem of minimising integrals in 1744. He began to use undetermined multipliers before Lagrange reinvented them. When Lagrange at the age of 23 sent his brand new method of tackling dynamical problems to the 54-year old Euler for comment, Euler found Lagrange's analytical method far superior to his semi-geometrical methods and immediately used it to solve one of the outstanding problems of the day, but did not publish it before he could convince Lagrange to publish his method first. Euler was always generously appreciative of the work of others. His treatment of his young rival Lagrange is one of the finest examples of unselfishness in the history of science. D'Alembert, Euler and Lagrange were great friends. The entire rigid body dynamics was Euler's one but small brainchild, which appeared in 1760 in the form of a book entitled *Theoria motus corpum solidorum seu rigidorum.* After one hundred years, another notable book *Dynamics of rigid bodies* by Edward John Routh truly surpassed Euler's work.

Apart from Euler and Routh, substantial contributions have come from Arnold Sommerfeld (1868 – 1951). While professor of Mathematics at the Bergakademie at Claustal, he began with Lord Klein in 1897 the preparation of a four volume classic treatise on the gyroscope, called *Theorie des Kreisels*, that was to take 13 years to complete. Joseph Lagrange, Edward Routh and Louis Poinsot have supplemented the Eulerian schemes. In fact, rigid bodies appear in so many different contexts and in so many different ways that there always remains a scope for completely solving even 'simple' problems like the motion of topsy-turvy tops, rotating pebbles, boomerangs etc. Contributions to specific problem oriented topics in rigid body dynamics are innumerable. Sometimes these are questions of correctly formulating the problem, if not finding solutions in closed forms.

12.1 DEGREES OF FREEDOM OF A FREE RIGID BODY

We already know that the distance between any two constituent particles of a ***rigid body*** remains fixed (by definition) throughout the motion of the body. In other words, the motion of a rigid body is constrained by the requirement that the distance between any two of its particles remain the same for all time. We have also seen that the rigidity constraint is holonomic.

The number of DOF of a free rigid body is the minimum number of independent coordinates required to describe all possible configurations of the rigid body. In the course of dynamical motions, a rigid body assumes various possible configurations maintaining, of course, the rigid body constraint. Let us assume that a rigid body has N particles in it ($N \geq 3$) and it has n DOF. If we now choose any particular particle in it, it can be translated to any desired point in the 3-D Euclidean space. Therefore, this particular particle must have three DOF. Let us now fix this particle at some point in 3-D space, so that we take away three degrees of freedom from the total number of DOF for the whole system, that is, if it had originally the number of DOF $= n$, now its number of DOF $= n - 3$.

Now let us choose a second particle in the rigid body. This particle should have had number of DOF $= 3$ before the fixation of the first particle, but since the first particle's location is fixed and the distance between the first and the second particle must remain unchanged due to the rigidity constraint, the corresponding constraint relation has to be satisfied. Hence the the number of DOF of the second particle, subject to the fixation of the first particle, is only 2. In fact, the second particle can now lie anywhere on the surface of a sphere of radius equal to the distance between the first and the second particle with the centre located on the first particle. Thus the second particle cannot translate at all but can only rotate about the first particle. If we now fix the second particle at some desired point on the sphere of its allowed 2-D motion, we further take away 2 degrees of freedom from the system. Hence the total number of DOF left for any rigid body having any two particles fixed in space is $n - 5$.

Let us now consider any third particle that may or may not lie on the line joining the first two particles. If the third particle lies on the previous line it cannot have any degree of freedom, in which case we have to go for the next and next particle until we choose a particle outside the above line. So long as these particles are chosen to lie on the same line defined by the first two particles, fixing these particles can be done without loss of any further degrees of freedom. As soon as we choose a particle that does not lie on the above line, this particle can move only in a circular track about the above line, because it has to satisfy two constraint relations, namely, its distance from the two previously fixed particles must remain constant. This is once again a 1-D rotational DOF. If we now fix this off-the-line particle, the system loses a total of 6 DOF and the number of DOF left is $n - 6$. Now after fixing three particles, lying on the vertices of a triangle, any fourth particle must satisfy three constraint relations, hence its number of DOF $= 0$. Any fifth particle will have to satisfy more than three constraint relations so for it also no DOF is left. This is true for all the rest of the particles implying that the rigid body is now left with no more DOF. Therefore $n - 6 = 0$, or, $n = 6$.

Thus any rigid body consisting of at least three particles, not arranged in one straight line, must have six DOF. In other words, any rigid body can have at most six DOF of which three are translational and the rest three are rotational DOF. The implication of this result is stated in the following points.

(i) Six generalised coordinates $(q_1, \cdots, q_6)$ are sufficient to describe the dynamical motion of any rigid body, out of which three are chosen for the location of any point fixed with respect to the rigid body and the other three for all possible rotations of the rigid body about this chosen point. Note that this point can be inside or outside the rigid body. If the point is chosen outside the physical boundary of a rigid body a suitable massless rigid pointer has to be firmly attached to the rigid body which will have the above point on its arrowhead. For the six generalised coordinates we need to define the corresponding generalised velocities $(\dot{q}_1, \ldots, \dot{q}_6)$, and canonical momenta $(p_1, \ldots, p_6)$, through a suitably defined Lagrangian function $\tilde{L} = \tilde{L}(q_1, \ldots, q_6, \dot{q}_1, \ldots, \dot{q}_6, t)$.

(ii) A rigid body must have $2n = 12$ independent constants of motion, of which 11 must be totally time independent. We shall see later that for a freely moving rigid body the constants of motion that can be easily identified are its total linear momentum (3), total angular momentum (3), translational kinetic energy (1), rotational kinetic energy (1) and the vector condition for Galilean invariance (3). The last three are in fact explicit functions of time, of which two can be made time independent by substituting the time dependence derived from the first. So in all these constitute 11 constants of motion. The twelfth independent constant of motion, unlike the other 11, may not always be expressed in closed form. This will become more apparent in section 12.14.

Just as the kinematical motions of a rigid body can now be studied without making any explicit reference to the motion of its N constituent particles, a full (dynamical) description of the rigid body is also possible without the specific details of its mass (or inertial) configuration, which, as we shall see later on, can be fully expressed in terms of only six independent quantities, constituting what is called the moment of inertia tensor. However it should be mentioned that this coincidence in number for the degrees of freedom and the independent components of the moment of inertia tensor corresponds to the fact that both are $n(n+1)/2$, where n is the number of the spatial dimension.

12.2 EULER'S AND CHASLES' THEOREMS

By a rigid displacement we mean any possible displacement of a rigid body in the real 3-D Euclidean space.

12.2.1 Euler's Theorem (1776)

Any rigid displacement is a combined result of rotation and translation.

This theorem can be rigorously proved using the properties of the Euclidean group which is shown to be isometric first with the operations of rigid displacements and then with the group of linear transformations corresponding to translation and rotation. However our approach will be geometric in nature.

Let us take any rigid body and note its location and configuration. We now give some arbitrary displacement to this body thus taking it to some final state. We note the final location and configuration. Now the question is, can there be a combination of translation and rotation that takes the rigid body from its initial state to its final state? What we must do first is to identify any specific particle in the rigid body, and translate the rigid body such that the chosen particle moves in a straight line from its position in the initial state to that in the final state. Now keeping the position of the particle fixed at this final position we just need to give a proper amount of rotation about a proper axis in order to make every particle in the body take up the position corresponding to the final state configuration. This can be done in one step, but can easily be done by a sequence of two rotations. For example, choose any second point in the body and rotate the body about the first point such that the second point coincides with its position in the final configuration. Then choose a third point, but not on the one on the line joining the first two points, and then perform a rotation about this line so as to make the third point go over to its position in the final configuration. This sequence of rotations will obviously make the whole body perfectly assume the final configuration. Since two successive rotations about a given point is equivalent to some single rotation about the same point, these two rotational operations can be regarded as a single unique rotational operation. This proves Euler's theorem by geometrical arguments.

Let us now put this proof in a mathematical form. The condition for rigidity is $|\boldsymbol{r}_i - \boldsymbol{r}_j| =$ constant for any pair of particles numbered with indices i and j. Let, due to any rigid displacement, $\boldsymbol{r}_i \to \boldsymbol{r}'_i$ and $\boldsymbol{r}_j \to \boldsymbol{r}'_j$. Then, by the condition of rigidity $|\boldsymbol{r}'_i - \boldsymbol{r}'_j| = |\boldsymbol{r}_i - \boldsymbol{r}_j|$.

Obviously, this condition is satisfied for the transformation $\boldsymbol{r}'_i = \boldsymbol{r}_i + \boldsymbol{a}$, where $\boldsymbol{a}$ represents uniform translation of the whole body.

Now let us try out another transformation which is linear, and is given by

$$(\boldsymbol{r}'_i)_p = \sum_{q=1}^{3} a_{pq}(\boldsymbol{r}_i)_q \qquad (\boldsymbol{r}'_j)_p = \sum_{s=1}^{3} a_{ps}(\boldsymbol{r}_j)_s \qquad p = 1,2,3$$

Hence,

$$|\boldsymbol{r}'_i - \boldsymbol{r}'_j|^2 = \sum_{p,s,q} a_{ps}[(\boldsymbol{r}_i)_s - (\boldsymbol{r}_j)_s]a_{pq}[(\boldsymbol{r}_i)_q - (\boldsymbol{r}_j)_q]$$

$$= a_{ps}a_{pq}[(\boldsymbol{r}_i)_s(\boldsymbol{r}_i)_q + (\boldsymbol{r}_j)_s(\boldsymbol{r}_j)_q - (\boldsymbol{r}_i)_s(\boldsymbol{r}_j)_q - (\boldsymbol{r}_j)_s(\boldsymbol{r}_i)_q]$$

This can be equated to $|\boldsymbol{r}_i - \boldsymbol{r}_j|^2$ if and only if

$$a_{pq}a_{ps} = \delta_{qs}$$

which means that the 3×3 matrix a_{pq} has to be orthogonal. Now, all orthogonal 3×3 matrices can be uniquely represented by some rotation in the 3-D Euclidean space. Hence any finite rotation is a possible rigid displacement satisfying the condition of rigidity.

The transformation represented by inversion, that is, $\boldsymbol{r}_i \rightarrow \boldsymbol{r}'_i = -\boldsymbol{r}_i$, also satisfies the condition of rigidity. But this is not a possible transformation, as it is discrete and cannot be effected by a succession of infinitesimal operations. There is no other operation known that can satisfy the rigidity condition. This completes the proof of Euler's theorem.

Note that the order of translation and rotation can be reversed, and that depending on the choice of the first particle, the amounts of required translation and rotation can also vary. But for a given translation, the rotation is uniquely fixed and vice versa. This fact is more precisely stated in Chasles' theorem.

12.2.2 Chasles' Theorem (1830)

Any rigid displacement can be uniquely expressed as a screw displacement where a screw displacement consists of the combination of a rotation with translation parallel to or along the same axis of rotation called the screw axis.

This theorem is not much used as it is essentially a variation of Euler's theorem. For Chasles' theorem one has to first find out the correct axis of rotation, give the right amount of vector rotation and then the right amount of translation along the axis of rotation. This axis of rotation may in general lie outside the rigid body.

These theorems could also have been proved rigorously by vector analysis but vectorial representation of any arbitrary but finite rotation involves Eulerian rotations and are somewhat complicated and tedious. However we know that there are at most six independent variables involved in the description of the velocity of any point in the rigid body. Equivalents of Euler's theorem and Chasles' theorem exist for the velocity representation and we now proceed to state and prove these by vectorial methods.

12.2.3 Euler's Second Theorem

If a rigid body is moving in any manner and B_o is any point of the body, then there exists at any instant a vector $\boldsymbol{\omega}$ such that the velocity of any particle B of the body at that instant is

$$\boldsymbol{v} = \boldsymbol{u}_o + \boldsymbol{\omega} \times \boldsymbol{\rho} \tag{12.1}$$

where $\boldsymbol{u}_o$ is the velocity of B_o relative to some fixed inertial frame outside the body and $\boldsymbol{\rho}$ is the position vector $\overrightarrow{B_oB}$ of B relative to B_o. Also $\boldsymbol{\omega}$ is unique and is independent of the choice of the point B_o. With respect to any fixed frame outside, there exists a velocity $\boldsymbol{u}$ at a given instant of time such that the velocity of any point B of the body with respect to the above fixed frame at that instant is given by

$$\boldsymbol{v} = \boldsymbol{u} + \boldsymbol{\omega} \times \boldsymbol{r} \tag{12.2}$$

where $\boldsymbol{r}$ is now the position vector of B with respect to the fixed frame.

Note that both $\boldsymbol{u}$ and $\boldsymbol{\omega}$ are claimed to have remained the same for any point of the rigid body at any given instant, so that $\boldsymbol{v}$ varies form point to point only because of differing $\boldsymbol{r}$. The six quantities representing the two vectors $\boldsymbol{u}$ and $\boldsymbol{\omega}$ fix the velocity $\boldsymbol{v}$ of any arbitrary point $\boldsymbol{r}$ in the rigid body at any given instant. With time both $\boldsymbol{u}$ and $\boldsymbol{\omega}$ may change, but at any instant, fixation of the above six quantities is sufficient to obtain the velocity of any point of the body at that instant, using Eq. (12.2).

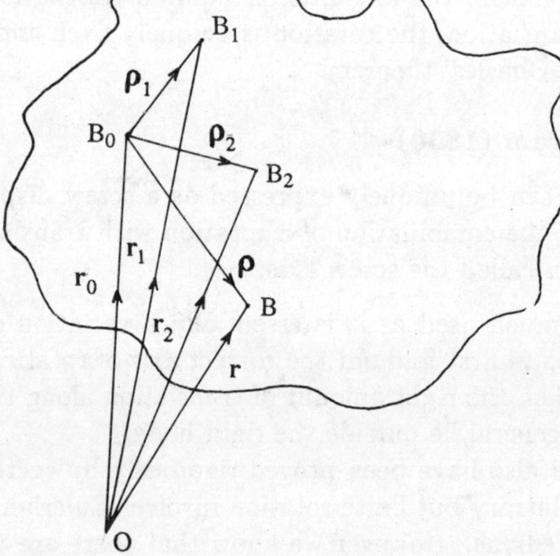

Fig. 12.1 Position vectors of the points B_1, B_2 and B of a rigid body with respect to an outside inertial frame at O and a body frame at B_o

Proof: Let O be the origin of the outside (inertial) reference frame and let us consider any two points B_1 and B_2 of the rigid body and B as any arbitrary point of the rigid body (see

Fig. 12.1). Take

$$\overrightarrow{B_oB_1} = \boldsymbol{\rho}_1 \qquad \overrightarrow{OB_o} = \boldsymbol{r}_o$$
$$\overrightarrow{B_oB_2} = \boldsymbol{\rho}_2 \qquad \overrightarrow{OB_1} = \boldsymbol{r}_1$$
$$\overrightarrow{B_oB} = \boldsymbol{\rho} \qquad \overrightarrow{OB_2} = \boldsymbol{r}_2$$
$$\text{and} \qquad \overrightarrow{OB} = \boldsymbol{r}$$

We shall also require a frame with its origin fixed at B_o and its axes always parallel to those of the inertial frame at O. From the definition of rigidity, we now have

$$|\boldsymbol{\rho}_1|^2 = \text{const.} \qquad |\boldsymbol{\rho}_2|^2 = \text{const.} \qquad |\boldsymbol{\rho}|^2 = \text{const.}$$
$$|\boldsymbol{\rho}_2 - \boldsymbol{\rho}_1|^2 = \text{const.} \qquad |\boldsymbol{\rho} - \boldsymbol{\rho}_1|^2 = \text{const.} \qquad |\boldsymbol{\rho} - \boldsymbol{\rho}_2|^2 = \text{const.}$$

Therefore, their time derivatives must vanish, that is,

$$\boldsymbol{\rho}_1 \cdot \dot{\boldsymbol{\rho}}_1 = \boldsymbol{\rho}_2 \cdot \dot{\boldsymbol{\rho}}_2 = \boldsymbol{\rho} \cdot \dot{\boldsymbol{\rho}} = \boldsymbol{\rho}_1 \cdot \dot{\boldsymbol{\rho}}_2 + \boldsymbol{\rho}_2 \cdot \dot{\boldsymbol{\rho}}_1 = 0$$
$$\boldsymbol{\rho}_1 \cdot \dot{\boldsymbol{\rho}} + \boldsymbol{\rho} \cdot \dot{\boldsymbol{\rho}}_1 = \boldsymbol{\rho}_2 \cdot \dot{\boldsymbol{\rho}} + \boldsymbol{\rho} \cdot \dot{\boldsymbol{\rho}}_2 = 0$$

Now,

$$\begin{aligned}\boldsymbol{\rho}_1 \times (\dot{\boldsymbol{\rho}}_1 \times \dot{\boldsymbol{\rho}}_2) &= (\boldsymbol{\rho}_1 \cdot \dot{\boldsymbol{\rho}}_2)\dot{\boldsymbol{\rho}}_1 - (\boldsymbol{\rho}_1 \cdot \dot{\boldsymbol{\rho}}_1)\dot{\boldsymbol{\rho}}_2 \\ &= (\boldsymbol{\rho}_1 \cdot \dot{\boldsymbol{\rho}}_2)\dot{\boldsymbol{\rho}}_1 + \mathbf{0} \\ &= -(\boldsymbol{\rho}_2 \cdot \dot{\boldsymbol{\rho}}_1)\dot{\boldsymbol{\rho}}_1\end{aligned}$$

So we get

$$\dot{\boldsymbol{\rho}}_1 = \frac{(\dot{\boldsymbol{\rho}}_1 \times \dot{\boldsymbol{\rho}}_2)}{(\dot{\boldsymbol{\rho}}_1 \cdot \boldsymbol{\rho}_2)} \times \boldsymbol{\rho}_1 \tag{12.3}$$

Similarly we can get

$$\dot{\boldsymbol{\rho}}_2 = \frac{(\dot{\boldsymbol{\rho}}_1 \times \dot{\boldsymbol{\rho}}_2)}{(\dot{\boldsymbol{\rho}}_1 \cdot \boldsymbol{\rho}_2)} \times \boldsymbol{\rho}_2 \tag{12.4}$$

A comparison of Eqs (12.3) and (12.4) indicates that the vector

$$\frac{(\dot{\boldsymbol{\rho}}_1 \times \dot{\boldsymbol{\rho}}_2)}{(\dot{\boldsymbol{\rho}}_1 \cdot \boldsymbol{\rho}_2)} = \boldsymbol{\omega} \qquad \text{say} \tag{12.5}$$

behaves like a common angular velocity vector for $\boldsymbol{\rho}_1$ and $\boldsymbol{\rho}_2$ giving velocities of pure rotations $\dot{\boldsymbol{\rho}}_1$, $\dot{\boldsymbol{\rho}}_2$. Should this $\boldsymbol{\omega}$ be the same for any arbitrary point, say B?

Using this expression for $\boldsymbol{\omega}$ let us now evaluate

$$\begin{aligned}(\boldsymbol{\omega} \times \boldsymbol{\rho} - \dot{\boldsymbol{\rho}}) \cdot \boldsymbol{\rho}_1 &= (\boldsymbol{\omega} \times \boldsymbol{\rho}) \cdot \boldsymbol{\rho}_1 - \dot{\boldsymbol{\rho}} \cdot \boldsymbol{\rho}_1 \\ &= -(\boldsymbol{\omega} \times \boldsymbol{\rho}_1) \cdot \boldsymbol{\rho} - \dot{\boldsymbol{\rho}} \cdot \boldsymbol{\rho}_1 \\ &= -\dot{\boldsymbol{\rho}}_1 \cdot \boldsymbol{\rho} + \dot{\boldsymbol{\rho}}_1 \cdot \boldsymbol{\rho} \\ &= 0\end{aligned}$$

Similarly

$$(\boldsymbol{\omega} \times \boldsymbol{\rho} - \dot{\boldsymbol{\rho}}) \cdot \boldsymbol{\rho}_2 = 0$$

Hence $\boldsymbol{\omega} \times \boldsymbol{\rho} = \dot{\boldsymbol{\rho}}$ unless $\boldsymbol{\rho}$ is coplanar with $\boldsymbol{\rho}_1$ and $\boldsymbol{\rho}_2$. When $\boldsymbol{\rho}$ is coplanar with $\boldsymbol{\rho}_1$ and $\boldsymbol{\rho}_2$ say $\boldsymbol{\rho} = \alpha_1\boldsymbol{\rho}_1 + \alpha_2\boldsymbol{\rho}_2$, α_1 and α_2 being scalars, we get

$$\begin{aligned}\boldsymbol{\omega} \times \boldsymbol{\rho} &= \alpha_1(\boldsymbol{\omega} \times \boldsymbol{\rho}_1) + \alpha_2(\boldsymbol{\omega} \times \boldsymbol{\rho}_2)\\ &= \alpha_1\dot{\boldsymbol{\rho}}_1 + \alpha_2\dot{\boldsymbol{\rho}}_2\\ &= \frac{d}{dt}(\alpha_1\boldsymbol{\rho}_1 + \alpha_2\boldsymbol{\rho}_2)\\ &= \dot{\boldsymbol{\rho}}\end{aligned}$$

Therefore, for any arbitrary point B, the vector $\overrightarrow{\mathrm{B_oB}} = \boldsymbol{\rho}$ satisfies a universal relation

$$\dot{\boldsymbol{\rho}} = \boldsymbol{\omega} \times \boldsymbol{\rho} \tag{12.6}$$

where $\boldsymbol{\omega}$ is the same for the whole body and is uniquely determined from the velocities and position vectors of any two points in the body, relative to any point B_o fixed in the body.

Now with this result we can write

$$\dot{\boldsymbol{\rho}} = \boldsymbol{\omega} \times \boldsymbol{\rho} \qquad \dot{\boldsymbol{\rho}}_1 = \boldsymbol{\omega} \times \boldsymbol{\rho}_1, \qquad \dot{\boldsymbol{\rho}}_2 = \boldsymbol{\omega} \times \boldsymbol{\rho}_2$$

where (see Fig. 12.1)

$$\boldsymbol{\rho} = \boldsymbol{r} - \boldsymbol{r}_o \qquad \boldsymbol{\rho}_1 = \boldsymbol{r}_1 - \boldsymbol{r}_o \qquad \boldsymbol{\rho}_2 = \boldsymbol{r}_2 - \boldsymbol{r}_o$$

Therefore, from Fig. 12.1 we further have

$$\dot{\boldsymbol{r}} - \dot{\boldsymbol{r}}_o = \boldsymbol{\omega} \times \boldsymbol{\rho}$$

or

$$\dot{\boldsymbol{r}} = \dot{\boldsymbol{r}}_o + \boldsymbol{\omega} \times \boldsymbol{\rho}$$

or

$$\boldsymbol{v} = \boldsymbol{u}_o + \boldsymbol{\omega} \times \boldsymbol{\rho} \tag{12.1}$$

where $\boldsymbol{v}$ is the velocity of the point B with respect to O and $\boldsymbol{u}_o$ is the velocity of B_o with respect to O.

Now to prove Eq. (12.2) consider

$$\begin{aligned}\dot{\boldsymbol{r}} &= \dot{\boldsymbol{r}}_o + \boldsymbol{\omega} \times \boldsymbol{\rho}\\ &= \dot{\boldsymbol{r}}_o + \boldsymbol{\omega} \times (\boldsymbol{r} - \boldsymbol{r}_o)\\ &= (\dot{\boldsymbol{r}}_o - \boldsymbol{\omega} \times \boldsymbol{r}_o) + \boldsymbol{\omega} \times \boldsymbol{r}\end{aligned}$$

Similarly

$$\dot{\boldsymbol{r}}_1 = (\dot{\boldsymbol{r}}_o - \boldsymbol{\omega} \times \boldsymbol{r}_o) + \boldsymbol{\omega} \times \boldsymbol{r}_1$$

and

$$\dot{\boldsymbol{r}}_2 = (\dot{\boldsymbol{r}}_o - \boldsymbol{\omega} \times \boldsymbol{r}_o) + \boldsymbol{\omega} \times \boldsymbol{r}_2$$

Since the part $(\dot{\boldsymbol{r}}_o - \boldsymbol{\omega} \times \boldsymbol{r}_o)$ is found to be a common velocity term for all particles, it can be set equal to, say,

$$\boldsymbol{u} \equiv \dot{\boldsymbol{r}}_o - (\boldsymbol{\omega} \times \boldsymbol{r}_o) = \boldsymbol{u}_o - (\boldsymbol{\omega} \times \boldsymbol{r}_o)$$

so that

$$\dot{\boldsymbol{r}} = \boldsymbol{u} + \boldsymbol{\omega} \times \boldsymbol{r}$$

or

$$\boldsymbol{v} = \boldsymbol{u} + \boldsymbol{\omega} \times \boldsymbol{r} \tag{12.2}$$

which is the most general result. It expresses the inertial velocity of any point in the rigid body at any instant, in terms of two universal vectors $\boldsymbol{u}$ and $\boldsymbol{\omega}$ which are the same for the whole rigid body. At any instant, $\boldsymbol{v}$ is different for different points in a rigid body only because $\boldsymbol{r}$ is different for different points.

Thus the inertial velocity of any point in the rigid body consists of two parts: one, the homogeneous translational velocity $\boldsymbol{u}$ which is the same for the whole body, and the other, a homogeneous rotation with the instantaneous angular velocity $\boldsymbol{\omega}$, which is also the same for the whole body. The latter quantity is also independent of the choice of the inertial reference frame. The existence of uniform translational and rotational velocities describing the actual velocity of any point of the rigid body proves the velocity analogue of Euler's theorem.

The screw motion view of the velocity vector can also be ascertained in the following way. Decompose $\boldsymbol{u}$ and $\boldsymbol{r}$ into components purely parallel (to the the screw axis) and perpendicular to the $\boldsymbol{\omega}$ vector, so that from Eq. (12.2)

$$\boldsymbol{v} = \left(\frac{\boldsymbol{u} \cdot \boldsymbol{\omega}}{\omega^2}\right)\boldsymbol{\omega} + \boldsymbol{u}_\perp + \boldsymbol{\omega} \times \boldsymbol{r}_\perp$$

Since both $\boldsymbol{u}_\perp$ and $\boldsymbol{\omega} \times \boldsymbol{r}_\perp$ are in the same plane perpendicular to $\boldsymbol{\omega}$, we can define a unique vector $\boldsymbol{R}$ in the plane perpendicular to $\boldsymbol{\omega}$ through the equation

$$\boldsymbol{u}_\perp = \boldsymbol{\omega} \times \boldsymbol{R} \tag{12.7}$$

The vector $\boldsymbol{r}_\perp$ can be written as

$$\boldsymbol{r}_\perp = \boldsymbol{r} - \left(\frac{\boldsymbol{\omega} \cdot \boldsymbol{r}}{\omega^2}\right)\boldsymbol{\omega}$$

Equation (12.7) gives

$$\boldsymbol{u}_\perp + (\boldsymbol{\omega} \times \boldsymbol{r}_\perp) = \boldsymbol{\omega} \times (\boldsymbol{R} + \boldsymbol{r}_\perp)$$

Hence

$$\boldsymbol{v} = \left(\frac{\boldsymbol{u} \cdot \boldsymbol{\omega}}{\omega^2}\right)\boldsymbol{\omega} + \boldsymbol{\omega} \times (\boldsymbol{R} + \boldsymbol{r}_\perp)$$

The first term corresponds to a translational velocity along the axis of rotation and the second term to a pure rotational velocity corresponding to some effective radius vector $(\boldsymbol{R} + \boldsymbol{r}_\perp)$ which lies perpendicular to the axis of rotation. Therefore, the velocity due to any rigid motion can be viewed as a screw velocity consisting of a translational velocity along the screw axis and a rotational velocity about the same axis.

12.2.4 Instantaneous Axis of Rotation

Now, how to find the instantaneous axis of rotation? Note that the equation $\dot{\boldsymbol{\rho}} = \boldsymbol{\omega} \times \boldsymbol{\rho}$ is valid in a frame of reference whose origin is at any arbitrary point B_o in the rigid body, the direction of its axes being fixed in space (that is, not rotating with the body). An observer sitting at B_o and moving with such a frame of reference will note, at any instant, $\boldsymbol{\omega}$ to be the instantaneous axis of rotation. Since $\boldsymbol{\omega}$ appears to pass through B_o, this observer will find himself or herself sitting on the instantaneous axis of rotation. But B_o is an arbitrary point and hence, the above statement will be true for every point in the rigid body.

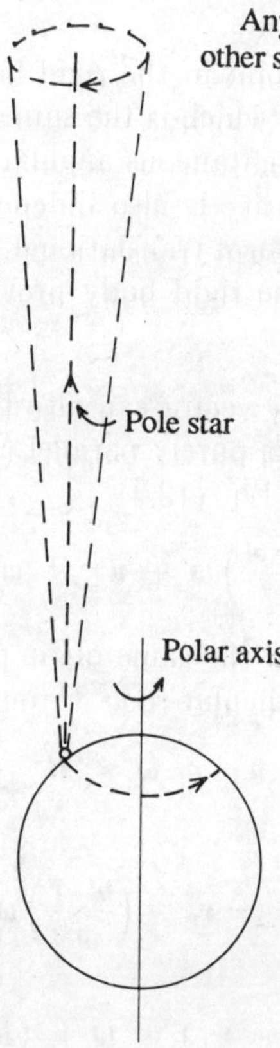

Fig. 12.2 A distant star is seen to revolve in the sky about the the celestial pole due to diurnal rotation of the earth

For example, consider an observer on earth, trying to find the location of the earth's axis of rotation by looking at only the most distant stars (see Fig. 12.2). Such an observer will find himself sitting always on the instantaneous axis of the earth's rotation as all distant stars would seem to be rotating about him/her. But we know for certain that for an observer in an outside fixed inertial frame, the earth's true axis of rotation passes through the centre of the earth. The problem is how to locate the actual line in space representing the instantaneous axis of rotation of any rigid body.

With reference to any outside fixed inertial frame of reference, the velocity of any point, say P, in the body, with position vector $\boldsymbol{r}$ is given by $\dot{\boldsymbol{r}} = \boldsymbol{u} + \boldsymbol{\omega} \times \boldsymbol{r}$. Now if the observer is displaced by $\boldsymbol{R}$ from the origin of the first inertial frame of reference to another, the position vector of P will now be read as $\boldsymbol{r}' = \boldsymbol{r} - \boldsymbol{R}$, and its velocity as $\dot{\boldsymbol{r}}' = \dot{\boldsymbol{r}} - \dot{\boldsymbol{R}}$, which means $\dot{\boldsymbol{r}} = \dot{\boldsymbol{r}}' + \dot{\boldsymbol{R}} = (\boldsymbol{u} + \boldsymbol{\omega} \times \boldsymbol{r}') + \boldsymbol{\omega} \times \boldsymbol{R}$. Since both the observers (frames) are fixed in space, $\dot{\boldsymbol{R}} = 0$, and therefore,

$$\dot{\boldsymbol{r}'} = (\boldsymbol{u} + \boldsymbol{\omega} \times \boldsymbol{R}) + \boldsymbol{\omega} \times \boldsymbol{r} \tag{12.8}$$

Now, if the second observer is sitting on the true axis of rotation of the body, the velocity of the body with respect to that observer is purely rotational plus the component of $\boldsymbol{u}$ parallel to the axis of rotation, if any. Therefore, we must have from Eq. (12.8),

$$\boldsymbol{u}_{\perp} + \boldsymbol{\omega} \times \boldsymbol{R} = 0 \tag{12.9}$$

If we try to solve Eq. (12.9) for $\boldsymbol{R}$ it will not be unique, but we shall get a definite locus for the tip of $\boldsymbol{R}$, which would exactly locate the *instantaneous axis of rotation* of the body (with respect to the first observer). So, we find that although the vector $\boldsymbol{\omega}$ may remain non-local for the kinematical description of the rigid body, it always has a well-defined location in space with respect to any fixed inertial frame. For the rigid earth, the true axis of its rotation passes approximately through its centre and the two geographical poles on its surface. Actually Euler's theorem is applicable only for rigid bodies. Since the distance between any two points on two different bogies of a train or between a point on the wheel or axle and a point on the bogie is not constant, a train as a whole is not a rigid body, but the individual bogies without their wheel systems are. So the instantaneous axes of rotation for these exist and pass through the centres of curvature of the track holding the boggies.

12.3 FRAMES OF REFERENCE USED TO DESCRIBE THE MOTION OF A RIGID BODY

We have already defined and used inertial frames having fixed Cartesian coordinate axes and origins lying outside the rigid body. We now proceed to define the so-called *body frames.* If we attach a frame of reference fixed with respect to a body which is moving in any manner with respect to any inertial frame of reference fixed in space, then the first frame of reference is called a body frame of reference. Obviously the origin of a body frame is fixed with respect to the body. A body frame is in general a simultaneously rotating and translating frame of reference. With respect to any body frame of reference, the matter distribution of the given rigid body and the orientation of all points of the body must remain unchanged for all time.

The instantaneous angular velocity of rotation is a vector quantity denoted usually by $\boldsymbol{\omega}$ and defined through Eq. (12.9). Note that $\boldsymbol{\omega}$ is measured always with respect to an inertial frame of reference. Its components can, however, be expressed in terms of the (instantaneous) unit vectors of any fixed or moving (translating and/or rotating) frame of reference, which may or may not be a body frame.

12.3.1 Deriving an Expression for Inertial Velocity of Any Particle of a Rigid Body With Respect To Any Body Frame Fixed in the Body

We have seen from Euler's theorem that the instantaneous *inertial* velocity of any particle of a rigid body is given by,

$$\boldsymbol{v} = \boldsymbol{u} + \boldsymbol{\omega} \times \boldsymbol{r} \tag{12.2}$$

where $\boldsymbol{u}$ and $\boldsymbol{\omega}$ are the same for the whole body, representing respectively uniform translation and uniform rotation. With respect to a frame fixed at a point B_o in the body and translating (but not rotating) with the body, the velocity of any point $\boldsymbol{v}$, defined through Eq. (12.2) is given by

$$\boldsymbol{v} = \boldsymbol{u}_o + \boldsymbol{\omega} \times \boldsymbol{\rho} \tag{12.1}$$

where $\boldsymbol{u}_o$ is the inertial velocity of the point B_o and $\boldsymbol{\rho}$ is the position vector of the point with respect to B_o. Here, $\boldsymbol{u}_o$ and $\boldsymbol{\omega}$ remain as the same vectors for the whole body. $\boldsymbol{\omega}$ in Eq. (12.1) is still the same angular velocity vector as measured with respect to an inertial frame. The forms of the two expressions (12.1) and (12.2) are the same except for the meanings of the entries that differ in the two cases.

Table 12.1 Various Interpretations of Eq. (12.2)

Frames	*Interpretations of* $\boldsymbol{u}$	$\boldsymbol{\omega}$	$\boldsymbol{r}$
I Space-fixed inertial frame S_o	Translational velocity of the whole rigid body with respect to S_o	Instantaneous angular velocity of the rigid body with respect to the unit vectors of S_o	Position vector of any particle of the rigid body measured from the origin of S_o
II A frame having fixed inertial directions for its axes but the origin translating with the rigid body (S_1)	Inertial velocity of the translating origin of S_1	Instantaneous angular velocity of the rigid body expressed in terms of the unit vectors of S_1	Position vector of any particle of the rigid body measured from the origin of S_1
III A body frame with all the axes fixed in the body and the origin fixed with respect to the body (S_2)	Inertial velocity of the translating origin of the frame S_2 expressed in terms of the unit vectors of S_2	Instantaneous angular velocity the rigid body with respect to S_o expressed in terms of the unit vectors of S_2	Position vector of any particle of the rigid body measured from the origin of S_2

As soon as we go to a *body frame* attached to the point B_o, this new frame will no longer be rotating, and obviously, an observer in the body frame will rather find the body nonrotating. However this does not prohibit us from expressing the vectors $\boldsymbol{\omega}$, $\boldsymbol{u}_o$, $\boldsymbol{v}$ and $\boldsymbol{\rho}$ as measured in an inertial frame in terms of the instantaneous basis vectors of the body frame. Thus we can use Eq. (12.1) to obtain the inertial velocity of a particle in the rigid body and express all the vectors occurring in it in terms of the instantaneous basis vectors of the body frame. Henceforth we shall always use Eq. (12.2) and mention the frame of reference whose basis vectors are used to express the vector quantities occurring in it. Table 12.1 summarises various interpretations of $\boldsymbol{u}$, $\boldsymbol{\omega}$ and $\boldsymbol{r}$ occurring in Eq. (12.2) for different frames of reference, the left hand side of which stands for the *instantaneous inertial velocity* of a particle of a rigid body that is moving in any possible manner.

For a rigid body rotating about a fixed point in it, the types II and III in the above table would be the most suitable frames with the origin chosen to be the fixed point and Eq. (12.2) reduces to

$$\boldsymbol{v} = \boldsymbol{\omega} \times \boldsymbol{r}$$

But the body frame is moving in any manner except that even when the axis of rotation of the body is passing through its origin, $\boldsymbol{u}$ is generally nonzero.

12.4 KINETIC ENERGY OF A ROTATING RIGID BODY

A rigid body is moving in any manner. We are interested in deriving an expression for its kinetic energy T at any instant with respect to any fixed outside inertial observer. Our starting formula would be

$$T = \frac{1}{2} \sum_{k=1}^{N} m_k |\boldsymbol{v}_k|^2 \tag{12.10}$$

where summation extends over all the N constituent particles of the rigid body and the individual terms represent the inertial kinetic energy of the individual particles. The expressions for the inertial velocity $\boldsymbol{v}_k$ must come from the general Eq. (12.2) which however can be interpreted in three different ways for the three different types of frames (see Table 12.1). So

$$\begin{aligned} T &= \frac{1}{2}\sum_k m_k |(\boldsymbol{u} + \boldsymbol{\omega} \times \boldsymbol{r}_k)|^2 \\ &= \frac{1}{2}u^2 \sum_k m_k + \boldsymbol{u} \cdot \sum_k m_k (\boldsymbol{\omega} \times \boldsymbol{r}_k) + \frac{1}{2}\sum_k m_k (\boldsymbol{\omega} \times \boldsymbol{r}_k) \cdot (\boldsymbol{\omega} \times \boldsymbol{r}_k) \\ &= \frac{1}{2}Mu^2 + \sum_k m_k \boldsymbol{r}_k \cdot (\boldsymbol{u} \times \boldsymbol{\omega}) + \frac{1}{2}\sum_k m_k \left[(\boldsymbol{\omega} \cdot \boldsymbol{\omega})(\boldsymbol{r}_k \cdot \boldsymbol{r}_k) - (\boldsymbol{\omega} \cdot \boldsymbol{r}_k)(\boldsymbol{\omega} \cdot \boldsymbol{r}_k)\right] \\ &= \frac{1}{2}Mu^2 + (\boldsymbol{u} \times \boldsymbol{\omega}) \cdot \sum_k m_k \boldsymbol{r}_k + \frac{1}{2}\sum_k m_k \left[\omega^2 r_k^2 - (\boldsymbol{\omega} \cdot \boldsymbol{r}_k)^2\right] \end{aligned}$$

$$= \frac{1}{2}Mu^2 + M\boldsymbol{R}_{\text{cm}} \cdot (\boldsymbol{u} \times \boldsymbol{\omega}) + \frac{1}{2}\sum_{k=1}^{N} m_k \sum_{i=1}^{3}\sum_{j=1}^{3} \{\omega_i\omega_j r_k^2 \delta_{ij} - \omega_i\omega_j (r_k)_i (r_k)_j\}$$

$$= \frac{1}{2}Mu^2 + M\boldsymbol{R}_{\text{cm}} \cdot (\boldsymbol{u} \times \boldsymbol{\omega}) + \frac{1}{2}\sum_{i=1}^{3}\sum_{j=1}^{3} I_{ij}\omega_i\omega_j$$

$$= T_t + T_m + T_r \quad \text{say} \tag{12.11}$$

where $M = \Sigma m_k =$ total mass of the body, $M\boldsymbol{R}_{\text{cm}} = \Sigma m_k \boldsymbol{r}_k$ defines the position vector $\boldsymbol{R}_{\text{cm}}$ of the centre of mass, and finally

$$I_{ij} = \sum_{k=1}^{N} m_k \{r_k^2 \delta_{ij} - (r_k)_i (r_k)_j\} \tag{12.12}$$

are defined to be the components of the *moment of inertia tensor* expressed with respect to the instantaneous position vectors of the constituent particles. Note that in Eq. (12.12) the index k represents the particle number that is the kth particle having mass m_k and instantaneous position $\boldsymbol{r}_k$ with Cartesian components $(r_k)_1$, $(r_k)_2$, $(r_k)_3$,or in the more compact form r_i or r_j. Since both i and j in Eq. (12.12) must run from 1 to 3, there are in all nine components of I_{ij}. It is easy to check that $I_{ij} = I_{ji}$, that is, the moment of inertia tensor is symmetric.

The first term T_t corresponds to the *translational kinetic energy* of the whole body at the given instant.

The second term T_m is a term having mixtures of rotational and translational velocities of individual particles and can therefore be termed as the mixed term. It simply vanishes if either the centre of mass is chosen to be the origin of the reference frame or the whole body translates in a direction parallel to the axis of rotation of the body.

The third term T_r is a purely rotational term, depending exclusively on the the components of the instantaneous angular velocity and the configuration of the whole body. This quantity T_r is taken to be the definition of the *rotational kinetic energy* of the rigid body.

With respect to the outside inertial frame the rigid body is changing its orientation. Therefore, the position vectors of all the constituent particles with respect to the outside inertial frame change continuously with time, thus making I_{ij}, as defined through Eq. (12.12), change with time. It is therefore customary to define I_{ij} with respect to a body frame (S_2) in the sense described in the section 12.3, and obviously we can still have the forms of Eqs (12.11) and (12.12) valid for the body frame. Only the interpretations of the position vectors, of the velocity components and therefore of the components of the moment of inertia tensor should be changed in order to reconcile them with the adopted frame for reference. So in the body frame, not only do all the expressions (12.11) and (12.12) remain the same, but also all the nine components of I_{ij} become static, that is, they do not change with time.

We now introduce the concept of angular momentum of a rigid body both from its Lagrangian and Newtonian definitions.

12.5 ANGULAR MOMENTUM

The *angular momentum* is defined to be the conjugate momentum corresponding to the angular velocity, that is, for a given Lagrangian $\tilde{L}$, the angular momentum

$$\boldsymbol{L} = \frac{\partial \tilde{L}}{\partial \boldsymbol{\omega}}$$

by definition. Since the Lagrangian is a quantity that ought to be evaluated in terms of the inertial kinetic and potential energies (which may however be conveniently expressed in terms of quantities defined in noninertial frames), we use Eq. (12.11) for the inertial kinetic energy, and also assume that the potential energy is independent of $\boldsymbol{\omega}$. We get for the *ith* Cartesian component of the angular momentum

$$L_i = \frac{\partial \tilde{L}}{\partial \omega_i} = \frac{\partial (T - V)}{\partial \omega_i} = \frac{\partial T}{\partial \omega_i} = \frac{\partial (T_m + T_r)}{\partial \omega_i}, \tag{12.13}$$

as $T = T_t + T_m + T_r$, and T_t does not depend on $\boldsymbol{\omega}$. Now

$$\begin{aligned}\frac{\partial T_m}{\partial \omega_i} &= \frac{\partial}{\partial \omega_i}[M\boldsymbol{R}_{\text{cm}} \cdot (\boldsymbol{u} \times \boldsymbol{\omega})] \\ &= M(\boldsymbol{R}_{\text{cm}} \times \boldsymbol{u})_i \\ &= \boldsymbol{R}_{\text{cm}} \times (M\boldsymbol{u})|_i\end{aligned}$$

The right hand side represents the moment of the linear part of the momentum of the whole body as if the whole body is effectively concentrated at the centre of mass of the body and is moving with a uniform translational velocity $\boldsymbol{u}$.

$$\frac{\partial T_r}{\partial \omega_i} = \frac{\partial}{\partial \omega_i}\left(\frac{1}{2}I_{ij}\omega_i\omega_j\right) = I_{ij}\omega_j \tag{12.14}$$

This corresponds to the rotational part of the angular momentum of the body. In the absence of rotation, $\boldsymbol{\omega} = 0$, and this component vanishes. Therefore, the ith component of the total angular momentum of the body is given by

$$L_i = [\boldsymbol{R}_{\text{cm}} \times M\boldsymbol{u}]_i + I_{ij}\omega_j \tag{12.15}$$

Now we want to see whether the angular momentum defined from the Lagrangian is the same as the moment of momentum of the body defined in the usual Newtonian manner. The moment of the total momentum of the body with respect to the origin of any fixed inertial frame is defined and given by

$$\begin{aligned}\boldsymbol{L}^{(m)} &= \sum m\boldsymbol{r} \times \boldsymbol{v} \\ &= \sum m\boldsymbol{r} \times (\boldsymbol{u} + \boldsymbol{\omega} \times \boldsymbol{r}) \\ &= \sum m\boldsymbol{r} \times \boldsymbol{u} + \sum[r^2\boldsymbol{\omega} - (\boldsymbol{r} \cdot \boldsymbol{\omega})\boldsymbol{r}]\end{aligned}$$

or its ith component is given by

$$\begin{aligned} L_i^{(m)} &= [\boldsymbol{R}_{\rm cm} \times M\boldsymbol{u}]_i + \sum m(r^2\omega_i - r_j\omega_j r_i) \\ &= [\boldsymbol{R}_{\rm cm} \times M\boldsymbol{u}]_i + \sum m(r^2\delta_{ij}\omega_j - r_i r_j \omega_j) \\ &= [\boldsymbol{R}_{\rm cm} \times M\boldsymbol{u}]_i + I_{ij}\omega_j \\ &= L_i \end{aligned}$$

Hence the Newtonian definition of the moment of momentum of any rigid body and the Lagrangian definition of its angular momentum as a quantity canonically conjugate to angular velocity refer to the same physical quantity.

Another point to note is that the angular momentum as measured with respect to any outside inertial frame about its origin contains two parts: a purely rotational part and a purely translational part. The translational part is nothing but the moment of the total linear momentum of the body as if the body has been shrunk to a point at the centre of mass and is moving with the inertial linear velocity of the CM. So this term will vanish if the observer is moving with the centre of mass of the system ($\boldsymbol{R}_{\rm cm}$). The second part, that is, the rotational part does not in general point towards the angular velocity, or in other words, the rotational part of the angular momentum vector may have a different direction compared to $\boldsymbol{\omega}$, unless I_{ij} is reduced to a scalar. This is, of course, one of the well-known properties of second rank tensors (see Appendix A3).

12.6 TRANSFORMATIONS OF AND THEOREMS ON THE MOMENT OF INERTIA TENSOR

The concepts of the centre of mass and moment of inertia were introduced by Euler.

Let us choose an arbitrary but fixed point in the rigid body and define a body frame with its origin at a point O in the body (see Fig. 12.3). Then the moment of inertia tensor about O can be defined through Eq. (12.12)

$$I_{ij} = \sum_{k=1}^{N} m_k \left[|\boldsymbol{r}_k|^2\delta_{ij} - (\boldsymbol{r}_k)_i(\boldsymbol{r}_k)_j\right] \tag{12.12}$$

The sum extends over all the N particles of the rigid body with the position vector of the kth particle given by $\boldsymbol{r}_k = \{(r_k)_1\hat{\boldsymbol{\imath}} + (r_k)_2\hat{\boldsymbol{\jmath}} + (r_k)_3\hat{\boldsymbol{k}}\} \equiv \{x_k\hat{\boldsymbol{\imath}} + y_k\hat{\boldsymbol{\jmath}} + z_k\hat{\boldsymbol{k}}\}$ expressed in terms of the given body frame basis vectors $(\hat{\boldsymbol{\imath}}, \hat{\boldsymbol{\jmath}}, \hat{\boldsymbol{k}})$.

Since the body does not rotate or translate with respect to the body frame, the position vector of the particles with respect to the body frame does not change with time. Thus the moment of inertia tensor, defined through Eq. (12.12), depends only on the mass distribution in the body and is a characteristic of the body itself. Further, note that if we choose a different point O$'$ in the body as the origin of the body frame, all the position vectors, in general, change. Consequently, the moment of inertia tensor, about different

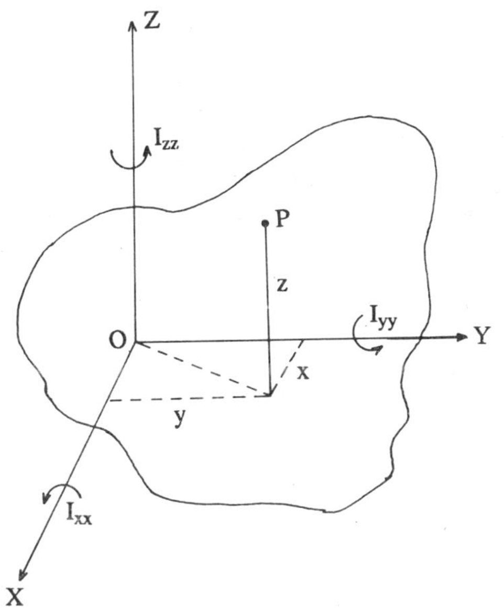

Fig. 12.3 Moments of inertia about the rectangular Cartesian coordinate axes of a body frame

points in the body is in general different. It is evident from Eq. (12.12) that

$$
\begin{aligned}
I_{xx} &= \sum_k m_k(r_k^2 - x_k^2) = \sum_k m_k(y_k^2 + z_k^2) = A \\
&= \text{moment of inertia about the x-axis} \\
I_{yy} &= \sum_k m_k(r_k^2 - y_k^2) = \sum_k m_k(z_k^2 + x_k^2) = B \\
&= \text{moment of inertia about the y-axis} \\
I_{zz} &= \sum_k m_k(r_k^2 - z_k^2) = \sum_k m_k(x_k^2 + y_k^2) = C \\
&= \text{moment of inertia about the z-axis}
\end{aligned}
\tag{12.16}
$$

These diagonal components of I_{ij} are called the moments of inertia of the body about the given point (fixed with respect to body from which the the quantities $\{x_k, y_k, z_k\}$ are measured as the rectangular Cartesian coordinates of the kth particle of the body) and the given set of the body axes. The relations (12.16) define the symbols A, B, and C. Further, we have,

$$
\begin{aligned}
I_{xy} &= -\sum_k m_k x_k y_k = I_{yx} = -D \\
I_{zx} &= -\sum_k m_k z_k x_k = I_{xz} = -F
\end{aligned}
$$

$$I_{yz} = -\sum_k m_k y_k z_k = I_{zy} = -G \tag{12.17}$$

These off-diagonal components of I_{ij} are called the products of inertia of the body about the given point and the given set of the body axes. Equations (12.17) are to be taken as the definitions of the symbols D, F and G.

The relations (12.17) show that the moment of inertia tensor is symmetric and therefore has only six independent components, namely A, B, C, D, F, and G. The details of the structural distribution of the N particles constituting the rigid body are therefore *not required* for studying the dynamics of a rigid body. Only six quantities, namely the three moments of inertia and the three products of inertia of the body, contain sufficient amount of information on the inertial structure of the rigid body, six generalised coordinates for its location and instantaneous orientation in space, and six generalised velocity components, namely $\boldsymbol{u}$ and $\boldsymbol{\omega}$, for the complete description of its instantaneous motion.

12.6.1 Properties of I_{ij}

(a) Changes of I_{ij} Under Translation

Usually all the six components of the moment of inertia tensor are available for a given point and a given set of body axes. Sometimes it is necessary to know the components of the inertia tensor about a different point in the body without of course changing the inertial directions of the body axes. This requires a translation of the origin of the body frame by a finite displacement vector, say $\boldsymbol{a}$. So let us transport the origin from O to O$'$ such that $\overrightarrow{OO'} = \boldsymbol{a}$ and $\boldsymbol{r}' = \boldsymbol{r} - \boldsymbol{a}$ for every particle in the body, but keep the directions of the axes parallel to the original ones. Therefore, the (ij)th component of the moment of inertia tensor at the new point O$'$ would be, by its definition,

$$\begin{aligned}
I'_{ij} &= \sum m(r'^2\delta_{ij} - r'_i r'_j) \\
&= \sum m\left[(r^2 - 2(\boldsymbol{r}\cdot\boldsymbol{a}) + a^2)\delta_{ij} - (r_i - a_i)(r_j - a_j)\right] \\
&= \sum m(r^2\delta_{ij} - r_i r_j) + \sum m(a^2\delta_{ij} - a_i a_j) \\
&\quad - 2\sum m(\boldsymbol{r}\cdot\boldsymbol{a})\delta_{ij} + \sum m(r_i a_j + a_i r_j) \\
&= I_{ij} + M(a^2\delta_{ij} - a_i a_j) - 2M(\boldsymbol{R}\cdot\boldsymbol{a})\delta_{ij} \\
&\quad + (\sum m r_i)a_j + (\sum m r_j)a_i
\end{aligned}$$

The above expression establishes a connection between the two sets of components of the moment of inertia tensor due to the translation of the origin by $\boldsymbol{a}$. If I_{ij} and $\boldsymbol{a}$ are known, the transformed M.I. tensor I'_{ij} can in general be obtained by using the above relation. The knowledge of the actual configuration of the body is also essential for evaluating the last two terms. However the above expression can be greatly simplified if we choose the first origin O to be at the centre of mass of the body. Then by definition, $\sum m r_i = M R_i = 0$, or $\sum m\boldsymbol{r} = 0$. Hence the last three terms in the above expression vanish, with the result that

$$I'_{ij} = I_{ij} + M(a^2\delta_{ij} - a_i a_j) \tag{12.18}$$

where I_{ij} is the moment of inertia tensor with respect to the centre of mass of the rigid body and $\boldsymbol{a}$ is the position vector of the new origin O′ with respect to the CM at O.

So it should be remembered that Eq. (12.18) is to be used for transforming between any two sets of moments of inertia if one of them is about the CM, not between any two arbitrary points. In order to transform the two sets of I_{ij} between any two arbitrary points, one has to do it in two steps: one has first to transform to the CM and then from the CM to the desired point, and this way one does not have to know the details of the structural distribution of the body more than once.

(b) Parallel Axes Theorem

This theorem comes out as a special case of the result derived in the last section.

Suppose that the axes at CM are so oriented that all the products of inertia vanish, that is, $I_{ij} = 0$, if $i \neq j$. Then the transport of the origin parallel to any of these coordinate axes makes only one of the three components of a_i's non-zero and the other two zero. Hence I'_{ij} remains diagonal under such transport of the body frame of reference. For example, $\boldsymbol{a} = (a_1, 0, 0)$, that is, translation parallel to the x-axis by a_1 from CM would give, using Eq. (12.18)

$$\begin{aligned} I'_{ij} &= I_{ij} \qquad \text{for} \quad i \neq j \\ I'_{11} &= I_{11} \\ I'_{22} - I_{22} &= I'_{33} - I_{33} = Ma_1^2 \end{aligned} \tag{12.19}$$

Thus, if the origin is shifted from the centre of mass by a distance a along any coordinate axis, then referred to the shifted axes, the products of inertia as well as the moment of inertia about the direction of displacement remain unchanged while the moments of inertia about the other two axes increase as if an additional point mass has been introduced at the old origin, that is the centre of mass.

(c) Perpendicular Axes Theorem

Consider a rigid body in the form of a thin sheet or a lamina, so that we can neglect its thickness in comparison with other dimensions and take it to have a planar mass distribution. In such cases the so-called perpendicular axis theorem applies, which states that the moment of inertia about the axis perpendicular to the plane of the body equals the sum of the moments of inertia about any two mutually perpendicular axes in the plane of the body (see Fig. 12.4).

From Eqs (12.16) we have

$$I_{xx} = \sum m(y^2 + z^2) \qquad \text{and} \qquad I_{yy} = \sum m(z^2 + x^2)$$

Therefore,

$$I_{xx} + I_{yy} = \sum m(x^2 + y^2 + 2z^2) = I_{zz} + 2\sum mz^2$$

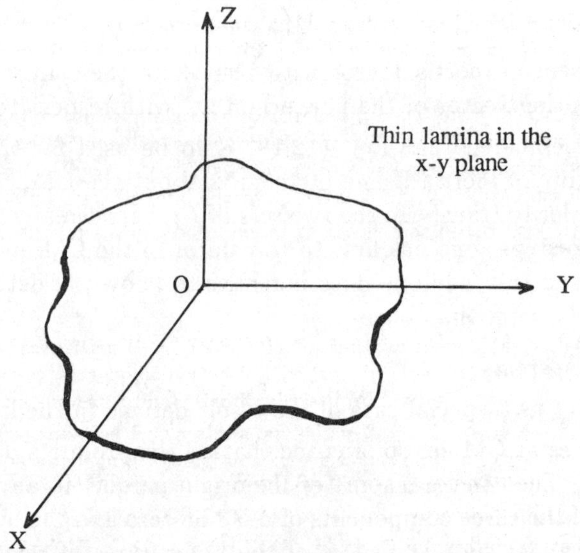

Fig. 12.4 A natural set of the rectangular Cartesian axes for a body frame attached to a thin lamina

This means, in general

$$I_{zz} \leq I_{xx} + I_{yy} \tag{12.20}$$

However, when the body is planar, $\sum mz^2 = 0$, and we get

$$I_{zz} = I_{xx} + I_{yy} \tag{12.21}$$

proving the above theorem.

The perpendicular axes theorem for a three dimensional rigid body may also be viewed as the invariance of the trace of the moment of inertia tensor.

(d) Principal Moments of Inertia

For any given mass distribution of a rigid body and a given origin and a set of rectangular Cartesian axes of the body frame, the moment of inertia tensor can be evaluated with its six independent components specifying the tensor. This set of I_{ij} will change under the rotation of the axes about the origin. Since any nonsingular 3×3 matrix can be diagonalised, it is always possible to find a set of axes (that is, the directions of the corresponding characteristic vectors) with respect to which all the products of inertia terms vanish leaving the diagonal terms as the three eigenvalues. Such a transformation (corresponding to the rotation of the axes) is called a principal axes transformation.

The characteristic equation for such a transformation is given by

$$\det \|I_{ij} - \lambda\delta_{ij}\| = 0 \tag{12.22}$$

which has at most three distinct solutions for λ, say $\lambda_1 = A$, $\lambda_2 = B$ and $\lambda_3 = C$. A, B and C are the diagonal elements of the diagonalised tensor (eigenvalues) and are called the *principal moments of inertia*. For these λ's the characteristic vectors (eigenvectors), namely $\boldsymbol{r}_1$, $\boldsymbol{r}_2$, and $\boldsymbol{r}_3$ specify the corresponding directions of the *principal axes*.

Remarks

(i) For each point of the rigid body there exists a set of principal axes and the corresponding principal moments of inertia.

(ii) If any two of the principal moments of inertia about some special point(s) in the body are equal then the rigid body is called a symmetric top. If all the three are identical then the body is called a spherical top. If all three are different for all points in the body, the rigid body is called an asymmetric top.

(iii) Again, if any two or more principal moments of inertia turn out to be the same, the normalised eigenvectors $\{\hat{\boldsymbol{n}}_1, \hat{\boldsymbol{n}}_2, \hat{\boldsymbol{n}}_3\}$ may not always be linearly independent and cannot be taken as the basis vectors of the new coordinate system. However, as argued in section 11.2.4, it is still possible to have a set of three mutually independent basis vectors, which can further be orthogonalised using Gram-Schmidt's orthogonalisation procedure. Of course, the choice of the characteristic vectors for the degenerate eigenvalues in the plane of degeneracy remains open.

(e) Moment of inertia about any arbitrary direction implied by a vector $\boldsymbol{x}$ passing through the origin

We choose the origin and the three rectangular Cartesian axes of the body frame for constructing the moment of inertia tensor of a body about the origin and the given axes. This is shown in Fig. 12.5. Now we choose an arbitrary direction OS passing through the origin O, about which we want to calculate the moment of inertia of the body. Obviously this quantity will just be a number and it should not depend on how we have chosen the orientations of the axes of the body frame. Such quantities are called scalars, as opposed to vectors or tensors. If we denote the direction OS by the vector, say $\boldsymbol{x}$, and the moment of inertia of the body about OS by I_x, then from the basic definition of the moment of inertia about an axis,

$$I_x = \sum_{\{P\}} m \, \mathrm{PN}^2$$

where the sum extends over all points P of the body, and rectilinear segment PN as shown in Fig. 12.5 corresponds to the normal distance of the point P from the given axis OS. Since $\overrightarrow{\mathrm{OP}} = \boldsymbol{r}$, and $\overrightarrow{\mathrm{OS}} = \boldsymbol{x}$, we can write PN^2 in terms of $\boldsymbol{r}$ and $\boldsymbol{x}$ as

$$\mathrm{PN}^2 = \left(\frac{\boldsymbol{r} \times \boldsymbol{x}}{x}\right)^2$$

where $x = |\boldsymbol{x}|$.

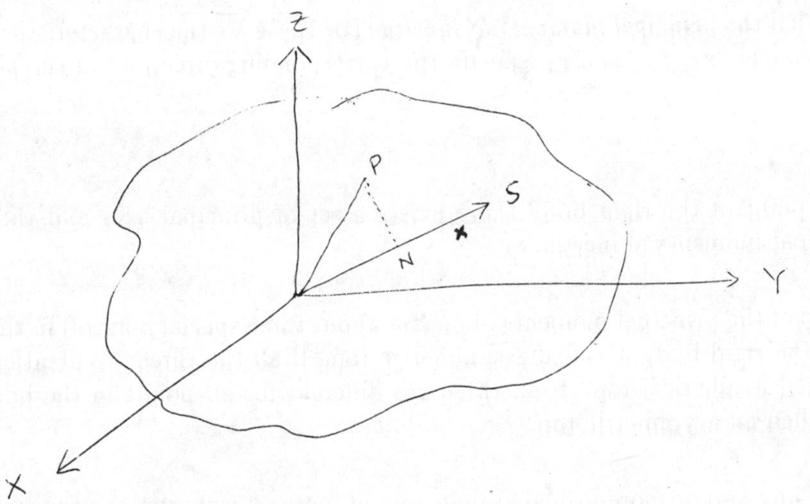

Fig. 12.5 A geometrical construction for calculating the moments of inetria of a rigid body about any line passing through the origin of the chosen body frame

Now consider

$$\begin{aligned} I_x x^2 &= \sum m |r \times x|^2 \\ &= \sum m \left[r^2 x^2 - (r \cdot x)^2 \right] \\ &= \sum m \left[r^2 x_i x_j \delta_{ij} - r_i x_i r_j x_j \right] \\ &= I_{ij} x_i x_j \end{aligned}$$

It is now obvious that I_x is a scalar formed out of the explicit knowledge of the direction OS and the moment of inertia tensor corresponding to the given origin and axes of the body frame, and its value is given by

$$I_x = \frac{\sum_{i,j} I_{ij} x_i x_j}{x^2} \tag{12.23}$$

or written explicitly,

$$I_x = \frac{1}{x^2} \left[I_{11} x_1^2 + I_{22} x_2^2 + I_{33} x_3^2 + 2 I_{12} x_1 x_2 + 2 I_{31} x_3 x_1 + 2 I_{23} x_2 x_3 \right]$$

(f) Ellipsoid of Inertia

The concept of ellipsoid of inertia was introduced by Cauchy.

We first note that Eq. (12.23) needs the specification of the direction of x and not the magnitude of $\boldsymbol{x}$. (To make this more apparent, note that

$$\frac{x_i x_j}{x^2} = l_i l_j$$

where (l_1, l_2, l_3) are the direction cosines of the direction $\boldsymbol{x}$ with respect to the Cartesian coordinate frame chosen as the body frame.) This means that we have the freedom of choosing the magnitude of $\boldsymbol{x}$ if that can serve any useful purpose. Indeed it can, if we choose the magnitude of $\boldsymbol{x}$ to be $1/\sqrt{I_x}$, so that

$$I_x x^2 = 1 = I_{ij} x_i x_j$$

that is,

$$I_{11}x_1^2 + I_{22}x_2^2 + I_{33}x_3^2 + 2I_{12}x_1x_2 + 2I_{23}x_2x_3 + 2I_{31}x_3x_1 = 1 \tag{12.24}$$

The above equation has the following form

$$ax^2 + by^2 + cz^2 + 2dxy + 2ezx + 2fyz = 1$$

where a, b, c, d, e, and f are constants. This is in fact an equation of an ellipsoid. This ellipsoid is generated by the tip of the vector $\boldsymbol{x}$ having the magnitude $x = 1/\sqrt{I_x}$. So what one has to do, in order to generate the above ellipsoid is to choose the directions of OS arbitrarily, find the moment of inertia about all such OS differently oriented and plot in the direction of OS the inverse of the square root of the moment of inertia of the body about that direction. The ellipsoid thus obtained is called the *ellipsoid of inertia*, or the *momental ellipsoid*, or simply the *inertial ellipsoid.*

The largest axis of the inertial ellipsoid corresponds to the direction about which the moment of inertia is minimum and the shortest axis of the ellipsoid of inertia must correspond to the direction about which the moment of inertia is maximum. Here, of course, one is referring to the moments of inertia about the set of axes passing through the origin of the coordinate frame. In order to obtain the inertial ellipsoid about the given origin of the body frame one can proceed as follows. Choose a large number of densely spaced directions (θ, ϕ) passing through the origin and $0 \leq \theta \leq \pi$ and $0 \leq \phi < 2\pi$. From the knowledge of I_{ij}, using Eq. (12.23) compute I_x for every chosen direction and plot a pair of points (for every direction) which lie at a distance $\pm 1/\sqrt{I_x}$ from the origin. All such points finally make the inertial ellipsoid.

Note that each point of the rigid body, as well as every point of the space surrounding the body which can be connected to the rigid body by a rigid rod, possesses a unique inertial ellipsoid. However, an inertial ellipsoid at any such point can be obtained rather easily from the knowledge of the inertial ellipsoid around the centre of mass of the body, and then using Eq. (12.18). Further, it is obvious that the axes of the inertial ellipsoid at any point define the principal axes of the moment of inertia tensor at that point. When the coordinate axes are set along the axes of the inertial ellipsoid, Eq. (12.24) becomes

$$I_x x^2 + I_y y^2 + I_z z^2 = 1 \tag{12.25}$$

as it should.

The concept of the inertial ellipsoid is a very useful one due to the symmetry it stands for. For example, for any spherical top, we have $I_x = I_y = I_z$ about the centre of mass of the top. A spherical top does not necessarily have to be spherical in geometry. It can as well be a homogeneous cube, for example, for which all the three principal moments of inertia are identical when referred to its centre of mass. The inertial ellipsoid about its centre of mass is a sphere of radius $1/\sqrt{I}$, $I = Ma^2/6$, a being the length of any side of the cube. Hence, the moment of inertia of the cube about any arbitrary axis passing through its centre of mass is the same, which appears rather surprising for an object like a cube. Surely, one would tend to intuitively think that the moment of inertia about an axis passing through the corner of the cube for example, would be different from that about an axis passing normally through the middle of any two parallel faces! Now if we shift the origin of the body frame to one of the corners of the cube, the ellipsoid of inertia no longer remains spherical. Along all the axes of the four-fold symmetry of the cube and the body diagonals, the transported origin would produce inertial ellipsoids as prolate spheroids, and in arbitrary directions the inertial ellipsoids become truly ellipsoids. After pointing out asymmetries about symmetric objects, let us give an example of symmetries for asymmetric bodies. Take any irregular body, and try to draw the ellipsoid of inertia about any arbitrary point of the body — it is still an ellipsoid. If you come to think of it, you may find a simple answer to it. In any case, due to various reflection symmetries of an ellipsoid, the momental ellipsoid can be cut into eight pieces equal in all respects. So there are eight directions, one in each piece, that will give the identical moment of inertia. And this is true for any arbitrary point chosen in any irregular body!

12.7 EXAMPLES OF THE CALCULATION AND THE EXPERIMENTAL MEASUREMENT OF THE MOMENT OF INERTIA TENSOR

1. A Homogeneous Right Triangular Pyramid with the Rectangular Base Sides a and Height 3a/2

Shown in Fig. 12.6 is a right triangular pyramid with reference to a fixed body frame.

We wish to obtain the moment of inertia tensor about the origin O. With $i, j = x, y, z$ we can write

$$I_{ij} = \int_0^{3a/2} dz \int_0^{a-(2z/3)} dy \int_0^{a-(2z/3)-y} dx\, \rho \begin{pmatrix} y^2+z^2 & -xy & -zx \\ -xy & z^2+x^2 & -yz \\ -zx & -yz & x^2+y^2 \end{pmatrix}$$

where ρ is the constant mass density of the triangular pyramid. ρ can be expressed in terms of the total mass M of the pyramid as

$$M = \rho \int_0^{3a/2} dz \int_0^{a-(2z/3)} dy \int_0^{a-(2z/3)-y} dx = \frac{1}{4}a^3\rho$$

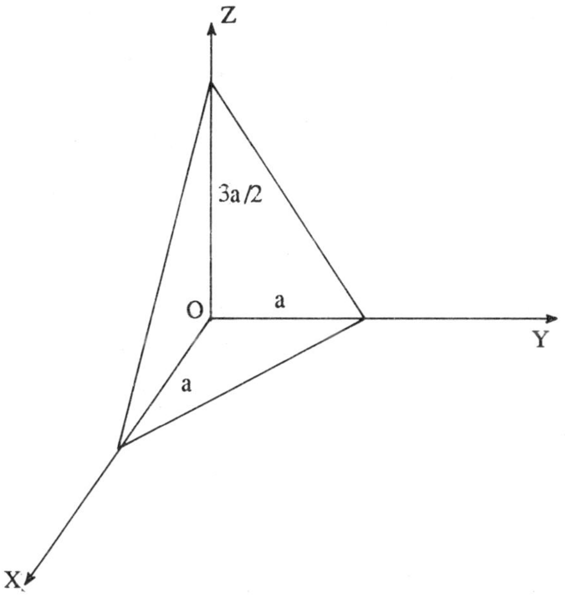

Fig. 12.6 A choice of the rectangular Cartesian axes and origin of a suitable body frame for a right triangular pyramid

Thus for the I_{ij} about O with respect to the xyz axes shown in Fig 12.6 we obtain

$$I_{ij} = \frac{Ma^2}{40}\begin{pmatrix} 13 & -2 & -3 \\ -2 & 13 & -3 \\ -3 & -3 & 8 \end{pmatrix} \tag{12.26}$$

In order to obtain the principal moments of inertia about O and the principal axes of inertia, we diagonalise the inertia tensor in Eq. (12.26) as described in section (12.6.1) (d). The result is

$$I_{ij}^{(p)} = \frac{Ma^2}{40}\begin{pmatrix} 15 & 0 & 0 \\ 0 & 5 & 0 \\ 0 & 0 & 14 \end{pmatrix} \tag{12.27}$$

with the eigenvectors for the principal axes

$$\begin{aligned} \hat{\boldsymbol{i}}_p &= \frac{1}{\sqrt{2}}(\hat{\boldsymbol{i}} - \hat{\boldsymbol{j}}) \\ \hat{\boldsymbol{j}}_p &= \frac{1}{\sqrt{6}}(\hat{\boldsymbol{i}} + \hat{\boldsymbol{j}} + 2\hat{\boldsymbol{k}}) \\ \hat{\boldsymbol{k}}_p &= -\frac{\sqrt{2}}{3}(\hat{\boldsymbol{i}} + \hat{\boldsymbol{j}}) + \frac{1}{\sqrt{3}}\hat{\boldsymbol{k}} \end{aligned} \tag{12.28}$$

where $\hat{\boldsymbol{i}}$, $\hat{\boldsymbol{j}}$ and $\hat{\boldsymbol{k}}$ are the unit vectors along the x, y and z axes shown in Fig. 12.6.

Note that we get

$$A : B : C = 15 : 5 : 14$$

where A, B and C are defined through Eq. (12.16), and are here the principal moments of inertia about the origin.

Thus the principal moments of inertia about O correspond to those of an asymmetric top. The ellipsoid of inertia about O is an ellipsoid with its axes in the ratio

$$\frac{1}{\sqrt{5}} : \frac{1}{\sqrt{14}} : \frac{1}{\sqrt{15}}$$

2. *A Homogeneous Ellipsoid having Semiaxes a, b and c*

The total mass M, expressed in terms of constant density ρ is

$$M = \frac{4\pi}{3}\rho abc$$

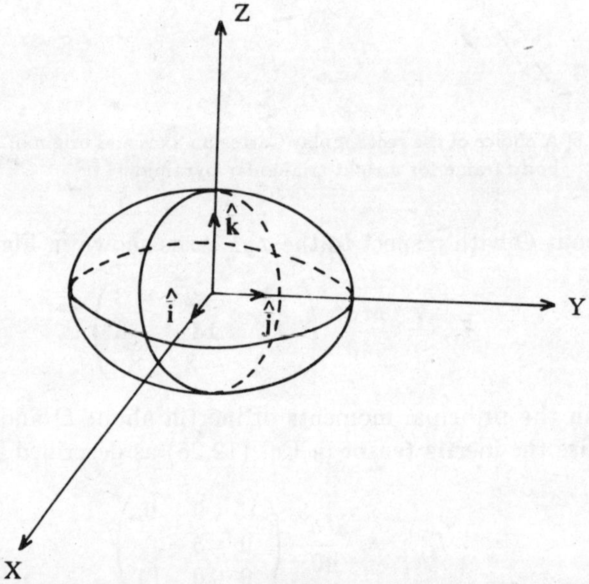

Fig. 12.7 A rectangular Cartesian body frame attached to the CM of a homogeneous ellipsoid

The moment of inertia tensor about O, with respect to x, y and z axes shown in Fig. 12.7 is

$$I_{ij} = \frac{M}{5}\begin{pmatrix} b^2 + c^2 & 0 & 0 \\ 0 & c^2 + a^2 & 0 \\ 0 & 0 & a^2 + b^2 \end{pmatrix} = I_{ij}^{(p)}$$

with the principal axes $\hat{\boldsymbol{i}}_p = \hat{\boldsymbol{i}}$, $\hat{\boldsymbol{j}}_p = \hat{\boldsymbol{j}}$ and $\hat{\boldsymbol{k}}_p = \hat{\boldsymbol{k}}$ with $\hat{\boldsymbol{i}}, \hat{\boldsymbol{j}}, \hat{\boldsymbol{k}}$ vectors as defined in Fig. 12.7.

3. The Earth Approximated to an Inhomogeneous Oblate Spheroid

The smooth mean sea level surface of the earth corresponds to a figure called geoid which is best approximated to an oblate spheroid with the equatorial semimajor axis $a = 6378137$m and the polar semiminor axis $c = 6356752$m, thus defining the geometrical flattening f to be

$$f = \frac{a - c}{a} = \frac{1}{298.257} = 0.00335281$$

This amount of flattening is known to be consistent with the hydrostatic equilibrium of the earth corresponding to its axial period of rotation. The seismic studies of the earth reveal that the interior part of the earth is quite inhomogeneous, both density and temperature increasing towards the centre. For any calculation of the moments of inertia of the earth, the knowledge of the density profile along the radial line is essential. However, it is also possible to measure the moments of inertia of the earth from the way it responds dynamically to the torques produced on earth, due to the action of the sun and the moon, or even from the details of the gravity measurements at different points of the earth, or from the details of the orbits of the thousands of geocentric artificial satellites.

We know that the principal moments of inertia of the earth about its centre of mass are

$$A = B = 0.329591\, Ma^2 \qquad C = 0.330674\, Ma^2 \tag{12.29}$$

with $Ma^2 = 2.4294 \times 10^{38}$ kg m^2, and a better defined quantity called the mass quadrupole moment of the earth, $J_2 = (C - A)/Ma^2 = 0.00108263$. When we shall be dealing with the forced precession of the axis of rotation of the earth in a forthcoming section of this chapter, we shall need the value of the following ratio

$$\frac{C - A}{C} = 0.00327401 = (305.436)^{-1} \tag{12.30}$$

Had the interior of the earth been homogeneous, one would have got for the principal moments about the centre of mass of the earth

$$A = B = \frac{1}{5}M(a^2 + c^2) \qquad C = \frac{2}{5}Ma^2 = 0.4\, Ma^2 \tag{12.31}$$

The difference between the two sets of values given in Eqs (12.29) and (12.31) is substantial, indicating once again that the interior of the earth is much more dense compared to its surface layers, which has led to great reduction of its moment of inertia about each of the geocentric principal axes. Moreover, for the homogeneous oblate earth,

$$\frac{C - A}{C} = \frac{a^2 - c^2}{2a^2} \simeq \frac{a - c}{a} = (298.257)^{-1} \tag{12.32}$$

which differs from the actual amount quoted in Eq. (12.30).

4. Experimental Determination of the Moment of Inertia Tensor of any Rigid Body About its Centre of Mass

This can easily be done by using the body as part of a torsional pendulum and measuring its period of oscillation. As shown in Fig. 12.8, the body should be mounted on the pendulum so as to make its CM lie on the line of the suspension wire. It is easily seen that the torsional period of oscillation (P) of the pendulum is given by

$$P = 2\pi\sqrt{\frac{I_z + I_f}{\phi}} \tag{12.33}$$

where I_z and I_f are the moments of inertia of the body and the frame used to mount the body (see Fig. 12.8) respectively and ϕ is the torsional constant of the suspension wire. I_f and ϕ can be determined, for example, by measuring periods of oscillation of two cylinders whose moments of inertia about their axes are known. Then, using Eq. (12.33), I_z can be found out. Repeating the same experiment by mounting the body in two orientations which are mutually perpendicular and also perpendicular to the z direction, one can determine I_x and I_y.

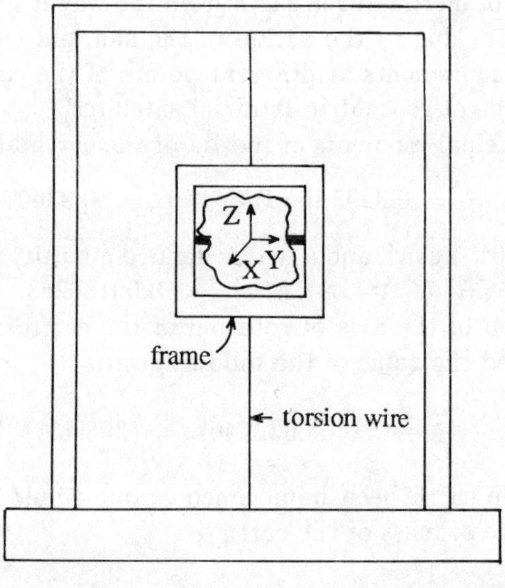

Fig. 12.8 An experimental set up for measuring the moments of inertia of a rigid body

To obtain the products of inertia, determine the moments of inertia, by the above procedure, about three arbitrary directions, all passing through the centre of mass. Expressing these in terms of I_{ij} and using Eq. (12.23) yield three algebraic equations in three unknowns, viz. I_{xy}, I_{zx}, and I_{yz}.

In Table 12.2 we give moments of inertia of bodies with various shapes and dimensions. The student is urged to actually compute and verify these formulae. The equations of the ellipsoid of inertia are given with respect to the point referred to in the caption of individual items and the principal axes. In order to transform the moment of inertia tensor and the equation of ellipsoid of inertia about any other point, one has to use the general transformation rules given in section 12.6.1.

Table 12.2 Moments of Inertia (MI) and Ellipsoids of Inertia (EI)

1. A straight filament AB of length l lying along the x-axis with its centre at the origin O

$$\text{MI}: \quad I_{xx}(\text{O}) = 0 \qquad I_{yy}(\text{O}) = I_{zz}(\text{O}) = \frac{Ml^2}{12}$$

$$\text{EI}: \quad \frac{Ml^2}{12}(y^2 + z^2) = 1 \qquad \text{an infinite cylinder}$$

$$\text{MI}: \quad I_{xx}(\text{A}) = 0 \qquad I_{yy}(\text{A}) = I_{zz}(\text{A}) = \frac{Ml^2}{3}$$

$$\text{EI}: \quad \frac{Ml^2}{3}(y^2 + z^2) = 1$$

2. A circular filament of radius r lying in the xy-plane with its centre at O

$$\text{MI}: \quad I_{xx}(\text{O}) = I_{yy}(\text{O}) = \frac{Mr^2}{2} \qquad I_{zz}(\text{O}) = Mr^2$$

$$\text{EI}: \quad \frac{Mr^2}{2}(x^2 + y^2 + 2z^2) = 1$$

3. A circular arc of radius r and angle 2θ, lying in the xy-plane with the axis of symmetry on the x-axis and the centre of the circle at the origin O

$$\text{MI}: \quad I_{xx}(\text{O}) = \frac{Mr^2}{2}\left(1 - \frac{\sin 2\theta}{2\theta}\right)$$

$$I_{yy}(\text{O}) = \frac{Mr^2}{2}\left(1 + \frac{\sin 2\theta}{2\theta}\right) \qquad I_{zz}(\text{O}) = Mr^2$$

$$\text{EI}: \quad \frac{Mr^2}{2}\left[\left(1 - \frac{\sin 2\theta}{2\theta}\right)x^2 + \left(1 + \frac{\sin 2\theta}{2\theta}\right)y^2 + 2z^2\right] = 1$$

4. An isosceles triangular lamina of height h and base b with base on the x-axis and the axis of symmetry on the y-axis

$$\text{MI}: \quad I_{xx}(\text{O}) = \frac{Mh^2}{6} \qquad I_{yy}(\text{O}) = \frac{Mb^2}{24} \qquad I_{zz}(\text{O}) = M\left(\frac{h^2}{6} + \frac{b^2}{24}\right)$$

$$\text{EI}: \quad \frac{Mh^2}{6}x^2 + \frac{Mb^2}{24}y^2 + M\left(\frac{h^2}{6} + \frac{b^2}{24}\right)z^2 = 1$$

5. A rectangular lamina of sides a and b with side a parallel to the x-axis and side b

parallel to the y-axis and the centre at the origin O

$$\text{MI}: \quad I_{xx}(\text{O}) = \frac{Mb^2}{12} \qquad I_{yy}(\text{O}) = \frac{Ma^2}{12} \qquad I_{zz}(\text{O}) = \frac{Ma^2 + Mb^2}{12}$$

$$\text{EI}: \quad \frac{Mb^2}{12}x^2 + \frac{Ma^2}{12}y^2 + \frac{Ma^2 + Mb^2}{12}z^2 = 1$$

6. A circular lamina of radius r lying in the xy-plane with its centre at the origin O

$$\text{MI}: \quad I_{xx}(\text{O}) = I_{yy}(\text{O}) = \frac{Mr^2}{4} \qquad I_{zz}(\text{O}) = \frac{Mr^2}{2}$$

$$\text{EI}: \quad \frac{Mr^2}{4}(x^2 + y^2 + 2z^2) = 1$$

7. An annular lamina of inner radius a and outer radius b lying in the xy-plane with its centre at the origin O

$$\text{MI}: \quad I_{xx}(\text{O}) = I_{yy}(\text{O}) = \frac{M(a^2 + b^2)}{4} \qquad I_{zz}(\text{O}) = \frac{M(a^2 + b^2)}{2}$$

$$\text{EI}: \quad \frac{M(a^2 + b^2)}{4}(x^2 + y^2 + 2z^2) = 1$$

8. An elliptical lamina whose boundary is defined by the equations $z = 0$ and $x^2/a^2 + y^2/b^2 = 1$ with its centre at the origin O

$$\text{MI}: \quad I_{xx}(\text{O}) = \frac{Mb^2}{4} \qquad I_{yy}(\text{O}) = \frac{Ma^2}{4} \qquad I_{zz}(\text{O}) = \frac{M(a^2 + b^2)}{4}$$

$$\text{EI}: \quad \frac{M}{4}[b^2x^2 + a^2y^2 + (a^2 + b^2)z^2] = 1$$

9. A spherical shell of radius r with its centre at the origin O

$$\text{MI}: \quad I_{xx}(\text{O}) = I_{yy}(\text{O}) = I_{zz}(\text{O}) = \frac{2}{3}Mr^2$$

$$\text{EI}: \quad \frac{2}{3}Mr^2(x^2 + y^2 + z^2) = 1$$

10. A cylindrical lamina of length l and radius r with its axis along the z-axis and centre at the origin O

$$\text{MI}: \quad I_{xx}(\text{O}) = I_{yy}(\text{O}) = M\left(\frac{r^2}{2} + \frac{l^2}{12}\right) \qquad I_{zz}(\text{O}) = Mr^2$$

$$\text{EI}: \quad \frac{M}{2}\left[\left(r^2 + \frac{l^2}{6}\right)(x^2 + y^2) + 2r^2z^2\right] = 1$$

11. A solid sphere (or hemisphere) of radius r with its centre at origin O

$$\text{MI}: \quad I_{xx}(\text{O}) = I_{yy}(\text{O}) = I_{zz}(\text{O}) = \frac{2Mr^2}{5}$$

$$\text{EI}: \quad \frac{2Mr^2}{5}(x^2 + y^2 + z^2) = 1$$

12. A hollow sphere of inner radius a and outer radius b with centre at origin O

$$\text{MI}: \quad I_{xx}(\text{O}) = I_{yy}(\text{O}) = I_{zz}(\text{O}) = \frac{2}{5}M\frac{b^5 - a^5}{b^3 - a^3}$$

$$\text{EI}: \quad \frac{2}{5}M\frac{b^5 - a^5}{b^3 - a^3}(x^2 + y^2 + z^2) = 1$$

13. A solid cylinder of radius r and length l with its axis along the z-axis and centre at the origin O

$$\text{MI}: \quad I_{xx}(\text{O}) = I_{yy}(\text{O}) = M\left(\frac{r^2}{4} + \frac{l^2}{12}\right) \qquad I_{zz}(\text{O}) = \frac{Mr^2}{2}$$

$$\text{EI}: \quad \frac{M}{4}\left[\left(r^2 + \frac{l^2}{3}\right)(x^2 + y^2) + 2r^2z^2\right] = 1$$

14. A hollow cylinder of length l, inner radius a and outer radius b with axis along the z-axis and centre at the origin O

$$\text{MI}: \quad I_{xx}(\text{O}) = I_{yy}(\text{O}) = M\left(\frac{a^2 + b^2}{4} + \frac{l^2}{12}\right), \quad I_{zz}(\text{O}) = \frac{M(a^2 + b^2)}{2}$$

$$\text{EI}: \quad \frac{M}{2}\left[\left(\frac{a^2 + b^2}{2} + \frac{l^2}{6}\right)(x^2 + y^2) + (a^2 + b^2)z^2\right] = 1$$

15. A solid right elliptical cylinder of height h and transverse axes $2a$ and $2b$ with longitudinal axis of the cylinder in the z-direction, major axis a in the x-direction, minor axis b in the y-direction and centre at the origin O

$$\text{MI}: \quad I_{xx}(\text{O}) = M\left(\frac{b^2}{4} + \frac{h^2}{12}\right) \qquad I_{yy}(\text{O}) = M\left(\frac{a^2}{4} + \frac{h^2}{12}\right)$$

$$I_{zz}(\text{O}) = \frac{M(a^2 + b^2)}{4}$$

$$\text{EI}: \quad \frac{M}{4}\left[\left(b^2 + \frac{h^2}{3}\right)x^2 + \left(a^2 + \frac{h^2}{3}\right)y^2 + (a^2 + b^2)z^2\right] = 1$$

16. A solid rectangular parallelepiped with sides a, b and c parallel to the $x-$, $y-$ and z-axes respectively and with centre at the origin O

$$\text{MI}: \quad I_{xx}(\text{O}) = \frac{M(b^2 + c^2)}{12} \qquad I_{yy}(\text{O}) = \frac{M(c^2 + a^2)}{12}$$

$$I_{zz}(\text{O}) = \frac{M(a^2 + b^2)}{12}$$

$$\text{EI}: \quad \frac{M}{12}\left[(b^2 + c^2)x^2 + (c^2 + a^2)y^2 + (a^2 + b^2)z^2\right] = 1$$

17. A solid right circular cone of height h and radius of base r with the symmetry axis in the z-direction and the base in the xy-plane with the centre at the origin O

$$\text{MI}: \quad I_{xx}(\text{O}) = I_{yy}(\text{O}) = \frac{M(3r^2 + 2h^2)}{20} \qquad I_{zz}(\text{O}) = \frac{3Mr^2}{10}$$

$$\text{EI}: \quad \frac{M}{20}\left[(3r^2 + 2h^2)(x^2 + y^2) + 6r^2z^2\right] = 1$$

18. A solid torus whose equation in cylindrical coordinates ρ, ϕ and z is given by $(\rho - b)^2 + z^2 = a^2$ where $b > a$ with the centre of symmetry at the origin O

$$\text{MI}: \quad I_{xx}(\text{O}) = I_{yy}(\text{O}) = \frac{M(5a^2 + 4b^2)}{8} \qquad I_{zz}(\text{O}) = \frac{M(3a^2 + 4b^2)}{4}$$

$$\text{EI}: \quad \frac{M}{8}\left[(5a^2 + 4b^2)(x^2 + y^2) + 2(3a^2 + 4b^2)z^2\right] = 1$$

12.8 ANGULAR MOMENTUM IN LABORATORY AND CENTRE OF MASS FRAMES

Laboratory frames are a class of idealised fixed inertial frames firmly attached to the earth or a laboratory in space, neglecting the effect of their rotation and acceleration, if any. For a colliding system, laboratory frame is usually defined to be the one in which either the heavier particle or the force centre is at rest. Let a system of N particles have masses m_i, position vectors $\boldsymbol{r}_i$ and velocities $\boldsymbol{v}_i$, with the total angular momentum about the origin of the laboratory frame as

$$\boldsymbol{L} = \sum_{i=1}^{N} \boldsymbol{r}_i \times \boldsymbol{p}_i$$

where $\boldsymbol{p}_i = m_i\boldsymbol{v}_i = m_i d\boldsymbol{r}_i/dt$ is the linear momentum of the ith particle in the laboratory frame. The position vector of the centre of mass and its velocity with respect to the laboratory frame are defined to be

$$\boldsymbol{R} = \frac{\sum m_i\boldsymbol{r}_i}{\sum m_i} = \frac{\sum m_i\boldsymbol{r}_i}{M} \qquad \boldsymbol{V} = \frac{\sum m_i\boldsymbol{v}_i}{\sum m_i} = \frac{\sum \boldsymbol{p}_i}{\sum m_i} = \frac{\sum \boldsymbol{p}_i}{M} \tag{12.34}$$

where M is the total mass of the system.

The centre of mass (CM) frame is, by definition, the frame in which the origin of the coordinate frame coincides with the centre of mass of the system. Consequently, the velocity of the centre of mass vanishes in the centre of mass frame. Let us denote the quantities measured with respect to the centre of mass frame by primes on the corresponding symbols, so that

$$\boldsymbol{r}'_i = \boldsymbol{r}_i - \boldsymbol{R} \qquad \boldsymbol{v}'_i = \dot{\boldsymbol{r}}'_i = \dot{\boldsymbol{r}}_i - \dot{\boldsymbol{R}} = \boldsymbol{v}_i - \boldsymbol{V} \qquad \boldsymbol{p}'_i = m_i(\boldsymbol{v}_i - \boldsymbol{V}) \tag{12.35}$$

It is easy to verify that

$$\sum m_i \boldsymbol{r}'_i = \boldsymbol{0} \qquad \text{and} \qquad \sum \boldsymbol{p}'_i = \boldsymbol{0} \tag{12.36}$$

The angular momentum in the CM frame about the CM is defined to be

$$\boldsymbol{L}' = \sum \boldsymbol{r}'_i \times \boldsymbol{p}'_i \tag{12.37}$$

There are two other equivalent ways of defining the same quantity, namely,

$$\boldsymbol{L}'_1 = \sum \boldsymbol{r}'_i \times \boldsymbol{p}_i \tag{12.38}$$

and

$$\boldsymbol{L}'_2 = \sum \boldsymbol{r}_i \times \boldsymbol{p}'_i \tag{12.39}$$

The equivalence of these three definitions can be easily established. Consider

$$\begin{aligned} \boldsymbol{L}' &= \sum \boldsymbol{r}'_i \times \boldsymbol{p}'_i = \sum \boldsymbol{r}'_i \times (\boldsymbol{p}_i - m_i \boldsymbol{V}) \\ &= \sum \boldsymbol{r}'_i \times \boldsymbol{p}_i - (\sum m_i \boldsymbol{r}'_i) \times \boldsymbol{V} = \sum \boldsymbol{r}'_i \times \boldsymbol{p}_i = \boldsymbol{L}'_1 \end{aligned}$$

Similarly,

$$\begin{aligned} \boldsymbol{L}' &= \sum \boldsymbol{r}'_i \times \boldsymbol{p}'_i = \sum (\boldsymbol{r}_i - \boldsymbol{R}) \times \boldsymbol{p}'_i \\ &= \sum \boldsymbol{r}_i \times \boldsymbol{p}'_i - \boldsymbol{R} \times \boldsymbol{p}_i = \sum \boldsymbol{r}_i \times \boldsymbol{p}'_i = \boldsymbol{L}'_2 \end{aligned}$$

Thus we get

$$\boldsymbol{L}' = \boldsymbol{L}'_1 = \boldsymbol{L}'_2$$

However, the angular momentum in the CM frame is not equal to the angular momentum in the laboratory frame. To see this, consider,

$$\begin{aligned} \boldsymbol{L}' &= \sum \boldsymbol{r}'_i \times \boldsymbol{p}'_i = \sum (\boldsymbol{r}_i - \boldsymbol{R}) \times (\boldsymbol{p}_i - m_i \boldsymbol{V}) \\ &= \sum \boldsymbol{r}_i \times \boldsymbol{p}_i - \boldsymbol{R} \times (\sum \boldsymbol{p}_i) - (\sum m_i \boldsymbol{r}_i) \times \boldsymbol{V} + \boldsymbol{R} \times \boldsymbol{V}(\sum m_i) \\ &= \boldsymbol{L} - M(\boldsymbol{R} \times \boldsymbol{V}) - M(\boldsymbol{R} \times \boldsymbol{V}) + M(\boldsymbol{R} \times \boldsymbol{V}) \\ &= \boldsymbol{L} - M(\boldsymbol{R} \times \boldsymbol{V}) \end{aligned} \tag{12.40}$$

The equation $\boldsymbol{L}' = \boldsymbol{L}$ is valid if (i) the observer is located at the centre of mass, or, (ii) the observer is moving (with respect to the lab frame) in such a way that either the centre of mass appears to be stationary, that is, $\boldsymbol{V} = \boldsymbol{0}$ or, (iii) $\boldsymbol{R}$ is parallel to $\boldsymbol{V}$, that is, the system is moving radially with respect to the lab frame.

Since a rigid body is a special case of an N-particle system, Eq. (12.40) should apply to it. Eq. (12.15) tells us that the angular momentum of a rigid body with respect to a fixed inertial frame outside (lab frame) is given by

$$\boldsymbol{L} = M\boldsymbol{R} \times \boldsymbol{u} + \sum_i (I_{ij}\omega_j)\hat{\boldsymbol{i}}$$

where $\boldsymbol{u}$ is the uniform translational velocity of the rigid body. (Such a mix-up of vector and tensor indices as above is allowed only if the coordinate frames involved are all of the rectangular Cartesian type.) Here L_i' may be identified with $\sum_j I_{ij}\omega_j$. However, for a proper comparison between Eqs (12.15) and (12.40), we must define a CM frame for the rigid body and this frame should also act as a body frame so that I_{ij}'s are not time varying. Such a frame is a body frame with its origin at the CM. Now, we can express the inertial velocity of any particle in the rigid body given by

$$\boldsymbol{v}_i = \boldsymbol{u} + \boldsymbol{\omega} \times \boldsymbol{r}_i$$

in terms of the instantaneous basis vectors of the CM frame defined above. Note again that all the quantities $\boldsymbol{v}_i$, $\boldsymbol{u}$, and $\boldsymbol{\omega}$ are measured in the lab frame (inertial frame) and $\boldsymbol{r}_i$ is the position vector of the particle with respect to the CM. Thus the linear momentum of the whole body is

$$\begin{aligned}\boldsymbol{P} &= \sum m_i\boldsymbol{v}_i = \sum m_i\boldsymbol{u} + \sum m_i(\boldsymbol{\omega} \times \boldsymbol{r}_i)\\ &= M\boldsymbol{u} + \boldsymbol{\omega} \times (\sum m_i\boldsymbol{r}_i)\\ &= M\boldsymbol{u}\end{aligned}$$

since $\sum m_i\boldsymbol{r}_i = 0$ (Eq. (12.36)). The inertial angular momentum about the CM turns out to be

$$\begin{aligned}\boldsymbol{L}' &= \sum m_i\boldsymbol{r}_i \times \boldsymbol{v}_i = \sum m_i\boldsymbol{r}_i \times (\boldsymbol{u} + \boldsymbol{\omega} \times \boldsymbol{r}_i)\\ &= M\boldsymbol{R} \times \boldsymbol{u} + \sum_{i,j} I_{ij}\omega_j\hat{\boldsymbol{i}}\\ &= \boldsymbol{L} \qquad \text{by Eq. (12.15)}\end{aligned}$$

Since the position vectors are with respect to the CM of the body, $M\boldsymbol{R} = \sum m_i\boldsymbol{r}_i = 0$ so that

$$\boldsymbol{L} = \boldsymbol{L}' = \sum_{i,j} I_{ij}\omega_j\hat{\boldsymbol{i}} \tag{12.41}$$

Notice that, here $\boldsymbol{L}$ and $\boldsymbol{L}'$ are both inertial quantities, $\boldsymbol{L}'$ being expressed in terms of the instantaneous basis vectors of the rotating CM frame and $\boldsymbol{L}$ is the same vector expressed in terms of the basis vectors of the fixed lab frame. Therefore in actual evaluation of $\boldsymbol{L}'$, time dependence is thrown into the basis vectors of the CM frame and I_{ij} do not vary with time, while for the evaluation of $\boldsymbol{L}$, I_{ij} vary with time and the basis vectors are fixed and therefore time independent.

12.9 TORQUE AND ITS RELATION TO ANGULAR MOMENTUM

If a system of N particles experience external forces the torque due to these forces about the origin of any inertial frame is defined by

$$\boldsymbol{\Gamma} = \sum \boldsymbol{r}_i \times \boldsymbol{F}_i = \sum m_i\boldsymbol{r}_i \times \ddot{\boldsymbol{r}}_i \tag{12.42}$$

The angular momentum about the same origin is defined as before

$$\boldsymbol{L} = \sum \boldsymbol{r}_i \times m\dot{\boldsymbol{r}}_i$$

Therefore,

$$\begin{aligned}\frac{d\boldsymbol{L}}{dt} &= \frac{d}{dt}\sum \boldsymbol{r}_i \times (m_i\dot{\boldsymbol{r}}_i) \\ &= \sum m_i\dot{\boldsymbol{r}}_i \times \dot{\boldsymbol{r}}_i + \sum m_i\boldsymbol{r}_i \times \ddot{\boldsymbol{r}}_i \\ &= \boldsymbol{\Gamma}\end{aligned} \tag{12.43}$$

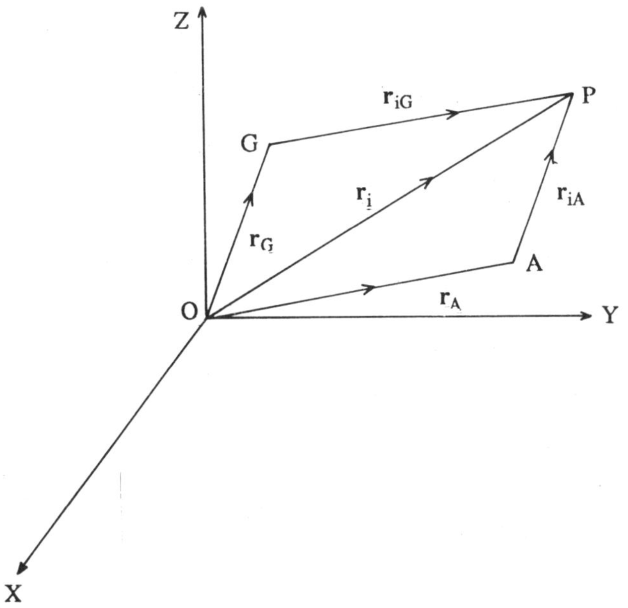

Fig. 12.9 Position vectors with respect to the origin O of an inertial frame, the centre of mass G, and an arbitrary particle at A, of a system of particles

This relation is the rotational equivalent of Newton's second law of motion and is valid when the moments are taken about the origin of any fixed inertial frame of reference. However, sometimes one has to compute the torque and angular momentum about a point which is not fixed, for example, about the moving centre of mass or some other fixed point of a body. Therefore, one must know under what conditions Eq. (12.43) is valid. Instead of taking moments about the fixed origin, let us take them about any arbitrary point A (see Fig. 12.9).

Consider a system of N particles. Let the ith particle sit at P and experience a total force $\boldsymbol{F}_i$. G is the centre of mass and $M = \sum m_i$ is the total mass of the system. From the geometrical constructs of Fig. 12.9 we can write

$$\begin{aligned} \boldsymbol{r}_i &= \boldsymbol{r}_A + \boldsymbol{r}_{iA} \qquad \boldsymbol{F}_i = m_i\ddot{\boldsymbol{r}}_i \\ \sum m_i\boldsymbol{r}_{iA} &= \sum m_i(\boldsymbol{r}_i - \boldsymbol{r}_A) = M(\boldsymbol{r}_G - \boldsymbol{r}_A) = M\boldsymbol{r}_{GA} \end{aligned} \tag{12.44}$$

The resultant moment of all forces about A is by definition the torque about A, that is,

$$\begin{aligned} \boldsymbol{\Gamma}_A &= \sum \boldsymbol{r}_{iA} \times (m_i\ddot{\boldsymbol{r}}_i) \\ &= \sum \boldsymbol{r}_{iA} \times m_i(\ddot{\boldsymbol{r}}_A + \ddot{\boldsymbol{r}}_{iA}) \\ &= \frac{d}{dt}\left(\sum \boldsymbol{r}_{iA} \times m_i\dot{\boldsymbol{r}}_{iA}\right) + \sum m_i(\boldsymbol{r}_{iA} \times \ddot{\boldsymbol{r}}_A) \\ &= \dot{\boldsymbol{L}}_A + M\boldsymbol{r}_{GA} \times \ddot{\boldsymbol{r}}_A \end{aligned} \tag{12.45}$$

where in the last step we have used Eq. (12.44). Here $\boldsymbol{L}_A = \sum m_i\boldsymbol{r}_{iA} \times \dot{\boldsymbol{r}}_{iA}$ is the angular momentum about the point A. So if we desire to have the torque angular momentum relation to be of the form Eq. (12.43), the second term on RHS of Eq. (12.45) must vanish and this happens when the point A

(i) has a constant velocity, or
(ii) is the CM itself implying $\boldsymbol{r}_{GA} = \boldsymbol{0}$, or
(iii) has acceleration parallel to $\boldsymbol{r}_{GA}$.

One could also start with another definition of $\boldsymbol{L}_A$ such as

$$\begin{aligned} \boldsymbol{L}'_A &= \sum \boldsymbol{r}_{iA} \times \boldsymbol{p}_i = \sum m_i\boldsymbol{r}_{iA} \times \dot{\boldsymbol{r}}_i \\ &= \sum m_i\boldsymbol{r}_{iA} \times (\dot{\boldsymbol{r}}_{iA} + \dot{\boldsymbol{r}}_A) \\ &= \boldsymbol{L}_A + M\boldsymbol{r}_{GA} \times \dot{\boldsymbol{r}}_A \end{aligned} \tag{12.46}$$

$\boldsymbol{L}'_A$ may be called the absolute angular momentum about A. In this case,

$$\begin{aligned} \boldsymbol{\Gamma}_A &= \dot{\boldsymbol{L}}_A + M\boldsymbol{r}_{GA} \times \ddot{\boldsymbol{r}}_A \\ &= \dot{\boldsymbol{L}}'_A - M\dot{\boldsymbol{r}}_{GA} \times \dot{\boldsymbol{r}}_A - M\boldsymbol{r}_{GA} \times \ddot{\boldsymbol{r}}_A + M\boldsymbol{r}_{GA} \times \ddot{\boldsymbol{r}}_A \\ &= \dot{\boldsymbol{L}}'_A + M\dot{\boldsymbol{r}}_A \times \dot{\boldsymbol{r}}_{GA} \\ &= \dot{\boldsymbol{L}}'_A + M\dot{\boldsymbol{r}}_A \times \dot{\boldsymbol{r}}_G \end{aligned} \tag{12.47}$$

If we want Eq. (12.47) to give the relation $\boldsymbol{\Gamma}_A = \dot{\boldsymbol{L}}'_A$, the fourth condition emerges, and that is, the point A (iv) has velocity parallel to that of the CM.

The importance of this exercise is that we are now in a position to use the Newtonian torque angular momentum relation for studying the motion of a rigid body as a special case of an N-particle system. If a rigid body is rotating in any manner, keeping one point, say A, fixed in space then $\boldsymbol{\Gamma}_A = \dot{\boldsymbol{L}}_A$ will be valid under any one the above four conditions. A most widely used case is to choose the centre of mass of the rigid body as the origin, (the condition (ii) above). However one must remember that $\boldsymbol{\Gamma}_A$ and $\boldsymbol{L}_A$ are both inertial quantities although they may have to be expressed in terms of the instantaneous basis vectors of a body frame which is rotating and translating with the body.

In chapter I, we have seen that internal forces do not manifest in the torque angular momentum relation, even though they can contribute to both the total torque and the total angular momentum. However, for rigid bodies, the internal forces are of the central force type, and therefore, do not contribute to the the torque or the angular momentum. Hence the torque in the above treatment can be taken to be equal to the total torque produced by the external forces only.

12.10 EULER'S EQUATION OF MOTION FOR RIGID BODIES

Consider a rigid body either rotating about a fixed point in space or moving in any manner with a body frame attached to the centre of mass. The angular momentum $\boldsymbol{L}$ about origin (in the first case the fixed point and in the second case the CM) and the instantaneous angular velocity $\boldsymbol{\omega}$ are the quantities that refer to a fixed inertial frame. When expressed in terms of the unit vectors of the rotating body frame, these are related as

$$L_i = I_{ij}\omega_j$$

The external forces $\boldsymbol{F}$ and the torque $\boldsymbol{\Gamma}$ about the origin, are also defined with respect to the inertial frames only. Therefore, Newton's second law of motion, that is,

$$\boldsymbol{\Gamma} = \frac{d\boldsymbol{L}}{dt} \quad \text{and} \quad \boldsymbol{F} = \frac{d\boldsymbol{P}}{dt}$$

where $\boldsymbol{P}$ is the total linear momentum of the rigid body, will be valid if d/dt is taken with respect to a fixed inertial frame only. We know from Eq. (3.1) that

$$\left(\frac{d}{dt}\right)_{\text{fixed}} = \left(\frac{d}{dt}\right)_{\text{rot}} + \boldsymbol{\omega} \times$$

is the relation between the time derivatives of a vector, taken with respect to a fixed and a rotating frame of reference respectively, if the latter rotates with an instantaneous angular velocity $\boldsymbol{\omega}$.

Therefore,

$$\boldsymbol{\Gamma} = \left(\frac{d\boldsymbol{L}}{dt}\right)_{\text{fixed}} = \left(\frac{d\boldsymbol{L}}{dt}\right)_{\text{rot}} + \boldsymbol{\omega} \times \boldsymbol{L} \tag{12.48}$$

and

$$\boldsymbol{F} = \left(\frac{d\boldsymbol{P}}{dt}\right)_{\text{fixed}} = \left(\frac{d\boldsymbol{P}}{dt}\right)_{\text{rot}} + \boldsymbol{\omega} \times \boldsymbol{P} \tag{12.49}$$

where $\boldsymbol{\omega}$, $\boldsymbol{L}$, $\boldsymbol{P}$, $\boldsymbol{F}$ and $\boldsymbol{\Gamma}$ are all expressed in terms of the instantaneous unit vectors

$\hat{\boldsymbol{i}}$, $\hat{\boldsymbol{j}}$, $\hat{k}$ of the rotating body frame with

$$\left(\frac{d\boldsymbol{L}}{dt}\right)_{\text{rot}} \equiv \sum_{i=1}^{3} \left(\frac{dL_i}{dt}\right) \hat{\boldsymbol{i}} \quad \text{and} \quad \left(\frac{d\boldsymbol{P}}{dt}\right)_{\text{rot}} \equiv \sum_{i=1}^{3} \left(\frac{dP_i}{dt}\right) \hat{\boldsymbol{i}}$$

Henceforth we shall drop the suffix 'rot' for convenience.

Equations (12.48) and (12.49) are called *Euler's equations of motion* for a rigid body moving in an arbitrary fashion. Note that both the translational and rotational motions are dealt with independently. Also if $\boldsymbol{\omega}$ is not parallel to $\boldsymbol{L}$ or $\boldsymbol{P}$ then in general $\boldsymbol{\Gamma} \neq d\boldsymbol{L}/dt$ and $\boldsymbol{F} \neq d\boldsymbol{P}/dt$. Further, even if $\boldsymbol{\Gamma}$ and $\boldsymbol{F}$ are zero, $d\boldsymbol{L}/dt$ and $d\boldsymbol{P}/dt$ need not vanish, that is, $\boldsymbol{L}$ and $\boldsymbol{P}$ can change with time even in the absence of $\boldsymbol{\Gamma}$ and $\boldsymbol{F}$, simply because one looks at them from a rotating body frame.

The form of Euler's equations of motion remains the same even for any arbitrary rotating frame having an instantaneous angular velocity of rotation $\boldsymbol{\Omega}$ ($\neq \boldsymbol{\omega}$, the instantaneous angular velocity of the rigid body, about its CM or any other fixed point under consideration), with $\boldsymbol{\omega}$ in Eqs (12.48) and (12.49) replaced by $\boldsymbol{\Omega}$. These equations of motion with respect to any arbitrary rotating frame are called *Euler's modified equations of motion.*

12.11 TIME VARIATION OF ROTATIONAL KINETIC ENERGY

The total kinetic energy is just the rotational kinetic energy if the rigid body is rotating about a fixed point. In any case, the rotational kinetic energy may vary with time with a rate, given by dT/dt, where

$$T = \frac{1}{2} I_{ij}\omega_i\omega_j = \frac{1}{2}\boldsymbol{\omega}\cdot\boldsymbol{L}$$

Therefore,

$$\begin{aligned}\frac{dT}{dt} &= \frac{1}{2} I_{ij}\dot{\omega}_i\omega_j + \frac{1}{2} I_{ij}\omega_i\dot{\omega}_j \\ &= I_{ij}\omega_i\dot{\omega}_j = \omega_i\frac{d}{dt}(I_{ij}\omega_j) \\ &= \boldsymbol{\omega}\cdot\frac{d\boldsymbol{L}}{dt}\end{aligned} \tag{12.50}$$

Note that the components of vectors used in this equation are with reference to the instantaneous basis vectors of the rotating body frame. Thus $d\boldsymbol{L}/dt$ occurring here is not the fixed frame $d\boldsymbol{L}/dt$. In fact in the absence of any external torque, $d\boldsymbol{L}/dt \neq 0$ in general. Does it then mean that the rotational kinetic energy may change with time even in the absence of any external torque? We aim to answer this question in the next section.

12.12 ROTATION OF A FREE RIGID BODY

We consider a freely rotating rigid body, that is, one in the absence of any net external torque. Since $\boldsymbol{\Gamma} = 0$, Eq. (12.48) becomes

$$\frac{d\boldsymbol{L}}{dt} + \boldsymbol{\omega} \times \boldsymbol{L} = \mathbf{0} \tag{12.51}$$

Taking a scalar product with $\boldsymbol{L}$, one gets

$$\boldsymbol{L} \cdot \frac{d\boldsymbol{L}}{dt} + \boldsymbol{L} \cdot (\boldsymbol{\omega} \times \boldsymbol{L}) = 0$$

or

$$\boldsymbol{L} \cdot \frac{d\boldsymbol{L}}{dt} = 0$$

or

$$\frac{d}{dt}(L^2) = 0$$

that is,

$$L^2 = \text{const.} \tag{12.52a}$$

Thus for $\boldsymbol{\Gamma} = 0$, even though $d\boldsymbol{L}/dt = \boldsymbol{L} \times \boldsymbol{\omega} \neq 0$ (unless $\boldsymbol{\omega}$ is parallel to $\boldsymbol{L}$), it is seen that L^2, or the magnitude of $\boldsymbol{L}$ remains constant. This is not surprising, because the $\boldsymbol{L}$ vector is actually fixed in space, (as $\boldsymbol{\Gamma} = 0$), but with respect to the body frame, only the direction of $\boldsymbol{L}$ appears to change without, of course, bringing in any change in its magnitude.

Again, if we take a scalar product with $\boldsymbol{\omega}$ on both the sides of Eq. (12.51), we obtain

$$\boldsymbol{\omega} \cdot \frac{d\boldsymbol{L}}{dt} + \boldsymbol{\omega} \cdot (\boldsymbol{\omega} \times \boldsymbol{L}) = 0 \quad \text{or} \quad \boldsymbol{\omega} \cdot \frac{d\boldsymbol{L}}{dt} = 0 \quad \text{or} \quad \frac{dT}{dt} = 0$$

that is,

$$T = \text{const.} \tag{12.52b}$$

Therefore, for freely rotating rigid bodies $\boldsymbol{\omega}$ and $d\boldsymbol{L}/dt$ are perpendicular to each other and the rotational kinetic energy T is a constant of motion. Thus there are two constants of motion, L^2 and T for rigid bodies rotating in any manner about a fixed point.

Now there are mainly two ways of dealing with the dynamics of the free rotation of any rigid body. One way is to follow Poinsot's geometrical construction (proposed by Poinsot in 1834), and the other is the analytical method of Euler. Of course, the Lagrangian approach would be yet another method of tackling the same problem. We shall see how these different methods enlighten the complementary aspects of the same problem.

12.13 POINSOT'S METHOD OF GEOMETRICAL CONSTRUCTION

Let us assume that a rigid body is rotating freely, that is, without any external torque acting on it, about a fixed point, say its centre of mass. Hence, the kinetic energy of its rotation, T, is a constant of motion. From the equation

$$T = \frac{1}{2} I_{ij}\omega_i\omega_j$$

where T is a constant and the summation over i, j are implied, we can write

$$I_{ij}\frac{\omega_i}{\sqrt{2T}}\frac{\omega_j}{\sqrt{2T}} = 1 \tag{12.53}$$

This equation looks like the equation of the ellipsoid of inertia provided we identify $\boldsymbol{\omega}/\sqrt{2T}$ with $\boldsymbol{x}$ in Eq. (12.24), that is,

$$x_i = \frac{\omega_i}{\sqrt{2T}} \tag{12.54}$$

Now, since T is constant, the surface of this inertial ellipsoid plotted in terms of the position vector $\boldsymbol{x}$ as defined above, must represent a surface of constant T, and by definition of $\boldsymbol{x}$ the direction of $\boldsymbol{x}$ is the same as that of the instantaneous angular velocity $\boldsymbol{\omega}$. The distance from the centre of this inertial ellipsoid to any point on its surface is simply $|\boldsymbol{\omega}|/\sqrt{2T}$. This inertial ellipsoid is depicted in Fig. 12.10.

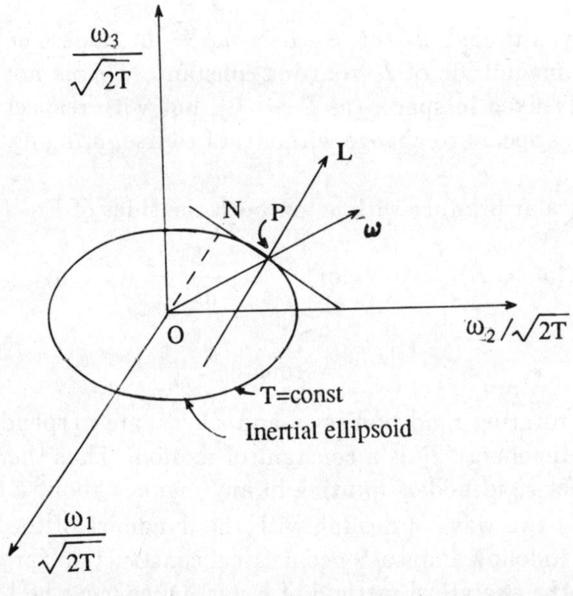

Fig. 12.10 Poinsot's geometrical construction for the motion of inertial ellipsoid in the $\boldsymbol{\omega}$-space

Let us elaborate on this new model of the inertial ellipsoid. It is an inertial ellipsoid because its equation contains all the elements of the inertial tensor. This inertial tensor is about the same point as the fixed point in the body about which the free rotation has been assumed to take place. If we fully expand Eq. (12.53), we can see that the space in which this equation stands for an ellipsoid is the space of instantaneous angular velocity. The higher the amount of rotational kinetic energy, the bigger is the size of this inertial ellipsoid. For a given constant kinetic energy of rotation, the longest axis of the ellipsoid (that is, the highest value of the instantaneous angular velocity) should correspond to the direction in the actual body of the smallest moment of inertia, which has to be one of the principal axes of the body about the point under consideration. This is sensible because if the body is rotating about an axis corresponding to the least moment of inertia, it has to rotate very fast (which means that it should point along the longest radius vector of this ellipsoid) in order to maintain the same kinetic energy of rotation. So if we choose any arbitrary point P on the ellipsoid and say that this point represents the instantaneous dynamical state of the rotating rigid body, it would immediately mean that the radius vector OP which corresponds to a unique direction in the actual body (because the principal axes of MI of the body are in some definite manner aligned with the geometrical axes of this ellipsoid) is the direction about which the body is currently rotating, and the length of OP is simply $|\boldsymbol{\omega}|/\sqrt{2T}$. If the freely rotating body changes the direction of $\boldsymbol{\omega}$ with time, as it usually should, the point P would be shifting on the surface of the ellipsoid, but it cannot go outside this surface because it maintains a constant rotational kinetic energy.

Now from the standard expression for T

$$\frac{\partial T}{\partial \omega_i} = I_{ij}\omega_j = L_i$$

A geometrical interpretation of this result in terms of the above inertial ellipsoid would be that the angular momentum vector

$$\boldsymbol{L} = \nabla_{\omega} T = \frac{1}{\sqrt{2T}} \nabla_x T, \tag{12.55}$$

where $\boldsymbol{x}$ is defined through Eq. (12.54). By Eq. (12.55) we see that $\boldsymbol{L}$ is directed perpendicular to the surface of constant kinetic energy depicted in the space of angular velocity (note that $\boldsymbol{x} \leftrightarrow \boldsymbol{\omega}$). Since the surface of the above kind of inertial ellipsoid represents a constant T surface, the normal to this ellipsoid at the point indicates the direction of the angular momentum vector $\boldsymbol{L}$. Again, since this is a case of free rotation, $\boldsymbol{L}$ is fixed in space, in direction and magnitude. But with respect to the body frame, the direction (but not the magnitude) changes as the body rotates. As the body rotates, its inertial ellipsoid must also rotate with it keeping, however, its origin fixed. Since the directions of the normal and the radius vector at any arbitrary point P on the ellipsoid are not parallel, the directions of $\boldsymbol{L}$ and $\boldsymbol{\omega}$ are also not parallel. This is all expected. For a spherical top, the moment of inertia tensor reduces to a single scalar, the inertial ellipsoid becomes spherical, and hence $\boldsymbol{L}$ and $\boldsymbol{\omega}$ must point in the same direction.

Let us now draw a tangent plane to the surface of the inertial ellipsoid at the point P (see Fig 12.10). The perpendicular distance of this plane from the origin of the inertial ellipsoid is given by

$$\begin{aligned} \text{ON} &= \text{OP} \cos(\angle \boldsymbol{\omega}, \boldsymbol{L}) \\ &= \frac{|\boldsymbol{\omega}|}{\sqrt{2T}} \frac{\boldsymbol{\omega} \cdot \boldsymbol{L}}{|\boldsymbol{\omega}|\,|\boldsymbol{L}|} = \frac{\sqrt{2T}}{|\boldsymbol{L}|} = \text{const.} \end{aligned}$$

If ON is fixed for all time, the tangent plane is also fixed in space for all time, that is, it must serve as an immovable or invariable plane for the dynamical study of free rotation. It does not change with time, although the inertial ellipsoid would change its orientation with time. In other words, the ellipsoid of inertia of any rigid body under free rotation always touches a fixed plane, known as the *invariable plane* the perpendicular to which drawn from the origin points always toward the fixed direction of the angular momentum of the body. This was the geometrical picture of a freely rotating rigid body suggested by Poinsot in 1834.

The fact that both $\boldsymbol{L}$ and the invariable plane are fixed in space has the following implication. Since the invariable plane has to meet tangentially the the inertial ellipsoid at some or other point, and since this point of contact determines the direction of the instantaneous angular velocity of the body (that is, the $\boldsymbol{\omega}$ vector), and since $\boldsymbol{\omega}$ changes with time, this point of contact on the surface of the inertial ellipsoid ought to change with time. However, we know that the invariable plane has to remain fixed in space for all time, and therefore the point of contact can change only if the inertial ellipsoid itself changes its orientation with time (keeping its origin fixed). Further, since $\boldsymbol{\omega}$ changes continuously with time the inertial ellipsoid has to roll over the invariable plane without slipping. Note that every point on the inertial ellipsoid corresponds to a different direction of $\boldsymbol{\omega}$ with respect to the body frame.

As the ellipsoid of inertia rolls without slipping over the invariable plane, the point of contact P between the ellipsoid of inertia and the invariable plane indicating the direction of instantaneous $\boldsymbol{\omega}$ with respect to the body as well as the fixed plane, traces a curve on the ellipsoid of inertia, called a *polhode.* Similarly, a curve is also traced on the invariable plane and is called a *herpolhode.*

12.13.1 Nature of Polhodes and Herpolhodes

The ellipsoid of inertia has got three principal axes. If the principal moments of inertia are labeled as $A < B < C$, the corresponding principal axes $\hat{\boldsymbol{x}}_1$, $\hat{\boldsymbol{x}}_2$, $\hat{\boldsymbol{x}}_3$ would correspond to the semiaxes satisfying $a > b > c$ for its ellipsoid of inertia. Now if the body is rotating with some angular velocity $\boldsymbol{\omega}$ about the principal axis $\hat{\boldsymbol{x}}_1$, then $\boldsymbol{\omega}$ must pass through $\hat{\boldsymbol{x}}_1$ and the ellipsoid of inertia must touch the invariable plane at the tip of $x_1 = a$. Since $x_1 = a$ is the farthest point on the ellipsoid from its centre, and since the invariable plane is fixed, the ellipsoid of inertia cannot move without detaching itself from the invariable plane. Hence only one solution is permissible, which is that $\boldsymbol{\omega}$ will never shift from the direction of its principal axis $\hat{\boldsymbol{x}}_1$. Also at this point the normal to the invariable plane coincides with the radius vector so that $\boldsymbol{L}$ is parallel to $\boldsymbol{\omega}$. Thus, the body rotates about its principal axis corresponding to the smallest principal moment of inertia, in quite a stable manner. A similar argument is also valid for the third principal axis having the largest principal moment of inertia (and hence the shortest semiaxis for its ellipsoid of inertia). The rotation about this axis is also stable, with the direction of $\boldsymbol{L}$ and $\boldsymbol{\omega}$ remaining coincident all the time. The rotation about the the intermediate principal axis is, however, very unstable. Having the length of its semiaxis intermediate between the two extreme ones, the point of contact can freely pass through this axis and the direction of $\boldsymbol{\omega}$ can change both with respect to the body and with respect to any outside inertial frame.

If the direction of the instantaneous angular velocity, $\boldsymbol{\omega}$, is somewhat away from the first and the third axes, the polhode is a closed curve encircling the nearest pole of the principal axes. Only at the pole of the intermediate principal axis, and at no other point, can two polhodes intersect. Polhodes are depicted in Fig. 12.11 on the surface of the inertial ellipsoid.

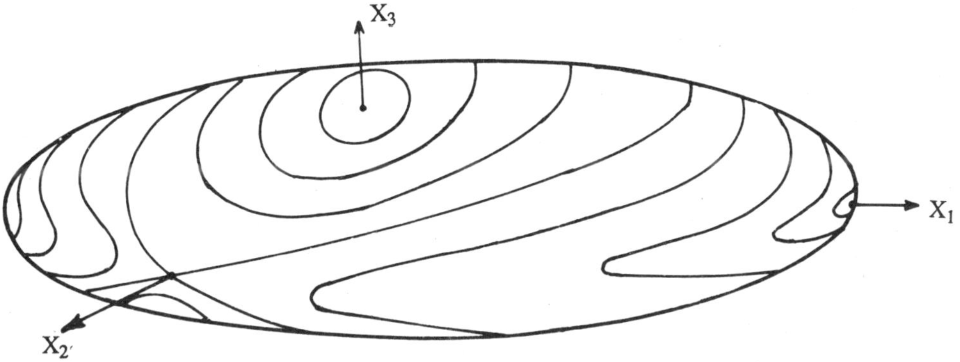

Fig. 12.11 Polhodes drawn on the surface of the inertial ellipsoid

Herpolhodes are drawn on the invariable plane as loci of the tip of the instantaneous $\boldsymbol{\omega}$ vector. From Fig. 12.11 one can see that

$$\mathrm{NP}^2 = \mathrm{OP}^2 - \mathrm{ON}^2 = \frac{\omega^2}{2T} - \frac{2T}{L^2}$$

Since L and T are constants, and ω is a measure of the radial distance from the centre to a point on the inertial ellipsoid, ω^2 and hence NP^2 are bounded. Therefore, herpolhodes are in general bounded rather than closed curves (see Fig. 12.12)

12.14 ANALYTICAL METHOD OF EULER FOR FREE ROTATION AND THE THIRD INTEGRAL OF MOTION

In this method one usually starts with Euler's equation for rotational motion (Eq. (12.51)) which provides us with the two Eulerian integrals of motion, namely L^2 = constant and $2T = \boldsymbol{L}\cdot\boldsymbol{\omega}$ = constant, for any rigid body freely rotating about a fixed point, $\boldsymbol{\omega}$ and $\boldsymbol{L}$ being expressed in terms of the unit vectors of any suitable body frame of reference.

Euler's equations of motion for a freely rotating rigid body referred to a body frame are given by

$$\frac{d\boldsymbol{L}}{dt} + \boldsymbol{\omega} \times \boldsymbol{L} = \mathbf{0} \tag{12.51}$$

If we choose the principal axes of the rigid body about the origin as the rectangular Cartesian axes of the body frame and the principal moments of inertia as $A \neq B \neq C$, then with $\boldsymbol{\omega} = (\omega_1, \omega_2, \omega_3)$ and $\boldsymbol{L} = (A\omega_1, B\omega_2, C\omega_3)$ with respect to the principal axes, Euler's

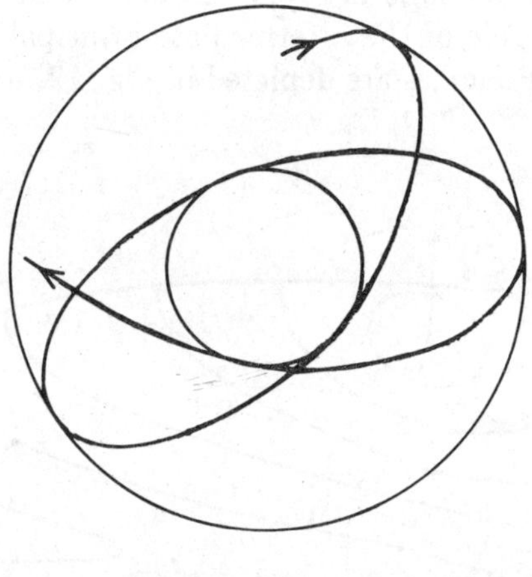

Fig. 12.12 Herpolhodes drawn on the invariable plane

equations of motion become

$$\begin{aligned} A\dot{\omega}_1 &= (B - C)\omega_2\omega_3 \\ B\dot{\omega}_2 &= (C - A)\omega_3\omega_1 \\ C\dot{\omega}_3 &= (A - B)\omega_1\omega_2 \end{aligned} \tag{12.56}$$

supplemented by the two Eulerian integrals of motion

$$L^2 = A^2\omega_1^2 + B^2\omega_2^2 + C^2\omega_3^2 \tag{12.57}$$

and

$$2T = A\omega_1^2 + B\omega_2^2 + C\omega_3^2 \tag{12.58}$$

One can eliminate ω_3 from Eqs (12.57) and (12.58) and from the resulting equation one can write ω_2 as a function of ω_1. Substituting this $\omega_2 = \omega_2(\omega_1)$ in either of Eqs (12.57) and (12.58) one obtains ω_3 as a function of ω_1, that is, $\omega_3 = \omega_3(\omega_1)$. Plugging these expressions for ω_3 and ω_2 in the first of Eqs (12.56) one gets a first order differential equation in ω_1 only, the general solution of which is available in the form of an elliptic integral. Repeating similar procedures for ω_2 and ω_3 one can find the complete solutions for ω_1, ω_2 and ω_3 as functions of A, B, C, L^2, T and the constants of integration or the initial value of $\boldsymbol{\omega}$.

Without going through the details of the solutions, one can, however, see that the rotation about the principal axes corresponding to the largest and smallest principal moments of inertia are stable and the remaining solution is unstable. Let ω_1, ω_2 and ω_3 correspond to the components along the axes for which we have the principal moments of inertia $A < B < C$ respectively. A particular solution such as $\omega_1 = \omega_2 = 0$ and $\omega_3 \neq 0$ satisfied by (12.56) suggests that $\dot{\omega}_3 = 0$ or $\omega_3 = \text{const.}$ The stability of such a solution can, however, be judged by allowing a small perturbation in ω_1 and ω_2 and noting how the perturbation evolves with time. For $A < B < C$, it can be shown that the perturbation grows with time for the initial conditions $\omega_1 \rightarrow 0$, $\omega_3 \rightarrow 0$ and $\omega_2 \neq 0$.

Therefore it is clear that if there are only two integrals of motion, they alone cannot give solutions to ω_1, ω_2 and ω_3 simultaneously. One then has to solve Euler's equations of motion quite explicitly in order to obtain the full solution. This is the reason why it is so important to have a third integral of motion for motions of the rigid bodies. It requires introduction of further symmetries to the problem. As we shall see later, even in the presence of gravitational torques, the rotation of symmetric tops about a fixed point in the body has two obvious integrals of motion. Long searches for the third integral of motion revealed the existence of the Poincaré integral (1892), Hess integral (1890), Kowalevski integral (1889), Tshapliguine integral (1901), and so on, under different restrictions imposed upon the symmetry of the body and in the choice of the fixed point about which the rotation should take place. Some of these are left as exercises (see problem 12.12).

In the next section we are planning to use the above analytical method for studying the free rotation of a symmetrical rigid body, such as the earth, for which the principal moments of inertia are $A = B < C$. The c-axis, which is the axis of the largest moment of inertia, is approximately the same as the axis of its geometrical symmetry. We show that the torque free rotation of the earth leads to a kind of wobbling in space, historically known as the *Chandler wobbling* of the earth, duly named after S. C. Chandler, who did the pioneering observational work on this phenomenon about a hundred years ago.

12.15 CHANDLER WOBBLING OF THE EARTH

The free rotation of a symmetric body such as the earth having its principal moments of inertia $A = B < C$ is described by Euler's equations of motion (Eq. (12.56)). Defining $k = (C - A)/A$, these equations become,

$$\dot{\omega}_1 + k\omega_2\omega_3 = 0 \qquad \dot{\omega}_2 - k\omega_1\omega_3 = 0 \qquad \text{and} \qquad \dot{\omega}_3 = 0 \tag{12.59}$$

where ω_1, ω_2 and ω_3 are the components of $\boldsymbol{\omega}$ along the principal axes of the MI ellipsoid.

The third equation is easily integrable to

$$\omega_3 = \text{const.}$$

that is, the component of the angular velocity in the direction of the inertial symmetry axis of the earth does not change with time.

Using the fact that ω_3 is constant and differentiating the first two of Eqs (12.59) with respect to time we get

$$\begin{aligned} \ddot{\omega}_1 &= -k\omega_3\dot{\omega}_2 = -(k^2\omega_3^2)\omega_1 \\ \ddot{\omega}_2 &= k\omega_3\dot{\omega}_1 = -(k^2\omega_3^2)\omega_2 \end{aligned} \tag{12.60}$$

The general solution of Eqs (12.60) can be written in the form

$$\omega_1 \pm i\omega_2 = a_\omega \, e^{\pm i(k\omega_3 t + \theta)} \tag{12.61}$$

Here a_ω and θ are two constants of integration. Since

$$\omega_1^2 + \omega_2^2 = (\omega_1 + i\omega_2)(\omega_1 - i\omega_2) = a_\omega^2$$

we have

$$\omega^2 = \omega_1^2 + \omega_2^2 + \omega_3^2 = a_\omega^2 + \omega_3^2 = \text{const.} \tag{12.62}$$

because a_ω and ω_3 are both constants of motion. Therefore, the tip of $\boldsymbol{\omega}$ (whose magnitude remains constant in time) is precessing about the inertial symmetry axis of the earth with ω_3 remaining constant.

Let us define

$$\tan \alpha_b = \frac{\sqrt{\omega_1^2 + \omega_2^2}}{\omega_3} = \frac{a_\omega}{\omega_3} \tag{12.63}$$

Obviously α_b is the angle between $\boldsymbol{\omega}$ and the symmetric axis. Since this angle α_b remains constant, the direction of the vector $\boldsymbol{\omega}$ must describe a cone of constant semiangle α_b about the inertial symmetry axis of the earth.

From Eq. (12.61), the angular velocity of precession of $\boldsymbol{\omega}$ about the symmetry axis of the body is given by

$$\Omega_b = k\omega_3 = \left(\frac{C - A}{A}\right)\omega_3 \tag{12.64}$$

For the earth, it is known that $A = B = 0.329591\ Ma^2$, $C = 0.330674\ Ma^2$, giving $k = (C - A)/A \simeq 1/304.4$. This gives, with the knowledge of ω_3 for earth as 7.292115×10^{-5} rad/s, for Ω_b a value of 2.39529×10^{-7} rad/s, which corresponds to a period of about 303.6 days.

Thus from the solution (12.61) it is apparent that the tip of the earth's angular velocity of rotation should describe a conical motion about the geometrical symmetry axis of the earth and that each revolution should take about 304 days. The sense of rotation of the tip is the same as that of the product $k\omega_3$. Since both k and ω_3 are positive in the case of the earth, the tip of $\boldsymbol{\omega}$ should move in an anticlockwise manner about the inertial or geometrical north pole of the earth when viewed from above the north pole.

In the second half of the last century, S. C. Chandler from Cambridge, U.S.A. collected the observational evidences for such a free wobbling of the earth. He found that the earth's axis of rotation is precessing about the geometrical pole of the earth at a separation of only a few meters and that the period of wobbling is not 304 days but much longer, about 435 days. For this measurement he did not have to go to the north or south pole of the earth. What he had to do was to measure very carefully the variation of the geographical latitude (same as the local altitude of the pole) of any place over a few years. From very accurate astronomical observations of the altitude of reference stars he found that the amplitude of wobbling in the latitude of a place was about 0.1 to 0.3 seconds of arc, a typical plot for the polar wandering being shown in Fig 12.13. The wobbling does not seem to be very regular and the average period over the past one hundred years has now been found to be about 433 days. Nevertheless the observed period of wobbling grossly disagrees with the expected period.

This discrepancy in the period of wobbling is believed to be due to the plasticity of the earth's interior, seasonal movement of the atmospheric masses, oceanic currents, response of the whole earth to the tidal forces due to the sun and the moon, etc., each causing a semi-irregular change in the moment of inertia of the earth. A proper quantitative analysis

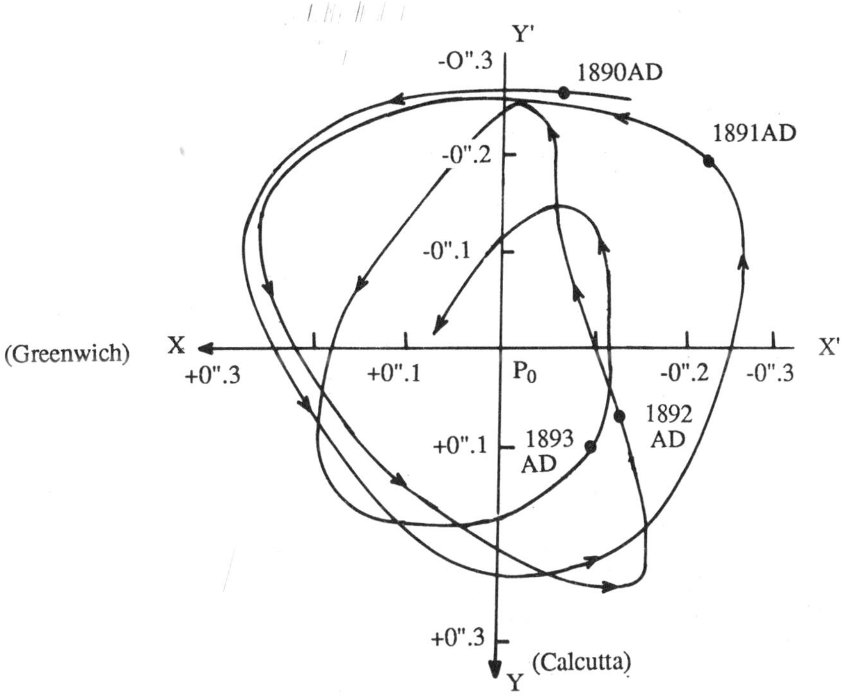

Fig. 12.13 Small wandering of the true inertial north pole of the earth about its mean position P_o

of all these effects is such a formidable task that even today we cannot claim that this discrepancy has been exactly explained.

12.16 MOTION OF ω IN SPACE FOR FREE ROTATION

We have already found that, with respect to an observer fixed to the body, the instantaneous $\boldsymbol{\omega}$ describes a cone about the inertial symmetry axis of the body with the semiangle

$$\alpha_b = \cos^{-1}\left(\frac{\omega_3}{\omega}\right)$$

and with a period

$$T = \frac{2\pi}{\Omega} = \frac{2\pi}{\omega_3}\frac{A}{C - A}$$

This cone may be termed as the *body cone* as it is traced on the rotating body.

Now let us see how an observer fixed in space would view this motion of $\boldsymbol{\omega}$. In a fixed inertial frame, the vector angular momentum $\boldsymbol{L}$ is fixed, as the net applied torque is zero. We also know that

$$2T = \boldsymbol{\omega} \cdot \boldsymbol{L} = \text{const.}$$

$$\omega = |\boldsymbol{\omega}| = \text{const.}$$
$$L = |\boldsymbol{L}| = \text{const.}$$

Hence,

$$\frac{\boldsymbol{\omega} \cdot \boldsymbol{L}}{|\boldsymbol{\omega}|\,|\boldsymbol{L}|} = \cos(\angle \boldsymbol{\omega}, \boldsymbol{L}) \quad \text{is a const.} \tag{12.65}$$

Let $\angle \boldsymbol{\omega}, \boldsymbol{L} = \alpha_s$ so that the angle α_s = angle between the fixed $\boldsymbol{L}$ and changing $\boldsymbol{\omega}$ is a constant. An expression for α_s can be obtained as

$$\begin{aligned} \cos\alpha_s = \frac{2T}{|\boldsymbol{\omega}|\,|\boldsymbol{L}|} &= \frac{A\omega_1^2 + B\omega_2^2 + C\omega_3^2}{\omega\sqrt{A^2\omega_1^2 + B^2\omega_2^2 + C^2\omega_3^2}} \\ &= \frac{Aa_\omega^2 + C\omega_3^2}{\sqrt{(a_\omega^2 + \omega_3^2)(A^2a_\omega^2 + C^2\omega_3^2)}} \end{aligned} \tag{12.66}$$

Since $\boldsymbol{L}$ and α_s are constants, $\boldsymbol{\omega}$ must describe another conical motion about the space fixed direction of $\boldsymbol{L}$ with the semiangle of the space fixed cone around $\boldsymbol{L}$ equal to α_s. This fixed space cone is naturally called the *space cone* for the free motion of any symmetric top. If

$$\frac{a_\omega}{\omega_3} \ll k = \frac{C - A}{A} \ll 1$$

as it is in the case of the Chandler wobbling of the earth, it can be shown that

$$\alpha_s \simeq \alpha_b\left(\frac{C - A}{C}\right) \simeq k\alpha_b$$

so that the space cone for the free rotation of earth is much smaller than its body cone by a factor k. Since the value of α_b for the free rotation of earth is about 0.1 to 0.3 arc second, the value of its α_s would be at most about a millisecond of arc.

The space and the body cones are always in touch with each other and the common tangent through the touching points is the direction of the instantaneous angular velocity $\boldsymbol{\omega}$. The space cone is fixed in space and hence the axis of the body cone which is the inertial symmetry axis of the body, must rotate around the axis of the space cone which is directed along the $\boldsymbol{L}$ vector. Since, again, the change of $\boldsymbol{\omega}$ with time is continuous, *the body cone must roll around the space cone without slipping.* As the radius of the space cone is smaller than that of the body cone by a factor of about k, the angular velocity of rotation of the space cone about the $\boldsymbol{L}$ vector is approximately ω_3, that is, practically as fast as the spin of the whole body about the symmetry axis. Hence, both $\boldsymbol{\omega}$ and the inertial symmetry axis $\hat{\boldsymbol{k}}$ must be revolving around the direction of the fixed $\boldsymbol{L}$ vector in space with an angular velocity approximately equal to ω_3.

We can see that the axes of the two cones and the direction of $\boldsymbol{\omega}$ must always lie in one plane and that this plane must rotate about the fixed axis of the space cone. So the angle between the axes of the two cones, say α, can have only two possible values, $\alpha = \alpha_b \pm \alpha_s$. Since

$$\cos\alpha = \frac{\boldsymbol{L} \cdot \hat{\boldsymbol{k}}}{L} = \frac{L_3}{L} = \frac{C\omega_3}{L}$$

it is easy to check from Eq. (12.63) that

$$\tan^2 \alpha = \frac{A^2}{C^2} \tan^2 \alpha_b$$

This means that if both α and α_b are acute angles, then

$$\alpha > \alpha_b \qquad \text{for} \quad C < A$$

and

$$\alpha < \alpha_b \qquad \text{for} \quad C > A$$

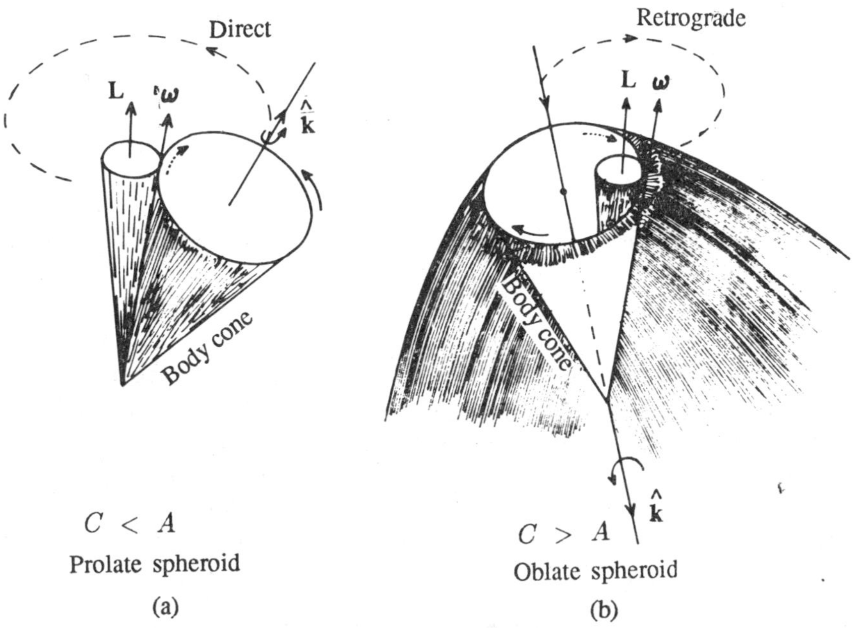

Fig. 12.14 Motion of body cones about the fixed space cones, showing the precession of both $\boldsymbol{\omega}$ and $\hat{\boldsymbol{k}}$ about the direction of $\boldsymbol{L}$, for two cases (a) prolate spheroid and (b) oblate spheroid

So for a prolate spheroid, $C < A$, and hence $\alpha = \alpha_b + \alpha_s$, that is, the two cones must touch externally as shown in Fig. 12.14a. On the other hand, for an oblate spheroid, such as the earth or a coin, $C > A$, and therefore, $\alpha = \alpha_b - \alpha_s$, that is, the space cone being smaller than the body cone should appear to touch on the inside surface of the body cone (Fig. 12.14b). However, it is practically impossible to insert the solid space cone inside the solid body cone. So, for Fig. 12.14b, a possible configuration would be to have the body cone as a hollow cone and the solid space cone touching from the hollow side of the body cone. Such a hollow body cone must have its axis pointing downward if, by definition, a solid space cone has its axis pointing upward ($\boldsymbol{L}$). With this revised configurational interpretation, now α can have only one choice, namely, $\alpha = \alpha_b + \alpha_s$, with α_s always acute angled, because physically the direction of the angular momentum vector $\boldsymbol{L}$ can never be very far from the direction of $\boldsymbol{\omega}$. So α_b can remain acute angled for Fig. 12.14a but has to be obtuse angled for Fig. 12.14b. These rearrangements are perfectly consistent with the formula $\tan^2\alpha = (A^2/C^2)\tan^2\alpha_b$, which implies $\alpha > \alpha_b$, or $\alpha = \alpha_b + \alpha_s$, for both the cases of $C < A$ and $C > A$. In the latter case, both α and α_b are obtuse angled (see Fig. 12.14b). The solid arrows near the circumference of the body cones represent the sense of its actual rotation and the dotted arrows indicate the sense of actual motion of $\boldsymbol{\omega}$ along the periphery of the respective body cones. The space cone remains fixed all the time and the body cone merely rolls on it without slipping. When $C < A$, the precessional motion of $\boldsymbol{\omega}$ around $\boldsymbol{L}$ is anticlockwise if the sense of rotation of the body cone about its own inertial axis of symmetry $\hat{\boldsymbol{k}}$ is anticlockwise. Hence the motion is called *direct*. But when $C > A$, this is just the opposite and the sense of the precessional motion of $\boldsymbol{\omega}$ around $\boldsymbol{L}$ becomes *retrograde*.

Obviously, for the free rotation of the earth it would be a case of retrograde precessional motion. Since the general direction of both $\boldsymbol{\omega}$ and $\boldsymbol{L}$ for the earth is towards the north pole, and both α and α_b have to be obtuse angled, the inertial symmetry axis $\hat{\boldsymbol{k}}$ of the earth should be directed along the south pole rather than the conventional north pole. From this point of view, the earth's axial rotation with respect to the above $\hat{\boldsymbol{k}}$ direction is clockwise. In Fig. 12.14b, the clockwise rotation of the body cone about the $\hat{\boldsymbol{k}}$ direction would give an anticlockwise precession of $\boldsymbol{\omega}$ around both the geometrical north pole and $\boldsymbol{L}$.

One can now see the conceptual correspondence between the set of polhode and herpolhode for free rotations of symmetric tops, and the set of the body and the space cones. It is the body cone that is responsible for the tracing of the polhode on the inertial ellipsoid, and the space cone is responsible for the tracing of the herpolhode on the invariable plane. Since the space cones and the body cones are closed circles, the polhodes and the herpolhodes are also the closed circular tracings for symmetric tops. As the inertial ellipsoid rolls without slipping on the invariable plane with $\boldsymbol{\omega}$ passing through the point of contact, the body cone also rolls on the surface of the space cone with $\boldsymbol{\omega}$ passing through their common tangent.

12.17 WHY SHOULD A FREELY ROTATING BODY PRECESS AT ALL?

Mathematically speaking, for a free rotation of a rigid body, one has

$$\left(\frac{d\boldsymbol{L}}{dt}\right)_{\text{inertial frame}} = \boldsymbol{\Gamma}_{\text{external}} = \boldsymbol{0}$$

$$= \left(\frac{d\boldsymbol{L}}{dt}\right)_{\text{body frame axes}} + \boldsymbol{\omega} \times \boldsymbol{L}\Big|_{\text{body frame axes}}$$

This extra $\boldsymbol{\omega} \times \boldsymbol{L}$ term, which may be regarded as a pseudotorque arising out of the noninertialness of the rotating body frame, is found to be responsible for the precession of the freely rotating rigid body. This is mathematically secured through keeping L^2 and $\boldsymbol{L}\cdot\boldsymbol{\omega}$ constant but neither of the vectors $\boldsymbol{L}$ and $\boldsymbol{\omega}$ conserved, as seen from the body frame.

We know that with respect to any rotating frame, a number of pseudoforces arise, namely the centrifugal force due to the circular motion of the particle tied rigidly to the rotating body, the Coriolis force due to any motion of the particle with respect to the rotating body frame and the Eulerian force due to any inertial change in $\boldsymbol{\omega}$ with time. Thus the particles of the rotating rigid body must experience the centrifugal force and the Eulerian force but not the Coriolis force because the particles are fixed in position with respect to the body frame. The total centrifugal torque experienced by the whole body is therefore given by

$$\begin{aligned}\boldsymbol{\Gamma}_{\text{centrifugal}} &= \sum \boldsymbol{r} \times [m(\boldsymbol{\omega} \times \boldsymbol{r}) \times \boldsymbol{\omega}] \\ &= \sum m(\boldsymbol{r}\cdot\boldsymbol{\omega})(\boldsymbol{\omega} \times \boldsymbol{r}) - \sum m\,[\boldsymbol{r}\cdot(\boldsymbol{\omega} \times \boldsymbol{r})]\,\boldsymbol{\omega}\end{aligned}$$

The second term on RHS vanishes because $\boldsymbol{r}$ is perpendicular to $\boldsymbol{\omega} \times \boldsymbol{r}$. Therefore,

$$\boldsymbol{\Gamma}_{\text{centrifugal}} = \sum m(\boldsymbol{r}\cdot\boldsymbol{\omega})(\boldsymbol{\omega} \times \boldsymbol{r}) \tag{12.67}$$

where the sum extends over all particles of the body.

In order to study the nature of this centrifugal pseudotorque, we choose the z-axis of the body frame to be along the instantaneous $\boldsymbol{\omega}$ vector, that is, $\boldsymbol{\omega} = \omega_3\hat{\boldsymbol{k}}$ in which case, from Eq. (12.67), $\Gamma_3 = 0$, but

$$\begin{aligned}\Gamma_1 &= -\sum m r_2 r_3 \omega_3^2 = I_{23}\omega_3^2 \\ \Gamma_2 &= \sum m r_3 r_1 \omega_3^2 = -I_{31}\omega_3^2\end{aligned}$$

Therefore,

$$\boldsymbol{\Gamma}_{\text{centrifugal}} = \omega_3^2(I_{23}\hat{\boldsymbol{i}} - I_{31}\hat{\boldsymbol{j}}). \tag{12.68}$$

This shows that the centrifugal torque does not vanish if the products of inertia of the body with respect to the chosen body frame axes (that defines the $\hat{\boldsymbol{k}}$ axis along the instantaneous axis of rotation) do not vanish. Or in other words, the rotations of the body about any of the principal axes will lead to the vanishing of the centrifugal pseudotorque. Hence such rotations being torque free, are expected to be in steady states, as we have seen earlier.

Now, consider

$$\begin{aligned}\boldsymbol{L} \times \boldsymbol{\omega}\Big|_{\text{body frame}} &= \sum(\boldsymbol{r} \times \boldsymbol{p}) \times \boldsymbol{\omega} \\ &= \sum [m\boldsymbol{r} \times (\boldsymbol{\omega} \times \boldsymbol{r})] \times \boldsymbol{\omega} \\ &= -\sum m\boldsymbol{\omega} \times \{\boldsymbol{r} \times (\boldsymbol{\omega} \times \boldsymbol{r})\} \\ &= \sum m(\boldsymbol{\omega}\cdot\boldsymbol{r})(\boldsymbol{\omega} \times \boldsymbol{r}) - \sum m\,[\boldsymbol{\omega}\cdot(\boldsymbol{\omega} \times \boldsymbol{r})]\,\boldsymbol{r} \\ &= \sum m(\boldsymbol{\omega}\cdot\boldsymbol{r})(\boldsymbol{\omega} \times \boldsymbol{r}) \\ &= \boldsymbol{\Gamma}_{\text{centrifugal}} \equiv \frac{d\boldsymbol{L}}{dt}\Big|_{\text{body frame}}\end{aligned}$$

or

$$\boldsymbol{\Gamma}_{\text{centrifugal}} + \boldsymbol{\omega} \times \boldsymbol{L}\Big|_{\text{body frame axes}} = \boldsymbol{0}$$

or

$$\left.\frac{dL}{dt}\right|_{\text{body frame axes}} + \omega \times L\Big|_{\text{body frame axes}} = \mathbf{0} \tag{12.51}$$

which gives back Euler's equations of motion for a freely rotating rigid body. One can also verify that the total pseudotorque due to the Eulerian force $\sum m r \times (r \times \dot{\omega})$ is precisely equal to $-\,dL/dt$ in the body frame; hence the sum of the two pseudotorques vanish in the absence of any external torque.

Similarly one can calculate the total amount of the centrifugal force that is experienced by the particles of the rotating rigid body.

$$\begin{aligned} F_{\text{centrifugal}} &= \sum m(\omega \times r) \times \omega \\ &= -\sum m\omega \times (\omega \times r) \\ &= \sum m\omega^2 r - \sum m(\omega \cdot r)\omega \\ &= \omega^2 M R_{\text{cm}} - M(\omega \cdot R_{\text{cm}})\omega \end{aligned}$$

Therefore, $F_{\text{centrifugal}}$ can vanish only if $R_{\text{cm}} = \mathbf{0}$, that is, if the rotation is taking place about the centre of mass of the rigid body. Otherwise, if pure rotation is taking place about a point other than the centre of mass , then

$$\begin{aligned} F_{\text{centrifugal}} &= \sum m(\omega \times r) \times \omega \\ &= \sum m v \times \omega = P_{\text{cm}} \times \omega \\ &= -\,\omega \times P_{\text{cm}} \end{aligned}$$

Therefore we get, remembering that

$$F_{\text{centrifugal}} \equiv \left.\frac{dP_{\text{cm}}}{dt}\right|_{\text{body frame}}$$

$$\frac{dP_{\text{cm}}}{dt} + \omega \times P_{\text{cm}} = \mathbf{0} \tag{12.69}$$

which is, again, Euler's equation for the motion of the centre of mass of any rotating rigid body, expressed in the unit vectors of the rotating body frame.

12.18 STEADY PRECESSION OF A UNIAXIAL BODY (SYMMETRIC TOP) UNDER THE ACTION OF AN EXTERNAL TORQUE

Let $\hat{k}$ be the unit vector along the symmetry axis of a uniaxial body say a 'top' (see Fig. 12.15) which makes an angle α with the inertial z-axis, the latter being aligned in the local vertical direction. O is the bottom tip of the body about which the body is rotating with an instantaneous angular velocity ω. The distance of the centre of mass of the body (which is the same as centre of gravity) from O is h.

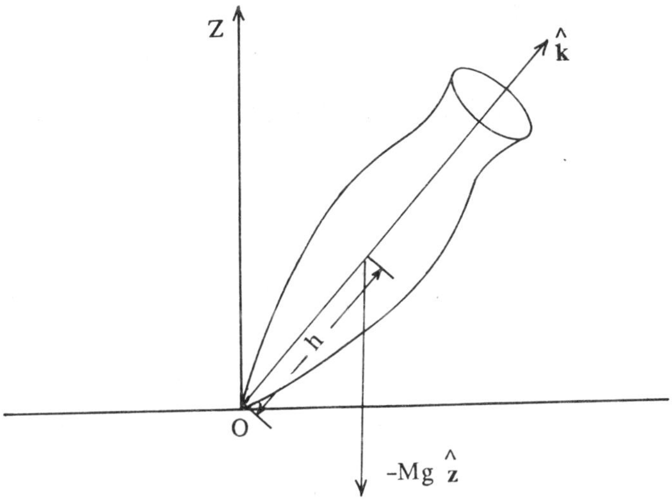

Fig. 12.15 A symmetric top under the action of gravitational torque about a fixed point O in the body

If the body's symmetry axis, that is, the direction of $\hat{\boldsymbol{k}}$ is changing with time with respect to the inertial frame, the tip of $\hat{\boldsymbol{k}}$ has a motion with respect to the inertial frame, given by (see Eq. (3.2))

$$\frac{d\hat{\boldsymbol{k}}}{dt} = \boldsymbol{\omega} \times \hat{\boldsymbol{k}}$$

so that

$$\hat{\boldsymbol{k}} \times \frac{d\hat{\boldsymbol{k}}}{dt} = \hat{\boldsymbol{k}} \times (\boldsymbol{\omega} \times \hat{\boldsymbol{k}}) = \boldsymbol{\omega} - (\boldsymbol{\omega} \cdot \hat{\boldsymbol{k}})\hat{\boldsymbol{k}} = \boldsymbol{\omega} - \omega_3 \hat{\boldsymbol{k}}$$

Therefore, the angular velocity of the body $\boldsymbol{\omega}$ is given by

$$\boldsymbol{\omega} = \hat{\boldsymbol{k}} \times \frac{d\hat{\boldsymbol{k}}}{dt} + \omega_3 \hat{\boldsymbol{k}} \tag{12.70}$$

Hence the angular momentum $\boldsymbol{L}$ is

$$\boldsymbol{L} = A\left(\hat{\boldsymbol{k}} \times \frac{d\hat{\boldsymbol{k}}}{dt}\right) + C\omega_3 \hat{\boldsymbol{k}} \tag{12.71}$$

and the total torque about the origin

$$\boldsymbol{\Gamma} = \frac{d\boldsymbol{L}}{dt} = A\hat{\boldsymbol{k}} \times \frac{d^2\hat{\boldsymbol{k}}}{dt^2} + C\omega_3 \frac{d\hat{\boldsymbol{k}}}{dt} + C\dot{\omega}_3 \hat{\boldsymbol{k}} \tag{12.72}$$

The angular momentum, torque and the angular velocity are all referred to the inertial frame.

Now let us assume that there is a steady precession of the body axis $\hat{\boldsymbol{k}}$ about the space fixed axis $\hat{\boldsymbol{z}}$, that is, the angle α remains the same but $\hat{\boldsymbol{k}}$ rotates about $\hat{\boldsymbol{z}}$ with an angular velocity $\boldsymbol{\Omega} = \Omega\hat{\boldsymbol{z}}$. This is called a pure precession of a rotating symmetric top under the action of, say, the usual gravitational torque. For such a steady precession, the motion of the tip of the unit vector $\hat{\boldsymbol{k}}$ is given by

$$\frac{d\hat{\boldsymbol{k}}}{dt} = \Omega(\hat{\boldsymbol{z}} \times \hat{\boldsymbol{k}})$$

so that

$$\begin{aligned}\frac{d^2\hat{\boldsymbol{k}}}{dt^2} &= \Omega\hat{\boldsymbol{z}} \times \frac{d\hat{\boldsymbol{k}}}{dt} = \Omega^2\hat{\boldsymbol{z}} \times (\hat{\boldsymbol{z}} \times \hat{\boldsymbol{k}}) \\ &= -\Omega^2\hat{\boldsymbol{k}} + \Omega^2(\hat{\boldsymbol{z}}\cdot\hat{\boldsymbol{k}})\hat{\boldsymbol{z}} = \Omega^2[\cos\alpha\,\hat{\boldsymbol{z}} - \hat{\boldsymbol{k}}]\end{aligned} \tag{12.73}$$

The maintenance of such a steady precession would require an external torque to be given by

$$\begin{aligned}\boldsymbol{\Gamma} &= A\hat{\boldsymbol{k}} \times \frac{d^2\hat{\boldsymbol{k}}}{dt^2} + C\omega_3\frac{d\hat{\boldsymbol{k}}}{dt} + C\dot{\omega}_3\hat{\boldsymbol{k}} \\ &= A\Omega^2\cos\alpha\,(\hat{\boldsymbol{k}} \times \hat{\boldsymbol{z}}) + C\omega_3\Omega(\hat{\boldsymbol{z}} \times \hat{\boldsymbol{k}}) + C\dot{\omega}_3\hat{\boldsymbol{k}} \\ &= \Omega(C\omega_3 - A\Omega\cos\alpha)(\hat{\boldsymbol{z}} \times \hat{\boldsymbol{k}}) + C\dot{\omega}_3\hat{\boldsymbol{k}}\end{aligned} \tag{12.74}$$

Now we ask the following question: can there be a steady precession of the top about the local vertical axis with and without an external torque acting on it?

Case (A): A Free Rotation of the Top (Top in a Spaceship!)

By definition $\boldsymbol{\Gamma} = 0$. Then the required conditions are from Eq. (12.74)

(i) $\dot{\omega}_3 = 0$,

that is, the component of the angular velocity along the symmetry axis is a constant of motion. We have seen this earlier in the context of the free rotation of the symmetric rigid bodies (Eq. (12.59)).

(ii) $C\omega_3 = A\Omega\cos\alpha$ or

$$\Omega = \frac{C\omega_3}{A\cos\alpha} \equiv \Omega_f \quad \text{say} \tag{12.75}$$

Thus a freely rotating symmetric top can precess with a steady precessional angular velocity Ω_f given by Eq. (12.75) about an axis which makes an angle α with the body's symmetry axis. Since ω_3, C, A and α are constants, Ω_f is also a constant of motion.

Now substituting for $d\hat{\boldsymbol{k}}/dt$ in Eq. (12.70) from Eq. (12.73), we obtain

$$\boldsymbol{\omega} = \Omega\hat{\boldsymbol{z}} + (\omega_3 - \Omega\cos\alpha)\hat{\boldsymbol{k}}$$

So $\boldsymbol{\omega}$ can be thought of as a combination of two vectors — one due to the angular velocity of steady precession about $\hat{\boldsymbol{z}}$ and the other a spin angular velocity about the body's symmetry axis $\hat{\boldsymbol{k}}$. This latter quantity is denoted as

$$\omega_3 - \Omega\cos\alpha \equiv \dot{\psi}$$

if ψ is defined to be the angle of body spin about $\hat{\boldsymbol{k}}$. Since ω_3 = constant for free rotation, it implies that

$$\omega_3 = \dot{\psi} + \Omega \cos\alpha = \text{const.}$$

and also that $\dot{\psi}$ is a constant because of the constancy of α and of $\Omega = \Omega_f$.

It is now easy to compare the motion with reference to the body and space cones. Obviously α is the angle between the axes of the two cones, and the spin angular velocity of the body cone about $\hat{\boldsymbol{k}}$ is simply $\dot{\psi}$. Since the body cone has the principal moments of inertia given by A, A and C, one can easily find its angular momentum $\boldsymbol{L}$ given by Eq. (12.71) to be

$$\boldsymbol{L} = A\Omega_f \hat{\boldsymbol{z}}$$

So the idea of the space and body cones is not at all fictitious. In fact, one can now show that the direction of $\boldsymbol{\omega}$ is actually along the line of contact of these two cones.

From Eq. (12.75), one can also verify that Ω_f is positive if α is acute angled and vice versa. So the sense of precession becomes retrograde for $\alpha > \pi/2$, in which case the body cone becomes oblate shaped with its $C > A$. Another point to note is that as $\alpha \to \pi/2$, the magnitude of the required precessional angular velocity $\Omega_f \to \infty$, unless $\omega_3 \to 0$.

Again, substituting for $\omega_3 = \dot{\psi} + \Omega\cos\alpha$ in Eq. (12.75), one obtains

$$\Omega = \frac{C\dot{\psi}}{(A - C)\cos\alpha}$$

This implies that for $\dot{\psi} > 0$, that is, for anticlockwise spinning about the symmetry axis, the precession will be retrograde if either of $(A - C)$ and $\cos\alpha$ is negative, and vice versa.

Case (B): A Steady Precessional Motion Under the Action of Gravity

The body will experience a torque due to the action of gravity given by

$$\boldsymbol{\Gamma} = h\hat{\boldsymbol{k}} \times (-Mg\hat{\boldsymbol{z}}) = Mgh(\hat{\boldsymbol{z}} \times \hat{\boldsymbol{k}}) \tag{12.76}$$

When inserted in Euler's equations of motion, this torque naturally satisfies

$$\dot{\omega}_3 = 0 \quad \text{or,} \quad \omega_3 = \text{const.}$$

because the torque has no component along the $\hat{\boldsymbol{k}}$ direction. A comparison of Eq. (12.76) with Eq. (12.74) yields

$$\Omega(C\omega_3 - A\Omega\cos\alpha) = Mgh$$

or

$$A\Omega^2\cos\alpha - C\Omega\omega_3 + Mgh = 0$$

or

$$\Omega = \frac{C\omega_3 \pm \sqrt{C^2\omega_3^2 - 4MghA\cos\alpha}}{2A\cos\alpha} \equiv \Omega_{2,1}$$

So this gives two solutions for Ω, say Ω_2 and Ω_1, for a given A, C, ω_3, Mgh and α.

However, we can also get a single value of Ω, say $\Omega_1 = \Omega_2 = \Omega_o$, only if

$$C\omega_3 = 2\sqrt{MghA\cos\alpha} \tag{12.77}$$

and, therefore,

$$\Omega_o = \frac{C\omega_3}{2A\cos\alpha} = \frac{1}{2}\Omega_f$$

Thus the steady precessional frequency of a symmetric top in the presence of a gravitational torque is just the half of the required value for its maintenance under a torque free condition of rotation, provided Eq. (12.77) is satisfied. Note that such a case is permissible only if $\alpha < \pi/2$, and further, no comparison should be made in terms of the space and body cones.

A pair of distinct real values for Ω exists only if

$$C\omega_3 > 2\sqrt{MghA\cos\alpha}$$

for every given $0 < \alpha < \pi/2$. So if the above condition is satisfied for each given α, then there exist two definite values (Ω_1, Ω_2) of the steady precessional rates, one of which would correspond to a *fast* precession (Ω_2) and the other to a *slow* precession (Ω_1) with $\Omega_1 < \Omega_2$.

In any case, in order that a steady precession under the action of gravity exist, we require

$$\omega_3 \geq 2\sqrt{\frac{MghA\cos\alpha}{C^2}} \tag{12.78}$$

that is, a fast enough rotation about the symmetry axis. This will be further discussed in section 12.23, case IV.

12.19 THE CASE OF ARBITRARY ROTATIONS

In the previous section we wanted to study the conditions under which steady precession is possible. But in general, the precession is neither steady nor does it maintain a constant angle α with the fixed vertical direction. Such general motions can be studied using Eulerian angles.

So far we have been dealing with general and special case solutions of rigid body rotations in terms of $\boldsymbol{\omega}$ or its components along the principal axes. Even if we have a complete solution in terms of $\boldsymbol{\omega}$ it may not first of all reveal what it means in terms of spin, precession, etc. Second, solutions in terms of $\boldsymbol{\omega}$ cannot be regarded as dynamically complete, because one would finally like to obtain the solutions in terms of the generalised coordinates, rather than the generalised coordinate velocities. And here lies the problem. The components of $\boldsymbol{\omega}$ are in general not expressible as the generalised velocities with reference to some physically meaningful generalised coordinates. Euler successfully devised a set of physically meaningful generalised coordinates for the description of the most general possible rotations of any rigid body.

Before we move on to the description of the Eulerian angles in section 12.21, we would like to introduce the various types of rotations that are used to describe the general rotations of any rigid body. Particularly the kinematical motion of an aeroplane in air can have all three degrees of freedom for rotation together with its translational motion. These are three basic rotations, called ***roll, pitch*** and *yaw* (see Fig. 12.16).

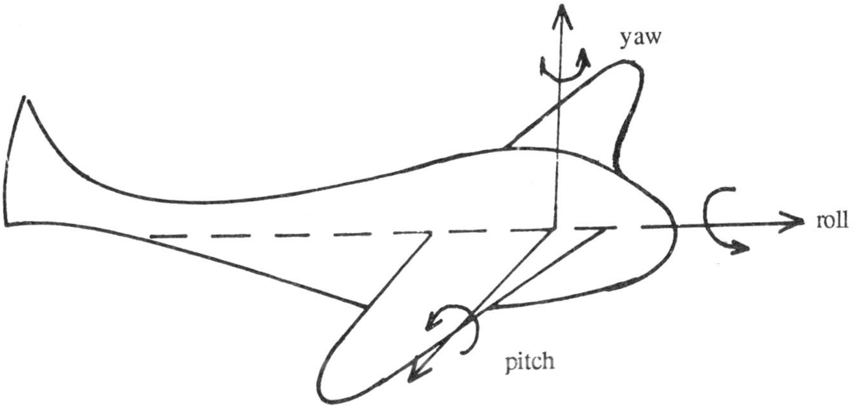

Fig. 12.16 Roll, pitch and yaw motions of an aeroplane

Roll is the rotation of the body about the longitudinal direction of the motion. For example, while swimming straight ahead if one decides to turn one's posture sidewise from supine to prone and back to supine, one has to perform a complete roll.

Pitch is the rotation about the transverse horizontal axis of the body. When one decides to dive up and down, so that one's nose goes up and down, or say a car wants to climb up or down on a hilly road, the rotation involved would be a pitch.

Yaw is the rotation about the transverse vertical axis of the body, so that the nose of the aircraft or swimmer can move sideways.

All these three basic types of rotations are essential for manoeuvring the orientation of any aircraft or kite, etc. with respect to the general direction of its translational motion. Since these three basic rotations are mutually independent of one another, and by Euler's theorem one requires three degrees of freedom for general rotation, Euler had defined the the so-called three Eulerian rotations in terms of roll, pitch and yaw. Thus any arbitrary spatial orientation of any rigid body can be thought of as a linear combination of yaw, pitch and roll about the centre of mass, or any given fixed point in the body.

A similar statement is also valid for the instantaneous angular velocity of any rigid body, that is, the latter can be thought of as a linear combination of the angular velocities due to yaw, pitch and roll. In order to see this, we prove in the following section a basic theorem on the vector addition of two angular velocities about a given point.

12.20 ADDITION OF TWO ANGULAR VELOCITIES

If a frame S_2 has an angular velocity $\boldsymbol{\omega}_2$ with respect to S_1 about their common origin O, and the frame S_1 has an angular velocity $\boldsymbol{\omega}_1$ with respect to an inertial frame S_o about the same common origin, then S_2 has an angular velocity of $\boldsymbol{\omega} = \boldsymbol{\omega}_1 + \boldsymbol{\omega}_2$ with respect to the inertial frame S_o.

To see this, let P be a point rigidly fixed to S_2. The velocity of P in S_2 is obviously zero, that is, $\boldsymbol{v}_2 = 0$. The velocity of P in S_1 is

$$\boldsymbol{v}_1 = \boldsymbol{v}_2 + \boldsymbol{\omega}_2 \times \overrightarrow{OP} = \boldsymbol{\omega}_2 \times \overrightarrow{OP}$$

The velocity of P in S_o is

$$\begin{aligned}\boldsymbol{v}_o &= \boldsymbol{v}_1 + \boldsymbol{\omega}_1 \times \overrightarrow{OP} \\ &= \boldsymbol{\omega}_2 \times \mathbf{OP} + \boldsymbol{\omega}_1 \times \overrightarrow{OP} \\ &= (\boldsymbol{\omega}_1 + \boldsymbol{\omega}_2) \times \overrightarrow{OP}\end{aligned}$$

This must be equal to $\boldsymbol{\omega} \times \overrightarrow{OP}$, if $\boldsymbol{\omega}$ is defined to be the angular velocity of P in S_o. Since P is an arbitrary point, we must have

$$\boldsymbol{\omega} = \boldsymbol{\omega}_1 + \boldsymbol{\omega}_2 \tag{12.79}$$

12.21 EULERIAN ANGLES

Let us consider a fixed inertial frame S_o with its z_o-axis pointing vertically upward. First we give a yaw ϕ about the z_o-axis so that the frame S_o changes to S_1 with their z_o-z_1 axes common and the axes x_o and y_o are rotated by an angle ϕ to assume the position of x_1 and y_1 axes in S_1 (see Fig. 12.17). Then we give a pitch θ about the new x_1-axis so that the frame S_2 now has x_1-x_2 as the common axis, called the *line of node*, and y_2-axis separates from y_1-axis and z_2-axis from z_1-axis, each by the same angle θ. Then we give a roll (or spin) about the z_2-axis by an angle ψ, keeping z_3 and z_2 axes coincident, but the x_2 and y_2 axes rotated by ψ, in their common plane, to the new x_3 and y_3 axes respectively. This forms the frame S_3. Usually the frame S_3 is identified with the body frame and S_o with the inertial frame. To compare them with the spherical polar coordinates (r, θ, ϕ) one can easily see the total resemblance between the two θ's and the two ϕ's, and the radial line ($\boldsymbol{r}$) having a roll about itself by an angle ψ, which cannot be realised in any usual spherical polar coordinate system. It is indeed a replacement of the length-like r-coordinate of the spherical polar coordinate system by an angular coordinate ψ in the Eulerian description.

Now consider the position vector of any given point P having coordinates (x, y, z) with respect to a rectangular Cartesian coordinate system. Suppose this coordinate system is rotated about its x-axis through an angle θ, so that with respect to the rotated coordinate frame the coordinates of the same point P become (x', y', z'). Denoting $\boldsymbol{X} \equiv (x, y, z)$ and $\boldsymbol{X}' \equiv (x', y', z')$ we have the relation in matrix notation

$$\boldsymbol{X}' = R_x(\theta)\boldsymbol{X}$$

where

$$R_x(\theta) = \begin{pmatrix} 1 & 0 & 0 \\ 0 & \cos\theta & \sin\theta \\ 0 & -\sin\theta & \cos\theta \end{pmatrix} \tag{12.80}$$

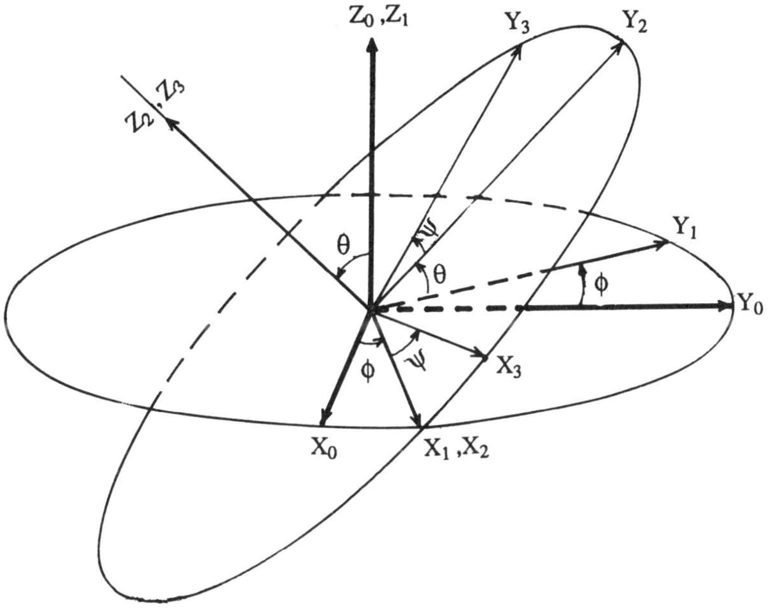

Fig. 12.17 Eulerian angles (ϕ, θ, ψ) as angles of elementary rotations of a rectangular Cartesian frame of reference in the sequence $S_o \to S_1 \to S_2 \to S_3$

If fully expanded, this transformation would look like

$$
\begin{aligned}
x_1' &= x_1 \\
x_2' &= x_2 \cos\theta + x_3 \sin\theta \\
x_3' &= -x_2 \sin\theta + x_3 \cos\theta
\end{aligned}
$$

Similarly, if we made a rotation by an angle θ about the y-axis instead of about the x-axis, we would have got

$$\boldsymbol{X}' = R_y(\theta)\boldsymbol{X}$$

with

$$R_y(\theta) = \begin{pmatrix} \cos\theta & 0 & -\sin\theta \\ 0 & 1 & 0 \\ \sin\theta & 0 & \cos\theta \end{pmatrix} \tag{12.81}$$

and for the rotation about the z-axis through an angle θ would give

$$\boldsymbol{X}' = R_z\boldsymbol{X}$$

with

$$R_z(\theta) = \begin{pmatrix} \cos\theta & \sin\theta & 0 \\ -\sin\theta & \cos\theta & 0 \\ 0 & 0 & 1 \end{pmatrix} \tag{12.82}$$

We can easily write the transformation matrices for the three Eulerian angles as

$$\begin{aligned} R_z(\phi) &= \begin{pmatrix} \cos\phi & \sin\phi & 0 \\ -\sin\phi & \cos\phi & 0 \\ 0 & 0 & 1 \end{pmatrix} \\ R_x(\theta) &= \begin{pmatrix} 1 & 0 & 0 \\ 0 & \cos\theta & \sin\theta \\ 0 & -\sin\theta & \cos\theta \end{pmatrix} \\ R_z(\psi) &= \begin{pmatrix} \cos\psi & \sin\psi & 0 \\ -\sin\psi & \cos\psi & 0 \\ 0 & 0 & 1 \end{pmatrix} \end{aligned} \tag{12.83}$$

The first one obviously corresponds to a rotation by ϕ about the z_o-axis, the second one to a rotation by θ about the first intermediate or the nodal x_1-axis, and finally the third one to a rotation by ψ about the body's z_3-axis.

When these three Eulerian rotations are performed in the sequence described above to give a final rotated frame S_3, the components of a vector in the S_o and S_3 frames are related by

$$X''' = R(\phi, \theta, \psi)X \tag{12.84}$$

where the *Eulerian rotation matrix*,

$$R(\phi, \theta, \psi) = R_z(\psi) \cdot R_x(\theta) \cdot R_z(\phi)$$

$$= \begin{pmatrix} \cos\psi\cos\phi - \cos\theta\sin\phi\sin\psi & \cos\psi\sin\phi + \cos\theta\cos\phi\sin\psi & \sin\psi\sin\theta \\ -\sin\psi\cos\phi - \cos\theta\sin\phi\cos\psi & -\sin\psi\sin\phi + \cos\theta\cos\phi\cos\psi & \cos\psi\sin\theta \\ \sin\theta\sin\phi & -\sin\theta\cos\phi & \cos\theta \end{pmatrix}$$

Since all the matrices are orthogonal, their inverses are simply equal to their transposes. We can therefore write

$$X = \tilde{R}(\phi, \theta, \psi)X''' \tag{12.85}$$

where $\tilde{R}(\phi, \theta, \psi)$ is the transpose of $R(\phi, \theta, \psi)$.

It is easy to see that the elementary Eulerian rotations are independent of each other in the sense that none of these can be effected by using the other two. We have seen that a rigid body has exactly three rotational degrees of freedom. Thus the three Eulerian angles (ϕ, θ, ψ) can be used as generalised coordinates to fix the orientation of a rigid body with respect to a given coordinate frame. In other words, if a coordinate frame with a set of rectangular Cartesian coordinates (x''', y''', z''') is obtained by rotating a frame having the rectangular Cartesian coordinates (x, y, z) about any arbitrary direction passing through the origin and through an arbitrary angle, it is possible to find a unique set of three Eulerian angles (ϕ, θ, ψ) such that the components of any given instantaneous position vector in both the frames are mutually related through the transformations (12.84) and (12.85).

The elementary angular velocities for the three elementary Eulerian operations are

$$\begin{aligned} \omega_\phi &= \dot{\phi}\hat{\boldsymbol{k}}_o = \dot{\phi}\hat{\boldsymbol{k}}_1 && \text{(between S}_o \text{ and S}_1) \\ \omega_\theta &= \dot{\theta}\hat{\boldsymbol{i}}_1 = \dot{\theta}\hat{\boldsymbol{i}}_2 && \text{(between S}_1 \text{ and S}_2) \\ \omega_\psi &= \dot{\psi}\hat{\boldsymbol{k}}_2 = \dot{\psi}\hat{\boldsymbol{k}}_3 && \text{(between S}_2 \text{ and S}_3) \end{aligned} \tag{12.86}$$

Hence by the theorem we proved in section 12.20, the total angular velocity of S_3 with respect to S_o is

$$\omega = \omega_\phi + \omega_\theta + \omega_\phi$$

or

$$\begin{aligned} \omega &= \dot{\phi}\hat{\boldsymbol{k}}_1 + \dot{\theta}\hat{\boldsymbol{i}}_1 + \dot{\psi}(-\sin\theta\hat{\boldsymbol{j}}_1 + \cos\theta\hat{\boldsymbol{k}}_1) && \text{in unit vectors of S}_1 \\ &= \dot{\phi}[\sin\theta\hat{\boldsymbol{j}}_2 + \cos\theta\hat{\boldsymbol{k}}_2] + \dot{\theta}\hat{\boldsymbol{i}}_2 + \dot{\psi}\hat{\boldsymbol{k}}_2 && \text{in unit vectors of S}_2 \\ &= \dot{\phi}[\sin\theta\sin\psi\hat{\boldsymbol{i}}_3 + \sin\theta\cos\psi\hat{\boldsymbol{j}}_3 + \cos\theta\hat{\boldsymbol{k}}_3] \\ &\quad + \dot{\theta}(\cos\psi\hat{\boldsymbol{i}}_3 - \sin\psi\hat{\boldsymbol{j}}_3) + \dot{\psi}\hat{\boldsymbol{k}}_3 && \text{in unit vectors of S}_3 \\ &= \dot{\phi}\hat{\boldsymbol{k}}_o + \dot{\theta}[\cos\phi\hat{\boldsymbol{i}}_o + \sin\phi\hat{\boldsymbol{j}}_o] \\ &\quad + \dot{\psi}[\sin\theta\sin\phi\hat{\boldsymbol{i}}_o - \sin\theta\cos\phi\hat{\boldsymbol{j}}_o + \cos\theta\hat{\boldsymbol{k}}_o] && \text{in unit vectors of S}_o \end{aligned} \tag{12.87}$$

Since the body frame is S_3 we shall be interested in expressing $\boldsymbol{\omega}$ in terms of the unit vectors of S_3, that is, from the third expression for ω in Eq. (12.87), given by

$$\begin{aligned} \omega_1 &= \dot{\phi}\sin\theta\sin\psi + \dot{\theta}\cos\psi \\ \omega_2 &= \dot{\phi}\sin\theta\cos\psi - \dot{\theta}\sin\psi \\ \omega_3 &= \dot{\phi}\cos\theta + \dot{\psi} \end{aligned} \tag{12.88}$$

for which the principal axes of the body are chosen to be the rectangular Cartesian axes of the frame S_3 with the unit vectors $(\hat{\boldsymbol{i}}_3, \hat{\boldsymbol{j}}_3, \hat{\boldsymbol{k}}_3)$, implying for example, $I_{11}^{(p)} = A$, $I_{22}^{(p)} = B$ and $I_{33}^{(p)} = C$, for any asymmetric top. Looking at the third equation of Eq. (12.88) and comparing it with the analysis presented in section 12.18, it is now easy to recognise ψ to be the angle of body spin, and ϕ as the angle of precession. The new angle θ is called the angle of nutation, which was of course represented by α in sections 12.16 and 12.18.

The vector transformations from one basis set to another basis set that are used in Eq. (12.87) are given as follows

Between S_o and S_1:

$$\hat{\boldsymbol{i}}_1 = \cos\phi\hat{\boldsymbol{i}}_o + \sin\phi\hat{\boldsymbol{j}}_o \qquad \hat{\boldsymbol{j}}_1 = -\sin\phi\hat{\boldsymbol{i}}_o + \cos\phi\hat{\boldsymbol{j}}_o \qquad \hat{\boldsymbol{k}}_1 = \hat{\boldsymbol{k}}_o$$

$$\hat{\boldsymbol{i}}_o = \cos\phi\hat{\boldsymbol{i}}_1 - \sin\phi\hat{\boldsymbol{j}}_1 \qquad \hat{\boldsymbol{j}}_o = \sin\phi\hat{\boldsymbol{i}}_1 + \cos\phi\hat{\boldsymbol{j}}_1 \qquad \hat{\boldsymbol{k}}_o = \hat{\boldsymbol{k}}_1$$

Between S_1 and S_2:

$$\hat{\boldsymbol{i}}_2 = \hat{\boldsymbol{i}}_1 \qquad \hat{\boldsymbol{j}}_2 = \cos\theta\hat{\boldsymbol{j}}_1 + \sin\theta\hat{\boldsymbol{k}}_1 \qquad \hat{\boldsymbol{k}}_2 = -\sin\theta\hat{\boldsymbol{j}}_1 + \cos\theta\hat{\boldsymbol{k}}_1$$

$$\hat{\imath}_1 = \hat{\imath}_2 \qquad \hat{\jmath}_1 = \cos\theta\hat{\jmath}_2 - \sin\theta\hat{k}_2 \qquad \hat{k}_1 = \sin\theta\hat{\jmath}_2 + \cos\theta\hat{k}_2$$

Between S_2 and S_3:

$$\hat{\imath}_3 = \cos\psi\hat{\imath}_2 + \sin\psi\hat{\jmath}_2 \qquad \hat{\jmath}_3 = -\sin\psi\hat{\imath}_2 + \cos\psi\hat{\jmath}_2 \qquad \hat{k}_3 = \hat{k}_2$$

$$\hat{\imath}_2 = \cos\psi\hat{\imath}_3 - \sin\psi\hat{\jmath}_3 \qquad \hat{\jmath}_2 = \sin\psi\hat{\imath}_3 + \cos\psi\hat{\jmath}_3 \qquad \hat{k}_2 = \hat{k}_3$$

These are simply the vectorial representations of the transformation matrices given in Eq. (12.83).

Now suppose we have a rectangular Cartesian frame S, and rotate the frame by a finite angle χ about an axis that is represented by the unit vector $\hat{n}$ and that passes through the origin to obtain it as a frame S′. Any arbitrary position vector $\boldsymbol{r}$ in the frame S would read in the frame S′ as

$$\boldsymbol{r} \to \boldsymbol{r}' = \boldsymbol{r}\cos\chi + \hat{n}(\boldsymbol{r}\cdot\hat{n})(1-\cos\chi) + (\boldsymbol{r}\times\hat{n})\sin\chi \tag{12.89}$$

This equation was possibly first derived by Gibbs in 1901. Here the angle χ represents, by Euler's theorem, the single composite angle of rotation for the operation of the three elementary Eulerian rotations in succession represented by the single vector Eq. (12.84), where $\boldsymbol{X}$ corresponds to $\boldsymbol{r}$ and $\boldsymbol{X}'''$ to $\boldsymbol{r}'$. One can solve uniquely for χ, n_1 and n_2 from these equations in terms of ϕ, θ and ψ, and of course, n_3 will be determined from the normalisation condition $n_1^2 + n_2^2 + n_3^2 = 1$, where $\hat{\boldsymbol{n}} = (n_1, n_2, n_3)$.

12.22 MOTION OF A HEAVY SYMMETRIC TOP ROTATING ABOUT A FIXED POINT IN THE BODY UNDER THE ACTION OF GRAVITY

Let the principal axes about the fixed point of rotation of a symmetric top be chosen as the body frame axes (see Fig. 12.15) so that

$$I_{11} = A = I_{22} = B \qquad \text{and} \qquad I_{33} = C$$

In terms of the Eulerian angles and their time derivatives, $\dot{\phi}$, $\dot{\theta}$ and $\dot{\psi}$, the instantaneous angular velocity of the top about the fixed point of rotation is given by

$$\boldsymbol{\omega} = \omega_1\hat{\imath} + \omega_2\hat{\jmath} + \omega_3\hat{k}$$

where $\hat{\imath}$, $\hat{\jmath}$ and $\hat{k}$ are the unit vectors along the principal axes (that is, the body frame axes) and therefore, ω_1, ω_2 and ω_3 are given by Eq. (12.88).

There are two ways of setting up the equations of motion.

12.22.1 The Lagrangian Method

One constructs the Lagrangian of the system from the expressions for kinetic and potential energies. We have, for the kinetic energy,

$$\begin{aligned} T &= \frac{1}{2} I_{ij}\omega_i\omega_j \\ &= \frac{1}{2}A\omega_1^2 + \frac{1}{2}A\omega_2^2 + \frac{1}{2}C\omega_3^2 \\ &= \frac{1}{2}A\left(\dot{\theta}^2 + \dot{\phi}^2\sin^2\theta\right) + \frac{1}{2}C\left(\dot{\phi}\cos\theta + \dot{\psi}\right)^2 \end{aligned} \tag{12.90}$$

and the potential energy

$$V = Mgh\cos\theta \tag{12.91}$$

where h is the distance of the CG from the point of support (the origin).

Therefore, the Lagrangian of this conservative system is given by

$$\tilde{L} = \frac{1}{2}A\left(\dot{\theta}^2 + \dot{\phi}^2\sin^2\theta\right) + \frac{1}{2}C\left(\dot{\phi}\cos\theta + \dot{\psi}\right)^2 - Mgh\cos\theta \tag{12.92}$$

This Lagrangian has three cyclic variables, namely t, ϕ and ψ. Hence the total energy E and two canonical momenta p_ϕ and p_ψ are constants of motion. These are

$$\begin{aligned} E &= T + V \\ &= \frac{1}{2}A\left(\dot{\theta}^2 + \dot{\phi}^2\sin^2\theta\right) + \frac{1}{2}C\left(\dot{\phi}\cos\theta + \dot{\psi}\right)^2 + Mgh\cos\theta \end{aligned} \tag{12.93}$$

$$p_\psi = \frac{\partial\tilde{L}}{\partial\dot{\psi}} = C\left(\dot{\phi}\cos\theta + \dot{\psi}\right) = \text{const.} = C\omega_3 \tag{12.94}$$

and

$$\begin{aligned} p_\phi &= \frac{\partial\tilde{L}}{\partial\dot{\phi}} = A\dot{\phi}\sin^2\theta + C\left(\dot{\phi}\cos\theta + \dot{\psi}\right)\cos\theta \\ &= \text{const.} = D \qquad \text{say} \end{aligned} \tag{12.95}$$

Using Eqs (12.94) and (12.95), $\dot{\phi}$ and $\dot{\psi}$ can be eliminated from the expression for the energy E given by Eq. (12.93), leaving it as a function of $\dot{\theta}$ and θ. Thus Eq. (12.93) reduces to a first order total differential equation in θ. Its solution $\theta(t)$, and hence the solutions $\phi(t)$ and $\psi(t)$ obtainable from the expressions for $\dot{\phi}$ and $\dot{\psi}$ in terms of $\dot{\theta}$ and θ, constitute the complete solution to the above problem.

12.22.2 The Eulerian Method

Alternatively, we can use Euler's equations of motion, namely,

$$\frac{d\boldsymbol{L}}{dt} + \boldsymbol{\omega} \times \boldsymbol{L} = \boldsymbol{\Gamma} \tag{12.48}$$

where $\boldsymbol{L}$ and $\boldsymbol{\Gamma}$ are the angular momentum of the top and the external torque applied on it, both expressed in terms of the unit vectors of the body frame. Here

$$\boldsymbol{\Gamma} = \boldsymbol{r} \times \boldsymbol{F} = h\hat{\boldsymbol{k}} \times (-Mg\hat{\boldsymbol{z}})$$

In terms of the Eulerian intermediate frames defined in the previous section (S_1,S_2,S_3) we have

$$\hat{\boldsymbol{k}} = \hat{\boldsymbol{k}}_3 \equiv (\hat{\boldsymbol{z}} \text{ in the } S_3 \text{ frame})$$

$$\hat{\boldsymbol{z}} = \hat{\boldsymbol{k}}_1 \equiv (\hat{\boldsymbol{z}} \text{ in the } S_1 \text{ frame})$$

Therefore,

$$\begin{aligned} \boldsymbol{\Gamma} &= -Mgh(\hat{\boldsymbol{k}}_3 \times \hat{\boldsymbol{k}}_1) \\ &= -Mgh(\hat{\boldsymbol{k}}_2 \times \hat{\boldsymbol{k}}_1) \\ &= -Mgh(-\hat{\boldsymbol{i}}_1) \\ &= Mgh(\cos\psi\hat{\boldsymbol{i}}_3 - \sin\psi\hat{\boldsymbol{j}}_3) \end{aligned} \tag{12.96}$$

Since $\Gamma_3 = 0$, the third of Euler's equations is

$$C\dot{\omega}_3 = \Gamma_3 = 0$$

which leads to

$$C\omega_3 = C\left(\dot{\phi}\cos\theta + \dot{\psi}\right) = \text{const.}$$

Again, since $\boldsymbol{\Gamma}$ is perpendicular to $\hat{\boldsymbol{k}}_1$, we have $\Gamma_\phi = 0$ leading correspondingly to p_ϕ = constant. And finally the energy E can also shown to be a constant of motion by differentiating Eq. (12.93) with respect to time and plugging Euler's equations of motion in it which leads to a cancellation of all the terms. These facts may then be used to solve the dynamical problem completely, as outlined at the end of the Lagrangian method. So once again one can see the superiority of the Lagrangian method over the Eulerian one, the latter being essentially a Newtonian scheme based on the concept of forces, torques, etc.

12.23 DETAILED STUDY OF THE MOTION OF A SYMMETRIC TOP

Let us now initiate the procedure outlined in the last paragraph of section 12.22.1. Eliminating $\dot{\phi}$ in Eq. (12.93) by using Eq. (12.95), we get

$$A\dot{\theta}^2 + A\left(\frac{D - C\omega_3\cos\theta}{A\sin^2\theta}\right)^2 \sin^2\theta + 2Mgh\cos\theta + C\omega_3^2 = 2E$$

Putting $2E - C\omega_3^2 = E'$,

$$A\sin^2\theta\,\dot{\theta}^2 + A\left(\frac{D - C\omega_3\cos\theta}{A}\right)^2 + 2Mgh\cos\theta\sin^2\theta = E'\sin^2\theta \tag{12.97}$$

The equation of motion expressed in Eq. (12.97) corresponds to a one dimensional motion in θ. One may regard $1/2A\dot{\theta}^2$ as the kinetic energy of the θ motion for which the effective potential energy $V_{\text{eff}}(\theta)$ is given by the rest of the terms, that is,

$$V_{\text{eff}} = \frac{1}{2}A\left(\frac{D - C\omega_3\cos\theta}{A\sin^2\theta}\right)^2 \sin^2\theta + Mgh\cos\theta = \frac{1}{2}E'$$

Obviously, Eq. (12.97) would give an elliptic integral as a general solution for θ in the form of $\theta(t)$.

However, without going into such elliptic integral solutions, one can study the behaviour of the solutions in the following way. Remember that, here, θ is the same angle as α in section 12.18.

Substituting $\cos\theta = z$ in Eq. (12.97), we get

$$A\dot{z}^2 + \frac{(D - C\omega_3 z)^2}{A} + (2Mghz - E')(1 - z^2) = 0$$

or

$$A\dot{z}^2 = E'(1 - z^2) - 2Mghz(1 - z^2) - \frac{(D - C\omega_3 z)^2}{A} \tag{12.98}$$

$$= f(z) \qquad \text{say}$$

The RHS of Eq. (12.98) is equated to $f(z)$, a function of z, which can be readily interpreted as the negative of an effective potential energy for a one-dimensional motion in z except for a positive constant factor. So the function $f(z)$ would have the following properties:

(i) The maxima of the function $f(z)$ (or the minima of $-f(z)$) would correspond to stable motion in z or equivalently in θ, that is, the top remains in a state of equilibrium with respect to θ, and θ does not change with time.

(ii) Since z is by definition $\cos\theta$, its physical range of variation must be limited to $-1 \le z \le +1$.

(iii) Since $A\dot{z}^2$ is always ≥ 0, so would the value of $f(z)$. Thus, the physically meaningful range of z corresponds to $|z| \le 1$ and $f(z) \ge 1$.

(iv) Since $f(z)$ is a cubic polynomial in z, $f(z) = 0$ has in general three roots implying that $\dot{z} = 0$ has at most three distinct solutions. It should be remembered that $\dot{z} = 0$ implies a turning point in the motion of z or equivalently of the angle θ.

We now make an assumption that $f(z)$ is positive and has a maximum so that it has two real roots (on each side of the maximum), at least one of which falls within $|z| \le 1$. Physically this means that the z-motion of the top has a point of equilibrium (stable or unstable) about which oscillations may be performed. Whether this is actually the case will depend on the coefficients of the cubic polynomial in z or on the specific values of the physical quantities like M, C, A, h and the dynamical constants E', ω_3 and D.

It is well known that a cubic polynomial has either three real roots, or one real root and a conjugate pair of complex roots. However, for a physically viable solution, the polynomial $f(z)$ given by Eq. (12.98) must have all the three roots real satisfying the further condition $|z| \le 1$.

Now it is easy to see that for $z \to +\infty$, $f(z) \to +\infty$; $z \to \infty$, $f(z) \to -\infty$; both at $z = +1$ and $z = -1$, $f(z) < 0$, provided $D \neq C\omega_3$. Therefore, in order that a root exists between $+1$ and -1, the graph of $f(z)$ must cross the abscissa twice between $+1$ and -1. The existence of two real roots implies the reality of the third. This situation is depicted in Fig. 12.18.

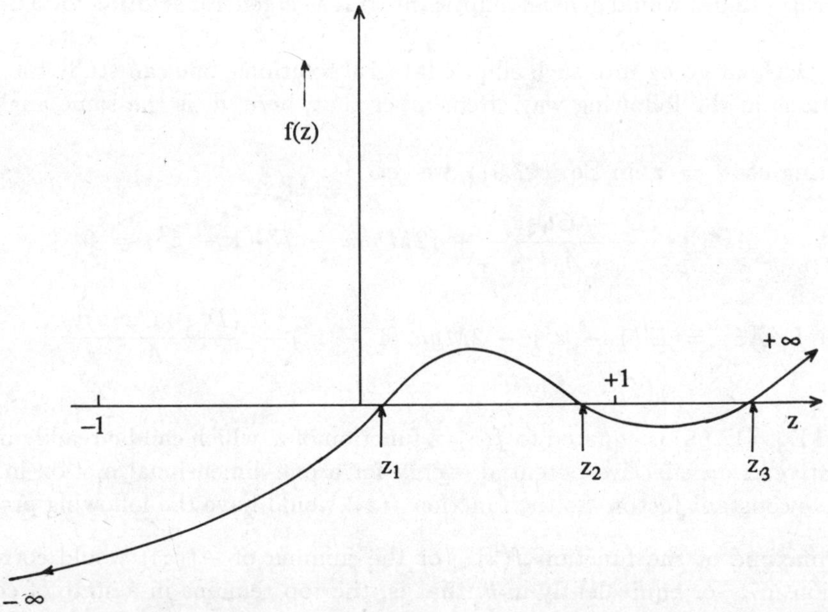

Fig. 12.18 Finding roots of the cubic equation $f(z) = 0$

Let us denote these three distinct real roots by z_1, z_2, z_3 with $z_1 < z_2 < z_3$. The change of sign of $f(z)$ between $z = +1$ and $z = +\infty$ implies either all the three or at least one root must lie above $z = +1$.

Since $f(z)$ must be ≥ 0 over the allowed range of z namely $|z| \leq 1$, it is imperative that there exist a range namely $z_1 \leq z \leq z_2$ for the allowed motion, implying that the motion must be bounded in θ between say, $\theta_1 \geq \theta \geq \theta_2$ corresponding to $z_1 \leq z \leq z_2$, so that only the third root z_3 can lie above $z = +1$, as shown in Fig. 12.18.

However, if the initial conditions are such that $D = C\omega_3$, $f(z_2) = 0$ for $z_2 = 1$ or $\theta_2 = 0$, meaning that the top becomes vertically aligned at some stage of its motion.

Again, since the top is spinning on a flat table or ground, the value of θ can never exceed $\pi/2$, hence z can never be negative (unless the top is hung like a gyroconical pendulum), so that the actual allowed range of θ is $0 \leq \theta \leq \pi/2$, or $1 \geq z \geq 0$.

Let us further introduce another function defined by

$$g(z) = \frac{f(z)}{1 - z^2} = -2V_{\text{eff}}(\theta)$$

so that

$$g(z) = A\dot{\theta}^2 = E' - 2Mghz - \frac{(D - C\omega_3 z)^2}{A(1 - z^2)} \tag{12.99}$$

As $z \to \pm 1$, $g(z) \to -\infty$ and the allowed solutions must have positive values of $g(z)$ (see Fig. 12.19) with, as before, only two possible zeroes between $z = \pm 1$.

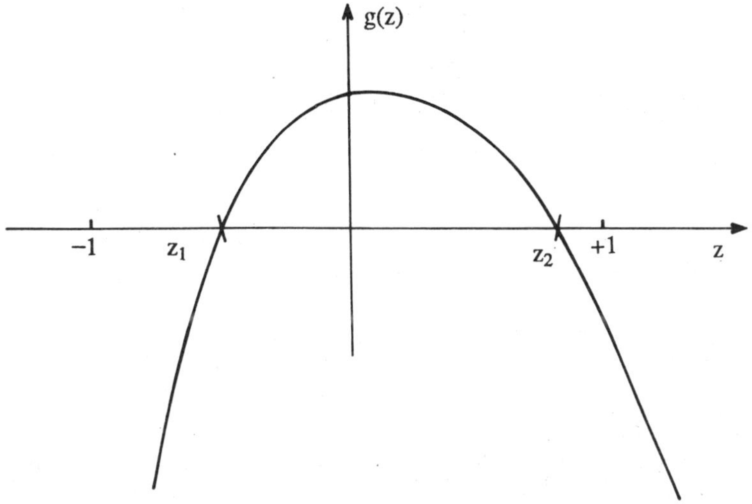

Fig. 12.19 Graphical representation of the function $g(z)$ showing the roots of the equation $g(z) = 0$

We now study in detail various cases of top motion.

Case I: $D = C\omega_3 z$ — The Rise and Fall of the Top

In this case θ_1 and θ_2 are the two distinct roots of $g(z) = 0$, so that for $\theta = \theta_1$ and $\theta = \theta_2$, $\dot{\theta} = 0$. Graphically this corresponds to three possible subcases as depicted in Fig. 12.20, depending whether the sign of $\dot{\phi}$ changes or not.

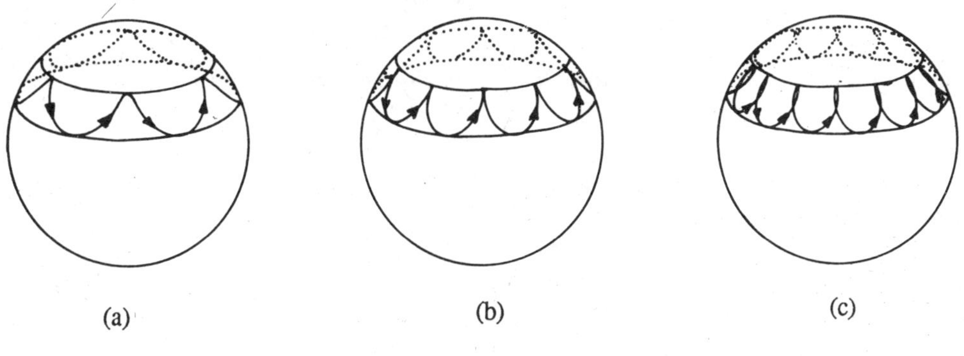

Fig. 12.20 Three cases of a precessing and nutating symmetric top. The rate of precession can be faster than, as in (a), equal to, as in (b), or slower than, as in (c), a critical value depending on initial conditions

In all the three subcases the variations of θ are drawn in such a way that the value of $\dot{\theta}$ at θ_1 and θ_2 is zero. So there will be a wobbling in the θ motion. Any periodic wobbling in θ motion is by definition called a nutation.

In the subcase (a), it can be seen from Fig. 12.20a that when $\dot{\theta}$ vanishes at the extremities of θ , $\dot{\phi}$ does not vanish and $\dot{\phi} > 0$. So the free upper end of the top describes a curve like the one shown in Fig. 12.20a.

In the subcase (b), the initial conditions are such that when $\dot{\theta}$ is at the lower extremity, that is, at the upper extremity for θ, $\dot{\phi} > 0$ at $\theta = \theta_1$; and $\dot{\phi} < 0$ for $\theta = \theta_2$. This will make the motion of the top wobbling like the one shown in Fig. 12.20b.

In the subcase (c), the initial conditions are given in such a balanced way that when $\dot{\theta}$ vanishes at $\theta = \theta_2$, the value of $\dot{\phi}$ also exactly vanishes, but at the other extremity of θ, namely at $\theta = \theta_1$, the value of $\dot{\phi}$ is positive. Under this situation, when the top reaches the uppermost point its kinetic energy is reduced to zero, because it moves neither in θ nor in ϕ. So the top must momentarily fall vertically forming a cusp at the topmost point. This is shown in Fig. 12.20c.

The required conditions on M, h, D, C, A, ω_3 and E' for satisfying any one of the above cases can in principle be derived, but the derivations are quite tedious. A book in four volumes was devoted to present various possible cases of top motion, by Arnold Sommerfeld and Klein, who pioneered the systematic study of these motions.

Case II: The Initial Conditions are such that $D = C\omega_3$ and $\dot{\theta} \neq 0$ at $\theta = 0$ (or $z = 1$)

For this case,

$$g(z) = E' - 2Mghz - \frac{C^2\omega_3^2}{A}\frac{(1 - z)}{(1 + z)} = A\dot{\theta}^2 \tag{12.100}$$

The equation $g(z) = 0$ is now quadratic in z with one root ¿ 1, because at $z = 1$,

$$g(1) = E' - 2Mgh = A\dot{\theta}^2 > 0 \tag{12.101}$$

by the chosen initial condition. Therefore, the allowed range of z is between $z = z_1$ (say) and $z = 1$ (see Fig. 12.21).

Hence, the axis of the top may periodically pass through the vertical and can come down as far as $z = z_1$, or $\theta = \theta_1$. As seen from above, the axis of the top may appear to trace a curve as shown in Fig. 12.22.

Case III: Sleeping Top — The Initial Conditions are such that $D = C\omega_3$, and $\dot{\theta} = 0$ when $\theta = 0$

If $\dot{\theta} = 0$ when $z = 1$, we get

$$g(z) = 0 = E' - 2Mgh \tag{12.102}$$

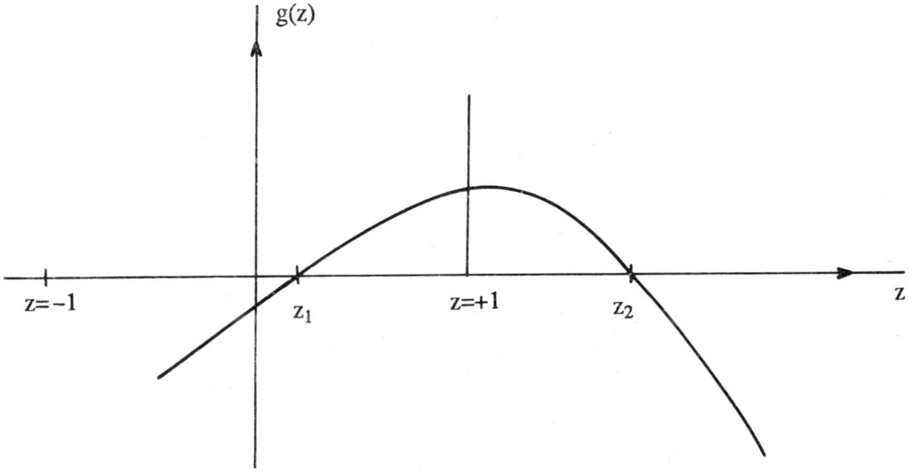

Fig. 12.21A case of the symmetric top motion in which any one root of the polynomial $g(z)$ exists in the interval $[-1,1]$

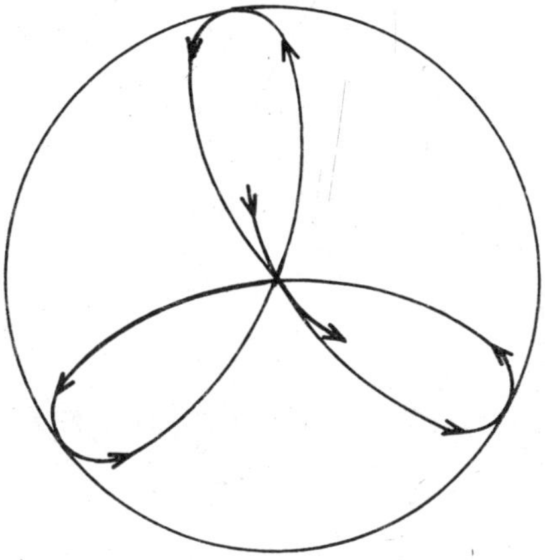

Fig. 12.22 A case of the symmetric top motion in which the axis of the top nutates and precesses through its upright posture while the motion remaining bounded by the surface of a cone

or

$$\begin{aligned} g(z) &= 2Mgh(1 - z) - \frac{C^2\omega_3^2}{A}\frac{1 - z}{1 + z} \\ &= (1 - z)\left[2Mgh - \frac{C^2\omega_3^2}{A(1 + z)}\right] \end{aligned} \tag{12.103}$$

Thus $g(z) = 0$ at $z = 1$ so that one root of $g(z) = 0$ is $z = 1$. But for $z = -1$, $g(z) = -\infty$; therefore, the other root may or may not lie in the range $-1 \le z \le +1$

(see Fig. 12.23).

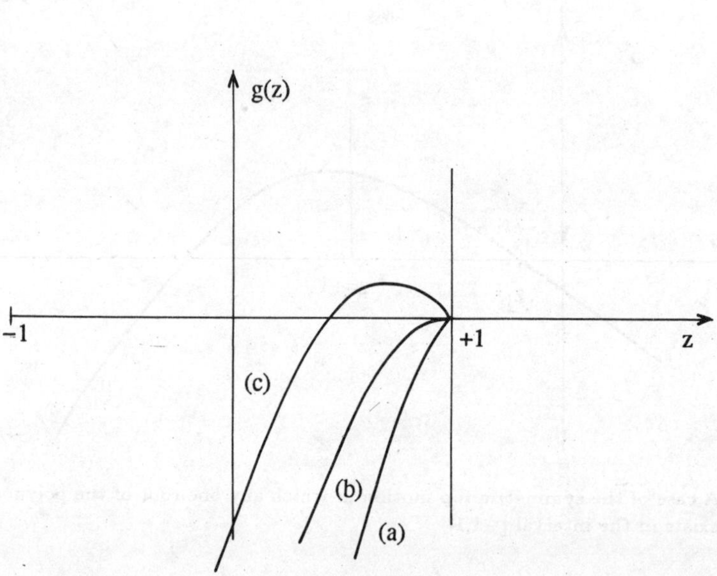

Fig. 12.23 Admissible solutions to $g(z) \geq 0$ with one solution at $z = 1$, for the cases: (a) $g'(z) \neq 0$ within $[-1, 1]$, (b) $g'(z) = 0$ at $z = 1$, and (c) $g'(z) = 0$ in the interval $(-1, 1)$

Now let us see what slope the function $g(z)$ has at $z = 1$. We have,

$$g'(z) = \frac{dg}{dz} = -\left[2Mgh - \frac{C^2\omega_3^2}{A(1+z)}\right] + (1-z)\frac{C^2\omega_3^2}{A(1+z)^2} \tag{12.104}$$

Therefore,

$$g'(z=1) = -2Mgh + \frac{C^2\omega_3^2}{2A} = \frac{C^2\omega_3^2 - 4MghA}{2A} \tag{12.105}$$

Depending on whether $g'(z) > 0$, $g'(z) = 0$, or $g'(z) < 0$, one can think of three subcases (a), (b) and (c) shown in Fig. 12.23 with the equivalent required conditions

$$\begin{aligned} C^2\omega_3^2 &> 4MghA \\ &= 4MghA \quad \text{and} \\ &< 4MghA \quad \text{respectively.} \end{aligned}$$

The upright vertical posture of the top as a possible solution is assured in all these three subcases (a), (b) and (c), with varying degrees of freedom to deviate from this upright posture. When the top can continue to spin, keeping its spin axis upright, the top in this spinning state is called a ***sleeping top***. For subcase (a),

$$C^2\omega_3^2 > 4MghA$$

and the sleeping top is stable; it simply cannot fall down due to the lack of any other possible value of θ as a solution. Sometimes a top in this state is also called a ***strong top***. The above condition can be rewritten for this case as

$$\frac{1}{2}C\omega_3^2 > 2\left(\frac{A}{C}\right)Mgh$$

This means that the amount of rotational kinetic energy is more than sufficient to raise the centre of mass of the top by a height $2h$. In fact, the stable static equilibrium posture of a top corresponds to a state of a freely hanging top, that is, $\theta = \pi$, and its CM has to be raised by a total height of $2h$ in order to make it upright or sleeping. Also in the sleeping state, the externally applied gravitational torque disappears, and therefore, the strong top continues in its sleeping state for an indefinite period. This is an example of dynamically stable equilibrium state of motion.

For subcase (b) as depicted in Fig. 12.23, the spin must have reduced from its value suitable for subcase (a) and now satisfies the condition

$$C^2\omega_3^2 = 4MghA$$

The top becomes critically unstable for maintaining its sleeping state any longer.

Due to unavoidable frictional loss of energy the spin rate continues to decrease further and case (c) is realised with the condition

$$C^2\omega_3^2 < 4MghA$$

The top now begins to slip down from its initial upright sleeping state. Such a top is called a ***weak top***, which cannot precess at a value of θ less than θ_o given by the condition

$$C^2\omega_3^2 = 4MghA\cos\theta_o$$

Since $g(z) = -2V_{\text{eff}}(\theta)$, the maximum of the function $g(z)$ must correspond to the minimum of $V_{\text{eff}}(\theta)$ and therefore, a weak top must wobble about some mean value of θ at which the maximum of the function $g(z)$ occurs.

Then with time, more and more frictional losses of the rotational kinetic energy of the top makes it wobble with a bigger and bigger amplitude in θ, until finally the top falls on to the ground and begins to roll on the ground instead of rotating about the fixed point on its apex.

Case IV: Steady Precessional Motion

It means that there is no nutation or wobbling in θ, that the motion is conical about the local vertical with a nonzero constant value of θ, and that the motion in ϕ along the surface of the conical precession is uniform. So mathematically, this case corresponds to $\dot{\theta} = \ddot{\theta} = 0$ for some value of $\theta = \theta_o \neq 0$ and the precessional frequency $\dot{\phi} = \Omega =$ constant.

In terms of $g(z) = A\dot{\theta}^2$, this means that both $g(z)$, and $g'(z)$ must vanish for some value of $z = z_o$ (see Fig. 12.24). For the condition $g'(z_o) = 0$, we get

$$Mgh - \frac{(D - C\omega_3 z_o)C\omega_3}{A(1 - z_o^2)} + \frac{z_o(D - C\omega_3 z_o)^2}{A(1 - z_o^2)^2} = 0 \qquad (12.106)$$

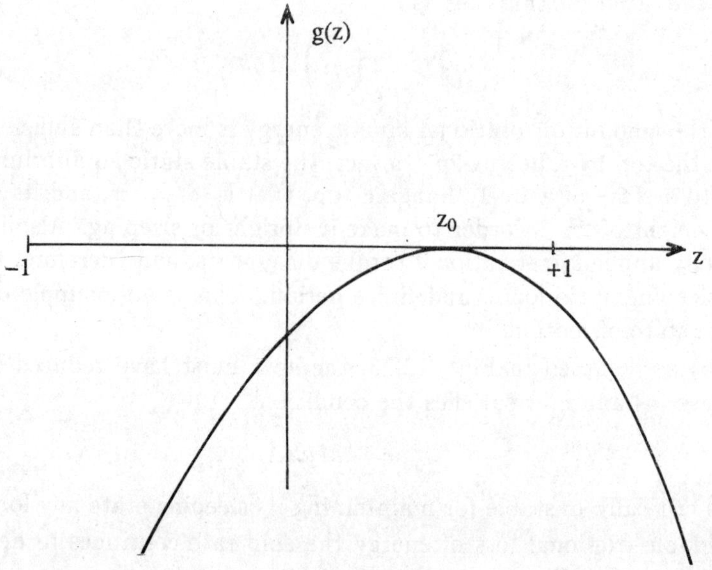

Fig. 12.24 A case for allowing steady precession with a one-point solution for $g(z) \geq 0$ at $z_o < 1$

and for the condition $g(z_o) = 0$, Eq. (12.99) gives

$$E' - 2Mghz_o - \frac{(D - C\omega_3 z_o)^2}{A(1 - z_o^2)} = 0 \tag{12.107}$$

it being the situation where $g(z) = 0$ has a single root z_o ($\neq 1$) depicted in Fig. 12.24. Using Eq. (12.95) we can further write

$$(D - C\omega_3 z_o) = A\dot{\phi}\sin^2\theta_o = A(1 - z_o^2)\dot{\phi} = A(1 - z_o^2)\Omega \tag{12.108}$$

Substituting Eq. (12.108) in Eq. (12.106),

$$Az_o\Omega^2 - C\omega_3\Omega + Mgh = 0 \tag{12.109}$$

which gives, for the roots of Ω,

$$\Omega = \frac{C\omega_3 \pm \sqrt{C^2\omega_3^2 - 4MghAz_o}}{2Az_o} \equiv \Omega_{2,1}$$

which are the same as derived in section 12.18.

Ω is real, provided

$$C^2\omega_3^2 \geq 4MghAz_o$$

and the double solution for Ω corresponds to (i) a slower steady precession represented by the smaller root $\Omega = \Omega_1$, say, and (ii) a faster steady precession for the larger root, say, $\Omega = \Omega_2$. In order to get the estimates for the slow and fast precession rates, we use the condition $C^2\omega_3^2 \gg 4MghAz_o$ in the exact expression for both Ω_1 and Ω_2 respectively, getting

$$\Omega_1 \simeq \frac{Mgh}{C\omega_3} \tag{12.110}$$

and

$$\Omega_2 \simeq \frac{C\omega_3}{A\cos\theta_o} = \Omega_f \tag{12.111}$$

This is the same Ω_f as obtained in Eq. (12.75).

The above results are quite interesting. If any fast spinning symmetric top is found to execute a steady precessional motion, the top must initially be set into motion with one of the two possible precessional rates given by Eqs (12.110) and (12.111) and then the top will continue its motion in that given steady precessional mode. The frequency of the slower mode is found to be independent of θ_o, hence for any chosen value of θ_o, the required precessional frequency is the same. The relation between the signs of spin and precession is obtained by substituting $\omega_3 = \Omega_1 \cos\theta_o + \dot{\psi}$ in Eq. (12.110) and then solving for $\Omega_1 = \Omega_1(\dot{\psi})$. One should remember that $\dot{\psi}$ not ω_3, stands for the spin angular velocity.

The frequency of the faster mode, on the other hand, is independent of the gravity g, but depends on θ_o, which is the angle between the axis of precession and the body's symmetry axis. Ω_2 is the same as that for a freely precessing symmetric object, namely Ω_f (see Eq. (12.75)). This is an extremely fast precession, almost as fast as ω_3, if not exceeding ω_3. The value of $\dot{\psi}$ or the spin angular velocity may become negligible compared to Ω_2. Practically the whole of the top's angular momentum is due to the precessional frequency, leaving hardly any room for spinning about the symmetry axis ($\Omega_2 \cos\theta_o \simeq C\omega_3/A$). Also Ω_2 changes sign as θ_o crosses $\pi/2$, and $\Omega_2 \to \infty$ as $\theta_o \to \pi/2$. In a gravity-free condition, only $\Omega_2 = \Omega_f$ exists and the required spin angular velocity is

$$\dot{\psi} = \frac{A - C}{C}\Omega_f \cos\theta_o$$

However, in the presence of gravity, the slower mode is selected in most natural phenomena involving steady precessions.

We now wish to study the stability of the above steady precessional motion.

Stability Analysis of Steady Precessional Motion: We know that

$$A\dot{\theta}^2 = g(z)$$

Differentiating with respect to time t,

$$2A\dot{\theta}\ddot{\theta} = g'(z)\dot{z} = g'(z)(-\sin\theta\,\dot{\theta}) = -\sqrt{1 - z^2}\,g(z)\dot{\theta}$$

Therefore,

$$2A\ddot{\theta} = -\sqrt{1 - z^2}\,g'(z) \tag{12.112}$$

For a steady precessional motion of the top, $g(z_o) = g'(z_o) = 0$ as $\dot{\theta} = \ddot{\theta} = 0$ at $\theta = \theta_o$.

To see how a small perturbation in θ grows around $\theta = \theta_o$, we take

$$\theta = \theta_o + \epsilon \tag{12.113}$$

where ϵ is small compared to θ_o, so that z becomes $z_o + \delta$, δ being small and given by,

$$z = z_o + \delta = \cos(\theta_o + \epsilon) = \cos\theta_o - \epsilon\sin\theta_o$$

or

$$\delta = -\epsilon\sin\theta_o = -\epsilon\sqrt{1 - z_o^2} \tag{12.114}$$

Substituting Eqs (12.113) and (12.114) in Eq. (12.112) we get

$$2A\ddot{\epsilon} = -\sqrt{1 - z_o^2}\, g''(z_o)\delta = (1 - z_o^2)g''(z_o)\epsilon \tag{12.115}$$

Here we have used

$$g'(z_o + \delta) = g'(z_o) + g''(z_o)\delta$$

which is justified because $\delta \ll z_o$.

Since $z_o^2 < 1$ and $g(z)$ is maximum at z_o (see Fig. 12.23), $g''(z_o) < 0$ and $(1 - z_o^2) > 0$. Therefore,

$$(1 - z_o^2)g''(z_o) < 0$$

Let us now define

$$p^2 \equiv -\frac{(1 - z_o^2)g''(z_o)}{2A} > 0 \tag{12.116}$$

so that Eq. (12.115) becomes

$$\ddot{\epsilon} + p^2\epsilon = 0 \tag{12.117}$$

with the solution

$$\epsilon = \epsilon_o\cos(pt + \alpha) \tag{12.118}$$

Thus we see that a small perturbation ϵ in steady precessional angle θ_o leads to small oscillations in θ around θ_o. Thus the steady precession obtained by requiring $g(z_o) = g'(z_o) = 0$ is stable. The small oscillation around θ_o with a frequency p is called nutation.

We now calculate the nutational frequency p for the slow mode of the steady precession given by Eq. (12.116). Differentiating Eq. (12.106) we get

$$\begin{aligned} g''(z) = &-\frac{2C^2\omega_3^2}{A(1 - z^2)} - \frac{2(D - C\omega_3 z)C\omega_3}{A(1 - z^2)} \\ &+ \frac{8C\omega_3 z}{A(1 - z^2)^2} - \frac{8z^2(D - C\omega_3 z)^2}{A(1 - z^2)^3} \end{aligned} \tag{12.119}$$

Now we put $z = z_o$ in Eq. (12.119) and use Eq. (12.108) to get

$$p^2 = \frac{(C\omega_3 - 2A\Omega z_o)^2 + A^2\Omega^2(1 - z_o^2)}{A^2} \tag{12.120}$$

Finally putting Eq. (12.110) in Eq. (12.120) we get

$$p = \frac{C}{A}\omega_3 \tag{12.121}$$

which is the required nutational frequency of the top motion. For $C \simeq A$, the nutational frequency is practically as high as ω_3.

Both Ω_1 and p are found to be independent of θ_o, but in order to have a steady precession possible the condition $C^2\omega_3^2 > 4MghAz_o$ has to be satisfied, that is, the top must spin at least as fast as it would require to have its rotational kinetic energy exceeding the difference of potential energy between the states for $-z_o$ and $+z_o$. For a sleeping top, this amounts to $2Mgh < 1/2\, C^2\omega_3^2$, or $C^2\omega_3^2 > 4Mgh$. Except for the factor C/A, the nutational frequency is roughly the same as the component of the total angular velocity along the symmetry axis of the top.

Case V: Rising Top

Sometimes a top becomes upright due to the couple produced by the frictional force acting on the hinge of the top. This couple has a vertical component which is responsible for causing an extra precession of the symmetry axis towards the vertical. The top, therefore, gradually becomes upright.

The effect of friction is twofold: the friction with the air that is responsible for slowing the spin down and that due to the contact of the peg with the ground, which makes the top rise towards the vertical. We study these two effects separately.

(i) The effect of the forces of friction with the air over the spinning surface of the top: Assuming that the top is spinning about its centre of mass and that the force of friction is linear in velocity (Stokes' law: $\boldsymbol{f} = -6\pi\eta r\boldsymbol{v}$), the couple provided due to the force of friction with air is

$$\begin{aligned}\boldsymbol{\Gamma}_a &= \sum_{\text{surface}} \boldsymbol{r} \times \boldsymbol{f} = -\lambda \sum_{\text{surface}} \boldsymbol{r} \times (\boldsymbol{\omega} \times \boldsymbol{r}) \\ &= -\lambda \sum_{\text{surface}} r^2\boldsymbol{\omega} + \lambda \sum_{\text{surface}} (\boldsymbol{r}\cdot\boldsymbol{\omega})\boldsymbol{r}\end{aligned} \tag{12.122}$$

where $\lambda = 6\pi\eta$, η being the viscosity of air.

By Euler's third equation, namely

$$\frac{dL_3}{dt} = (\Gamma_a)_3$$

we can write

$$C\dot{\omega}_3 = -\lambda \sum_{\text{surface}} r^2\omega_3 + \lambda \sum_{\text{surface}} (\boldsymbol{r}\cdot\boldsymbol{\omega})(\boldsymbol{r}\cdot\hat{\boldsymbol{k}})$$

or

$$C\dot{\omega}_3 = -\lambda \sum_{\text{surface}} r^2\omega_3 + \lambda \sum_{\text{surface}} \omega_3(\boldsymbol{r}\cdot\hat{\boldsymbol{k}})^2 + \lambda \sum_{\text{surface}} (\omega_\perp r_\perp) r_\parallel$$

Due to the symmetry about the $\hat{\boldsymbol{k}}$-axis all the terms in the last sum will cancel pairwise, making it zero. The above equation can then be written as

$$C\dot{\omega}_3 = -\lambda'\omega_3$$

so that

$$\omega_3 = (\omega_3)_o \exp\left(-\frac{\lambda'}{C}t\right) \tag{12.123}$$

where λ' is a constant.

Thus the spin rate about the symmetry axis decreases exponentially with time. For a slow top the air resistance due to precessional motion of the top axis, that is, due to the component of $\boldsymbol{\omega}$ perpendicular to $\hat{\boldsymbol{k}}$ is negligible.

A sleeping top loses its spin rate essentially due to air friction. At some stage it starts precessing and nutating, then falls flat on the ground and begins to roll.

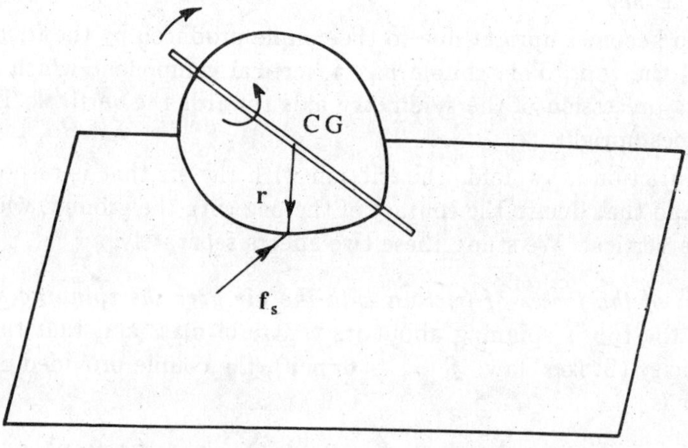

Fig. 12.25 Frictional forces on a rotating symmetric top

(ii) Friction with a horizontal rough surface: When a rapidly spinning top is placed on a rough horizontal surface with its symmetry axis in general at some angle with the vertical, the area of the contact surface with the ground is appreciable (see Fig. 12.25). The net force of sliding that acts on the top would be horizontal and directed opposite the velocity of the top at the point of contact. The net torque is

$$\boldsymbol{\Gamma}_s = \boldsymbol{r} \times \boldsymbol{f}_s = (\boldsymbol{r}_{\parallel} + \boldsymbol{r}_{\perp}) \times \boldsymbol{f}_s \tag{12.124}$$

the suffix s is to mean sliding. Here $\boldsymbol{r}_{\parallel}$ and $\boldsymbol{r}_{\perp}$ are, respectively, the components of $\boldsymbol{r}$ parallel and perpendicular to the $\hat{\boldsymbol{k}}$ direction, that is, the symmetry axis of the top. The second term in Eq. (12.124) reduces the spin rate ω_3 as the force of friction with the air does. But the first term in Eq. (12.124) gives a torque acting perpendicular to the spin axis and the top should start precessing about $-\boldsymbol{f}_s$. The direction of the torque $\boldsymbol{r}_{\parallel} \times \boldsymbol{f}_s$ is towards the vertical line and it sets in a precessional motion of the $\hat{\boldsymbol{k}}$-axis in that direction.

As a result the top rises towards the vertical. This phenomenon is called the rising top.

As the top rises, its potential energy increases at the expense of the rotational kinetic energy; so the rotational speed decreases. If the top is initially given a very high spin, a rising top will finally settle in a sleeping top, as in this state $\boldsymbol{r} \times \boldsymbol{f}_s$ vanishes and the precession stops. However, the loss of spin rate due to the other components of frictional torque continues to act. On the other hand, if the sleeping state of the top on the ground stops before the top becomes vertical, the rolling of the top takes over.

12.24 EXAMPLES OF TOPS AND THEIR ANALOGUES

12.24.1 Tippe Top (Topsy-turvy Top)

This delightful toy top has the fascinating property that, given sufficient spin about its axis of symmetry in the statically stable orientation, it will turn itself upside down and then behave like a sleeping top. No matter what the orientation of the top was with respect to the initial vertical spin, it will end up standing on its leg. People like Sir William Thomson and Niels Bohr were interested in this problem, but the first correct explanation came to light in the early 1950's by C. M. Braams and W. A. Pliskin.

Tippe top has the shape of a part of a sphere with a small stem added to it (Fig. 12.26). When this top is spun on its head (Fig. 12.26a), such that the centre of mass C lies below the centre O of the spherical part, it gradually proceeds to flip over and finally it rotates on its stem (Fig. 12.26b). If we compare the initial and the final positions of the top, we notice that

1. the CM rises indicating an increase in the P.E. at the final position,

2. the sense of rotation of the top with respect to an axis (Z axis in the figure) fixed in the body of the top changes in the process of flipping, so as to keep the direction of angular momentum unchanged.

The former point implies that there must be corresponding decrease in the K.E., that is, a decrease in the vertical component of the angular momentum. The decrease must be caused by an external vertical torque which can be nothing other than the torque due to the force of sliding friction (air friction is neglected).

Having argued qualitatively about the cause of toppling, let us now try to get a picture of how the frictional force actually does the job. To do so, we fix up rectangular Cartesian coordinate system XYZ in the body of the top with the origin at C. Let Z_o be a vertical axis.

Consider the top at any instant during the motion so that CX is perpendicular to ZCP plane as shown in Fig. 12.26c. The forces acting on the system are

1. force ($\boldsymbol{W} = -W\hat{\boldsymbol{z}}_o$) of gravity through C, which produces no torque about C,

2. force ($\boldsymbol{F}_n = W\hat{\boldsymbol{z}}_o$) of reaction vertically upward (along $\hat{\boldsymbol{z}}_o$) at the point of contact (P). This produces a torque $\boldsymbol{N}_n$ about C given by,

$$\boldsymbol{N}_n = \boldsymbol{r} \times \boldsymbol{F}_n = (a\hat{\boldsymbol{z}} - R\hat{\boldsymbol{z}}_o) \times (W\hat{\boldsymbol{z}}_o) = -Wa\sin\theta\hat{\boldsymbol{x}}$$

3. force ($\boldsymbol{F}_f$) of friction acting at P opposite to the instantaneous velocity of the top at

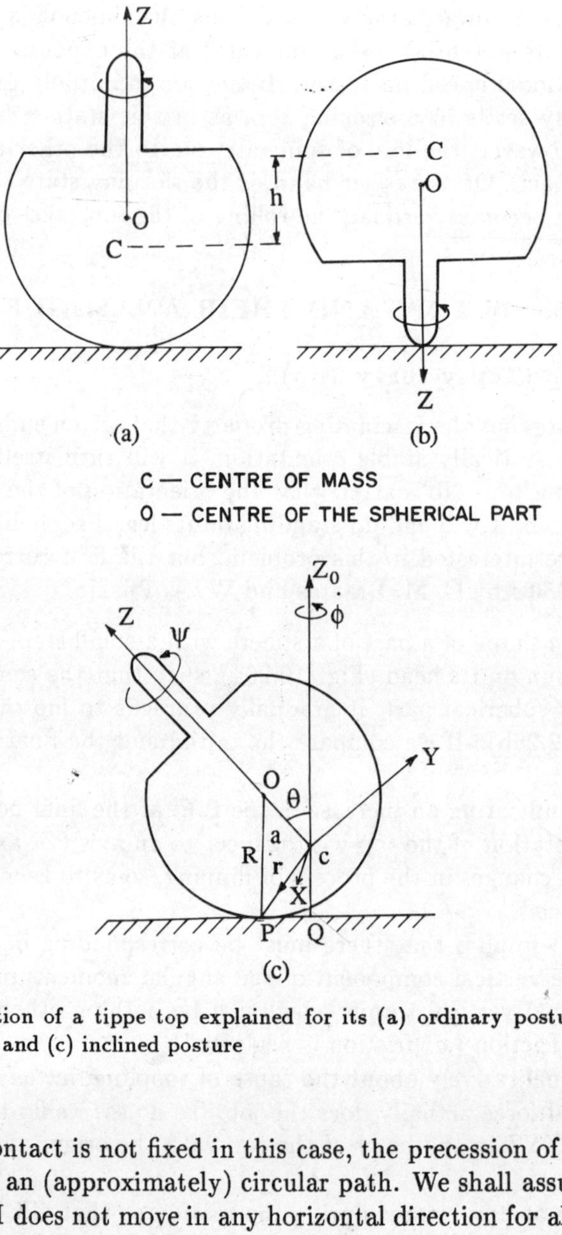

Fig. 12.26 The motion of a tippe top explained for its (a) ordinary posture, (b) inverted posture, and (c) inclined posture

P.

Since the point of contact is not fixed in this case, the precession of the top would cause the point P to move in an (approximately) circular path. We shall assume that the friction is small so that the CM does not move in any horizontal direction for all practical purposes, and thus the velocity at P with respect to the CM is tangential to the circular path, that is, normal to the PCZ plane, or along the X axis. So, the direction of the frictional force is along the negative X axis. The corresponding torque is,

$$\boldsymbol{N}_f = \boldsymbol{r} \times \boldsymbol{F}_f = (a\hat{\boldsymbol{z}} - R\hat{\boldsymbol{z}}_o) \times (-F_f\hat{\boldsymbol{x}})$$
$$= F_f\{(R\cos\theta - a)\hat{\boldsymbol{y}} - R\sin\theta\hat{\boldsymbol{z}}\}$$

Let $\boldsymbol{\omega}$ be the angular velocity of the XYZ frame. For small friction, we shall assume that the top topples slowly, so that the Eulerian angle θ changes slowly, that is,

$$\frac{d\theta}{dt} = \omega_x \ll \omega_y, \omega_z$$

so that

$$\boldsymbol{\omega} \simeq \omega \hat{\mathbf{z}}_o$$

This means

$$\omega_z = \omega \cos\theta \qquad \text{and} \qquad \omega_y = \omega \sin\theta$$

or

$$\frac{\omega_z}{\omega_y} = \cot\theta$$

The expression for the frictional torque reveals that

(a) for $\theta < \cos^{-1}(a/R)$, the y-component of the torque is positive. Hence ω_y increases. On the other hand ω_z decreases due to the negative torque. The last equation above implies that θ must increase in this case.

(b) for $\theta > \cos^{-1}(a/R)$, ω_y decreases, but in practical cases ω_z decreases at a faster rate than ω_y. So, the angle θ still goes on increasing until the stem touches the ground.

As soon as the stem touches the ground, the force of reaction on the stem gradually increases, whereas it decreases on the head. Ultimately, the top rests on the stem. A similar analysis, however, can easily show that the top should now rise on its stem (identical as a rising top) provided it has sufficient kinetic energy.

12.24.2 Wobbling of the Christmas Tree Toy

A hollow cone-shaped Christmas tree is divided into four separate vertical sections, each section hinged at the bottom to a plastic circular base and held together with a single rubber band connected internally to each section (see Fig. 12.27). The tree is set in rotation about its axis of symmetry. All these tree sections widen out about the hinge point at the bottom, due to centrifugal action of rotation, and as a result a hiding Santa Claus becomes visible from within. Eventually as the rotation slows down, the tree sections begin to close, but interestingly enough, they do not close monotonically; the effect of nutation is distinctly visible. During the last stage of closing, the final round of the nutational motion allows the tree sections to close completely first and then reopen to complete the nutational cycle, letting the Santa Claus out for a brief final view.

The analysis of this symmetric top motion can be done by the Euler-Lagrange method. The input expressions are

the kinetic energy $T = 2I\,(\dot{\theta}^2 + \sin^2\theta\dot{\phi}^2)$

the gravitational PE $V_1 = 2MghR\cos\theta$ and

the spring PE $V_2 = 4kb^2\sin^2\theta$

where I is the moment of inertia of each section about the point O. One may use the effective potential for the θ motion to study the stability of the precessional motion.

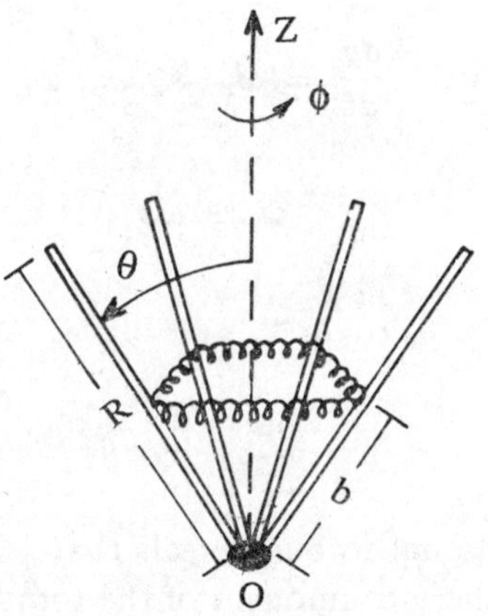

Fig. 12.27 Christmas tree toy

12.24.3 Motion of a Boomerang

Boomerangs are the famous wooden weapons used by the Australian aboriginals. These are made out of thin discs of wood, usually given a shape of the letter V with the bottom part rounded (see Fig. 12.28). Boomerangs are thrown into the air with a rotation in the plane of the disc. It is slightly convex on one side and more decidedly convex on the other. It is held at one end and thrown over the shoulder by a right handed thrower with the nearly flat side vertically up and the more convex side turned down. The missile is set into rotational motion about a normal to the mean plane and it finally returns to the thrower tracing a closed loop in the air. A professional thrower can make the boomerang complete a number of loops before it is caught at the same position as it was thrown.

The cross-section of the boomerang's arm is an aerofoil section, much like an aeroplane wing, and therefore it generates a lift force when it moves through the air. At the same time the boomerang spins rapidly in the vertical plane as it flies forward. These two facts enable one to have a quantitative explanation of why a boomerang returns to the thrower when it is thrown.

As the boomerang spins, the relative velocity of the air over each arm is larger when it advances into the air stream and smaller when it retreats during the other half of its cycle. The lift force on the arm depends on this velocity and so is larger during one half cycle. This results in a net torque acting on the spinning boomerang. The boomerang responds to this torque like a gyroscope, by precessing. This change of orientation is what makes the flight path curve.

For a detailed analysis one may read the article 'The aerodynamics of boomerangs' by Felix Hess, *Scientific American*, Nov. 1968, p. 214. The interesting result from Hess' analysis seems to be that the radius of curvature of the path of a boomerang is independent of both the linear speed and the angular spin of throw, and depends only on the boomerang's shape and mass. Even a straight boomerang should move in an arc, but of much larger radius

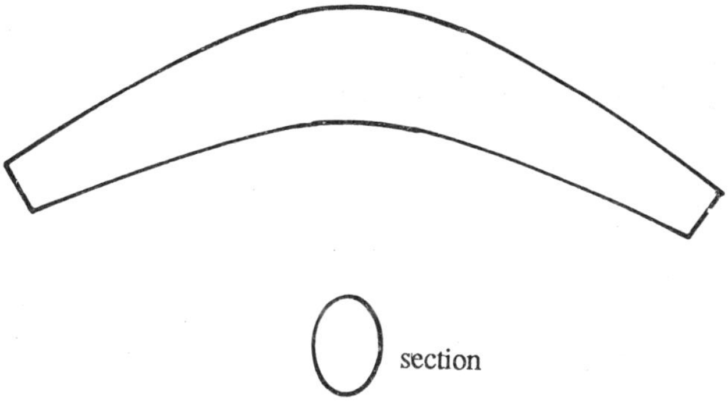

Fig. 12.28 Longitudinal and transverse sections of a boomerang

of curvature. So one can combine two straight boomerangs into one X- or V-shaped one and decrease the radius of curvature of its path by a factor of two.

12.24.4 Manoeuvre of the Motion of a Motorcycle

The wheels of a motorcycle at high speed may be regarded as two fast-rotating flywheels with their axes of rotation pointing horizontally to the left of the rider. Let us now determine out the sequence of operations that the rider has to follow in order to take a left turn. From experience, we know that it involves two steps of actions. First, the handle bars are twisted clockwise, that is, to the right (the wrong way!) in order to make the vehicle incline to the left, the vehicle automatically begins to take the left turn on the road. The rider allows it to continue till the entire curve is negotiated, just by keeping the handle bars in the normal position. Second, when the left turn is over, the vehicle is to be returned to its upright posture for which a leftward twist on the handle bars (again the wrong way!) is applied.

The initial twist to the right produces a vertically downward couple acting on the flywheel. Since the initial angular momentum was to the left (horizontal) of the rider, the tip of $\boldsymbol{L}$ moves a bit vertically downward. This makes the vehicle lean towards the left. As the vehicle leans towards the left, the gravitational couple begins to act on the system. The direction of the gravitational couple is in the backward (horizontal) direction of the instantaneous motion. Hence the tip of $\boldsymbol{L}$ must change in that direction, so that the plane of the motorcycle wheels keeps on turning to the left. This is how the left turn is accomplished by the vehicle. Once the negotiation of the curve is over, the vehicle has to be made upright for which the tip of the $\boldsymbol{L}$ vector is to be pushed upward. This can be effected simply by exerting a leftward twist on the handle bars.

12.25 FORCED PRECESSION OF THE EARTH'S AXIS OF ROTATION

As the flattened body of the earth revolves around the sun in a fixed plane called the ecliptic, with its axis of rotation inclined to the ecliptic by 66° 34′, the equatorial bulge of the earth experiences a couple that acts perpendicular to the plane formed by the earth's axis of rotation and the normal to the plane of the ecliptic. Such a torque results in a slow but steady precession of the earth's axis of rotation (about the normal to the ecliptic), keeping, of course, the angle between the axis of rotation of the earth and the plane of the ecliptic constant. The orbit of the moon also lies very close to the plane of the ecliptic. The moon also exerts a similar torque but of somewhat greater magnitude than the sun.

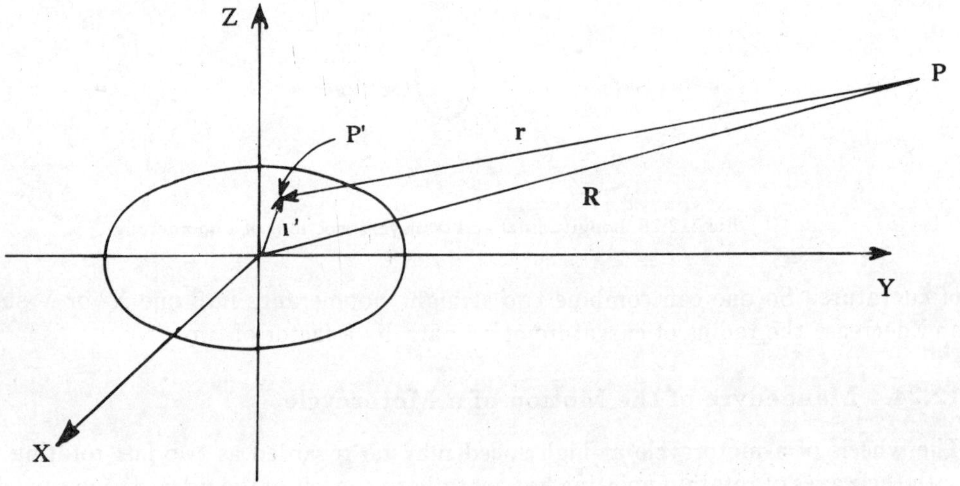

Fig. 12.29 Geometrical construction for finding the gravitational potential of the oblate-spheroid-shaped earth due to a point mass located outside

In order to study this effect, one must first know the potential energy that the oblate earth acquires due to any distinct point mass at say $P(x, y, z)$ with respect to the origin at the centre of the earth O (see Fig. 12.29). Let $\hat{\boldsymbol{z}}$ be the symmetry axis of the earth and P′ be any arbitrary point inside the earth having position vector $\boldsymbol{r}'$. From Fig. 12.29, we see that

$$\boldsymbol{r} = \boldsymbol{R} - \boldsymbol{r}' \quad \text{and } |\boldsymbol{r}| = \sqrt{R^2 + r'^2 - 2\boldsymbol{r}' \cdot \boldsymbol{R}} \tag{12.125}$$

The potential energy of the earth due to a point mass M at P is therefore

$$V(R) = -GM \int \frac{\rho(\boldsymbol{r}')}{|\boldsymbol{r}|} dx' dy' dz' \tag{12.126}$$

The integral in Eq. (12.126) is to be taken over the total volume of the earth. To proceed further, we expand $|\boldsymbol{r}|^{-1} = |\boldsymbol{R} - \boldsymbol{r}'|^{-1}$ in a Taylor's series

$$\frac{1}{|\boldsymbol{r}|} = \frac{1}{|\boldsymbol{R} - \boldsymbol{r}'|} = \frac{1}{R}\left(1 + \frac{\boldsymbol{r}' \cdot \boldsymbol{R}}{R^2} + \frac{3(\boldsymbol{r}' \cdot \boldsymbol{R})^2 - r'^2 R^2}{2R^4} + \cdots\right) \tag{12.127}$$

Substituting Eq. (12.127) in Eq. (12.126) we get

$$V(\boldsymbol{R}) = -\frac{GM}{R^2}\int\int\int \rho(x',y',z')\Big[1 + \frac{1}{R^2}(x'x + y'y + z'z) + \frac{3}{2R^4}(x'^2x^2 + y'^2y^2 + z'^2z^2 + 2x'xy'y + 2z'zx'x + 2y'yz'z) - \frac{r'^2}{2R^2} + \cdots\Big]\,dx'dy'dz' \tag{12.128}$$

Assuming that the earth's density distribution is symmetric about the origin, all terms containing a single x', y', z' are integrated to zero, as the integrand becomes an odd function of its arguments. Thus we are left with

$$\begin{aligned} V(\boldsymbol{R}) &= -\frac{GM}{R}\int\int\int \rho(x',y',z')\Big[1 + \frac{1}{2R^4}\{(3x'^2 - r'^2)x^2 \\ &\quad + (3y'^2 - r'^2)y^2 + (3z'^2 - r'^2)z^2\} + \cdots\Big]\,dx'dy'dz' \\ &= -\frac{GMm}{R} - \frac{GM}{2R^5}(I_3 - I_1)(R^2 - 3z^2) + \cdots \end{aligned} \tag{12.129}$$

Here we have taken $I_1 = I_2$ and m as the mass of the earth.

Now, with respect to an observer on the earth, the sun is moving in a nearly circular orbit fast enough compared to the precessional rate of the earth's rotation axis that we are interested in. Therefore, the sun may be assumed to be moving in a nearly circular orbit with a ring distribution of mass around the earth. The sun's angular frequency of revolution around the earth is

$$n = \sqrt{\frac{GM}{R^3}} \tag{12.130}$$

From Fig. 12.30, we see that the instantaneous position of the sun is given by

$$\begin{aligned} x &= R\cos(nt + \phi) \\ y &= -R\cos\theta\sin(nt + \phi) \\ z &= R\sin\theta\sin(nt + \phi) \end{aligned} \tag{12.131}$$

Substituting Eq. (12.131) into Eq. (12.129) we get

$$V(\boldsymbol{R}) = -\frac{GMm}{R} - \frac{GM}{2R^3}(I_3 - I_1)[1 - 3\sin^2(\phi + nt)\sin^2\theta] \tag{12.132}$$

If we now take a time average of $V(\boldsymbol{R})$ over a sufficiently long period of time compared to $2\pi/n$, the factor $\sin^2(\phi + nt)$ averages to $1/2$, so that

$$V(\boldsymbol{R}) = -\frac{GMm}{R} - \frac{GM}{2R^3}(I_3 - I_1)\left[1 - \frac{3}{2}\sin^2\theta\right] \tag{12.133}$$

The torque on the earth resulting from $V(\boldsymbol{R})$ in Eq. (12.133) is

$$\Gamma_x = \boldsymbol{R} \times (-\nabla V(\boldsymbol{R}))\big|_x = \frac{3}{2}\frac{GM}{R^3}(C - A)\sin\theta\cos\theta \tag{12.134}$$

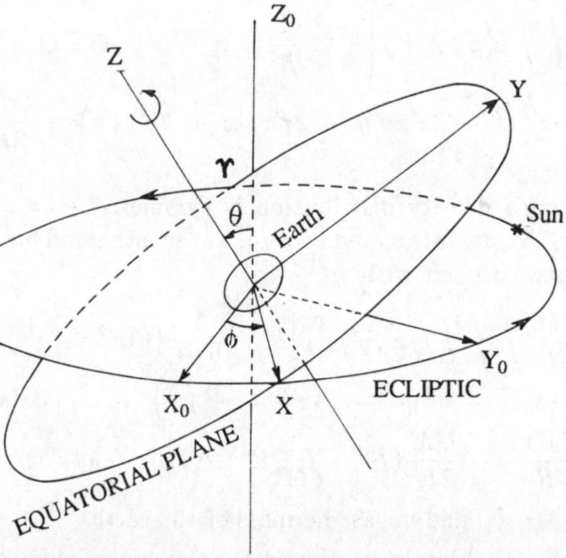

Fig. 12.30 Geometrical configuration of the apparent orbit of the sun in relation to earth's figure and its axis of rotation

having neglected the first term which does not produce any precession. Now the Lagrangian for the earth's motion is

$$L = \frac{1}{2}\left[I_1(\dot{\theta}^2 + \sin^2\theta\dot{\phi}^2) + I_3(\dot{\phi}\cos\theta + \dot{\psi})^2\right] + \frac{GM}{2R^3}(I_3 - I_1)\left(1 - \frac{3}{2}\sin^2\theta\right) + \frac{GMm}{R} \quad (12.135)$$

Since ϕ and θ are cyclic,

$$p_\phi = \frac{\partial L}{\partial \dot{\phi}} = (I_1 \sin^2\theta + I_3\cos^2\theta)\dot{\phi} + I_3\cos\theta\dot{\psi} = \text{const.}$$

and

$$p_\psi = \frac{\partial L}{\partial \dot{\psi}} = I_3(\dot{\phi}\cos\theta + \dot{\psi}) = \text{const} \quad (12.136)$$

Since $\dot{\phi} \ll \dot{\psi} \equiv \omega =$ the angular velocity of earth due to its diurnal rotation, we have

$$p_\phi = I_3\omega\cos\theta \qquad \text{and} \qquad p_\psi = I_3\omega \quad (12.137)$$

implying that

$$\theta = \text{const.}$$

Using Eq. (12.135) and neglecting $\dot{\phi}$ in comparison with ω, the equation of motion in θ

reads as

$$I_1\ddot{\theta} + I_3\omega\dot{\phi}\sin\theta + \frac{3GM}{2R^3}(I_3 - I_1)\sin\theta\cos\theta = 0 \tag{12.138}$$

If the precession is uniform with θ = constant, then $\ddot{\theta} = 0$ so that Eq. (12.138) becomes

$$\dot{\phi} = -\frac{3GM}{2R^3}\frac{I_3 - I_1}{I_3}\frac{\cos\theta}{\omega}$$

$$= -\frac{3}{2}\Omega^2_{\text{sun}}\left(\frac{I_3 - I_1}{I_3}\right)\frac{\cos\theta}{\omega_{\text{earth}}}$$

where, as seen from Fig. 12.30, θ is the obliquity of the ecliptic, and Ω_{sun} = the angular velocity of the apparent revolution of the sun around the earth.

For the total precessional angular velocity of the earth's axis of rotation, we get (since the moon is also almost on the ecliptic)

$$\dot{\phi} = \dot{\phi}_{\text{sun}} + \dot{\phi}_{\text{moon}} = -\frac{3}{2}(\Omega^2_{\text{sun}} + \Omega^2_{\text{moon}})\left(\frac{I_3 - I_1}{I_3}\right)\frac{\cos\theta}{\omega_{\text{earth}}} \tag{12.139}$$

This gives a steady precessional rate of 50.29 arc second per year and is retrograde in nature. Thus at this rate one complete revolution of the equinox along the ecliptic takes about 25,800 years. The earth's axis of rotation does a conical precession in space with respect to the stars and completes one revolution in the same number of years, while the plane of the ecliptic remains almost fixed except for small perturbations due to Jupiter.

Since the moon does not lie exactly on the ecliptic, it sets in a nutational motion in θ of amplitude 9.3 arc seconds over a period of about 18.6 years. This periodicity matches with the period of revolution of the node of the moon's orbit around the earth (see Fig. 12.31).

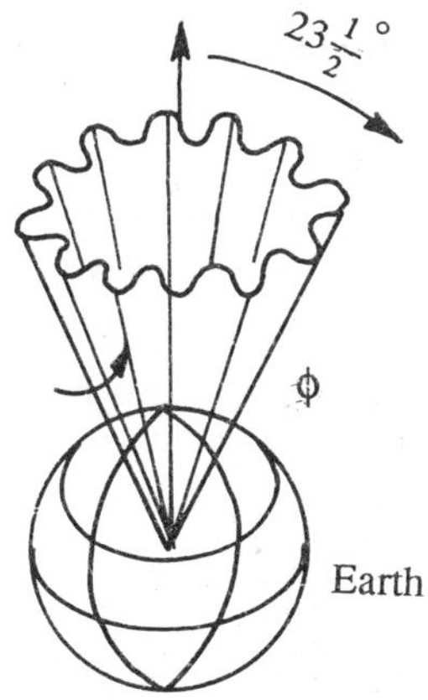

Fig. 12.31 Forced precession and nutation of the earth's axis of rotation

12.26 FOUCAULT'S GYROSCOPE

A gyroscope is a heavy symmetrical top spinning very fast about its axis of symmetry, the top being mounted on a set of mutually rotating frames so as to allow the axis of rotation of the top to have any arbitrary orientation in space. Circular frames are hierarchically pivoted in such a way that the pivots on the fixed frame enable the whole system internal to it (top1, top2, top3) to be able to freely rotate about the vertical line. Then the inner frame which is pivoted on top1 (see Fig. 12.32) allows top2 and top3 to rotate freely about a horizontal axis, called the nodal line. Finally, top3 pivoted to top2 allows the former to rotate about the nodal line. Top3 is a symmetric flywheel or a symmetric top which can spin about a direction perpendicular to the nodal line. Hence the flywheel can execute all the angular motions corresponding to the three Eulerian angles ϕ, θ and ψ. A gyroscope in its steady operation, that is, its flywheel spinning very fast and at a constant rate $\dot{\phi}$, has got the property that the spin axis always points towards a fixed direction in space even if the entire set up of the gyroscope is allowed to move slowly, in any manner one likes. This property is a consequence of the fact that the spin axis of the flywheel coincides with a principal axis of the moment of inertia tensor of the flywheel about its centre of mass.

The famous French experimentalist Léon Foucault used this property of the gyroscope in order to demonstrate the rotation of the earth. The precessing simple pendulum under the action of the Coriolis force due to earth's rotation was the first experiment of its kind to demonstrate the rotation of the earth in a laboratory in 1851. This classic experiment was reasonably successful, and was performed at the Pantheon in Paris, and also in the cathedrals of Amiens and Rheims. Very soon Foucault devised a second method (in 1852) based on the principle of a gyrostat which was not an immediate success though. It had, nevertheless, the potential of demonstrating the rotation of the earth experimentally in just a few minutes as opposed to his day long ordinary pendulum experiment. Not only would one save time this way but also reduce the size of the instrument and eliminate the problem of maintenance of free motion for long enough periods.

Foucault's gyroscope can have two versions, of which only one is described here. It is simply a fast spinning symmetric top, the axis of which is constrained to move in a vertical plane passing through the local meridian (that is, through the zenith and the poles). At any instant, its spin axis (the z-axis) makes an angle θ with the earth's axis of rotation. We define the x-axis to be in the vertical plane, perpendicular to the z-axis and y-axis perpendicular to both the x and z axes so that the y-axis can point in the east direction (see Fig. 12.33). On the surface of the earth this triad x-y-z is a rotating frame rotating with an angular velocity $\boldsymbol{\Omega}'$ which is close to that of the earth. This rotating frame is not the body frame of the flywheel. However, Euler's equations of motion are still applicable to this (first) frame of reference where $\boldsymbol{\omega}$ has now to be replaced by $\boldsymbol{\Omega}'$ in the Eq. (12.48) as $\boldsymbol{\Omega}'$ is the rotational angular velocity in space (see last paragraph of section 12.10). Such a replacement of $\boldsymbol{\omega}$ by $\boldsymbol{\Omega}'$ can work simply because, as the flywheel rotates about its own axis, having a geometrical symmetry about it, the principal moments of inertia A and B remain identical for any frame arbitrarily rotating about the symmetry axis. In this modified form,

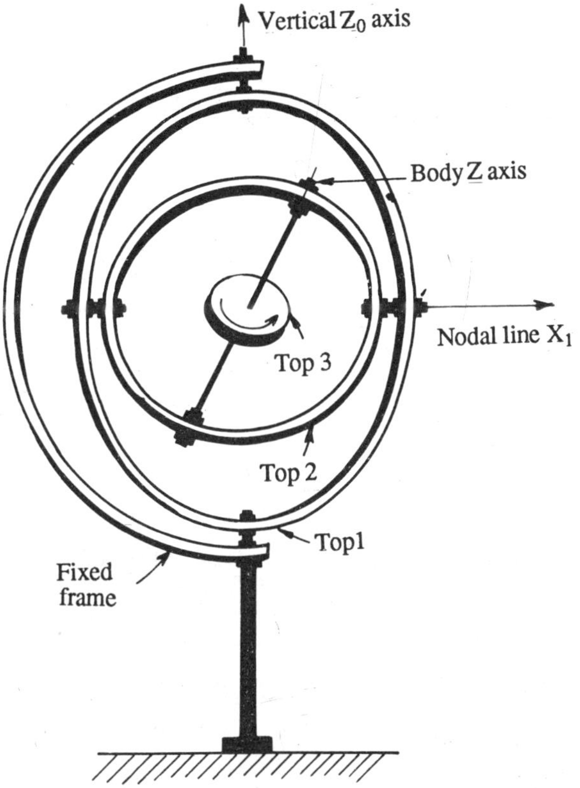

Fig. 12.32 A schematic drawing of gyroscope showing its three independent Eulerian axes of rotation

Euler's equations look like

$$\frac{d\boldsymbol{L}}{dt} + \boldsymbol{\Omega}' \times \boldsymbol{L} = \boldsymbol{\Gamma} \tag{12.140}$$

where all the quantities $d\boldsymbol{L}/dt$, $\boldsymbol{\Omega}'$, $\boldsymbol{L}$ and $\boldsymbol{\Gamma}$ are expressed in terms of the instantaneous unit vectors of the rotating frame which is rotating with the angular velocity $\boldsymbol{\Omega}'$. Obviously,

$$\boldsymbol{\Omega}' = \left(-\,\Omega \sin\theta,\ \frac{d\theta}{dt},\ \Omega\cos\theta\right) \tag{12.141}$$

and the angular velocity of the top $\boldsymbol{\omega}$ is

$$\boldsymbol{\omega} = \left(-\,\Omega \sin\theta,\ \frac{d\theta}{dt},\ \omega_o\right)$$

where ω_o is the spin angular velocity of the top about its z-axis and Ω is the earth's angular speed of rotation. Hence the angular momentum vector is

$$\boldsymbol{L} = \left(-\,A\Omega \sin\theta,\ A\frac{d\theta}{dt},\ C\omega_o\right)$$

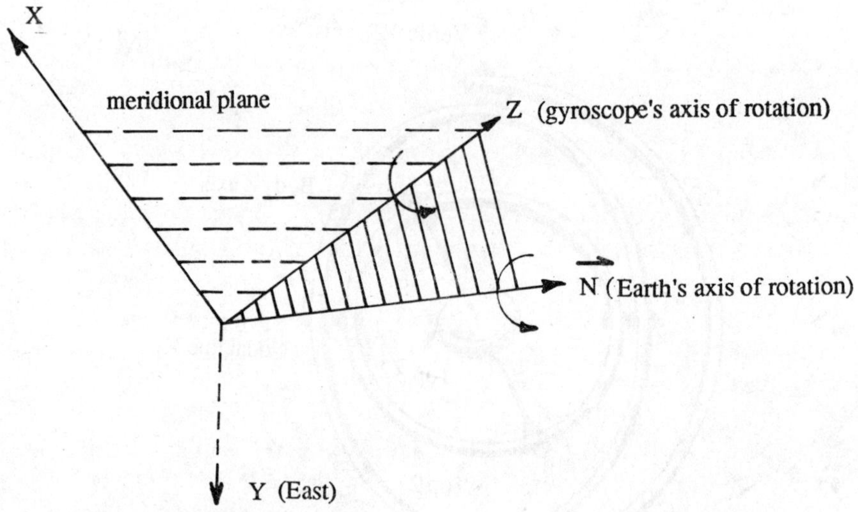

Fig. 12.33 Orientation of the axis of rotation of Foucault's gyroscope

and the modified Euler's equations become

$$\Gamma_x = -A\Omega\cos\theta\dot{\theta} + C\omega_o\dot{\theta} - A\Omega\cos\theta\dot{\theta}$$

$$\Gamma_y = A\ddot{\theta} - A\Omega^2\sin\theta\cos\theta + C\Omega\omega_o\sin\theta$$

$$\Gamma_z = C\frac{d\omega_o}{dt}$$

Now this gyroscope is constrained to move in the vertical plane. This constraint on the spin axis z produces a couple only in the x direction, hence $\Gamma_y = \Gamma_z = 0$, giving

$$\omega_o = \text{const.}$$

and

$$\ddot{\theta} + \frac{C}{A}\Omega\omega_o\sin\theta - \Omega^2\sin\theta\cos\theta = 0$$

The Ω^2 term is negligibly small compared to the $\omega_o\Omega$ term. Hence

$$\ddot{\theta} + \frac{C}{A}\Omega\omega_o\sin\theta = 0$$

For small θ this equation gives the motion of an SHM so that the gyroscope will perform oscillations about a line parallel to the earth's axis of rotation with a period

$$T = 2\pi\sqrt{\frac{A}{C\Omega\omega_o}}$$

If $\theta = 0$, that is, if the axis of the gyroscope coincides with that of the earth, there will be no oscillations and the axis of the gyroscope will point steadily towards the earth's axis of rotation, thus enabling one to determine the latitude of the place. However, if θ is small, the period of oscillation T can be made quite small by having larger ω_o. With ω_o roughly about 1000 rpm one gets an oscillation period of about one minute. These angular speeds were not difficult to meet even in the days of Foucault.

12.27 STABILITY CONDITIONS FOR MOTIONS OF RIGID BODIES IN ROTATING FRAMES

We have seen in chapter 11 that small oscillations occur about any point of stable equilibrium of a dynamical system and that this stable equilibrium occurs at a point of absolute minimum of the potential energy function. Now suppose we move to a frame of reference S′ that is rotating about its origin in the same manner as an inertial frame of reference S with an angular velocity $\boldsymbol{\Omega}$. What will be the condition for stable equilibrium of any rigid body motion from the point of view of the rotating frame of reference?

Let $\boldsymbol{r}$ be the position vector of any point in the rigid body measured with reference to S′. The velocity of the point measured with respect to S is then (see chapter 3)

$$\boldsymbol{v} = \boldsymbol{u} + \boldsymbol{\Omega} \times \boldsymbol{r}$$

where $\boldsymbol{u} = d\boldsymbol{r}/dt$ is the velocity with respect to S′. So the kinetic energy in S is given by

$$\begin{aligned} T &= \frac{1}{2}\sum mv^2 = \frac{1}{2}\sum mu^2 + \sum m\boldsymbol{\Omega}\cdot(\boldsymbol{r} \times \boldsymbol{u}) + \frac{1}{2}\sum m|\boldsymbol{\Omega} \times \boldsymbol{r}|^2 \\ &= T' + \boldsymbol{\Omega}\cdot\boldsymbol{L}' + \frac{1}{2}I_{ij}\Omega_i\Omega_j \end{aligned} \tag{12.142}$$

and the total angular momentum in S is

$$\boldsymbol{L} \equiv \frac{\partial T}{\partial \boldsymbol{\Omega}} = \sum m(\boldsymbol{r} \times \boldsymbol{v}) = \boldsymbol{L}' + I_{ij}\Omega_j\hat{\boldsymbol{i}}$$

where T' is the kinetic energy relative to the rotating axes, $\boldsymbol{L}'$ is the vector moment of momentum relative to the rotating axes. Thus we get

$$T = T' + \boldsymbol{\Omega}\cdot\boldsymbol{L} - \frac{1}{2}I_{ij}\Omega_i\Omega_j \tag{12.144}$$

Now we plan to set up the Euler-Lagrange equations of motion for this system with reference to quantities measured in the rotating frame of reference. We also assume $\boldsymbol{\Omega}$ to be constant so that $\boldsymbol{\Omega} = \dot{\psi}\hat{\boldsymbol{n}}$. Then apart from the coordinate ψ, we shall require $n - 1$ generalised coordinated , say $q_1, \ldots, q_{n-1}$, if the the number of DOF of the system is n, so that for these $n - 1$ coordinates we have

$$\boldsymbol{r} = \boldsymbol{r}(q_1, \ldots, q_{n-1}) \qquad \boldsymbol{u} = \frac{d\boldsymbol{r}}{dt} = \frac{\partial \boldsymbol{r}}{\partial q_s}\dot{q}_s$$

$$\frac{\partial \boldsymbol{u}}{\partial \dot{q}_s} = \frac{\partial \boldsymbol{r}}{\partial q_s} \qquad \text{and} \qquad \frac{d}{dt}\left(\frac{\partial \boldsymbol{r}}{\partial q_s}\right) = \frac{\partial \boldsymbol{u}}{\partial q_s}$$

Therefore,

$$\frac{\partial \boldsymbol{L}'}{\partial \dot{q}_s} = \sum m \left(\boldsymbol{r} \times \frac{\partial \boldsymbol{u}}{\partial \dot{q}_s} \right) = \sum m \left(\boldsymbol{r} \times \frac{\partial \boldsymbol{r}}{\partial q_s} \right)$$

$$\frac{d}{dt}\left(\frac{\partial \boldsymbol{L}'}{\partial \dot{q}_s} \right) = \sum m\dot{\boldsymbol{r}} \times \frac{\partial \boldsymbol{r}}{\partial q_s} + \sum m\boldsymbol{r} \times \frac{d}{dt}\left(\frac{\partial \boldsymbol{r}}{\partial q_s} \right) = \sum m\boldsymbol{u} \times \frac{\partial \boldsymbol{r}}{\partial q_s} + \sum m\boldsymbol{r} \times \frac{\partial \boldsymbol{u}}{\partial q_s}$$

$$\frac{\partial \boldsymbol{L}'}{\partial q_s} = \sum m\boldsymbol{r} \times \frac{\partial \boldsymbol{r}}{\partial q_s} + \sum m \frac{\partial \boldsymbol{r}}{\partial q_s} \times \boldsymbol{u}$$

thus giving

$$\frac{d}{dt}\left(\frac{\partial \boldsymbol{L}'}{\partial \dot{q}_s} \right) - \frac{\partial \boldsymbol{L}'}{\partial q_s} = 2\sum m\boldsymbol{u} \times \frac{\partial \boldsymbol{r}}{\partial q_s} = 2\sum m \left(\frac{\partial \boldsymbol{r}}{\partial q_p} \times \frac{\partial \boldsymbol{r}}{\partial q_s} \right) \dot{q}_p \equiv \boldsymbol{B}_{ps}\dot{q}_p$$

Clearly from the above definition of $\boldsymbol{B}_{ps}$, it is an antisymmetric (axial) vector. For constant $\boldsymbol{\Omega}$, the Lagrangian equations of motion

$$\frac{d}{dt}\left(\frac{\partial T}{\partial \dot{q}_s} \right) - \frac{\partial T}{\partial q_s} = -\frac{\partial V}{\partial q_s} + Q'_s$$

in terms of the quantities defined in the rotating frame for $s = 1, \ldots, n - 1$ generalised coordinates take the form

$$\frac{d}{dt}\left(\frac{\partial T'}{\partial \dot{q}_s} \right) - \frac{\partial T'}{\partial q_s} + \boldsymbol{\Omega} \cdot \left[\frac{d}{dt}\left(\frac{\partial \boldsymbol{L}'}{\partial \dot{q}_s} \right) - \frac{\partial \boldsymbol{L}'}{\partial q_s} \right] - \frac{1}{2}\frac{\partial I_{ij}}{\partial q_s}\Omega_i\Omega_j = -\frac{\partial V}{\partial q_s} + Q'_s$$

or

$$\frac{d}{dt}\left(\frac{\partial T'}{\partial \dot{q}_s} \right) - \frac{\partial T'}{\partial q_s} + (\boldsymbol{\Omega} \cdot \boldsymbol{B}_{ps})\dot{q}_p = -\frac{\partial}{\partial q_s}\left(V - \frac{1}{2}I_{ij}\Omega_i\Omega_j \right) + Q'_s \qquad (12.145)$$

where $V = V(q_s)$ is the ordinary potential energy due to externally applied conservative forces and Q'_s are nonpotential force components, if any.

So these equations of motion differ from the case with $\boldsymbol{\Omega} = 0$ in two respects: first by the presence of the gyroscopic terms $(\boldsymbol{\Omega} \cdot \boldsymbol{B}_{ps})\dot{q}_s$ and the second by $V(q_s) - \frac{1}{2}I_{ij}\Omega_i\Omega_j$ replacing the potential energy function $V(q_s)$.

The equations of motion for the nth generalised coordinate, that is ψ, is given by

$$\frac{d}{dt}\left(\frac{\partial T}{\partial \dot{\psi}} \right) - \frac{\partial T}{\partial \psi} = G \qquad \text{giving} \qquad \frac{dL}{dt} = \boldsymbol{G} \qquad (12.146)$$

where $\boldsymbol{G}$ is the couple needed to maintain the constant angular velocity $\boldsymbol{\Omega}$.

When the system is in equilibrium, that is, $\dot{q}_1 = \ldots = 0$,

$$\frac{\partial}{\partial q_s}\left(V - \frac{1}{2}I_{ij}\Omega_i\Omega_j \right) = Q'_s$$

and if there are no nonpotential forces, the condition for stable equilibrium in a uniformly rotating frame of reference will be

$$\frac{\partial}{\partial q_s}\left(V - \frac{1}{2}I_{ij}\Omega_i\Omega_j\right) = 0 \qquad (12.147)$$

or

$$\frac{\partial}{\partial q_s}\left(V - \frac{1}{2}I_o\Omega^2\right) = 0$$

where I_o is the moment of inertia about the direction of $\mathbf{\Omega}$. The usual potential $V(q_s)$ is now replaced by the function

$$V(q_s) - \frac{1}{2}I_o\Omega^2$$

the extremum (actually minimum) of which should now correspond to (stable) equilibrium.

Example: A spherical bowl of radius a is made to rotate with a constant angular speed Ω and a small spherical shot is set free to roll on the inside surface of the bowl.

The possible configuration for equilibrium is to be decided by the condition

$$\frac{\partial}{\partial\theta}\left(V - \frac{1}{2}\Omega^2 I\right) = -\frac{\partial}{\partial\theta}\left[mga\cos\theta + \frac{1}{2}m\Omega^2a^2\sin^2\theta\right] = 0$$

giving either $\theta = 0$ (unstable equilibrium) or $\cos\theta = g/\Omega^2 a$ (stable equilibrium), θ being the angle made at the centre of the bowl between the particle and the assumed vertical axis of rotation.

12.28 DYNAMICS OF SOME GAMES AND SPORTS

In this section we plan to give rough estimates of the relevant physical quantities involved in walking, running, jumping, cycling, throwing, swimming, etc.

First of all we must know the basic physical statistics of an average athlete.

12.28.1 Physical Statistics of an Average Athlete

(i) Mass of the body (M). This is an essential quantity, which is taken to be 50 kg, unless otherwise stated. The centre of mass of the body lies quite close to one's navel, the average position being about 5 cm below the navel and about as much inside the body. The average density of the body is minimally less than that of water, except for the head.

(ii) Surface area of the body (A). The knowledge of this quantity for different parts of the body is essential for different types of sports activities, but it is not at all easy to estimate with great accuracy. Perhaps one can take a wide roll of nonsticking bandage cloth, wrap it around the whole body without overlap and estimate the total surface area to an accuracy on the order of 1%. In order to reach a 5% accuracy, one can divide the whole body broadly into 4 sections — head and neck, trunk, hands and legs, assuming their shapes roughly as spheres or, cylinders or, truncated cones as the case may be. At a still more crude level, the area of the whole body can be taken as approximately three times the area of the trunk. A widely used formula seems to be $A = (M/30\text{kg})^{0.7}$ metre^2. The proportional distributions for head and neck : trunk : hands : legs ratios for an average male athlete are 0.09 : 0.33 : 0.20 : 0.38 for the surface area, and 0.07 : 0.57 : 0.09 : 0.27 for the mass; whereas for female athletes these ratios are 0.09 : 0.31 : 0.17 : 0.43 and 0.07 : 0.52 : 0.07 : 0.34 respectively. For the total surface area, the formula is the same for women except for the constant for normalisation which replaces 30 kg by 33 kg.

(iii) Principal moments of inertia of the body about its centre of mass (I_{xx}, I_{yy}, I_{zz}) for different symmetric configurations. The body frame axes x, y, z are defined as follows:
x-axis: back to front (horizontal forward) about which cartwheeling is performed
y-axis: right to left (horizontal sidewise) about which somersault is performed
z-axis: bottom to top (vertically upward) about which twist is performed.

Table 12.3 shows the principal moments of inertia of an average athlete of 60 kg body weight.

Table 12.3 Moments of Inertia of Human Body under Different Configurations

Configuration	Layout, arms at sides	Layout, arms overhead	Layout, arms out	Layout, twists thrown	Relaxed
I_{xx} (kg m^2)	13.5	17.9	16.6	15.0	10.8
I_{yy} (kg m^2)	12.0	16.0	13.3	13.5	10.3
I_{zz} (kg m^2)	01.5	01.5	03.5	01.3	04.4

(iv) Body's rate of expenditure of energy (K in Cal/hr/kg of bodyweight). There are basically two types of food as well as replenishable material in our body that are capable of delivering energy to or out from the body. One is fat (oily substances) with its calorie value 7700 Cal/kg (1 Cal = 1000 cal = 4200 J) and the other is carbohydrate with its calorie value 3500 Cal/kg. It means that if you eat 100 gm of any oil/fat or 220 gm of sugar/carbohydrate you gain about 770 Cal, and that if you work physically worth 770 Cal you will lose 220 gm of body's sugar content or 100 gm of body's stored fat in case sugar is not readily available. Here is a table for the energy expenditure rate (K) for various activities in Cal/hr/kg of bodyweight (see Table 12.4).

In total, a typically hard-working person accounts for a daily expenditure rate of energy of about 30 Cal/kg of bodyweight on various items listed in the above table. The other major losses are due to required supply of heat of evaporation of sweat and the heat loss of the body to the surroundings in order to maintain the temperature difference between the body and the immediate surrounding.

12.28.2 Strolling or Leisurely Walking

When one walks in a leisurely fashion, one does not exert much effort consciously. The

Table 12.4 Power Consumption in various Human Activities

Slow Activities	K (Cal/hr/kg)	Fast Activities	K (Cal/hr/kg)
Sleeping	1.00	Walking(4.5km/hr)	3.3
Sitting still	1.30	Carpentry	3.8
Standing relaxed	1.55	Active exercise	4.2
Sewing by hand	1.65	Fastwalking(6.5km/hr)	4.4
Dressing/undressing	1.75	Going down steps	5.0
Singing	1.85	Loading heavy objects	5.5
Typewriting	2.00	Heavy exercise	6.0
Washing dishes	2.10	Tennis play/swimming	7.2
Sweeping	2.20	Very heavy exercise	9.0
Light exercise	2.75	Going up steps	15.

process of such walking can be approximated to the natural pendulum-like oscillations of the legs about the respective hip joints. If the centre of mass of the legs of length L lies a distance d below the hip joint and the two legs make a maximum angle 2θ at the apex during walking, the half period of oscillation of the legs is simply

$$T_o = \pi\sqrt{\frac{d}{g}}$$

and during this time, the person moves through a distance x_o, the length of stride,

$$x_o = 2L\sin\theta \tag{12.148}$$

Thus the average speed of walking leisurely is

$$v_o = \frac{x_o}{T_o} = \frac{2L\sin\theta}{\pi}\sqrt{\frac{g}{d}} = \frac{2}{\pi}\sqrt{\frac{gL}{\lambda}}\sin\theta \tag{12.149}$$

where λ is defined through $d = \lambda L$, $\lambda < 0.5$.

Therefore, (i) the longer the legs the faster is the speed of walking, (ii) the bigger the stride the faster is the speed, (iii) the speed is independent of the weight of the body, and (iv) walking on the surface of the moon will be about 2.5 times slower than that on earth, because of the reduced g-factor.

Taking $\lambda = 0.4$ $\quad L = 0.8$m, and small θ, one gets

$$v_o = 2.8 \times \theta \text{ m/s} \simeq 10 \times \theta \text{ km/hr}$$

If $\theta \simeq 15^o$ $\quad v_o \simeq 2.6$ km/hr.

Now when the two legs are farthest apart (2θ), the centre of gravity of the body is lowered by $h = L(1 - \cos\theta)$. So the work done in walking through a total distance D is given by

$$W_o = Mgh\left(\frac{D}{2L\sin\theta}\right) \simeq \frac{MgD\theta}{4} \tag{12.150}$$

So the total work done is proportional to the distance walked as well as to the length of stride or the speed of walking.

12.28.3 Race Walking

The difference between walking and running is that, in walking either of the legs must continue to keep in touch with the ground. As one tends to walk fast, one moves the legs with conscious effort and the motion can no longer be approximated to the natural oscillation of the legs. In race walking the objective is to increase the speed of walking to the maximum extent. Equation (12.149) suggests that the increase of speed can be achieved by increasing the length of stride or θ. But as θ increases, the total vertical amplitude of the up and down motion of the CM, that is, h increases as θ^2, and the requirement of power also increases as θ^2. For a stride length of about $\theta = 30^o$, the waddling amplitude of the CM from the previous formula becomes as high as 10.7 cm for $L = 0.8$ m. During fast walking, the legs begin to bend forward sufficiently at the knees, the CM begins to experience a free fall through a height of h, and the time interval T_o between the strides is approximately given by

$$T_o = 2\sqrt{\frac{2h}{g}}$$

with the exception that for bent legs , the expression for h can no longer be given by $h = L(1 - \cos\theta)$. Keeping h as a free parameter, the speed of race walking now becomes

$$v_o = \frac{2L\sin\theta}{T_o} = L\sin\theta\sqrt{\frac{g}{2h}} \tag{12.151}$$

Equation (12.151) suggests that the athlete cannot increase the speed of his/her race walking without increasing θ or decreasing h, which under normal circumstances does not go in the desired opposite way. Moreover, for $\theta = 30^o$, $L = 0.8$ m, and $v_o = 5$m/s (= 18 km/hr), the required value of h must not exceed 3 cm !

Therefore, the art of race walking is to learn how not to allow the waddling of the CM increase with the increase of the length of stride. This is accomplished by athletes with a calculated movement of their hips which is fast enough to arrest the rapid free fall of the CM of the whole body but slow enough for throwing their legs to have as big a stride as possible.

12.28.4 Maximum Speed of Running

A runner usually accelerates in each stride in the beginning and in about a dozen strides achieves the full speed of running. Now each leg comes to rest for a while when it touches the ground. The kinetic energy of the trunk of the body continues with full speed once this maximum is achieved, but the leg's rotational kinetic energy about the feet and the hip joints vary alternately between zero and a maximum value of $I\omega_o^2/2$, where I is the average MI of the leg about either end and ω_o is the maximum angular velocity of both the legs in each stride. The constant supply of this energy comes from the work done by the thrust of reaction acting on the forward leg that rests on the ground and bends at the knee, and the force acts over a push-off length s of the bent leg. If the maximum force available in the form of the thrust of reaction from the ground available is μ times the body's weight Mg, the energy equation simply gives

$$2 \times \frac{1}{2} I\omega_o^2 \leq \mu Mgs \tag{12.152}$$

where ω_o is given by

$$\omega_o = \frac{v_o}{L}$$

v_o being the maximum speed of the runner and L being the length of each leg.

Here the uncertain parameters are I, μ and s. However, one can perhaps take

$$I = \frac{1}{3} m_l L^2 \qquad \mu = 1.5 \quad \text{and} \quad \frac{M}{m_l} = 7 - 7.5$$

where m_l is the mass of each leg. For an estimate of s, which is approximately the separation between a fully extended leg and a bent one, or the distance through which the CM of the body moves while the leg is on the ground, one can assume the location of the knee to be at the middle point of the leg and the maximum bending of the leg at the knee is as large as 90°, giving

$$s \simeq \frac{(2 - \sqrt{2})L}{2} \simeq 0.3L$$

So finally we get, for an average athlete,

$$v_o \leq \sqrt{3\left(1 - \frac{1}{\sqrt{2}}\right) \mu g L \left(\frac{M}{m_l}\right)} \simeq 8.7\text{m/s} \tag{12.153}$$

In order to increase the value of v_o further, a professional runner must have longer ($L \simeq 1$ m) but lighter legs ($M/m_l \simeq 8$), relatively longer forelegs compared to thigh (for achieving larger value of s) and strong enough to produce larger thrust ($\mu \simeq 1.5$) so that

$$v_o \simeq 10.2 \text{ m/s}$$

or in other words, for a 100 m run, the runner would take about 9.8 s.

However, using certain drugs such as steroids, one can illegally increase the strength factor μ, which was the reason for Mr. Ben Johnson's earning notoriety in the 100 m men's running event, in the 1988 Olympics.

Since the work done by the legs during each stride is $W_o = \mu Mgs$ and the final kinetic energy of the runner becomes

$$\frac{1}{2} M v_o^2 = \frac{3}{2} \frac{\mu M^2 gs}{m_l} = \frac{3}{2} \left(\frac{M}{m_l}\right) W_o \simeq (10 - 12) \times W_o \tag{12.154}$$

It means that the runner can accelerate himself/herself to his/her maximum speed of running at the end of the first 10 — 12 strides. This is universally true for all runners, amateur or professional, as it depends simply on the ratio of M and m_l.

12.28.5 Maximum Range of Long Jump

We have seen that at the end of about a dozen strides, the athlete gains the maximum speed of horizontal running. For a long jump (also called broad jump) the runner has to throw himself off the ground with an angle of elevation say θ_i in order to increase the range of his jump. In absence of any drag, the horizontal range of the runner as a projectile is

$$R_l = \frac{V_o^2}{g} \sin 2\theta_i \tag{12.155}$$

where V_o is the speed just before taking off the ground. Obviously, R_l is maximum for $\theta_i = \pi/4$, giving $R_l = V_o^2/g$. However note that $\partial R_l/\partial\theta_i = 0$ for $\theta_i = \pi/4$, so achieving maximum value of R_l near $\theta_i = \pi/4$ is relatively insensitive to θ_i. For a range of θ_i between 40° and 50°, the variation of R_l remains within about 2%.
Putting $V_o = 10$ m/s, $R_l = 10$ m, and even if $\theta_i = 30^o$, R_l reduces only to 8.7 m.

It seems that the best runner would also succeed as the best champion of broad jump. But this is not so simple. The art of this game is to produce the right take off angle which should be no less than 30°. The entire linear momentum of the body has to change its direction during the last stride only. It requires a special technique so that the last push off becomes sufficiently long. The vertical component of the momentum generated in the final push off has to be comparable to its horizontal component, the one that has been achieved in about 10 strides. Usually the runner lowers the level of his/her CG and thrusts himself/herself up and the duration of the last push τ is made to be the longest possible one.

Now, after n ($n < 12$) strides on the ground before the final one, the horizontal speed becomes

$$v_{\parallel} = \sqrt{2n\mu g s}$$

During the last stride the gain in the vertical component of the velocity can be approximated to

$$v_{\perp} = \mu g\tau = \mu g\frac{\beta L}{v_{\parallel}} \tag{12.156}$$

where β, defined through the above relation, corresponds to an effective length of the final stride. We can treat β as a constant only if $v_{\parallel} \gg 0$, which is true for broad jumps but not for high jumps. Since $\tan\theta_i = v_{\perp}/v_{\parallel}$ and $V_o^2 = v_{\parallel}^2 + v_{\perp}^2$, we can substitute it back in Eq. (12.155), and get

$$R_l = 2\mu\beta L$$

and

$$\theta_i = \tan^{-1}\left[\frac{\beta}{(2-\sqrt{2})n}\right] \tag{12.157}$$

The extra parameter β plays a crucial role in determining R_l apart from μ and L. The current world record of long jump $R_l \simeq 8.9$ m requires a value of $\beta \simeq 3$, and hence $\theta_i \simeq 27^o$ for $n \simeq 10$.

12.28.6 Maximum Height of Vertical Jump

In this game, it is the centre of gravity of the athlete that has to be lifted as high as possible by generating the maximum amount of the vertical component of the impulse using the maximum possible thrust received from the ground. The separation between the lifted CG and the reference horizontal bar (h') is also to be minimised. We know that the CG of the upright body lies inside the body, but if the body is given a shape of an inverted 'V', the CG will not only come out of the body but also remain in a low position. It is known that one can topple over a horizontal fencing keeping the CG all the time slightly below the upper boundary of the fencing. So an athlete can in practice achieve $h' \leq 0$ in high jumps.

Suppose just before the final take off the athlete brings his/her CG down by a height $h_o\delta$ ($\delta < 1$) from its usual original height h_o. Then the athlete exerts maximum possible thrust on the ground so that the force of reaction μMg begins to act on the body. It can continue to act so long as the feet remain on the ground, that is, the CG does not go off above its normal height h_o. Since the work done on the whole body is $\mu Mgh_o\delta$, after the take off the CG will continue to rise a further height of $\mu h_o\delta$. Hence the total height of the CG above the ground at its peak of climbing becomes

$$H + h' = h_o(1 + \mu\delta) \tag{12.157}$$

where H is the height of the reference bar from the level of the ground.

For a typical athlete, $h_o = 1$ m, $\delta = 0.6$, $\mu = 1.5$ and $h' = 0$, thus giving

$$H = 1.9 \text{ m}$$

By stretching all the parameters to the extreme, one can perhaps achieve $h_o = 1.1$ m, $\delta = 0.75$, $\mu = 1.6$, $h' = -0.05$ m in which case $H = 2.47$ m, the present world record of high jump being 2.44 m, held by Javier Sotomayor of Cuba.

The interesting point to note is that in Eq. (12.157) the value of g scales out from both sides, and therefore, the statistics of high jump will hardly improve on any other celestial object where the value of g is markedly different, except that the value of the μ-factor might be substantially higher in conditions of lower gravity.

12.28.7 Throwing

In throwing a javelin, discus or shot put, the muscular strength of the athlete's hands becomes the most important factor. From weightlifting statistics, it is known that the highest limit of lifting a dead load W_d lies somewhere between 4 and 5.2 depending on the weight class of the weightlifters, the ratio being highest for weightlifters having body weights 60 – 70 kg. Since the weights are lifted by hands, the limits strongly depend on the cross section of the weakest joint in the arm (A_w) and the total surface area of the feet that supports the reaction, apart from the strength of the muscle fibres of the arms and legs. Hence the muscular strength of the hands for sustaining a maximum pressure can be expressed by the ratio W_d/A_w, where A_w is the cross-section of the wrist.

Now in all kinds of throwing processes the hand makes a final swing before the projectile is thrown out in the air. Hence the entire arm, due to the circular motion of the final swing, must experience an outward centrifugal force and the shoulder joint has to experience a tremendous amount of centrifugal pressure. This happens even when one attempts to throw a small stone chip, let alone a javelin, discus or shot put. During weightlifting, the outward pressure is maximum at the point of smallest cross-section, that is the wrist joint, but for throwing, the outward centrifugal pressure becomes maximum at the shoulder joint, which is given by

$$P_{\text{cf}} = \frac{1}{A_a}\int_0^{L_h} A(l)\rho(l)\omega^2 dl$$

where L_h is the length of the hand, $A(l)$ and $\rho(l)$ are respectively the cross-section and mass density at a distance l below the shoulder joint, ω is the approximately constant angular speed of the arm at a given instant and A_a is the cross-section at the shoulder joint ($l = 0$). So

$$P_{\text{cf}} \simeq \frac{\bar{A}\bar{\rho}L_h^2\omega^2}{2A_a} \simeq \frac{1}{2}\frac{v^2 m_h}{L_h A_a} \tag{12.158}$$

where m_h is the mass of the hand and v is the speed of swing of the projectile held in the hand.

At the time of release, the maximum speed of throw v_{max} can reach high enough to satisfy the following equation

$$P_{\text{cf}} = \frac{W_d}{2A_w}$$

as the weightlifting is done by using both the hands. Taking $W_d = \mu' Mg$, we get

$$v_{\text{max}}^2 = \frac{L_h A_a W_d}{m_h A_w} = \mu'\left(\frac{M}{m_h}\right)\left(\frac{A_a}{A_w}\right) gL_h = \gamma g L_h$$

where γ and μ' are defined through the above relations.

It is desirable that the thrower have the largest possible value of γ. We can take $\mu' = 5$, $(M/m_h) = 20$ and $(A_a/A_w) = 1.5$, giving $\gamma = 150$. This means that a swinging hand can sustain a maximum outward centrifugal acceleration of the hand of about 150 times the value of g.

Combining Eqs (12.155) and (12.158), it is now easy to find out the maximum possible range of throwing a stone chip, for example (without of course imparting any CM motion of the body to the projectile), which becomes

$$R_{\text{sc}} = \gamma L_h \tag{12.159}$$

or about 150 times the length of the hand. If $L_h = 0.65$ m, the maximum range of throwing a stone chip without running becomes a little less than 100 m. If by just one swing of hand you can throw up to a distance of say 50 m, you know that you can achieve a centrifugal acceleration on the order of $75g$, which also implies that after the act of throwing you would feel your hand to have become tired, as if it had lifted a dead load from the ground, weighing about 2.5 times your body weight. This proves not only that our arm muscles are generally very strong, but also that their actions are extremely swift. According to Eq. (12.158), a good thrower should have a relatively lighter, longer and stronger arm.

Now if you run to bring the speed of your CM to v_o before you throw the stone chip, the maximum range would become, using Eqs (12.155) and (12.158),

$$R_m = \frac{(v_{\max} + v_o)^2}{g} \sin 2\theta_i + R_o \tag{12.160}$$

the extra term R_o being a small correction due to the nonzero height at the moment of the throw (h_i). Usually $R_o \simeq h_i$. For $v_o = 8$ m/s, $v_{\max} = 30.9$ m/s and $R_o = 1$ m, $R_m = 155$ m.

(i) Throwing a Javelin

The javelin is basically a long but light rod pointed at one end. Since it is long and held in hand at the arm's length, it will produce an extra centrifugal pressure at the hinge point of the swinging arm. One has therefore to add a term to our expression for P_{cf} before equating to $W_d/2A_w$. The whole effect can be viewed as an increase in the effective mass of the hand m_h. An extra factor α_f by which the value of m_h increases would depend on the mass and length of the javelin, the point where the javelin is held in hand and its orientation with respect to the straightened arm. Since one is allowed to run before throwing the javelin, one would have from Eqs (12.158) and (12.160)

$$R_m = \frac{1}{g}\left[\sqrt{\frac{\gamma g L_h}{\alpha_f}} + v_o\right]^2 \sin 2\theta_i + R_o \tag{12.161}$$

which for $v_o = 8$ m/s, $\alpha_f = 1.7$ gives $R_m = 104$ m, assuming that at the moment of throwing the initial height R_o of the CG of the javelin was about 1.5 m above the ground. The current world record seems to stand at 104 m, set by Uwe Hohn of GDR.

(ii) Throwing a Shot Put

In this game a 16 lb lead shot is to be thrown from within a small marked circular zone on the ground without lifting at any time both the legs from the ground. With this heavy shot in one hand, the value of α_f in Eq. (12.161) becomes 4.8 or so, and the effective value of γ does not quite reach 150 in just little more than half a swing. The thrower also attempts to achieve as high a forward centre of mass speed (v_o) as possible. This is done by turning back, then skidding backward on one leg (which makes him attain a forward CM motion), and finally making a half swing of the body as well as of the shot which follows a calculated spiral orbit before release. At the same time much effort is spent to raise the CM of the body so as to impart maximum possible vertical component of velocity to the shot. The typical values of $v_o \simeq 2$ m/s, $\gamma \simeq 120$ and $R_o = 1.5$ m giving

$$R_m \simeq 23.3 \text{ m}$$

the current world record being about 22.9 m.

(iii) Throwing a Discus

A discus is not much heavier than a javelin, but because of its characteristic shape it requires a spin which endows it with a gyroscopic stability in its long route of directed motion through air. It being unlike a small cricket ball, adequate spin cannot be imparted just by the use of fingers and the thrower makes one or two complete turns about himself/herself before the discus is thrown. With $\alpha_f = 1.8$, $v_o = 3$ m/s, $\gamma = 150$ and $R_m = 1$ m, Eq. (12.161) gives $R_m = 70$ m.

12.28.8 Cycling

Cycling is performed by exerting muscular power of the leg on the pedals of a bicycle. In order to find the maximum speed of cycling achievable by a professional cyclist in a race, we must first know what maximum power is available from the trust of the legs on the pedals. We can take this from the performance of an athlete in a 100 m race, for example. The configuration of legs during fast running suggests that the length of the strides is about $L/\sqrt{2}$, for the expression that we have used for s in the subsection on running. Hence using Eqs (12.152) and (12.153), the maximum power spent running in a race per unit mass of the body is given by

$$K_r = \frac{\sqrt{2}}{3}\left(\frac{m_l}{M}\right)\frac{v_o^3}{L} \simeq 0.4(\mu g)^{1.5}\left(\frac{M}{m_l}\right)^{0.5} L^{0.5} \tag{12.162}$$

For an average athlete, $K_r \simeq 54$ W/kg (= 46 Cal/hr/kg for easy comparison with various entries in Table 12.4) of the body weight. Since running with such a high power lasts only for 10—100 sec, a 60 kg person shall not lose more than 8–80 Cal. The maximum power of leg thrusting on hard ground can thus become 2.7 kW for a 50 kg athlete, which is about 3.6 HP!

If the bicycle racer keeps on feeding power at this rate to the cradle of the bicycle, the speed should keep on increasing endlessly. But as it gains speed the losses become more important. For a runner on the ground, the loss was mainly due to periodic acceleration and deceleration of the legs. We calculated the final steady speed of running by equating this rate of loss to the pumping rate from the thrusting of legs on the ground. In cycling too, the loss due to periodic acceleration and deceleration of the legs on pedal is unavoidable, but it is now about 10 or 15 times smaller than the pumping rate (the exact factor depends on the diameter of paddling wheel, height of the bicycle, length of the legs and the speed ratio of the wheel to the cradle). The main loss is however due to combating the air drag. In the speed range we are interested in, the drag law is a quadratic one and is given by

$$F_D = \frac{1}{2} C_D \rho_a A v^2 \tag{12.163}$$

where F_D is the drag force experienced by the moving system (= rider + bicycle), A is the frontal cross-section of the whole system, $C_D = 0.9$, ρ_a = density of air and v is the speed of the system. The loss of power due to this drag is $F_D v$. Keeping a factor λ (slightly greater than unity) in order to include the losses by the legs and a possible difference in the value of μ for thrusting on pedals rather than on ground, we can have for the maximum attainable speed v_b in bicycle races

$$v_b = \left(\frac{2\sqrt{2}}{3\lambda C_D}\frac{m_l}{\rho_a A L}\right)^{\frac{1}{3}} v_o \tag{12.164}$$

where v_o is the maximum speed of the athlete as a runner in, say, a 100 m race. The ratio of v_b to v_o seems to be fairly independent of the athlete's capacities, as m_l is nearly proportional to the product AL. For an athlete keeping his/her head vertically up while cycling, the net frontal area is approximately

$$A = 0.5 \left(\frac{M}{60 \text{ kg}} \right)^{0.7} \text{m}^2$$

the numerical factor 0.5 becomes about 0.45 if both the trunk and the head lean sufficiently forward. Obviously such a posture is helpful in achieving higher speed as A occurs in Eq. (12.164) in its denominator. For an average athlete the constant of proportionality in Eq. (12.164) becomes about 2.51 for ($\lambda = 1.1$), thus giving

$$v_b = 21.8 \text{ m/s}$$

the present world record of maximum speed in bicycling being about 22 m/s.

12.28.9 Swimming

Swimming is a dynamical process in which the swimmer gains a net horizontal momentum by throwing parts of the body in and out while the body remains entirely supported by a pool of water. Since there is no component of gravity (the external force) that can act in the horizontal direction, the centre of mass of the body cannot acquire any horizontal component of linear momentum by merely performing any number of internal motions, such as throwing hands and legs, etc. So one has to transfer a net horizontal component of momentum to the surrounding medium, so that the body can receive an equivalent amount as a reaction. During running the momentum is transferred to the earth as an action and during swimming it is transferred to the surrounding water medium. In both the cases the body receives the reaction which is capable of producing the motion of the centre of mass of the body.

There are four different styles of swimming depending on the mode of generating the required thrust on water. In *freestyle*, strokes by hands are performed longitudinally and alternately. In *butterfly stroke*, longitudinal strokes of hands are made in unison. In *breast-stroke*, the hand strokes go sideways with hands remaining fully outstretched. In *backstroke*, the hand strokes are quite similar to those of the freestyle mode, but the body is now kept always in the prone position. Here we shall consider the butterfly mode for reasons of simplicity.

Let us analyse a case when the strokes are produced both by hands and legs. The hand strokes begin with both the hands stretched in the forward direction. Let γg be the constant acceleration of the tip of the hand, produced by the muscles of the hand, and as a result, at time t, θ be the angle that each arm make with the forward direction. Assuming as before the hands to be uniform rods of length L_h, mass m_h and longitudinal vertical cross-section A_h (that effectively faces the force of drag from water), the centre of mass of each hand would experience a net horizontal force as the sum of $F_{\text{ext}} = m_h \gamma g/2$ and the drag force $F_d = -2\, C_D \rho_w A_h v_{\text{cm}}^2/3$, where $C_D =$ drag coefficient (for swimming speeds $C_D = 0.7$), $\rho_w =$ density of water, and $v_{\text{cm}} =$ the instantaneous speed of the CM of the hand. Since

$F_d \propto v_{\rm cm}^2$, it wins over the muscular force at some stage after which deceleration takes over and brings the hands to rest with respect to the shoulder joint say at $t = t_o$ when $\theta = \theta_{\max}$, say. Since both the final and initial values of $v_{\rm cm}$ with respect to the body are zero, the hands must have transferred all the momentum they gained in between, to the surrounding water.

The net horizontal forward component of this momentum of each hand that goes to the water in each stroke is

$$p_h = -\int_o^{t_o} m_h \dot{v}_{\rm cm} \sin\theta dt$$

The equation of motion can be exactly solved in order to get expressions for p_h, $\theta_{\max}$ and t_o in terms of γ, g, m_h, C_D, A_h and ρ_w. The whole body receives the momentum $-p_h$ as a reaction and moves forward with a final speed V_f (starting from zero, of course) at the end of $t = t_o$, given by

$$V_f = \frac{5\pi}{2^{5/2}3^{3/4}}\left(\frac{m_h}{M}\right)\sqrt{\gamma g L_h \theta_{\max}} \simeq 1.22\left(\frac{m_h}{M}\right)\sqrt{\gamma g L_h \theta_{\max}} \qquad (12.165)$$

and time taken

$$t_o = \frac{3^{1/4}\pi}{2\sqrt{2}}\sqrt{\frac{L_h\theta_{\max}}{\gamma g}} \simeq 1.46\sqrt{\frac{L_h\theta_{\max}}{\gamma g}} \qquad \text{where} \qquad \theta_{\max} = \frac{2\sqrt{3}\, m_h}{C_D \rho_w A_h L_h} \qquad (12.166)$$

Note that the most uncertain parameter A_h is eliminated using the expressions for the directly observable quantity $\theta_{\max}$. The above expressions will be valid also for the leg strokes with appropriate values of the γ factor, L and m_l. Since a leg can exert a maximum of force $\mu M g$, its lower tip, that is foot, can produce a maximum acceleration of $2\mu Mg/m_l \equiv \gamma' g \simeq 22g$. Also note that in the opening out phase of the legs, the body is retarded, while in the returning phase the body gains a forward momentum, if both are performed by thrusting water.

The return strokes of the hands could retard the whole body almost exactly by the same amount as it had accelerated in their forward strokes, but the return strokes are carried out in air instead of in water, and therefore retardation of the body due to muscular efforts for resetting the hands back to the original positions are avoided. It is the drag force of water that acts on the whole body during both the onward and return parts of the strokes and continues to retard the motion of the CM. For maximum gain in thrust, the hands should open out in water, but the legs should open out in air. If the swimmer fails to do so, or does it the wrong way, the efforts of the legs will simply reduce the speed of swimming to a great extent. From Eq. (12.165), one can achieve $V_f \simeq 1.2$ m/s at the end of each stroke of the hands if $\theta_{\max} = 30^o$, and can go up to 1.7 m/s if $\theta_{\max} = 60^o$.

It is obvious that the maximum average speed V_c achieved by the swimmer will depend on the values of V_f, the total surface area of the body that experiences the drag and the relative lengths of the passive intervals between two successive active phases of the strokes. During each active part of the stroke by hands, the momentum of the whole body should follow the following equation of motion

$$\dot{P} = -\dot{p}_h - \frac{1}{2}C_D\rho_w A_o \left(\frac{P}{M}\right)^2$$

where A_o is the effective surface area of the whole body that produces the drag. And during the passive part of the strokes,

$$\dot{P} = -\frac{1}{2}C_D\rho_w A_o \left(\frac{P}{M}\right)^2$$

Under steady state conditions, the time average of $\dot{P}$ over the full period of a stroke must vanish. Since the solution for p_h as a function of t is given by

$$p_h(t) = \frac{5}{12}\gamma m_h g t + \frac{m_h}{8}\sqrt{\frac{3m_h\gamma g}{C_D\rho_w A}}\sin\left(\sqrt{\frac{C_D\rho_w A\gamma g}{3m_h}}\, t\right) \qquad \text{for } t \le t_o$$

the time average over a period $2t_o$ under the steady state conditions will give

$$\frac{5}{12}\gamma m_h g = \frac{1}{2}C_D\rho_w A_o < V^2 > \tag{12.167}$$

However in actual practice the return part of the stroke is made slightly longer than t_o, in which case, the coefficient 0.5 on the right hand side of Eq. (12.167) will effectively increase. As seen from the above expression for $p_h(t)$, the instantaneous velocity of the body V will approximately vary sinusoidally with an amplitude V_f over the average speed of swimming V_c, which would give, after averaging

$$< V^2 > = V_c^2 + \frac{1}{2}V_f^2$$

Since both the legs and hands are producing the strokes, a more correct equation would be

$$< V^2 > = V_c^2 + \frac{1}{2}(V_f^2)_{\text{hand}} + \frac{1}{2}(V_f^2)_{\text{leg}} \tag{12.168}$$

Substituting Eq. (12.168) in Eq. (12.167) and using the expressions for V_f's, we get

$$V_c^2 = \frac{5\gamma m_h g}{6C_D\rho_w A_o}\left[1 - \frac{5\pi^2}{16}\left(\frac{m_h}{M}\right)^2\left(\frac{A_o}{A_h}\right) - \frac{5\pi^2}{16}\frac{\gamma_l m_l}{\gamma m_h}\left(\frac{m_l}{M}\right)^2\left(\frac{A_o}{A_l}\right)\right] \tag{12.169}$$

neglecting other types of relatively minor contributions coming from the thrusts produced by the chest and head.

Putting $A_o = 0.6\ \text{m}^2$, $A_h = 0.02\ \text{m}^2$, $A_l = 0.09\ \text{m}^2$, $M = 50\ kg$, $\gamma = 150$, $M/m_l = 7.25$, $\gamma_l = 22$, $M/m_h = 23$, $C_D = 0.7$, $\rho_w = 1000\ \text{kg/m}^3$, we get for the maximum attainable speed of swimming under most favourable cases

$$V_c = 2.0\ \text{m/s}$$

The Olympic records till the present suggest $V_c = 2.0$ m/s in the free style, $= 1.86$ m/s in butterfly mode, $= 1.80$ m/s in backstroke, and $= 1.59$ m/s in the breaststroke.

For different styles of swimming, the exact numerical coefficient 5/6 in the leading term of Eq. (12.169) would vary a great deal, apart from the changes in the values of A_o and A_h.

However, it should be noted that the treatment presented above is by no means complete. The physics of a complicated art like swimming has still remained a matter of research.

12.28.10 Playing Tennis, Golf, Ping Pong and Base Ball

Small and light weight balls are hit by hand-held tennis rackets for playing tennis, by hand-held golf sticks for playing golf, etc. The speed of the spinning balls often acquires a maximum exceeding 30 m/s. At such high speeds, two types of drag forces are experienced by the spinning balls, one is the usual *quadratic law of drag force*

$$\boldsymbol{F}_d = -\frac{1}{2}C_D\rho_a A v\boldsymbol{v}$$

and the other called the *Magnus force of lift* (after H. G. Magnus who discovered it in 1853) acts always perpendicular to the the flying ball's velocity vector $\boldsymbol{v}$ and its axis of spinning $\hat{\boldsymbol{n}} = \boldsymbol{\omega}/\omega$

$$\boldsymbol{F}_m = \frac{1}{2}C_L\rho_a Ar(\boldsymbol{\omega} \times \boldsymbol{v})$$

where $\boldsymbol{v}$ is the instantaneous velocity of the ball, r = radius of the ball, $A = \pi r^2$ = effective cross-section of the ball, $\boldsymbol{\omega}$ = angular velocity of rotation, ρ_a = air density, C_D = drag coefficient for linear speed, and C_L = drag coefficient for the Magnus force. The last two quantities are given by the following approximate empirical formulae

$$C_D = 0.508 + \left[22.503 + 4.196\left(\frac{\omega r}{v}\right)^{-2.5}\right]^{-0.4}$$

$$C_L = \left[2.202 + 0.981\left(\frac{\omega r}{v}\right)^{-1}\right]^{-1}$$

Hence the equation of motion of the centre of mass of the ball is simply

$$m\dot{\boldsymbol{v}} = m\boldsymbol{g} + \boldsymbol{F}_D + \boldsymbol{F}_m$$

Usually a constant spin angular speed is assumed for the entire trajectory, and the equation of motion is integrated numerically, using the method of quadrature. It is found that the effect of backspin is to increase the range of the ball. For attaining maximum range, the back spin rate should be as high as possible and the optimum launch angle should decrease with the increase in the initially given spin rate. Since the Magnus force always acts perpendicular to the direction of motion, it cannot affect the speed but the motion does not remain confined in one plane. It moves either to the right or to the left depending on the sign of the spin.

12.28.11 Playing Acrobatics

Acrobatics involve basic rotations such as somersault, twist and cartwheeling of the body in various configurational states of the body, namely, arms laid out on sides, or overhead, or in twists, or in relaxed or outstretched conditions. Table 12.3 gives an idea of the principal moments of inertia about the centre of mass of the body under the above mentioned operations.

If the body is thrown in air, gravity cannot produce any net external torque on the body. So the torque free rotation of the body can be described by Euler's equations of motion given by

$$\left(\frac{dL}{dt}\right)_{\text{bodyframe}} = -\boldsymbol{\omega} \times \boldsymbol{L}\Big|_{\text{bodyframe}}$$

where $\boldsymbol{L}$ is the angular momentum of the body and is given by

$$\boldsymbol{L} = I_{xx}\omega_x\hat{i} + I_{yy}\omega_y\hat{j} + I_{zz}\omega_z\hat{k}$$

The solutions of ω_x, ω_y and ω_z can be obtained by numerically integrating these equations of motion.

12.28.12 Performance of Women in Sports

This requires an understanding of some subtle and gross differences between men and women in terms of strength, constitution and organisation of the body. The same is true for cartoons and line drawings that bring out subtle features that enable one to easily distinguish between men, women and children, apart from the quite obvious ones. For performance in sports, the following differences may be noted.

(i) Smaller feet and lighter body weight. Women are capable of producing less thrust on the ground than men do. The μ factor seems to be about 1.25. If we substitute this value of μ, most of the Olympic statistics for women can easily be explained.

(ii) Wavy outline of the body due to constricted waist and greatly extended hip. This has happened during the course of biological evolution that enabled women to carry and nurture babies before and after birth. So the centre of gravity of their body lies well inside the body. This gives more stability to performing odd rotations of the body in space.

(iii) Fat content. An average woman has about 40% of the body weight in the form of fat, compared to about 25% for men. They are mainly located in the abdomen, hips, thighs and breasts. However, all these fatty components are considered to be an absolute nuisance for a woman athlete particularly for running, swimming and performing gymnastics, because during all swift movements of the body, these locations try to displace in the same direction adding to great imbalance of the body.

(iv) Hands and legs. It is only during adolescence that a girl between 12 and 16 becomes generally taller than boys of the same age. The centre of mass of the legs begins to move upward, the hands and legs become about 5% taller than those of the boys. These factors do help compensate to some extent the deficiencies caused by the lower values of μ and γ for girls of the above age group over their male peers.

12.28.13 Controlling Bodyweights

Most people are concerned with gaining a control over their accelerating or decelerating bodyweights. With your normal daily intake of food and daily routine for work including exercises, you find your bodyweight Mg is either increasing or decreasing with time, or remaining quite steady. If the rate of increase is $\dot{M} = dM/dt$, which is for all practical purposes the same as the rate of fat deposition in the body, you must either increase the degree of your daily exercise or reduce the daily calorie intake from food or both in order to neutralise the effect, so that

$$\dot{M}g \times 7000 \text{ Cal} = -\Delta K_e W + \Delta Q_f$$

where ΔK_e is the induced change in the daily average of K in terms of extra exercises, say, by selecting items from Table 12.4, and Q_f is the intended changes in the daily intake of food calories. You can make $\dot{M} = 0$ by suitably adjusting the two terms on the right hand side of the equation.

To give an example, suppose you noticed that your bodyweight (say 50 kg at the time) was increasing at a rate of 1kg per month, and you wanted to keep it steady at about 50 kg only by increasing the level of your daily exercise. Now, 1 kg of fat per month implies 32 gm/day $= 0.032 \times 7700$ Cal/day $= 250$ Cal/day, or $= 5$ Cal/day/kg of bodyweight. From Table 12.4, the requirement can be satisfied by an extra exercise of say playing tennis or swimming for 45 minutes or very fast walking (of average speed 6.5 km/hr) for about an hour and a quarter.

However, we would like to add a cautionary remark. Most people, particularly young women, are quite conscious of either achieving or maintaining a slim figure. This is good so long as the fat reserve in the body does not go below a critical level. Recent studies have revealed that if the fat content drops below 30% of the body weight, the natural cycle of ovulation becomes irregular, and it stops or cannot even begin for the first time if the fat content remains below 25%.

12.29 SUMMARY

We have seen that the degrees of freedom for any arbitrary motion of a rigid body is six, implying that its configuration space is six-dimensional. It therefore becomes extremely difficult to perceive motions of rigid bodies in all their richness with our limited power of vision, which encompasses only up to 3 dimensions. So when we restrict the motion of a rigid body to rotating about a fixed point in the body, there is hope for visualising all the richness of its motion. Hence the latter sections are devoted to studying such motions.

Since the definition of rigidity and the definition of distance in Euclidean space are conceptually identical, the general motions of a rigid body form a group isomorphous to the Euclidean group. This means that like the basic Euclidean operations, the motions of rigid bodies can be decoupled into translations and rotations, which is guaranteed by Euler's theorem.

The existence of three translational degrees of freedom of a rigid body allows the rigid body as a whole to behave like a particle. The other three degrees of freedom that constitute what is called rotation of a rigid body, are completely new in kind. For their dynamical descriptions, the knowledge of total mass, again a particle concept, is no longer sufficient. The structural details of the rigid body are coded in the six independent components of the moment of inertia tensor. Through various theorems on the moment of inertia and the properties of ellipsoid of inertia, the symmetries of the moment of inertia tensor are brought out.

Since the moment of inertia of a body can remain steady only with reference to body frames, there is a necessity for developing a scheme for tackling dynamical problems with reference to body frames, which are generally rotating and are therefore grossly noninertial. The generalisations of the Newonian schemes in retaining the torque angular momentum relationship or developing the relevant equations of motion were successfully carried out by Euler. The addition of a centrifugal term in Euler's equations of motion has been justified in the text in several ways.

Free rotations of rigid bodies with Poinsot's geometrical interpretations in terms of polhodes and herpolhodes, Euler's analytical solutions in terms of Eulerian angles, and a combination of both in terms of body cones and space cones bring out all the subtle features of free rotations.

The motions of symmetric tops under the action of gravitational torques about a fixed point in the rotating body are found to retain the same number of first integrals of motion as a freely rotating rigid body has. This property makes them ideally suited as the first step of extension towards understanding, as well as applying to, many natural examples of top motions in an analytic fashion. The introduction of the Eulerian angles help interpret the motions in terms of most fundamental rotations, such as precession, nutation and axial spin.

Lastly, the motivation behind our consideration of a simplified dynamics of some sports and games has been to illustrate the richness of the motions of the human body as a rigid body. The physics of complicated events are usually not so complicated as they appear to be. Through these examples we have also tried to demonstrate how one would go about in order to formulate a physical problem, be it as complicated as the process of running or swimming.

PROBLEMS

12.1 A sphere can roll without slipping on a given plane horizontal surface. Find the equations for the nonholonomic rolling constraint, if (i) the surface is at rest, and (ii) the surface is a uniformly rotating heavy platform.
Show that in the second case, the ball will make circular orbits with respect to the outside inertial observers.

12.2 A sphere of radius a is pressed between two perfectly smooth parallel plates and made to revolve with uniform angular speeds Ω_1 and Ω_2 about some fixed axes perpendicular to their planes. Determine the motion of the sphere, and show that the path of the centre of the sphere is a circle described with uniform speed.

12.3 A right circular cone of semivertical angle α rolls on a horizontal plane with its vertex at O. A second cone of semivertical angle $\pi/2 - 2\alpha$ rotates with its axis vertical and vertex at O, in rolling contact with the first cone. If the line of contact of the first cone with the plane makes a complete circuit around the vertical in time T, determine the angular velocity of the second cone.

12.4 If $\boldsymbol{r}(t)$ denotes the position vector of any particle in a rigid body with respect to a fixed point O in the body about which the body turns, show that the motion that sends $\boldsymbol{r}(0)$ into $\boldsymbol{r}(t)$ may be reproduced as a single rotation of magnitude $\theta(t)$ about an axis with unit vector $\hat{\boldsymbol{n}}(t)$, and the Rodgrigue's formula for finite rotation vector $\boldsymbol{\beta}$ satisfies

$$\boldsymbol{\omega}(t) = \left(1 + \frac{1}{4}\beta^2\right)^{-1}\left(\dot{\boldsymbol{\beta}} + \frac{1}{2}\boldsymbol{\beta} \times \dot{\boldsymbol{\beta}}\right)$$

where $\boldsymbol{\omega}$ = instantaneous angular velocity vector, provided

$$\boldsymbol{\beta} = 2\tan\left(\frac{\theta}{2}\right)\hat{\boldsymbol{n}}$$

Also show that

$$\boldsymbol{r}(t) = \left(1 + \frac{1}{4}\beta^2\right)^{-1}\left[\left(1 - \frac{1}{4}\beta^2\right)\boldsymbol{r}(0) + \frac{1}{2}(\boldsymbol{\beta}\cdot\boldsymbol{r}(0))\boldsymbol{\beta} + \boldsymbol{\beta}\times\boldsymbol{r}(0)\right]$$

12.5 Prove the following theorems on centre of mass and moment of inertia
(i) Lagrange's theorem (1783): If $\boldsymbol{R}$ be the position vector of the centre of mass at G of any given object measured from any arbitrarily chosen point O in the body, then prove that

$$MR^2 = \sum_{i=1}^{n} m_i r_i^2 - \frac{1}{2}\sum_{i=1}^{n}\sum_{j=1}^{n} m_i m_j |\boldsymbol{r}_i - \boldsymbol{r}_j|^2$$

where $\boldsymbol{r}_i$ is the position vector of the ith particle, and M = total mass of the body. Use this theorem to find out the centre of mass of a regular pyramid.
(ii) If x, y, z are three mutually perpendicular intersecting axes set in a given body, prove that the sum of the MI about the three axes is given by

$$I_{xx} + I_{yy} + I_{zz} = 2\sum m_i r_i^2$$

or in other words, prove that the trace of the moment of inertia tensor is invariant. Use this theorem to show that the moment of inertia of a circular hoop of mass M and radius R about an axis 45° with respect to the symmetry axis is $3MR^2/4$.
(iii) Express the mass quadrupole tensor $D_{ij} = \sum m(3r_i r_j - r^2\delta_{ij})$ in terms of the moment of inertia tensor I_{ij}.

12.6 An object of mass M and moment of inertia I is initially at rest on a frictionless surface. If F be a force of constant magnitude whose line of application is always at a distance d from the centre of mass and its orientation with respect to the body remains always the same, show that the trajectory of the centre of mass of the object is a Cornu's spiral.

12.7 What is the height-to-diameter ratio of a right circular cylinder such that the inertial ellipsoid at the centre of the cylinder is a sphere. Is it possible to have a suitable height to diameter ratio for a right circular cone that would make the inertial ellipsoid about its vertex a sphere?

12.8 A homogeneous sphere is thrown on the floor with a speed v_o such that it slides initially. Calculate the speed at which rolling will occur using the torque angular momentum relationship according to section 12.9 about (i) the centre of mass, and (ii) about the point of contact with the floor. Show that both these frames give the identical answer, namely $v = 5v_o/7$.

12.9 We know that the total electrostatic energy retained in the electrostatic field of a static electron of mass m and charge e exceeds the value mc^2 if the radius of the electron is assumed to be smaller than $2r_o/3$, where $r_o = \mu_o e^2/4\pi m$ = the classical radius of the electron. Since the electron is known to have a spin angular momentum $|\boldsymbol{S}| = \sqrt{s(s+1)}\hbar$, $s = 1/2$, show the speed required on the equator of the classical electron exceeds about 440 times the speed of light, that is, if the electron is assumed to be a rigid sphere of radius $2r_o/3$, and rotating uniformly. This is one reason why one says the spin of an electron is quantum mechanical. However, knowing that an electron also has a magnetic moment $\boldsymbol{\mu} = -(e/m)\boldsymbol{S}$, the region outside the electron must produce both an electric field $\boldsymbol{E}$ and a magnetic dipole field $\boldsymbol{H}$, the combination of which will produce an effective angular momentum $\boldsymbol{L}$ totally outside the electron, defined through the energy flux interpretation of the Poynting vector. Show that $\boldsymbol{L} = \boldsymbol{S}$ if we integrate the angular momentum density due to the Poynting vector over the entire space from infinity down to $r = 2r_o/3$!

12.10 Einstein and de Haas devised the following experiment in 1916. Suppose you take an iron wire of say 5 cm length and 1mm diameter, suspended with its axis vertical, and free to rotate about the axis. The wire is suddenly magnetised by a magnetic field applied parallel to the axis and the resulting increase in its angular velocity was measured. How large was the effect?

12.11 A horizontal circular disc of mass M is pivoted about a point on its rim, so that it is free to rotate about a vertical axis passing through the point. If a cat of mass m walks once around the rim, show that the disc turns through an angle α, given by

$$\alpha = \int_0^{\pi} \frac{4m\cos^2\theta d\theta}{(3M/2) + 4m\cos^2\theta}$$

12.12 A body is rotating about a fixed point O in space under the action of gravity. The directions of the principal moments of inertia of the body are given by the triad OXYZ $(\hat{\boldsymbol{i}}, \hat{\boldsymbol{j}}, \hat{\boldsymbol{k}})$. Let the direction of the vertical be represented by the unit vector $\hat{\boldsymbol{z}}$ $(\equiv p\hat{\boldsymbol{i}} + q\hat{\boldsymbol{j}} + r\hat{\boldsymbol{k}})$, and the position vector of the centre of gravity G be $\overrightarrow{OG} = \mathbf{h}\hat{\boldsymbol{i}} + \mathbf{k}\hat{\boldsymbol{j}} + \mathbf{l}\hat{\boldsymbol{k}}$. Find the two usual integrals of motion.
Show that a third integral of motion exists provided
(i) $k = 0$ and $(Ah^2 + Cl^2)/AC = (h^2 + l^2)/B$, giving the Hess' integral $Ah\omega_1 + Cl\omega_3 = 0$.
(ii) $A = B = 2C$ and $l = 0$, giving the Kowalevski's integral $\omega_1^2 - \omega_2^2 -$

$ghp/C)^2 + (2\omega_1\omega_2 - ghq/C)^2 = \text{const.}$
(iii) $A = B = 4C$, $k = l = 0$, giving the Tshapliguine's integral $\omega_3(\omega_1^2 + \omega_2^2) - gh\omega_1 r/C = \text{const.}$

12.13 (i) Show that polhodes are closed curves.
(ii) Show that steady rotations about the principal axes of any asymmetric top are stable except for the intermediate principal axis.

12.14 A cone of semiangle α_b is rotating without slipping on the surface of a stationary cone of semiangle α_s keeping their vertices at a common point. If the precessional angular speed of the axis of the first cone be $\dot{\phi}$, find the instantaneous axis of rotation $\hat{\boldsymbol{n}}$, instantaneous total angular velocity $\boldsymbol{\omega}$ and the axial spin rate $\dot{\psi}$ of the rolling cone about its body frame principal axes. Assume α_s and α_b to be acute angles. What happens when α_b becomes obtuse? (These cones describe precisely the rolling of the body cone over the space cone and the analogy is, in every sense, a realistic one.)

12.15 A uniform right circular cylinder , whose length is 3 times the radius of its circular section and is set spinning with an angular velocity $\boldsymbol{\Omega}$ about an axis passing through its centre and a point on the rim of one of its plane ends, is thrown into the air. If the air resistance is neglected, prove that the times taken by the instantaneous axis of rotation to describe the herpolhode and polhode cones are in the ratio 3 : 5.

12.16 If a constant couple N be applied about the axis of symmetry of a body supported at its centre of mass, and initially rotating about an axis perpendicular to that of symmetry, determine the motion completely and show that the cone described in the body by the instantaneous axis of rotation has the equation

$$2AN\left[x^2 + y^2)\tan^{-1}\left(\frac{y}{x}\right)\right] = C(A - C)\Omega^2 z^2$$

where Ω is the initial angular speed of rotation.

12.17 A flywheel of mass m and radius a is executing a free rotation about a fixed point on its shaft. If its precessional angular velocity $\Omega\hat{\boldsymbol{z}}$ and the total angular velocity $\boldsymbol{\omega}$ make an angle α, find the locations of the body cone, space cone and the time to make one complete revolution of the body cone around the space cone. What happens to the motion if a constant gravity force is switched on along $-\hat{\boldsymbol{z}}$?

12.18 A pair of locomotive wheels of radius r on the respective rails are negotiating a curve in the railway track, that has a radius of curvature R. If the speed of the locomotive remains constant at v_o, find the angular velocity of precession of the system and the torque required for this negotiation. Show that the torque can be produced by increasing the elevation of the outer track gently over the total length l of the bend. Find the condition for equalisation of the two torques if h = superelevation of the outer track and s = track gauge.

12.19 If the surface of a sphere is vibrating slowly in such a way that the principal moments of inertia are harmonic functions of time

$$I_{zz} = \frac{2mr^2}{5}(1 + \epsilon \cos \omega t) \qquad I_{xx} = I_{yy} = \frac{mr^2}{5}(2 - \epsilon \cos \omega t)$$

where $\epsilon \ll 1$. The sphere is simultaneously rotating with angular velocity $\boldsymbol{\Omega}(t)$. Show that the z-component of $\boldsymbol{\Omega}$ remains approximately constant. Show also that $\boldsymbol{\Omega}(t)$ precesses around the z-axis with a precession frequency $\omega_p = (3\epsilon\Omega_z/2)\cos \omega t$ provided $\Omega_z \gg \omega$.

12.20 A symmetrical top is spinning with its vertex in contact with a rough horizontal plane. Initially the axis of the top is at rest and makes an angle $\pi/3$ with the upward vertical, the spin about the axis being $2\sqrt{Mgh/C}$. Prove that after the axis is released its inclination to the vertical oscillates between $\pi/3$ and $\pi/2$, and that in the latter position the angular velocity of precession is $\sqrt{Mgh/A}$.

12.21 If the outer surface of the earth is assumed to be an oblate spheroid (equatorial radius a, polar radius c) with the principal moments of inertia about its centre A, A and C, and it rotates with an angular velocity Ω about the polar axis, show that the expressions for the effective acceleration due to gravity g_{eff} at the poles g_p and at the equator g_e are given by

$$g_e = \frac{GM}{a^2}\left(1 + \frac{a - c}{c} - \frac{3}{2}\frac{\Omega^2 a^3}{GM}\right) \quad \text{and} \quad g_p = \frac{GM}{a^2}\left(1 + \frac{\Omega^2 a^3}{GM}\right)$$

where M is the mass of the earth and G the Newtonian constant of gravitation.

12.22 (i) Show that the condition for secular stability of a freely rotating rigid body (that is, with the angular momentum $\boldsymbol{L}$ = constant) having a moment of inertia I is given by the absolute minimum of the effective potential

$$V_{\text{eff}} = V + \frac{1}{2}\frac{L^2}{I}$$

(ii) Consider the example given at the end of section 12.27. Show that for $\omega^2 < g/a$, the effective potential has an absolute minimum at $\theta = 0$, but for $\omega^2 > g/a$, the minimum shifts to $\theta = \theta_c = \cos^{-1}(g/\omega^2 a)$. Will the shot suddenly jump to the new state of stable equilibrium or do it gradually, if the above critical limit in ω is crossed from below? Solve the equation of motion and describe the path it follows.

12.23 Determine the period of small amplitude oscillations of a uniform hemisphere which lies on a smooth horizontal surface in the field of gravity, keeping its plane surface up. Consider also the more general case in which the sphere is arbitrarily cut by a horizontal plane and is made to oscillate about the symmetry axis.

12.24 Do a better analysis of the power demand in walking. Suppose the power P is spent not only in raising the CG of the body (P_1) in each stride but also in accelerating and decelerating the legs ($P_2 = P - P_1$) in each stride. Consider also the effect of finite foot length a_f in considering the length of strides a. Find the functional form for P as $P(v,a)$ and show that P has a minimum for some intermediate length of strides.

12.25 Show that a backspinning ball while bouncing off from a surface always experiences a greater decrease in both translational kinetic energy and in total energy than a forward spinning ball, so that the ball slows down to a great extent. This is why a backspinning cricket ball gives rise to a very slow catch within yards of the striker.

12.26 (i) Show that the maximum range of a triple jump is approximately twice the maximum range of the long jump.
(ii) If the maximum height of a high jump is H and the maximum attainable speed in horizontal running v_o, find the maximum height achieved in a pole vault.

12.27 (i) Why do you prefer to locate a spacious flat surface of a rock to sit upon, while during diving you prefer to use the minimum area of the water surface to dip in?
(ii) Cats and monkeys jump from a height with any arbitrary initial configuration and always land safely on the ground having rotated their bodies in flight by the right amount. Does this violate the principle of conservation of angular momentum? If not, how?
(iii) While walking, why do your hands swing in opposite directions?
(iv) How will you explain the larger total surface area of the body of a man than that of a woman of the same body weight?

12.28 A chain is suspended keeping both the ends at the same elevation. One end is released. Show that the free end can fall with an acceleration exceeding g.

12.29 Prove the following theorem on elastic collision of two rigid bodies:
The component of relative velocity of points of impact along the impulse direction is exactly reversed.

12.30 It is known that a doubly asymmetric round pebble when left spinning on a flat surface about one of its asymmetric axes suddenly reverses its sense of spinning. This problem has been completely solved by Hermann Bondi only a few years ago. You can give it a try.

13

Elasticity

13.0 INTRODUCTION

In reality no body is strictly rigid but many solid bodies undergo small deformations and return to their original size or configuration when the deforming agency is removed. Such bodies are known as elastic bodies and the property is known as elasticity. Thus a rigid body becomes a *solid body* when the rigidity constraints are minimally relaxed. But then, a solid body consisting of N particles must have assume $3N$ degrees of freedom. Since the displacement of each particle is small, the immediate neighbourhood of the constituent particles is minimally disturbed. In this chapter we study the elastic properties of any solid body assuming that the body is a continuous medium consisting of an infinite number of particles and therefore having infinite degrees of freedom. Thus each point in the body changes its position under deformation. The deformations are assumed to be generally small compared to the extent of the body. A knowledge of tensors is a prerequisite for reading this chapter.

The first law of elastic displacements came from Robert Hooke (1635 – 1703). A weak boy from birth, he suffered throughout his life, from chronic inflammation of his frontal sinuses in childhood, to severe indigestion, giddiness and insomnia in later years. No portrait of his exists today. When he was 30, in a meeting of the Royal Society, someone described him as 'one who is the most, and promises the least, of any man in the world that I ever saw'. At the age of 18, he entered Oxford university as a student, and assisted Robert Boyle in designing air pumps. Boyle's law was possibly due to Hooke! In 1660, he conceived the fundamental idea of a simple spring to control the oscillations of a balance wheel in a watch. A few years later, he invented the spiral spring, but lost to Huygens in the claim of priority. He published *Lectures de Potentia Restitution or of Spring* in which he stated his law of elasticity and its implications.

However, the major stalwarts of this field are once again Euler, Lagrange, Cauchy, Lamé, Young and Poisson. Like Euler, Augustine Louis Cauchy (1789 – 1857) was a prolific writer of papers, producing more than 700 original papers, many of which are longer than 100 pages. However, the modern treatment of elasticity in terms of tensor notations got its basic motivation from Albert Einstein, who used the concept of the stress-energy tensor in his formulation of the general theory of relativity. Landau and Lifshitz's book on elasticity is strongly recommended for a detailed and complete exposition of the subject.

13.1 DISPLACEMENT VECTOR AND THE STRAIN TENSOR

Let us assume that the position vector of any given point of an elastic body, say $\boldsymbol{r} = (x_1, x_2, x_3)$ before deformation, changes to a new position vector $\boldsymbol{r}' = (x_1', x_2', x_3')$ under the action of some deforming agent. The *displacement vector* defined by (see Fig. 13.1)

$$\boldsymbol{u} = \boldsymbol{r}' - \boldsymbol{r} \tag{13.1}$$

can be regarded as a continuous vector field defined over the whole body, so that

$$u_i = x_i' - x_i = u_i(x_1, x_2, x_3) \tag{13.2}$$

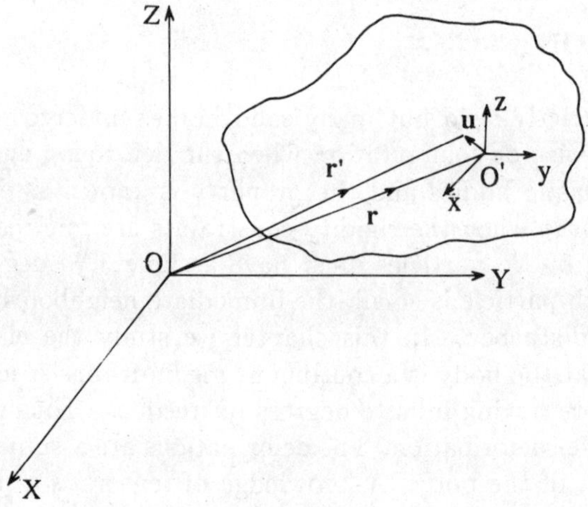

Fig. 13.1 Displacement vector field $\boldsymbol{u}(\boldsymbol{r}) = \boldsymbol{r}' - \boldsymbol{r}$, defined over the region of 3-D space occupied by the elastic body

Let us now expand the displacement $u_i(x_1, x_2, x_3)$ at any point in the body with position vector $\boldsymbol{r}$, in a Taylor's series about the origin O. This gives

$$u_i(x_1, x_2, x_3) = u_i(0,0,0) + \left(\frac{\partial u_i}{\partial x_k}\right)_{\boldsymbol{r}=0} x_k + \frac{1}{2}\left(\frac{\partial^2 u_i}{\partial x_j \partial x_k}\right)_{\boldsymbol{r}=0} x_j x_k + \cdots \tag{13.3}$$

We further assume that for enough small elastic displacements, the linear terms are dominant over the second and higher order terms. In that case we get

$$u_i(x_1, x_2, x_3) = u_i(0,0,0) + a_{ik} x_k \tag{13.4}$$

where

$$a_{ik} = \left(\frac{\partial u_i}{\partial x_k}\right)_{\boldsymbol{r}=0}$$

are constant coefficients, independent of x_1, x_2, x_3. It is now easy to see that apart from a constant, the elastic displacements are linearly homogeneous in x_k, that is,

$$u_i(x_1, x_2, x_3) = u_i(0,0,0) + \frac{\partial u_i}{\partial x_k} x_k \tag{13.5}$$

where

$$a_{ik} = \left(\frac{\partial u_i}{\partial x_k}\right) = \left(\frac{\partial u_i}{\partial x_k}\right)_{\boldsymbol{r}=\boldsymbol{0}} \quad \text{i.e. } a_{ik}\text{'s are independent of } \boldsymbol{r}$$

Thus, under this assumption, the displacement *at any arbitrary point* (x_1, x_2, x_3) of the body is the sum of the displacement at the origin of the coordinate frame and some linearly dependent expansion terms. The first term in Eq. (13.5) is just an additive constant which is the same for all points in the body. So one can interpret the first term in Eq. (13.5) as the uniform displacement of the whole body. Such a uniform displacement is nothing but a translation for the whole body, which cannot be regarded as a deformation. A deformation, by definition, implies displacement differing from point to point; otherwise, the configuration remains identical. Therefore, without loss of generality we can drop the first term from the expansion in Eq. (13.5) as we are interested in elastic deformations. Thus we get, for the displacement at any arbitrary point in the body,

$$u_i(x_1, x_2, x_3) = \left(\frac{\partial u_i}{\partial x_k}\right) x_k = a_{ik} x_k \tag{13.6}$$

Here we have defined the set of quantities a_{ik} for the purpose of the rest of the chapter. These are the rates at which non-translational displacements change for a unit shift of the position. Such quantities are by definition ***strains***, the deformation over any unit distance. Since $\boldsymbol{u}$ is a vector, $\boldsymbol{x}$ is another vector, and a_{ik} are constants (see Eq. (13.5)), the quotient theorem of tensors suggests that a_{ik} must be a tensor. Since the individual components of a_{ik} are nothing but strain like quantities, the full set of nine quantities a_{ik}, $i = 1, 2, 3$, $j = 1, 2, 3$ is called the ***strain tensor***. So for homogeneous linear deformations, Eq. (13.5) requires in total 12 quantities to be fixed. Hence such a body has only 12 degrees of freedom, out of which 3 DOF are due to the translation of the whole body.

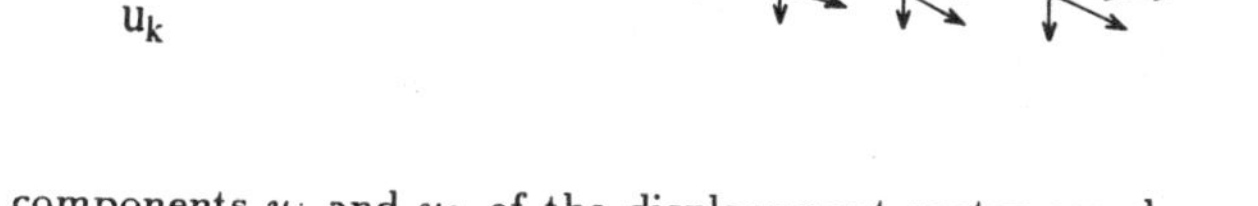

Fig. 13.2 The components u_i and u_k of the displacement vector are shown to vary along the $\hat{\boldsymbol{k}}$-axis, suggesting a possible tensor character of the coefficients a_{ik}

The individual component a_{ik} is the strain produced in the ith component of the deformation if one moves in the direction of the kth axis (see Fig. 13.2). From Eq. (13.6), we can write

$$\begin{aligned} u_i &= \frac{1}{2}(a_{ik} + a_{ki})x_k + \frac{1}{2}(a_{ik} - a_{ki})x_k \\ &= \frac{1}{2}\left(\frac{\partial u_i}{\partial x_k} + \frac{\partial u_k}{\partial x_i}\right)x_k + \frac{1}{2}\left(\frac{\partial u_i}{\partial x_k} - \frac{\partial u_k}{\partial x_i}\right)x_k \\ &= e_{ik}x_k + \omega_{ik}x_k \end{aligned} \tag{13.7}$$

Here $e_{ik} = (a_{ik} + a_{ki})/2$ is the symmetric part of the tensor a_{ik} and $\omega_{ik} = (a_{ik} - a_{ki})/2$ is the antisymmetric part.

Let us take

$$\boldsymbol{r}' = \boldsymbol{r} + \delta\boldsymbol{\theta} \times \boldsymbol{r}$$

so that

$$u_i = \epsilon_{ijl}\delta\theta_j x_l \tag{13.8}$$

Therefore

$$\begin{aligned} \omega_{ik}x_k &= \frac{1}{2}\left(\frac{\partial u_i}{\partial x_k} - \frac{\partial u_k}{\partial x_i}\right)x_k \\ &= \frac{1}{2}[\epsilon_{ijk}\delta\theta_j x_k - \epsilon_{kji}\delta\theta_j x_k] \\ &= \epsilon_{ijk}\delta\theta_j x_k \\ &= u_i \end{aligned} \tag{13.9}$$

Equation (13.9) means that the antisymmetric part of a_{ik} corresponds to a pure rotation of the body as a whole. Proceeding in a similar manner, we obtain for e_{ik}

$$e_{ik}x_k = 0 \tag{13.10}$$

from the definition of u_i given by Eq. (13.8). Thus pure rotation corresponds to no strain at all, which is intuitively obvious.

Thus ω_{ik} corresponds to pure rotation and a pure rotation does not contribute to e_{ik}. Since pure rotation does not bring about any deformation in the body, this part of a_{ik} does not correspond to any straining. Note further that any antisymmetric tensor of second rank can be viewed as an axial vector, say $\boldsymbol{\omega}$, which in this case is given by

$$\boldsymbol{\omega} = \frac{1}{2}\boldsymbol{\nabla} \times \boldsymbol{u} \tag{13.11}$$

Thus the symmetric part e_{ik} of the tensor a_{ik} represents the strain tensor in the true sense of the term.

13.1.1 Properties of e_{ik}

(i) It is a real and symmetric tensor of second rank. Therefore, it can have at most six independent nonzero components. So out of 9 independent components of a_{ik}, 3 independent components are required for the antisymmetric part representing rotation, and the remaining six for purely elastic strain.

(ii) This tensor can be diagonalised by a principal axes transformation. All it means is that one can choose a rectangular triad at the origin in the body, so that only the diagonal components e_{ii} exist and $e_{ij} = 0$ for $i \neq j$.

(iii) Any arbitrary rotational transformation (which is an orthogonal transformation) leaves the trace of the e_{ij} matrix

$$\Delta = e_{11} + e_{22} + e_{33}$$

invariant. Note that

$$\Delta = e_{11} + e_{22} + e_{33} = \frac{\partial u_i}{\partial x_i} = \boldsymbol{\nabla} \cdot \boldsymbol{u} \tag{13.12}$$

13.1.2 Dilation

The rotationally invariant quantity defined by Eq. (13.12) is called *dilation.* The meaning of this term will be apparent from the following considerations.

Let a volume element dV change to dV' under elastic deformation. Let us assume that the tensor a_{ik} can be diagonalised, and choose the principal axes to be the coordinate axes. Let x_i' be the component of the displacement vector along the ith principal axis. Then,

$$x_i' = a_{ii} x_i$$

or

$$dx_i' = dx_i(1 + a_{ii}) \qquad (i \text{ not summed over})$$

Therefore

$$\begin{aligned} dV' &= dx_1' dx_2' dx_3' \\ &= dx_1 dx_2 dx_3 (1 + a_{11} + a_{22} + a_{33}) \\ &= dV(1 + e_{11} + e_{22} + e_{33}) \\ &= dV(1 + \Delta) \end{aligned} \tag{13.13}$$

Now we know that by definition the *volume strain* or the *bulk strain* of the body is given by

$$\frac{dV' - dV}{dV} = \Delta = \boldsymbol{\nabla} \cdot \boldsymbol{u} \tag{13.14}$$

where we have used Eq. (13.13). Thus Δ is simply the volume strain of the body.

Again, it is to be noted that since the antisymmetric part of a_{ik} is given by a curl of some vector, it cannot contribute to the divergence of $\boldsymbol{u}$ as the divergence of the curl of any vector is zero. This result is consistent with the fact that if a body simply rotates through an angle, its volume does not change.

Therefore, when $\Delta = 0$ the volume of the body is not affected by the process of straining.

Another way of looking at the meaning of Δ is the following. By a well known corollary of the divergence theorem we get

$$\Delta = \text{div}\, \boldsymbol{u} = \lim_{V \to 0} \left[\frac{1}{V} \oint_S \boldsymbol{u} \cdot d\boldsymbol{S} \right]$$

where S is the boundary surface of the body. However, since $\boldsymbol{u}$ is the displacement vector field, the surface integral in the above equation is the change in volume δV enclosed by the surface S due to deformation. Therefore,

$$\Delta = \operatorname{div} \boldsymbol{u} = \lim_{V \to 0} \frac{\delta V}{V} \tag{13.15}$$

Assuming that this limit exists and (for the homogeneous strain) is the same for the whole body, we see that Δ is, by definition, the bulk strain of the whole body.

13.1.3 Shearing Strain

Let us assume that for a given solid and a given vector field $\boldsymbol{u}$ defined on it, the strain tensor a_{ik} is symmetric, that is, ω_{ik} in Eq. (13.7) is zero. For a given solid, we say such a vector field $\boldsymbol{u}$ represents a purely strain producing displacement. We can then write,

$$\begin{aligned} u_i &= e_{ik} x_k \\ &= (e_{ik} - \frac{1}{3}\Delta\delta_{ik}) x_k + \frac{1}{3}\Delta\delta_{ik} x_k \\ &= b_{ik} x_k + \frac{1}{3}\Delta\delta_{ik} x_k \end{aligned} \tag{13.16}$$

Here Δ is as defined by Eq. (13.12) and δ_{ik} is the Kronecker δ symbol. Equation (13.16) defines a new tensor b_{ik}. It is easy to see that the tensor b_{ik} is traceless:

$$b_{ii} = b_{11} + b_{22} + b_{33} = \sum e_{ii} - \sum \frac{1}{3}\Delta\delta_{ii} = \Delta - \frac{1}{3}\Delta\, 3 = 0 \tag{13.17}$$

Since b_{ik} is traceless the first term in Eq. (13.16) does not have any dilation, that is, it does not give rise to any change in volume. We know that any nonzero strain that does not induce any change in volume is going to change the shape. Such a strain is called a ***shearing strain*** or a ***shear*** for short. Thus b_{ik} represents the shearing strain.

The second term in Eq. (13.16) namely $(\delta_{ik}\Delta/3)$ is isotropic in nature, with only nonvanishing diagonal components, each equal to $\Delta/3$, so that its trace amounts to Δ or dilation. Thus the tensor $(\delta_{ik}\Delta/3)$ corresponds to the entire bulk strain.

Thus any strain producing displacement can be decomposed into two parts; one related to the shearing strain and the other related to the isotropic bulk strain.

However, in general, any arbitrary infinitesimal displacement leading to a homogeneous strain given by Eq. (13.5) can have four components:

(i) translation of the whole body (number of DOF = 3),

(ii) rotation represented by the antisymmetric part of a_{ik} (number of DOF = 3),

(iii) an isotropic change $\frac{1}{3}\delta_{ik}\Delta x_k$ corresponding to a change in volume without any change in shape (number of DOF = 3) and

(iv) a shear given by $b_{ik}x_k$ corresponding to a change in shape without any change in volume (number of DOF = 3).

Note that the first two motions also apply to a rigid body. Thus the extra degrees of freedom possessed by a homogeneously strained elastic body show up through motions given in (iii) and (iv) above. That a change in volume corresponds to 3 DOF is obvious. Since the strain is homogeneous the displacements u_i at any two points in the body are not independent. In fact, once the shearing displacement u_i at the origin is fixed, those at any other point in the body are also fixed, through the first term of Eq. (13.16) giving rise to 3 DOF for the shear. Thus the total number of DOF for a homogeneously strained body is 12.

There may be a case of straining called *torsion* which falls in the category of shear, and which may not produce any visible change in shape, if the body is under torsion about its symmetry axis. This is in fact a case in which straining occurs internally, without showing any change in the size or the external shape of the body.

In the case of pure strain, that is, when $\omega_{ik} = 0$, Eq. (13.11) gives $\nabla \times \boldsymbol{u} = 0$. Therefore, $\boldsymbol{u}$ can be conveniently derived from a scalar potential function called *strain potential* $\phi(x_1, x_2, x_3)$ through the relation

$$\boldsymbol{u} = -\nabla\phi \tag{13.18}$$

Equation (13.18) means that the displacement $\boldsymbol{u}$ is always perpendicular to the equipotential surface for the strain potential ϕ. Further, for pure shear $\Delta = \nabla \cdot \boldsymbol{u} = 0$ giving

$$\nabla^2\phi = 0 \tag{13.19}$$

which means that, for pure shear, ϕ is a harmonic function.

13.1.4 Strain Ellipsoid

Let us draw a unit sphere about the origin (taken at an arbitrary point in the body) and see how it looks like after a small homogeneous elastic deformation has taken place throughout the body. For simplicity we choose the axes to be the principal axes of the strain tensor e_{ik}. Let the principal components of e_{ik} be e_1, e_2 and e_3 respectively. The displaced coordinate x'_i along the ith principal axis, for any point on the unit sphere, is then given by

$$x'_i - x_i = u_i = e_i x_i$$

or

$$x'_i = x_i(1 + e_i) \qquad (i \text{ is not summed})$$

This gives, for the radius of the sphere,

$$1 = x_1^2 + x_2^2 + x_3^2 = \frac{x'^2_1}{(1 + e_1)^2} + \frac{x'^2_2}{(1 + e_2)^2} + \frac{x'^2_3}{(1 + e_3)^2} \tag{13.20}$$

Hence the deformed unit sphere is an ellipsoid. This ellipsoid is called the *strain ellipsoid* (see Fig. 13.3). The volume of the strain ellipsoid is $1 + \Delta$. Hence a sphere of radius $1 + \frac{1}{3}\Delta$ will have approximately the same volume as that of the strain ellipsoid.

If $e_1 \neq e_2 \neq e_3$, the directions of $\boldsymbol{r}'$, $\boldsymbol{r}$ and $\boldsymbol{u}$ are all different (see Fig. 13.3) except when $\boldsymbol{r}$ is along any one of the principal axes. Hence, in general there is shear. But the geometrical structure of a general shear is not a simple one. The circles of intersection between the strain ellipsoid and the sphere of radius $R = (1 + (\Delta/3))$ form the bases of two cones about which a general shear occurs (see Fig. 13.3).

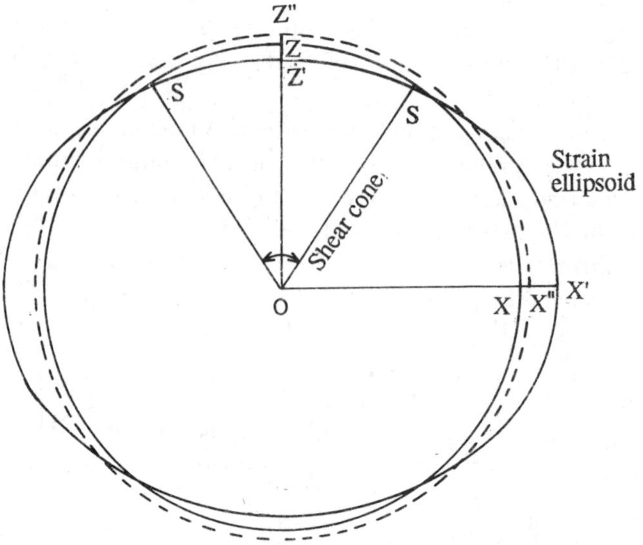

Fig. 13.3 A section of the strain ellipsoid in the x-z plane. The original circle (actually sphere) is deformed to an ellipse (ellipsoid) with a change in area (volume), keeping however, certain directions (on the surface of a cone) undeformed

It is customary to express general shear as a combination of three simple shears about any three mutually perpendicular (triad) axes, with respect to which e_{ij}s are available with nonzero off-diagonal elements. Any off-diagonal term e_{ij} corresponds to a pure shear about the shearing axis $\hat{\boldsymbol{k}} = \hat{\boldsymbol{i}} \times \hat{\boldsymbol{j}}$ with the amount of shear equal to $2e_{ij}$, which, by definition, is the angle of shear. A symmetric pair of e_{ij} terms ($e_{ij} = e_{ji},\ i \neq j$) imply no stretch along the $\hat{\boldsymbol{k}} = \hat{\boldsymbol{i}} \times \hat{\boldsymbol{j}}$ direction. In this case a stretch of amount e_{ij} along the positive bisector of the $\hat{\boldsymbol{i}}$-$\hat{\boldsymbol{j}}$ axes equals the stretch of amount e_{ij} along the negative bisector of the $\hat{\boldsymbol{i}}$, $\hat{\boldsymbol{j}}$ axes. The combination of these three simple shears (that is, off-diagonal elements of e_{ij} tensor) is somewhat difficult to imagine, but Fig. 13.4 may help visualise such a case.

In Fig. 13.4, □ OPRQ → □ OP'R'Q' after shearing in the plane of the diagram due to the terms e_{ij} and e_{ji}.

$$\begin{aligned}\text{Angle of shear} &= \angle \text{POQ} - \angle \text{P'OQ'} \\ &= \frac{\pi}{2} - \theta \\ &= e_{ij} + e_{ji} = 2e_{ij}\end{aligned}$$

The change in area due to shear is given by (see Fig. 13.4)

$$\square\text{OP'R'Q'} - \square\text{OPRQ} = x_i x_j - x_i x_j (1 - e_{ij}^2) = x_i x_j e_{ij}^2 \tag{13.21}$$

This change is of second order in e_{ij} which implies that the shear does not change the

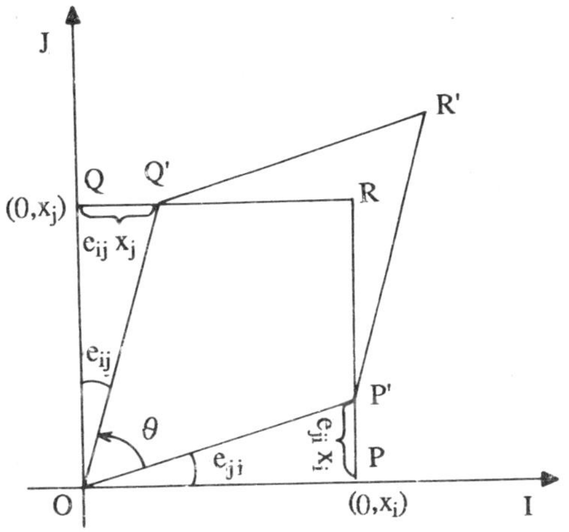

Fig. 13.4 Angle of shear explained. One can verify that pure shearing does not result in a change of volume. Here the rectangle has deformed into a rhombus with a change in area only at the level of the second order of smallness

volume to the first order.

13.2 STRESS TENSOR

In this and later sections we analyse the forces causing deformations and their relations with the resulting strain and other physical attributes of the body.

If the force on any element of volume dV of a body is proportional to dV, or proportional to the amount of matter contained in dV, it is called a *body force*. Examples are gravity, centrifugal force, etc.

A force that is acting on a surface and is in general proportional to the surface area for infinitesimal surface elements is called a *surface force.*

Stress is defined to be the surface force exerted per unit area of the surface. Examples are pressure, force per unit area of sliding friction, etc.

The external forces acting on the outer boundary of the body produce the external stress.

The internal stress is caused by inter-molecular forces. In equilibrium the total internal force inside any volume element is zero. Even the total force between any pair of the nearest neighbour molecules at rest is zero. Under deformation, the restoring forces operate in the form of internal stress. Each part of the body exerts an internal stress through the boundary surface on its adjacent part, in the form of a restoring force per unit area of the separating surface between the two parts of the body, which is deformed infinitesimally.

We now know that, by definition, the stress is the restoring force per unit area of any deformed body. This area element can be placed anywhere inside the body giving any orientation to it. The normal component of stress acting on a given area element in the body is called the normal stress and the tangential component is called the shearing stress.

The stress tensor gives us the full information on the nature of the restoring forces that operate at any given point inside the body specifying both the normal and the shearing stresses acting on all the sides of an infinitesimal cubic volume centred about the given point. We use the Cartesian axes for specifying the directions and the surfaces of the elementary cube.

The stress tensor is a tensor of second rank, so that it requires two indices to specify its elements. The first index stands for the component of the force that it represents and the second index specifies the surface on which the above force component acts. The index for a surface is given by the index for the outward drawn normal to the surface. Thus the ijth component, σ_{ij}, of the stress tensor σ corresponds to the ith component of the force that acts on a unit area of a surface having an outward normal parallel to the jth axis. Obviously σ_{xx}, σ_{yy}, σ_{zz} are the normal stresses while σ_{xy}, σ_{yx}, ..., σ_{zx}, σ_{xz} are the shearing stresses (see Fig. 13.5). Some books however, follow an opposite convention for indexing ij namely, the first index i for the surface and the second index j for the force component. To specify all the elements of the tensor σ_{ij}, note that for i, j running over x, y, z axes, we have

σ_{ij} = Force in the ith direction acting on unit surface area perpendicular to the j axis.

By definition

$$\begin{aligned}\sigma_{ij} &= \lim_{\Delta S_j \to 0} \frac{\Delta f_i}{\Delta S_j} \\ &= \lim_{\Delta S_j \to 0} \frac{i\text{th component of the force acting on the the surface area } \Delta S_j}{\Delta S_j}\end{aligned}$$

Therefore

$$\Delta f_i = \sigma_{ij} \Delta S_j \qquad \text{where} \quad \Delta S_j = \epsilon_{jkl} \Delta x_k \Delta x_l \tag{13.22}$$

Since both Δf_i and ΔS_j are components of vector quantities which are not parallel in general, by the quotient theorem, σ_{ij} must be a tensor of the second rank. However, unlike the strain tensor e_{ij}, the stress tensor σ_{ij} need not always be a symmetric tensor. Now, being a vector by nature, any arbitrary surface (area) element $\boldsymbol{dS}$ can be decomposed into three rectangular components such as

$$\boldsymbol{dS} = dS_1 \hat{\boldsymbol{i}} + dS_2 \hat{\boldsymbol{j}} + dS_3 \hat{\boldsymbol{k}}$$

The net force $\boldsymbol{dF}$ on the surface area element $\boldsymbol{dS}$ due to stresses σ_{ij} is given by the components

$$dF_i = \sigma_{ij} dS_j \tag{13.23}$$

Therefore, the total surface force, acting on the volume V enclosed by the total surface area S is given by

$$F_i = \oint_S \sigma_{ij} dS_j$$

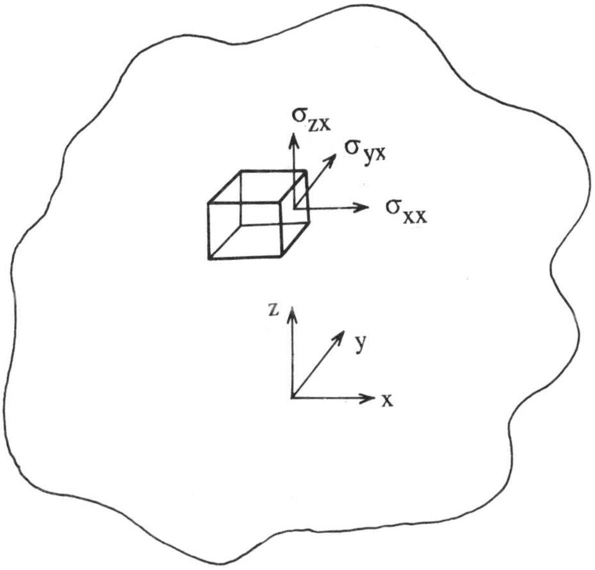

Fig. 13.5 Our adopted convention of defining the indices of a stress tensor explained, namely the first index for the force component, and the second index for the direction of the outward surface normal

which by Gauss' divergence theorem transforms to

$$F_i = \int_V \frac{\partial \sigma_{ij}}{\partial x_j} dV \tag{13.24}$$

Writing $F_i = \int_V f_i dV$ we define

$$f_i = \frac{\partial \sigma_{ij}}{\partial x_j} \tag{13.25}$$

to be the ith component of the volume density of force at any point.

When two bodies are pressed together, the stress acting on one due to the other through the surface of contact is obviously negative, as the force exerted acts along the inward drawn normal to the surface of the latter. So all negative stresses are classified as *pressure*. On the other hand, if the two bodies attract each other through their surface of contact, the stress is positive, and such a stress is called a *traction*. For example, when a rubber band is stretched outward, the internal stress developed over any section of the rubber band is of the traction type.

13.2.1 Conditions for Translational Equilibrium of Elastic Bodies

Consider a portion of continuously deformed elastic medium having volume V enclosed by a surface S. Then the total surface force exerted on this volume V by its surrounding is given by Eq. (13.24). If this volume V also experiences a body force of some external origin say the force of gravity per unit mass $\boldsymbol{F}$, then the ith component of the the total body force experienced by the volume V is

$$\int_V \rho F_i dV$$

Here i stands for the ith component of the body force and ρ stands for the mass density. Hence the ith component of the total force on the enclosed volume V is

$$\int_V \left(\frac{\partial \sigma_{ij}}{\partial x_j} + \rho F_i \right) dV$$

which must vanish if this enclosed portion is to be in translational equilibrium. As V is arbitrary, the condition for translational equilibrium at any point of any continuously deformed elastic body is given by

$$\frac{\partial \sigma_{ij}}{\partial x_j} + \rho F_i = 0 \tag{13.26}$$

where $\boldsymbol{F}$ is the external body force per unit mass of the body. In the absence of such an external body force, the condition for translational equilibrium reduces to

$$\frac{\partial \sigma_{ij}}{\partial x_j} = 0 \tag{13.27}$$

The conditions (13.26) or (13.27) are a set of three scalar equations, each containing 3 terms due to the implied summation over j.

13.2.2 Conditions for Rotational Equilibrium of Elastic Bodies

Let us take the total moment $\boldsymbol{\Gamma}$ of the forces about the origin, that act on a chosen domain of the elastic body enclosing a volume V with a boundary surface S. We have,

$$\Gamma_i = \int_V \rho(\boldsymbol{r} \times \boldsymbol{F})_i dV + \oint_S \epsilon_{ijk} x_j \sigma_{kl} dS_l$$

The second integral can be transformed using Gauss' divergence theorem, so that

$$\begin{aligned}
\Gamma_i &= \int_V \epsilon_{ijk} x_j F_k \rho dV + \int_V \frac{\partial}{\partial x_l} (\epsilon_{ijk} x_j \sigma_{kl})\, dV \\
&= \int_V \epsilon_{ijk} x_j F_k \rho dV + \int_V \epsilon_{ijk} x_j \frac{\partial \sigma_{kl}}{\partial x_l} dV + \int_V \epsilon_{ijk} \delta_{jl} \sigma_{kl} dV \\
&= \int_V \epsilon_{ijk} x_j \left(\rho F_k + \frac{\partial \sigma_{kl}}{\partial x_l} \right) dV + \int_V \epsilon_{ijk} \sigma_{kj} dV
\end{aligned} \tag{13.28}$$

Now let us assume that the body is in translational equilibrium or, in other words, there is no net force on the body. The first of the above integrals vanishes. Now such a body cannot experience a net torque, which requires that $\Gamma_i = 0$. Hence the integrand $\epsilon_{ijk} \sigma_{kj}$ summed over all j and k must vanish. This means

$$\sigma_{jk} = \sigma_{kj} \tag{13.29}$$

In other words, the stress tensor must be symmetric in order that the conditions of translational and rotational equilibrium be simultaneously satisfied. These conditions are fairly basic conditions since the body must remain in a rotational equilibrium state in the absence of any net force acting on the body. Thus if we derive a stress tensor which is not symmetric to start with, we must symmetrise it before using it for studying a physical situation involving a stress tensor. Another way to look at the above result is that, if $\sigma_{jk} \neq \sigma_{kj}$, then the torque produced by the σ_{jk} component will not be balanced by that produced by the σ_{kj} component. An equal but opposite torque is produced by σ_{kj} provided Eq. (13.29) is satisfied.

Since σ_{ij} is a symmetric tensor of second rank it can have at most six independent components.

Again, just like the strain tensor e_{ij}, σ_{kj} should also have the following properties.

1. It can be diagonalised by a principal axes transformation, reducing only to the normal stresses (that is, all shearing stresses vanish for the planes perpendicular to the principal axes). So at every point inside an elastic body, one can orient the infinitesimal cube centred at the point in such a way that the cube does not experience any shearing stress. The axes of this cube are then the principal axes of the stress tensor at the given point.

2. The stress tensor also forms an ellipsoid similar to the strain ellipsoid. The *stress ellipsoid* represented by the equation

$$\psi \equiv \sigma_{ij} x_i x_j = 1 \tag{13.30}$$

is called *Cauchy's stress quadric*. The axes of the ellipsoid correspond to the direction of principal tractions and obviously there is no tangential stress in any of the principal planes.

13.3 Strain Energy

A strained body acquires some energy due to the work done on the body during the process of deformation. We imagine the process of this deformation to be of the virtual type, that is, we only allow the displacement but no instantaneous velocity of the displacement (the latter can happen only if finite real time is allowed to elapse). However, if we account for this velocity, it will contribute to the energy of the system in the form of kinetic energy, and as soon as the body reaches an equilibrium configuration under the action of deformation forces, the kinetic energy part disappears. As our main interest is to find the energy of strain, we drop the kinetic energy associated with the actual process of straining and wait until it reaches the equilibrium state. This is what we mean here when we assume the displacement to be *virtual*.

Consider an elastic body occupying a volume V, enclosed by a surface S before the deformation takes place. The virtual work done on this elastic body due to deformation, resulting in an virtual displacement field u_i is given by

$$\delta W = \int_V \rho F_i \delta u_i dV + \oint_S \sigma_{ik} dS_k \delta u_i \tag{13.31}$$

where, for a given point x_k in the body $u_i = a_{ik}x_k$ so that

$$\delta u_i = (\delta a_{ik})x_k \tag{13.32}$$

and F_i is the external body force per unit mass of the body. Equation (13.32) gives

$$\frac{\partial}{\partial x_k}(\delta u_i) = \delta a_{ik} = \delta\left(\frac{\partial u_i}{\partial x_k}\right) \tag{13.33}$$

Note that δu_i is the variation of the displacement u_i at the same point x_k where the body is deformed infinitesimally. Substituting Eq. (13.33) in (13.31) and transforming the second integral in Eq. (13.31) by Gauss' divergence theorem,

$$\begin{aligned} \delta W &= \int_V \rho F_i \delta u_i dV + \int_V \frac{\partial}{\partial x_k}(\sigma_{ik}\delta u_i)dV \\ &= \int_V \left(\rho F_i + \frac{\partial \sigma_{ik}}{\partial x_k}\right)\delta u_i dV + \int_V \sigma_{ik}\delta a_{ik} dV \end{aligned}$$

The first integral vanishes by virtue of the requirement of translational equilibrium, and therefore,

$$\delta W = \int_V \sigma_{ik}(\delta e_{ik} + \delta\omega_{ik})dV$$

Since σ_{ik} is symmetric and ω_{ik} is antisymmetric,

$$\sum_{i,\,k} \sigma_{ik}\delta\omega_{ik} = 0$$

and hence,

$$\delta W = \int_V \sigma_{ik}\delta e_{ik} dV \tag{13.34}$$

Equation (13.34) gives the work done on the system due to an infinitesimal deformation δu_i. Therefore, the work done by the system per unit volume around any given point in the deformed body is

$$\delta W' = -\lim_{V\to 0}\frac{\delta W}{V} = -\sigma_{ik}\delta e_{ik} \tag{13.35}$$

We have already seen that $-\sigma_{ik}$ plays the role of pressure in the process of straining. Now if we assume the process of straining to be an infinitesimal reversible thermodynamic process carried out at constant temperature T' and pressure p' we can identify $(-\sigma_{ik}de_{ik})$ with $p'dV'$, where dV' is the differential change in the volume. Thus we can write for the total differential of the internal energy $E'(S', V')$ of the body,

$$dE' = T'dS' - p'dV' = T'dS' + \sigma_{ik}de_{ik} \tag{13.36}$$

Similarly for straining at constant pressure p' and entropy S', the total differential of the free energy $F(T', V')$ of the body can be written as

$$dF' = -S'dT' - p'dV' = -S'dT' + \sigma_{ik}de_{ik} \tag{13.37}$$

and for straining at constant entropy and volume, the total differential of the Gibbs function $G'(T', p')$ becomes

$$dG' = -S'dT' + V'dp' = -S'dT' - e_{ik}d\sigma_{ik} \tag{13.38}$$

From Eqs (13.36) and (13.37) we get

$$\sigma_{ik} = \left(\frac{\partial E'}{\partial e_{ik}}\right)_{S'} = \left(\frac{\partial F'}{\partial e_{ik}}\right)_{T'} \tag{13.39}$$

and from Eq. (13.38),

$$e_{ik} = -\left(\frac{\partial G'}{\partial \sigma_{ik}}\right)_{T'} \tag{13.40}$$

These are the basic relations obeyed by the stress and strain tensors through the thermodynamic potentials. If a thermodynamic potential, such as the free energy for any deformed elastic body, is known as an explicit function of the strain tensor e_{ik}, then the stress tensor for such a body can be found out by using Eqs (13.39).

We expect that F' should be an explicit function of T' and e_{ik}, say

$$F' = F_o'(T') + C_{ik}(T')e_{ik} + \frac{1}{2!}C_{iklm}(T')e_{ik}e_{lm} + \frac{1}{3!}C_{iklmpq}(T')e_{ik}e_{lm}e_{pq} + \cdots$$

when expanded in Taylor's series of e_{ik}.

13.4 POSSIBLE FORMS OF FREE ENERGY AND STRESS TENSOR FOR ISOTROPIC SOLIDS

By definition, the physical properties of any isotropic solid should not depend on any specific orientation of the body in space. More specifically, under any arbitrary rotation the physical properties of an isotropic body, say the total free energy content of the body (which is a scalar), must remain invariant. However, by Eq. (13.37), free energy depends on the tensorial quantities, such as the stress and strain tensors, the components of which strictly depend on the choice of orientation of coordinate axes in space. Thus it is necessary that we express the free energy as functions of scalars only; these scalars may be formed out of the e_{ik} tensor.

We know that of all the scalars formed out of a second rank tensor, its trace and magnitude are the only two scalars that have no terms in the cubic or higher order products of the individual elements of the tensor. Therefore, these two quantities, given by

$$e_{ii} = e_{11} + e_{22} + e_{33}$$

and

$$(e_{ik})^2 = e_{ik}e_{ik} = e_{11}^2 + e_{22}^2 + e_{33}^2 + 2e_{12}^2 + 2e_{13}^2 + 2e_{23}^2 \tag{13.41}$$

do not change under arbitrary rotations.

How would be the explicit dependence of F' on e_{ik}? Since in equilibrium (in the absence of any external stress) $e_{ik} = 0$ and $\sigma_{ik} = 0$, from the definition of σ_{ik} given by Eq.

(13.39), F' must not contain any term having a linear dependence on e_{ik}. Thus the simplest form for F' for small isothermal deformations is obtained from the second order terms (by dropping higher order terms) given by

$$F' = F'_o + \frac{1}{2}\lambda(e_{ii})^2 + \mu(e_{ik})^2 \tag{13.42}$$

where only two arbitrary isothermal constants $\lambda(T')$ and $\mu(T')$ are introduced as there are the only two independent bilinear invariant quantities that one could form out of the e_{ik} tensor. These coefficients λ and μ are called *Lamé's coefficients*, after Gabriel Lamé, who introduced these in 1852. F' may be rewritten as

$$F' = F'_o + \frac{1}{2}\lambda(e_{ik}\delta_{ik})^2 + \mu(e_{ik})^2$$

leading to, using Eq. (13.39),

$$\sigma_{ik} = \left(\frac{\partial F'}{\partial e_{ik}}\right)_{T'} = \lambda\delta_{ik}\Delta + 2\mu e_{ik} \tag{13.43}$$

Again, since $\partial F'/\partial e_{ik} = 0$ at $e_{ik} = 0$ which must correspond to a stable equilibrium, F' must be a minimum at $e_{ik} = 0$. Therefore, the conditions

$$\frac{\partial^2 F'}{\partial e_{ik}^2} > 0$$

result in $\lambda+2\mu > 0$ for differentiation with respect to the diagonal elements of e_{ik}, and $\mu > 0$ otherwise. These may be combined to say that the conditions for existence of isothermal stability with respect to small elastic deformations are that both $\lambda > 0$ and $\mu > 0$.

13.5 ELASTIC MODULI FOR ISOTROPIC SOLIDS

The relation between the stress and strain tensors for any isotropic solid given by Eq. (13.43) is a linear relationship and as $e_{ik} \rightarrow 0$, $\Delta \rightarrow 0$ and $\sigma_{ik} \rightarrow 0$. Equation (13.43) can be used to find various elastic moduli for isotropic solids in terms of Lame's coefficients λ and μ, so that λ and μ can in turn be expressed in terms of any two of the elastic moduli.

13.5.1 Young's Modulus and Poisson's Ratio

When an elastic body is subject to a uniform isothermal normal traction in any one direction, that is, producing a stress tensor σ_{ij} of the type $\sigma_{11} \neq 0$ and $\sigma_{ij} = 0$, for all other combinations of i, j, *Young's modulus* is, by definition,

$$Y = \frac{\sigma_{11}}{e_{11}} \tag{13.44}$$

that is, the ratio of the normal longitudinal stress and the longitudinal strain (stretch) produced in the same direction. We can therefore write

$$\begin{aligned} 0 \neq \sigma_{11} &= \lambda\Delta + 2\mu e_{11} \\ 0 = \sigma_{22} &= \lambda\Delta + 2\mu e_{22} \\ 0 = \sigma_{33} &= \lambda\Delta + 2\mu e_{33} \\ 0 = \sigma_{ij} &= 2\mu e_{ij} \qquad \text{for } i \neq j \end{aligned}$$

The second and third of these equations give

$$e_{22} = e_{33} = -\frac{\lambda\Delta}{2\mu} = -\frac{\lambda(e_{11} + e_{22} + e_{33})}{2\mu}$$

so that

$$e_{22} = e_{33} = -\frac{\lambda}{2(\lambda + \mu)} e_{11}$$

Hence from Eq. (13.44)

$$Y = \frac{\sigma_{11}}{e_{11}} = \frac{\mu(2\mu + 3\lambda)}{\lambda + \mu} \tag{13.45}$$

Poisson's ratio is given by

$$\sigma' = \frac{\text{transverse strain}}{\text{longitudinal strain}} = \left|\frac{e_{22}}{e_{11}}\right| = \frac{\lambda}{2(\lambda + \mu)} \tag{13.46}$$

13.5.2 Bulk Modulus

Here the body is stretched uniformly in all directions so that

$$\sigma_{11} = \sigma_{22} = \sigma_{33} \neq 0 \qquad \text{but } \sigma_{ij} = 0 \text{ for } i \neq j$$

The bulk modulus K is, by definition, the ratio of the normal stress and the isothermal volume strain or the isothermal dilation Δ that is produced, that is,

$$K = \frac{\sigma_{11}}{\Delta} \tag{13.47}$$

Using Eq. (13.43)

$$\sigma_{11} = \lambda\Delta + 2\mu e_{11} \qquad \sigma_{22} = \lambda\Delta + 2\mu e_{22} \qquad \sigma_{33} = \lambda\Delta + 2\mu e_{33}$$
$$0 = \sigma_{ij} = 2\mu e_{ij} \qquad \text{for } i \neq j$$

Therefore $e_{ij} = 0$ for $i \neq j$ and as $\sigma_{11} = \sigma_{22} = \sigma_{33}$, $e_{11} = e_{22} = e_{33} = \Delta/3$, giving $\sigma_{11} = \lambda\Delta + 2\mu\Delta/3$ and therefore,

$$K = \frac{\sigma_{11}}{\Delta} = \lambda + \frac{2}{3}\mu \tag{13.48}$$

13.5.3 Modulus of Rigidity

In this case one must apply a shearing stress say, $\sigma_{12} \neq 0$. But this shearing stress alone cannot keep the body in rotational equilibrium. Hence one must also have $\sigma_{12} = \sigma_{21} \neq 0$. Let us now set all the remaining components $\sigma_{ij} = 0$. From Eq. (13.43),

$$e_{12} = e_{21} = \frac{\sigma_{12}}{2\mu}$$

and all other $e_{ij} = 0$.

Now the above conditions produce a shear about the third axis and in the plane of the axes numbered 1 and 2 of an amount $2e_{12}$. Therefore, by definition, the *modulus of rigidity*

$$= \frac{\text{shearing stress}}{\text{shearing strain}} = \frac{\sigma_{12}}{2e_{12}} = \mu$$

Hence Lame's second coefficient μ is itself the *modulus of rigidity* of any isotropic body. Note that, from Eq. (13.43) we can write

$$\begin{aligned}\sigma_{ik} &= \lambda\Delta\delta_{ik} + 2\mu\left(e_{ik} - \frac{1}{3}\Delta\delta_{ik}\right) + \frac{2\mu}{3}\Delta\delta_{ik} \\ &= \left(\lambda + \frac{2\mu}{3}\right)\Delta\delta_{ik} + 2\mu\left(e_{ik} - \frac{1}{3}\Delta\delta_{ik}\right) \\ &= K\Delta\delta_{ik} + 2\mu b_{ik}\end{aligned} \tag{13.49}$$

Equation (13.49) makes the meanings of K and μ more obvious in terms of the isotropic and shearing parts of the strain.

Even though no solid can be ideally isotropic, any homogeneous polycrystalline or amorphous substance can very closely approximate it. The elastic properties of isotropic solids will therefore be applicable to these substances.

13.6 ELASTIC PROPERTIES OF GENERAL SOLIDS: HOOKE'S LAW AND STIFFNESS CONSTANTS

For general solids there may be symmetries in their structure but certainly not as unrestricted as an ideal isotropic solid would have. Any solid which is a single crystal must exhibit the symmetry properties conforming to any one of the seven broadly classified crystal systems, namely, cubic, tetragonal, hexagonal, trigonal, orthorhombic, monoclinic and triclinic systems, ordered from the most symmetric to the least symmetric ones. Although the cubic system is regarded as an optically isotropic system, mechanically it is not so. However let us now consider a most general solid, that is, one belonging to the triclinic system and try to construct the free energy of such a solid as an explicit function of the strain tensor e_{ik}.

Since at equilibrium the condition of no stress should yield no strain, the free energy must not contain any linear terms in e_{ik}. Therefore, one can write F' in a Taylor's series,

$$F' = F'_o + \frac{1}{2!}C_{ijkl}e_{ij}e_{kl} + \frac{1}{3!}C_{ijklmn}e_{ij}e_{kl}e_{mn} + \cdots$$

For small deformations, e_{ij}'s would be small and one can drop the cubic and higher order terms. Since e_{ij} is a tensor of the second rank, C_{ijkl} must be a tensor of the fourth rank, and is called the most general stiffness constant. The stress tensor σ_{ij} corresponding to this free energy is given by

$$\sigma_{ij} = \left(\frac{\partial F'}{\partial e_{ij}}\right)_{T'} = C_{ijkl}\, e_{kl} \tag{13.50}$$

Thus, for small deformations, the stress tensor depends linearly on the strain tensor e_{kl} since C_{ijkl} are constants. This is called the generalised *Hooke's law of elasticity*. Robert Hooke gave this law in its simplest from in 1675.

In order to arrive at this law we had to neglect the cubic and higher order terms in e_{ij} in our expression for the free energy. So we can turn around to say that if Hooke's law is to be accepted as an empirical law of nature, the cubic and higher order terms in e_{ij} in the expression for F' should not dominate the quadratic terms. In fact, there are cases in which, even for small e_{ij}'s, the coefficients C's are such that the cubic terms become comparable to the quadratic ones.

As it stands C_{ijkl} has $3^4 = 81$ components all of which need not be independent. The maximum number of independent components in C_{ijkl} tensor depends crucially on the symmetry properties of σ_{ij} and e_{kl} which in turn depend on the geometrical symmetries of the solid under consideration.

We shall follow Voigt's analysis of the symmetry properties of C_{ijkl}. To start with, Voigt in 1887 introduced a new system of indexing. Noting that both σ_{ij} and e_{ij} are symmetric, we have only six independent components for each of the tensors so that one can treat them as six dimensional vectors. According to Voigt's notation e_{ij} $(i, j = 1, 2, 3)$ is replaced by S_i $(i = 1, 2, \ldots, 6)$ and σ_{ij} by T_i $(i = 1, 2, \ldots, 6)$ with the correspondence

$$11 \to 1,\ 22 \to 2,\ 33 \to 3,\ 23 \to 4,\ 31 \to 5,\ 12 \to 6$$

We can therefore express the free energy in Voigt's notation as

$$F' = F'_o + \frac{1}{2} C_{ij} S_i S_j \tag{13.51}$$

for small deformations S_i. C_{ij} are the elastic stiffness constants which now number 36 in all instead of 81 according to the previous notation. The generalised Hooke's law (13.50) now takes the form

$$T_i = \frac{\partial F'}{\partial S_i} = C_{ij} S_j \qquad i, j = 1, 2, \ldots, 6 \tag{13.52}$$

Since the free energy is a scalar, one could also write it as

$$F'_o + \frac{1}{2} C_{ji} S_j S_i$$

as both i and j are summed; but it would now give $T_i == C_{ji} S_j$ implying that C_{ij} should be a six-dimensional symmetric tensor of rank 2.

Therefore, the total number of independent components in C_{ij} is $6^2 - {}^6C_2 = 36 - 15 = 21$. If a solid is devoid of any symmetry as is the case with triclinic system, the maximum number of independent stiffness constants would be 21.

Again, since the free energy F' has to be a minimum around F'_o for a stable equilibrium against any arbitrary small deformation, the matrix C_{ij} must be positive definite, and therefore, nonsingular and invertible. Thus there exists an inverse of Hooke's law

$$S_i = C'_{ij}T_i \tag{13.53}$$

such that C'_{ij} is the matrix inverse of C_{ij}. The coefficients C'_{ij} are thus called the *compliance constants*.

For a monoclinic system there would be, in total, eight symmetry restrictions to be imposed. This leads to 13 independent stiffness constants. Similarly, there will be only 9 independent stiffness constants for orthorhombic, 6 for trigonal and hexagonal, 5 for tetragonal and 3 for cubic crystals. For example, a cubic crystal would have the following nonzero stiffness constants:

$$C_{ij} = \begin{pmatrix} C_{11} & C_{12} & C_{12} & 0 & 0 & 0 \\ C_{12} & C_{11} & C_{12} & 0 & 0 & 0 \\ C_{12} & C_{12} & C_{11} & 0 & 0 & 0 \\ 0 & 0 & 0 & C_{44} & 0 & 0 \\ 0 & 0 & 0 & 0 & C_{44} & 0 \\ 0 & 0 & 0 & 0 & 0 & c_{44} \end{pmatrix}$$

Therefore, for cubic crystals,

$$\begin{aligned} F' = F'_o &+ \frac{1}{2}C_{11}(S_1^2 + S_2^2 + S_3^2) + C_{12}(S_1S_2 + S_2S_3 + S_3S_1) \\ &+ \frac{1}{2}C_{44}(S_4^2 + S_5^2 + S_6^2) \end{aligned} \tag{13.54}$$

The three independent stiffness constants are, C_{11}, C_{12}, and C_{44}.

For isotropic solids, there is one more symmetry with respect to the cubic case namely the choice of the axes. In the case of a cubic crystal the choice of the rectangular axes cannot be arbitrary, but for an isotropic solid this also becomes arbitrary. Hence in the expression for the free energy an extra condition appears in the form of

$$C_{11} - C_{12} = C_{44}$$

One can now easily identify C_{12} with λ, C_{44} with 2μ and C_{11} with $\lambda + 2\mu$ for isotropic solids.

13.7 ELASTIC PROPERTIES OF ISOTROPIC SOLIDS

The two independent elastic constants for isotropic solids are Lame's constants, λ and μ. Since μ is the rigidity modulus, in some sense, it should also define the ***rigidity***. If μ is everywhere infinite so that e_{ij} vanish for any finite σ_{ij}, the substance is an ideal rigid body. If μ is finite but nonzero then the substance is a perfect solid. Finally, if $\mu = 0$ the substance is a perfect fluid, that is, there cannot be any shearing stress developed in the motion of this fluid. Only the nonzero normal stress components will exist and correspond to the hydrostatic pressure p, so that for ideal fluids, from Eq. (13.43) with $\mu = 0$, and

$\lambda = K$,

$$\sigma_{ij} = -p\delta_{ij} = K\Delta\delta_{ij} \tag{13.55}$$

We know that

$$\Delta = \frac{\text{final volume} - \text{initial volume}}{\text{initial volume}}$$

For an ideal gas the final volume is finite but the unstrained initial volume is infinite. Hence $\Delta = -1$ giving

$$p = K \tag{13.56}$$

Thus the isothermal bulk modulus for an ideal gas is equal to its hydrostatic pressure.

13.7.1 Interrelations Between Elastic Constants

Since only two constants are independent, all others can be expressed in terms of the chosen first two. For example,
In terms of μ and λ,

$$Y = \frac{\mu(2\mu + 3\lambda)}{\mu + \lambda} \qquad \sigma' = \frac{\lambda}{2(\lambda + \mu)} \qquad K = \lambda + \frac{2\mu}{3} \tag{13.57}$$

In terms of K and μ,

$$Y = \frac{9K\mu}{3K + \mu} \qquad \sigma' = \frac{1}{2}\frac{3K - 2\mu}{3K + \mu} \tag{13.58}$$

In terms of Y and σ' (Poisson's ratio),

$$\lambda = \frac{Y\sigma'}{(1 + \sigma')(1 - 2\sigma')} \qquad K = \frac{Y}{3(1 - 2\sigma')} \qquad \mu = \frac{Y}{2(1 + \sigma')}. \tag{13.59}$$

13.7.2 Limits of Poission's Ratio

The free energy $F'(T', V')$ of an elastic body must be at a minimum when the body is in a thermodynamically stable state. From the relation

$$dF' = -S'dT' - p'dV'$$

we get

$$p' = -\left(\frac{\partial F'}{\partial V'}\right)_{T'}$$

Therefore, the *isothermal bulk modulus*,

$$K = -V'\left(\frac{\partial p'}{\partial V'}\right)_{T'} = V'\left(\frac{\partial^2 F'}{\partial V'^2}\right)_{T'}$$

Since V' and $(\partial^2 F'/\partial V'^2)_{T'}$ are both positive for a thermodynamically stable state, we see that the isothermal bulk modulus K must also be positive. We have already seen that the rigidity modulus μ should similarly be a positive constant. Hence putting $K > 0$ and

$\mu > 0$ we get for Poisson's ratio, from Eq. (13.58),

$$-1 \leq \sigma' \leq \frac{1}{2} \tag{13.60}$$

However, Eq. (13.57), coupled with the conditions $\lambda \geq 0$ and $\mu \geq 0$ gives

$$0 \leq \sigma' \leq \frac{1}{2} \tag{13.61}$$

Observationally, no substance has been found with a negative value of σ', confirming the general validity of the condition (13.61) in preference to (13.60). For a rubber-like object $\sigma' \to 1/2$, for earth-like solids $\lambda \simeq \mu$ giving $\sigma' = 1/4$.

13.7.3 Interrelation Between σ_{ik} and e_{ik}

Equation (13.43), written in terms of (K, μ) and (Y, σ') respectively look like,

$$\sigma_{ik} = \left(K - \frac{2}{3}\mu\right) \Delta\delta_{ik} + 2\mu e_{ik} \tag{13.62}$$

or

$$\sigma_{ik} = \frac{Y}{1 + \sigma'}\left[e_{ik} + \frac{\sigma'}{1 - 2\sigma'}\Delta\delta_{ik}\right] \tag{13.63}$$

Inverting Eq. (13.43) we get

$$e_{ik} = \frac{1}{2\mu}\left[\sigma_{ik} - \lambda\Delta\delta_{ik}\right]$$

To express Δ in terms of σ_{ik} we define the trace of the stress tensor

$$\Sigma = \sigma_{ii} = \sigma_{11} + \sigma_{22} + \sigma_{33} = \lambda\Delta\delta_{ii} + 2\mu e_{ii} = \Delta(3\lambda + 2\mu) \tag{13.64}$$

Using Eq. (13.64) we get

$$e_{ik} = \frac{1}{2\mu}\left[\sigma_{ik} - \frac{\lambda\Sigma}{3\lambda + 2\mu}\delta_{ik}\right] \tag{13.65}$$

This expresses e_{ik} in terms of the σ_{ik}, if the latter components are known *a priori.*

13.7.4 Conditions for Translational Equilibrium Applied to Isotropic Solids

The condition for translational equilibrium of an isotropic solid under the action of an external body force $\boldsymbol{g}$ per unit mass is given by Eq. (13.26),

$$\rho g_i + \frac{\partial \sigma_{ik}}{\partial x_k} = 0$$

Using Eq. (13.43) alongwith the definitions of e_{ik} and Δ, we can write,

$$\begin{aligned}
\frac{\partial \sigma_{ik}}{\partial x_k} &= \lambda\delta_{ik}\frac{\partial \Delta}{\partial x_k} + \mu\frac{\partial}{\partial x_k}\left(\frac{\partial u_i}{\partial x_k} + \frac{\partial u_k}{\partial x_i}\right) \\
&= \lambda\delta_{ik}\frac{\partial \Delta}{\partial x_k} + \mu\frac{\partial^2 u_i}{\partial x_k^2} + \mu\frac{\partial}{\partial x_i}\left(\frac{\partial u_k}{\partial x_k}\right) = \lambda\frac{\partial \Delta}{\partial x_i} + \mu\frac{\partial^2 u_i}{\partial x_k^2} + \mu\frac{\partial \Delta}{\partial x_i} \\
&= (\lambda + \mu)\frac{\partial \Delta}{\partial x_i} + \mu\nabla^2 u_i \qquad \left[\nabla^2 \equiv \sum_k \frac{\partial^2}{\partial x_k^2} \ : \text{Laplacian operator}\right]
\end{aligned}$$

Therefore the condition for translational equilibrium is

$$\rho \boldsymbol{g} + (\lambda + \mu)\nabla(\Delta) + \mu\nabla^2\boldsymbol{u} = \boldsymbol{0} \tag{13.66}$$

Note that $\nabla^2\boldsymbol{u}$ is a vector quantity with components $\nabla^2\boldsymbol{u}_i$ $(i = 1,2,3)$. Again, using a well known vector identity for 'curl of curl' we get

$$\nabla \times (\nabla \times \boldsymbol{u}) = \nabla(\nabla\cdot\boldsymbol{u}) - \nabla^2\boldsymbol{u} = \nabla(\Delta) - \nabla^2\boldsymbol{u}$$

or

$$\nabla^2\boldsymbol{u} = \nabla(\Delta) - \nabla \times (\nabla \times \boldsymbol{u})$$

Substituting in Eq. (13.66) gives

$$\rho \boldsymbol{g} + (\lambda + 2\mu)\nabla(\Delta) - \mu\nabla \times (\nabla \times \boldsymbol{u}) = \boldsymbol{0} \tag{13.67}$$

which is another form of the translational equilibrium condition (Eq. (13.66)). Yet another form can be obtained by taking the divergence of Eq. (13.67) which gives

$$\rho\nabla\cdot\boldsymbol{g} + (\lambda + 2\mu)\nabla^2(\Delta) = 0. \tag{13.68}$$

For a gravitational field $\nabla\cdot\boldsymbol{g}$ is given by Poisson's equation, that is, $\nabla\cdot\boldsymbol{g} + 4\pi G\rho = 0$, so that for any isotropic solid resting in a gravitational field we must have

$$\nabla^2(\Delta) = \frac{4\pi G\rho^2}{\lambda + 2\mu}$$

Usually $G\rho^2 \ll \lambda + 2\mu$, giving $\nabla^2(\Delta) \simeq 0$. We can further operate a Laplacian ∇^2 on both sides of Eq.(13.66) to get

$$\nabla^4\boldsymbol{u} = \boldsymbol{0} \tag{13.69}$$

that is, a biharmonic equation is satisfied by the displacement vector field u_i. Equation (13.68) is also valid for $\boldsymbol{g}$ = constant throughout the body.

13.8 PROPAGATION OF ELASTIC WAVES IN ISOTROPIC ELASTIC MEDIA

In this case the body is no longer in translational equilibrium but each point of the solid responds with an acceleration $\partial^2\boldsymbol{u}/\partial t^2$, where $\boldsymbol{u}$ is the displacement at an arbitrary point

(x, y, z).

The equations of motion are

$$\rho \frac{\partial^2 u_i}{\partial t^2} = \rho g_i + \frac{\partial \sigma_{ik}}{\partial x_k} \tag{13.70}$$

or, in vector notation and using Eq. (13.66),

$$\rho \frac{\partial^2 \boldsymbol{u}}{\partial t^2} = \rho \boldsymbol{g} + (\lambda + \mu)\boldsymbol{\nabla}(\Delta) + \mu \nabla^2 \boldsymbol{u} \tag{13.71}$$

or

$$\rho \frac{\partial^2 \boldsymbol{u}}{\partial t^2} = \rho \boldsymbol{g} + (\lambda + 2\mu)\boldsymbol{\nabla}(\Delta) - \mu \boldsymbol{\nabla} \times (\boldsymbol{\nabla} \times \boldsymbol{u}) \tag{13.72}$$

Now taking the divergence of Eq. (13.72), we get

$$\rho \frac{\partial^2 \Delta}{\partial t^2} = \rho(\boldsymbol{\nabla} \cdot \boldsymbol{g}) + (\lambda + 2\mu)\nabla^2(\Delta) \tag{13.73}$$

and taking the curl of Eq. (13.71) gives

$$\rho \frac{\partial^2 \boldsymbol{\omega}}{\partial t^2} = 2\rho(\boldsymbol{\nabla} \times \boldsymbol{g}) + \mu \nabla^2 \boldsymbol{\omega} \tag{13.74}$$

where we have used Eq. (13.11) for the definition of $\boldsymbol{\omega}$.

Equations (13.73) and (13.74) represent the wave equations for the propagation of a Δ-wave and an $\boldsymbol{\omega}$-wave respectively. The first one is a wave of dilation and compression and the second one is a wave of rotational displacement. It is to be noted that if $\boldsymbol{g}$ corresponds to the gravitational field $\boldsymbol{\nabla} \times \boldsymbol{g} = 0$ and $\boldsymbol{\nabla} \cdot \boldsymbol{g} = -4\pi G\rho$, so that Eq. (13.74) becomes independent of the existence of any external field derivable from any potential, such as gravity,

$$\rho \frac{\partial^2 \boldsymbol{\omega}}{\partial t^2} = \mu \nabla^2 \boldsymbol{\omega} \tag{13.75}$$

and in Eq. (13.73) one may neglect div $\boldsymbol{g}$ term if $G\rho^2 \ll \lambda + 2\mu$, then,

$$\rho \frac{\partial^2 \Delta}{\partial t^2} = (\lambda + 2\mu)\nabla^2(\Delta) \tag{13.76}$$

and the general Eq. (13.71) takes the form

$$\rho \frac{\partial^2 \boldsymbol{u}}{\partial t^2} = (\lambda + \mu)\boldsymbol{\nabla}(\boldsymbol{\nabla} \cdot \boldsymbol{u}) + \mu \nabla^2 \boldsymbol{u} \tag{13.77}$$

Obviously, from Eq. (13.76), the speed of propagation of the compressional wave in an isotropic solid is

$$C_l = \sqrt{\frac{\lambda + 2\mu}{\rho}} = \sqrt{\frac{K + 4\mu/3}{\rho}} \tag{13.78}$$

and from Eq. (13.75) the speed of propagation of the torsional wave is

$$C_t = \sqrt{\frac{\mu}{\rho}} < C_l \tag{13.79}$$

For an ideal fluid medium, $\mu = 0$, $C_t = 0$ and

$$C_l = \sqrt{\frac{K}{\rho}} = \sqrt{\frac{p}{\rho}} \tag{13.80}$$

which is the isothermal speed of sound. So ideal fluids cannot transmit any torsional wave. However, in any isotropic solid, the speed of propagation of compressional (longitudinal) waves always exceeds that of torsional waves.

13.8.1 Nature of Plane Wave Solutions

We force a plane wave solution on the differential Eq. (13.77) and see what conditions are needed to be satisfied. In any case, Eqs (13.75) and (13.76) allow a plane wave solutions directly for Δ as well as for $\boldsymbol{\omega}$. Here we use Eq. (13.77) with a general plane wave solution for $\boldsymbol{u}$ given by (see the plane wave solutions of Eq. (10.51))

$$\boldsymbol{u} = \boldsymbol{f}(\boldsymbol{k}\cdot\boldsymbol{r} - \omega' t) \equiv \boldsymbol{f}(\theta) \qquad \text{(say)} \tag{13.81}$$

where $\theta = \boldsymbol{k}\cdot\boldsymbol{r} - \omega' t$, $\boldsymbol{k}$ being the wave vector and ω' the angular frequency of propagation in the direction of $\boldsymbol{k}$.

Now this form of $\boldsymbol{u}$ gives

$$\frac{\partial^2 \boldsymbol{u}}{\partial t^2} = \omega'^2 \frac{\partial^2 \boldsymbol{f}}{\partial \theta^2} \qquad \nabla^2 \boldsymbol{u} = k^2 \frac{\partial^2 \boldsymbol{f}}{\partial \theta^2} \qquad \text{and } \boldsymbol{\nabla}(\Delta) = \boldsymbol{k}\left(\boldsymbol{k}\cdot\frac{\partial^2 \boldsymbol{f}}{\partial \theta^2}\right)$$

and Eq. (13.77) becomes

$$\rho\omega'^2 \frac{\partial^2 \boldsymbol{f}}{\partial \theta^2} = (\lambda + \mu)\boldsymbol{k}\left(\boldsymbol{k}\cdot\frac{\partial^2 \boldsymbol{f}}{\partial \theta^2}\right) + \mu k^2 \frac{\partial^2 \boldsymbol{f}}{\partial \theta^2} \tag{13.82}$$

Taking a scalar product of $\boldsymbol{k}$ with both sides of Eq. (13.82), one obtains the condition for existence of plane wave solution to Eq. (13.77), given by

$$\left[\rho\omega'^2 - (\lambda + 2\mu)k^2\right]\left(\boldsymbol{k}\cdot\frac{\partial^2 \boldsymbol{f}}{\partial \theta^2}\right) = 0 \tag{13.83}$$

This condition is satisfied provided either

(a) $$\rho\omega'^2 = (\lambda + 2\mu)k^2 \quad \text{or} \quad \frac{\omega'^2}{k^2} = \frac{\lambda + 2\mu}{\rho} \equiv C_l^2 \tag{13.84}$$

or

(b) $$\boldsymbol{k}\cdot\frac{\partial^2 \boldsymbol{f}}{\partial \theta^2} = 0 \tag{13.85}$$

When the condition (13.84) is satisfied, Eq. (13.82) becomes

$$k^2 \frac{\partial^2 \boldsymbol{f}}{\partial \theta^2} \doteq \boldsymbol{k}\left(\boldsymbol{k} \cdot \frac{\partial^2 \boldsymbol{f}}{\partial \theta^2}\right) \tag{13.86}$$

which can be satisfied only if the propagational wave vector $\boldsymbol{k}$ is parallel to $\boldsymbol{u}$, the displacement vector. This means that the displacement takes place in the same direction as the plane wave propagates. Such a wave is called a *longitudinal wave* and its speed of propagation is $C_l = \sqrt{(\lambda + 2\mu)/\rho}$ which is the same as the speed of propagation of rarefaction and compression, (see Eq. (13.78)).

For the case (b) we need $\boldsymbol{k}\cdot(\partial^2 \boldsymbol{f}/\partial\theta^2) = 0$ which means that $\boldsymbol{f}\ (\equiv \boldsymbol{u})$ is perpendicular to $\boldsymbol{k}$, if the form of $\boldsymbol{f}$ is that of a plane sinusoidal wave. So the displacement $\boldsymbol{u}$ is transverse to the direction of propagation ($\boldsymbol{k}$). These are the so called *transverse waves.* Now from Eq. (13.82) with condition (b) above, we get,

$$\rho \omega'^2 = \mu k^2 \tag{13.87}$$

so that the speed of propagation of the transverse waves is

$$\frac{\omega'}{k} = \sqrt{\frac{\mu}{\rho}} \equiv C_t$$

It is also possible to eliminate all the vector components of $\partial^2 \boldsymbol{f}/\partial\theta^2$ from the vector Eq. (13.82) and a general dispersion relation $\omega'(\boldsymbol{k})$ can be obtained in the form of a secular equation. Such a dispersion relation turns out to be a sixth degree polynomial in ω' with the solutions given by

$$\frac{\omega'}{k} = \pm\, C_l, \ \pm\, C_t \text{ and } \pm\, C_t$$

implying that there can be two independent transverse modes and one longitudinal mode of elastic waves, each being capable of propagating in both the forward and backward directions (for each mode), in any isotropic solid. These two transverse modes mimic those of light waves propagating in vacuum in the sense that both cases require two degrees of freedom for the description of their polarizations. They are normally referred to as SH (secondary horizontal) and SV (secondary vertical) polarization states for the transverse mode of elastic wave propagations in isotropic solid media.

13.8.2 Seismic Waves

The message of an earthquake is transmitted through the solid body of the earth in the form of propagating elastic waves. One can approximate the earth as an isotropic solid with $\lambda \simeq \mu$ and $\sigma' \simeq 0.25$ so that $C_l : C_t \simeq \sqrt{3} : 1$. In the language of seismology the longitudinal or compressional waves are called P waves (push wave, or primary wave or pressure wave) and the torsional waves are called S waves (shake wave, secondary wave, or shear wave). Obviously P waves arrive earlier than S waves. The time difference of their arrival at a seismic station carries the information of its distance from the centre of the earthquake.

Sound waves, like light waves, undergo regular reflections and refractions across the boundary between two layers of the earth having different density structures. The relative intensities of the seismic waves that are detected at a large number of stations distributed all around the world, can give the most useful information on the density structure of the interior of the earth. We also know that S waves cannot propagate through any perfect fluid. Hence the intricate pattern of the various reflected and refracted P and S waves from different layers of the earth's interior, can also suggest whether the whole of the interior is in the solid state or not.

For example, it is observationally found that no seismic centre receives any strong P wave signal from any earthquake centre if the epicentre of the earthquake lies between 105° and 142° (of the geometric arc) from the receiving centre. This zone is known as the *shadow zone* of the seismic P wave and results from the reflection of P and S waves from a surface of major discontinuity in density and structure lying at a depth of 2900 km from earth's surface. This boundary is called the core mantle boundary across which the speed of P waves drops abruptly from 13.6 km/sec to 8.1 km/sec and that of the S wave from 7.3 km/sec to practically zero. It means that the earth's core is in a fluid state. However, there are certain other complicated features of the P and S wave reflections, that suggest the existence of an inner central core (radius = 1250 km) in a rather solid state.

13.9 SUMMARY

When compared to rigid bodies, homogeneously and linearly strained solid bodies have twice as many degrees of freedom. Out of these 12 degrees of freedom, three are for translation, three for rotation, three for dilation and the rest three for shearing. Dilation corresponds to the trace of the strain tensor, and the shearing is contributed by the off diagonal terms. In the same way as the concept of inertial ellipsoid was introduced in chapter 12 for motions of rigid bodies, the idea of strain ellipsoid is useful for the description of homogeneous elastic strains in elastic bodies. Stress is viewed as a tensor of the second rank. If the rotational equilibrium is a desirable consequence of translational equilibrium of a strained solid body, the stress tensor has to be symmetric. Again, since stresses are supposed to produce strains, the two must be related. For small deformations, this relation is universally linear in nature and gives rise to what is called the generalised Hooke's law of elasticity. But the directions of strains are not, in general, parallel to the directions of applied stresses, requiring that the constants of proportionality in Hooke's law must behave as tensors of the fourth rank. Voigt's ingenious scheme of notation are used to clearly demonstrate that most general solids with least symmetries in its lattice structure will have at most 21 independent elastic constants. The solids of the cubic class have three and the isotropic solids have only two independent elastic constants.

The propagation of elastic waves in an isotropic solid medium can take place in all three perpendicular directions; the longitudinal one is a propagation of the pressure wave and the two degenerate transverse modes correspond to the rotational or shear waves. The speed of propagation of the first one, called P wave, is considerably higher than those of the shear waves called the S waves. This fact is used for inferring the distances to the epicentres of the earthquakes from the seismic stations.

PROBLEMS

13.1 Derive the expressions for strain tensor e_{ij} for finite deformations taking $\boldsymbol{r} \to \boldsymbol{r}' = \boldsymbol{r} + \boldsymbol{u}(\boldsymbol{r})$ and using the Lagrangian definition of e_{ij} given by the line element $dl^2 = (\delta_{ij} + 2e_{ij})dx_i dx_j$. In the Eulerian scheme, the finite deformations are represented by $\boldsymbol{r} \to \boldsymbol{r}' = \boldsymbol{r} + \boldsymbol{u}'(\boldsymbol{r}')$, that is, the displacement vector as a function of the displaced position of the particles. Find the expression for the strain tensor e'_{ij} using the Eulerian definition of e'_{ij} given by $dl^2 = (\delta_{ij} - 2e'_{ij})dx'_i dx'_j$.

13.2 Given a set of a_{ij} $(i, j = 1, 2, 3)$, show that the following six compatibility conditions have to be satisfied in order that the a_{ij}'s represent a possible physical displacement vector field:

$$\frac{\partial^2 a_{ii}}{\partial x_j^2} + \frac{\partial^2 a_{jj}}{\partial x_i^2} = 2\frac{\partial^2 a_{ij}}{\partial x_i \partial x_j}$$

and

$$\frac{\partial^2 a_{ii}}{\partial x_j \partial x_k} = \frac{\partial}{\partial x_i}\left(-\frac{\partial a_{jk}}{\partial x_i} + \frac{\partial a_{ik}}{\partial x_j} + \frac{\partial a_{ij}}{\partial x_k}\right)$$

where i, j, k are not summed and $i \neq j \neq k$.

Suppose $a_{11} = \alpha(x_1^2 - x_2^2)$, $a_{22} = \alpha x_1 x_2$, $a_{12} = a_{21} = \beta x_1 x_2$, where $\alpha = 3 \times 10^{-5}$ and $\beta = 3.5 \times 10^{-5}$. Is the above strain compatible?

13.3 Express the components of the strain tensor e_{ij} in cylindrical polar coordinates (r, ϕ, z) in terms of the u_r, u_ϕ, u_z for the given u_x, u_y, u_z.

A long solid rod of circular cross section undergoes the following displacements $u_r = ar + b/r$, $u_\phi = crz$, $u_z = ez$ (a, b, c, e are constants). Find the expression for the components of the strain tensor, the rotation tensor and dilation.

13.4 The vector field of elastic displacement in a solid is given as follows:

$$u_x = \epsilon(x + 2y + 3z)$$
$$u_y = \epsilon(-2x + y)$$
$$u_z = \epsilon(x + 4y + 2z)$$

where ϵ is a small quantity. Calculate the dilation, rotation and shear. Also find the principal strains and the corresponding principal axes.

13.5 The most general strain tensor representing pure shear in the x-y plane is given by

$$e_{ij} = \begin{pmatrix} a & b & 0 \\ b & -a & 0 \\ 0 & 0 & 0 \end{pmatrix}$$

Find the principal axes of the strain and the corresponding principal strains. Obtain the components of the strain tensor in a frame which is rotated through an angle θ about the z-axis. Using the components find the directions of maximum and minimum (algebraically) extension as well as the maximum angle of shear. Also find the direction in which the length is preserved as well as those lines for which the directions are preserved.

13.6 Consider the following situations of homogeneous strain and stress in an isotropic elastic body and find the remaining normal components of stress and strain tensor:
(i) $\sigma_{11} \neq 0, \ \sigma_{22} \neq 0, \ \sigma_{33} = 0$ as in a thin sheet stressed in its own plane.
(ii) $\sigma_{11} \neq 0, \ e_{22} = 0, \sigma_{33} = 0,$ that is, zero stress and zero extension in two perpendicular directions normal to the stress σ_{11}.

13.7 A rod of length l made of an elastic isotropic solid is hanging vertically under its own weight. Show that the following elastic displacements field maintain the equilibrium

$$u_1 = -\sigma' g\rho x_1 x_3/Y$$
$$u_2 = -\sigma' g\rho x_2 x_3/Y$$
$$u_3 = \frac{\rho g}{2Y}(x_3^2 - l^2) + \frac{\sigma' \rho g}{2Y}(x_1^2 + x_2^2)$$

where σ' = Poisson's ratio, Y = Young's modulus and ρ = density.

13.8 A vertical strut, having length l and a square cross-section with side a, is firmly fixed to the ground. Show that the maximum weight it can carry on its free end without bending is given by $W = \pi^2 a^4 Y/48\, l^2$, Y = Young's modulus for the material of the strut.

13.9 A thin uniform chimney is pivoted at its low end. As the chimney falls, a section through the chimney at some point undergoes a flexion stress and the chimney breaks. Calculate the most probable point of rupture during its fall.

13.10 The displacement vector field $\boldsymbol{u}$ in a plane irrotational wave propagating in a uniform isotropic medium is given by

$$\boldsymbol{u} = A\hat{\boldsymbol{n}} \sin(kx_1 - \omega' t)$$

where $\hat{\boldsymbol{n}}$ is the unit vector parallel to $\boldsymbol{u}$.
State what the direction of $\hat{\boldsymbol{n}}$ is and obtain an expression for e_{ij} and σ_{ij}. Express σ_{22}/σ_{11} in terms of Poisson's ratio. Does the stress σ_{ij} correspond to a uniform hydrostatic compression?

13.11 Assume that the speed of seismic waves in the mantle c_p = 10.85 km/s and c_s = 6.31 km/s, and in the liquid core (radius of the core mantle boundary being 3480 km) c_p = 9.02 km/s and c_s = 0.
(i) After an earthquake, a seismic station records the time delay between the arrival of the S wave following the P wave as 2 min 11 s. Find the distance between the epicentre of the earthquake and the seismic station.
(ii) Calculate the angular radius of the beginning of the shadow zone for direct transmissions of the seismic waves through the mantle.

14

Fluid Dynamics

14.0 INTRODUCTION

In this chapter we deal with motion of matter in a continuous form that exists in the fluid phase, where any relative motion between various parts of the system is permissible. Obviously the number of degrees of freedom becomes virtually infinite, and discrete mechanics cannot handle the situation. An entirely new technique is required, which was primarily developed by Daniel Bernoulli and Leonhard Euler.

Daniel Bernoulli (1700 – 1782), son of Jean Bernoulli, was born in Netherlands. Having got his doctorate in medicine, he became a professor of mathematics at St. Petersburg Academy in 1725. He immediately invited Euler to join the same institute, and both of them had a good time there. It was during his stay in St. Petersburg that Daniel finished his book *Hydrodynamica sive de viribus et motibus fluidorum commentarii* in thirteen chapters, which was finally published in 1738. Having had enough of Euler and Russia, he returned to Basel in Switzerland to become a professor of anatomy and botany and of natural philosophy. However, his father, Jean Bernoulli did not like his son's book on hydrodynamics, particularly the *ad hoc* nature of the equation of motion (the so called Bernoulli's equations of motion), and began to criticise the book openly, in spite of the fact that Bernoulli's equation did explain a lot of natural phenomena.

So D'Alembert got interested in the study of the motion of fluids from the mechanical point of view, following the criticism of Jean Bernoulli, and published a book in 1744 entitled *Traité de l'équilibre et du mouvement des fluides.* D'Alembert also studied the vibrations of strings and obtained the second order partial differential equation for propagating waves in 1747, together with the most general solution. (All these are duly named after D'Alembert.)

Real progress took place only when Euler became interested in fluid dynamics, and decided to resolve the crises raised by the works of Bernoulli and D'Alembert. In 1755, Euler presented a number of papers to the Berlin Academy on the theory and practice of hydrostatics. There he derived his famous equation of motion for perfect fluids, and as a special case derived the Bernoulli equation in a rigorous manner. Even today, people feel uncomfortable about the Bernoulli equation which defies common sense in many respects. We shall try to justify this with the most recent interpretations.

Apart from Bernoulli and Euler, significant contributions have come from Lagrange, Cauchy, Poiseuille, Jacobi, Reynolds, Stokes, Kelvin, Helmholtz, and innumerable other workers. Inclusion of viscosity, turbulence and chaotic behaviour has made modern fluid dynamics flourish in all its diversity, and it is at present one of the most rapidly developing branches of classical physics. Its immediate application to plasma physics and magnetohydrodynamics bring it to the focal point of all such studies, and therefore, one should be properly introduced to the subject, which is the aim of this chapter.

14.1 A FEW BASIC DEFINITIONS

Basic Fluid Dynamical Variables: We assume the system to be a continuous medium and at each point of such a medium there exist scalar point functions, namely the *pressure* $p(x, y, z, t)$ and the *density* $\rho(x, y, z, t)$. If these are also functions of time, the medium must be in a dynamic state. The specification of the state of motion of any constituent particle at any point (x, y, z) is made by defining a vector point function (a vector field) called the *velocity vector field* $\boldsymbol{q}(x, y, z, t)$. The coordinates of any point are always referred to with respect to a fixed frame of reference. These five quantities $\rho(\boldsymbol{r}, t)$, $p(\boldsymbol{r}, t)$ and $q_i(\boldsymbol{r}, t)$, $i = 1, 2, 3$, are regarded as the five basic dynamical variables of the fluid system in motion.

Fluid: A fluid is a continuous medium which has the property that, when it is in (dynamical) equilibrium, the shearing stress must vanish at every point and the pressure function must completely specify the stress tensor. A fluid is said to be in equilibrium when the quantities ρ, p and $\boldsymbol{q}$ do not change with time for an observer moving with a given element of the fluid (see below).

Liquid: A fluid is said to be a liquid if it is possible to confine it in such a way that it exhibits a free boundary surface while it is in equilibrium.

Gas: A fluid is said to be a gas, if any attempt to confine it in a given bounded region defined by rigid boundaries makes it expand to the extent of completely filling the container.

Compressibility: When an increase in the stress acting on a fluid results in a decrease in volume or a proportionate increase in the density, the fluid is said to be *compressible*. If no change in volume occurs subject to any finite change in the value of the stress, the fluid is said to be *incompressible*. To a first approximation most liquids can be regarded as incompressible.

Hydrodynamics: It is the study of motion of incompressible fluids. In fact any prefix *hydro* implies the assumption of incompressibility. This definition of hydro is applicable even to magnetohydrodynamics.

Hydrostatics: It is the study of the properties of incompressible fluids in equilibrium.

Fluid Dynamics: This deals with the motion of both compressible and incompressible fluids.

Perfect Fluid: We have seen that a fluid in equilibrium cannot develop any tangential stress in it. Some fluids can still satisfy this condition even if they are not in a state of equilibrium. Such fluids are called perfect or ideal fluids. Those fluids which develop shearing stresses while having a differential motion are called imperfect or non-ideal fluids. There are further classifications of imperfect fluids which we shall introduce later. For the present we shall assume that the fluid is perfect, that is, the relation,

$$\sigma_{ij} = -p\delta_{ij}$$

is valid for all possible states of motion of the fluid.

14.2 THE CENTRAL PROBLEM OF FLUID DYNAMICS

When the fluid is in motion, its dynamical state at any instant can be completely specified by the knowledge of the five quantities ρ, p, q_1, q_2, q_3. Each of these is a function of $\boldsymbol{r}$ and t. The central problem of fluid dynamics is to determine the explicit dependence of these five dynamical variables on $\boldsymbol{r}$ and t. Thus five non-trivial equations relating these variables are needed in order to solve for them. Specifications of an equation of state, an equation of continuity and one equation of motion in vector form usually satisfy these basic requirements.

14.3 EQUATION OF STATE

An equation of state, by definition, is an explicit relation between the pressure and the density of any given fluid, that is, p as a function of ρ. But more often such a relation also involves other parameters, such as temperature, entropy, etc. This invariably means an increase in the number of variables involved and hence one has to look for extra equations. An ideal gas, for example, has an equation of state $p = \rho RT'/\mu$, where μ is the mean molecular weight of the gas, T' the temperature and R the gas constant. If we want to keep p as a function of ρ alone, we must consider either an isothermal, (that is, T' =constant) case or an adiabatic (that is, isentropic) case, for which $p \propto \rho$ and $p \propto \rho^\gamma$ are respectively valid, with $\gamma = c_p/c_v$, the ratio of the two specific heats. For simplicity one can parametrise the relationship in the form of $p \propto \rho^\gamma$, where γ can be regarded as a constant but adjustable (floating) index. A physicist prefers to call an equation of state 'hard' if $\gamma > 2$, and 'soft' if an effective $\gamma < 2$. However, when $\gamma = 1$, it is the value of the constant of proportionality that defines the hardness of the state. For an incompressible fluid the equation of state is simply ρ = constant, where the constant is independent of p. A fluid for which pressure p depends only on the density is called a *barotropic fluid.*

14.4 TYPES OF TIME RATES OF CHANGE OF QUANTITIES

Before we move on to derive the equation of continuity, we need to introduce three kinds of time derivatives that usually appear in the description of the motion of any fluid.

(i) The *local* rate of change of any quantity is defined to be the rate of change of the quantity measured at a given point in the fluid that is fixed with respect to a fixed frame. If P is a fixed point with coordinates (x, y, z) referred to the fixed frame then the local rate of change of any quantity, say ρ, at P is given by

$$\lim_{\triangle t \to 0} \left(\frac{\triangle \rho}{\triangle t} \right)_{x,y,z=\text{const.}}$$

which is by definition the partial time derivative $\partial \rho / \partial t$. Similarly, for p and $\boldsymbol{q}$, the local rates are $\partial p / \partial t$ and $\partial \boldsymbol{q} / \partial t$, respectively. These are sometimes called the *Eulerian time derivatives.*

(ii) The *substantial* time derivative of a quantity at a point is defined to be the time rate of change of the quantity with respect to an observer moving with the fluid element at the concerned point. This time derivative is also called the *comoving* time derivative or the *Lagrangian* time derivative, and is denoted by D/Dt. Thus if at a given point $\boldsymbol{r}$ and time t, the fluid particle is moving with velocity $\boldsymbol{q}$, then at time $t + \triangle t$, the fluid particle must move to $\boldsymbol{r} + \boldsymbol{q} \triangle t$. Hence, by definition, the comoving time derivative of any quantity, say ρ at $\boldsymbol{r}$ and at time t, is given by

$$\begin{aligned} \frac{D\rho(\boldsymbol{r},t)}{Dt} &= \lim_{\triangle t \to 0} \frac{\rho(\boldsymbol{r} + \boldsymbol{q} \triangle t, t + \triangle t) - \rho(\boldsymbol{r},t)}{\triangle t} \\ &= \frac{\partial \rho}{\partial t} + q_i \frac{\partial \rho}{\partial x_i} \\ &= \frac{\partial \rho}{\partial t} + (\boldsymbol{q} \cdot \nabla) \rho \qquad (14.1) \end{aligned}$$

Similarly for the other derivatives

$$\frac{Dp}{Dt} = \frac{\partial p}{\partial t} + (\boldsymbol{q} \cdot \nabla) p \qquad (14.2)$$

$$\frac{D\boldsymbol{q}}{Dt} = \frac{\partial \boldsymbol{q}}{\partial t} + (\boldsymbol{q} \cdot \nabla) \boldsymbol{q} \qquad (14.3)$$

(iii) The *total* time derivative is the time derivative of any quantity measured with respect to an observer moving with any arbitrary velocity $\boldsymbol{v}$, where $\boldsymbol{v}$ is measured with respect to a fixed frame. This is denoted simply by d/dt. Therefore,

$$\frac{d\rho}{dt} = \frac{\partial \rho}{\partial t} + (\boldsymbol{v} \cdot \nabla) \rho \qquad (14.4)$$

and similarly for p and $\boldsymbol{q}$. Note that when $\boldsymbol{v} = \boldsymbol{q} =$ the velocity of the fluid at $(\boldsymbol{r}, t)$, the total and comoving time derivatives become identical.

To illustrate with an example, let us assume that a fish is watching the flow of water in a river and wishes to know how the pressure changes at a given point. If the fish is fixed with respect to the shore, the time rate of change of pressure at the given point, noted by the fish, is the local rate $\partial p / \partial t$. Now if the fish allows itself to drift with the current so that all the fluid elements in the immediate neighbourhood of the fish appear to remain unchanged to it, the fish will find the pressure changing with time at a rate Dp/Dt. The comoving pressure can change simply because the depth, the flow velocity, etc. may all change with time as the fish drifts along the stream. Lastly, the total time derivative is applicable to the measurement of the rate of change when the fish is moving with any arbitrary velocity, that is, when it prefers to swim. If $\boldsymbol{v}$ is the velocity of the swimming fish with respect to the shore (or any other fixed frame), then

$$\frac{dp}{dt} = \frac{\partial p}{\partial t} + (\boldsymbol{v} \cdot \nabla)p \tag{14.5}$$

Again a few more definitions:

Steady State: A quantity is said to be in a steady state if its local time derivative is zero, that is, $\partial/\partial t = 0$. In other words, at any fixed point the quantity does not change with time.

Equilibrium or Stationary State: A quantity is said to be in equilibrium or stationary state, if its comoving time derivative is zero, that is, $D/Dt = 0$. That is, if one moves with the element of fluid, the quantity under consideration does not seem to change with time.

When the entire fluid motion is in the steady state, none of the quantities p, ρ and $\boldsymbol{q}$ seems to change locally, although they may have different values at different points. That is, they do not have explicit time dependence in their functional form. On the other hand, when the entire fluid is in stationary state (that is, for an equilibrium flow), none of the quantities p, ρ and $\boldsymbol{q}$ should change with respect to any comoving observer associated with any specific fluid element.

14.5 EQUATION OF CONTINUITY

Let a region of space having a total volume V and a boundary surface S be fixed with respect to time. Let a quantity $\psi = \psi(\boldsymbol{r}, t)$ be defined at all points of the fluid and represent a density of some physical quantity (that is, mass density, momentum density, energy density, etc.). The net local rate of this quantity integrated over volume V is, by definition:

$$\frac{\partial}{\partial t} \int_V \psi(\boldsymbol{r}, t) dV$$

This must equal the total rate of its influx through the boundary surface S which consists of two components, one due to the motion of the quantity along with the motion of the fluid through the boundary surface S, that is,

$$-\oint_S (\psi \boldsymbol{q}) \cdot d\boldsymbol{S}$$

and a second component due to a generating flux $\boldsymbol{J}_\psi$ of the quantity at every point of the fluid, giving an influx of

$$-\oint_S \boldsymbol{J}_\psi \cdot d\boldsymbol{S}$$

A total generation of the quantity inside the volume V at a rate g_ψ is also possible which amounts to an increase in the quantity inside V given by

$$\int_V g_\psi dV$$

Thus the equation for the net balance becomes:

$$\frac{\partial}{\partial t}\int_V \psi dV = -\oint_S (\psi \boldsymbol{q})\cdot d\boldsymbol{S} - \oint_S \boldsymbol{J}_\psi \cdot d\boldsymbol{S} + \int_V g_\psi dV \tag{14.6}$$

where g_ψ stands for the rate of creation of ψ per unit volume and $\boldsymbol{J}_\psi$ is the accompanying momentum density (or flux) of the created ψ. It is of course possible to have $g_\psi \neq 0$ but $\boldsymbol{J}_\psi = 0$ (all ψ is created statically), but it would be difficult to imagine a case of $\boldsymbol{J}_\psi \neq 0$ but $g_\psi = 0$.

Now by Gauss' divergence theorem, the RHS of Eq. (14.6) can be transformed to get

$$\int_V \left[\frac{\partial \psi}{\partial t} + \nabla\cdot(\psi\boldsymbol{q}) + \nabla\cdot\boldsymbol{J}_\psi - g_\psi\right] dV = 0 \tag{14.7}$$

Since Eq. (14.7) must hold for any arbitrary volume V, the integrand must vanish at each point inside V, that is,

$$\frac{\partial \psi}{\partial t} + \nabla\cdot(\psi\boldsymbol{q}) + \nabla\cdot\boldsymbol{J}_\psi + g_\psi = 0 \tag{14.8}$$

Equation (14.8) is called the most general form of the equation of continuity, as it is applicable to flux of mass, momentum, energy, heat, etc. Usually the creation factors g_ψ and $\boldsymbol{J}_\psi$ are absent and the equation of continuity takes the form

$$\frac{\partial \psi}{\partial t} + \nabla\cdot(\psi\boldsymbol{q}) = 0 \tag{14.9}$$

Expanding the divergence,

$$\frac{\partial \psi}{\partial t} + \boldsymbol{q}\cdot\nabla\psi + \psi\nabla\cdot\boldsymbol{q} = 0$$

Combining the first two terms,

$$\frac{D\psi}{Dt} + \psi\nabla\cdot\boldsymbol{q} = 0 \tag{14.10}$$

Equations (14.9) and (14.10) are the two standard forms of the equation of continuity when no creation of ψ is taking place in a given region.

Now taking ψ to be the mass density ρ, Eqs (14.9) and (14.10) become

$$\frac{\partial \rho}{\partial t} + \nabla\cdot(\rho\boldsymbol{q}) = 0 \tag{14.11}$$

$$\frac{D\rho}{Dt} + \rho\nabla\cdot\boldsymbol{q} = 0 \tag{14.12}$$

respectively, representing the equation of continuity for mass densities.

Two special cases may be mentioned. First, if the motion is *steady*, that is, $\partial\rho/\partial t = 0$, then $\rho(\boldsymbol{r})$, that is, ρ is no longer an explicit function of time, and the equation of continuity for mass is

$$\nabla\cdot(\rho\boldsymbol{q}) = 0 \tag{14.13}$$

This would mean $\nabla\cdot\boldsymbol{q} = 0$ only if the fluid is incompressible so that ρ is constant throughout.

Second, if the motion is *stationary*, that is, $D\rho/Dt = 0$, then

$$\nabla \cdot \boldsymbol{q} = 0 \tag{14.14}$$

which is valid for any fluid, be it compressible or incompressible, ideal or nonideal.

14.6 APPLICATION TO LIOUVILLE'S THEOREM

Consider the phase space of a conservative system. Under the natural motion of the phase space, the velocity $\boldsymbol{v}$ of any point $(q_1, q_2, \cdots, q_n; p_1, p_2, \cdots, p_n)$ in the phase space is given by the components $\dot{q}_1, \dot{q}_2, \cdots, \dot{q}_n$ and $\dot{p}_1, \dot{p}_2, \cdots, \dot{p}_n$ where n is the number of DOF of the system. Therefore, the divergence of $\boldsymbol{v}$ taken over the $2n$ dimensions of the phase space is:

$$\begin{aligned}
\nabla \cdot \boldsymbol{v} &\equiv \sum_{i=1}^{n} \left(\frac{\partial v_i}{\partial q_i} + \frac{\partial v_i}{\partial p_i} \right) \\
&\equiv \sum_{i=1}^{n} \left(\frac{\partial \dot{q}_i}{\partial q_i} + \frac{\partial \dot{p}_i}{\partial p_i} \right) \\
&= \sum_{i=1}^{n} \left[\frac{\partial}{\partial q_i} \left(\frac{\partial H}{\partial p_i} \right) - \frac{\partial}{\partial p_i} \left(\frac{\partial H}{\partial q_i} \right) \right] \\
&= 0
\end{aligned} \tag{14.15}$$

where $H(q_1, q_2, \cdots, q_n; p_1, p_2, \cdots, p_n; t)$ is the Hamiltonian of the system. If the density of the 'phase fluid' at any instant is ρ, then

$$\frac{D\rho}{Dt} = -\rho(\nabla \cdot \boldsymbol{v}) = 0 \tag{14.16}$$

Hence ρ is stationary, that is, the comoving density of the phase fluid does not change with time. So a region of the phase space containing the particles evolves as a whole but the density of the phase fluid remains unchanged. This is the essence of Liouville's theorem (1838).

14.7 EQUATIONS OF MOTION

We apply Newton's second law of motion to any control volume V bounded by the surface S comoving with the fluid. This gives

$$\begin{aligned}
\int_V \rho \frac{Dq_i}{Dt} dV &= \text{Total force on the boundary surface } S + \text{the body force inside } V \\
&= \int_V \left(\frac{\partial \sigma_{ik}}{\partial x_k} + \rho g_i \right) dV
\end{aligned} \tag{14.17}$$

where σ_{ik} is the stress tensor and $\boldsymbol{g}$ is the externally applied body force per unit mass (see

Eqs (13.24) and (13.26)). Since V is arbitrary we must have

$$\rho\frac{Dq_i}{Dt} = \frac{\partial \sigma_{ik}}{\partial x_k} + \rho g_i. \tag{14.18}$$

Now since $\sigma_{ik} = -p\,\delta_{ik}$ (for a perfect fluid)

$$\frac{\partial \sigma_{ik}}{\partial x_k} = -\frac{\partial p}{\partial x_k}\delta_{ik} = -\frac{\partial p}{\partial x_i}$$

giving

$$\rho\frac{D\boldsymbol{q}}{Dt} = -\boldsymbol{\nabla} p + \rho\boldsymbol{g} \tag{14.19}$$

The vector equation Eq. (14.19) is called *Euler's equation* of fluid motion. It was first derived by Euler in 1755. Note that when the fluid is in equilibrium, that is, $D\boldsymbol{q}/Dt = \boldsymbol{0}$, we get

$$\boldsymbol{\nabla} p = \rho\boldsymbol{g} \tag{14.20}$$

Thus the gradient of pressure has the same direction as that of the externally applied body force at any point. Further when $\boldsymbol{g} = \boldsymbol{0}$ we see that $\boldsymbol{\nabla} p = \boldsymbol{0}$, so that the pressure is constant in space and time. We shall deal with the equilibrium situation later.

Writing $D\boldsymbol{q}/Dt$ explicitly, Eq. (14.19) becomes:

$$\rho\frac{\partial \boldsymbol{q}}{\partial t} + \rho(\boldsymbol{q}\cdot\nabla)\boldsymbol{q} = -\boldsymbol{\nabla} p + \rho\boldsymbol{g} \tag{14.21}$$

Using

$$\boldsymbol{\nabla}(\boldsymbol{q}\cdot\boldsymbol{q}) = 2(\boldsymbol{q}\cdot\nabla)\boldsymbol{q} + 2\boldsymbol{q}\times(\boldsymbol{\nabla}\times\boldsymbol{q})$$

Eq. (14.21) becomes

$$\frac{\partial \boldsymbol{q}}{\partial t} + \frac{1}{\rho}\boldsymbol{\nabla} p + \frac{1}{2}\boldsymbol{\nabla}(q^2) - \boldsymbol{q}\times(\boldsymbol{\nabla}\times\boldsymbol{q}) - \boldsymbol{g} = \boldsymbol{0} \tag{14.22}$$

This is another form of Euler's equation of motion for a perfect fluid.

14.8 PRESSURE POTENTIAL

Let us define the quantity

$$P = \int_{p_0}^{p} \frac{dp'}{\rho} \tag{14.23}$$

to be the pressure potential of the fluid at any given point $\boldsymbol{r}$ and time t. If the equation of state is known and is in the form of p as a function of ρ only (that is, for barotropic fluids), one can determine the pressure potential P. From this definition of P it follows that

$$dP = \frac{dp}{\rho}$$

or

$$\nabla P = \frac{1}{\rho}\nabla p \tag{14.24}$$

For an incompressible fluid ρ = constant, therefore,

$$P = \frac{p - p_0}{\rho} \tag{14.25}$$

One would now like to know whether P signifies some known physical quantity or is just a mathematical object.

From thermodynamics we know that the enthalpy function H' satisfies the following differential relation

$$dH' = T'\,dS' + V'\,dp = T'\,dS' + \frac{dp}{\rho}$$

since $V' = 1/\rho$. This gives the relation

$$(dH')_{S'=\text{const.}} = \frac{dp}{\rho} = dP \tag{14.26}$$

For any adiabatic fluid flow, that is, a flow without loss of heat due to thermal conduction, viscosity, etc. (which is guaranteed by the motion of a perfect fluid), the entropy remains constant. Thus we may say that the motion of perfect fluid corresponds to an ***isentropic*** flow. For such motions of the fluid $P = H'$, that is, the pressure potential is nothing else but the enthalpy of the system.

However, if the motion is ***isothermal***, consider the Gibbs potential function satisfying

$$dG' = -S'\,dT' + V'\,dp = -S'\,dT' + \frac{dp}{\rho}$$

so that, for constant temperature,

$$(dG')_{T'=\text{const.}} = \frac{dp}{\rho} = dP \tag{14.27}$$

Thus the pressure potential may be identified with the Gibbs potential G' if the fluid flow takes place at a constant temperature. Such a fluid flow may even have viscous losses, or in other words, the fluid may even be imperfect in nature.

14.9 EXTERNAL FORCE FIELD

If the external force field is conservative in nature, $\boldsymbol{g}$ may be derived from a potential function, say Ω. That is

$$\boldsymbol{g} = -\nabla\Omega \tag{14.28}$$

For example, the force of gravitation and the centrifugal force of rotation can be derived from suitable potential functions. Hence for a wide variety of situations, Eq. (14.28) would be quite useful. Using Eqs (14.24) and (14.28), Euler's equation (Eq. (14.22)) can be transformed to the following form

$$\frac{\partial \boldsymbol{q}}{\partial t} - \boldsymbol{q} \times (\boldsymbol{\nabla} \times \boldsymbol{q}) = -\boldsymbol{\nabla}\left(\frac{1}{2}q^2 + P + \Omega\right) \tag{14.29}$$

If $\partial \boldsymbol{q}/\partial t = 0$ and $\boldsymbol{\nabla} \times \boldsymbol{q} = 0$, it follows that

$$\boldsymbol{\nabla}\left(\frac{1}{2}q^2 + P + \Omega\right) = \mathbf{0}$$

implying that

$$\frac{1}{2}q^2 + P + \Omega = \text{const.} \tag{14.30}$$

throughout the fluid. This is *Bernoulli's equation*. We shall discuss about it in more detail later.

14.10 CASES OF EQUILIBRIUM FLUID DISTRIBUTION IN PRESENCE OF EXTERNAL FIELDS

These are static cases, in which $D\boldsymbol{q}/Dt = 0$ leading to Eq. (14.20). As noted before, this ascertains that, in equilibrium, the direction of the pressure gradient is the same as that of the external body force at any point. Hence the equipotential surfaces for a conservative external field are also isobaric surfaces.

As water is a fluid, the steady surface of the ocean water must follow the equipotential surface of earth's gravity. Similarly, since the atmosphere is also a fluid, a static atmosphere must produce the same pressure at the mean sea level over any place on earth.

For the earth's constant gravity field $\boldsymbol{g} = -g\hat{\boldsymbol{k}}$, and Eq. (14.20) gives

$$\frac{\partial p}{\partial z} = -\rho g$$

or, on integration along a vertical column,

$$p = p_0 - \int_0^z \rho(z')g\, dz' \tag{14.31}$$

where $p = p_0$ at $z = 0$. For incompressible fluids ρ is constant, and

$$p - p_0 = \rho g h \tag{14.32}$$

for $z = -h$. This is the usual hydrostatic theorem for pressure variation with depth, say, in water.

Even for gases, such as the atmosphere, both ρ and g are positive quantities. Hence $\partial p/\partial z$ is negative, implying that the static pressure of the atmosphere must decrease monotonically upward irrespective of its density variations. Moreover, for an isothermal atmosphere $p = \rho RT'/\mu$ with RT'/μ = constant, so that the pressure variation would be given by

$$\frac{\partial p}{\partial z} = -p\,\frac{\mu\, g(z)}{RT'}$$

Now, if g is assumed to be constant,

$$p = p_0 e^{-\mu g z/RT'} \tag{14.33}$$

and

$$\rho = \rho_0 e^{-\mu g z/RT'} \tag{14.34}$$

where $(\mu g/RT')^{-1}$ is the scale height of the atmosphere, which is 8.8 km for $T' = 300K$, $\mu = 28.8$ and $g = 9.81$ ms^{-2}. Such an exponential (isothermal) atmosphere must extend up to infinity and the pressure and density must drop by a factor of $e = 2.7182$ every 8.8 km above the ground. One can of course find more realistic formulæ, using $p = \rho^\gamma$ (adiabatic variation) and $g = GM/(R_\oplus + z)^2$ instead of a constant.

14.11 BERNOULLI'S THEOREM

14.11.1 A Few More Definitions

(*i*) *Vorticity Vector*: This is defined as

$$\boldsymbol{\omega} = \frac{1}{2}\nabla \times \boldsymbol{q} \tag{14.35}$$

where $\boldsymbol{\omega}$ is a vector point function (vector field) representing the rotation of the fluid.

(*ii*) *Scalar Velocity Potential*: For irrotational motion of the fluid $\boldsymbol{\omega} = \boldsymbol{0} = \nabla \times \boldsymbol{q}$, which means that $\boldsymbol{q}$ can be expressed as the gradient of some scalar potential function $\phi(\boldsymbol{r}, t)$ called the *scalar velocity potential*

$$\boldsymbol{q} = -\nabla\phi \tag{14.36}$$

For an incompressible fluid we have seen that $\nabla \cdot \boldsymbol{q} = 0$. Hence, for an incompressible fluid having an irrotational motion, the scalar velocity potential must satisfy

$$\nabla^2\phi = 0$$

or, more explicitly

$$\frac{\partial^2\phi}{\partial x^2} + \frac{\partial^2\phi}{\partial y^2} + \frac{\partial^2\phi}{\partial z^2} = 0 \tag{14.37}$$

Hence ϕ is a harmonic function for any perfect incompressible fluid that has an irrotational motion.

(*iii*) *Velocity Vector Potential*: For the steady motion of an incompressible fluid flow $\nabla \cdot \boldsymbol{q} = 0$. This means that $\boldsymbol{q}$ can be expressed as the curl of some vector point function, say $\boldsymbol{A}(\boldsymbol{r}, t)$ so that

$$\boldsymbol{q} = \nabla \times \boldsymbol{A} \tag{14.38}$$

where $\boldsymbol{A} = \boldsymbol{A}(\boldsymbol{r}, t)$ is called the *velocity vector potential*. Such fluid flow can have vorticity given by

$$\begin{aligned}\boldsymbol{\omega} &= \frac{1}{2}\nabla \times \boldsymbol{q} \\ &= \frac{1}{2}\nabla \times (\nabla \times \boldsymbol{A}) \\ &= \frac{1}{2}\left[\nabla(\nabla \cdot \boldsymbol{A}) - \nabla^2 \boldsymbol{A}\right]\end{aligned} \tag{14.39}$$

(*iv*)*Streamlines*: If a curve drawn in the fluid at any given instant is such that the direction of the tangent at any point of the curve coincides with that of the velocity of the fluid particle at that point and at that instant, then the curve is called a *streamline*.

If $\hat{\boldsymbol{t}}_s$ is the unit tangent vector to a streamline at a given point, the vector equation for the streamline is given by

$$\hat{\boldsymbol{t}}_s \times \boldsymbol{q} = \mathbf{0} \tag{14.40}$$

as $\hat{\boldsymbol{t}}_s = \boldsymbol{q}/|\boldsymbol{q}|$ by definition. The pattern of the streamlines changes with time for a non-steady motion for which $\partial \boldsymbol{q}/\partial t \neq \mathbf{0}$.

(*v*) *Vortex lines*: A vortex line is a curve drawn in the fluid at any given instant such that the direction of the tangent at any point of the curve coincides with that of the vorticity of the fluid at that point at that instant.

If $\hat{\boldsymbol{t}}_v$ is the unit tangent vector to a vortex line at a point on it, the equation for the vortex line is given by

$$\hat{\boldsymbol{t}}_v \times \boldsymbol{\omega} = \mathbf{0} \tag{14.41}$$

since $\hat{\boldsymbol{t}}_v = \boldsymbol{\omega}/|\boldsymbol{\omega}|$ by definition.

(*vi*) *Stream Tube*: The set of all streamlines that pass through any given closed curve inside the fluid forms a stream tube. (See Fig. 14.1).

(*vii*) *Vortex Tube*: The set of all vortex lines that pass through any given closed curve inside the fluid forms a vortex tube. (See Fig 14.1).

14.11.2 Bernoulli's Theorem

Bernoulli's theorem states that if

(a) the body forces are conservative ,

(b) the density of the fluid is a function of pressure only, (that is, the fluid is barotropic),

(c) the fluid is ideal, and

(d) the flow is steady,

then the quantity

$$\psi = \Omega + P + \frac{1}{2}q^2 \tag{14.42}$$

is constant along every streamline and every vortex line. This theorem was enunciated by Daniel Bernoulli in 1738.

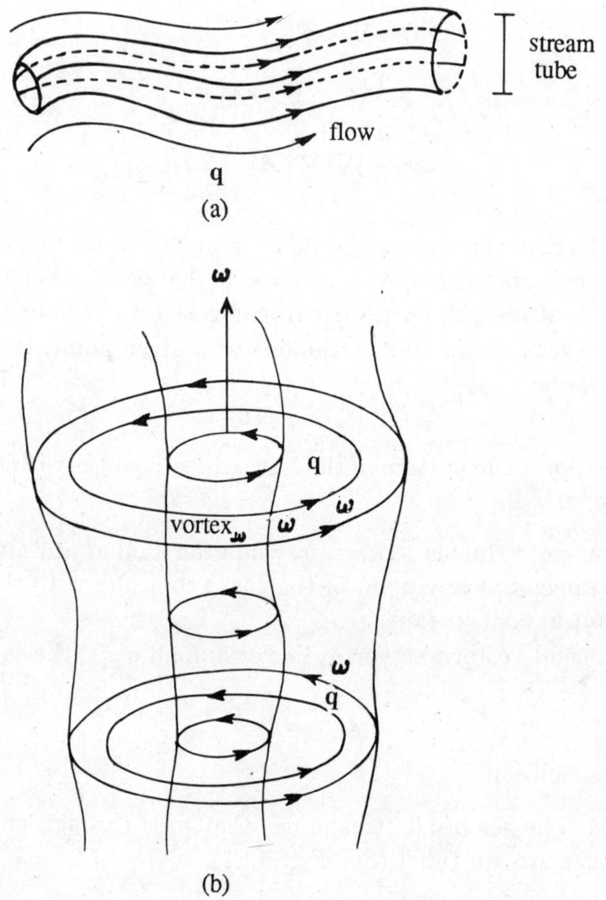

Fig. 14.1 (a) Stream tube and (b) vortex tube

Proof: Euler's equation of motion, Eq. (14.29), gives

$$\frac{\partial \boldsymbol{q}}{\partial t} - \boldsymbol{q} \times (\nabla \times \boldsymbol{q}) = -\nabla \psi$$

where ψ is defined by equation Eq. (14.42). Since the flow is steady $\partial \boldsymbol{q}/\partial t = 0$, and hence

$$2\boldsymbol{q} \times \boldsymbol{\omega} = \nabla \psi \tag{14.43}$$

Taking the scalar product of the above with $\hat{\boldsymbol{t}}_v = \boldsymbol{\omega}/|\boldsymbol{\omega}|$, we get

$$\hat{\boldsymbol{t}}_v \cdot \nabla \psi = 0 \tag{14.44}$$

Now along the vortex line, $d\boldsymbol{r} = |d\boldsymbol{r}|\hat{\boldsymbol{t}}_v$. Let the corresponding change in ψ be $d\psi$. Then by

Eq. (14.44),

$$d\psi = \nabla\psi \cdot d\boldsymbol{r} = \nabla\psi \cdot (|d\boldsymbol{r}|\,\hat{\boldsymbol{\imath}}_v) = |d\boldsymbol{r}|\,(\nabla\psi)\cdot\hat{\boldsymbol{\imath}}_v = 0 \tag{14.45}$$

Therefore along every vortex line, ψ is a constant.

Similarly, taking the scalar product of Eq. (14.43) with $\hat{\boldsymbol{\imath}}_s = \boldsymbol{q}/|\boldsymbol{q}|$, one gets

$$\hat{\boldsymbol{\imath}}_s \cdot \nabla\psi = 0 \tag{14.46}$$

If $d\boldsymbol{r}$ is directed along the tangent to a streamline then by definition $d\boldsymbol{r} = |d\boldsymbol{r}|\,\hat{\boldsymbol{\imath}}_s$. Then a calculation similar to Eq. (14.45), using Eq. (14.46), gives the change in ψ along the streamline to be zero. So ψ remains constant along every streamline. This completes the proof of Bernoulli's theorem.

The function ψ defined by equation Eq. (14.42) is called the *stream function.*

Special cases other than Bernoulli's theorem arise in the following:

(*i*) The motion is steady as well as irrotational, that is, $\boldsymbol{\omega} = 0$ and $\partial\boldsymbol{q}/\partial t = \boldsymbol{0}$. In this case Euler's equation (Eq. (14.29)) becomes

$$\nabla\psi = \nabla\left(\Omega + P + \frac{1}{2}q^2\right) = \boldsymbol{0} \tag{14.47}$$

This means that a displacement in any arbitrary direction by an amount $d\boldsymbol{r}$ results in a corresponding change in ψ by an amount $d\psi = \nabla \cdot d\boldsymbol{r} = 0$, implying that ψ does not change along the arbitrary direction of $d\boldsymbol{r}$. Hence $\psi = \Omega + P + \frac{1}{2}q^2$ has the same constant value at every point of the fluid, at every instant of time. Note that ψ is time independent because motion is steady.

(*ii*) The motion is only irrotational but not steady. Here, $\boldsymbol{\omega} = \nabla\times\boldsymbol{q} = \boldsymbol{0}$ and $\partial\boldsymbol{q}/\partial t \neq \boldsymbol{0}$. In this case $\boldsymbol{q} = -\nabla\phi$ and therefore

$$\frac{\partial\boldsymbol{q}}{\partial t} = -\frac{\partial}{\partial t}(\nabla\phi) = -\nabla\left(\frac{\partial\phi}{\partial t}\right)$$

Hence Euler's equation becomes

$$\nabla\left(\Omega + P + \frac{1}{2}q^2 - \frac{\partial\phi}{\partial t}\right) = \boldsymbol{0}$$

Thus the quantity

$$\psi' = \Omega + P + \frac{1}{2}q^2 - \frac{\partial\phi}{\partial t} \tag{14.48}$$

has the same value at all points but as $\phi = \phi(\boldsymbol{r}, t)$ is a function of time ψ' is in general a function of time.

(*iii*) A steady, irrotational and incompressible fluid. Such a fluid, because of the equation of continuity, (see Eq. (14.37)) satisfies $\nabla^2\phi = 0$, where ϕ is the scalar velocity potential. The solution ϕ of this equation is a harmonic function. Then $\boldsymbol{q} = -\nabla\phi$ gives the velocity distribution at any given point. Since ψ is constant throughout the fluid (from case(*i*) above), we can obtain the pressure distribution by substituting expressions for $\boldsymbol{q}$, Ω and

$P \,(= (p - p_0)/\rho)$ in the equation

$$\psi = \left(\Omega + P + \frac{1}{2}q^2\right) = \text{const.} \tag{14.49}$$

14.11.3 Interpretation of Bernoulli's Theorem

Bernoulli's theorem introduces a constant of motion for ideal barotropic fluids having steady flows, under any system of conservative body forces. As already stated, this constant of motion is called the stream function and is given by Eq. (14.42).

It can be easily seen that Eq. (14.42) is a kind of energy expression, the individual energy terms consisting of the total potential Ω for the externally applied body forces, the pressure potential P and the kinetic potential $\frac{1}{2}q^2$. So far, particle dynamics or even rigid body dynamics have made us aware of only two terms, namely Ω and $\frac{1}{2}q^2$. It is only in the context of fluid dynamics that we come across a new type of energy term P. In fact the existence of such a term is highly justified for the fluid motions, because apart from the translational kinetic energy of the body of the fluid per unit mass ($= \frac{1}{2}q^2$) and the potential energy per unit mass ($= \Omega$) due to the externally applied conservative body forces, the fluid may have a store of internal energy in the form of enthalpy or Gibbs' potential. This energy is due to internal motion of the particles arising due to the random motions that exist at the atomic or molecular level, which do not contribute to the mechanical motion of the fluid as a whole. As soon as the rigidity constraint is released, the individual particles can have internal degrees of freedom in the form of vibrations, rotations and random translations, and the corresponding internal energy no longer remains decoupled from the conditions of the microscopic motion. For point particles and rigid bodies there were no degrees of freedom left for their internal energy in the form of rotation, vibration and random motion of the constituent particles. Therefore, the corresponding equation for energy balance never contained any such internal energy term. However, for fluid motion, the internal energy term appears in the form of enthalpy for the case of isentropic flows and as Gibbs' free energy for isothermal motions.

Although the above interpretation can readily be appreciated for gas flows, one may still feel uncomfortable while applying Bernoulli's theorem to the steady, irrotational motion of incompressible fluids such as water or any other liquid well below their boiling points. For such incompressible fluids, ρ is constant and, therefore, the pressure potential P is $(p - p_0)/\rho$. If we can set $p_0 = 0$ or disregard the constant term $-p_0/\rho$, P is simply given by $P = p/\rho$. The stream function then reduces to

$$\psi = \Omega + \frac{p}{\rho} + \frac{1}{2}q^2 = \text{const.} \tag{14.50}$$

for every streamline (vortex line) of the fluid at all instants of time. For motions under the gravitational field of earth, $\Omega = gh$ near its surface, (where g is the acceleration due to the earth's gravity), leading finally to

$$\psi = gh + \frac{p}{\rho} + \frac{1}{2}q^2 = \text{const.} \tag{14.51}$$

Again, for motions confined to a horizontal plane and assuming h to be very small, (for example, a liquid in a shallow stream), we face the intuitively most puzzling aspect of Bernoulli's theorem; that is

$$\frac{p}{\rho} + \frac{1}{2}q^2 = \text{const.} \tag{14.52}$$

It simply means that if the flow velocity increases downstream, the pressure of the fluid on the same horizontal level must decrease, and vice versa.

Since the fluid is perfect, the pressure at any point is isotropic, that is, the same in all directions, and is defined to be the normal force per unit area exerted on any imaginary surface passing through the point, by either side of the fluid on the other. How can this force change with the speed of the fluid? The fluid is moving in one direction, but the pressure by definition has to remain isotropic, and yet its value changes with the speed of the fluid when the external forces are ineffective (due to the smallness of h).

One way of looking at this problem is to consider energy conservation. The energy (per unit mass) associated with the system having volume V and pressure p is $pV = p/\rho$. In the absence of any other external energy source, the speed of the fluid can increase only at the expense of the energy p/ρ so that Eq. (14.52) can remain valid along every streamline. But this explanation does not say how exactly this transformation takes place. The question still is: what is the mechanism behind the release of the isotropic pressure leading to increase in the speed for the one dimensional motion of the fluid? Actually the whole process of acceleration of the fluid accompanied by a general reduction of pressure is ultimately connected with the geometry of the flow, determined by the geometrical constraints imposed upon the system, which invariably produces extra forces of constraints in the following way.

The equation of continuity for mass motion requires that the total flow rate Q across any surface through which the entire flow is taking place must be the same. If we want to increase the speed of the flow we must constrict the effective cross-sectional area of the flow. This implies the convergence of the streamlines toward the higher speed side of the stream (see Fig. 14.2). The fluid particles following the respective streamlines must experience centrifugal forces acting outwards, while following the bend of the streamlines. This outwardly acting centrifugal force has two effects. Its normal component due to the symmetry of the configuration cannot produce any net effect, but the horizontal component acts to accelerate the fluid and at the same time the pressure is reduced due to the acceleration. (We know that the pressure exerted on the floor of a lift by a person standing motionless with respect to the lift, is reduced if the lift is accelerating in the direction of the applied force. It is due to the same reason that an outwardly moving wall causes a drop in pressure as well as in temperature of a gas during the adiabatic expansion of its container.)

14.12 APPLICATIONS OF BERNOULLI'S THEOREM

For a steady irrotational flow of any incompressible, ideal, barotropic fluid under constant gravitational potential, Bernoulli's theorem takes the form of Eq. (14.52). This implies low pressure at the point of highest velocity of the flow and highest pressure at the point where

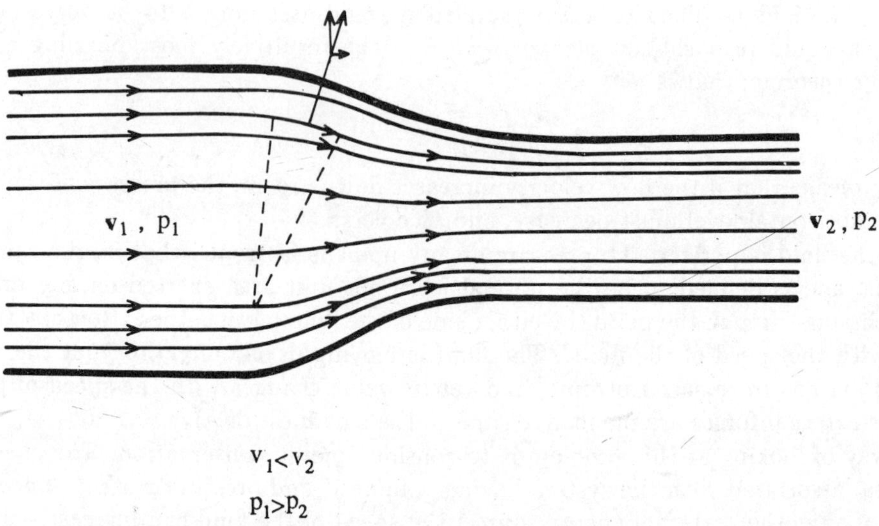

Fig. 14.2 Implication of the curvature of streamlines for accelerating/decelerating the motion of fluid near a constriction, which ought to justify the equation of continuity

the flow becomes momentarily stagnant before taking a turn. Some examples are given here from everyday experience.

(*i*) Pressure on the river banks due to flowing water. Apart from the Coriolis effect the river banks are eroded also due to the pressure exerted by the water wherever its flow is arrested and has to change its direction. A mass of water exerts a tremendous pressure on anything that impedes its flow. For the same reason, during storms the high speed of winds can uproot even a house or a tree due to the pressure of its momentary stagnation.

(*ii*) The opposite phenomena, namely sucking effects come into play when the flow is suddenly released and the pressure drops. If the wind is moving at a very high speed parallel to a particular wall of a house, a sudden opening of the door or window on that side results in a rushing of all light-weight paper material or linen materials in the room towards that door or window. Walking by the side of a railway line can be dangerous, because when a fast moving train passes by, the air very close to it starts moving with a very high speed resulting in a substantial drop in pressure. A passer-by may be immediately sucked in because of the resulting pressure difference. Note that in applying Eq. (14.51) to air motion, we assume that the local density varies negligibly with space and time.

We now give a few scientific applications of the Bernoulli's theorem

(*i*) *Venturimeter*: This device is used to monitor the rate of flow of any incompressible fluid, say water or oil, in the supply pipes (which usually lie underground) without interrupting the flow. The flow is constricted at one place, thereby reducing the area of cross-section from A_1 to A_2 (see Fig. 14.3). This results in a decrease of pressure and a consequent increase in the flow velocity in the constricted part. The equation of continuity requires that the total flow rate Q remain the same everywhere, that is,

$$Q = q_1 A_1 = q_2 A_2$$

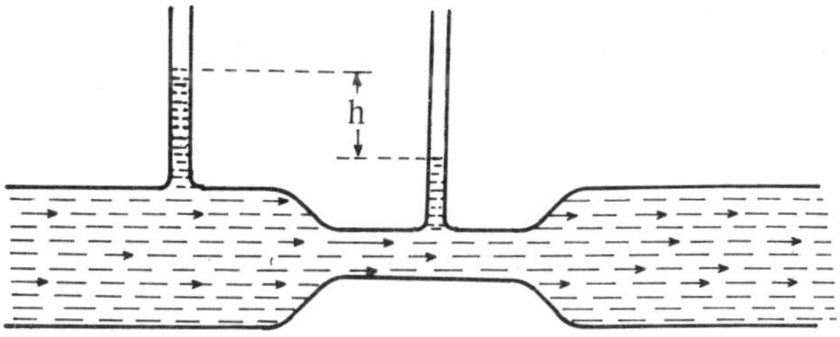

Fig. 14.3 Working principle of venturimeter

Therefore the pressure difference is

$$p_1 - p_2 = \frac{1}{2}(q_2^2 - q_1^2)\rho$$

If a manometer reads the pressure difference in terms of the difference in height h as shown in Fig. 14.3, then

$$p_1 - p_2 = \rho g h$$

giving

$$2hg = Q^2 \left(\frac{1}{A_2^2} - \frac{1}{A_1^2} \right)$$

or

$$Q = \sqrt{2hg \frac{A_2^2 A_1^2}{A_1^2 - A_2^2}} \propto \sqrt{h} \tag{14.53}$$

Therefore the flow rate can be directly checked and measured by noting the manometer readings.

(*ii*) *Bunsen's Jet Exhaust Pump*: A strong jet of air is passed through a sealed tube connected to a chamber to be evacuated (see Fig. 14.4). The high speed of air at the narrow end of the muzzle creates a low pressure region, which sucks in the gas inside the chamber. A vacuum cleaner also works on the same principle.

(*iii*) *One dimensional flow of gas through a nozzle*: Let the x-axis be the axis of the nozzle whose cross-section decreases from left to right, ending finally into the narrow opening of the nozzle through which the fluid comes out with high speed (see Fig. 14.5). Let p_0, ρ_0, q_0 and A_0 be respectively the pressure, density, speed and the cross-sectional area of the fluid

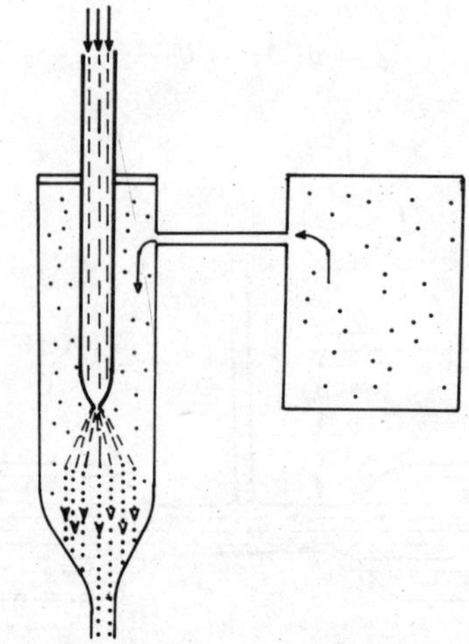

Fig. 14.4 Bunsen's jet exhaust pump

at the mouth of the nozzle (that is, at $x = x_0$ in Fig. 14.5), and let p, ρ, q and A denote the same quantities at some arbitrary value of x. By the equation of continuity we require that the total flow rate Q across any surface through which the entire flow is taking place must remain constant. This means,

$$A\rho q = \text{const.}$$

where q is the x-component of the velocity $\boldsymbol{q}$. Equivalently,

$$\ln A + \ln \rho + \ln q = \text{const.}$$

or differentiating,

$$\frac{1}{A}\frac{dA}{dx} + \frac{1}{\rho}\frac{d\rho}{dx} + \frac{1}{q}\frac{dq}{dx} = 0 \tag{14.54}$$

Assuming the effect of the gravitational potential to be negligible, Bernoulli's theorem gives

$$\frac{1}{2}q^2 + \int_{p_0}^{p} \frac{dp}{\rho(p)} = \text{const.}$$

Noting that p is in general a function of x and that p_0 is a constant, we get, by Leibniz's rule for differentiation of an integral

$$\frac{d}{dx}\int_{p_0}^{p} \frac{dp}{\rho(p)} = \frac{1}{\rho(p)}\frac{dp}{dx}$$

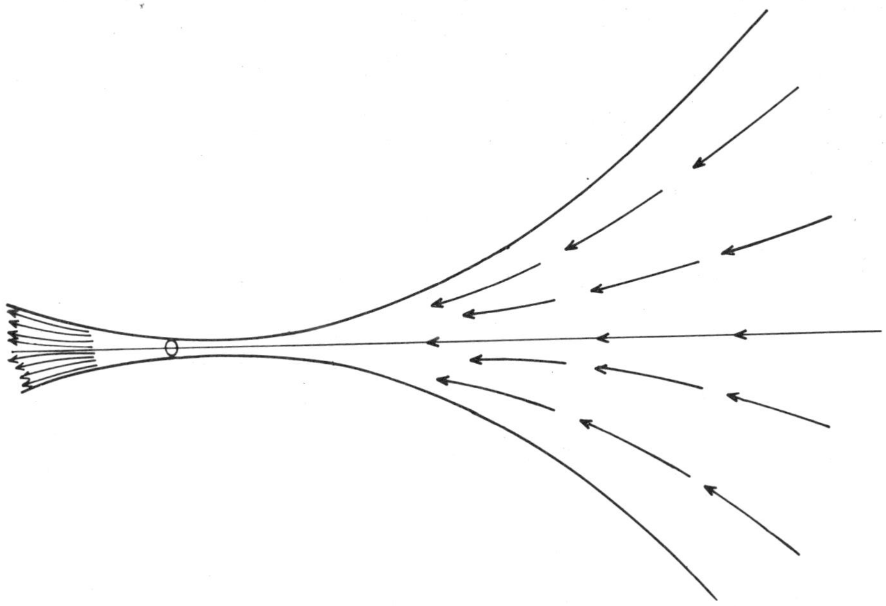

Fig. 14.5 Flow through a constriction

Therefore differentiating Bernoulli's equation with respect to x we get

$$q\frac{dq}{dx} + \frac{1}{\rho}\frac{dp}{d\rho}\frac{d\rho}{dx} = 0 \qquad \text{or} \qquad q\frac{dq}{dx} + \frac{c^2}{\rho}\frac{d\rho}{dx} = 0 \tag{14.55}$$

where $c = \sqrt{(dp/d\rho)}$ is the speed of sound in the medium in question. Using Eq. (14.55), Eq. (14.54) can be written as

$$\frac{1}{A}\frac{dA}{dx} = \frac{1}{q}\left(\frac{q^2}{c^2} - 1\right)\frac{dq}{dx} \tag{14.56}$$

The ratio of the speed of fluid and the speed of sound is called the *Mach number*, denoted by $M \equiv q/c$. Obviously,

(a) $M < 1$ means $q < c$, that is, the flow is *subsonic*,
(b) $M = 1$ means $q = c$, that is, the flow is *sonic*,
(c) $M > 1$ means $q > c$, that is, the flow is *supersonic*.

Thus, from Eq. (14.56)

$$\frac{1}{A}\frac{dA}{dx} = \frac{1}{q}(M^2 - 1)\frac{dq}{dx} \tag{14.57}$$

or

$$\frac{dq}{dA} = \frac{q}{A(M^2 - 1)} \tag{14.58}$$

Now we deal separately with three possible cases.

(a) *Subsonic flow*: For this case $M < 1$, which by Eq. (14.58) implies $dq/dA < 0$. Thus the velocity of the fluid decreases as the cross-sectional area increases. Hence, as the fluid approaches the mouth of the nozzle while having subsonic velocities all the time, the velocity of the flow increases.

(b) *Sonic flow*: Here $M = 1$. Using Eq. (14.57) we get $dA/dx = 0$ for $M = 1$. It means that when the fluid passes through the sonic point, the cross-sectional area of the flow remains unchanged.

(c) *Supersonic flow*: $M > 1$, for which $dq/dA > 0$ by Eq. (14.58). In this case the flow velocity increases with the cross-sectional area, which is quite contrary to its subsonic behaviour.

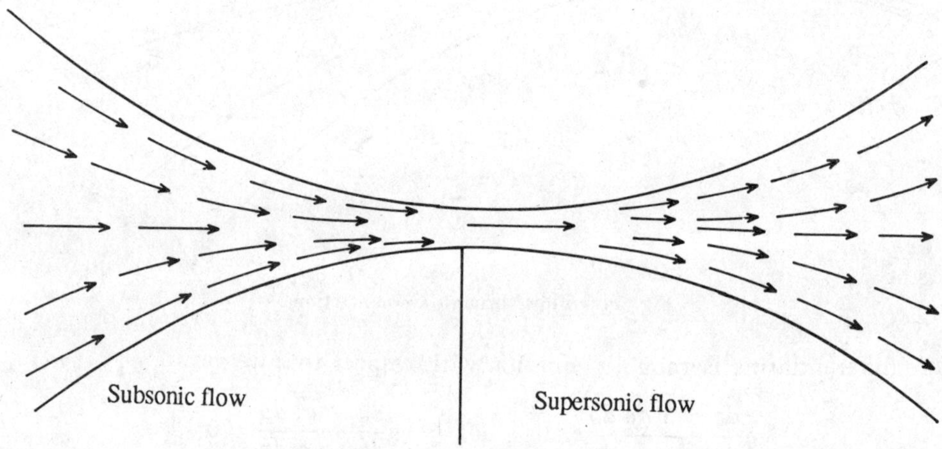

Fig. 14.6 A subsonic flow can become a supersonic one while passing through a narrow enough constriction

The above analysis suggests a way to accelerate the flow speed past the sonic point (see Fig. 14.6). A nozzle is constructed, which opens out on both sides, and the dimension of its neck is such that for some initial velocity field of the gas the flow reaches the sonic point at the most constricted zone. In that case the flow of the fluid can easily be accelerated to large supersonic values of the Mach number M. Since the flow becomes supersonic the density structure no longer remains continuous and a surface of discontinuity of density (called a shock front) develops.

14.13 GRAVITY WAVES AND RIPPLES

14.13.1 Gravity Waves

Suppose a train of waves is propagating on the surface of a pond, lake or sea. The whole column of the water right from the bottom to the free surface, has to take part in it, and such waves are called *body waves*. Since water is incompressible, the wave pattern that we see on the surface cannot be produced just by the vertical oscillation of each liquid molecule. This will defy the equation of continuity. Thus any rise and fall of water seen on the surface must also be accompanied by horizontal motions of the fluid particles. In fact, the passage of a train of waves on an otherwise calm water surface is equivalent to the motion of each fluid particle describing a circle in the vertical plane, with a uniform circular speed $v = 2\pi a/T = 2\pi ac/\lambda$, where a and c are respectively the amplitude and the speed of the wave, T is the time period of one complete circular motion and λ denotes the wavelength. This can be proved as follows (see Fig. 14.7):

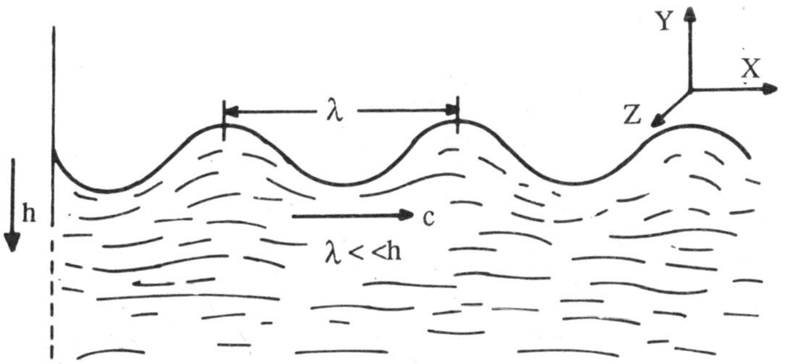

Fig. 14.7 Deep water gravity waves, a case when the wavelength of the waves $\ll$ depth of water

Let $\boldsymbol{u}$ denote the displacement in the vertical plane (that is, the x-y plane). Then the equation

$$\frac{\partial^2 \boldsymbol{u}}{\partial t^2} = c^2 \frac{\partial^2 \boldsymbol{u}}{\partial x^2} \tag{14.59}$$

describes the propagation of displacement in the x-direction with speed c. Now with

$$\begin{aligned} u_x &= a\cos(\omega t - kx + \delta) \\ \text{and} \qquad u_y &= a\sin(\omega t - kx + \delta) \end{aligned} \tag{14.60}$$

$\boldsymbol{u} = u_x\hat{\boldsymbol{i}} + u_y\hat{\boldsymbol{j}}$ satisfies Eq. (14.59). This means that the displacement at an any point (x, y) corresponds to a circular motion of the particle at that point.

Since a wave is propagating in the fluid, it is not in a steady state. In order that the fluid motion appear steady, one has to move with the waves, that is, with a speed c along the positive direction of the x-axis. To such an observer, the fluid motion is steady and the velocity at any point is a function of x alone, not of time. For example,

the velocity at the crest $= v - c = (2\pi ac/\lambda) - c$

and

the velocity at the trough $= -(v + c) = -(2\pi ac/\lambda) - c$

Therefore, Bernoulli's theorem can be applied to the wave motion for an observer moving with the same speed as of the wave and therefore keeping in phase with it.

Let us consider the body waves of very short wavelengths (compared to the depth h of the fluid). The pressure at the trough can be taken to be approximately equal to the pressure at the crest, which again is the same as the atmospheric pressure at that level. So there is no change in pressure over the surface of the wave. But the gravity head has changed by $2a$ between the crest and the trough. Hence by Bernoulli's theorem we must have

$$\frac{1}{2}q_1^2 + \frac{p_1}{\rho} + \Omega_1 = \frac{1}{2}q_2^2 + \frac{p_2}{\rho} + \Omega_2 \tag{14.61}$$

As $p_1 = p_2$, $q_1 = (2\pi ac/\lambda) - c$, $q_2 = -(2\pi ac/\lambda) - c$ and $\Omega_1 - \Omega_2 = 2ga$, the above equation reduces to

$$2ga = \frac{1}{2}\left[\left(\frac{2\pi ac}{\lambda} + c\right)^2 - \left(\frac{2\pi ac}{\lambda} + c\right)^2\right] = \frac{4\pi ac^2}{\lambda}$$

or

$$c = \sqrt{\frac{\lambda g}{2\pi}} \tag{14.62}$$

Thus the speed of the gravity waves, (that is, waves for which $\lambda \ll h$), is independent of amplitude but depends on wavelength. Indeed the longer the wavelength, the higher the speed. Thus very long wavelength deep sea waves will arrive at the shore in the least time. So, if there is a volcanic eruption under the sea, the water waves of longer wavelength will carry the message faster. The same is true for sea storms, such as hurricanes or psunamis, where the sea propagates the message in the form of sending huge deep water waves out to the shore.

14.13.2 Ripples

Ripples are deep water waves of extremely small wavelengths for which the surface tension effects are not negligible. Due to surface tension, the pressure just below the surface of the fluid is different from that on the free surface, which is the atmospheric pressure p_0. The pressure difference due to surface tension T across any surface of a fluid is given by,

$$p = T\left(\frac{1}{R_1} + \frac{1}{R_2}\right) \tag{14.63}$$

where R_1 and R_2 are the two radii of curvature of the surface in two perpendicular sections, both normal to the free surface.

In the above case, in one section (in the y-z plane) the curvature is zero but in the other section (in the x-z plane) the curvature is given by

$$\frac{1}{R} = \left|\frac{d^2y/dx^2}{(1 + dy/dx)^{\frac{3}{2}}}\right|$$

Since the curvature is maximum at the trough as well as at the crest, where $dy/dx = 0$, using Eq. (14.60) we get

$$\frac{1}{R} = \frac{4\pi^2 y}{\lambda^2} \tag{14.64}$$

Therefore, at the crest, the pressure just inside the surface is

$$p_0 + \left|\frac{T}{R}\right| = p_0 + \frac{4\pi^2 aT}{\lambda^2} = p_1$$

Similarly at the trough, the pressure just inside the surface is

$$p_0 - \left|\frac{T}{R}\right| = p_0 - \frac{4\pi^2 aT}{\lambda^2} = p_2$$

Now for this case, Bernoulli's equation takes the following form

$$2ag + \frac{8\pi^2 Ta}{\lambda^2 \rho} = \frac{4\pi ac^2}{\lambda} \tag{14.65}$$

which gives

$$c = \sqrt{\frac{\lambda g}{2\pi} + \frac{2\pi T}{\lambda\rho}} \tag{14.66}$$

For small enough wavelengths the above reduces to

$$c = \sqrt{\frac{2\pi T}{\lambda\rho}} \tag{14.67}$$

which is controlled by the surface tension only. Such small wavelength waves are called ripples. Since the speed of the wave c according to Eq. (14.66) increases both for large and small λ, its value will assume a minimum for some $\lambda = \lambda_{\text{critical}}$ (see Fig. 14.8).

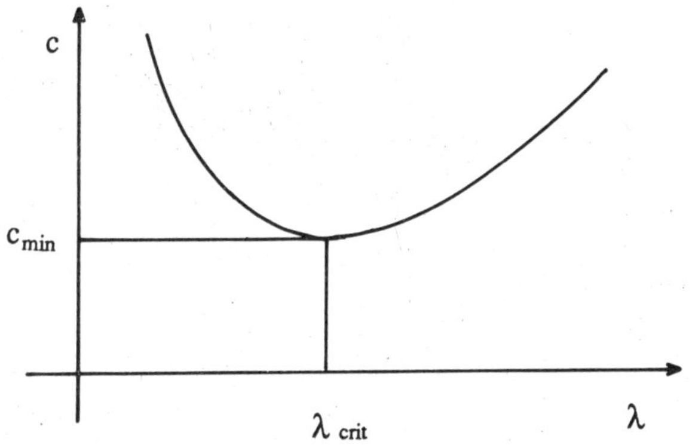

Fig. 14.8 The minimum speed of propagation of surface waves for the critical wavelength of propagation

One can show that

$$\lambda_{\text{critical}} = 2\pi\sqrt{\frac{T}{\rho g}} \quad \text{and} \quad c_{\min} = \left(\frac{4gT}{\rho}\right)^{\frac{1}{4}} \tag{14.68}$$

For water $T = 7.0 \times 10^{-2}$ N/m and $\rho = 10^3$ kg/m^3, therefore

$$\lambda_{\text{critical}} = 0.0172 \text{ m} \qquad \text{and} \qquad c_{\min} = 0.231 \text{ m/s} \tag{14.69}$$

For $\lambda \gg \lambda_{\text{critical}}$, the waves are gravity waves; and for $\lambda \ll \lambda_{\text{critical}}$, the waves are capillary waves or ripples.

The group velocity of these waves is given by

$$v_g = \frac{d\omega}{dk} = \frac{1}{2}c \qquad \text{for gravity waves}$$

$$= \frac{3}{2}c \qquad \text{for ripples}$$

Thus on the water surface, the wave groups raised by a boat or a swarm of fish will travel at half of the speed of the individual crests if $\lambda > 0.02$ m. Similarly, the wave groups will travel faster than the individual crests for $\lambda < 0.015$ m.

Suppose a stream is flowing with a speed $c > 0.23$ m/s and a stone is sticking out of the water surface. The capillary waves formed at the stone will be found to travel up the stream and the gravity waves will propagate down the stream. But if the velocity of the stream is less than 0.23 m/s, no such waves are formed.

14.13.3 Shallow Water Waves

This case applies where the wavelength of the waves λ is very large compared to the depth of the fluid h. The fluid velocity $\boldsymbol{q}$ is then taken to be uniform over any vertical cross-section of the fluid, but $\boldsymbol{q}$ varies with x, the direction of propagation of the waves (see Fig. 14.9a). Let η be the elevation of the wave (see Fig 14.9b). If Bernoulli's theorem is to be applied the observer must move with a speed c which is that of wave propagation. In this case, Bernoulli's theorem gives

$$\frac{1}{2}(q-c)^2 + g(h+\eta) = \frac{1}{2}c^2 + gh$$

and the equation of continuity is

$$(q+c)(h+\eta) = ch$$

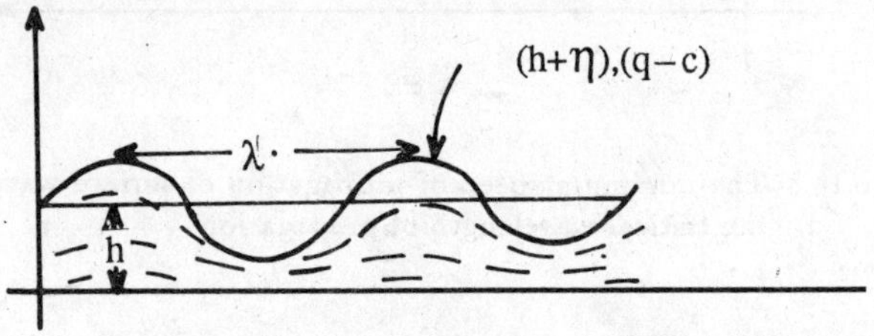

Fig. 14.9 Breakers or shallow water waves; a case when the wavelength of propagation ≫ depth of water

The above two equations give (neglecting $(\eta/h)^2$ and $(q/c)^2$)

$$-qc + g\eta = 0, \qquad \text{and} \qquad qh - c\eta = 0$$

Solving for c, we get

$$c = \sqrt{gh} \tag{14.70}$$

The wave velocity is now independent of both the wave amplitude and wavelength. The speed depends only on the depth h of the water.

If the depth of the water is 10 m, the wave speed is about 10 m/s. This speed decreases, as the wave gradually approaches the shore. One can easily notice how the speed of wave propagation diminishes as the breakers approach the shore line.

14.13.4 The Most General Case

The above three special cases can be derived from the most general result for the speed of the waves given by

$$c^2 = \left(\frac{g\lambda}{2\pi} + \frac{2\pi T}{\lambda\rho}\right)\tanh\left(\frac{2\pi h}{\lambda}\right) \tag{14.71}$$

where h is the depth of the water, T is the surface tension and λ the wavelength. This is left as an exercise.

14.13.5 Streaming and Shooting Flows

When a river is flowing steadily in a straight, uniform, horizontal channel of constant width, the flows can have interesting properties. Let the depth of the water flow be h, and its velocity $\mathbf{q}$. Let us also assume, for convenience, that the width of the flow is unity. Therefore, the discharge rate Q, which is defined to be the volume of liquid flowing per unit width per unit time, is given by

$$Q = qh \tag{14.72}$$

Bernoulli's theorem says that

$$gh + \frac{1}{2}q^2 = \text{const.} = gH \qquad \text{(say)} \tag{14.73}$$

Eliminating q from Eqs (14.72) and (14.73) we get,

$$h^3 - Hh^2 + \frac{Q^2}{2g} = 0 \tag{14.74}$$

Let us define two dimensionless quantities by

$$F = \frac{q}{\sqrt{gh}} = \frac{Q}{\sqrt{gh^3}} \qquad \text{and} \qquad k = \frac{8gH^3}{Q^2} \tag{14.75}$$

In terms of F and k, Eq. (14.74) can be expressed as

$$(2 + F^2)^3 = kF^2 \tag{14.76}$$

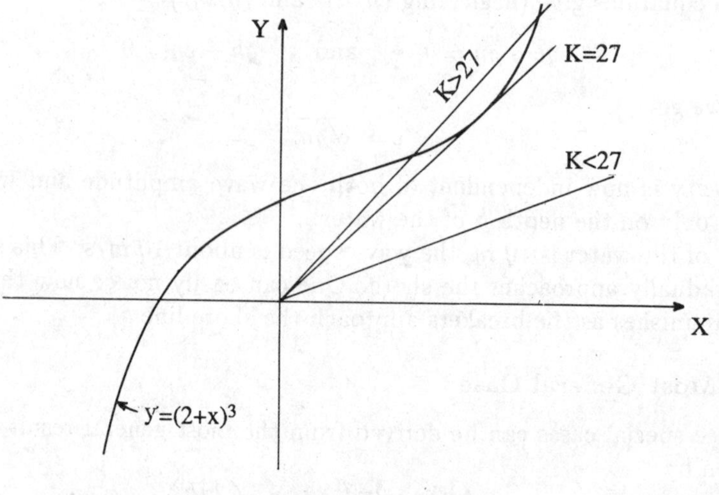

Fig. 14.10 Graphical solution of two simultaneous equations $y = kx$ and $y = (2+x)^3$. No solution exists for $k < 27$, but two discrete solutions do for $k > 27$

This is a transcendental equation and can be solved graphically. Putting $F^2 = x$, the solutions to Eq. (14.76) are given by the intersection of the curves $y = kx$ and $y = (2+x)^3$, shown in Fig. 14.10. Note that if $k < 27$ these two curves never intersect, and therefore there is is no solution. If $k = 27$, the curves touch at $x = 1$ and $y = 27$, which corresponds to the unique solution

$$Q_{\max} = \sqrt{\frac{8gH^3}{27}} \tag{14.77}$$

which in turn implies $q = \sqrt{gh}$. If $k > 27$, there are two points of intersection for $x > 0$, both of which correspond to a value of $Q < Q_{\max}$. One of them is for $F^2 < 1$ implying $q < \sqrt{gh}$, and the other for $F^2 > 1$ implying $q > \sqrt{gh}$. Thus these two solutions classify the stream flows into two distinct types: the former with velocity less than $\sqrt{gh}$ is called the ***streaming flow***, and the latter with velocity greater than $\sqrt{gh}$ is called the ***shooting flow*** (see Fig. 14.10).

This effect is in fact seen in shallow water streams where suddenly the shooting solution jumps to the streaming solution. This happens, for example, near a dam or barrier, where there is a sudden jump in the height of the water column. Loosely speaking, this can be thought of as a fluid mechanical analogue of the quantum jump from one possible eigenstate (of the stream velocity) to the other.

14.14 TWO-DIMENSIONAL STEADY IRROTATIONAL FLOW OF INCOMPRESSIBLE FLUIDS

Since the flow is irrotational we must have $\boldsymbol{q} = -\nabla\phi$, where ϕ is the scalar velocity potential, and since the flow is steady and the fluid is incompressible, $\nabla \cdot \boldsymbol{q} = 0$. Combining these two conditions we have $\nabla^2 \phi = 0$, that is, ϕ satisfies Laplace's equation in two dimensions

$$\frac{\partial^2 \phi}{\partial x^2} + \frac{\partial^2 \phi}{\partial y^2} = 0 \tag{14.78}$$

Similarly, taking divergence of Eq. (14.47), $\nabla^2 \psi = 0$. Therefore ϕ and ψ are harmonic functions.

A planar flow means that the flow extends in two dimensions, say x and y, but the thickness in the z-direction remains constant. Since the description is two-dimensional, a representation of the velocity potential in the complex plane is possible. A large and important class of functions of complex variables z $(= x + iy)$ exists, such that both their real and imaginary parts satisfy Eq. (14.78). The properties of such functions, called analytic functions, can be profitably used to obtain the solution $\phi(x, y)$ of Eq. (14.78). This $\phi(x, y)$ then determines the flow pattern by the relation $\boldsymbol{q} = -\nabla \phi$.

14.14.1 Condition for Analyticity of a Complex Function

Let $f(z)$ be a complex valued function of the complex variable $z = x + iy$ with $f(z) = \phi(x, y) + i\psi(x, y)$, where $\phi(x, y)$ and $\psi(x, y)$ are some real functions of x and y. $f(z)$ is said to be differentiable at z if the limit

$$\lim_{z' \to z} \frac{f(z') - f(z)}{z' - z} \tag{14.79}$$

exists. However, this limit will, in general, depend on the manner in which z' approaches z. In order that $f(z)$ be differentiable at z this limit should not be dependent on the direction of approach. A function $f(z)$ is said to be analytic at a point z if it is differentiable at z and also at every point in some neighborhood of z in the complex plane.

If we evaluate the above limit along the direction of the real and imaginary axes, we obtain respectively

$$\lim_{x' \to x} \frac{f(z') - f(z)}{(x' + iy) - (x + iy)} = \frac{\partial f}{\partial x} = \frac{\partial \phi}{\partial x} + i\frac{\partial \psi}{\partial x}$$

$$\lim_{y' \to y} \frac{f(z') - f(z)}{(x + iy') - (x + iy)} = \frac{1}{i}\frac{\partial f}{\partial y} = \frac{1}{i}\left(\frac{\partial \phi}{\partial y} + i\frac{\partial \psi}{\partial y}\right) = \frac{\partial \psi}{\partial y} - i\frac{\partial \phi}{\partial y}$$

For $f(z)$ to be analytic these two limits ought to be equal. This gives us the following conditions

$$\frac{\partial \phi}{\partial x} = \frac{\partial \psi}{\partial y} \quad \text{and} \quad \frac{\partial \psi}{\partial x} = -\frac{\partial \phi}{\partial y} \tag{14.80}$$

These are called the Cauchy-Riemann conditions for the analyticity of $f(z)$. Note that in the above we have only shown that these conditions are necessary. However they can also be shown to be sufficient.

From Eq. (14.80) it is obvious that the real and imaginary parts of an analytic function

$f(z)$, namely $\phi(x,y)$ and $\psi(x,y)$, satisfy

$$\frac{\partial^2 \phi}{\partial x^2} + \frac{\partial^2 \phi}{\partial y^2} = 0 \quad \text{and} \quad \frac{\partial^2 \psi}{\partial x^2} + \frac{\partial^2 \psi}{\partial y^2} = 0 \tag{14.81}$$

Next consider the integral of $f(z)$ along a curve C in the complex plane

$$\int_C f(z)dz = \int_C (\phi + i\psi)(dx + idy)$$
$$= \int_C (\phi\, dx - \psi\, dy) + i \int_C (\psi\, dx + \phi\, dy)$$

This integral will be independent of the chosen path C and will be a function only of the endpoint coordinates, if and only if the quantities in the parentheses are perfect differentials. This is so if and only if the Cauchy-Riemann conditions Eq. (14.80) are satisfied. Thus the functions ϕ and ψ are conservative and irrotational. Note that the above analysis also implies that $\oint_C f(z)dz = 0$ if the function $f(z)$ is analytic in the region bounded by the closed curve C.

Now it is easy to see that at all points

$$\begin{aligned}\nabla\phi \cdot \nabla\psi &= \left(\hat{\boldsymbol{i}}\frac{\partial \phi}{\partial x} + \hat{\boldsymbol{j}}\frac{\partial \phi}{\partial y}\right) \cdot \left(\hat{\boldsymbol{i}}\frac{\partial \psi}{\partial x} + \hat{\boldsymbol{j}}\frac{\partial \psi}{\partial y}\right) \\ &= \frac{\partial \phi}{\partial x}\frac{\partial \psi}{\partial x} + \frac{\partial \phi}{\partial y}\frac{\partial \psi}{\partial y} \\ &= 0\end{aligned} \tag{14.82}$$

by virtue of the Cauchy-Riemann conditions. Thus the equipotential surfaces for ϕ and ψ at each point are perpendicular to each other. If $\phi(x,y)$ is taken to be the velocity potential, then the velocity $\boldsymbol{q} = -\nabla\phi$ must be along the line of the constant ψ. Bernoulli's theorem says that the stream function is constant along all streamlines. The streamlines are along the direction of instantaneous velocity or along $-\nabla\phi$. So ψ can be treated as the stream function for the problem.

On the other hand, since all analytic functions have to satisfy the Cauchy-Riemann conditions, the real part ϕ and the imaginary part ψ of any analytic function must represent the velocity potential and the stream function pair for some steady, planar, irrotational flow of incompressible fluids.

Examples

Let us now pick up some analytic functions and see what type of flow patterns they represent.

(i) $f(z) = z^2 = (x^2 - y^2) + i\, 2xy$. Thus

$$\phi(x,y) = x^2 - y^2 \quad \text{and} \quad \psi(x,y) = 2xy$$

The flow pattern is depicted in Fig. 14.11.
This is the flow pattern expected around a rectangular corner. (Combine a half y-axis and a half x-axis to form a rectangle.)

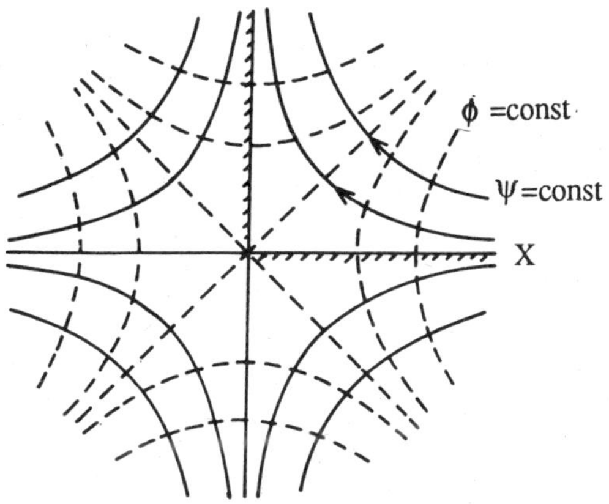

Fig. 14.11 Two-dimensional flow around a 90° corner

(ii) $f(z) = z^n, \quad n > 2$. Here

$$f(z) = (r\, e^{i\theta})^n = r^n\, e^{in\theta} = r^n \cos(n\theta) + i\, r^n \sin(n\theta) \equiv \phi + i\psi$$

This corresponds to a flow pattern around an angle $\alpha = \pi/n$. The case with $n = 3$ is shown in Fig. 14.12.

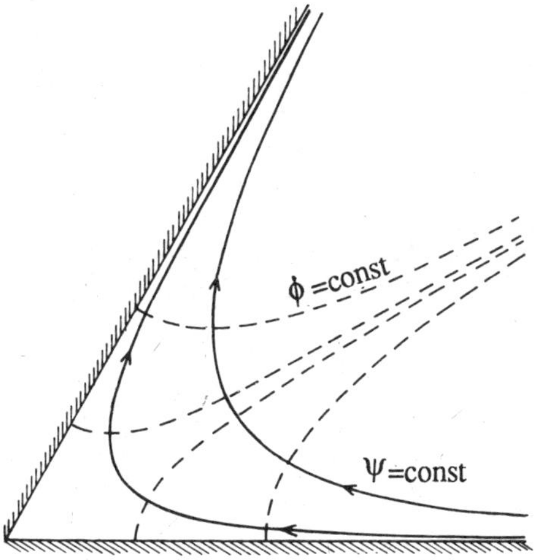

Fig. 14.12 Two-dimensional flow around a 60° corner

(iii) $f(z) = A\sqrt{z}$, A being a real constant. Here,

$$\phi(x,y) = A\sqrt{r}\,\cos(\theta/2) \qquad \text{and} \qquad \psi(x,y) = A\sqrt{r}\,\sin(\theta/2)$$

This gives

$$\frac{2\phi^2}{A^2} = 2r\cos^2(\theta/2) = r(1 + \cos\theta) = r + x$$

and

$$\frac{2\psi^2}{A^2} = 2r\sin^2(\theta/2) = r(1 - \cos\theta) = r - x$$

Hence, ϕ = constant and ψ = constant are the confocal and coaxial parabolas respectively (See Fig. 14.13). This corresponds to a flow turning around the edge of a semi-infinite plane sheet.

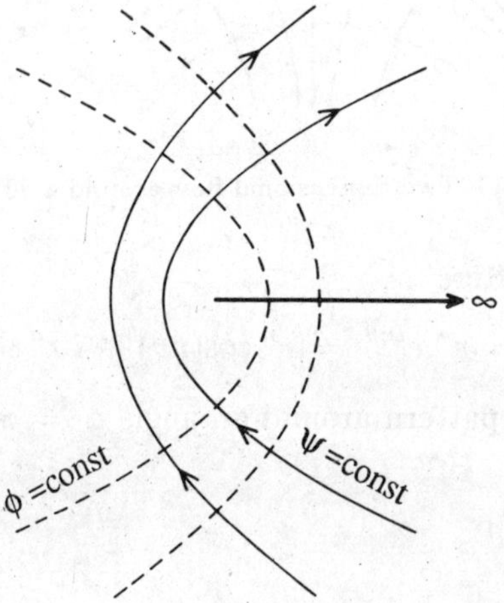

Fig. 14.13 Two-dimensional flow around a semi-infinite straight line

(iv) $f(z) = -M/(2\pi z)$, M being a real constant. This gives

$$\phi = -\frac{M\cos\theta}{2\pi r} \quad \text{and} \quad \psi = \frac{M\sin\theta}{2\pi r}$$

The resulting flow pattern is shown in Fig. 14.14.

This flow represents a doublet source with a source and sink sitting at the origin. The streamlines are like that of some dipole field lines. The source strength M is like the dipole moment of the source flow.

(v) $f(z) = q_o z$. This gives a uniform stream with stream velocity q_o in the direction of the negative x-axis.

14.14.2 Flow around Bodies of Simple Shape

The flow around any axisymmetric body can be reproduced by embedding a distribution of sources and sinks in a uniform translational flow along the axis of the body. For a single

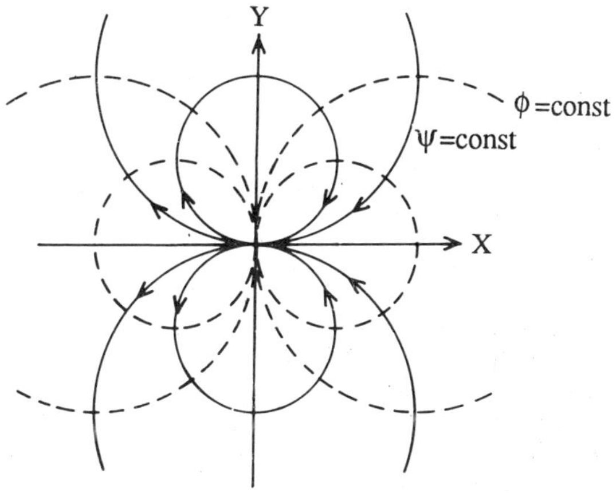

Fig. 14.14 The pattern of flow around a 2-D doublet source consisting of a source and a sink of equal strength, at an infinitesimal separation

spherical source of strength M placed in a uniform stream of velocity q_o, the stream lines are shown in Fig. 14.15. The strength M of a source is defined so as to represent the total mass emitted per second by $4\pi\rho M$, ρ being the density of the incompressible fluid.

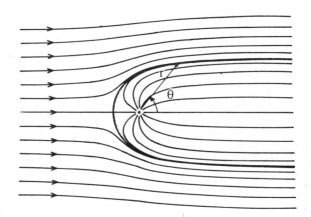

Fig. 14.15 Streamlines around an axially symmetric obstacle, constructed by a method similar to the method of images used in electrostatics

Since there is no flow across the stream lines, the flow just outside the body must reproduce the shape of the body. The position of the dividing streamline defines the shape of the body in question. For this type of a flow an approximate choice of the stream function would be

$$\psi(r,\theta) = -\frac{1}{2}q_o r^2 \sin^2\theta + M\cos\theta \qquad (14.83)$$

and similarly for the velocity potential,

$$\phi(r,\theta) = -q_o r\cos\theta + \frac{M}{r} \tag{14.84}$$

Note that the velocity potential ϕ in equation Eq. (14.84) can be obtained from the stream function (Eq. (14.83)) using the Cauchy-Riemann conditions.

14.14.3 Flows Around More Complex Axially Symmetric Shapes

One can put a number of sources and sinks along the symmetry axis and follow the method similar to that of the method of images in electrostatics to produce the desired position of the dividing streamline which corresponds to the profile of the body.

For a number of sources and sinks put along the symmetry axis,

$$\psi(r,\theta) = -\frac{1}{2}q_o r^2\sin^2\theta + \sum_{i=0}^{n-1} M_i\cos\theta_i \tag{14.85}$$

and

$$\phi(r,\theta) = -q_o r\cos\theta + \sum_{i=0}^{n-1}\frac{M_i}{r_i} \tag{14.86}$$

where M_i is the strength of the ith source and θ_i is the angle that the radius vector $\mathbf{r}_i$ makes with the symmetry axis.

At the position of the dividing stream line (that is, where $\theta = \pi$), the value of the stream function is

$$\psi_o = -\sum_{i=0}^{n-1} M_i \tag{14.87}$$

Now putting this value of ψ_o in Eq. (14.85), one can obtain the equation of the dividing streamline $r(\theta)$ as

$$-\sum_{i=0}^{n-1} M_i = -\frac{1}{2}q_o r^2\sin^2\theta + \sum_{i=0}^{n-1} M_i\cos\theta_i \tag{14.88}$$

because at all points of the dividing streamline, ψ must have the value given by Eq. (14.87).

Applying numerical procedures one can make guesses about M_i and θ_i in such a way that Eq. (14.87) graphically resembles the shape of the given object (obstacle). In general fewer than about 20 guesses or iterations are required to generate a curve that matches the desired one with precision typically within 5 per cent. Once the correct distribution of M_i, r_i and θ_i are guessed, the expression for $\phi(r,\theta)$ yields the velocity distribution at any given point and $\psi(r,\theta)$ gives the equations for the streamlines.

14.14.4 Aerodynamic Lifting Force on Aerofoils

The shape of an aerofoil is shown in Fig. 14.16. When it moves through air, the surrounding air appears to stream past the foil, with a pattern of streamlines also shown in Fig. 14.16.

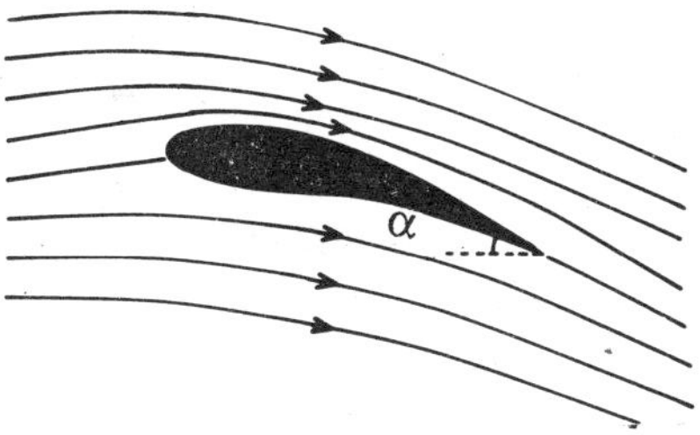

Fig. 14.16 Flow around an aerofoil and the angle of attack

The velocity of air streaming along the aerofoil is greater on the upper side than on the lower side. Small distances between the streamlines on the upper side indicate high velocity and vice versa. Hence the pressure is lower on the upper side than on its lower side. Thus there acts a resulting upward force on the wing, called the *lifting force*. The distribution of forces that act on the surface of the aerofoil is shown in Fig. 14.17, with the direction and relative magnitudes represented by the arrowed lines.

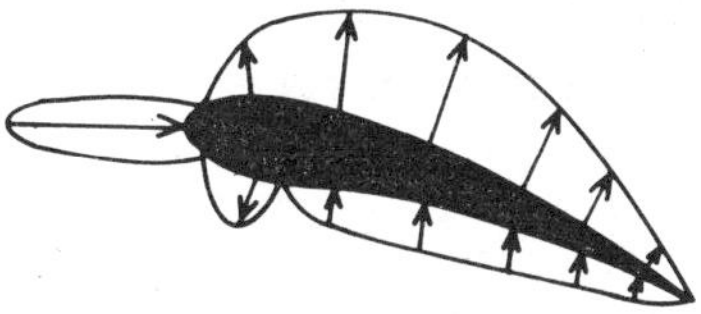

Fig. 14.17 Pressure distribution around an aerofoil moving through the air. The net upward force on the aerofoil provides the lift

Obviously, this distribution of pressure force is created due to the particular shape of the aerofoil which forces the streamlines to follow its specific curved surface. The low pressure at the upper side is actually a consequence of the nature of the curved surface. An element of air following this curved path must experience centrifugal forces. So with the streamlines having a radius of curvature R we have the general formula for the pressure gradient developed due to streaming (given by Euler in 1754),

$$\frac{dp}{dR} = \frac{\rho q^2}{R} \tag{14.89}$$

where q is the streaming velocity and ρ the density of the fluid.

If the longitudinal axis of the aerofoil is inclined upward by an angle α with the horizontal called the *angle of attack*, the lifting force is found to increase with α up to about $\alpha = 25^o$. The blades of ceiling fans, table fans and pumping sets are set to have an angle of attack close to the above figure in order to produce maximum pressure difference across the blades.

14.15 KELVIN'S AND HELMHOLTZ'S THEOREMS

We start with the definition of a quantity called *circulation* around a closed curve. Let Γ denote any closed curve drawn in the fluid at time t. Then

$$c = \oint_{\Gamma} \boldsymbol{q} \cdot \boldsymbol{dl} = \oint_{\Gamma} \boldsymbol{q} \cdot \hat{\boldsymbol{t}}\, dl \tag{14.90}$$

is called the *circulation* around the closed curve Γ at time t, l being the parameter chosen to describe the closed path Γ.

14.15.1 A Theorem on null circulation

If the motion of a fluid in a simply connected region is irrotational at any instant, the circulation around any closed curve in that region at that instant is zero.

Proof: By Stokes' theorem,

$$c = \oint_{\Gamma} \boldsymbol{q} \cdot \boldsymbol{dl} = \int_{S} (\nabla \times \boldsymbol{q}) \cdot \boldsymbol{dS} = 0$$

The converse of this theorem is also true. In general, the strength of a vortex tube is equal to the circulation around any circuit surrounding the tube.

14.15.2 Kelvin's Theorem on Circulation

The circulation around any closed curve comoving with the fluid does not change with time if the external field of force (if any) is conservative and ρ is a function of p alone (that is, the fluid is barotropic).

Proof: Let $\boldsymbol{r}$ denote the vector function giving the position vectors of all the points on the curve at any given time. Since the curve moves so as to contain the same fluid particles at all times, dl remains invariant, but not $\boldsymbol{dr}$ which can change with time because we only require

$$|\boldsymbol{dr}| = |D\boldsymbol{r}| = dl$$

Therefore,

$$\begin{aligned} \frac{Dc}{Dt} &= \frac{D}{Dt} \oint_{\Gamma} \left(\boldsymbol{q} \cdot \frac{D\boldsymbol{r}}{dl} \right) dl \\ &= \oint_{\Gamma} \frac{D}{Dt} \left(\boldsymbol{q} \cdot \frac{D\boldsymbol{r}}{dl} \right) dl \\ &= \oint_{\Gamma} \left[\frac{D\boldsymbol{q}}{Dt} \cdot \frac{D\boldsymbol{r}}{dl} + \boldsymbol{q} \cdot \frac{D}{dl} \left(\frac{D\boldsymbol{r}}{Dt} \right) \right] dl \end{aligned}$$

But $D\boldsymbol{r}/Dt = (\boldsymbol{q}\cdot\nabla)\boldsymbol{r} = \boldsymbol{q}$, so that using Eq. (14.19),

$$\frac{Dc}{Dt} = \oint_\Gamma \left\{-\nabla(\Omega + P)\cdot\frac{D\boldsymbol{r}}{dl} + \boldsymbol{q}\cdot\frac{D}{dl}(\boldsymbol{q})\right\} dl$$

$$= \oint_\Gamma \frac{D}{dl}\left\{-\Omega - P + \frac{1}{2}q^2\right\} dl$$

$$= \oint_\Gamma D(-\Omega - P + \frac{1}{2}q^2)$$

For a closed path comoving in the fluid this integral is zero so that

$$\frac{Dc}{Dt} = 0 \tag{14.91}$$

which implies that the circulation c is a constant of motion.

Thus if the motion of a non-viscous fluid is initially irrotational, it remains irrotational, provided the body forces are conservative and the fluid is barotropic.

14.15.3 Helmholtz's Vorticity Theorem

If the body forces are conservative and p is a function of ρ alone, then

$$\frac{D}{Dt}\left(\frac{\boldsymbol{\omega}}{\rho}\right) = \left(\frac{\boldsymbol{\omega}}{\rho}\cdot\nabla\right)\boldsymbol{q}$$

where $\boldsymbol{\omega} = \frac{1}{2}\nabla \times \boldsymbol{q}$ is the vorticity of the fluid at any instant and at any point. This theorem was originally stated by Helmholtz in 1858.

Proof: Taking the curl of both sides of Euler's equation of motion (Eq. (14.19)) we get

$$\frac{\partial\boldsymbol{\omega}}{\partial t} - \nabla \times (\boldsymbol{q} \times \boldsymbol{\omega}) = \mathbf{0}$$

or

$$\frac{\partial\boldsymbol{\omega}}{\partial t} - \{(\nabla\cdot\boldsymbol{\omega})\boldsymbol{q} + (\boldsymbol{\omega}\cdot\nabla)\boldsymbol{q} - (\nabla\cdot\boldsymbol{q})\boldsymbol{\omega} - (\boldsymbol{q}\cdot\nabla)\boldsymbol{\omega}\} = \mathbf{0}$$

Now since $\nabla\cdot\boldsymbol{\omega} = 0$, and from the equation of continuity (Eq. (14.12)) and using

$$\frac{D\boldsymbol{\omega}}{Dt} = \frac{\partial\boldsymbol{\omega}}{\partial t} + (\boldsymbol{q}\cdot\nabla)\boldsymbol{\omega}$$

we can finally have

$$\frac{D\boldsymbol{\omega}}{Dt} - (\boldsymbol{\omega}\cdot\nabla)\boldsymbol{q} - \frac{1}{\rho}\left(\frac{D\rho}{Dt}\right)\boldsymbol{\omega} = \mathbf{0}$$

Multiplying by ρ^{-1} we then get,

$$\frac{D}{Dt}\left(\frac{\boldsymbol{\omega}}{\rho}\right) = \left(\frac{\boldsymbol{\omega}}{\rho}\cdot\nabla\right)\boldsymbol{q} \tag{14.92}$$

Hence for a nonequilibrium fluid flow, vorticity generally evolves as the fluid proceeds and this evolution depends on the distribution of $\boldsymbol{q}$ at any given instant. This is like the time variation of the magnetic induction related to the space variation of the electric field, in the theory of electromagnetism.

Some other properties of the vorticity motion emerge from Helmholtz's theorem. Taking a dot product of both sides of Eq. (14.92) with $\boldsymbol{\omega}/\rho$, we get

$$\frac{1}{2}\frac{D}{Dt}\left(\frac{\omega^2}{\rho^2}\right) = \left\{\left(\frac{\boldsymbol{\omega}}{\rho}\cdot\nabla\right)\boldsymbol{q}\right\}\cdot\left(\frac{\boldsymbol{\omega}}{\rho}\right)$$

Let us define

$$\frac{\boldsymbol{\omega}}{\rho} = \left|\frac{\boldsymbol{\omega}}{\rho}\right|\hat{\boldsymbol{n}}$$

$\hat{\boldsymbol{n}}$ being the unit vector along $\boldsymbol{\omega}$. Then,

$$\frac{D}{Dt}\left\{\ln\left(\frac{\omega^2}{\rho^2}\right)\right\} == 2(\hat{\boldsymbol{n}}\cdot\nabla)\boldsymbol{q}\cdot\hat{\boldsymbol{n}} \tag{14.93}$$

If $\boldsymbol{q}$ has to have continuous first partial derivatives, we must have

$$|(\hat{\boldsymbol{n}}\cdot\nabla)\boldsymbol{q}\cdot\hat{\boldsymbol{n}}| \leq Q_o \tag{14.94}$$

where Q_o is a positive constant. Hence

$$-Q_o \leq (\hat{\boldsymbol{n}}\cdot\nabla)\boldsymbol{q}\cdot\hat{\boldsymbol{n}} \leq Q_o \tag{14.95}$$

Now if at time t_o, the vorticity is $\boldsymbol{\omega}_o$ and the density is ρ_o, then from Eq. (14.93)

$$\ln\left(\frac{\omega^2}{\rho^2}\right) - \ln\left(\frac{\omega_o^2}{\rho_o^2}\right) \leq \int_{t_o}^{t} 2Q_o\,dt' = 2Q_o(t - t_o) \tag{14.96}$$

Hence

$$\frac{\omega^2}{\rho^2} \leq \frac{\omega_o^2}{\rho_o^2}\exp\{2Q_o(t - t_o)\} \tag{14.97}$$

This result can be interpreted as

(i) If the vorticity of a particle is ever zero at any instant it must always be zero. Thus a motion with non-zero vorticity cannot be generated in a barotropic ideal fluid by conservative body forces if the motion is initially irrotational. Thus,

(ii) the motion with vorticity cannot be generated in a barotropic ideal fluid initially at rest.

Now taking the lower bound on $(\hat{\boldsymbol{n}}\cdot\nabla)\boldsymbol{q}\cdot\hat{\boldsymbol{n}} \geq -Q_o$, we get

$$\frac{\omega^2}{\rho^2} \geq \frac{\omega_o^2}{\rho_o^2}\exp\{-2Q_o(t - t_o)\} \tag{14.98}$$

Hence , we have, as further interpretations,

(iii) a particle which initially has nonzero vorticity can never at any instant lose all of its vorticity,

(iv) the vorticity vector of a particle can never reverse its direction, and

(v) the rate of change of vorticity in two dimensions for motions of incompressible fluids is given by Eq. (14.92) which, for two dimensions, reduces to

$$\frac{D\boldsymbol{\omega}}{Dt} = (\boldsymbol{\omega} \cdot \nabla)\boldsymbol{q} = \omega_3 \frac{\partial \boldsymbol{q}}{\partial x_3}$$

since $\boldsymbol{\omega}$ does not have any x, y components for planar motion. But since $(\partial \boldsymbol{q}/\partial x_3) = \boldsymbol{0}$ by definition of a planar flow, we must have for planar flows

$$\frac{D\boldsymbol{\omega}}{Dt} = \boldsymbol{0}$$

Thus for a planar (two dimensional) motion of an incompressible fluid the vorticity of any particle remains constant.

An Application

A body of incompressible liquid rotates with constant angular velocity about the vertical axis under constant gravity. We want to find the free surface of its revolution and the vorticity at any point in the liquid.

Let $\boldsymbol{\Omega}$ be the constant angular velocity of rotation about the z-axis so that $\boldsymbol{\Omega} = \Omega\hat{\boldsymbol{k}}$ (see Fig. 14.18).

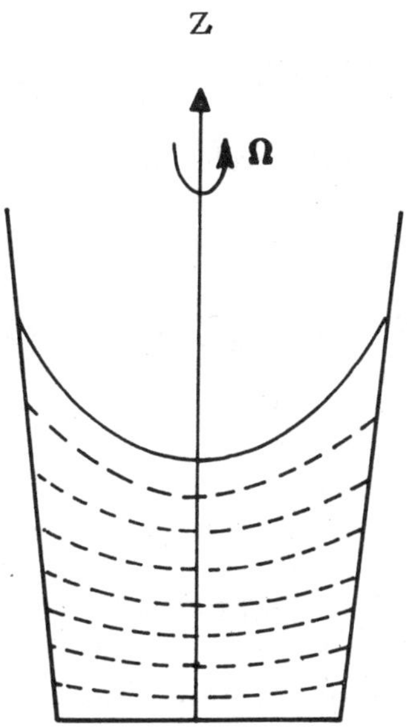

Fig. 14.18 Liquid in a rotating bucket assumes a paraboloidal surface

Now the velocity $\boldsymbol{q}$ of a particle at $\boldsymbol{r}$ at time t is

$$\boldsymbol{q}(\boldsymbol{r}, t) = \boldsymbol{\Omega} \times \boldsymbol{r} \qquad \text{where} \qquad \boldsymbol{r} = x\hat{\boldsymbol{i}} + y\hat{\boldsymbol{j}} + z\hat{\boldsymbol{k}}$$

Therefore,

$$\frac{D\boldsymbol{q}}{Dt} = \boldsymbol{\Omega} \times \frac{D\boldsymbol{r}}{Dt} = \boldsymbol{\Omega} \times \boldsymbol{q} = \boldsymbol{\Omega} \times (\boldsymbol{\Omega} \times \boldsymbol{r})$$

$$= (\boldsymbol{\Omega}\cdot\boldsymbol{r})\boldsymbol{\Omega} - \Omega^2\boldsymbol{r} = -\,\Omega^2(x\hat{\boldsymbol{i}} + y\hat{\boldsymbol{j}}) \tag{14.99}$$

$$= -\frac{1}{2}\Omega^2\boldsymbol{\nabla}(x^2 + y^2)$$

In order to construct Euler's equation of motion we note that the external body force is the gravitational force,

$$\boldsymbol{F} = -\,g\hat{\boldsymbol{k}} = -\,\boldsymbol{\nabla}(gz) \tag{14.100}$$

and the pressure potential is given by Eq. (14.25) for incompressible fluids. Therefore, using Eqs (14.99), (14.100) and (14.25), Euler's equation reduces to

$$-\frac{1}{2}\Omega^2\boldsymbol{\nabla}(x^2 + y^2) = -\,\boldsymbol{\nabla}\left(gz + \frac{p - p_o}{\rho}\right)$$

or

$$\Omega^2(x^2 + y^2) - 2gz - \frac{p - p_o}{\rho} = \text{const.} \tag{14.101}$$

Since the surface of rotation under consideration is a free surface for which $p = p_o$, its equation would be given by

$$z = \left(\frac{\Omega^2}{2g}\right)(x^2 + y^2) + \text{const.} \tag{14.102}$$

This is an equation for a paraboloid of revolution about the z-axis, which represents the free surface of a rotating mass of incompressible liquid with a constant angular velocity.

The vorticity of the liquid at any point and at any instant is

$$\boldsymbol{\omega} = \frac{1}{2}\boldsymbol{\nabla} \times \boldsymbol{q} = \frac{1}{2}\boldsymbol{\nabla} \times (\boldsymbol{\Omega} \times \boldsymbol{r}) = \Omega\hat{\boldsymbol{k}} \tag{14.103}$$

Thus the vorticity at each point of the fluid is the same as the angular speed of rotation of the liquid mass. This gives a direct physical interpretation of vorticity, as the angular velocity of rotation of a body of fluid mass.

14.16 REPRESENTATION OF VORTICES BY COMPLEX FUNCTIONS

A representative two-dimensional vortex is a cylindrical vortex. By definition, a *cylindrical vortex* of radius a implies a constant vorticity $\boldsymbol{\omega}$ throughout $r < a$, but vortices vanish outside. The strength of such a vortex is defined to be $k = -\,\omega a^2/2$. The fluid inside the vortex is as if it were a solid cylinder rotating with an angular velocity $\boldsymbol{\omega}/2$. Outside the tube the motion is irrotational.

The complex function that represents such a vortex motion, is given by

$$f(z) = i\,k\,\ln(z) \tag{14.104}$$

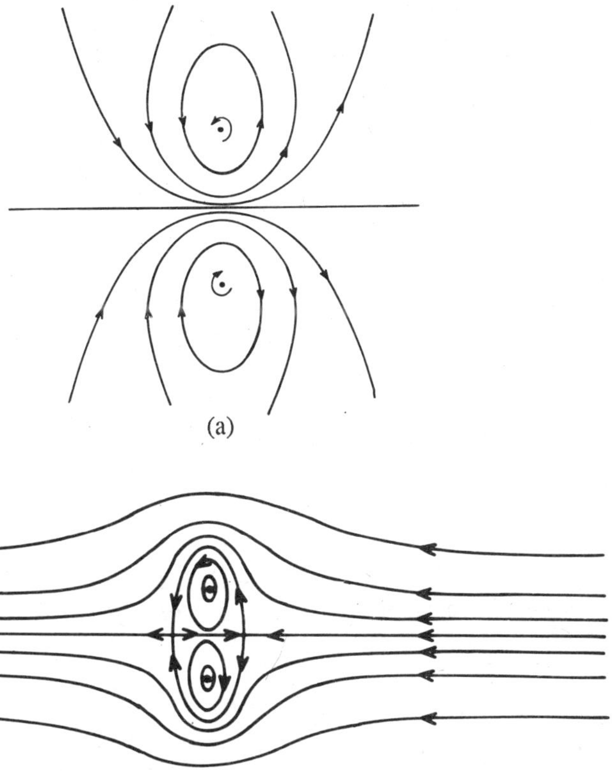

(a)

(b)

Fig. 14.19 Natural drifting a pair of vortices having equal but opposite strengths, shown in (a). When such a pair of vortices is put in a stream having a velocity equal but opposite to that of natural drifting of the pair, the pair of vortices remains stationary, shown in (b).

where k is the strength of a vortex. However, the function $f(z)$ defined in Eq. (14.104) actually represents a circular vortex that has shrunk to the origin in such a way that its strength k has remained constant. Such a concentrated vortex is called a *vortex filament* or *point vortex.*

Two equal and opposite vortices, separated by $\pm\, a$ from the x-axis but oriented along the y-axis, can be represented by a complex function

$$f(z) = i\,k\,\ln\left(\frac{z - ia}{z_* + ia}\right) \tag{14.105}$$

The distance between the two vortices remains constant, but both the vortices move to the right with the same horizontal velocity equal to what is called their induced velocity given by $k/2a$. Here k is the strength of each vortex (see Fig. 14.19(a)).

These two vortices may remain stationary, if they are placed in a uniform stream having complex potential $(k/2a)z$ so that (see Fig. 14.19(b))

$$f(z) = \frac{k}{2a}z + i\,k\,\ln\left(\frac{z - ia}{z + ia}\right) \tag{14.106}$$

14.17 FLOW OF IMPERFECT FLUIDS

We know that fluids at rest do not develop any shearing stress. Perfect fluids do not develop any shearing stress even in motion. But in reality all fluids show some amount of shearing forces in order to control the shearing motions. Fluids that develop finite shearing stresses for differential tangential motions are called imperfect fluids.

For solids the shearing displacements are defined in terms of shearing strains where strains are defined to be the space gradients of the elastic displacements . For fluids any amount of displacement between two different equilibrium conditions is possible, without developing any restoring forces. However, these displacements do not correspond to steady velocities. For fluids, the space gradient of velocities play a similar role as the space gradients of the elastic displacements do for the elastic solids . Let $\boldsymbol{q}$ be the velocity vector field defined over the extent of the fluid motions. Then the *rate of strain tensor*, $\tilde{e}_{ij}$ is defined as

$$\tilde{e}_{ij} = \frac{1}{2}\left(\frac{\partial q_i}{\partial x_j} + \frac{\partial q_j}{\partial x_i}\right) \tag{14.107}$$

The stress tensor σ_{ij} can now have two terms, one is $-\,p\delta_{ij}$ for its isotropic pressure, and a second term, say σ'_{ij}, for the imperfectness of the fluid, so that

$$\sigma_{ij} = -\,p\delta_{ij} + \sigma'_{ij} \tag{14.108}$$

This σ'_{ij} is taken to be related to $\tilde{e}_{ij}$ in a fashion quite similar to that between σ_{ij} and e_{ij} for isotropic solids. In fact, σ'_{ij} is connected to $\tilde{e}_{ij}$ by the following relation:

$$\sigma'_{ij} = \tilde{\lambda}\tilde{\Delta}\delta_{ij} + 2\tilde{\mu}\tilde{e}_{ij} \tag{14.109}$$

where

$$\tilde{\Delta} = \tilde{e}_{11} + \tilde{e}_{22} + \tilde{e}_{33} = \boldsymbol{\nabla}\cdot\boldsymbol{q} \tag{14.110}$$

It is to be noted that if the fluid is incompressible, $\boldsymbol{\nabla}\cdot\boldsymbol{q} = 0$ so that $\tilde{\Delta} = 0$. However we can write Eq. (14.109) as

$$\begin{aligned}\sigma'_{ij} &= \tilde{\lambda}\tilde{\Delta}\delta_{ij} + 2\tilde{\mu}\left\{\left(\tilde{e}_{ij} - \frac{1}{3}\tilde{\Delta}\delta_{ij}\right) + \frac{1}{3}\tilde{\Delta}\delta_{ij}\right\} \\ &= \left(\tilde{\lambda} + \frac{2\tilde{\mu}}{3}\right)\tilde{\Delta}\delta_{ij} + 2\tilde{\mu}\tilde{b}_{ij} \\ &= \xi\tilde{\Delta}\delta_{ij} + 2\eta\tilde{b}_{ij}\end{aligned} \tag{14.111}$$

where $\xi = \tilde{\lambda} + 2\tilde{\mu}/3$ is called the *coefficient of bulk viscosity* and $\eta = \tilde{\mu}$ the *coefficient of shearing viscosity*. For incompressible fluids, the stress due to bulk viscosity vanishes as

$\tilde{\Delta} = 0$. Both ξ and η are positive constants.

The incompressible liquids that follow Eq. (14.111) (with $\tilde{\Delta} = 0$, of course) are called Newtonian liquids. They simply obey $\sigma'_{ij} = 2\eta\tilde{b}_{ij} = 2\eta\tilde{e}_{ij}$, as $\tilde{\Delta} = 0$. Here η is called the *coefficient of dynamic viscosity.*

14.17.1 Navier-Stokes' Equation for Imperfect Fluids

The general equation of motion for any fluid is given by

$$\rho\frac{Dq_i}{Dt} = \rho g_i + \frac{\partial\sigma_{ij}}{\partial x_k} \tag{14.112}$$

Now

$$\begin{aligned}\frac{\partial\sigma_{ik}}{\partial x_k} &= \frac{\partial}{\partial x_k}(-p\delta_{ik}) + \tilde{\lambda}\delta_{ik}\frac{\partial\tilde{\Delta}}{\partial x_k} + \tilde{\mu}\frac{\partial}{\partial x_k}\left(\frac{\partial q_i}{\partial x_k} + \frac{\partial q_k}{\partial x_i}\right)\\ &= -\frac{\partial p}{\partial x_i} + \tilde{\lambda}\frac{\partial}{\partial x_i}\left(\frac{\partial q_k}{\partial x_k}\right) + \tilde{\mu}\frac{\partial^2 q_k}{\partial x_k\partial x_i} + \tilde{\mu}\frac{\partial^2 q_i}{\partial x_k^2}\\ &= -\frac{\partial p}{\partial x_i} + (\tilde{\lambda} + \tilde{\mu})\frac{\partial^2 q_k}{\partial x_i\partial x_k} + \tilde{\mu}\nabla^2 q_i\\ &= -\frac{\partial p}{\partial x_i} + \left(\xi + \frac{1}{3}\eta\right)\frac{\partial^2 q_k}{\partial x_i\partial x_k} + \eta\nabla^2 q_i\end{aligned}$$

Therefore, the most general equations of motion for viscous fluids are given by

$$\rho\left(\frac{\partial q_i}{\partial t} + q_j\frac{\partial q_i}{\partial x_j}\right) = -\frac{\partial p}{\partial x_i} + \left(\xi + \frac{1}{3}\eta\right)\frac{\partial}{\partial x_i}(\nabla\cdot q) + \eta\nabla^2 q_i - \rho\frac{\partial\Omega}{\partial x_i} \tag{14.113}$$

where Ω is the conservative body force potential given by $\boldsymbol{g} = -\nabla\Omega$. Written in vector notation, Eq. (14.113) becomes

$$\frac{\partial \boldsymbol{q}}{\partial t} + (\boldsymbol{q}\cdot\nabla)\boldsymbol{q} = -\frac{1}{\rho}\nabla p - \nabla\Omega + \frac{1}{\rho}\left(\xi + \frac{1}{3}\eta\right)\nabla(\nabla\cdot\boldsymbol{q}) + \frac{\eta}{\rho}\nabla^2\boldsymbol{q}$$

or using the identity appearing just after Eq. (14.21),

$$\frac{\partial \boldsymbol{q}}{\partial t} - \boldsymbol{q}\times(\nabla\times\boldsymbol{q}) = -\nabla\left(\Omega - \frac{\xi + \eta/3}{\rho}\nabla\cdot\boldsymbol{q} + \frac{1}{2}q^2\right) + \frac{\eta}{\rho}\nabla^2\boldsymbol{q} - \frac{1}{\rho}\nabla p \tag{14.114}$$

For incompressible fluids

$$\frac{\partial \boldsymbol{q}}{\partial t} + (\boldsymbol{q}\cdot\nabla)\boldsymbol{q} = -\frac{1}{\rho}\nabla p - \nabla\Omega + \frac{\eta}{\rho}\nabla^2\boldsymbol{q} \tag{14.115}$$

Eq. (14.115) is called *Navier-Stokes' equation.* The coefficient $\eta/\rho = \nu$ is sometimes called the *kinematic viscosity* of the fluid as ν does not contain any mass factor in its physical dimension.

14.17.2 Flow in a Pipe: Poiseuille's Formula

An incompressible viscous fluid flows steadily in an axially symmetric pipe of radius R, in the x direction.

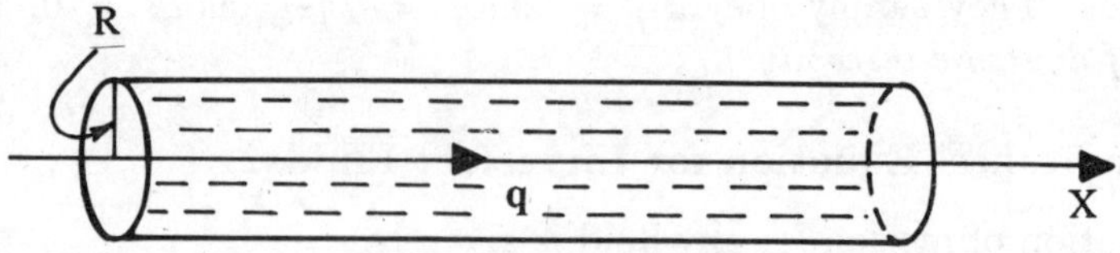

Fig. 14.20 Flow of a viscous fluid in a tube

From Fig. 14.20, it is clear that $\boldsymbol{q} \equiv (q, 0, 0)$. Since the flow is steady we must have $\partial \boldsymbol{q}/\partial t = 0$. Further we have

$$(\boldsymbol{q} \cdot \nabla)\boldsymbol{q} \equiv (q\frac{\partial q}{\partial x}, 0, 0)$$

The very fact that the velocity only has an x-component means that we have neglected the effect of the gravitational force (which is in the negative z-direction) on the flow. We can do this if $\boldsymbol{q}$ is large enough. This amounts to putting $\nabla\Omega = 0$. Since the fluid is incompressible, $\nabla \cdot \boldsymbol{q} = 0$, which in the present case becomes $\partial q/\partial x = 0$, implying that q is only a function of y and z, that is, $\boldsymbol{q} = q(y, z)$. Thus Navier-Stokes' equations for the flow as depicted in Fig. 14.20 become

$$0 = -\frac{\partial p}{\partial x} + \eta\nabla^2 q \qquad 0 = \frac{\partial p}{\partial y} \qquad \text{and} \qquad 0 = \frac{\partial p}{\partial z} \tag{14.116}$$

The last two of Eqs (14.116) imply that the pressure p depends only on x, that is, $p = p(x)$. Now the first of Eqs (14.116) gives

$$\frac{\partial p}{\partial x} = \eta\left(\frac{\partial^2 q}{\partial y^2} + \frac{\partial^2 q}{\partial z^2}\right)$$

Since LHS is a function of x only and RHS a function of y and z only, they can be set equal to a constant independent x, y and z.

$$\frac{\partial p}{\partial x} = \text{const.} = -\alpha \qquad \text{(say)}$$

Here $-\alpha$ is nothing but the constant pressure gradient along the x-axis, giving

$$\frac{\partial^2 q}{\partial y^2} + \frac{\partial^2 q}{\partial z^2} = -\frac{\alpha}{\eta} \tag{14.117}$$

In terms of polar coordinates the above equation becomes

$$\frac{1}{r}\frac{d}{dr}\left(r\frac{d}{dr}\right)q = -\frac{\alpha}{\eta}$$

or

$$r\frac{dq}{dr} = -\frac{\alpha r^2}{2\eta} + \beta$$

or

$$q = -\frac{\alpha r^2}{4\eta} + \beta \ln r + \gamma$$

where β and γ are constants of integration.

Now for $r = 0$, q must be finite. Therefore, $\beta = 0$. For $r = R$, $q = 0$ which means $\gamma = \alpha R^2/4\eta$. Thus

$$q(r) = \frac{\alpha}{4\eta}(R^2 - r^2) \tag{14.118}$$

Now the flow rate is

$$Q = 2\pi\rho \int_0^R rq\, dr = \frac{2\pi\rho\alpha}{4\eta} \int_0^R (R^2 - r^2) r\, dr = \frac{\pi\rho R^4 \alpha}{8\eta}$$

where α is the horizontal pressure gradient,

$$\alpha = \frac{\Delta p}{l}$$

$$= \frac{\text{pressure difference between any two transverse vertical sections}}{\text{separation between the above two sections}}$$

Therefore we finally have for the flow rate

$$Q = \frac{\pi\rho R^4 \Delta p}{8\eta l} \tag{14.119}$$

Equation (14.119) is called *Poiseuille's formula*, derived by Jean Léon Poiseuille in 1840 (also independently by Hagen perhaps two years earlier).

14.17.3 Reynolds' Number

Osborne Reynolds (1883) introduced a dimensionless number to characterise the state of the viscous flow, defined by

$$R_e = \frac{\rho v l}{\eta} \tag{14.120}$$

where R_e is *Reynolds' number*, ρ is the density of the fluid, v is the velocity of the fluid, l is the characteristic length of the flow, and η is the dynamical viscosity. For a given Reynolds' number the motion is expected to be dynamically similar, irrespective of the wide range of variations in ρ, v, l and η. In order to have dynamically similar states for a given Reynolds' number, a high velocity flow must be considered in a smaller spatial extent, whereas a low velocity flow can continue in a dynamically similar state for a larger spatial extent. Similarly, more viscous fluids can support a dynamically similar state for either higher velocities or over larger dimensions.

Now what is it that changes with the flow velocity or increasing Reynolds' number? Reynolds characterised the flow in two qualitative states. At lower Reynolds' number the flow is streamlined or what is called *laminar*. Beyond a critical value of Reynolds' number the flow becomes *turbulent*. Eddies develop in the flow, with nonvanishing circulation at all points, or in other words, dissipative vortices can develop in a random fashion. For example, for Poiseuille's type of viscous flow in a pipe the critical Reynolds' number is about 2800. The transition from laminar to turbulent flow takes place at different critical Reynolds' number for different types of geometry of the flow.

14.17.4 Drag Coefficient for the Motion of a Sphere Moving in a Fluid

A smooth sphere of cross-sectional area A is moving with speed v through a fluid having density ρ_f. The quadratic law of drag force is

$$F_D = \frac{1}{2} C_D \rho_f A v^2 \tag{14.121}$$

where C_D is called the *drag coefficient* which, for a sphere, is a function of Reynolds' number

$$R_e = \frac{2r\rho_f v}{\eta_f}$$

r being the radius of the sphere and η_f the viscosity of the fluid. For laminar flow, $R_e < 1$,

$$C_D = \frac{24}{R_e}$$

in which case

$$F_D = 6\pi\eta_f r v \tag{14.122}$$

This is called *Stokes' law of viscous drag force* and can be used to determine η_f by measuring v at various values of r. Remember that Stokes' law is valid if $R_e < 1$. For a rigorous proof of Stoke's law,see Routh's book, for example.

The tdransition from laminar to turbulent flow can occur in the range of Reynolds' number $1 < R_e < 10^3$, an approximate numerical fit to the observational results is given by

$$\log C_D = \log(0.37) + 0.21\{\log R_e - \log(4400)\}^{1.68}$$

For turbulent flows, $10^3 < R_e < 2 \times 10^5$, and $C_D = 0.5$.
The above values of C_D correspond to the motion of a sphere in a fluid.

A quadratic drag law is quite valid for motion of vehicles that have to overcome the aerodynamic drag forces. Typically for a

heavy truck, $C_D = 1.00$,
bus, $C_D = 0.65$,
good car, $C_D = 0.30$,
motorcycle, $C_D = 0.90$, and
light aircraft, $C_D = 0.12$

At very large Reynolds' numbers, $R_e \gg 10^3$, the flow is characterised by the presence of an extremely irregular variation of velocity with time at each point of the flow. The velocity at each point is seen to fluctuate around some mean value, but the amplitude of fluctuation is not small as compared to the magnitude of the mean velocity itself. Turbulent eddies are formed which also change in size and finally disappear, and this process continues leading to substantial dissipation of power. This phenomenon is called turbulence and appears to develop if the Reynolds' number for the given flow dimensions exceeds a few thousands.

14.18 SUMMARY

The central problem of fluid dynamics is to formulate a sufficient number of independent equations, required for solving all the unknowns. For perfect barotropic fluids, there are five unknowns, namely the vector field for the flow velocity and the scalar fields for the density and pressure of the fluid. Euler's vector equation of motion, the continuity equation and the equation of state constitute the five required equations for a complete solution to the problem.

Bernoulli's equation is shown to be a special case of Euler's equation. Both macroscopic and microscopic interpretations of Bernoulli's equation are suggested. The examples of its applications given in the text should clarify its meaning further.

The study of water waves as gravity waves, ripples and shallow water waves establishes the versatility of Bernoulli's equation. The shooting and streaming flows are unique in their character leading to discrete solutions similar to those one often comes across in quantum mechanics. These ideas could have tremendous potential in astrophysical situations, where detailed stability analyses show that discrete solutions may indeed give rise to shocks.

Irrotational planar flows are studied in some detail, just to emphasize that complex functions and their analyticity can represent natural flow patterns in two dimensions. It is also shown that vorticity and circulation in ideal fluid flows are conserved. The stagnation of flows around obstacles always causes enormous thrust on the obstacles. The origin of the aerodynamic lift force which is essential for modern aerial navigation, due to a particular shape of the aerofoil, is explained.

The chapter ends with a derivation of Navier-Stokes' equation of motion for imperfect fluids. The details of its implications have not been discussed due to want of space. The concept of Reynolds' number has just been introduced. For further studies, enthusiastic readers are referred to Landau and Lifshitz's classic book on fluid dynamics.

PROBLEMS

14.1 A liquid flows along a horizontal pipe AB. The difference between the levels of the liquid in two side tubes stemming up vertically from the central axis of the tube (as shown in Fig. 14.21) is 0.10 m. The diameters of the tubes are the same. Determine the velocity of the liquid flowing in the pipe. If it were an open water stream instead of a flow in a pipe and the tube were sealed from the top with a small orifice on its lid at a height h_o from the free water surface, then how high would the jet be?

14.2 A horizontally oriented tube AB of length l rotates with a constant angular velocity $\boldsymbol{\omega}$ about a stationary vertical axis OO′ passing through the end A. The tube is filled with an ideal liquid. The end A of the tube is open, and the closed end B has

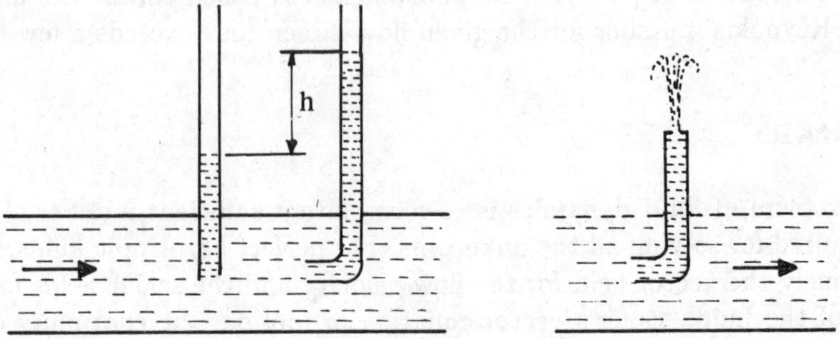

Fig. 14.21 Diagram for problem 14.1

a small orifice. Find the velocity of the fluid relative to the tube as a function of the remaining column length h (see Fig. 14.22).

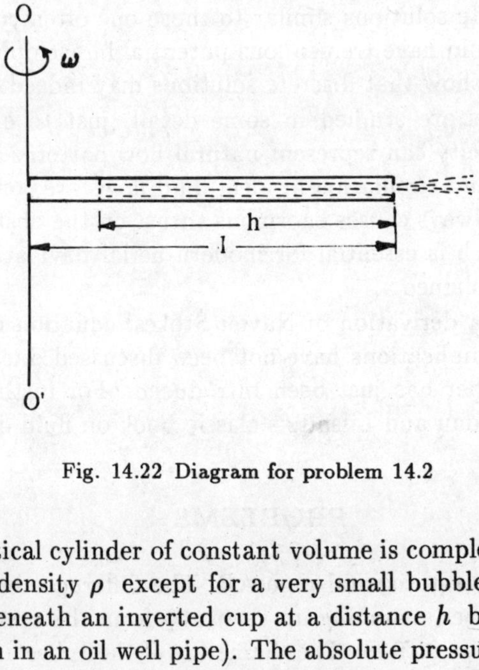

Fig. 14.22 Diagram for problem 14.2

14.3 A long closed vertical cylinder of constant volume is completely filled with an incompressible fluid of density ρ except for a very small bubble of an insoluble ideal gas that is trapped beneath an inverted cup at a distance h below the top of the liquid (as it may happen in an oil well pipe). The absolute pressure in the liquid at the top of the cylinder is P_o and at the site of the bubble $P_b = P_o + \rho gh$. The cup is now overturned and the bubble is allowed to escape. What happens to the pressure at various levels, for example, at the top, at the bottom of the cup, and at the bottom of the well.

14.4 Show that

(i) in the plane two-dimensional motion of an incompressible fluid, the vorticity of any particle remains constant,

(ii) an isothermal atmosphere in the actual gravity field of the earth can extend to infinity remaining nonzero,
(iii) $\nabla^2 \boldsymbol{q} = 0$, if the vorticity of an incompressible fluid is constant throughout,
(iv) $(\boldsymbol{q} \cdot \nabla)\boldsymbol{\omega} = (\boldsymbol{\omega} \cdot \nabla)\boldsymbol{q}$, if the motion of an incompressible fluid is constant throughout,
(v) Navier-Stokes' equation in vorticity $\boldsymbol{\omega}$ has the following form

$$\frac{\partial \boldsymbol{\omega}}{\partial t} = \nabla \times (\boldsymbol{q} \times \boldsymbol{\omega}) + \frac{\eta}{\rho}\nabla^2 \boldsymbol{\omega}$$

(vi) the circulation c around any closed path satisfies

$$\frac{Dc}{Dt} = \frac{\eta}{\rho}\nabla^2 c$$

14.5 Find the steady flow pattern of a two-dimensional irrotational flow of an ideal fluid, represented by the following complex potentials:
(*i*) $f(z) = -az + \exp(-ikz)$ (*ii*) $f(z) = -A \ln z$ and
(*iii*) $f(z) = \{ik/(2\pi)\} \ln z$ where a, k and A are real constants and $z = x + iy$.

14.6 Tar is continuously poured on an inclined (plane) road of width b, at a discharge rate (= volume flux) Q per unit width. Find the equilibrium thickness of the tar, if the tar is incompressible and has a viscosity η.

14.7 Show that the kinetic energy of a body of homogeneous fluid within a closed surface S, moving irrotationally is

$$T = \frac{1}{2}\rho \oint_S \phi \nabla \phi \cdot d\boldsymbol{S}$$

ϕ being the velocity potential.

14.8 If $\boldsymbol{q}$ and $\boldsymbol{q}'$ are the velocities of some fluid particle relative to two frames of reference S and S′, moving in any manner, the angular velocity of S′ relative to S being $\boldsymbol{\omega}_o$, show that the vorticity vector transforms as

$$\boldsymbol{\omega}' = \boldsymbol{\omega} - \boldsymbol{\omega}_o$$

and the circulation in a given closed contour,

$$c' = c - 2\omega_o A$$

where A is the area enclosed by the projection of Γ on the plane perpendicular to $\boldsymbol{\omega}_o$.

14.9 Express (i) the equation of continuity in the spherical polar and cylindrical polar coordinates. (ii) the equations of motion of a perfect fluid with respect to a frame of reference that is rotating with angular velocity $\boldsymbol{\omega}_o$ and translating with velocity $\boldsymbol{u}_o$.

14.10 If a moving fluid is bounded by a fixed surface $g(\boldsymbol{r}) = 0$, then show that the boundary condition is $\boldsymbol{q} \cdot \nabla g = 0$. However, if the boundary surface is itself moving and is given by $g(\boldsymbol{r}, t) = 0$, show that the boundary condition is now given by

$$\frac{\partial g}{\partial t} + \boldsymbol{q} \cdot \nabla g = 0$$

14.11 If a body of liquid is revolving about a vertical axis with an angular velocity $\boldsymbol{\omega} = f(r)\hat{\boldsymbol{k}}$, then show that the motion can be irrotational if $\boldsymbol{q} = rf(r)\hat{\boldsymbol{\theta}}$, and $f(r) \propto r^{-2}$.

14.12 Water from a running faucet is found to be tapering downwards until it breaks up into fast-moving droplets. How does the diameter of the continuous part of the flow change with distance from the mouth of the faucet?

14.13 When water is running out of a tap with sufficient speed, it is seen to form a nice circular halo of streaming water on the flat surface of the basin, due to a sudden changeover from shooting to streaming flow. Can you find the radius of transition? It might well be a research problem.

14.14 Find the equilibrium distribution of the acceleration due to gravity, and density of a perfect fluid near the surface of a star (assume a parallel atmosphere, that is, neglect the effect of the finite radius of curvature of the surface of the star).

14.15 A horizontally oriented circular plate is rotated with a very high angular speed. Another identical plate is almost on top of it with a small parallel gap between the two. The top disc will corotate with the bottom one due to frictional coupling. Now the centrifugal force acting on the gas molecules reduces the pressure of air inside, and the plates are attracted to each other. What is the magnitude of the force that will be required to keep the plates separated with a fixed gap?

14.16 The normal functioning of a heart requires that all heart muscles receive the supply of fresh blood in adequate amount. During a heart block, one of the coronary arteries develops an obstruction. As a remedy, a surgeon removes a piece of vein from some other part of the patient's body and grafts it across the coronary obstruction. This grafted coronary bypass restores the normal flow of blood to the heart muscle. Assume that the flow rate after the obstruction develops drops from Q to Q_a. Using Poiseuille's equation for viscous flow in a pipe, find the required length and diameter of the grafted vein.

APPENDIX A1

Coordinate Frames

All natural phenomena occur in space and in the course of time. In order to characterise a point in space where an event occurs, every point in space has to be labeled. It is assumed that free space or vacuum is homogeneous and isotropic, that is, all points in free space and all directions in it are equivalent. Points in space are labeled by means of a coordinate system. Any point in space can be chosen to be the origin of the coordinate frame. Thus each coordinate frame must have an origin. The origin of any physical coordinate frame is always associated with a material particle. We shall now describe a few types of coordinate systems that are useful for descriptions of natural phenomena.

In the three dimensional Euclidean space where we live, any point can be uniquely specified by an ordered set of three real numbers called, by definition, the coordinates of the point. A coordinate frame is designed in such a manner that this assignment of the coordinates to all points in the 3-D Euclidean space is unambiguously performed. However, there can be coordinate frames that are restricted to a limited region of space. Now, at any given point, it is possible to find out a set of three lines (curved or straight lines) along which alternately only one of these three coordinates changes while the other two coordinates remain constant. Such a set of three lines, known as coordinate lines, exist for every point in the space over which the coordinate frame is defined. If these coordinate lines at all points are found to be mutually perpendicular, the coordinate frame under consideration is called an *orthogonal* coordinate frame, and the system of coordinates are called *orthogonal* coordinates. Furthermore, if any or all coordinate lines are found to be not straight lines (in the Euclidean sense), the system of coordinates are called *curvilinear* coordinates.

A1.1 ORTHOGONAL COORDINATE FRAMES

A1.1.1 Rectangular Cartesian Coordinate Frame

It is the simplest and most natural coordinate system. It is constructed by tracing from the origin O three mutually perpendicular straight lines, denoted by OX, OY and OZ and called x-, y- and z-axes respectively (see Fig. A.1). Choosing some convenient units, these axes are graduated, so that any point on these axes has a measure of length expressed as a number in the above unit, representing the distance from the origin, of the point along the axis concerned. If the point is not on any one of these axes, then the rectangular projections of the line OP are drawn on these axes giving, say, OL $= x$, OM $= y$ and ON $= z$, respectively. The ordered set of these three numbers (x, y, z) are by definition called the rectangular Cartesian coordinates of the point P with respect to the given Cartesian coordinate frame OXYZ. The coordinate lines drawn through any point P are always parallel to the respective coordinate axes, which are by definition mutually perpendicular. Hence, this is an orthogonal coordinate frame.

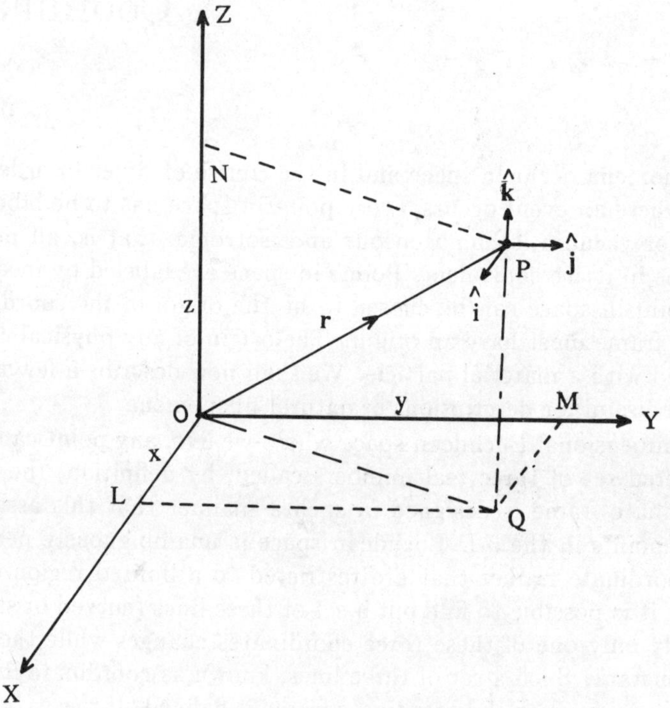

Fig. A.1 Rectangular 3-D Cartesian coordinate frame

Sometimes one may like to define a direction in space for point P. In that case, a knowledge of distance OP $= r$ is redundant. Instead one defines ratios $n_1 =$ OL/OP $= x/r$, $n_2 =$ OM/OP $= y/r$ and $n_3 =$ ON/OP $= z/r$. The set (n_1, n_2, n_3) is called the *direction cosines* of the direction OP. Obviously they satisfy $n_1^2 + n_2^2 + n_3^2 = 1$, implying that only two of them are independent, which is perfectly justified as a direction requires only two independent coordinates to be specified.

Since vectors are defined to be directed magnitudes, $\overrightarrow{\mathrm{OP}} \equiv \boldsymbol{r}$ will be the most natural notation for position vector of the point P with reference to the origin. So a unit vector in a given direction is the vector having unit magnitude. Let us use hats for representing the unit vectors, for example $\hat{\boldsymbol{r}}$ for the unit vector along $\boldsymbol{r}$. We use the unit vectors $\hat{\boldsymbol{\imath}}$, $\hat{\boldsymbol{\jmath}}$ and $\hat{\boldsymbol{k}}$ for the x-, y- and z-axes respectively. They constitute an orthogonal basis set of vectors. We know from the rules of addition of vectors that several vectors can be added simply by either constructing parallelepipeds with sides and directions given by the vectors or by following from tip to tip of the vectors in succession (the latter operation is allowed by the very definition of vectors; being simply the directed magnitudes, they can be transported parallel to themselves to anywhere in space), thus giving

$$\boldsymbol{r} = x\hat{\boldsymbol{i}} + y\hat{\boldsymbol{j}} + z\hat{\boldsymbol{k}} \qquad (A1.1)$$

and

$$\hat{\boldsymbol{r}} = n_1\hat{\boldsymbol{i}} + n_2\hat{\boldsymbol{j}} + n_3\hat{\boldsymbol{k}}$$

The rectangular Cartesian frames that have axes pointing towards fixed directions in space with the origin not accelerated with respect to most distant stars and galaxies are the nearest approximations to inertial frames.

Very often, one needs to construct a number of rectangular Cartesian frames with their origins separated and axes rotated by fixed amounts. The coordinate relations between the sets of coordinates, (x_1, x_2, x_3) and (x'_1, x'_2, x'_3), in two such rectangular Cartesian frames, say S and S′ respectively, are given by

$$x'_i = \sum_{j=1}^{3} a_{ij}x_j + b_i \qquad i = 1, 2, 3 \qquad (A1.2)$$

where $\boldsymbol{b} = \overrightarrow{\mathrm{OO'}} = b_1\hat{\boldsymbol{i}} + b_2\hat{\boldsymbol{j}} + b_3\hat{\boldsymbol{k}}$ is the the separation between the two origins and $a_{ij} = \cos\angle\hat{\boldsymbol{i}}',\hat{\boldsymbol{j}}$ are the direction cosines between unit vectors along coordinate axes x'_i and x_j. The derivation of the inverse relation, namely $x_i = \sum_j a_{ji}x'_j + c_i$, is left as an exercise.

It should however be pointed out that rectangular Cartesian coordinate frames are just a special class of all possible Cartesian coordinate frames. A Cartesian frame, by definition, has all the axes as straight lines fixed in space. The angular relation between the axes is a matter of choice. When the axes are not mutually perpendicular at the origin, such a Cartesian frame is called an *oblique Cartesian frame*. We shall briefly discuss them in section A1.2.

A1.1.2 Spherical Polar Coordinate Frame

In this frame any two of the rectangular Cartesian coordinate axes are retained intact, and the third coordinate axis is defined directly along the direction of the point whose coordinates are to be found out. So depending on the location of the point P, this new axis, called the *radial* axis, would have to orient itself in that direction (see Fig. A.2). So the radial axis is not a fixed axis in space, and therefore any such frame cannot be regarded as an inertial frame. Then out of the two Cartesian coordinate axes, one (usually the z-axis) is marked as the *polar* axis, and the other (usually the x-axis) as the *equatorial* reference axis in the equatorial or azimuthal plane of the frame. Being Cartesian in nature, both the polar axis and the azimuthal plane are fixed in space.

Now the *spherical polar coordinates* are defined as follows: The *radial coordinate* r is the projection of OP on to itself, the radial axis. Hence, r = OP. The *polar coordinate* θ is defined to be the angle between the polar axis and OP, that is, $\theta = \angle$ZOP. So θ is zero

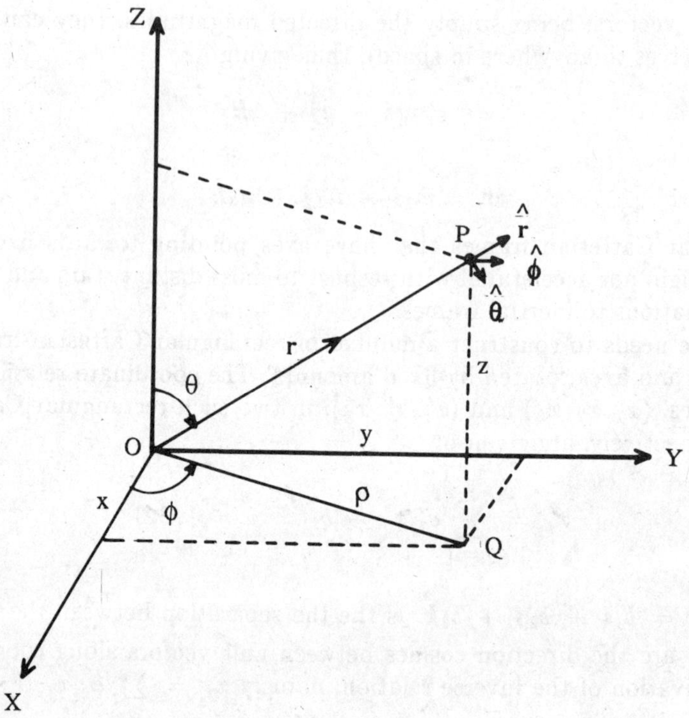

Fig. A.2 Spherical polar coordinate system

when OP is aligned with the z-axis, is $\pi/2$ when OP lies in the equatorial plane, and attains its maximum value of π when pointing towards the $-z$ axis. The *azimuthal coordinate* ϕ, the third, is defined to be the angle between the x-axis and the equatorial projection of OP. This can vary between 0 and 2π. So r = constant defines the surface of a sphere, θ = constant defines the surface of a cone with the apex at the origin and axis coinciding with the polar axis, and ϕ = constant represents a half plane bounded on one side by the entire polar axis. So through any point P, out of the three coordinate lines, only the radial coordinate line is a straight line, the other two are circular arcs. Hence, this is a curvilinear coordinate system.

Now, if the equatorial projection of OP is denoted by $OQ = \rho$, it is easy to see that $\rho = r\sin\theta$. So the geometrical correspondence between the rectangular Cartesian and the spherical polar coordinate systems with a common origin and z-axis as the polar axis is

$$x = r\sin\theta\cos\phi \qquad y = r\sin\theta\sin\phi \qquad \text{and} \qquad z = r\cos\theta \tag{A1.3}$$

and in vector notation

$$\boldsymbol{r} = r\hat{\boldsymbol{r}} \tag{A1.4}$$

Obviously,

$$\hat{\boldsymbol{r}} = \sin\theta\cos\phi\hat{\boldsymbol{i}} + \sin\theta\sin\phi\hat{\boldsymbol{j}} + \cos\theta\hat{\boldsymbol{k}} \tag{A1.5}$$

One can define two other unit vectors in the spherical polar coordinate system in the same spirit as they are defined for the rectangular Cartesian frame. For example, $\hat{\boldsymbol{\theta}}$ should be defined to point in the direction at P in which only the θ-coordinate increases, which is in fact given by

$$\hat{\boldsymbol{\theta}} = \hat{\boldsymbol{r}}(\theta + \frac{\pi}{2}, \phi) = \cos\theta\cos\phi\hat{\boldsymbol{i}} + \cos\theta\sin\phi\hat{\boldsymbol{j}} - \sin\theta\hat{\boldsymbol{k}} \tag{A1.6}$$

Similarly, $\hat{\boldsymbol{\phi}}$ is defined to point in the direction from P in which only the ϕ-coordinate increases. This direction lies in a plane parallel to the equatorial plane, hence

$$\hat{\boldsymbol{\phi}} = \hat{\boldsymbol{r}}(\theta = \frac{\pi}{2}, \phi + \frac{\pi}{2}) = -\sin\phi\hat{\boldsymbol{i}} + \cos\phi\hat{\boldsymbol{j}} \tag{A1.7}$$

It is now easy to check that the three unit vectors $(\hat{\boldsymbol{r}}, \hat{\boldsymbol{\theta}}, \hat{\phi})$ defined at the point P are locally tangential to the coordinate lines and are also perpendicular to each other, and hence form a complete set of locally orthogonal basis (unit) vectors. So the spherical polar coordinate systems are *orthogonal curvilinear coordinate systems.*

A1.1.3 Cylindrical Coordinate Frame

In this frame, the z-axis and x-axis are as usual kept intact, but the third axis, called the cylindrical radial axis, is redefined so as to point along OQ, the equatorial projection of OP. So the *cylindrical radial coordinate* becomes OQ $= \rho$. The azimuthal coordinate ϕ of the spherical polar coordinate system continues to be the same except for a change of its name to *cylindrical polar coordinate.* The third coordinate is chosen to be the original Cartesian z-coordinate. So in terms of the cylindrical polar coordinates (ρ, ϕ, z),

$$x = \rho\cos\phi \qquad y = \rho\sin\phi \qquad \text{and} \qquad z = z \tag{A1.8}$$

and in vector notation

$$\boldsymbol{r} = \rho\cos\phi\hat{\boldsymbol{i}} + \rho\sin\phi\hat{\boldsymbol{j}} + z\hat{\boldsymbol{k}}. \tag{A1.9}$$

The distinction between the nomenclatures of 'spherical polar' and 'cylindrical polar' arises from the fact that r = constant represents the surface of a sphere but ρ = constant represents the surface of an infinite cylinder. They are 'polar' because of the symmetry about the polar z-axis. Proceeding similarly, the orthogonal set of unit vectors at the point P for the cylindrical polar coordinate frame is given by

$$\hat{\boldsymbol{\rho}} = \cos\phi\hat{\boldsymbol{i}} + \sin\phi\hat{\boldsymbol{j}} \qquad \hat{\boldsymbol{\phi}} = -\sin\phi\hat{\boldsymbol{i}} + \cos\phi\hat{\boldsymbol{j}} \qquad \text{and} \qquad \hat{\boldsymbol{k}} \tag{A1.10}$$

So this is also a case of a curvilinear orthogonal coordinate system.

In fact, one can slightly redefine the instantaneous coordinate axes of the cylindrical polar frame as the same old rectangular Cartesian frame but rotated about its z-axis by an angle ϕ, so that the cylindrical radial axis is redefined as the new x-axis, say x'-axis. Therefore, the new Cartesian y-axis, say y'-axis will also be rotated by an angle ϕ in the common plane of x-y and x'-y' axes. The unit vectors $(\hat{\boldsymbol{i}}', \hat{\boldsymbol{j}}')$ are just the same as $(\hat{\boldsymbol{\rho}}, \hat{\boldsymbol{\phi}})$, and hence from Eq. (A1.10)

$$x' = x\cos\phi + y\sin\phi \qquad \text{and} \qquad y' = -x\sin\phi + y\cos\phi \tag{A1.11}$$

Equation (A1.11) can also be obtained from Eq. (A1.2) for the above rotation by an angle ϕ about the z-axis.

The plane polar frames are just a special case of both the spherical polar and cylindrical polar frames, as they are confined to the equatorial plane. The set (ρ, ϕ) are the coordinates.

A1.1.4 Orthogonal Parabolic Coordinate Frame

We move from the cylindrical polar coordinate frame to an orthogonal parabolic coordinate system having the coordinates χ, ζ and ϕ. This is effected by the relations

$$z = \frac{1}{2}(\chi - \zeta) \qquad \rho = \sqrt{\chi\zeta} \tag{A1.12}$$

The coordinates χ and ζ take values from 0 to ∞. The surfaces of constant χ and ζ are two families of paraboloids of revolution, with the z-axis still as the axis of symmetry. These equations can be rewritten in terms spherical polar radial coordinate $r = \sqrt{\rho^2 + z^2} = (\chi + \zeta)/2$, as

$$\chi = r + z \qquad \text{and} \qquad \zeta = r - z \tag{A1.13}$$

A1.1.5 Prolate Spheroidal Orthogonal Coordinate Frame

The prolate spheroidal coordinates (ξ, η, ϕ) are defined as

$$\begin{aligned} x &= \frac{d}{2}\sqrt{(\xi^2 - 1)(1 - \eta^2)}\cos\phi \\ y &= \frac{d}{2}\sqrt{(\xi^2 - 1)(1 - \eta^2)}\sin\phi \\ z &= \frac{d}{2}\xi\eta \end{aligned} \tag{A1.14}$$

where $1 \leq \xi < \infty$, $-1 \leq \eta \leq 1$, $0 \leq \phi < 2\pi$, and $d =$ interfocal distance.

The surfaces of constant ξ are confocal ellipsoids $4z^2/d^2\xi^2 + 4\rho^2/d^2(\xi^2 - 1) = 1$, of which, say F and F′ are the foci. The surfaces of constant η are the hyperboloids $4z^2/d^2\eta^2 - 4\rho^2/d^2(1 - \eta^2) = 1$, also with the same foci F and F′. The distances r_1 and r_2 to points F and F′ on the z-axis for which $z = \pm d/2$, are given by

$$r_1 = \sqrt{\left(z - \frac{d}{2}\right)^2 + \rho^2} \qquad \text{and} \qquad r_2 = \sqrt{\left(z + \frac{d}{2}\right)^2 + \rho^2}$$

which means

$$r_1 = (\xi - \eta)/2 \qquad \text{and} \qquad r_2 = (\xi + \eta)/2. \tag{A1.15}$$

Some of the most important orthogonal curvilinear coordinate systems are introduced here in detail, because orthogonality will be found to be the most important criterion for separability of coordinates for solving the Hamilton-Jacobi partial differential equation of motion, to be discussed in chapter 10.

A1.2 NONORTHOGONAL OR OBLIQUE COORDINATE FRAMES

When one or a few or all the coordinate lines of a coordinate system deviate from the condition of being mutually perpendicular, the coordinate system is called nonorthogonal or oblique. In such cases, the unit vectors defined along the coordinate lines are not mutually orthogonal at all points. We know that any three linearly independent vectors can form a basis set that is sufficient to describe any arbitrary vector in the 3-D Euclidean space. But the choice of the basis set is not quite unique for oblique coordinate frames. The coordinates will obviously depend on the choice of the *base vectors*. Hence one can have more than one choice of the set of coordinates for any given point, depending on the choice of the basis set. One obvious choice of the basis set is of course the standard one, namely the unit vectors along the coordinate lines, and the coordinates obtained correspondingly are called *contravariant* coordinates, and the base vectors are called *covariant* basis vectors. The other equally feasible choice of the basis vectors is to take the normal directions to the coordinate surfaces at the point under consideration (coordinate surfaces at a point are those surfaces over which a particular coordinate remains constant). In the case of orthogonal coordinate systems, the normal to the coordinate surface for any coordinate at any point is perfectly aligned with the local tangent to the coordinate line for the same coordinate. So one may argue, why should not the normals to the coordinate surfaces be considered for the candidate of the base vectors? In fact, if we have to deal with vectors of all possible kinds arising in diverse physical situations, one cannot help but accept two mutually complementary basis sets of vectors at each point of the space under any frame of reference, particularly for the oblique ones. The latter basis set of vectors, called the *contravariant* base vectors, are used to define the *covariant* coordinates of the same point, as well as the covariant components of any vector in general.

A1.2.1 Oblique Cartesian Coordinate Frame

This is the most simple case of a nonorthogonal coordinate frame having all the axes as straight lines fixed in space, but the angles between the axes are in general not right angles. We demonstrate a case in two dimensions (see Fig. A.3). OX and OY are the rectangular Cartesian axes. Let us choose OY′ as an oblique axis that makes an angle α ($\neq \pi/2$) with the axis OX, so that XOY′ can represent an oblique Cartesian frame.

The directions of the two sets of basis vectors at an arbitrary point P are shown in the figure. We have followed the standard conventions for denoting contravariant and covariant components of any vector, say the position vector, with a superscript index for contravariance and subscript index for covariance. The directions of the covariant base vectors are denoted in the figure by $\boldsymbol{g}_1$ and $\boldsymbol{g}_2$, whereas for contravariant ones by $\boldsymbol{g}^1$ and $\boldsymbol{g}^2$, as we are dealing with a 2-D case. The base vectors need not be unit vectors, in fact, in most cases they are not. In this particular example, we have for the position coordinates of P

$$\begin{aligned} x^1 &= x - y\cot\alpha \qquad & y^1 &= y_1 \csc\alpha \\ x_1 &= x & y_1 &= x\cos\alpha + y\sin\alpha \end{aligned} \tag{A1.16}$$

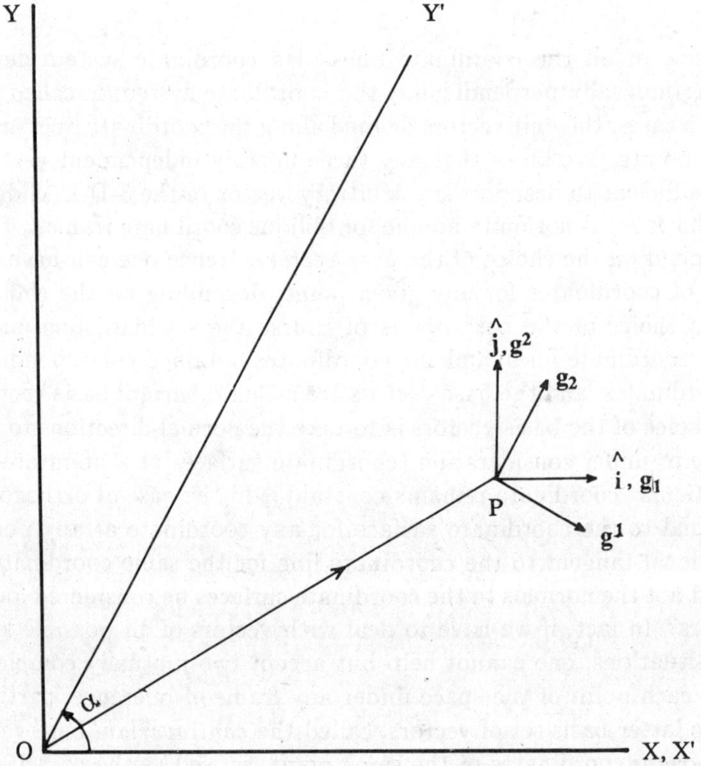

Fig. A.3 Oblique 2-D Cartesian coordinate frame showing covariant and contravariant basis vectors

where x, y are the rectangular Cartesian coordinates, x^1, y^1 are the contravariant position coordinates, and x_1, y_1 are the covariant position coordinates in the oblique Cartesian frame, of the same point P.

Obviously, for $\alpha = \pi/2$, all these definitions are equivalent. So there is no ambiguity in defining the rectangular Cartesian coordinates of any point. In orthogonal curvilinear coordinate frames, the directions of the two basis sets of vectors are also identical but these, not always being unit vectors, have usually different magnitudes, the determination of which will be considered in Appendix A2.

We cite just one example of nonorthogonal curvilinear coordinate frames.

A1.2.2 A 2-D Nonorthogonal Parabolic Frame

Consider the following parabolic coordinates u and v in the first quadrant of a rectangular Cartesian frame defined in a plane, given by

$$x = uv \quad \text{and} \quad y = \frac{1}{2}(u^2 + v^2) \tag{A1.17}$$

The coordinate curves for both u and v are parabolas of varying latus recta with the focal points evenly distributed on the y-axis, and therefore, intersect at all possible angles.

The criteria for checking nonorthogonality will be discussed in Appendix A2.

APPENDIX A2

Vector Calculus

The vector formulation started appearing in physics through the work of Josiah Willard Gibbs (*Vector Analysis* 1901) and is extremely useful in representing and dealing with physical quantities having both magnitude and direction. In this appendix we summarise the necessary parts of vector calculus which will be used in the main text of the book. We shall be dealing with ordinary vectors without making any distinction between the contravariant and covariant types until we come to section A2.9. In orthogonal coordinate systems such distinctions are not so important.

A2.1 INTRODUCTION TO KRONECKER DELTA AND LEVI-CIVITA SYMBOLS

We would like to introduce Kronecker's δ_{ij} symbol through the following elementary scalar product relations.

$$\delta_{ij} \equiv \hat{\boldsymbol{\imath}} \cdot \hat{\boldsymbol{\jmath}} \qquad (A2.1)$$

where $\hat{\boldsymbol{\imath}}$ and $\hat{\boldsymbol{\jmath}}$ are any two orthogonal basis vectors (unit vectors) in a 3-D Euclidean space, so that

$$\begin{aligned} \delta_{ij} &= 1 \qquad \text{provided} \quad i = j \\ &= 0 \qquad \text{otherwise} \end{aligned} \qquad (A2.2)$$

So δ_{ij} represents the unit matrix of rank 3.

The following properties of δ_{ij} can easily be proved:

$$\delta_{ij} = \delta_{ji} \qquad \delta_{ij}\delta_{kl} \neq \delta_{ik}\delta_{jl} \qquad \delta_{ij}\delta_{jk} = \delta_{ik} \qquad \text{and} \quad \delta_{ii} = 3 \qquad (A2.3)$$

where Einstein's summation convention, namely the repeated index in a term implying a sum over that index running from 1 to 3, is assumed. So when we use Einstein's summation convention to express any vector $\boldsymbol{a}$, it would simply be $\boldsymbol{a} = a_i\hat{\boldsymbol{\imath}}$, as i being the repeated index here implies the sum $a_1\hat{\mathbf{1}} + a_2\hat{\mathbf{2}} + a_3\hat{\mathbf{3}}$. One should keep in mind that $\hat{\mathbf{1}} \equiv \hat{\boldsymbol{\imath}}$, $\hat{\mathbf{2}} \equiv \hat{\boldsymbol{\jmath}}$ and $\hat{\mathbf{3}} \equiv \hat{\boldsymbol{k}}$, if we link them with the notations used in Appendix A1. So following this new convention, the scalar product of any two vectors $\boldsymbol{a}$ and $\boldsymbol{b}$ in a 3-D Euclidean space would be given as

$$\boldsymbol{a} \cdot \boldsymbol{b} = (a_i\hat{\boldsymbol{\imath}}) \cdot (b_j\hat{\boldsymbol{\jmath}}) \qquad i, j = 1, 2, 3$$

Bringing the scalar coefficients together and using Eqs (A2.1) – (A2.3), we get

$$\boldsymbol{a} \cdot \boldsymbol{b} = a_i b_j (\hat{\boldsymbol{\imath}} \cdot \hat{\boldsymbol{\jmath}}) = a_i b_j \delta_{ij} = a_i b_i \qquad (A2.4)$$

which obviously agrees with the usual definition of the scalar product of two vectors. Note that $b_j\delta_{ij} \equiv \Sigma_{j=1}^{3} b_j\delta_{ij} = b_i$.

We would like to define the Levi-Civita symbol ϵ_{ijk} through the equation

$$\epsilon_{ijk} = \hat{\boldsymbol{i}}\cdot(\hat{\boldsymbol{j}} \times \hat{\boldsymbol{k}}) \tag{A2.5}$$

where $\times$ symbolises the usual vector product.

It is easy to check that ϵ_{ijk} is antisymmetric in i, j, k, that is, it changes sign under any odd permutation of i, j, k. Thus, $|\epsilon_{ijk}| = 1$ only if all the indices i, j and k are different, while $\epsilon_{ijk} = 0$ if any two or all the indices are identical. So out of a total of $3 \times 3 \times 3 = 27$ elements of ϵ_{ijk}, only 6 survive, and the rest 21 elements are simply zeros. For a right handed coordinate system, $\epsilon_{ijk} = +1$ if i, j, k are in cyclic order of 1,2,3 and $\epsilon_{ijk} = -1$ if i, j, k are in the reverse cyclic order of 1,2,3. For a left-handed system, the above rules are exactly opposite.

Now the ith component of the vector (cross) product of any two arbitrary vectors $\boldsymbol{a}$ and $\boldsymbol{b}$ can be written as

$$(\boldsymbol{a} \times \boldsymbol{b})_i \equiv \hat{\boldsymbol{i}}\cdot(\boldsymbol{a} \times \boldsymbol{b}) = \hat{\boldsymbol{i}}\cdot[(a_j\hat{\boldsymbol{j}}) \times (b_k\hat{\boldsymbol{k}})] \qquad i, j, k = 1, 2, 3$$

giving

$$(\boldsymbol{a} \times \boldsymbol{b})_i = \hat{\boldsymbol{i}}\cdot(\hat{\boldsymbol{j}} \times \hat{\boldsymbol{k}})a_j b_k = \epsilon_{ijk}a_j b_k \tag{A2.6}$$

Here in Eq. (A2.6), i is not a repeated index on the right-hand side, but both j and k are. On expansion, this actually represents nine terms but only two of them would be surviving, thus matching with the expectation from a vector product. Levi-Civita symbols are also known as 'permutation symbols', as they are used to define the determinant of any say 3×3 matrix **A**, as follows

$$\det\|\mathrm{A}\| = \epsilon_{ijk}A_{i1}A_{j2}A_{k3}$$

The Levi-Civita symbols are connected to the Kronecker delta symbols through the following identity

$$\epsilon_{ijk}\epsilon_{lmn} = \text{det of} \begin{pmatrix} \delta_{il} & \delta_{im} & \delta_{in} \\ \delta_{jl} & \delta_{jm} & \delta_{jn} \\ \delta_{kl} & \delta_{km} & \delta_{kn} \end{pmatrix} \tag{A2.7}$$

Equation (A2.7) readily leads to the following identities

$$\begin{aligned} \epsilon_{ijk}\epsilon_{ilm} &= \delta_{jl}\delta_{km} - \delta_{jm}\delta_{kl} \\ \epsilon_{ijk}\epsilon_{ijl} &= 2\delta_{kl} \\ \epsilon_{ijk}\epsilon_{ijk} &= 2\delta_{kk} = 6 \end{aligned} \tag{A2.8}$$

Using the first of the Eqs (A2.8), the following identity can easily be established

$$\epsilon_{ijk}\epsilon_{ilm} + \epsilon_{ijm}\epsilon_{ikl} + \epsilon_{ijl}\epsilon_{imk} = 0 \tag{A2.9}$$

It is also easy to check that $\epsilon_{ijk}\delta_{jk} = 0$. Most of these relations will be required in chapter 9. It may be noted that all polar vectors, such as position vector, velocity vector, etc., can be expressed without involving any ϵ_{ijk} symbol, but all axial vectors, such as angular velocity, angular momentum, magnetic field, etc., will irreducibly involve an ϵ_{ijk} factor in their expressions. In fact, the matrix representation of ϵ_{ijk} explicitly reflects the handedness of the coordinate frame used. Since the product of two ϵ_{ijk} matrices is always expressible in terms of the Kronecker delta symbols, the product of any two axial vectors gives a polar vector. Arguing similarly, we can say that the scalar product between an axial vector and a polar vector cannot give an absolute scalar, but a pseudoscalar, whose sign would depend on the handedness (right or left) of the coordinate frame.

Exercise

Use Kronecker delta and Levi-Civita symbols to prove the following identities

(i) $\boldsymbol{a}\cdot(\boldsymbol{b}\times\boldsymbol{c}) = \boldsymbol{b}\cdot(\boldsymbol{c}\times\boldsymbol{a}) = \boldsymbol{c}\cdot(\boldsymbol{a}\times\boldsymbol{b})$
(ii) $\boldsymbol{a}\times(\boldsymbol{b}\times\boldsymbol{c}) = (\boldsymbol{a}\cdot\boldsymbol{c})\boldsymbol{b} - (\boldsymbol{a}\cdot\boldsymbol{b})\boldsymbol{c}$
(iii) $(\boldsymbol{a}\times\boldsymbol{b})\cdot(\boldsymbol{c}\times\boldsymbol{d}) = (\boldsymbol{a}\cdot\boldsymbol{c})(\boldsymbol{b}\cdot\boldsymbol{d}) - (\boldsymbol{a}\cdot\boldsymbol{d})(\boldsymbol{b}\cdot\boldsymbol{c})$
(iv) $(\boldsymbol{a}\times\boldsymbol{b})\times(\boldsymbol{c}\times\boldsymbol{d}) = [\boldsymbol{a},\boldsymbol{c},\boldsymbol{d}]\boldsymbol{b} - [\boldsymbol{b},\boldsymbol{c},\boldsymbol{d}]\boldsymbol{a} = [\boldsymbol{a},\boldsymbol{b},\boldsymbol{d}]\boldsymbol{c} - [\boldsymbol{a},\boldsymbol{b},\boldsymbol{c}]\boldsymbol{d}$
where $[\boldsymbol{a},\boldsymbol{b},\boldsymbol{c}]$ stands for the scalar triple product $\boldsymbol{a}\cdot(\boldsymbol{b}\times\boldsymbol{c})$.

A2.2 PARTIAL DIFFERENTIATION OF VECTORS AND SCALARS

Let $\phi(\boldsymbol{x})$ be a scalar valued function of a vector argument $\boldsymbol{x} = (x\hat{\boldsymbol{i}}, y\hat{\boldsymbol{j}}, z\hat{\boldsymbol{k}})$ where (x, y, z) are the rectangular Cartesian coordinates of the point defining $\boldsymbol{x}$ with respect to a given orthonormal basis $(\hat{\boldsymbol{i}}, \hat{\boldsymbol{j}}, \hat{\boldsymbol{k}})$ of the 3-D Euclidean space. We define an operator ∇ operating on ϕ and yielding a vector $\nabla\phi$ through,

$$\nabla\phi = \frac{\partial\phi}{\partial x}\hat{\boldsymbol{i}} + \frac{\partial\phi}{\partial y}\hat{\boldsymbol{j}} + \frac{\partial\phi}{\partial z}\hat{\boldsymbol{k}} \tag{A2.10}$$

and therefore,

$$d\phi = \frac{\partial\phi}{\partial x}dx + \frac{\partial\phi}{\partial y}dy + \frac{\partial\phi}{\partial z}dz = \nabla\phi\cdot d\boldsymbol{r}$$

For a given magnitude of $d\boldsymbol{r}$, $d\phi$ is maximum only if $d\boldsymbol{r}$ is aligned parallel to $\nabla\phi$, or in other words, the direction of the vector $\nabla\phi$ is that in which the space rate of change of ϕ is maximum. This is the reason why $\nabla\phi$ is often called 'grad ϕ' or the *gradient* of ϕ. It is now obvious that

$$(\nabla)_i = \hat{\boldsymbol{i}}\cdot\nabla = \frac{\partial}{\partial x_i} \qquad \text{and} \qquad \frac{\partial x_i}{\partial x_j} = \delta_{ij}$$

which is another definition of δ_{ij}. Note that we have returned to the notation of (x_1, x_2, x_3) for (x, y, z). The divergence of a vector field $\boldsymbol{A}(\boldsymbol{x})$ is defined to be a scalar product of ∇ operator and the vector field $\boldsymbol{A}(\boldsymbol{x})$:

$$\nabla\cdot\boldsymbol{A} = \frac{\partial A_i}{\partial x_i} \tag{A2.11}$$

Carl Gauss proved in 1839 that the divergence of a vector field at a given point represents the net flux of the vector field across any arbitrarily small closed surface around the point.

The ith component of the *curl* of a vector field $\boldsymbol{A}(\boldsymbol{x})$ at a given point is defined by the vector product of the operator ∇ and $\boldsymbol{A}$:

$$(\text{curl } \boldsymbol{A})_i = \hat{\boldsymbol{i}} \cdot (\nabla \times \boldsymbol{A}) = \epsilon_{ijk} \frac{\partial A_k}{\partial x_j} \tag{A2.12}$$

In 1854, George Stokes gave a physical meaning to the curl operation. The quantity corresponding to the curl of a vector is the circulation of the flow of any vector field (for example, the circulation of fluid flow).

One can now easily prove all the ∇ operator identities, using δ_{ij} and ϵ_{ijk}. We demonstrate here with an example.

$$\begin{aligned}
\nabla \cdot (\boldsymbol{A} \times \boldsymbol{B}) &= \frac{\partial}{\partial x_i} (\boldsymbol{A} \times \boldsymbol{B})_i = \frac{\partial}{\partial x_i} (\epsilon_{ijk} A_j B_k) \\
&= \epsilon_{ijk} \frac{\partial A_j}{\partial x_i} B_k + \epsilon_{ijk} \frac{\partial B_k}{\partial x_i} A_j \geq' 6'6 \geq \frac{\partial B_k}{\partial x_i} A_j \\
&= (\nabla \times \boldsymbol{A})_k B_k - (\nabla \times \boldsymbol{B})_j A_j \\
&= \boldsymbol{B} \cdot (\nabla \times \boldsymbol{A}) - \boldsymbol{A} \cdot (\nabla \times \boldsymbol{B})
\end{aligned}$$

where $\boldsymbol{A}(\boldsymbol{x})$ and $\boldsymbol{B}(\boldsymbol{x})$ are any two vector fields defined over the same region of space.

Exercise

Prove the following vector identities involving the ∇ operator

(i) $\nabla(r^n) = n r^{n-2} \boldsymbol{r}$ (ii) $\nabla \cdot \boldsymbol{r} = 3$ (iii) $\nabla \times (\omega \times \boldsymbol{r}) = 2\omega$

(iv) $\nabla \cdot (\phi \boldsymbol{A}) = (\nabla \phi) \cdot \boldsymbol{A} + \phi (\nabla \cdot \boldsymbol{A})$ (v) $\nabla \times (\nabla \phi) = 0$

(vi) $\nabla \times (\phi \boldsymbol{A}) = (\nabla \phi) \times \boldsymbol{A} + \phi (\nabla \times \boldsymbol{A})$ (vii) $\nabla \cdot (\nabla \times \boldsymbol{A}) = 0$

(viii) $\nabla \times (\boldsymbol{A} \times \boldsymbol{B}) = (\boldsymbol{B} \cdot \nabla)\boldsymbol{A} - \boldsymbol{B}(\nabla \cdot \boldsymbol{A}) - (\boldsymbol{A} \cdot \nabla)\boldsymbol{B} + \boldsymbol{A}(\nabla \cdot \boldsymbol{B})$

(ix) $\nabla(\boldsymbol{A} \cdot \boldsymbol{B}) = (\boldsymbol{B} \cdot \nabla)\boldsymbol{A} + (\boldsymbol{A} \cdot \nabla)\boldsymbol{B} + \boldsymbol{B} \times (\nabla \times \boldsymbol{A}) + \boldsymbol{A} \times (\nabla \times \boldsymbol{B})$

Show that if both divergence and curl of a vector field $\boldsymbol{A}(\boldsymbol{r})$ are specified, that is, if $\nabla \cdot \boldsymbol{A} = \rho(\boldsymbol{r})$ and $\nabla \times \boldsymbol{A} = \boldsymbol{H}(\boldsymbol{r})$ are given, the solution for $\boldsymbol{A}$ is unique apart from a trivial constant vector and is given by $\boldsymbol{A}(\boldsymbol{r}) = \frac{1}{3}(\rho\, \boldsymbol{r}) - \frac{1}{2}(\boldsymbol{r} \times \boldsymbol{H})$.

A2.3 ORDINARY DIFFERENTIATION OF VECTORS

Let $\boldsymbol{r} \equiv \boldsymbol{r}(t)$ be a vector function depending on a single parameter t. One obvious interpretation of $\boldsymbol{r}(t)$ in physical situations would be the position vector of a particle as an explicit function of t as time. We can write $\boldsymbol{r}$ as $(x(t), y(t), z(t))$ where (x, y, z) are the rectangular Cartesian coordinates of the particle at time t. The instantaneous velocity and acceleration of the particles are then defined as

$$\boldsymbol{v}(t) = \frac{d\boldsymbol{r}}{dt} = \left(\frac{dx(t)}{dt}, \frac{dy(t)}{dt}, \frac{dz(t)}{dt} \right) \tag{A2.13}$$

and

$$\boldsymbol{a}(t) = \frac{d^2 \boldsymbol{r}(t)}{dt^2} = \left(\frac{d^2 x(t)}{dt^2}, \frac{d^2 y(t)}{dt^2}, \frac{d^2 z(t)}{dt^2} \right) \tag{A2.14}$$

If $\boldsymbol{A}(t)$ and $\boldsymbol{B}(t)$ are two vector functions of a single parameter t and ϕ is a scalar valued function, then

$$\frac{d}{dt}(\boldsymbol{A} \times \boldsymbol{B}) = \frac{d\boldsymbol{A}}{dt} \times \boldsymbol{B} + \boldsymbol{A} \times \frac{d\boldsymbol{B}}{dt} \quad \text{and} \quad \frac{d}{dt}(\phi \boldsymbol{A}) = \frac{d\phi}{dt}\boldsymbol{A} + \phi\frac{d\boldsymbol{A}}{dt} \qquad (A2.15)$$

From the Eqs (A2.15), it is now easy to see the following vector conditions for constancy of vectors and of their magnitudes:
(i) if $d\boldsymbol{A}/dt = \boldsymbol{0}$, $\boldsymbol{A} = \text{const.}$
(ii) if $\boldsymbol{A} \cdot (d\boldsymbol{A}/dt) = 0$, then $|\boldsymbol{A}| = \text{const.}$ and
(iii) if $\boldsymbol{A} \times (d\boldsymbol{A}/dt) = \boldsymbol{0}$, then $d\boldsymbol{A}/dt$ is parallel to $\boldsymbol{A}$ implying that $\boldsymbol{A}$ has constant direction.

Further, we have for $\boldsymbol{a} = \boldsymbol{A}(\boldsymbol{r}, t)$

$$d\boldsymbol{A} = \frac{\partial \boldsymbol{A}}{\partial x}dx + \frac{\partial \boldsymbol{A}}{\partial y}dy + \frac{\partial \boldsymbol{A}}{\partial z}dz + \frac{\partial \boldsymbol{A}}{\partial t}dt = (d\boldsymbol{r} \cdot \boldsymbol{\nabla})\boldsymbol{A} + \frac{\partial \boldsymbol{A}}{\partial t}dt$$

or

$$dA_i = \frac{\partial A_i}{\partial x_j}dx_j + \frac{\partial A_i}{\partial t}dt \qquad (A2.16)$$

A2.4 VECTOR INTEGRATION

This involves integration of a vector field specified over a region of space in R^3 or a region on a surface or on a segment of a curve. These integrals are expressed as multiple integrals over the parameters describing the regions of space which then are evaluated. We shall not pause here to detail this theory of integration and the important integral theorems like Green's theorem (1828), Gauss' divergence theorem (1838) and Stokes' theorem (1854). We merely give the statements of the above theorems. Their proofs and the problems based on them have to be dealt as a part of an independent course on vector calculus. In everything that follows we shall assume that all functions are C^1, that is, these functions have continuous partial derivatives.

Green's Theorem

Let

$$\boldsymbol{F}(x, y) = (P(x, y), Q(x, y))$$

denote a vector field defined over a region in a plane. Let $C : [a, b] \rightarrow U$ be a curve in this region parametrised by a parameter t. Then we have

$$\int_C \boldsymbol{F} \cdot d\boldsymbol{r} = \int_a^b F(C(t)) \cdot C'(t)dt = \int_C P(x, y)dx + Q(x, y)dy \qquad (A2.17)$$

The last integral is abbreviated as $\int_C P\,dx + Q\,dy$.

Now the statement of Green's theorem is as follows:
Let P, Q be C^1 functions on a region A which is the interior of a closed piecewise C^1 path

C parametrised counterclockwise. Then

$$\int_C P\,dx + Q\,dy = \int\int_A \left(\frac{\partial Q}{\partial x} - \frac{\partial P}{\partial y}\right) dy\,dx \tag{A2.18}$$

Gauss's divergence theorem

Following is the statement of the theorem.

Let U be a region in 3-space, forming the inside of a surface S which is smooth except for a finite number of smooth curves. Let $\boldsymbol{F}$ be a C^1 vector field on a region containing U and S. Let $\hat{\boldsymbol{n}}$ be the unit outward normal to S. Then

$$\int_S \boldsymbol{F}\cdot\hat{\boldsymbol{n}}\,d\sigma = \int_U (\nabla\cdot\boldsymbol{F})\,dV \tag{A2.19}$$

where the expression on the RHS is the triple integral of the function div $\boldsymbol{F}$ over the region U.

It is one of the most fundamental theorems used extensively in practically all domains of physics. The right hand side of Eq. (A2.19) represents a volume integral for the integrand div $\boldsymbol{F}$, a scalar function formed out of a vector field $\boldsymbol{F}$. So it requires the knowledge of the vector field $\boldsymbol{F}$ over each and every point of the region U. But look at the integral on the left hand side of Eq. (A2.19). For its evaluation it does not require any knowledge of the values of $\boldsymbol{F}$ at any inside point of the region U, instead, only the values of $\boldsymbol{F}$ on the bounding surface U suffice. To stress upon its importance, let us take $\boldsymbol{F}$ to be the gravity field $\boldsymbol{g}$ of the earth. Obviously, we can hardly have any direct measurement of $\boldsymbol{g}$ for most part of the earth's interior. Yet, the volume integral of $\nabla\cdot\boldsymbol{g}$ over the entire earth can be evaluated, by Gauss' theorem, from the closed surface integral of $\boldsymbol{g}$, the integration being performed over the surface the bounds its interior, for which the values of $\boldsymbol{g}$ are readily available. It appears amazing simply because without opening a box, you are speaking correctly of its content. You can find it yourself from any book on vector calculus that gives a proof of Gauss' theorem, and see how and at what point of the proof, the volume integral changes to a surface integral. Obviously, you have to integrate in one dimension, and the very definition of divergence of a vector helps it do so.

The left hand side of Eq. (A2.19) corresponds to the total flux of $\boldsymbol{F}$, that come out of the closed surface bounding the region U. The flux of a vector $\boldsymbol{F}$ over any piece of surface S, is defined as

$$\text{Flux} = \int_S \boldsymbol{F}\cdot\hat{\boldsymbol{n}}\,d\sigma \tag{A2.20}$$

Since the total flux of a vector tells us about how much of it is coming out of the closed surface, then by Gauss' theorem, $\nabla\cdot\boldsymbol{F}$ at any inside point must say how much of the flux it really generates at that point. So Gauss' theorem is a book-keeping theorem on flux conservation.

Similarly, Stokes' theorem converts an open surface integral into a line integral, the line being the boundary of the open surface. In this case, it is the book keeping of circulation or vortices (which are always 'curly' in appearance), rather than the flux. Intuitively speaking, the concept of flux has to involve a surface integral, whereas a circulation has its business done on a curve.

Stokes' Theorem:

Let S be a smooth surface in R^3 bounded by a closed curve C. Assume that the surface is orientable and that the boundary curve is oriented so that the surface lies to the left of the curve. Let $\boldsymbol{F}$ be a C^1 vector field in a region containing S and its boundary. Then

$$\int_S (\nabla \times \boldsymbol{F}) \cdot \hat{\boldsymbol{n}}\, d\sigma = \int_C \boldsymbol{F} \cdot d\boldsymbol{l} \tag{A2.21}$$

There are other usable forms of Gauss' and Stokes' theorems, namely

$$\int_V (\nabla \times \boldsymbol{F})\, dV = \int_S d\boldsymbol{S} \times \boldsymbol{F} \quad \text{and} \quad \int_C \phi\, d\boldsymbol{r} = \int_S d\boldsymbol{S} \times \nabla\phi \tag{A2.22}$$

Also Green's theorem can be developed into two identities, namely

$$\int_V (\phi\nabla^2\psi + \nabla\phi \cdot \nabla\psi)\, dV = \int_S (\phi\nabla\psi) \cdot d\boldsymbol{S} \tag{A2.23}$$

and

$$\int_V (\phi\nabla^2\psi - \psi\nabla^2\phi) dV = \int_S (\phi\nabla\psi - \psi\nabla\phi) \cdot d\boldsymbol{S} \tag{A2.24}$$

A2.5 TANGENT, PRINCIPAL NORMAL AND BINORMAL OF ORBITS

Let $\boldsymbol{r}(s)$ represent the orbit of a particle, which is a curve in the 3– D Euclidean space parametrised by s, the arc length measured along the curve from some chosen point on the orbit. Any neighbouring point on it has a position vector, say $\boldsymbol{r} + d\boldsymbol{r}$. Obviously, $|d\boldsymbol{r}| = ds$, and hence $d\boldsymbol{r}/ds$ is a unit vector pointing along the tangent at the point and toward the increasing value of s. Thus, the unit vector (see Fig. A.4)

$$\hat{\boldsymbol{t}} = \frac{d\boldsymbol{r}}{ds} \tag{A2.25}$$

evaluated at a point on the orbit having the parameter value $s = s_o$ defines the direction of the tangent to the curve at the point $\boldsymbol{r}(s_o)$. It is called the unit tangent vector.

Now since $\hat{\boldsymbol{t}} \cdot \hat{\boldsymbol{t}} = 1$, on differentiation with respect to s it gives

$$0 = \frac{d\hat{\boldsymbol{t}}}{ds} \cdot \hat{\boldsymbol{t}}$$

which means that $d\hat{\boldsymbol{t}}/ds$ is perpendicular to $\hat{\boldsymbol{t}}$. Thus we can write

$$\frac{d\hat{\boldsymbol{t}}}{ds} = \kappa\hat{\boldsymbol{n}} \tag{A2.26}$$

where $\hat{\boldsymbol{n}}$ is a unit vector in the direction of $(d\hat{\boldsymbol{t}}/ds)$ and hence perpendicular to $\hat{\boldsymbol{t}}$. This definition of $\hat{\boldsymbol{n}}$ also suggests that $\hat{\boldsymbol{n}}$ must lie in the tangent plane passing through an infinitesimal segment of the curve at the point concerned. Hence $\kappa = |d\hat{\boldsymbol{t}}/ds|$ is called

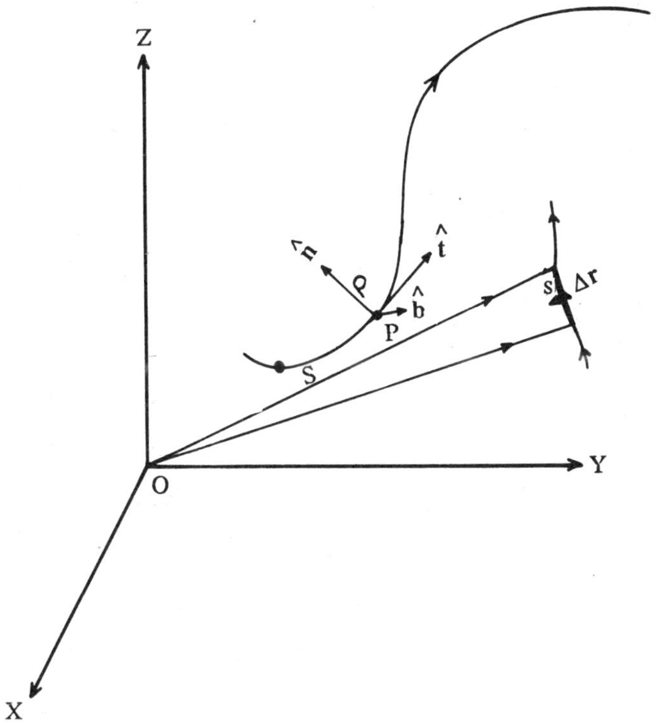

Fig. A.4 Directions of unit tangent, unit normal, and unit binormal vectors at any point of the trajectory of a particle in 3-D space

the *curvature* of the orbit or of the curve $\mathbf{r}(s)$. κ^{-1} would be, by definition, the radius of curvature of the orbit. $\hat{\boldsymbol{n}}$ is called the *principal normal* unit vector.

Exercise

Show that if an orbit lies in a plane and is described by a curve $\mathbf{r}(s)$ in terms of arc length s and its slope angle θ, the curvature $\kappa = |d\hat{t}/ds| = d\theta/ds$.

Since we have been able to define two unit vectors at a point mutually orthogonal, the third unit vector orthogonal to both these unit vectors can be uniquely defined through the vector product $\hat{\boldsymbol{t}} \times \hat{\boldsymbol{n}}$. This is how the *binormal* unit vector $\hat{\boldsymbol{b}}$ is defined,

$$\hat{\boldsymbol{b}} = \hat{\boldsymbol{t}} \times \hat{\boldsymbol{n}}$$

Again, using the fact that $\hat{\boldsymbol{b}} \cdot \hat{\boldsymbol{b}} = 1$, we get $0 = \hat{\boldsymbol{b}} \cdot (d\hat{\boldsymbol{b}}/ds)$ implying that $(d\hat{\boldsymbol{b}}/ds)$ is perpendicular to $\hat{\boldsymbol{b}}$. Also since $\hat{\boldsymbol{t}} \cdot \hat{\boldsymbol{b}} = 0$, we get on differentiation,

$$\frac{d\hat{\boldsymbol{t}}}{ds} \cdot \hat{\boldsymbol{b}} + \hat{\boldsymbol{t}} \cdot \frac{d\hat{\boldsymbol{b}}}{ds} = 0$$

of which the first term vanishes, proving finally the orthogonality of $\hat{\boldsymbol{t}}$ and $d\hat{\boldsymbol{b}}/ds$. This means that $d\hat{\boldsymbol{b}}/ds$ must be parallel to $\hat{\boldsymbol{n}}$ and we can write

$$\frac{d\hat{\boldsymbol{b}}}{ds} = \tau\hat{\boldsymbol{n}} \tag{A2.27}$$

The above equation defines another scalar constant τ, which is called the *torsion* of the orbit or curve $\boldsymbol{r}(s)$ at the given instant. Further, since $\hat{\boldsymbol{t}}$, $\hat{\boldsymbol{n}}$ and $\hat{\boldsymbol{b}}$ form an orthonormal triad

$$\hat{\boldsymbol{n}} = \hat{\boldsymbol{b}} \times \hat{\boldsymbol{t}}$$

we get,

$$\frac{d\hat{\boldsymbol{n}}}{ds} = \frac{d\hat{\boldsymbol{b}}}{ds} \times \hat{\boldsymbol{t}} + \hat{\boldsymbol{b}} \times \frac{d\hat{\boldsymbol{t}}}{ds} = -\tau\hat{\boldsymbol{b}} - \kappa\hat{\boldsymbol{t}} \tag{A2.28}$$

Equations (A2.25) to (A2.28) are known as the Frenet-Seret formulae.

We shall now use these formulae to study an important genera of curves called *evolutes* and *involutes*. At the moment, these concepts may appear quite abstract, but will find a place in chapter 7.

Definition

If there is a one-to-one correspondence between the points of two curves C_1 and C_2 such that the tangent at any point of C_1 is a normal at the corresponding point of C_2, then C_1 is called an *evolute* of C_2 and C_2, an *involute* of C_1.

Suppose the equation for the evolute curve C_1 is given as $\boldsymbol{r} = \boldsymbol{f}(s)$. We want to find out the equation for its involute C_2. If the distance P_1P_2 (see the Fig. A.5) is taken to be u, the position vector OP_2 will be $\boldsymbol{R} = \boldsymbol{r} + u\hat{\boldsymbol{t}}$, where $\boldsymbol{r} = \boldsymbol{f}(s)$ and $\hat{\boldsymbol{t}} = d\boldsymbol{r}/ds$. Therefore,

$$\frac{d\boldsymbol{R}}{ds} = \left(1 + \frac{du}{ds}\right)\hat{\boldsymbol{t}} + u\kappa\hat{\boldsymbol{n}}$$

Since $d\boldsymbol{R}/ds$ is parallel to the tangent at P_2, which is normal to $\hat{\boldsymbol{t}}$, $d\boldsymbol{R}/ds$ must be perpendicular to $\hat{\boldsymbol{t}}$. Therefore,

$$1 + \frac{du}{ds} = 0 \quad \text{or} \quad u = u_o - s \tag{A2.29}$$

Hence, the equation for the involute will be

$$\boldsymbol{R} = \boldsymbol{f}(s) + (u_o - s)\frac{d\boldsymbol{f}}{ds}$$

for any given evolute $\boldsymbol{r} = \boldsymbol{f}(s)$. Actually, for each value of u_o, there will be an involute. So for a given evolute, there exists a family of an infinite number of involutes. The same is true for a given involute.

The simplest realisation of involutes to a given evolute is the case of winding strings on the surface of any object. The open end of the string, if forced to remain stretched during the process of winding, will describe an involute to the curve on the body traced by the winding thread. The latter is an evolute as the string touches it tangentially, and the open end of the

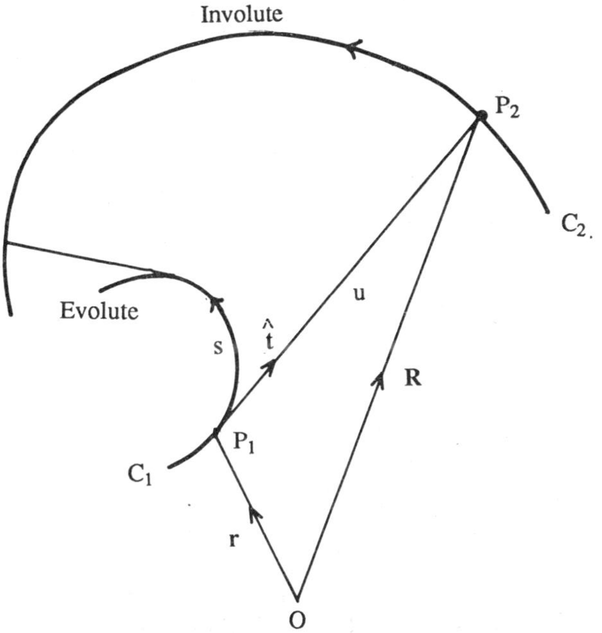

Fig. A.5 A construction for finding the equation of an involute C_2 for a given evolute C_1 and vice versa

string must move in a direction perpendicular to the string itself. Equation (A2.29) suggests that the length of the string u used up in winding is just equal to the increase in arclength s of the evolute along which the winding takes place. So the involute of a circle is a spiral (see problem I.39). In fact, there are families of curves such that both the evolutes and involutes belong to the same family, such as cycloids, hypocycloids and epicycloids. The involutes of any cycloid are themselves cycloids. Such families of self-replicating evolute-involute curves are said to form *tesserals*. We shall see more of them in chapter 7.

A2.6 KINEMATICS OF PARTICLE MOTION

We can now express the kinematical quantities like velocity, acceleration and jerk of a particle in terms of the complete set of orthonormal basis vectors $(\hat{\boldsymbol{t}}, \hat{\boldsymbol{n}}, \hat{\boldsymbol{b}})$. Let the curve traced by the particle be $\boldsymbol{r}(s)$, where s is the measure of the arc length along the curve. We then have for the velocity

$$\boldsymbol{v} = \frac{d\boldsymbol{r}}{dt} = \frac{d\boldsymbol{r}}{ds} \cdot \frac{ds}{dt} = \frac{ds}{dt}\hat{\boldsymbol{t}} = v\hat{\boldsymbol{t}} \tag{A2.30}$$

and the acceleration

$$\boldsymbol{a} = \frac{d\boldsymbol{v}}{dt} = \frac{d^2 s}{dt^2}\hat{\boldsymbol{t}} + \frac{ds}{dt}\frac{d\hat{\boldsymbol{t}}}{ds}\frac{ds}{dt} = \frac{dv}{dt}\hat{\boldsymbol{t}} + v^2\kappa\hat{\boldsymbol{n}} \tag{A2.31}$$

where $v = ds/dt$ is the speed or the magnitude of velocity of the particle. Similarly, the 'jerk'

$$\boldsymbol{j} \equiv \frac{d^3\boldsymbol{r}}{dt^3} = -\kappa^2\hat{\boldsymbol{t}} + \frac{d\kappa}{ds}\hat{\boldsymbol{n}} - \kappa\tau\hat{\boldsymbol{b}} \tag{A2.32}$$

So one can easily see that the acceleration has two components, one component is due to the acceleration in the direction of motion, and the other component is the centripetal acceleration, and this is valid for all possible trajectories of the particle. The acceleration does not involve the torsion of the orbit, but the jerk does.

The values of κ and τ can be obtained from the following two expressions

$$\left[\frac{d\boldsymbol{r}}{dt}, \frac{d^2\boldsymbol{r}}{dt^2}, \frac{d^3\boldsymbol{r}}{dt^3}\right] = -\kappa\tau v^3 \tag{A2.33}$$

and

$$\left|\frac{d\boldsymbol{r}}{dt} \times \frac{d^2\boldsymbol{r}}{dt^2}\right| = v^3\kappa \tag{A2.34}$$

As an illustration, we consider the motion of a charged particle in the field of a constant magnetic induction $\boldsymbol{B}$. We wish to find the curvature and the torsion of the spiralling path of the charged particle at any instant. The equation of motion is

$$m\frac{d\boldsymbol{v}}{dt} = e(\boldsymbol{v} \times \boldsymbol{B})$$

which implies

$$\boldsymbol{v} \cdot \frac{d\boldsymbol{v}}{dt} = 0$$

so that $|\boldsymbol{v}| = \text{constant} = v_o$, say. The solution to the equation of motion is

$$\boldsymbol{v} = \boldsymbol{v}_o + \frac{e}{m}\{(\boldsymbol{r} - \boldsymbol{r}_o) \times \boldsymbol{B}\}$$

which gives

$$\boldsymbol{v} \cdot \boldsymbol{B} = \boldsymbol{v}_o \cdot \boldsymbol{B} = v_o B \cos\theta$$

where θ is the angle between $\boldsymbol{v}_o$ and $\boldsymbol{B}$. Taking the vector product with respect to $\boldsymbol{v}$ on both sides of the original equation of motion we get

$$\boldsymbol{v} \times \frac{dv}{dt} = \frac{e}{m}\boldsymbol{v} \times (v \times \boldsymbol{B}) = \frac{e}{m}[(v \cdot \boldsymbol{B})v - v^2\boldsymbol{B}]$$

Similarly differentiating the same equation of motion once with respect to t, we get

$$\boldsymbol{j} = \frac{d^2\boldsymbol{v}}{dt^2} = \frac{e^2}{m^2}[(v \cdot \boldsymbol{B})\boldsymbol{B} - B^2\boldsymbol{v}]$$

We can now obtain the curvature (κ) and the torsion (τ) as

$$\kappa = \frac{e}{m}\frac{B\sin\theta}{v_o} \quad \text{and} \quad \tau = \frac{e}{m}\frac{B\cos\theta}{v_o} \tag{A2.35}$$

Taylor's Series Expansion of r(s), Where s is Small

Let $\boldsymbol{r}(s)$ be a vector function of the scalar arclength parameter s. Then $\boldsymbol{r}(s)$ can be expanded for small s around $s = 0$ as

$$\begin{aligned}\boldsymbol{r}(s) &= \boldsymbol{r}(0) + s\left.\frac{d\boldsymbol{r}}{ds}\right|_{s=0} + \frac{s^2}{2!}\left.\frac{d^2\boldsymbol{r}}{ds^2}\right|_{s=0} + \frac{s^3}{3!}\left.\frac{d^3\boldsymbol{r}}{ds^3}\right|_{s=0} + \cdots \\ &= \boldsymbol{r}_o + s\hat{\boldsymbol{t}}\Big|_{\boldsymbol{r}_o} + \frac{s^2}{2!}\kappa\hat{\boldsymbol{n}}\Big|_{\boldsymbol{r}_o} + \frac{s^3}{3!}\left[-\kappa^2\hat{\boldsymbol{t}} + \frac{d\kappa}{ds}\hat{\boldsymbol{n}} - \kappa\tau\hat{\boldsymbol{b}}\right]_{\boldsymbol{r}_o} + \cdots\end{aligned} \qquad (A2.36)$$

A2.7 KINEMATICS IN SPHERICAL POLAR AND OTHER COORDINATE FRAMES

Figure A.2 shows the orthogonal basis vectors $(\hat{\boldsymbol{r}}, \hat{\boldsymbol{\theta}}, \hat{\boldsymbol{\phi}})$ respectively for the spherical polar coordinates (r, θ, ϕ). The relation between the sets $(\hat{\boldsymbol{r}}, \hat{\boldsymbol{\theta}}, \hat{\boldsymbol{\phi}})$ and $(\hat{\boldsymbol{i}}, \hat{\boldsymbol{j}}, \hat{\boldsymbol{k}})$, the set of Cartesian basis vectors is given in Eqs (A1.5) – (A1.7). On differentiation with respect to time, one gets

$$\dot{\hat{\boldsymbol{r}}} = \dot{\theta}\hat{\boldsymbol{\theta}} + \dot{\phi}\sin\theta\hat{\boldsymbol{\phi}} \quad \dot{\hat{\boldsymbol{\theta}}} = -\dot{\theta}\hat{\boldsymbol{r}} + \dot{\phi}\cos\theta\hat{\boldsymbol{\phi}} \quad \text{and} \quad \dot{\hat{\boldsymbol{\phi}}} = -\dot{\phi}[\sin\theta\hat{\boldsymbol{r}} + \cos\theta\hat{\boldsymbol{\theta}}] \qquad (A2.37)$$

Thus we can express the velocity and acceleration of a particle in spherical polar coordinates as

$$\boldsymbol{v} = \frac{d}{dt}(r\hat{\boldsymbol{r}}) = \dot{r}\hat{\boldsymbol{r}} + r\dot{\theta}\hat{\boldsymbol{\theta}} + r\sin\theta\dot{\phi}\hat{\boldsymbol{\phi}} \qquad (A2.38)$$

and

$$\begin{aligned}\boldsymbol{a} = \frac{d\boldsymbol{v}}{dt} &= (\ddot{r} - r\dot{\theta}^2 - r\sin^2\theta\dot{\phi}^2)\hat{\boldsymbol{r}} + (r\ddot{\theta} + 2\dot{r}\dot{\theta} - r\sin\theta\cos\theta\dot{\phi}^2)\hat{\boldsymbol{\theta}} \\ &\quad + (r\sin\theta\ddot{\phi} + 2\dot{r}\dot{\phi}\sin\theta + 2r\dot{\theta}\dot{\phi}\cos\theta)\hat{\boldsymbol{\phi}}\end{aligned} \qquad (A2.39)$$

The kinetic energy (T) and the moment of momentum $(\boldsymbol{L})$ can be written as

$$T = \frac{1}{2}mv^2 = \frac{1}{2}m[\dot{r}^2 + r^2\dot{\theta}^2 + r^2\sin^2\theta\dot{\phi}^2] \qquad (A2.40)$$

$$\boldsymbol{L} = m\boldsymbol{r} \times \boldsymbol{v} = -mr^2\sin\theta\dot{\phi}\hat{\boldsymbol{\theta}} + mr^2\dot{\theta}\hat{\boldsymbol{\phi}} \qquad (A2.41)$$

so that

$$L^2 = m^2r^4[\dot{\theta}^2 + \dot{\phi}^2\sin^2\theta] \qquad (A2.42)$$

The above expressions for various kinematical quantities can be reduced to the special case of plane polar coordinates by forcing $\theta = \pi/2$ (the equatorial plane) and setting $r = \rho$. Hence the velocity and acceleration in plane polar coordinates become

$$\boldsymbol{v} = \dot{\rho}\hat{\rho} + \rho\dot{\phi}\hat{\boldsymbol{\phi}}$$

and

$$\boldsymbol{a} = (\ddot{\rho} - \rho\dot{\phi}^2)\hat{\rho} + (\rho\ddot{\phi} + 2\dot{\rho}\dot{\phi})\hat{\phi} \qquad (A2.43)$$

Note that for simple rotation about the z-axis, $\dot{\rho} = 0$ and $\dot{\phi}\hat{\boldsymbol{k}} = \boldsymbol{\omega}$ (a constant vector, called the angular velocity vector), one obtains

$$\boldsymbol{v} = \boldsymbol{\omega} \times \boldsymbol{\rho} \tag{A2.44}$$

In the expression for acceleration (A2.43), one can easily recognise the radial, centripetal, Euler (actually negative) and the Coriolis (actually negative) terms as one goes from left to right.

Note also that acceleration in spherical polar coordinates has no longer any simple form like that in the Cartesian coordinates. Thus the acceleration in the Cartesian coordinates $\boldsymbol{a} = \ddot{x}\hat{\boldsymbol{i}} + \ddot{y}\hat{\boldsymbol{j}} + \ddot{z}\hat{\boldsymbol{k}}$ does not take an equivalent simple form, namely $\ddot{r}\hat{\boldsymbol{r}} + r\ddot{\theta}\hat{\boldsymbol{\theta}} + r\ddot{\phi}\hat{\boldsymbol{\phi}}$. The fictitious forces like the centripetal, Euler and Coriolis forces appear for the rotating frame. We shall see more of it in chapter 3.

The expressions for $\boldsymbol{r}$, $\boldsymbol{v}$ and $\boldsymbol{a}$ in cylindrical polar coordinates can be obtained by adding $z\hat{\boldsymbol{k}}$, $\dot{z}\hat{\boldsymbol{k}}$ and $\ddot{z}\hat{\boldsymbol{k}}$ to the respective expressions obtained in plane polar coordinates.

A few other useful vectorial quantities are defined below.

Areal Velocity

Given any two vectors $\boldsymbol{A}$ and $\boldsymbol{B}$, $\boldsymbol{A} \times \boldsymbol{B}$ gives the area of the parallelogram spanned by $\boldsymbol{A}$ and $\boldsymbol{B}$. Hence $\boldsymbol{A} \times \boldsymbol{B}$ is called the 'area vector'. This is an axial vector since its sign depends on the sense of rotation or the handedness of the frame used to define it. In Fig. A.6, $\boldsymbol{r}$ and $\boldsymbol{r} + d\boldsymbol{r}$ are the position vectors of two adjacent positions of the particle on its path. By definition, $\boldsymbol{r} \times d\boldsymbol{r}$ = area of the parallelogram spanned by $\boldsymbol{r}$ and $d\boldsymbol{r}$. The areal velocity is therefore given by

$$\text{Areal velocity} = \frac{1}{2}\boldsymbol{r} \times \frac{d\boldsymbol{r}}{dt} = \frac{d\boldsymbol{S}}{dt} = \frac{1}{2}(\boldsymbol{r} \times \boldsymbol{v}) = \frac{\boldsymbol{L}}{2m} \tag{A2.45}$$

Except for the factor $1/2m$, areal velocity is the kinematical counterpart of the moment of momentum $\boldsymbol{L}$.

Solid Angle

Referring to Fig. A.7 we have an element of area vector $d\boldsymbol{S}$ characterised by its magnitude dS and a direction chosen to be a normal $\hat{\boldsymbol{n}}$ drawn on the surface element:

$$d\boldsymbol{S} = \hat{\boldsymbol{n}}\, dS = dS_x\hat{\boldsymbol{i}} + dS_y\hat{\boldsymbol{j}} + dS_z\hat{\boldsymbol{k}} \tag{A2.46}$$

where

$$dS_x = dS\cos\alpha \quad dS_y = dS\cos\beta \quad dS_z = dS\cos\gamma \quad \hat{\boldsymbol{n}} = \cos\alpha\hat{\boldsymbol{i}} + \cos\beta\hat{\boldsymbol{j}} + \cos\gamma\hat{\boldsymbol{k}}$$

and $\cos\alpha$, $\cos\beta$ and $\cos\gamma$ are the direction cosines for $\hat{\boldsymbol{n}}$.

Now, $\boldsymbol{r}\cdot d\boldsymbol{S} = dS(\hat{\boldsymbol{n}}\cdot\boldsymbol{r}) = r\,dS\cos\theta$, where $\theta = \angle\hat{\boldsymbol{n}},\hat{\boldsymbol{r}}$. If dS_o is the projection of $d\boldsymbol{S}$ onto the plane perpendicular to $\boldsymbol{r}$, the solid angle $d\Omega$ subtended by $d\boldsymbol{S}$ at O is defined by

$$d\Omega \equiv \frac{dS_o}{r^2} = \frac{dS\cos\theta}{r^2} = \frac{\boldsymbol{r}\cdot d\boldsymbol{S}}{r^3} \tag{A2.47}$$

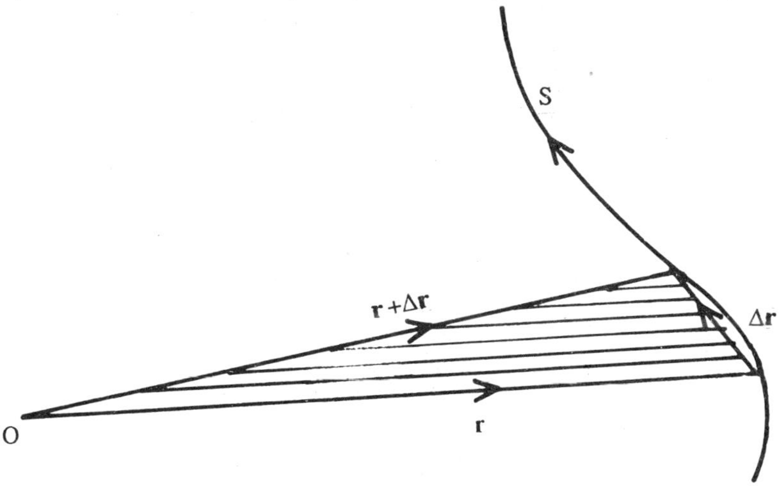

Fig. A.6 Definition of an infinitesimal area vector, spanned by the changing position vector

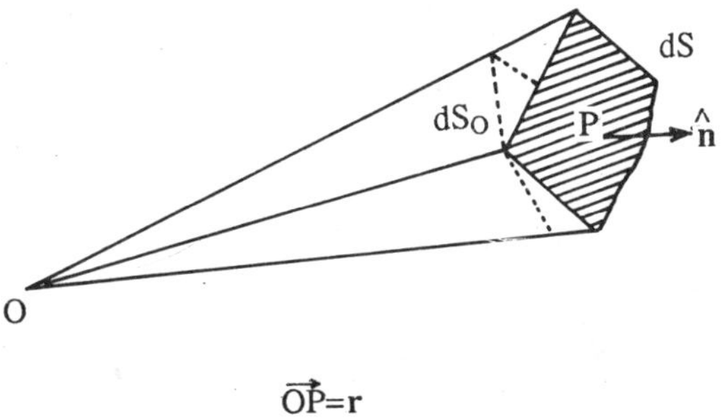

Fig. A.7 An element of solid angle subtended by a given area element with respect to a given point, say O

A2.8 VECTORS IN ORTHOGONAL CURVILINEAR COORDINATE SYSTEMS

A system of curvilinear coordinates, say (u, v, w), given as functions of rectangular Cartesian coordinates $(x, y, z\ :\ \boldsymbol{r})$ in the form of either

$$u = u(\boldsymbol{r}) \quad v = v(\boldsymbol{r}) \quad w = w(\boldsymbol{r}) \qquad \text{or the inverse relations} \quad \boldsymbol{r} = \boldsymbol{r}(u, v, w) \quad (A2.48)$$

is said to be *orthogonal* if the three coordinate surfaces (or equivalently the coordinate lines) at every point are mutually perpendicular (see Fig. A.8). The relations (A2.48) are assumed to be single-valued, continuous, continuous in first partial derivatives and with a nonzero

Jacobian determinant. Such transformation relations between two sets of coordinates are called *admissible* coordinate transformations defined over a given region of space. Just to refresh our memory, given any point, one can draw a curve passing through the point in such a way that only one of the the three curvilinear coordinates changes along the curve and the values of the other two coordinates remain constant. For three curvilinear coordinates one can draw three such curves, all passing through the given point and mutually intersecting at right angles. Each is called a *coordinate curve*, and the surface passing through the point and showing a constant value of a particular coordinate is called a *coordinate surface*.

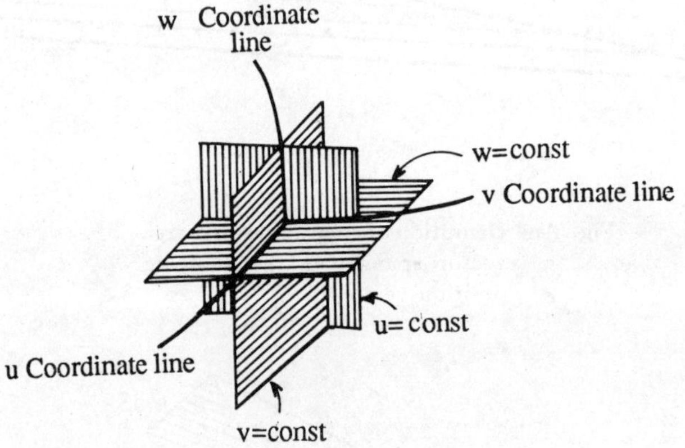

Fig. A.8 The network of coordinate lines and coordinate surfaces at any arbitrary point, defining a curvilinear coordinate system

Let the equation for the coordinate curves at a point ($u = u_o$, $v = v_o$, $w = w_o$) be

$$\boldsymbol{r} = \boldsymbol{r}(u, v_o, w_o) \qquad \boldsymbol{r} = \boldsymbol{r}(u_o, v, w_o) \qquad \text{and} \qquad \boldsymbol{r} = \boldsymbol{r}(u_o, v_o, w) \tag{A2.49}$$

The tangents to the coordinate curves are parallel to the vectors

$$\frac{\partial \boldsymbol{r}(u, v_o, w_o)}{\partial u}, \frac{\partial \boldsymbol{r}(u_o, v, w_o)}{\partial v}, \frac{\partial \boldsymbol{r}(u_o, v_o, w)}{\partial w}$$

respectively. Orthogonality of these vectors requires that

$$\frac{\partial \boldsymbol{r}}{\partial u} \cdot \frac{\partial \boldsymbol{r}}{\partial v} = \frac{\partial \boldsymbol{r}}{\partial u} \cdot \frac{\partial \boldsymbol{r}}{\partial w} = \frac{\partial \boldsymbol{r}}{\partial v} \cdot \frac{\partial \boldsymbol{r}}{\partial w} = 0 \tag{A2.50}$$

The differential displacement along any arbitrary path of a particle is given by

$$d\boldsymbol{r} = \frac{\partial \boldsymbol{r}}{\partial u} du + \frac{\partial \boldsymbol{r}}{\partial v} dv + \frac{\partial \boldsymbol{r}}{\partial w} dw \tag{A2.51}$$

thus giving the differential length of the path in the form of line element

$$
\begin{aligned}
ds^2 &\equiv d\boldsymbol{r}\cdot d\boldsymbol{r} = \left(\frac{\partial \boldsymbol{r}}{\partial u}\right)^2 du^2 + \left(\frac{\partial \boldsymbol{r}}{\partial v}\right)^2 dv^2 + \left(\frac{\partial \boldsymbol{r}}{\partial w}\right)^2 dw^2 \\
&\equiv h_1^2 du^2 + h_2^2 dv^2 + h_3^2 dw^2
\end{aligned}
\tag{A2.52}
$$

where h_1, h_2 and h_3 are defined through the above equation.

Again let the coordinate surfaces be

$$u = u(x,y,z) \qquad v = v(x,y,z) \qquad \text{and} \qquad w = w(x,y,z)$$

where (x,y,z) are the Cartesian coordinates with respect to some rectangular Cartesian frame. The normals to the coordinate surfaces are given by $(\boldsymbol{\nabla}u, \boldsymbol{\nabla}v, \boldsymbol{\nabla}w)$, which owing to the orthogonality, must satisfy

$$0 = (\boldsymbol{\nabla}u)\cdot(\boldsymbol{\nabla}v) = (\boldsymbol{\nabla}u)\cdot(\boldsymbol{\nabla}w) = (\boldsymbol{\nabla}v)\cdot(\boldsymbol{\nabla}w) \tag{A2.53}$$

We can now take the fundamental triad as

$$\hat{\boldsymbol{a}} = \frac{\boldsymbol{\nabla}u}{|\boldsymbol{\nabla}u|} \qquad \hat{\boldsymbol{b}} = \frac{\boldsymbol{\nabla}v}{|\boldsymbol{\nabla}v|} \quad \text{and} \quad \hat{\boldsymbol{c}} = \frac{\boldsymbol{\nabla}w}{|\boldsymbol{\nabla}w|} \tag{A2.54}$$

Let $d\boldsymbol{r}_1$, $d\boldsymbol{r}_2$, and $d\boldsymbol{r}_3$ be the differential displacements along the u, v and w coordinate lines respectively. We then have

$$(\boldsymbol{\nabla}u)\cdot(d\boldsymbol{r}_1) = |\boldsymbol{\nabla}u||d\boldsymbol{r}_1| = du$$

$$(\boldsymbol{\nabla}v)\cdot(d\boldsymbol{r}_2) = |\boldsymbol{\nabla}v||d\boldsymbol{r}_2| = dv$$

and

$$(\boldsymbol{\nabla}w)\cdot(d\boldsymbol{r}_3) = |\boldsymbol{\nabla}w||d\boldsymbol{r}_3| = dw$$

Further,

$$ds^2 = |d\boldsymbol{r}|^2 = dr_1^2 + dr_2^2 + dr_3^2 = \frac{du^2}{|\boldsymbol{\nabla}u|^2} + \frac{dv^2}{|\boldsymbol{\nabla}v|^2} + \frac{dw^2}{|\boldsymbol{\nabla}w|^2} \tag{A2.55}$$

Comparing the Eqs (A2.52) and (A2.55) we get

$$
\begin{aligned}
h_1 &= \frac{1}{|\boldsymbol{\nabla}u|} = \sqrt{\left(\frac{\partial \boldsymbol{r}}{\partial u}\right)^2} \quad \text{implying} \quad \hat{\boldsymbol{a}} = h_1\boldsymbol{\nabla}u \\
h_2 &= \frac{1}{|\boldsymbol{\nabla}v|} = \sqrt{\left(\frac{\partial \boldsymbol{r}}{\partial v}\right)^2} \quad \text{implying} \quad \hat{\boldsymbol{b}} = h_2\boldsymbol{\nabla}v \\
h_3 &= \frac{1}{|\boldsymbol{\nabla}w|} = \sqrt{\left(\frac{\partial \boldsymbol{r}}{\partial w}\right)^2} \quad \text{implying} \quad \hat{\boldsymbol{c}} = h_3\boldsymbol{\nabla}w
\end{aligned}
\tag{A2.56}
$$

An example

For spherical polar coordinates we identify $u = r$, $v = \theta$ and $w = \phi$, where

$$r = \sqrt{x^2 + y^2 + z^2} \quad \theta = \cos^{-1}\left(\frac{z}{\sqrt{x^2 + y^2 + z^2}}\right) \quad \text{and} \quad \phi = \tan^{-1}\left(\frac{y}{x}\right)$$

This gives $h_1^{-1} = |\nabla r| = 1$, $h_2^{-1} = |\nabla\theta| = r^{-1}$ and $h_3^{-1} = |\nabla\phi| = (r\sin\theta)^{-1}$. Therefore,

$$ds^2 = h_1^2 dr^2 + h_2^2 d\theta^2 + h_3^2 d\phi^2 = dr^2 + r^2 d\theta^2 + r^2\sin^2\theta d\phi^2$$

Also, the fundamental triad is

$$\hat{\boldsymbol{a}} = \hat{\boldsymbol{r}} \quad \hat{\boldsymbol{b}} = \hat{\boldsymbol{\theta}} \quad \text{and} \quad \hat{\boldsymbol{c}} = \hat{\boldsymbol{\phi}}$$

We can also invert the transformation to go from (r, θ, ϕ) to (x, y, z) coordinates treating, formally, (x, y, z) to be the curvilinear coordinates, in which case we have

$$x = r\sin\theta\cos\phi \quad y = r\sin\theta\sin\phi \quad \text{and} \quad z = r\cos\theta$$

This gives

$$h_1 = \sqrt{\left(\frac{\partial x}{\partial r}\right)^2 + \left(\frac{\partial y}{\partial r}\right)^2 + \left(\frac{\partial z}{\partial r}\right)^2} = 1$$

$$h_2 = \sqrt{\left(\frac{\partial x}{\partial \theta}\right)^2 + \left(\frac{\partial y}{\partial \theta}\right)^2 + \left(\frac{\partial z}{\partial \theta}\right)^2} = r$$

$$h_3 = \sqrt{\left(\frac{\partial x}{\partial \phi}\right)^2 + \left(\frac{\partial y}{\partial \phi}\right)^2 + \left(\frac{\partial z}{\partial \phi}\right)^2} = r\sin\theta$$

which are identical to those already obtained from the forward transformations. Finally we write down a few more quantities expressed in terms of curvilinear coordinates:
Gradient of a scalar function $\phi(u, v, w)$ w.r.t. Cartesian triad $(\hat{\boldsymbol{i}}, \hat{\boldsymbol{j}}, \hat{\boldsymbol{k}})$

$$\begin{aligned}\nabla\phi &= \frac{\partial\phi}{\partial u}\nabla u + \frac{\partial\phi}{\partial v}\nabla v + \frac{\partial\phi}{\partial w}\nabla w \\ &= \left(\frac{1}{h_1}\frac{\partial\phi}{\partial u}\right)\hat{\boldsymbol{a}} + \left(\frac{1}{h_2}\frac{\partial\phi}{\partial v}\right)\hat{\boldsymbol{b}} + \left(\frac{1}{h_3}\frac{\partial\phi}{\partial w}\right)\hat{\boldsymbol{c}}\end{aligned} \tag{A2.57}$$

Divergence of a vector function $\boldsymbol{f}(\boldsymbol{r}) = f_1(\boldsymbol{r})\hat{\boldsymbol{a}} + f_2(\boldsymbol{r})\hat{\boldsymbol{b}} + f_3(\boldsymbol{r})\hat{\boldsymbol{c}}$ with $\boldsymbol{r} = \boldsymbol{r}(u, v, w)$

$$\nabla\cdot\boldsymbol{f} = \frac{1}{h_1h_2h_3}\left[\frac{\partial(f_1h_2h_3)}{\partial u} + \frac{\partial(f_2h_3h_1)}{\partial v} + \frac{\partial(f_3h_1h_2)}{\partial w}\right] \tag{A2.58}$$

and similarly the curl of $\boldsymbol{f}(\boldsymbol{r})$ is given by

$$\nabla\times\boldsymbol{f} = \frac{1}{h_1h_2h_3}\begin{vmatrix} h_1\hat{\boldsymbol{a}} & h_2\hat{\boldsymbol{b}} & h_3\hat{\boldsymbol{c}} \\ \frac{\partial}{\partial u} & \frac{\partial}{\partial v} & \frac{\partial}{\partial w} \\ h_1f_1 & h_2f_2 & h_3f_3 \end{vmatrix} \tag{A2.59}$$

The Laplacian operator, in the curvilinear coordinates becomes

$$\nabla^2\phi \equiv \boldsymbol{\nabla}\cdot(\boldsymbol{\nabla}\phi) = \frac{1}{h_1h_2h_3}\left[\frac{\partial}{\partial u}\left(\frac{h_2h_3}{h_1}\frac{\partial\phi}{\partial u}\right) + \frac{\partial}{\partial v}\left(\frac{h_3h_1}{h_2}\frac{\partial\phi}{\partial v}\right) + \frac{\partial}{\partial w}\left(\frac{h_1h_2}{h_3}\frac{\partial\phi}{\partial w}\right)\right] \tag{A2.60}$$

The volume element dV, in terms of curvilinear coordinates is

$$dV = |d\boldsymbol{r}_1||d\boldsymbol{r}_2||d\boldsymbol{r}_3| = h_1h_2h_3\; du\; dv\; dw \tag{A2.61}$$

Exercise

Obtain the expressions for $\boldsymbol{\nabla}\phi$, $\boldsymbol{\nabla}\cdot\boldsymbol{f}$, $\boldsymbol{\nabla}\times\boldsymbol{f}$, $\nabla^2\phi$ and dV in terms of spherical polar and cylindrical polar coordinates.

A2.9 VECTORS IN GENERAL CURVILINEAR COORDINATES

Since we shall now be dealing with covariant and contravariant vectors, let us use the curvilinear coordinates $u^i(x^1, x^2, x^3)$ as functions of rectangular Cartesian coordinates (x^1, x^2, x^3) with superscript notations for the assumed contravariant nature of the coordinates, even though for rectangular Cartesian coordinates this distinction does not exist. Let us assume further that transformations between the two sets of coordinates are admissible. An infinitesimal displacement or separation between two points at location P defined by the rectangular Cartesian position vector $\boldsymbol{r}$ can be given as

$$d\boldsymbol{r} = \frac{\partial x^i}{\partial u^j}du^j\hat{\boldsymbol{i}} = \frac{\partial \boldsymbol{r}}{\partial u^j}du^j \equiv \boldsymbol{g}_j du^j \tag{A2.62}$$

where $\boldsymbol{g}_j$'s are defined through the above equation, and are called the *covariant base vectors* at point P.

These must be the base vectors for the (differential) curvilinear coordinates du^i because the vector $d\boldsymbol{r}$ can be interpreted as having three components (du^1, du^2, du^3) along the set of base vectors only. Now the Euclidean line element ds^2 becomes

$$ds^2 \equiv d\boldsymbol{r}\cdot d\boldsymbol{r} = (\boldsymbol{g}_j du^j)\cdot(\boldsymbol{g}_k du^k) = (\boldsymbol{g}_j\cdot\boldsymbol{g}_k)du^j du^k \equiv g_{jk}du^j du^k \tag{A2.63}$$

It is easy to see that g_{jk} as defined in Eq. (A2.63) are nine functions of curvilinear coordinates. As a 3×3 matrix, it can readily be checked that it is a symmetric matrix. This is known as the *Euclidean metric tensor* for any system of curvilinear coordinates. The expression for g_{jk} is

$$g_{jk} = \sum_{i=1}^{3}\frac{\partial x^i}{\partial u^j}\frac{\partial x^i}{\partial u^k} \tag{A2.64}$$

where x^i's are just the ordinary rectangular Cartesian coordinates of the point P at which the metric tensor is determined.

Obviously, if the curvilinear coordinates are orthogonal, $\boldsymbol{g}_i$'s will be orthogonal, and therefore, the Euclidean metric tensor will be diagonal, otherwise not. So just by looking at an expression for the Euclidean metric tensor in terms of any given set of curvilinear coordinates, one can decide its orthogonality. This is extremely useful information for solving dynamical problems. First of all, with the knowledge of the metric tensor, one can straightaway express the kinetic energy term in the expression for Lagrangian for a single particle, as

$$\frac{1}{2}mv^2 = \frac{1}{2}m\left(\frac{ds}{dt}\right)^2 \tag{A2.65}$$

where ds comes from the line element. Second, the orthogonality will guarantee the separability of coordinates in HJ theory, existence of action-angle variables, etc. The velocity $\boldsymbol{v}$ of a particle at P is

$$\boldsymbol{v} = \frac{d\boldsymbol{r}}{dt} = \frac{\partial \boldsymbol{r}}{\partial u^i}\frac{du^i}{dt} = \boldsymbol{g}_i \dot{u}^i \tag{A2.66}$$

Similarly, one can find an expression for acceleration by differentiating Eq. (A2.66) once more with respect to time t. Third, the Jacobian determinant for the transformation from the curvilinear set of coordinates to the set of rectangular Cartesian coordinates is just the determinant of the matrix representing the Euclidean metric tensor, that is,

$$J_{u \to x} = \det \|g_{jk}\| \tag{A2.67}$$

For admissible transformations, J cannot be zero, but it can be either positive or negative. If it is positive, the transformation is said to be *proper*, that is, a right-handed coordinate system is transformed into a right-handed one, otherwise the opposite, an *improper* one. This happens because of the presence of an ϵ_{ijk} factor sitting in the expression of the Jacobian and keeping track of the handedness.

Now in many situations, the external forces $\boldsymbol{F}$ are conservative in nature, and are hence derivable from a scalar potential function, say $\phi(\boldsymbol{r})$. Using the transformation equations, the arguments of ϕ can easily be converted into curvilinear coordinates, and then an expression for force in terms of u^i 's can be obtained as follows

$$\boldsymbol{F} = -\nabla\phi = -\frac{\partial\phi}{\partial\boldsymbol{r}} = -\frac{\partial\phi}{\partial u^i}\left(\frac{\partial u^i}{\partial\boldsymbol{r}}\right) \tag{A2.68}$$

The entry in (A2.68) after the last equality sign has its first factor resembling an ith component of the 'force' related to the ith curvilinear coordinate, and the second factor, a full vector, appears in the reverse order of partial differentiation when compared to definition of $\boldsymbol{g}_i$. It is therefore compelling to write the Eq. (A2.68) in the form of

$$\boldsymbol{F} = \boldsymbol{g}^i F_i^{(u)} \qquad \text{with} \qquad \boldsymbol{g}^i = \frac{\partial u^i}{\partial\boldsymbol{r}} = \frac{\partial u^i}{\partial x^j}\hat{\boldsymbol{j}} = \nabla u^i \tag{A2.69}$$

thus defining the *contravariant base vectors* which are most suitable for expressing force components in curvilinear coordinates. Since $\boldsymbol{g}^i$ is the gradient of u^i, it means that $\boldsymbol{g}^i$ must point in a direction normal to the level surfaces represented by u^i = constant, which is precisely the definition of the coordinate surface for the coordinate u^i.

So it is now established that $\boldsymbol{g}_i$'s correspond to the covariant base vectors pointing tangentially to the coordinate lines, and that the contravariant base vectors $\boldsymbol{g}^i$'s point normally to the coordinate surfaces. Also we have known that the components of a vector along the contravariant base vectors give its covariant components, and vice versa. So if we try to express $\boldsymbol{dr}$ in terms of the base vectors $\boldsymbol{g}^i$'s instead of $\boldsymbol{g}_i$'s, we would get the set of differentials of *covariant* curvilinear coordinates du_i for the same $\boldsymbol{dr}$, and these are given by

$$\boldsymbol{dr} = \boldsymbol{g}^i du_i \qquad (A2.70)$$

Since the transformations are invertible, one can easily show that

$$\boldsymbol{g}_i \cdot \boldsymbol{g}^j = \delta_i^j \qquad (A2.71)$$

the same Kronecker delta matrix representing the unit matrix, but now in mixed suffices, one contravariant, the other covarint. This result can be used to show further that

$$ds^2 = du_i du^i \qquad (A2.72)$$

Exercise
Find the expressions for the Euclidean metric tensor, and the free particle Lagrangian for all the coordinate systems described in Appendix A1.

The main message of this section is that all vectors have basically two natural sets of coordinate components in any system of curvilinear coordinates. This fact remained unnoticed for long because they merely become degenerate in all rectangular Cartesian coordinate systems and are therefore not so obvious in any orthogonal coordinate system.

APPENDIX A3

Tensors

A3.1 FORMAL CONCEPTS OF SCALARS AND VECTORS

We are coming back to vectors again and again, but this time we shall study them from the point of view of the properties of coordinate transformations. Scalars and vectors are just special cases of tensors, the former being tensors of rank zero, and the latter of the rank one.

It is often convenient to formulate laws of physics in some coordinate system. However, the equations expressing laws of nature should have an invariant meaning when we make coordinate transformations, just as we expect them to have an invariant meaning under changes of systems of units.

In this section, we shall study 3-D Cartesian vectors and scalars. These geometric objects are useful in study of many natural phenomena.

A3.1.1 Scalars

A quantity is called *scalar* if it has only a single component, say ϕ, in terms of any one system of coordinates and a single component, say ϕ', in the variables of any other system of coordinates (the two systems of coordinates being connected by an admissible transformation), and if ϕ and ϕ' are numerically equal at the corresponding points. It can be called a true scalar, if the physical quantity can be represented by a single number, which has the same value in all coordinate frames, and has no explicit or implicit dependence on any coordinate frame. For its representation one needs only a system of units in order to express its magnitude or value. To the best of our present-day knowledge, the examples of true scalars are the speed of light in vacuum, Planck's constant, the electric charge of an electron, etc.

There are scalars which are independent of some particular type of coordinate frames, but not in others. Such scalars are named after the general type of coordinate frames with respect to which they are independent. So, the *Cartesian* scalars are those that are independent of Cartesian frames, for example, the distance between two points in 3-D Euclidean space, speed, energy and mass of particles, etc., along with the list of true scalars. However, when we move to special relativistic dynamics, most of these above mentioned Cartesian scalars do not behave as scalars. The scalars in the domain of the theory of special relativity have to be Lorentzian scalars, supposedly independent of the Lorentzian transformations between 4-D Minkowskian coordinate frames. Examples of Lorentzian scalars include the invariant line element or the 4-D Minkowskian distance between any two events, rest mass of particles, etc. The 3-D distance between two points, mass and energy of particles are no longer scalars in Minkowskian frames. In fact, the relativistic mass of a particle behaves as a tensor of rank two.

A3.1.2 Cartesian Vectors

The conceptual development of vectors depends intimately on how the idea of scalars is perceived. For example, when one wants to build the idea of Lorentzian vectors in the 4-D Minkowskian space, the central scalar in the development is either the speed of light in vacuum or the invariance of the 4-D Minkowskian line element, the 4-D distance between two neighbouring events. Naturally, for Cartesian vectors, some Cartesian scalar has to play the key role, and this is chosen to be the Euclidean line element, or in simple words, the distance between any two points in the 3-D Euclidean space.

The positions of any two arbitrary points, say P and Q, in a given rectangular Cartesian frame OXYZ, are expressed by two unique sets of ordered numbers, say (x_1, x_2, x_3) and (y_1, y_2, y_3). The Cartesian distance between these two points is defined as $d(\mathrm{P,Q}) = \sqrt{\sum(y_i - x_i)^2}$. Since this is a Cartesian scalar, it should be, by definition, independent of all rectangular Cartesian frames. When we move to a new rectangular Cartesian frame OX′Y′Z′ having the origin still at O, we must have another unique set of three numbers for each point in space, say (x'_1, x'_2, x'_3) and (y'_1, y'_2, y'_3) for P and Q respectively, such that

$$d^2(\mathrm{P,Q}) = \sum_{i=1}^{3}(y_i - x_i)^2 = \sum_{i=1}^{3}(y'_i - x'_i)^2 \qquad (A3.1)$$

If the connection between the old and new sets of coordinates for any point, say P, with (x_1, y_1, z_1) and (x'_1, x'_2, x'_3), can be expressed by any explicitly prescribed global function of the coordinates, then such functions are said to represent a coordinate transformation. Since the distance between two points are not allowed to change, the transformations should be homogeneous functions of coordinates of degree not exceeding one. Homogeneous functions of degree zero correspond to a globally uniform translation, which is prevented here by the choice of keeping the origins of the two frames coincident at O. So the only alternative left for the transformation is to be homogeneously linear in coordinates, that is,

$$x'_i = \sum_{j=1}^{3} a_{ij}x_j \qquad \text{with all } a'_{ij}\text{s real const.} \qquad (A3.2)$$

Since this transformation is global, that is, valid for the entire 3-D space, we must have $y'_i = \sum a_{ij}y_j$, and the condition (A3.1) can be satisfied (for details see the proof of Euler's theorem in section 12.2), provided

$$\sum_{i=1}^{3} a_{ij}a_{ik} = \delta_{jk} \qquad (A3.3)$$

where δ_{jk} is the unit matrix in Kronecker's delta notation.

This is precisely the condition for the matrix $\mathbf{A} = \{a_{ij}\}$ to be orthogonal, namely its transpose being equal to its inverse. The message that comes out of this exercise is that the

Cartesian or Euclidean distance between any pair of points in 3-D space is not disturbed by any homogeneously linear orthogonal transformation whatsoever.

Now if the distance between every possible pair of points in 3-D Euclidean space remains unchanged, the relational structure of the entire space remains intact, and therefore the relative orientation of any point with respect to all other points (and the distances as well) remain unchanged. Thus we can safely conclude that in relation to every other point in space $\overrightarrow{OP}$, the directed line segment OP, or for that matter $\overrightarrow{OQ}$ or $\overrightarrow{PQ}$, all remain relationally unaffected by any homogeneously linear orthogonal transformation of merely the coordinates.

Now a *Cartesian vector* is defined to be a mathematical entity that has the following properties:

(i) It can be represented in an arbitrary rectangular Cartesian frame S by a set of three numbers (P_1, P_2, P_3 say) called the components of the the Cartesian vector $\boldsymbol{P}$ in the frame S.

(ii) If S and S$'$ are two rectangular Cartesian frames connected by an orthogonal transformation then the components of the vector in the two frames are related to each other in the same way as are the rectangular Cartesian coordinates with respect to S and S$'$ of any arbitrary point P.

Thus if (P_1, P_2, P_3) and (P_1', P_2', P_3') are components of $\boldsymbol{P}$ in the two frames, we require

$$P_i' = a_{ij} P_j \tag{A3.4}$$

where the matrix **A** is a 3×3 orthogonal matrix satisfying the property given in Eq. (A3.3).

This definition of a vector is modeled on the position vector. Thus a vector is rightly identified as a directed line segment, or a directed physical quantity, the magnitude of which retains the physical dimension. So we can represent any vector by a notation like $\boldsymbol{P}$. Such a compact notation did not exist in previous centuries. Obviously, if you do not have such a notation, you would explicitly write its component(s) in some direction(s), or in some special coordinate frames, and then you cannot *a priori* judge it to be a vector from its appearance. We shall identify a physical quantity to be a Cartesian vector, only if it satisfies the transformation equations given by Eqs (A3.4). For this, what experiments do you have to perform? Take a rectangular Cartesian frame S, measure the components of the quantity along its axes. Then rotate the Cartesian frame S about its origin about some axis by some angle to let it become another Cartesian frame S$'$. Now measure the components of the same quantity along these new axes. Arrange the original components in the form of a column matrix **P**, and similarly the final components also in the form of another column matrix **P**$'$. Now suppose you could construct a 3×3 matrix **A**, such that the matrix product **AP** is just **P**$'$. Now check whether the transpose of **A** is the same as its inverse. If it is, the matrix **A** is proved to be orthogonal. Now you have to show that, no matter how you choose the orientation of S$'$, the corresponding matrix **A** is always orthogonal, and the physical quantity under test is qualified as a Cartesian vector. This actually proves that the physical quantity points to the same direction with the same magnitude, even though components get changed due to rotation of the frame. It is a proof of its physical reality, and therefore deserves to be represented merely by its name, say just by $\boldsymbol{P}$, without reference to any specific coordinate frame. However, its direction cannot be expressed without using a coordinate frame. If you specify its direction in any one coordinate frame, it can be uniquely specified in all other frames provided only the coordinate transformation (which is a set of geometrical relations and has nothing to do with the vector) between the two are known.

A large number of physical quantities, such as velocity, acceleration, linear momentum, angular momentum, force, electric field, magnetic field, etc. are found to satisfy the above transformation property, and are therefore examples of Cartesian vectors.

Here we have defined vectors with respect to an O(3) group. Any transformation within this group preserves the distance between every pair of points in 3-D Euclidean space. But when we go to the Minkowskian 4-D space, the concept of distance and invariance of line element are not exactly Euclidean. Hence the vectors defined in Minkowskian space satisfying Lorentz transformations will no longer be Cartesian vectors.

A3.1.3 Contravariant and Covariant Vectors

We have seen towards the end of both Appendices A1 and A2 that nonorthogonal curvilinear frames give rise to two types of position coordinates, one of contravariant type and the other of covariant type. If the vectors are to be modeled on the position vectors, we would naturally have two types of representations of any given vector.

Another point of concern would be to seek for a possible extension of the notion of vectors in non-Cartesian, that is, generally curvilinear, coordinate frames. Obviously, the transformation equations in curvilinear coordinates are not generally linear. (See Eqs (A1.3) or (A1.8) for spherical polar and cylindrical polar coordinates.) However, if we take the differentials of the coordinates, they seem to provide us with a homogeneously linear set of relations over infinitesimally small regions of space. This can be proved as follows. Suppose the transformation between the rectangular Cartesian coordinates $\{x^i\}$ and any complete set of curvilinear coordinates, say $\{x'^i\}$, is given by

$$x'^i = x'^i(x^1, x^2, x^3) \qquad i = 1, 2, 3 \tag{A3.5}$$

then

$$dx'^i = \frac{\partial x'^i}{\partial x^j} dx^j = \frac{\partial x'^i}{\partial x^1} dx^1 + \frac{\partial x'^i}{\partial x^2} dx^2 + \frac{\partial x'^i}{\partial x^3} dx^3 \tag{A3.6}$$

The partial derivatives evaluated at the point under consideration can be taken as constants over a sufficiently small region of space. Now if the distance between any two infinitesimal points before and after transformation is to be kept independent of the transformations, that is, if we impose the condition of the invariance of infinitesimal line elements, we would now have the orthogonality of the matrix

$$A_{ij} \equiv \frac{\partial x'^i}{\partial x^j} \tag{A3.7}$$

which also satisfies Eq. (A3.2). Obviously, the matrix $\mathbf{A}$ is the Jacobian matrix for the above coordinate transformation.

So now we can define vectors in curvilinear coordinate systems in the model of the differentials of the position coordinates, preserving still the Cartesian notion of invariance of distances between neighbouring points, so that the components $\{P^i\}$ and $\{P'^i\}$ of any vector $\boldsymbol{P}$ in the two frames are defined to follow the rule of transformation, given by

$$P'^i = \frac{\partial x'^i}{\partial x^j} P^j \tag{A3.8}$$

But there are in general two different types of position coordinates — one is contravariant and the other covariant for the same point P. Hence, for any given vector also, there should be contravariant and covariant forms of the vector with two different set of components for the same set of curvilinear coordinates. In section A2.9, we defined the covariant set of coordinates as components with respect to the contravariant basis set, which point normal to the coordinate surfaces. The equations for coordinate surfaces are scalar functions of coordinates, say $\phi(x^1, x^2, x^3) =$ constant. Normals to such surfaces are decided by $\boldsymbol{\nabla}\phi$. So we should model the covariant vectors in the model of the transformation of $\boldsymbol{\nabla}\phi$, where ϕ is any Cartesian scalar point function of coordinates. So we have

$$d\phi = \frac{\partial \phi}{\partial x'^i} dx'^i$$

and also

$$d\phi = \frac{\partial \phi}{\partial x^j} dx^j = \frac{\partial \phi}{\partial x^j} \frac{\partial x^j}{\partial x'^i} dx'^i$$

and comparing the two

$$\frac{\partial \phi}{\partial x'^i} = \frac{\partial \phi}{\partial x^j} \frac{\partial x^j}{\partial x'^i} \quad \text{or} \quad (\nabla'\phi)_i = \frac{\partial x^j}{\partial x'^i} (\boldsymbol{\nabla}\phi)_j$$

Therefore, if $\{P_i\}$ and $\{P'_i\}$ are the covariant components of the vector $\boldsymbol{P}$ in the two frames, we can define the covariant vector transformations given by

$$P'_i = \frac{\partial x^j}{\partial x'^i} P_j \tag{A3.9}$$

The transformation Eqs (A3.8) are taken to be the definition of the contravariant vector transformations. Unlike Eq. (A3.7), the matrix of the transformation in Eq. (A3.9) corresponds to the Jacobian matrix for the inverse transformation of coordinates.

Thus a vector is said to be contravariant if it transforms like the differentials of the coordinates (but not as whole coordinates) of any coordinate system under consideration. A vector is covariant if it transforms as a gradient of a scalar potential function or scalar function.

A3.2 Tensors

A3.2.1 Addition and Multiplication of Two Vectors

Two vectors can be added if their physical dimensions and the covariance (or contravariance) nature are identical. So any two covariant (or contravariant) vectors of the same physical dimension are allowed to be added in order to give another covariant (or contravariant) vector.

However, the multiplication of two ordinary Cartesian vectors, depending on the rule of multiplication, can result in a scalar, vector or a tensor of rank two. The scalar product is defined as an inner product, and the vector product is a peculiar operation giving a vector pointing in a direction perpendicular to the plane of vectors. There is however another type of product, called thee outer product of two vectors, that gives rise to a tensor of rank two. These three somewhat arbitrary rules of multiplication had been invented through the years in order to understand the variety of natural processes. Such arbitrariness was unavoidable because people did not make any distinction between covariant and contravariant vectors. Once these distinctions were made clear, the rule of vector multiplication became simple, and it has just one rule. You write the two vectors side by side and transform them individually according to their transformation rules, and see how the product behaves.

A3.2.2 Tensors

Any physical quantity whose transformation properties can be identified with those of the product of some number of vectors, all defined in the same region of space with the same specified rules of coordinate transformations, is by definition a tensor. Vectors are considered as tensors of rank one. The rank of a tensor is determined depending on the number of vectors and on their nature of covariance/contravariance.

The product of a covariant vector with a contravariant one, both described in the same region of space, can give a scalar (not always), but the product of two covariant (or contravariant) vectors would give what is by definition a covariant (or contravariant) tensor of rank two. It has nine components in 3-D, and sixteen in 4-D. Similarly, a product of three vectors of the same type would give a tensor of rank three. So the product of two vectors can either give a scalar or a tensor of rank two. Then you may ask what happens to the conventional notion of a vector product. Well, it is easy to see that any antisymmetric 3×3 matrix has only three independent elements. So 3-D antisymmetric tensor of rank two can be viewed as an axial vector. This only shows the total integrity of the tensorial operations in formulating the physical laws.

So one can define the transformations of the second rank covariant and contravariant and mixed tensors as follows:

$$\begin{aligned} S'^{ij} \equiv P'^{i}Q'^{j} &= \frac{\partial x'^{i}}{\partial x^{k}}\frac{\partial x'^{j}}{\partial x^{l}}P^{k}Q^{l} \\ &= \frac{\partial x'^{i}}{\partial x^{k}}\frac{\partial x'^{j}}{\partial x^{l}}S^{kl} \end{aligned} \qquad (A3.10)$$

$$\begin{aligned} S'_{ij} \equiv P'_{i}Q'_{j} &= \frac{\partial x^{k}}{\partial x'^{i}}\frac{\partial x^{l}}{\partial x'^{j}}P_{k}P_{l} \\ &= \frac{\partial x^{k}}{\partial x'^{i}}\frac{\partial x^{l}}{\partial x'^{j}}S_{kl} \end{aligned} \qquad (A3.11)$$

$$\begin{aligned} S'^i_j \equiv P'^i Q'_j &= \frac{\partial x'^i}{\partial x^k}\frac{\partial x^l}{\partial x'^j} P^k Q_l \\ &= \frac{\partial x'^i}{\partial x^k}\frac{\partial x^l}{\partial x'^j} S^k_l \end{aligned} \tag{A3.12}$$

If we now take the trace of the matrix representation of any mixed tensor,

$$S'^i_i = \frac{\partial x'^i}{\partial x^k}\frac{\partial x^j}{\partial x'^i} S^k_j = \delta^j_k S^k_j = S^j_j \tag{A3.13}$$

it becomes totally independent of the coordinate frames, as the coordinate transformations are invertible and nonsingular. Eq. (A3.13) also defines the Kronecker delta symbol in the form of a mixed tensor. This is the correct form of the Kronecker delta symbol. That this is a mixed tensor can be proved by putting it back in Eq. (A3.12). However, the most important message that emerges from Eq. (A3.13) is that the trace of the matrix representation of any mixed tensor is a scalar. This process of reducing a mixed tensor into a scalar is called the 'contraction of indices'. A contravariant index, usually denoted by an upper index, can always be contracted with a covariant index, usually denoted by a lower one, by taking a trace with reference to the indices contracted. While playing with the tensors, scalars are always formed by the process of contraction of indices alone, leaving behind no indices that are not repeated. Scalars are obviously tensors of rank zero.

A3.2.3 Properties of Tensors

(i) If all the components of a tensor vanish in one coordinate frame, then they vanish in all coordinate frames, which are in one-to-one correspondence with the given system.

(ii) The sum or difference of two tensors of the same physical dimension and rank is again a tensor of the same physical type and rank.

(iii) If a tensor equation is true in one coordinate system, then it is true in all other coordinate systems, which are in one-to-one correspondence.

So it is now apparent that most physical quantities have a tensorial character. If the laws of nature are expressed in the form of equations or relations in terms of tensors, their physical reality and transformation properties can immediately be inferred, and applied or adapted to the physical conditions under which they can be tested or further experimented.

A3.2.4 Concept of Tensors Simplified

The way we have introduced the concept of tensors here might appear quite formal. We can perhaps tone down a little bit, and talk about these in a more informal way.

Let $\boldsymbol{P}$ denote a Cartesian vector in the 3-D Euclidean space with components (P_1, P_2, P_3) with respect to a rectangular Cartesian coordinate system. Let this coordinate system be rotated (that is, transformed orthogonally) to a new coordinate frame with respect to which the components of $\boldsymbol{P}$ are (P'_1, P'_2, P'_3). We know that these two sets are related by

$$P' = A_{ik} P_k$$

where $\mathbf{A} = [A_{ik}]$ is an orthogonal matrix, that is $\tilde{\mathbf{A}} = \mathbf{A}^{-1}$.

Now let $\boldsymbol{P}$ and $\boldsymbol{Q}$ be two Cartesian vector quantities in the 3-D Euclidean space whose components with respect to a rectangular Cartesian frame are related as

$$P_i = T_{ij} Q_j \qquad i = 1,2,3 \tag{A3.14}$$

Here T_{ij} is the set of nine coefficients occurring in the set of three equations above. Many laws of nature are expressed in this form. For example, $\boldsymbol{P}$ may be a displacement vector at a point in an elastic body and $\boldsymbol{Q}$ the position vector of that point. Then the relation between their components have the same form as Eq. (A3.14). Another example is $\boldsymbol{P}$ and $\boldsymbol{Q}$ being the angular momentum and the angular velocity of a rigid body with the origin of the coordinate frame at the CM of the body. As a last example, $\boldsymbol{P}$ and $\boldsymbol{Q}$ may be the electric polarization and the applied electric field at a point in an anisotropic dielectric medium. In all these cases, $\boldsymbol{P}$ and $\boldsymbol{Q}$ point in different directions. The geometrical meaning of the product of a 3×3 matrix with a column vector implies that the resulting column vector points in a different direction, unless it satisfies the eigenvalue equation, namely $\mathbf{A}X = \lambda X$, that is, X is such that the transformed column vector is parallel to the original column vector. We now want to investigate whether the transformation matrix $\mathbf{T}$ is a representation of some second-order Cartesian tensor or not.

We now transform the coordinate system orthogonally as before, so that the components of $\boldsymbol{P}$ and $\boldsymbol{Q}$ change over to $\{P_i'\}$ and $\{Q_j'\}$, $i,j = 1,2,3$ respectively. However, we require that the relation between these new components of $\boldsymbol{P}$ and $\boldsymbol{Q}$ must have the same form as Eq. (A3.14). Thus we must have

$$P_i' = T_{ij}' Q_j' \tag{A3.15}$$

However, we know that

$$P_i' = A_{ik} P_k \qquad \text{and} \qquad Q_j' = A_{jm} Q_m$$

Substituting into Eq. (A3.15), we get

$$A_{ik} P_k = T_{ij}' A_{jm} Q_m$$

Written in the matrix form,

$$\mathbf{AP} = \mathbf{T}'\mathbf{AQ} \tag{A3.16}$$

Multiplying on the left of Eq. (A3.16) by $\mathbf{A}^{-1}$, and comparing Eq. (A3.16) with the matrix form of Eq. (A3.14), we immediately get

$$\mathbf{T}' = \mathbf{ATA}^{-1} \qquad \text{or} \qquad T_{ik}' = A_{im} T_{mn} A_{nk}^{-1} \tag{A3.17}$$

where $\mathbf{A}$ is the orthogonal transformation matrix for the coordinate transformation.

Eq. (A3.17) is taken to be the definition of the 3-D second rank tensor with reference to rectangular Cartesian transformations. The rank of the tensor is as usual the number of suffices required to specify its elements. Thus any quantity having nine components which transform according to Eq. (A3.17) under the orthogonal transformation of the rectangular Cartesian coordinate system is, by definition, a Cartesian tensor of the second rank.

Now a physical law may relate the product of the components of more than one vector to the components of a single vector. Thus, given three vectors $\boldsymbol{P}$, $\boldsymbol{Q}$ and $\boldsymbol{S}$, we may have

$$P_i = T_{ijk} Q_j S_k \tag{A3.18}$$

If we now require that the form of Eq. (A3.19) remain invariant under the aforementioned coordinate transformation, we get

$$T_{ijk} = A_{il}^{-1} T'_{lmn} A_{mj} A_{nk} \tag{A3.19}$$

where again $\mathbf{A}$ is the transformation matrix for the orthogonal coordinate transformation. Equation (A3.19) defines a 3-D Cartesian tensor of the third rank. The above procedure can be generalised in a straightforward way to define 3-D Cartesian tensors of arbitrary rank. The general transformation defining an rth rank Cartesian tensor is

$$T_{ijkl\cdots} = A_{im}^{-1} T'_{nopq\cdots} A_{nj} A_{ok} A_{ql} \cdots \tag{A3.20}$$

Any physical quantity labeled by r indices having 3^r components, which transform according to Eq. (A3.20) under the orthogonal transformation of Cartesian coordinates, is called a Cartesian tensor of rank r.

A3.2.5 Importance of Tensor Analysis

Every big discovery in physics or in any other branch of science leads essentially to a claim for having found a link between two different ideas or phenomena. A physical law is merely a statement of this new link between two not-so-obvious ideas or phenomena. In order to express the law in an abstract form or say in terms of mathematical logic, an equation is developed, the left-hand side of which comes from one set of assumptions and logic, and the right-hand side originates from another set. First of all, the two sides must have the same physical dimensions. It is a necessity. Second, it is desirable that the form of the equation have general validity with respect to any frame of reference. This is possible only if every term in the equation has the same tensor characteristics. If this condition is not satisfied, a simple change of coordinate system will destroy the form of the relationship.

Tensor analysis is in fact as important as dimensional analysis in formulating physical laws. Two physical quantities cannot be equated unless they have same dimensions, that is, any physical equation cannot be correct unless it is invariant with respect to a change of fundamental units.

The use of tensors enables us to have a unified treatment, which is good for any curvilinear coordinates — orthogonal or nonorthogonal. This is achieved at the expense of recognising the distinction between contravariance and covariance. Each physical vector has two tensor images: one contravariant and the other covariant, depending on how the components are resolved. The distinction between contravariance and covariance disappears if the transformations are restricted to only rectangular Cartesian coordinate systems. So when only the rectangular Cartesian coordinates are considered, sometimes all the indices are written as subscripts.

Given any tensor of second or higher rank, it is possible to define vectors and scalars from it by merely devising some process of contraction of the indices. So even if a quantity on one side of the equation representing a law to be proposed, has an apparently mismatching rank with that of the right-hand side, the valid scheme of contracting tensorial indices and or coupling with the metric tensor is of paramount significance. It helps one build a valid tensor equation out of tensorial quantities which have non-agreeing ranks to start with. It is much like the process of matching the dimensions between the two sides of an equation by invoking a constant factor which absorbs the required balance of the physical dimensions.

All the transformation laws defining tensors, Cartesian or otherwise, are based on some given coordinate transformation, which, in turn, is valid in some region of space. This, in general, makes the components of a tensor change as one scans through the points of the underlying space. Thus each component of a tensor becomes a function, whose domain is the region of space over which the tensor is defined and whose range is the set of real numbers R. When this function is specified for every tensor component (explicitly or implicitly), we say that we have defined a tensor field. For example, the moment of inertia tensor of a rigid body is a Cartesian tensor field defined over the finite extension of the rigid body.

APPENDIX B

Sample of Short Questions

These questions were actually set for the first year students of the TIFR – PU joint M. Sc. programme in physics during Aug – Dec 1987. We adopted a system of evaluation giving 40% of the course credit to an internal assessment and the rest to the end of semester final examination. Again, the internal part of the assessment had two parts; three quarters of it was based on the average of performances in monthly tests, and a quarter on problem solving and attendance to weekly tutorials for problem solving. One had to qualify in both the internal and end of semester assessments. Out of about 60 students, about one fifth used to be nationally selected, who were usually graded in A, while the local students had to struggle for securing the minimum qualification.

Class Test I

All questions are to be attempted.

1. A simple pendulum is swinging without any sign of damping. Justify whether it can be regarded as a closed and/or a conservative system. Which are the quantities that are not conserved?
2. A rigid cylinder rolling on the horizontal floor of a hall comes across a vertical wall and starts slipping against the wall and the floor, with the coefficient of dynamical friction μ_k. Find the forces of friction and show that the effective weight is reduced. Do these reaction forces depend on the instantaneous angular velocity of the cylinder?
3. Determine the kinetic energy of a tractor crawler belt of mass m, if the tractor is moving with speed v and the crawler, having been geared with two wheels, rolls over the road without slipping.
4. Using the principle of conservation of linear momentum, derive the equation of motion of a rocket of (continuously varying) mass m, burning fuel at a rate dm/dt and ejecting the exhaust gas with velocity $\boldsymbol{u}_o$ with respect to the rocket. Under what condition of the rocket orientation will the speed of the rocket remain unchanged in spite of the rocket action?
5. A pencil of length l placed vertically falls down. What will be the angular velocity at the end of the fall?
6. How can one derive the constraint forces from a given set of constraint relations?
7. Define virtual displacement and show that virtual work done by holonomic constraint forces is zero.

8. An incline is accelerated horizontally in order to prevent the frictionless sliding of a block sitting on the incline. Using D'Alembert's principle, calculate how much horizontal acceleration is needed, if the incline makes an angle α with the horizontal.
9. Show that all the gyroscopic forces can be included in the definition of generalised potential. Just cite an example.
10. Construct the Lagrangian of a bicycle rolling down an incline.
11. A rigid rod of length l is constrained to move in such a way that both of its ends always maintain physical contact with the inside surface of a hemispherical bowl of radius R ($> r$). Find the degrees of freedom of the system. Why do nonholonomic systems require a larger number of generalised coordinates than the number of degrees of freedom?
12. Give an example where the constraint is not only holonomic but also rheonomic and bilateral. Are all the scleronomic systems conservative?
13. Why should a Lagrangian be computed only with reference to inertial frames? How is this requirement satisfied when one wants to construct the Lagrangian for the motion of a particle in a rotating frame?
14. Using δ_{ij} and ϵ_{ijk} evaluate the gradients of the following scalars : $|\boldsymbol{\omega} \times \boldsymbol{r}|^2$ and $\boldsymbol{v} \cdot (\boldsymbol{\omega} \times \boldsymbol{r})$, where $\boldsymbol{\omega}$ is a constant vector and $\boldsymbol{v}$ does not explicitly depend on $\boldsymbol{r}$.
15. Compare the qualitative effects of the Coriolis forces in the two geographical hemispheres of the earth for (a) vertical free fall of any object, (b) rivers flowing east, and (c) a pendulum swinging in a vertical plane.
16. Show that the time rate of change of any vector quantity $\boldsymbol{A}$ in a rotating frame differs from its inertial counterpart by a term $\boldsymbol{\omega} \times \boldsymbol{A}$, where $\boldsymbol{\omega}$ is the angular velocity of rotation of the rotating frame with respect to the inertial frame.
17. Why does a plumbline usually indicate the true vertical line at any place, even though the earth is not truly spherical in shape and the centrifugal forces due to earth's rotation are not negligible compared to the gravitational forces?
18. Derive the condition for Galilean invariance and show that the Lagrangian for a free particle changes under Galilean transformation only by a totally differentiable function with respect to time.
19. Following Noether's symmetry arguments, prove that the total angular momentum of any closed system is conserved due to the isotropy of space.
20. Write down the Lagrangian of a free particle in the rectangular Cartesian, spherical polar and cylindrical polar coordinates, and interpret the significance of the changes in the number of cyclic coordinates in each of them.

Class Test II

All questions are to be attempted.

1. What do you mean by closure, boundedness and stability of orbits under central forces? State their necessary conditions.
2. Analyse the following forces to find whether they are central or not : uniform gravity field, tidal force field of moon acting on the ocean water on earth, and force of impact

during isotropic elastic collision of two neutral atoms.

3. How many independent integrals of motion are there for a planet orbiting around the sun? State them, both in terms of the orbital elements and in terms of the first integrals of motion.
4. Explain the fact that the actual force exerted by moon on any drop of ocean water on earth is about 30 times larger than the tidal force that is responsible for the origin of oceanic tides.
5. A heavy horizontal turntable is rotating with a uniform angular velocity $\boldsymbol{\omega}_d$. A sphere is let rolling on it without slipping. If its initial centre of mass velocity is $\boldsymbol{v}_o$ with respect to an inertial observer, how will the force $\boldsymbol{F}$ acting on it change with time in the same inertial frame? Is this a central force?
6. Explain with diagrams what are meant by differential scattering cross-section, extinction and impact parameter.
7. What is the virial of an interacting N-particle system? Using the virial theorem derive the equation of state of any ideal monatomic gas.
8. State the conditions under which Hamilton's and Maupertuis' principles of least action are valid. What are the independent arguments of Hamilton's characteristic and principal functions?
9. Prove the following : $d(\delta q) = \delta(dq)$ and $\delta\dot{q} = d(\delta q)/dt$. Explain what do you mean by the quantity δH.
10. Find the equation of the curve if it satisfies $\delta \int_1^2 y\, ds = 0$, where s is measured along the curve (in two dimensions only) and y is measured vertically downward.
11. What are brachistochrones and tautochrones? Under what conditions do the two become identical? Define and draw cycloids and hypocycloids.
12. Find the Hamiltonian $H(\boldsymbol{r},\boldsymbol{p})$ for a relativistic particle that has its Lagrangian $L(\boldsymbol{r},\boldsymbol{v}) = -c^2 m_o(1 - v^2/c^2)^{1/2} - V(|\boldsymbol{r}|)$.
13. Show that $L(q,\dot{q},t)$ and $L'(q,\dot{q},t) = L(q,\dot{q},t) + dF(q,t)/dt$ produces the same equations of motions. Show that the transformation is canonical. Use $F_2(q,P) = qP - F(q,t)$.
14. What is a Routhian? Find the expression for energy in terms of the Routhian function only. When is the knowledge of Routhian important?
15. Show that the Runge-Lenz vector for planetary motion is a constant of motion. Why is it also called the eccentricity vector?
16. The Hamiltonian of a charged particle moving in an electromagnetic field is $H(\boldsymbol{r},\boldsymbol{p},t) = (\boldsymbol{p} - e\boldsymbol{A})^2/(2m) + e\phi$, where $\boldsymbol{A}(\boldsymbol{r},t)$ and $\phi(\boldsymbol{r},t)$ are the electromagnetic potentials. Show that the energy is $E = (mv^2/2) + e\phi$.
17. Show that for a simple 2-D phase space transformation from (q,p) to (Q,P), the Jacobian is unity if the transformation is canonical. Why is it an important result?
18. Mention any six examples of physically interesting canonical transformations, and at least one which is much used as a point transformation but is itself not canonical. Show that an exchange transformation is canonical. What is its significance?
19. Show that under any point transformation $q_i = q_i(Q_1,\ldots,Q_n,t)$ $i = 1,\ldots,n$. the

momentum and energy change in the following way :

$$p'_j = p_i \frac{\partial q_i}{\partial Q_j} \text{ and } E' = E - p_i \frac{\partial q_i}{\partial t}$$

20.. Find the generating function $F_2(q, P)$ and the transformed Hamiltonian $K(P, Q)$, if $F_1(q, Q) = \frac{1}{2}\sqrt{km}\, q^2 \cot Q$ and $H(p, q) = (p^2/2m) + (kq^2/2)$

Class Test III

All questions are to be attempted.

1. Show that for a 3-D isotropic harmonic oscillator, the Runge-Lenz tensor $A_{ij} = p_i p_j/2m + kx_i x_j/2$ is a constant of motion, that is, its PB with the Hamiltonian $H = |\boldsymbol{p}|^2/2m + k|\boldsymbol{r}|^2/2$ is zero.
2. If $H = |\boldsymbol{p}|^2/2m + V(x_1, x_2, x_3)$ and $\boldsymbol{L}$ is the angular momentum, show that the Poisson bracket $[\boldsymbol{L}, H] = \boldsymbol{\Gamma} =$ torque about the origin $= \boldsymbol{r} \times \boldsymbol{F} = -\boldsymbol{r} \times \nabla V$
3. Prove Jacobi's theorem for the time-dependent Hamilton-Jacobi theory.
4. What are the advantages of having the H-J equation separated in all variables?
5. What are action variables and under what conditions are they integrals of motion? Why should they be called 'angle' and 'action' variables?
6. For planetary orbits, define J_r, J_θ and J_ϕ and specify the suitable range of integrations for r, θ and ϕ respectively. Show that the frequencies of oscillation in r, θ, ϕ are degenerate, since $(J_r + J_\theta + J_\phi)^2 E + 2\pi^2 G^2 M^2 m^3 = 0$ is satisfied. How would you remove these degeneracies?
7. What do you mean by libration, rotation and adiabatic invariants?
8. Cite any three examples of adiabatic invariants.
9. Show that potential energy has to be minimum for a stable equilibrium.
10. Mercury fills a U tube up to a total column length L. The tube is rocked so that mercury begins to oscillate. Find the period of oscillation.
11. Find the conditions under which a normal mode of small amplitude oscillation is possible for a system having n degrees of freedom. The characteristic equation is $(b_{ij} - p^2 a_{ij})\, A_j = 0$, A_js are the complex amplitudes and p is the frequency.
12. What do you mean by normal coordinates, principal oscillations and the normal modes of small amplitude oscillations?
13. Find the number of degrees of freedom of the following rigid bodies :
    (a) Your ball point pen, when you are drawing a diagram on a plane sheet of paper (will there be any difference if you use a fountain pen?),
    (b) a table lamp stand that has two totally flexible joints both connected via rigid rods (the base being immovable),
    (c) a rigid cylinder rolling without slipping on a plane surface.
14. Find the location of the instantaneous axis of rotation of the following bodies :
    (a)the front wheel of your bicycle while in motion,
    (b) a spinning sphere at a great distance showing you no more than half of its surface,
    (c) a bus taking a left turn along any gentle curve of a road.

15. Interpret different meanings of the expression $\boldsymbol{v} = \boldsymbol{u} + \omega \times \boldsymbol{r}$ for the description of any rigid body moving in any manner.
16. Suppose you know the moment of inertia tensor of a given rigid body about a given point which is not its centre of mass. Find the moment of inertia tensor about the centre of mass.
17. Find the principal moments of inertia and the corresponding principal axes about the centre of a Christian 'cross' made up of two thin bars of unequal lengths.
18. Draw the inertial ellipsoid of a thin circular disc about any point on the rim of the disc.
19. Derive the conditions under which the usual torque angular momentum relation, namely $\boldsymbol{\Gamma} = d\boldsymbol{L}/dt$, is valid.
20. A disc is rolling vertically without slipping on a horizontal plane. Why is its total kinetic energy is taken to be the sum of its translational and rotational components? Why should the mixed component be zero? Is there any point on the disc about which only the rotational component exists?

Class Test IV

All questions are to be attempted.

1. Explain why a cyclist does not fall under the action of gravity when it takes a turn either to the left or to the right. How could an expert cyclist dare leave the control on the steering even when taking a turn?
2. Under what conditions does a polhode reduce to a point and a circle? Show that herpolhodes are in general bounded curves.
3. Why is it said that a body cone always lies outside the space cone for any freely rotating symmetric top?
4. If a spinning ball is made to bounce from a rough horizontal surface with an angle of incidence θ_1 with the horizontal, find its angle of reflection.
5. Given the Lagrangian of a system
$$L = \frac{1}{2}A(\dot{\theta}^2 + \dot{\phi}^2 \sin^2\theta) + \frac{1}{2}C(\dot{\phi}\cos\theta + \dot{\psi})^2 - mgh\cos\theta$$
find the effective potential $V_{\text{eff}}(\theta)$ for its θ-motion.
6. Interpret the condition for sleeping top, $C\omega_3 > 2\sqrt{mgh}$. Differentiate between a strong and a weak top. What is the mathematical argument for the stability of a sleeping top? (Just mention it.)
7. What are the effects of friction on a fast spinning top?
8. What is a gyroscope? State the essential property of a gyroscope. How did Foucault use it to demonstrate the rotation of the earth?
9. An isotropic elastic body (Lamé's elastic constants λ, μ) is under tension in one direction. Find its Young's modulus and the dilation.
10. If $\boldsymbol{u}$ is the deformation vector for a homogeneous elastic solid, show that $\nabla \cdot \boldsymbol{u}$ is its dilation. How will you find the shearing part of its strain b_{ik}? What happens if b_{ik} is tried for diagonalisation?

11. Explain the meanings of e_{yz} and σ_{yz}. Show that the condition $\sigma_{yz} = \sigma_{zy}$ is good enough for the rotational equilibrium about the x-axis. Demonstrate geometrically that $e_{yz} = -e_{zy}$ corresponds to pure rotation, but that $e_{yz} = e_{zy}$ produces a pure shear to be given by an angle $2e_{yz}$
12. Show that a general elastic solid can have at most 21 independent elastic constants, if the deformation follows the generalised Hooke's law. How is it that a cubic crystal is less symmetric than an isotropic body, although cubic crystals are known to exhibit isotropic optical properties?
13. Starting from the equation

$$\rho\frac{\partial^2 \boldsymbol{u}}{\partial t^2} = (\lambda + \mu)\nabla(\triangle) + \mu\nabla^2\boldsymbol{u}$$

show that two transverse and one longitudinal mode of wave propagation are possible through any isotropic elastic medium.
14. Show that the motion of the phase fluid under conservative forces is equivalent to that of an incompressible fluid.
15. Show that (i) $D\boldsymbol{r}/Dt = \boldsymbol{q}$, (ii) pressure potential for barotropic fluids is either the enthalpy or Gibb's free energy function, and (iii) for incompressible fluid flows $\nabla\cdot\boldsymbol{q} = 0$
16. State and prove Bernoulli's theorem of fluid dynamics. Define stream tubes and vortex tubes.
17. Show that in any supersonic jet, the speed of the fluid increases as the fluid is allowed to expand laterally.
18. Show that the group velocity of deep water gravity waves is exactly one half of their phase velocity, the latter being given by $c = \sqrt{g\lambda/2\pi}$, but for the ripples the group velocity is one and a half times larger than the phase velocity $c = \sqrt{2\pi T/\lambda\rho}$, where T is the surface tension of the medium.
19. Draw the two dimensional flow pattern for a steady irrotational flow of an incompressible fluid, represented by the complex analytic function $f(z) = z^3$, where $z = x + iy$, x and y being real.
20. With regard to the shape of an aeroplane, explain the origin of the lift force against gravity, while in motion. What are its basic orientational manoeuvrings, called yaw, pitch and roll?

Final Examination

Attempt any *ten* questions.

1. State only the conditions under which
   (a) the work done by the constraint forces vanishes
   (b) the total energy becomes an integral of motion.
   Show that all the gyroscopic forces can be included in the generalised potential $U(q, \dot{q}, t)$. Demonstrate this with an example.
2. Find the effective potentials due to centrifugal and Coriolis forces.
   Show that the plane of oscillation of Foucault's pendulum rotates in the opposite sense

to that of the rotation of the earth.
Assume that the river Mutha is flowing northward (say, near the Mhatre bridge in Pune) with a speed of 10 km/hr (latitude $\lambda = 18^o$ N). What will be the height difference of its water level between the two banks due to Coriolis force, if the width of the river is 100 m?

3. If $\boldsymbol{L}$ be the total angular momentum of a planet, show that $L^2 = p_\theta^2 + p_\phi^2/\sin^2\theta$. Find the location on the orbit where the radial component of the orbital velocity is maximum. Find the eccentricity of the transfer orbit for launching a geostationary satellite from a circular orbit around the earth, that has a radius 6600 km. (Radius of the earth is 6380 km, and mass 6×10^{24} kg.)
4. Show that the virial of a system of particles moving under mutual central force potentials satisfies the translational invariance. Apply the virial theorem to prove that a star becomes unstable if the ratio of the two specific heats c_p/c_v of its constituent gas is less than 4/3.
What is the form of the virial theorem for particles moving in their mutual gravitational fields?
5. Find the Lagrangian and the Hamiltonian for a ray of light traveling in any optical medium having refractive index $n(\boldsymbol{r}, \boldsymbol{p})$. Find the equation of motion of its path. Show that the path followed by the light ray is a brachistochrone.
6. Find the frequency of small oscillation of any rigid homogeneous hemisphere kept upside down on a horizontal table. Find the frequencies of the normal modes of oscillation of a system if its Lagrangian is given by $L(x, y, \dot{x}, \dot{y}) = (\dot{x}^2 + \dot{y}^2)/2 - (k_1 x^2 + k_2 y^2)/2 + axy$; k_1, k_2 and a being constants.
7. Show that all the univalent canonical transformations do form a group. Mention at least three methods of testing whether a given phase space transformation is canonical or not. Show that the electromagnetic gauge transformation $\boldsymbol{A}' = \boldsymbol{A} + \nabla f(\boldsymbol{r}, t)$, $\phi = \phi - \partial f/\partial t$ effected by a generating function $F_2(\boldsymbol{r}, \boldsymbol{P}) = \boldsymbol{r} \cdot \boldsymbol{P} - ef(\boldsymbol{r}, t)$ can be regarded as a canonical transformation from $(\boldsymbol{r}, \boldsymbol{p})$ to $(\boldsymbol{r}, \boldsymbol{P})$
8. Differentiate between libration and rotation.
Determine the action-angle variables for a one-dimensional harmonic oscillator. Is there any adiabatic invariant of the system?
Evaluate the Poisson bracket $[v_i, v_j]$ for a charged particle moving with velocity $\boldsymbol{v}$ in a field of magnetic induction $\boldsymbol{B}$.
9. How are the time-dependent and time-independent solutions of the Hamilton-Jacobi theory for any conservative system related to each other? What are Hamilton's principal and characteristic functions? What kind of action principles do they follow from? State the conditions under which Hamilton's principle is valid. Just mention what sort of curves you get from the following variational principles: $\delta \int_1^2 ds = 0$, $\delta \int_1^2 dt = 0$ and $\delta \int_1^2 y ds = 0$
10. Show that a dynamical system having n degrees of freedom can have at most $2n - 1$ independent constants of motion. How are they determined by the methods such as due to (i) Euler-Lagrange (ii) Hamilton (iii) Hamilton-Jacobi and (iv) by the method of Poisson brackets? Outline the Hamilton-Jacobi method to find all the constants of

motion for a particle moving in the potential field $V = \boldsymbol{a} \cdot \boldsymbol{r}/r^3$, $\boldsymbol{a}$ being a constant vector.

11. Show that (i) polhodes are closed curves, (ii) herpolhodes are bounded curves and (iii) steady rotations about the principal axes of any asymmetric top are stable except for the intermediate principal axis.
12. Explain with diagrams the properties of the following : body cone and space cone, Foucault's gyroscope, sleeping top, tippe top, Chandler's wobbling of the earth and boomerang.
13. A bicycle rider is moving with a constant speed v_o along a horizontal circular track of radius R. The total mass of the bicycle and the rider is M, the radius of the wheels r_o and the mass of the two wheels m. Find the angular velocity of precession and the total kinetic energy of the system. Why does the bicycle rider not fall due to the action of the gravitational couple?
14. Give reasons why

    (i) any elastic body which is capable of producing homogeneous elastic deformation has 12 degrees of freedom,

    (ii) isotropic solids have only two independent elastic constants and

    (iii) P-wave component of the earthquakes should always travel faster than the S-wave component.

    Find the rotation, dilation and shear due to an elastic displacement function $\boldsymbol{u} = \epsilon[(2 - 3x + 4y - 2z)\hat{\imath} + (1 + 2x - 5y + 7z)\hat{\jmath} + (x - 2y - 2z)\hat{k}]$, ϵ being a small dimensionless quantity.
15. (i) Explain the significance of Bernoulli's theorem for fluid motions.

    (ii) Apply it to find the speed of gravity waves propagating in a deep ocean and having a wavelength of 100 m.

    (iii) Draw the pattern of the planar, steady and irrotational flow of an incompressible fluid given by the complex potential $f(z) = z^2$, where $z = x + iy$.

APPENDIX C

Hints and Answers to Selected Problems

Introduction

I.1 Solve for the four unknowns in four independent dimensional equations. The Planck mass $m_P = \sqrt{\hbar c/G} \sim 10^{-8}$ kg, Planck length $l_P = \sqrt{G\hbar/c^3} \sim 10^{-35}$ m, Planck time $t_P = l_P/c$, and Planck temperature $T_P = m_P c^2/k$. All the wavelengths are comparable to one another.

I.2 Solve for the motions of the car and ball and show that they meet. If wheels have got appreciable mass, it shares some kinetic energy of rotation, so the car will proceed slower than the ball along the incline.

I.3 Set up the equations of motion of the chair and of the rider separately, assuming masses m and M for the chair and rider respectively, and T as the tension in the rope and a as the acceleration of the rider. Eliminate T to get $N = (M - m)(a + g)/2$. For upward acceleration, we need $M > m$, but if $m > M$, the rider will be lifted out of the chair.

I.4 Set up the equation of motion of the massive object in terms of tensions in two segments, $T_1 - (T_2 + Mg) = Ma$. Now, $a \simeq 0$, for quasistatic pull, but for sudden jerk, it is possible to produce $a < -g$, and hence the results.

I.5 The spring term is 0 for $r \leq L$, the equilibrium length, and is $K(r - L)$ otherwise. Solve the equations of motion. In x, and y, the motion is simple harmonic about the origin, but for the z-axis, the motion is that of a displaced harmonic oscillator.

I.6 Collision means identical position vectors at some instant t, and this leads you to arrive at a vector condition of the form $\boldsymbol{a} = \boldsymbol{b}\,t$. Define a vector product in order to eliminate t.

I.7 You ought to get an answer virtually independent of the original height of dropping. Terminal velocity $v_T \simeq 13$ m/s. After bounce it has to again encounter drag forces and the height is reduced by a factor of ln 2, giving the final height at bounce 5.4 m

I.9 1.3 watt

I.10 First, from the given temperature difference, calculate the radiation loss per day using Stefan's law of radiation. (In section 12.28.1 the surface area of human beings is given.) Second, calculate the total heat of evaporation of sweat per day. Now compare the sum with the total calorie value of the food you take every day. From your daily intake of calorie, calculate how many grammes of carbon can be burned, which becomes CO_2 on oxidation, e.g., for 2000 kcal, the total amount of oxygen to be inhaled is about 16.6 moles, for which so many (?) litres of air to be inhaled? The required lung capacity turns out to be about 270 cc.

I.11 One million volts! Find the mass of rain drop. Every 18 gm of water contains Avogadro's number of water molecules. Each water molecule contains how many electrons and hence how much total negative charge? The earth receives the equivalent amount of positive charge, and then apply the formula for the gain in potential of a uniformly charged spherical conductor.

I.12 This problem can be formulated and solved in three different ways. Each turn of the tape can be viewed as a term of an AP series, or as a differential increment in length as well as in thickness of the tape (that is, handle the problem through formulating integrals), or by simply considering the increase in the volume of the disk as the tape winds. The radii are 1.80 cm and 2.26 cm, ans.

I.13 This problem is given in order to test your ability to formulate a differential equation. Set up the differential equation in the form of $dv/dt + kv = kat$ and solve it.

I.14 Don't be afraid of black holes. You may learn a lot of black hole thermodynamics from this problem. You have the temperature and surface area of the black hole. Use Stefan's law of radiation to calculate the power of emission of radiation. Energy loss also means mass loss ($\dot{E} = -\dot{M}c^2$). Written fully, it is nothing but a differential equation in M, whose solution will give you the lifetime of the blackhole $t_o = 5120G^2M^3/\pi^3\hbar c^4$.

I.15 Take the mass-radius relation of black holes from the previous problem. The density of the universe $\rho = 3c^2/8\pi GR^2 \simeq 8 \times 10^{-27}$ kg/m^3, and the total number of galaxies about 2×10^{11}.

I.16 The collapse time is $t = \sqrt{3\pi/32G\rho}$. If this problem is inverted, it corresponds to the big bang, instead of big crunch. The age-density relation for the hot big bang universe is just the same as the above one! So, no wonder, you would get the age of the universe if you plug in the present mass density of the universe in the above formula. Ans. 29.5 min, 14.9 min, 19.2 min and 21 billion years.

I.17 The angular momentum remains conserved, $I_1\omega_1 = I_2\omega_2$, before and after collapse. During the collapse, gravitational energy is released. The minimum radius of the contracting sun will be achieved when the centrifugal force becomes strong enough to completely neutralise the force due to gravitational attraction on the equator. This gives the radius of the pulsar to be $R \geq 4\pi^2 R_\odot^4/GM_\odot T_\odot^2 \simeq 15$ km, and its period $T \geq R^2 T_\odot/R_\odot^2 \simeq 1$ millisecond. The increase in rotational kinetic energy is by a factor of 2×10^9.

I.18 Since all the forces involved are conservative in nature, you can solve the problem by setting up the energy equation. On hitting the ground the stone loses all its energy content, about 5.85 cal.

I.19 Solve the equations of motion in (x, y) coordinates, eliminate t, and express v_o^2 as a function of θ_o, h and L. Minimise v_o with respect to θ_o, which gives you the required relation.

I.21 Power = magnitude of force × speed. Power lost to combat the force of drag with water during swimming is $\sim$ 150 W, but the swimmer actually loses more than 10 times that for coördinating the limbs for swimming.

I.22 It is a lengthy calculation, but will surely give you an opportunity to recapitulate certain integrations and tricky algebra. Best of luck!

I.23 The effect of rotation is to effectively increase the mass! This is the lesson, if you have not already realised. Ans. 253 J.

I.24 However quietly you step on the platform of any spring type weighing machine, the initial deflection is always twice the one that it will finally settle in! Very strange, isn't it? Solve the problem first for $h =$ 1 m, and get the correct answer $x = .221$ m. The general formula is a solution to the quadratic equation $x^2 - 2x_o(x + h) = 0$ (this comes from the energy equation).

I.25 Carbon. Find the mass ratio of the target and the projectile from the given data.

I.27 This is a practical method of isotope separation followed in most nuclear plants. Heavier isotopes experience higher centrifugal force and hence have lower centrifugal potential energy. In gas phase with an equilibrium thermal distribution at a given temperature, the particles with higher energy must have lower density (Boltzmann's $e^{-E/kT}$ rule). So towards the rim of the centrifuge, hexafluorides of U^{238} will be more populated than those of U^{235}. The abundance ratio of isotopes at radius r is given by

$$\left(\frac{N_1}{N_2}\right)_r = \left(\frac{N_1}{N_2}\right)_o e^{\frac{1}{2}\omega^2 r^2 (m_1 - m_2)/kT}$$

Since $(N_1/N_2)_o = 139 : 1$, $m_1 = 352$ amu and $m_2 = 349$ amu, the enrichment factor for the heavier isotope near the wall is 1.27 (in a single run). So the higher isotope fraction should be separated about 20 times in succession in the centrifuge in order to obtain a mixture containing up to 80% of the light uranium isotope.

I.28 Change in the length of the spring $\Delta l = 4a\sin^2\alpha/2$. Work done for the compression of the springs must equal to the work done by the centrifugal forces that has moved the weights through a distance of $a\sin\alpha$, thus giving $\tan\alpha/2 = \sqrt{m\omega^2/2k}$. You could also set up the force equations for the balls of the governor, the component forces being the centrifugal force, the tension in the links and the elastic forces in the spring (the governor is rotating with constant angular speed with constant α). The equilibrium corresponds to zero force condition. Since the expression does not contain g, the acceleration due to gravity, the device should equally work in the condition of weightlessness.

I.29 (i) $v = \sqrt{2mgh/(m + I/r^2)}$, (ii) $I_1 = mr^2/2$, $I_2 = m(r^2 + r_1^2)/2$, (iii) $t = 2h/v \sin\alpha$, giving $t_1 = 0.78$ s and $t_2 = 0.88$ s

I.30 Preventing from sliding downward means the frictional force is acting upward. Equate the balancing forces to obtain $\omega_1^2 = g\tan(\alpha - \phi)/R\sin\alpha$, where $\tan\phi = \mu_s$. Note that preventing from sliding upward would give you another condition on ω. What would be the state of the object if the value of ω were set in between?

I.31 Just at the time when the drop breaks from the wire, force due to surface tension must equal the weight of the drop. Ans. 34 cm

I.32 Write down the equation of motion of the centre of mass (include the force of friction $(-f\hat{\boldsymbol{i}})$ and the force of reaction $(N\hat{\boldsymbol{j}})$, where $f = \mu N$. Write also the torque equation for the cm and solve for $\omega(t)$. Show that the motion of cm reverses at time $t_1 = v_o/\mu g$. Then sliding stops and rolling begins at, say, time t_2, when $\boldsymbol{\omega} \times R\hat{\boldsymbol{j}} = \boldsymbol{v} =$ instantaneous velocity of cm. Now show that $t_2 > t_1$ is possible only if $\omega_o > v_o/R$

I.33 At the two lines of contact, calculate the normal forces and the respective forces of friction from which the net torque can be calculated. Form the torque equation and solve it. Remember that the frictional force developed at the vertical line of contact changes the normal force at the horizontal line of contact, and vice versa. So you either apply the principle of balancing forces, or end up in summing two series of terms. Try both the methods.

I.34 Cylinder will detach if the component of the centrifugal force, in the vertical direction, exceeds its weight. Use the principle of energy conservation in order to calculate the magnitude of the centrifugal force, while rolling over the edge. The energy equation for rolling over the edge gives $v^2 = v_o^2 + 4gR(1 - \cos\theta)/3$.

I.35 Find the condition for detachment and use energy conservation $(T = -V)$ or balance of forces. Note that the absolute angular speed of the rolling ball is not the same as the one inferred from the motion with respect to the point of contact.

I.36 Set up the equation of motion from the fact that at any instant only a part of the chain is accelerated uniformly due the driving force provided by the weight of another part of the chain. You must express acceleration in terms of dv/dx and integrate the equation of motion. Ans. $v = \sqrt{2gh\ln(l/h)}$.

I.37 Apply Eq. (I.27) for the variable mass problem. Since the magnitude of force is constant and acts in a direction perpendicular to the motion, the curvature of the path is constant. Ans. $\alpha = (u/v_o)\ln(m_o/m)$

I.38 Use Eq. (I.27) with $\boldsymbol{F}_{\text{ext}} = 0,\ -mg\hat{\boldsymbol{k}},\ -\hat{\boldsymbol{k}}\,GMm/z^2$, for the three cases.

I.39 It is a problem of evolute and involute. See Appendix A2 of the book. Ans. $t = l_o^2/2v_oR$.

I.40 If the bit of mud leaves the rim at height y from the ground and with the vertical component of the speed v_y, the maximum height it gains is $h = y + (v_y^2/2g)$. Now maximise h with respect to the initial location, say θ. Why does $h_{\max} \to \infty$ as $v_o \to 0$? There comes the critical speed $v_o = \sqrt{bg}$.

I.41 During hitting, the angular momentum about the hinge remains conserved. Maximum swing can be obtained from the energy balance. Answer to part (a): $v \simeq (M/m)\sqrt{2gl/3}\,\sin(\alpha/2)$, part (b) $mvx(mx + Ml/2)/(mx^2 + Ml^2/3)$. The impact transfers momentum to the support through the reaction at the fulcrum.

I.43 Curvature $\kappa = 2bs/a^3$ and the total acceleration $= a\sqrt{1 + (4bs^2/a^3)^2}$.

I.44 If v_o and v are the velocities of the small ball before and after collision with the big ball, then $A = v/v_o$, where A^2 is the height amplification factor. Speed before bouncing $v_o = \sqrt{2gh}$; the larger ball bounces with a speed $V_1 = e_1 v_o$; momentum balance after collision with small ball on top of the large ball $e_1 M v_o - m v_o = MV + mv$ and their relative velocities before and after collision must obey the relation $v - V = e_2(V_1 + v_o)$, by definition of the coefficient of restitution. Thus, if $e_1 = e_2 = 1$, and $m \ll M$, $A = v/v_0 = 3$. For three balls in succession, show that $A = 7$

I.45 Express F_{linear} and $F_{\text{quadratic}}$ in terms of v and respective terminal speeds v_T, and show that their ratio is just v/v_T, and since $v < v_T$, hence the conclusion.

I.46 Show that $dg(r)/dr = 4\pi G\{\rho(r) - 2\bar{\rho}(r)/3\}$, from which the result follows.

I.47 Show that at a depth z, the gravity anomaly $\Delta g(z) = 4\pi G_\infty \rho\alpha\{1 + 0.5\lambda(1 - e^{-z/\lambda})\}$.

I.48 Characteristic vectors for diagonalising M represents the lab to cm transformation of velocities.

I.49 Calculate the work done by frictional forces.

I.50 The matrix solution e^{At} represents the most general solution for forced damping, and as $\omega \rightarrow \lambda$, the solution approaches that in the limit of critical damping.

Chapter 1

1.1 (i) $x_1^2 + y_1^2 + z_1^2 = x_2^2 + y_2^2 + z_2^2 = R^2$, $(x_2 - x_1)^2 + (y_2 - y_1)^2 + (z_2 - z_1)^2 = l^2$
(ii) $d(\mathrm{OP}) + d(\mathrm{O'P}) = l_o - l$
(iii) $d(\mathrm{OP}) = R(t)$: holonomic, rheonomic, nonconservative and bilateral. In the second case, equality is replaced by $\geq$, which makes the constraint unilateral.
(iv) See the problem solved in section 2.16
(v) Each hinge acts as a centre with its emerging stem as the radius of the sphere over which its other end of the stem can freely move. The subtle difference between a coiled and a straight filament is that when rotated about their axes the former changes configuration but not the latter. So the latter would have an extra constraint relation compared to the former.
(vi) At the hinge point, the motion of the crank is planar (instead of spherical when compared to the hinges of the previous problem), which means one constraint relations for this hinge.

1.2 $\sum m_i \ddot{\boldsymbol{r}}_i \cdot d\boldsymbol{r}_i = dT$, hence the result.

1.3 If you have solved problem I.35, translate it into Cartesian coordinates.

1.4 Write down the constraint relation in 2-D Cartesian coordinates and proceed.

1.5 The first part is solved in many text books. For the second part, force of sliding friction is involved. Without slipping, the loss in pot. energy = gain in translational and rotational kin. energy. But during slipping, a constant frictional torque acts, the work done by the torque is simply the product of the torque and the net angular slip. The angular slip can be calculated from solving the rotation under constant torque.

1.6 The length of the wire is manipulated to change periodically. The constraint is rheonomic. Virtual displacement will not have any radial component. Take the general expression for acceleration $\boldsymbol{a} \equiv \ddot{\boldsymbol{r}}$ in say, spherical polar coordinates, $\boldsymbol{F}_{\text{ext}} = -mg\hat{\boldsymbol{k}}$, and then apply D'Alembert's principle $(\boldsymbol{F}_{\text{ext}} - m\boldsymbol{a}) \cdot \delta\boldsymbol{r} = 0$. Now in this equation substitute $r = a + b\cos\omega t$.

1.7 You may consult Whittaker's book.

1.8 Since $\boldsymbol{r}(\lambda)$ is given, set up Lagrange's equation of the first kind, by doubly differentiating $\boldsymbol{r}(\lambda)$ with respect to time and so on, and arrive at an equation of the form $\ddot{\lambda} =$ constant. Obtain a solution in the form $\lambda = \lambda(t)$, and substitute in $\boldsymbol{r}(\lambda)$ in order to get the complete solution. Repeat the procedure for the second example.

Chapter 2

2.1 The number of constraints can be found from the hints to 1.1, and hence the number of DOFs. Wherever constant distances occur as constraints, one may use polar coordinates as generalised coordinates.

2.2 The concept of DOF of molecular systems is extremely useful in thermodynamics of gas and of phase transitions. Remember that helium is monatomic, nitrogen is diatomic and a water molecule triatomic. The number of DOFs released during vaporisation is 3, 5 and 6 respectively. Heat of vaporisation includes the effect of releasing the molecular bonds between molecules (the bond energy $\sim$ 5 eV/bond), the effect of releasing the DOFs (translation and rotational), and the work done by the vapour while rapidly expanding its volume under constant pressure.

2.3 Start from D'Alembert's principle. $\delta T + Q_i \delta q_i = d(p_i \delta q_i)/dt$.

2.4 Convert into generalised coordinates in steps quite similar to ones you follow in order to derive Euler-Lagrange's equations of motion. Instead of T , you come up with S, both are initially defined in Cartesian coordinates only. The equivalence of the two will become obvious.

2.5 Do this problem in order to have clear idea of generalised forces.

2.6 Define the usual generalised coordinates θ and ϕ for the double pendulum. Find the expressions for generalised forces from infinitesimal virtual works due to virtual displacements $\delta\theta$ and $\delta\phi$

2.7 (i) $L = (m_1 + m_2)\dot{r}^2/2 + m_1 r^2\dot{\theta}^2/2 - m_2 g(r - l)$
(ii) $L = M\dot{x}^2/2 + m(\dot{x}^2 + l^2\dot{\theta}^2)/2 - ml\dot{x}\dot{\theta}\cos\theta + mgl\cos\theta$
(iii) 2 DOF, say the angle ϕ made at the centre of the wire by the instantaneous position of the bead on the wire and the rotating line joining the centre of rotation (a point on the wire) and the centre of the wire, and the angle θ made by the rotating centre at the hinge of rotation with respect to a fixed direction in space. Show that $L = T = \frac{1}{2}mR^2\{(\dot{\theta} + \dot{\phi})^2 + \dot{\theta}^2 + 2\dot{\theta}(\dot{\theta} + \dot{\phi})\cos\phi\}$
(iv) A nonholonomic case with 2 DOF and 2 nonholonomic constraints in 4 generalised coordinates, say (x, y) the Cartesian planar coordinates of the cm, ϕ the coordinate angle of rotation in the plane of the disc, and ψ the coordinate angle that defines the orientation of the plane of the disc with respect to the space-fixed x-axis. The constraint relations are $\dot{x}^2 + \dot{y}^2 - R^2\dot{\phi}^2 = 0$, and $\dot{x}\sin\psi - \dot{y}\cos\psi = R\dot{\phi}$. This gives the Lagrangian as $L = (I\dot{\phi}^2 + J\dot{\psi}^2)/2 + m(\dot{x}^2 + \dot{y}^2)/2$, I and J being moments of inertia about the axes defining the angles ϕ and ψ respectively. The final solution corresponds to the displaced circular orbit of the CM.
(v) Can be found in many text books.

2.8 The problem is not trivial, particularly if you take the gradual drop in the height of cm of the winding roll from the surface of the incline. This will also contribute to both kinetic and potential energy terms. Divide the whole length of the tape into two parts: unwound and to be unwound. The remaining number of turns (n) and the length (L_2) to be unwound are related to the thickness of the tape k by a relation $L_2 \simeq \pi n^2 k$. Follow the moving location of the cm both along the incline (x-axis) and perpendicular to it (y-axis). Note that unfolding of the tape is possible even when α is negative with $\alpha > \tan^{-1}(3/2\pi n_o)$.

2.9 The inclusion of the rotational kinetic energy term in the problem leads to the expected difference. $2L = m(R - r)^2\dot{\theta}^2 + IR^2\dot{\theta}^2/r^2 - 2mg(R - r)(1 - \cos\theta)$, θ being the angle of the bob with the vertical.

2.10 At some stage expand in terms of a small parameter, say $\alpha = k/2m_o c^2$, and finally obtain the period $P \simeq 2\pi\sqrt{m_o/k}(1 + 3\alpha a^2/8)$, a being the amplitude of oscillation.

2.11 DOF $= 1$, θ = polar angle with respect to the vertical axis of rotation. $V = -gr_o(1 - \cos\theta)$, $T = r_o^2(\dot{\theta}^2 + \omega^2\sin^2\theta)/2$. Hence, $\dot{\theta}(\partial L/\partial\dot{\theta}) - L = \text{constant} \neq T + V = E$.

2.12 If necessary, consult Greenwood's book.

2.13 You must know how to differentiate a definite integral with respect to a variable that occurs as one of its limits. This complicated looking Lagrangian gives the same equation of motion as that for a 1-D simple harmonic oscillator.

2.14 The force of friction guides the translational motion of the cm; it also provides the torque for rolling; and rolling without slipping obeys the standard nonholonomic constraint relations. With the help of these three vector equations, find the frictional force to be given by $\boldsymbol{F} = \{mk^2/(1 + k^2)\}\boldsymbol{\omega} \times \boldsymbol{v}$, k being the radius of gyration of the ball. Then show that motion under this $\boldsymbol{F}$ is always circular. In the mid 1940's, Einstein was asked about this problem, namely the motion of a marble on a turntable. A careful experiment was performed in 1979. It is now your turn to work out the theory.

2.15 1 DOF, say the angle of swing (θ) with respect to the vertical. The length of suspension $l(t)$ is variable: the constraint is rheonomic. The Lagrangian $L = m(\dot{l}^2 + l^2\dot{\theta}^2)/2 - mgl\cos\theta$. In the equation of motion $\dot{l}$ controls the effect of damping. When $\dot{l}$ is negative, it becomes a case of negative damping, implying that the oscillation should increase with time. In a child's swing, pulling of the chord at the right time will increase its amplitude of oscillation.

2.16 For any closed system in n-dimensional space, the number of energy integrals = 1, number of angular momentum integrals (each for two axes at a time) $= {}^nC_2 = n(n - 1)/2$, number of linear momentum integrals $= n$ and number of centre of mass motion integrals $= n$

2.17 Potentials are either given or can be formulated. You have to construct the kinetic energy terms either in spherical polar, or cylindrical polar coordinates, as it seems appropriate. It would be fun to derive these integrals of motions, not all being trivial. If you cannot derive them by the Lagrangian method, simply differentiate with respect to time and show that they vanish.

2.18 Use the expressions for transformation of generalised momenta and Jacobi integral under generalised coordinate transformations, namely $J' = J - p_j \partial q_j/\partial t$, and $p_i' = p_j \partial q_j/\partial Q_i$.

Chapter 3

3.1 The problem is similar to problem 2.14, but here it is a case of sliding with negligible friction. Start with the general equation of motion given by Eq. (3.6). The general solution in terms of complex numbers: $z(t) = \{z(o) + v_o t + z(o)i\omega t\}exp(-i\omega t)$. If the particle is thrown from the centre of the disc with initial speed v_o, the track on the disc would thus appear as a spiral.

3.2 Represent rotation by a matrix of transformation. Obviously, $a_{ij}b_{jk} \neq b_{ij}a_{jk}$, even though both the matrices are orthogonal. But for infinitesimal transformations, $x_i' = \epsilon_{ijk}(\delta\theta)n_j x_k$. Now demonstrate the commutability of two infinitesimal rotations. For the rest of the problem, all necessary guidelines are given in the text of the problem.

3.3 Set $\boldsymbol{g} = 0$, and rename the variables $\boldsymbol{v}$, t and $2\boldsymbol{\omega}$ as $\boldsymbol{R}$, θ and $-\hat{\boldsymbol{n}}$ respectively.

3.4 In order to calculate the kinetic energy of the system, one has to find out the true inertial velocities of the two point masses of the dumbbell. Apply the most general formula (3.33) to the case, and deal the problem in spherical polar coordinates about both cm of the dumbbell and the centre of the circular track.

3.5 The conservation of angular momentum gives $m\omega_o(R + h)^2 = m\omega(R + h - gt^2/2)$, which on integration yields $\theta = \int_o^T \omega\, dt \simeq \omega_o T + \omega_o g T^3/3R$. Hence the result.

3.8 Use the formulae (3.33) and (3.34). For example, for the tip of instantaneously located horizontal blade ($\boldsymbol{r} = r_o\hat{\boldsymbol{j}}$, $\boldsymbol{R} = R_o\hat{\boldsymbol{i}}$, $\hat{\boldsymbol{i}}$ pointing towards the outward axis of blades and $\hat{\boldsymbol{k}}$ vertically upward), the inertial velocity and accelerations are

$\boldsymbol{v}_o = \omega_o R_o \cos\Omega t\hat{\boldsymbol{j}} - \omega_o r_o \cos\Omega t\hat{\boldsymbol{j}} + \omega_1 r_o\hat{\boldsymbol{k}}$, and

$\boldsymbol{a}_o = (\omega_o\Omega r_o \sin\Omega t - \omega_o^2 R_o \cos^2\Omega t)\hat{\boldsymbol{i}} - (\omega_o^2 r_o \cos^2\Omega t + \omega_1^2 r_o)\hat{\boldsymbol{j}}$

For the tip of an instantaneously located vertical blade ($\boldsymbol{r} = r_o\hat{\boldsymbol{k}}$ and $\boldsymbol{R} = R_o\hat{\boldsymbol{i}}$)

$\boldsymbol{v}_o = (\omega_o R_o \cos\Omega t - \omega_1 r_o)\hat{\boldsymbol{j}}$, and $\boldsymbol{a}_o = (2\omega_o\omega_1 r_o \cos\Omega t - \omega_o^2 R_o \cos\Omega t)\hat{\boldsymbol{i}} - \omega_1^2 r_o\hat{\boldsymbol{k}}$

3.9 These are Eulerian rotations. Try without looking at section 12.21

3.10 The KE does not change in this example, whereas in Foucault's pendulum, the average KE is one half of the maximum speed at the centre. However, you should solve the equation of motion, which just contains the Coriolis term.

Chapter 4

4.1 This problem is often referred to 'Jack and the sky hook', because of its similarity with 'Jack and the bean stalk', the bean stalk appearing to be self-supported. So Jack must be located on the equator, the total centrifugal force applied over the entire bean stalk has to balance its total weight. Since gravity changes with distance as r^{-2} and the centrifugal force as $\omega^2 r$, the length of the bean stalk is obtained by solving for L in the equation $GM\{R^{-1} - (R + L)^{-1}\} = \omega^2(L^2 + 2RL)/2$, R and M being the radius and mass of the earth. The equation for tension T would satisfy the differential equation $dT/dr = \mu \times$ the net downward force per unit mass, μ being the mass per unit length of the rope. For free support, the tension should vanish at both the ends of the rope. Similarly, calculate the total energy E = KE + PE. You would get $E > 0$, which means that given a slight perturbation, the rope will finally escape!

4.2 Take the origin at the centre of mass and proceed. Express the equations of motion of each body in terms of the position vector of that body. $E_2 = m_1 E_1/m_2$, $\boldsymbol{L}_2 = m_1\boldsymbol{L}_1/m_2$

4.3 (a) Use Eqs (4.15) and (4.16). In the second case, you have to derive the equations of motion, satisfying the given constraint and then an expression for $V_{\text{eff}}(r)$, in plane polar coordinates. Ans. $r < \frac{1+\sqrt{5}}{2}a$, the

famous golden ratio. For further discussion read Hestenes's book.
(b) The equation for a vertically placed cone (apex pointing downward) with semivertex angle α is given by $r = z\tan\alpha$, kinetic energy $T = \frac{1}{2}m(\dot{r}^2 + r^2\dot{\theta}^2 + \dot{z}^2)$, potential energy $V = mgz$, angular momentum $h = mr^2\dot{\theta}$. Find $V_{\text{eff}}(r)$ and analyse the stability of circular orbits.

4.4 For the origin at a point on the circumference of a circle, the equation of the circle in plane polar coordinates becomes $r = 2a\cos\theta$. Find the angular momentum integral $H = r^2\dot{\theta}$, and show that the radial component of acceleration from $f(r)\hat{r} - r\dot{\theta}^2 = -8a^2H^2r^{-5}$, an attractive force varying as the inverse of the fifth power of the radial separation. Find that the total energy = KE + PE = 0! What does it mean?

4.5 Some more examples similar to the above one. Exactly similar procedure. (i) inverse cubic, (ii) inverse quintic power law of radial distance.

4.6 (i) $\boldsymbol{j} = 2KHr^{-5}(dr/d\theta)\hat{r} - KHr^{-4}\hat{\theta}$
(ii) $\cos\theta_m = (-1 \pm \sqrt{1 + 48e^2})/8e$
(iii) The sidereal period of revolution $P = S/(S-1)$, for superior planets ($a > 1$ AU), and $P = S/(S+1)$, for inferior planets, S being the synodic period (= the time interval between successive return of any planet with respect to the moving sun-earth line). Use Kepler's third law.

4.7 Use the standard conic equation for parabola, and show $\dot{\theta} = Hr^{-2} = 4\sqrt{K/p^3}\cos^4(\theta/2)$, p being the semilatus rectum of the parabolic orbit. Integrate this equation to obtain the time spent by the comet inside earth's orbit, $t_o = 2\sqrt{(2r - p)/K}(p + r) \simeq 76.6$ days for the given problem.

4.8 (a) Differentiate Eq. (4.43), substitute in Eq. (4.24), use Eq. (4.40), eliminate ν and r by means of Eq. (4.42), in order to obtain $2\pi dt/P = (1 - e\cos E)dE$, which on integration gives Kepler's equation.
(b) $\nu = g + 2e\sin g + \frac{5}{4}e^2\sin 2g + \frac{1}{12}e^3(13\sin 3g - 3\sin g) + \frac{1}{96}e^4(103\sin 4g - 44\sin 2g) + \cdots$,
$E = g + e\sin g + \frac{1}{2}e^2\sin 2g + \frac{1}{8}e^3(3\sin 3g - 3\sin g) + \frac{1}{6}e^4(2\sin 4g - \sin 2g) + \cdots$

4.9 Grav. force $F_g = GM_{\odot}m_e/r^2$, Force due to radiation pressure $F_p = \sigma_{\text{th}} < s > /c$, σ_{th} = Thompson cross-section for electron $= 8\pi(e^2/m_ec^2)^2/3$, $< s >$ = average energy flux from the sun $= L_{\odot}/4\pi r^2$, $L_{\odot}$ = Luminosity of sun $= 3.86 \times 10^{26}$ W. See that $F_g/F_p \simeq 40$, the electron cannot escape from the solar system. Setting the radiation pressure on an electron equal to the weight of a proton, one obtains the Eddington limit of maximum possible equilibrium stellar luminosity, corresponding to $L_*/M_* = 1.5\, Gm_pm_e^2c^5/e^4$.

4.10 Assuming a circular orbit of earth, v_{esc} from the orbit $= \sqrt{2}v_{\text{orb}}$. The excess speed required in the direction of earth's orbital motion $(\sqrt{2} - 1)v_{\text{orb}} \equiv v_{\text{excess}}$. In order to achieve this, the speed at which the object has to be thrown from the surface of the earth $v = \sqrt{v^2_{\text{excess}} + v^2_{\text{esc,earth}}} = \sqrt{(12.1)^2 + (11.2)^2} =$ 16.4 km/s, since $v_{\text{orb}} = 29.8$ km/s.

4.11 Because $\sqrt{M_{\odot}/M_{\oplus}} = 574 >$ (dist of sun/dist of moon) = 390, the force on the moon due to earth < force on the moon due to the sun. Hence, the net centripetal force on moon is always acting towards the sun (or its vicinity) irrespective of the location of the earth. The orbit of moon is therefore always concave towards the sun.

4.12 $< r >_t = \int_o^P r dt/P = a(1 + e^2/2)$, $< r >_\theta = a\sqrt{1 - e^2}$, $< r >_s = \int_o^L r ds/\int_o^L ds = a$. For the last one you should use Eq. (4.42) and change the variable of integration to the eccentric anomaly E.

4.13 Transfer orbit is assumed to be Keplerian. In order to meet the counter-earth, its period has to be $T = T_{\oplus}(2n + 1)/2n$, n being any positive integer. Most satisfactory choice is $n = 1$. Answer to the last part is approximately $4e$ radian or 3.3 degrees of arc.

4.14 $r_1 = 1.0$ AU, $r_2 = 1.51$ AU. The required speed for sending from the surface of the earth = 11.56 km/s. In-flight time = 256.8 days.

4.15 Since the intended orbit was a bound one and the launching speed (hence KE, and also total energy) did not change, it will still be an elliptical one. Calculate the total energy for the intended orbit, which gives using Eq. (4.38) the length of the semi-major axis $a = R_{\oplus} + h$. Since the distance between two foci via any point on the orbit is $2a$, and given that the distance from one focus = a, the satellite must be on the semi-minor axis. Then from the property of reflection angle (see section 4.10) $\tan\phi = b/ae$, giving $e = \cos\phi$.

4.16 Distance to nearest approach from prime focus = radius of the star, and the initial speed of the particle = the speed of light = c. So, $R_{\text{ns}} = a(e - 1) = |(GM_{\text{ns}}/2E')|(\csc\frac{\psi}{2} - 1)$. Taking the given values of R_{ns} and M_{ns}, the classical deflection of light $\psi = 2\sin^{-1}(GM_{\text{ns}}/(GM_{\text{ns}} + R_{\text{ns}}c^2)) = 20°.96$.

4.17 For hard sphere of radius r, the scattering cross-section $\sigma(\psi) = r^2/4$. Effective focal length of Rutherford scattering is $f = |K/4E'|$.

4.18 First calculate how many neutrinos (actually $\bar{\nu}_e$) are emitted by the supernova = total energy available/energy per neutrino. If they are emitted equally in all directions, then at such a far off distance, how many of them passed through per square metre of normal area (that is, integrated flux at earth), say N particles/m^2. Now if there are N' protons in the Ćerenkov detector and σ_ν is the reaction cross-section between protons and $\bar{\nu}_e$, then the number of antineutrinos caught in the detector $N_c = NN'\sigma_\nu$. Knowing N, N' and N_c, show that $\sigma_\nu \sim 10^{-47}$ m^2.

4.20 (i) $\Omega_p = a^2(1-e^2)\omega_p/2d^2$, (ii) $\Omega_p = \omega_p\delta(1-\sqrt{1-e^2})/e^2$, (iii) $\Omega_p = 6(K'/Ka^3)(1+e^2/4)/(1-e^2)^3$

4.21 See *Am. J. Phys.* 44, p687, (1976).

4.22 Ans. A sphere of radius 15 fm.

4.23 Use the formula (4.79). Answer is 6.7×10^{12} kg/year.

4.24 This is basically due to a simple geometrical property of prolate spheroids.

4.25 The Roche lobe radius $R_{\rm rl} = (16\rho_p/\rho_s)^{1/3}R_p \simeq 2.51\, R_p$. A satellite is broken into pieces to form rings if it comes closer than $R_{\rm rl}$.

4.26 Add the rotational part, due to centrifugal potential energy.

Chapter 5

5.1 If the Lagrangian is linearly dependent on velocity, the Hamiltonian vanishes, and vice versa! The latter is true for light rays and ultrarelativistic particles.

5.2 All $\dot{q}_i$'s have to be expressed as explicit functions p_j's. For this invert the equations obtained from $p_i = \partial L/\partial \dot{q}_i$

5.3 These strongly resemble the creation and annihilation operators defined in the context of quantised harmonic oscillators. Then, how about the Hamiltonian equations of motion expressed in terms of creation and annihilation operators?

5.4 These look very similar to Dirac's formulation of constraint dynamics. We shall talk more about them in chapter 9.

5.5 These are six independent constants of motions. The first three correspond to the conservation of angular momentum, the case being one of the central forces.

5.6 (i) $H(x,p) = p^2/2(1+2\beta x)^2 + \omega^2x^2/2 + \alpha x^3$
(ii) If you treat $z(t)$ as rheonomic variable, $H(\theta, p_\theta) = (p + ml\dot{z}\sin\theta)^2/2ml^2 - mgl\cos\theta - m\dot{z}^2/2 - mgz$, otherwise it would be a very complicated expression for $H = H(\theta, z, p_\theta, p_z)$
(iii) $H(q,p,t) = [p - F(q,t)]^2/2G(q,t) + V(q,t)$
(iv) $H(x,p) = p^2/[2m\{1 + (df/dx)^2\}] + mgf(x)$

5.7 (i) $R(r,\dot{r},p_\theta) = -\mu\dot{r}^2/2 + p_\theta^2/2\mu r^2 - GMm/r$, the last two terms being the effective potential for r-motion.
(ii) $R(\theta,\dot{\theta},p_\phi,p_\psi) = p_\psi^2/2I_3 + (p_\phi - p_\psi\cos\theta)^2/2I_1\sin^2\theta - I_1\dot{\theta}^2/2 + mgl\cos\theta$, the second and fourth terms constitute the effective potential for θ-motion.

5.8 $\boldsymbol{r}_i' = \boldsymbol{r}_i + \boldsymbol{\epsilon}$, and $\boldsymbol{p}_i' = \boldsymbol{p}_i$ for the $i^{\rm th}$ particle, $\boldsymbol{\epsilon}$ being a small constant infinitesimal translation. The condition for invariance: $H(\boldsymbol{r}_i,\boldsymbol{p}_i) = H(\boldsymbol{r}_i',\boldsymbol{p}_i')$. On substitution for $\boldsymbol{p}_i'$ and $\boldsymbol{r}_i'$, the rhs becomes $H(\boldsymbol{r}_i,\boldsymbol{p}_i) - \boldsymbol{\epsilon}\cdot\Sigma\dot{\boldsymbol{p}}_i$, which means $\Sigma\boldsymbol{p}_i$ = constant, as $\boldsymbol{\epsilon}$ is arbitrary. In a similar way prove the second part.

5.9 (i) $\boldsymbol{v} \equiv \dot{\boldsymbol{r}} = \partial H/\partial\boldsymbol{p} = c^2(\boldsymbol{p} - e\boldsymbol{A})/D$, where $D = \sqrt{c^2(\boldsymbol{p}-e\boldsymbol{A})^2 + m_o^2c^4}$,
$\dot{\boldsymbol{p}} = \{c^2e[(\boldsymbol{p}-e\boldsymbol{A})\cdot\nabla]\boldsymbol{A} + c^2e(\boldsymbol{p}-e\boldsymbol{A})\times(\nabla\times\boldsymbol{A})\}/D - e\nabla\phi = e(\boldsymbol{E} + \boldsymbol{v}\times\boldsymbol{B})$
(ii) $\dot{q} = \partial H/\partial p = p/(2m\omega\sin^2\omega t)$ and $\dot{p} = -(\partial H/\partial q) = p\omega\cot\omega t + m\omega^2 q$

5.10 From Eq. (5.26), it is easy to see that $\boldsymbol{p}$ changes only in the direction of $\boldsymbol{\nabla}\mu$, so that only p_z will be affected due to the vertical gradient of μ. For horizontally grazing incidence of light, $p_z \ll p$, and one can take p to be practically constant. Differentiating Eq. (5.25) with respect to time and eliminating $\dot{p}_z$ using Eq. (5.26), one can easily establish $\ddot{z} \simeq (c/\mu^3)(d\mu/dz)$. Thus, for μ decreasing upwards, the curvature of the trajectory will be convex upward (inverted mirage) and vice versa.

5.11 Just algebra.

Chapter 6

6.1 You have to minimise potential energy, which can be formulated to appear in the form $\delta \int_1^2 y\, ds = 0$. The solution corresponds to catenary: $y = a\cosh(x/a)$

6.2 This is a problem of shortest route on the surface of a sphere: $\delta \int_1^2 ds = 0$, $ds^2 = R_\oplus^2(d\lambda^2 + \cos^2\lambda\, d\phi^2$, λ = geographical latitude, and ϕ = geographical longitude. Define $\lambda' = d\lambda/d\phi$, and arrive at the equation of geodesic in the form $\int \phi\, d\phi = \int C_o d\lambda/\cos\lambda\sqrt{\cos^2\lambda - C_o^2}$, C_o being a constant of integration. Acceptable solution exists for $\cos^2\lambda > C_o^2 = \cos^2\lambda_o$, say. Thus at $\lambda = \lambda_o$, the path will always be convex towards the nearer pole. One can also find λ'', and show that $\lambda'' < 0$, at $\lambda' = 0$, and $\lambda > 0$.

6.3 Express $L = m\dot{z}^2 - V$, and minimise $\int_0^{t_o} Ldt$ with respect to variations of A and C.

6.4 Here both x and t are transformed, with the result that the Lagrangian would transform according to Eq. (6.29). It is not so apparent that the form of the Lagrangian would remain unchanged, but not surprisingly, covariance would demand it.

6.5 This is also an interesting property of the given Lagrangian. Most useful in the field theories. Straightforward algebra. $dt = \lambda dT$, $\dot{q} = \lambda^{-1}dq/dT$, and set $\delta W = (\partial W/\partial\lambda)\delta\lambda = 0$

6.6 Since at the surface of discontinuity, the potential is changed abruptly, the normal component of momentum would change abruptly and the tangential component remains continuous, that is, $v_1 \sin i = v_2 \sin r$. For electromagnetic waves, the boundary conditions for electric and magnetic fields are such that the speed relation is just the opposite.

6.7 Use $\mathbf{r}' = \mathbf{r} + \epsilon\mathbf{u}$, $t' = t + \epsilon$, ϵ being a small quantity. This leaves the argument of V invariant. Then apply Noether's theorem (Eq. (6.40))

6.8 For infinitesimal transformations, choose $\beta_1 = 1+\epsilon$, and $\beta_2 = 1+\gamma\epsilon$. Now, $\delta W = 0$ implies $\gamma = 2$ and $n = -2$. The final result follows from the application of Noether's theorem.

6.9 We know that for free particles, $Ldt = -m_o c\, ds$. In the general theory of relativity, all motions are free and follow geodesics, even though gravity is present (gravity is considered to be as fictitious as centrifugal or Coriolis forces are). So the form of the Lagrangian from the above relation is something that varies as the ratio ds over dt. From the given metric, find ds/dt, and hence the form of the Lagrangian L (per unit mass) for motion of test particles in the gravitational field of the heavy object, given by

$$L \simeq \frac{1}{2}v^2 - \phi + \frac{1}{2}\phi^2 - \frac{1}{2}\phi v^2 - \frac{1}{8}v^4 + \phi\frac{(\mathbf{r}\cdot\mathbf{v})}{r^2} + \cdots, \quad \phi = \frac{GM}{r}$$

Once L is known, you can derive the equation of motion. You should, however, remember that $dr/dt = v_r$, not v, and that $v^2 = \dot{r}^2 + r^2\dot{\theta}^2 + r^2\sin^2\theta\dot{\phi}^2$

6.10 Assume that g_{ik} are functions of coordinates. Write down Lagrange's equations of motion. For each term do the necessary differentiations and finally arrange the equations of motion in the form prescribed in the problem. The relevance of the last two exercises will be clear only when you would study tensor calculus and general theory of relativity. However, remember that L is defined in a configuration space, but ds and g_{ik} for metric spaces only. So the analogy that this problem tries to impress upon you is valid only for free particle dynamics, for which the configuration space is indeed a metric space.

Chapter 7

7.1 Ans. $l = 4R$.

7.2 Use $ds^2 = dx^2 + dy^2$, $r^2 = x^2 + y^2$ and $s = 0$ at $r = r_0$.

7.3 Show that the relation (7.10) satisfies the differential equation (7.8)

7.4 Ans. $L = 2\theta(2\pi - \theta)R/\pi^2$, $H = R\theta/\pi$, $P_{\text{hypocycloid}} : P_{\text{straight}} = \sqrt{\theta(2\pi - \theta)} : \pi$

7.5 Derive the Lagrangian for the motion of the disc: $L = 3m\dot{u}^2/2 - mgy$, u being the measure of distance along the curve, y the height of the cm. For tautochronous motion, we must have the potential energy term $\propto u^2$, suggesting y to have a form $y = a + bu^2$. Since $dx^2 = du^2 - dy^2$, this gives an idea of the nature of dx^2. Show that they satisfy the equation of a cycloid.

7.6 The effective radius increases, which becomes infinite when the effective gravity vanishes on the surface of the earth for $\omega \simeq 17\omega_o$

7.7 This is a case for which brachistochrone is a circular arc! Travel time $= 2\sqrt{m/c}\ln[x_o + \sqrt{x_o^2 + y_o^2}/y_o]$

7.8 $ds^2 = \rho_o^2 d\phi^2 + dz^2$, $v^2 = 2g(z_o - z)$. Define a parameter $\zeta = \rho_o\phi$, and proceed. The travel time along the brachistochrone $t_b = \theta_o \csc(\theta_o/2)\sqrt{z_o/2g}$, where θ_o is the solution of the equation $(1 - \cos\theta_o)/(\theta_o - \sin\theta_o) = z_o/\zeta_o$, $\zeta_o = \rho_o\phi_o$

Chapter 8

8.1 Use Eqs (8.10) and (8.12 – 14)

8.2 Follow a method similar to ones used in section 8.3

8.3 $\boldsymbol{P} = (-p_1, p_2, p_3)$

8.4 $F_2 = R_{ij}x_j p_i'$ and $p_i = R_{ij}p_j'$

8.5 The Jacobian for the first transformation is not unity. $p^2 = p_r^2 + p_\theta^2/r^2 + p_\phi^2/(r^2\sin^2\theta)$

8.6 (i) Make use of the relations (8.15). (ii) See Whittaker's book.

8.7 (i) Use the condition (8.17).
(ii) Use the first of the conditions (8.15) and finally obtain $\alpha\beta q^{2\alpha - 1} = 1$. Since q is arbitrary, $\alpha = 1/2$ and $\beta = 2$
(iii) Use the elementary PB relations as given in problem 8.6 (i).
(iv) The same conditions as above.
(v) Keeping $t =$ constant, use the conditions (8.17).
(vi) – (x) Use the elementary PB relation.

8.8 (i) $Q = \tan^{-1}(m\omega q/p)$, $P = (p^2 + m^2\omega^2 q^2/2m\omega$, $K = \omega P(1 + \dot{\omega}\sin Q\cos Q/\omega^2)$
(ii) $Q = \tan^{-1}(m\omega q/p - F(t)/\omega p)$, $P = p^2/2m\omega + m\omega(q - F(t)/m\omega^2)^2/2$
$K = \omega P + \sqrt{2P/m\omega^3}[\omega F(t)\sin Q - \dot{F}(t)\cos Q] + F^2(t)/2m\omega^2$
(iii) $Q = p + m\omega q$, $P = (p - m\omega q)/2m\omega$, $K = (Q^2 + 4m^2\omega^2P^2)/4m$
(iv) $Q = \ln(1 + \sqrt{q}\cos p)$, $P = 2(1 + \sqrt{q}\cos p)\sqrt{q}\sin p$
$K = \frac{1}{2m}\{\tan^{-1}[P/2e^Q(e^Q - 1)]\}^2 + \frac{1}{2}m\omega^2[(e^Q - 1)^2 + P^2/4e^{2Q}]^2$

8.10 Since the particle is moving under $V = -mgz$, $Q(t) = q(t+\tau) = q(t) + p(t)\tau/m + g\tau^2/2$ and $P(t) = p(t+\tau) = p(t) + mg\tau$, satisfying the relations $p = \partial F_1/\partial q$ and $P = -\partial F_1/\partial Q$

8.11 The transformed Hamiltonian is desired to have the form $K(Q,P) = P^2/2 + \omega^2Q^2/2$. From the given F_2, one can obtain using (8.12) and rearranging the terms with Taylor expansions, $p \simeq P + 2aQP$ and $q \simeq Q - aQ^2 - 3bP^2$. Substituting in H and equating K with H, obtain $\alpha = a$ and $\beta = 3b - 2a$. Now the solutions in terms of Q and P are perfectly harmonic, and the anharmonic solutions for q and p can be obtained from those for Q and P by the transformation $q \simeq A\cos\omega t - \alpha A^2\cos^2\omega t - (\beta + 2\alpha)\omega^2 A^2\sin^2\omega t$, and so on.

8.12 $dy - pdx = d(y - px) + xdp \equiv \lambda(dY - PdX)$ say, where $(x, y, p) \rightarrow (X, Y, P)$ so that the contact nature is preserved. Taking $\lambda = 1$, one can have $X = p$, $Y = y - px$, and also $x = -P$, $y = -PX + Y$, which make a contact transformation between (x, y) and (X, Y)

Chapter 9

9.1 All the rules given in Eqs (9.1) – (9.7) are in fact common. Ans. 0 and $[[A, C], [B, D]]$

9.2 (i) $\boldsymbol{a}\cdot\boldsymbol{b}$, (ii) $2\boldsymbol{a}(\boldsymbol{a}\cdot\boldsymbol{r})$, (iii) $-\,\boldsymbol{r}\times\boldsymbol{\nabla}V = \boldsymbol{\Gamma} =$ torque, (iv) $(\boldsymbol{g}\times\boldsymbol{f})\cdot\boldsymbol{L} + [f_i, g_j]L_iL_j$.

9.3 $[L_i, A_{jk}] = \epsilon_{ijl}A_{lk} + \epsilon_{ikl}A_{lj}$, $[A_{jk}, A_{il}] = (\epsilon_{klm}\delta_{ij} + \epsilon_{jlm}\delta_{ik} + \epsilon_{kim}\delta_{jl} + \epsilon_{jim}\delta_{kl})L_m$

9.4 The starting point is the relation $m\boldsymbol{v} = \boldsymbol{p} - e\boldsymbol{A}(\boldsymbol{r}, t)$.

9.5 To show A as a constant of motion, prove $[A, H] = 0$

$[A_i, A_j] = \epsilon_{ijk}L_k$, $[L_i, A_j] = \epsilon_{ijk}A_k$ and $[A_i, H] = 0 = [L_i, H]$. These are in fact generators of Lie algebra $O(4) = O(3)\times O(3)$ for $E < 0$ and $L(3,1)$ for $E > 0$.

9.6 Write the usual Taylor series expansion and use Poisson's theorem (Eq. (9.14)).

9.7 Show that $\Delta p_i = -(\partial u/\partial q_i) = (dp_i/d\theta)\Delta\theta = -(\partial w/\partial q_i)\Delta\theta = [p_i, w]\Delta\theta$. Similarly for Δq_i. Then use the relation (9.7) for any $f = f(q, p)$:

$$\frac{df}{d\theta} = \sum\frac{\partial f}{\partial p_i}\frac{dp_i}{d\theta} + \sum\frac{\partial f}{\partial q_i}\frac{dq_i}{d\theta} = \sum\frac{\partial f}{\partial p_i}[p_i, w] + \sum\frac{\partial f}{\partial q_i}[q_i, w] = [f, w]$$

9.8 Starting relations are Poisson's theorem (Eq. (9.14)) for Q_i and P_i, and the definitions of Q_i and p_i from F_2. Then evaluate using the basic definition of PB relation (Eq. (9.1)) the PB $[Q_i, \partial F_2/\partial t]$ and at an intermediate stage you should obtain $[Q_i, \partial F_2/\partial t] = \partial^2F_2/\partial P_i\partial t + (\partial^2F_2/\partial q_j\partial t)(\partial q_i/\partial P_i)$, which will finally reduce to $\partial Q_i/\partial t$

9.9 $dQ/dT = -\,dq/dt = -\,\partial H(q,p)/\partial p = -\,\partial H(Q,-P)/\partial(-P) = \partial K/\partial P$. Similarly, $dP/dT = dp/dt = -\,\partial K/\partial Q$

So Hamilton's equations of motion are preserved. But the PB relation $[Q, P] = -1 \neq [q, p]$

Chapter 10

10.1 Show that $(d/dt)(\partial S/\partial\alpha_i) = (\partial H/\partial\alpha_i)$. Since $H = E = \alpha_n$, $\partial S/\partial\alpha_i = 0$ for $i = 1, \ldots, n-1$ and $\partial S/\partial\alpha_n = t + \text{const.}$

10.2 $W(x, y, z, t, p_1, p_2, E) = -\,Et + p_1x + p_2y - \frac{2}{mg}\sqrt{E - p_1^2/2m - p_2^2/2m - mgz}$ and $\beta_1 = \partial W/\partial E$, $\beta_2 = \partial W/\partial p_1$, $\beta_3 = \partial W/\partial p_2$ are also constants by Jacobi's theorem.

10.3 The Hamiltonian is $H(p, x) = (p^2\mathrm{sech}^2x + x^2)/2$ and the complete integral for W is

$W(x, E, t) = -\,Et + \int\sqrt{2E - x^2}\cosh x\,dx$. Now find and solve the equations of motion by both the methods.

10.4 The HJ equation in $F_2 = S(q, P)$ would be $(1/2m)(\partial S/\partial q)^2 + m\omega^2q^2/2 = f(P)$ with $p = \partial S/\partial q$ and $Q = \partial S/\partial P$. Solution to HJ equation gives $S(q, P) = \{f(P)/\omega\}\sin^{-1}\sqrt{m\omega^2q^2/2f(P)} + \frac{1}{2}q\sqrt{2mf(P) - m^2\omega^2q^2}$. Now $Q = \partial S/\partial P = \{f'(P)/\omega\}\sin^{-1}\sqrt{m\omega^2q^2/2f(P)}$, thus giving the CT

$q = \sqrt{2f(P)/m\omega^2}\sin(\omega Q/f')$, $p = \sqrt{2mf(P)}\cos(\omega Q/f')$

10.5 Write the Hamiltonian. On comparison with Eq. (10.17) $a(r) = 0$, $b(\theta) = a\cos\theta$, and therefore the complete integral for HJ equation takes the form (see Eq. (10.18))

$$W(r, \theta, \phi, E, \beta, p_\phi, t) = -\,Et + p_\phi\phi \pm \int\sqrt{\beta - 2\mu a\cos\theta - \frac{p_\phi^2}{\sin^2\theta}}d\theta \pm \int\sqrt{2\mu E - \frac{\beta}{r^2}}dr$$

where the first integrals of motion are E, p_ϕ and β. Since the angular momentum $L = \sqrt{p_\theta^2 + (p_\phi^2/\sin^2\theta)}$, $\beta = L^2 + 2\mu a\cos\theta$, and therefore L is not conserved but its ϕ-component p_ϕ is. A particle can fall into the centre if $p_r = m\dot{r} = -\sqrt{2mE - (\beta/r^2)} \to -\infty$ as $r \to 0$, that is, if $\beta < 0$. Hence the impact parameter satisfies $s^2 < a\cos\theta/E$ leading to the cross-section $\sigma = (\pi a/E)\cos\alpha$, $\alpha = \angle(\boldsymbol{v}_\infty, \boldsymbol{a})$. Averaging over all possible orientations of $\boldsymbol{a}$, $<\sigma> = \pi a/4E$

$L^2 > 0$, but for a given β and E, L^2 becomes negative for $\cos\theta > \beta/2\mu a$, and all such particles are absorbed.

10.6 Derive the Hamiltonian and show that the HJ equation is

$$\frac{\partial W}{\partial t} + \frac{2}{m(u + v)}\left[u\left(\frac{\partial W}{\partial u}\right)^2 + v\left(\frac{\partial W}{\partial v}\right)^2 + \frac{1}{4}\left(\frac{1}{u} + \frac{1}{v}\right)\left(\frac{\partial W}{\partial \phi}\right)^2 + k^2 + \frac{E}{4}(u^2 - v^2)\right] = 0$$

and proceed for the separation of variables as demonstrated in section 10.4. Note that E is not energy here, but the magnitude of the electric field.

10.7 The action variable $J = (1/\pi)\int_{q_1}^{q_2}\sqrt{2m(E - V_o\tan^2(\alpha q)}\,dq$, where the limits q_1 and q_2 are given by $q_1 = -q_2$, and $\tan^2(\alpha q_2) = E/V_o$. On integration, this results in $J = (\sqrt{2m(E + V_o)} - \sqrt{2mV_o})/\alpha$, and the angle variable $\omega = \nu t + \beta$, where the frequency $\nu = \partial E/\partial J = \alpha\sqrt{2(E + V_o)/m}$ and the angular frequency $= 2\pi\nu$

10.8 $J_\phi = 2\pi\alpha_\phi$ and $J_r = \oint\sqrt{2mE + 2mk/r - \alpha_\theta^2/r^2}\,dr$. These are the same as those for the Kepler problem (see Eqs (10.41) – (10.43). But $J_\theta = \oint\sqrt{\alpha_\theta^2 - \alpha_\phi^2\csc^2\theta - \beta^2\sec^2\theta}\,d\theta$ which is different. Substitute $u = \tan^2\theta$ and do a contour integral (branch cut from u_1 to u_2) to evaluate $J_\theta = \pi(\alpha_\theta - \alpha_\phi - \beta)$ and finally $J_r = -2\pi\alpha_\theta + \sqrt{2\pi^2mk^2/(-E)}$. Show that $E = -2\pi^2mk^2/(J_r + 2J_\theta + J_\phi + 2\pi\beta)^2$, giving $\nu_r = \nu_\phi = 4\pi^2mk^2/(J_r + 2J_\theta + J_\phi + 2\pi\beta)^3 = \nu_\theta/2$, implying that the particle completes two oscillations in θ during each orbit.

10.9 The form of the Hamiltonian would be like the one shown in Eq. (10.16) with the condition that $V(r) \neq 0$ only at $r = a$, the radius of the sphere. It is the last integral in Eq. (10.18) that would appear in the integral for J_r. $J_r = (1/2\pi)\int_{r_m}^{a}\sqrt{2mE - (L^2/r^2)}dr$, $L=$ angular momentum, and $E =$ energy. Thus $J_r = J_r(Ea^2, L)$. Thus for adiabatic changes in the radius a, we must have $Ea^2 =$ const., and for the angle of incidence α, $\sin\alpha = r_m/a = L/a\sqrt{2mE}=$ const.

10.10 Set up the HJ equation. The constant of separation for the ϕ-variable will be $\alpha_\phi = p_\phi^2/2mr^2\sin^2\theta - eBp_\phi/2m$ and its corresponding action variable $J_\phi = 2\pi\alpha_\phi$. Other action variables are $J_\theta = J_\theta(p_\phi, \beta)$, $J_r = J_r(E + eBp_\phi/2m, \beta)$. When B is slowly changed, p_ϕ, β and $E + eBp_\phi/2m$ should remain constant.

Chapter 11

11.1 Ans. $\omega_o = \sqrt{2pV/md^2}$ for isothermal oscillations, and $= \sqrt{2\gamma pV/md^2}$ for adiabatic oscillations, $V =$ volume of the enclosed gas, $2d =$ length of the gas column, $p =$ gas pressure at equilibrium, and $\gamma = c_p/c_v$

11.2 The equation of motion of the particle along the curve is given by $m\ddot{s} = -mg\sin\theta = -mg\,dy/ds \equiv -\omega^2 s$, hence the required equation of the curve becomes $y = \omega^2/2g)s^2$.

11.3 The flywheel of the watch drags some amount of air with it due to the viscosity of air, and hence the effective moment of inertia of the flywheel is slightly higher on the ground that at a high altitude.

11.4 Let $r_o =$ radius of the ball, $R_c =$ radius of the circular track for the ball-track contact, $r_c =$ contact radius of the ball on the track $= r_o/\sqrt{2}$ for say 90° trough, $m =$ mass of the ball, $R_g =$ radius of gyration of the track, $\phi =$ angular displacement of the CM of the track from the vertical, $\psi =$ instantaneous angular displacement of the centre of the ball from the vertical. There are 2 DOF (no nonholonomic constraints). KE $= T = \frac{1}{2}MR_g^2\dot{\phi}^2 + \frac{1}{2}mr^2\dot{\psi}^2 + \frac{1}{5}(r_o/r_c)^2(R_c\dot{\phi} - r\dot{\psi})^2$, and PE $= V = MgR(1 - \cos\phi) + mgr(1 - \cos\psi)$

Set up Euler-Lagrange's equations of motion and seek for the normal mode solutions $\phi = A_1\cos\omega t$, $\psi = A_2\cos\omega t$. Because of the coupled nature of the equations of motion, there would be dramatic starts and stops.

11.5 Set up the Lagrangian $L = I\dot{\theta}^2/2 + mgr\cos(\theta + \phi) - m'gr\theta +$ constant, giving the period $P = 2\pi\sqrt{I/mgr\cos\phi}$

11.6 Ans. $P \simeq 2\pi\sqrt{m_o/k}[1 + 3ka^2/16m_oc^2]$ for the first case.

$$P = 2\pi\sqrt{m/k}[1 + \theta_o^2/16 + 11\theta_o^4/3072 + 173\theta_o^6/45 \times 2^{14} + \cdots]$$

11.7 Set up the Lagrangian and the Routhian in order to find the effective potential for the θ-motion given by $V_{\text{eff}}(\theta) = p_\phi^2/2m^2l^4\sin^2\theta - (g/l)\cos\theta$. For steady motion, $V'_{\text{eff}}(\theta_o) = 0$ giving $\sec\theta_o\sin^4\theta_o =$

(p_ϕ^2/m^2l^3g) and the angular frequency of oscillation in θ about θ_o is given by $\omega = \sqrt{(\partial^2 V_{\text{eff}}(\theta_o)/\partial\theta^2)} = \sqrt{g(1 + 3\cos^2\theta_o)/l\cos\theta_o} \longrightarrow = \sqrt{2g/l}$ for $\theta_o \longrightarrow 0$.

11.8 Ans. $\omega_{1,2,3} = \omega_o\sqrt{3}, -\omega_o\sqrt{3}, 0$ where $\omega_o = \sqrt{k/m}$.

11.9 The Lagrangian for the system is $L = \frac{1}{2}m(\dot{u}_1^2 + \dot{u}_2^2) - \frac{1}{2}k[u_1^2 + (u_2 - u_1)^2]$, so that the b-matrix is not diagonal. This problem is quite similar to the one worked out in section 11.2.5.

11.10 In the first case, b-matrix is not diagonal and in the second case a-matrix is not diagonal. Procedures are once again straightforward.

11.11 Make the bob out of any ferro-magnetic substance and apply a strong magnetic field in order to change the spring constant. You would need about 0.03 Tesla of magnetic field which can be created inside a solenoid of diameter about 0.1 m carrying a dc electric current of about 5 A, to be applied on a bob made up of soft iron of mass about 8 g.

11.12 The pyramid can be suspended from a spring of known spring constant, say k_1, and the system is made to settle in a normal mode oscillation given by $\omega^4 - \omega^2\{(k_1 + k_o)/m_1 + k_o/m_o\} + k_1k_o/m_1m_o = 0$, where m_o = mass of the bob, m_1 = mass of the pyramid, k_o = spring constant of the support spring, $\omega_o = \sqrt{k/m_o}$. Measurement of ω_o, ω, and the total mass $M = m_1 + m_o$ gives m_o.

11.13 You have to rock it vertically with a frequency twice the natural frequency of the noninverted pendulum.

Chapter 12

12.1 The inertial velocity of the point of contact is given by $\dot{\boldsymbol{r}} = \dot{\boldsymbol{r}}_{\text{cm}} + \boldsymbol{\omega} \times (\boldsymbol{r} - \boldsymbol{r}_{\text{cm}})$. The equation for rolling constraint (without slipping) is (i) $\dot{\boldsymbol{r}} = 0$ and (ii) $\dot{\boldsymbol{r}} = \boldsymbol{\Omega} \times \boldsymbol{r}$, $\boldsymbol{\Omega}$ = angular velocity of the rotating platform.

12.2 If G be the centre of the sphere, its velocity $\boldsymbol{v} = \frac{1}{2}\hat{\boldsymbol{k}} \times (\Omega_1\boldsymbol{r}_1 + \Omega_2\boldsymbol{r}_2) = \frac{1}{2}(\Omega_1 + \Omega_2)\hat{\boldsymbol{k}}[(\Omega_1\boldsymbol{r}_1 + \Omega_2\boldsymbol{r}_2)/(\Omega_1 + \Omega_2)] \equiv \boldsymbol{\Omega} \times \boldsymbol{R}$, which corresponds to circular motion with angular velocity $\frac{1}{2}(\Omega_1 + \Omega_2)\hat{\boldsymbol{k}}$ and a radius R.

12.3 Ans. $\omega_2 = -(2\pi/T)\cot\alpha\tan 2\alpha$.

12.4 Use the results from the problems 3.2 and 3.3, and/or see Konopinski's book.

12.5 (iii) $D_{ij} = I_{kk}\delta_{ij} - 3I_{ij}$

12.6 Euler's equation of motion gives $I\ddot{\theta} = Fd$, giving $\theta(t) = (Fd/2I)t^2$. The equation of motion of the cm: $\ddot{x} = (F/m)\cos\theta(t)$ and $\ddot{y} = (F/m)\sin\theta(t)$. These are the parametric equations for Cornu's spiral.

12.7 For cylinder $h = \sqrt{3}a$ and for the cone $h = a/2$.

12.9 Poynting vector $\boldsymbol{N} = \boldsymbol{E} \times \boldsymbol{H}$ = energy density $\times$ c, where the electric field $\boldsymbol{E} = -e\boldsymbol{r}/(4\pi\varepsilon_o r^3)$, the magnetic induction due to a magnetic dipole $\boldsymbol{B} = (1/4\pi\varepsilon_o c^2)[(\boldsymbol{\mu}\cdot\boldsymbol{r})/r^5 - \boldsymbol{\mu}/r^3]$. The volume density of linear momentum $\boldsymbol{p}$ = energy density $/c = \boldsymbol{N}/c^2$, the volume density of angular momentum about the centre of the electron is $\boldsymbol{l} = \boldsymbol{r} \times \boldsymbol{p}$, and hence, the total angular momentum along the z-axis $L_z = \int \boldsymbol{l}\cdot\hat{\boldsymbol{k}}\, dV = S_z$

12.10 At saturation of magnetisation, each atom of iron has roughly two electrons with line up spins. The sum total of all the spin angular momentum of the lined up electrons results in the increase in the total angular velocity of the body. Ans. 0.008 rad/s.

12.11 Let B be the point fixed on the rim of the disc about which the disc can pivot. α is the angle through which the disc travels, and $\beta = 2\theta$ = the angle through which the cat travels on the disc. So the angular momentum of the disc about B at any instant is given by $L_d = \frac{3}{2}MR^2\dot{\alpha}$, and the angular momentum of the cat about B = $L_c = (\dot{\alpha} - \dot{\beta}/2)4R^2 m\sin^2(\beta/2)$. Since the total angular momentum before the cat began walking was zero, the sum $L_d + L_c$ will always remain zero.

12.12 See Routh's book.

12.13 (i) Polhodes are intersections two ellipsoids in $\boldsymbol{\omega}$-space, one for the constant kinetic energy surface and the other for constant angular momentum L^2

12.14 Can be found in the book.

12.15 $I_{11} = I_{22} = 2I_{33} = Mr^2$, the initial angular velocity $\boldsymbol{\omega} = (2\Omega/\sqrt{13}, 0, 3\Omega/\sqrt{13})$ giving $L = 5Mr^2\Omega/(2\sqrt{13})$ and $2T = 17Mr^2\Omega^2/26$. Therefore, $\alpha_b = \sin^{-1}(2/\sqrt{13})$, $\alpha_s = \cos^{-1}(17/5\sqrt{13})$, and $\sin\alpha_s : \sin\alpha_b = 3:5$

12.16 Show first that the general solutions for Euler's equations of motion gives $\omega_3 = Nt/C$, $\omega_1 + i\omega_2 = K\exp(i\lambda t^2/2)$, $\lambda = N(A - C)/AC$. The initial conditions are, say, $\omega_3 = 0$, $\omega_1 = \Omega$, $\omega_2 = 0$. For the equation for $\boldsymbol{\omega}$, assume $\boldsymbol{\omega}$ parallel to $\boldsymbol{r}$, so that $x = \alpha\Omega\cos(\lambda t^2/2)$, $y = \alpha\Omega\sin(\lambda t^2/2)$ and $z = \alpha Nt/C$, α being the constant of proportionality between $\boldsymbol{\omega}$ and $\boldsymbol{r}$. Eliminate t and α in order to derive the desired relation.

12.17 See section 12.18.

12.19 Start with Euler's equation.

12.20 A variation of the symmetric top problem.

12.21 The effective potential due to a rotating spheroid is given by $V_{\text{eff}}(\boldsymbol{r}) = V(\boldsymbol{r}) - \frac{1}{2}|\boldsymbol{\Omega} \times \boldsymbol{r}|^2$, where $V(\boldsymbol{r})$ is given by Eq. (12.129), that is, $V(\boldsymbol{r}) = -GM/r + (GM/2r^3)(C - A)\{3(\hat{\boldsymbol{r}}\cdot\hat{\boldsymbol{k}}) - 1\}$. The surface of the earth being a geoid is defined by $V_{\text{eff}}(\boldsymbol{r}) = \text{const.} = K$, say. The const. K can be evaluated by setting $\boldsymbol{r} = c\hat{\boldsymbol{k}}$ or $\hat{\boldsymbol{r}}\cdot\hat{\boldsymbol{k}} = 1$. Finally derive $\boldsymbol{g}_p = -\nabla V_{\text{eff}}$ evaluated at $\boldsymbol{r} = c\hat{\boldsymbol{k}}$, and similarly $\boldsymbol{g}_e$ at $\boldsymbol{r} = a\hat{\boldsymbol{i}}$.

12.23 Ans. $T = 2\pi\sqrt{\{28R^5/15 - 4R^3h^2 + 11R^2h^3/3 - 5Rh^4/4 + 3h^5/20\}/gh^2(R - h/2)^2}$, where h is the central thickness of the missing flat. For $h = R$, that is, a hemispherical cut, $T = 2\pi\sqrt{26R/15g}$

12.24 $P = P_1 + P_2$, $P_1 \propto Mgv(a - a_f)^2/La$, $P_2 \propto Mv^3/a$. The constants of proportionalities α_1 and α_2 for P_1 and P_2 can be taken as 0.05 and 0.1 respectively. So P becomes minimum for $a \simeq 0.7$ m.

12.25 For a spinning ball (spin axis transverse to the motion of the ball, forward spinning = spin axis going from right to left), the change in the translational kinetic energy $\Delta T_t = -2m(6v_o^2 - 5R\omega_o v_o - R^2\omega_o^2)/49$ and the change in the rotational kinetic energy $\Delta T_r = m(5v_o^2 + 4R\omega_o v_o - 9R^2\omega_o^2)/49$. Obviously, for the forward spinning case, $\omega_o > 0$ and for the backward spinning case, $\omega_o < 0$. The changes are bigger for the bounce of backspinning balls off the level ground.

12.26 (i) Ans. $(\beta + 2\sqrt{2})L \simeq 2\beta L$, as $\beta \simeq 3$
(ii) Maximum height for pole vault $H_{\text{pv}} = v_o^2/2g + h_o \simeq 6$ m

12.27 (i) Total force of reaction (= body weight) will produce more pressure if it has to act over a smaller surface area. During diving, the force of reaction is due to the drag force which depends on area of contact and velocity. For a given speed, the drag force is minimum if the area of cross-section with water is minimum.
(ii) Internal forces can produce a net torque as well as net angular momentum, without violating the torque-angular momentum relation.
(iii) Two identical pendula coupled by the shoulder link oscillate in exactly opposite phase in their normal mode of oscillation.
(iv) Given a volume, the surface area is minimum for a sphere. More round the configuration, less must be the enclosing surface area.

12.28 PE $= V = -\frac{1}{4}\mu g(L^2 + 2Lx - x^2)$, x being the vertical drop of the free end of the chain from its original level, μ the mass per unit length, L the total length of the chain. KE $= \frac{1}{4}\mu(L - x)^2\dot{x}^2$. Now show that $\ddot{x} = g + \dot{x}^2/2(L - x) > g$. The physical reason is that there is some amount of tension in the chain that pulls the free end down in addition to gravity.

12.29 See *Am. J. Phys.* **57**, p40 (1989).

12.30 See *Proc. Royal Society of London* **A405**, p265 (1986).

Chapter 13

13.1 $dl_i = \delta x_i + (\partial u_i/\partial x_j)\delta x_j = (\delta_{ij} + \partial u_i/\partial x_j)\delta x_j$ and hence from the Lagrangian definition of e_{ij}, we have $e_{ij} = (\partial u_i/\partial x_j + \partial u_j/\partial x_i)/2 + (\partial u_k/\partial x_i)(\partial u_k/\partial x_j)/2$. Similarly, from the Eulerian definition of $\boldsymbol{u}'$, $dl_i = \delta x_i = (\delta_{ij} - \partial u_i'/\partial x_j')\delta x_j'$, and hence, $e_{ij}' = (\partial u_i'/\partial x_j' + \partial u_j'/\partial x_i')/2 - (\partial u_k'/\partial x_i')(\partial u_k'/\partial x_j')/2$

13.2 Take the definition of a_{ij} from Eq. (13.6), differentiate twice and prove the relations. The given strains are not compatible.

13.3 Use $u_x = u_r \cos\phi - u_\phi \sin\phi$, $u_y = u_r \sin\phi + u_\phi \cos\phi$, $u_z = u_z$. $e_{rr} = \partial u_r/\partial r$, $e_{\phi\phi} = u_r/r + r^{-1}\partial u_\phi/\partial\phi$, $e_{zz} = \partial u_z/\partial z$, $e_{r\phi} = \frac{1}{2}(r^{-1}\partial u_r/\partial\phi + \partial u_\phi/\partial r - u_\phi/r)$, $e_{zr} = \frac{1}{2}(\partial u_r/\partial z + \partial u_z/\partial r)$, $e_{z\phi} = \frac{1}{2}(r^{-1}\partial u_z/\partial\phi + \partial u_\phi/\partial z)$. For the given problem, $e_{rr} = a - b/r^2$, $e_{\phi\phi} = a + b/r^2$, $e_{zz} = e$, $e_{r\phi} = e_{zr} = 0$, $e_{z\phi} = cr/2$; the dilation $\Delta = e_{rr} + e_{\phi\phi} + e_{zz} = 2a + e$; the components of the rotation vector $\omega_r = -cr/2$, $\omega_\phi = 0$, $\omega_z = cz$

13.4 $e_{ij} = (e_{11}, e_{22}, e_{33}, e_{12}, e_{13}, e_{23}) = \epsilon(1, 1, 2, 0, 2, 2)$, dilation $\Delta = 4\epsilon$, rotation $\boldsymbol{\omega} = \epsilon(2\hat{\boldsymbol{i}} + \hat{\boldsymbol{j}} - 2\hat{\boldsymbol{k}})$, and shear: about x-axis by an angle 4ϵ, and about y-axis by an angle 4ϵ. The principal strains $\lambda_1 = \epsilon$ along $\boldsymbol{r}_1 = \hat{\boldsymbol{i}} - \hat{\boldsymbol{j}}$, $\lambda_{2,3} = (3 \pm \sqrt{33})\epsilon/2$ along $\boldsymbol{r}_{2,3} = \hat{\boldsymbol{i}} + \hat{\boldsymbol{j}} \pm 8\hat{\boldsymbol{k}}/(\sqrt{33} \mp 1)$.

13.5 The principal strains are $0, \pm\sqrt{a^2 + b^2}$ and the corresponding principal axes are defined by $\hat{\boldsymbol{k}}, (a \pm \sqrt{a^2 + b^2})\hat{\boldsymbol{i}}/b + \hat{\boldsymbol{j}}$. If we rotate by an angle θ about the z-axis, the strain tensor e_{ij} transforms to $e'_{11} = a\cos\theta + b\sin\theta = -e'_{22}$, $e'_{12} = -a\sin\theta + b\cos\theta = e'_{21}$, $e'_{13} = e'_{31} = e'_{23} = e'_{32} = 0$. Thus maximum positive extension occurs along the angles $\theta = \tan^{-1}(b/a)$ and maximum negative extension along the directions $\theta = \tan^{-1}(-a/b)$ with respect to the x-axis, all lying in the x-y plane. The maximum of shear of magnitude $2\tan^{-1}\{b/(1 + a)\}$ takes place about the z-axis with $\theta = \frac{1}{2}\tan^{-1}(-a/b)$ with respect to the x-axis lying in the x-y plane. There is no strain (that is, the length is preserved) along $\pm\hat{\boldsymbol{k}}$. Similarly, the directions are preserved with non-zero strains along $\pm(a\hat{\boldsymbol{i}} + b\hat{\boldsymbol{j}})$, $\pm(b\hat{\boldsymbol{i}} - a\hat{\boldsymbol{j}})$

13.6 (i) $e_{11} = \{\sigma_{11} - \lambda(\sigma_{11} + \sigma_{22})/(3\lambda + 2\mu)\}/2\mu$, $e_{22} = \{\sigma_{22} - \lambda(\sigma_{11} + \sigma_{22})/(3\lambda + 2\mu)\}/2\mu$, $e_{33} = \lambda(\sigma_{11} + \sigma_{22})/2\mu(3\lambda + 2\mu)$
(ii) $e_{11} = \sigma_{11}(\lambda + 2\mu)/4\mu(\lambda + \mu)$, $e_{33} = -\sigma_{11}\lambda/4\mu(\lambda + \mu)$, $\sigma_{22} = \lambda\sigma_{11}/2(\lambda + \mu)$

13.7 Use the translational equilibrium equations (13.26), the stress-strain relations (13.43) and solve for the strain tensor fields, namely $e_{ij} = e_{ij}(x_1, x_2, x_3)$ with appropriate boundary conditions.

13.8 Calculate the bending moment through a section of the strut at a height x to be given by $N = Ya^4/12R$, R= radius of curvature of the strut at height x. Neglect dy/dx compared to 1, and set up the differential equation, knowing that N must also be equal to the torque of the weight about the point at x, given by $N = W(y_o - y)$, where y_o = projected horizontal extension or the horizontal coordinate of the point at x. Then show that the solution will have the form $y = y_o(1 - \cos\omega x)$ with the auxiliary condition $y_o \cos\omega l = 0$, where $\omega^2 = 12W/Ya^4$. So for $\omega l < \pi/2$, y_o must be zero, that is, no deviation of the strut from its vertical orientation. But as soon as ωl becomes equal to $\pi/2$ due to increase in W, the above condition for instability can be approached.

13.9 When the chimney is falling as a whole, it rotates by an angle $\theta(t)$ about its base point satisfying $ML^2\ddot{\theta}/3 = (MgL/2)\sin\theta$. If the chimney breaks at a distance x from the base, its lower end satisfies an equation $Mx^3\ddot{\theta}/3L = (Mgx^2/2L)\sin\theta + xF - \Gamma$, where F is the force of shear developed at the breaking point and Γ is the internal flexion torque at the point x. Similarly, the rotation of the upper broken portion about its own cm satisfies an equation $[M(L - x)^3/12L]\ddot{\theta} = [L - x]F/2 + \Gamma$. So using these three equations one can solve for F and Γ, as functions of x, the distance to the breaking point. For a thin chimney $\Gamma \gg$ product of F with the width of the chimney, and then Γ is maximum at $x = L/3$. (The last two problems are taken from the Chicago university problem book.)

13.10 Irrotational plane waves belong to the compressional longitudinal mode. The phase factor $kx_1 - \omega' t$ suggests that the direction of propagation is along the x-axis with $\omega' k = (\lambda + 2\mu)/\rho$, $e_{11} = \partial u_1/\partial x_1 = Ak\cos(kx_1 - \omega' t)$, all other $e_{ij} = 0$. Thus, $\sigma_{11} = A\omega'\rho\cos(kx_1 - \omega' t)$, $\sigma_{22} = \sigma_{33} = \lambda e_{11}$, and $\sigma_{22}/\sigma_{11} = k\lambda/\rho\omega'$

13.11 (i) Distance d =1975 km (ii) Angular radius = 114°.

Chapter 14

14.1 Ans. 1.4 m/s, height of the jet $h = \sqrt{v^2/2g} - h_o$

14.2 Ans. $v = \omega h\sqrt{2lh - 1}$

14.3 Since the liquid is incompressible by nature, the pressure inside the bubble cannot change. Ans. The pressure at various levels assume the following values: $P_o + 2\rho gh$ at the top, $P_o + \rho(h + H)$ at the bottom, and $P_o + \rho gh$ at the level of the cup, H being the total height of the cylinder.

14.4 (i) Since $\boldsymbol{q}$ is planar, $\boldsymbol{\omega}$ is perpendicular to the plane, and the result follows from the Kelvin-Helmholtz theorem.
(ii) $\rho = \rho_o \exp\{\frac{\mu GM_\oplus}{RT}\left(\frac{1}{r} - \frac{1}{R_\oplus}\right)\}$, the density thus not falling to zero at infinity.
(iii) Start with $\nabla \times \boldsymbol{q} = 0$
(iv) Start with the Kelvin-Helmholtz theorem.
(v) Take the curl of both sides of Eq. (14.113)
(vi) Proceed similar to the derivation of Kelvin's theorem with Euler's equation replaced by Navier-Stokes'.

14.5 Draw the flow patterns for visualisation.

14.6 Ans. The thickness of the flow $d = (3\eta Q/\rho gb \sin\theta)^{1/3}$

14.7 Start from the right hand side and apply Green's theorem.

14.8 Use $\boldsymbol{q}' = \boldsymbol{q} - \boldsymbol{\omega}_o \times \boldsymbol{r}$, and find its curl and circulation.

14.9 Use the expressions for divergence of vectors in orthogonal curvilinear coordinates (see section A2.8).

14.10 Motion of the fluid near the boundary ought to be normal to ∇g. For moving boundaries, $(\boldsymbol{q}-\boldsymbol{u})\cdot\nabla g = 0$, where $\boldsymbol{u}$ is the velocity of the boundary at the given point.

14.11 Since $\boldsymbol{\omega}$ is given, $\boldsymbol{q} = \boldsymbol{\omega} \times \boldsymbol{r}$. Find $\nabla \times \boldsymbol{q}$, which vanishes only if $r^2 f(r)=$ const.

14.12 Ans. $y(x) = D(1 + 2gx/v_o^2)^{-1/4}$, $D =$ diameter of the mouth of the faucet.

14.13 Find the conditions for instability. This can be a good research problem for graduate students.

14.14 $g = -\sqrt{8\pi\rho_c GRT}\tanh(z\sqrt{2\pi\rho_c G/RT})$, $\rho = \rho_c \mathrm{sech}^2(z\sqrt{2\pi\rho_c G/RT})$, $\rho_c =$ central density, $R =$ gas constant, and $T =$ temperature of the star (assumed to be isothermal).

14.15 Ans. $F = \pi\rho R^4\omega^2/4$, $\rho =$ density of air outside, $R =$ radius of the discs, and $\omega =$ angular velocity of rotation.

14.16 Define the equivalent resistance (electrical type) of the Poiseuille flow in a tube of diameter D and length L by $R = \Delta P/Q = (128\eta/\pi)L/D^4$, η being the viscosity of the fluid and Q the flow rate. Let the flow rate through the original artery drop to $Q_a = \Delta P/R_a$, and after the graft of the bypass the total flow rate becomes $Q = \Delta P[R_g^{-1} + (R_o + R_a)^{-1}]$, R_o being the resistance of the obstruction developed and R_g the resistance of the graft. Thus $Q/Q_a = 1 + (R_o + R_a)/R_g =$ the improvement ratio of the flows after and before the graft $=$ function of only L_a, D_a, L_g, D_g, L_o and D_o. The ratio can be about 28 for a choice of $L_o/L_a = 0.2$, $D_o/D_a = 0.5$, $L_a/L_g = 0.4$ and $D_g/D_a = 2$, for example.

APPENDIX D

Physical Constants

Universal Constants

speed of light in vacuum	c	299 792 458	ms^{-1}
permeability of vacuum	μ_0	$4\pi \times 10^{-7}$	NA^{-2}
		= 12.566 370 614...	10^{-7} NA^{-2}
permittivity of vacuum, $1/\mu_0 c^2$	ϵ_0	8.854 187 817...	10^{-12} Fm^{-1}
Newtonian constant of gravitation	G	6.672 59(85)	10^{-11} m^3 kg^{-1} s^{-2}
Planck constant	h	6.626 075 5(40)	10^{-34} J s
in electron volts, h/e		4.135 669 2(12)	10^{-15} eV s
$h/2\pi$	$\hbar$	1.054 572 66(63)	10^{-34} J s
in electron volts, $\hbar/e$		6.852 122 0(20)	10^{-16} eV s

Atomic and Nuclear Constants

elementary charge	e	1.602 177 33(49)	10^{-19} C
fine-structure constant, $\mu_0 ce^2/2h$	α	7.297 353 08(33)	10^{-3}
Bohr radius, $\alpha/4\pi R_\infty$	a_0	0.529 177 249(24)	10^{-10} m
electron mass	m_e	9.109 389 7(54)	10^{-31} kg
		5.485 799 03(13)	10^{-4} amu
in electron volts, $m_e c^2/e$		0.510 999 06(15)	MeV
Compton wavelength, $h/m_e c$	λ_c	2.426 310 58(22)	10^{-12} m
$\lambda_c/2\pi = \alpha a_0 = \alpha^2/4\pi R_\infty$	$\bar{\lambda}_c$	3.861 593 23(35)	10^{-13} m
classical electron radius, $\alpha^2 a_0$	r_e	2.817 940 92(38)	10^{-15} m
Thomson cross-section, $(8\pi/3)r_e{}^2$	σ_e	0.665 246 16(18)	10^{-28} m^2
electron magnetic moment	μ_e	928.477 01(31)	10^{-26} JT^{-1}
in Bohr magnetons	μ_e/μ_B	1.001 159 652 193(10)	
proton mass	m_p	1.672 623 1(10)	10^{-27} kg
		1.007 276 470(12)	amu
in electron volts, $m_p c^2/e$		938.272 31(28)	MeV
neutron mass	m_n	1.674 928 6(10)	10^{-27} kg
		1.008 664 904(14)	amu
in electron volts, $m_n c^2/e$		939.565 63(28)	MeV
Avogadro's constant	N_A, L	6.022 136 7(36)	10^{23} mol^{-1}
atomic mass constant			

$m_u = \frac{1}{12}m(^{12}C)$	m_u	1.660 540 2(10)	10^{-27} kg
in electron volts, $m_u c^2/e$		931.494 32(28)	MeV
molar gas constant	R	8.314 510(70)	J mol^{-1} K^{-1}
Boltzmann constant, R/N_A	k	1.380 658(12)	10^{-23} J K^{-1}
in electron volts, k/e		8.617 385(73)	10^{-5} eV K^{-1}
in hertz, k/h		2.083 674(18)	10^{10} Hz K^{-1}
in wavenumbers, k/hc		69.503 87(59)	m^{-1} K^{-1}
Stefan-Boltzmann constant, $(\pi^2/60)k^4/\hbar^3 c^2$	σ	5.670 51(19)	10^{-8} W m^{-2} K^{-4}

Astronomical Constants

heliocentric gravitational constant	$GM_\odot$	1.327 124 38	10^{20} m^3 s^{-2}
geocentric gravitational constant	$GM_\oplus$	3.986 004 48	10^{14} m^3 s^{-2}
Astronomical unit	1 AU	1.495 978 706 6	10^{11} m
equatorial radius of the sun	$R_\odot$	6.959 9	10^8 m
equatorial radius of the earth	$R_\oplus$	6.378 137	10^6 m
angular velocity of the earth	$\omega_\oplus$	7.292 115 146 7	10^{-5} s^{-1}
mass ratio of the earth and the moon	$M_\oplus/M$	81.300 813	
radius of the moon	R	1.738 2	10^6 m

Bibliography

Abraham, R., and J. E. Marsden, *Foundations of Mechanics*, Benjamin/Cummings Publ. Co. Inc, Massachusetts, 1978 (2nd revision).

Barger, V., and M. Olsson, *Classical Mechanics: A Modern Perspective*, McGraw-Hill Book Co., Inc., New York, 1973.

Bell, E. T., *Men of Mathematics*, Dover Publ., Inc., New York, 1937.

A. B., Bhatia, and R. N. Singh, *Mechanics of Deformable Media*, Adam Hilger, Bristol, 1986.

Brancazio, P. J., *Sport Science*, Simon and Schuster, New York, 1984.

Clagett, M., *Science of Mechanics in the Middle Ages*, The University of Wisconsin Press, Madison, 1959.

Cole, G. H. A., *Fluid Mechanics*, John Wiley and Sons, Inc., New York, 1962.

Desloge, E. A., *Classical Mechanics*, Vol. I and II, John Wiley and Sons, Inc., New York, 1982.

Easthrope, C. E., *Three Dimensional Dynamics*, Butterworths Scientific Publ., London, 1958.

Fetter, A. L., and J. D. Walecka, *Theoretical Mechanics: A Modern Perspective*, McGraw-Hill Book Co., Inc., New York, 1980.

Feynman, R. P., R. B. Leighton, and M. Sands, *The Feynman Lectures on Physics*, Vol. I, II, and III, Addison-Wesley Publ. Co., Inc., Massachusetts, 1965.

Fung, Y. C., *Foundations of Solid Mechanics*, Prentice-Hall, Inc., New Jersey, 1965.

Gantmacher, F. R., *Analytical Mechanics*, Mir Publishers, Moscow, 1975.

Goldstein, H., *Classical Mechanics*, Addison-Wesley Publ. Co., Inc., Massachusetts, 1950.

Gray, A., *A Treatise on Gyrostatics and Rotational Motion*, Dover Publ., Inc., New York, 1959 (original 1918).

Greenwood, D. T., *Classical Dynamics*, Prentice-Hall, Inc., New Jersey, 1977.

Griffing, D. F., *The Dynamics of Sports — Why That's the Way the Ball Bounces*, Mohican, Ohio, 1982.

Gupta, K. C., *Classical Mechanics of Particles and Rigid Bodies*, Wiley Eastern Ltd, New Delhi, 1988.

Gupta, B. D., and S. Prakash, *Classical Mechanics*, Kedar Nath Ram Nath, Meerut, 1985.

Halfman, R. L., *Dynamics* Vol I and II, Addison-Wesley Publ. Co., Inc., Massachusetts, 1962.

Halliday, D., and R. Resnick, *Fundamentals of Physics*, John Wiley and Sons, Inc., New York, 1970 (2nd Ed).

Hestenes, D., *New Foundations for Classical Mechanics*, D. Reidel Publ. Co., Dordrecht, 1986.

Housner, G. W., and D. E. Hudson, *Applied Mechanics Dynamics*, D. van Norstrand Co. Inc., NY, 1959 (2nd Ed).

Ishlinski, A. Yu., *Mechanics of Gyroscopic Systems*, NASA, Washington, 1965.

Jammer, M., *Concept of Force*, Harvard Univ Press, Harvard, 1957.

Jammer, M., *Conceptual Development of Quantum Mechanics*, McGraw-Hill Book Co., Inc., New York, 1961.

Kane, T. R., and D. A. Levinson, *Dynamics: Theory and Applications*, McGraw-Hill Book Co., Inc., New York, 1985.

Kibble, T. W. B., *Classical Mechanics*, McGraw-Hill Book Co., Inc., New York, 1966.

Kilmister, C. W., *Hamiltonian Dynamics*, Longman, Green and Co. Ltd., London, 1964.

Konopinski, E. J., *Classical Descriptions of Motion*, W. H. Freeman and Co., San Francisco, 1969.

Kotkin, G. L., and V. G. Serbo, *Collections of Problems in Classical Mechanics*, Pergamon Press, Oxford, 1971.

Lamb, H., *Hydrodynamics*, Dover Publ., Inc., New York, 1945.

Lanczos, C., *The Variational Principles of Mechanics*, Univ. of Toronto Press, Toronto, 1949.

Landau, L. D., and E. M. Lifshitz, *Course of Theoretical Physics*, Vol. I: *Mechanics*, Vol. VI: *Fluid Mechanics*, Vol. VII: *Theory of Elasticity*, Pergamon Press, Oxford, 1960.

Leech, J. W., *Classical Mechanics*, Methuen & Co. Ltd., London, 1958.

Lin, C. C., *The Theory of Hydrodynamic Stability*, Cambridge University Press, Cambridge, 1955.

Lovelock, D., and H. Rund, *Tensors, Differential Forms, and Variational Principles*, John Wiley and Sons, Inc., New York, 1975.

Mach, E., *The Science of Mechanics*, The Open Court Publ. Co., London, 1893.

Marion, J. B., *Classical Dynamics of Particles and Systems*, Academic Press, New York, 1970 (2nd ed).

McCusky, S. W., *An Introduction to Advanced Dynamics*, Addison-Wesley Publ. Co., Inc., Massachusetts, 1953.

McLeod, E. B., *Introduction to Fluid Dynamics*, Pergamon Press, Oxford, 1963.

Møller, C., *The Theory of Relativity*, Clarendon Press, Oxford, 1972.

Narayan, S., and J. N. Kapur, *A Text Book of Vector Calculus*, S. Chand and Co. Ltd., New Delhi, 1955.

Parcival, I., and D. Richards, *Introduction to Dynamics*, Cambridge University Press, Cambridge, 1982.

Park, D., *Classical Dynamics and Its Quantum Analogues*, Springer-Verlag, Berlin, 1979.

Pars, L. A., *Introduction to Dynamics*, Cambridge University Press, Cambridge, 1953.

Patharia, R. K., *The Theory of Relativity*, Pergamon Press, New York, 1974.

Prandtl, L., *Essentials of Fluid Dynamics*, Blackie and Son Ltd., London, 1952.

Prescott, J., *Mechanics of Particles and Rigid Bodies*, Longman, Green and Co. Ltd., London, 1929.

Rasband, S. N., *Dynamics*, John Wiley and Sons, Inc., New York, 1983.

Raychaudhuri, A. K., *Classical Mechanics — A Course of Lectures*, Oxford University Press, Calcutta, 1983.

Resnick, R., *Basic Concepts in Relativity and Quantum Theory*, John Wiley and Sons, Inc., New York, 1972.

Resnick, R., and D. Halliday, *Physics Part I*, John Wiley and Sons, Inc., New York, 1960.

Richtmyer, F. K., E. H. Kennard, and J. N. Cooper, *Introduction to Modern Physics*, Tata McGraw-Hill Publ. Co., Ltd., New Delhi, 1976 (6th ed).

Routh, E. J., *Dynamics of a System of Rigid Bodies, Part I and II*, Dover Publ., Inc., New York, 1955 (original 1860).

Savet, P. H., *Gyroscopes; Theory and Design*, McGraw-Hill Book Co., Inc., New York, 1961.

Serway, R. A., *Physics for Scientists and Engineers*, Saunders College Publ., Philadelphia, 1982.

Serway, R. A., and J. S. Faughn, *College Physics*, Saunders College Publ., Philadelphia, 1985.

Sommerfeld, A., *Mechanics*, Academic Press, New York, 1952.

Spiegel, M. R., *Theoretical Mechanics*, Schaum Series, New York, 1967.

Stacey, F. W., *Physics of the Earth*, John Wiley and Sons, Inc., New York, 1977.

Sudarshan, E. C. G., and N. Mukunda, *Classical Dynamics: A Modern Perspective*, John Wiley and Sons, Inc., New York, 1974.

Symon, K. R., *Mechanics*, Addison-Wesley Publ. Co., Inc., Massachusetts, 1971.

Synge, J. L., *Relativity: The Special Theory*, North Holland Publ. Co., New York, 1972.

Takwale, R. G., and S. Puranik, *Introduction to Classical Mechanics*, Tata McGraw-Hill Publ. Co. Ltd., New Delhi, 1980.

Temple, G., *An Introduction to Fluid Dynamics*, Clarendon Press, Oxford, 1958.

Ter Haar, D., *Elements of Hamiltonian Mechanics*, North Holland Publ. Co., New York, 1961.

Ugarov, V. A., *Special Theory of Relativity*, Mir Publishers, Moscow, 1979.

Valentine, H. R., *Applied Hydrodynamics*, Butterworths Scientific Publ., London, 1959.

van de Kamp, P., *Elements of Astromechanics*, W. H. Freeman and Co., San Francisco, 1963.

von Laue, M., *History of Physics*, Academic Press, Inc., New York, 1950.

Webster, A. G., *The Dynamics of Particles and of Rigid, Elastic, and Fluid Bodies*, Hatner Publ. Co. Inc., New York. 1949.

White, H. E., *Modern College Physics*, D. Von Nostrand Co., Inc., Princeton, 1966 (5th ed).

Whittaker, E. T., *A Treatise on the Analytical Dynamics of Particles and Rigid Bodies*, Dover Publ., Inc., New York, 1944.

Williams, T. I., *A Biographical Dictionary of Scientists*, John Wiley and Sons, Inc., New York, 1982.

Young, H. D., M. W. Zemansky, and F. W. Sears, *University Physics*, Addison-Wesley Publ. Co., Inc., New York, 1982.

Yourgran, W., and S. Mandelstam, *Variational Principles in Dynamics and Quantum Theory*, Dover Publ., Inc., New York, 1979.

Index

Nicholas Copernicus
1473-1543

Galileo Galilei
1564-1642

Johannes Kepler
1571-1630

Leonard Euler
1703-1783

Joseph Louis Lagrange
1736-1813

Pierre-Simon Marquis de Laplace
1749-1827

Pierre de Fermat
1608-1665

Sir Isaac Newton
1642-1727

Gottfried Wilhelm Leibniz
1646-1716

Augustine-Louis Cauchy
1789-1867

Carl Gustav Jacob Jacobi
1804-1851

Sir William Rowan Hamilton
1805-1865

(Adapted from David Eugene Smith, *Portraits of Eminent Mathematicians with Biographical Sketches,* Vol. I & II, Scripta Mathematica, New York, 1938)